ROAD TRIP USA

Cross-Country Adventures on America's Two-Lane Highways

Jamie Jensen

AVALON
TRAVEL

When you come to a fork in the road, take it.

—Yogi Berra

On the Road

The journeys in this book are as wild and varied as the landscapes they traverse. All celebrate the notion that freedom and discovery await us on the open road. Poets and artists from Walt Whitman to Muddy Waters have long sung the praises of rolling down the highway, and no matter how times have changed we still believe there's nothing more essentially American than hitting the road and seeing the country.

America has always been a nation on the move. From colonial times onwards, each generation pushed relentlessly westward, until the outward frontier finally closed around the turn of the 20th century. Taking advantage of the internal combustion engine, and inspired by the slogan "See America First," Americans began to explore a new frontier, the system of highways that developed between the Atlantic and Pacific coasts. The first transcontinental route, the Lincoln Highway from New York to San Francisco, was completed in 1915, and motor courts, diners, and other new businesses soon sprang up along the roadside to serve the passing trade.

The half-century from the 1920s until the arrival of the Interstate highway system was the golden age of American motor travel, but this book is not especially motivated by nostalgia. Almost all of the places described in *Road Trip USA*—soda fountains and town squares, neon-signed motels and minor-league baseball teams—are happily thriving in the modern world, and better yet, they are close at hand. The simple act of avoiding the soulless interstates, with their soggy franchises and identikit chains, opens up a vast, and much friendlier, two-lane world. You'll chance upon monuments marking the actual sites of things you last thought about in high school history classes, or kitschy little souvenir stands flaunting giant dinosaurs outside their doors, and inside still selling the same postcards as they have for decades.

After traveling well over 400,000 miles in search of the perfect stretches of two-lane blacktop, this is the book I wish I'd had with me all along. So, whether you're a biker, an RVer, a road warrior, or a Sunday driver, hop on board, turn the key—and hit the highway.

Jamie Jen

Contents

pg. 15

Bellingham
Everett

Port
Angeles

Olympic
National Park

Olympia

n Beach

370 mi

WASHINGTON

Portland

Salem

pg. 34

Cape Perpetua

Eugene

Burns

300 mi

OREGON

Medford

I

Avenue of
the Giants

Redding

pg. 49

235 mi

Chico

Elko

Ren

Sacramento

San Francisco

pg. 60

San Francisco

NEVADA

180 mi

San
Jose

Fresno

pg. 77

Hearst Castle

Las Vegas

Bakersfield

Los
Angeles

Santa
Barbara

320 mi

San Diego

San Diego

pg. 100

CALIFORNIA
HIGHWAYS

Yuma

Vancouver

PACIFIC COAST

The amazing thing about the West Coast is that it is still mostly wild, open, and astoundingly beautiful country, where you can drive for miles and miles and have the scenery all to yourself.

Between Olympic National Park and San Diego, California

For some reason, when people elsewhere in the country refer to the **Pacific Coast**, particularly **California**, it's apparent that think it's a land of kooks and crazies, an overbuilt suburban desert supporting only shopping malls, freeways, and body-obsessed airheads. All this may be true in small pockets, but the amazing thing about the Pacific Coast—from the dense green forests of western **Washington** to the gorgeous beaches of Southern California—is that it is still mostly wild, open, and astoundingly beautiful country, where you can drive for miles and miles and have the scenery all to yourself.

Starting at the northwest tip of the United States at **Olympic National Park,** and remaining within sight of the ocean almost all the way south to the Mexican border, this 1,500-mile, mostly two-lane route takes in everything from temperate rainforest to near-desert. Most of the Pacific Coast is in the public domain, freely if not always easily accessible, and protected from development within national, state, and local parks, which provide habitat for such rare creatures as mountain lions, condors, and gray whales.

Heading south, after the rough-and-tumble logging and fishing communities of Washington State, you cross the mouth of the Columbia River and follow the comparatively peaceful and quiet **Oregon** coastline, where recreation has by and large replaced industry, and where dozens of quaint and not-so-quaint communities line the ever-changing shoreline. At the midway point, you pass through the great redwood forests of Northern California, where the tallest and most majestic living things on earth line the "Avenue of the Giants," home also to some of the best (meaning gloriously kitsch) remnants of the golden age of car-borne tourism: drive-through trees, drive-on trees, houses carved out of trees, and much more. The phenomenally beautiful coastline of Northern California is rivaled only by the incredible coast of **Big Sur** farther south, beyond which stretch the beachfronts of Southern California. The land of palm trees, beach boys, and surfer girls of popular lore really does exist, though only in the southernmost quarter of the state.

Along with the overwhelming scale of its natural beauty, the West Coast is remarkable for the abundance of well-preserved historic sites—most of which haven't been torn down, built on, or even built around—that stand as vivid evocations of life on what was once the most distant frontier of the New World. While rarely as old as places on the East Coast, or as impressive as those in Europe, West Coast sites are quite diverse and include the Spanish colonial missions of California, Russian and English fur-trading outposts, and the place where Lewis and Clark first sighted the Pacific after their long slog across the continent.

Last but certainly not least are the energizing cities—**Seattle** in the north, **San Francisco** in the middle, and **Los Angeles** and **San Diego** to the south—which serve as gateways to (or civilized respites from) the landscapes in between them. Add to these the dozens of small and not-so-small towns along the coast, with alternating blue-collar ports and upscale vacation retreats, and you have a great range of food, drink, and accommodation options. Local cafés, seafood grills, and bijou restaurants abound, as do places to stay—from youth hostels in old lighthouses to roadside motels (including the world's first, which still stands in lovely San Luis Obispo, California) to homespun B&B inns in old farmhouses.

WASHINGTON

The coast of Washington is a virtual microcosm of the Pacific Northwest, containing everything from extensive wilderness areas to Native American fishing villages and heavily industrialized lumber towns. Starting at splendid **Port Townsend,** US-101 loops west around the rugged Olympic Peninsula, passing near the northwesternmost point of the continental United States while allowing access to the unforgettable natural attractions—sandy, driftwood-strewn beaches, primeval old-growth forests, and pristine mountain lakes and glaciated alpine peaks, to name just a few—of **Olympic National Park.** The roadside landscape varies from dense woods to clear-cut tracts of recently harvested timber, with innumerable rivers and streams perhaps the most obvious signs of the immense amount of rainfall (up to 12 feet) the region receives every year. Scattered towns, from **Port Angeles** in the north to the twin cities of **Grays Harbor** on the coast, are staunchly blue-collar communities almost wholly dependent upon natural resources—not only trees, but also salmon, oysters, and other seafood. Though the tourism trade has been increasing steadily, visitor services are still few and far between, so plan ahead.

Though it's not on the ocean, the Puget Sound port city of Seattle makes a good starting or finishing point to this Pacific Coast road trip.

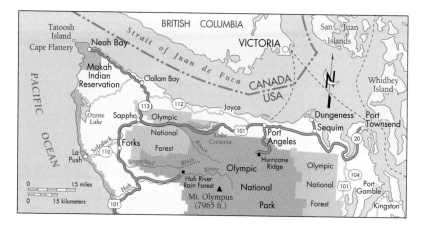

Port Townsend

Few places in the world can match the concentration of natural beauty or the wealth of architecture found in tiny **Port Townsend** (pop. 8,727). One of the oldest towns in Washington, Port Townsend was laid out in 1852 and reached a peak of activity in the 1880s. But after the railroads focused on Seattle and Puget Sound as their western terminus, the town sat quietly for most of the next century until the 1960s, when an influx of arts-oriented refugees took over the waterfront warehouses and cliff-top mansions, converting them to galleries, restaurants, and comfy B&Bs while preserving the town's turn-of-the-20th-century character.

The Waterstreet Hotel

Port Townsend is neatly divided into two halves: Multi-story brick warehouses and commercial buildings line Water Street and the wharves along the bay, while lovely old Victorian houses cover the bluffs above. It's basically a great place to wander, but there are a couple of sights worth seeing, particularly the landmark **City Hall** along the east end of Water Street at 210 Madison Street. Half of this eclectic gothic pile now houses a local historical **museum** (daily; donations accepted), with three floors of odds and ends tracing Port Townsend history, including the old city jail where Jack London spent a night on his way to the Klondike goldfields in 1897. The City Hall is also a starting point for Joyce Webb's expertly guided **walking tours** (daily by appointment; $10; 360/385-1967) of the waterfront district.

Not surprisingly, considering the extensive tourist trade, Port Townsend has a number of good restaurants and bars. You'll find many of the best places at the east end of town near the corner of Water and Quincy Streets. For breakfast or lunch, try the **Salal Cafe** (360/385-6532), at 634 Water Street. For dinner, one of the best seafood places is the **Silverwater Cafe** (360/385-6448), at 237 Taylor Street near the Quincy Street dock. The lively neighborhood also holds a pair of restored 1880s hotels: the **Waterstreet Hotel** ($50 and up; 360/385-5467 or 800/735-9810), at 635 Water Street, and the quieter **Palace Hotel** ($95 and up; 360/385-0773 or 800/962-0741), 1004 Water Street, where the room names play up the building's past use as a brothel.

Fort Worden, on the north side of Port Townsend, is a retired military base that served as a location for the Richard Gere movie *An Officer and a Gentleman*. It now hosts an excellent series of annual music and arts festivals; contact the Centrum at 360/385-5320 for schedules and more information.

Toward Seattle: Port Gamble

You have a number of options if traveling to or from Port Townsend. You can follow US-101 around the western Olympic Peninsula, or take a ferry via Whidbey Island and explore it and the even prettier San Juan Islands to the north. Last, but not least, you can take a middle route across the Kitsap Peninsula, then catch a ferry to Seattle (see pages 450–451).

This last route, which includes a trip on the very frequent (and frequently crowded) Washington State Ferry ($13; 206/464-6400) between Kingston and Edmonds, has the great advantage of taking you through the lovely old logging town of **Port Gamble**, a slice of New England on the shores of Puget Sound. The entire town is a historic district, with dozens of immaculate Victorian buildings standing along maple tree–lined streets. After wandering past the saltbox houses, have a look inside the large General Store, which includes a barber shop, a seashell museum, and a small café; or visit the photo-filled **historical museum** ($2.50; 360/297-8074) across the street.

The most comfortable accommodations in Port Townsend are the many 1880s-era B&Bs dotting the bluffs above the port area, including the ever-popular **Old Consulate Inn** ($110 and up; 360/385-6753), 313 Walker Street, where the plush rooms come with a view of Mt. Olympus and a hearty multi-course breakfast. For less-pricey lodging, there's a **campground** (360/344-4400) and the **HI Olympic Hostel** (360/385-0655) in the old Army barracks at Fort Worden, on the coast two miles north of town, with dorm beds for $14 members, $17 nonmembers; private rooms are available for around $40.

Sequim and Dungeness

A half hour southwest of Port Townsend via Hwy-20 and US-101, **Sequim** (pop. 4,334; pronounced SKWIM) sits in the rain shadow of the Olympic Mountains and so tends to be much drier and sunnier than spots even a few miles west. Though it retains its rural feel, Sequim's historic farming-and-fishing economy is quickly switching over to tourism, with tracts of new homes filling up the rolling, waterfront landscape, and a new freeway bypassing the center of town. It's ideal cycling country, for the moment at least, with acres and acres of lavender farms lining quiet country roads.

Coming in from the east on two-lane US-101, the first thing you pass is the large, modern **John Wayne Marina**, built on land donated by the Duke himself, who spent a lot of time in Sequim cruising around on his converted U.S. Navy minesweeper, the *Wild Goose*. The US-101 frontage through town is lined by the usual franchised fast-food outlets and some unique variations, like the ersatz but enjoyable **Hi-Way 101 Diner** (360/683-3388), at 392 W. Washington Street in the heart of town.

The natural cut of the **Hood Canal** on the east side of the Olympic Peninsula is one of the West Coast's prime oyster-growing estuaries, source of the gourmet Quilcenes, Hama Hamas, and other varieties available at roadside stands, shops, and restaurants throughout the region.

Just north of US-101 at 175 W. Cedar Street, the **Sequim-Dungeness Museum** (Tues.–Sun. 8 AM–4 PM; donation; 360/683-8110) houses everything from 12,000-year-old mastodon bones discovered on a nearby farm, to exhibits of Native American cultures and pioneer farm implements. From the museum, a well-marked road winds north for 10 miles before reaching the waterfront again at **Dungeness,** where a seven-mile-long sand spit, the country's longest, protects a shellfish-rich wildlife refuge. All that remains of the abandoned fishing community that existed here through the 1890s is an old schoolhouse, though the excellent **Three Crabs Restaurant** (360/683-4264), overlooking Dungeness Harbor, has been serving up fresh fish and local Dungeness crab for over 25 years.

The Indian-owned **7 Cedars Casino** stands above US-101 at the foot of Sequim Bay, fronted by totem poles.

Sequim's annual **Irrigation Festival,** held every May, is Washington's oldest community celebration.

The well-signed **Olympic Game Farm** (daily in summer; $9; 360/778-4295), five miles northwest of Sequim, is a 90-acre retirement home for former animal actors and other creatures, great and small. Visitors are very welcome.

Stay in Sequim at **Groveland Cottage** ($90–125; 360/683-3565), a quaint B&B just a half mile from the harbor at 4861 Sequim-Dungeness Way, or at the popular waterfront **Juan de Fuca Cottages** ($150; 360/683-4433), two miles to the west at 182 Marine Drive.

Port Angeles

A busy, industrial city at the center of the northern Olympic Peninsula, **Port Angeles** (pop. 18,397) makes a handy base for visiting the nearby wilderness of Olympic National Park. The town is slowly but surely recovering from its traditional dependence on logging, and the waterfront, which once hummed to the sound of lumber and pulp mills, is now bustling with tourists wandering along a six-mile walking trail and enjoying the sealife (sea slugs, eels, starfish, and octopuses) on display at the small but enjoyable **Marine Life Center** (daily; $2.50), on the centrally located City Pier.

Weather on the Olympic Peninsula varies widely from place to place. The peaks and coastal valleys of Olympic National Park receive as much as 200 inches of rainfall each year, while the town of Sequim, a mere 30 miles away, garners an average of just 17 inches annually.

Malls, gas stations, and fast-food franchises line the US-101 frontage through town, but life in Port Angeles, for locals and visitors alike, centers on the attractive downtown area, two blocks inland from the waterfront around Lincoln Avenue and 1st Street. Here cafés like **First Street Haven** (360/457-0352), at 107 E. 1st Street, offer good, inexpensive soup-and-salad lunches and dinners, and amiable bars and pubs like **Peaks,** around the corner on Lincoln Avenue, draw bikers, hikers, and loggers with their pub-grub and good beers. Across from Peaks, occupying a terra-cotta building that used to be a fire station, **Bonny's Bakery** (360/457-3585) serves coffees and pastries on a (sometimes) sunny front patio at 215 S. Lincoln Avenue. If you're waiting for a ferry, or are fresh off of one, a number of places to eat and drink surround the ferry terminal, including the attractive **Landings Restaurant** (360/457-6768), at 115 E. Railroad Avenue, with great fish-and-chips.

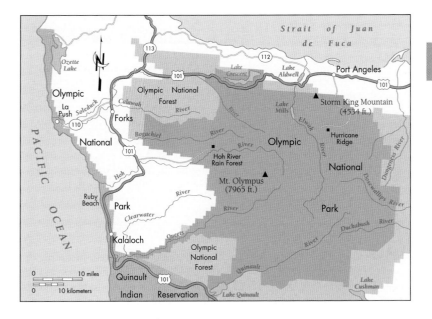

Olympic National Park

Olympic National Park, in the heart of the Olympic Peninsula, is a diversely beautiful corner of the country, combining features of Maine's rocky coast and the snowcapped peaks of the Rocky Mountains with the unique rainforests covering the park's Pacific coastal valleys. The rugged, million-acre landscape, ranging from rocky shores to impassably dense forests, resisted exploitation and development until the turn of the 20th century, when local conservationists persuaded Teddy Roosevelt to declare most of the peninsula a nature preserve, a movement that eventually resulted in the establishment of Olympic National Park in 1939.

There are no roads and few trails across the peninsula, so you have to choose your points of entry depending upon what you want to see. The different areas of Olympic National Park are covered in the following pages, but the most popular part of the park is Hurricane Ridge, which rises high above Port Angeles and offers great views of the silvery peaks and the many glaciers that flank them. At the northwestern corner of the park, Lake Crescent sits serenely amidst the forests and peaks, while on the western slopes, the temperate rainforests of the usually wet and rainy river valleys hold some of the world's largest trees, all draped with a thick fabric of mosses. At the edge of the peninsula, the almost completely undeveloped Pacific Ocean coastline, added to the park in 1953, offers miles of sandy beaches and rocky headlands, littered only with driftwood logs and vibrant tidepools.

Ferries to Victoria, British Columbia

From Port Angeles, a pair of ferries—the **MV** *Coho,* carrying cars and passengers ($33 per car one-way, plus $9 per person; 360/457-4491); and the faster, summer-only **Victoria Express**, carrying passengers only ($12.50 per person each way; 360/452-8088 or 800/633-1589)—shuttle across the water to and from pretty Victoria, the provincial capital of British Columbia, one of Canada's most popular destinations. Both ships leave Port Angeles at the middle of the attractively landscaped waterfront, and arrive very near the center of Victoria, making for a great day-trip from either place. At the Port Angeles dock there's a very helpful information center packed with maps and brochures on Victoria and the rest of B.C., or you can call **Tourism Victoria** at 800/663-3883.

Places to stay in Port Angeles vary. You'll find highway motels, including the **Quality Inn Uptown** ($80–160; 360/457-9434), at 101 E. 2nd Street, and the **Red Lion** ($90–150; 360/452-9215), on the water at the foot of Lincoln Street. There are also many characterful B&Bs; for details of these, and for more general information, phone the **North Olympic Peninsula Visitors and Convention Bureau** at 800/942-4042, or stop by the Port Angeles **tourist office** (360/452-2363)at the ferry terminal, 121 E. Railroad Avenue.

Hurricane Ridge

High above Port Angeles, **Hurricane Ridge** provides the most popular access to **Olympic National Park**. A paved road, open year-round during daylight hours, twists and turns 17 miles up a steep 7 percent grade to the mile-high summit, where, on a clear day, you can gape at the breathtaking 360-degree views of mountain, valley, and sea. A summer-only lodge at the crest provides food and drink, and a concession offers ski and snowshoe rentals on winter weekends. Trails lead down into the backcountry, where you're likely to spot marmots, deer, and bald eagles—and if you're lucky, maybe an elk or a mountain lion. Thrill-seeking drivers and mountain bikers may get a kick out of the Obstruction Point Road, a twisting gravel road that continues (without guardrails!) for another eight miles along the crest from the Hurricane Ridge parking lot. Obstruction Point Road ends at a trailhead; drivers will have to turn around. In winter, the snowed-in road becomes a popular cross-country skiing trail.

Apart from the area right around Hurricane Ridge, most of the Olympic National Park backcountry is fairly wet and rugged, and if you plan to camp overnight, be prepared, and be sure to get a **permit** from the Olympic National Park **ranger station** (360/565-3130) in Port Angeles, two blocks south of US-101 on the road up to Hurricane Ridge. This is also the best place to pick up general information on the rest of the park, which extends all the way west to the rainforest areas along the coastal valleys (see below for more).

Lake Crescent

One of the most idyllic spots in the entire Pacific Northwest, the fjord-like **Lake Crescent**, over eight miles long and some 625 feet deep, lies right alongside two-lane US-101, just 20 miles west of Port Angeles. Powerboats are banned, and the placid surface reflects the clouds and surrounding peaks, including 4,534-foot Storm King Mountain; you can rent **rowboats** ($9 an hour) from the Lake Crescent Lodge and float around under your own steam. Also from the lodge, a popular mile-long hike follows a well-maintained nature trail up to the delicate cascade of 90-foot **Marymere Falls,** while along the north shore an abandoned railroad grade is open to hikers and mountain bikers.

Incomparably situated along US-101 on the lake's southeast shore, **Lake Crescent Lodge** ($80–160, open April–Oct. only; 360/928-3211) was originally built in 1916 and has been hosting visitors ever since. Fairly rustic rooms are available in the old lodge, which also has a cozy dining room; more modern accommodations are available in the adjacent cabins and

> In the forested hills above US-101, **Sol Duc Hot Springs Resort** ($90 and up; 360/327-3583) has family-friendly cabins and a restaurant set around a swimming pool and natural hot spring ($11 for non-guests).

motel, though the whole place is booked solid on summer weekends, so reserve as soon as you can. Another nice place to stay is the **Log Cabin Resort** (360/928-3325), three miles north of US-101 on the northeast shore, with motel rooms and waterfront A-frame cabins from around $100 a night in summer.

Hwy-112: Strait of Juan de Fuca

The Strait of Juan de Fuca, the narrow inlet that links the open Pacific with Puget Sound and divides the United States from Canada, was named for the Greek sailor (real name: Apostolos Valerianus) who first mapped it while working for the Spanish Crown in 1610. On a clear day, you can get some great views across the strait from Hwy-112, which runs along the shore from US-101 all the way to the tip of the Olympic Peninsula at Neah Bay. Though it looks like a great drive on the map, Hwy-112 is a very narrow and winding road with some surprisingly steep hills and thick woods that block much of the view, all of which (in addition to the plentiful logging trucks) can make it less than ideal for bicycling or even a scenic drive.

The fish-headed, human-legged, sneaker-wearing statue that stands outside the Clallam Bay General Store is known alternately as "The Running Fish," "Gill," and "The Fishman," for obvious reasons.

Neah Bay and Cape Flattery

From the crossroads Sappho on US-101, Hwy-113 leads north, linking up with Hwy-112 on a long and winding 40-mile detour through **Clallam Bay** (home of the nearly-world-famous *Running Fish* statue) to **Cape Flattery,** the northwesternmost tip of the continental United

States. The highway is paved as far as the town of **Neah Bay**, a tiny and somewhat bedraggled community that's the center of the Makah Indian Reservation. Salmon fishing, both by Makah and by visitors, is about the only activity here, though the tribe does have the impressive and modern **Makah Museum** (daily in summer, closed Mon. and Tues. the rest of the year; $5; 360/645-2711), one of the best anthropological museums in the state. Most of the displays are of artifacts uncovered in 1970, when a mudslide revealed the pristine remains of a 500-year-old coastal village—the Pompeii of the Pacific Northwest. Other galleries display finely crafted baskets, a full-scale longhouse complete with recorded chants, and a whaling canoe from which fearless Makah harpooners would jump into the surf and sew up the jaws of dying whales, to keep them from drowning and sinking. If you want a special souvenir, the museum gift shop displays and sells a variety of high-quality arts and crafts made by Makah people.

> In the late 1990s, as part of an effort to preserve tribal traditions and instill pride in younger Makah, the **Makah tribe** resumed small-scale hunting of migratory gray whales, which they voluntarily ceased when the whales became endangered a century ago. Though the hunting was largely ceremonial, the news raised the hackles of wildlife organizations, which filed lawsuits and staged loud protests to prevent whales from being killed.

The Hwy-112/113 route twists along the rocky and wooded shore of the Strait of Juan de Fuca, but reaching the actual cape itself isn't difficult. From Neah Bay, the well-maintained western half of the Cape Loop Road winds along the Pacific to a parking area which gives access to a trail that brings you to the top of a 65-foot-high cliff overlooking the crashing surf and offshore **Tatoosh Island.** On a sunny day it's a gorgeous vista, but if the weather's less than perfect (which it often is) your time would be much better spent inside the Makah Museum.

Forks

Bending southwest along the banks of the Sol Duc River, US-101 passes through miles of green forests under ever-gray skies to reach **Forks** (pop. 3,120), the commercial center of the northwestern Olympic Peninsula. Named for its location astride the Sol Duc and Bogachiel Rivers, Forks is a die-hard lumber town grappling with the inevitable change to more ecologically sustainable alternatives, mainly tourism. Visitors come to fish for steelhead during the late-summer runs, to beachcomb along the rugged coast, or to visit the remarkable rainforests of Olympic National Park to the southeast. The main attraction in Forks proper is the quirky **Timber Museum** (daily; donations; 360/374-9663), on US-101 on the south edge of town, packed with handsaws, chainsaws, and other logging gear as well as antique cooking stoves and displays telling the town's characterful history. There's also a forest-fire lookout tower perched outside the upper floor gallery.

> The old-growth forests of Olympic National Park provide prime habitat for the northern spotted owl, an endangered species whose preservation has sparked heated debate throughout the Pacific Northwest.

With four gas stations and four motels, Forks is not a metropolis by any stretch of the imagination, but it does offer the best range of services between

Port Angeles and Aberdeen. **Sully's** at 220 N. Forks Avenue is a good burger stand on US-101 at the north end of town, and there are also two Chinese and two Mexican places, plus the great smoked salmon sandwiches at the **Smoke House Restaurant.** Stay at the **Forks Motel** ($50–90; 360/374-6243), at 351 S. Forks Avenue, or a more peaceful B&B, the **Miller Tree Inn** ($75–175; 360/374-6806), which sits on 30 acres at 654 E. Division Street, five blocks east of Forks's solitary stoplight.

South of Forks along US-101, **Bogachiel State Park** has over 100 forested acres of very nice campsites (with showers!) along the Bogachiel River. Sites are first-come, first-served, and cost around $10 for tents, $15 for RV hookups (360/374-6356).

For more-complete information, contact the Forks **visitors center** (800/443-6757), next to the Timber Museum.

Hoh River Rainforest

If you have time to visit only one of the lush rainforest areas of Washington's northwest coast, head for the **Hoh River Rainforest,** 12 miles south of Forks then 18 miles east along a well-signed and well-paved road. Not only is this the most easily accessible of these incredibly lush, old-growth areas, the Hoh River forest is also among the least disturbed, with a thick wet blanket of vibrant green ferns, mosses, and lichens covering every inch of the earth at the foot of massive hemlocks, cedars, and towering Sitka spruce. Displays inside the **visitors center** tell all about the forest's flora and fauna. There's also a wheelchair-accessible nature trail and a wide range of hiking trails, including the quickest access to the icy summit of 7,965-foot Mt. Olympus, 22 miles away in the glacier-packed alpine highlands at the heart of the park.

> If you're very lucky, you might spy one of the rare Roosevelt elk, for whose protection Olympic National Park was established; if you're unlucky, you might also come face-to-face with a mountain lion, which can be dangerous but generally avoids contact with humans.

The closest services to the Hoh River Rainforest are in Forks, but budget travelers may want to take advantage of the $12-a-night bunks at the amiable **Rain Forest Hostel** (360/374-2270), 23 miles south of Forks along US-101 (between milemarkers 169 and 170), midway between the Hoh River Rainforest and the coast at Ruby Beach.

Kalaloch and the Pacific Beaches

Looping around the northern Olympic Peninsula, US-101 finally reaches the coast 27 miles south of Forks at **Ruby Beach,** where a series of wave-sculpted sea stacks frame a photogenic, driftwood-strewn cove. From Ruby Cove, US-101 runs south through the wild coastal section of Olympic National Park,

Ruby Beach

which is almost always foggy and cool, even when the weather's sunny and hot just a mile inland. While almost the entire coast south from Cape Flattery is protected within the national park, this is the only easily accessible stretch. Parking areas along the highway, numbered from Beach 6 to Beach 1 north to south, give access to 20 miles of generally deserted beach, backed by rocky bluffs and packed with tidepools and an incredible variety of flotsam and jetsam.

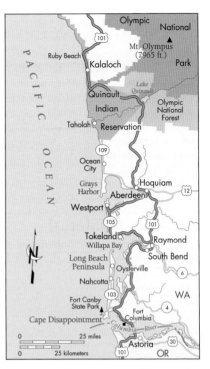

At the southern end of this short but sweet stretch of coastline, between Beach 2 and Beach 3, 25 miles north of Lake Quinault, **Kalaloch Lodge** ($120–250; 360/962-2271) is a modern resort, with a coffee shop and a nice restaurant overlooking a picturesque cove. There's also a gas station, a summer-only **ranger station** across US-101, and an oceanside **campground** just to the north.

South of Kalaloch (pronounced KLAY-lock), US-101 turns inland along the northern border of the massive Quinault Indian Reservation, not reaching the Pacific again until the mouth of the Columbia River.

Lake Quinault

Spreading in a broad valley at the southwest corner of Olympic National Park, **Lake Quinault** offers lush rainforest groves within a short walk or drive of most creature comforts. The lake has served for decades as a popular resort destination—cabins, lodges, and stores dating from the 1920s line the southern shore, just outside the park boundary—and the old-growth forests here have survived intact, though the naked tracts of clear-cut timber along US-101 north and south of the lake give a good sense of what the area might have looked like had Teddy Roosevelt and friends not stepped in to protect it around the turn of the 20th century.

From US-101 at Hoquiam, Hwy-109 runs west and north along the Pacific Ocean through a series of fishing ports and beach resorts to the heavily logged lands of the **Quinault Indian Reservation**.

The best first stop is the USFS **ranger station** (360/956-2400) on the south shore, where you can get details of the many excellent hikes in the Lake Quinault area, and pick up a map of the guided driving tour around the lake, including the location of the many record-size trees. The roughly four-mile-long **Quinault Loop Trail** winds on a paved path from the ranger station along crashing Cascade Creek up through an old-growth rainforest of alders and bigleaf maples, whose leaves grow upwards of 12 inches across. Midway along, the trail crosses a raised wooden boardwalk through a fecund cedar swamp, then drops down again along another creek before returning by way of the lakeshore.

The nicest place to stay, right next to the ranger station, is historic **Lake Quinault Lodge** ($80–180; 360/288-2900), with a rustic but spacious lobby opening onto lakefront lawns and a very nice restaurant, the Roosevelt Room, serving gorgeous grilled salmon, oysters, and other local delicacies. Besides offering comfortable and reasonably priced accommodations and very good food, the nearby **Rain Forest Village** (360/288-2535 or 800/562-0948), at the east end of the lake, also holds the **World's Largest Spruce**, a 191-foot giant.

Grays Harbor: Hoquiam and Aberdeen

The Olympic Peninsula is cut off from the southern Washington coast by the spade-shaped bay of **Grays Harbor,** named for the early American sea captain and explorer, Robert Gray. Long the state's prime lumber port, Grays Harbor still processes huge piles of trees, but in many ways what's most interesting is the contrast between the two towns here, Hoquiam and Aberdeen.

At the western end of Grays Harbor, tidy **Hoquiam** (pop. 9,097; kind of rhymes with requiem) celebrates its lumber-based history with an annual Logger's Playday bash, complete with ax-throwing and tree-climbing competitions, the second weekend in September. The rest of the year, get a feel for the bygone days of the lumber industry at red-shingled **Hoquiam's Castle** (daily; $4; 360/533-2005), on a hillside three blocks off US-101 at 515 Chenault Avenue, a 20-room mansion built in 1897 by a local lumber baron. If you like the looks of it, you can stay overnight in a B&B room for $90–150. Another grand old timber-magnate mansion now houses the **Polson Museum** (Wed.–Sun; $2; 360/533-5862), on US-101 at 1611 Riverside Drive. It's devoted to the history of logging.

East of Hoquiam along the Chehalis River at the head of Grays Harbor, **Aberdeen** (pop. 16,600) is much more heavily industrialized and thus has been even harder hit by the continuing downturn in the Northwest timber industry. The downtown area has more than a few rough edges, but it also holds one of the more high-profile of the state-sponsored efforts to move from timber to tourism:

> Grunge-rock hero and Nirvana lead singer **Kurt Cobain**, who killed himself at age 28, grew up in and around Aberdeen.

The *Lady Washington* is a replica of one of the first American ships to explore the West Coast.

Grays Harbor Historical Seaport (daily; $3; 360/532-8611), a half mile east of US-101. A reconstruction of American explorer (and Grays Harbor namesake) Capt. Robert Gray's ship, the *Columbia Rediviva,* can be toured—when she's not off on one of her regular "goodwill" cruises. The original ship was the first American vessel to visit the area, way back in 1788, and the replica was completed here in 1989 to celebrate the Washington State centennial. When the *Columbia Rediviva* is in port, you can hop on board for an unforgettable trip ($40).

Across the river from Aberdeen, the region's largest employer, a Weyerhaeuser pulp mill, looms alongside US-101 through the inappropriately named town of Cosmopolis, before the road cuts inland toward Raymond and Willapa Bay.

Heading east from Aberdeen, US-12 cuts inland, passing the Satsop nuclear power plant and one of the most heavily logged areas in Washington before joining the I-5 freeway at the state capital of Olympia. Midway along, the **Grays Harbor HI Hostel** in Elma (360/482-3119) has $14-a-night beds (and a small golf course!).

Hwy-105: Westport and Tokeland

Between Hoquiam and Raymond, US-101 cuts inland from the coast, while an alternative route, Hwy-105, loops to the west past miles of cranberry bogs (and occasional wild elk) through the salmon-fishing town of **Westport.** Once called "The Salmon Capital of the World," and still a prime place for watching migrating gray whales, Westport is a very busy port—and one of Washington's few good surfing and surf-kayaking beaches. The whole place really comes to life during the Labor Day seafood festival. For details on Westport or anywhere along Hwy-105, contact the very helpful **visitors center** (360/268-9422 or 800/345-6223).

One of coastal Washington's best-loved destinations, the seaside red-cedar Dunes Restaurant south of Westport in Grayland, burned to the ground in 1997—with no insurance, and therefore no chance of rebuilding. Now, the only

real place nearby with anywhere near comparable character is the 120-year-old **Tokeland Hotel** (360/267-7006), off Hwy-105 on the north shore of Willapa Bay, with $65 rooms and a very nice dining room.

Willapa Bay: Raymond and South Bend

One of the country's prime oystering grounds, **Willapa Bay** is sheltered from the Pacific by the Long Beach Peninsula and fed by the Nasalle, Willapa, and North Fall Rivers. There are very few towns or even villages on this stretch of US-101, which winds past tidal marshes, cattle ranches, and some engaging roadside sculptures of people canoeing, bird-watching, cycling, fishing, and generally enjoying the Great Outdoors. The landscape is also marked by extensively clear-cut forests—which billboards proclaim to be "America's first industrial tree farm," giving dates of harvest, planting, and re-harvest, on a roughly 40-year cycle.

If the weather's right for a picnic, fresh shellfish can be had at bargain prices—by the bite or by the half gallon—from the area's many producers, wholesalers, and roadside stands; look for them all along US-101. Willapa Bay produces nearly one-sixth of all the oysters consumed in the United States.

At the northeast corner of Willapa Bay, on the south bank of the Willapa River, stand two towns that jointly embody the natural resource–based history and economy of the Pacific Northwest: **Raymond** (pop. 2,975) has the lumber mills, while **South Bend** (pop. 1,807) calls itself the "Oyster Capital of the World"—a claim supported by the piles of oyster shells flanking the road outside packing houses like Bendickson's Seafood on the north side of town. South Bend's other claim to fame is its landmark **Pacific County Courthouse** (Mon.–Fri. only), which since 1910 has loomed like a mini–Taj Mahal on a hill just east of US-101. Step inside for a look at the 30-foot stained-glass dome above the rotunda, and wander through the lushly landscaped park next door.

If you want to stretch your legs, Raymond and South Bend are linked by a nice walking and cycling path, which follows an old railroad right-of-way along the Willapa River.

Long Beach Peninsula

On the western side of Willapa Bay, the **Long Beach Peninsula** stretches for 28 miles of hard-packed sandy beaches along the roiling Pacific Ocean. Away from the few small towns, beaches and breakers abound along here, and you won't have any problem finding peace and solitude. The center of activity on the Long Beach Peninsula is the town of **Long Beach,** two miles west of US-101, with a wanderable collection of crafts galleries and souvenir shops, and one of the coast's best B&Bs, the historic **Shelburne Inn** ($125–185; 360/642-2442), in the Seaview neighborhood at Pacific Way (aka Hwy-103, the main road) and 45th Street. The Shelburne also houses a friendly pub and a very good res-

Toll-free **hiking and camping information** for Washington's state parks is available by calling 800/233-0321.

taurant, **The Shoalwater,** rated by many as the best on the Washington coast. At the other end of the taste range, Long Beach is also the home of the "World's Largest Frying Pan," which hangs on a rack in front of the one-of-a-kind **Marsh's Free Museum,** a totally tacky (and wonderfully kitsch) collection of postcards, peep shows, and old-time arcade games on Pacific Way near 10th Street.

The rest of the peninsula is quite quiet, dotted with cranberry bogs and historic fishing and oystering towns. In **Nahcotta**, a dozen miles north of Long Beach, **The Ark** (360/665-4133) is another of Washington's most highly regarded restaurants, and you can stay overnight at the cozy **Moby Dick Hotel and Oyster Farm** ($75–120; 360/665-4543), at 25814 Sandridge Road. Just north, **Oysterville** is the peninsula's oldest community, with some nifty historic homes dating back to the 1850s. The peninsula comes to an end in the north at **Leadbetter Point State Park**, a great place for watching gulls, hawks, eagles, and migratory seabirds passing through on the Great Pacific Flyway.

For further information on the Long Beach Peninsula, contact the **visitors bureau** (360/642-2400 or 800/451-2542) at the US-101/Hwy-103 junction.

"World's Largest Frying Pan"

Cape Disappointment

The high headland marking the place where the Columbia River finally merges into the Pacific Ocean, **Cape Disappointment** was named by the early explorer Capt. John Meares, who in 1788 incorrectly interpreted the treacherous sandbars offshore to mean that, despite reports to the contrary, there was neither a major river nor any mythical Northwest Passage here.

A pair of statues sculpted by chain saws in a small state park, three miles west of the US-101 bridge across the Columbia River, marks the site where Lewis and Clark camped in December 1805 before heading south in search of better weather—which is about the only thing they never found on their epic trip.

Besides the grand view of the raging ocean, the best reason to visit the cape is to tour the small but worthwhile **Lewis and Clark Interpretive Center** (daily; free; 360/642-3029), incongruously built atop a WW II–era artillery emplacement a short walk from the end of the road. On November 7, 1805, after five months and more than 4,000 miles, the explorers finally laid eyes on the Pacific from this point; they sat through nine days of continuous rain before fleeing south to Oregon. Displays inside the museum give the overall context for their journey of discovery, walking you through the different stages of their two-year round-trip. The small "Cape D" **lighthouse** stands atop the 60-foot-high cliff, a half-mile walk from the museum.

The entire area around the cape is protected from development within **Cape Disappointment State Park,** and the nearest services—gas stations and a couple of cafés—are in nearby **Ilwaco,** a small rough-and-tumble fishing port two miles west of US-101.

Southeast of Cape Disappointment, toward the Oregon border, US-101 winds along the north bank of the Columbia River. Along with good views of the river's five-mile-wide mouth, the road passes through the quaint town of **Chinook,** home of "Washington's First Salmon Hatchery," which started here way back in 1893.

OREGON

Rarely losing sight of the Pacific Ocean during its 365-mile jaunt along the Oregon coast, US-101 winds past rockbound coast, ancient forests, and innumerable towns and villages. While the region also has its share of strip towns and places where the timber boom went bust, the beach loops, historic restorations, and more state parks per mile than any place in the country soften its few hard edges. Every 20 miles or so, you'll pass through attractive, if moderately touristy, towns populated by at most a couple thousand people, but as a general rule it's the mileage between these hamlets that explains why most people visit: To take in one of the most dramatic meetings of rock and tide in the world.

Starting in the north along the Columbia River at historic **Astoria,** one of the oldest settlements in the western United States, the route winds along the ocean past the very different beachfront hamlets of **Seaside** and **Cannon Beach** before edging slightly inland through the rich dairy lands of **Tillamook County.** Midway along, the popular vacation spots of **Lincoln City, Newport,** and **Florence** form the most developed corridor along the coast, but it's still easy to reach unpeopled stretches, especially at the remarkable **Oregon Dunes** stretching to the south. The dunes end abruptly at the heavily industrial port of **Coos Bay,** beyond which the natural beauty returns with a string of state parks and the diverse coastal towns of **Bandon, Port Orford, Gold Beach,** and **Brookings.**

Astoria

The oldest American city west of the Missouri River, **Astoria** (pop. 9,813) is an upbeat mix of lovingly preserved past and busy contemporary commerce. Houses perched atop high hills overlook the Columbia River, creating a favorite backdrop for Hollywood movies. Despite its picturesque appearance, Astoria supports an active commercial fishing fleet and dozens of tugboats guide tankers and

container ships across the treacherous sand-bars. As more than a few Astoria bumper stickers proclaim, "We Ain't Quaint." Founded by and named after fur-trade magnate John Jacob Astor in 1811, Astoria protected the tenuous American claim to the Pacific coast until the opening of the Oregon Trail brought substantial settlement. By the turn of the 20th century, Astoria was still Oregon's second-largest city, but the downturn in both salmon fishing and logging since the end of World War II has caused an economic decline which, as always, town officials look to tourism to overcome.

By state law, there is no self-service gasoline in Oregon; all stations have attendants who pump the gas for you. There's no sales tax, either.

US-101 crosses across the Columbia River on the toll-free, high-level Astoria Bridge, completed in 1966, which drops you at the west end of the downtown waterfront. To get a sense of the lay of the land, follow the signs along 16th Street up Coxcomb Hill to the **Astoria Column** (daily 8 AM–dusk; $1) for a view of the Columbia meeting the ocean, the coastal plain south to Tillamook Head, and the snowcapped Cascade Range (including, on a clear day, Mt. St. Helens) on the eastern horizon. A mosaic chronicling local history is wrapped like a ribbon around the column, tracing the many significant events in the town's past. A spiral staircase climbs to the top.

Back downtown at 441 8th Street, **Flavel House** (daily in summer; $5) is a red-roofed Queen Anne–style Victorian showplace restored as an elegantly furnished museum of Astoria's first millionaire, Columbia River pilot George Flavel. A half mile east, near the foot of l7th Street on the north side of waterfront Marine Drive, the **Columbia River Maritime Museum** (daily; $8; 503/325-2323) displays a large and very impressive collection that tells the story of the lifeblood of this community: the Columbia River.

To find out about local issues and current events on the northern Oregon coast, pick up a copy of the excellent Daily Astorian newspaper (50 cents), or tune to commercial-free KMUN 91.5 FM for NPR news and diverse programming.

Fortify yourself at one of the many good seafood places along the water, starting at the ever-popular **Columbian Cafe** (503/325-2233), 1114 Marine Drive, where chef Uriah Hulsey prepares all sorts of ultra-fresh food in an impossibly cramped galley kitchen, just a countertop away from his legions of foodie fans. Meals are massive yet reasonably priced, so be sure to arrive with an appetite; breakfast and lunch are served daily, dinner Wednesday–Saturday. Other Astoria eating options include the casual **Cafe Uniontown** or the pub-like **Ship Inn,** both under the bridge at Marine Drive and 2nd Street. Gourmets might want to visit adjacent **Josephson's Smokehouse** (503/325-2190), at l06 Marine Drive, to sample the delicious array of smoked salmon, which is prepared on the premises and sold all over the country.

To absorb a full portion of Astoria's addictive ambience, stay the night at the riverview **Crest Motel** ($55–120; 503/325-3141), three miles east of town along US-30 at 5366 Leif Erickson Drive, or at one of Astoria's handful of nice

B&Bs like the 1890s **Astoria Inn** ($80–100; 503/325-8153), at 3391 Irving Avenue. For detailed listings or further information, contact the **Astoria Chamber of Commerce** (503/325-6311), located at 111 W. Marine Drive.

Fort Clatsop

In the conifer forests six miles south of Astoria and three miles east of US-101, the **Fort Clatsop National Memorial** (daily; $5 per car; 503/861-2471) is a credible reconstruction of the encampment Lewis and Clark and company constructed during the winter of 1805–06. A range of exhibits in the visitors center, a full-scale replica of the 50- by 50-foot log fort, and summertime living history reenactments help conjure the travails of that time. The expedition spent three miserable months near here, mingling occasionally with the native Clatsop and Chinook tribes but mostly growing moldy in the incessant rain and damp while being bitten by fleas, sewing new moccasins, and making salt in preparation for the return journey across the continent.

Fort Stevens, off US-101 on the way to Fort Clatsop, was the only continental U.S. fortification bombed during WW II, sustaining a shelling from a Japanese submarine on June 21, 1942.

Gearhart

Just north of boisterous Seaside, but a world away in character and ambience, the tiny town of **Gearhart** (pop. 995) was the home of influential chef and cookbook author James Beard. Beard's culinary legacy lives on in the **Pacific Way Bakery and Cafe** (503/738-0245), a half mile west of US-101 at 601 Pacific Way, which offers the coast's best coffees and croissants, along with four-star lunches and dinners. Like many places along the Oregon coast, it's closed Tuesday and Wednesday

Seaside

Nothing along the Oregon coast prepares you for the carnival ambience of downtown **Seaside** (pop. 5,900), Oregon's oldest seafront resort. Ben Holladay, who built the place in 1873, included a racetrack, zoo, and plush hotel to lure

The End of the Lewis and Clark Trail

Portlanders to ride his rail line to the beach. Come during spring break, or on a weekend during July or August, and join the hordes wandering among the saltwater-taffy stands and video-game arcades along Broadway, or cruising the concrete boardwalk (called The Prom) along the beach.

Where Broadway meets the beach, a small traffic circle known locally as The Turnaround is marked by a statue and a sign proclaiming Seaside "The End of the Lewis and Clark Trail." South of here, between Beach Drive and The Prom, is a replica of the Lewis and Clark **salt cairn**, where the explorers boiled seawater nonstop for seven weeks to produce enough salt to preserve meat for their return trip east.

For food, sample the clam chowder at **Dooger's** (503/738-3773), at 505 Broadway.

A half mile north of downtown, housed in a wood-shingled old motor court on the banks of the Necanicum River, the **HI Seaside Hostel** (503/738-7911), at 930 Holladay Drive, has $19-a-night dorms, $46 private rooms, canoes and kayaks, an espresso bar—and nightly movies. There are dozens of inexpensive motels and a handful of B&Bs; for listings and other information, contact the **Seaside Visitors Bureau** (503/738-3097 or 888/306-2326), at 7 N. Roosevelt Drive.

This part of the Pacific Coast marks the beginning of our **Oregon Trail** route, which runs east across the country along a combination of US-6, US-20, and US-26. Coverage of the route begins on page 532; Portland, just over an hour or so inland from Seaside and Cannon Beach, is covered on pages 536–537.

Ecola State Park

Just north of Cannon Beach, a mile south of the junction between US-101 and US-26 from Portland, the rainforested access road through **Ecola State Park** (day use only; $3 per car; 503/436-2844) leads you to one of the most photographed views on the coast: Looking south you can see Haystack Rock and Cannon Beach with Neahkahnie Mountain looming above them. Out to sea, the sight of **Tillamook Rock Lighthouse** to the northwest is also striking. Operational from 1881 to 1957, the lighthouse is now used as a repository for the ashes of people who've been cremated.

The rest of Ecola State Park protects a series of rugged headlands stretching for nine miles along the coast, with many forested hiking trails including some of the most scenic portions of the Oregon Coast Trail System. The park also marks the southernmost extent of Lewis and Clark's cross-country expedition. Clark and a few other members of the Corps of Discovery expedition traversed the area in search of supplements to their diet of hardtack and dried salmon. The word "ecola" means whale in the Chinookan tongue and was affixed to this region by the Lewis and Clark expedition, who found one of these leviathans washed up on a beach. They happily bought 300 pounds of tangy whale blubber from local Indians, but these days you'd better bring your own lunch to picnic atop bluffs with sweeping views of the rock-strewn Pacific.

South of Cannon Beach at **Oswald West State Park**, a half-mile trail winds beneath the highway through an ancient forest to driftwood-laden Short Sands Beach and Smuggler's Cove.

Cannon Beach

Unlike many Oregon coast towns, **Cannon Beach** (pop. 1,588) is hidden from the highway, but it's one place you won't want to miss. Though it's little more than a stone's throw south of boisterous Seaside, Cannon Beach has long been known as an artists' colony, and while it has grown considerably in recent years thanks to its popularity as a weekend escape from Portland, it retains a rustic atmosphere. The view from the top of **Tillamook Head,** which rises

Haystack Rock

1,200 feet above the sea between Seaside and Cannon Beach, was memorialized by explorer William Clark as "the grandest and most pleasing prospect" he had ever beheld.

At the start of summer, Cannon Beach hosts the largest and most enjoyable **sand castle competition** on the West Coast, with some 10,000 spectators and as many as 1,000 participants turning out with their buckets and spades. But in terms of traditional "tourist attractions," there's not a lot to do, but Cannon Beach is an unbeatable place in which to stop and unwind, or to take long walks along the seven-mile strand and then retreat indoors to the many good galleries, cafés, and restaurants. For breakfast or brunch, fill up on eggs Benedict at the **Lazy Susan Cafe** (closed Tues. and Wed. in winter; 503/436-2816), at 126 N. Hemlock Street; they also serve a stupendous array of ice cream at their "scoop shop" up the street. Reasonably priced rooms near the beach and town can be found at the **McBee Motel Cottages** ($69–129; 503/436-2569), at 888 S. Hemlock.

South of Cannon Beach, the Beach Loop, an extension of Hemlock, runs along a spectacular grouping of volcanic plugs, notably 235-foot-high **Haystack Rock.**

For further information, or details on the annual events and festivals, contact the Cannon Beach **visitors bureau** (503/436-0434), at 201 E. 2nd Street.

Neahkahnie Mountain and Manzanita

South of Cannon Beach, US-101 rises 700 feet above the Pacific. Nowhere else along the Oregon coast does the roadbed sit so high above an ocean view. Soaring another thousand feet above you on the other side of this WPA-built stretch of highway is **Neahkahnie Mountain.** Of the dozen marked scenic overlooks and hiking trails in the next 20 miles, your itinerary should include **Neahkahnie Wayside,** which looks southward at the Nehalem Valley and the ocean between Manzanita and Cape Meares. South of the mountain, and thus spared much of the stormy coastal weather (annual rainfall hereabouts averages 80 inches), is the upscale resort town of **Manzanita,** where you'll find one of the coast's best restaurants, the **Blue Sky Cafe** (Wed.–Sun. dinner only, no credit cards; 503/368-5712), at 154 Laneda Avenue. The multi-ethnic, seasonally changing seafood specialties here can be very expensive, but are worth it for celebrating special occasions—like a road trip along the Oregon coast.

South of Manzanita, **Nehalem Bay State Park** (503/368-5154) has a large campground with hundreds of sites and plenty of hot showers. US-101 continues through a series of small towns before winding inland past the sloughs and dairy country along Tillamook Bay.

Tillamook

With cows outnumbering people by more than two to one, **Tillamook** (pop. 4,352) sprawls over lush grasslands at the southern end of Tillamook Bay. Its motto, "Cheese, trees, and ocean breeze," conjures a clear sense of the place. Tillamook (a Salish word meaning land of many waters) is dominated by

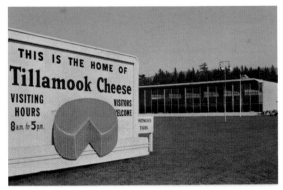

Tillamook Cheese Factory

the **Tillamook Cheese Factory** at the north end of town, one of the busiest tourist draws in the state. Inside, a self-guided tour with informational placards traces Tillamook cheese-making from the last century to the present, and a glassed-in observation area lets you watch the stuff being made and packaged.

Tillamook's other odd attraction is east of US-101 and south of town. One of the world's largest wooden structures—300 feet wide, 1,100 feet long, and nearly 200 feet tall—has been preserved as the **Tillamook Air Museum** (daily; $9.50 adults, under 7 free; 503/842-1130), wherein the story of the WW II surveillance blimps built and maintained here by the U.S. Navy is recounted. There are also displays about these dirigible craft as well as other vintage airplanes, a theater, and a restaurant, all making for a fascinating and unusual stop. This used to be one of a pair of hangars, but the other one burned down.

Three Capes Loop

US-101 veers inland for 50 miles between Tillamook and Lincoln City, the next sizeable town south. If time and weather are on your side, head west along the coast via the well-signed, 35-mile-long **Three Capes Loop.** Running northwest from Tillamook, the loop reaches the mouth of Tillamook Bay at **Cape Meares State Park,** which has a restored 1890 lighthouse and an oddly contorted Sitka spruce known as the Octopus Tree.

Seven miles south of Tillamook, a turnoff east follows a bumpy, one-mile access road leading to the highest waterfall in Oregon's Coast Range, 266-foot **Munson Creek Falls.** From the parking area at the end of the road, a short trail leads to this year-round cascade.

Heading south through the coastal villages of **Oceanside** and **Netarts,** the loop proceeds through dairy country until it climbs onto the shoulder of **Cape Lookout,** where a small sign proclaiming Wildlife Viewing Area marks the beginning of a 2.5-mile trail that leads through an ancient forest to the tip of the cape, 100-plus feet above the water. Besides the coastal panorama, in winter and spring this is a prime place to view passing gray whales. From the trailhead, the middle path leads to the cape, while others to the left and right lead down to the water. **Cape Lookout State Park** (800/551-6949) has the area's most popular campground, with hot showers and other creature comforts costing around $18 a night per campsite, less in winter.

The Oregon coast's most famous promontory, **Cape Kiwanda**, sees some of the state's wildest surf battering the sandstone headland. Across from the cape is **Haystack Rock**, a 327-foot sea stack a half mile offshore. Along the beach south of the cape, surfers ride waves while fisherfolk skid their small dories along the sands every afternoon: a sight worth hanging around to see. The southernmost settlement on this scenic alternative to US-101 is neighboring **Pacific City**, where two great places to eat, the **Grateful Bread Bakery** (503/965-7337) and **The Riverhouse** (503/965-6722), sit beachside on Brooten Road.

Lincoln City

The most overdeveloped section of the Oregon coast stretches for miles along US-101 through **Lincoln City** (pop. 7,437), seven miles of strip malls, outlet stores, motels, and fast-food franchises. With more than 1,000 oceanside rooms, Lincoln City does offer some of the coast's cheapest lodging, especially in the off-season when sign after sign advertises rooms for as low as $25 a night. Apart from cheap rooms, with so much scenic splendor nearby there's no great reason to stop—unless you're a cheeseburger fanatic, in which case you ought to stop by the **Dory Cove** (541/994-5180), a marshland shack at 5819 Logan Road off US-101 near **Road's End State Park**. They also make great pies, as many as a dozen different kinds every day, so bring an appetite.

South of Lincoln City, 2.5 miles east of US-101, the **Drift Creek Covered Bridge** is the oldest of some 50 such structures in the state.

Five miles northeast of Lincoln City, just east of US-101 on Hwy-18, the **Otis Cafe** (541/994-2813) immortalizes American road food, offering excellent waffles and other breakfast treats along with epicurean lunches and berry pies for dessert. It's open for breakfast and lunch daily, plus dinner Thursday–Sunday.

Seven miles south of Lincoln City, a sign announces the **Salishan Lodge** (541/764-3600 or 800/452-2300), a beautifully landscaped rustic resort with good off-season value packages (three nights for $239), a five-star dining room, and a surprisingly affordable coffee shop, **The Sun Room**. Down the hill across US-101, **Siletz Bay** is a birdwatcher's paradise.

Depoe Bay

Depoe Bay has an appeal, but so much of its natural beauty is obscured from the highway by gift shops or intruded upon by traffic that you've got to know where to look. In his book *Blue Highways*, William Least Heat-Moon wrote "Depoe Bay used to be a picturesque fishing village; now it was just picturesque." While it's true that most of the commercial fishing is long gone, you can still park your car along the highway and walk out on the bridge to watch sportfishing boats move through the narrow

Depoe Bay was originally known as Depot Bay, named after a local Siletz Indian who worked at the local U.S. Army depot and called himself **Charlie Depot**.

45TH PARALLEL HALFWAY BETWEEN THE EQUATOR AND NORTH POLE

channel to what the *Guinness Book of World Records* rates as the world's smallest navigable harbor. South of the bridge is another record-setter, the Oregon coast's largest secondhand bookstore, the **Channel Bookstore** (541/765-2352).

The **Sea Hag** restaurant (541/765-2734), on US-101 in downtown Depoe Bay, is a time-tested seafood place, as is **Whale Cove Inn** (541/765-2255), two miles south of town overlooking a picturesque inlet formerly used by bootleggers during Prohibition.

Cape Foulweather and the Devil's Punchbowl

Between Depoe Bay and Newport, the roadside scenery along US-101 and the parallel "old road," now signed as the Otter Crest Loop, is dominated by miles of broad beaches and sandstone bluffs, including the 453-foot headland of **Cape Foulweather**, named by Capt. James Cook and offering a 360-degree coastal panorama. (The Otter Crest Loop has frequently been closed by slides and reconstruction efforts, but you can reach it from many access roads.)

Farther south, midway between Depoe Bay and Newport, the aptly named

Devil's Punchbowl gives a ringside seat on a frothy confrontation between rock and tide. In the parking area you'll find a small lunch café (a branch of Newport's **Mo's**) graced by a chair where "The Boss" (singer Bruce Springsteen) sat on June 11, 1987.

Newport

Another old fishing community turned tourist nexus, **Newport** (pop. 9,532) started in the 1860s on the strength of sweet-tasting Yaquina Bay oysters, which were in demand from San Francisco to New York City and are still available at local restaurants. Oysters, crabs, and clams, along with sea otters, sharks, and seabirds, are the stars of the show at the large and modern **Oregon Coast Aquarium** (daily; $12; 541/867-3474), south of Newport across the Yaquina Bay Bridge. The aquarium includes an aquatic aviary, where sea lions, tufted puffins, and other shorebirds cavort in a simulat-

The coast and inland forests along the Siletz River near Newport were the primary location of the **Ken Kesey** novel (and Paul Newman film) *Sometimes a Great Notion*.

ed rockbound coastal habitat, and over 40,000 square feet of similarly eco-friendly exhibits.

On the north side of the US-101 bridge over Yaquina Bay, turn onto Hubert Street and head for the bayfront, where boatyards and fish-packing plants service a working harbor. Though it's still the state's second-largest fishing port, much of Newport's bayfront has been consumed by souvenir shops, a wax museum, a Ripley's Believe It or Not, and other tourist traps. But you'll find the original **Mo's** (541/265-2979), a locally famous seafood restaurant, at 622 Bay Boulevard; it and its annex across the street are the area's best dining values.

Dining options can also be found at **Nye Beach,** a mélange of old-fashioned beach houses and destination resorts north of the harbor; just look for signs on the western side of US-101. **Don Petrie's** (541/265-3663), serves excellent Italian food at 613 NW 3rd Street. Nye Beach is also home to the bohemian **Sylvia Beach Hotel** ($80–180; 541/265-5428), 267 NW Cliff Street, *the* place to stay in Newport for anyone of literary bent. If you can't afford the private rooms—with decor evocative of different authors, including a scary Edgar Allan Poe room based on "The Pit and the Pendulum"—there are dormitory bunk beds for around $25 a night. All rates include breakfast.

> The old-growth forests of the **Drift Creek Wilderness** east of Waldport are prime nesting areas for the endangered northern spotted owl.

The very helpful **Newport Information Center** (800/262-7844), at 555 SW Coast Highway, has complete accommodations listings and other useful information.

Waldport

If you want to avoid lines and general tourist bustle, **Waldport** is a nice alternative to the resort towns surrounding it. Tourism is low-key here, and you can still sense the vestiges of the resource-based economy, a by-product of the town's proximity to rich timber stands and superlative fishing. Stop along US-101 at the **Alsea Bay Bridge Interpretive Center** (541/563-2002) for interesting exhibits on coastal transportation and the local Alsea tribe, as well as a telescope trained on waterfowl and seals in the bay. The center sits at the south foot of the modern span that, in 1991, replaced the historic (circa 1936) art deco–style bridge. From the north end of the bridge, you can follow Hwy-34 seven miles upstream to the **Kozy Kove Kafe** (541/528-3251), a floating restaurant with good food and bucolic riverside ambience.

Four miles south of Waldport, **Beachside State Park** (800/551-6949) has a very popular campground, with hot showers, RV hookups, even a laundromat.

Yachats

On the way into **Yachats** (pop. 617; pronounced YA-hots), beach loops on either side of the Yachats River give a sense of why the area is called "the gem of the Oregon coast." It's a great place to wander and get lost and found again, but one place to catch up on life hereabouts is on US-101 at 4th Street, where the **New Morning Coffeehouse and Bookstore** has good espresso and a (sometimes) sunny outdoor deck-cum-sculpture garden. For the past 25 years, **Leroy's Blue Whale** (541/547-3399), on US-101 at 580 Coast Highway, has been serving breakfast, lunch, and dinner every day, featuring fluffy pancakes, fresh chowders, and fine fish-and-chips.

The word "cottage" is a popular lodging label here, usually referring to a moderately priced, self-contained cabin or duplex with kitchen. On US-101 between Waldport and Yachats are a half dozen different cottage complexes, each fronting the beach. **Cape Cod Cottages** ($55–95; 541/563-2106), two-plus miles south of Waldport at 4150 US-101, is a good choice for location and comfort. If you want more than a simple place to spend the night, the **Oregon House** ($75–175; 541/547-3329) on US-101 nine miles south of Yachats has spacious apartment-like rooms, some with fireplaces and ocean views, and all with access to the well-tended grounds and trails leading down the bluffs to a gem of a sandy cove.

Cape Perpetua

For nearly 400 miles along the Oregon coast, US-101 abounds with national forests, state parks, and viewpoints. But unless you have a lifetime to spend here, **Cape Perpetua,** two miles south of Yachats, deserves most of your attention. Stop first at the **Siuslaw National Forest visitors center** (541/547-3289), just east of US-101, for seacoast views, and exhibits on forestry and area history. From the visitors center, trails lead across the highway past wind-bent trees, piles of seashells and other artifacts left behind by native peoples, excellent tidepools, and two rock formations, Spouting Horn and the Devil's Churn. During stormy seas, both shoot huge spouts of foam into the air. The friendly folks at the visitors center can also point you toward Cape Perpetua's small, summer-only **campground** ($12), which has bathrooms but no showers or hookups.

You can reach the top of 800-foot-high Cape Perpetua itself by following a two-mile-long road, marked by Cape Perpetua Viewpoint signs and leaving US-101 100 yards or so north of the visitors center. Once atop the cape, walk the **Trail of the Whispering Spruce,** a half-mile loop around the rim of the promontory that yields, on a clear day, 150-mile views of the Oregon coast from a rustic, WPA-built stone observation point.

Heceta Head and the Sea Lion Caves

Halfway between Cape Perpetua and Florence, a small bridge just south of Carl Washburne State Park marks the turnoff to **Heceta Head Lighthouse,** perhaps the most photographed beacon in the United States. Built in 1893, it was named for the Spanish mariner who is credited with being the first European to set foot in the region. You'll have to be content with gazing at it across the cove from a small but rarely crowded beach, unless you stay at the quaint old lighthouse keeper's quarters, restored as an unforgettable B&B ($150 and up; 541/547-3696).

Farther along US-101, 10 miles north of Florence, traffic slows to a stop at the gift shop that serves as the entrance to **Sea Lion Caves** (daily; $8). You can ride an elevator down to America's largest sea cave and the only mainland rookery for the Steller sea lion. Fall and winter offer the best times to see (and smell!) these animals. They are visible for free from a viewpoint 100 yards up US-101.

Florence

If first and last impressions are enduring, **Florence** is truly blessed. As you enter the city from the north, US-101 climbs high above the ocean; coming from the south, travelers are greeted by the graceful **Siuslaw River Bridge**, perhaps the most impressive of a half dozen WPA-built spans designed by Conde McCullough and decorated with his trademark Egyptian obelisks and art deco stylings. Unfortunately, the rest of town, visible from US-101, is a bland highway sprawl of motels, gas stations, and franchised restaurants.

The best part of Florence, **Old Town,** is just upstream from the bridge along the north bank of the river. Here, among Bay Street's three blocks of interesting boutiques and galleries, you'll find a number of cafés and seafood restaurants. Old Town Florence is also home to the very welcoming **Edwin K. B&B** ($100–150; 541/997-8360) at 1155 Bay Street, a lovely white Craftsman-style home built in 1914 by one of the town's founders.

"Dune Country": Oregon's Sahara

For nearly 50 miles south of Florence, US-101 has an extensive panorama of oceanfront dunes. Though the dunes are often obscured from view by forests, roadside signs indicate access roads to numerous dunescapes on both sides of the highway. Coming from the north, the first of these access points is **Honeyman State Park,** 10 miles south of Florence, where rhododendrons line a half-mile trail leading to a 150-foot-high dune overlooking a mirage-like lake. A longer trek, leaving from the very pleasant **Tahkenitch Lake campground** (reservations essential; 800/452-5687), gives a more in-depth look at the dunes' diverse flora and fauna, including swans and occasional black bears. Perhaps the best introduction is at **Umpqua Dunes,** nine miles south of the visitors center in Reedsport. From **Eel Creek Campground,** a 1.5-mile trail leads across small marshes and conifer groves en route to the sea, negotiating lunar-like dunes soaring 300–500 feet—some of the tallest in the world.

Before setting out on any extended exploration, your first stop should be the USFS-run **Oregon Dunes visitors center** (541/271-3611) at the junction of US-101 and Hwy-38 in **Reedsport,** along the Umpqua River midway between Florence and Coos Bay at the heart of the dunes. The helpful rangers can provide detailed information on hiking and camping throughout the park. Reedsport itself has a line of motels and burger joints—**Don's Diner,** on US-101 at 2115 Winchester Avenue (541/271-2032), has legions of fans—and you'll find one more interesting option in the **Gardiner Guest House** (541/271-4005), which offers comfortable B&B rooms in a restored Victorian home at 401 Front Street.

Giant rhododendrons and tumble-down shacks which rent out dune buggies and ATVs line US-101 between Florence and Coos Bay. One of the best of these rental places is **Sandland Adventures** (541/997-8087), a mile south of Florence's Siuslaw River bridge, which also offers thrilling, sand-in-your-mouth guided dune buggy tours.

Coos Bay

Even if you race right through, it's quite apparent that **Coos Bay** (pop. 15,374), once the world's largest lumber port, retains a core of heavy industry. Though many of the big mills have closed, you can still watch huge piles of wood chips, the harbor's number-one export, being loaded onto factory ships in the harbor east of US-101. The chips are sent to Asia where they're turned into low-grade paper. You can also get a sense of Coos Bay's seagoing heritage by visiting the tiny, church-run **Seamen's Center,** a block west of US-101 at 171 N. Broadway, where old salts mingle with foreign sailors and make model ships almost every evening. The handy Coos Bay **visitors bureau** (541/269-0215 or 800/824-8486), at 50 Central Avenue, has maps and information on the entire "Bay Area" region.

Behind the Coos Bay visitors bureau, a monument remembers the region's favorite son, middle-distance runner **Steve Prefontaine,** *who electrified the athletic world before his sudden death at age 24 in 1974. There's also an annual 10K memorial run every September.*

Big breakfasts, eclectic but inexpensive lunches and dinners, great pies, and a good range of microbrews are served at **The Blue Heron** (541/267-3933), at 100 Commercial Avenue, across from the visitors bureau. There's no shortage of easy-to-find lodging, including **Motel 6** ($45–65; 541/267-7171) on US-101 at 1445 N. Bayshore.

Shore Acres State Park

The historical antecedents for Coos Bay port development were laid a century ago by the Simpson Lumber Company, whose ships transported Oregon logs around the world. The ships returned with seeds that were planted in the Simpson estate's garden, 12 miles west of Coos Bay via the Cape Arago Highway, three miles beyond the busy commercial and sportfishing port of **Charleston.** Though the Simpson house burned to the ground in 1923, the 750-acre gardens are still a floral fantasia, now open to the public as **Shore Acres State Park** (daily 9 AM–dusk; $3 per car). Besides the formal gardens, which are illuminated during the Christmas holiday season, there's an observation tower above wave-battered bluffs and a trail down to a delightful beach.

On the way to Shore Acres from Coos Bay is **Sunset Bay State Park,** *Oregon's best swimming beach. Beyond Shore Acres is* **Cape Arago State Park,** *complete with tidepools and seals on offshore rocks.*

Bandon

There's no sharper contrast on the Oregon coast than the difference between industrial Coos Bay and earthy **Bandon** (pop. 2,833), 23 miles to the south. Here, in the **Old Town** section along the banks of the Coquille River, are several blocks of galleries, crafts shops, and fine restaurants, marked by a gateway arch off US-101. Start a tour of Old Town at the corner of 1st and Baltimore, where Big Wheel Farm Supply houses the **Bandon Driftwood Museum** (daily; free). The combination of

Bandon Lighthouse

sculpted tree roots and fertilizer displays gives a good sense of Bandon's back-to-the-land, hippie ethos. A more academic introduction to the town and region can be had at the new and improved **Coquille River Museum** (Mon.–Sat., plus Sun. in summer; $2; 541/347-2164), at 270 Fillmore Street. Its exhibits on area history, cranberries, and local color are artfully done, and the building on US-101 is easy to find, so be sure to stop. South of town from 1st Street, a **Beach Loop** runs along a ridge overlooking a fantastic assemblage of coastal monoliths.

For fish-and-chips along the waterfront, the **Bandon Fish Market** (541/347-4282), at 249 1st Street, is cheap and cheerful; for more sit-down fare and a view of the lighthouse, head to **Bandon Boatworks** (541/347-2111), 275 SW Lincoln Avenue.

Outside of town, the exclusive (but open to the public) new **Bandon Dunes Golf Resort** (golf $225/round, rooms $250 and up; 541/347-4380 or 888/345-6008) has been drawing raves from golfers and well-heeled vacationers alike. Designed to preserve the "natural" landscape in the style of Scottish "links" courses rather than the anodyne green swathes that characterize most country club courses, Bandon Dunes also offers select accommodations and a nice restaurant.

> South of Bandon and 11 miles north of Port Orford, **Cape Blanco** is considered—by Oregonians, at least—the westernmost point of land in the contiguous United States. Named by early Spanish explorers for the white shells encrusting the 245-foot cliff face, the cape is also the site of Oregon's oldest (circa 1870) and highest lighthouse.

Port Orford and Humbug Mountain

Pastoral sheep ranches, cranberry bogs, berry fields, and Christmas tree farms dominate the 25-mile stretch south of Bandon, but as you pull into **Port Orford** (pop. 1,025), you'll notice a huge volcanic plug abutting the crescent-shaped shoreline. Known as **Battle Rock,** it's where early settlers fought off a party of hostile Indians; the rock is most impressive from the harbor below. Due to the southwest orientation, which subjects the harbor to turbulent winds and constant waves, fishing boats have to be lowered into the water by crane.

A nice place to stay in Port Orford is the **Home by the Sea B&B** ($90–120; 541/332-2855 or 800/480-2144), at 444 Jackson Street, within walking distance to town along a stunning stretch of coastline.

Six miles south of Port Orford you'll come to **Humbug Mountain,** whose 1,756-foot elevation flanks the west side of the highway. It's the coast's highest peak rising directly off the beach, and its steep contours and tree-covered slopes impart an eerily beautiful quality to the light on this section of US-101. The mountain's name was bestowed by prospectors who found that tales of gold deposits here were just "humbug."

> People who keep track of these things say that tiny Port Orford is the "Most Westerly Incorporated City in the Continental United States," as well as the rainiest place on the Oregon coast.

Prehistoric Gardens

On the west side of the highway, midway between Port Orford and Gold Beach, you'll come across one of the Oregon coast's tackiest but most enduring and enjoyable tourist traps, the **Prehistoric Gardens** (daily; $7 adults, under 3 free; 541/332-4463). Standing out like a sore thumb on this otherwise unspoiled stretch of US-101, a collection of brightly colored, more or less life-sized dinosaur sculptures inhabits the evocatively lush green forest. Since 1953, when amateur paleontologist E. V. Nelson sculpted his first concrete *T. rex,* two dozen more have been added to the forest menagerie.

Gold Beach

Gold Beach was named for the nuggets mined from the area's black sands during the mid-19th century, but despite its name this is one coastal town where the action is definitely *away* from the beach. The **Rogue River** defines the northern city limits and is the town's economic raison d'être. During salmon season, Gold Beach hotels and restaurants fill up with anglers, while **jet-boat tours** of the wild river are also a draw. Along with many other operators hawking their services with billboards next to the highway, **Jerry's Jetboats** ($39; 541/247-4571 or 800/451-3645), by the bridge at the north end of town, takes passengers upstream to the isolated hamlet of **Agness,** where a homespun mountain lodge serves family-style fried-chicken lunches and dinners (though the food is not included in the price of the jet-boat ride). Other trips head farther upstream to the Rogue River rapids and the roadless wilderness areas of the **Siskiyou National Forest;** these cost $50–75.

Southern Oregon's coastal forests yield the increasingly rare **Port Orford cedar,** a very valuable, fragrant, lightweight but strong wood popular for use in Japanese home construction.

Oceanview rooms are available at **Ireland's Rustic Lodges,** on US-101 at 1120 S. Ellensburg Avenue ($60–100; 541/247-7718). For a more memorable visit, try the **Tu Tu Tun Lodge** ($90–250; 541/247-6664 or 800/864-6357), 96550 North Bank Rogue. Set on a hill above the Rogue River, seven miles upstream from the coast, this upscale fishing lodge (pronounced ta-TWO-tun) has plushly rustic rooms and a great restaurant.

Mt. Emily, just east of Brookings, was bombed by a submarine-launched Japanese seaplane in September 1942. Though the Japanese plans to ignite the entire coastline in a massive forest fire fizzled, the attack weakened a short-lived secession movement by southern Oregonians and Northern Californians to establish a new state called **Jefferson**.

Samuel Boardman State Park

Between Gold Beach and Brookings, US-101's windy, hilly roadbed is studded with the cliffside ocean vistas, giant conifers, and boomerang-shaped offshore rock formations of **Samuel Boardman State Park.** The park covers most of the "Fabulous 50" miles between the two towns, and all of the above-mentioned features come together at **Natural Bridges Cove,** just north of the Thomas Creek Bridge, the highest bridge on the coast north of San Francisco's Golden Gate. Despite being signed, this turnout is easy to miss because, from the highway, it appears to be simply a parking lot fronting some trees; from the south end of the lot, however, a short trail through an old-growth forest leads to a viewpoint several hundred feet above three natural rock archways standing out from an azure cove.

South of the bridge, just north of suburban Brookings, one final piece of nature has been preserved at **Harris Beach State Park,** across US-101 from the Oregon Welcome Center. Here you can walk down to a driftwood-laden beach and look out at numerous bird-infested islands.

Brookings

The drive through **Brookings's** malled-over main drag offers only fleeting glimpses of the Pacific, and after the last 350-plus miles of coastal Oregon's scenic splendor, the final few miles south to California are somewhat anticlimactic. Just over the border, however, is Redwood National Park, truly one of the West Coast's great places.

CALIFORNIA

Stretching along the Pacific Ocean for roughly a thousand miles from top to tail, the California coast includes virgin wilderness, the cutting edge of cosmopolitan culture, and the full spectrum in between. For almost the entire way, coastal roads give quick and easy access to the best parts, with panoramic views appearing so often you'll simply give up trying to capture it all.

Starting in the north, the green forests of the Pacific Northwest continue well beyond the state border, forming a mountainous seaside landscape that lasts until the edge of metropolitan San Francisco. Along this stretch you'll find a number of old logging and fishing towns, varying from the burly blue-collar likes of **Eureka** and **Crescent City** to the upscale ambience of **Mendocino,** in and amongst endless acres of redwood forest.

At the approximate midpoint of the California coast sits **San Francisco,** deservedly ranked among the world's favorite cities. The 100 miles of coast stretching south from San Francisco hold numerous remnants of the Spanish and Mexican eras, exemplified by the town of **Monterey** and the beautiful mission at **Carmel.** Beyond here is another stretch of wild coastline, the rugged country of **Big Sur.**

Beyond the southern edge of Big Sur, opulent **Hearst Castle** marks the start of what most people consider Southern California, the rivers and trees of the north giving way to golden beaches, grassy bluffs, and considerably denser populations. A pair of very pleasant small cities, Midwestern-feeling **San Luis Obispo** and ritzy **Santa Barbara,** make excellent stops in themselves, smoothing the transition into the environs of **Los Angeles,** the unwieldy megalopolis that, seen from the I-5 freeway that links Los Angeles and **San Diego,** seems like one monstrous, 100-mile-long suburb. While it's true that the natural beauty that brought so many people to Southern California in the first place is increasingly endangered, some lovely, almost untouched places remain, hidden away but within easy access of the fast lane. We've pointed them out; enjoy them while they last.

Jedediah Smith Redwoods State Park

The northernmost of the great redwood groves, **Jedediah Smith Redwoods State Park** covers nearly 10,000 acres of virgin forest along the banks of the Smith River. Stretching east of US-101, and most easily accessible from US-

The Smith River and Jedediah Smith Redwoods State Park were named in memory of the legendary mountain man **Jedediah Strong Smith**, who in 1826 at the age of 27 led the first party of Americans overland to California.

199, the park offers over 20 miles of usually uncrowded hiking trails through the pristine wilderness, and is considered by many to be the most perfect of all the redwood forests. One of the most enjoyable trails leads through **Stout Grove,** past the park's tallest tree and a number of summertime swimming holes along the Smith River.

The park is jointly managed by the state and federal governments, and you can get full hiking and camping information from the **ranger station** (707/464-6101) along US-199 at the main entrance to the park, four miles east of US-101. There's also a good **campground** (800/444-7275) with hot showers.

Crescent City

The county seat and largest city in Del Norte County, **Crescent City** (pop. 4,006) is best treated as a base from

Outside Crescent City, California's most violent long-term criminals are kept behind bars in the state-of-the-art **Pelican Bay State Prison,** built in 1990.

which to explore the surrounding wilderness. The foggy weather that helps the redwoods thrive makes the city fairly depressing and gray, and what character it developed since its founding in 1853 has been further eroded by storms; a giant tidal wave, caused by the 1964 earthquake off Alaska, destroyed nearly the entire city.

Crescent City includes the usual motels and restaurants, like the **Beacon Burger** (707/464-6565), at 160 Anchor Way. There's one unique spot 10 miles north of town: the **Ship Ashore** (707/487-3141), a gift shop, restaurant, and motel along US-101, marked by a grounded ship.

Crescent City does have the headquarters for **Redwood National Park**

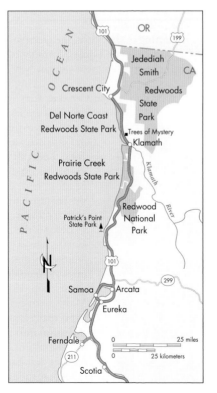

(707/464-6101); a block east of US-101 at 1111 2nd Street, this is the best source of information for southbound travelers.

Del Norte Coast Redwoods State Park

Spreading south from the Jedediah Smith redwoods, **Del Norte Coast Redwoods State Park** runs along the Pacific Ocean (and US-101) for about 10 miles, containing more than 6,000 acres of first- and second-growth redwoods as well as brilliant blooms of rhododendrons, azaleas, and spring wildflowers. Del Norte also protects miles of untouched coastline, the best stretch of which is accessible from the end of **Enderts Beach Road,** which cuts west from US-101 just north of the park entrance. From here, a 30-mile trail follows the coast to Prairie Creek.

The state park area is bounded on the south by an undeveloped section of **Redwood National Park.** Amongst the trees, the **HI Redwood Hostel** (707/482-8265), 12 miles south of Crescent City and two miles north of the Trees of Mystery at 14480 US-101, is housed in a historic farmhouse and offers cozy dormitory accommodations and a few private rooms for about $15 per person for members, $18 nonmembers.

Trees of Mystery and Klamath

Hard to miss along US-101, thanks to the massive statues of **Paul Bunyan and Babe the Blue Ox** looming over the highway, the **Trees of Mystery** (daily 8 AM–dusk; $12; 707/482-2251) are literally and figuratively the biggest tourist draws on the Northern California coast. Along the "Tall Tales Trail," chainsaw-cut figures, backed by audio-taped stories,

stand in tableaux at the foot of towering redwoods. There's also a Sky Trail gondola lifting passengers up into the treetop canopy, a huge gift shop, and a small free museum of Native American art and artifacts. Across the highway, **Motel Trees** (707/482-3152) has standard rooms from $60 and a coffee shop.

Along the banks of the mighty Klamath River, four miles south of the Trees of Mystery, the town of **Klamath** (pop. 650) is a brief burst of highway sprawl, supported by anglers who flock here for the annual salmon runs. At the south end of town, drive through the **Tour-Thru Tree** ($2), then cross the Klamath River on a bridge graced by a pair of gilded cement grizzly bears.

All the land along the Klamath River is part of the extensive **Hoopa Valley Indian Reservation,** which stretches for over 30 miles upstream from the Pacific Ocean.

Prairie Creek Redwoods State Park

The largest of the trio of north coast redwood parks, **Prairie Creek Redwoods State Park** is best known for its large herd of endangered **Roosevelt elk,** which you can usually see grazing in the meadows along US-101 at the center of the park, next to the main **ranger station** (707/464-6101). A new freeway carries US-101 traffic around, rather than through, the Prairie

Creek redwoods; to reach the best sights, detour along the well-signed Newton B. Drury Scenic Parkway, which follows Prairie Creek along the old US-101 alignment through the heart of the park.

Another elk herd can be spotted among the coastal dunes at **Gold Bluffs Beach**, which stretches for 11 miles through untouched wilderness; there's a primitive **campground** and trails leading from US-101, or you can follow Davison Road northwest from US-101, three miles south of the ranger station. Apart from the elk, Prairie Creek offers the usual mix of old-growth redwood trees, which here, more than in the other parks, mingle with dense growths of Sitka spruce and Douglas firs to form a near rainforest of greenery.

Redwood National Park

Established in 1968, and later enlarged at a total cost of over $500 million, **Redwood National Park** protects some 100,000 acres of redwood forest, including the 30,000 acres previously preserved in the adjacent Smith, Del Norte, and Prairie Creek State Parks. To be honest, apart from the adjacent state parks, the trees preserved here aren't

The groves of giant trees in Redwood National Park were used as a location for the Star Wars film *Return of the Jedi*, in which the characters cruised through the forest on airborne cycles. More recently, Patrick's Point played a starring role in the first *Jurassic Park*.

by any means the oldest, largest, or most beautiful; in fact, much of the federal parkland is second- or third-growth timber, clear-cut as recently as the 1960s.

Though redwoods are the fastest-growing softwoods on earth—growing three to five feet a year when young—the groves here are rather disappointing compared to those in nearby areas, and serve more as an environmental buffer zone than a tree-lover's pilgrimage site.

That said, Redwood National Park does hold two special sights, including the **Lady Bird Johnson Grove**, on Bald Hill Road a mile east of US-101, where the new park was dedicated in 1969. Ten miles further up this road, and a long hike beyond that, the Tall

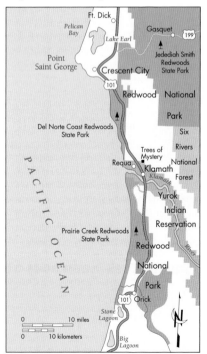

Trees Grove holds the **world's tallest tree,** the 370-plus-foot Libbey Tree, whose trunk measures over 14 feet across.

At the south end of the park, enjoy Teutonic breakfasts at the German-run **Rolf's Park Cafe,** attached to the handy **Prairie Creek Motel** ($70; 707/488-3841), which for over 15 years has made a good budget-travelers' base for exploring Redwood National Park and environs. The roadside-strip town of **Orick** stretches south toward the coast, where the main Redwood National Park **visitors center** (707/464-6101) stands at the mouth of Redwood Creek.

Patrick's Point State Park

If your idea of heaven is sitting on a rocky headland listening to the roar of the Pacific while watching the sunset or looking for passing gray whales, you won't want to pass by **Patrick's Point State Park.** Three different 200-foot-high promontories at the heart of the park provide panoramic views, while the surrounding acres hold cedar and spruce forests (no redwoods), open pastures bright with wildflowers, great tidepools, a wide dark-sand beach, and two **campgrounds** (800/444-7275) with hot showers. There's also preserved and restored remnants of a Yurok village; obtain further information and camping reservations from the **visitors center** (707/677-3570).

Continuing south, US-101 becomes a four-lane freeway along the ocean to Arcata and Eureka, but the old US-101 alignment winds along the cliff tops between Patrick's Point and the small town of Trinidad. Along this road you'll find some nice older motels, like the **Patrick's Point Inn** (707/677-3483 or 800/354-7006) at 3602 Patrick's Point Drive, just a half mile from the park entrance, with oceanside rooms from around $60 a night. Also here is the excellent **Larrupin Cafe** (707/677-0230), at 1658 Patrick's Point Drive, which serves up bountiful portions of very fresh all-American food in a friendly, homey ambience—it's California cuisine without the snooty pretense you sometimes find farther south. It's open for dinner only, nightly except Tuesday and Wednesday, and is cash-only; two can dine very well for around $60.

Arcata

The most attractive and enjoyable town on the far north coast of California, **Arcata** (pop. 16,651) makes the best first (or last, depending upon the direction you're traveling) overnight stop south of the Oregon border. The presence of Humboldt State University's campus on the hills above US-101 accounts for the town's youthful, non-conformist energy, especially in the cafés, bookstores, bars, and crafts shops that surround the lively **Town Plaza,** two blocks west of US-101 at 9th and G Streets, incongruously graced by palm trees and a statue of President McKinley. The *Utne Reader* recently rated Arcata as "the most enlightened small town in California," and spending even a little time in this vibrant, cooperative Ecotopia may make you wonder whether or not you really do have to race back to the big-city 9-to-5 grind.

The author **Bret Harte** was run out of Arcata by angry townspeople in 1860, after writing an editorial in the local paper criticizing a massacre of a local Wiyot tribe.

You can admire the town's many elaborate Victorian-era cottages, hunt wild mushrooms, clamber over sand dunes, or hike in the redwoods; afterwards, relax with a cup of tea or, better yet, a soak in a hot tub at homey **Cafe Mokka,** the coast's only combo sauna and espresso bar, at 5th and J Streets (707/822-2228). Microbrews flow from the taps of Arcata's amiable bars, many of which feature live music; for food, drink, and entertainment all under one roof, try the **Humboldt Brewery** (707/826-2739), just off the plaza at 856 10th Street. For a complete selection of foodstuffs and supplies, and more insight into the local community, head to the large and stylish **North Coast Co-op,** at 8th and I Streets uphill from the plaza.

For a place to stay, the centrally located **Hotel Arcata** ($60–90; 707/826-0217 or 800/344-1221) is right on the plaza at 708 9th Street, or you can take your pick of the usual motels along US-101.

Eureka

Inland from Arcata along scenic US-299, the town of **Willow Creek** claims to be the heart of "Bigfoot Country," boasting a large statue of the furry beast to prove it. US-299 continues east over the coast range through the beautiful Trinity Alps to **Weaverville,** well-preserved site of a mid-1850s gold rush, before linking up with I-5 at Redding.

Evolving into a lively artists' colony from its roots as a fairly gritty and industrial port, **Eureka** (pop. 26,128) was well known to fur-trappers and traders long before it became a booming lumber and whaling port in the 1850s. Thanks to the lumber trade, Victorian Eureka grew prosperous, building elaborate homes, including the oft-photographed but closed to the public **Carson Mansion** along the waterfront at 2nd and M Streets, two blocks west of US-101. Along with dozens of well-preserved Victorian houses, Eureka has done a fine job of finding new uses for its many ornate commercial buildings, most of which have been preserved to house art galleries, cafés, and restaurants in what's now called **Old Town,** a half-dozen blocks between the waterfront and US-101. This historic downtown quarter has a number of good places to eat and drink, including **Ramone's Bakery** (707/445-2923) at 209 E Street, the pub-like **Cafe Waterfront** (707/443-9190) at 1st and F Streets, and the popular **Sea Grill** (707/443-7187), a block from US-101 at 316 E Street. Another good place is the no-frills **Seafood Grotto** (707/443-2075), south of Old Town along US-101 at 6th and Broadway, whose motto is "We Ketch 'em, Cook 'em, Serve 'em".

Accommodation options range from roadside motels to upscale places like the **Carter House Inn** ($125 and up; 707/445-1390) at 1033 3rd Street, a re-created Victorian manor with spacious rooms and a big breakfast in the morning. For a more authentic Victorian experience, stay at one of California's most delightful B&Bs, the **Elegant Victorian Mansion** ($120 and up; 707/444-3144), at 1406 C Street. A real treasure in a land of nice B&Bs, this magnificently restored 1888 Eastlake-style home has been opulently decorated with real antiques and Bradbury & Bradbury wallpapers by the hospitable Belgian-born innkeeper, Lily Vieyra.

For further information, contact the **Eureka! Humboldt County Convention and Visitors Bureau** (707/443-5097 or 800/346-3482), 1034 2nd Street.

Kinetic Sculpture Race

Arcata's creative community comes alive every Memorial Day weekend for the world-famous Kinetic Sculpture Race, in which participants pedal, paddle, and otherwise move themselves and their handmade vehicles on a multiple marathon across land and sea. Part art, part engineering, and part athletic competition, the kinetic sculpture race is like nothing you've seen before. Beginning midday Saturday and running around the clock until Monday afternoon, a mind-boggling array of mobile contraptions—past winners have included everything from dragons and floating flying saucers to Egyptian pyramids (named "Queen of Denial") and a Cadillac Coupe de Ville—make their way over land, sand, and sea from the town square of Arcata to the main street of Ferndale, twice crossing chilly Humboldt Bay.

Rule Number One of the Kinetic Sculpture Race is that all of the "sculptures" must be people-powered; beyond that, imagination is the primary guide. Many "rules" have developed over the years since the race was first run in 1969, including such pearls as: "In the Event of Rain, the Race Is Run in the Rain," but most of these emphasize the idea that maintaining style and a sense of humor are at least as important as finishing the fastest. Since the Grand Prizes are valued at somewhere around $14.98, racers take part solely "for the glory," but prizes are awarded in many categories: First- and last-place finishers are winners, and the racer who finishes in the exact middle of the pack gets the coveted Medio-Car Award—a broken-down old banger.

Spectators are expected to be active participants, too, so be prepared to shout and scream and applaud the competitors, or even jog or bike or kayak alongside them. There are many great vantage points along the route, but you have to be in the right place on the right day. The Kinetic Sculpture Race begins at noon on Saturday with a pre-race line-up around Arcata's Town Square, from where racers wind along country roads to the sandy Samoa Peninsula before spending the first night in downtown Eureka. Sunday morning the racers head across Humboldt Bay from Field's Landing, then camp out overnight along the ocean. Monday's trials include another water crossing and the muddy mess of the Slimey Slope, culminating in a mad dash down the Main Street of Ferndale surrounded by cheering multitudes. It's all good fun, and a great focus for a visit to this remarkable corner of the world.

For further information, call the Eureka visitors bureau at 800/346-3482.

"Just for the Halibut": racing along Samoa Peninsula

Samoa

Even if you're just passing through, don't miss the chance to visit the busy mill town of **Samoa**, across the bay from Eureka but easily reachable via the Hwy-255 bridge. Follow the signs past the piles of logs and belching mill chimneys to the unique **Samoa Cookhouse** (707/442-1659), built at the turn of the 20th century by the Louisiana Pacific lumber company, which still owns most of the peninsula. Inside the cookhouse, which is packed with logging memorabilia, take a seat at one of the 20-foot-long tables (redwood, of course, covered in checkered oilcloth) and dig into the family-style feast. There are no menus, just huge platters of food at ridiculously low prices.

One unique thing to see in Eureka are the **Romano Gabriel Wooden Sculptures,** displayed in a plate-glass showcase at 315 Second Street. This brilliantly colorful folk-art extravaganza of faces and flowers originally stood in the front yard of local gardener Romano Gabriel, who made them out of discarded packing crates and other recycled materials over a period of some 30 years before his death in 1977.

Ferndale

Well worth the 10-mile detour west of US-101, the historic town of **Ferndale** (pop. 1,382) is an odd fish along the woodsy Northern California coast, a century-old dairy town that would look more at home in middle America. The three-block-long, franchise-free **Main Street** includes a fully stocked general store (the Golden Gait/Gate Mercantile), and whitewashed farmhouses dot the pastoral valleys nearby. Ferndale's diverse history is well-documented inside the **Ferndale Cultural Center** (hours vary; 707/786-4466), off Main Street at Shaw and 3rd Streets, where some of the wacky racers that take part in the annual Kinetic Sculpture Race (see sidebar) are displayed.

Ambling along Main Street is the best way to get a feel for Ferndale, and if you build up an appetite, there are many good places to eat. One of the oldest cafés in the West, **Poppa Joe's** (707/786-4180), is housed in a Victorian storefront at 409 Main Street, while the self-proclaimed "Oldest Hotel" is now a family-friendly Italian restaurant, **Ivanhoe** (707/786-9000), open for dinner only at 315 Main Street.

The area around Ferndale has been hit by numerous earthquakes, including a destructive tremor in April 1992 that registered 6.9 on the Richter scale.

Ferndale is equally well-supplied with places to stay. Right off the heart of Main Street is the clean and tidy **Fern Motel** ($75; 707/786-5000) at 332 Ocean Avenue, while for the full Victorian experience, *the* place to stay (or at least to see) in Ferndale is the lushly landscaped **Gingerbread Mansion** (707/786-4000) at 400 Berding Street, with deluxe rooms in a fabulously ornate home starting around $120 a night. Also nice is the **Shaw House** (707/786-9958), an 1854 American Gothic masterpiece with B&B rooms and bikes for rent at 703 Main Street.

Pick up free walking-tour maps and other visitor information inside the Cultural Center, or contact the volunteer-run **chamber of commerce** (707/786-4477).

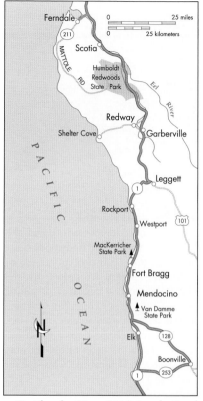

The Lost Coast

Between Ferndale and Mendocino, the main US-101 highway heads inland along the Eel River, but if you have time and a taste for adventure, head west from Ferndale along the narrow, winding Mattole Road, which loops around Cape Mendocino through the northern reaches of the so-called **Lost Coast,** a 100-mile stretch of shoreline justly famous for its isolated beauty. By road, you can only get close to the ocean at a few points—the few miles south of Cape Mendocino, and again at the fishing resort of **Shelter Cove,** west of Garberville—but hikers can have a field day (or week) exploring the extensive coastal wilderness. Some 50 miles of rugged, untouched coastline, packed with tidal pools and driftwood-strewn beaches, have been preserved in a pair of parks, the **Kings Range National Conservation Area** in the north, and the **Sinkyone Wilderness State Park** farther south.

Besides the Hwy. 211/Mattole Road, which makes a 73-mile loop between Ferndale and the Rockefeller Forest section of Humboldt Redwoods State Park, a network of rougher and even more remote routes allows auto access to the Lost Coast, linking the hamlet of Honeydew with coastal Hwy-1 near Rockport. If you do explore this wild (and very rainy) region, take a good map and plenty of food and water, and be careful.

For further information on the Lost Coast, contact the **Bureau of Land Management** (707/825-2300); their office is at 1695 Heindon Road in Arcata.

The Lost Coast area was the site of the first oil wells in California, which were drilled in the 1860s near the town of **Petrolia** but are now long gone.

Scotia

Back along US-101, on the banks of the Eel River midway between the coast and the Humboldt Redwoods, **Scotia** is the only true company town left in California. The Pacific Lumber Company (aka "PALCO") built it and still owns everything, from the two huge mills to the 10 blocks of pastel-painted houses, church, and schools that constitute this little community of about 1,000 people.

Stop first at the small **museum,** housed in the redwood Greek Revival former bank at the center of town, to pick up passes for self-guided **tours** (Mon.–Fri. 7:30 AM–2 PM; free) of the world's largest redwood mill. Following a yellow painted line through the mill at your own pace, you can gawk at (and listen to—it's a noisy business) every stage of the milling process. First, cut logs get de-barked by a powerful jet of water, then laser-guided band saws slice the logs into rough boards, which are turned into finished lumber. A raised catwalk runs through the center of the mill, and signs explain what's happening at each stage.

The one place to stay in town is the rustic **Scotia Inn** ($120 and up; 707/764-5683), which has B&B rooms and a very good restaurant; it's on Main Street, a block from the museum.

Humboldt Redwoods State Park

The protection of the mighty redwood forests of Northern California was made possible not by the state or federal governments but primarily by the efforts of the **Save the Redwoods League,** a private organization that has raised, since its founding in 1918, millions of dollars to buy or preserve over 160,000 acres of redwood forest. To support these efforts, write to 114 Sansome Street, Room 605, San Francisco, CA 94104, or call 415/362-2352.

Sheltering the biggest and best collection of giant coastal redwoods anywhere in the world, **Humboldt Redwoods State Park** is an exceptionally breathtaking corner of an exceptionally beautiful region. Covering 50,000 acres along the Eel River, this is the true heart of redwood country, containing the largest and most pristine expanses of virgin forest as well as some of the largest, tallest, and most remarkable trees.

Even if you're just passing through, be sure to turn onto the amazing **Avenue of the Giants,** 32 miles of old highway frontage between Jordan Creek and Phillipsville. This sinuous old road snakes alongside, and sometimes under, the faster and busier US-101 freeway, which is carried on concrete stilts through the park. At the north end of the park you'll find an impressive collection of trees in the well-marked **Founders Grove,** where a half-mile nature trail leads past the 362-foot-tall, 1,600-year-old **Dyerville Giant,** lauded as the world's tallest tree before it fell during the winter of 1991. West of Founder's Grove, across US-101, the 13,000-acre **Rockefeller Forest** is one of the largest old-growth forests in the world, and includes two of the park's champion trees, each over 360 feet tall and some 17 feet in diameter. In and amongst the natural wonders along the Avenue of the Giants are a handful of man-made ones: The **Eternal Treehouse** in Redcrest and the **Shrine Drive-Thru Tree** in Myers Flat are just two of the many good-natured "tourist traps" in this neck of the woods.

The best source of information on the park is the **visitors center** (707/946-2263), midway along the Avenue of the Giants in **Weott.** There's a pleasant **campground** (800/444-7275) with showers right next door. You may have to drive a ways north (to Ferndale, Eureka, or Arcata) or south (to Garberville) from the park to find a good meal, though there are a few nice places to stay, like the **Redcrest Resort** ($55–75; 707/722-4208), across from the Eternal Treehouse. Midway along the

Avenue of the Giants

The stretch of historic US-101 through the redwood country of Humboldt County, frequently called the "Avenue of the Giants," is lined by pristine groves of massive trees and provides boundless opportunities to come face-to-face with your own insignificance in nature's greater scheme of things. If you tire of this display of natural majesty, or simply want to keep it in context with the modern "civilized" world, you're in luck: Every few miles, amongst the stately trees, you'll come upon shameless souvenir stands selling redwood burl furniture and chainsaw sculptures, as well as wonderfully tacky tourist traps like the "Legend of Bigfoot" or "Hobbittown USA," in Phillipsville. None of these is big or bold enough to detract from the main event—the big trees—and since they've been in operation since the early days of car-borne tourism, they're as much a part of the redwood experience as the trees themselves. Most charge only a few dollars' admission, so there's not a lot to lose.

While you're encouraged to stop at any and all of them—at least long enough to buy a postcard or two—some of the more tried-and-true attractions are the **Trees of Mystery,** marked by huge statues of Paul Bunyan and Babe the Blue Ox along US-101 in Klamath; the One-Log House in Phillipsville, a mobile home carved from a single, 32-foot redwood log; and the Drive-Thru Tree, 13078 Avenue of the Giants (old US-101) in Myers Flat, which wagon-borne travelers drove through more than a century ago. In the south, near the town of Leggett, are two more. One of the best stops in Redwood Country, **Confusion Hill** ($4) is one of those places where water runs uphill and the rules of physics seem not to apply; there's also a little railway train here that chugs uphill to a very nice grove of trees. Finally, at the **Chandelier Drive-Thru Tree,** south of Leggett off old US-101 on Drive-Thru Tree Road, $3 buys you the chance to drive your car through a 315-foot redwood tree, still growing strong despite the gaping hole in its belly.

at the end of Leggett, the "original" Drive-Thru Tree

Avenue of the Giants, the historic **Myers Inn** (707/943-3259) in Myers Flat has B&B rooms from around $125, while farther south the hamlet of Miranda holds the pleasant **Miranda Gardens Resort** ($50–140; 707/943-3011), with motel rooms and rustic cabins.

Garberville and Redway

Since its recurring presence in the national media during the government's high-profile, late-1980s raids on local marijuana plantations, **Garberville** has returned to its previous sleepy self. The US-101 freeway bypasses the town, which stretches for a half-dozen blocks along Redwood Drive, the well-signed business loop off the highway.

Enjoy an early-morning breakfast with the old-time locals at the **Eel River Cafe** (707/923-3783) at 801 Redwood Avenue, or enjoy an espresso and healthy food at the **Woodrose Cafe** (707/923-3191), a block south at 911 Redwood Avenue. Garberville also has all the motels you could want, including the **Motel Garberville** (707/923-2422) at 948 Redwood Drive.

The annual **Reggae on the River** festival, organized by the Mateel Community Center (707/923-3368), attracts top performers and thousands of fans to French's Campground near Piercy every August.

Just west of Garberville on the old highway, **Redway** is worth the short side trip for breakfast, lunch, or dinner at the **Mateel Cafe** (707/923-2030), a health-conscious gourmet haunt along Redwood Avenue at the center of town.

Along US-101, four miles south of Garberville, one of the region's most characterful places is the stately **Benbow Inn** ($100–200; 707/923-2124), a circa 1926 mock Tudor hotel with a nice restaurant offering afternoon tea and scones on a sunny terrace overlooking Lake Benbow.

Leggett: The Drive-Thru Tree

No longer even a proverbial wide spot in the road since the US-101 freeway was diverted around it, **Leggett** marks the southern end of the Humboldt redwoods. At the south end of "town," a mile from the US-101/Hwy-1 junction along the old highway, stands one of the redwood region's most venerable and worthwhile roadside attractions, the "original" **Drive-Thru Tree** (daily 8 AM–dusk; $3). In addition to the famous tree, which had the hole cut through it in the 1930s, there's an above-average gift shop with a broad range of books, postcards, and schlocky souvenirs.

South of Leggett, US-101 runs inland, while scenic Hwy-1 cuts west over the coastal mountains to Mendocino, winding south along the Pacific to San Francisco.

Rockport and Westport

From US-101 at Leggett, Hwy-1 twists up and over the rugged coastal mountains before hugging the coast through the weatherbeaten logging and fishing communities of **Rockport** and **Westport**. The small and informal **Howard Creek Ranch** (707/964-6725) in Westport offers comfortable B&B rooms, an outdoor hot tub, and easy access to the driftwood-laden beach. Farther south, **MacKerricher State Park** protects seven miles of rocky coast and waterfront pine forest; there's also a nice campground (800/444-7275).

Fort Bragg

Cruising south along Hwy-1, the first real town you come to, **Fort Bragg** (pop. 7,026), has a burly, blue-collar edge that comes as something of a shock on the otherwise undeveloped, touristy Mendocino coast. Home to a large Georgia Pacific lumber mill and the region's largest commercial fishing fleet, Fort Bragg takes a mostly no-frills approach to the tourist trade, leaving the dainty B&B scene to its upscale neighbor, Mendocino. However, there are a few down-to-earth places to eat: Very good omelettes and other eggy dishes are available at the appropriately named **Egghead's Restaurant** (707/964-5005) at 326 N. Main Street, while **The Wharf** (707/964-4283), along the Noyo River at 780 N. Harbor Drive, serves good-value seafood dinners. Perhaps the most popular place in town is **North Coast Brewing** (707/964-2739) at 455 N. Main Street, which serves a full range of food and pints of their tasty Red Seal Ale.

Fort Bragg also has many inexpensive (by Mendocino standards, at least) motels, including the **Beachcomber Motel** ($59–199; 707/964-2402), at 1111 N. Main Street, which boasts the coast's only beachfront accommodation options (apart from camping).

For more information on the Fort Bragg/Mendocino area, contact the **North Coast Chamber of Commerce** (707/961-6300 or 800/726-2780), located at 332 N. Main Street.

> From Fort Bragg, the **California & Western Railroad** runs a number of historic steam- and diesel-powered "Skunk Trains" over the mountains to Willits and back. Half-day and full-day trips ($25—35; 707/964-6372) run year-round.

Mendocino

One of the prettiest towns on the California coast (as seen in TV shows like *Murder, She Wrote* and numerous movies), **Mendocino** (pop. 1,100) is an artists' and writers' community par excellence. Now firmly established as an upscale escape for wage-slaving visitors from San Francisco (hence the local nickname, "Spendocino"), the town was originally established as a logging port in the 1850s. In recent years, Mendocino has successfully preserved its rugged sandstone coastline—great for wintertime whale-watching—while converting many of its New England–style clapboard houses into super-quaint B&B inns. The area is ideal for leisurely wandering, following the many paths winding through **Mendocino Headlands State Park,** which wraps around the town and offers uninterrupted views across open fields, heathers, and other coastal flora to the crashing ocean beyond. For field guides, maps, or a look at Mendocino in its

Mendocino

lumbering heyday, stop by the **visitors center** in the historic Ford House (707/937-5804) at 735 Main Street.

Along with its many fine art galleries and bookshops, Mendocino also has a delicious collection of bakeries, cafés, and restaurants. If you're not getting a breakfast at a B&B, come to the hippy-dippy **Mendocino Cafe** (707/937-2422), at 10451 Lansing Street, where locals have been starting their days for nearly 20 years. Lunch or dinner at the **Moosse Cafe** (707/937-4323), at 390 Kasten at Albion Street, is always unforgettable, and for a total splurge, try one of California's best restaurants, **Cafe Beaujolais** (707/937-5614), two blocks from the waterfront at 961 Ukiah Street, which serves a world-famous prix fixe gourmet feast of California cuisine delicacies for dinner, nightly 6–9 PM.

Places to stay in Mendocino are rather expensive but generally delightful. The lovely **MacCallum House** ($150 and up; 707/937-0289), at 45020 Albion Street, includes a beautiful garden, good breakfasts, and a cozy nighttime bar and restaurant. Another place to stay is the circa 1858 **Mendocino Hotel** ($95 and up; 707/937-0511), on the downtown waterfront at 45080 Main Street.

Van Damme State Park

South of Mendocino at the mouth of the Little River, **Van Damme State Park** stretches for five miles along the coastal bluffs and beaches and includes some 1,800 acres of pine and redwood forest. The park's unique attribute is the oddly contorted **Pygmy Forest,** a natural bonsai-like grove of miniature pines, cypress, and manzanita, with a wheelchair-accessible nature trail explaining the unique ecology; the trailhead is four miles east of Hwy-1. There's also a small, very popular campground, and a **visitors center** (707/937-0851) housed in a New Deal–era recreation hall.

Anderson Valley

From Hwy-1 south of Mendocino, Hwy-128 cuts diagonally across to US-101 through the lovely **Anderson Valley,** home to numerous fine wineries (including Husch, Navarro, and Kendall-Jackson) and the *Anderson Valley Advertiser,* one of California's most outspoken local newspapers. Anderson Valley also has its own regional dialect, called "Boontling," combining English, Scots-Irish, Spanish, and Native American words into a lighthearted lingo created, some say, simply to befuddle outsiders—or "shark the bright-lighters," in the local lingo.

To find out more, stop in the valley's tiny main town, **Boonville,** at the "All That Good Stuff" gift shop and ad-hoc information center, alongside the Horn of Zeese coffee shop. Fans of local food and wine will want to cross the highway to the **Boonville Hotel** ($85 and up; 707/895-2210), a wonderful restaurant (dinner only, alas) and wine bar. The historic building has upstairs rooms filled with art and furniture made by local craftspeople. Beer fans can make a pilgrimage east of town to the solar-powered home of the **Anderson Valley Brewing Company** (707/895-BEER), 17700 Hwy-253, where you can sample some of the world's best beers, including the legendary Boont Amber Ale.

Elk

While the coastal scenery is stupendous all the way, one place worth keeping an eye out for on the drive along Hwy-1 is the tiny roadside community of **Elk** (pop. 450), 15 miles to the south of Mendocino. Elk is a wonderful little wide-spot-in-the-road, with what must be one of the oldest and most characterful service stations in California (the Elk Garage, in business since 1901) alongside a great little veggie-friendly breakfast-and-lunch road-food stop: **Queenie's Roadhouse Café** (707/877-3285). Elk also boasts a general store, some quirky cliffside cabins, and a steep trail leading down to the Pacific shore at Greenwood Cove.

Point Arena and Gualala

The southernmost 40 miles of Mendocino coastline are almost totally undeveloped and virtually uninhabited, with green forests and coastal coves as far as the eye can see. The westernmost point here, **Point Arena,** is about five miles northwest of Hwy-1 via Lighthouse Road (the namesake lighthouse, built in 1870, stands 10 stories tall).

15 miles further south, situated at the very southern edge of Mendocino County, the old logging port of **Gualala** (pop. 1,500) has one truly remarkable feature: the Russian Orthodox domes of **St. Orres** (707/884-3303), now a B&B inn and Francophile gourmet restaurant glowing with polished wood and stained glass, above Hwy-1 on the north side of town. Tiny Gualala has at least two more culinary landmarks as well. **Pangaea** (Wed.–Sun. dinner only; 707/884-9669) is one of the coast's most popular new restaurants, serving everything from beefy burgers to crab cakes with Thai curry sauce.

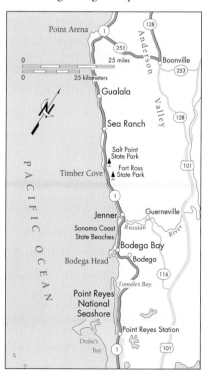

You'll also find inexpensive lodging (rooms for around $75 a night, a real rarity in these parts) and a locally popular restaurant at the **Gualala Hotel** (707/884-3441) right in town. Great **camping** and an incredible coastal panorama can be yours at **Gualala Point Regional Park** (707/785-2377), on the south side of the Gualala River.

Sea Ranch

Midway between Mendocino and the San Francisco Bay Area, located astride the San Andreas Rift Zone, the vacation-home community of

Sea Ranch was laid out in the mid-1960s by an enthusiastic group of then-young architects and planners, including Lawrence Halprin and the late Charles Moore, who hoped to show that development need not destroy or negatively impact the natural beauty of the California coast. Strict design guidelines, preserving over half the 5,000 acres as open space and requiring the use of muted natural wood cladding and other barn-like features, made it an aesthetic success, which you can appreciate for yourself at the **Sea Ranch Lodge** ($160 and up; 707/785-2371), near the south end of the development.

The rest of Sea Ranch, however, is strictly private, which has raised the hackles of area activists, who after years of lawsuits finally forced through a few coastal access trails in the mid-1980s; these, such as **Walk-On Beach** at milepost 56.5, are marked by turnouts along Hwy-1.

Salt Point State Park

The many sheltered rocky coves of **Salt Point State Park** make it ideal for undersea divers, who come to hunt the abundant abalone. Along the five miles of jagged shoreline, pines and redwoods clutch the water's edge, covering some 6,000 acres on both sides of Hwy-1. Though parts of the park were badly burned in a 1994 fire, Salt Point is still a prime place for hiking and camping. For more information, or for a guide to the many remnants of the Pomo tribal village that stood here until the 1850s, contact the **visitors center** (707/847-3221).

One of the few positive effects of cutting down the native redwood forests that once covered the Northern California coast has been the emergence of giant-sized rhododendrons in their place. You'll find the most impressive display at the **Kruse Rhododendron Preserve,** high above Hwy-1 at the center of Salt Point State Park, where some 350 acres of azaleas and rhododendrons, some reaching 15 feet in height, burst forth in late spring, usually peaking around the first week of May.

Fort Ross State Historic Park

Russian Orthodox Chapel at Fort Ross

If you're captivated by California's lively history, one of the most evocative spots in the state is **Fort Ross State Historic Park,** the well-restored remains of a Russian fur-trapping outpost built here in 1812. During a 30-year residency, the Russians farmed wheat and potatoes, traded with native tribes, and trapped local seals and sea otters for their furs, which commanded huge sums on the European market. By 1840, the near-destruction of the sea otter population caused the company to shut down operations and sell the fort to Sacramento's John Sutter, who went bankrupt to finance the purchase. Later, the abandoned fort was badly damaged by the 1906 San Francisco earthquake and later fires, but the state has completed a high-quality restoration and reconstruction project, using hand-hewn lumber and historically accurate building methods to replicate the original barracks and other buildings, including a luminous redwood chapel.

Outside the fort's walls, a modern **visitors center** (daily; $6 per car; 707/847-3286), traces the site's natural, native, and Russian history, and offers information on the park's many fine hiking trails.

Jenner, Guerneville, and the Russian River

South of Fort Ross, Hwy-1 climbs high above the rugged coastline, offering breathtaking vistas of the Pacific Ocean hundreds of feet below. Twelve miles south of Fort Ross, Hwy-1 reaches the low-key resort community of **Jenner** (pop. 300), which stretches along the broad mouth of the Russian River. Harbor seals and sea lions sun themselves on the beach at Goat Rock, houses climb the steep hillsides, and there's also a gas station, a post office (inside a mobile home), and the excellent **River's End** (707/865-2484), which has a range of great food (everything from burgers to Indonesian-spiced seafood) and oceanview tables (inside and outside, depending on the weather).

Bohemian Grove, the world's most exclusive men's club, covers 2,500 acres of redwood forest just south of the Russian River outside the village of Monte Rio.

In between Salt Point and Fort Ross, Beniamo Bufano's 72-foot *Peace* statue looms like a shiny silver missile alongside Hwy-1 above craggy **Timber Cove,** where there's also a nice restaurant and lodge (707/847-3231).

From Jenner, Hwy-116 runs east along the river, passing through forests, vineyards, and popular summertime resort towns, the largest of which is **Guerneville,** 12 miles away, with a number of worthwhile cafés and an alternative-minded (read: gay and lesbian) population. **Fife's** ($65 and up; 800/734-3371) is the largest gay-oriented resort here, famous for its clothing-optional sunbathing, and can be found at 16467 River Road. A more traditional place, with boat rentals, cabins, and riverfront camping, is **Johnson's** (707/869-2022) at 16241 1st Street. After 35-odd miles, Hwy-116 eventually links up with the US-101 freeway to and from San Francisco, providing a faster alternative to coastal Hwy-1.

the closing of the Russian River ferry, c. 1931

Sonoma Coast Beaches State Park

South of Jenner and the Russian River, Hwy-1 hugs the coast along 10 miles of rocky coves and sandy beaches, collectively protected as **Sonoma Coast Beaches State Park** (707/875-3483). Starting with Goat Rock at the southern lip of the Russian River mouth, a bluff-top trail leads south past intriguingly named and usually unpopulated pocket strands like Blind Beach, Schoolhouse Beach, Shell Beach, Wright's Beach (site of the park's main beachfront campground; 800/444-7275), and Salmon Creek Beach.

While hiking along the Sonoma Coast, be careful: Over 75 people have been drowned by "sleeper" waves, which rise unannounced and sweep people off the rocky shore.

At the southernmost end, Sonoma Coast Beaches State Park broadens to include the wildflower-covered granite promontory of **Bodega Head,** which juts into the Pacific and provides a great vantage point for watching the gray whale migrations in winter.

Bodega Bay and Valley Ford

Protected by the massive bulk of Bodega Head, the fishing harbor of **Bodega Bay** has grown into an upscale vacation destination, with Sea Ranch–style vacation homes lining the fairways of golf resorts, and deluxe hotels overlooking the still-busy commercial wharves. On the waterfront, the **Lucas Wharf Deli** at 595

Hwy-1 dishes up fish-and-chips and clam chowder; the nearby **Tides Wharf** is bigger and has a large fresh-fish market.

South of Bodega Bay, Hwy-1 cuts inland around the marshy coastal estuaries, passing by the photogenic small town of **Bodega,** whose church Alfred Hitchcock used for many of the scariest scenes in his 1960 movie, *The Birds.* The next town you pass through, **Valley Ford,** is another quaint little spot that holds a great old family-run roadhouse, **Dinucci's** (707/876-3260), serving huge portions of unreconstructed Italian food—minestrone, fresh bread, salad, and pasta—for around $12 per person. Dinner only, plus lunch on Sundays.

Point Reyes

Between Bodega Bay and the Golden Gate Bridge, Hwy-1 slices through one of the country's most scenically and economically wealthy areas, **Marin County.** Though less than an hour from San Francisco, the northwestern reaches of the county are surprisingly rural, consisting of rolling dairylands and a few untouched small towns; Hwy-1 follows a slow and curving route along the usually uncrowded two-lane blacktop.

A sign outside the small white garage on Main Street in Point Reyes Station claims that it is the oldest Chevrolet dealer in California.

After looping inland south of Bodega Bay, Hwy-1 reaches the shore again at oyster-rich **Tomales Bay,** around which it

winds for 20 miles before reaching the earthy but erudite town of **Point Reyes Station.** Here the excellent **Station House Cafe** (415/663-1515) at 3rd and Main Streets serves incredibly good breakfasts and delicious lunches that include great-tasting local oysters, on the half-shell or barbecued.

West from town, the 74,000-acre **Point Reyes National Seashore** offers an entire guidebook's worth of hiking and cycling trails, broad beaches, dense forests, and more; stop at the Bear Valley **visitors center** (daily; free; 415/464-5100) for more information. At the west end of Sir Francis Drake Boulevard, the photogenic lighthouse at the tip of Point Reyes gives great views over the coast, and in winter and spring (Dec.–June) the steep headland makes an ideal spot for watching migrating gray whales.

Eight miles from the visitors center, the **HI Point Reyes Hostel** (415/663-8811), at 1380 Limantour Road, has dorm beds in an old farmhouse on the road to Drake's Bay.

Dozens of delightful inns and restaurants operate in and around Point Reyes, but because they're a mere 20 miles from San Francisco, they're often booked solid weeks in advance. Everything from tree-top rooms to waterfront cabins can be found through **Inns of Marin** (415/663-2000).

Bolinas and Stinson Beach

Sitting at the southern end of the Point Reyes peninsula, **Bolinas** is a small town with a well-earned reputation for discouraging tourists; the signs leading you here from Hwy-1 are regularly torn down by locals bent on keeping the place—little more than a general store, a bakery, and a bar—for themselves. Bolinas also boasts one of the coast's best tidepool areas in **Duxbury Reef,** which curves around the western edge of Bolinas.

In contrast, the broad strands of **Stinson Beach,** four miles south along Hwy-1, are the Bay Area's most popular summertime suntanning spots. A grocery store and deli, the

Livewater Surf Shop (which rents boards and the essential wetsuits), and a couple of outdoor bar-and-grills along Hwy-1 form a short parade at the entrance to the beach. The best place to eat hereabouts is the **Parkside Cafe** (415/868-1272), at 43 Arenal Avenue; if you want to stay overnight, try the basic but cheap **Stinson Beach Motel** ($65 and up; 415/868-1712), at 3416 Hwy-1.

If you have the chance to plan ahead, try to book a night at the **Steep Ravine Cabins** (800/444-7275), just over a mile south of Stinson Beach on the ocean side of Hwy-1. Now part of Mt. Tamalpais State Park, these 10 rustic redwood cabins are very basic roofs-over-the-head (bring sleeping bags and food; water faucets are just outside the door) in an absolutely beautiful coastal chasm. These very popular cabins (originally owned by Bay Area bigwigs like Dorothea Lange) sleep up to 5 people and cost around $60 a night.

Mt. Tamalpais, Muir Woods, and Muir Beach

From the coast, a pair of roads—Panoramic Highway and the Shoreline Highway (Hwy-1)—twist up and over the slopes of **Mt. Tamalpais** (elev. 2,586), the signature peak of the San Francisco Bay Area. Known usually as "Mt. Tam," the whole mountain has been protected in semi-natural state within a series of state and national parks, and its voluptuous slopes offer incredible views of the urbanized Bay Area and the untouched coastline; drive to within 100 yards of the top for a 360-degree panorama, or stop at the Pan Toll **ranger station** (415/388-2070) for a map of Mt. Tam's hiking routes and fire roads.

The all-terrain mountain bike, which now accounts for half of all bikes on (and off) the roads, was invented in the late 1970s by a group of daredevil Marin cyclists intent on cruising down the fire roads of Mt. Tamalpais at the highest possible speed.

A deep, dark valley between the coast and Mt. Tamalpais holds the last surviving stand of Marin County redwoods, preserved for future generations as the **Muir Woods National Monument** (daily 8 AM–dusk; free), and named in honor of turn-of-the-century naturalist John Muir. A paved, mile-long trail takes in the biggest trees, but since the park is often crowded with busloads of sightseeing hordes making the tour from San Francisco, you may want to explore the farther-flung areas, climbing up Mt. Tamalpais or following Muir Creek two miles downstream to the crescent-shaped cove of **Muir Beach**, along Hwy-1. Besides stunning scenery, Muir Beach is also home to the welcoming **Pelican Inn** (415/383-6000), an "Olde English"–style pub serving food and fine beers.

Another enjoyably ersatz experience awaits at the junction of Hwy-1 and the US-101 freeway, where a historic roadside restaurant has been resurrected as the **Buckeye Roadhouse,** near Mill Valley at 15 Shoreline Highway (415/331-2600), where you can feast on fine BBQ, great steaks and burgers, and delicious desserts in a lively, retro–Route 66 atmosphere.

Marin Headlands

If you can avoid the magnetic pull of the Golden Gate Bridge and San Francisco, take the very last turnoff from US-101 (northbound drivers take the second turnoff after crossing the bridge) and head west to the **Marin Headlands,** a former military base that's been turned back into coastal semi-wilderness. A tortuous road twists along the face of 300-foot cliffs, giving incredible views of the bridge and the city behind it. The road continues west and north to the **visitors center** (415/331-1540), housed in an old chapel, with a reconstructed Miwok shelter and details on hiking and biking routes. And if you're so inclined, on Wednesday–Friday afternoons you can tour an intact but no longer functioning Nike missile silo (free).

Every June since 1905, one of the country's wildest foot races, the **Dipsea,** has followed a rugged 7.1-mile route from the town of Mill Valley over Mt. Tamalpais to Stinson Beach. For more information, call the Dipsea hotline at 415/331-3550.

Nearby, the barracks of old Fort Barry have been converted into the very peaceful **HI Marin Headlands Hostel** (415/331-2777), which has dorm beds and private rooms for around $20 per person.

Across San Francisco

From the north, Hwy-1 enters **San Francisco** across the glorious **Golden Gate Bridge,** where parking areas at both ends let you ditch the car and walk across the elegant two-mile-long span. South from the bridge, Hwy-1 follows 19th Avenue across Golden Gate Park, then runs due south through the outer reaches of San Francisco, finally reaching the coast again at the often-foggy town of Pacifica. The most scenic alternate is the **49-Mile Drive,** the best part of which heads west from the bridge through **Presidio National Park,** along Lincoln Boulevard and Camino del Mar, following the rugged coastline to **Land's End,** where you can hike around and explore the remains of Sutro Baths, eat at the wonderful new Cliff House, or experience the wonders of the Camera Obscura.

From Land's End, this scenic route runs south along the oceanfront Great Highway, which eventually links back up with Hwy-1 near the

the opening of the Golden Gate Bridge, 1937

San Francisco

San Francisco is easily the most enjoyable city in the United States. Its undulating topography turns every other corner into a scenic vista, while its many distinctive neighborhoods are perfect for aimless wandering. Museums document everything from Gold Rush history to cutting edge modern art, while stellar restaurants offer the chance to sample gourmet food from around the world—all in an easily manageable, densely compact small city.

If there's one place in the city you should stop to get your bearings, it's **Fort Point**, a massive, photogenic Civil War fort standing along the bay, directly beneath the Golden Gate Bridge. You can wander at will through the honeycomb of corridors, staircases, and gun ports, watch the fearless surfers and windsurfers offshore, and take in a panoramic view of the City by the Bay. From here you can walk up to and across the Golden Gate Bridge, or head west to Land's End or back into town via a popular bayfront walking and cycling trail.

If there's one other place that ought to be on your S.F. itinerary, it's **Alcatraz**. Aptly known as The Rock, from 1934 until 1963 this was America's most notorious prison. Now preserved as a historical park, the island is worth a visit as much for the views of San Francisco as for its grim past. To reach Alcatraz, take one of the Red & White Fleet ferries that leave throughout the day from Pier 41 at the east end of Fisherman's Wharf. Alcatraz is one of the city's prime tourist destinations, so buy your tickets as far in advance as possible (800/229-2784).

The **San Francisco Giants** (415/467-8000) play at retro-modern SBC Park, in downtown's South of Market district, while the **Oakland Athletics** (510/638-5100) play across the bay near Oakland Airport.

Practicalities

San Francisco is one of the few American cities on the West Coast where you really don't need a car, since distances are short and public transportation quite extensive; the gridded street plan makes it easy to find your way around. San Francisco's Municipal Railway's ("Muni"; 415/673-6864) network of public transit buses, trams, and cable cars will take you all over the city.

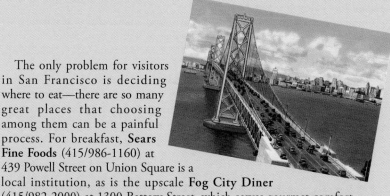

The only problem for visitors in San Francisco is deciding where to eat—there are so many great places that choosing among them can be a painful process. For breakfast, **Sears Fine Foods** (415/986-1160) at 439 Powell Street on Union Square is a local institution, as is the upscale **Fog City Diner** (415/982-2000) at 1300 Battery Street, which serves gourmet comfort food (and the world's best French toast) in a stainless steel supper club. Two more S.F. culinary landmarks are the **Swan Oyster Depot** (weekdays till 6 PM only; 415/673-1101 or 415/673-2757), a half block north of the California Street cable car at 1517 Polk Street, a simple oyster bar serving the city's freshest shellfish and coldest Anchor Steam beer; and **Sam's Grill** (415/421-0594), downtown at 374 Bush Street, with incredible grilled meat and fish dishes, melt-in-your-mouth shoestring fries, and ancient-looking 1930s wooden booths that seem like set pieces from a Sam Spade mystery.

Given San Francisco's worldwide popularity, it's no surprise that room rates run pretty high—expect to pay around $200 a night (including taxes).If you're here for a honeymoon or other romantic reason, the nicest place in town is the swanky **Mandarin Oriental** ($350 and up; 415/276-9600) at 222 Sansome Street, which fills the top floors of a Financial District skyscraper and has 270-degree bay views (even from the bathtubs!). The best budget options are the two HI hostels, one on the bay at Fort Mason (415/771-7277), another downtown at 312 Mason Street (415/788-5604); both cost about $20 a night. In between there are some nice motels on the outskirts of downtown, like the nouveau retro **Hotel del Sol** ($99 and up; 415/921-5520), in the Marina District at 3100 Webster Street.

The San Francisco Convention and Visitors Bureau (415/974-6900) publishes a good free street map and offers extensive listings of attractions, accommodations, and restaurants.

small but enjoyable **San Francisco Zoo** (daily; $10; 415/753-7080). Across from the zoo, a semi-contentious landmark to the Bay Area's proletarian past—a giant, sleepy-eyed dachshund that years ago was the emblem of the Doggie Diner fast-food chain—stands next to the **Carousel** diner (415/564-6052), at 2750 Sloat Boulevard.

Since driving and parking in San Francisco can be frustrating and expensive (Steve McQueen could never make *Bullitt* in today's traffic!), consider parking out here in the 'burbs and taking public transportation into the center of town. The N-Judah MUNI trolley line runs between downtown and the coast just south of Golden Gate Park, where parking is plentiful.

San Francisco is the start of our cross-country road trip along US-50, **The Loneliest Road**, beginning on page 636. The route crosses high mountains and red-rock deserts before winding up at Ocean City, Maryland.

San Mateo Coast

From the San Francisco city limits, Hwy-1 runs along the Pacific Ocean through the rural and almost totally undeveloped coastline of San Mateo County. The first eight miles or so are high-speed freeway, but after passing through the suburban communities of Daly City and Pacifica, the pace abruptly slows to a scenic cruise. **Pacifica,** which has a long pier, a popular surfing beach, a bowling alley, an oceanview Taco Bell, and a handy Holiday Inn Express motel, makes a good edge-of-town base for seeing the San Francisco area; south of here, two-lane Hwy-1 hugs the decomposing cliff tops for the next few miles before reaching **Montara,** where the old but still functioning lighthouse has been partly converted into the **HI Point Montara Hostel** (650/728-7177).

South of Montara, Hwy-1 bends inland around the rugged shores of the **James Fitzgerald Marine Preserve** (650/728-3584), a wonderful (but very fragile) tidepool area filled with anemones and other delicate sea creatures; look, but don't touch!

Looking for the world's biggest waves? Head down to **Maverick's,** an offshore reef area a half mile off Pillar Point, three miles north of Half Moon Bay. In winter, when conditions are right, 35-foot mega-waves draw expert surfers from all over the world. For a report, and a safety advisory to warn off any wannabes, call **Maverick's Surf Shop** at 650/726-0469. They're located at 530 Main Street in Half Moon Bay.

The first sizeable coastal town south of San Francisco, **Half Moon Bay** is 25 miles from the city but seems much more distant. A quiet farming community that's slowly but surely changing into a Silicon Valley suburb, Half Moon Bay still has an all-American Main Street a block east of the Hwy-1 bypass, lined by hardware stores, cafés, bakeries, and the inevitable art galleries and B&Bs. The main event here is the annual **Pumpkin Festival,** held mid-October, which celebrates the coming of Halloween with a competition to determine the world's largest pumpkin—winning gourds weigh as much as a half ton!

Pescadero and Pigeon Point Lighthouse

The 50 miles of coastline between Half Moon Bay and Santa Cruz are one of the great surprises of the California coast: The virtually unspoiled miles offer rocky tidepools and driftwood-strewn beaches beneath sculpted bluffs topped by rolling green fields of brussels sprouts, pumpkins, cabbages, and artichokes. The biggest town hereabouts, **Pescadero** (pop. 500), is a mile or so inland from Hwy-1, and well worth the short detour for a chance to sample the fresh fish, great pies, and other home-cooked treats at **Duarte's Tavern**, 202 Stage Road (650/879-0464), open daily

Pigeon Point Lighthouse

for breakfast, lunch, and dinner at the center of the block-long downtown.

Ten miles south of Pescadero, the photogenic beacon of **Pigeon Point Lighthouse** has appeared in innumerable TV and print commercials; the graceful, 115-foot-tall brick tower is open for **tours** (Sun. 10 AM–3 PM; $2 donation), and the adjacent lighthouse quarters function as the very popular **HI Pigeon Point Hostel** (650/879-0633), with a hot tub perched above the crashing surf.

Año Nuevo State Reserve

One of nature's more bizarre spectacles takes place annually at **Año Nuevo State Reserve** (8 AM–dusk daily; $6 per car; 650/879-2025), where each winter hundreds of humongous northern elephant seals come ashore to give birth and mate. The males reach up to 20 feet head-to-tail, weigh as much as three tons, and have dangling proboscises that inspired their name. These blubbery creatures were hunted almost to extinction for their oil-rich flesh. In 1920, fewer than 100 were left in the world; their resurgence to a current population of more than 100,000 has proved that protection does work.

Every December, after spending the summer at sea, hordes of male elephant seals arrive here at Año Nuevo, the seals' primary onshore rookery, ready to do battle with each other for the right to procreate. It's an incredible show, with the bulls bellowing, barking, and biting at each other to establish dominance; the "alpha male" mates with most of the females, and the rest must wait till next year. Pups conceived the previous year are born in January, and mating goes on through March. During the mating season, ranger-led **tours** ($5; 800/444-4445) are the only way to see the seals; these tours are very popular, so plan ahead and try to come midweek. The 3-mile walk from the parking area to the shore is worth doing at any time of year, since it's a very pretty scene and some of the seals are resident year-round.

The only accommodation option along this stretch of coast is two miles north of Año Nuevo at **Costanoa** ($30–250; 650/879-1100). A stylish retro-modern resort, open since 1999 on the inland side of Hwy-1, Costanoa has everything from a luxurious lodge to tent cabins and a campground (complete with saunas!). There's also a very nice grocery store and small café, open for breakfast, lunch, and dinner every day.

Though the San Mateo coastline is quite beautiful, the waters are very cold—and home to a hungry population of great white sharks, which have been known to attack surfers as well as seals.

Midway between Año Nuevo State Reserve and Santa Cruz, the **Davenport Cash Store**, on the east side of Hwy-1 in the village of Davenport, serves hearty breakfasts and lunches. Tiny Davenport is also the birthplace of the Odwalla fresh fruit-juice company.

Big Basin Redwoods State Park

The oldest and largest of California's state parks, **Big Basin Redwoods State Park** ($6 per car; 831/338-8860) protects some 16,000 acres of giant coastal redwoods. Established in 1902, the park has many miles of hiking and cycling trails high up in the mountains. The heart of the park is most easily accessible from Santa Cruz via Hwy-236, but a popular trail winds up from the coast to the crest, starting from Hwy-1 at **Waddell Creek Beach,** a popular haunt for kite-surfers and sailboarders, who sometimes do flips and loops in the wind-whipped waves.

Santa Cruz

The popular beach resort and college town of **Santa Cruz** (pop. 54,593) sits at the north end of Monterey Bay, a 90-minute drive from San Francisco, at the foot of a 3,000-foot-high ridge of mountains. Best known for its Boardwalk amusement park, which holds the only surviving wooden roller coaster on the West Coast, and for the large University of California campus in the redwoods above, Santa Cruz takes its name from the ill-fated mission settlement begun here in 1777 but wiped out by an earthquake and tidal wave in 1840. Modern Santa Cruz was all but leveled by another earthquake in 1989 but has since recovered its stature as one of the most diverting stops on the California coast.

Natural Bridges State Park, two miles north of Santa Cruz via West Cliff Drive, has a natural wave-carved archway and, in winter, swarms of monarch butterflies.

The downtown area lies a mile inland, so from Hwy-1 follow the many signs pointing visitors toward the wharf and the beach, where plentiful parking is available. Walk, rent a bike, or drive along the coastal Cliff Drive to the world's first **Surfing Museum** (Wed.–Mon. noon–4 PM; donations), which is packed with giant old redwood boards and newer high-tech cutters, as well as odds and ends tracing the development of West Coast surfing. Housed in an old lighthouse, it overlooks one of the state's prime surfing spots, Steamer Lane, named for the steamships that once brought day-tripping San Franciscans to the wharf.

Surfboard designs have come a long way.

A large part of the Santa Cruz economy still depends upon visitors, and there are plenty of cafés, restaurants, and accommodation options to choose from. Eating and drinking places congregate west of Hwy-1 along Front Street and Pacific Avenue in downtown

Santa Cruz, which has a number of engaging, somewhat countercultural book and record shops along with cafés like **Zoccoli's** (831/423-1711) at 1534 Pacific Avenue, which has great soups and sandwiches. The best burgers, veggie burgers and fries are a block west of Pacific at **Jack's Hamburgers** (831/423-4421), 202 Lincoln Street.

Motels line Hwy-1, and older, funkier ones stand atop Beach Hill, between the Boardwalk and downtown, where you can also avail yourself of the **HI Santa Cruz Hostel** (831/423-8304) at 321 Main Street, with dorm beds in an immaculate 1870s cottage for less than $20 per person. Another characterful old place is the **Capitola Venetian Hotel** ($180 and up; 831/476-6471), a 1920s mission-style complex right on the beach at 1500 Wharf Road in **Capitola**, three miles east of Santa Cruz. Among the many nice B&Bs is the rustic **Babbling Brook** ($189 and up; 831/427-2437 or 800/866-1131) at 1025 Laurel Street.

> Santa Cruz has just about fully recovered from the 1989 Loma Prieta earthquake, which had its epicenter in the hills southeast of the city.

For more-complete listings or other information, contact the **Santa Cruz Visitors Council** (831/425-1234 or 800/833-3494), with an office at 1211 Ocean Street.

Santa Cruz Boardwalk

The bayfront **Santa Cruz Boardwalk** should really be your main stop; besides the dozens of thrill rides and midway games, it boasts the art deco Cocoanut Grove ballroom, where throughout the summer swing bands still play the sounds of the 1930s and 1940s, and two rides that are such classics of the genre they've been listed as National Historic Landmarks. The biggest thrill is the **Giant Dipper** roller coaster, open since 1924, a senior citizen compared to modern rides but still one of the Top 10 coasters in the country—the clattering, half-mile-long tracks make it seem far faster than the 40 mph maximum it reaches. Near the roller coaster is the beautiful Charles Looff **carousel,** one of only six left in the country, with 70 hand-carved wooden horses doing the same circuit they've followed since 1911; grab for the brass rings while listening to music pumped out by the 342-pipe organ, imported from Germany and over 100 years old.

Along with these and many other vintage arcade attractions, the amusement park also features a log flume ride, a sky ride, a two-story miniature-golf course installed inside the old bathhouse, plus a bowling alley and all the shooting galleries, laser tag, and virtual reality machines you could want. The Boardwalk, which has been paved but retains a great deal of charm and character, is open daily in summer, and weekends only during the rest of the year. Admission is free and individual rides vary in cost, with the Giant Dipper costing about $4 a trip and all-day passes priced about $25. For more information, call 831/423-5590.

the roller coaster at Santa Cruz

Mystery Spot

In the hills above Santa Cruz, two miles east of Hwy-1 at 1953 Branciforte Drive, the **Mystery Spot** (daily; $5; 831/423-8897) is one of those fortunate few tourist traps that actually gets people to come back again. Like similar places along the Pacific coast, the Mystery Spot is a section of redwood forest where the usual laws of physics seem not to apply (trees grow in oddly contorted corkscrew shapes, and balls roll uphill). Among those who study vortexes and other odd geomantic places, the Mystery Spot is considered to be the real thing, but you don't have to take it seriously to enjoy yourself.

Watsonville, Castroville, and Moss Landing

Between Santa Cruz and Monterey, Hwy-1 loops inland through the farmlands fronting Monterey Bay. Part freeway, part winding two-lane road, Hwy-1 races through, and to be honest there's not a lot worth stopping for: The beaches can be dreary, and the two main towns, Watsonville and Castroville, are little more than service centers for the local fruit and vegetable packers. **Watsonville** is still

reeling from the 1989 earthquake, which destroyed half of the downtown area, though **Castroville**—where in 1947, then-unknown **Marilyn Monroe** reigned as "Miss Artichoke" during Castroville's Artichoke Festival, still celebrated each September—does have one odd sight: the "World's Largest Artichoke," a concrete statue outside a very large fruit stand at the center of town.

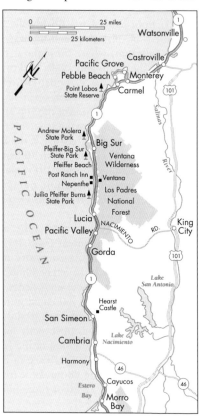

Back on the coast, midway along Monterey Bay, the port community of **Moss Landing** is a busy commercial fishery, with lots of trawlers and packing plants—not to mention pelicans aplenty. Moss Landing sits alongside Elkhorn Slough, the largest wetlands area in Monterey Bay, and is home to the research arm of the Monterey Bay Aquarium, to an obtrusively huge electricity generating plant, and to **The Whole Enchilada** (831/633-3038), which has spicy seafood and a

Coastal farms along **Monterey Bay** grow nearly 85 percent of the nation's artichokes, which you can sample along with other produce at stands along Hwy-1.

popular Sunday jazz brunch right on Hwy-1, just south of the power plant.

Much of the bayfront north of Monterey formerly belonged to the U.S. Marine Corps base at Fort Ord. Almost the entire parcel was turned over to the State of California to house the **California State University at Monterey Bay,** which opened its doors in 1995.

San Juan Bautista

Away from the coast, 15 miles inland from Monterey Bay via Hwy-129 or Hwy-156, stands one of California's most idyllic small towns, **San Juan Bautista** (pop. 1,549). It centers upon a grassy town square bordered by a well-preserved mission complex, complete with a large church and monastery, standing since 1812. Two other sides of the square are lined by hotels, stables, and houses dating from the 1840s through 1860s, preserved in their entirety within a state historic park (daily; $2; 831/623-4881).

Completing the living history lesson, the east edge of the square is formed by one of the state's few preserved stretches of El Camino Real, the 200-year-old Spanish colonial trail that linked all the California missions with Mexico. Adding to the interest, the trail runs right along the rift zone of the San Andreas Fault, and a small seismograph registers tectonic activity. (Incidentally, San Juan Bautista was where the climactic final scenes of Hitchcock's *Vertigo* were filmed—though in the movie, they added a much more prominent bell tower with a seemingly endless staircase.)

The town's Main Street is a block from the mission, and is lined by a handful of antique shops, Mexican restaurants, and cafés like the **Mission Cafe** at 300 3rd Street.

North of San Juan Bautista, at the southern fringe of the Bay Area's famed Silicon Valley, **Bonfante Gardens** at 3050 Hecker Pass Road (daily in summer only; $30; 408/840-7100), is five different gardens on 100-plus acres, offering a taste of everything from early California agriculture to topiary animals—plus a few thrill rides, of course.

Monterey

The historic capital of California under the Spanish and Mexican regimes, **Monterey** (pop. 31,954), along with its peninsular neighbors Carmel and Pacific Grove, is one of the most satisfying stops in California. Dozens of significant historical sites have been well preserved, most of them concentrated within a mile-long walk called the Path of History that loops through the compact downtown area. Park in the lots at the foot of Alvarado Street, Monterey's main drag, and start your tour at **Fisherman's Wharf,** where bellowing sea lions wallow in the water, begging for popcorn from tourists. Next stop should be the adjacent **Custom House,** the oldest governmental building in the state, recently restored as the **Monterey State Historic Park visitors center** (daily; 831/649-2836); here you can pick up maps or join walking tours of old-town Monterey.

From the Custom House, which is now surrounded by the modern Doubletree Hotel complex, you can follow the

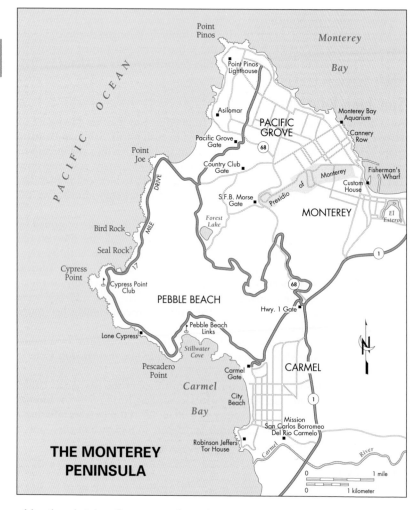

**THE MONTEREY
PENINSULA**

old railroad right-of-way west along the water to **Cannery Row**, where abandoned fish canneries have been gussied up into upscale bars and restaurants—most of them capitalizing on ersatz Steinbeckian themes. The one real attraction here is the excellent **Monterey Bay Aquarium** (daily; $19.95; 831/648-4800), 886 Cannery Row, housed in a spacious modern building and loaded with state-of-the-art tanks filled with over 500 species of local sealife. The aquarium is rated by many as the best in the world: Displays let visitors touch tidepool denizens, watch playful sea otters, gaze into the gently swaying stalks of a three-story-tall kelp forest, be hypnotized by brilliantly colored jellyfish, or face truly weird creatures that usually live thousands of feet below the surface of the bay.

Along Hwy-1 on the northwest edge of Monterey, the elegant **Hotel Del Monte**, a grand resort that attracted the first wealthy tourists in the 1880s, is now part of the large **U.S. Navy Postgraduate School**.

It's also worth noting that the internationally famous **Monterey Jazz Festival** is held every year at the end of summer. For performers, dates, and other information, phone 800/307-3378.

Monterey Practicalities

Because Monterey gets a considerable tourist trade, there's no shortage of restaurants, though good food at reasonable prices can be hard to find. One good bet is the **Old Monterey Cafe** (831/646-1021), 489 Alvarado Street, serving large portions at breakfast and lunch. For seafood, catch an early-bird special (before 6 PM) at one of the dozen restaurants on the wharf—**Cafe Fina** (831/372-5200) has the best food, including good pizzas. Top of the scale is flashy **Montrio** (831/648-8880), located at 414 Calle Principal, which serves San Francisco–style grilled chicken and fish in a converted fire station; reservations are essential, ever since *Esquire* magazine rated it Restaurant of the Year for 1995.

The writer John Steinbeck lived in and around the Monterey Peninsula for many years, and set many of his stories here, though things have changed so much in recent years that his beloved Cannery Row is hard to recognize. Steinbeck was born and is buried in **Salinas**, east of Monterey on US-101, and after spurning him for most of his lifetime, the town recently opened the **National Steinbeck Center** at 1 Main Street as a memorial to its literary son.

Places to stay vary widely, starting with the new **HI Monterey Hostel** ($19; 831/649-0375), in historic Carpenters Union Hall off Cannery Row at 778 Hawthorne Street, four blocks from the aquarium. Moderate motels line Munras Street along the old US-101 highway frontage south toward Carmel, while prices in downtown Monterey hover in the $200 range. One exception to the generally high prices is the refurbished and centrally located **Monterey Hotel** ($100; 831/375-3184 or 800/727-0960) at 406 Alvarado.

Many other nice places can be found in neighboring Pacific Grove or Carmel (see below for more). For additional information on anything from Monterey south to Big Sur, contact the Monterey County **visitors bureau** (831/649-1770 or 888/221-1010).

Pacific Grove

Perched at the tip of the Monterey Peninsula, **Pacific Grove** (pop. 16,117) is a quiet throwback to old-time tourism, dating from the late 1880s when the area was used for summertime Methodist revival meetings. The revivalists' tents and camps later grew into the West Coast headquarters of the populist Chautauqua educational movement, based in upstate New York. The town still has a curiously midwestern feel, from its many small churches to the rows of well-maintained Victorian cottages lining its quiet streets. Besides the many fine old buildings, the best reason to come here is the beautiful, fully accessible shoreline, which boasts some of the coast's best tidepools, sunset views, and endless opportunities for winter whale-watching.

Hotel Del Monte, California, on Road of a Thousand Wonders

Pacific Grove's main street, Lighthouse Avenue, runs through the 15-mph commercial district of galleries, movie theaters, and cafés like **Toastie's** (831/373-7543), a comfy breakfast and lunch place at 702 Lighthouse Avenue. Nearby **Pepper's** (831/373-6892), at 170 Forest Avenue, serves very good, fresh Mexican food, while a range of fairly priced fish dishes are on the menu at **The Fishwife** (831/375-7107), overlooking **Asilomar State Beach** at 1996 Sunset Drive.

Pacific Grove is the best-known of about 20 places in California where millions of monarch butterflies spend the winter months. From October until March, the butterflies congregate on the "Butterfly Trees," a grove of pines on Ridge Road off Lighthouse Avenue, well-signed from downtown.

Places to stay in Pacific Grove are more reasonably priced than in Monterey or Carmel: **Andril's Fireplace Cottages** ($90–150; 831/375-0994), is a lovingly maintained set of old-fashioned motor-court cabins, all with fireplaces and just two blocks from the ocean at 569 Asilomar Boulevard. Rustic **Asilomar Conference Center** ($95 and up; 831/372-8016), at 800 Asilomar Boulevard, has a modern lodge and some lovely woodsy, Julia Morgan–designed cabins, but the former YWCA summer camp is often filled with church groups or convention-goers. For a romantic getaway, it's hard to beat the jointly-run pair of Victorian-era B&Bs overlooking the Pacific from Lover's Point: **Grand View** and **Seven Gables** ($175 and up; 831/372-4341), at 555–557 Ocean View Boulevard.

One event that brought Pebble Beach to national attention was the annual golf tournament hosted by Bing Crosby; originally an informal get-together, it grew into one of the main events of the professional circuit and is now the **AT&T Pebble Beach National Pro-Am** held each winter. Every August for nearly 50 years, Pebble Beach has drawn classic car collectors from around the world to show off their immaculately restored automobiles at the annual **Concours d'égance.**

17-Mile Drive and Pebble Beach

Spanning the coast between Pacific Grove and Carmel, the **17-Mile Drive** is one of the most famous toll roads in the nation. Opened in the 1880s, the route initially took guests of Monterey's posh Hotel Del Monte on a scenic carriage ride along the coast through the newly planted Del Monte Forest between Carmel and Pacific Grove. Guided by Samuel F. B. Morse, son of the inventor, the formerly wild area underwent development beginning in the 1920s, first with golf courses like Pebble Beach and Cypress Point, and since then with resort hotels and posh homes.

Enter the drive at any of the gates, where you'll pay the toll ($8.50) and be given a map and guide to the route, pointing out all the scenic highlights, especially the trussed-up old **Lone Cypress,** subject of so many Carmel postcards. It's definitely worth doing, if only to say you have, but to be honest, the views from the drive are no more or less splendid than they are from the toll-free drives, like Ocean View Boulevard in Pacific Grove, Scenic Drive in Carmel, or Hwy-1 through Big Sur. You do, however, get to stop at the Lodge, where your toll will be deducted from the price of lunch or dinner. If you're in the mood to splurge on wanton luxury, you can also stay overnight at either of two extremely plush golf and tennis resorts: the modern, suburban-style country

the Lone Cypress

club of the **Inn at Spanish Bay,** which is also home to an Ansel Adams photography gallery, or the stately, old-money **Lodge at Pebble Beach.** Both resorts charge upwards of $500 a night; for details on accommodations (or golfing fees and tee times), call 831/647-7500.

Carmel

The exclusive enclave of **Carmel-by-the-Sea** (to give its complete name) began life in the early years of the 20th century as a small but lively bohemian colony inhabited by the literary likes of Sinclair Lewis, Mary Austin, and Upton Sinclair. However, with a few arts-and-craftsy exceptions, by the 1950s Carmel had turned into the archly conservative and contrivedly quaint community it is today—a place where Marie Antoinette would no doubt feel at home, dressing down as a peasant, albeit in Chaps by Ralph Lauren. Preserving its rural feel by banning street addresses (and skateboards and home mail delivery . . .), Carmel simultaneously loves and abhors the many thousands of tourists who descend on it every weekend to window-shop its many designer boutiques and galleries that fill the few blocks off Ocean Avenue, the main drag through town. Though most of Carmel's many art galleries seem directed at interior decorators, a few are worth searching out, including the **Photography West Gallery** on the southeast corner of Dolores and Ocean Streets, and the **Weston Gallery** on Sixth Avenue near Dolores Street, featuring the works of Edward Weston, Ansel Adams, and other Carmel-based photographers.

Carmel's leading light, **Clint Eastwood,** seems ever-present: Besides once serving as mayor, he owns the Carmel Mission Ranch resort. As a filmmaker, he used Carmel as the location for one of his most disturbing movies, the psychopathic 1970s *Play Misty for Me.*

Though it's easy to be put off by the surface glitz, Carmel does have a lot going for it. The water is too cold and treacherous for swimming, but broad **City Beach** at the foot of Ocean Avenue gleams white against a truly azure cove. To the south, aptly named **Scenic Drive** winds along the rocky coast, past poet Robinson Jeffers's dramatic **Tor House** (tours Fri. and Sat. 10 AM–3 PM; $7; 831/624-1840). Jeffers, who lived here between 1914 and 1962, built much of what you see here out of boulders he hauled up by hand from the beach.

At the south end of the Carmel peninsula, another broad beach spreads at the mouth of the Carmel River; this usually unpopulated spot, part of **Carmel River State Park,** is also a favorite spot for scuba divers exploring the deep undersea canyon.

Above the beach, just west of Hwy-1 a mile south of central Carmel, **Carmel Mission** (daily; donations) was the most important of all the California missions, serving as home, headquarters, and final resting place of Father Junipero Serra, the Franciscan priest who established Carmel and many of the 20 other California missions, and who is entombed under the chapel floor. The gardens—where on weekends wedding parties alight from limos to take family photos—are beautiful, as is the facade with its photogenic bell tower; this is the mission to visit if you visit only one.

Carmel Practicalities

Dozens of good and usually expensive restaurants thrive in Carmel, but one place to see, even if you don't eat there, is the tiny, mock-Tudoresque **Tuck Box Tea Room** (closed Mon. and Tues.; 831/624-6365), on Dolores Street near 7th Avenue. Rebuilt after a fire but still dollhouse-cute, it serves up bacon-and-eggs breakfasts and dainty plates of shepherd's pie and Welsh rarebit for lunch. If you'd rather join locals than mingle with your fellow tourists, head to **Katy's Place** (daily 7 AM–2 PM; 831/624-0199) on Mission Street between 5th and 6th, serving delicious waffles and some of the world's best eggs Benedict.

Carmel has only one place to stay approximating a budget option, the very pleasant **Carmel River Inn** (831/624-1575 or 800/882-8142), just west of Hwy-1 near the Carmel Mission, but even here rates average well over $100 a night. However, if you want to splurge on a bit of luxury, Carmel is a good place to do it. Besides the golf course resorts of nearby Pebble Beach, Carmel also has the commodious, 1920s-era, mission-style **Cypress Inn** at Lincoln and 7th ($150–250; 831/624-3871 or 800/443-7443), partly owned by dog-loving Doris Day (and featuring posters of her movies in the small bar off the lobby). A relaxing spot away from downtown is the historic, Clint Eastwood-owned **Carmel Mission Ranch** ($110 and up; 831/624-6436 or 800/538-8221) at 26270 Dolores Street, within walking distance of the beach and mission and offering full resort facilities and a very good restaurant.

Point Lobos State Reserve

The sculpted headland south of Carmel Bay, now protected as **Point Lobos State Reserve** (daily; $8 per car; 831/624-4909), holds one of the few remaining groves of native Monterey cypress, gnarled and bent by the often stormy coastal weather. The name comes from the barking sea lions *(lobos del mar)* found here by early Spanish explorers; hundreds of seabirds, sea lions, sea otters, and—in winter—gray whales are seen offshore or in the many picturesque, sea-carved coves.

The entrance to the reserve is along Hwy-1, three miles south of Carmel Mission, but in summer the park is so popular that visitors sometimes have to wait in line outside the gates. If possible, plan to come early or during the week. Whenever you can, come: Point Lobos has been lauded as the greatest meeting of land and sea in the world, and crowded or not it's definitely a place you'll want to see. Point Lobos has endless vistas up and down the rocky coast, and if you don't mind a short hike, there are a number of magical beaches hidden away at its southern end.

Big Sur

Stretching 90 miles south of Carmel from Point Lobos all the way to Hearst Castle, Big Sur is one of the most memorable sections of coastline on the planet, with 5,000-foot-tall mountains rising up from the Pacific Ocean. Early Spanish missionaries dubbed it El País Grande del Sur, the "Big Country of the South," and the rugged land has resisted development or even much of a population—the current total of around 1,500 is roughly the same as it was in 1900, and for the 3,000 years before that.

Hwy-1, the breathtaking drive through Big Sur, was finally cut across the very steep cliffs in 1937 after 20 years of convict labor and several fatalities. Named the state's first scenic route, so dedicated by Lady Bird Johnson in 1966, it's an incredible trip. Like the Grand Canyon and other larger-than-life natural wonders, Big Sur boggles the mind and, in an odd way, can be hard to handle; you have to content yourself with staring in awestruck appreciation, taking pictures, or maybe toasting the natural handiwork with a cold beer or glass of wine at one of the few but unforgettable cafés and restaurants along the way.

However beautiful the drive along Hwy-1, it's also narrow, twisting, packed with sluggish RVers on holiday weekends, and often closed by mud slides and washouts during torrential winter storms. In 1983, the biggest storm in recent memory closed the road for over a year, and in 1998, 70 miles of it were blocked for over four months; sections of it are closed almost every year.

There are also very few services, and most of the overnight accommodations are booked solidly during the peak summer season. Spring brings wildflowers, while fall gets the most reliably good weather. No matter when you come, even if you just drive through in an afternoon, be sure to stop whenever possible and get out of the car; scenic viewpoints line the roadside, and dozens of trails lead off into the wilds. The best basic guide to Big Sur is an annual free newspaper, *El Sur Grande,* published by Monterey County and available at ranger stations and many other locations in and around Big Sur.

Andrew Molera State Park

Spreading along the coast at the mouth of the Big Sur River, 21 miles south of Carmel, **Andrew Molera State Park** is a grassy former cattle ranch on the site of one of Big Sur's oldest homesteads. In the 1850s, immigrant John "Juan Bautista" Roger Cooper bought the land and built a cabin, which still stands along Hwy-1 near the park entrance. Well-blazed trails wind along both banks of the river down to the small beach, horses are available for hire (831/625-5486), and there are quite a few nice places to **camp** (walk-in only). In winter, the park is also a popular resting spot for migrating Monarch butterflies.

Big Sur Village

South of Andrew Molera, Hwy-1 cuts inland toward the heart of **Big Sur,** the deep and densely forested valley carved by the Big Sur River. Consisting of little more than three gas stations, a couple of roadside markets, and a number of lodges and restaurants, the mile-long village of Big Sur (pop. 950) represents the only real settlement between Carmel and Hearst Castle.

The photogenic **Bixby Creek Bridge,** 15 miles south of Carmel, was the largest concrete bridge in the world when it was built in 1932. The old coast road runs along the north bank of the creek, linking up again with Hwy-1 near Andrew Molera State Park.

At the north end of "town," the **Big Sur River Inn** (831/667-2700) has moderately priced, rustic rooms in the lodge and in the motel across the highway; there's also a woodsy, warm, and unpretentious restaurant overlooking the river. Next door is a small complex that includes crafts galleries, a grocery store with burrito bar, and the homey **Big Sur Village Pub,** which features good beers, pizzas, and pub grub. Continuing south, the next mile of Hwy-1 holds Big Sur's main family-oriented resorts, all offering rustic cabins and campgrounds along the river: **Riverside** (831/667-2414), **Ripplewood** (831/667-2242), and **Fernwood** (831/667-2422).

Pfeiffer–Big Sur State Park

Roughly a half mile south of Big Sur village, **Pfeiffer–Big Sur State Park** is the region's main event, an 810-acre riverside forest that's one of the most pleasant (and popular) parks in the state. Besides offering a full range of visitor services—restaurant, lodge, campground, and grocery store—the park includes one of Big Sur's best short hikes, a two-mile loop on the Valley View trail that takes in stately redwoods as well as oak and madrone groves, a 40-foot waterfall, and a grand vista down the Big Sur valley to the coast. Campsites cost $15–20 (800/444-7275); for cabins or rooms at the lodge, call 831/667-3100.

The northern stretches of Big Sur are marked by the volcanic hump of **Point Sur,** 19 miles south of Carmel, a symmetrical dome capped by a 100-year-old lighthouse.

The park also has the main **ranger station** (831/667-2315) for all the state parks in the Big Sur area. Just south of the park entrance, a USFS **ranger station** (831/667-2423) on the east side of Hwy-1 has information on hiking and camping opportunities in the mountains above Big Sur, including the isolated (but poison oak–ridden) **Ventana Wilderness.**

Pfeiffer Beach

South of Pfeiffer–Big Sur State Park, halfway up a long, steep incline, a small road turns west and leads down through dark and heavily overgrown Sycamore Canyon, eventually winding up at Big Sur's best beach, **Pfeiffer Beach.** From the lot at the end of the road, a short trail runs through a grove of trees before opening onto the broad white sands, loomed over by a pair of hulking offshore rocks. The water's way too cold for

swimming, but the half-mile strand is one of the few places in Big Sur where you can enjoy extended beachcombing strolls. The beach's northern half attracts a clothing-optional crew, even on cool, gray days.

Ventana and the Post Ranch Inn

South of Sycamore Canyon, roughly three miles from the heart of Big Sur village, Hwy-1 passes between two of California's most deluxe small resorts. The larger of the two, **Ventana** (831/667-2331 or 800/628-6500), covers 1,000 acres of Big Sur foothills and offers saunas, swimming pools, and four-star accommodations in 1970s-style cedar-paneled rooms and cabins. Rates range $200–800 a night, and there's also a very fine restaurant with incredible views and reasonable prices, to which guests are ferried in a fleet of golf carts.

Completed in 1992 and directly across Hwy-1 from Ventana, the **Post Ranch Inn** (831/667-2200 or 800/527-2200), a low-impact but ultra-high-style luxury resort hanging high above the Big Sur coast, is at the forefront of eco-tourism. In order to preserve Big Sur's untarnished natural beauty, the Post Ranch Inn is designed to be virtually invisible from land or sea: The 24 accommodations—all featuring a king-sized bedroom and a whirlpool bath with built-in massage table—blend in with the landscape, disguised either as playful tree houses raised up in the branches of the oaks and pines, or as underground cabins carved into the cliff top. Rates start at $300 a night, but if you want to have a look and plan for a future escape, free tours of the resort are given Monday–Friday at 2 PM.

The landmark red farmhouse along Hwy-1 at the entrance to Ventana was built in 1877 by pioneer rancher **W. B. Post**, whose descendants developed the Post Ranch Inn.

Nepenthe

One of the most popular and long-lived stopping points along the Big Sur coast, **Nepenthe** (831/667-2345) is a rustic bar and restaurant offering good food and great views from atop a rocky headland a thousand feet above the Pacific. The hilltop where Nepenthe now stands was previously the site of a rustic cabin that Orson Welles bought for his wife, Rita Hayworth, in 1944. Named for the mythical drug that causes one to forget all sorrows, Nepenthe looks like something out of a 1960s James Bond movie, built of huge boulders and walls of plate glass. The menu too is somewhat dated; burgers, steaks, and fried fish predominate.

A decade ago, the mighty California condor was all but extinct in the wild. Now, thanks to a successful captive breeding program, these massive birds can be seen soaring over the Ventana Wilderness that rises above Big Sur.

Sharing a parking lot, and taking advantage of similar views, the neighboring **Cafe Kevah** (831/667-2344) serves a veggie-friendly range of soups, salads, and quesadillas, plus good teas and coffees and microbrews on a rooftop deck; you'll find a gift shop downstairs selling top-quality arts and crafts and knitwear by Kaffe Fassett, who grew up here and whose family owns the place.

Right along Hwy-1, at a sharp bend in the road just south of Nepenthe, the **Henry Miller Memorial Library** (irregular hours, usually daily in summer;

831/667-2574) carries an erratic but engaging collection of books by and about the author, who lived in Big Sur for many years in the 1950s.

A half mile south of Nepenthe on the east side of the highway, one of the oldest and most atmospheric places to stay is **Deetjen's Big Sur Inn** ($80–180; 831/667-2377), a rambling and rustic redwood lodge built by a Norwegian immigrant in the 1930s and now a nonprofit, preservationist operation. Deetjen's also serves Big Sur's best breakfasts and hearty dinners.

Julia Pfeiffer Burns State Park

If for some untenable reason you only have time to stop once along the Big Sur coast, **Julia Pfeiffer Burns State Park** (dawn–dusk daily) should be

the place. Spreading along both sides of Hwy-1, about 14 miles south of Big Sur village, the park includes one truly beautiful sight: a slender waterfall that drops crisply down into a nearly circular turquoise-blue cove. This is the only waterfall in California that plunges directly into the Pacific.

Julia Pfeiffer Burns was a Big Sur pioneer whose family lived near Pfeiffer Beach and homesteaded much of this rugged, isolated area. In 1915, she married John Burns, a Scottish orphan who lived with the nearby Post family, and they continued to live and ranch at what is now Julia Pfeiffer Burns State Park until Julia's death in 1928.

From the parking area, east of the highway, a short trail leads under the road to a fine view of the waterfall, while another leads to the remnants of a pioneer mill, complete with a preserved Pelton wheel. Other routes climb through redwood groves up to the chaparral-covered slopes of the Santa Lucia Mountains.

About six miles south of Nepenthe, or a mile north of the parking area at Julia Pfeiffer Burns State Park, a steep fire road drops down to **Partington Cove**, where ships used to moor in the protected anchorage. The last stretch of the route passes through a 100-foot-long tunnel hewn out of solid rock.

Lucia and the Nacimiento Road

*Three miles south of Julia Pfeiffer Burns State Park, the New Age **Esalen Institute** offers a variety of "Human Potential" workshops; they also have an incredible set of natural hot springs, right above the ocean and sometimes open to the public midnight—5am. For information or reservations, phone 831/667-3000.*

The southern reaches of the Big Sur coast are drier and more rugged, offering bigger vistas but fewer stopping places than the northern half. The road winds along the cliffs, slowing down every 10 miles or so for each of three gas station/café/motel complexes, which pass for towns on the otherwise uninhabited coast. The first of these, 25 miles south of Big Sur village, is **Lucia**, which has a very good restaurant and lantern-lit cabins. High on a hill just south of Lucia, marked by a slender black cross, is the Benedictine **New Camaldoli Hermitage**, open to interested outsiders as a silent retreat. For details, phone 831/667-2456.

Five miles south of Lucia, the narrow Nacimiento Road makes an unforgettable climb up from Hwy-1 over the coastal mountains. Though ravaged in places by recent wild fires, it's a beautiful drive, winding through hillside chap-parel and dense oak groves before ending up near King City in the Salinas Val-ley. One real highlight here is **Mission San Antonio de Padua** (daily 8 AM–5 PM; 831/385-4478), a well preserved church and monastery that is still in use by a Catholic religious community. Because the road passes through sections of Fort Hunter-Liggett Army Base, you may need to show valid car registration and proof of insurance.

Near the foot of the Nacimiento road are two of the most accessible oceanside campsites in Big Sur: **Plaskett Creek** and **Kirk Creek,** operated by the U.S. Forest Service (831/667-2423).

Continuing south, Hwy-1 runs through **Pacific Valley,** the hills above which are a popular hang-gliding spot, then passes by a number of small but pretty beaches and coves before reaching **Gorda,** the southernmost stop on the Big Sur coast. Beyond here, a series of small state parks lines the highway, but the next services are 25 miles farther south in San Sime-on, at the entrance to Hearst Castle.

In order to help prevent erosion and mud slides, the roadside along Hwy-1 in the southern half of Big Sur has been planted with odd-looking bunches of pampas grass that helps keep the hills from washing away but has become an intrusive pest, crowding out local flora.

San Simeon: Hearst Castle

At the south end of Big Sur, the mountains flatten out and turn inland, and the coastline becomes rolling, open-range ranch land. High on a hill above Hwy-1 stands the coast's one totally unique attraction, **Hearst Castle.** Locat-ed 65 miles south of Big Sur village and 43 miles northwest of San Luis Obispo, Hearst Castle is the sort of place that you really have to see to believe, though simple numbers—144 rooms, including 36 bedrooms—do give a sense of its scale.

Even if Hearst's taste in interior design (or his megalomania, which by all accounts was understated by his fictional portrayal in Orson Welles's *Citizen Kane*) doesn't appeal, Hearst Castle cries out to be seen. One of this centu-ry's most powerful and influential Americans (the Rupert Murdoch of his day), Hearst inherited the land, and most of his fortune, from his father George Hearst, a mining mogul, and began work on his castle following the death of his mother in 1919. With the help of the great California architect Julia Morgan, who designed the complex to look like a Mediterranean hill town with Hearst's house as the cathedral at its center, Hearst spent 25 years working on his "castle," building, rebuilding, and filling room after room with furniture, all the while enter-taining the great and powerful of the era, from Charlie Chap-lin to Winston Churchill.

A small **museum** (daily; free) in the visitors center, next to where you board the trams that carry you up to the house, details Hearst's life and times. If you want to go on a **tour,** the Introductory Tour (Tour 1, which costs around $20) gives the best first-time overview, taking in the main house and the two swimming pools, plus a 45-minute movie giving the background on Hearst and his house-building. Other tours (2, 3, and 4) specialize in different aspects of the house and gardens; each one costs $12 and takes around two hours. Advance reservations (800/444-4445) are all but essential, especially in summer.

Since Hearst Castle is rather isolated, it's a good idea to stay the night before or after a visit at nearby San Simeon, which has grown into a massive strip of motels. One of the nicest ones here is the **San Simeon Lodge** ($40–140; 805/927-4601) at 9520 Castillo Drive.

Cambria

Without Hearst Castle, **Cambria** would be just another farming town, but being next to the state's number-two tourist attraction (after Disneyland) has turned Cambria into quite a busy little hive. Apart from a few hokey, tourist-trapping souvenir shops at the north end of town, it's a casual, walkable, and franchise-free community of arts and crafts galleries, boutiques, and good restaurants; from Hwy-1, Main Street makes a three-mile loop around to the east, running through the heart of town.

Above Cambria, a folk-art landmark known as **Nit Wit Ridge** ($10; 805/927-2690) was built by the eccentric artist Art Beal, who used old Busch beer cans, sea shells, roof tiles, and broken-down car parts to build, over 50 years starting in the late 1920s, what is often called a "Poor Man's Hearst Castle." The sprawling three-story house, with great views and intriguing details, is now open for tours at 881 Hillcrest Drive.

Back in town, hearty breakfasts are available at the **Redwood Cafe** (805/927-4830) at 2094 Main Street, while well-prepared multiethnic and vegetarian food is on the menu at **Robin's** (805/927-5007), a half block off Main Street at 4095 Burton Drive. For BBQ, check out the **Main Street Grill** (805/927-3194), at 603 Main Street. Places to stay range from standard motels like the Bluebird Inn ($70 and up; 805/927-4634), at 1880 Main Street, to the spacious suites and cabins at rustic **Cambria Pines Lodge** ($140 and up; 805/927-4200), on a hill above Hwy-1 at 2905 Burton Drive.

Five miles south of Cambria, **Harmony** (pop. 18) is a former dairy town turned arts and crafts colony, with a range of galleries and a small wedding chapel. Another diverting little town, **Cayucos**, sits along the coast 10 miles farther south.

Morro Bay

Marked by the Gibraltar-like monolith of Morro Rock, which was noted by Juan Cabrillo in 1542 and now serves as a peregrine falcon preserve and nesting site, **Morro Bay** (pop. 10,350) surrounds a busy commercial fishing harbor, a half mile west of Hwy-1. A thin, six-mile-long strip of sand protects the bay from the Pacific Ocean, forming a seabird-rich lagoon that's included within **Morro Bay State Park,** a mile southeast of Morro Rock. There's an informative museum with displays on local wildlife, and the park also contains the friendly **Bayside Cafe** (805/772-1465), serving lunch and dinner. Next door, when the weather's nice, you can rent **kayaks** ($6 an hour) and paddle around the estuary.

The rest of Morro Bay is pretty quiet; one unusual sight is a giant **outdoor chessboard** (with waist-high playing pieces), at the foot of Morro Bay Boulevard on the waterfront in City Park.

The **James Dean memorial,** 27 miles east of Paso Robles near the junction of Highways 46 and 41, is the site where the talented and rebellious actor crashed his silver Porsche and died on September 30, 1955.

San Luis Obispo

Located midway between San Francisco and Los Angeles at the junction of Hwy-1 and US-101, **San Luis Obispo** (pop. 44,174) makes a good stopping-off point, at least for lunch if not for a lengthier stay. Like most of the towns along this route, San Luis, as it's almost always called, revolves around an 18th-century mission, here named **Mission San Luis Obispo de Tolosa,** which is said to

be the place where Franciscan missionaries first developed California's traditional red-tiled roofs. Standing at the heart of town, at Chorro and Monterey Streets, the mission overlooks one of the state's liveliest small-town downtown districts, with dozens of shops and restaurants backing onto Mission Plaza, a two-block park on the banks of Mission Creek.

Besides the mission and the lively downtown commercial district that surrounds it, not to mention the nearly 20,000 students buzzing around the nearby campus of Cal Poly San Luis Obispo, San Luis holds a singular roadside attraction, the **Madonna Inn** ($80–180; 805/543-3000 or 800/543-9666), which stands just west of US-101 at the foot of town. One of

Another San Luis landmark, the world's first motel, opened at 2223 Monterey Street in 1925. Originally called the Milestone Motel, the Spanish revival structure was later renamed the Motel Inn, but it went out of business long ago and now stands, forlorn but not forgotten, next to US-101 on the grounds of the Apple Farm restaurant and motel.

El Camino Real and the California Missions

While the American colonies were busy rebelling against the English Crown, a handful of Spaniards and Mexicans were establishing outposts and blazing an overland route up the California coast, along the New World's most distant frontier. Beginning in 1769 with the founding of a fortress and a Franciscan mission at San Diego, and culminating in 1776 with the founding of another outpost at what is now San Francisco, a series of small but self-reliant religious colonies was established, each a day's travel apart and linked by El Camino Real, "The King's Highway," a route followed roughly by today's US-101.

Some of the most interesting missions are listed below, north to south, followed by the dates of their founding.

San Francisco Solano de Sonoma (1823). The only mission built under Mexican rule stands at the heart of Sonoma, a history-rich Wine Country town.

San Juan Bautista (1797). This lovely church forms the heart of an extensive historic park, in the town of the same name (see page 67).

San Carlos Borromeo (1770). Also known as Carmel Mission, this was the most important of the California missions (see page 71).

San Antonio de Padua (1771). This reconstructed church, still in use as a monastery, stands in an undeveloped valley inland from Big Sur in the middle of Hunter Liggett Army base. Monks still live, work, and pray here, making for a marvelously evocative visit.

San Miguel Arcangel (1797). The only mission not to have undergone extensive renovations and restorations—almost everything, notably the vibrantly colorful interior murals, is as it was.

Mission San Fernando from Memory Garden, and Father Junipero Serra Statue

La Purisima Concepción (1787). A quiet coastal valley is home to this church, which was restored in the 1930s using traditional methods as part of a New Deal employment and training project (see page 83).

Santa Barbara (1782). Called the "Queen of the Missions," this lovely church stands in lush gardens above the upscale coastal city (see page 85).

San Gabriel Arcangel (1771). Once the most prosperous of the California missions, it now stands quietly and all but forgotten off a remnant of Route 66 east of Los Angeles.

San Juan Capistrano (1776). Known for the swallows that return here each year, this mission has lovely gardens, but the buildings have been badly damaged by earthquakes and the elements, meaning they've been under scaffolding for years (see page 97).

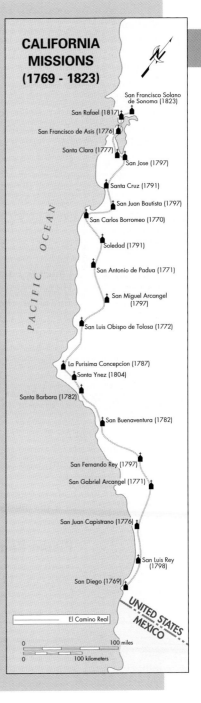

**CALIFORNIA
MISSIONS
(1769 - 1823)**

San Francisco Solano de Sonoma (1823)
San Rafael (1817)
San Francisco de Asis (1776)
Santa Clara (1777)
San Jose (1797)
Santa Cruz (1791)
San Juan Bautista (1797)
San Carlos Borromeo (1770)
Soledad (1791)
San Antonio de Padua (1771)
San Miguel Arcangel (1797)
San Luis Obispo de Tolosa (1772)
La Purisima Concepcion (1787)
Santa Ynez (1804)
Santa Barbara (1782)
San Buenaventura (1782)
San Fernando Rey (1797)
San Gabriel Arcangel (1771)
San Juan Capistrano (1776)
San Luis Rey (1798)
San Diego (1769)

PACIFIC OCEAN

UNITED STATES
MEXICO

El Camino Real

0   100 miles
0   100 kilometers

California's most noteworthy pop culture landmarks, the Madonna Inn is a remarkable example of what architecturally minded academic types like to call vernacular kitsch. Created by local contractor Alex Madonna, who died in 2004, the Madonna Inn offers over 100 unique rooms, each decorated in a wild barrage of fantasy motifs: There's the bright pink honeymoon suites known as "Just Heaven" and "Love Nest", the "Safari Room" covered in fake zebra skins with a jungle-green shag carpet, and the cave-like "Cave Man Room." *Roadside America* rates it as "the best place to spend a vacation night in America," but even if you can't stay, at least stop for a look at the gift shop, which sells postcards of the different rooms. Guys should head down to the men's room, where the urinal trough is flushed by a waterfall.

A pedestrian walkway in downtown San Luis Obispo, off Higuera Street between Garden and Broad Streets, has become known around the world as Bubble Gum Alley. Since the 1950s, local kids have written their names and allegiances on the brick walls, using chewing gum rather than the more contemporary spray paint.

Though the Madonna Inn has a huge, banquet-ready restaurant—done up in white lace and varying hues of pink—the best places to eat are located downtown, near the mission. **Linnaea's Cafe** (805/541-5888), at 1110 Garden Street off Higuera, serves coffee and tea and sundry snack items all day and night; there's also the lively, multi-culti **Big Sky Cafe** (805/545-5401) at 1121 Broad Street, and the usual range of beer-and-burger bars you'd expect from a college town.

Along with the Madonna Inn, San Luis has a number of good places to stay, with reasonable rates that drop considerably after the summertime peak season. Besides the national chains, try the **La Cuesta Inn** ($79–120; 805/543-2777 or 800/543-2777), at 2074 Monterey Street. There's also the **HI San Luis Obispo Hostel** (805/544-4678), near downtown and the Amtrak station at 1617 Santa Rosa Street.

Also worth noting: Every Thursday evening, the main drag of San Luis Obispo, Higuera Street, is closed to cars and converted into a very lively farmers market and block party, with stands selling fresh food and good live bands providing entertainment.

For more information, contact the **San Luis Obispo Chamber of Commerce** (805/781-2777), near the mission at 1039 Chorro Street, or pick up a copy of the free weekly *New Times*.

Pismo Beach

At the south end of Pismo Beach, Nipomo Dunes State Preserve holds endless acres of sand dunes and marshlands, as well as the buried remains of a movie set used in C. B. DeMille's The Ten Commandments.

South of San Luis Obispo, Hwy-1 and US-101 run along the ocean past **Pismo Beach** (pop. 8,551), a family-oriented beach resort where the main attraction is driving or dune-buggying along the sands. Pismo was once famous for its clams, now over-harvested to the point of oblivion, but you may still see people pitchforking a few small ones out of the surf. The area has grown significantly in the past decade, thanks mainly to an influx of retired people housed in red-roofed townhouses, but Price Street, the old main road, offers a wide range of motels and fast-food restaurants.

Guadalupe and Santa Maria

South of Pismo Beach, the highways diverge. Hwy-1 cuts off west through the still-agricultural areas around sleepy **Guadalupe** (pop. 5,659), where produce stands sell cabbages, broccoli, and leafy green vegetables fresh from the fields. The town itself feels miles away from modern California, with a four-block Main Street lined by Mexican cafés, bars, banks, and grocery stores. A great place to get a feel for Guadalupe is at the **Far Western Tavern** (805/343-2211), open daily for breakfast, lunch, and dinner at 899 Guadalupe Street. Try the steaks, which are awesome.

If you opt to follow US-101, shopping malls and tract-house suburbs fill the inland valleys through **Santa Maria**, a town best known these days for the sad saga of pop star Michael Jackson. Before his child-abuse trials, however, Santa Maria was famous for its thick cuts of salsa-slathered barbecued beef, which can be sampled at the large and historic **Santa Maria Inn** (805/928-7777), a half mile west of US-101 at 801 S. Broadway.

In the late 1930s, Nipomo was the place where **Dorothea Lange** took that famous photograph of a migrant mother huddling with her children in a farmworker camp.

Lompoc and La Purisima Mission

The rolling valleys around Lompoc are famed for their production of flower seeds, and consequently the fields along Hwy-1 are often ablaze in brilliant colors. Apart from colorful murals adorning downtown buildings, **Lompoc** as a town is not up to much, despite the unusual nature of the area's two main nonagricultural employers. One is a minimum-security federal prison; the other is Vandenburg Air Force Base, site of numerous missile tests, the aborted West Coast space shuttle port, and the $60 billion "Son of Star Wars" National Missile Defense program.

With its long arcade reaching across the floor of a shallow, grassy valley, **Mission La Purisima** (daily; $4 per car; 805/733-3713) gives a strong first impression of what the missions may have looked like in their prime. Four miles northeast of Lompoc, between Hwy-1 and US-101 on Hwy-246, the mission here was originally built in 1812 but fell to ruin before being totally reconstructed as part of a WPA make-work scheme in the New Deal 1930s. During the restoration, workers used period techniques wherever possible, hewing logs with

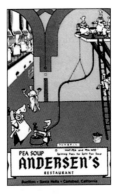

The town of **Buellton**, a block west of US-101 at the Solvang exit, holds one of California's classic roadside landmarks, **Andersen's Pea Soup Restaurant** (805/688-5581), advertised up and down the coast. Another Buellton landmark, the **Hitching Post** restaurant (805/688-0676), starred in the recent wine-loving road-trip movie, *Sideways*.

hand tools and stomping mud and straw with their bare feet to mix it for adobe bricks. Workers also built most of the mission-style furniture that fills the chapel and the other rooms in the complex. Also here: a functioning aqueduct, many miles of hiking trails, and a small museum.

Solvang

America's most famous mock-European tourist trap, the Danish-style town of **Solvang** (pop. 5,332) was founded in 1911. Set up by a group of Danish immigrants as a cooperative agricultural community, Solvang found its calling catering to passing travelers. The compact blocks of cobblestoned streets and Old World architecture, highlighted by a few windmills and signs advertising the "Hamlet Motel" among many more suspicious claims to Danishness, now attract tourists by the busload. Many other U.S. towns (Leavenworth, Washington, and Helen, Georgia, to name two) have been inspired by Solvang's success, but to be honest there's nothing much to do here apart from walking, gawking, and shopping for pastries.

Local sybarites love to soak in the naturally hot waters of **Las Cruces hot spring**, tucked away up a canyon just south of the US-101/Hwy-1 junction.

Just east of Solvang's windmills and gables, the brooding hulk of **Mission Santa Ynez** stands as a sober reminder of the region's Spanish colonial past. Built in 1804, it was once among the more prosperous of the California missions, but now is worth a visit mainly for the gift shop selling all manner of devotional ornaments.

Pop singer Michael Jackson's Neverland Ranch lies here in the foothills of the Santa Ynez Valley, southeast of Solvang via the truly scenic Hwy-254, which loops inland south to Santa Barbara.

Gaviota and Refugio State Beaches

Between Solvang and Santa Barbara, US-101 follows the coast past some of California's most beautiful beaches. Dropping through a steep-sided canyon, US-101 reaches the coast at **Gaviota State Beach,** where a small fishing pier and campground are overwhelmed by the massive train trestle that runs overhead. Continuing south, US-101 runs atop coastal bluffs past prime surfing beaches, usually marked by a few VWs pulled out along the west side of the highway. Midway along this stretch of coast, some 22 miles north of Santa Barbara, **Refugio State Beach** has groves of palm tress backing a clear white strand. There's also a small, summer-only store, and a number of attractive campsites with hot showers.

Rancho del Cielo, the ranch of former President Ronald Reagan, spreads along the crest of the coastal hills above Refugio State Beach.

Reservations for camping at Gaviota or Refugio, or at any California state beach, should be made in advance by calling 800/444-7275.

Santa Barbara

The geographical midpoint of California may well be somewhere near San Francisco, but the Southern California of popular imagination—golden beaches washed by waves and peopled by blond-haired surfer gods—has its start, and perhaps best expression, in Santa Barbara. Just over 100 miles north of Los Angeles, **Santa Barbara** (pop. 92,325) has grown threefold in the last 60 years, but

for the moment, at least, it manages to retain its sleepy seaside charm. Much of its character comes from the fact that, following a sizeable earthquake in 1929, the town fathers—caught up in the contemporary craze for anything Spanish Revival—required that all buildings in the downtown area exude a mission-era feel, mandating red-tile roofs, adobe-colored stucco, and rounded arcades wherever practicable. The resulting architectural consistency gives Santa Barbara an un-American charm; it looks more like a Mediterranean village than the modern city that, beneath the surface, it really is.

For a good first look at the city head down to the water, where **Stearns Wharf** sticks out into the bay, bordered by palm tree–lined beaches populated by joggers, inline skaters, and volleyball players. From the wharf area, follow State Street away from the sands to the downtown district, where Santa Barbarans parade among the numerous cafés, bars, and boutiques. At the north end of downtown is the excellent **Museum of Art** (closed Mon.; $7, free Sun.; 805/963-4364), at 1130 State Street. A block east on Anacapa Street, the **County Courthouse** is one of the finest public buildings in the state, a handcrafted Spanish Revival monument set in lush semitropical gardens, with an observation tower (daily 9 AM–5 PM; free) giving a fine view over the red-tiled cityscape.

Santa Barbara's reigning attraction, **Mission Santa Barbara** (daily; $4; 805/682-4713), stands atop a shallow hill a well-posted mile up from State

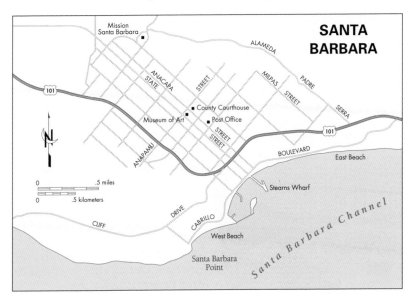

Street, looking out over the city and shoreline below. Called the "Queen of the Missions" by the local tourist scribes, Mission Santa Barbara is undeniably lovely to look at, its rose-hued stone facade perfectly complemented by the roses and bougainvillea that frame the well-maintained gardens and lawns.

Santa Barbara has perhaps the coast's best variety of places to eat. State Street holds the most lunch and dinner places, like the old-fashioned burgers and beer on tap in the dark-wood dining room of **Joe's Cafe** (805/966-4638) at 536 State Street. Finally, some of the world's best hole-in-the-wall Mexican food is served a half mile east of State Street at **La Super-Rica** (805/963-4940) at 622 N. Milpas Street, where such distinguished foodies as Julia Child have come to chow down on a variety of freshly made soft tacos and delicious seafood tamales. It's not cheap, but the food is great (fresh tortillas, traditional *adobado*-marinated pork, and spicy chorizo), and the *horchata* is the creamiest you'll taste. Yum.

*Santa Barbara is one of many great places along the coast to go on a **whale-watching cruise**, on the Condor Express or other boats, to see migrating gray whales in winter and jumping humpbacks in summer. Trips take a half day or full day, and some head out to the Channel Islands; call 805/963-3564 or 888/779-4253 for details or reservations.*

The city's accommodations, however, are among the central coast's most expensive, especially in summer when even the most basic motel can charge as much as $150 a night. One of the nicest of many motels is the **Franciscan Inn** ($90 and up; 805/963-8845), just a short walk from the beach and wharf at 109 Bath Street. At the top of the scale, the **Simpson House** ($215 and up; 805/963-7067 or 800/676-1280) at 121 E. Arrellaga Street offers comfortable, centrally located B&B rooms. Off the scale completely, money's-no-object visitors can enjoy the deluxe facilities of the **San Ysidro Ranch** ($395 and up; 805/969-5046), in the hills above neighboring Montecito, where Jackie and JFK spent some of their honeymoon. Somewhat ironically, considering the generally high prices here, international budget chain Motel 6 got its start in Santa Barbara, where they now have five properties, including one near the beach at 443 Corona Del Mar ($80; 805/564-1392).

For further details on Santa Barbara, stop into the **Visitor Information Center** (805/966-9222 or 800/676-1266), near Stearns Wharf at 1 Santa Barbara Street.

Channel Islands National Park

South of Santa Barbara, US-101 widens into an eight-lane freeway along the coast. Looking out across the Pacific, beyond the partially disguised offshore oil wells, you can't miss seeing the sharp outlines of the Channel Islands, whose rocky shores are protected as a national park.

Consisting of eight islands altogether, they sit from 12 to nearly 50 miles off the mainland. Numerous scenic cruises around the Channel Islands start from Santa Barbara, but only the smallest and closest, Anacapa Island, is easily accessible to the public, via daily trips from Ventura Harbor, offered by **Island Packers** ($42; 805/642-1393).

Ventura

Midway between Malibu and Santa Barbara, **Ventura** (pop. 100,916) is an offbeat little place, its three-block Main Street lined by enough thrift shops (seven at last count) to clothe a destitute retro-minded army. Apart from searching out vintage couture, the main reason to stop is the small and much-reconstructed **Mission San Buenaventura** (daily; donations), standing at the center of Ventura at 225 E. Main Street, just east of the US-101 freeway. This was the ninth in the California mission chain, and the last one founded by Father Serra, in 1782. A block from the mission at 113 E. Main Street, the **Albinger Archaeological Museum** (closed Mon.; free) collects a wide range of artifacts—the oldest from 1500 BC, the most recent from early American settlers—all excavated from a single city block–sized site alongside the mission.

Ventura doesn't get anything like the tourist trade that Santa Barbara draws, but it does have the very pleasant **Bella Magiore Inn** ($90 and up; 805/652-0277 or 800/523-8479), offering good-value B&B rooms in a nicely restored 1920s courtyard house at 67 S. California Street, between downtown and US-101.

South of Ventura, US-101 heads inland through the San Fernando Valley to Hollywood and downtown Los Angeles, while Hwy-1 heads south through the 10 miles of stop-and-go sprawl that make up the rapidly suburbanizing farming community of **Oxnard** (pop. 170,358), then continues right along the coast through Malibu and West Los Angeles.

> Ventura is the birthplace and headquarters of the outdoor equipment and clothing company **Patagonia**, started and still owned by legendary rock climber **Yvon Chouinard**.

Simi Valley

If you opt to follow US-101 rather than coastal Hwy-1 into Los Angeles, be sure to check out the somnolent suburb of **Simi Valley,** 20 miles east of Ventura. Home to the jury that acquitted the LAPD officers who beat Rodney King, it's also where the hilltop **Ronald Reagan Presidential Library** (daily; $5; 805/522-8444) fills 150,000 square feet of Spanish-style stucco. The "Great Communicator" was interred here following his death in 2004; to get here, take US-101 to Hwy-23 North, exit at Olsen Road, and follow the signs.

The other Simi Valley sight to see is **Bottle Village** (donations; 805/583-1627), a complex of small buildings and sculptures built out of glass bottles, TV sets, hubcaps, and assorted other recycled refuse in the 1940s and 1950s by the late Tressa Prisbey. Badly damaged in the 1992 Northridge earthquake, and subject of a heated battle between preservationists and those who think it's a pile of junk, the village can be viewed from the road or by occasional guided tours; it's at 4595 Cochrane Street, a mile south of the Hwy-118/210 freeway between the Tapo Canyon and Sterns Road exits.

Pacific Coast Highway Beaches

Running right along the beach, the Pacific Coast Highway (Hwy-1) heads south from Oxnard around the rocky headland of **Point Mugu** (ma-GOO), where the U.S. Navy operates a missile testing center and the Santa Monica Mountains rise steeply out of the Pacific Ocean. Most of these chaparral-covered granite mountains have been protected as parkland, with hiking, cycling, and riding trails offering grand views and a surprising amount of solitude. Before or after a hike in the hills (or a Harley ride along the coast, the preferred mode of arrival), the ramshackle **Neptune's Net** restaurant (310/457-3095) at 42505 Pacific Coast Highway is a great place to hang out and "star"-gaze while enjoying fresh seafood, served up on paper plates for that down-home Hollywood feel.

South from here, a series of state-owned beaches mark your progress along the coastal road, but this stretch is basically natural wilderness—apart from the highway, of course. Biggest and best of the beaches hereabouts is the lovely **Leo Carrillo State Beach**, which has a sandy strand, some great tidepools, and a sycamore-shaded campground (800/444-7275).

South of Leo Carrillo, which marks the Los Angeles County line, there are many more public beach areas, including (in roughly north-to-south order) Nicholas Canyon County Beach, El Pescador, El Matador (where episodes of TV's *Baywatch* have been filmed), and big, brash Zuma Beach, where the highway bends inland.

Malibu

South of Zuma Beach, houses begin popping up along Hwy-1 to block the oceanfront views, and more-elaborate multimillion-dollar homes dot the canyons above as well, forming the sprawling exurbia and movie-star playground of **Malibu**, which stretches along Hwy-1 for the next 27 miles into Santa Monica and metropolitan Los Angeles. It's hard to get more than a glimpse of the garage doors or wrought-iron gates of these palaces, but this is the address of choice for the movers and shakers of the entertainment world: If you can name them, they probably own property here. Most of the truly huge estates are hidden away on ranches high up in the mountains.

The main route inland from the coast, Malibu Canyon Road, was the setting of the key murder scene in **James M. Cain's** thriller *The Postman Always Rings Twice*.

One of the few accessible hideaways has been evolving since 1993, when Barbra Streisand donated her 22-acre ranch for use as a botanical preserve. Called **Ramirez Canyon Park**, and located at 5750 Ramirez Canyon Road, it's managed by the Santa Monica Mountains Conservancy and is open to visitors only on a weekly guided tour (Wed. at 1 PM; $35; 310/589-2850) of the delightful gardens, finishing with an afternoon tea.

From Hwy-1, the most prominent sight is the **Pepperdine University** campus, which was described by the late, great architect Charles Moore as "an overscaled motel set in obscenely vivid emerald lawns." (Pepperdine is also the place Clinton-chasing Special Prosecutor Kenneth Starr agreed to be Dean of the Law School, only to quit in continuing pursuit of Monica

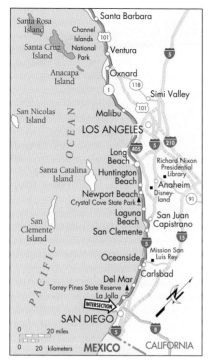

Lewinsky a few days later.) Below the bluff-top campus, the legendary **Malibu Colony** of celebrity homes stretches along the coast in high-security splendor.

About the only place in Malibu where it's fun (and legal) to explore is the area around the landmark **Malibu Pier,** which juts into the ocean at the heart of Malibu's short and rather scruffy commercial strip. North of the pier, which was used most famously in TV's *The Rockford Files,* stretches **Surfrider Beach,** site of most of those Frankie Avalon and Annette Funicello beach blanket babylon movies made during the 1950s. The pier and the beach are part of **Malibu Lagoon State Park,** which also protects the historic **Adamson House** (Wed.–Sat. 11 AM–2 PM; $3; 310/456-8432) at 23200 Pacific Coast Highway, a lovely old circa-1929 Spanish Revival courtyard home, right on the beach and full of gorgeous tile work and other architectural features. Tours of the house are given throughout the day, and fascinating exhibits portray Malibu history and the Rindge family, who once owned the entire region.

Between Malibu and Santa Monica, **Topanga Canyon** is home to an alternative community of hippies and New Agers. South of Topanga, and once again open to the public after 10 years of remodeling, are the world-famous antiquities of the **J. Paul Getty Museum** (daily; free). Over 1,200 priceless classics are displayed in the Getty Villa, where the oil magnate's art collection was housed prior to the construction of the massive Getty Center complex above Brentwood. To reach the new Getty Center from the shore, follow winding Sunset Boulevard 10 miles east to the San Diego Freeway (I-405), but call first for parking reservations (310/440-7300), which are essential. From Sunset Boulevard south to Santa Monica, the Pacific Coast Highway (Hwy-1) runs along the wide-open sands of **Will Rogers State Beach,** gifted to the public by the Depression-era humorist.

Santa Monica marks the western start of legendary **Route 66,** which winds between Southern California and Chicago. Our road trip coverage begins on page 784.

Crossing Los Angeles

From Malibu and Topanga Canyon, Hwy-1 swoops along the shore, running along the beach as far as the landmark Santa Monica Pier before bending inland through a tunnel and metamorphosing quite unexpectedly into the I-10 Santa Monica Freeway. The second exit off this freeway

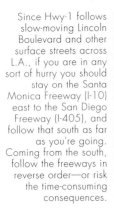

(which has been officially dubbed the Christopher Columbus Transcontinental Highway, running all the way east to Jacksonville, Florida) takes you to Lincoln Boulevard, which carries the Hwy-1 moniker south through Venice and Marina del Rey to Los Angeles International Airport (LAX), where it runs into Sepulveda Boulevard.

Since Hwy-1 follows slow-moving Lincoln Boulevard and other surface streets across L.A., if you are in any sort of hurry you should stay on the Santa Monica Freeway (I-10) east to the San Diego Freeway (I-405), and follow that south as far as you're going. Coming from the south, follow the freeways in reverse order—or risk the time-consuming consequences.

After passing through a tunnel under the airport runways—worth the drive just for the experience of seeing 747s taxiing over your head—Sepulveda emerges in the Tarantino-esque communities of L.A.'s "South Bay," which utterly lack the glamour of chichi Santa Monica and Malibu. At Hermosa Beach, one of a trio of pleasant if surprisingly blue-collar beach towns, Sepulveda Boulevard changes its name to Pacific Coast Highway, then bends inland to bypass the ritzy communities of the Palos Verdes Peninsula, passing instead through the industrial precincts of San Pedro that border the Los Angeles/Long Beach harbor, one of the busiest on the West Coast.

Long Beach

Directly south of downtown Los Angeles, the city of **Long Beach** (pop. 461,522) is the second-largest of L.A.'s constituent cities, but it feels more like the Midwest than the cutting-edge West Coast. Long Beach is probably best known as the home of the cruise ship RMS *Queen Mary,* one of the largest and most luxurious liners ever to set sail. Impossible to miss as it looms over Long Beach harbor, the stately ship is open for self-guided tours ($25; 562/435-3511).

In place of Howard Hughes's famous "Spruce Goose" airplane, which used to stand next door, there's now a Cold War–era submarine, and across the bay on the main downtown Long Beach waterfront, the **Aquarium of the Pacific** (daily; $18.95; 562/590-3100) explores the diverse ecosystems of the Pacific Ocean, from tropical coral reefs (shown off in an amazing, 360,000-gallon display) to the frigid waters of the Bering Sea. The tanks full of jellyfish of all kinds, colors, and sizes are the main event.

Along with the annual Toyota Long Beach Grand Prix, an Indy Car race held on the city streets every April, other Long Beach attractions include the **world's largest mural**, a 115,000-square-foot painting of whales on the outside of the

Long Beach Arena, and the self-proclaimed **Skinniest House in the USA,** at 708 Gladys Avenue.

Long Beach also marks the southern end of L.A.'s reborn streetcar and subway system, and you can ride the Blue Line north to downtown. It's an inexpensive base for exploring the Los Angeles area, especially if you avail yourself of the $15-a-night **HI South Bay Hostel** (310/831-8109), on a hill overlooking the harbor area at 3601 S. Gaffey Street. There's also a **Best Western** ($80; 562/599-5555) at 1725 Long Beach Boulevard, directly across from a Blue Line train stop.

For more information, contact the Long Beach **visitors bureau** (562/436-3645 or 800/452-7829).

Huntington Beach

Winding south and east from Long Beach, Hwy-1 continues along the coast past a series of natural marshlands and small-craft marinas. The first real point of interest is the town of **Huntington Beach** (pop. 189,594), one of the largest communities in Orange County. Founded in 1909 by Henry Huntington as a stop along his legendary Pacific Electric "Red Car" interurban railway network, Huntington Beach is best known as the place where **surfing** was first introduced to the U.S. mainland. To attract Angelenos down to his new town, Huntington hired Hawaiians to demonstrate the sport, which at the time made use of huge solid wooden boards, 15 feet long and weighing around 150 pounds. Huntington Beach, especially around the pier, is still a very popular surfing spot—though contemporary surfers slice through the waves on high-tech foam-core boards, a third the size of the original Hawaiian long boards and weighing under 10 pounds. The history and culture of West Coast surfing, with examples of boards then and now (plus special collections highlighting "surf" movies and the creation of "surf music" by local heroes Leo Fender and Dick Dale), is recounted in the small but enthusiastic **International Surfing Museum** (daily noon–5 PM; $2; 714/960-3483), two blocks from the pier at 411 Olive Avenue, in the heart of the lively downtown business district.

Nearby, within a few blocks of the pier at 421 8th Street, is the handy **Colonial Inn Youth Hostel** (714/536-3315), with dorm beds for $13 and double rooms for $30.

Disneyland

Like a little bit of middle America grafted onto the southern edge of Los Angeles, inland Orange County used to feel like a totally different world. Though the demographics have changed considerably in the past decade or two, in contrast to L.A.'s fast-paced, edgily creative multiethnic stew, Orange County in the 1950s and 1960s was suburban America writ large—mostly white, mostly well-off, and absolutely, totally bland. In short, a perfect place to build the ultimate escapist fantasy, the self-proclaimed "Happiest Place on Earth," **Disneyland.**

Los Angeles

Love it or hate it, one thing you can't do about L.A. is ignore it. Thanks to Hollywood in all its many guises (movies, television, the music industry), the city is always in the headlines. Without falling too deeply under the spell of its hyperbole-fueled image-making machinery, it's safe to say that L.A. definitely has something for everyone. In keeping with its car-centered culture, however, our suggested tour ignores the many individual attractions and focuses instead on a pair of quintessential LA drives.

Gay and Happy Beach Crowds Bathing in the Pacific, Santa Monica

Winding along the crest of the Hollywood Hills, **Mulholland Drive** is the classic L.A. cruise. Starting in the east within sight of the Hollywood Sign and the Hollywood Bowl, this ribbon of two-lane blacktop passes by the city's most valuable real estate, giving great views on both sides, both by day and after dark, ending up eventually at the north end of Malibu on Pacific Coast Highway (PCH).

Another classic L.A. cruise, running from the scruffy fringes of downtown all the way west to the coast, **Sunset Boulevard** gives glimpses into almost every conceivable aspect of Los Angeles life. Starting downtown, the historic core of colonial Los Angeles and now a showcase of contemporary architecture thanks to a stunning new cathedral and concert hall, Sunset Boulevard's 27-mile course then winds west past Echo Park and Hollywood to West Hollywood, where it becomes the "Sunset Strip," still the liveliest nightclub district in town. Continuing west, Sunset winds through Beverly Hills, Brentwood, and Bel-Air, lined by the largest mansions you're likely to see, before ending up at the edge of the Pacific Ocean.

Practicalities

Most flights into Los Angeles arrive at Los Angeles International Airport (LAX), on the coast southwest of downtown, where you'll find all the usual shuttles and rental car agencies. Other useful L.A. airports include Burbank, Long Beach, Ontario, and John Wayne, in Orange County.

Before choosing a place to stay, think about where you want to spend your time, and settle near there. High-end places abound, but character can be hard to come by. Along the coast, recommended accommodations range from the handy **Santa Monica HI Hostel** (310/393-9913), a block from the beach at 1436 2nd Street, where dorm beds cost $25 and private rooms are $65; to the unique **Hotel Queen Mary** in Long Beach ($109 and up; 562/435-3511), offering understandably cramped quarters in the fabulous old luxury liner. For mid-range with a great mid-city location, try the **Farmer's Daughter** ($99 and up; 800/334-1658), at 115 S. Fairfax Avenue, a very friendly 1950s-style motel with tons of charm and the city's hottest new shopping mall and entertainment complex, The Grove, across the street next to the historic Farmer's Market. Downtown, the most fabulous place to stay is the retro-1960s **Downtown Standard** ($175–up; 213/892-8080), 550 S. Flower Street, with the world's coolest rooftop, poolside bar.

For food, one place I always try to stop is the **Apple Pan** (310/475-3585), at 10801 W. Pico Boulevard, an ancient (circa 1947) landmark on the west L.A. landscape, serving the best hamburgers on the planet—though I'll admit to being biased, since I grew up eating them. Take a seat at the counter, and be sure to save room for a slice of their wonderful fruit pies. Late at night, the huge sandwiches and heart-warming soups at **Canter's Deli** (open daily 24 hours; 213/651-2030), 419 N. Fairfax Avenue, draws all kinds of night owls to a lively New York–style deli in the heart of the predominantly Jewish Fairfax District. Downtown, in the heart of old L.A. at 1001 Alameda, **Philippe's French Dip Sandwiches** (213/628-3781) is a classic workingman's cafeteria, offering good food at impossibly low prices, with character to spare.

The **Los Angeles Dodgers** (323/224-1471) play at beautiful Dodger Stadium, on a hill above downtown.

The usual array of information about hotels, restaurants, tickets to TV show tapings and all other L.A.-area attractions is available through the **Los Angeles Convention and Visitors Bureau** (213/689-8822 or 800/228-2452), with an office at 685 S. Figueroa Street.

The phenomenon of Disneyland has been done to death by all sorts of social critics, but the truth is, it can be great fun—provided you visit out of season and get there early to avoid the crowds, and really immerse yourself in the extroverted, mindless joy of it all. Most of the rides are great, each in different ways (I like "Pirates of the Caribbean" best), but there can be little forgiveness for "It's a Small World." Avoid it like the plague, or risk having the song ringing in your head for days afterward.

If you haven't been before, or not for a while at any rate, here are some useful tidbits of information: Disneyland is 20 miles south of downtown L.A., right off I-5 in the city of Anaheim—you can see the Matterhorn from the freeway. The park is open daily; in summer, it remains open until midnight. Admission to the park, which includes all rides, costs around $50 per person per day, with discounts for extended visits; kids under 12 save 20 percent. For further park details, including opening hours, call Disneyland at 714/781-7290.

Disneyland opened in 1955, when there was nothing surrounding it; in intervening years, an entire metropolis has grown up around it, and in 2001 the park was joined by the much smaller, more grown-up–oriented **California Adventure**. Instead of cuddly cartoon characters, this billion-dollar park has thrill rides like "California Screamin'," a 60-mph roller coaster, and the excellent "Soaring Over California" motion simulator, offering an airborne tour of the Golden State from Yosemite Falls to the Malibu beaches. California Adventure is totally separate from Disneyland, but the hours and admission are about the same.

The Anaheim Angels (714/940-2000) play at Angel Stadium on Gene Autry Way.

The whole Disney ensemble includes an upscale resort-hotel complex, surrounded by motels and yet more motels, and it's well worth staying overnight so you can get an early start, go "home" for a while, and come back for the nightly fireworks show. A highly recommended place to stay is the **Coast Anaheim Hotel** (714/750-1811), a block from Disneyland at 1855 S. Harbor Boulevard, offering spacious modern rooms (and a nice pool) from $90 per night, with free parking and free shuttles every half hour to and from Disneyland. For more lodging and other travel information, call the **Anaheim Convention and Visitors Bureau** at 714/765-8888.

Richard Nixon Presidential Library

If you've already done the Disneyland thing, or just want a foil to the empty-headed fun, there is one other Orange County attraction you really shouldn't miss: the **Richard Nixon Presidential Library** (daily; $5.95; 714/993-5075), 18001 Yorba Linda Boulevard, 10 miles northeast of

Disneyland off Hwy-91. The library is built on the very ground where the former president was born in 1913; it's also where he and his wife, Pat, are buried, side by side next to the restored Craftsman-style bungalow where Nixon grew up. No matter what your feelings toward him, the spare-no-expense displays do a fascinating job of putting his long career into the distorted perspective you'd expect from the only president ever forced to resign from office. If you can take the show at face value, highlights are many, such as the pictures of the pumpkin patch where Whittaker Chambers concealed the microfilm that Nixon used to put Alger Hiss in prison as a Communist spy, next to photos of Nixon and JFK as chummy freshman U.S. senators sharing sleeping compartments on a train. The best-selling item in the gift shop? Postcards of Nixon greeting Elvis Presley, also available as place mats, china, and fridge magnets.

Newport Beach

Back on the coast, if you want to get a sense of what wealthy Orange Countians do to enjoy themselves, spend some time along the clean white strands of **Newport Beach.** Located at the southern edge of Los Angeles's suburban sprawl, Newport started life as an amusement park and beach resort at the southern end of the L.A. streetcar lines. In the 1930s and 1940s, thousands of Angelenos spent summer weekends at the **Balboa Pavilion,** at the southern tip of the slender Balboa peninsula, where a few remnants of the pre–video game amusements survive—a Ferris wheel, a merry-go-round, and those odd "Pokerino" games in which you win prizes by rolling rubber balls into a series of numbered holes.

To return to Hwy-1 from Balboa Peninsula, you can either backtrack around the harbor or ride the **Balboa Ferry,** which shuttles you and your car from the pavilion across the harbor past an amazing array of sailboats, power cruisers, and waterfront homes.

Midway along the peninsula, near 23rd Street, Newport Pier is flanked by another holdout from the old days: the **dory fleet,** where almost every day small boats set off to catch rock cod and more exotic fish that, starting around noon, are sold straight from the boats at an outdoor market right on the sands.

A mile south of Balboa Pavilion, next to the breakwater at the very southern end of Balboa peninsula, **The Wedge** is one of the world's most popular and challenging bodysurfing spots, with well-formed waves often twice as high as anywhere else on the coast.

Crystal Cove State Park

Midway between Newport and Laguna Beaches, amidst the ever-encroaching Orange County sprawl, **Crystal Cove State Park** (daily dawn–dusk; $6 per car) protects one of Southern California's finest chunks of coastline. With three miles of sandy beaches and chaparral-covered bluff lined by well-marked walking trails, it's a fine place to enjoy the shoreline without the commercial trappings. Originally home to Native Americans, the land here was later part of Mission San Juan Capistrano and, until 1979 when the state bought it, the massive Irvine Ranch, which once covered most of Orange County.

The main parking area for Crystal Cove is at **Reef Point** (daily dawn–dusk; $10 per car; 949/494-3539) near the south end of the park, where there are bathrooms and showers plus excellent tidepools, a fine beach, and a well-preserved collection of 1920s beach cottages, where you can stay overnight for $50–150. (The cottages were slated to be "developed" into an upscale resort by the creators of Big Sur's Post Ranch Inn, but local preservationists managed to keep the place in public hands). There is also a large section inland from Hwy-1, through the oakland glade of **El Moro Canyon,** which gives a vivid sense of Orange County's rapidly vanishing natural landscape.

Laguna Beach

Compared with much of Orange County, **Laguna Beach** (pop. 23,727) is a relaxed and enjoyable place. Bookstores, cafés, and galleries reflect the town's beginnings as an artists' colony, but while the beach and downtown area are still very attractive, the surrounding hills have been covered by some of the world's ugliest tracts of "executive homes."

During the annual **Pageant of the Masters,** Laguna Beach residents re-create scenes from classical and modern art by forming living tableaux, standing still as statues in front of painted backdrops. Held every summer, it's a popular event and proceeds go to good causes, so get tickets ($15–80; 949/497-6582 or 800/487-3378) well in advance.

Right across Hwy-1 from the downtown shopping district, which is full of pleasant cafés and a wide range of art galleries, Laguna's main beach (called simply Main Beach) is still the town's main draw, with a boardwalk, some volleyball courts where the standard of play is very high, and a guarded swimming beach with showers.

Many other fine but usually less crowded and quieter beaches are reachable from Cliff Drive, which winds north of downtown Laguna past cove after untouched cove; follow the signs reading Beach Access.

Adjacent to the beach, right on Hwy-1, is **Greeter's Corner Cafe** (949/494-0361), locally famous thanks to an elderly gentleman named Eiler Larsen, now deceased, who used to stand out front and wave at the passing traffic. The food is fine, and you can eat outside on the broad deck overlooking the beach. Another place worth searching out is the small **Taco Loco** (949/497-1635), 640 S. Hwy-1 at the south end of the downtown strip, where the ultra-fresh Mexican food includes your choice of three or four different seafood tacos, from shark to swordfish, in daily-changing specials from about $1.50 each.

Places to stay are expensive, starting at around $100 a night, and include the centrally located, somewhat older **Hotel Laguna** (949/494-1151) at 425 S. Hwy-1, and the beachfront **Laguna Riviera Hotel and Spa** (949/494-1196), 825 S. Hwy-1. At the top end of the scale, the newish **Montage Resort** (866/271-6953), at 30801 S. Hwy-1, is California's only Mobil five star–rated spa and resort, with everything you could want from a hotel—all yours for $750 a day.

South of Laguna Beach, Hwy-1 follows the coast for a final few miles before joining up with the I-5 freeway for the 40-mile drive into San Diego.

San Juan Capistrano

Of the 21 missions along the California coast, **Mission San Juan Capistrano** (daily; $6; 949/234-1300) has been the most romanticized. When the movement to restore the missions and preserve California's Spanish colonial past was at its apogee in the late 1930s, its main theme tune was Leon Rene's "When the Swallows Come Back to Capistrano," popularizing the legend that these birds return from their winter migration every St. Joseph's Day, March 19th. After wintering in Goya, Argentina, they do come back to Capistrano, along with several thousand tourists, but the swallows are just as likely to reappear a week before or a week after—whenever the weather warms up, really.

The mission, which has lovely, bougainvillea-filled gardens, stands at the center of the small, eponymously named town, a short detour inland along I-5 from the coast. Besides the birds, the main attractions include the small **chapel**, the last surviving church where the beatified Father Serra said Mass, widely considered to be the oldest intact church and perhaps the oldest building of any kind in California, and the ruins of the massive **Stone Church**, a finely carved limestone structure that collapsed in an earthquake in 1812, just six years after its completion. Many visitors to the chapel are terminally ill patients saying prayers to St. Pereguin, the patron saint of medical miracles.

To get a sense of the huge scale of the Stone Church, a full-sized replica called the New Church has been constructed behind the mission, and now serves as the official mission church, open to visitors except during religious services. Across the street from the New Church, a Michael Graves–designed local **library** gives an intriguing postmodern take on the mission style.

In the block between the Mission and I-5, the **Walnut Grove Restaurant** and **Mission Inn Motel** are two of the few survivors of old-style San Juan Capistrano, holding out against the relentless suburbanizing that has leveled many of the surrounding historic commercial structures. Another unique spot is the **Coach House** (949/496-8930) at 33157 Camino Capistrano, one of Southern California's best small clubs for listening to live music.

San Clemente

At the southern tip of coastal Orange County, **San Clemente** marks the midway point between San Diego and Los Angeles. A sleepy beachside community, with frequent Amtrak train service and a nicely undulating stretch of old US-101 (El Camino Real) running through its heart, San Clemente is probably best known as the site of Casa Pacifica, the one-time "Western White House" of former president Richard Nixon, who lived here following his election in 1968 until after his impeachment in the mid-1970s. The white-walled, mission-style house at the south end of Avenida del Presidente (the western frontage road to I-5) is more easily visible from the beach below, though the 25 acres of trees have grown up to obscure it in recent years.

Twelve miles south of San Clemente, alongside the prominent nuclear power plant at San Onofre, one of Southern California's better surfing beaches has been home to the friendly, family-run **Pascowitz Surf Camp** (949/728-1000) every summer since 1972.

Within a quick walk uphill from the handful of cafés and bars on and around the pier, **The Beachcomber** ($100–125; 949/492-5457) is a tidy, old-fashioned motor-court motel, facing onto the open ocean. San Clemente also has a handy **HI Hostel** (949/492-2848), just a short walk from the beach at 233 Avenida Granada, and a great breakfast place: **Duke's Griddle and Grill,** 204 S. El Camino Real in the Mission-style downtown business district.

Mission San Luis Rey de Francia

In the sun-bleached hills above the blue Pacific, four miles east of the ocean off the I-5 along Hwy-76, **Mission San Luis Rey de Francia** (daily; $5) was among the largest and most successful of the California missions. Its lands have been taken over by Camp Pendleton, and most of the outbuildings have disappeared, but the stately church at the heart of the complex survives in fine condition, worth a look for the blue-tinted dome atop the bell tower and for the haunting carved stone skull that looks down from the cemetery gate.

A long but worthwhile detour inland from San Luis Rey brings you to the least visited but perhaps most evocative of all the California missions, **Mission San Antonio de Pala** (sometimes closed Mon.; $2; 760/742-1600). Located on the Pala Indian Reservation, 20 miles east of San Luis Rey along Hwy-76, then another 100 yards north along a well-marked side road, Mission San Antonio de Pala is the only California mission still serving its original role of preaching to the native people, and gives an unforgettable impression of what California's mission era might have been like.

Oceanside

At the southern edge of 125,000-acre Camp Pendleton Marine Corps Base, **Oceanside** (pop. 161,029) is the largest city between Los Angeles and San

Diego, but offers little to attract the casual visitor—apart from guided tours of Camp Pendleton's amphibious-assault training exercises, and the state's longest fishing pier. But if you're in the mood to shop for camouflage gear, watch the muscle cars cruise Hill Street, get a $3 G.I. Joe haircut, or drink beer with a gang of young recruits, this is the right place.

Oceanside is also home to one of the last survivors of the old pre–I-5, Coast Highway businesses: The **101 Café** (760/722-5220) at 631 S. Coast Highway has been open for classic road food since 1928, and often hosts "classic car" rallies and generally glows with neon-lit nostalgia.

South from Oceanside, all the way to San Diego, a very pleasant alternative to the often-clogged I-5 is the old alignment of US-101, now signed as County Road S21 (and occasionally, "Coast Highway 101"). Slower than the freeway but still in regular use, the old road is now the main drag of quaint beachfront towns like Carlsbad, Leucadia, Encinitas, and Del Mar. If you have the time, it's a great drive, in sight of the ocean for most of the way.

> The northwest corner of San Diego County is taken up by the U.S. Marines Corps' massive **Camp Pendleton** training base, which fills 125,000 acres, running for 20 miles along the coast and 15 miles inland. Camp Pendleton (the base motto is "No Beach out of Reach") is the largest undeveloped section of the Southern California coast.

Carlsbad: La Costa and Legoland

Named for the European spa town of Karlsbad, in Bohemia of what's now the Czech Republic, **Carlsbad** (pop. 78,247) was established in the 1880s and had a brief heyday as a spa town until the 1930s. A few remnants of the historic resort area, including the circa-1887 landmark **Neiman's Restaurant** (760/729-4131) at 2978 Carlsbad Boulevard, still survive along old US-101 in the center of town. A few flower and strawberry fields surround the town, surviving against the ever-expanding tide of sprawl, but these days Carlsbad is best known as the home of **La Costa Resort and Spa** ($225 and up; 760/438-9111), a 500-room complex of luxurious rooms, health spas, golf courses and tennis courts covering 400 acres of hills on the inland side of I-5.

Carlsbad's other main attraction, since its opening in early 1999, is the first American outpost of the popular European children's theme park **Legoland** (adults $42, children $35; 760/918-5346). Built out of more than 30 million Lego bricks, and covering 128 acres above the Pacific Ocean, the park is divided up into three main areas, including Mini-Land, where miniature landscapes modeled on New York, New Orleans, New England, and the Northern California coast have all been constructed using the trademark plastic bricks.

> Some of the best views of the Southern California coastline can be had from the windows of the frequent **Coaster commuter trains** (800/COASTER), which run right along the shore between San Juan Capistrano and Del Mar. The full trip between San Diego and Los Angeles takes about two hours.

model of San Francisco made entirely from Lego blocks

San Diego

Set along a huge Pacific Ocean harbor at the southwestern corner of the country just a few miles from the Mexican border, San Diego embodies the Southern California ideal. Around the turn of the 20th century, it rivaled Los Angeles as a boomtown based on wild real estate speculation, but while L.A. continued to expand by leaps and bounds, San Diego grew comparatively slowly. Instead of Hollywood

glamour, San Diego's economy has long been based around the U.S. Navy, as evidenced by the massive former USS *Midway* moored right downtown. (San Diego successfully mixed its military and Hollywood influences in the movie *Top Gun*.) Despite a metropolitan population of nearly 3 million people, San Diego still feels small and anything but urban.

The main things to see in San Diego are in **Balboa Park,** a lushly landscaped 1,150-acre spread on downtown's northwest edge, which was laid out and constructed as part of the 1915 International Exposition celebrating the completion of the Panama Canal. The many grand buildings, all built in gorgeous Spanish Revival style by architect Bertram Goodhue, have been preserved in marvelous condition, and now house sundry museums, ranging from automobiles to fine art to a functioning replica of Shakespeare's Globe Theatre.

Balboa Park is also home to the **San Diego Zoo** (daily; $20-32; 619/234-3153), one of the largest and most popular in the world. With over 4,000 animals kept in settings that simulate their natural habitats, you can see koalas and komodo dragons, panda bears and polar bears, plus gorillas, giraffes—you name it, if it's anywhere outside in the wild, it'll be here amidst the zoo's lushly landscaped 100 acres. Sports fans may be interested to know that the **San Diego Padres** (619/795-5000) play at retro-modern Petco Park downtown.

Practicalities

The city of San Diego bends diagonally around its natural harbor, which makes orientation occasionally confusing. The main airport, Lindbergh Field, is on the waterfront just north of downtown—and has one of the swiftest final approaches of any urban American airport. Because it is small and relatively compact, San Diego is easy to get around. Downtown is walkable, and on a bike you could see most everything in a day. Buses operated by San Diego Transit ($1; 619/234-1060) fan out from downtown, while the light rail Tijuana Trolley ($2) runs south from downtown to the Mexican border.

Though you may feel the need to duck when planes land at nearby Lindbergh Field, for breakfast try the **Hob Nob Hill** (619/239-8176) at 2271 First Avenue, a classic old coffee shop with great pecan waffles. San Diego's most popular old-style Mexican place is the **Old Town Cafe** (619/297-4330), at 2489 San Diego Avenue near the Old Town historic park. Also good—for huge margaritas and unforgettable fried ice cream desserts—is the courtyard of the **Casa de Bandini** (619/297-8211), nearby at 2754 Calhoun Street. In Balboa Park, soak up San Diego's Spanish Revival splendor while enjoying a meal at **Prado** (619/557-4441) in the original House of Hospitality.

Places to stay are generally modern, clean, and comfortable, though rates vary with seasons and conventions. For top-of-the-line accommodations, or just to appreciate the historic architecture, head to the wonderful old **Hotel Del Coronado** ($235–600; 619/435-6611), across the bridge from downtown on Coronado Island at 1500 Orange Avenue. Rising up in turreted glory, this fabulously grand Victorian-era resort hotel still caters, as it always has, to the four-star trade. It has been seen in many movies, including the great Peter O'Toole flick *The Stunt Man.* It's also where England's King Edward VIII first met the femme fatale who inspired him to give up his throne: Mrs. Simpson, whose husband was commander of the local navy base. The cheapest beds are at the **HI San Diego Hostel** (619/525-1531), in the historic downtown Gaslamp District at 521 Market Street; there's also **HI Point Loma Hostel** (619/223-4778) northwest of downtown, at 3790 Udall Street. Both hostels offer dorm bunks (around $20) and family rooms ($55). Near the beach and Point Loma at 5142 W. Point Loma Boulevard, the **Ocean Villa Motel** ($90 and up; 619/224-3481) has oceanview rooms, while for downtown style at a moderate rate, try the hip **500 West** ($89 and up; 619/234-5252), a boutique restoration of a 1920s YMCA at 500 West Broadway.

The best range of information is available from the **San Diego Visitors Center** (619/236-1212) at 1040 W. Broadway.

For information on visiting Carlsbad, contact the **visitors bureau** (760/434-6093 or 800/227-5722).

South Carlsbad State Park ($6 per car; 760/438-3143) three miles south of town, is one of the nicest and most popular places to camp on the Southern California coast, with its spacious campsites with hot showers ($20–25) spread out along a sandstone bluff above a broad beach. However, swimming can be dangerous because of strong riptides. If you don't want to camp, or pay the parking fee, leave your car at the park entrance, which is well-marked on a surviving stretch of the old US-101 highway.

Del Mar and Torrey Pines State Reserve

Most of the time, **Del Mar** (pop. 4,860) is a sleepy little upscale suburb of San Diego, with big houses backing onto a fine, four-mile-long beach. But in late summer, it comes to life for the thoroughbred racing season at beautiful **Del Mar Racetrack**, built by Hollywood types like Bing Crosby, and seen in *The Grifters* and many other Hollywood movies. The waves here are well suited to bodysurfing, but the sands can be hard to reach in summer because of a lack of parking—weekdays it's less of a problem.

A Torrey Pine, San Diego, Cal.—9

South along the Camino Del Mar coast road from Del Mar, hang-gliders, tidepoolers, surfers, and beachcombers flock to the nearly 2,000 acres of bluffs and beaches protected in **Torrey Pines State Reserve.** Named for the long-needled pines that grow naturally only here, the reserve is crisscrossed by hiking trails leading down steep ravines between the bluffs and the sands. Besides hang-gliders, Torrey Pines is prime air space for remote-controlled model gliders, which float gracefully in the nearly constant onshore breeze. The primary launching spot is the small city park at the south end of the reserve.

Overlooking the Pacific from atop a bluff at the south end of the reserve, the **Salk Institute** is one of the world's most important centers for research in the life sciences. Founded by the late Jonas Salk, designed by Louis Kahn, and modeled in part on the gardens of the Alhambra in Granada, the institute is open for **tours** Monday–Friday at 10 AM, 11 AM, and noon (free; 760/453-4100).

Stretching inland and south from the Salk Institute, the hills are covered with faceless business parks around the spacious campus of **University of California at San Diego** (UCSD), beyond which spreads La Jolla and the greater San Diego area.

La Jolla

The richest and most desirable part of San Diego, La Jolla sits along the coast northwest of the city proper, gazing out over azure coves to the endless Pacific. Besides the gorgeous scenery, great surfing (head to Windansea for the best waves), beachcombing, and skin diving, a big draw here is the recently renovated **Museum of Contemporary Art** (daily; $4; 858/454-3541), overlooking the ocean at 700 Prospect Avenue. Tons of good cafés and restaurants have long made La Jolla an all-around great day out, suiting all budgets—especially those with no upper limit.

Start the day off right at La Jolla's **Cottage** (858/454-8409), at 7702 Fay Avenue, where delicious food (including a divine buttermilk coffee cake) is served up on a sunny patio. For a memorable lunch or dinner, the very plush **Tapenade** (858/551-7500) at 7612 Fay Avenue is one of the best restaurants in Southern California, offering a deluxe mix of Mediterranean dishes. To continue the swaddled-in-luxury SoCal experience, stay the night at the elegant, Craftsman-style **Lodge at Torrey Pines** ($199 and up; 858/453-4420), a modern re-creation of California's turn-of-the-20th-century Golden Age located at 1148 N. Torrey Pines Road.

Between La Jolla and San Diego at **Belmont Park** (619/491-2988), the Giant Dipper wooden roller coaster survives as the sole remnant of a 1920s beachfront amusement park.

San Diego is also the beginning of our cross-country **Southern Pacific** route, along US-80, which runs east across Arizona all the way to Tybee Island, Georgia. See page 724.

Driving San Diego

From La Jolla south, the US-101 highway is pretty well buried by the I-5 freeway. Old US-101 can still be followed, however, by following Pacific Highway past Mission Bay and Lindbergh Field toward San Diego Bay, where it becomes Harbor Drive—where the light rail Tijuana Trolley now runs.

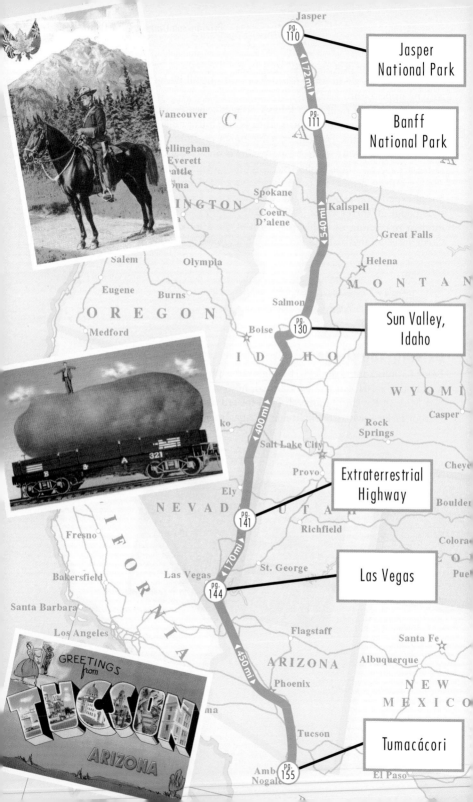

Jasper
pg. 110

Jasper
National Park

pg. 111

Banff
National Park

172 mi

540 mi

Vancouver

C

Bellingham
Everett
Seattle
Tacoma

Spokane

Coeur
D'alene

Kalispell

Great Falls

A

Helena

INGTON

Salem

Olympia

M O N T A N

Eugene

Burns

OREGON

Medford

Salmon

Boise

Sun Valley,
Idaho

pg. 130

I D A H O

W Y O M I

400 mi

Rock
Springs

Casper

Salt Lake City

Cheye

Ely

Provo

Extraterrestrial
Highway

N E V A D

U T A H

pg. 141

Richfield

Boulder

Colora

Fresno

170 mi

St. George

Las Vegas

O

Bakersfield

IFORNIA

Las Vegas

pg. 144

Pue

Santa Barbara

Flagstaff

Santa Fe

Los Angeles

A R I Z O N A

Albuquerque

450 mi

Phoenix

N E W
MEXICO

GREETINGS from

TUCSON

ARIZONA

ma

Tucson

Tumacácori

pg. 155

Amb
Nogal

El Paso

BORDER TO BORDER

Besides offering up-close looks at mile after mile of almost completely <u>untouched wilderness</u>, US-93 also takes you right through the <u>neon heart</u> of Las Vegas, Nevada.

Between the Canadian Rockies and the Rio Grande

The western half of North America is often described as a land of contrasts, and no route across it gives a sharper sense of the region's extremes than Highway 93. Starting in the north, across the Canadian border at **Jasper National Park** in the heart of the Rocky Mountains, and winding up south-of-the-border in the Sonora Desert twin towns of **Nogales,** this route, which retains the number 93 despite the different international jurisdictions, traverses some of the wildest and most rugged lands imaginable: mighty mountains, glaciated valleys, raging rivers, and two very different deserts. Besides offering up-close looks at mile after mile of magnificent and almost completely untouched wilderness, US-93 also takes you right through the neon heart of what is surely the most extreme (and most extremely visual) example of our contemporary "civilization": Las Vegas.

The route divides into two almost unrecognizably different halves. The northern section, from the Canadian Rockies wonderland of **Banff** and **Jasper** south as far as **Sun Valley, Idaho,** is pure alpine majesty. Passing the western flanks of **Glacier National Park,** US-93 runs along river valleys through diverse communities where skiing, hiking, and sightseeing have replaced mining and lumbering as the economic engines. South of **Kalispell,** the highway winds across the **Flathead Indian Reservation** along the western shores of Flathead Lake to **Missoula,** located at the heart of the bountiful country captured in the film *A River Runs Through It.* Western Montana's natural beauty reaches a peak in the **Bitterroot Valley,** which stretches south from Missoula all the way to the Idaho border. Besides scenery, the valley also abounds in history, holding many key sites pertaining to the explorers Lewis and Clark, the first whites to set foot in the region, and other sites related to the epic struggle of Chief Joseph and the Nez Percé tribe.

As you pass over the Bitterroots into Idaho across the **Continental Divide,** the scenery remains impressive as US-93 winds along the banks of the Salmon River, all the way to its source in the serrated Sawtooth Mountains, then drops down swiftly into Sun Valley, the oldest and most upscale ski resort in the country.

South of Sun Valley, however, everything changes very suddenly. Roaring rivers and mountain forests give way to lava flows and empty deserts as US-93 races across the inhospitable landscape of the Snake River plain. This was the most difficult portion of the historic Oregon Trail, though the biggest difficulty facing today's travelers is the struggle to stay alert—there's very little to look for, apart from acres of potato farms reclaimed from the arid desert. The one real sight is the **Snake River** itself, which has carved itself into a deep gorge near Twin Falls.

Continuing south into Nevada, US-93 embarks on what is truly, if not officially, the "Loneliest Road in America," traveling across 500 miles of Great Basin Desert. Though not for the faint-hearted (or those with unreliable cars!), it's an unforgettably beautiful journey; after hours (or days) of existential solitude, you drop down into the frenetic boomtown of **Las Vegas.**

Crossing Hoover Dam into Arizona, the route crosses old Route 66 west of the **Grand Canyon,** then races southeast across the lush Sonora Desert—known as the "world's greenest desert" because of its abundant flora and fauna—through **Phoenix** and **Tucson** to the Mexican border. This last stretch is among the most fascinating 200 miles of highway in the country, taking you past such intriguingly diverse and unique sights as the controversial Biosphere 2 scientific research center, the country's only intact Cold War–era missile silo, and a pair of centuries-old churches, two of the most captivating pieces of architecture in the western United States.

CANADIAN ROCKIES

At its northernmost extreme high up in the Canadian Rockies, Highway 93 passes through some of the most famous vacation areas in North America: the Canadian national parks of Banff and Jasper. Popular with skiers and snowboarders in winter, and hikers and sightseers in summer, these resort towns date back over 100 years and remain among the most beautiful places on earth. Between **Jasper** and **Lake Louise,** Hwy-93 is known as the Icefields Parkway, an amazing drive, with endless panoramas of glaciers and towering peaks, and dozens of turnouts and trailheads to tempt you out from behind the wheel. Over 140 miles (225 km) long, the Icefields Parkway runs right alongside the Continental Divide, the rugged crest that separates the Atlantic and Pacific watersheds. South of the Icefields Parkway, our route passes through the world-renowned resort towns of **Banff** and Lake Louise, taking in their unforgettable alpine scenery—and historic landmark hotels.

Southwest from Lake Louise, Hwy-93 winds through **Kootenay National Park,** another incredible assembly of mountain scenery, before dropping down out of the mountains for the run south to the border, following the broad Kootenay River all the way to Montana.

Town of Jasper

The northernmost point on Hwy-93, at the junction of the Icefields Parkway with the cross-country Yellowhead Highway (Hwy-16), which links Edmonton with Prince Rupert, the town of **Jasper** (pop. 4,800) preserves its frontier character intact. Unlike Banff, which exudes wealth and comfort, Jasper (which became an incorporated entity only in 2001, and is officially referred to as "Town of Jasper" to differentiate it from Jasper National Park) is a rough-and-ready, workaday sort of place. Founded on fur-trading and mining, Jasper boomed when a cross-Canada railroad came through in 1911, but since the establishment of the national park in 1930, Jasper has served primarily as a handy base for exploring the wilds that surround it.

The park's main attractions are covered below under the Jasper National Park heading, but a few others are located

Prices in the Canadian sections are given in Canadian dollars, which at time of writing cost about 75 cents in American money. Also, the colloquial Canadian equivalent of "buck" (for a dollar) is **"loonie,"** thanks to the image of a loon (a bird) on the dollar coin.

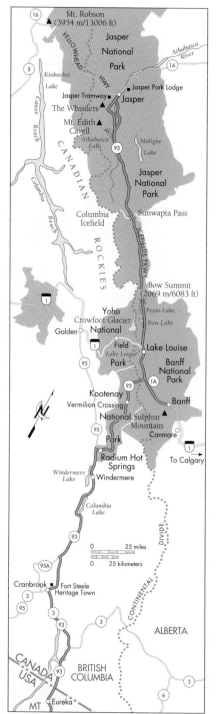

very close to town. First and foremost of these is probably the **Jasper Tramway** (daily; $C21; 780/852-3093), which lifts passengers 3,500 vertical feet (1,067 meters) up the steep north face of the Whistlers in under 10 minutes. From the upper terminal of the tramway, you can follow a half-mile (.8 km) path to the 8,100-foot (2,468-meter) summit for a breathtaking panorama south to the Columbia Icefield, and (on a clear day) northwest to Mt. Robson, the highest point of the Canadian Rockies, at 13,006 feet (3,964 meters) above sea level.

The other big draw is **Maligne Canyon,** a 100- to 150-foot-deep (30- to 46-meter) limestone canyon that's so narrow in places that squirrels can leap from rim to rim. Trails lead around and across it, and in winter you can join an unforgettable guided tour ($C40; 780/852-5595) and wander along the bottom of the narrow, ice-covered gorge. Beyond Maligne Canyon is one the prettiest lakes in the Canadian Rockies, **Maligne Lake.** Hiking trails lead along the shore and to panoramic viewpoints, but it is the **cruise** ($C35; 780/852-3370) to Spirit Island that attracts most visitors.

Jasper's compact center, sandwiched between the west bank of the Athabasca River and a wide bench of land dotted with forest-encircled lakes, holds all the cafés and gift shops you could want within a block of the main drag, Connaught Drive. The **Soft Rock Cafe** (780/852-5850), at 632 Connaught Drive, has cinnamon buns, great fresh-fruit waffles, and anything else you need to start the day off right; **Jasper Pizza Place** (780/852-3225), two blocks north at 402 Connaught

The Last Frontier

The Canadian Rockies are farther north than anything else in *Road Trip USA*, but for indefatigable adventurers there's at least one additional destination: Alaska, "The Last Frontier." It's a mere 2,500 miles from Jasper to Anchorage, via the legendary Alaska Highway. Running from the oil- and gas-producing center of Dawson Creek (no connection with the TV show) in British Columbia, the Alaska Highway was constructed in 1942, in just nine months, an amazing engineering feat fueled by fears of a Japanese invasion during World War II. Much improved in the years since, it's now paved all the way, but is still quite an adventure, with endless miles (and miles, and miles) of forests, rivers, and mountains.

If you're going, plan ahead carefully and keep a lookout for a few places you won't want to miss. One of these is roughly midway, in Watson Lake right on the BC/Yukon border right along the highway: the world-famous **Signpost Forest,** a collection of city limits signs from around the globe. The "forest" was started in 1942 by Carl Lindley, a U.S. soldier working to build the highway. When ordered to fix an official road sign, he added another of his own making, pointing the way and the distance to his home in Danville, Indiana. Others followed his lead, and over the years, have added sign upon sign to  create the current collection, which at last count totalled 51,843.

In the middle of the Signpost Forest is the very helpful **Visitor Reception Centre** (daily in summer; 867/536-7469) with practical information and historical exhibits.

Drive, has wood-fired ovens and walls covered in photos of Jasper in the early days. Another lively spot is the bar and grill on the ground floor of the **Athabasca Hotel** ($C109–149; 780/852-3386) at 510 Patricia Street, which also has Jasper's least expensive in-town lodging. Jasper's most expensive place to stay is the **Jasper Park Lodge** ($C549 and up; 780/852-3301), a grand mountain resort dating back to 1921 but now a mostly modern resort offering 450 rooms, plus golfing and horseback riding, on a lovely site across from town on the other side of the Athabasca River.

Budget travelers may want to take advantage of the hostels around Jasper, including the 80-bed **Jasper International Hostel** ($C20–25 per person) five miles (eight km) south of Jasper on the road to the Jasper Tramway, and the smaller and more rustic **Maligne Canyon Hostel** ($C13–18 per person) a short walk from the canyon. Reservations for either hostel, and for other hostels in Jasper National Park, can be made by phone, 780/852-3215. There are also two large **campgrounds,** Whistlers and Wapiti, along Hwy-93 on the south side of Jasper, with over 1,000 sites altogether, some with RV hookups.

For details on hiking and camping options, or to purchase the required entrance passes and backcountry camping permits, go to the Parks Canada **information center** (780/852-6176) in a lovely old stone building off Connaught Drive in Athabasca Park; for more-complete information, including listings of rooms available in private homes, talk to the folks at the Jasper **visitors center,** which shares the space (780/852-3858).

Jasper National Park

Running from the Town of Jasper all the way to Lake Louise 144 miles (232 km) to the south, this section of Hwy-93 is known as the Icefields Parkway. Like many roads in American national parks, the Icefields Parkway was initially built as a relief project during the Great Depression and was completed in 1940.

The four contiguous Canadian Rockies national parks—Jasper, Banff, Yoho, and Kootenay, along with neighboring wilderness areas—jointly protect a 7,000-square mile (18,000-square km) area that has been declared a UNESCO World Heritage Site for its ecological importance.

Without a doubt one of the world's great drives, this sinuous ribbon winds along the banks of a series of icy rivers between glaciers and towering Rocky Mountain peaks, with almost no development to mar the views. The northern half of the highway passes through Jasper National Park, alongside the milky green Athabasca River.

While the Icefields Parkway makes a great drive, a worthwhile detour follows an older alignment of the highway, Hwy-93A, which runs parallel and slightly to the west. One of the best concentrations of scenery surrounds Mt. Edith Cavell, easily reached by Mt. Edith Cavell Road that turns off Hwy-93A about four miles (six km) south of the Town of Jasper. From the winding road, you can choose from fairly short day-hikes up to wildflower-rich alpine meadows, with views of Angel Glacier, or longer overnight treks into the backcountry, including the **Tonquin Valley Lodge** (780/852-3909), a 15-mile (24 km) hiking or cross-country skiing trip from the trailhead. Right at the trailhead there's the handy **Mt. Edith Cavell Hostel** (June–Nov. only; $C13–18 per person; 780/852-3215).

Passes are required for each person entering any of the Canadian Rockies national parks and are available at park gates and at visitors centers. They're valid for one day ($C7 per person) or all year ($C45 per person).

About 15 miles (24 km) south of the Town of Jasper, Hwy-93A and the Icefields Parkway rejoin at **Athabasca Falls,** where the river is forced through a narrow gorge and over a cliff into a cauldron of roaring water; numerous viewpoints above and below the falls let you get up close and personal with the thundering torrent. There's a rustic **hostel** (877/852-0781) a short walk away from the falls.

At the southern end of Jasper National Park, 60 miles (97 km) south of the Town of Jasper, the massive Columbia Icefield rises high above the west side of the Icefields Parkway.

Columbia Icefield

Rising to the west of Sunwapta Pass, the dividing line between Banff and Jasper Parks, the massive **Columbia Icefield** is what the Icefields Parkway is all about:

The Brewster Boys

Few guides in the Canadian Rockies were as well known as Jim and Bill Brewster. In 1892, at the ages of 10 and 12 respectively, they were hired by the Banff Springs Hotel to take guests on a tour of local landmarks. As their reputations grew so did their business, which expanded to include a livery and outfitting company, a pair of hotels, and a ski lodge. Today, their legacy lives on in Brewster, where their tour and transportation company has become an integral part of the Canadian Rockies experience for many visitors. The Brewster company operates a fleet of tour buses, a Banff hotel, and the famous Ice Explorers that take tourists out onto the Columbia Icefield.

the largest icefield and most accessible glacier in the Canadian Rockies, seemingly endless square miles of solid ice sitting high atop the Continental Divide. Visibly shrinking throughout the 20th century, the icefield is still immense, and you can get an up-close look by joining the very popular "Ice Explorer" tours ($C30; 877/423-7433) operated by the Brewster company, which leave every 15 minutes and travel out onto Athabasca Glacier.

Overlooking the icefield from across the Icefields Parkway is the modern **Columbia Icefield Centre** (daily May–Oct.; free), a mini-museum of glacial lore operated by Parks Canada. If you want to experience the icefield up close, buy a ticket and take one of the Ice Explorer tours; don't simply walk across the highway and clamber up, since it only takes one false step to fall to your death into one of the very deep but invisible crevasses that crisscross the glacier.

The **Icefields Parkway** is kept open year-round, but gas, food, and lodging services are available pretty much only near the towns of Banff, Jasper and Lake Louise. Wide shoulders and frequent HI hostels (780/852-3215) along the Parkway make it an excellent bicycling route, too.

Banff National Park

Roughly midway along the Icefields Parkway, the Columbia Icefield and Sunwapta Pass mark the boundary between Jasper and Banff National Parks, and the dividing line between the Arctic and Atlantic watersheds. South of the pass, the first worthwhile stop is the **Weeping Wall,** a 350-foot cliff of gray limestone down which a series of waterfalls tumble. Frozen in winter, it's a prime spot for ice-climbing thrill-seekers.

Though it may well sound like empty hyperbole, the list of candidates for the most beautiful sight in **Banff National Park,** and perhaps the entire Canadian Rockies, has to

The Icefields Parkway drops down into Bow Valley.

include jewel-like **Peyto Lake,** an iridescently glowing blue-green glacial lake that reflects the surrounding snow-capped peaks. The often mirror-smooth waters of this small, oblong lake change color from a deep blue to jade green as the proportion of glacial silt in the water increases with the snowmelt from summer to fall. The short trail to the usually crowded Peyto Lake overlook starts from the parking area along the Icefields Parkway at 6,803-foot (2,069-meter) **Bow Summit.**

Bow Summit is one of the highest points reachable by road in Canada; south of here, the Icefields Parkway drops down into the Bow Valley, which is dominated by the sparkling waters of **Bow Lake** and the views across it to Crowfoot Glacier. At the north edge of the lake, historic **Simpson's Num-Ti-Jah Lodge** ($C210–255; 403/522-2167) is a giant octagonal log cabin, with well-priced rooms and a rustic restaurant, that marks the start of a popular trail to spectacular **Bow Glacier Falls;** it's a fairly level, two-mile (three-km) one-way hike.

From the lodge, the Icefields Parkway winds along the east shore of Bow Lake, then along the banks of the Bow River, which flows south through Lake Louise, Banff, and on through Calgary, eventually ending up in Hudson Bay.

Yoho National Park

From the village of Lake Louise, the Trans-Canada Highway cuts off from Hwy-93, running west through Kamloops toward Vancouver. The first 25 miles (40 km) of this highway, west from Lake Louise and the Icefields Parkway, passes through **Yoho National Park,** the smallest and least-known, but perhaps most feature-packed, of the contiguous Canadian Rockies parks. It's impossible to do justice to the park in a paragraph or two, but if you like the other parks, and particularly if you enjoy backpacking, think about spending some time here, too.

From Lake Louise, Trans-Canada Hwy-1 climbs quickly over Kicking Horse Pass before reaching the **Spiral Tunnel Viewpoint,** where you can learn about the amazing engineering feat that allowed trains to travel through this rugged region. Five miles (eight km) farther, the next swing north takes you up, and up, and up, along a *very* tight series of hairpin turns, to **Takkakaw Falls,** perhaps the most impressive waterfall in the Canadian Rockies. You can see the 1,400-foot (427-meter) falls from the parking lot, but a short trail leads to the Yoho River, where you can appreciate the view in all its rainbow-refracting glory.

Farther west along Trans-Canada Hwy-1, about a dozen miles (20 km) from the Icefields Parkway in the hamlet of **Field,** you come to the Yoho National Park **information center** (250/343-6324), which can tell you all about the park's natural attractions. Contained in the back of Field's general store, **Truffle Pigs Café** (250/343-6462) is a charming little eatery serving up healthy and hearty breakfasts and lunches.

Three miles (five km) west of Field, a turnoff to the north leads into the wilderness to the **Emerald Lake Lodge** (403/410-7417 or 800/663-6336), a rustic, upscale resort that dates back to 1902. Sitting on the shores of one of the Canadian Rockies' most magnificent lakes, the lodge is open year-round, offering food and lodging ($C300–475 a night, depending on season) as well as swimming, boating, and horseback riding.

Lake Louise

The sight of **Lake Louise,** spreading in a deep aquamarine pool at the foot of silvery snow-capped peaks, is worth traveling around the world to see. Which is exactly what many people do: If you come here in summer, you'll be among an international gaggle of tourists for whom Lake Louise really *is* the Canadian Rockies. A small village with the same name sits along Trans-Canada Hwy-1, but the 1.5-mile-long (2.4-km) and very cold lake itself is about two miles (three km) west, at the end of Lake Louise Drive. Besides the summer sightseeing, the Lake Louise area offers world-class downhill skiing and snowboarding: Three mountains (over 3,000 vertical feet, 900 vertical meters) are yours for the price of a Lake Louise lift ticket ($C58; 403/522-3555). One of the lifts operates throughout the summer as well, offering a grand Canadian Rockies panorama.

Like the town of Banff to the south, Lake Louise was developed over a century ago as a tourist resort by the Canadian Pacific Railway. As in Banff, the landmark here is a magnificent hotel, the **Fairmont Chateau Lake Louise** (403/522-3511), which stands 10 stories high above the lakeshore. Taking on a Swiss Alps theme—staff wear lederhosen, while yodelers and harmonica players perform in the hotel lobbies and bars, and all day long a funny old man stands along the shore blowing a 15-foot alpine horn which echoes back and forth in the canyons across the lake—the 520-room Chateau Lake Louise has every service and comfort you could want, at rates ranging in the neighborhood of $C420–1,200 per night.

Of course, there's no charge to explore the hotel or walk along the lake and enjoy the views. You can rent canoes and paddle out onto the lake, and from the hotel a popular trail climbs over 1,000 feet (305 meters) in about two miles (three km) to **Bridal Veil Falls,** continuing a short way farther to **Lake Agnes,** where a rustic teahouse serves sandwiches (and teas!).

Immediately below the lake, the family-owned, summer-only **Paradise Lodge and Bungalows** (403/522-3595) is smaller and friendlier, with cozy log cabins and modern lodge rooms (many with fireplaces) running $C195–300 per night.

Back down in Lake Louise Village, at the northwest end of Village Road, the **HI Lake Louise Alpine Centre** (403/670-7580) is a very large, modern log-built lodge, with $C34–38 dorm beds and the very nice **Bill Peyto's Cafe,** the area's least expensive place to eat, open daily 7 AM–9 PM. There are gas stations, gift shops, a grocery store, cafés, and the popular **Laggan's Mountain Bakery**

Originally built by the Canadian Pacific Railway, the **Banff Springs Hotel, Chateau Lake Louise,** and **Jasper Park Lodge** (and some 25 others across Canada) are all owned and operated by the same company, Fairmont Hotels and Resorts. For rates and reservations, call 800/257-7544.

calm, spectacular Moraine Lake

(great pastries and coffee), in the hard-to-miss Samson Mall. There's also a large **campground** along the Bow River a half mile (.8 km) south of town; one section has electricity hookups. The whole place tends to fill up most days despite having over 400 campsites total.

Smaller, less-visited, but every bit as spectacular as Lake Louise, **Moraine Lake** sits at the end of a summer-only road, six miles (10 km) south of the midpoint of Lake Louise Drive. Despite the name, Moraine Lake is not in fact formed by a glacial moraine, but by a rockfall; nevertheless it's a gorgeous spot, the placid lake reflecting the jagged surrounding peaks. From the lakeside, a two-mile (three-km) trail climbs up to **Larch Valley,** where you can see fall color extraordinaire courtesy of the namesake trees, which are prolific here.

Town of Banff

Fifteen miles (24 km) southeast of Lake Louise, Hwy-93 and the Trans-Canada Hwy-1 diverge, with Hwy-93 cutting due south through **Kootenay National Park** across southeastern British Columbia toward the U.S. border. That is the route we follow, all the way south to Mexico eventually, but anyone in his or her right mind will want to make the 15-mile (24-km) trip southeast along Hwy-1 to visit the beautiful Town of Banff, home of the landmark Fairmont Banff Springs Hotel, the biggest and most impressive of the grand old Canadian Pacific hotels. When it opened in 1888, this was the largest hotel in the world, with a grand total of 250 rooms; over the years, the hotel has been rebuilt and expanded to currently hold 846 rooms, most of which are booked up months in advance. Spreading between the hotel and Hwy-1, the Town of Banff has grown into the tasteful but bustling commercial center of the Canadian Rockies, with a year-round population of some 7,500 people, plus many times that many visitors daily during the peak summer season. Though the commercialism can detract from the natural splendor, Banff is definitely a very pleasant place to while away some time.

For the most spectacular introduction to Banff, head up Mountain Avenue, where the **Banff Gondola** (daily; $C22; 403/762-2523) will take you 2,300 feet (700 meters) up Sulphur Mountain for a grand view over the entire Bow Valley. The "springs" in the Fairmont Banff Springs Hotel's name refer to actual hot springs; to take a soak, visit the **Upper Hot Springs** ($C7.50; 403/762-1515), at the foot of the Banff Gondola. The original hot springs that spurred the growth of Banff have been closed and converted into the **Cave and Basin National Historic Site** (daily; $C4; 403/762-1566), west of town at the end of Cave Avenue, where exhibits detail the underlying geology that makes hot springs happen.

The main drag of town, Banff Avenue, has all the cafés, restaurants, and shopping you could want (for suggestions, see Town of Banff Practicalities below), but if the weather's bad (and if

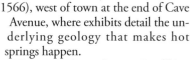

historic Banff Springs Hotel

it's not, you really ought to be outdoors, enjoying Mother Nature!), you can learn about Banff and the Canadian Rockies in a trio of museums. Best first stop is the **Banff Park Museum** (daily; $C4), near the river at the foot of Banff Avenue, a Victorian-era remnant (it was built in 1903) that displays the taxidermied remains of typical park wildlife. Around the corner, a half block down from pleasant, riverside Central Park at 111 Bear Street, the **Whyte Museum of the Canadian Rockies** (daily; $C6) has an expansive collection of historic books, postcards, paintings, and photographs, all capturing various aspects of the mountains and their inhabitants. Last but not least, the stockade-like **Luxton Museum** (daily; $C6), across the river at 1 Birch Street, details the cultures of the native peoples who inhabited the Canadian Rockies long before there were any Canadians. Inside there's an intricately decorated tepee, bows and arrows and other hunting equipment, and some peace pipes; the museum gift shop is also worth a browse.

One of many cultural events that take place in Banff is the **Banff Mountain Film Festival** (403/762-6675), where the world's best adventure-travel and mountain-climbing films are shown every November.

Town of Banff Practicalities

So long as you plan ahead, and can afford to enjoy some of Canada's most expensive hotels and restaurants, the Town of Banff makes a great place to visit. Because the Town of Banff is located within the confines of Banff National Park, development has been limited—so much so that summertime accommodations here can be hard to come by, and very expensive. Throughout the summer, hotels are booked up solidly well in advance, and rates start around $C200 for a basic room. (Winter rates are usually less than half that.) A dozen places are within a short walk of downtown: **Brewster's Mountain Lodge** (403/762-2900) at 208 Caribou Street has spacious rooms starting around $C200 a night in summer, while rooms at the landmark **Fairmont Banff Springs Hotel** ($C500 and up; 403/762-2211 or 800/441-1414), when available, climb quickly into the four-digit range.

If you have trouble finding an affordable room in Banff, consider taking a trip farther east to **Canmore,** a lively little city on Hwy-1, just east of the park's boundary, where the nonprofit Alpine Club of Canada operates the $C23-a-night **HI Canmore Hostel** (403/678-3200).

While Trans-Canada Hwy-1 is faster, the **Bow Valley Parkway** is a more scenic alternative between Banff and Lake Louise. Running parallel and to the east, it also gives access to some very nice spots, including the waterfalls of Johnston Canyon, where **Johnston Canyon Resort** (C$129-229; 403/762-2971) has inexpensive rooms in a quiet, woodland setting.

Restaurants in Banff are plentiful, good, and wide-ranging—there are over 100, which works out to one for every 70 residents. One of the most popular places, with locals and visitors alike, is **Melissa's** (daily; 403/762-5511) on the west side of downtown at 218 Lynx Street. Housed in a 1928 log building, Melissa's serves great pancakes (with real maple syrup) and beefy burgers, and has a nice bar and outdoor deck. Along with two good Italian places (**Guido's** and **Giorgio's,** at 116 and 219 Banff Avenue, respectively), downtown Banff also has many Japanese places, a Greek café, and the ever-popular **Wild Bill's Saloon,** which has good food and drink (mostly the latter).

Parks Canada operates three **campgrounds** along Tunnel Mountain Road, two miles (three km) east of downtown, which have over 1,000 sites altogether; all the campgrounds have hot showers, and many sites have full or partial RV hookups. Also on Tunnel Mountain Road is the large **HI Banff Alpine Centre** ($C29–33; 403/762-4122).

For comprehensive information on Banff, head to the large **visitors center,** downtown at 224 Banff Avenue, which is home to both the commercially oriented Banff/Lake Louise Tourism Bureau (403/762-8421) and the rangers of Banff National Park (403/762-1550).

Kootenay National Park

Though Banff and Jasper seem to get all the attention, neighboring **Kootenay National Park** draws a breed of traveler who prefers to experience wilderness without having to wait in line. It was originally known as the "Highway Park," since the land was deeded to the federal government in exchange for it building (and paying for!) the 65-mile-long (105-km) Banff-Windermere Road that now runs through the heart of the park. Completed in 1922, this was the first road over the Canadian Rockies, and linked the prairies and the west coast of British Columbia for the first time. Fortunately for visitors, Hwy-1, which runs through Yoho to the north, now carries most of the through traffic.

Kootenay National Park spreads for five miles (eight km) to either side of the highway. As in all the Canadian Rockies parks, grizzly bears still roam the Kootenay backcountry, and black bears, bighorn sheep, and moose are regularly seen along the roadside. A number of stops along the way offer great short hikes. Two of the most enjoyable, **Marble Canyon** and **Paint Pots,** are at the north end of the park, well-signed along the north side of the highway. Marble Canyon is an amazing sight (and sound): a 100-foot-deep, very narrow slot canyon carved in the shiny white dolomite limestone by the thundering cascade of Tokumn Creek. A half-mile (.8 km) trail leads back and forth on a series of man-made and natural bridges over the gorge. Two miles (three km) south, the Paint Pots are much more sedate, displaying a handful of brightly colored mud puddles dyed varying shades of red and yellow by oxidizing minerals in the natural springs.

At **Vermilion Crossing** at the center of the park, about 15 miles (24 km) south of the Paint Pots and 40 miles (64 km) from Radium, you'll find the park's only overnight accommodations at **Kootenay Park Lodge** ($C90–130; 403/762-9196), which in summer has a handful of cabins, a restaurant, a gas station, a seasonal visitors center, and a general store. From here south, the road follows the broad banks of the Vermilion and Kootenay Rivers before cutting west over Sinclair Pass, where a viewpoint offers a stunning high-country panorama. At the southern end of the park, the road winds through the narrow gorge of Sinclair Canyon before running suddenly into the roadside sprawl of Radium Hot Springs.

You can drive through Kootenay without charge, but if you want to stop en route you need to buy a park pass ($C7 per person per day) from the entrance stations. Park maps and details of Kootenay's hiking and camping options are available from the very helpful **information center** (250/347-9515) in Radium Hot Springs at the park's southwestern edge, or from the Parks Canada centers further north in Banff and Jasper.

Radium Hot Springs

At the west edge of Kootenay National Park, the town of **Radium Hot Springs** is a swift change from the natural idyll. Block after block of motels, cafés, and gas stations line Hwy-93, and apart from satisfying your fuel-and-food needs, there's not a lot here. The one good place to eat is **The Springs** restaurant, west of town on the golf course. Motels here include the $C90-a-night **Alpen Motel** (250/347-9823) and the family-friendly **Radium Resort** ($C135–285; 250/347-9311 or 800/667-6444).

The actual hot springs from which the town takes its name are just east, inside the park boundary in a heavily developed complex (daily; $C7), with two pools (a small one at 103°F, another at 84°F), and an artery-clogging café. Unfortunately, the water is heavily chlorinated, and there are no "natural" springs left.

Fort Steele Heritage Town

South of Radium Hot Springs, Hwy-93 runs along the western foot of the Rocky Mountains, but the natural beauty of the national parks doesn't really return until you cross the border and visit Glacier National Park, a good 200 miles (322 km) away. That said, it's a wide-open drive, passing a few towns, some golf resorts, and two big lumber mills, following the banks of the Kootenay River all the way.

The one real attraction along this stretch of road is the resurrected frontier community of Fort Steele, roughly midway between Radium and the border crossing. Containing more than 60 preserved and reconstructed buildings, **Fort Steele Heritage Town** (daily; $C11; 250/426-7352) recreates the boomtown that stood here from 1890 until 1898, servicing the silver, gold, and lead mines of the East Kootenays. Along with the buildings, which house interpretive exhibits as well as an ice cream store, a bakery and restaurant, and a general store selling top hats and other period essentials, you can enjoy theater performances or ride on a steam train—though there are extra charges for these activities.

If you're passing through Radium Hot Springs, be sure to stop for a look at the amazing array of signs and sculptures outside Swiss-born artist Rolf Heer's **Radium Wood Carvers** on a hill just east of the Hwy-93/95 junction.

MONTANA

From the Canadian border, US-93 runs south and east along the Tobacco River valley, then cuts through the **Flathead National Forest** to the logging and ski resort towns of **Whitefish** and **Kalispell.** Continuing south along the shores of **Flathead Lake,** the route passes through the college town and cultural nexus of **Missoula,** south of which US-93 passes through some of the most beautiful terrain in the country, winding through broad valleys at the foot of the Bitterroot Mountains, past alpine lakes and snowcapped peaks all the way south to the Idaho border.

Eureka

Like British Columbia, Montana's northwest corner, where Canadian Hwy-93 ends and US-93 begins, is an isolated land of dense forests, broad rivers, and glaciated valleys. Besides providing natural habitat for herds of moose, elk, bison, and bighorn sheep, not to mention mountain lions, wolves, and grizzly bears, the thick groves of cedars, pines, and firs support the Northwest's other endangered species—the logger—whose angular clear-cuts and mono-crop tree plantations are also apparent as you pass through the region.

*Hwy-37 is an official Scenic Byway that winds along the **Kootenai River** and **Lake Koocanusa** from Eureka to the town of Libby, where it intersects US-2.*

The first sizeable town, 15 miles south of the border, is **Eureka** (pop. 1,200), a sleepy little place with a pair of gas stations, a couple of cafés, and **Tobacco Valley Historical Village** (open summer only), a fascinating collection of pioneer buildings, preserved and moved to a small park along US-93 at the south end of town.

Whitefish

A major division point on the historic Great Northern railroad, whose tracks are still in use by Amtrak and the Burlington Northern Santa Fe, **Whitefish** (pop. 5,032) was originally known as Stumptown because of the intensive logging operations centered here. Despite its proud industrial history, the blue-collar base has long since been eclipsed by tourism, and the city now calls itself the "Recreational Capital of Montana," with alpine lakes, fishing streams, hiking trails, great skiing, and endless mountain scenery right on its doorstep. The main attraction in Whitefish, for skiing in winter and hiking and mountain biking in summer, is **Big Mountain,** the 6,770-foot peak (with a 2,170-foot vertical drop!) that looms over the northwest shore of Whitefish Lake.

*For a truly unusual experience, spend the night in the former **USFS fire lookout** atop Webb Mountain, 20 miles southwest of Eureka. It's very popular, and costs a mere $25 a night; for details and rental availability, contact the USFS ranger station in Eureka (406/296-2536).*

Besides giving access to the surrounding great outdoors, Whitefish is a pleasant place to stop and stretch your legs, and has everything you could want from a resort town—without the rampant tourist-pandering and real estate speculation that has ruined so many other places. A small **museum** (daily; free) inside the rustic Great Northern train station, which stands in a pleasant park at the north end of Central Avenue, gives a historical overview of Whitefish.

Across the park from the station there's a new theater, a new library, and a new home for **Black Star Brewing,** whose hoppy products you can sample in a small tasting room, or in any Whitefish bar.

The heart of town is a few blocks of Central Avenue, running south from the railroad tracks to Montana's one and only Frank Lloyd Wright building, an early 1950s bank and of-fice complex on the east side of Cen-tral Avenue between 3rd and 4th Streets called, directly enough, the **Frank Lloyd Wright Building.** In between you'll find some great bars and saloons, the **Bookworks** book-store on 3rd and Spokane Streets, art galleries, and the **Big Mountain Trading Company,** a pawn shop where you can bargain for anything from saddles to DVDs.

The best place to start the day in Whitefish is along 3rd Street, east of Central Avenue, where the **Buffalo Cafe** (406/862-2833), 514 E. 3rd Street, is a popular breakfast and lunch spot, locally famous for its huevos rancheros. Back on Central, across from the FLW Building, at 334 Central Avenue, the **Whitefish Times** (406/862-2444) is an erudite and relaxing coffeehouse, with maga-zines and books and overstuffed sofas. Lunch and dinner places line up along Central Avenue, where you can get great burgers and cheap beers at the rowdy **Bulldog Saloon,** Mexican food at **Serrano's,** wood-fired pizza at upscale **Truby's,** or simply quaff a beer or two at **The Palace,** White-fish's oldest and most ornate bar—all in the same block.

Besides the extensive resort accom-modations available year-round at the **Big Mountain Resort** ($85 and up; 406/862-1960 or 877/754-3474), you can choose from numerous motels along US-93 south of town. Two more accommodation options are walkably close to downtown: the attractive and comfortable **Garden Wall B&B** ($95–150; 406/862-3440 or 888/530-1700), a Craftsman-era cottage at 504 Spokane Avenue, and the tidy **Non-Hostile Hostel** (406/862-7447), at 300 E. 2nd Street, where bunk beds in a converted Elks lodge go for $15 a night.

For further listings or information, contact the Whitefish **visitors bureau** (406/862-3501); their office is at 6475 S. US-93, south of downtown.

Kalispell marks the junction of US-93 and the the **Great Northern** route along US-2 (see page 462), which runs east through Glacier National Park and west across Idaho and Washington to the Pacific Ocean (full coverage on pages 446–528).

Kalispell

The nearest thing to an urban center in northwestern Montana, **Kalispell** (pop. 14,223) spreads across the northern Flathead Valley at the junction of the Stillwater, Whitefish, and Flathead Rivers. Cut by two main thoroughfares, east–west US-2 and north–south US-93, it ain't quaint by any stretch of the imagination; at first glance it looks like yet another lumber mill-and-mining town, but the historic downtown area is full of interesting spots, such as the engaging **Hockaday Center for the Arts** (closed Sun, Mon.; $5), housed in the old Carnegie Library on 3rd Street, two blocks east of Main Street (US-93). Another few blocks east stands the impressive, perfectly preserved **Conrad Mansion,** built by pioneer trader and Kalispell founder Charles Conrad in 1895 and now open for guided tours (daily in summer; $7; 406/755-2166).

Chief Charlo

Breakfasts don't get much better than those served at **Norm's News** (406/756-5446), a historic soda fountain luncheonette at 34 Main Street where you can also get killer milk shakes and a wide variety of newspapers and magazines; upstairs is the old Kalispell Opera House. Kalispell also has an above-average range of taverns, including the venerable **Moose's Saloon** (406/755-2337), near the junction of US-2 and US-93 at 173 N. Main Street, famous for pizza and occasional live music.

There are the usual national motels, but *the* place to stay in Kalispell is the **Kalispell Grand Hotel** ($65 and up; 406/755-8100 or 800/858-7422), a conveniently located historic downtown hotel at 100 Main Street with nice, clean rooms.

For more information, contact the **visitors center** (406/756-9091 or 800/543-3105), on Main Street (US-93) at the south edge of town.

Flathead Lake

The largest natural freshwater lake west of the Mississippi River, deep-blue **Flathead Lake** is a magnet for outdoor recreation in western Montana. US-93 winds along the lake's hilly western shore, passing through a number of state parks and small resort communities that enjoy grand views of the Rocky Mountains to the east and the green foothills of the Flathead National Forest to the west.

Along US-93 at the north end of the lake, **Somers** is a neat old timber town with some well-preserved turn-of-the-20th-century buildings, one of which holds **Tiebuckers Pub** (406/857-3335), a beer bar and good restaurant. From Somers, you can detour east onto Hwy-82 for a trip along the eastern shore of Flathead Lake, where you can enjoy the upscale resort town of **Bigfork** and the acres of cherry orchards that line the lakeshore.

Polson: Miracle of America Museum

The southern half of Flathead Lake is surrounded by the Flathead Indian Reservation, home to a mixed population of Flathead Salish, Kootenai, and Caucasians, who make up around 80 percent of the reservation's population. The large reservation covers a 1.2 million-acre area, roughly 35 by 65 miles, hemmed in by the Mission and Cabinet Mountains, but apart from a few small towns, it's mostly prairie and riverside wetlands.

The largest of these towns, **Polson,** at the bottom end of the lake where the Flathead River flows south, is a predominately white retirement community, with 24-hour gas stations, the area's only ATMs, a Safeway supermarket, and chain motels. Polson is also home to the deluxe lakefront **Best Western KwaTaqNuk Resort** ($65–135; 406/883-3636), at 303 US-93 East and owned and operated by the Salish-Kootenai tribe, with two pools, an on-site casino, a boat dock, and direct access to the lake.

Just two miles south of Polson along US-93, the bizarre but fascinating **Miracle**

Elmo, at the north edge of the Flathead Reservation, hosts the annual **Standing Arrow PowWow** on the third weekend in July (406/849-6018). Arlee, at the southern edge of the reservation, hosts the **4th of July PowWow,** one of the most popular Native American gatherings in Montana. For more information, call the Confederated Salish and Kootenai Tribal Council (406/675-2700), or stop by the People's Center in Pablo, four miles south of Polson.

A River Runs Through It

Missoula has long been something of a literary center, thanks in part to the late Norman MacLean, whose novella *A River Runs Through It* rhapsodizes over the surrounding Rocky Mountain country and the larger-than-life lives lived there. The book, which was faithfully adapted into a film by Robert Redford, makes a great traveling companion, full of vivid description and insightful humor—MacLean writes that while growing up he soon discovered that the world is "full of bastards, the number increasing rapidly the farther one gets from Missoula, Montana." He lovingly uses the art of fly-fishing as an essential metaphor for a life well lived.

of America Museum (daily in summer, shorter hours rest of the year; $3; 406/883-6804), which calls itself "Western Montana's Largest Museum," displays a mixed bag of kitchen appliances, toys, tractors, armored tanks, and framed newspaper clippings to give a unique (to say the least!) view of America's industrial, military, and cultural history. If you'd enjoy things like a motorized toboggan or a collection of tractor seats, count on spending an hour at least—twice that long if you also like music, because the museum doubles as the **Montana Fiddler's Hall of Fame.**

St. Ignatius and the National Bison Range

The wildly angular Mission Mountains, rising to the east of the Flathead Reservation, were named for a Catholic mission established in the 1850s at **St. Ignatius,** a small town midway between Polson and Missoula. Like most reservation communities, it's a poor and fairly depressed place, worth a look for the imposing **St. Ignatius Mission church** (daily in summer; donations), just east of US-93. Built by Flathead laborers in 1891, the church holds over 50 religious frescoes painted by Fr. Joseph Carignano, the mission cook.

Along with the church, St. Ignatius holds the **Flathead Indian Museum and Trading Post** (daily; 406/745-2951), a large gift shop, motel, and drive-through espresso stand right on US-93. There's also a friendly campground, real tepees you can sleep in, and some dormitory bunks at **Hostel of the Rockies** (around $14; 406/745-3959). The dorm beds are in a passive-solar earthlodge built out of old tires coated in adobe mud.

West of St. Ignatius, 18,500 acres of natural rolling prairie have been set aside since 1908 as the **National Bison Range,** protected home of the 500 or so resident bison (aka buffalo) along with deer, elk, pronghorns, and mountain goats. Allow around two hours to drive a complete circuit of the park; the entrance and visitors center are on the west side of the reserve, off Hwy-200 six miles west of the crossroads town of **Ravalli.**

On US-93 in Ravalli, the **Bison Inn** (406/745-4268) has good food for breakfast, lunch, and dinner; the house specialty is (you guessed it) buffalo burgers, and in summer, huckleberry milk shakes.

Missoula

Spreading along the banks of the Clark Fork of the Columbia River at the mouth of Hell Gate Canyon, **Missoula** (pop. 57,053) is an engaging mix of college-town sophistication and blue-collar grit. The two industries that built the city, railroads and lumber mills, have both diminished considerably since their turn-of-the-20th-century heyday, but still form the foundation of the local economy. The University of Montana campus has given Missoula a literate and left-leaning air not usually found in this neck of the woods.

The mountains, rivers, and canyons around Missoula are Montana at its best, and downtown Missoula, stretching along the north bank of the river, contains a large number of elegant turn-of-the-20th-century brick buildings housing a buoyant range of businesses, from department stores to bike shops. Missoula's other social nexus, the **University of Montana** campus, spreads south of the river at the foot of dusty brown Mt. Sentinel (the one marked with the large "M") and the Sapphire Mountains. It's a pleasant place to walk around—in summer at least, when cyclists and inline skaters outnumber pedestrians on the many paths—keeping an eye out for posters advertising local events.

> East of Missoula, scenic Hwy-200 runs along the **Clearwater River** to Clearwater Junction, where a giant steer welcomes travelers to town.

Missoula's number one attraction, the **Smokejumpers Aerial Fire Depot** (Mon.–Fri. in summer; donations; 406/329-4934), is seven miles west of town at the end of Broadway. Displays include dioramas, old photographs, and antique fire-fighting gear; hourly guided tours are led by the very people who jump out of airplanes to battle raging forest fires.

Missoula Practicalities

Thanks to the student population, Missoula has a wider than usual range of places to eat. Start the day at **Bernice's Bakery** (406/728-1358), at 190 S. 3rd Street West, which has great pastries. Right downtown at 139 W. Main Street, the landmark **Missoula Club** (406/728-3740) is a perfectly preserved 1940s burgers-and-beer bar; for an even grittier Missoula scene, it's hard to beat the round-the-clock **Oxford Club** (406/549-0117), 337 N. Higgins Street, where the brave try the eggs-and-brains, and everyone else drinks too much Bud.

There's no shortage of accommodations in Missoula, though it's always a good idea to book a room in advance. The nicest place to stay is **Goldsmith's** ($80–130; 406/728-1585), a very comfortable downtown B&B along the river at 803 E. Front Street. A half dozen motels line I-90 and US-93 (which follows Broadway west of Missoula, and Brooks Street south of town), including the usual national chains.

> If you're a fan of hot springs, or want to unwind after a day of cross-country skiing, you won't want to miss the idyllic **Lolo Hot Springs Resort** (406/273-2290), in the mountains 26 miles southwest of Missoula via scenic US-12. Moose wander through the wooded grounds, and the hot springs ($6/day), where Lewis and Clark soaked themselves, have been extensively but attractively developed.

For more information on visiting Missoula and the surrounding country, contact the **visitors center** (406/721-4750 or 800/526-3465), at 121 E. Broadway.

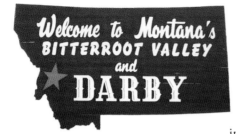

The Bitterroot Valley

South of Missoula toward the Idaho border, US-93 runs along the banks of the beautiful Bitterroot River through a broad valley bordered by parallel ridges of 8,000-foot peaks. Once you get past the log-home manufacturers and tract-house suburbs of Missoula that increasingly fill the valley's northern end, the US-93 roadside is lined by groves of cottonwood trees and occasional hamlets like **Florence,** where **Glen's Cafe** (406/273-2534), tucked away just west of the highway, is renowned throughout Montana for its carb-loaded pancakes and incredibly good double-crusted fresh berry pies.

South of Florence, a well-marked alternative route, the **East Side Highway** (Hwy-203 and Hwy-269), runs parallel to US-93 a half mile to the east, passing rolling ranch lands, pioneer homesteads—some of which are among the oldest in the state—and occasional prefab trailers. This side of the valley is mostly open countryside, with a few small hamlets like **Stevensville,** Montana's oldest town. It was founded by Jesuits in 1841 around the still intact **St. Mary's Mission** (daily in summer; $3; 406/777-5734), at the end of 4th Street, two blocks west of Main.

Hamilton

The Bitterroot Valley's sole sizeable town, **Hamilton** (pop. 3,705) stands at the southern end of the valley, where US-93 and the East Side Highway rejoin. Hamilton was laid out in the 1890s as a planned community by the multimillionaire "Copper King" **Marcus Daly.** Daly's elegant 42-room Georgian mansion, now a **museum** (daily in summer; $6, 406/363-6004), is set in 50 acres of lushly landscaped gardens ($1).

At the north end of the Bitterroot Valley, where Lolo Creek empties into the Bitterroot River, **Lewis and Clark** set up camp at what they called **Traveler's Rest** in September 1805 and again on their return in July 1806. A marker along US-93, a mile south of the US-12 junction, tells more of the story.

Hamilton's other main draw is the large **Ravalli County Museum** (closed Tues., Wed.; free; 406/363-3338), housed in a 100-year-old former courthouse on the corner of 3rd and Bedford, two blocks south of Main Street. Besides an above-average collection of fishing flies, pioneer clothing, and Native American artifacts, the museum has an entire room dedicated to **Rocky Mountain spotted fever ticks**—Hamilton, home of the Rocky Mountain National Laboratory, was where the spotted fever was discovered—and you owe it to yourself to study the 2-foot-tall tick model and the diagrams tracing the tick's life cycle.

Hamilton has some great places to eat, like the very popular **Coffee Cup**

Cafe and the newer **Mangy Moose,** both on US-93 on the south side of town. The more upscale **Banque** (406/363-1955) serves steaks in an old bank at 225 W. Main Street. The best burgers are at **Nap's Grill,** 220 N. 2nd Street.

One of many highway motels in Hamilton, the **Best Western Hamilton** ($60–80; 406/363-2142) is on US-93 at 409 S. 1st Street. Besides its convenience as a stopover, Hamilton is also the gateway to outdoor activities (hunting, fishing, and riding, mainly) in the Bitterroots; for details, contact the **visitors center** (406/363-2400) at 105 E. Main Street.

Bitterroot Mountains

South of Hamilton, the serrated peaks and forested foothills of the **Bitterroot Mountains** close in along US-93 as the valley narrows sharply, the towns shrink in size, and woodlands (and campgrounds) replace farmlands (and commerce) along the roadside. Just 17 miles south of Hamilton, the pioneer village of **Darby** has a couple of cafés, a log-cabin public library, and an only-in-Montana combination: a liquor store that sells secondhand books and used fishing flies. Darby also has a helpful **ranger station** (406/821-3913), the best source of information on hiking and camping in the Bitterroots.

> The Big Hole National Battlefield (406/689-3155), where 800 Nez Percé warriors, women, and children were attacked by the U.S. Army on August 9, 1877, lies east of the Continental Divide near the hamlet of Wisdom, 20 miles east of Lost Trail Pass via Hwy-43.

South of Darby, US-93 cuts away from the Bitterroot River at the hamlet of **Sula,** beyond which the highway continues its slow climb up through seven miles of sub-alpine landscape to another of Montana's many pleasant resorts, **Lost Trail Hot Springs** (406/821-3574 or 800/825-3574), at 8321 Hwy-93 South, open year-round with hot springs pools ($6), an attractive variety of moderately priced rooms and cabins, and good on-site restaurant. Lost Trail is especially popular with cross-country skiers, who can traverse many miles of nearby trails, including the route followed by Chief Joseph and the Nez Percé in 1877 while fleeing from the U.S. Cavalry.

From Lost Trail Hot Springs, US-93 climbs up to 6,995-foot **Lost Trail Pass,** which Lewis and Clark crossed in 1805 on their return from the impassable Snake River, and which now marks the border with Idaho. The pass also serves as a low-key downhill ski area ($24; 406/821-3211), with 1,200 vertical feet of groomed runs.

IDAHO

In 1938, the WPA *Guide to Idaho* described the state's section of US-93 as "miles of beautiful mountains, ranging from soft flanks voluptuously mounded to the lean and glittering majesty of toothed backbones." Though the official US-93 route was redirected around the mountains, not much else has changed since then: The old road is still in place, and still gives an unmatched tour of the best of what Idaho has to offer.

Entering the state through a historic pass in the beautiful Bitterroot Mountains, the route drops down to follow the mighty Salmon River to its headwaters over 100 miles away near the frontier resort of **Stanley,** high up in the Sawtooth Mountains. South of the Sawtooths, the route plunges into the plush resort community of **Sun Valley,** then races across the Snake River plain through Twin Falls to the Nevada border.

Salmon River: North Fork

Beginning at the Montana border, atop Lost Trail Pass, US-93 winds steeply downhill through the 1.7-million-acre **Salmon National Forest.** Another 26 miles south of the pass, US-93 passes by the village of North Fork—where the **North Fork General Store** (208/865-2412) is a combination café/motel/post office that has everything a traveler could want, from great pies to an RV park. Here US-93 crosses the Salmon River, which is often called the "River of No Return" because, without a jet boat to help you along, it is navigable only in a downstream direction. Running swiftly for nearly 300 miles west through the heart of the most extensive wilderness left in the lower 48 states, the Salmon River has carved one of the deepest gorges in North America, a full 1,000 feet deeper than the Grand Canyon.

From North Fork, a paved road leads 17 miles west along the riverside to the tiny hamlet of **Shoup,** beyond which a number of rough roads and hiking trails lead to ghost towns and the **Frank Church Wilderness,** deep in the rugged mountains.

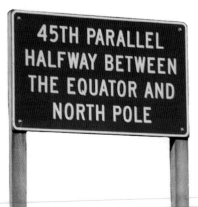

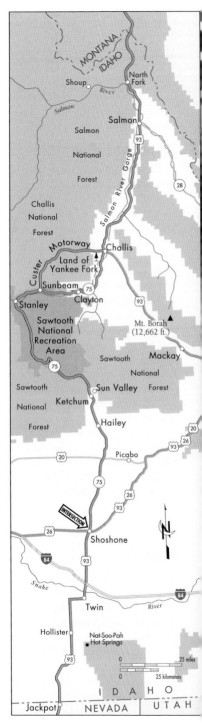

Salmon

Surrounded by ranch lands in a broad valley between the Bitterroot and Yellowjacket Mountains, **Salmon** (pop. 3,122) is a picturesque place that has turned increasingly to tourism and outdoor recreation as its timber and ranching industries have faded. Not surprisingly, it makes a better base from which to explore the surrounding scenery than it does a destination in itself. Main Street, which US-93 follows through town, holds a good variety of places to eat, including the **Salmon River Coffee Shop** (208/756-3521) at 606 Main Street, and **Bertram's Brewery** (208/756-3391) at 101 S. Andrews. Just off US-93, the quiet **Motel DeLuxe** ($40–60; 208/756-2231) at 112 S. Church Street offers inexpensive rooms. Rafting, hunting, and fishing guides are all over; the **visitors center** (208/756-2100 or 800/727-2540), next to City Hall at 200 Main Street, has complete lists.

> Across Idaho, towns and services are few and far between, and during the peak summer season it's a good idea to make arrangements for accommodations well in advance.

Salmon River Gorge

South of Salmon, US-93 continues beside the Salmon River, climbing slowly through a landscape that alternates from open meadows to sheer canyons. Nearly 100 miles later, the route arrives at the river's headwaters high up in the Sawtooth Mountains. Apart from a few cottonwoods, there are few trees and no real towns along this stretch of US-93, and traffic still has to stop for the occasional cattle drive, but it's a very pretty drive, and you can stop almost anywhere for a quick walk or picnic along the river. The appearance of the Salmon River canyon varies tremendously, but for most of the way it is dry and brown—a real shock compared to the dense green forests of Montana, just an hour to the north.

> Around Salmon, tune to **KSRA 92.7 FM** or **960 AM**, for an eclectic broadcast of oldies, country music, ABC News, and reports on life in the Salmon and Big Hole region.

Challis and the Land of Yankee Fork State Park

The only town for 50 miles in any direction, **Challis** is an old mining camp that has grown into a miniature version of Salmon—albeit without the water or the tourists. Apart from boasting the all-time Idaho record for least rain in a year (seven inches), Challis is a very quiet market center for local cattle ranchers, with more bars—and barber shops—than you'd expect of a town this small.

On the south side of Challis, at the junction of US-93 and Hwy-75, the excellent, modern **Land of Yankee Fork State Park visitors center** (daily in summer, closed Sun. rest of year; 208/879-5244) has extensive displays of local mining history and maps to guide visitors to many evocative ghost towns and other relics sprinkling the surrounding hills. Gold was first discovered in the region in the 1870s, and nearby mines and mining camps boomed for the next 25 years, though by 1905 the last mine had closed. A few gold mines have reopened in recent years, though all of these are hidden away in isolated areas and protected behind high-security walls and fences; none is open to the public.

US-93: Mackay and the Lost River Valley

At Challis, our main route follows the 1940s alignment of US-93, heading west into the Sawtooth Mountains, but today's US-93 swings southeast toward Arco and the Craters of the Moon National Monument through the Lost River Valley. The scenery here remains spectacular, with the mountains towering over the ranches of the valley floor, but it can't compare with the glories of the old road route.

But if you're in a rush, or there's been a recent storm blocking the mountain passes, or you just want to see another corner of Idaho, US-93 will be there for you. Mountaineers follow US-93 on their way to climb 12,662-foot **Mt. Borah,** the highest point in Idaho and a demanding though not technically difficult summit to reach. The trailhead is at the end of the well-signed Borah Peak Access road, roughly halfway between Challis and Mackay. For details, contact the **USFS ranger station** (208/588-2224) in Mackay.

In 1805, explorers **Lewis and Clark** became the first Americans to cross the Continental Divide when they climbed over **Lemhi Pass,** 25 miles southeast of Salmon. Hoping to follow the Salmon River west to the Pacific, they found it was impassable and continued north over **Lost Trail Pass,** roughly along the route of US-93.

The rough and ready town of **Mackay** (pop. 575; rhymes with wacky) is the valley's hub. You can stay at the **Wagon Wheel** (208/588-3331), where rooms with kitchenettes go for as little as $40 a night. Mackay also hosts an annual rodeo, the Custer County Fair, and a mountain bike race, but it's best known for its famous **free barbecue** on the 3rd Saturday in September, when hundreds of people come here for general fun and games and massive amounts of free food ("Tons of Meat—Mackay's Treat" say the signs).

South of Mackay, US-93 continues to Arco, then elbows west through the eerie Craters of the Moon, rejoining Hwy-75 at Shoshone.

Clayton and Sunbeam

On October 28, 1983, one of the most powerful earthquakes ever to hit North America rumbled the Lost River Valley, instantly dropping the valley floor as much as 14 feet, and forming dramatic escarpments still visible in places throughout the region.

Though US-93 swings to the southeast from Challis, the original alignment, now Hwy-75, winds west into the mountains through the 2,000-foot-deep canyon carved by the Salmon River. You're deep in the forest by the time you reach **Clayton** (pop. 26), a riverside wide spot with a gas station and a biker-friendly tavern. Farther west, some 50 miles upstream from Challis, you come to the small but pleasant year-round resort of **Sunbeam,** which overlooks the confluence of the Yankee Fork and Salmon Rivers. There's a café and campground at the junction, and just a half mile upstream you'll find the area's greatest attraction: the natural **hot springs,** steaming wildly on cold days and forming rock pools of varying temperatures in the Salmon River, marked by a stone bathhouse built during the New Deal 1930s but no longer in use.

From Sunbeam, it's only another 15 miles to Stanley, heart of the glorious Sawtooth mountains.

Custer Motorway

If you're here in summer and have a few hours to spare, take the rough (no RVs, please!) but very scenic alternative to Hwy-75, built by the Civilian Conservation Corps in the 1930s and called the **Custer Motorway,** which winds west from Challis into the Yankee Fork mining district, passing the remains of old stagecoach stations and stamp mills before reaching the ghost town of **Custer.** Undergoing restoration as the centerpiece of the Land of Yankee Fork State Park, Custer now consists of a half-dozen mining shacks and log cabins, the Empire saloon, and the small but engaging **Custer Museum,** housed in the old one-room schoolhouse. Beyond Custer, a well-maintained gravel road follows the Yankee Fork of the Salmon River south to Hwy-75, passing an abandoned gold dredge and other relics of mining operations, past and present, before rejoining the highway at Sunbeam, on the banks of the Salmon River.

Further details, and free maps of Custer and the Custer Motorway, are available from the Land of Yankee Fork State Park visitors center in Challis (see above).

Stanley

Set in a broad basin at the eastern foot of the angular Sawtooth Mountains, 58 miles west of Challis, **Stanley** is a tiny (pop. 69; elev. 6,260 feet), isolated town that makes an excellent base for exploring the surrounding two-million-plus acres of alpine forest. In summertime, the population swells to around 500, including visitors, so although it's just 60 miles north of busy Sun Valley there's still plenty of room to move. Hikers and mountain bikers in summer, and cross-country skiers in winter, should have no trouble finding solitude in the 10,000-foot peaks; the **ranger station** (208/774-3000), four miles south of town on Hwy-75, can supply details of trails and campgrounds as well as rafting trips along the Middle Fork of the Salmon River.

Places to eat, drink, and be merry stand along Ace of Diamonds Avenue, the main street of Stanley proper, southwest of the Hwy-21/75 junction: Enjoy budget beers-and-burritos and frequent live music at the **Rod & Gun Club Saloon,** and the steaks and chops at the **Kasino Club,** 21 Ace of Diamonds Avenue.

If you're not camping, a popular, locally owned and semi-historic accommodation is **Danner's Log Cabins** ($80 and up; 208/774-3539), along Hwy-21 at the center of town. If the log cabins are full, the modern **Mountain Village Resort** ($60 and up; 208/774-3661) at the junction of Hwy-75 and Hwy-21 offers motel rooms, a decent restaurant, and a gas station.

Sawtooth National Recreation Area

Stanley and Sunbeam both stand along the northern border of the 750,000-acre **Sawtooth National Recreation Area,** which extends south for over 20 miles of untrammeled meadows, forests, and lakes, and includes the headwaters of many major Idaho rivers. It also holds one of the nicest places to stay in the Rockies: the historic **Redfish Lake Lodge** (May–Sept. only; 208/774-3536), seven miles south of Stanley on Hwy-75 on the east shore of Redfish Lake, which has rustic, log-walled rooms in the main lodge from around $60 a night, and spacious cabins for $90–200. The lodge also has a very good restaurant.

There are two main **visitors centers** for the Sawtooth NRA: a summer-only one near Redfish Lake, and the headquarters (208/727-5013) on the north side of Ketchum.

South of Redfish Lake, Hwy-75 switchbacks steeply up to 8,752-foot **Galena Summit,** which gives a grand view over the surrounding mountains, before dropping steeply down toward Sun Valley along the headwaters of the Wood River. About five miles south of the pass, 20-odd miles before you reach the resort area, there's one last stop worth making: **Galena Lodge** (208/726-4010), which dates back to the mining era of the 1880s and has been resurrected as a cross-country ski lodge, with food service, ski or snowshoe rentals, and the Sun Valley area's most extensive system of groomed trails. The lodge also maintains a system of backcountry "yurts": tent-like structures with wood-burning stoves, bunks for up to six people—and dinner delivered to your door.

Sun Valley

The first, and still among the most famous, destination ski resorts in the United States, **Sun Valley** was developed by Union Pacific railroad tycoon Averill Harriman in the 1930s. Harriman built a large mock-Tyrolean chalet, the **Sun Valley Lodge** ($150 and up; 208/622-4111 or 800/635-8261), at 1 Sun Valley Road, and began to cultivate Sun Valley's exclusive reputation—reinforced by high prices for lift tickets rapidly approaching $100 a day, and five-star facilities, including golf courses, tennis courts, and gourmet restaurants. Though Colorado's Vail and other resorts now compete for the top-dollar trade, Sun Valley still attracts well-heeled clientele, if the private jets parked at the local airport are any indication.

While the resort itself isn't huge, Sun Valley has come to stand for the larger area, including the towns of Ketchum and Hailey and much of the nearby wilderness. Somewhat surprisingly, the Sun Valley area is quite barren and treeless—ideal for skiing, perhaps, though not particularly beautiful. Besides skiers in winter, Sun Valley also draws golfers in summer and fall, not to mention anglers, who rate the Wood River as one of the nation's best.

Sun Valley isn't all about money, however; for details on hiking, camping, or mountain biking in the nearby forests, stop by the Sawtooth National Forest **ranger station** (208/622-5371), a mile east of Ketchum on Sun Valley Road.

Ernest Hemingway is probably the most famous name associated with Sun Valley. Hemingway first came here in the 1930s, and worked on *For Whom the Bell Tolls* while staying at the Sun Valley Lodge. He returned in 1960, and a year later shot himself; he's now buried in a simple plot in the middle-rear section of Ketchum's small cemetery. Hemingway is also remembered by a small and surprisingly kitschy memorial along Trail Creek, a mile east of the resort.

Ketchum

Though both places preexisted Sun Valley, the two old mining and sheep-ranching towns of Ketchum and Hailey have more or less lost themselves in the upmarket resort aura of their famous neighbor. **Ketchum** (pop. 3,873), the more touristy of the two, has wall-to-wall art

galleries and T-shirt shops lining its traffic-jammed streets.

It also supports dozens of very expensive resort hotels and restaurants that cater to Sun Valley's country club set, plus a handful of more interesting and affordable places along Main Street. **Whiskey Jacques'** (208/726-5297), at 251 N. Main Street, serves good pizzas and has frequent live music. The Harley-friendly **Casino** (208/726-9901) is a local institution, serving beers and burgers in one of Ketchum's oldest buildings at 220 N. Main Street. There's a very good coffeehouse, **Java on Fourth,** a block west of Main Street at 191 4th Street.

Most central and affordable of Ketchum's accommodations is the **Bald Mountain Lodge** ($65 and up; 208/726-9963 or 800/892-7407), a rustic former hot springs resort at 151 S. Main Street. For more listings, stop by the handy **visitors bureau** (208/726-3423 or 800/634-3347) at 4th and Main.

Hailey

Hailey, 10 miles south of Ketchum and linked by a popular rail-trail bike path, was founded originally in the 1880s as a supply center for local silver and lead mines, and is now the home base of all those workers who make the resorts run smoothly and ski in-between shifts. Hailey feels much more friendly and low-key than Ketchum or Sun Valley, and the eating options are much more down-to-earth. For breakfast or lunch, head to diner-style **Shorty's** (208/578-1293), at 126 S. Main Street, owned by local mom and movie star Demi Moore. When the sun goes down, you can hang out with the local ski bums and bikers at the venerable **Hailey Hotel** (208/788-3140), 201 S. Main Street, which has a lively bar downstairs and the region's cheapest beds—around $40 a night with shared bath.

In contrast to the civic love affair Sun Valley has with the legacy of Ernest Hemingway, Hailey takes little notice of the fact that it was the birthplace (in 1885, in a house that still stands at Pine Street and 2nd Avenue) of another noteworthy literary figure, **Ezra Pound.** His parents were here working for the U.S. government, but fled the snowy winters just two years later.

Shoshone marks the junction of US-93 with our cross-country **Oregon Trail** route (see page 552), which runs along US-20/26 between Boise and the Craters of the Moon National Monument. For full coverage, see pages 532–633.

Shoshone: Ice Caves

South of the Sun Valley area, Hwy-75 runs across 60 miles of south-central Idaho's rocky black lava flows. Halfway between Sun Valley and Twin Falls,

dinosaur at Shoshone Ice Caves

eight miles north of the town of Shoshone, the **Shoshone Ice Caves** (daily in summer; $6; 208/886-2058) present a series of lava tubes developed into a low-key tourist trap. Just west of the highway, their constant cool temperatures (as low as 28°F) do make a pleasant contrast to the often-scorching summer heat. (The "ice" in the name is created by air currents flowing through the tubes, causing subterranean water to freeze.) The only way to explore the caves is through guided tours, which take about 45 minutes. The gift shop and mineral museum will satisfy anyone's needs for tourist-trap trash.

Just down the road, **Mammoth Cave** is much more basic and undeveloped; for serious spelunkers, there are over a dozen other caves and lava tubes nearby. Contact the **BLM office** (208/732-7200) at 400 W. F Street in Shoshone for details.

The only town along this stretch of road, **Shoshone** (pop. 1,395) is a ranching and railroad center that marks the junction of Hwy-75 with US-93. Some of its buildings have been constructed from local volcanic rock, and though it's a fairly timeworn place, Shoshone looks great at sunset, when its steel water tower glows and places like the neon-signed **Manhattan Cafe** (208/886-2142) along the railroad tracks look especially appealing.

Minidoka Internment National Monument

Between Shoshone and Twin Falls, the potato-growing Snake River plains hold a surprising remnant of a moment in time many Americans would just as soon forget: the forcible arrest and deportation of 110,000 Americans of Japanese descent during the early 1940s. Moved from their homes in California, Washington, and Oregon—but not Hawaii, where they were a key segment of the workforce—entire families were uprooted and relocated to desolate, middle-of-nowhere places where they were made to live in makeshift shacks. Here at **Minidoka Internment National Monument,** 17 miles northeast of Twin Falls, more than 13,000 American citizens were held as prisoners between 1942 and the end of World War II three years later. The 73-acre site preserves a handful of buildings, including the guard house, but it's the isolation that endures most. The site has no services, and can be hard to reach; head east from US-93 along Hwy-25 for 9.5 miles, then north along Hunt Road for another 2.5 miles. (The visitors center is in Hagerman, 20 miles away; see page 549.)

Evel Knievel and the Snake River Canyon

No one who lived through the 1970s could forget the name Evel Knievel, the ultimate thrill seeker who became rich and famous performing dangerous and virtually impossible feats on a motorcycle. Born in Butte, Montana, in 1939, Knievel dropped out of high school and worked a dozen different jobs before finding his true calling as a motorcycle daredevil. In 1965 he made his first jump, flying over a caged mountain lion and boxes of rattlesnakes at Moses Lake, Washington. Within a few years he hit the big time: leaping over the fountains at Caesar's Palace and jumping 50 cars at the L.A. Coliseum. Though he broke nearly every bone in his body as a result of his numerous crash landings, Knievel's feats were always bigger, better, and more dangerous than the last; as he liked to say, "Where there's little risk, there's little reward."

Banned by the government from attempting a leap over the Grand Canyon, Knievel set his sights on the Snake River Canyon in southern Idaho, leasing the land so no one could stop him, then building a massive ramp and working out the details of his custom-made, rocket-powered Harley-Davidson X-2 Skycycle. On September 8, 1974, some 30,000 people turned out, along with many millions more watching on TV, for Evel's big leap. Unfortunately, one of his parachutes deployed on takeoff, and he floated gently down into the bottom of the gorge, safe and sound, and proud of having the guts to try—even if he didn't quite make it.

Twin Falls

Named for a pair of 200-foot cascades in the Snake River, both of which have long been diverted for irrigation or to generate electricity, **Twin Falls** (pop. 34,469) is the heart of the extensive "Magic Valley" of highly productive irrigated croplands that cover half a million acres of south-central Idaho. Best known to people outside Idaho as the place where, in 1974, daredevil Evel Knievel tried and failed to ride a rocket-powered motorcycle across the Snake River canyon, Twin Falls is both a quiet farming community and a busy highway town—with a barrage of backlit and neon signs around the junction of US-93 and the I-84 freeway.

The one unique attraction of Twin Falls, the site of **Evel Knievel's** aborted motorcycle jump, is a mile north of town on US-93, south of I-84. There's a large parking area and a visitors center at the south foot of the delicate Per-

Many of Idaho's famous potatoes are grown in the Magic Valley area around Twin Falls; harvest season is late September. To learn everything you ever wanted to know about spuds, take a trip east via US-26 to Blackfoot, Idaho, and the **World Potato Exposition** ($3; 208/785-2517), at 130 N.W. Main Street.

341. Twin Falls on the Snake River, near Twin Falls, Idaho.

rine Memorial Bridge, and it's well worth stopping for, not only to see the remains of his launch pad (a triangular pile of dirt, on private property a mile or so east of the bridge) or the stone monument that calls him "Robert 'Evel' Knievel—Explorer, Motorcyclist, Daredevil." The views down into the 500-foot-deep gorge, the floor of which has been irrigated and filled with a bright green golf course, are also impressive, especially at sunset when the whole scene takes on an otherworldly glow.

Though the town can make a good jumping-off point for Sun Valley and the mountain wilderness farther north, there's not a lot to *do* in Twin Falls. The waterfalls for which the town is named are worth a look if you have the time: **Shoshone Falls,** taller than Niagara, may still impress, especially in spring. Check them out from the park at the end of Falls Avenue, seven miles east of US-93. Without its namesake waterfalls, however, Twin Falls has little to offer travelers apart from a chance to fill the gas tank, eat, or get a night's sleep. For breakfast or a lunchtime burger, head to **Kelly's Diner** (208/733-6466), at 110 N. Main Avenue, or the 24-hour **Depot Grill** (208/733-0710), along downtown's diagonal main drag at 545 S. Shoshone Street. Sleep at your choice of two **Best Westerns,** a **Comfort Inn,** an **Econo Lodge,** a **Super 8,** or any of a dozen others along US-93 or I-84.

Nat-Soo-Pah Hot Springs

South of Twin Falls, there's a whole lot of nothing in the 47 miles before you reach the Nevada border at Jackpot. One place worth a stop is the summer-only **Nat-Soo-Pah hot springs** ($5; 208/655-4337), halfway to Nevada, where you'll find a giant (125 by 50 foot!) spring-fed swimming pool, a 90-foot waterslide, a tree-shaded picnic area and snack bar, and a $12-a-night **campground.** Nat-Soo-Pah is about a mile south of Hollister, then three miles east on a well-signed road. There are a number of other natural springs in the area, so if you enjoy being in hot water, southern Idaho is a great place to explore.

NEVADA

US-93 runs south along the eastern edge of Nevada for 520 miles, 500 of which take you through an exceptional degree of desolation—endless straight and narrow valleys, two-car traffic jams, and towns few and far between. From the gambling oasis of Jackpot on the Idaho border to where the highway crosses into Arizona atop Hoover Dam, US-93 is at least as lonely as its Nevada sibling US-50, the official Loneliest Road in America. Towns like **Wells,** along I-80 in the northern half of the state, are big events; south of here it's 130 miles to

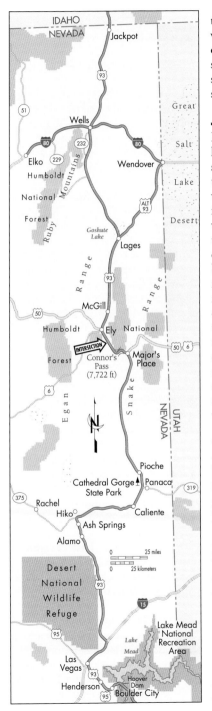

the next watering hole, **Ely,** beyond which the old mining camp of **Pioche** and the desert hot springs resort of **Caliente** are the only wide spots in the road before you hit the staggering city of **Las Vegas.**

Jackpot

In every respect but one, **Jackpot** belongs more to Idaho than Nevada—a somewhat incongruous introduction to US-93 in the Silver State. Jackpot's visitors and workers mostly come from Idaho, as do its power and water; even its clocks are set to Idaho time. The one little exception, however, is pure Nevada: border-town gambling. Jackpot was founded in 1956, mere months after Idaho banned slot machines, which didn't, to be sure, reduce the demand. In fact, Jackpot has thrived, as a pit stop in any of the town's casinos will attest. Jackpot is compact enough to give long-distance travelers just enough lights, action, and comfort to satisfy more immediate needs and then send them on their way again.

Cactus Pete's ($50 and up; 775/755-2321) is the 10-story tower you can see for miles; along with the big casino, it has a great snack bar, a buffet, a sit-down restaurant, showroom, and more of the same in the **Horseshu** across the street.

If you're heading south from Jackpot, be sure to fill the tank before hitting the road; the next gas is over an hour away.

Wells

Some lone peaks, a stretch of badlands and buttes, and a couple of north-south–trending ranges usher US-93 down a long basin toward the little junction town of **Wells** (pop. 1,346). Just under 70 miles from Jackpot at

Bonneville Speedway

Located in the middle of nowhere, west of the Great Salt Lake on the Utah/Nevada border, the vast salt flats of Bonneville cover some 150 square miles. Since the 1930s, Bonneville's broad, hard, flat and unobstructed surface has made it a mecca for efforts to set ever-faster land speed records. The earliest speed records were set at Daytona Beach, Florida (see page 424), but as top speeds increased, racers needed more room to maneuver safely. In 1931, Ab Jenkins set Bonneville's first world record in his bright red Mormon Meteor, and racers have converged on Bonneville's 10-mile-long drag strip in pursuit of record-breaking speed ever since.

Craig Breedlove, in his car "Spirit of America," was the first to exceed the 400, 500, and 600 mph marks, but in recent years, problems with water dissolving the salt have made Bonneville less than ideal, so racers like Richard Noble, whose team set the current record of 763 mph in 1996, have opted for the Black Rock Desert, 150 miles north of Reno, Nevada. Still, every summer hundreds of thrill-seekers descend on Bonneville, racing their hot rods in a series of time trials.

the interchange of US-93 and the I-80 freeway, Wells was named by the Central Pacific Railroad, which chose the site for a depot and town to make use of the plentiful springs in the hills a few miles northeast. The old downtown—take a right on 6th Street and another right at the light—is the most intact abandoned **railroad row** on the entire mainline across northern Nevada. Wells provides an explicit illustration of the West's transition from rail to road to superhighway: The newest action in town is at the east and west exit ramps of I-80; the "strip" between the exits is 6th Street (old US-40), the vintage, pre-interstate place for action in the 1950s and even 1960s, but now derelict around the edges. Commerce along the 125-year-old tracks is, of course, extinct.

Wells is situated at the northeastern base of the scenic **East Humboldt Range.** To get into the mountains, go under Wells's west exit ramp and follow the signs; the paved road climbs to 8,400 feet, passing one campground and terminating at another. For details, contact the USFS **ranger station** (775/752-3357) at the west end of town.

Continuing down US-93 affords a different view of the East Humboldts. Ten miles south of Wells, you can take a right on Hwy-232, which makes a loop through luxuriant Clover Valley at the eastern base of the mountains, one of the most bucolic basins in Nevada. About six miles in from the highway is a right turn onto a rough dirt track. Look up to see **Hole-in-the-Mountain Peak.** The tallest peak in the East Humboldts (11,276 feet), it features a 30- by 25-foot natural window in the thin rock 300 feet below its summit, which gives you a spectacular little patch of blue (or silver, orange, or purple, depending on the time of day) right through the top of the range. Compelling.

Wendover

At I-80, US-93 becomes the hypotenuse of an alternative route, which runs for 60 miles southeast to the Utah border at **Wendover,** then another 60 miles southwest to rejoin the mainline US-93 at Lages. Wendover, like Jackpot, is a thriving Nevada border town, with new golf course–view subdivisions and at least five major casino-hotels—try the **Red Garter** (775/664-2111). Wendover's other claims to fame include **Wendover Will,** the huge cowboy outside the Stateline casino who welcomes you to Nevada along the Utah state line; the **Bonneville Salt Flats** and speedway, where most of the world's land-speed records have been set over the past 80 years; and **Wendover Air Force Base,** where in 1945 the crew of the *Enola Gay* trained to drop an atomic bomb on Japan.

Wendover Will

The Ruby Mountains and Elko

It's a long, solitary, 140 miles from Wells to Ely. US-93 shoots down Clover Valley to the southern edge of the East Humboldts where Hwy-229, a maintained gravel road, cuts off southwest toward the **Ruby Mountains,** also known as the Nevada Alps. This is one of Nevada's most scenic ranges: 100 miles long, with more than a dozen peaks over 9,000 feet.

The best access to the Ruby Mountains is through the engaging small city of **Elko,** 50 miles west of Wells via I-80. Besides maintaining its Basque culture, Elko is home to the **Western Folklife Center,** which hosts the very popular **Cowboy Poetry Gathering** every January, a **Cowboy Music Gathering** the last weekend in June, and a 4th of July celebration. Take advantage of some of the fine family-style Basque restaurants like the **Star Hotel** (775/738-9925), near the railroad tracks at 246 Silver Street, which is worth the drive for the delicious lamb chops and other dishes.

For more information, contact the **Elko Convention and Visitors Bureau** (775/738-7135 or 800/428-7143), at 140-5 Idaho Street.

Between Wells and Ely, US-93 bends away from the heart of the Ruby Mountains, running southeast through Steptoe Valley on a marathon drive down an elongated basin, hemmed in by the Schell Creek Range on the east and the Egan Range on the west. The only signs of civilization on this stretch are two roadhouses: one at Lages (78 miles south of Wells) and the other at Schellbourne (40 miles north of Ely).

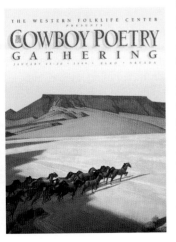

McGill

Tiny **McGill,** 128 miles south of I-80 and 12 miles north of Ely, is the classic Nevada company town, its workaday life revolving for the first 50 years of the 20th century around a giant copper smelter. Mining company officials lived in the fancy houses around the "Circle" at the top of the hill just below the factory, while workers were housed according to their ethnic origins. The saloon and jail were conveniently built right next door to each other, and steam from the copper furnaces was piped to heat the town's houses. The company's been gone for more than 15 years, but the layout remains, along with acres of fenced-off brick factory buildings painted with fading signs encouraging workers to behave safely.

The McGill smelter's last sky-scraping smokestack was felled in September 1993. At 750 feet, it was the tallest structure in Nevada.

A few of McGill's buildings have been converted to current uses, but most are closed and quite forlorn. US-93, which runs at the foot of town, attracts most of the businesses, including a **Frosty** stand (for burgers and shakes) and the **McGill Club,** right on US-93 down the street in the old Cyprus Hall. "The Oldest Back Bar in the State," the latter is considered one of Nevada's finest by connoisseurs of Silver State–licensed establishments. (The McGill jail, however, is now in Ely.)

Another semi-survivor along this short stretch of US-93 is the **McGill Drug Store** (open by appointment or good luck; 775/235-7082), long-closed but preserved as an ad-hoc museum under the care of the White Pine Historical Museum in neighboring Ely. If you can't arrange a tour, peer in through the windows at a soda fountain and shelves stocked full of 1950s-era merchandise.

Ely marks the junction of US-93 and US-50, the legendary **Loneliest Road** in America. See pages 636–721; Ely is described on page 653.

Connors Pass and Major's Place

Southeast of Ely, US-93, spliced together with US-50 and US-6 into a single two-lane highway, continues for 25 miles before crossing the narrow waist of the Schell Creek at **Connors Pass** (elev. 7,722 feet), one of only two fractions of US-93 in Nevada that climb above the tree line. (Unlike most of the rest of the country, the tree line in Nevada has a lower, as well as an upper, limit: No trees grow below roughly 4,000 feet.) As you ascend toward the pass, the air cools and freshens, the single-leaf piñon and Utah juniper appear and thicken, and, cresting the summit, the mighty Snake Range, including 13,061-foot Wheeler Peak, comes into view.

At **Major's Place** (where there's a roadhouse), US-93 splits off from US-50 and US-6, the latter two heading east toward Utah, while US-93 cuts south, heading 80 long, solitary miles to the next contact with humans at Pioche. Once again, the highway rolls along taffy-pulled Spring and Lake Valleys, ushered on its way by the Schell Creek, Fairview, Bristol, and Highland Ranges on the west, and the Snake and Wilson Creek Ranges on the east.

Pioche

The only places that are more than a ghostly outline of civilization in the nearly 300 miles of Great Basin Desert that US-93 crosses between Ely and Las Vegas are the wildly different towns of Caliente, Panaca, and Pioche. The oldest and most northerly of the three, **Pioche** (pop. 800; pronounced pee-OACH, which means "pick-axe" in French), is a one-time mining boomtown that had its heyday well over a century ago. Being so remote—back then exponentially more than now—during the 1870s Pioche descended to a level of anarchy that rivaled Bodie and Tombstone, and over 75 men were killed before anyone died of natural causes.

Corruption, too, was the order of the day, and you can tour Pioche's "Million Dollar" **Lincoln County Courthouse** on Lacour Street for a graphic example of it. Designed in 1871 at an estimated cost of $26,000, the courthouse wasn't completed until 1876, to the tune of $88,000. Then, unable to pay off the principal, the county commissioners kept refinancing the debt, while interest accrued, year after year; by the time it was paid off in 1937, the courthouse had cost a million bucks and been replaced by a more modern structure. Now restored, the old courthouse is open for self-guided **tours** (daily; donations; 775/962-5182) of the offices, the courtroom, and the old jail.

The eclectic **Lincoln County Historical Museum** (daily; free; 775/962-5207), on Main Street at the center of town, is another good stop, as are nearby historic buildings such as the **Thompson Opera House** and the **Commercial Club.** The rusting remains of the **aerial tramway** that ran through Pioche, carrying ore to the stamp mills, can be explored—cables, cars, and all—from various points in town. Two state parks to the east (Echo Canyon and Spring Valley, 12 and 20 miles respectively) round out your Pioche-area sightseeing.

Panaca and Cathedral Gorge

Panaca, 11 miles south of Pioche and a mile east of US-93 on Hwy-319, was founded in 1864 by Mormon farmers, attracted to the valley by the plentiful water of Panaca Spring, in what was then a part of Utah. The mining strikes at nearby Bullionville and Pioche disturbed their peace briefly, but Panaca—which has a single gas station/minimart, plus a school and lots of houses—has a strong sense of tranquility and timelessness rarely felt in the rest of Nevada.

Panaca Spring, a fine local swimming hole with warm, sweet water, is found just outside the town of Panaca: Take 5th Street north past the baseball diamond and a rusty old steam engine, toward a big cottonwood tree about a half mile beyond where the pavement ends.

Just west of US-93, two miles north of Panaca, **Cathedral Gorge State Park** is a mini–Grand Canyon of eroded mud. A lake once covered this deep gully, and silt and clay were washed to the bottom by streams and creeks. The lake dried up, exposing the sediments, and erosion (which never sleeps) sculpted them into the fantastic procession of formations that you see today. The **campground** ($14 per site; 775/728-4460) here has shade trees, flush toilets, even showers.

Caliente

To Pioche's mining and Panaca's farming, **Caliente** (pop. 1,100), 15 miles south, adds railroading. This small town was built around the San Pedro, Los Angeles, and Salt Lake Railroad tracks in the early 1900s, a short while before Las Vegas itself was founded. The **Union Pacific Depot,** which was built in 1923 and still gets Amtrak service on the Las Vegas–Salt Lake City line, is the nerve center of Caliente, being restored to house government offices and a local history and art gallery.

The town supports two gas stations and a half dozen motels, the best of which is the **Hot Springs Motel** ($55; 775/726-3777), off US-93 on the north side of Caliente. Here your room comes with use of Roman baths, whose fire-hydrant faucets can fill the five-foot-square, four-foot-deep tubs in three minutes flat with scalding-hot 115°F water. Road food, however, is limited to two choices: the **Knotty Pine** coffee shop and casino (775/726-3194) at 690 Front Street, and the very pleasant **Brandin' Iron** café (775/726-3164), across from the depot at 190 Clover Street.

Rainbow Canyon, south of Caliente on Hwy-317, is one of Nevada's most scenic and least-known drives: Colorful, high volcanic-tuff cliffs, railroad trestles, and idyllic farms and ranches line Meadow Wash. The pavement ends after 21 miles, but in dry weather you can continue 38 miles through Kane Springs Valley to connect back up with US-93.

South from Caliente, US-93 bends due west for 43 miles. Newman Canyon just outside of town has high, sheer, smooth, volcanic-tuff walls similar to Rainbow Canyon's. You twist and climb out of the canyon to cross the Delmar Range at **Oak Springs Summit** (6,237 feet), where the juniper trees are a welcome change from the low desert scrub. Beyond is an even rarer sight, not only for this highway but for any highway: a little interface zone in which the junipers grow right next to Joshua trees. This is the first indication of the change from Great Basin Desert, which lies to the north, to the front edge of the Mojave Desert, which spreads south and west. Pahroc Summit is next (just under 5,000 feet), then Six Mile Flat, and then **Hiko,** where Hwy-375 heads northwest to US-6 and Tonopah.

Ash Springs and Alamo

From the Hwy-375 junction, US-93 turns due south again and enters some unexpectedly lush country, in the midst of which three large and faithful springs provide plentiful water for alfalfa farms and cattle ranches, as well as for the only bona fide lakes that US-93 encounters in more than 400 miles of its Nevada leg. **Ash Springs**—consisting of a single gas station and convenience store called R Place—is named after the nearby water source, which is believed to be part of a vast aquifer underlying much of eastern Nevada.

The extraterrestrial issues surrounding Area 51 are nothing compared to the actual explosive truth of what has happened there over the years. If you doubt this, visit the new **Atomic Testing Museum** (daily; $10; 702/794-5151), at 755 E. Flamingo Road in Las Vegas.

Twelve miles south of Ash Springs is **Alamo,** whose two motels, two truck stops, and 24-hour Mexican restaurant, Del Pueblo, are the only real services between Caliente and Las Vegas. Four miles south of town is **Upper Pahranagat Lake;** an old road runs along the eastern shore, with camping and picnic sites and big cotton-

The Extraterrestrial Highway

West of US-93, stretching nearly to Death Valley and the California border, the U.S. government has turned the 3.5-million-acre expanse of Nellis Air Force Range into its most top-secret laboratory and testing ground. H-bombs, U-2 spy planes, Stealth bombers, you name it—this is where projects no one is supposed to know about exist.

It's not so surprising that, like Roswell, New Mexico, this lonely corner of the world has become the focus of an ongoing controversy pitting government secrecy against allegations that the Air Force has been using a corner of the base known as Area 51 to study UFOs and extraterrestrials. Fueled in part by tabloid stories claiming an E.T.-like creature is being kept alive at Area 51 in a high-security compound underneath Groom Lake—and also by local businesspeople's realization that UFO tourism could mean big money—the hoopla has focused on the tiny village of Rachel, which has become to UFO-spotters what the grassy knoll is to JFK conspiracy theorists.

Rachel (pop. 99), the only community along the 100-mile stretch of Hwy-375 (now officially known as the Extraterrestrial Highway, promoted by the state along the lines of the "Loneliest Road" campaign), is a block-long strip that holds the lighthearted **Little A-Le-Inn,** a typical back-of-beyond bar and grill where you can munch on "Alien Burgers," down drinks like the "Beam Me Up, Scotty" (Jim Beam, 7UP, and Scotch) or peruse UFO-related key chains, fridge magnets, and T-shirts. The Little A-Le-Inn also has rooms (775/729-2515) for around $40 a night.

woods—one of the most idyllic spots on the whole Nevada portion of US-93. The water is close enough to the source at Ash Springs that it's relatively warm year-round. Lower Pahranagat Lake, a bit farther south, freezes in the winter.

Upper Pahranagat Lake is also home to the administration and maintenance facilities for the **Desert National Wildlife Refuge,** at 1.5 million acres the largest refuge in the Lower 48. Elusive desert bighorn sheep enjoy protection within this huge habitat, alongside of which US-93 travels for the length of the aptly named Sheep Range. The road descends gradually into rocky and barren desert until finally, 70 miles from Alamo and 125 miles from Caliente, US-93 merges with the I-15 freeway for the high-speed haul into the Big Glow: Las Vegas.

Driving Las Vegas

Las Vegas has to be the easiest city in the world to drive around: Everything lines up along, or in relation to, one big road—**The Strip.** Recently dubbed an official "All-American Highway," along with such scenic landmarks as the Blue Ridge Parkway and the stretch of Hwy-1 through California's

Big Sur, this 10-mile-long, traffic-clogged barrage of bright lights and architectural extravagance is also known as South Las Vegas Boulevard, and runs parallel to I-15 between the compact downtown area and the airport. Other roads in Las Vegas are named after the big hotels near their junction with The Strip, hence you have Sahara Avenue, Flamingo Road, and Tropicana Avenue one after another.

Almost everybody who drives into Las Vegas comes by way of the I-15 freeway, which runs between Los Angeles and Salt Lake City, and which connects with US-93 some 20 miles northwest of The Strip. From the south and Hoover Dam, use the new I-515 freeway, which carries US-93 and US-95 on a snaking S-figure between Henderson and Fremont Street in downtown Las Vegas.

US-93 actually bypasses The Strip, veering southeast along Fremont Street and the Boulder Highway—or along I-515—but it's all but required that you drive at least a little of The Strip before you can say you've been to Las Vegas. Don't expect to get anywhere very quickly, though; The Strip is like one big, slow cruise, with 10 lanes of traffic moving past all those casino lights at about 10 mph, day or night.

Time the drive into Las Vegas so you arrive around dusk, when the western sky sports a purple sunset, and the horizon shines brightly from a billion amber street lights stretching from one end of the valley to the other.

The world's highest amusement park stands atop the Stratosphere Tower, where 4 different roller coasters and thrill rides hang, spin, and twirl you 1,000 feet above The Las Vegas Strip.

Henderson

Southeast of Las Vegas, US-93 joins courses with US-95 along Nevada's newest freeway, I-515, which connects Las Vegas with the rapidly growing industrial city of **Henderson.** Henderson itself is relatively young, even by Nevada standards. In 1941, the War Department selected this site, due to its proximity to unlimited electricity generated by the then-six-year-old Hoover Dam, for a giant factory to process magnesium, needed for bombs and airplane components. Within six months, 10,000 workers arrived, and the plant and a town for 5,000 people had been built. After the war ended, the factory was subdivided for private industry, and since then, Henderson has grown to be the third-largest city in Nevada, behind Las Vegas and Reno—the only three population centers in Nevada with more than 100,000 residents.

Though it doesn't even try to compete with the attractions of Las Vegas, Henderson does have a number of casinos (including the world's largest bingo parlor), a Ritz-Carlton hotel, and the very good **Clark County Heritage Museum** (daily; $1.50; 702/455-7955), located two miles south of town at 1830 S. Boulder Highway.

South of Henderson, US-93/95 climbs up and over 2,367-foot Railroad Pass, and just beyond is the junction where US-95 cuts south, heading along the Colorado River to Laughlin, Nevada; Needles, California; and Yuma, Arizona. US-93 continues east, and a little north, to Boulder City.

Boulder City

Like Henderson, **Boulder City** (pop. 14,966) was founded and built by the federal government to house workers at Hoover Dam, what was then the largest construction project ever undertaken. Though the dam was completed in 1935, Boulder City continued under the Feds' ownership and management for another 25 years; in 1960, an Act of Congress conferred independent municipal status on the town. Long-time residents purchased their houses and alcohol consumption was permitted for the first time in the town's history, though gambling remained forbidden. To this day, almost a half century since "independence," Boulder City remains the only town in Nevada that expressly prohibits gambling, which may explain why it feels more like the Midwest than a suburb of Sin City.

If you're interested in the men and machines involved in building the dam, spend some time at the **Boulder City/Hoover Dam Museum,** inside the historic (and newly restored) **Boulder Dam Hotel** ($99–149; 702/293-3510) at 1305 Arizona Street; the hotel also has a good dining room. There is a handful of motels and fast-food outlets in town—a run of 1950s-style cafés and motels lines the Nevada Highway/US-93 Business Route through town—but the real draws are just below Boulder City. At the dam, of course, and the lake behind it.

Heading south across Hoover Dam into Arizona, you'll pass no towns or services for some 75 miles, until you reach Kingman on old Route 66, so stock up and fill up in Boulder City before proceeding.

Hoover Dam and Lake Mead

Approaching **Hoover Dam** from the Nevada side, in the eight miles from Boulder City you pass a Nevada Welcome Center, a National Park Service visitors center for **Lake Mead National Recreation Area,** and a peculiar parade of electrical generators, transformers, and capacitors all secured by cyclone fencing topped by razor wire and barbs to keep out intruders.

Next up is the parking lot for the **visitors center** (daily; $10, plus $5 parking; 702/294-3517), which finally opened in 1995, 10 years behind schedule and $100 million over budget. The steep admission price buys you a half-hour film, a self-guided museum tour, and an elevator ride down inside the dam to gape at the humming turbines, which at peak times generate some 2000 megawatts of electricity, enough to supply a million homes and still have enough juice left over to light up the Las Vegas Strip. Beyond the visitors center, US-93 rolls right over the top of the gargantuan wedge of Hoover Dam: nearly a quarter-mile

Las Vegas

Viva Las Vegas! Since its founding 100 years ago, Las Vegas has been the biggest, brightest, and brazenest boomtown in the history of the world. In the past 20 years, the population has more than tripled (rapidly approaching 2 million people in the metropolitan area), and over a dozen major hotels and mega-resorts have re-created everything from ancient Egypt to Venice (complete with canals and gondoliers), Paris (a mock Eiffel Tower), and New York City (with a Coney Island roller coaster and fake steam puffing up from fake sidewalks). More numbers: With nearly 150,000 rooms, the city has as many as New York and Chicago combined, and 40 million visitors lose close to $10 billion in the casinos here every year.

In addition to gambling, Las Vegas casinos have all the rooms, restaurants, and recreational opportunities you can imagine (and then some). If you're staying overnight, you'll enter the wacky and somewhat wicked world of Las Vegas lodging. Rooms aren't the dirt-cheap bargains they were

a decade or more ago; rates vary depending on the time of year, time of the week, and sometimes even the time of day, but count on spending at least $50 for a decent hotel room, 5 times that for something special. You should definitely make reservations as early as you can; on Friday nights, or during a big convention or boxing match, the whole town is often sold out. A final note: If you'll be schlepping a lot of luggage, Las Vegas hotel rooms are a long way from parking spaces in the high-rise garages and huge lots, but parking is free. Here are a few of the many places you can play:

Caesars Palace (702/731-7110 or 800/634-6001): Long before there was a Mirage; a New York, New York; a Bellagio; or a Venetian, there was Caesars Palace. From the day it opened in 1966 as the first "themed" hotel in Las Vegas, Caesars Palace has been the classiest and most famous place in town.

Hard Rock Hotel/Casino (4555 Paradise Road; 702/693-5000 or 800/473-7625): For anyone under 60, this is the coolest place in town. Off the Strip and small by Vegas standards, but where else can you listen to nonstop classic rock 'n' roll while playing Jimi Hendrix slot machines (a line of "Purple Haze" pays $200), or drinking a cocktail at the swim-up bar?

Luxor (3900 Las Vegas Boulevard South; 702/262-4000 or 800/288-1000): The most distinctive, housed inside a mammoth (29-million-cubic-foot) glass pyramid at the southern end of the Strip. Above the casino, stage sets of city streets hold high-tech attractions: motion simulators, 3-D and IMAX movies, and virtual reality arcade games.

The Mirage (3400 Las Vegas Boulevard South; 702/791-7111 or 800/627-6667): Has its own rainforest, a 50,000-gallon aquarium, and white tigers on display (this is the home of Siegfried and Roy). Next door, at Treasure Island, a theatrical (and free) pirate show is staged right on the Strip every 90 minutes or so all day long.

Wynn Las Vegas (3131 Las Vegas Boulevard South; 702/770-7100 or 888/320-WYNN): Brought to you by the creator of Mirage and Bellagio, on the site of the historic Desert Inn (where billionaire recluse Howard Hughes used to live), this ultra-fashionable 2,700-suite oasis is the last word in high-end indulgence, with an on-site Ferrari dealership and some of the best restaurants in the country.

across, 726 feet high, 660 feet thick at the base, all accomplished with a mere seven million tons (that's 14 billion pounds) of concrete. If you just want to see the dam, you can walk across it for free and peer down at the lake or distant river below; because of security concerns, pedestrians are banned after dark.

Hoover Dam marks the border between Nevada and Arizona, and between the Pacific and Mountain time zones, so set your clocks and watches accordingly (and remember, Arizona does not use daylight saving time).

Upstream from the dam spreads Lake Mead, the largest man-made lake in the western hemisphere. Containing roughly 30 million acre-feet or just over nine *trillion* gallons, Lake Mead irrigates some 2.5 million acres of land in the United States and Mexico, while helping to control the river's seasonal flooding. The lake is a very popular recreation site, with thousands of water-skiers and others flocking to its 500 miles of shoreline year-round.

ARIZONA

Coming into Arizona across the top of Hoover Dam, US-93 cuts southeast across the length, and half the breadth, of the state, covering nearly 500 miles of desiccated desert. Starting at the Nevada border, US-93 makes a diagonal beeline toward the old Route 66 town of **Kingman,** one of the few watering holes in Arizona's northwest quarter.

South of Hoover Dam, US-93 runs parallel to the older version of the highway, with numerous old bridges and sections of gravel roadway standing along the modern four-lane freeway.

Joshua trees and ghost towns far outnumber gas stations in this part of the state, so fill up before setting off into these great wide-open spaces. From Kingman, the route cuts south across another huge stretch of desert, passing through the dude-ranch resort town of **Wickenburg.** In the middle of Arizona spreads **Phoenix,** the state's capital and largest city. From this sprawling megalopolis, our route bends east into the mountains, following backroads past the otherworldly Biosphere 2 "space station" before hitting **Tucson,** another hugely horizontal city. South of here you'll enjoy the most feature-packed part of the trip, passing by the historic Spanish colonial communities of **Tubac** and **Tumacácori** before winding up at the enjoyable twin border town of **Ambos Nogales.**

Lake Mead Recreation Area

Most people come from the Las Vegas area to visit Lake Mead, which covers some 160,000 acres and includes over 500 miles of shoreline, on the extensively developed Nevada side. In contrast, the only access on the Arizona side is from **Temple Bar,** 19 miles south of Hoover Dam, then another 27 miles northeast on a good paved road. Here you'll find a small marina with boat rentals and a motel (800/752-9669).

Stretching to both sides of Hoover Dam, the **Lake Mead Recreation Area** also incorporates the smaller **Lake Mojave,** clearly visible from US-93 and accessible at **Willow Beach** on the Colorado River, 14 miles south of Hoover Dam and four miles west of US-93.

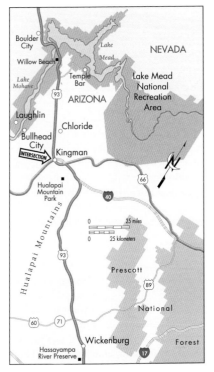

Laughlin, Nevada

Between Hoover Dam and Kingman, a detour heads west to the Nevada side of the Colorado River to **Laughlin, Nevada,** a place that epitomizes the anything-goes character of Nevada gaming. Laughlin, a booming gambling resort that in many ways seems even more mirage-like than Las Vegas, may lack glitz and pizzazz, but makes up for it with cheaper rooms ($20 is not uncommon) and the almost unheard-of attraction of river views from the casino floors.

The history of Laughlin—or rather, the lack of it—is impressive even by Nevada standards. Starting with a run-down bait shop he bought in the mid-1960s, Michigan-born entrepreneur Don Laughlin envisioned the fantasyland you see today, opening his **Riverside Hotel** (702/298-2535 or 800/227-3849), which is still a local favorite, in the late 1970s, and drawing visitors from all over Arizona and Southern California. Laughlin's independent mini-empire was eclipsed in the 1980s by the big shots: First **Harrah's** came, then Circus Circus opened the steamboat-shaped **Colorado Belle,** then the **Flamingo** added a 2,000-room palace. Fortunes have ebbed and flowed ever since, but Laughlin is still well worth a look or an overnight stay.

For further information, contact the **Laughlin Chamber of Commerce** (702/298-2214 or 800/4-LAUGHLIN).

> Laughlin is one of the hottest inhabited places in the country, with an all-time high temperature of 125°F, registered here in 1994.

Chloride

Marked by a big "C" inscribed in the hillside above it, the near-ghost town of **Chloride** (pop. 352), 53 miles south of Hoover Dam and 15 miles north of Kingman, then four miles east of the highway on a paved, well-marked road, is the oldest and among the most evocative former mining camps in Arizona. Following the discovery of silver here in the 1860s, mining activities continued through the 1940s; the town is now preserved by its dedicated residents.

A couple of stores and cafés still cling to life, and occasional festivals and flea markets draw sizeable crowds of visitors. Mostly what there is to see are the odd bits of "folk art" so often found in the American desert: strange sculptures made of rusting metal and odd bits of junk, plus comical tributes to the mythology of the Wild West, like a fake "Boot Hill" cemetery with laconic epitaphs and hand-painted signs playing up the apocryphal legacy of the local "Hangin' Judge" Jim Beam.

Before I-40 bypassed it in the 1970s, Kingman was a vital desert oasis; it marks the intersection of US-93 and **Route 66**. This route begins on page 784; Kingman is described on page 795.

Hualapai Mountain Park

East from Kingman, US-93 follows I-40 for over 20 miles before turning south again, but parallel to the freeway a well-marked 14-mile road leads up from the desert to **Hualapai Mountain Park,** where pines and firs cover the comparatively cool slopes of the 8,417-foot peak. Hiking trails wind through the wilderness, and there's a **campground** and a few rustic **cabins** built by the CCC during the New Deal 1930s.

For detailed information or to make reservations, contact the **ranger station** (928/757-3859), near the park entrance.

Wickenburg

In the middle of the Arizona desert, 60 miles northwest of Phoenix and 130 miles from Kingman, **Wickenburg** (pop. 5,082) grew up as a gold-mining camp in the 1860s and has survived as a low-key resort community. A few crusty prospectors still search for a strike, and cowboys are often seen riding through town, which makes Wickenburg a pleasant place to get a feel for the Old West, especially during the winter months when temperatures are mild and the sun shines nearly every day.

North of Wickenburg, US-93 is known as the Joshua Tree Parkway because it passes through one of the world's densest concentrations of these odd trees (members of the lily family, apparently, and found only here).

Wickenburg's Wild West ambience and reliably good winter weather accounts for the number of **dude ranches** dotting the surrounding desert, most of which are intended for long stays (a week at least) rather than passing travelers. Wickenburg is also home to the gold-mining ghosts of the Vulture Mine, which produced some $200 million before its closure in the 1940s. For complete details on the region, contact the Wickenburg **visitors center** (928/684-5479), in the old railroad depot on Frontier Street, a block west of US-93.

Two blocks south along Frontier Street and the railroad tracks, at the US-60/US-93 junction and Wickenburg's only stoplight, the **Desert Caballeros Western Museum** (daily; $5; 928/684-2272) gives a broad overview of regional history, and contains a surprisingly good collection of Western art and sculpture (from George Catlin to Charley Russell), plus the usual rocks and rusty relics.

Most of the places to eat and sleep are lined up along east–west US-60 (Wickenburg Way); try the **Gold Nugget**

the Santa Fe Depot, Wickenburg

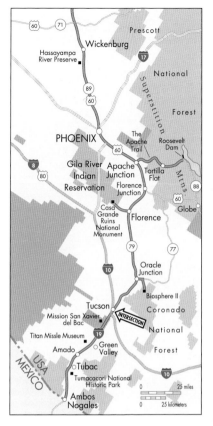

coffee shop at 222 E. Wickenburg Way, across from the **Best Western Rancho Grande** motel ($80 and up; 928/684-5445 or 800/528-1234).

Hassayampa River Preserve

One of Arizona's very few stretches of riverside ecology preserved in its natural state, the **Hassayampa River Preserve,** three miles southeast of Wickenburg on US-60/89, is a great place to break a journey. For most of its way, the Hassayampa River runs underground, but here it rises to irrigate a dense forest of willows and cottonwood trees, which in turn shelter an amazing variety of birds—over 200 species, from songbirds to raptors, are listed in the preserve's birders' guide.

The Nature Conservancy, which owns and operates the preserve, runs a small **visitors center** (Wed.–Sun. 8 AM–5 PM in winter, limited hours in summer; $5 donation; 928/684-2772), where you can pick up trail guides and maybe join a guided walk.

Across Phoenix

From the northwest, our route arrives in ever-growing metropolitan **Phoenix** by way of US-60/89, which passes through the retirement communities of Surprise and Sun City. The historic route follows Grand Avenue all the way to the downtown area, where you can follow the old main road, Van Buren Street, but if you're in a hurry hop onto the freeway system and hope you don't get too lost—it's a crazy and confusing city, so spread out it can seem to take forever to get anywhere.

Superstition Mountains and the Apache Trail

East of Phoenix, US-60 runs as a four-lane freeway through suburban Tempe and Mesa, but the sprawl fades as you approach the angular **Superstition Mountains,** some 40 miles east of downtown. Protected within the massive **Tonto National Forest,** this area of volcanic crags, desert cactus, and Ponderosa pines is best seen by traveling

Phoenix

Nearly four million people have settled in and around the Arizona capital, Phoenix, all but obliterating any sense that the land here ever was, and still is, a desert. Golf courses, swimming pools, lakes, and fountains are everywhere, with only a few carefully coiffed cacti remaining to testify to the natural state of things. But there is something oddly charming about the place—an anything-goes, Wild West spirit manifest in the highest rate of car theft in the country, and a truly phoenix-like ability to grow and thrive despite the almost total lack of natural advantages.

The best thing about visiting Phoenix is the chance to explore the marvelous **Heard Museum** (daily; $7; 602/252-8840), at 2301 N. Central Avenue, among the best museums anywhere devoted to the native cultures of the Southwestern United States. The permanent galleries trace the history and diversity of prehistoric peoples and contemporary tribes, while changing exhibitions focus on specific themes. Don't miss the amazing collection of Hopi kachina dolls, collected by hotelier Fred Harvey and the late U.S. Senator Barry Goldwater. Just down the street is the **Phoenix Art Museum** (daily; $9, free Thurs; 602/257-1222), at 1625 N. Central Avenue, with the largest art collection in the Southwest.

Another treat: **Taliesin West** (Thurs.–Mon.; $12–16; 480/860-2700), at 108th Street at the east end of Cactus Road, where every winter from 1937 until his death in 1959, Frank Lloyd Wright lived, worked, and taught, handcrafting the complex of studios, theaters, and living quarters that survives as an architecture school.

The biggest thing to see in downtown Phoenix is Chase Field, home of the **Arizona Diamondbacks** (602/514-8400). It's the only major league ballpark with its own outfield swimming pool.

Practicalities

Phoenix really is a sprawling mess, expanding by many acres every day, with no end (or beginning or middle, for that matter) in sight. The I-10 freeway cuts through the center, and a spaghetti bowl of local freeways, such as the Hwy-202 Loop, Hwy-51, and the US-60 "Superstition Freeway" complete the high-speed overlay. Though there is a skeletal bus service, trying to get around town without a car is hazardous to your health. In a word, drive.

Phoenix is actually made up of many separate surrounding cities, each of which has its own character—Mesa, for example, was founded by Mormons, and is now bigger than Minneapolis. Not surprisingly, considering its well-deserved reputation as a winter oasis, the Phoenix area is home to a number of gorgeous resort hotels; rates quoted here are for winter, and summer prices are much lower. The historic **Arizona Biltmore** ($250 and up; 602/955-6600 or 800/950-0086), on the north side of Phoenix at 24th and Missouri Streets, is an absolutely beautiful, Frank Lloyd Wright–style resort complex tucked away on spacious grounds. More fun for families can be had at the many water park–style resorts, like the **Pointe Hilton Tapatio Cliffs Resort** (180 and up; 602/866-7500) at 11111 N. 7th Street, which has large suites and four large swimming pools. Downtown, the **San Carlos Hotel** ($75 and up; 602/253-4121), at 202 N. Central Avenue, is a well-maintained older hotel with a rooftop swimming pool, and the **HI Phoenix Hostel** (602/254-9803), 1026 9th Street, has dorm beds for around $20 a night.

The classic road food stop in Phoenix is the **Tee Pee** (602/956-0178), at 4144 E. Indian School Road, a characterful and always-crowded place serving huge and very cheap plates of old-style Ameri-Mexican food. For something a bit hotter, brave the salsa at **Los Dos Molinos** (602/243-9113), at 8646 S. Central Avenue in the old Tom Mix house. Phoenix also boasts an unexpected treat: **Pizzeria Bianco** (dinner only; 602/258-8300), 623 E. Adams Street, where transplanted New Yorker Chris Bianco cooks up delicious wood-fired designer pizzas in an historic downtown storefront.

The Phoenix area **visitors bureau** (877/225-5749) puts out the usual hotel and restaurant listings and other practical information for travelers; visit them downtown at 50 N. 2nd Street.

State Capitol, Phoenix, Arizona

Spring Training: Cactus League Baseball

The arrival of the Arizona Diamondbacks in 1998 culminated a long but limited history of baseball in the Grand Canyon State. Though it never before had a major league team of its own, Arizona has welcomed out-of-state teams for pre-season spring training since 1947, when the Cleveland Indians and New York Giants first played at Tucson's HI Corbett Field (now home to the Colorado Rockies). Every March, hundreds of ball players at all levels of the game come to Arizona to earn or keep their places on professional teams, and the daily workouts and 20-odd exhibition games of what's known as the Cactus League attract thousands of hard-core baseball fans as well.

The metropolitan Phoenix area hosts the bulk of the teams and the tourists, but Tucson gets a fair share as well. Though they're not necessarily played to win, Cactus League games are played in modern 10,000-seat stadia that approach the major leagues in quality, and the smaller sizes allow an up-close feel you'd have to pay much more for during the regular season. (And your chances of snagging balls during batting practice are infinitely better, too.) Most teams have extensive training facilities adjacent to their home stadium, and morning workouts and practice sessions are usually free and open to the general public.

The best central source of Cactus League schedules, information, and tickets is the Mesa visitors bureau (480/827-4700 or 800/283-6372). Tickets for games cost $5–15, and are available through Ticketmaster (480/784-4444), at the stadium box offices, and online. Be aware, however, that March is peak tourist season all over Arizona, so make accommodation arrangements long before game time.

along Hwy-88, the scenic **Apache Trail** which winds along the Salt River, the region's lifeblood. Named for the Indian tribe that dominated the area a century ago, and now an official National Scenic Byway, the Apache Trail is a 78-mile, 4-hour loop, but even a short trip along it will take you far away from the fast lane.

A mere five miles north of US-60, the Phoenix suburbs give way to the wild desert of **Lost Dutchman State Park** ($5; 480/982-4485), named for a legendary gold mine located nearby. Two miles farther is the overlook for the 4,535-foot phallus of Weaver's Needle, beyond which the road passes several reservoirs before reaching the entertaining tourist-trap hamlet of **Tortilla Flat** (pop. 6), 18 miles from US-60 and named after the Steinbeck novella—which has nothing to do with Arizona, but who cares?

Beyond Tortilla Flat, the road turns to dirt and twists and turns through spectacular desert country for the next 27 miles to Roosevelt Dam, then heads southeast to rejoin US-60 near Globe, at the western edge of the San Carlos Apache Indian Reservation, 50 miles east of Phoenix.

In springtime in particular, another great attraction of the Apache Trail region is the **Boyce Thompson Arboretum State Park** (daily; $7.50; 520/689-

2811), the state's oldest and largest botanical exhibit, covering 323 acres with a full array of Sonora Desert cactus and wildflowers. The arboretum is right on US-60, 20 miles west of Globe near the copper-mining town of Superior.

Hwy-79: Florence and Casa Grande Ruins National Monument

From Apache Junction, US-60 runs southeast for 15 miles to Florence Junction, where Hwy-79 (old US-89) cuts off to the south at **Florence.** One of Arizona's oldest towns, but now best-known as the site of the state's largest prison, Florence has a pleasant, non-touristy Main Street of bars, general stores, and junk shops, parallel to and a half mile west of the highway. The penal history is documented in gruesome detail at the **Pinal County Historical Museum** (Wed.–Sun. noon–4 PM; donations; 520/868-4382) at 715 S. Main Street, where an actual hangman's noose and chairs from the retired gas chamber are displayed along with photos of people put to death.

West of Florence, some of the state's largest and most perplexing prehistoric remains are preserved in the **Casa Grande Ruins National Monument** (daily; $3; 520/723-3172), off Hwy-287 midway between Florence and I-10. A small **visitors center** at the entrance gives some background on the Hohokam people who built the four-story "big house" and the surrounding village, but no one knows what it was used for, or why it was abandoned.

Biosphere 2

One of the most ambitious, controversial, and just plain bizarre schemes to hatch in recent years, **Biosphere 2** stands in the Arizona desert at the northern foot of snow-capped Mt. Lemmon. Developed in the 1990s by a New Age group called "Synergia Ranch," and funded by Texas billionaire Ed Bass, Biosphere 2 was originally intended to simulate the earth's entire ecosystem, in order to test the possibility of building self-sustaining colonies on other planets. A crew of four "biospherians" spent two not entirely self-sustained years sealed inside, but amidst allegations of corruption and deceit, the project has since been redirected to focus on research into the effects of "greenhouse gases" and other ecosystem changes. Media attention and tourist traffic have died down considerably, but you can still visit the very pretty site and take a self-guided **tour** (daily; $19.95, kids under 5 free; 520/838-6200). To reach Biosphere 2, follow Hwy-79 to Oracle Junction, 25 miles north of Tucson, then turn east onto Hwy-77 for six miles and follow the signs.

Cowboy actor **Tom Mix** died on October 12, 1940, when he crashed his 1937 Cord Phantom into a ditch along Hwy-79 and was decapitated by his suitcase. The site is marked by a statue of a riderless horse, in a rest area 18 miles south of Florence.

South of Florence, Hwy-79 follows the **Pinal Pioneer Parkway,** the old main road between Phoenix and Tucson. The route is now lined by a series of signs pointing out palo verde trees, saguaros, and other desert flora.

Tucson marks the junction of the US-93 route with our cross-country **Southern Pacific** route along US-80 (see page 732). Around Tucson, Saguaro National Park, and Tombstone are covered on pages 732–737.

Across Tucson

From Oracle Junction, Hwy-77/Oracle Road winds around the western Catalina Mountains, following a series of one-way surface streets into compact downtown Tucson. The fastest way around Tucson is I-10, which runs diagonally along the western and southern edges of the city, while some of the more interesting "old road" routes around town include the Miracle Mile, north of downtown, and 6th Avenue, the main highway before the Interstate was built. South of Tucson, 6th Avenue becomes the Old Nogales Highway, the old road to Mexico, which veers in various alignments among extensive pecan groves while crisscrossing I-19.

The environmental activist and author **Edward Abbey,** *who died in 1989, spent his last years living in the Arizona desert near Oracle Junction.*

Mission San Xavier del Bac

Among the most strikingly memorable of all the Spanish colonial missions in the Southwest, **Mission San Xavier del Bac** was built over 200 years ago and still serves the native Tohono O'odham (aka Papago) people. Known as the "White Dove of the Desert" because of the gleaming white plaster that covers its adobe walls, balustrades, and twin bell towers—one of which is domed, the other not—this landmark edifice was designed and built by Franciscan missionaries beginning in 1778.

Rising up from the flat desert plain, San Xavier presents an impressive silhouette, but what's most unforgettable is the Mexican folk-baroque interior, covered in intensely wrought sculptures and paintings of saints and religious imagery. Currently under restoration by a team brought in from Italy, these paintings and figurines are among the country's finest example of folk art, using painted mud to simulate marble, tiles, and crystal chandeliers.

The mission (daily; donations; 520/294-2624) is well-signed and easy to reach, just 10 miles south of downtown Tucson off I-19 exit 92, then a half mile west. Across the plaza from the church is a small Tohono-owned and -operated complex of craft galleries, plus a very good taco stand.

Titan Missile Museum

In just 15 miles south of San Xavier, you can travel from the colonial 1700s to the Cold War 1960s by stopping at the **Titan Missile Museum,** the only Intercontinental Ballistic Missile (ICBM) silo preserved intact and open to the public anywhere in the world. On the north side of the sprawling stucco retirement community of Green Valley (pop. 17,283), just west from I-19 off exit 69 on Duval Mine Road, the silo was in active use from 1963 until 1982, was declared a National Historic Landmark in 1994, and is now open for **tours** (daily; $8.50; 520/625-7736). The tours, which take around an hour, involve donning a hard hat and descending stairs into the control room of the hardened silo, which still contains a 110-foot-tall Titan missile.

Tubac

Another good place to stop between Tucson and the Mexican border is **Tubac,** 45 miles from Tucson, just east of I-19 at exit 34. One of the first European outposts in what's now Arizona, Tubac was established as a Spanish presidio (fort) in 1751, and a century later boomed with the opening of gold mines nearby.

Scattered around a dusty central plaza, just west of the presidio park, Tubac has developed into a small but diverting arts-and-crafts colony, with a number of good shops and cafés. Local artists are frequently showcased in the **Tubac Center for the Arts** on the north side of the plaza.

Tumacácori National Historic Park

The preserved ruins of an impressive Spanish colonial mission stand at the center of **Tumacácori National Historic Park** (daily; $3; 520/398-2341), 42 miles from Tucson, 19 miles north of Nogales, and just three miles south of Tubac, off I-19 exit 29. The site was used by missionaries as early as 1691, but it wasn't until 1800 that they set to work building the massive adobe church. Though never finished, thanks to Apache raids and the Mexican Revolution, Tumacácori stands as an impressive reminder of the religious passion of the friars and their efforts to convert local tribes.

In Amado, just west of I-19 at the Arivaca Road exit, a huge concrete cow's skull marks the entrance to the **Longhorn Grill** restaurant and cantina (520/398-3955), one in a long series of businesses that have tried to make a go of this unique location.

Directly across the highway from Tumacácori is a rare sight—a Greek café—and a half mile north is **Wisdom's** (520/398-2397), which serves reliable Mexican and American food.

Nogales

Arizona's busiest border crossing, Nogales is also perhaps the most pleasant of all the "international" cities along the U.S.–Mexico border. Despite being divided by an ugly corrugated steel fence, it gets promoted as **Ambos Nogales,** "Both Nogales." The twin cities are economically co-dependent, especially post-NAFTA, as Mexicans come across to shop at Safeway and Wal-Mart, and Americans while away evenings drinking cerveza in south-of-the-border cantinas. Apart from the intriguing little **Pimeria Alta Historical Society Museum** (Thurs.–Sun.; donations; 520/287-4621), which documents cross-border history in the storefront-sized Old City Hall at 136 N. Grand Avenue, 400 yards north of the border crossing, there are few real sights to see, but if you just want to spend an hour or two shopping for souvenirs and practicing your Spanish, Nogales, Mexico, is a painless place in which to do it.

To save hassle (and time) crossing the border, drivers should park on the streets or in the $5-a-day lots on the U.S. side and walk across. Border formalities are minimal, and U.S. dollars are accepted on both sides.

Tucson

Though it's less than half the size of
Phoenix, Tucson (pop. 486,000) is at least
twice as nice a place to visit. With a lively
university community, some of the most
beautiful desert landscapes anywhere on
earth, and more palpable history than
anywhere in the Southwest outside
New Mexico, Tucson is well worth
taking the time to get to know. It also
makes an excellent jumping-off point
for visiting the Wild West towns of
Tombstone and Bisbee in the state's
southeast corner.

However, with daytime temperatures averaging over 100°F,
Tucson is hotter than heck during the summer months (early May to late
September), so try to visit during the rest of the year. Spring is especially
nice, with wildflowers blooming and spring training baseball bashing away,
but this is also the most expensive time to be here—room rates in March
are easily double those the rest of the year.

Many of Tucson's biggest attractions (Biosphere 2, Mission San Xavier
del Bac, the Arizona Sonora Desert Museum, and Saguaro National Park)
are outside the city limits and covered under various road trips, but the
downtown area is worth a wander for the many historic buildings that have
been spared the redeveloper's wrecking ball, including a recently restored
Fox movie palace.

East of downtown, the nicely landscaped 350-acre **University of Arizona**
campus, which spreads between Speedway Boulevard and 6th Street, holds
the engaging historical exhibits of the **Arizona State Museum** (daily; $3;
520/621-6302) and one of the country's preeminent photography collections in the **Center for Creative Photography** ($2; 520/621-7968), nearby
at 1030 N. Olive Road.

In the foothills of the Santa Catalina Mountains that rise north of Tucson, **Sabino Canyon** (daily; 520/749-2861), with its seasonal waterfalls and
a nearly year-round creek, is a great place to stretch your legs while getting a
sense of how pretty and vibrant the desert can be. Sabino Canyon is 17
miles east of downtown, well-signed off Tanque Verde Road.

Practicalities

The main I-10 freeway runs diagonally from northwest to southeast along
the usually dry Santa Rita River at the western edge of town. Tucson
stretches east from here for over 10 miles, and north toward the foothills of
the Santa Catalina mountains. The main east-west route across town is

Speedway Boulevard, along with numerous parallel roads.

In addition to the usual highway motels, Tucson has some characterful places to stay, from restored downtown hotels to luxurious vacation resorts. One of the latter is the **Hacienda del Sol** ($90 and up; 520/299-1501), 5601 N. Hacienda del Sol Road, a historic guest ranch built as a posh girl's school in the 1920s and now a quiet, intimate getaway, with a pool, tennis courts, great sunset views, and one of Tucson's best restaurants (The Grill). Another historic property, the **Arizona Inn** ($120 and up; 520/325-1541 or 800/933-1093), at 2200 E. Elm Street, is perhaps the classic Arizona resort, little-changed since the 1920s, when it was a favorite winter haunt of the Rockefellers and other elites. The Arizona Inn offers very comfortable accommodations on lovingly landscaped grounds near the University campus.

Fans of roadside Americana may want to check out the **Ghost Ranch Lodge** ($50 and up; 520/791-7565), at 801 W. Miracle Mile, where a cool sign and 8-acre cactus garden has been welcoming weary travelers since the 1940s.

One of the most enjoyable places to eat in all of Arizona is the quirky **Cafe Poca Cosa** (520/622-6400), right downtown at 88 E. Broadway. Adventurously creative Mexican food, served up in large portions at reasonable prices, is the specialty here—try anything in a mole sauce, and you won't be disappointed. Nearby at 151 N. Stone Street, the Little Cafe Poca Cosa is open for breakfast and lunch versions of the same delicious stuff. On the west side of downtown is **El Charro** (520/622-1922), at 311 N. Court Avenue, "the oldest family-operated Mexican restaurant in the USA," so they say, serving up inexpensive food (and margaritas) since 1922 in a turn-of-the-20th-century house.

And when the summer heat begins to hit, Tucson families flock to **Austin's** (520/327-3892), 2920 E. Broadway, where huge dishes of house-made ice cream, thick shakes, and even a few sandwiches have been served up for more than 50 years.

The **Metropolitan Tucson Visitors Bureau** (520/624-1817 or 800/638-8350), at 100 S. Church Avenue, has tons of information on Tucson and the surrounding regions.

Bird's-Eye View of Tucson, Arizona

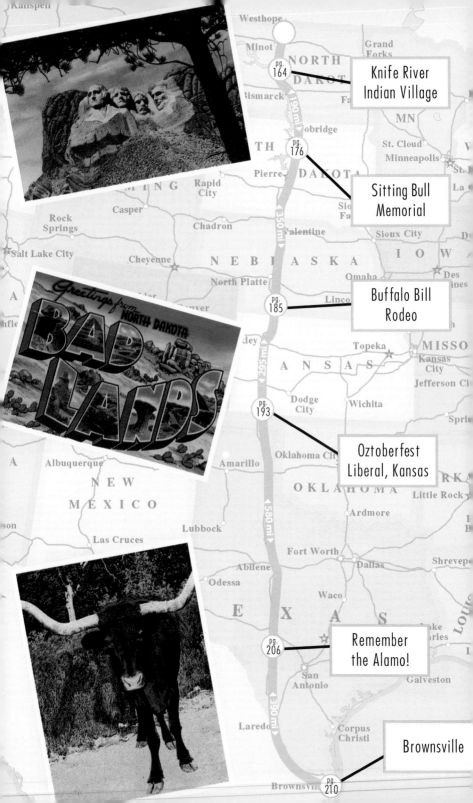

Westhope

Minot

NORTH

pg.
164

Knife River
Indian Village

Grand
Forks

Bismarck

DAKOT

Fa

MN

TH

obridge

St. Cloud

Minneapolis

MN

St.

pg.
176

Pierre

DAKOTA

Sitting Bull
Memorial

Siou
Fa

La

ING

Rapid
City

Casper

Chadron

Valentine

Sioux City

IOWA

Rock
Springs

Salt Lake City

Cheyenne

North Platte

NEBRASKA

Omaha

Des
ines

Denver

ley

pg.
185

Buffalo Bill
Rodeo

Linc

Topeka

MISSO

ANSAS

Kansas
City

Jefferson Ci

Dodge
City

Wichita

Spri

pg.
193

Oztoberfest
Liberal, Kansas

Albuquerque

NEW
MEXICO

Amarillo

Oklahoma City

OKLAHOMA

RKA

Little Rock

Ardmore

Las Cruces

Lubbock

son

Fort Worth

Dallas

Shrevep

Abilene

Odessa

Waco

E

X

A

S

LOUI

ake
rles

pg.
206

Remember
the Alamo!

San
Antonio

Galveston

Laredo

Corpus
Christi

pg.
210

Brownsville

Brownsv

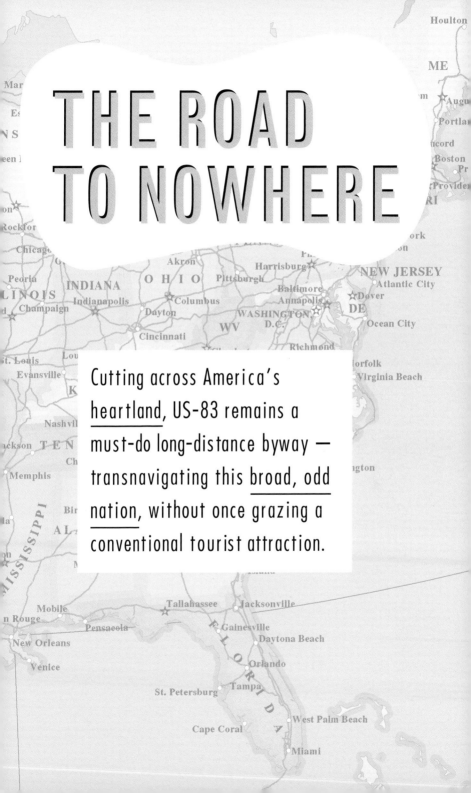

THE ROAD TO NOWHERE

Cutting across America's heartland, US-83 remains a must-do long-distance byway — transnavigating this broad, odd nation, without once grazing a conventional tourist attraction.

Between North Dakota and Matamoros, Mexico

Once the only entirely paved route from Canada to "Old Mexico" (as hard-to-find postcards along the route still say), US-83 is still likely the shortest—from Swan River, Manitoba, dead south to Brownsville, Texas, and beyond to Matamoros, Mexico, seemingly without turning once. Its grim moniker, "The Road to Nowhere," is alternately unfair and then not severe enough, for the route navigates some of the widest and most aesthetically challenged landscapes in the country: the yawn-inducing rolling grasslands of the northern Great Plains, the beefy expanses of western Nebraska and Kansas, and the mesmerizing heat of the Texas/Oklahoma Panhandle, before following the lower Rio Grande south to the Gulf of Mexico. Yet on US-83 you'll also take in some phenomenal country: verdant farmland dotted with truly small towns, endlessly shifting prairie grassland, winding Missouri River roadways, and plain, isolated, where-the-hell-am-I agricultural expanses.

Following roughly along the 100th Meridian, US-83 marks the historic divide between the "civilized" eastern United States and the arid western deserts. Physiography aside, this route's cultural landscape centers around small but self-sufficient farm or cattle communities that date back to the last days of the Wild West and that are far enough off the tourist trail to retain an unself-conscious, aw-shucks quaintness. For endless miles in every direction, telephone and power poles provide some of the only signs of life between the highway and the distant horizon, though the towns—where average speeds drop suddenly from 70 mph to radar-enforced 25 mph or slower—are spaced just often enough along the highway to serve your food-and-fuel needs.

Perhaps best of all, US-83 manages to transnavigate this broad, odd nation, albeit north-to-south, without once grazing a conventional tourist attraction. Here in the nation's heartland, conversations over a daybreak breakfast, afternoons spent cooling off by municipal swimming pools, and twilight American Legion baseball games provide the stuff of truly memorable Road Trip diversions, and for that reason alone, US-83 remains a must-do long-distance byway.

NORTH DAKOTA

Beginning at the U.S. border with Manitoba, Canada, US-83's route across North Dakota is a 285-mile-long rehash of childhood back-of-station-wagon dream-scapes: epic plains too green or golden-hued for your eyes to process rationally, and endless cultivated fields punc-tuated by umpteen farmers' cooperatives, storage bins, silos, and grain eleva-tors. Hay bales of all shapes and sizes dry perilously close to the roadside, and Stetsoned figures in dusty pickups or mighty tractors amiably lift their index fingers off steering wheels in back-forty greetings.

US-83 doesn't really follow a straight plumb line south—it just seems that way. After meandering from the border across the fertile residuals of ancient Lake Souris near lonely **Westhope**, the route seems to fall straight down the map while crossing the drift prairie south to **Minot**. Continuing south across the neck of giant **Lake Sakakawea**, US-83 winds across slightly more ambitious hills and plateaus along a historic and hardly changed stretch of the mighty Mis-souri River to **Bismarck**, the state capital and a better-than-expected place to spend some time. South of Bismarck, US-83 cuts away from the riverfront through a pastry-rich pastoral landscape settled around the turn of the 20th century by German immigrants—including the parents of dance-meister Lawrence Welk—while a recommended detour follows the Missouri River across the huge, historic **Standing Rock Indian Reservation** that stretches into South Dakota.

Westhope

US-83 begins winding its way from the Canadian border at the small United States entrance station (daily 9 AM–10 PM only) six miles north of **Westhope** (pop. 575). Westhope, named by an optimistic Great Northern Railway official, is a good example of North Dakota's small agrarian towns. A few motels, cafés, and gas stations, a sparse two-block-long downtown, and that's about it. The **Gateway Inn** motel/lounge (701/245-6264) has tourist information on the area.

Six miles south of Westhope, US-83 zig-zags west along Hwy-5 for five miles before sharply banking south. The next 37 miles to Minot are a straight shot south, passing nothing save two sweeping wildlife refuges and a lonely **Domino's Pizza**, all by itself apart from occasional A-10s thundering overhead to and from Minot Air Force Base.

A half-hour side trip east from US-83 along Hwy-5 brings you to the town of Dunseith, where a giant turtle named Wee'l has been constructed out of 200 old car and truck wheels. If you like what you see, nearby Bottineau, North Dakota, has a statue of a giant turtle riding a snowmobile.

Minot

Snug in the Souris River Valley at the junction of US-2 and US-83, **Minot** (pop. 36,567; rhymes with "Why not?") grew so rapidly after the Great Northern Railroad came through in 1887 that it was dubbed "Magic City," though perhaps "Event Capital" would be more apropos today, for despite the city's importance in other areas, most people visit during the huge **state fair** (third week in July) and during October's burgeoning **Norsk Hostfest,** "North America's Largest Scandinavian Festival." The fairgrounds, along the grandly named Burdick Expressway (Business US-2) a half mile east of downtown, also hold the small **Pioneer Village and Museum** (daily in summer only), the usual assembly of turn-of-the-20th-century buildings and artifacts gathered from all over the county.

On US-83 south of town, Minot's newest attraction, **Scandinavian Heritage Park** (daily; free; 701/852-9161) at 1020 S. Broadway is set in a pleasant, tree-shaded city park, and includes all sorts of things tracing—guess what?—Minot's Scandinavian heritage: a 230-year-old house from Sigdal, Norway; a Danish windmill; a statue and eternal flame honoring famous Scandinavian skiers like Casper Oimoen and Sondre Norheim; a number of waterfalls, and a statue of that famous Viking wanderer, Leif Ericsson. Towering over the whole ensemble is a beautiful (and huge!) wooden replica of the medieval Gol Stave Church in Oslo, Norway, and right along US-83 there's a 20-foot-tall red Dala horse, symbolizing Minot's Swedish heritage.

*What look like high-security parking lots in the fields west of Minot may actually be underground missile silos under the command of **Minot Air Force Base.** In the post—Cold War era, most of these structures have been demolished.*

In summer, when daytime highs hover in the mid-90s, Minot's most enticing attractions are the expansive gardens of **Roosevelt Park,** along the banks of the Souris River between the fairgrounds and downtown Minot. Named, like everything else in North Dakota, for Teddy Roosevelt—there's a larger-than-life statue of him, astride a horse in full Rough Rider regalia—the shady green space also holds a large **swimming pool** ($2.50) with a 350-foot-long water slide, a slacker's dream of a skateboard park, a rideable miniature train ($2), and a 20-acre **zoo** (daily; $5) with a Northern Plains habitat.

To rent bikes and explore the trails of Roosevelt Park, try **Val's Cyclery** (701/839-4817) at 222 E. Central Avenue.

Minot Practicalities

Along with the usual crossroads barrage of franchised fast-food places, Minot supports a couple of local cafés, including **Charlie's Main Street Cafe** (701/839-6500) at 113 S. Main Street and **Ebenezer's** (701/839-0758) at 300 E. Central Avenue. Charlie's is right downtown, its fluorescent-lit pink vinyl booths full of gossiping Minot ladies, while Ebenezer's is three blocks east, near the train tracks and grain elevators, its fluorescent-lit brown vinyl booths and next-door bar full of gossiping Minot men; the food's good at both, and you get a pot of coffee when you order a cup. Another attraction of Minot is the wide range of cowboy hats and Western wear in the downtown stores.

After dark, choose from any of over a dozen haunts, from bingo parlors and low-stakes casinos to country-western honky-tonks and low-key beer bars like the **Blue Rider** (701/852-9050) at 118 1st Avenue SE, a smoke-free pub with what may be rural North Dakota's best selection of bottled brews—look for the Grain Belt Beer sign.

Motels are scattered along the congested arteries of both US-83 and US-2, so you shouldn't have trouble finding a place to sleep (except perhaps during the state fair). The nicest place to stay is the **International Inn** ($60–80; 701/852-3161), on US-83 at 1505 N. Broadway. East of downtown Minot near the fairgrounds, there's a new **Holiday Inn** and less-expensive local motels like the clean and quiet **Fairview Lodge** ($40–75; 701/852-4488 or 800/836-2047) at 1900 E. Burdick Expressway.

To cope with the extreme weather on the northern Great Plains (winter cold and summer heat), locals seek relief at the **Splashdown Dakota** water park, shopping mall, and Sleep Inn motel ($90 and up; 701/837-3100), 2400 10th Street, where room rates include free use of the water slides, swimming pools, and hot tubs.

The Minot **visitors center** (701/857-8206 or 800/264-2626), on US-83 south of downtown near the Scandinavian Heritage Park at 1020 S. Broadway, has more-complete listings and detailed information on events and activities. Being so central to the state, Minot hosts everything from chili cook-offs to the state softball championships, and there's usually *something* going on.

East of Minot on US-2, the town of **Rugby** is nearly the geographical center of North America.

In range for an hour or more in all directions, Minot's **KRRZ 1390 AM** broadcasts oldies from the 1950s and 1960s, along with Minnesota Twins baseball games.

Minot marks the junction of US-83 and the **Great Northern** route along US-2 (see page 477), which runs cross-country from Seattle to Acadia National Park in Maine. For full coverage, see pages 446–528.

Lake Sakakawea Dam

Even though ongoing drought has shrunk it down, at nearly 200 miles long and with 1,600 miles of shoreline along the dammed Missouri River, **Lake**

Sakakawea is one of the largest man-made "lakes" in the United States. There are countless things to do on the water, most of them involving fishing. The pleasant town of **Garrison** (pop. 1,530), on the north shore of the lake and six miles west of US-83 on Hwy-37, serves as lake headquarters, with a pair of red-roofed water towers labeled Hot and Cold, and a photogenic fiberglass statue of Wally-the-26-Foot-Walleye.

At the south end of Lake Sakakawea, and 12 miles west of US-83 via Hwy-200, the Missouri River backs up behind wide but low-slung **Garrison Dam,** the third-largest earth-filled dam in the United States. The powerhouse is enmeshed within a labyrinth of huge power stanchions, high-voltage lines, and transformers. In the adjacent **fish hatchery** on the downstream side of the dam, tanks hold hundreds of thousands of walleye, bass, and northern pike, plus rainbow and brown trout.

*Lake Sakakawea is one of many places in the northwestern United States named for the legendary Shoshone Indian woman, also known as **Sacagawea,** who accompanied the Lewis and Clark expedition across the Rocky Mountains.*

South of Garrison Dam, roadside interest along US-83 focuses on leviathan testimonials to engineering prowess. Huge tractors and bulldozers raise clouds of dust at the extensive **coal mining** operations around Underwood—the whole area on both sides of US-83 has been strip-mined and restored, though current operations are hard to get a good look at—and most of the valuable black rock ends up at electricity generating plants like the 1,100-megawatt **Coal Creek Station,** six miles north of Washburne and two miles off the roadway but *readily* apparent. This is the largest lignite-fired coal plant in the country, boasting a **four-mile-long coal conveyor belt,** which passes over the highway in a tube.

However, unless you have an abiding interest in fossil fuels, a more interesting alternative to driving this stretch of US-83 is to follow the river's western bank south of Lake Sakakawea, where it reverts to its naturally broad and powerful self for the next 75 miles.

Knife River Indian Village National Historic Site

Between Garrison Dam and Washburn, scenic Hwy-200 passes two of North Dakota's most significant historic sites: Fort Clark and the Knife River Indian Village, both of which, though small, saw key scenes of the late 18th- and early-19th-century interactions between Native Americans and interloping European traders and explorers. Downstream from Garrison Dam along the west bank of the Missouri River, the **Knife River Indian Village National Historic Site** (daily; free; 701/745-3309) is one of North Dakota's most fascinating historic places, and the only federally maintained site devoted to preservation of the Plains tribes' cultures. Standing above the Missouri floodplain, on the site of what was the largest and

most sophisticated village of the interrelated Hidatsa, Mandan, and Arikara tribes, the park protects the remains of dozens of terraced fields, fortifications, and earth lodges, remnants of a culture that lived here for thousands of years before being devastated by disease within a few short decades of European contact.

Knife River Indian Village

A highlight of the park is an **earth lodge,** reconstructed using traditional materials, which gives a vivid sense of day-to-day Great Plains life. Measuring over 50 feet across, and 12 feet high at its central smoke hole, the earth lodge looks exactly as it would have when the likes of George Catlin and Karl Bodmer were welcomed by the villagers during the 1830s. Just north of the earth lodge spread circular depressions in the soil—which are all that remains of the Hidatsa community where, in 1804, the Lewis and Clark Corps of Discovery was joined by the French fur-trapper Charbonneau and his wife, Sacagawea.

The modern **visitors center,** well-signed off Hwy-200 at the south edge of the park, has high-quality reproductions of the drawings and paintings that Catlin, Bodmer, and others made of the Knife River Indian Village, along with archaeological and anthropological summaries that help bring to life these intriguing Native American peoples. The center also has information on the many annual events, festivals, and powwows held at Knife River throughout the year, including the **Northern Plains Indian Culture Fest** in late July.

A half mile south of the visitors center, the tiny town of **Stanton** (pop. 517) has two cafés, two bars, and two gas stations along its three-block main drag. For breakfast or lunch before or after a hike around the Knife River Indian Village site, stop off at **Glo's Kitchen** (701/745-3535) on Hwy-31 in tiny, tidy "downtown" Stanton; Glo's specializes in homemade ice cream sundaes, but also dishes up a mean sandwich or boxed lunch for those more inclined to pack up a picnic to nosh on down by the river. The **Mercer County Courthouse,** at the center of Stanton, displays arrowheads and other Indian artifacts.

Fort Clark

Seven miles downstream from the Knife River site, well-signed off Hwy-200, **Fort Clark Historical Site** (daily April–Oct.; free; 701/328-3467) is as eerily isolated as can be. One of three major fur-trading posts on the upper Missouri River, Fort Clark was founded by the American Fur Company circa 1831, primarily to trade with the Mandan Indians. The fort was visited by other tribes, as well as the usual roll-call of adventurers, explorers, and frontier luminaries such as Prince Maximilian, George Catlin, and Karl Bodmer; unfortunately, the steamboats that plied the waters to bring supplies also brought smallpox, and in one tragic winter in 1837, the Mandan tribe's population was cut from 1,600 to 100. After the fur trade declined, Fort Clark was abandoned in 1860.

Today the tranquil site, approached on a narrow gravel-and-dirt road, is devoid of anything—it's a somber, quiet piece of history stretching out on a grassy, flat-topped bluff overlooking the Missouri River. Unfortunately, the silence and emptiness of the place are marred by the presence of a smoky Basin Electric Power Company coal plant up the river. A walking trail has markers designating the locations of eight original buildings, and depressions from an earth lodge village and primitive fortifications are still apparent, but you really need to use your imagination to see very much.

The Lewis and Clark Expedition

Following the instructions of President Thomas Jefferson, Meriwether Lewis and William Clark set off across the continent in 1804 to explore the vast territory recently acquired from France in the Louisiana Purchase. Part of their mission was to find a viable trade route from the Mississippi River to the Pacific Ocean.

Sharing command of what was officially known as the Corps of Discovery, which included 33 soldiers and experienced "mountain men," plus the legendary Sacagawea, her husband Toussaint Charbonneau, and their infant Pomp, not to mention Lewis's Newfoundland dog, Seaman, Lewis and Clark blazed a route up the Missouri River, crossed the Rocky Mountains, and made their way west down the Columbia River, returning to St. Louis after two and a half years and over 8,000 miles of unprecedented travel.

Along with their copious journals, many good books have been written documenting the Lewis and Clark expedition and tracing their route, which has been declared the **Lewis and Clark National Historic Trail.** Much of the land they traversed has been altered beyond recognition, though thanks to recent bicentennial celebrations, numerous historic sights along the way have been preserved or protected as parks or museums. The best of these are:

Jefferson National Expansion Memorial is an excellent museum underneath the Gateway Arch in St. Louis (see page 252).

In Sioux Falls, the **Floyd Monument** is a stone obelisk marking the grave of the only expedition member to lose his life, from appendicitis (see page 572).

On-a-Slant Indian Village has been reconstructed atop the remains of a Mandan village (see page 172).

Fort Mandan, where the expedition spent the winter of 1804–05, has been reconstructed downstream from the original site (see page 168).

Knife River Indian Village National Historic Site, along the banks of the Missouri River, holds the remains of the Hidatsa village where Sacagawea lived before joining the Corps of Discovery (see page 164).

Lemhi Pass, on the Idaho/Montana border, is where the expedition first crossed the Continental Divide (see page 128).

The River of No Return is an impassable portion of the Salmon River (see page 126).

Traveler's Rest, in the Bitterroot Valley south of Missoula, was such an idyllic spot that the Corps of Discovery camped here on both the outbound and return legs of their journey (see page 124).

Fort Canby, overlooking the mouth of the Columbia River, has a small museum on the spot where the expedition first saw the Pacific Ocean.

Fort Clatsop, a full-scale reconstruction of the wooden fort where the expedition spent a miserable winter in 1805–06, sits in lush forest along the Oregon coast (see page 27).

Tillamook Head, rising high above the Pacific Ocean, is the farthest point the expedition reached (see page 28).

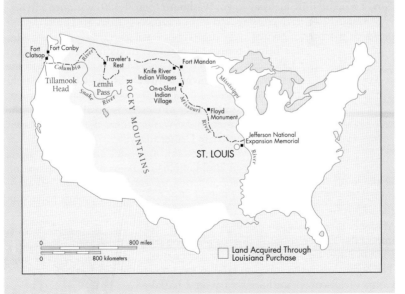

Fort Mandan

Back on the east bank of the Missouri River, north of Washburn and two miles west of US-83, **Fort Mandan** is a reconstruction of Lewis and Clark's winter quarters in 1804–05. Arriving here at the end of October after a tediously diffi-cult six-month slog upstream from St. Louis, the expedition set up camp, which consisted of rough-hewn log cabins arranged to form a triangular palisade, sur-rounded by an 18-foot-high wall. Here the 44 men spent the winter, making friendly contact with nearby Indian tribes, most significantly those of the Knife River site—where Lewis and Clark hired the French fur-trap-per Charbonneau and his young wife, the legendary Saca-gawea, who helped guide them across the Rockies.

As it flows across the south-central corner of North Dakota, the Missouri River also marks the dividing line between the central and mountain time zones.

The actual site of Lewis and Clark's encampment, some 10 miles upstream across the river from the site of Fort Clark, was long ago washed away by the ever-shifting Missouri River, but this full-scale, historically accurate replica fort, was built in 1969 by local history buffs and recently restored and expanded as part of the Lewis & Clark Interpretive Center in Washburn. Constructed and fur-nished, with some original pieces, to look how it did when Lewis and Clark camped here, the fort gives a good sense of the difficulties the explorers faced. History aside, the wild Missouri River frontage is a great place to play Tom Sawyer—on summer afternoons you'll see barefoot kids, shirtless in overalls, fishing and mucking along the banks. Another insight into local life is provided by the visitors center, which is constructed almost entirely out of recycled by-products of the coal-mining industry.

Washburn: Lewis & Clark Interpretive Center

Now a tranquil little highway town, **Washburn** (pop. 1,389) was once a frenet-ic Missouri River ferry crossing, served by steamboats from St. Louis, the last of which has been mounted on a concrete pedestal at the base of the bridge that helped to make it obsolete. In addition to nearby Fort Clark, across the river, and Fort Mandan, two miles to the northwest—not to mention the **Lewis and Clark Cafe** right downtown, where you can rent a canoe or a kayak to experi-ence the Missouri River as closely as possible to how the Corps of Discovery did—Washburn has the excellent **Lewis & Clark Interpretive Center** (daily; $5; 701/462-8535). It's located at the intersection of US-83 and North Dakota Hwy-200A, an ideal jumping-off point for your exploration of the lower Missouri River valley. Offering the hard-to-find combination of informative exhibits (including a full set of the detailed watercolors painted in the 1830s by explorer-artist Karl Bodmer), great Missouri River views, an excellent gift shop, and impeccably clean restrooms, this is a place you will want to linger for at least an hour (or maybe two). The highly interactive museum exhibits let curious Corps of Discovery enthusiasts try on a buffalo

Billboards all around North Dakota relay the state's provocative tourism slogan: "Lewis & Clark Slept Here—146 Times," part of the 2004—2006 bicentennial celebrations of the Corps of Discovery's amazing expedition.

Detour: The Enchanted Highway

Standing out against the badlands of western North Dakota, the world's largest collection of roadside statuary enlivens an otherwise unexciting swathe of the northern Great Plains. Standing along a quiet country road outside the town of Regent (pop. 268), some 32 miles south of I-94 exit 72, the unexpected visual delights of the Enchanted Highway have earned it a place in the Guinness Book of World Records (as the "World's Largest Scrap Metal Sculpture"), as well as in the hearts of many a long-distance road-tripper. Created over the past 15 years by former schoolteacher and self-taught metal sculptor Gary Greff, these are some of the largest works of art in the world—a flock of geese reaches over 100 feet into the air, while the "Tin Family" stands some 50 feet tall along the roadside. The Enchanted Highway is, well, simply enchanting, and definitely worth the detour.

robe, program their own museum-browsing background music (selecting from a variety of period fiddle music and Native American chant tracks), or trace the dramatic shifts in the river's course over the past 200 years.

Cross Ranch State Park

Across the Missouri River, six miles southwest of Washburn via Hwy-1806, **Cross Ranch State Park** ($2 per car; 701/794-3731) is set among 560 acres of cottonwood-shaded Missouri River bottomland with numerous hiking trails, canoe rentals, and fine camping, with sites for RVs and tents. There's also a fully furnished **log cabin,** in which you can stay for around $35 a night; for details, phone the **visitors center,** which also has information on the annual **Missouri River Bluegrass Festival,** held here Labor Day weekend.

Next to the campground, the remains of the pioneer town of **Sanger** stand as a mute memorial to Great Plains history. Founded in the 1880s, Sanger was the county seat and a major steamboat and railroad town, with a population of some 400 people. By World War II, Sanger had effectively been bypassed by the modern age, and the post office closed down in the mid-1950s; by the 1970s, the last residents had moved out, but a half-dozen buildings still line Main Street, urgently awaiting some visionary effort to preserve and protect them for future generations.

From the state park, enticing trails lead into the Nature Conservancy's **Cross Ranch Nature Preserve** (daily dawn–dusk; free; 701/794-8741). One of the richest surviving native Missouri River valley ecosystems, the preserve includes floodplain prairie and riparian forest, plus a resident herd of bison and some undisturbed Native American archaeological sites.

Bismarck

In his best-selling travelogue *Travels with Charley,* writer John Steinbeck wrote about Bismarck: "Here is where the map should fold. Here is the boundary between east and west. On the Bismarck side it is eastern landscape, eastern grass,

In winter, the steps of the North Dakota state capitol are so treacherously icy that workers pile snow onto them to prevent people from walking up them.

with the look and smell of eastern America. Across the Missouri on the Mandan side it is pure west, with brown grass and water scorings and small outcrops. The two sides of the river might well be a thousand miles apart."

Like many towns across the Great Plains, **Bismarck** (pop. 55,532) was named after a wealthy European, in this case the chancellor of Germany, in order to lure much-needed capital investment. The town grew exponentially following booms in the railroad industry, gold, and, most recently, oil and synthetic fuels; but it's still economically and culturally dependent upon its status as North Dakota's state capital. It's one of the smallest of the 50 in the United States, but as state capitals go, Bismarck rates quite highly for its size, with thousands of parkland acres, well-preserved historic districts, and an old-time boat ride along the Missouri River.

Thirty miles west of Bismarck, the **"World's Largest Cow"** stands along I-94 in New Salem.

Bureaucratic Bismarck seems intent on glossing over its bawdy historical peccadilloes by building monuments to modernity, like the capitol building, 19 stories of angular art deco nicknamed the "Skyscraper of the Prairies." The white limestone and classical symbolism seem out of place on the plains, but free **tours** highlight the ornate interior's woodwork, stonecarving, and metalsmithing.

On the grounds you'll find the usual memorial statues of noteworthy North Dakotans, starting with a large statue of **Sacagawea,** the guide of Lewis and Clark, carrying her newborn baby Pomp and looking sternly forward; nearby is another popular subject, a **buffalo,** here rendered out of rusty steel reinforcing rod. A short walk away, the **North Dakota Heritage Center** (daily; donations; 701/328-2666) has an informative array of historical and cultural exhibits, tracing the development of North Dakota from its geological underpinnings to its

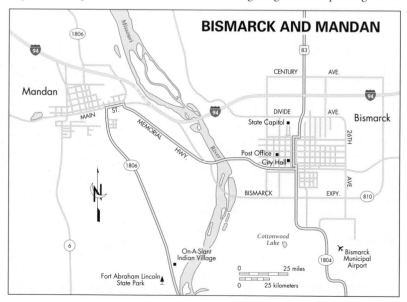

BISMARCK AND MANDAN

contemporary industries.

Though Bismarck is the state capital, the selection of places to eat is on the meager side, with a few old buildings turned into ersatz but suddenly upscale pubs-cum-restaurants like **Peacock Alley** (701/255-7917), serving pasta and Cajun dishes at 422 E. Main Street. For a truly otherworldly experience that combines pretty tasty American and Tex-Mex with Jetsonesque, space-age decor, the **Space Aliens Cafe** (701/223-6220), at 1304 E. Century Avenue on the US-83 strip north of downtown, is your logical destination. "Earthlings welcome," proclaims the telltale sign; this lively joint may get a bit too cute with its nomenclature, but it does deliver on flavor with its "Planet of the Zombies" taco burger, "Martian Munchies" BBQ platter, and "Outer Space" appetizer.

> Between the two state capitals of Bismarck, North Dakota, and Pierre, South Dakota, the Missouri River has been dammed to form 200-mile-long **Lake Oahe**.

Along with the clusters of motels on the northern fringes of US-83 and along I-94, accommodation options include a nice **Holiday Inn** (701/255-6000) at 605 E. Broadway, within walking distance of the state capitol.

For further information, contact the Bismarck **visitors center** (701/222-4308 or 800/767-3555), 523 N. 4th Street.

Missouri River Tour: Hwy-1806

An outstanding alternative to US-83 between Bismarck and the South Dakota border is the narrow but well-maintained Hwy-1806, which meanders along the Missouri River taking in views of great hillocks and easy bluffs off to the left, or scintillating blue water ribboning beneath stark-white, standing-driftwood trees. Round a bend and you'll see a lagoon or a morass. Or admire a great panorama of 2,000-foot buttes to the west, all the way across the state line. Be sure to fill up on gas and supplies before you set off since it's a 100-mile drive with few services along the way.

Mandan

Cross-river sibling to the state capital, **Mandan** (pop. 16,718) is a shipping and warehousing center that grew up swiftly in the years after 1882, when the Northern Pacific railroad completed a bridge from Bismarck. Everything in Mandan, from cafés to beauty parlors, seems to be named after Lewis and Clark—apart from the string of windowless, cowboy-themed beer bars along Main Street (choose among Silver Dollar Lounge, the Buckhorn Bar, and a number of others). The main things to see in Mandan are two statues, one a **25-foot-tall Indian** figure carved from a cottonwood tree, standing at 601 S.E. 6th Avenue, the other the requisite **Teddy Roosevelt,** in front of the train station on Main Street; these aside, the real reason to stop in Mandan is to enjoy a sandwich and a milk shake (or a rare cup of espresso!) at the

Theodore Roosevelt, Roughrider

lunch counter of the truly marvelous Americana-rich **Mandan Drug** (daily; 701/663-5900) at 316 W. Main Street.

Mandan marks the beginning of the wild western United States, and for a quick trip back to the 1880s, when the Northern Pacific Railroad made its epic push across the Great Plains, visit the **North Dakota State Railroad Museum** (daily 1–5 PM; 701/663-9322), at 3102 37th Street NW. In addition to a wide array of old railroad photographs, the museum includes restored cabooses, boxcars, tankers, and flatcars from the Soo, Great Northern, and Burlington Northern lines. Model railroad enthusiasts will also enjoy the display of 200 different model hopper cars, and a miniature train sometimes carries passengers.

George Armstrong Page Custer

Fort Abraham Lincoln State Park

Heading south along Hwy-1806 from Mandan along the west bank of the Missouri River, the first place you'll reach is sprawling **Fort Abraham Lincoln State Park** (daily except winter; $5 per car; 701/667-6340), which was originally established by the Northwest Company as a fur-trading post in 1780. It eventually fell into the hands of the U.S. Army, which in 1872 changed the fort's name to the present one. Soon afterwards, General Custer arrived to take over the reins of command, and in 1876 the fort was placed squarely on the map and in the national press as the departure point for the doomed general and his 250 men, who met their demise at Little Big Horn. Abandoned in 1891, the fort was dismantled by settlers who salvaged the wood and bricks to build their own homes, and most everything here today is a reconstruction.

The modern park covers nearly 1,000 acres and contains a number of barracks, stables, and stores, plus a replica of **Custer's house** (daily; $4), where paid sycophants will lead you around, calling you "General" while conducting guided tours. Best of all is the **On-A-Slant Indian Village,** near the north end of the park, an excavated Mandan village dating from the mid-17th century, where you can explore four full-scale earth lodges re-created by the Civilian Conservation Corps in 1933–34.

If you like the idea of *not* driving for a change, the **Fort Lincoln Trolley** (daily 1–5 PM in summer; $4) runs along the river between Mandan and Fort Abraham Lincoln, departing every hour or so for the 4.5-mile trip, leaving Mandan from a depot at 2000 S.E. 3rd Street. You can also stay at the park overnight, either in a small sleeping **cabin** (summer only; $30) or in the adjacent **campground;** make reservations for these well ahead (800/807-4723) so you don't miss out on the Missouri River sunrise views.

US-83: Linton, Strasburg, and the Lawrence Welk Birthplace

bandleader Lawrence Welk

While the scenery is superior along the Hwy-1806 detour, the trek south of Bismarck along US-83 is redeemed by one totally unique Road Trip destination: the **Ludwig Welk Farmstead** (daily in summer, by appointment rest of year; $4; 701/336-7687), boyhood home of Lawrence Welk. Located a mile north of the town of **Strasburg,** then 2.5 miles west from US-83 following well-signed dirt roads, this is the preserved homestead where the world-famous band leader and accordion player was born in 1903.

Though the Lawrence Welk connection is the main draw for most visitors, the farm is intended as a memorial to his parents, who as part of an exodus of Bavarian-born Catholic farmers fled the Ukraine during the 1870s and 1880s when exemptions from military service were threatened. The promise of land brought the Welks to North Dakota in the 1890s. The clapboard house that stands today began as a sod house—the mud walls can still be seen in places—and is now full of odds and ends of furniture and memorabilia donated by the Welk family, who still own the place. Hand tools, a windmill, and farming implements are arranged around the yard, while in the hayloft a mannequin dressed as young Lawrence squeezes out polkas on the accordion—apparently, his early playing was so bad that he was banned from practicing in the house, though now his recordings are broadcast nonstop from a *M*A*S*H*-like speaker system strung around the grounds.

Much of southern North Dakota is still predominantly populated by descendants of the original wave of these immigrant "Germans from Russia" who homesteaded the region in the 1890s. Their influence is clearly apparent in the town of **Linton** (pop. 1,410), on US-83 18 miles north of the Welk homestead, where the **Model Bakery** (701/254-4687), at 117 N. Broadway, bakes up delicious, creamy custard kuchen and Germanic cakes and cookies Tuesday–Friday, while in Strasburg (pop. 600), Welk's parents are buried in the cemetery behind the absolutely huge Catholic church that dwarfs the tiny town.

The primary tourist attraction on the Standing Rock Indian Reservation is the surreal **Prairie Knights casino,** on Hwy-1806, 44 miles south of Mandan. To sample this little bit of Vegas-on-the-Plains, contact the resort at 800/425-8277.

Both Linton and Strasburg also have the only-in-North-Dakota attractions of what must be the **world's smallest bowling alleys:** One is tucked away in back of the **Linton Cafe** (701/254-9077) at 105 N. Broadway, while Strasburg's four-laner is behind the **Pin Palace Cafe** at 714 Main Street (701/336-9616).

Standing Rock Indian Reservation: Fort Yates

Genuinely huge hills start to appear around the **Standing Rock Indian Reservation,** home to approximately 4,500 Sioux and spreading across the state line with a total of 880,000 acres. For outsiders, the main draw to the reservation, besides the fantastic roadside views and the glitzy Prairie Knights casino, is the original burial site of **Sitting Bull** in **Fort Yates** (pop. 183), the reservation headquarters. Though Sitting Bull was originally buried here, two miles west of Hwy-1806, the unimpressive site, marked by a boulder on a dusty side road, is certainly not what one would expect for the great warrior. He is now more suitably interred near Mobridge, South Dakota.

The border between North and South Dakota is marked by 720 **stone monuments**, each seven feet tall but half-buried in the ground every half mile. They were erected by the federal government in 1892; one stands right alongside Hwy-1804, on the eastern shore of Lake Oahe.

Across from the agency headquarters is another site sacred to the Sioux, the **Standing Rock** from which the reservation takes its name. In the correct angle of sunlight, the stone resembles a seated woman wearing a shawl. Legend holds that the woman, jealous of her husband's second wife, refused to move when the tribe decamped; a search party later found her, turned to stone.

South of Fort Yates, the scenery and the driving (or riding) are magnificent. Flawless blacktop winds through valleys and up ambitious, swooping hills of grazing land, and you'll be confronted by one gorgeous landscape after another, especially at dusk, when the intense Western sun illuminates the bands of sunflower fields, turns the dry, grassy hills a reddish shade of ochre and casts angular shadows beneath the darting sandpipers, who whisk their brown-and-white forms along the roadway, buzzing the lone car on the road in an extended game of highway tag. You won't even realize you're in South Dakota until you notice the gold border on the highway signs.

SOUTH DAKOTA

Crossing mostly level but never slate-flat topography, and passing through what's known as the "Great Lakes" region of the state, most evident in and around Pierre, 254 miles of US-83 cut through eastern South Dakota's broad expanse. Instead of a multi-lane, transcontinental highway, US-83 across South Dakota resembles a country road, giving an up-close-and-personal look at farming and grazing lands, with an occasional jutting hill, ravine, or serpentine creek bed to break up the monotony. Classic South Dakota—no pretensions.

Wild pheasants and other beautifully plumed game birds scurry about in the grassy verges along US-83 across the Dakotas.

To either side of the North Dakota border, US-83 is little more than a beeline across the plains. Sadly, the Missouri River is well out of eyeshot, so we highly recommend following a scenic detour across the river through the huge Standing Rock Indian Reservation, linking up with US-83 again at Mobridge. After that you'll pass through small farm towns before reaching the state capital, Pierre, at the center of South Dakota.

Standing Rock Indian Reservation: Mobridge

Since US-83's route across northern South Dakota doesn't offer much stimulation for the senses, if you've got the time to spare, detour west along the Missouri River, leaving North Dakota via the Lewis and Clark Highway,

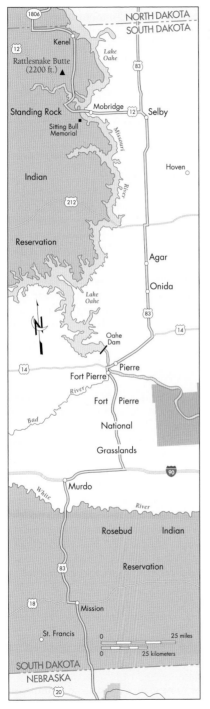

Hwy-1806. This scenic route brings you across the middle of **Standing Rock Indian Reservation**, which falls mainly in South Dakota but stretches about 30 miles over the border.

On Hwy-1806, at tiny **Kenel**, a historical marker points out the site of fur-trading **Fort Manuel**, where Lewis and Clark's guide Sacagawea may have died of fever in 1812, at the age of 25. South of Kenel, the road runs straight south, away from the winding Missouri River and toward imposing 2,200-foot Rattlesnake Butte. After 20 miles or so, you'll cross on sweeping bridges over Lake Oahe's huge bays, then roll into **Mobridge** (pop. 3,574), the biggest town between the North and South Dakota capitals. (The town's name stems from a hasty telegraph message transmitted in 1906 by an operator who needed a quick and clear reference to the area. He chose, at random, Mo for the Missouri River, and bridge, referring to the one then under construction by the Milwaukee Railroad.)

Mobridge, once a village of the Arikara tribe, is heavily dependent on the anglers who come to pluck the lunkers, walleye, and even 20-pound northern pike from Lake Oahe, here many miles wide. The area's earlier history and Native American culture is celebrated on the walls inside the **Scherr-Howe Arena** (Mon.–Fri. only; free), at 212 Main Street, where bold 16- by 20-foot murals depict Sioux history and culture.

The most interesting food option is **Rick's Award-Winning Chili and Burgers Cafe** (605/845-5300), in downtown Mobridge at the end of Main Street. Alternatives include the equally self-descriptive **Missouri River Pins & Pizza** (605/845-3924),

where the typically wedged-into-downtown Plains bowling alley creates the right vibe for you to appreciate the place's filling (if not thrilling) pizza offerings. The **Wrangler Motor Inn** ($50 and up; 605/845-3641), located a half mile west on US-12 at 820 W. Grand Crossing, is the best overnight stop on the stretch, with two dining rooms, a coffee shop, and a heated pool. The **Super 8** (605/845-7215), also on US-12 West, is a little cheaper.

Sitting Bull Memorial

A ten-minute trip from Mobridge, six miles west on US-12 and then four miles south on a paved road, will bring you to the **Sitting Bull Memorial.** This is the final resting place of the great Sioux Indian leader, after his body was disinterred in 1953 from Fort Yates in a surreptitious and still-controversial move. Whatever injustice or disrespect exhuming his body may have incurred, this magnificent view, high atop a palisade hilltop looking southeast over the river, is at least worthier than the previous site. The massive granite bust that serves as Sitting Bull's tombstone was carved by the late Korczak Ziolkowski, the sculptor who began the quixotic Crazy Horse Mountain carving near Mt. Rushmore.

US-83: Selby

Twenty-odd miles east and slightly south of Mobridge, US-83 passes through diminutive **Selby** (pop. 707), the kind of sleepy, middle American hamlet with grain elevators and water towers, populated with children riding bikes home at dusk, and teenagers rumbling down Main Street in their muscle cars. Downtown Selby has an old "opera house" theater, and the comfortable, inviting **Berens Cafe** (605/649-7621) on Main Street. Berens serves home-cooked meals downstairs in a humble, friendly setting that will make you want to linger as long as you can.

Another place that may encourage you to hang around is on the northwest edge of town, near the US-12 and US-83 intersection: oasis-like **Lake Hiddenwood State Park** ($3), with picturesque deep swales and oak and cedar trees surrounding, as the name implies, a secluded swimming hole. If you mentally transport yourself back a century and a half, when explorers crossed these bone-dry parts and stumbled accidentally onto this lushness, the name's quite apt.

Agar and Onida

Between Selby and Pierre, there's nothing of dramatic importance. Highway hypnosis is kept at bay by the **Bangor Monument,** a roadside marker five miles south of Selby, standing on the site of the vanished town of Bangor; farther south, then 13 miles east of US-83, the very large **Cathedral on the Prairie** looms over the hamlet of **Hoven** (pop. 522).

And then, finally, a town . . . or at least some grain elevators and a turquoise water tower. **Agar** (pop. 82), "Home of the 1977 State B Track Champions," is a classic, single-sidewalk leg-stretch where the Pepsi machine seems as large as the filling station it rests against. The same goes for little **Onida** (pop. 761), with a handsome onion-domed courthouse, a water tower emblazoned with a sunflower, and a cute city park complete with swimming pool and horseshoe courts. You'd hardly guess that this was once a thriving homesteader boomtown, full of transplanted New Yorkers who named it after Oneida, with no apparent reason for the change in spelling.

Pierre

The second smallest and by far the sleepiest state capital in the country, **Pierre** (pop. 13,876; pronounced PEER), is an odd amalgam of South Dakota characteristics. Part farm town, part railroad town, and best of all, part river town, Pierre accurately embodies South Dakota's dominant activities. Located at nearly the geographic center of the state, quiet, easy Pierre is filled with natural attractions, and totally lacking in the usual power-broker trappings of other state-capital cities.

Pierre's one not-to-be-missed stop is the excellent **South Dakota Cultural Heritage Center** (daily; $3; 605/773-3458) at 900 Governor's Drive, built into the side of a hill on the north side of town. A startling and beautiful structure, it is designed to be a modern evocation of a traditional, energy-efficient Native American dwelling. Inside, the museum has the usual interpretive historical displays of native and pioneer cultures, with a focus on the Sioux tribes and the battles for the Black Hills region. A glass case holds the actual lead plate which the brothers Louis-Joseph and Francois Verendrye, the first Europeans to explore what's now South Dakota, left behind when they claimed the entire territory for France in 1743.

At the center of town, the state **capitol** grounds are a verdant island of tranquillity with an arboretum, walking trails, and the **Fountain Memorial,** dedicated to Korean and Vietnam War veterans. The fountain sits on a lake that is home to thousands of migrating winter waterfowl.

Also worth a look is the **South Dakota National Guard Museum** (Mon.–Fri. 1–5 PM; free), 301 E. Dakota, which you can't miss because of the Sherman tank, the A-70 Corsair, and the artillery pieces on the boulevard. You can also see General Custer's dress sword here. For travel-weary road hogs, the coolest museum is the hands-on **South Dakota Discovery Center and Aquarium** (daily; $4; 605/224-8295), in the old Pierre Municipal Power & Light building at 805 W. Sioux Avenue, with loads of science exhibits.

Locally known as Houck's, the **Triple U Buffalo Ranch,** 25 miles northwest of Pierre on Hwy-1806, is a 53,000-acre spread supporting about 3,500 head of bison, some of whom were seen in the movie *Dances with Wolves.* A small gift shop (605/567-3624) sells buffalo steaks, jerky, hides, skulls and other products.

Spreading across the plains south of Pierre along both sides of US-83, the 116,000 acres of the **Fort Pierre National Grasslands** are home to deer, pronghorn, jillions of waterfowl, and one of the most pervasive stretches of prairie dog towns in the region. The grassland doesn't offer developed campsites, but it does have great fishing at some of the hundreds of small dams dotting the landscape.

WALL DRUG

America's most famous roadside business began with free ice water. Ted Hustead bought this tiny South Dakota town's drug store in 1931. For five years, Ted and his wife Dorothy struggled to survive during the depths of the Depression. Then Dorothy had a brainstorm: Hundreds of people drove past Wall every day on US-16, the main route across South Dakota, battling the dusty dirt road and 90-degree summer heat. Why not give them an excuse to stop? Once in the store, maybe they'd buy an ice cream, or an aspirin.

So in the summer of 1936, Ted Hustead erected roadside signs to tempt travelers off the highway and into his store. Spaced at intervals along the highway, like the famous Burma Shave ads, the signs read:

> GET A SODA
> GET ROOT BEER
> TURN THE CORNER
> JUST AS NEAR
> TO HIGHWAY 16 AND 14
> FREE ICE WATER
> WALL DRUG

Before he could return to the store, the tourists were already arriving. And they're coming still: some 20,000 per day in the summer, well over a million a year. Proud South Dakotans have covered foreign landscapes with signs proclaiming the mileage to Wall Drug, and the Husteads themselves have advertised on London buses, Amsterdam canals, and French bistros.

Museums aside, nature is really what draws folks to Pierre. Bordering the town to the south is the long **La Framboise Isle Nature Area,** a perfect place to while away time, recuperating from the drive along the beautiful bay. If you're interested in biking or paddling along the Missouri River, you can rent bikes and boats at **Pedal & Paddle** (605/224-8955), 411 S. Pierre Street.

Pierre Practicalities

If you look under Hotels in the Pierre Yellow Pages, you'll find only one listing (and that's a Days Inn!), but there are the usual assorted motels on US-83 as it swoops in from the north and follows the wide landscaped boulevards beyond downtown. Along US-83, west of the state capitol building, are lots of locally owned places: the **Governor's Inn** ($60; 605/224-4200 or 800/341-8000), 700 W. Sioux Avenue, is at the top end of the price and comfort scale, and this same can't-miss-it main drag holds that noteworthy **Days Inn,** ($50 and up; 605/224-0411) at 520 W. Sioux Avenue.

The downtown hole-in-the-wall **D & E Cafe** (605/224-7200), at 115 W. Dakota Avenue, seemingly lifted out of celluloid cliché into real life, includes

Before the 1960s era of "highway beautification" banned most billboards, Wall Drug touted its free ice water on 3,000 billboards in all 50 states.

But what's waiting at the end of all those billboards?

Originally, not much, apart from that glass of water. But today's 50,000 square-foot Wall Drug is a different story: it can feed, clothe, and entertain the entire family for hours. Photo opportunities abound, thanks to the 80-foot-long dinosaur, 6-foot fiberglass jackalope and Mt. Rushmore replica, a 520-seat cafe, and shops for everything from postcards to cowboy boots. A younger generation of Husteads still runs Wall Drug, the ice water's still free, and the coffee still costs a nickel. Drop in sometime!

Wall Drug (605/279-2175) is at 510 Main Street, at the center of Wall, South Dakota (pop. 800), just north of I-90 exit 110. Apart from Wall Drug, the other reason to visit is the chance to tour a real-life nuclear missile silo, at the **Minuteman Missile National Historic Site** (daily; 605/433-5552), off I-90 exit 131.

original smoky floors and walls with forgotten wainscoting abused by multiple coats of coffee-brown paint. The food is classic short-order with gum-cracking service on the side. At the opposite end of the culinary spectrum is **La Minestra** (605/224-8090), 106 E. Dakota Avenue, a surprisingly cozy and elegant dinner-only bistro; the sophisticated Italian specialties make this one of the nicest restaurants you'll find along the 100th Meridian.

The gregarious staff at the **chamber of commerce** (605/224-7361 or 800/962-2034) at 800 W. Dakota Avenue are chock-full of helpful information.

Fort Pierre

South of Pierre, US-83 crosses the Missouri River, then takes you into **Fort Pierre** (pop. 1,900). It's not much now, but it has a rich history. As far back as 1817, it was known as Fort Pierre Chouteau, an American Fur Company trading post; and before that it was Ree and Arikara tribal lands. Located at the mouth of the Bad (Teton) River, Fort Pierre once was a thriving port. But it is better known as the site where Joseph La Framboise, a French fur-trader, stopped and erected a driftwood shelter out of necessity, establishing the area's first white settlement.

Visit the old fort, now a National Park Service landmark spread out over 1.3 acres near town. At 115 N. Main Street in the center of town you'll find the **Verendyre Museum** (daily in summer only), which has collections of South Dakota pioneer artifacts and a duplicate of the plate the Verendyre brothers, the first white men to enter South Dakota, planted here in 1743 to claim the land for France. The original plate is in the state Heritage Center in Pierre; the Verendyre brothers themselves are commemorated with a monument in small **Centennial Park,** off US-83 at the center of town.

Immediately south of Fort Pierre, typical South Dakota topography resumes: rolling black and green hills and twisting creek beds beneath sharp vertical drops of million-year-old geology.

Murdo

One of the duller stretches of US-83 is this 20-mile leg along the mind-numbing I-90 artery between the Fort Pierre grasslands and **Murdo** (pop. 700). Once a stop on the legendary Texas Cattle Trail and also used by stagecoaches, the town was named for cattle baron Murdo McKenzie, whose ranch pushed through some 20,000 head of cattle a year. Today, the town of Murdo still lives on the cattle industry.

The one place that's definitely worth a stop is smack-dab at the diesel-blue polluted confluence of US-83 and I-90, where nostalgists will find the **Pioneer Auto Museum and Antique Town** (daily; $8.50; 605/669-2691); pricey, maybe, but it's a 10-acre, 39-building collection of about 250 antique cars, with tons of other great items. Classic cars include a rare Tucker (the 1940s car with the central pivoting headlamp; Francis Ford Coppola made a movie about it). There's also a nifty White Co. motor home from 1921, one of the earliest RVs, and the "General Lee" muscle car from TV's *Dukes of Hazzard.* Star of the show: Elvis Presley's 1976 Harley-Davidson Electra Glide 1200 motorcycle. Pure Americana.

If you're thinking about driving along US-83 during August, be aware that you may have to share the road with hordes of Harley riders bound for the annual get-together in **Sturgis**, at the edge of the Black Hills.

The public swimming pool across the street, and the **Tee Pee Restaurant** down the road at 303 5th Street ("We Will Sell No Coffee Over a Half-Hour Old") can round off your Murdo visit.

Rosebud Indian Reservation

There's nothing much south of I-90 and Murdo until you come across a picturesque dale while crossing the White River, sheltering the first grove of trees in too long a time. South of White River, US-83 bumpity-bumps its way across the **Rosebud Indian Reservation.** After the signing of the Fort Laramie Treaty in 1868, the Sicangu Lakota, under the guide of Spotted Tail, were moved five times before finally being settled on this reservation, one of the smallest on the Great Plains. The first town you'll encounter is **Mission,** the reservation's trading center. It's a strip of gas stations and a Rosebud/Sioux arts and crafts cen-

ter. The heart of the reservation is **Rosebud,** five miles west of Mission on US-18, then 10 miles southwest on BIA-1. Most of the reservation's activities, including weekend **rodeos** and **powwows,** are centered around the tribal headquarters here (605/747-2381). The biggest powwow is the **Rosebud Sioux Tribal Fair and Powwow** in late August, where you can feast on a traditional buffalo dinner.

Another eight miles southwest is tiny **St. Francis,** which has the **Buechel Memorial Lakota Museum** (daily June–Sept.; free; 605/747-2745), a museum dedicated to the Teton Sioux culture and begun by Fr. Eugene Buechel, a German Jesuit, avid botanist, and dedicated student of the culture.

Back on US-83, 23 miles south of Mission, is the tribe's most recent economic endeavor, the **Rosebud Casino,** which has an attached **Quality Inn** motel ($65–85; 605/378-3360). The complex sits right on the Nebraska state line, which shows where their prospective gamblers are coming from.

NEBRASKA

The 257 miles from South Dakota to Kansas encompass two distinct regions: typical Midwestern wheat and cattle ranches, and the fascinating grass-coated sand dunes of central Nebraska's Sand Hills region. Contrary to popular belief, Nebraska isn't mostly corn, but beef, lots and lots of it. US-83 passes by more cattle than it does people, with scant few communities along the way.

The powers that be don't neglect to mention your entrance into Nebraska, and for those coming from the north the differences may well be very welcome: Suddenly there are trees, trees, and more trees, as you drop down from the scorched South Dakota plains into the evergreen-studded **Niobrara River Valley.** (Along with these changes in topography, the roadbed also improves.) Your first stop south of the border is **Valentine,** then you cross the rolling Sand Hills region toward the railroad town of **North Platte,** former home of "Buffalo" Bill Cody. From North Platte, it's a straight shot south across acres of corn to Kansas.

Valentine

Just west of the 100th Meridian, the small town of **Valentine** (pop. 2,826) is a center of the extensive cattle ranching industry of the Sand Hills region, and the kind of tiny but prideful town that makes road-tripping fun. Seat of enormous Cherry County and situated at the northern edge of the 20,000-square-mile Sand Hills region, Valentine, which takes its name from a U.S. congressman, is a broad, well-maintained place that pays its bills with beef cattle fed to tenderness on the 800 species of grasses coating the region.

Considering the long stretches of road ahead, it's prudent to check out what the town's got, and there's quite a bit.

Thanks to its cupidic name, Valentine is a popular place to mail greeting cards for delivery on February 14. If you want a special **"With Love on Valentine's Day"** postmark, in early February pack up your stamped, addressed Valentine's cards in a larger envelope and send them to "The Postmaster, Valentine Re-Mailing, Valentine NE 69201."

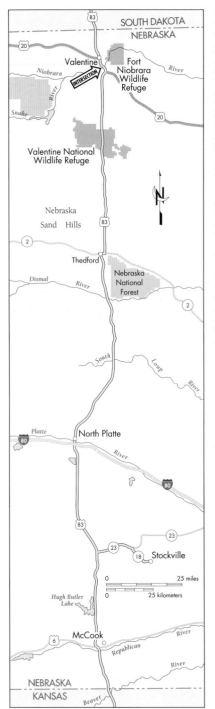

Downtown—where the streetlights are hung with red and white banners emblazoned with the unsurprising town motto "Valentine, Heart of the Sand Hills"—the facade of the First National Bank holds the **largest brick mural** in Nebraska, with 1,200 square feet of images of longhorn cattle and the building of the transcontinental railroad built out of dark brown bricks. Of Valentine's **museums**, the most intriguing is **Sawyer's Sand Hills Museum** (daily in summer; $2), on US-20 four blocks west of US-83. The museum offers a broad display, including some legitimately historical stuff, as well as a two-headed calf and a great collection of antique cars that still run. The **Cherry County Historical Society Museum,** next door to the visitors center at the US-20/US-83 junction, is much more traditional. Four miles southeast of Valentine on US-20/83, an absolutely *huge* old railroad trestle bridges the broad Niobrara River.

Valentine has the usual motels scattered along US-20 and US-83, including the **Trade Winds Motel** ($40 and up; 402/376-1600 or 800/341-8000); there's also a Comfort Inn and a new Holiday Inn Express. The place most people go for a sit-down meal is the **Peppermill** (402/376-1440), 112 Main Street, featuring steaks, seafood, and alfresco dining in summer.

For details on camping, eating, sightseeing, sleeping, and anything else in and around Valentine, contact the pharmaceutically clean and well-stocked **visitors center** (402/376-2969 or 800/658-4024), 239 S. Main Street at the US-20/US-83 junction.

Valentine marks the junction of US-83 and the east-west **Oregon Trail** along US-20. See page 570. For full coverage of this road trip, see pages 532–633.

Fort Niobrara Wildlife Refuge

One of Valentine's sightseeing highlights is the massive old railroad bridge over the broad Niobrara River. Just two miles south of downtown along US-20/83, rising on trestles 150 feet above the water, the bridge now carries a hiker-biker trail that follows the old railroad right-of-way across the state. This stretch of the Niobrara River is protected within the **Fort Niobrara Wildlife Refuge** (402/376-3789), and offers top-notch canoeing and tubing. The refuge is named for old Fort Niobrara, semi-famous for never fighting a battle during its 27 years on the Wild West prairie; today, elk, bison and Texas longhorns roam its 19,000-plus acres of gorgeous, rolling dune prairie.

Nature-lovers score well at other sites around Valentine. Seasoned canoeists and keen trout anglers will want to tackle the rough **Snake River** some 15 miles southwest of town, near the short but powerful **Snake River Falls.** A good local outfitter is **Yucca Dune** (402/376-3330), at 148 E. 1st Street in downtown Valentine, which rents bikes, rafts, canoes, and kayaks and sells a variety of outdoor clothing, and climbing and camping gear.

Nebraska Sand Hills

South of Valentine are two fine natural areas, preserving and highlighting the unique ecosystems of the Nebraska Sand Hills. South along US-83 is the large **Valentine National Wildlife Refuge,** which, thanks to water seeped from the world's biggest aquifer, the Ogalala Aquifer, is home to both native rolling dune prairie and lowlands of lake, marsh, and sub-irrigated meadow. Lots of curlews, sandpipers, terns, and mule deer are found on the drives and hikes through the vaulted hills and long spiny grasses, and along the lakeshores.

The Sand Hills of northwestern Nebraska form one of the largest areas of rolling dune geology in the world. They're also the largest tract of mid- to tall-grass prairie in North America, and, in the right light (sunrise or sunset), at the right time of year (spring especially), they are absolutely beautiful.

Beyond this, the Sand Hills occasionally flatten out into simple, absolutely open range, with perhaps a ridge jutting out. The aspect of the land here shows itself as much more scabrous than the Dakotas. Mauve, tan, and cream cows fleck the land, as do a few windmills: great, stark, American Gothic windmills, not the pseudo-efficient energy spinners seen elsewhere.

US-83 joins with Hwy-2 approximately 30 miles after leaving the Valentine Wildlife Refuge. Swinging east will take you to one of the three huge districts of the **Nebraska National Forest,** among the largest man-made forest tracts in the world (20,000 acres total), all planted by hand more than a century ago.

Thedford and Scenic Hwy-2

Sleepy little **Thedford** (pop. 243) stretches west of US-83, lining up along the Burlington Northern railroad tracks. The town—not much more than a few little houses, some loud cicadas, a Rodeway Inn motel, and a combination Conoco station and road-food restaurant—does mark the junction of US-83 and scenic Hwy-2, which runs west–east across the heart of Nebraska, abounding in wildflowers, ultra-quaint but totally unself-conscious small towns, and pastoral beauty from horizon to horizon. At the south edge of the Sand Hills, 100 miles west of Thedford at the end of Hwy-2, the totally unique **Carhenge**—the finest Detroit wheels, stacked on top of each other to form a steel Stonehenge—stands just outside the town of Alliance (see page 569).

South of Thedford, US-83 jumps and descends for another 65 miles toward North Platte with very, very little to occupy your time other than scenic overlooks along the Dismal and South Loup Rivers.

North Platte

It can take some time getting into **North Platte** (pop. 24,500), but despite the heavy-industrial initial appearances there is a lot here to enjoy. The northern approach along US-83 crosses over the North Fork of the Platte River, taking a leisurely little swoop up and over it, passing scenic bluffs, then flashing back through a living history of the days when the train was king. Rusty old weed-filled tracks and abandoned shops and warehouses lie off to the side, steel and brick remnants of North Platte's blue-collar trade and transportation heyday. From the south the entrance is less memorable, crossing the I-80 strip with its plastic signs and anonymous franchise architecture.

Originally the site of a Union Pacific construction camp, North Platte nearly expired when the workers decamped for Colorado; but the town's 300 permanent residents were spared when the railroad chose it as a division point, securing its future. The city is still proud of its **Bailey Yard**, recently decreed by the *Guinness Book of World Records* as the largest railroad classification yard in the world. A high-tech visitors center (complete with 15-story Golden Spike Tower) is on the drawing boards, but for now you can view the trains from a high platform three miles west of town on Front Street. (Get directions from the visitors bureau, as it can be hard to find.)

Many of the city parks feature railroad displays, including 90-acre **Cody Park** along US-83. Within the confines rests **Big Boy**, one of the world's largest steam locomotives.

Before the railroad came through, North Platte was a key stop on both the Oregon Trail, which followed the Platte River west past Scotts Bluff and into Wyoming, and the Pony Express. At the dawn of the Automobile Age, North Platte played a starring role along the historic Lincoln Highway, the first transcontinental road, which followed the Oregon Trail route west along what's now US-30, eventually ending up in San Francisco.

But North Platte is most widely known as the home of Buffalo Bill Cody. The huge **Buffalo Bill Scout's Rest Ranch**, (daily; $2.50 per car; 308/535-8035), four miles northwest via US-30 and Buffalo Bill Avenue, is a state historical park with original dwellings on 16 of the original 4,000-acre spread. Cody's house, and some outbuildings, look much the way they did when Buffalo Bill lived here, from 1879 to 1913. This is where Buffalo Bill originated his rodeo with the "Old Glory Blowout" in 1882 and later housed his Wild West Show when not on the road. Tours are available, and the buffalo stew cookouts ($5) are popular. The town still whoops it up with the **Buffalo Bill Rodeo** in June.

Buffalo Bill

Besides Buffalo Bill memorabilia, North Platte has an interesting WW II canteen mock-up (preserved intact from the days when North Platte was a whistlestop for troop trains), a great Railroad Town, and an eight-million-year-old, 200-pound, fossilized land tortoise, all on display at the **Lincoln County Museum** (daily; 308/534-5640), adjacent to the Scout's Rest Ranch at 2403 Buffalo Bill Avenue.

Downtown North Platte, on the south side of the railroad tracks, has largely been superseded by the surrounding Interstate sprawl, but the brick-paved streets here still hold some grand old buildings and a few nifty old neon signs, including one for the landmark **Fox Theater**, at 5th and Bailey Streets. Just north of I-80 is one last great Buffalo Bill stop: the giant **Fort Cody Trading Post** (free; 308/532-8081), a massive postcard and souvenir store with a very good selection of books on Western Americana and, best of all, a fabulously detailed miniature working model of Buffalo Bill's Wild West Show, complete with dancing bears, jumping horses, and hundreds of cowboys and Indians.

Fifty miles east of North Platte along I-180 or the old Lincoln Highway, the town of **Cozad** has a big sign proudly proclaiming its place along the 100th Meridian, the historic dividing line down the middle of America.

South of North Platte on US-83, you'll pass a country road, going east and south, that leads to the **Sioux Lookouts**, one of the highest points above the Platte Valley.

Because Interstate 80 whips through North Platte, there's no shortage of fast food or places to stay, including a **Motel 6** (308/534-6200) on the south side of town at the US-83/I-80 junction.

You can find out more about the town and region at the North Platte **visitors bureau** (308/532-4729 or 800/955-4528) at 219 S. Dewey Street, between downtown and I-80.

The Great Platte River Road Archway Monument

The north–south US-83 route takes you through the heart of North Platte, but historically the main way through was heading west. First along the Oregon Trail, then along the Pony Express, the Union Pacific railroad, and up to today's I-80 freeway, the Platte River has long been one of the country's most important transportation throughways. Paying tribute to all stages of the river corridor's long history, the **Great Platte River Road Archway Monument** (daily; $10; 308/237-1000) is an expansive new interactive museum dedicated to America's freedom of mobility. The museum actually spans I-80 at exit 272, just east of the town of Kearney (pronounced CAR-knee), an hour east of North Platte.

South of Kearny is another great monument to America: **Harold Warp's Pioneer Village** (daily; $10; 800/445-4447), a Middle America version of Henry Ford's Greenfield Village, with a much better sense of fun. The 20-acre site preserves dozens of historic structures along with the "world's oldest steam-powered merry-go-round", 350 classic cars, trucks, and airplanes, and some 50,000 other items of varying historical interest. Almost everything here dates from 1830–1950, illustrating Mr. Warp's sense of history: "For thousands of years man lived quite simply. Then like a sleeping giant our world was awakened. In a mere hundred and twenty years of eternal time man progressed from open hearth, grease lamps, and ox carts to television, super sonic speed, and atomic power. We have endeavored to show you the actual development of this astounding progress as it was unfolded by our forefathers and by ourselves."

The I-80 route replaced one of the country's first cross-country roads, the Lincoln Highway, and if you've got some time (and an appetite!), take a little trip along the old Lincoln Highway (US-30). You'll find a number of old motels and cafés; 12 miles west of North Platte, along US-30 in the town of Hershey, **Butch's** (308/368-7231) serves some of the country's best prime rib and pork chops, so tender you can cut 'em with a fork.

Wellfleet: Dancing Leaf Earth Lodge

South of North Platte, there's nothing much, community-wise, in the 70-odd miles along US-83 until you reach McCook, but the road and rolling landscape will definitely hold your interest. You're privy to the few acres of genuine Nebraska corn, which eventually fold into encroaching knobby little rises, hollows full of oaks, or open range. Though there are no real sights to look out for, a detour east of the highway brings you to one truly unique place: the **Dancing Leaf Earth Lodge,** located amongst cottonwood trees along the banks of Medicine Creek, midway between North Platte and McCook in the town of **Wellfleet,** 2 miles east of US-83 at 6100 E. Opal Springs Road. An as-authentic-as-possible re-creation of a Native American dwelling, the 20- by 20-foot lodge is the heart of a "cultural learning center" that endeavors to give visitors a total immersion into the lifeways and spirituality of ancient Plains Indians. Constructed by hand from willows and grasses and plastered with thick mud, the two earth lodges stay cool in summer and warm in winter, and provide primitive but comfortable accommodations and an unforgettable experience of what life might have been like before the arrival of European cultures.

Guided **tours** (daily; $7; 308/963-4233) give a good overall introduction to Plains Indian traditions, but nothings beats an overnight stay. Families and groups are especially welcome at the Dancing Leaf, where rates, including a buffalo stew dinner and a soothing session in the sweat lodge, start at $90 a night for up to three people. The lodges each sleep a maximum of 15 people, and guests need to bring sleeping bags. Even if you don't stay overnight, tours of the lodges and nearby archaeological remains, plus informal instruction in tool-making, basket-weaving, hunting, fishing, and cooking, are also available from the hosts, Les and Jan Hosick.

McCook

Fifteen miles north of the Kansas border, patches of corn grow in the fertile loam of the undulating Republican River Valley around **McCook** (pop. 7,994), the market center for much of southwest Nebraska. With the arrival of the railroad, the town (which is still served by Amtrak's Zephyr and numerous freight trains) grew into a farm trade center, and now is a sedate, content-enough place, with at least two good excuses for a brief stop, both of them on the hill above downtown. The **High Plains Museum** (closed Mon.; free; 308/345-3661), in a large modern building at 421 Norris Avenue, includes excellent fossil collections, some WW II prisoner-of-war artwork, a room dedicated to Sen. George Norris, and an old drugstore replicated in the very building where Kool-Aid was developed. Up the street, the **George W. Norris Home** (daily; $3), 706 Norris Avenue, is devoted to McCook's favorite son, the Nebraska senator who founded the Tennessee Valley Authority and promoted rural electrification during the New Deal 1930s. Norris also authored the 20th Amendment to the Constitution, which ended the traditional "lame duck" sessions of Congress and moved the date of presidential inaugurations from March to January.

In between the two museums, at 602 Norris Avenue, stands Nebraska's only Frank Lloyd Wright–designed house, still a private residence and not open for tours.

> McCook sits at the crossroads of US-83 and US-6, which used to be the longest cross-country highway in the United States, running from the tip of Cape Cod all the way to Long Beach, California. South of McCook, US-83 turns grandly scenic (it's even marked as such on some maps). Just north of the Nebraska/Kansas state line, the highway crosses the Beaver River, passing over an old trestle bridge.

KANSAS

Kansas is no mere geographical expression, but a "state of mind," a religion, and a philosophy in one.
—Carl Becker, *Kansas* (1910)

I like Kansas—that is, natural Kansas—better than I had expected to. . . .
—Horace Greeley, *An Overland Journey* (1859)

The clichés have told you wrong: US-83 across much of Kansas—surprise, surprise —is actually a treat, not at all the interminable tedium of grainfield stretches you might expect. Yes, the physiography through most of the intrastate span is still predominantly flat, dry Northern High Plains, but it's compensated for, particularly in the north, with extensive irrigation that coaxes lusher patches of vegetation out of the dark rich soil.

US-83 ushers you along gaping, horizon-filled stretches broken by isolated lakes and occasional oases such as **Oberlin** and **Oakley,** home of the nearly

famous **Prairie Dog Town.** Continuing south across the windblown plains and limestone hills, US-83 passes through the cow towns of **Scott City** and **Garden City** before crossing the Arkansas River into the baked-clay watercolor that stretches south into Oklahoma and Texas. One final Kansas stop is perhaps the best: **Liberal,** self-declared home of Dorothy from *The Wizard of Oz.*

Oberlin

Funky little **Oberlin,** 12 miles south of the Nebraska state line, is definitely worth a stop. A picture-postcard town, with awnings covering storefronts along the two blocks of red-brick downtown streets, it has a mini-cinema (called the Sunflower, of course) playing Hollywood hits, and a Social Realist sandstone statue of a pioneering family marking its northern edge.

The peace and quiet of today's Oberlin is in stark contrast to its past: Oberlin was the site of the last Indian raid in Kansas on September 29, 1878, after a fierce skirmish had erupted between Chief Dull Knife's Northern Cheyenne, heading to regain their lands in the Dakotas, and an infantry contingent from Fort Dodge at what is today Lake Scott State Park, near Scott City 80 miles to the south. The Oberlin cemetery contains a memorial to the 19 settlers who were killed in Cheyenne attacks, and the town has the late-September **Mini-Sapa Days,** a two-day festival commemorating the event. Downtown along S. Penn Avenue, the worthwhile **Decatur County/Last Indian Raid Museum** (closed Mon.; $3; 785/475-2712) has eight preserved buildings, including a sod house.

Colby

Out of Oberlin, US-83 sweeps through beautiful farmlands, often paralleling railroad tracks, and passes through low, one-horse towns with towering feed elevators. The road banks sharply west and then south, at which point you can either continue on US-83 until the road crosses I-70 near Oakley, or head west along US-24 to the I-70 junction at ambitious **Colby,** which calls itself "The Oasis of the Plains." The town is simply a service center for the wheat belt, but it does have the fairly huge **Prairie Museum of Art and History** (closed Mon. in winter; $5; 785/462-4590) at 1905 S. Franklin Street. The museum is a sprawling, 24-acre complex that includes rare porcelains, china dolls, assorted historical stuff, a complete home decorated as it would have been in the 1930s, and the **Cooper Barn,** one of the largest barns in the state—over 7,000 square feet!

Traveling US-83 across the Midwest, you'll notice that most of the roadside services are found along the east-west crossroads, especially the major old transcontinental highways like US-6, US-30, or US-40, or today's Interstate superslabs. North–south travelers have always been a rare species.

Oakley

Back on US-83, amid the olfactory assault of I-70, stands possibly the most bizarre tourist trap the highway has to offer: **Prairie Dog Town** (daily May–Oct.; $5.95 adults, under-10s $2.95; 785/672-3100). This collection—"Home of the 8,000-lb. Prairie Dog," as the old roadside signs say—is a combination petting zoo and freak show, with collections of the eponymous little dogs as well as dozens of birds, snakes, bobcats, bison, and other Great Plains critters, many taken in as orphans. There's even a five-legged cow.

The rest of **Oakley** (pop. 1,993), south and west of I-70 and lined up along historic US-40, turns out to be an old, big-time ranching and railroad town, featuring lots of utilitarian architecture, massive diesel engines, farm supply stores, and railroad tracks. It's unassuming but important, situated as it is at the junction of three major highways.

Right off US-83, the **Fick Fossil Museum** (daily; free), at 700 W. 3rd Street, features some unique exhibits: 11,000 fossilized shark teeth, a sod house, collections of pressed wildflowers, and some perfectly garish mosaics, including the Great Seal of the President of the United States, made entirely out of the aforementioned shark's teeth. It was created by—who else?—Mrs. Fick. The local history and paleontology exhibits are quite good, too.

The I-70 Business Loop (old US-40) offers the usual array of cafés and motels. The favorite local place to go for dinner and a drink is the very friendly **Scotts Bluff** (785/672-8892), a private club with great steaks and sandwiches at 310 S. Freeman Avenue. Oakley is a "dry" town, but motel guests get complimentary "membership" at the Scotts Bluff, and there's no better place to hang out and overhear cowgirls, cattlemen, and assorted other bull-shippers shooting the breeze over a beer or two.

Chalk Pyramids/Monument Rocks

South of Oakley, the road bolts straight for over 20 miles, passing between an enormous sea of yellow flowers (in early summer) on one side and expanses of

Monument Rocks

open range on the other. Later, the scenery peters out into a prickly dry, faintly yellow, rocky desolation that signals the fringes of the Smoky Hills region.

The prime topographical feature of the Smoky Hills is the surreal **Chalk Pyramids,** also known as **Monument Rocks;** they are referred to in the old WPA *Guide to Kansas* as the "Kansas Pyramids." Whatever you call them, these highly eroded geological formations, which reach heights of 70 feet above the plains, are composed of layers of ancient seabed from the Cretaceous period and were originally formed 80 million years ago. The impressive spires, karst-like formations, and shaley cliffs farther on have yielded thousands of excellent fossils of sharks, shark's teeth, fish, and reptiles. Although the pyramids are on private land, access is not restricted; however, there are no facilities. To get there, drive 26 miles south of Oakley, or 18 miles north from Scott City, then east from US-83 for 6.5 miles, then 2.5 miles north.

You can get some good maps and directions to the Rocks themselves at the friendly **Keystone Gallery** (620/872-2762), "conveniently located in the middle of nowhere" midway between Oakley and Scott City along US-83; the gallery also has a display of fossils from the Monument Rocks, and you can enjoy a sampling of local art and sculpture as well.

Lake Scott State Park and Scott City

Midway across Kansas, south of the Monument Rocks and west of US-83, **Lake Scott State Park** (daily dawn–dusk; $5 per car; 620/872-2061) is a true spring-fed oasis sheltering cottonwoods, ash, hackberry, and willow in open high-sky rangeland. Beyond offering a lovely and relaxing spot in which to unwind, Lake Scott includes Kansas's most intriguing historical site, **El Cuartelejo** ("The Old Barracks"), the only Pueblo Indian community in Kansas and the farthest north of any in the country.

Originally settled in the 1660s by Taos Pueblo people fleeing the Spanish in New Mexico, the area became home to the Picuris about 30 years later. Both

migrant groups joined with the local Plains Apache clan, but the oasis and the ruined pueblo buildings continued to be used for occasional nomadic squatting by the Pawnee, and later by Spanish and French explorers and traders, before eventually eroding away. In the late 1880s the site was discovered accidentally by Herbert Steele, who stumbled onto the extensive irrigation ducts leading from spring areas to crop patches. Further excavation eventually revealed the pueblo sites, now considered the first permanent-walled structures in the state. The park has a few other historical points of interest, including a marker on the site of the fateful last battle between the U.S. Cavalry and escaping

Cheyenne Indians led by Chief Dull Knife. The park also has herds of elk and bison, and visitors can see the preserved home of Herbert Steele, full of pioneer furniture and farming implements.

South of Lake Scott State Park, US-83 continues across the High Plains, with not a whole lot to disrupt the continuity until Garden City, another 45 miles south. The only town of any size is **Scott City** (pop. 3,800), with its miles and miles of cattle fencing, feed lots, innumerable cattle companies, and big American flags greeting you (or waving good-bye) at the town limits. It's a hardy, industrious place, with everyone busy working. Hard.

Garden City stands at the junction of US-83 and coast-to-coast US-50, **The Loneliest Road** in America (see page 677). Full coverage of this road trip begins on page 636.

Garden City

One of the biggest towns in this part of the Great Plains, **Garden City** (pop. 28,451) is best known for its huge public **swimming pool:** 337 feet by 218 feet, with over 2.5 million gallons of water. It's south of US-50 at the end of 4th Street, near the Arkansas River in Finnup Park, and it's free! Next to the swimming pool is a small historical museum and the nice **Lee Richardson Zoo** (620/276-1250), with rhinos, elephants, giraffes, and zebras; it's free for people on foot, but costs $3 for a drive-thru tour.

North of the zoo in the brick-paved downtown, which unlike many places shows few signs of businesses fleeing to the highway frontages, you can window-shop (or even buy something) at the department stores and antique shops, see a movie at the classic **State Theatre** on Main Street, or get a bite to eat at cafés like **Herb's Hamburgers** (620/276-8021; good burgers!) at 110 W. Kansas Avenue or **Traditions Sodas and Sandwiches** (620/ 275-1998) at 121 Grant Avenue, a block west of Main. The classic Windsor Hotel downtown is a hotel no longer, but after its construction in 1886 this "Waldorf of the Prairies" drew lots of cowpoke-luminaries, including Buffalo Bill Cody.

Garden City also supports the usual gas stations, motels, and fast food, but, best of all, the 4,000-acre **State Buffalo Preserve**, which may be viewed along the west side of US-83, south of town for about five miles.

Farther south, across the often dry-as-a-bone Arkansas River, oil pumps languidly dip their heads. This is where the stereotypical Kansas landscape comes in: either stark desolation or—thanks to money and modernity—vast irrigation efforts. Prior to the advent of reliable irrigation from the

Garden City was founded in 1879 by **C. J. "Buffalo" Jones,** one of many larger-than-life characters who populated the Wild West, and a pal of writer **Zane Grey,** who based the novel *Last of the Plainsmen* on his life. One of Jones's many achievements was the capture and preservation of a small herd of buffalo, the descendants of which populate the Buffalo Preserve on the south side of town.

The Dust Bowl

Though it may not have been the biggest migration in U.S. history, it was certainly the most traumatic—entire families packing up their few belongings and fleeing the Dust Bowl of the Depression-era Great Plains. Beginning in 1933 and continuing year after year until 1940, a 400-mile-long, 300-mile-wide region roughly bisected by US-83—covering 100 million acres of western Kansas, eastern Colorado, and the "Panhandles" of Oklahoma and Texas—was rendered uninhabitable as ceaseless winds carried away swirling clouds of what had been agricultural land.

The "Dust Bowl," as it was dubbed by Associated Press reporter Robert Geiger in April 1935, was caused by a fatal combination of circumstances. This part of the plains was naturally grassland and had long been considered marginal at best, but the rise in agricultural prices during and after World War I made it profitable to till and plant. Farmers invested in expensive machinery, but when the worldwide economic depression cut crop and livestock prices by as much as 75 percent, many farmers fell deeply in debt. Then, year after year of drought hit the region, and springtime winds carried away the fragile topsoil, lifting hundreds of tons of dust from each square mile, and dropping it as far east as New York City.

By the mid-1930s, many of the farmers had been forced to abandon their land, and while some were able to rely upon a series of New Deal welfare programs, many more fled for California and the Sunbelt states. In this mass exodus, as recorded by photographers like Dorothea Lange, and most memorably in John Steinbeck's 1939 novel *Grapes of Wrath*, some 100,000 people each year packed up their few possessions and headed west, never to return.

Nowadays, thanks to high-powered pumps that can reach down to the Ogalala Aquifer, much of what was the Dust Bowl is once again fertile farmland, no longer as dependent on the vicissitudes of the weather. Much of the rest of the land was bought up by the U.S. government, and some four million acres are now protected within a series of National Grasslands that maintain the Great Plains in more or less their natural state.

Ogalala Aquifer, over-eager farmers almost ruined the region's fortunes plowing up the fragile buffalo grass for a one-season crop, before the wind blew the topsoil away. The hills that stood here prior to the Dust Bowl are gone completely now, and the landscape is endless, see-forever plains, marked by grain elevators a deceptive 10 miles away.

At the Brookover feed lot along US-83 on the northwest side of Garden City, a huge sign standing atop a pair of grain elevators reads: "Eat Beef Keep Slim." From the comfort of your car you can hear the hundreds of cattle burping and mooing up a storm.

Liberal

First, the name. It's said that a munificent early settler came and dug a well, and whenever a dusty emigrant would offer money for a drink or the chance to wash his neck, the settler would say, "Water is always free here." One day the reply came, "That is mighty liberal." Bob Dole probably wouldn't approve of the word choice, but the name stuck, and now the town's stuck with it.

Second, the adjectives: hot, dusty, treeless, flat. The approach into town reveals the drab side of Liberal's oil, gas (the town lies on the eastern edge of an enormous natural gas field), and meatpacking industries.

But the sights do improve. Honest. There is one significant draw, the top-notch **Mid-America Air Museum** (daily; $5; 620/624-5263), at 2000 W. 2nd Street, on the site of the old Liberal Army Airfield. It's one of the largest air museums in the United States and has amassed an astonishingly diverse collection of aircraft covering the entire history of flight, including military fighters and bombers from World War II and the Korean and Vietnam Wars.

A dozen miles north of Liberal, the majestic **Rock Island Line Railroad Bridge** *crosses the Cimarron River. The "Mighty Sampson," at 1,200 feet long and 100 feet above the river, is among the largest of its kind.*

Otherwise, there's a lot of **Ozmania** in town. Though there's not even the most tenuous connection between Liberal and the film or the book, apart from them all being set in Kansas, an annual **Oztoberfest** blowout is held at so-called **Dorothy's House**, also known as the **Coronado House,** (daily; $5; 620/624-7624), a block north of US-54 at 567 E. Cedar Street. This combination historical museum and re-creation of the movie's Kansas sets displays a mock-up of Dorothy's bedroom from the movie, a mini–Yellow Brick Road lined by models of the film's animal heroes, as well as a horse bit from the expedition of Don Francisco Vasquez de Coronado and his troops, who passed through in 1541 searching for the fabled Seven Cities of Cibola.

The city's most unusual attraction happens annually on Shrove Tuesday (aka Mardi Gras), when it holds its annual, international, soon-to-be-famous **Liberal Pancake Race,** a competition between local housewives and their counterparts from Olney, England. They race a 415-yard, S-shaped course, each flipping a pancake along the way. The Olney event purportedly

Visit — DOROTHY'S HOUSE from the Wizard Of Oz

LIBERAL, KS.

dates from 1445, when a woman rushed to church with her pan still in her hand; the Liberal race has taken place since 1950.

US-83 and US-54, which is known as Pancake Boulevard, claim the majority of places to eat and sleep.

OKLAHOMA

On its beeline to Texas, US-83 doesn't just cross Oklahoma; it forsakes it, merely nipping the panhandle for a 37-mile dash. When crossing the border three miles south of Liberal, among the first things you see are a trailer park, a couple of bars, and a bingo hot-spot. They're inauspicious sights at best. And that's not even mentioning the slate-flat, wicked badlands, with temperatures high enough in summer to occlude your vision of the blistering pavement, and preclude a drive at top speeds. After a while, you're unable to conjure up synonyms for "endless," though there's plenty of time for it. Even the historical marker you think you eventually see winds up being in Texas.

The first town you come up to is diminutive **Turpin**, comprising a Phillips filling station now usurped by a Shamrock, farm equipment places, and a motel or two sans signs. Oh yes—there's a stop sign at Balko, where US-83 crosses US-412.

And that's it. *Finito.* You keep stretching the atlas over the steering wheel (no danger in these parts), wondering where the hell **Gray** is, and why you care. It's supposed to be on this highway. You're sure of it. But for some reason it never appears. Before you know it, Texas looms outside the windshield, and suddenly, there are lots of trees, and hills, and that historical marker you've been dreaming of.

TEXAS

The old WPA *Guide to Texas* says that "no other route across Texas offers such differences in topography, produce, climate, and people" as does US-83, which is still very true today. Starting at the Oklahoma border on the southern edge of the Great Plains, your route winds along the foot of the Cap Rock escarpment, then opens out onto the cattle country of **Edwards Plateau** where numerous river canyons provide respite from the mesquite scrubland, and finally ends up some 900 miles later at the **Gulf of Mexico**. Besides diverse landscapes, US-83 also passes through a virtual survey of Texas history: the prehistoric pictographs of **Paint Rock;** Mexican-American battlegrounds along the **Rio Grande;** 100-year-old frontier towns built of red brick around their central courthouses; and the modern Gulf Coast resort of **South Padre Island.** As you'll soon learn if you're perusing other Texas travel literature, this section of the state is, for the most part, ignored. Thus, you're definitely among an elite company, traveling along truly unbeaten paths.

In its 900-plus-mile crossing of Texas, US-83 is known as the **Vietnam Veterans Memorial Highway**. It forms the longest stretch of U.S. highway through any of the lower 48 states.

Perryton

After passing by wheat fields and ranch lands, then negotiating a verdant allée of foliage, you arrive at medium-sized, agreeable **Perryton** (pop. 7,607), seven miles south of the Oklahoma border. The town was formed in 1919 when the Santa Fe Railroad came through; people in nearby towns simply picked up their stuff—buildings included—and shifted them here. Ochilton, eight miles south off US-83/Hwy-70, was one such town, before some 600 people moved the whole infrastructure. If you ignore the industrial oil-well litter on the outskirts, Perryton's not bad-looking, with spacious, tree-lined streets. The self-styled "Wheatheart of the Nation," Perryton is also the hometown of Mike Hargrove, former American League Rookie of the Year and later manager of the Cleveland Indians.

South from Perryton, the landscape changes radically from the plains stretches, offering instead classic ranches with miles of fencing and great white gates à la *Dallas,* a few oil wells, small canyons with innumerable creekbeds, and craggy, fluted bluffs peppered with veldt-like vegetation.

Canadian

Coming from the north, **Canadian** (pop. 2,233) offers an auspicious view as you descend toward it. You plow through an imposing tunnel of trees and then cross the namesake river, once an important route for early explorers; the crossing itself runs alongside anachronistic railroad trestles. Besides sustaining the only trees for miles, contemporary Canadian also has the interesting

River Valley Pioneer Museum (daily; 806/323-6548) on US-83 at 118 S. 2nd Street.

For food, Main Street holds some doughnut shops and lunch stands complete with the quintessential advertisement proclaiming "Good Eats." There are motels on the north side of town, but a couple of blocks east of the chamber of commerce, at 103 N. 6th Street, is an alternative place to stay, the **Emerald House Bed and Breakfast** (806/323-5827).

Ten miles east of Canadian via paved Hwy-2266, the **Black Kettle National Grassland** maintains one of the few surviving portions of the natural landscape that once covered the Great Plains—where the deer and the antelope once played, and millions of buffalo roamed. Camping is available at Lake Marvin (580/497-2143). Four miles south of Canadian, along the east side of suddenly four-lane highway that jointly carries US-60 and US-83, a huge **brontosaurus** stands atop a high bluff. Her name is Aud; don't ask me why.

At Shamrock, US-83 crosses the legendary **Route 66** (see page 816). This full L.A.-to-Chicago odyssey is covered on pages 784–839.

Shamrock

Once a major oil pumping and refining center, **Shamrock** is a dusty, rusty old industrial town, off I-40 and a mile south of historic Route 66, which survives as the "Business Loop" of I-40 through town. Though it's not a particularly lovely place, Shamrock does have at least one real highlight: the lovely old **Tower Gas Station** and **U Drop Inn** café, standing together in full art deco glory on the northeast corner of US-83 and Route 66. Following a long-overdue $1.2-million restoration, these landmark buildings look great, but instead of selling gas or serving food, they now dispense generous portions of helpful advice, courtesy of the friendly local **visitors bureau** (806/256-2501).

Playing up the Irish connection, Elmore Park in the Route 66 town of Shamrock exhibits a reportedly genuine sliver of the **Blarney Stone**, encased in a hip-high hunk of green concrete, and there's an annual St. Patrick's Day parade and celebration, but no green bee—Shamrock is a dry town.

To discover more about Shamrock, visit the old brown-brick Reynolds Hotel, south of Route 66 and east of US-83 at 204 N. Madden Street, where the better-than-you-might-expect **Pioneer West Museum** (Mon.–Fri. free) has two dozen rooms full of bygone goodies, including the complete interiors, fixtures, and fittings of a dentist's office, a barber shop, and a general store. There's also an exhibit honoring Apollo astronaut Alan Bean, who lived nearby in his youth.

Wellington and the Rocking Chair Mountains

South of Shamrock, US-83 passes over the Salt Fork of the Red River, which definitely deserves its name, running a muddy red throughout the rainy season. West of the highway rise the **Rocking Chair Mountains,** named after a large cattle ranch established west of here in the 1880s by a group of aristocrats, mainly younger sons of noble Scottish families. The only visible sign of their Hibernian legacy survives in place-names like Aberdeen, Clarendon, and **Wellington** (pop. 2,450), 25 miles south of Shamrock. Wellington is now a major market town for the surrounding cotton plantations, and during the harvest the gins run round the clock. The center of town is west of the highway, but the US-83 frontage holds four gas stations and four cafés, including the popular **Roberson Restaurant** (806/447-2951) alongside a dilapidated Quonset-hut machine shop.

Childress

A vintage Texas town built around an old Spanish zocalo (town square), **Childress** (pop. 6,778) is an important shipping and supply point for surrounding grain and cattle ranches, and serves as the market town for area cotton farmers. Located at the junction of US-83 and US-287, Childress was named after George Childress, the author of the Texas Declaration of Independence; it is also the hometown of eight-time world champion calf roper Roy Cooper.

The once-picturesque downtown still houses the small but engaging **Childress County Heritage Museum** (closed Sun.; free) at 10 3rd Street NW (follow the signs). The downtown is one short step from dry, depressed implosion—the result of every business relocating to the congested, annoying fringe highways—but the elaborate 100-year-old facades provide ample opportunities for nostalgic photography and aimless wandering. Depending on your time of arrival, the brick-cobbled streets and empty shells of formerly grand buildings smack more of a ghost town, but there are a few good antique shops taking advantage of the historic charm.

The Goodnight Trail, the famed frontier cattle trail, passed through Childress.

Virtually every motel in town lines US-287 (Avenue F) east and west of the junction with US-83, but thanks to their highway-side location, they all suffer from a lack of quiet and privacy.

Paducah

South of Childress, US-83 passes through a magnificent landscape of rich red and gold canyonlands covered with vast groves of trees. **Paducah,** 30 miles south of Childress at the junction of US-70, is a modest cotton town proudly arrayed around a New Deal–era central courthouse modeled after an Egyptian temple. Brick-paved streets front abandoned stores and the huge old Cottle Hotel, which stands as a dormant reminder of better times, when harvest season or round-up would bring hundreds of transient field hands, cowboys, and card sharps into town. Nowadays Paducah offers little in the way of restaurants other than a doughnut shop and **Cracker's Steakhouse** (806/492-3171), at 1112 Easley Street. You can find a room at three motels west of US-83 along US-70; other options will require more than an hour's drive, so if it's quitting time, check out **The Town House** (806/492-3595), 1301 Easley, the best of the lot.

West of Paducah along US-70 spreads the **Matador Ranch,** once one of the largest in Texas, with 450,000 acres of fenced pasture and thirsty gullies amid semiarid canyons dotted with cedars and mesquite.

Hamlin and Swedona

Deep in the heart of Texas, surrounded by miles and miles of green grass, red earth, mesquite and juniper trees, windmills, pump supplies, and peanut driers, the tidy town of **Hamlin** (pop. 2,248; "Home of the Pied Pipers") is full of charming folks and streets lined by locust trees. There's not much here, but on the north side of town the blue-roofed **Hatahoe Restaurant** (325/576-2464), despite its ominous chainlike appearance, serves copious, cheap, and quite good meals. Standing next to the only stoplight in town, this is *the* place to meet the area's characters over breakfast.

Seven miles west of Hamlin on Hwy-92 stood **Swedona** (swee-DOAN-ya), a farming community founded by Swedish immigrants in 1877 that held fast to the ways of the Old Country for over 50 years. All that remains today is a tranquil cemetery.

Anson marks the junction of US-83 and US-80, part of the cross-country **Southern Pacific** route (see page 751). This road trip is described more fully beginning on page 724.

Anson

Eighteen miles southeast of Hamlin, at the junction of US-180, sits **Anson,** named in honor of Dr. Anson Jones, the last president of the Republic of Texas. Anson was also a stop on the legendary Butterfield Stage U.S. Mail route that ran between St. Louis and San Francisco from 1858 to 1861, but these days it feels more like a stage set for *The Last Picture Show*, with handsome blocks of brick-fronted buildings forming a square around the stately Jones County Courthouse at the center of town. Anson is still a center for the local cotton industry, but its main claim to fame is the **Cowboys' Christmas Ball**, described in an 1890 poem by William Lawrence "Larry" Chittenden and recently re-awakened by the involvement of country-folk singer Michael Martin Murphey, who did a Christmas show here in 1995.

Many of the smaller, usually dirt, roads in Texas are labeled "FM," for farm-to-market, or "RM," for ranch-to-market, before their route numbers: e.g., "RM-1208." For simplicity's sake, we have labeled them "Hwy-XX."

You can see almost all of Anson by driving through on US-83, but if you want to learn more, stop by the **Anson Jones Museum** (Wed.–Sun. 2–4:30 PM), a block southeast of the courthouse. For more information, contact the Anson **visitors bureau** (325/823-3259).

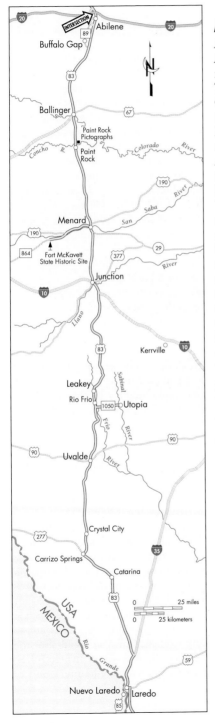

Abilene

At the junction of US-83 and I-20, **Abilene** (pop. 115,930) sits approximately in the geographic center of Texas. Abilene's fundamentalist Christian seminaries and the tame (for Texas) demeanor of its citizens have earned it the much-used nickname, "Buckle of the Bible Belt." Abilene, Texas, originally named after the raucous cowboy town of Abilene, Kansas, grew from nothing once the Texas and Pacific Railway came through in the 1870s. Then as now, cattle played a predominant economic role, though Abilene's economy has diversified into less-classically Texas endeavors, such as the unavoidable military air base and petroleum refinery. Abilene supports big-city amenities, including a symphony, though its indigenous fundamentalism precludes more libertine nocturnal notions; in 1925, the town fathers made it a misdemeanor, in the eyes of the law, to "flirt in a public place."

Abilene's downtown area, marked by a pair of 10-story towers, is not quite gentrified, but obviously galvanized for the attempt. The grand old Grace Hotel, now refurbished and known as the **Museums of Abilene** (closed Sun.; $5, free on Thursday; 325/673-4587), at 102 Cypress Street, houses an art museum, an engaging historical museum, and a children's museum. It's air-conditioned and well worth a look.

If you choose to spend some time in Abilene, you won't want for excursions. The **Abilene Zoo** (daily; $3) yields the **Discovery Center**, which features a great exhibit on southwest habitats, comparing veldts and plains of places as diverse as Africa and the United States. West of town is the

Cowboys' Christmas Ball

All along US-83, but especially in the Panhandle area of northern Texas, you pass through town after time-worn town that has clearly seen more prosperous times. Stately courthouse squares, massive old hotels, and blocks of all-but-abandoned storefronts testify to the depopulation of many rural areas in the wake of agricultural mechanization and a myriad of related economic and social changes. Looking at the photogenic remains of these once-bustling towns, it's hard not to imagine what life would have been like here during harvest, round-up, or holiday festivities, when every able-bodied man, woman, and child for miles would come to town to buy supplies, sell their goods, and socialize with friends and neighbors. An excerpt from an entertaining poem written about Anson, Texas, in 1890 by William Lawrence "Larry" Chittenden captures the vitality of these occasions, and gives a strong sense of the creative phraseology that animates Cowboy Poetry to this day.

Way out in Western Texas, where the Clear Fork's waters flow,
Where the cattle are a-browsin' and the Spanish Ponies grow;
Where the Northers come a-whistlin' from beyond the Neutral Strip;
And the prairie dogs are sneezin', as though they had the grip;

Dyess Air Force Base and its **Linear Air Park,** a collection of aircraft from World War II to Desert Storm; it's free and you paid for it, so you may as well check it out. Dyess AFB also served as command center for 1960s Atlas Missile silos, 5 of which line the "Atlas ICBM Highway" (Hwy-604), east of Abilene and south of I-20 exit 301.

Abilene Practicalities

The best place for food is the upscale **Cypress Street Station** (325/676-3463), at 158 Cypress Street next to the museums in the heart of downtown Abilene. If you'd prefer to search out some local flavor, aim for the classic Texan BBQ of **Joe Allen's** (11 AM–9 PM daily; 325/672-6082), 1233 S. Treadway Boulevard (US-83 Business) at S. 13th Street south of downtown in an unpromising industrial district. Joe Allen's interior looks straight out of some beer commercial (and they have galvanized tubs full of iced Texan Shiner Bock beers, as well as the other usual suspects); the food is excellent, especially the ribs, and they also serve mesquite-grilled staples such as chicken, sausage, or brisket, plus rib eye steaks cut to order, as thick as you want 'em. For more roadside fun, you could also stop at the local **Sonic Drive-In** (325/692-1014), 3856 S. Clark, where roller-skating waitresses won a Top Ten place in the Travel Channel's poll of "World's Best Fast Food."

The only real alternative to all-news, Tejano, or twangy country-western on your radio dial is Abilene's KCWS 102.7 FM, which plays a mixed bag of 1970s hits—Jefferson Airplane, Creedence Clearwater Revival, and the odd New Wave tune.

Where the coyotes come a-howlin' round the ranches after dark,
And the mockin' birds are singin' to the lovely medder lark;

Where the 'possom and the badger and the rattlesnakes abound,
And the monstrous stars are winkin' o'er a wilderness profound;
Where lonesome, tawny prairies melt into airy streams,
While the Double Mountains slumber in heavenly kinds of dreams;
Where the antelope is grazin' and the lonely plovers call,
It was there I attended the Cowboys' Christmas Ball.
The town was Anson City, old Jones' county seat,
Where they raised Polled Angus cattle and waving whiskered wheat;
Where the air is soft and balmy and dry and full of health,
Where the prairies is explodin' with agricultural wealth;
Where they print the Texas Western, that Hall McCann supplies
With news and yarns and stories, of most amazin' size . . .

—Larry Chittenden, From *Songs of the Cowboys,*
compiled in 1908 by Jack Thorp

    With most of the accommodation options lined up along I-20 or the older US-80 strip along the railroad tracks, Abilene motels include a **Motel 6** ($40; 325/672-8462) at 4951 W. Stamford, off I-20 at exit 282, not far from the junction with US-83; and the plusher **Kiva Inn** ($80; 325/695-2150) at 5403 S. 1st Street.

Buffalo Gap

If you're passing through Abilene, don't miss the re-stored frontier town of **Buffalo Gap** (daily; $5; 325/572-3365), 14 miles southwest of town via Hwy-89. It's not completely a tourist trap; cowpokes still reside here, and a courthouse and jail are just two of 20-odd buildings dating from the late 1800s, when Buffalo Gap, then the county seat, had over 1,200 residents and Abilene was barely a blip on the map. Other buildings are done up as Wild West souvenir stands, and there's at least one good restaurant: **Perini Ranch** (325/572-3339) for steak and chicken.

Ballinger

The first large town you come to, 53 miles south of Abilene among the rolling sheep-herding hills of the fantastic Edwards Plateau, is **Ballinger** (pop. 4,243). It's a lively little town with many of its brick and sandstone buildings dating from its inception in 1886 as Hutchins City, when the railroad came through. Standing along the banks of the Colorado River, the town now supports itself with agriculture. Catercorner to the **Coppini Cowboy Statue** on the courthouse square, Ballinger has the incredibly cheap and always packed **Texas Grill** (325/365-3314), open 24 hours at the corner of US-83 and Hwy-67. The courthouse is a Texas classic, built in 1883 in opulent, Second Empire style.

the Coppini Cowboy statue at Courthouse Square in Ballinger

Paint Rock Pictographs

Fifteen miles south of Ballinger, just west of US-83, the **Paint Rock Pictographs** are the largest concentration of prehistoric drawings in Texas, with well over 1,500 brightly colored images covering a limestone bluff along the north bank of the Concho River. These images, which range in size from a few inches to over five feet tall, are on ranchland owned since the 1870s by the family of Kay Campbell, who offers 2-hour guided tours through **Paint Rock Excursions** ($6 adults, $3 children, with a $15 minimum; 325/732-4376). Many of the paintings were made in the frontier days of the 19th century, when Comanche Indians lived in the region, but some are believed to date back over 1,000 years, to the time when Kiowa and Apache forebears settled here.

South of Ballinger along US-83, keep an eye out for the massive **stainless steel cross,** set on a hill east of the highway.

Menard

South of Paint Rock, US-83 winds through another 40 miles of scrubby hills before reaching the fascinating old wool-products market town of **Menard** (pop. 1,775; muh-NARD), standing in a lush valley along the San Saba River. A trading post and stop on the old cattle trails, Menard was originally founded by Franciscan missionaries in 1757, and many of its early structures survive or have been restored.

It's an eerily picturesque little town, with huge trees and a wide, wide bridge over the river. **Menardville Museum,** housed in the old Santa Fe railroad depot, contains a 150-year-old wooden bar from the now-defunct Legal Tender Saloon. A block south of the main drag, the **Historic Ditch Walk** follows the 10-mile Vaughn Agricultural and Mechanical Canal, a fancy name for an irrigation ditch that has served local farmers since 1876. The canal features remains of the old waterworks and colorful flower plantings, and the walk passes the 1899-vintage **Sacred Heart Catholic Church.**

Several historic limestone buildings in town date to the turn of the 20th century. The Luckenbach Building (built in 1903) contains the **Burnham Brothers Co.** (325/396-4572), the oldest U.S. retailer of game calls, from simple wooden instruments to state-of-the-art computerized devices that lure turkey, deer, elk, duck, and other animals.

During Menard's annual **Jim Bowie Days** in late June, visitors and residents gather for arts and crafts shows, mock gunfights, live music, and the outdoor production of *Song of Silver,* a musical patterned after Bowie's life story.

On the main highway, **Sideoats Bakery & Café** (325/396-2069), 509 US-83, serves up tasty, health-conscious baked goods and breakfast items, and there are a couple of basic motels: the **Motel 83** ($30; 325/396-4549) and the **Hilltop** ($45; 325/396-2075).

San Saba Mission

Two miles west of Menard, off US-190 on the banks of the river, a cemetery and foundations of a few buildings are all that's left of the **Santa Cruz de San Saba Mission.** Established in 1757 as Spain's northernmost outpost in the Apache and Comanche lands of what is now Texas, the mission was abandoned in 1768 after repeated Comanche attacks. Now a county park next to a golf course along Hwy-29, the rebuilt chapel houses a small museum, and portions of a later stone fort, named **Real Presidio de San Saba,** also survive. A simple inscription, "BOWIE," on the stone gate is thought to have been carved by Jim Bowie of Alamo fame. Bowie lived at the presidio ruins while searching for buried Spanish silver during the early 1800s.

Fort McKavett State Historic Site

Further along US-190, 17 miles from Menard, then another six miles south on Hwy-864, **Fort McKavett** (daily; $2; 325/396-2358) was established in 1852 as the "Camp on the San Saba" by the 8th Infantry. It was soon renamed in honor of a U.S. Army colonel who was killed in the Battle of Monterrey during the war with Mexico. As with other west Texas forts, Fort McKavett served as a first line of defense against Comanche raids along the Texas frontier and provided protection for travelers along the Upper San Antonio–El Paso Trail. Temporarily abandoned in 1859, the post was re-established in 1868 by the 4th Cavalry after local residents lobbied for Army protection. The cavalry was soon replaced by the 38th Infantry, a company of African-American troops. All four of the Army's black units, whose ranks came to be known as "**Buffalo Soldiers**" by the Indians, eventually served at McKavett, including the famous 9th and 10th Cavalries. Fourteen of the original 40 buildings have been restored, including the officers' quarters, barracks, hospital, school, bakery, and post headquarters. Seven other buildings lie in ruins, and the rest are gone. The hospital ward serves as a visitors center and contains interpretive exhibits explaining the natural and military history of the area. A nature trail leads to the old fort kiln and the Government Springs.

Junction

After passing through the attractively rugged but shallow canyonlands south of Menard—which make US-83 into a roller coaster of a road, by Texas standards—the two-lane road crosses high-speed I-10 at the aptly named town of Junction. Once a major crossing where the east–west Chihuahua Trail met a branch of the north–south Chisholm Trail (now I-10 and US-83 respectively), **Junction** (pop. 2,618) sits at the edge of Texas's famed Hill Country, where the Edwards Plateau crumbles into limestone canyons and cliffs along the Balcones Escarpment. As in the areas to the immediate north, wool and mohair production are the main means of local livelihood, supplemented by pecan farming.

From Junction, I-10 continues southeast to San Antonio, passing through the Hill Country town of Kerrville, which hosts the very popular **Kerrville Folk Festival** around Memorial Day. For information, call 830/257-3600 or 800/435-8429.

Places to eat line Main Street (US-83) through town—try Mexican places like **La Familia** (915/446-2688), at 1927 N. Main Street; or, in summer especially, the **Milky Way Drive Inn** (915/446-4683) at 1619 Main Street. Motels, including a nice Days Inn, congregate around the I-10/US-83 junction, a mile east of downtown.

To continue south along US-83, you can wind along Main Street or follow I-10 southeast for one exit, roughly two miles, to rejoin the old road. Another nice drive is along US-377, which traces a scenic route along the Llano River southwest of Junction, bisecting typical Edwards Plateau tableaus of limestone arroyos studded with mesquite, oak, prickly pear, and yucca. **South Llano River State Park** (325/446-3994), four miles southwest of Junction off US-377, protects 507 wooded acres and abundant wildlife (white-tailed deer, Rio Grande turkey, blue birds, finches, and javelina), and offers facilities for picnicking, camping, hiking, mountain-biking, canoeing, and swimming.

Leakey and the Frio Canyon

Below Junction, US-83 continues southward through 55 beautiful miles of rolling ranches and native pecan orchards, entering a verdant, spring-filled region that was one of the last strongholds of the Lipan Apaches and Comanches. The rolling hills around **Leakey** (pop. 420; LAY-key) hold limestone caves, some of which the Confederates mined for saltpeter—an essential ingredient of gunpowder—during the Civil War. At 1,600 feet above sea level, this is one of US-83's prettiest reaches through Texas, as the road follows the clear, cold Frio River through 17 miles of cypress, pecan, live oak, cedar, walnut, wild cherry, piñon, and mountain laurel. Some areas also have bigtooth maple and sycamore, a major tourist attraction in the late fall when the leaves change color.

You'll find a dozen or more camps and lodges—including tin-roofed, wooden-sided **Welcome Inn Motor Hotel** ($50 and up; 830/232-5246) on US-83 in the center of Leakey—between the highway and the river, which is popular for fishing and tubing.

East of Leakey, there's a wonderful drive into the Hill Country along Hwy-337 to **Lost Maples State Park,** north of Vanderpool. The road gets especially rugged (and popular with proto–Lance Armstrong cyclists) around Medina, midway to San Antonio. Back on US-83, heading south along the eponymous river, the hamlet of **Rio Frio** (pop. 50) boasts the largest live oak tree in Texas. The centuries-old tree stands alongside Hwy-1120 on the east side of the Frio River.

About 10 miles south of Rio Frio along US-83, the very pretty 1,420-acre **Garner State Park** (830/232-6132) offers campgrounds, cabins, hiking trails, canoe rentals, pedal boats, river swimming, and a popular summertime dance terrace on the banks of the Frio River. On summer weekends, the park reaches capacity early in the mornings, so to make the most of it get here as soon as you can or stay overnight. Just south of the park entrance, the **Frio Canyon Smoke Shack** (830/232-6605) serves up the "best burgers between Canada and Mexico," along with traditional Texas BBQ brisket.

Utopia

Fifteen miles east of Rio Frio via Hwy-1050, on the Sabinal River, is the town of **Utopia** ("This is Paradise—Keep it Nice," a sign says). Seven churches and a population of only 250 represent a legacy left by frontier circuit preachers who found this spot a heavenly place to hold camp meetings and save souls. Playing up the heavenly connections, Utopia's best place to eat is the **Garden of Eatin'** (830/966-3391), at 301 Main Street, serving simple, fresh sandwiches and a full range of breakfasts; there's also a pizza place.

> To get a taste of South Texas culture, tune in to "Tejano 102," **KUVA 102.3 FM**, for nonstop Tejano and traditional country-western tunes.

The **Sabinal Canyon Museum** (Sat. 10 AM–4 PM, Sun. 1–4 PM; 830/966-3747) down Main Street displays local arts and crafts, including antique handmade quilts, historic photos, farm implements, arrowheads, spurs, and other artifacts that outline Bandera County history.

Uvalde

Forty miles south of Leakey, US-83 crosses US-90 (the former San Antonio–El Paso Trail) at **Uvalde** (pop. 14,292), founded in 1855 and still centered around a broad square that originally served as a wagonyard for teamsters and travelers. Now a mostly Hispanic town, with a wide variety of buildings lining lushly verdant streets, Uvalde has seen its civic life migrate from downtown out toward the highway frontages. Uvalde was the home of a Western legend, the late, great celluloid cowgirl Dale Evans; and the town's most famous native son, John Nance "Cactus Jack" Garner, served as Franklin Delano Roosevelt's first- and second-term vice president (1933–41). After retiring from politics, Garner returned to Uvalde and lived here until his death in 1967 at age 98. His home at 333 N. Park is now owned by the University of Texas, and

> Five miles west of Uvalde on US-90, a large roadhouse-style dance hall called **The Purple Sage** (830/278-1006) offers two floors of bars, live country-western swing bands, and dance floors. It's open weekends only; minors are admitted.

contains the **John Nance Garner Museum** (closed Sun. and Mon.; 830/278-5018), a repository of memorabilia from Garner's political career. The 1891 **Grand Opera House,** on the square at 104 W. North Street, has been restored to a 390-seat live performance venue; it's open weekdays for free guided tours.

For good Mexican and American food or a cold drink (thick milk shakes a specialty), head to Uvalde's soda fountain, inside the **Rexall Drug Store** (830/278-2589) at 201 N. Getty Street. A number of motels line US-90 (Main Street) east of the town square, including the **Inn of Uvalde** ($40 and up; 830/278-4511), at 920 E. Main Street.

Detour: The Alamo

One of the great icons of the American Southwest, The Alamo sits about 70 miles east of US-83, at the center of the city of San Antonio. "Remember the Alamo!" was never a question, but a pledge of allegiance that inspired frontier-era Texans to fight and win their independence from Mexico. The significance of the Alamo varies depending upon how you look at it—some see at the first triumph of Yankee imperialism, others as a sad case of mighty, slave-holding southerners spreading their dominion—but from any angle, the story is quite compelling. The Alamo itself is a small Mexican church, which was built in 1724 and taken over in 1836 by a band of American mercenaries and soldiers led by Davy Crockett. They were besieged and eventually killed by the Mexican Army. Other Americans then defeated the Mexican Army and established the Republic of Texas, which briefly existed as an independent nation before joining the United States in 1845. The **Alamo church** (daily; free; 210/225-1391), right downtown at 300 Alamo Plaza, still stands much as it has for 160-odd years, and is a pilgrimage spot—one of the most visited sites in the country.

To soak it all up, stay the night at the historic **Menger Hotel** ($150 and up; 210/223-4361), across the street at 204 Alamo Plaza. The surrounding city of San Antonio is very attractive in its own right, with the lively River Walk winding through downtown, and numerous other sites and attractions. **Austin**, the Texas state capital, is just a way's up the road from "San Antone." Between San Antonio and US-83, the **Texas Hill Country** is perhaps the most beautiful part in the Lone Star State.

For more information, contact the San Antonio visitors bureau (800/447-3372).

South of Uvalde: Crystal City

As US-83 continues south from Uvalde, the highway descends farther onto the mostly flat Rio Grande Plain, entering a subtropical zone of seemingly endless chaparral. Amidst "brush country"—marked by a mixture of thorny cacti, mesquite, dwarf oak, black bush, and huisache—spread large irrigated farms known as the "Winter Garden of Texas" for the bounty of spinach and citrus crops they produce. Forty miles south of Uvalde sits **Crystal City** (pop. 7,190), the Zavala County seat and self-proclaimed "Spinach Capital of the World," where a photo-friendly statue of Popeye stands on the town square. Three miles south of Crystal City, the seasonal **Espantosa Lake** once served as an important water stop along the colonial mission trail between Mexico and Texas.

Laredo

Founded as the first non-missionary, nonmilitary Spanish settlement in North America in 1755, **Laredo** (pop. 176,576) is surrounded by some of the oldest ranch lands in the United States. With a population that is about 90 percent Hispanic, the city is growing rapidly (more than doubling in the past 20 years) due to its position as the largest international trade center along the U.S.–Mexico border. The I-35 corridor feels as anonymous and fast-paced as anywhere in the United States, but the center of town still holds on to its historic personality.

At the heart of downtown Laredo, a block north of the Rio Grande, is the **Villa de San Agustín Historical District,** site of the original 1755 Spanish settlement of Villa de San Agustín. Numerous historic buildings surround the plaza, including a small stone building next to La Posada Hotel that served as the capitol of the short-lived Republic of the Rio Grande. It now houses a **museum** (closed Mon.; $1;

Eighteen miles north of Laredo, US-83 merges with I-35, then crosses the Rio Grande to meet Mexico 85 (the Pan-American Highway), forming a continuous road between Canada and the Panama Canal, via Mexico and Central America.

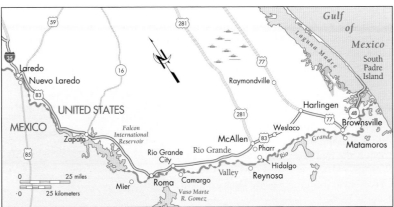

Zapata!

956/727-3480) containing a collection of memorabilia from the separatist movement of 1840.

Laredo and its Mexican neighbor, Nuevo Laredo, go crazy for several weeks in February and March in honor of George Washington's Birthday, a tradition dating back to 1898. The annual party now spawns an array of parades, pageants, street parties, balls, concerts, fireworks, a carnival, jalapeño-eating contest and even an air show.

For food, there's a good café and a more expensive Latin American restaurant, the Tack Room, inside the plaza's stately **La Posada Hotel** ($100 and up; 956/722-1701). On the old US-83 route, just west of the I-35 freeway, the timeless **La Reynera Bakery & Restaurant** (956/722-6641), at 1819 San Bernardo Avenue, has been serving breakfast tacos (here called "*margaritas*"), plus *pan dulce* (sweet pastries) and lunch specials since 1928.

Southeast from Laredo: Roma

South of Laredo, US-83 follows a route parallel to the Rio Grande that was originally cut through the dry chaparral by Gen. Zachary Taylor's soldiers during the 1846–48 Mexican-American War. The 1953 construction of 87,000-acre **Falcon International Reservoir** submerged the town of Zapata but provides hydroelectric power, flood control, and recreation along US-83.

The lower Rio Grande area is both the fastest-growing and most Hispanic area in the United States; Starr County, around Rio Grande City, has doubled in population in recent years, and is 98 percent self-described Hispanic.

US-83 continues southeast along the Rio Grande, passing through several Texas border towns held together by a common historical and cultural thread: All were settled by Spanish colonists in the mid-18th century as part of the famous José de Escandón land grant.

The surviving 19th-century Spanish- and Creole-style architecture in **Roma,** 40 miles southeast of Zapata, once the end of the line for steamboats sailing up the Rio Grande from the Gulf of Mexico, inspired director Elia Kazan to use the town as a film location for the 1952 movie *Viva Zapata!* starring Marlon Brando and Anthony Quinn. Many of the town's buildings have been quietly restored, but the town is *so* quiet you can sometimes hear roosters crowing across the river in the Mexican town of **Mier,** where the narrow sandstone streets, old churches, and plazas haven't changed in centuries.

Farther south along US-83 comes **Rio Grande City,** another former riverboat terminal. Among the historic buildings downtown is the renovated **LaBorde House** ($50; 956/487-5101), at 601 E. Main Street, a Creole-style inn designed by Parisian architects in 1899.

If it's fruit, you'll find it here.

Crossing the Border

At dozens of sleepy little towns across Southern California, Arizona, New Mexico, and Texas, the temptation to nip across the border and see something of our southern neighbor can be strong. It's only a hop and a skip away, and the crossing is usually simple and hassle-free, but in these days of Homeland Security it's good to know a few things about international customs—small "c" and big "C," before you go.

For years, all that a U.S. citizen needed to cross the border for 72 hours or less (and be re-admitted to the United States afterwards!) was some proof of citizenship. Often, you could get by with just a driver's license, or simply an American-looking face, but in this age of increased security new rules are being implemented. Effective January 1, 2008, all travelers returning from Mexico or Canada will need a valid, current passport to re-enter the United States.

If you're thinking of heading south to stock up on Mexican beers or a rug or other handicrafts, the NAFTA treaty did nothing to change what you can bring back: All merchandise is subject to a $400 duty-free limit, above which U.S. customs will charge a 10 percent duty based on fair retail value. Alcohol imports by individuals are limited to a whopping liter every 30 days—about two cans of beer—and it is illegal to import Mexican versions of trademarked items (perfumes, watches, even cans of Coke!) that are also sold in the United States. So don't risk having to leave something behind at the border—ask before you buy.

Because of insurance and other legal concerns, you should definitely leave your car on the United States side of the border and cross into Mexico on foot. Driving is not worth the hassle, especially with the long lines to cross back into the United States.

Rio Grande Valley

Southeast of Rio Grande City, the river and US-83 curve eastward toward the Gulf of Mexico through a broad delta region known as the **Rio Grande Valley**, despite the fact there are no nearby mountains to make it a true valley. Citrus orchards, interspersed with date palms planted as windbreaks, line the highway, while lush plantings of bougainvillea and poinsettias drape many of the houses in the string of towns that appear every few miles all the way to the Gulf. The population of the valley, which sits at the same latitude as the Florida Keys, swells with the arrival each winter of over 100,000 "Winter Texans" fleeing the colder midwestern states. This "snowbird" presence is highlighted by weekly square dance festivals and perhaps the nation's highest

The influx of "snowbirds" is perhaps most noticeable at the weekly open-air promenades held each Monday in McAllen, in the weeks leading up to the annual **Texas Square Dance Jamboree**. As many as 10,000 people take part, making McAllen the unofficial "Square Dance Capital of the World."

concentration of RV and mobile home parks. In McAllen, the westernmost, oldest, and largest of the valley towns, the **visitors bureau** (956/682-2871), at 1200 Ash Street, has information on the entire Rio Grande Valley region.

South of McAllen on the Mexican border, the town of Hidalgo has proclaimed itself the **"Killer Bee Capital of the USA"** and has a hundred-times-larger-than-life statue of one of these ferocious-looking critters, in front of the library at the center of town, to prove it.

The McAllen area's unique attraction is **Los Ebanos ferry,** the last hand-pulled ferry across the Rio Grande. To get there, drive west from McAllen on US-83 to Hwy-886 (between Havana and Sullivan City), then turn left (south) and follow the mazelike road until you hit the river. In service daily 7 AM–3 PM, the ferry can carry three cars and a small number of pedestrians on each crossing.

About eight miles southwest of McAllen via Hwy-374 (west) and Hwy-2062 (south), **Bentsen-Rio Grande Valley State Park** (956/585-1107) preserves 588 acres of Rio Grande riparian ash and elm woodlands and *matorral* (thorn scrub), adjacent to 1,700 acres of the riverside **Santa Ana National Wildlife Refuge.** The park is also home to the World Birding Center, which helps bird-watchers find their way around the dozen different wildlife refuges along the lower Rio Grande, where some 500 different species are regularly seen and heard.

Harlingen

For only the second time in its 2,000-mile journey from the Canadian border to the Gulf of Mexico, US-83 continues as a full-fledged, multi-lane freeway between McAllen and **Harlingen** (pop. 57,564). At the junction of US-83 and US-77 you'll find a **Texas Travel Information Center,** the best source of tourist information for this part of the state.

Harlingen's **Rio Grande Valley Historical Museum Complex** (closed Mon.; $2; 956/430-8500), three miles north of town at Boxwood and Raintree near the Harlingen airport, contains exhibits interpreting the history of the valley. At the private Marine Military Academy, next to the airport, the **Iwo Jima**

the original Iwo Jima Memorial sculpture

Memorial is the original sculpture (first made of plaster, now protected in fiberglass) from which the famous bronze statue of the flag-raising WW II Marines was made. There's also a small museum (Mon.–Fri.; donations; 800/365-6006) documenting the experience of Iwo Jima veterans.

Brownsville

South of Harlingen, US-83 merges with US-77 for the final 26 miles to **Brownsville,** where you may well feel like you've unknowingly crossed the border into Mexico. One of the most historic cities in Texas, Brownsville retains its Spanish and Mexican heritage more than most places, particularly in the architecture of the downtown district around **Elizabeth Street,** which runs northwest from the 24-hour border crossing at **Matamoros, Mexico.** U.S.-Mexico trade supports the local economy via a Union Pacific rail terminus connected with Mexico's national railway over the Rio Grande; also, a 17-mile deep-sea channel in the river delta links the city with the U.S. Inland Waterway System and the Gulf of Mexico.

Besides the historic downtown, another must-see is the well-endowed **Gladys Porter Zoo** (daily; $8.50; 956/546-2177) at Ringgold and 6th Streets, named by zoo professionals as one of the country's 10 best zoological facilities.

> **Raymondville**, 23 miles north of Harlingen via US-77, has been a boot-making center since at least the turn of the 20th century. Tom Mix, Ronald Reagan, and many more western heroes have had pairs made here.

For an authentic Tex-Mex meal, one of the popular places in town is **Los Camperos Char Chicken** (956/546-8172), at 1440 International Boulevard, open daily for lunch and dinner. The house specialty is smoked, charbroiled chicken served with corn tortillas and red and green salsas.

Sabal Palm Grove Sanctuary

The last remaining grove of endangered Sabal palms in the Rio Grande delta (they are the only palm tree native to the continental United States) is protected for future generations in the 527-acre **Sabal Palm Grove Sanctuary,** which is run by the National Audubon Society and located about five miles southeast of Brownsville. Bird-lovers flock here to catch a glimpse of the rare green jays, as well as the colorful parakeets and hummingbirds that make their homes in the dense jungle-like growth.

To reach the reserve from Brownsville, take Boca Chica Boulevard (Hwy-4) east, then turn right (south) on Hwy-3068. From the end of the road, turn right (west) on Hwy-1419 and follow the marked road to the sanctuary. The **visitors center** (daily; $5; 956/541-8034) has maps and natural history guides to the sanctuary, which is open from dawn to dusk.

South Padre Island

Twenty-six miles northeast of Brownsville via Hwy-48 and the Queen Isabella Causeway, **South Padre Island** provides a strong contrast to the sleepy, historic towns of the Rio Grande Valley. Only the southernmost five miles of this 30-mile Gulf of Mexico barrier island are developed; sand dunes and tidal marshes dominate the remainder.

In the developed zone, multi-story hotels and condominiums line white-sand beaches on both the Gulf and Laguna Madre sides of the island. Rooms are easy to come by except during the annual spring break (mid-March) when some 200,000 college kids from all over Texas and the Midwest fill the hotels and beaches with round-the-clock revelry. Drinking is legal on the beaches here; you have been warned. To dive in, try the **Padre Island Brewery** (956/761-9585), at 3400 Padre Boulevard, for great seafood, sports on TV, pool tables, and microbrews; another popular spot is **Louie's Backyard** (956/761-6406), at 2305 Laguna Boulevard, a bayside bar "as seen on MTV."

Call the helpful **South Padre Visitor and Convention Bureau** (956/761-6433 or 800/343-2368) for a listing of hotels, condos, and beach home properties.

THE GREAT RIVER ROAD

Old Man River, Father of Waters, "body of a nation," Big Muddy— by any name the mighty Mississippi River cuts a mythic figure across the American landscape.

Mississippi Headwaters
pg. 215

World's Largest Six-Pack
pg. 227

Mark Twain's Hometown
pg. 244

Elvis Presley's Graceland
pg. 261

Delta Blues Museum
pg. 263

Cajun Country
pg. 279

NORTH DAKOTA
Grand Forks
Bemidji
Duluth
MN
St. Cloud
Minneapolis
St. Paul
Green Bay
Oshkosh
Saginaw
WISCONS
Madison
Milwaukee
Lansing
Detr
Falls
Sioux City
Dubuque
Rockford
NE
SKA
IOWA
Cedar Rapids
Peoria
ILLINO
Omaha
Des Moines
Lincoln
Springfield
Chai
MISSOURI
Joseph
Spring
St. Louis
Evansvi
Kansas City
Jefferson City
SAS
Wichita
Springfield
Nashville
KLAHOMA
Smith
ARKANSAS
Chattanooga
Huntsville
Ardmore
Little Rock
emphis
TENNESSEE
Ashe
Pine Bluff
renada
Atla
Worth
Dalla
ackson
MISSISSIPPI
E
Waco
LOUISIANA
Lake Charles
Baton Rouge
M
A
Austin
Houston
ayette
New Orl
Cajun Country
pg. 279

Royal Street in New Orleans' French Quarter

475 mi
325 mi
425 mi
80 mi
360 mi
PAUL BUNYAN

Between Lake Itasca and the Gulf of Mexico

Old Man River, Father of Waters, "body of a nation," Big Muddy: By any name, the mighty Mississippi River cuts a mythic figure across the American landscape. Who hasn't read Mark Twain or listened to *Showboat* and not dreamt of a trip down the Mississippi? If you're tired of waiting for somebody to buy you passage aboard the *Delta Queen* or to help you paddle among the 1,500-ton barges, then do what Huck Finn would have done if he'd had a driver's license: Tag alongside the Mississippi on the Great River Road.

Created in 1938 from a network of federal, state, and local roads, the Great River Road—also known as the River Road, and commonly abbreviated to "GRR"—forms a single route along the Mississippi from head to toe. Designed to show off the 10 states bordering the Mississippi from its headwaters to its mouth, the GRR is nothing if not scenic, and anyone who equates the Midwest with the flat Kansas prairie will be pleasantly surprised. Sure, farms line the road, but so do upland meadows, cypress swamps, thick forests, limestone cliffs, and dozens of parks and wildlife refuges.

Of course it isn't all pretty. There's enough industry along the Mississippi for you to navigate the river by the flashing marker lights on smokestacks, and a half-dozen major cities compete with their bigger cousins on the coasts for widest suburban sprawl and ugliest roadside clutter. A pandemic of tacky strip malls has infected the region, too, but apart from the astounding growth in casinos (you'll never be more than 100 miles from a slot machine from one end of the Mississippi to the other) the GRR resists the developers' bulldozers because its meanders are shunned by a century increasingly drawn to the straight, fast, and four-lane.

A full 50 percent longer than the comparable route along the interstates, the GRR changes direction often, crosses the river whenever it can, dallies in towns every other road has forgotten, and altogether offers a perfect analog to floating downstream. If the road itself isn't your destination, *don't* take it. For those who do travel it, the GRR spares you the fleets of hurtling 40-ton trucks and that Interstate parade of franchised familiarity, and rewards you with twice the local color, flavor, and wildlife (two- and four-legged) found along any alternate route. Lest these tangibles be taken too much for granted, every so often the GRR will skip over to a freeway for a stretch to help you sort your preferences. Savor, and enjoy.

MINNESOTA

The Great River Road begins in **Lake Itasca State Park** and stair-steps along occasionally unpaved but well-graded backcountry roads through a mix of northern boreal forest, tree farms, and hayfields, all the while staying as close to its namesake as possible. By **Grand Rapids**, only 130 road miles from its source, the Mississippi has been transformed from a grassy brook barely deep enough to canoe to an industry-sustaining river fed by a half dozen of the state's 10,000 lakes. Farther south, the red and white pines, paper birch, and bigtooth aspen give way to more farms while the route breaks from the surveyor's section lines to curve with the river across the glacially flattened state. By **St. Cloud,** the GRR enters an increasingly developed corridor that culminates in the hugely sprawling Twin Cities of St. Paul and Minneapolis, south of which the road slips into rural Wisconsin.

If the rivers were being named today, the Mississippi River would flow into the Missouri River and not vice versa, since the Missouri is by far the longer of the two.

Lake Itasca State Park

The GRR begins here among the cattails and tall pines, in the park that protects the headwaters of the mighty Mississippi River. The small, clear brook tumbling out of the north end of Lake Itasca will eventually carry runoff from nearly two-thirds of the United States and enough silt to make the muddy plume at the river's mouth visible from space. But at its headwaters, 2,550-odd meandering miles from the Gulf of Mexico, you can not only wade across the Mississippi, you can see the bottom. Here, drinking the river water won't cause cancer—an increasingly rare claim, unfortunately.

*Throughout the upper Midwest, Friday night is the traditional night for a **fish fry**. Look for the backlit signboards or hand-lettered banners stuck out in front of the local VFW post or social club for a sample of the truly local variety.*

The Mississippi's humble beginnings were the object of chest-thumping adventurers and the subject of not-so-scholarly debate for decades before explorer Henry Rowe Schoolcraft, led by Ojibwa native Ozaawindib, determined this lake to be the true source of the nation's most legendary river in 1832. Schoolcraft's story, the tale of the battle to protect the park against logging, and lots of

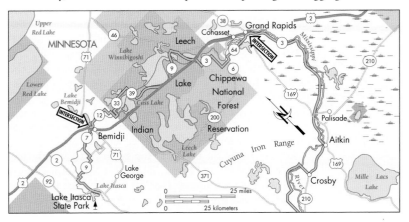

Navigating the Great River Road

The Great River Road (or GRR) is identified on signs by a green pilot's wheel with a steamboat pictured in the middle. Quality and quantity of route markers vary considerably from state to state: Some states, like Minnesota and Illinois, are well-marked, with advance warning of junctions and confirmation after turns, while other states, like Louisiana and Mississippi, seem committed to hiding GRR signs miles from where they would serve any conceivable good. Adding to the confusion are the many variations—signposted as "Alternate" or "State Route"—and spurs, denoted by a brown pilot's wheel, which lead off the GRR to various points of interest.

Though most people will be able to find their way along the riverside without too many dead-ends, trying to travel the length of the GRR just by following the signs is not recommended for perfectionists; part of the fun is getting slightly lost, and making your own way. To ease your journey, order a **detailed map** of the entire GRR, and a guide to local happenings in each of the states along the route, by sending $3 to the Mississippi River Parkway Commission, PO Box 59159, Minneapolis, MN 55459-8257, or call 763/212-2560. Their very helpful, ad-free website is www.mississippiriverinfo.com.

other Mississippi facts are found at the **interpretive center** just inside the park's north entrance (open year-round; $7 per car; 218/266-2114). Skeptics will also find out why professional geographers don't consider the two smaller lakes and the five creeks that feed Itasca competition for the headwaters title.

The fact that the lakeshore has been "improved" from its naturally marshy state, the surrounding old-growth pine forest—the most extensive stand of virgin timber left in the state—and outdoorsy amenities such as paved bike trails and boat launches all contribute to Itasca's popularity; rangers and bulletin boards at either entrance can explain what's going on when. Bike and boat rentals are available spring through fall opposite the park's headquarters. If you plan to camp, be sure to pack repellent for ticks and mosquitoes; other accommodations include the grand turn-of-the-century **Douglas Lodge,** where rooms cost $50–80 a night, and assorted lakeside cabins (all overnight reservations can be made at 800/246-2267).

Just steps from the bike path and beach you'll find the immaculate, friendly, and bargain-priced **HI Mississippi Headwaters Hostel** (year-round; 218/266-3415), which has rooms for families and couples as well as single travelers. When not

Explorer Henry Schoolcraft christened Lake Itasca with syllables from the Latin veritas caput, *meaning "true head." The native Ojibwa called it Omushkos, their word for elk, while the French trappers knew it as Lac La Biche, or Elk Lake. It's a local legend that if you make a wish while stepping over Lake Itasca's Mississippi River headwaters, your wish will come true when the waters reach the Gulf of Mexico—about three months later.*

fishing or foraging for your meals, consider the Douglas Lodge dining room, where the menu includes regional blueberries, wild rice, and walleye pike.

 Between Bemidji and Grand Rapids, the Great River Road follows a slower but more scenic parallel to transcontinental US-2 (see page 482). This **Great Northern** route across Minnesota is detailed on pages 446–528.

Bemidji

Less than a century ago, the northern forests of Minnesota were chock-full of lumber boom camps, with hundreds of mills and lumber works whining night and day, and dozens of saloons, brothels, and boardinghouses catering to the rough-and-tumble logging trade. The ravenous cutting wiped out the stands—virtually nothing remains of Minnesota's primeval pine forests—and the camps disappeared as quickly as they sprang up, but the woods have repeatedly grown back, to be harvested on a more sustainable basis while still providing an eye-pleasing backdrop to the region's literally thousands of lakes.

If you're practicing your **Lake Wobegon** language skills, be sure to say "You bet" in place of "You're welcome."

North Woods Public Radio broadcasts NPR news and other arts and cultural programming on a series of stations across northern Minnesota, including **KAXE 91.7 FM** in Grand Rapids.

From its boomtown roots, **Bemidji** (pop. 11,917) has long since settled down into a picturesque community—i.e., looking just as it did when Hubert Humphrey first ran for Congress—its compact and charismatic business district filling a half-dozen blocks along the south shore of lovely Lake Bemidji. With large mills still busily turning trees into wood products, Bemidji is a typically industrious lumber town, remarkable mainly for having assisted in the birth of that well-loved legendary duo of logging lore, Paul Bunyan and his blue ox, Babe (see sidebar "The Legends of Paul Bunyan").

The main course of US-2 wraps around downtown Bemidji, so be sure to follow the Business Loop (old US-2), which passes up and over both the Mississippi River and Lake Bemidji while winding to downtown and a park where the town's big tourist draw, leviathan statues of **Paul Bunyan** and **Babe the Blue Ox,** have stood along the lakefront since their construction in 1937.

Along with Paul and Babe, Bemidji offers endless opportunities for water-skiing, canoeing, fishing, ice-fishing, and autumnal leaf-peeping. It also has more than enough cafés to detain the most discerning road-tripper. Top of the list are the **Southside** (218/751-5110), part of Pete's Truck Stop at 3417 Washington Avenue, and the **Maid-Rite Diner** (218/444-7224), at 1602 Bemidji Avenue across from the lake near the information center. A classic diner, it's open from 7:30 AM for hearty meals

The Legends of Paul Bunyan

Like most other myths born on the American frontier, the legend of Paul Bunyan is obscured in the mists of time. The stories describing Paul's life—such as that when he was born it took five storks to deliver him and it took a whole herd of cows to keep him fed; that at just a week old he was big enough to wear his father's clothes; that he once bent a crowbar and used it as a safety pin to hold his pants together; that he was able to fell trees an acre at a time, and he used to whistle through a hollowed-out log—are impossible to trace, though their widespread popularity is due primarily to a public relations man at the Red River Lumber Company, William Laughead.

Beginning in 1914, and continuing for the next 20 years, Laughead and the lumber company, which was owned by the Walker family (founders of the Walker Art Center in Minneapolis), published a series of illustrated booklets recounting the stories already in general circulation around the logging camps. The booklets bore the full title: *The Marvelous Exploits of Paul Bunyan as Told in the Camps of the White Pine Lumberman for Generations, During Which Time the Loggers Have Pioneered the Way through the North Woods from Maine to California, Collected from Various Sources and Embellished for Publication.*

The first large statue of Paul and Babe was built in 1937 in Bemidji, where they now stand along the lake. Statues of Paul and Babe were later built in nearby Brainerd, Minnesota, and others can be found in logging towns from coast to coast, like Klamath, California, and Bangor, Maine.

and homemade rhubarb pies. For a nice lunch or dinner try **Union Station** (218/751-9261), in the old railroad building at 128 W. 1st Street, a bar and restaurant serving pastas, steaks, the ever-present walleye, and the best wild-rice salad around. For late-night dining, **Dave's Pizza** (218/751-3225) at 15th and Irvine is open till 11 PM, until midnight on weekends.

Walleye pike is a mild white fish sought by Midwest anglers from May through the cold of February. The walleye found in Minnesota restaurants all come from Red Lake, site of the only commercial walleye fishing allowed by law.

Bemidji's many motels include the family-oriented **Hampton Inn** ($50–70; 218/751-3600 or 800/776-3343), appropriately situated on the lake at 1015 Paul Bunyan Drive, with its own beach and complimentary canoes available to guests. For more info, stop by the recently remodeled **visitors center** (218/751-3541 or 800/458-2223), next to Paul and Babe on the lakeshore. Besides boasting a fireplace made with stones from every U.S. state (apart from Alaska and Hawaii, which weren't states when the fireplace was first built), the visitors center shares space with a small **museum** ($1.25) of taxidermied wildlife and odd historical items—including Paul Bunyan's ax and oversized underwear.

Bemidji to Grand Rapids: The Big Fish

Leaving downtown Bemidji along the edge of the lake, the GRR makes a series of backcountry loops past tree farms and at least 6 of the state's 10,000 lakes, crossing US-2 twice before snaking into Grand Rapids 100 miles later. The road hugs red pine- and aspen-wooded shores and crosses the ever-widening Mississippi eight times, while numerous signs point to unseen resorts, which in Minnesota don't offer luxury so much as proximity to good fishing. Fishing is serious business hereabouts, as is evident from the frequency of signs advertising Leeches-Minnows-Nightcrawlers.

If you're just passing through, one place to search out is about halfway along, in the hamlet of Bena. Right along US-2, a 65-foot-long tiger muskie, with a 14-foot-wide mouth, welcomes customers to the popular **Big Fish Supper Club** (218/665-2333). As seen in that classic Chevy Chase road-trip movie, *National Lampoon's Vacation,* the friendly café is open for three meals a day in summer, shorter hours the rest of year.

Big Fish Supper Club

Grand Rapids

Navigational headwaters of the Mississippi River, **Grand Rapids** (pop. 7,764) is a small Frank Capra–esque kind of place, known for its four large in-town lakes (there are over 1,000 in this part of the state) and a great bridge over the river. The town—which is proud of its recent rating as the "47th Best Small Town in America"—can be a bit confusing in its layout, but its compact size makes sightseeing manageable.

Grand Rapids is very proud of its most famous daughter, **Judy Garland**, and whoops it up every July with a festival in her honor.

The city sits along the western edge of the famed Mesabi Iron Range and includes viewing sites at a handful of **open pit mines.** The iron mines are a thing of the past, but Grand Rapids is still a major lumber town, and you can tour the impossible-to-miss **Blandin Paper Mill** (free; 218/327-6302). One of the world's largest paper producers, Blandin owns most of the surrounding forests and turns the trees into the stock onto which magazines like *Time* and *Sports Illustrated* are printed.

Three miles southwest of Grand Rapids, well-signed along the Great River Road and equidistant via US-169 or US-2, the fine **Forest History Center** (daily in

Cass Lake was home to Ka-Be-Nah-Gwey-Wence, whose Anglicized name was John Smith, a Chippewa who lived to be 129 years old. It is said he never slept in a bed. It may be unrelated, but the lake enjoys a reputation for having some of the most beautiful and serene camping in the state.

West of Grand Rapids, near Cohasset, a low ridge divides this area of Minnesota and distributes the rivers and streams into three watersheds: south to the Gulf of Mexico, north to the Hudson Bay, and east to the Great Lakes.

summer, weekends only rest of the year; $6; 218/327-4482) is a living-history replica of a 19th-century logging camp, complete with nature trails through the surrounding woods and energetic lumberjacks rolling logs and telling tall tales.

In the center of town, the **Itasca Heritage and Arts Center** ($4; 218/327-1843) is housed in a squat, three-story Victorian Romanesque-style grade-school building at the crossroads of US-2 and US-169. Here you'll find the county historical museum, with the usual "Main Street" of banks, stores, services, and pell-mell displays of farm equipment and logging gear.

Upstairs, however, is the real draw: the self-proclaimed **"World's Largest Collection of Judy Garland Memorabilia,"** she of ruby-slipper fame having been born in Grand Rapids on June 10, 1922. Truly a cradle-to-grave biographical assembly, the collection displays everything from her first crib to photos of her early performances as part of the Gumm Sisters, a family vaudeville group, to fading images of the London house where she died of an overdose of sleeping pills on June 22, 1969, and a final shot of her tomb in Hartsdale, New York. There are posters from most of her movies, and a copy of her costume from *The Wizard of Oz*, complete with ruby slippers. In front of the building, right along US-2, is a miniature "Yellow Brick Road" dedicated by some of the surviving "munchkins" who worked on the picture.

And if that's not enough, you can visit the house where she was born, which has been moved to a site south of downtown and restored as the **Judy Garland Museum** ($6; 218/327-9276), 2727 S. US-169.

The Grand Rapids **visitors center** (800/355-9740) is downtown at N.W. 3rd Street in the circa-1898 Great Northern Railroad depot.

Aitkin

South of Grand Rapids, the land rivals Kansas for flatness, yet the mix of farms and forest continues to lend visual interest to what could otherwise be achingly monotonous. The GRR alleviates boredom with its sinuous irregularity, the curves always hinting at the proximity of the Mississippi. For most of the way the river itself remains hidden, although regular signs for boat landings confirm its presence, and on occasion its broad channel and tree-lined banks roll into view.

Some of the best pies in the land of great pies can be had 20 miles north of Aitkin in the riverside town of Palisade (pop. 150), where the wonderful **Palisade Café** (218/845-2214) at 210 Main Street sells all sorts of fresh homemade pies.

For nearly 70 miles south of Grand Rapids you will have this rural road to yourself; then at the single stoplight in **Aitkin** (pop. 1,770), the GRR joins busy Hwy-210, at the edge of the mid-state lakes region. Aitkin is best known as the site of the annual **Fish House Parade,** in which ice fishermen show off their one-of-a-kind refuges from the winter cold; this unique event is held every year on the Friday following Thanksgiving. Year-round, Aitkin is a nice, all-American town, with a still-in-use 1930s movie palace (The Rialto, on Minnesota Avenue), and the very good **Aitkin Bakery**, at 14 NW 2nd Street.

Crosby

Watch your compass needle for signs of deflection as you proceed to the small but tidy town of **Crosby**, the center of Minnesota's "forgotten" iron range, the Cuyuna. The flood-prone mines have died out, but the surrounding landscape still bears evidence of mining's heyday, with lakes and hills created by subsidence and strip mining, and also by contemporary gravel quarrying. Crosby itself has a nice park fronting onto Serpent Lake, complete with a brightly colored Chinese dragon, while **Croft Mine Historical Park** (daily in summer; tour $3.50; 218/546-5466), well-posted on the edge of Crosby, profiles the iron-mining industry and an era, covering immigration and labor issues as well as the actual mining process. Machinery, period buildings, a gift shop, and a simulated underground tour round out the site's features.

South of Crosby, the GRR leaves the truck traffic and takes to the cornfields and sumac-laced forests again, passing as many barns as houses, the occasional lakeside hideaway, and some rural town halls; for a thumbnail overview of the area's settlement history, keep an eye peeled for the historical markers along the way.

> Between Grand Rapids and Brainerd, the official GRR takes a slow and somewhat scenic route along country lanes, though you'll save many hours (and not miss that much) by taking US-169 and Hwy-210.

Brainerd

At roughly the geographical center of the state, **Brainerd** (pop. 13,178) is a medium-sized Minnesota town that played a starring role in that offbeat Coen brothers movie, *Fargo*. The 4th of July in Brainerd is a big event, with marching bands, rock bands, and parades—plus a rubber duck race down the Mississippi River.

A huge Potlatch paper mill along the banks of the river notwithstanding, the economy of this part of the state benefits greatly from recreation. In Minnesota this means lakes: over 400 within a 50-mile radius, with over 150 resorts or campgrounds on their shores. Brainerd, the commercial center of it all, began life in 1871 when the Northern Pacific Railroad chose to cross the Mississippi River here. The rail yards are still in the heart of town beneath the giant water tower, which resembles a Las Vegas–style medieval castle. The historic downtown has

Twin Cities: Minneapolis and St. Paul

The Twin Cities share the Mississippi River, but have little else in common. In general, Minneapolis has fashion, culture, and reflective glass, while St. Paul has a greater small-town feel, more enjoyable baseball, and the state Capitol. Together, the Twin Cities are a typically sprawling American metropolis with an atypically wholesome reputation: safe, liberal-minded, welcoming to strangers, and inclined to go to bed early. Don't fret, there's enough to keep the visitor fully entertained.

The best place to stop and get a feel for the Twin Cities is at the **Minneapolis Sculpture Garden,** on Lyndale Avenue along I-94 (daily 6 AM–midnight; free). This is one of the city's finer urban oases, with over 40 works of art ranging from Henry Moore to Claes Oldenburg's Pop Art "Spoonbridge with Cherry." Running over the I-94 freeway, a sculptural footbridge adorned with words from a John Ashbery poem connects the sculpture garden to Loring Park and the pedestrian greenway to downtown (a roller blader's heaven). Next to the garden is the **Walker Art Center** (closed Mon.; $6; 612/375-7622), rightfully renowned as one of the nation's finest contemporary art museums, and an architectural marvel.

Across the Mississippi in St. Paul, the **Minnesota History Center** (closed Mon.; $8; 651/296-6126), off I-94 at 345 W. Kellogg Boulevard, will further convince you there's more to Minnesota than meets the eye. Start with the Tales of the Territory historical exhibit on the third floor, to ground yourself in the mid-19th century setting in which the state of Minnesota rapidly emerged out of a thickly forested Indian territory. There's also a truly interactive Music in Minnesota section, where you can record your own version of the Twin Cities' disco smash, "Funkytown," or dance in a re-created 1940s swing ballroom. Exhausting? Maybe. Worth it? You bet!

One advantage of visiting the Twin Cities: Baseball fans have a choice. The major-league **Minnesota Twins** play indoors at the **Hubert Humphrey Metrodome** ($5–25; 612/338-9467), off I-35W at the 3rd Street exit. The unaffiliated, independent, and generally anarchic **St. Paul Saints** play outdoors at usually sold-out **Midway Stadium** ($4–10; 651/644-3517), 1771 Energy Park Drive, north of I-94 at the Snelling Avenue exit. The fun-loving Saints fans cheer as freight trains rumble past the outfield fences, and take an inordinate amount of pleasure from the fact the team is sponsored by trash collection company WMI.

Practicalities

The Twin Cities are on opposite sides of the Mississippi River, at the crossing of the I-35 and I-94 freeways. Located seven miles south, the Minneapolis–St. Paul International Airport (MSP) is served by 10 major airlines, with Northwest Airlines exercising the home field advantage. Drivers here, like all Minnesotans, are friendly and helpful, and the city grids are easy enough to navigate by car, although on-street parking becomes more scarce as you approach the downtown areas. There are many parking garages (called "ramps"), and rates vary considerably.

Eating is perhaps the area where the Twin Cities really show off their multi-cultural vitality to best advantage. There are large Central American, Carribean, Somali, and Hmong populations here, and the traditional dominance of meaty northern and eastern European cuisine is being challenged by a bumper crop of new and different places to eat all over town. For a sample, head to **Chino Latino** (612/824-7878), 2916 S. Hennepin Avenue, where the "Sushi Loco" selections capture all the complexity and contradiction underlying the Twin Cities' calm surface. For a taste of old-style Minnesota, there's still **Nye's Polonaise Room** (612/379-2021), just over the bridge from downtown at 112 E. Hennepin Avenue, a dimly lit, plush-boothed, 1950s surf-and-turf restaurant with nightly sing-along Polka concerts. For another touch of the Twin Cities' past, nearby **Kramarczuk's Sausage** (612/379-3018), 215 E. Hennepin Avenue, has fat wursts and borscht, as well as *varenyky, nalesnyky,* and *holubets* (aka dumplings, crepes, and cabbage rolls), all served up cafeteria-style beneath coffered tin ceilings and the gaze of a giant Miss Liberty holding aloft her lamp.

Without doubt, the best road-food place is the decidedly ungentrified, 24-hour **Mickey's Dining Car** (651/222-5633), right in downtown St. Paul at 36 7th Street, opposite the bus station. Haute cuisine it ain't, and half the regulars treat it as a social service agency, but this 1937 O'Mahony is a fine example of what has become an endangered species since the proliferation of double arches.

If you're traveling on an expense account, downtown Minneapolis has the hotel for you: the sleek, modern **Le Meridien** ($199 and up; 800/543-4300), at 601 N. First Avenue. In St. Paul, the **St. Paul Hotel** ($160 and up; 651/292-9292 or 800/292-9292), at 350 Market Street, across from the beautiful Ordway Music Theatre, is a 1910 gem built for the city's rail and mill tycoons, and has a rooftop gym. For a unique stay, try the **Covington Inn** ($140–200; 651/292-1411), a tugboat B&B moored on the Mississippi opposite downtown St. Paul. Otherwise, look to the Interstate beltways for the national chains, particularly I-494 between the airport and Bloomington's 100-acre **Mall of America**, the nation's largest.

The **Greater Minneapolis Convention and Visitors Association**, 40 South 7th Street (612/661-4700), can provide complete information on hotels, restaurants, and attractions.

Cream of Wheat is one of the many cereals made in Minneapolis.

been badly "malled" by outlying shopping plazas, but among the discount merchandisers, pawn shops, and empty storefronts there are still a few points of light, such as the **Front Street Cafe** (218/ 828-1102), at 616 Front Street, across the tracks from that faux piece of Camelot. With free seconds on soups, mile-high meringue on the pies, and unbelievably low prices—plus a collection of commemorative plates to which words cannot do justice—the Front Street Cafe sets a hip standard for square meals.

West of the river, don't be put off by the unprepossessing location of the **West Side Cafe** (218/829-5561) at 801 W. Washington Street: the fact that it's in a gas station doesn't detract a whit from the fact that it serves some of the best pies for miles around, in a setting akin to an old Woolworth's lunch counter. From seasonal rhubarb to tangy cherry to unusual carrot, none is too sweet, and the superb flaky crusts are baked to a full golden brown—for a dollar and change, it doesn't get much better than this. Open daily 6 AM–10 PM, they serve unlimited cups of coffee for 75 cents an hour—with weekly rates available on request.

South of Little Falls, the GRR continues on its meandering way, but you can switch over to the uglier but much faster US-10 or I-94 freeways for the ride into the Twin Cities without missing anything significant.

East of downtown Brainerd, the Paul Bunyan statue seen in the movie Fargo has moved to a new home at **Paul Bunyan Land** (daily in summer; 218/764-2524) at 17553 Hwy-18, part of the 35-acre kid-friendly rural-history theme park called This Old Farm.

Many chain motels are clustered on Hwy-210 heading west out of Brainerd, while there's an **EconoLodge** and a **Holiday Inn** right on the GRR (Hwy-371) on the town's southern outskirts. The cheapest decent sleep in town is the aging **Riverview Motel** (218/829-8871), at 324 Washington Street, smack-dab in the tacky commercial stretch just west of the Mississippi crossing.

For a free vacation planner and complete guide to the area's family-oriented resort accommodations—or simply the latest local weather report—contact the Brainerd Lakes Area Chamber of Commerce's **information center** (800/450-2838), 124 N 6th Street.

Crow Wing State Park and Little Falls

South of Brainerd, the GRR speeds along Hwy-371, which yearns to be an Interstate for the 30-odd straight miles it takes to reach Little Falls. Exceedingly flat and awash in a sea of corn, it gives no hint of the Mississippi except at **Crow Wing State Park** ($5; 218/825-3075), with trails, picnic area, and camping beside the confluence of the Mississippi and Crow Wing Rivers. Native Americans, missionaries, fur-trappers, and lumberjacks made this a thriving and mostly inebriated 19th-century town, but the forced removal of the Indians

Charles Lindbergh

and the shift of trade to the rail crossing at Brainerd turned Crow Wing into a ghost town; only cellar holes and cemeteries remain around the old townsite.

At **Little Falls** the GRR neatly misses the fast food and gas claptrap that has sprung up on the Hwy-371 bypass, proceeding instead through the heart of town, which would probably still be recognizable to Charles Lindbergh, who spent his boyhood summers here. Running along the west bank of the river, the GRR passes by the **Charles A. Lindbergh House and History Center** (daily in summer, limited hours rest of the year; $6; 320/632-3154) a mile south of town. The house, which sits on a beautiful stretch of the Mississippi, bears the unusual distinction of having been restored with the meticulous guidance of the aviator himself. Lindy wanted the site to honor his father, a five-term U.S. congressman, as well as himself, and so it does. Exhibits also illustrate the junior Lindbergh's life and achievements after his historic solo flight across the Atlantic. There is little mention of Lindy's public admiration for Adolf Hitler, but the museum does display Lindy's 1959 VW Beetle, which he drove over 170,000 miles on 4 continents.

Driving the Twin Cities

South of Little Falls, agriculture continues to dominate the landscape, but as our route approaches the junction with I-94 at St. Cloud, the loss of farms foreshadows what is to come downriver. For nearly 100 miles, the GRR does its best to offer a scenic alternative, but sprouting subdivisions and suburban mini-malls make it hard to enjoy. I-94 parallels the GRR and the Mississippi River all the way through the heart of the Twin Cities, and for better or worse is pretty much the closest you'll get to a riverside highway; if you were hoping to follow the river through this stretch (by car, at least), you're out of luck.

WISCONSIN

Heading out of St. Paul along the industrialized Mississippi riverbanks, the GRR crosses the St. Croix River at Prescott, Wisconsin, and wends south on Hwy-35 across a portion of the glacial plain whose rolling hills, sown in corn, account for an important part of the nation's breadbasket. The fertile soil here, as throughout the Midwestern grain belt, is a product of drift: pulverized soil left by mile-thick ice sheets scouring the ancient sediments of an inland sea for about two million years. Farther south, however, the GRR enters a very different landscape, known as

Across the Mississippi from Monticello, 2.5 miles downstream from Elk River off US-10, the **Oliver H. Kelley Farm** preserves the 40 acres where the Patrons of Husbandry, an agricultural education and lobbying organization better known as The Grange, was founded in 1867.

The Burma-Vita Company, based just west of Minneapolis, began erecting advertising signs along Hwy-61 near Red Wing and Hwy-65 near Albert Lea back in 1925. Over the next 38 years, these signs and their witty rhymes appeared in nearly every state in the United States and made **Burma-Shave** one of the most recognized brand names in American business.

On the Minnesota side of the Mississippi River, US-61 runs as a very fast and fairly scenic freeway, four lanes wide with near-continuous river views almost all the way south to La Crosse, Wisconsin. One place along here worth a linger is the town of **Wabasha**, as seen in the Walter Matthau/Jack Lemmon film *Grumpy Old Men*. Another is **Lake City**, where banners and billboards proclaim it the "Birthplace of Water Skiing."

On an island near Red Wing, Minnesota, the **Prairie Island Nuclear Power Plant** is the northernmost of a half-dozen atomic-powered generating stations located along the Mississippi.

the **Driftless Region**, an area of limestone bluffs and rocky uplands bypassed by all that rototilling glaciation. Stretching south into Illinois, and covering an area four times the size of Connecticut, the Driftless Region affords dramatic views, wildlife habitat, and a setting for one of the more painful episodes in Native American history, the devastating Black Hawk War.

The GRR follows two-lane Hwy-35 from Prescott south for nearly 100 miles, staying within closer view of the Mississippi for longer stretches than almost anywhere else on the route.

Hwy-35: Main Street USA

At **Maiden Rock**, about 50 miles southeast of St. Paul, Hwy-35 enters the heart of the Driftless Region, picking its way between steep bluffs and the wide Mississippi. Small towns, populations numbering only in the hundreds, cling to the margin, competing for the distinction of having the longest Main Street in the nation, if not the world; for some of these long hamlets the GRR is nearly the *only* street. These towns wear their age well, too busy with fishing or loading up barges to make themselves pretty for tourists, or to tear down every old building that no longer seems useful. Most of these towns have at least a gas station, open late, and a roadhouse with Old Style or Pabst neon in the windows, open even later. Along with the riverside scenery, most also have a single tourist attraction: Amish crafts in **Stockholm,** a cheese factory in **Nelson,** and **Alma** has an observation platform and small café over Lock and Dam No. 4, where you can watch river traffic "lock through." In **Pepin**, midway between Maiden Rock and Alma (and roughly midway between Minneapolis and La Crosse), there's a replica of the log cabin where Laura Ingalls Wilder was born in 1867. Her first book, *Little House in the Big Woods,* was set here, though it's hard now to imagine that back then this was still the wild northwestern frontier (but it was); Pepin also has a small, summer-only museum dedicated to her. Also here in Pepin: the very popular **Harbor View Cafe** (715/442-3893) near the marina (surprise, surprise).

Trempealeau

At the sleepy hamlet of **Trempealeau** (pop. 1,319), the GRR would have you zig-zag right through town, but detour a block down toward the river's edge to find the **Historic Trempealeau Hotel, Restaurant & Saloon** ($50 and up; 608/534-6898), sole survivor of an 1888 downtown fire—maybe that's why the whole joint is smoke-free. The hotel dining room offers a surprisingly eclectic menu, from steak and seafood to Tex-Mex and vegetarian dishes; just head for the "Delicious Food" neon sign. The rooms are nice (and cheap!), and the hotel also

sponsors an excellent annual outdoor music series beginning with a Reggae Sunsplash the second weekend of May and featuring bands you've heard of throughout the summer (Steppenwolf and Asleep at the Wheel have appeared more than a few times). They rent canoes and bicycles to hardy souls desiring to try either the **Long Lake Canoe Trail** or the 100-mile network of **paved bikeways** that passes through town.

Shortly south of Trempealeau, the GRR crosses US-53. Consider taking this interstate-wannabe into La Crosse to avoid the uninteresting 12 miles of stop-and-go traffic through Holman and Onalaska, La Crosse's northern abutters.

La Crosse

La Crosse (pop. 51,818) was named by fur-traders who witnessed local Winnebago Indians playing the game. It's an attractive place, but you wouldn't know that coming into town from the north; thanks to the town's location astride the I-90 freeway, mile after mile of food-gas-lodging establishments compete for attention. Successfully run the gauntlet and your reward will be finding the century-old downtown, the tidy residential neighborhoods, and the leafy University of Wisconsin—La Crosse campus. Slap *Spartacus* on the theater marquee and the whole place could easily be mistaken for a giant Eisenhower-era time capsule.

The biggest sight to see in La Crosse is the **World's Largest Six-Pack,** right on the GRR on the south side of downtown. La Crosse–based Heileman was widely recognized around the upper Midwest for its "Old Style" brand beer, and its brewery was famous for its giant fermenta-

World's Largest Six-Pack at Heileman's Brewery

Six miles east of La Crosse, **West Salem** was the boyhood home of Pulitzer Prize—winning novelist **Hamlin Garland**, whose bittersweet stories of 1860s Wisconsin farm life have earned him a reputation as one of the finest American authors. His honest, social-realist books include the autobiographical *Son of the Middle Border* and an excellent collection of stories, *Main-Traveled Roads.*

tion tanks painted to look like the world's largest six-pack. Alas, a few years ago Heileman's brewery was bought out by Miller, which immediately whitewashed over what had long been a cherished local landmark. Then a local company took over the brewery, and brought back the big Six Pack, which when full holds enough beer to fill 7 *million* real-life six-packs.

The best overview of La Crosse is two miles east of downtown at the end of Main Street: **Grandad Bluff**, a lofty 590 feet over the city, gives a grand view of the Mississippi and the two states along its opposite shore. The view is a balm to any aesthete jangled by the commercial neon carpet that welcomes travelers, too, for La Crosse actually looks rather attractive from above. Listen closely and you might hear the University of Wisconsin marching band practicing below.

La Crosse Practicalities

La Crosse food tends toward the hearty and all-American: Heart-stopping omelettes, plus melt-in-your-mouth doughnuts so good they were featured on David Letterman, are on the menu at **Mr. D's** (608/784-6737), at 1146 State Street. For good ol' drive-in burgers, root beers, and milk shakes, nothing beats **Rudy's** (608/782-2200), northeast of downtown at 10th and La Crosse Streets, where roller-skating carhops feed you 10 AM–10 PM daily, March–October.

The Pearl (608/782-6655), a polished-to-perfection confectionery at 207 Pearl Street, offers such indulgences as fluorescent Blue Moon ice cream while the Andrews Sisters harmonize in the background. More grown-up pleasures, in the shape of some 200 bottled beers (or a dozen microbrews on draught), await you at the awesome **Bodega Brew Pub** (608/782-0677), right downtown at 122 S. 4th Street. Travelers seeking something wholesome, fresh, and filling should head to the deli of the **People's Food Co-op**, on 5th Avenue between Cass and King.

For accommodations, look to I-90 for the national chains, while local motels line Hwy-35/US-61 (the GRR, sometimes aka Mormon Coulee Road), such as the **Bluff View Inn** ($50 and up; 608/788-0600), 3715 Mormon Coulee Road.

For a complete lodging and attractions guide, with map, call the La Crosse Area Convention and Visitors Bureau (608/782-2366 or 800/658-9424) or visit their **information center** in leafy green Riverside Park, where a

Black Hawk War

One name recurs frequently as you travel along the northern Mississippi River: Black Hawk, who was leader of the Sauk and Mesquakie Indians of northern Illinois during the feverish era of American expansion into the newly opened Louisiana Purchase in the late 1820s. 19th-century Americans held frontier Indian fighters in high esteem: Consider that a number of U.S. Army officers sent against Black Hawk later became President, including William Henry Harrison, Zachary Taylor, Abraham Lincoln, Jefferson Davis, and Andrew Jackson. After Jackson rode his Indian-fighter reputation into the White House, Black Hawk and his people were forced to leave their rich Illinois cornfields as settlers and lead miners moved in.

In 1832, as newspapers around the United States demanded the extermination of any and all Indians, Black Hawk (who was around 65 years old at the time) moved back to Illinois to regain the tribe's lost lands along the Rock River. In response, Jackson sent in the army, and as Black Hawk and his 300 or so supporters tried to withdraw back across the Mississippi, soldiers and frontier militias attacked them at what became known as the **Battle of Bad Axe,** near the present town of Victory, midway between La Crosse and Prairie du Chien. When Black Hawk and his men came forward under a white flag, an Army gunboat opened fire on them while many of the Indian women and children who had succeeded in riding log rafts across the river were slaughtered on the other side. By various accounts, some 150 of Black Hawk's people were killed. Black Hawk himself was soon captured and imprisoned, then paraded around the United States in chains. After he died, his skeleton was displayed in the governor's mansion in Iowa, like a trophy.

25-ton, 25-foot-tall statue of Hiawatha greets river traffic with arms crossed and a politically incorrect plaque reading "Me Welcome You to Visitor Center."

Spring Green

Frank Lloyd Wright's famous country house and studio, **Taliesin** (tally-ESS-en), is in **Spring Green,** 70 miles east of Prairie du Chien via Hwy-60. Fully guided tours of the private residence and architecture school are offered daily May–October; ticket prices vary, depending on what's included in the tour ($15–75; 608/588-7900). Spring Green is also home to the state's biggest tourist trap, the incredible **House on the Rock** (daily; $20; 608/935-3639)

Between Minneapolis and La Crosse, Winona State University's **KQAL 89.5 FM** plays an excellent range of commercial-free pop, punk, and world beat music.

with its "World's Largest" merry-go-round, kitschy collections of everything from dolls to replicas of the Crown Jewels, and the eponymous house, standing atop a 450-foot-high rock.

Hwy-35

For most of the nearly 60 miles between La Crosse and Prairie du Chien, the GRR (Hwy-35) is again confined to the margin between the tall gray and yellow bluffs and the impressively wide, lake-like Mississippi. At times the roadway is so narrow that the few houses have to climb three stories up the irregular wooded slopes, while the railroad tracks on your right are suspended over the water on viaducts. About halfway along, there's a maze of small islands around the mouth of the Bad Ax River, with the occasional blue heron poised like a Giacometti sculpture in algae-covered sloughs. Dotting the curves alongside the road are a series of historical markers old enough to be artifacts themselves; most are related to the tragic **Black Hawk War** of 1832.

South of Prairie du Chien, across from McGregor, Iowa, is the spot where **Louis Joliet** and his Jesuit companion **Jacques Marquette**, after coming down the Wisconsin River in 1673 while searching for a route to the Orient, caught their first sight of what became known as the Mississippi River.

Midway along this scenic stretch of highway, 34 miles north of Prairie du Chien between the riverside hamlets of De Soto and Genoa, the **Great River Roadhouse** (608/ 648-2045) at 1006 Hwy-35 is a great place to stop and stretch your legs—and your stomach, feasting on the roast chickens, good pizza, tangy BBQ, and cold beers.

Prairie du Chien

Named by early 19th-century French voyagers, **Prairie du Chien** (duh-SHEEN) could be re-christened Prairie du Kwik-Stop or Prairie du Pabst by the modern traveler cruising along the GRR on downtown's West Blackhawk Avenue. The town's main attraction is the posh **Villa Louis** (daily May–Oct.; $8.50; 608/326-2721), which embodies the wealth that could be made in the fur trade back when every European dandy's head sported beaver-pelt hats. Built by the state's first millionaire, the house boasts one of the finest collections of domestic Victoriana in the country; signs point you here from all over town.

IOWA

In its 140-mile course across Iowa, the GRR passes swiftly but unmistakably across the cultural and geographic North-South Divide. Separated by the Mississippi River from the rough topography of Wisconsin's Driftless Region, the southeastern corner of Iowa offers instead a taste of the state's trademark rolling plains covered with corn and soybeans. Menus are different, too: Cattle here are raised for meat instead of milk, and Iowa is a leading producer of hogs (one of the state lottery games is called "Bring Home the Bacon," while radio ads encourage you to "eat more pork—the other white meat"). So say goodbye to walleye and hello to BBQ.

Running along the western bank of the Mississippi, our route tends to the tops of the bluffs, too, rather than to their base, which means the river is often spied from a distance and seems unrelated to the rolling landscape; fortunately it continues to guide the curves of the road. Other than Dubuque, our route passes through towns so far from the beaten path they don't even rate a fast-food strip or Wal-Mart—appreciate this while it lasts.

Marquette: Effigy Mounds National Monument

Immediately across, and effectively underneath, the long bridges over the Mississippi from Prairie du Chien, **Marquette** is a homey, work-a-day community that verges on quaint—so long as you manage to turn a blind eye to the garish pink elephant advertising its Isle of Capri Riverboat Casino complex. Unless you're a gambler, the main reason to visit is three miles north of Marquette, right along the riverbank: the **Effigy Mounds National Monument** ($5 per car; 563/873-3491), which preserves 2,500 acres of natural riverside ecosystems plus nearly 200 distinct burial mounds, many shaped like birds and animals. The unusual mounds are traces of the native people who lived along the Mississippi from around 500 BC to the time of first European contact; for more on these fascinating if little-known prehistoric Americans, see "The Mound Builders" sidebar. The visitors center has exhibits on the archaeology of the mounds, and a dozen miles of hiking trails reach from the river to restored vestiges of the native tallgrass prairie.

Forty-six miles west of McGregor is the Bohemian (as in Czechoslovakia, not bearded poets) town of **Spillville**, where **Antonin Dvorak** completed his symphony, From the New World, in 1893. The Main Street house (319/562-3569) where he stayed now leads a double life: Displays on Dvorak are upstairs, while downstairs is an incredible show of wooden clocks carved by the Bily brothers, depicting everything from the Twelve Apostles to Charles Lindbergh.

Effigy Mounds National Monument

McGregor

Just south of Marquette, near the foot of the "original" Pike's Peak—Zebulon Pike came up the Mississippi before he went out west to Colorado—**McGregor** is a river town whose enticing old saloons and storefronts are a fine reason to stop and stretch your legs, watching the boat and barge traffic or simply wandering along the water. The slogan of McGregor's tourism promotion effort is "Intriguing Stores on Historic Shores," and for once the copywriter prose is about right. A number of browsable antique-and-collectible shops line the GRR through the four-block main business district,

McGregor was the hometown of the five children who grew up to found the **Ringling** Brothers circus.

and right at the center of town is **Ringlings,** a very agreeable combo café-and-pub on the ground floor of the historic **Alexander Hotel** ($45–95; 563/873-3454) at 213 Main Street. McGregor also boasts about the only riverside hotel on the entire Great River Road: the family-friendly **Holiday Shores Motel** ($50–80; 563/873-3449) at the foot of Main Street.

Just south of town, the 500-foot-high limestone bluff known as Pike's Peak is one of the highest points anywhere along the Mississippi River, and has been protected at the center of spacious green **Pike's Peak State Park** (563/873-2341), with hiking trails, scenic viewpoints, and a campground with a small store, hot showers, and RV hookups.

Guttenberg

Atop the bluffs, tidy frame farmhouses dot the landscape, with white barns, silos, and farmland aroma accompanying US-18 and US-52 as they loop inland south toward **Guttenberg** (pop. 1,987), another postcard-pretty old river town whose downtown lines the Mississippi. In fact, it's one of the few Mississippi riverfronts where the river itself is not hidden away behind levees, and a long green riverside park, just a quick two blocks east of the main highway, makes the downtown area a particularly pleasant place to stroll.

Guttenberg is indeed named in honor of Johannes Gutenberg, 15th-century inventor of printing from moveable type. Local legend has it that an official of French descent purposely added the extra "t" after German residents won a vote to change the town's name from the original Prairie la Porte. Germanic surnames still predominate the local phone book, and the two main streets, which run perpendicular to the Mississippi, are named Schiller and Goethe.

On the north side of town, where the GRR takes an up-close look at the prairie's geological underpinnings as it cuts down to the river's edge, the first of Guttenberg's two Phillips 66 stations stands adjacent to the reliable **Rausch's Cafe** (563/252-2102). From the downtown area, it's a quick walk upriver to the concrete walls of Lock and Dam No. 10. Besides giving a sense of the massive engineering that attempts to tame the Mississippi, the locks are also home to an **aquarium** (daily in summer; free; 563/252-1156) that offers a quick biology lesson through displays of live specimens of many of the river's fish and invertebrate species.

There are great views to be had in the first few miles of Iowa's GRR route south of Guttenberg. About 10 well-signed miles south of Guttenberg, you can take the Cassville ferry (see below) across the Mississippi from Millville and visit the unique Dickeyville Grottoes, or stay on the Iowa side and cruise through the Germanic eyeblink towns that dot the rolling uplands between Guttenberg and Dubuque: Midway along, tiny **Balltown** in particular is worth a stop to sample the food and decor at **Breitbach's** (563/552-2220), a bar and restaurant that's so old President Millard Fillmore issued the permit allowing it to open.

Gutenberg is the finish line for the trans-Iowa **RAGBRAI,** a 500-mile, week-long mass bike ride that sees 10,000 cyclists cruising past the cornfields every July.

Dickeyville Grottoes

Across the river from Dubuque, the Wisconsin town of Dickeyville is home to one of the most interesting folk-art environments along the Mississippi: the **Dickeyville Grottoes** ($1 suggested donation; 608/568-3119). Started by Father Mathias Wernerus in 1920 as a memorial to three local boys killed in World War I, and worked on as a community project by his followers up through the 1960s, the Dickeyville Grottoes consist of a series of caves, alcoves, and shrines made of poured concrete almost completely covered in shells, shards, minerals, and costume jewelry. Along with the expected Catholic religious themes, parts of the Grottoes also exhibit a unique vein of patriotic Americana—highlighted by the "Patriotism in Stone" memorial to Christopher Columbus, George Washington, and Abraham Lincoln. Maintained as a public park, with almost no commercialization,

Dickeyville Grotto

the Grottoes are open 24 hours every day at 305 W. Main Street, adjacent to the Holy Ghost Catholic Church, a block west of US-61.

Dickeyville can be reached a number of ways. It's a quick shot north along US-151 from Dubuque, or from Prarie du Chien, you can follow scenic Hwy-133 along the east bank of the Mississippi. If it's summertime and you want an up-close look at the Mississippi, make your way to Cassville, a historic frontier town that holds one of the river's few surviving car ferries (daily 9 AM–9 PM, Memorial Day–Labor Day, weekends only in May and October; $10 per car; 608/725-5180 for 24-hour information).

Dubuque marks the junction of the Great River Road and our cross-country route US-20, **The Oregon Trail** (see page 576). This road trip is covered in full detail beginning on page 532.

Dubuque

At the southern end of a very enjoyable ride, cruising up and down sculpted hills and winding past miles of Iowa prairie and river towns, the GRR rolls into **Dubuque** (pop. 57,686), named for the 18th-century French voyageur Julien Dubuque, who unsuccessfully mined lead on land acquired from the Spanish. Finding lead wasn't the problem—Indians had dug lead by hand as early as 1680 for trade with the English—but getting it to market was. After the steamboat's invention and forced removal of native tribes in the late 1820s, mineral wealth became a major catalyst to settlement of the tri-state area around Dubuque, as town names like Potosi, Mineral Point, New Diggings, and Lead Mine attest. During the Civil War, just five counties around here supplied all the lead for the entire Union war effort.

On the inland side of the compact downtown, a grand view of the city and the Mississippi valley can be had from the top of the **Fenelon Place Elevator,** a historic funicular cable car that proudly holds the title of "world's steepest, shortest scenic railway" (daily April–Nov.; $1 each way). Still hauled up and down the hill by a 15-hp motor in the head house, the elevator is a mini version of those in Pittsburgh and the Swiss Alps. Hop on at the east end of 4th Street, and ride up to the plush residential district on the hilltop.

If you're looking for a hit of Deep Purple's "Smoke on the Water" to accompany you along the river, tune in to Dubuque's headbanging **KGRR 97.3 FM.**

On the other side of downtown, the Dubuque waterfront has been recharged by the **National Mississippi River Museum** (daily; $9.75; 563/557-9545), 350 E. 3rd Street, one of the two biggest and best museums dedicated to the history and culture of Old Muddy (the other one is on River Island in Memphis, see page 258). A large collection of historic riverboats is highlighted by the steamboat *William M. Black,* an official National Landmark, while other galleries include a National Rivers Hall of Fame that tells the stories of explorers and adventurers like Lewis and Clark and John Wesley Powell. The introductory film, *River of Dreams,* is narrated by Mr. Lake Wobegon himself, Garrison Keillor.

The ball field created for the movie Field of Dreams *has become a minor tourist mecca for rural* **Dyersville,** *30 miles due west of Dubuque via US-20. You can also reach Dyersville via the surprisingly scenic, gravel-paved* Heritage Trail, *which runs along an old railroad west from Dubuque.*

The museum complex is at the heart of the "America's River" complex, which also has docks for scenic sightseeing and gambling boats, a nice riverside promenade, plus the **Grand Harbor Resort** ($99 and up; 563/690-4000), a deluxe hotel and 25,000-square-foot water park right on the river. Also here is the main Dubuque **visitors center** (563/566-4372 or 800/798-8844).

Dubuque is a very meat-and-potatoes place when it comes to food, and as in most of the Midwest, you should plan to dine early to catch restaurants before they close. Basic coffee-shop breakfasts, lunches, and dinners are on the menu at **Dottie's Cafe** (563/556-9617), downtown at 5th and Central, while the landmark **Bridge** steakhouse (563/557-7280), on Main Street at the foot of the US-20 bridge (look for the neon "Good Food" sign), is a step or two up in price and quality. Near the Fenelon Place Elevator, the **Shot Tower Inn** (563/556-1061) at 390 Locust Street is a pizza place with an upstairs deck and beer by the pitcher.

A highly recommended 15-mile side trip is to **Galena,** *southeast of Dubuque via US-20. Spawned by the early 19th-century lead rush,* Galena *was the early social and cultural capital of the Upper Mississippi, and is now one of the best-preserved historic towns in the country.*

South of Dubuque, the GRR follows US-52 back up the bluffs past Julien Dubuque's original lead workings and across 45 miles of upland farms and wooded bottoms until the next Mississippi crossing at Sabula.

St. Donatus

Fifteen undulating agricultural miles south of Dubuque, the tiny hamlet of **St. Donatus** is widely advertised as a historic and picturesque Luxembourg village, mainly thanks to the handsome masonry of the **Gehlen House** (563/773-8200), a 150-year-old home now used as a restaurant and B&B. Other eye-catching structures are the Catholic church and **Pietà Chapel** atop the adjacent

Calvary Hill; if you wish to make a pilgrimage up the Way of the Cross, start behind the church burial ground, east of the Kalmes General Store. There's a nice view from the top—the other set of spires across the valley belongs to the German Lutheran St. John's Church.

Bellevue and Sabula

The GRR (US-52) returns to the Mississippi valley at **Bellevue**, with its lengthy Main Street and Riverfront Park beside Lock and Dam No. 12. Bellevue earns its name when you sit on the porch of the restored **Mont Rest B&B** ($135 and up; 563/872-4220), at 300 Spring Street, and take in the sweeping 270-degree panorama over the Mississippi. Continuing south, the GRR stays in sparsely populated wooded lowlands through **Sabula**, an island of a town created by the Corps of Engineers when the pool above Lock and Dam No. 13, 16 miles downstream, flooded out the surrounding plains. Sabula takes its name from the Latin sabulum, meaning "sand." The river here is nearly four miles wide. Sabula's encompassing levees provide fine wetlands bird-watching, especially for bald eagles.

From the end of November to the beginning of March, the **American bald eagle** nests along the middle and upper Mississippi. The best place to catch sight of one is below any of the dams, where turbulence keeps the river from icing over and fish injured or stunned by the dams make easy prey for the great bird.

ILLINOIS, IOWA, AND MISSOURI

The Great River Road route along the middle Mississippi starts in northwestern Illinois, at the southern edge of the Driftless Region, and proceeds through sandy floodplain and fertile prairie, nipping back and forth across the ever-locked and dammed Mississippi between Illinois, southern Iowa, and the generally more-developed Missouri uplands. Here, small towns bypassed by much of the 20th century are more likely to be forlorn than quaint, a prelude to those southern states in which local ordinances appear to require the public display of rusty appliances. With a few exceptions—such as the historic Mormon town of **Nauvoo** or Mark Twain's hometown of **Hannibal**—our route now mostly runs through communities whose best years may have passed. This stretch of the GRR also includes one of the most dramatic sections of the entire route: the 25 miles around **Grafton, Illinois**, at the northern doorstep of **St. Louis**.

South of St. Louis, I-55 is the recommended route, as it bypasses a long string of auto dealerships, appliance stores, shopping centers, and other prefab conveniences lining old US-61. Passing by the enticing old river town of **Sainte Genevieve**, the GRR crosses the Mississippi once again, ambling back to the corn, soybeans, and cicadas of Southern Illinois. Accents, "Bar-B-Q" signs, and Baptist churches leave no doubt that our route has entered the South; in summer the heat and humidity confirm this with a vengeance. Fortunately, after leaving the "American Bottom" the GRR skirts the edge of the **Shawnee National Forest**, whose shade brings up to 25° of relief from the temperatures

The names **Black Hawk, Marquette**, and **Joliet** continue to crop up along this stretch of the Mississippi River. South of the Quad Cities you'll see more of Abraham Lincoln, too, as the GRR shares the road with Illinois's **Lincoln Heritage Trail**.

along the roadside fields on a sunny July day. Occasional levees, raised roadbeds, and brackish seasonal ponds are reminders that the mile-wide Mississippi is only temporarily out of sight of the GRR, which finally crosses into Kentucky beside the giant turbid confluence of the Mississippi and Ohio Rivers at Cairo.

Savanna: Mississippi Palisades

Across the Mississippi from Iowa, **Savanna**, Illinois, is an old railroad town that has grown into an antiques center, offering three antique mini-malls along the main drag. Savanna maintains a few pretty Victorian mansions up on the heights, but for a truly attractive vista take a detour north along Hwy-84 from the end of the Iowa bridge to the 2,500-acre **Mississippi Palisades State Park** (815/273-2731), with its great eroded bluffs (popular with rock climbers), 13 miles of hiking trails (brilliant fall color in the forested ravines), and fine river views. There's camping, too, with hot showers and RV hookups.

Between Savanna and the I-80 beltway around the Quad Cities are nearly 50 flat miles of river valley, dotted with small historic river and railroad towns mixed in with new commercial and residential construction. Agriculture is conspicuous, too, and the sandy soils between Savanna and Thomson are particularly known for their melon crops. While the Mississippi for the

Thomson, 20 miles south of Savanna on Hwy-84, is the self-proclaimed Watermelon Capital of the World, and celebrates its **Melon Days festival** every Labor Day weekend. Country music, carnival rides, watermelon-eating contests, and free watermelon are the traditional highlights.

most part stays invisible from the GRR, the industry on its banks is clearly evident, especially at night. River access is at hand via a handful of **recreation areas** in the **Upper Mississippi National Fish and Wildlife Refuge.**

View of Mississippi River from Bluffs at SAVANNA ILL.
Publisher for A. O. Elliott, Savanna, Ill.

Le Claire, Iowa

On the northeastern edge of the Quad Cities, just off the I-80 freeway, lies the little town of **Le Claire** (pop. 2,734), famous once for its river pilots but now best remembered as William F. "Buffalo Bill" Cody's home. The **Buffalo Bill Museum** (daily in summer, weekends only the rest of the year; $2; 563/289-5580), on the waterfront at 200 N. River Drive, is dedicated to Cody's life.

The welcome sign for Le Claire alludes to a "famous green tree," a sight familiar in Mark Twain's day, but now long gone. The tree was the gathering point for the specialized "rapids pilots" who would guide boats through the 14-mile-long Moline Rapids that began below Le Claire.

The **Faithful Pilot** (563/289-4156), at 117 N. Cody Road on Le Claire's main street (US-67), is one of the best restaurants in the entire Quad Cities region, with creative, high-quality cuisine, a good wine list, and fine microbrews, all at prices you'd expect. The small bar at the back has views of the river, and the friendliest bartender along its banks.

The Amana Colonies

Some 80 miles west of the Quad Cities via I-80, the Amana Colonies were a utopian agricultural community established by German immigrants in the 1850s. Many of the original homes, churches, barns, and communal kitchen buildings still stand in a series of small villages sprinkled around the original 20,000-acre site. The community ended its collective economy in the 1930s, and is now a bevy of private enterprise (one of which developed the Amana brand of home appliances and in 1967 introduced the Radarange, the first domestic microwave oven).

Though attracting and catering to tourists is now the major industry, most of the 1,700-or-so Amana residents are descended from the original utopian colonists, and Amana communities still share a rather austere religious approach to life. However, as in the better-known Amish communities of the Pennsylvania Dutch Country, the Amana Colonies have become best known for hearty, family-style German meals (all the sauerkraut and strudel you can eat!), served up at shared tables in restaurants like the **Colony Inn** (319/622-6270) at 741 47th Avenue. Aficionados of German-style beers should keep an eye out for local products of the Millstream Brewing Company,

In **Walcott**, 15 miles west of Le Claire along I-80, the **World's Largest Truck Stop** (563/284-6961) is now home to the Trucking Hall of Fame, displaying 20,000 square feet of big rigs and mementoes of the men and women who drive them.

brewed in Amana and available both at the Old Colony and many other fine establishments.

The Quad Cities

Straddling the Mississippi at its confluence with the Rock River, the **Quad Cities**—Moline and Rock Island, Illinois, and Davenport and Bettendorf, Iowa—encompass an enormous sprawl of some 400,000 residents. While much of the cityscape is dominated by heavy industry, particularly on the Iowa side, points of interest are sprinkled throughout.

Along the river at the heart of the Quad Cities, adjacent to downtown Rock Island, is the former namesake of that city, now called Arsenal Island for the U.S. Army facility based there. Despite the look of the gatehouse at the southern entrance, the island is open to the public; besides an arsenal museum and Civil War cemeteries, there's a very good **Corps of Engineers visitors center** (daily; free) on the island right next to Lock and Dam No. 15, where the operation of the locks can be seen from a penny-pitch away.

The first railroad bridge over the Mississippi linked Rock Island and Davenport in 1856. The railroad was promptly sued by a steamboat company whose craft was mortally attracted to the bridge piers. The plaintiffs argued that bridges violated their navigation rights; the defense lawyer's elegantly simple—and successful—rebuttal was to claim that a person has as much right to cross a river as to travel upon it. That lawyer was Abraham Lincoln. Today the railroad crosses the river on the upper deck of the old iron Government Bridge, which swings open for the tows entering the locks; cars crossing between Rock Island and Davenport can ride the humming lower deck for free or take the modern concrete highway span below the dam for a 50-cent toll.

The **Davenport Museum of Art** (closed Mon.; 563/326-7804), at 1737 W. 12th Street, has a good regional collection featuring Thomas Hart Benton and Grant Wood, along with parodies of Wood's most famous painting, *American Gothic.* Davenport is also home to the new **River Music Experience** (daily; $4; 563/326-1333), 131 W. 2nd Street, an interactive museum exploring the many different sorts of music that have grown up along the Missisippi River. Frequent, free live concerts are held on the plaza outside.

Davenport celebrates the music legacy of native son and cornetist Leon Beiderbecke with the annual **Bix Beiderbecke Memorial Jazz Festival,** held at the end of July. A statue of Bix stands along the river, next to wonderful old (circa 1930) John O'Donnell Stadium, where the minor-league **Quad Cities River Bandits** (tickets $3–6; 319/324-2032) play their home games. (Unless, of course, the Mississippi is flooding as it did in 2001, when the stadium spent the month of May underwater).

coronetist Leon Beiderbecke

Quad Cities Practicalities

In downtown Davenport, which is the only large Mississippi River city not cut off from Ol' Muddy by a flood wall, look to Harrison and Brady Avenues within the first few blocks of both the casino landing and convention center to find several eateries and **Theo's Java Hut** (563/323-5282), 221 Brady Street. Off I-80 exit 292, the **Iowa Machine Shed Restaurant** (563/391-2427), at 7250 Northwest Boulevard, draws families from near and far for its huge portions of roast pork and other Midwest faves.

Downtown Moline is but a half-dozen blocks along 5th Avenue between I-74 and 14th Street; among its offerings are **Le Mekong** (309/797-3709) at 1606 5th Avenue, the **Cafe Piccalo** (309/764-3459) at 421 14th Street, and for re- plenishing your backseat car buffet, **Heritage Natural Foods** up at 1317 6th Avenue near 14th Street. Also in downtown Moline is the extraordinary **Lagomarcino's** (309/764-1814), at 1422 5th Avenue, a soda fountain that still uses those conical paper cups in solid metal holders and serves drinks like "phosphates" in a setting virtually un- changed since it opened in 1908. Order a strawberry shake here and the flavor will come from scoops of real strawber- ries ladled over freshly made vanilla ice cream.

The headquarters of tractor manufacturers **Deere & Company** is located on a rural stretch of John Deere Road (Hwy-5) in southeast **Moline**.

Rock Island's old downtown, 2nd Avenue, has experienced something of a revival with the appearance of a riverboat casino a block away; one pleasant result is "the District," centered around the 2nd Avenue pedestrian

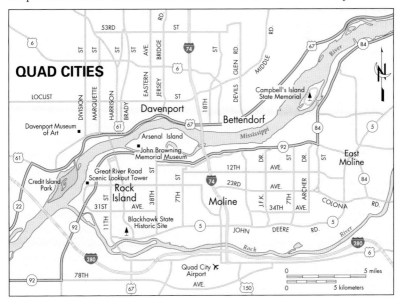

mall. At 1806 2nd Avenue is **All Kinds of People Espresso Bar & Bookshop** (309/788-2567), serving fine yuppie sandwiches, soup, baked goods, and beverages (including microbrews), at not-so-yuppie prices; travelers may feel like they've found a magic doorway back to the Beat Generation when they see the book and journal selection in the back. Neighbors include the **Blue Cat Brew Pub** (309/788-8247), around the corner at 113 18th Street, with salads, seafood, and desserts that go way beyond your average pub fare and beers that range from traditional to an esoteric orange coriander concoction.

For a truly regional diner experience, make your way to a **Maid-Rite Cafe;** there's one in Moline at 2036 16th Street (309/764-1196). A strictly upper-Midwest phenomenon whose faded logo, "Since 1926," can often be seen on old brick buildings or historic commercial storefronts up through Minnesota, the local Maid-Rites are unusually bright and polished, and come heartily recommended.

All the major chain **motels** are in the Quad Cities. Besides the familiar spots, the Quad Cities also has one of the most unusual places to stay in the Midwest: the **Abbey Hotel** ($99–165; 319/355-0291 or 800/438-7535), at 1401 Central Avenue in Bettendorf. Housed in a recently converted, circa-1917 Carmelite nunnery on a bluff overlooking the river, the hotel offers a full range of comforts while preserving the serenity of its original incarnation. (The chapel survives and is used for weddings, and one of the original cell-like rooms is kept as a mini-museum, complete with a nun's habit and straw-filled mattress.)

If you want more information, there are two **Welcome Centers** nearby (one on I-80 eastbound, the other on I-80 westbound); contact the Quad Cities **visitors bureau** (800/747-7800), or pick up a free copy of the monthly *River Cities Reader.*

Through the Yellow Banks

For nearly 100 miles south of the Quad Cities, the GRR picks its way along a series of back roads through Illinois floodplain and prairie, most of which is under cultivation. Frequent small towns serve as reminders of the need for frequent stops by early stages, steamboats, and railroads. Most of the towns seem not to have changed much since the last steamboat or train whistle blew, although now there's neon in the bars, vinyl and aluminum siding on the houses, and farmers with high-powered four-by-fours on the roads. All the big towns sit on the opposite side of the Mississippi, a product of the enormous 19th-century expansion of the American frontier. On the west bank were all the embarkation points for settlers heading across the great prairie and Plains trails—the Oregon, the Mormon, the Santa Fe—so it was around those places that supply towns grew. Illinois could only sit and watch.

Nearly 45 miles south of the Quad Cities beltway, the GRR passes tiny **New Boston,** at the mouth of the Iowa River. The town is a historical footnote these days, having been surveyed by the young Abraham Lincoln after his stint in the army—a tour of duty during which his only combat was against mosquitoes, he later recalled.

Steamer G.W. Hill landing at Burlington Iowa c. 1900

Along the river farther south, near **Keithsburg,** a sign welcomes travelers to **Yellow Bank country,** named for the deep layer of sand exposed in the river valley in this region. Because of this deposit, visitors can find sandburs and even cactus in the Big River State Forest south of town. Keithsburg used to be one of a number of button manufacturing centers located along the middle Mississippi: Freshwater clams were dredged from the river bottom and their shells were used for making pearl buttons. Clamming is still the commercial occupation of a few hardy divers, although now the shells are almost exclusively used for "pearl seed," the sand-sized implant injected into commercial pearl oysters in the Pacific.

Burlington and Niota

Across the Mississippi River via an austere modern suspension bridge, **Burlington** was the frontier capital of Iowa, founded in 1808 and holding many Victorian homes and commercial buildings. Awarded the "Great American Main Street" status from the National Trust for Historic Preservation in 2004, Burlington also has a riverboat casino, a great Maid-Rite diner (112 W. Division Street), and very busy downtown rail yards—home base of the Burlington Northern Santa Fe (BNSF) railroad conglomerate.

At **Niota,** the ghost of a town that marks the next crossing south of Burlington, a nifty old double-decker swing bridge (trains below, cars on top) crosses the Mississippi, landing on the west bank next to a huge old state prison at the historic town of Fort Madison.

Nauvoo

Founded in 1839 by the Church of Jesus Christ of Latter-day Saints (LDS), the town of **Nauvoo**—a Hebrew-sounding word its founding father was told meant "the beautiful location"—was named by Mormon leader Joseph Smith, 12 years after he received the Book of Mormon from the Angel Moroni. Smith and many of his followers had spent the previous winter jailed in Liberty, Missouri, and by 1846 they were effectively exiled to Utah, but for a few years Nauvoo was among the largest settlements on the western frontier, with hundreds of log cabins and brick buildings and a population of some 6,000 Mormon believers. After 150 years of relative peace and quiet, in the 1990s the Mormon church started a massive, $30-million program of historic preservation, turning Nauvoo into

In **Oquawka, Illinois,** 10 miles northeast of Burlington, Iowa, a roadside marker points out the spot where in 1971 a circus elephant (named **Norma Jean Elephant!**) was killed by lightning.

Mormons in Illinois

If you're passing through Nauvoo, you'll have plenty of opportunities to learn about Mormon history and religion. Nauvoo is Mecca for Mormons, or "Latter-day Saints" (LDS), as church members prefer to call themselves. In 1839, a dozen years after receiving their new gospel via the Angel Moroni, the Mormons purchased a large tract of swampy land along the Mississippi River, then set about draining swamps and building a city. Within a few years, Nauvoo was not only the largest LDS settlement in America, but the 10th-largest city in the United States. The emergence of such a powerful little theocracy (with its own well-armed militia) generated resentment among outnumbered neighbors, and even some internal dissent. The friction escalated to violence on both sides, finally culminating in the 1844 arrest of Joseph Smith Jr., church founder and president, for having sanctioned the destruction of printing presses used by some church members to question his leadership. While in the nearby Carthage jail, Smith was lynched by a mob and so became one of the Mormons' first martyrs. Amid ensuing disputes over church succession and renewed hostilities with non-Mormon neighbors, most residents followed Brigham Young across the Mississippi on the famous exodus to Salt Lake City.

Given Smith's martyrdom, the fact that he's buried here, and the Brigham Young migration's roots in the town, it's little wonder that Nauvoo attracts Mormon pilgrims by the busload. The Utah-based LDS have sponsored a massive restoration of old Nauvoo buildings, and the town now ranks as one of the capitals of historic preservation in the United States. Most of old Nauvoo is operated essentially as a big museum, totally free and open to the non-LDS public.

a top destination for Mormon pilgrims and retirees. The "restoration" of Mormon Nauvoo, and the influx of well-heeled Mormon immigrants, has been on such a big scale that many non-Mormons have felt under siege. Visitors to Nauvoo will certainly have plenty of opportunities to learn about Mormon history and religion, but for the moment at least the part-preserved, part-restored townscape has a broad interest as a mostly non-commercialized reminder of what frontier America looked like in the years before the Wild West was finally "won."

The biggest change in Nauvoo has been the reconstruction of the original Mormon **temple**, which, from the time it was finished in 1846 until it was burned down in 1848, was the largest building west of Philadelphia. An exact replica of the original, the new temple took more than 3 years to complete, and was dedicated in 2002. The temple, located at 50 Wells Street, has a remarkable series of stone capitals carved with sunburst motifs, and a 165-foot-high steeple capped by a statue of the Angel Moroni. Other interesting Mormon-related sites include the store run by Joseph Smith, and the home of Brigham Young. The home and workshop of Jonathon Browning, inventor of the repeating rifle, has been restored along Main Street, south of the present downtown area. There's also a massive **outdoor pageant** (8 PM Tues.–Sat.; free; 800/453-3860) every July; recent ones have celebrated the 200th birthday of LDS founder Joseph Smith.

Nauvoo Practicalities

For a map of the town and visitor information, stop by the huge **LDS Visitors Center** (daily; free; 888/453-6434), at the north end of Main Street. The town operates its own info center, too: the **Nauvoo Chamber of Commerce** (217/453-6648), at 1295 Mulholland Street, opposite the historic Hotel Nauvoo.

The annual **Nauvoo Grape Festival,** held each Labor Day weekend, celebrates the wine business that arose after European immigrants moved onto farms abandoned by the Mormon exodus; the town also acquired a blue-cheese industry in the 1920s, after Prohibition shut down the wine-making trade. The centerpiece of the festival is a combination custom car show and the "Wedding of the Wine and Cheese," a medieval-style pageant borrowed from Roquefort, France.

Restaurants and lodgings are clustered along Mulholland Street (Hwy-96, aka the GRR) within the few blocks of downtown Nauvoo. For picnic supplies, try the **Nauvoo Mill and Bakery** (217/453-6734) at 1530 Mulholland Street near the Shell station. For fried chicken, cold beers, or a Friday night fish fry, try the **Draft House** (217/453-6752) at 1360 Mulholland Street. The circa-1840s **Hotel Nauvoo** (217/453-2211), at 1290 Mulholland Street, is particularly well-regarded for its belt-straining buffets, and is also the town's most characterful place to stay (rooms run $49–99).

Warsaw

For a scenic dozen miles south of Nauvoo, the GRR returns after long absence to the banks of the Mississippi, shaded by native hickory and oak, and then sidesteps yet another opportunity to enter Iowa, this time via US-136 west to Keokuk. Staying on the east bank, we follow a series of farm roads past gravel pits and fields for most of the 40-mile run down to Quincy.

Warsaw lends its name to a variety of geode found locally in profusion; inside, **Warsaw geodes** grow calcite crystals. Across the Mississippi, **Keokuk geodes** grow quartzite crystals inside their stony spheres.

First stop south of Nauvoo is what used to be the town of **Warsaw.** Patrons of the bars along the main drag probably think it still *is* Warsaw, but blocks of empty windows and shuttered doorways tell a different story. At the end of town the GRR threatens to turn amphibious as it rolls down past a towering grain elevator to the Mississippi's edge, bends south along the base of the bluffs past old house trailers, scruffy fields full of wildlife—including wild turkeys and river turtles waddling along the roadside—and old kilns visible in the limestone, and passes, finally, into cornfields planted in the fertile floodplain of the river.

Quincy

Midway between the Quad Cities and St. Louis, **Quincy** (pop. 40,366) is a modest-sized city, Germanic enough in its heritage to consider Pizza Hut an ethnic restaurant. A bastion of abolitionists before the Civil War, Quincy was also home to anti-abolitionist Stephen Douglas, the incumbent Illinois senator whose campaign debates with Abraham Lincoln put that tall country lawyer on the path to the White House.

Drop the top on your convertible and maybe you can land yourself a travel companion during the **World Free Fall**, an annual skydiving event that fills Quincy's skies with thousands of jumpers from all over the planet. Held at Baldwin Field between the first two weekends in August, the Free Fall is the legacy of one Thomas Baldwin, whose pioneering parachute jump from a balloon into a Quincy park in 1887 earned him two world exhibition tours.

The GRR follows the riverfront and again the pilot's wheel is missing, but the giant span of the Bayview bridge over the Mississippi will leave no doubt as to which way to turn to stay on track. However, most of the city perches on the tall bluffs above the GRR and is worth a drive-through, if only to sample its textbook variety of residential architecture. Check out the **Gardner Museum of Architecture and Design** (Wed.–Sat. 1–5 PM; $2; 217/224-6873), in the old public library downtown on Maine and 4th, for an overview of both those topics. Then take a walk or drive through the East End, an area roughly bounded by Maine and State Streets between 16th and 24th. Filled with historic mansions along quiet tree-canopied streets, it's the perfect place to practice distinguishing your Queen Anne from Tudor, and your Prairie Style from Gothic Revival.

If you have thus far avoided the tried-and-true cooking of the **Maid-Rite** chain, Quincy gives you a chance to fix this oversight: There's one at 507 N. 12th Street (217/222-7527). For something even more strictly local and down-home, slide back down to the waterfront under the bridge for some fried fresh fish at the **Sky Ride Inn** (217/222-9703) on Front Street, marked by a multi-colored neon sign.

If you plan to spend the night, you'll find the national chains downtown out on Broadway near I-172. If you prefer antiques to HBO in your room, try the **Kaufmann House** ($45–65; 217/223-2502), in the heart of the historic mansions at 1641 Hampshire Street.

For more information, call or drop by their tourist information center in the **Villa Kathrine** (800/978-4748), that hard-to-miss, turn-of-the-20th-century Moorish residence on the bluffs overlooking the Mississippi, just south of the US-24 bridge.

Hannibal

It doesn't take a literature professor to figure out who **Hannibal's** most famous resident was: His name prefaces half the signs in town, and the names of his characters preface the other half. Cross the Mississippi River on the I-72 Mark

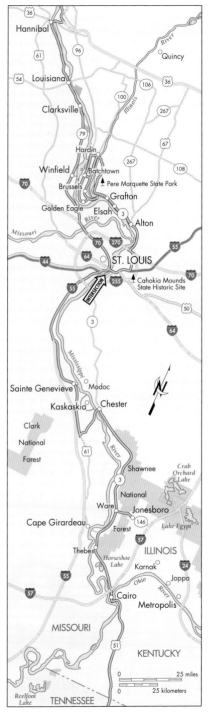

Twain Memorial Bridge, shop at the Huck Finn Mall or swim at Mark Twain Lake, then spend the night at Injun Joe's Campground or the Tom N' Huck Motel. Turn onto 3rd Street (the Great River Road) near the Hotel Clemens and park yourself in the heart of historic old Hannibal, and visit the Mark Twain Home and Mark Twain Museum. Take a very expensive ride on the almost miniature *Mark Twain* riverboat, docked at the Center Street Landing; browse through books by and about Twain at the Becky Thatcher Bookshop; or eat Mark Twain Fried Chicken at the Mark Twain Dinette. Not to detract from the credit due him, but don't look for any subtlety or modesty surrounding Mark Twain's achievements here.

Most of this Twainery is located downtown, within a few blocks of the Mississippi River, and enjoyment requires at least a passing familiarity with (and fondness for) *Tom Sawyer,* Twain's fictionalized memoir of his boyhood here. A statue of Tom and Huck stands at the foot of Cardiff Hill, and two blocks south, the white picket fence featured in that book still stands in front of the **Mark Twain Boyhood Home** (daily; $6; 573/221-9010), at 208 Hill Street, where young Samuel Clemens (Twain's real name) grew up in the 1840s. The historic site preserves a half dozen buildings, including his father's law offices and the drug store above which the Clemens family also lived. The home of Tom Sawyer's "girl next door," Becky Thatcher, is actually across the street, and the upstairs parlor and bedrooms have been recreated to evoke the era. The main

The Twain mania is so overwhelming that little is made of Hannibal's other famous sons. Baseball lovers searching for some mention of Joseph Jefferson "Shoeless Joe" Jackson will look in vain; there is none. Neither is there much mention of Bill Lear, inventor of the car radio and the Lear jet, who was born here in 1902.

Mark Twain Museum recently moved into a much larger space in an ornate Victorian building two blocks away at 415 N. Main Street, but is still part of the same operation. Exhibits, including a steamboat pilot's wheel and numerous first editions, bring to life scenes from Twain's Mississippi novels.

A pair of high hills bookend **Hannibal** (pop. 17,757), and climbing up either (or both) gives a grand overview of the town and the broad Mississippi, its historic lifeblood. On the north side, climb up the staircase from the Tom & Huck statue to the top of Cardiff Hill, where the **Mark Twain Memorial Lighthouse**, built in 1935 to celebrate the centenary of Twain's birth, offers a fine view. South of town, **Lover's Leap** is higher and more breathtaking—best visited by car or bike. Further south of downtown along the GRR (Hwy-79) is Hannibal's most hyped attraction: the **Mark Twain Cave** (daily; $12), where costumed guides spin tales about Tom and Huck on an hour-long tour.

Hannibal Practicalities

To immerse yourself fully in the Mark Twain experience, try the Mark Twain memorial chicken (or a Mississippi Mud milk shake) served all day at the **Mark Twain Dinette** (573/221-5511), at 400 N. 3rd Street, adjacent to the Mark Twain Home in what looks suspiciously like a converted A&W. A step up the culinary scale, **Ole Planters Restaurant** (573/221-4410) at 316 Main Street has a full range of lunches and dinners; dessert fans will want to sample the German chocolate pie, a specialty of the house. This species, like rhubarb, is predominantly found in pie cases along the middle Mississippi, so if you're planning a scientific sampling, start now. Away from downtown, the **Riverview Cafe** (daily 11 AM–8 PM; 573/221-8292), in Sawyer's Landing along Hwy-79 south of Hannibal, has possibly the best kitchen in town, with a view that may indeed be worth the slightly higher prices (some entrées are over $10). Don't let the surrounding kitsch of Sawyer's Creek arcades and gift shops keep you from venturing in.

Consistent with its status as an international tourist attraction, Hannibal has plenty of motels, B&Bs, and campgrounds. The **Hotel Clemens** ($60–90; 573/248-1150 or 800/528-1234), at 401 N. 3rd Street, sits downtown at the foot of the old US-36 bridge. The national chains line up along busy US-61 west of downtown.

For a complete list of lodgings, restaurants, events, and tourist traps,

pick up a free guide from the Hannibal **visitors center** (573/221-2477 or toll-free 1-TOM-AND-HUCK), at 505 N. 3rd Street. The most popular annual festival is **Tom Sawyer Days,** held the weekend nearest to the 4th of July, when children take part in the National Fence Painting Championship (a whitewashing homage to *Tom Sawyer*), a frog-jumping competition (remembering Twain's Gold Rush–era short story, the *Celebrated Jumping Frog of Calaveras County*), and the very messy Mississippi Mud Volleyball Championships.

Louisiana and Clarksville

For the first 20-odd miles south from Hannibal, the GRR ascends and descends the densely wooded tops of bluffs, pausing at scenic turnouts for views across the Mississippi Valley, here many miles wide. In October, the upland forests are blazing with fall color that compares with any outside New England, and if you roll down the windows or stop to stretch your legs during the summer, listen for the omnipresent buzz of cicadas in the tangled undergrowth.

Another icon of the lower Mississippi, one that has extended its range north, like the cicadas (and the fire ant), is the huge and pungent Hercules Chemical plant on the south side of the town of **Louisiana** (pop. 3,363). The town itself, like a Hannibal without Mark Twain, is full of 100-year-old brick cottages and warehouses, but looks like it has just about lost the battle against extinction—its Dairy Queen closed and up for sale, 15-year-old cars everywhere, and thrift stores lining up downtown—just the kind of place *aching* to attract a glittering riverboat casino.

A short ways farther south, **Clarksville** (pop. 480) is another GRR town with more of a past than a future, but some optimistic restorers of the riverfront historic block are counting on tourism to improve the town fortunes. Along 1st Street, down by the river and the railroad tracks, two blocks of ornate old buildings hold a doctor's office, a VFW post, a dance studio, and the **Dugout** bar.

Claiming preeminence as the highest point along this stretch of the Mississippi River, 600-foot **Pinnacle Peak** is also noteworthy for the rusty remains of its old "Sky Ride" chair lift, which once carried riders over the GRR all the way to the top. Clarksville also boasts what may be the largest concentration of **bald eagles** in the lower 48 states; in winter months they feed by the hundreds below Lock and Dam No. 24, on the northern edge of town.

Winfield Ferry

Swinging away from the river south of Clarksville, the GRR reenters the corn belt in great straight stretches of road over prairie still hilly enough that you can play peek-a-boo with approaching traffic over the miles of ups and downs, passing towns that often comprise little more than a few houses around a gas station and a grain elevator on a rarely used railroad siding.

Twain was a bit of an impractical investor, losing lots of money on lots of harebrained schemes while missing at least one spectacular opportunity, the telephone. Or so hindsight teaches us—but how much would you invest in a new invention by a guy who flies tetrahedral kites and makes devices to detect metal in the body? Twain said no, so **Alexander Graham Bell** took his invention to **J. P. Morgan** instead.

If you've been keeping track, you'll have noticed the lock and dam numbering skipped No. 23 between Hannibal and Clarksville. There are 29 Army Corps of Engineers—operated **locks and dams** on the Mississippi, from the unnumbered ones in the Twin Cities to No. 27 at St. Louis.

At the hamlet of Winfield, 100 yards north of the only stop sign on this stretch of the GRR, there's a clearly visible sign for the **ferry** (daily year-round; $6; 618/396-2535), which crosses the Mississippi about three miles east of town, just below Lock and Dam No. 25, and shuttles across to Calhoun County, Illinois. There are no fixed departure times: The operator leaves when all the customers waiting are aboard, or when the ferry is full, and returns when there's a fare to bring back or when he or she spots you waiting—so drive right up to where you can be seen, and if it's after dark, keep your lights on.

If the ferry isn't running, St. Louis's suburban edge is 20 miles south along Hwy-79.

Calhoun County

Wedged between the Mississippi and Illinois Rivers, the rural peninsula of **Calhoun County** is one of the best-kept secrets in the state of Illinois. Cut off from the rest of the "Land of Lincoln," and connected to neighboring Missouri by ferry only, Calhoun County is a world of its own. A third of the state's substantial peach crop is grown here on farms that have changed hands only a few times, if at all, since they were given out as land grants to veterans of the War of 1812; bypassing the summer farm stands, especially when the baseball-sized, plum-sweet tomatoes are in season, borders on criminal. A lucky few St. Louisians have weekend getaways here, too, alongside shacks and trailers that seem to accumulate debris like the Corps' dams accumulate Mississippi mud.

From the end of the Winfield ferry access road, detour north to **Batchtown**, stopping at **Friedel's Grocery** (618/396-2538) at 14 Main Street for a shake or malt as whim or muggy weather may demand. Farther south, in the town of **Brussels** (pop. 150), whose public phone booth is possibly the town's sole civic improvement since the Coolidge administration, a handful of cafés and bars is evidence of its popularity with weekenders from St. Louis. The most popular haunt in Brussels is the venerable **Wittmond Hotel** (618/883-2345) across from the water tower and post office at the heart of Brussels. The dining room here serves delicious, all-you-can-eat, family-style meals (very popular on Sunday). They also rent rooms (around $50 a night), have a timeless bar, and an even more ancient-looking general store—complete with dusty old merchandise that looks like it dates back to when the enterprise opened in 1847.

Getting to and around Calhoun County is a bit of an adventure. The main access is from the southeast, across the Illinois River via the state-run, round-the-clock Brussels Ferry; there's also a bridge at Hardin 14 miles upstream. From the northern St. Louis area, the privately operated *Golden Eagle* (618/883-2217) runs across the Mississippi River from a landing outside St. Charles to **Golden Eagle**, Illinois. Last but not least is the ferry across the Mississippi from Winfield, described above. Most of the ferries cease operation in the winter, but during summer they run more or less from dawn to midnight, sell local maps, and can offer basic visitor information. Road signs in Calhoun County are almost nonexistent, but just driving (or cycling!) around, getting lost and found, and lost and found again, is by far the best way to get a feel for this preserved-in-amber island in time.

The Illinois River and Père Marquette State Park

At the south end of Calhoun County, the Brussels Ferry takes all of two or three minutes to cross the narrow Illinois River, along which Marquette and Joliet returned to Canada after their failure to find a westward-flowing river to the rich lands of Cathay and the Far East. René-Robert Cavelier, Sieur de La Salle, came down the Illinois eight years later in 1681, on the first expedition to specifically target the Mississippi. It was La Salle who claimed the Mississippi territory for his sponsor, King Louis XIV of France, and who went all the way down to the Gulf of Mexico (Marquette and Joliet turned back after the confluence of the Arkansas River).

> While the Mississippi may be muddy and less than pristine, at least one man is working to clean it up: **Chad Pregracke**, who spends his days hauling old tires, sunken refrigerators, and other light industrial discards out of the water. You can follow the progress at www.livinglandsand waters.org.

If you're equipped for some hiking or biking, **Père Marquette State Park** is a short, well-signed, and definitely worthwhile three-mile detour upstream from the Brussels Ferry landing. The handsome **park lodge,** built by the Civilian Conservation Corps in the late 1930s, is noted for its 700-ton stone fireplace, massive tree-trunk roof supports, decorative ironwork, and outsized chess set in front of the ox-sized hearth that definitely can create a congenial chalet atmosphere, particularly if you time your arrival for evenings, midweek, or off-season to avoid the crowds. Cabins and lodge rooms are available for reasonable rates (from $99 for two; 618/786-2331). Expect holiday and fall foliage weekends to be booked up a year in advance; camping and tent rentals are also available (618/786-3323).

Following an old railroad route for much of the way, the 20-mile **Sam Vadalabene Bike Trail** between Père Marquette State Park and Alton is unquestionably the best venue for appreciating the scenery, even for a short walk, for Hwy-100 is a fast, divided highway whose drivers don't appreciate slowpokes.

Grafton and Elsah

North of St. Louis on the Illinois side of the Mississippi, the high-speed section of the GRR between Grafton and Alton is widely considered one of its most scenic stretches. Towering limestone bluffs, their curving faces pocked with caves and overhangs, push the road to the edge of the broad lake formed by Lock and Dam No. 26. Before or after the drive, stop at the south edge of Grafton, where **Elsah's Landing Restaurant** (closed Mon.; 618/786-7687), at 420 E. Main Street, has something of a monopoly on good food in these parts; its made-from-scratch ethic pays off in all departments.

EXCURSION STEAMER "CAPITOL" ON THE MISSISSIPPI.

STRECKFUS STEAMBOAT LINE, SAINT LOUIS.

Photo by Underwood & Underwood, N.Y.

Atop the bluffs over Elsah is the very Tudor campus of **Principia College,** the world's only Christian Science institution of higher education.

Speeding along Hwy-100 south of Grafton, it's easy to miss the turnoff for **Elsah,** but even if you have to turn around and come back, it's worth it to check out this tiny hamlet tucked away in a cleft in the palisades. Light years away from St. Louis, but only a half hour's drive away, Elsah is listed in the National Register of Historic Places in its entirety and is an architectural gem, with 19th-century cut-stone and clapboard buildings and narrow lanes reminiscent of some idyllic English country village. Two small B&Bs and the **Green Tree Inn** ($90–150; 618/374-2821) offer what most people would consider romantic getaways; the inn even has a tandem bike for guests.

South of Elsah, before the bluffs give way to grain elevators at Alton, you'll catch a glimpse of the **Piasa Bird** (PIE-a-saw) high on the wall of an old roadside quarry. Marquette and other early explorers mention a pair of huge pictographs on the cliff face, representations of the Illini Indians' legendary "bird that devours men." Faded by the 1840s, the original site was destroyed by quarrying. The current 20- by 40-foot replica, based on various eyewitness descriptions, resembles something from the notebook of an adolescent Dungeons and Dragons fan.

In May 2005, an Alton fisherman pulled a **125-pound blue catfish** out of the Mississippi River, a world-record catch.

Alton

At **Alton,** 20 miles northeast of St. Louis, the riverfront turns decidedly urban. The GRR races along the water, past busy tugboat docks, sulfurous chemical plants, and towering concrete grain elevators, all along a great protective levee under a thicket of high-tension power lines. The main attraction here is the vivid green-and-orange (and hugely lucrative) *Alton Belle* casino boat, the first in Illinois when riverboat gambling was made legal in 1991.

A life-sized statue of **Robert Pershing Wadlow,** the world's tallest human, stands on the campus of the **Southern Illinois University Dental School,** on College Avenue (Hwy-140) a mile or so east of the river. The Alton-born "gentle giant" was 8 feet 11 3/4 inches when he died at age 22.

Inland from the waterfront, however, Alton is surprisingly peaceful and quiet, its redbrick streets lined by mature trees and a range of modest but well-maintained 19th-century houses. Near 5th and Monument Streets at the south end of town, high on a hill above the riverfront, Alton's cemetery is dominated by a large column topped by a winged figure—a monument to one of Alton's most important individuals, the abolitionist newspaper editor **Elijah Lovejoy.** Widely considered to be the nation's first martyr to freedom of the press and freedom of speech, Lovejoy, a newspaper publisher and preacher, was lynched in Alton in 1837 by a mob of pro-slavery Missourians.

Six miles south of Alton, near the village of Hartford, keep an eye out for the signs to the **Lewis & Clark Historical Site,** a reconstruction of the winter campsite of the Corps of Discovery in 1803–04. Recently expanded with a large state-run museum (closed Mon. and Tues.; free; 618/251-5811), the site sits opposite the confluence of the Missouri and Mississippi Rivers, which roll together in a muddy tide between swampy wooded banks.

ONE OF THE MAGNIFICENT EIGHT-HORSE HITCHES OF INTERNATIONAL CHAMPION CLYDESDALES USED BY THE LARGEST BREWERY IN THE WORLD — ANHEUSER-BUSCH, INC., ST. LOUIS, MO. — BREWERS OF THE FAMOUS BUDWEISER, KING OF BOTTLED BEER.

The GRR Across St. Louis

The Great River Road has many routes in, around, and across St. Louis, and they're all so poorly marked that you're sure to get lost trying to follow any of them. From Alton, US-67 crosses just below Lock and Dam No. 26, taking first the Clark Bridge (over the Mississippi) and then the Lewis Bridge (over the Missouri River). No prizes for guessing what *those* names refer to, since you enter the city on Lewis and Clark Boulevard (Hwy-367).

A good main, non-freeway route across St. Louis is Kings Highway, which runs north to south past many of the city's main destinations, including Forest Park and the Missouri Botanical Gardens, before ending up at Gravois Avenue, part of old Route 66. From here, numerous roads give direct access to I-55 and US-61, both of which link up with the scenic GRR route south to Sainte Genevieve.

St. Louis is the only city where three of our *Road Trip USA* routes coincide—the Great River Road, US-50, and Route 66. For the intersection with **US-50**, see page 693; for the junction with **Route 66**, see page 833.

Sainte Genevieve

South of St. Louis, to avoid the sprawling suburbia, take I-55 as far as exit 162, where you can rejoin the GRR by picking up US-61 south. If you don't blink, you may even catch sight of one of Missouri's rare pilot's-wheel signs as the busy road ascends a ridge with a fine western panorama. About 55 miles south of St. Louis's I-270/255 beltway, the GRR reaches the outskirts of **Sainte Genevieve,** one of several French trading posts established along the Mississippi in the wake of La Salle's 17th-century expedition. The town's new trade is tourism, as the B&Bs, "fine dining," and shops clearly illustrate, but the beauty of Sainte Genevieve lies in its restored 18th- to 19th-century remnants, including a brick belle of a **Southern Hotel** ($80 and up; 573/883-3493), at 146 S. 3rd Street, one of the oldest hotels west of the Mississippi River. **Sara's Ice Cream** (573/883-5890), down toward the water at 124 Merchant Street, provides yet more tasteful distractions, with great handmade ice cream cones, old-fashioned soda fountain drinks and milkshakes.

252 THE GREAT RIVER ROAD

St. Louis

Founded by French fur trappers in 1764, St. Louis served for most of its first century as a prosperous outpost of "civilization" at the frontier of the Wild West. It was the starting point for the explorations of Lewis and Clark, and much later Charles Lindbergh, whose *Spirit of St. Louis* carried him across the Atlantic. Unfortunately, like many other American cities, St. Louis has suffered from years of decline and neglect; the population, which peaked at over 850,000 in 1950, is now less than half that. Although it has all the cultural and institutional trappings of a major city, not to mention the landmark Gateway Arch, St. Louis is at heart a city of small neighborhoods, such as bluesy Soulard south of downtown, the Italian-American "Hill" (boyhood home of Yogi Berra), and the collegiate West End district near verdant Forest Park.

One thing you have to see when in St. Louis (you literally cannot miss it) is the **Gateway Arch** (daily; 314/655-1700), on the riverfront at the foot of Market Street. Rising up from the west bank of the Mississippi River, Eero Saarinen's stunning 630-foot stainless steel monument still dominates the city skyline, despite the disrespectful rise of nearby office towers. Under the legs of the Arch, which is officially called the Jefferson National Expansion Memorial, the free and fascinating Museum of Westward Expansion chronicles the human wave that swept America's frontier west to the Pacific. A small elevator-like tram ($10) carries visitors up the arch to an observation chamber at the very top.

The **St. Louis Cardinals** (314/421-2400), one of the country's most popular baseball teams, play at brand-new retro-modern Busch Stadium, right downtown with views of the river and Gateway Arch. Games are broadcast on **KMOX 1120 AM**.

West of downtown around the Washington University campus, in Forest Park's 1,300 beautifully landscaped acres, museums of fine art, history, and science fill buildings that date back to the 1904 World's Fair, St. Louis's world-class swan song.

Practicalities

Freeways and high-speed arteries reminiscent of Los Angeles make a car handy for navigating the St. Louis area—unless you have oodles of money for cab fares—and thanks to the city's sad history of replacing its landmark buildings with blacktop, you'll find plenty of parking lots around downtown.

For food, The Hill neighborhood is hard to beat: **Gian-Tony's** (314/772-4893), at 5356 Daggettt Avenue, is perhaps the best of a dozen classic neighborhood Italian places. Wherever you go, try the toasted ravioli, a local treat. Across I-55 from the Budweiser factory, the wild **Venice Cafe** (314/772-5994), 1903 Pestalozzi Street, matches anarchic Gaudi-meets-the-Merry-Pranksters decor with lots of live music and a menu that leans heavily toward Jamaican jerk chicken, served up indoors—where poets linger over bottles of beer—or in the backyard garden.

Another great place is the slightly kitschy **Blueberry Hill** (314/727-0880), at 6504 Delmar Boulevard, a retro-1950s diner that has an excellent jukebox, very good burgers, and enough real-life credibility to sometime attract the likes of St. Louis–born father of rock 'n' roll, Chuck Berry, to play impromptu gigs.

No one leaves St. Louis without cruising old Route 66 southwest from downtown to **Ted Drewe's** (314/481-2652), 6726 Chippewa Avenue, a local institution famous for its many flavors of "concrete"—a delicious frozen dairy-and-egg-custard concoction so thick you can turn it upside down and not spill a drop.

St. Louis doesn't have that much of a tourist trade (the muggy weather here in summer keeps most sensible people far away), so places to stay are relatively cheap. **Hampton Inn at Gateway Arch** ($90 and up; 314/621-7900) at 333 Washington Avenue, and the larger **Adam's Mark** ($85 and up; 314/241-7400) at 112 N. 4th Street, are two of the more popular downtown hotels. Away from the Arch, at the **Hyatt Regency at Union Station** ($99 and up; 314/231-1234 or 800/233-1234), 1820 Market Street, the opulently restored lobby, formerly the great rail center's vaulted waiting room, is worth seeing even if you aren't a guest. In another historic reincarnation, a quartet of stately old warehouses has been converted to house the **Westin St. Louis** ($150 and up; 314/621-2000), near the Arch, the river, and the baseball stadium at 811 Spruce Street.

The **St. Louis Convention & Visitors Commission** (314/241-1764 or 800/916-0092) operates a well-stocked information center downtown at 308 Washington Avenue, near the river and I-70.

Get a feel for St. Louis listening habits by tuning in to commercial-free **KDHX 88.1 FM.**

George Rogers Clark's fame as a war hero, Indian fighter, and explorer put him at the top of Thomas Jefferson's short list for leading an expedition into what became the Louisiana Purchase, but the aging Clark nominated his younger brother instead. Thus did **William Clark** join **Meriwether Lewis** for their historic journey to the Pacific.

Where the Great River Road hops onto the I-55 freeway for its final approach into St. Louis, a clearly marked "GRR Spur" leads to **Cahokia Mounds,** the remains of the largest prehistoric American city north of Mexico.

Since US-61 doesn't enter town, follow the small blue Tourist Information signs down to the old waterfront to find the area's historic places, and visit the **Great River Road Interpretive Center** (daily; free; 573/883-7097 or 800/373-7007) at 66 S. Main Street to learn about the town's past and present.

To head south, go north: the **Mississippi River-Modoc Ferry** (daily; $8; 573/883-7382) to Modoc, Illinois, is almost three miles out of town. Follow Main Street north until it dead-ends at the ferry landing. On the Illinois side, twelve rural crop-lined miles from the Modoc Ferry we rejoin the GRR, heading south on Hwy-3 toward Chester.

Kaskaskia, Illinois

Fifteen miles south of Sainte Genevieve, signposted off US-61, is old **Kaskaskia**, the first Illinois state capital and the only Illinois town now *west* of the Mississippi, thanks to an 1881 flood. "Town" is a generous overstatement: Originally consisting of only a church and a handful of farmhouses, the community has been all but washed away numerous times in its 250-year history. Cut off from the Missouri shore by huge levees and a swampy river channel, Kaskaskia is now a ghost town with an illustrious past: It was here, during the American Revolution, that George Rogers Clark and his tiny force of Kentucky "**Long Knives**" launched their attack against British control of the huge, formerly French territory between the Mississippi and Ohio River Valleys, a campaign so stunningly successful that it effectively doubled the size of the United States. After capturing Fort Kaskaskia (now across the river), the victorious Americans rang the 600-pound bell that hung in the French Catholic church; this bell, now in its own spartan iron-barred chapel, is called "the Liberty Bell of the West."

Chester

The GRR neatly skips around **Chester,** "Home of Popeye," via a pleasant riverbank detour, returning to Hwy-3 on the downstream side of town. **Popeye** first appeared in print in 1929, and a memorial to local boy Elzie Segar, creator of the spinach-guzzling scrapper, stands in a picnic area beside the bridge to Missouri; if you miss it, you'll have to turn around on the other side of the Mississippi. Chester locals Frank "Rocky" Fiegel and William "Windy Bill" Schuchert were the inspiration for Popeye the Sailor and Wimpy the Hamburger Fiend. If you pass through on the

second weekend of September, drop by Popeye's birthday party, with its big flea market of all the Popeye collectibles you never imagined existed.

South of Chester, the GRR passes by a couple of old barns painted with fading signs advertising "Meramec Caverns—US-60—Stanton MO" (see page 831).

Hwy-3: Shawnee National Forest

No town of any consequence impedes the GRR's 90-mile leg along the southern tip of Illinois. The roadside landscape continues to be fields of heat-loving corn and leafy soybean, while the bluffs of the **Shawnee National Forest** (618/253-7114), whose recreational offerings are invitingly signposted with names like Oakwood Bottoms, Turkey Bayou, and Pine Hills, appear to the east. Much of the forested uplands are a botanical crossroads: glacier-borne northern species like the sumac and partridge berry; warmth-seeking southern species like the short-leaf pine; eastern species held back by the Mississippi, such as Virginia willow and silver bell; and western species with a toehold in the east, like Missouri primrose and Ozark coneflower. All count southern Illinois as the edge of their natural ranges. When John James Audubon passed through this region in the early 1800s, he recorded seeing thousands of bright green, red, and yellow-striped parakeets. They are all long-extinct; gone, too, are the native panther and black bear.

> Absent-minded and lead-footed drivers beware: Some cash-strapped counties of southern Illinois are known to use speed traps to help make ends meet.

Jonesboro

Just under 50 miles south of Chester, 8 miles east of the GRR via Hwy-146, is the small town of **Jonesboro**, whose **Dixie Barbecue** (618/833-6437), at 205 E. Broad Street, is definitely worth a side trip. In September 1858, Jonesboro hosted the third of the seven senate campaign debates between challenger Abe Lincoln and incumbent Stephen Douglas, who tried to portray Lincoln as being out of touch with the people over the issue of slavery. Although Illinois was a designated free state, this area had strong sympathies with the South.

Hwy-146 roughly marks the route of the **Trail of Tears,** the 1838 winter death march of the Cherokee nation. Six years after wiping out Indians of the upper Mississippi in the Black Hawk War, President Andrew Jackson ordered the "Five Civilized Tribes" of the Cherokee removed to the arid plains of Oklahoma from their lands in the fertile Tennessee River valley. Some five thousand Cherokee died along this thousand-mile journey, which passed through the state near here. On the Missouri side of the river, 10 miles north of Cape Girardeau, the 3,400-acre **Trail of Tears State Park** (573/334-1711) preserves one scene along this marathon tragedy, with a two-mile section of the historic "trail" and interpretive plaques marking the wooded, riverside bluffs.

Back on Hwy-3, just north of I-57 and the town of Cairo, the GRR passes **Horseshoe Lake Conservation Area,** an example of what happens when the river shifts to a new channel and leaves an oxbow lake behind. Now prime winter habitat for over a million migrating geese and ducks, its tupelo gum

> Cape Girardeau, on the Missouri side of the Mississippi River, was the boyhood hometown of radio talk-show host Rush Limbaugh, whose father and grandfather were local lawyers. In 2003, a $100-million, 100-foot-wide suspension bridge over the Mississippi replaced its narrow, rusting predecessor.

trees, bald cypress, and swamp cottonwoods foreshadow the scenery found downstream among the bayous of the Mississippi Delta.

Cairo

"A grave uncheered by any gleam of promise" was but one of Charles Dickens's unsympathetic descriptions of **Cairo** (CARE-oh or "K"-ro), the town that presides over—and sometimes under—the meeting of the Mississippi and Ohio Rivers. Routinely submerged by floodwaters until the Corps of Engineers ringed the town with a massive stockade of levees and huge steel floodgates, Cairo's star shone briefly in the steamboat era and during the Civil War, when General Grant quartered his Army of the Tennessee here and Union ironclads were berthed along the waterfront. A few Victorian mansions built by boat captains remain, and the circa-1872 **Customs House** has been turned into a small museum, but unless you have a fondness for wrack and ruin, the GRR's passage through town is best enjoyed with your eyes stuck firmly to the road.

What *is* worth seeing is the confluence of the two mighty rivers. Unless there's a flood in progress, do your watching from a small platform in **Fort Defiance State Park,** at the foot of the bridge that carries US-60 between Missouri and Kentucky, lasting but a quarter mile in Illinois.

Metropolis: Home of Superman

The town of Metropolis, Illinois (pop. 6,700), along the Ohio River 25 miles northeast of Cairo but most easily accessible via Paducah, Kentucky, takes pride in its adopted superhero son, Superman. An impressive and photogenic 15-foot-tall bronze statue of the "Man of Steel" stands downtown, on the north side of the Massac County Courthouse. Nearby are a quick-change telephone booth, the "offices" of the Daily Planet newspaper, and every June a festival celebrates his crime-fighting efforts. For more information, and a look at one of the most extensive collections of Superman artifacts and memorabilia anywhere, visit the **Super Museum** (daily; $3; 618/524-5518) at 519 Market Street.

Metropolis, Illinois, the hometown of **Superman,** is also associated with another famous figure: **Robert F. Stroud,** the "Birdman of Alcatraz," is buried in the Masonic Cemetery.

The other big attraction is the 40,000-square-foot **Harrah's Metropolis Casino,** down on the banks of the Ohio River at the base of the railroad bridge.

KENTUCKY AND TENNESSEE

Most of the GRR's 60-odd miles across Kentucky are quite scenic, populated by only a handful of small towns, none of which has been overrun by tacky commercial strips. Continuing south across the Tennessee line, the route retains its rural, slow-road feel as it

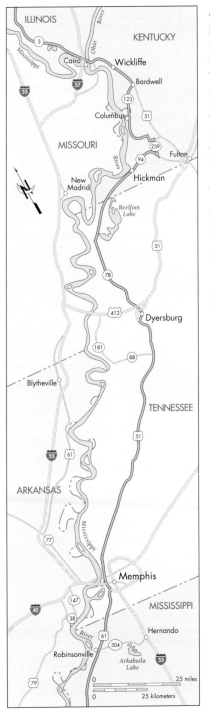

winds along the cultivated bottom-lands around earthquake-created Reelfoot Lake. Midway to Memphis, the GRR comes back to the modern world, crossing the I-55 freeway then rejoining four-lane US-51 as it races to downtown Memphis, passing pine woods and cotton fields mixed with mobile homes, suburban ranch houses, and gas stations that double as the local video stores.

Wickliffe, Hickman, and the New Madrid Earthquake

Skipping from the banks of the Ohio River, the GRR stays with US-51 southbound through small, thoroughly industrial **Wickliffe** (pop. 794), then takes an attractive 40-mile meander away from the rivers through wooded hill country, returning to the edge of the Mississippi at **Hickman,** a dozen miles from the Tennessee line.

West from Hickman, there's a small ferry to Missouri, landing near the town of **New Madrid** (MAD-rid), where one of the strongest earthquakes ever struck on December 16, 1811. The Richter scale wasn't around to measure it, but the quake was felt as far away as Boston.

Reelfoot Lake Area

Leaving Kentucky, the GRR follows Hwy-78 across a 40-mile stretch of low-lying bottomlands, passing the roadhouse bars and bait shops near **Reelfoot Lake,** a 25,000-acre recreation area and wildlife refuge created by the New Madrid earthquake. From here south to Memphis, US-51 does its level best to mimic an interstate, rendering the final 75 miles a forgettable blur.

Memphis

Memphis's gifts to American culture include the supermarket, the drive-in restaurant, the Holiday Inn, Elvis Presley, and Federal Express, and if you detect a pattern here you'll understand why the city is at once entertainingly kitsch and supremely captivating. This is not to say Memphis (pop. 599,000) lacks a coherent character—just the opposite—but its charms can have unpredictable side effects.

Beale Street, downtown between 2nd and 4th Streets, has been Memphis's honky-tonk central ever since native son W. C. Handy set up shop in the early 1900s with the blues he'd learned in Mississippi. Beale Street has been sanitized for your protection, turning it into a new! & improved! version of its old self, and a massive shopping mall and flashy new arena for the Grizzlies basketball team has transformed the entire south side of downtown Memphis; slap an adhesive name tag on your lapel and you'll fit right in with the tour bus crowd strolling at night along the block of clubs—including **B. B. King's** at 147 Beale Street (901/527-5464), marked by a giant neon guitar.

Fortunately, a number of other music-related museums and attractions capture a more authentic Memphis: The original **Sun Records** studio (daily; $9.50; 901/521-0664), where Elvis, Johnny Cash, Roy Orbison, and many others recorded their historic tracks in the 1950s, is a short walk northeast at 706 Union Avenue; while the site of **Stax Records** studio (daily; $9; 888/942-7685), at 926 E. McLemore Avenue, is now a museum documenting the soulful impact of Sam & Dave and Otis Redding during the 1960s.

If there's one place that shouldn't be missed, it's the eloquent **National Civil Rights Museum** (closed Tues.; $10; 901/521-9699), at 450 Mulberry Street, south of Beale Street behind the restored facade of the Lorraine Motel, where Dr. Martin Luther King Jr. was assassinated in 1968. Aided by extensive video newsreels and life-sized dioramas, museum exhibits let you step as far as you like into the powerful history of the civil rights movement. However, unless you're a conspiracy nut, you might want to miss out on the disturbingly expensive displays about Dr. King's assassination, housed in the old rooming house across the street, where James Earl Ray fired the fatal shots.

Another key Memphis destination is the **Center for Southern Folklore** (daily; 901/525-3655), in Pembroke Square at 119 S. Main Street, a great place to immerse yourself in southern lifeways, with a captivating collection of folk art plus frequent live music, a fine café, and all sorts of fun events. Elvis's favorite roller coaster, the Zippin' Pippin', lives on at **Libertyland** (about $25; 901/274-1776), south of Central Avenue at the Mid-South Fairground.

On the north side of downtown Memphis, **Mud Island** is a real island in the middle of the Mississippi River, connected to downtown by a pedestrian bridge and a monorail. This 50-acre island holds a five-block-long mock-up of the Mississippi River, with the Gulf of Mexico played by a huge, 1.3-million-gallon public swimming pool. Also here: the excellent **Mississippi River Museum.**

Right in downtown Memphis, but just a step away from the majors, the **Memphis Redbirds** ($5–15; 901/721-6050), Class AAA farm club for the St. Louis Cardinals, play at AutoZone Park at 200 Union Avenue.

Practicalities

As it is with live music, food is one area where Memphis can still surpass just about any other American city, and if your taste buds prefer improvisation and passion to over-refined "perfection," Memphis is sure to satisfy. **Buntyn Restaurant** (Mon.–Fri. 11 AM–8 PM; 901/458-8776), at 3070 Southern Avenue east of the Mid-South Coliseum, invites you to sit down to the kind of cookery that has made the South famous: veggies boiled with fatback pork, excellent batter-fried chicken, heaps of mashed potatoes with thick brown gravy, and sweet pies with crusts as white as snow. **Rendezvous Ribs** (901/523-2746) at 52 S. Second Street, with its main entrance through a downtown alley, is a cavernous place, frequently ranked as one of the best rib joints in a city that considers itself the BBQ capital of the world. Another of the many other candidates for "Best BBQ in the Universe" is **Interstate BBQ** (901/775-2304), at 2265 S. 3rd Street just north of where US-61 crosses I-55, where you can munch on fabulous ribs.

Except during the city's many music and food festivals, Memphis accommodations are priced very reasonably. The whole alphabet of major chains—from Best Western to Super 8—is spread around the I-240 beltway, and again along I-55 in neighboring Arkansas. One convenient place to stay is the **Holiday Inn,** 164 Union Avenue ($75-115; 901/527-4100). Across the street, The Peabody, 149 Union Avenue ($99-up; 901/529-4000 or 800/732-2639) is Memphis's premiere downtown hotel, whose sparkling lobby is home to the Mississippi's most famous mallards: Twice daily, at 11 AM and 5 PM, the red carpet is rolled out for the Peabody Ducks to parade (waddle, really) to and from the lobby fountain. And if you're planning a vigil at Graceland, consider **Elvis Presley's Graceland Motel,** 3677 Elvis Presley Boulevard ($65-95; 901/332-1000 or 800/945-7667). Owned by his heirs and across from his former lair, it features a 24-hour in-room Elvis movie channel.

For tourist information contact the friendly and thorough Memphis Convention and Visitors Bureau, 47 Union Avenue (901/543-5300 or 800/873-6282), or drop by their information booth at 340 Beale Street.

Driving Across Memphis

Fans of pop-culture kitsch will love what the GRR offers you in Memphis: The main road from the north (US-51) is Danny Thomas Boulevard; south of downtown, this turns into Elvis Presley Boulevard, and runs right past the gates of Graceland. (However, if you're continuing on to the Mississippi Delta, from Graceland you should switch onto US-61, which runs about two miles to the west.)

MISSISSIPPI

Ecologically speaking, the Mississippi Delta is the vast alluvial plain between Cairo and the Gulf of Mexico, but "The Delta" of popular myth is much more circumscribed, occupying the 250-mile-long realm of King Cotton, between Memphis and Vicksburg. As important as its proper boundaries is its legacy as the cradle of nearly every American musical style from gospel, blues, and jazz to country and rock 'n' roll. The backbone of our route, US-61, is also legendary as the path of the "Great Migration," the mass exodus to the industrialized northern United States of some five million black sharecroppers in the decades after World War I.

> The word Mississippi comes from the Algonquin word *misezibi* meaning "water from land all over," or "great water."

As the Great River Road cuts inland and drops like a plumb line across the cotton fields, we recommend a number of side trips to landmarks of this rich cultural heritage. Where the Delta ends at Vicksburg's bluffs, our route begins mingling with ghosts from the South's plantation and Civil War past, then finally rolls into Louisiana.

All across Mississippi, away from the main roads on the sleepier section of the GRR, the towns are filled with shotgun shacks, low-slung Creole-style bungalows, and old trailers that some people have nicknamed "doghouses" without any attempt at irony. What look like oil drums mounted on garden carts in the odd front yard are smokers, for doing barbecue just right; their presence sometimes implies the proximity of a social club or juke joint that may do only weekend business. Local stores, if they exist, are where men in overalls sit and stand in clusters, keeping an eye on the world. In autumn when the cotton is ready for harvest, huge truck-sized bales sit in the cleared muddy margins of the fields, and white fluff accumulates in drifts on the narrow loose shoulder, swirling in small eddies in your wake.

> Turn off the GRR toward the Commerce Landing casinos to find the vestiges of **Robinsonville**, hometown of musician **Robert Johnson**, who according to blues legend traded his soul to Satan at "The Crossroads" of Highways 49 and 61 to become king of the blues guitar. In Johnson's day, of course, any guitar-pickin' "musicianer" was thought to be in cahoots with the Devil.

Meanwhile the Mississippi River does its snaky shuffle off to the Gulf of Mexico behind a continuous line of levees, a bayou here and cut-off lake there as proof of past indirections.

In Search of Elvis

Scratch the surface of Memphis, and you'll always turn up a little Elvis, like pennies and pocket lint in an old sofa. That guy behind the counter? His mom used to give piano lessons to Elvis's step-brothers. That woman at the next table? Her after-school job was in the Libertyland amusement park, which Elvis would rent out in its entirety just so he could ride the Zippin' Pippin' roller coaster for hours on end. A frequent Graceland visitor during the Elvis years collected fuzz from the shag carpet to give to friends; maybe the woman paying for her coffee still has her tuft. Even the owner of the greasiest old pizza joint will tell you how Elvis would come in with his band, "back when he was nothin'." Get used to it: Elvis is everywhere.

The font of all this meta-Elvisness is, of course, **Graceland** (daily; 901/332-3322 or 800/238-2000), on Elvis Presley Boulevard (US-51) about a mile south of I-55 amid a clutter of burger joints and muffler shops. At age 21, flush with his early success, Elvis paid $100,000 for Graceland, which was one of the more fashionable houses in Memphis in 1957, and seeing what happens when Elvis's poor-white-boy taste and Hollywood budget run amok is well worth the price of admission. You can buy tickets to each part of the Graceland complex, or splurge on a $29 combination "Platinum Tour" ticket that gives admission to the mansion as well as the other "collections," such as the King's private jet or his car collection. (Many of his cars, including his famous pink 1955 Cadillac, are arrayed as if at a drive-in movie—with a big screen playing his race car scenes from *Viva Las Vegas* on a continuous loop—it's my favorite stop in the whole shebang.)

A visit to Graceland says very little about Elvis's music (though there is a room showing off an 80-foot wall full of gold and platinum records), but speaks volumes about his mystique. Elvis is buried on the property, alongside his father and mother, in the Meditation Garden.

Northwest Mississippi: Casino Country

Leaving Memphis via US-61, the GRR enters De Soto and Tunica Counties; the place-names memorialize Hernando de Soto, the first European to see the Mississippi, and the combative Tunica tribe who forced the Spanish conquistador's mosquito- and snake-bitten expedition to flee across the river hereabouts in 1542. Outfitted with cannon, priests, slaves, pigs, war dogs, and 1,000 soldiers, de Soto spent years marching through southern swamps in quest of gold—but he was 450 years too early. Tunica County, long one of the

Mississippi law doesn't require casinos to be riverboats, it merely requires them to float. All appearances to the contrary, the giant Las Vegas–style casinos in Tunica County are indeed floating, mostly in ponds dredged specifically to meet the letter of the law.

most destitute places in America, only became a gold mine after the state legalized gambling in 1992. Several billion dollars of investment later, Tunica is the third-largest gambling center in the country, and every big name in casinos lines the levee here. Bugsy Siegel would be proud, but as ever outsiders have benefited much more than the still-poor local residents.

To aid the influx of people anxious to part with their money, US-61 has been turned into a high-volume, four-lane highway. And motels, fast-food places, and gas stations have popped up like mushrooms after a spring rain.

South of the casino area along US-61, the GRR brings you to the classic grits-and-gravy, steak-and-potatoes **Blue & White Cafe** (662/363-1371), at 1355 N. US-61. Offering a true taste of the Delta with its buffets and local specialties, including deep-fried pickles, the Blue and White has hardly changed since the day it opened in 1937. South from Tunica, US-61 makes a 35-mile beeline through the cotton fields to Clarksdale.

Moon Lake

Twenty miles south of Tunica's casinos, just west of US-61, **Moon Lake** was home to one of the South's most famous Prohibition landmarks, the **Moon Lake Club.** Unlike speakeasies associated with thugs and tarts, this club was a family destination where parents could dance and gamble while the kids played by the lake. In a place and time when planes were still so rare the sound of their engines could interrupt work and empty classrooms, the club flew in fresh Maine lobster and Kansas City steak for its clientele of rich white Memphians.

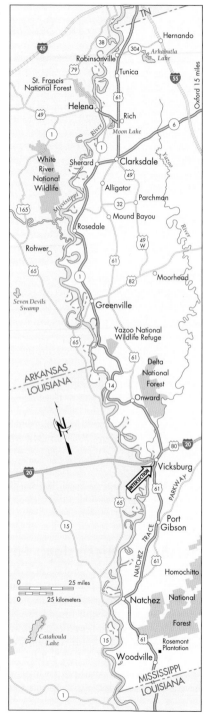

Moon Lake has a literary history, too, appearing in a number of Tennessee Williams's dramas. Williams knew it well: Not only was the club property owned by a cousin, but as a boy he had been a frequent guest, accompanying his grandfather, the Reverend Dakin, on parish calls throughout the county.

Helena, Arkansas

About a dozen miles west of the GRR and Moon Lake via US-49 is **Helena, Arkansas**, "the most deadly place on the river" to Union regiments in the Civil War, stopped in their tracks by the festering malarial swamps that once surrounded the town. It began building a different reputation back in the 1940s when local radio station KFFA 1360 AM began broadcasting the "King Biscuit Flour Hour," a live blues show; originally hosted by harmonica legend Sonny Boy Williamson, the show is still on the air every day at 12:15 PM. In early October, the **King Biscuit Blues Festival** (870/338-8798 for info) attracts fans by the tens of thousands to hear one of the best lineups of live gospel and blues in the nation. The rest of the year, the **Delta Cultural Center** daily; free; 870/338-4350), at 141 Cherry Street (in the renovated train depot downtown), with its fine historical displays on the lives of Delta inhabitants, is an equally compelling reason to visit this small river town.

St. Louis likes to claim **Tennessee Williams** as a native son, but while the family did indeed move there when Tom was in the fourth grade, the Mississippi-born playwright hated St. Louis "with a purple passion."

Clarksdale

The blues were born in the Delta, but they grew up in **Clarksdale**. The census rolls for this small town read like a musical hall of fame: Ma Rainey, W. C. Handy, Bessie Smith, Sam Cooke, Ike Turner, Muddy Waters, Wade Walton, John Lee Hooker, Big Jack Johnson, and many others whose achievements are described—and may be heard—in the **Delta Blues Museum** (closed Sun.; $7; 662/627-6820) in the circa-1918 railroad depot at the heart of Clarksdale's "Blues Alley" district downtown. The museum offers maps of blues landmarks around town and around the state, a calendar of blues events, and all sorts of helpful information. In short, this is the best place to start your journey through the Delta blues world.

Thomas Harris, author of *The Silence of the Lambs,* hails from the tiny hamlet of **Rich,** just east of the junction of US-61 and US-49.

Ever since W. C. Handy traded his steady gigs in Clarksdale for a career on Beale Street in Memphis, the Mississippi Delta has exported its blues musicians to places where they receive wider recognition and a living wage, but come on a Friday or Saturday night and you'll see Clarksdale still cooks up some good hot blues. Many of the most "authentic" juke joints are in a very dilapidated part of town around Sunflower Avenue and Tallahatchie Street, but for a first stop try the **Ground Zero Blues Club** (662/621-9009), across from the Delta Blues Museum. If you're in town during August, it would be a shame to miss the

Unlike the spreading deltas of the Orinoco or Nile, the Mississippi cuts a deeper channel as it rolls south, the deceptively smooth surface hiding a flow four times greater than it was at the St. Louis Arch.

Getting the Blues

If serious blues hounds sniff around enough, they can still find the kind of swaggering, sweaty, Saturday-night juke joint that will always be synonymous with real Delta blues. You know the place: bottles of Budweiser on ice in a plastic cooler, clouds of cigarette smoke, some rough customers, hot dancing, and honest gut-wrenching blues played with an intensity that rattles your fillings. Yes, such places exist, but they don't run display ads in the local paper, or make the list of area attractions given out by local chambers of commerce.

The really homegrown variety announces itself with hand-lettered signs on telephone poles and launderette bulletin boards, if at all. They have no phone numbers, no advance tickets (usually); you have to show up to find out who, if anyone, is playing. Ask around: the convenience store clerk, the person next to you at the BBQ counter. Keep in mind that the blues are rooted in a condition of the Delta's black community that is no bed of roses; voyeurs slumming as tourists-to-hardship will be politely stonewalled at best. Rest assured, though: with perseverance, and the proper attitude (and especially for women, a companion), you'll find what you're looking for. Once you get there, out-of-towners needn't worry about the reception: Blues musicians welcome an appreciative audience, period.

Weekends, again mostly Saturday nights, are also about the only time you'll catch blues in the more commercial juke joints and clubs, simply because so many musicians have other jobs during the week. If you really want to be sure of hearing some blues, time your travels to coincide with one of the big annual blues festivals, like these:

Sunflower River Blues and Gospel Festival
mid-August; Clarksdale, MS (662/627-7337 or 800/626-3764)

Memphis Music and Heritage Festival
Labor Day weekend; Memphis, TN (901/525-3655)

Mississippi Delta Blues Festival
mid-September; Greenville, MS (662/335-3523 or 800/467-3582)

King Biscuit Blues Festival
early October; Helena, AR (870/338-8798)

Sunflower River Blues and Gospel Festival, organized by the Delta Blues Museum and staged at venues around town.

The rest of downtown Clarksdale is well worth exploring for its lazy ambience and wealth of history. The old **Delta Cinema**, downtown at 11 3rd Street, still shows current releases in a 1920s theater; there's a steamboat-shaped store around the corner, across the street from the Sunflower River; and funky art galleries like **Cat Head Blues and Folk Art** (662/624-5992), at 252 Delta Avenue, showcase local culture and events.

Clarksdale has plenty of fast food, but the barbecue is better: Try the **Ranchero** (662/624-9768), on US-61 at 1907 N. State Street, or **Abe's Bar-B-Q** (662/624-9947), at 616 State Street in the center of town, cooking up tangy 'cue since 1924. For a surprising dose of Lebanese-Italian food amid the pork palaces, check out **Chamoun's Rest Haven** (closed Sun.; 662/624-8601) at 419 S. State Street, on US-61 just south of the Big Sunflower River.

US-61, aka State Street, is also where you'll find Clarksdale's motels, from a **Days Inn** across from the Ranchero to a **Comfort Inn** at the southern end of town.

For more information on visiting the Clarksdale area, contact the **visitors bureau** (662/627-7337), on US-49 at 1540 De Soto Street.

Clarksdale's old **Afro-American Hospital** at 615 Sunflower Avenue is where blues vocalist **Bessie Smith** died in 1937 after a car wreck out on US-61.

About 30 miles south of Clarksdale on US-49 is **Parchman**, infamous home to the state prison farm memorialized in songs like bluesman **Bukka White's** "Parchman Farm." The **"Midnight Special,"** another oft-heard allusion in Delta blues lyrics, was the weekend train from New Orleans that brought visitors to the prison.

Oxford

Do you need a break from the Delta yet? Has counting pickup trucks, propane tanks, and barbecued ribs induced a bad imitation drawl? How far would you detour for a well-stocked bookstore, or a restaurant that doesn't immerse everything in boiling oil? Sixty-two miles east of Clarksdale on Hwy-6 is the college town of **Oxford**, whose cultural amenities, though common to college towns from Amherst to Berkeley, set it in a world apart from most of Mississippi. The college in question is "Ole Miss," otherwise known as the **University of Mississippi**, whose pleasant campus holds such treasures as B. B. King's entire personal collection of records, posters, photos, and more in the **Ole Miss Blues Archive** (Mon.–Fri. only), in Farley Hall across from Barnard Observatory. The renovated antebellum observatory houses the **Center for the Study of Southern Culture** (Mon.–Fri. only; 662/232-5993), which sponsors exhibits, lectures, and screenings.

Elsewhere under the leafy old oaks you'll find a large collection of primitive **Southern folk art** in the University Museums (closed Mon.), and a collection of William Faulkner first editions in the J. D. Williams Library. Faulkner was a resident of Oxford for most of his life; readers of his novels will recognize in surrounding Lafayette County (luh-FAY-it) elements of Faulkner's fictional Yoknapatawpha. A statue of him was recently placed in the square at the center of Oxford, and **Rowan Oak** (Tues.–Sat. 10 AM–noon and 2–4 PM, Sun. 2–4 PM; free; 662/234-3284), his house on Old Taylor Road off S. Lamar Avenue, remains as he left it when he died in 1962, with the bottle of whiskey next to the old typewriter in his study almost, but not quite, empty. Visit his gravesite by following the signs from the north side of the courthouse square; near the cemetery entrance lie other family members who didn't affect adding the "u" to their surname, including the brother whose untimely death Faulkner mourned in his first novel, *Soldier's Pay.*

Oxford Practicalities

When respects have been paid to Southern culture and it's time to eat, there's a lot to choose from. The central Courthouse Square is surrounded by good restaurants, ranging from the homespun **Ajax Diner** to the eclectic "New Southern" cuisine of the plush **City Grocery** (662/232-8080), at 152 Courthouse Square, where traditional dishes like bread pudding and shrimp 'n' grits are complemented by fine wines and a full bar. And thanks to all the Ole Miss students, you can enjoy a range of fast food, pizza places, and live music along Lamar Street, south of the square.

Accommodations in Oxford include a **Holiday Inn** ($90 and up; 662/234-3031), north of the courthouse at 400 N. Lamar, and the comfortably worn **Oliver-Britt House** ($60 and up; 662/234-8043), a redbrick B&B at 512 Van Buren Avenue.

The **Oxford Tourism Council** (662/234-4680) will happily provide more information and a calendar of cultural events; they also operate a **visitors center** in a tiny cottage next to City Hall on the central square. Another good source of information is **Square Books,** on the south side of the same square; this is one of the country's great independent book stores, with a full range of local and international authors, plus a nice café.

Hwy-1: Great River Road State Park

Between Clarksdale and Greenville, the Great River Road winds west of the much-busier US-61, looping next to the Mississippi River along Hwy-1. It's a rural road, running past soybean, cotton, and "pond cat" farms—catfish farming is big business hereabouts. Midway along, the GRR runs past **Great River Road State Park,** near the town of Rosedale. Located inside the Mississippi River levee, the park offers unique views of the "Father of Waters" from a 75-foot-high overlook tower.

Further south, at the north edge of Greenville, the 1,000-year-old, 55-foot-high earthen cones next to the highway are the remnants of the prehistoric "Moundbuilder" people who lived here a millennium ago.

East of the GRR on Hwy-61 is small **Mound Bayou,** the oldest black town in the state. A man named **Isaiah Montgomery,** inspired by Booker T. Washington's prescriptions for black self-improvement, founded the all-black community in 1888 with support from his former employer, Jefferson Davis.

Now preserved as the **Winterville Mounds,** the two dozen ancient mounds here are thought to have been sacred ceremonial sites, but little is known about the enigmatic people who built them (and hundreds of others) along the banks of the Mississippi and Ohio rivers.

Greenville

The Delta's largest city, **Greenville** (pop. 41,633) is one of the largest river ports in the state, but instead of cotton-shipping wharves, its levees are now lined by floating casinos. Hwy-1 through Greenville takes top honors for the least attractive strip of gas stations and mini-marts along the GRR, but appearances can be deceiving, as the city has some fine cultural traditions, from the anti–Ku Klux Klan editorializing of Hodding Carter's *Delta-Democrat Times* during the 1950s and 1960s to the great steaks and hot tamales at **Doe's Eat Place** (662/334-3315). In the big white building at 502 Nelson Street (follow N. Broadway to the brick churches, then turn toward the river), Doe's is known throughout the state for its good food and honest prices, and for the fact that you have to enter through the kitchen. (Other Doe's Eat Place restaurants have opened around the South; the one in Little Rock, Arkansas, is a favorite of former President Bill Clinton.)

Second to Clarksdale in the Delta blues galaxy, Greenville comes alive in mid-September during the annual **Mississippi Delta Blues Festival.** The rest of the year, visit the more accessible beer-and-blues bar inside the **Walnut Street Bait Shop** (662/332-0315), at 128 Walnut Street in the historic downtown area, across from the levee-lining casinos.

For accommodations, look along US-82 near the junction with US-61, east of town: **Days Inn, Best Western, Ramada,** and **Hampton** are all there.

For more information contact the Greenville **visitors bureau** (662/378-3141) at 915 Washington Avenue.

Highway 61 Revisited

Between Greenville and Vicksburg, the GRR continues along Hwy-1 through the cotton-rich bottomlands, the landscape as unvarying as the country music that dominates the radio dial. Before the Civil War, this land was nearly uninhabitable hardwood forests and fever-riddled swamps, home to snakes, panthers, and mosquitoes. After Reconstruction, the valuable oaks, sweetgum, and hickory were logged off, the swamps drained, and levees built; now just the snakes and mosquitoes remain. It's a long, slow ride, while US-61 races along to the east.

East of Greenville, just west of US-61, the town of Leland was the boyhood home of Muppet-master Jim Henson. There's now a small and suitably warm-spirited museum, on the north side of US-82 at Deer Creek, honoring him, Kermit the Frog, and his other creations.

The 50 miles of US-82 between Greenville and Greenwood pass through the heart of Delta blues country, and a number of nearby towns feature high on any "blues pilgrimage" itinerary: Holly Ridge holds the grave of **Charley Patton** ("Voice of the Delta," 1891–1934);

Across the Mississippi from Rosedale in a cotton field off Hwy-1 is **Rohwer, Arkansas,** where 8,500 Japanese-Americans were forced from their California homes and imprisoned for the duration of World War II.

About 30 miles east of Greenville, **Moorhead** is known in blues geography as the place "where the Southern crosses the Dog," an allusion to the Southern and Yazoo-Delta (aka Yellow Dog) Railroads. Nearby **Money,** Mississippi, was the location of the notorious 1955 murder of 15-year-old **Emmett Till,** a key moment in the burgeoning Civil Rights Movement.

Hearing Delta blues live can be as big a challenge as finding it on the radio. Helena, Arkansas's historic **KFFA 1360 AM** plays at least an hour at lunchtime, and you can catch more-contemporary music on Greenville's **WBAD 94.3 FM.**

Birth of the Teddy Bear

About 30 miles north of Vicksburg along US-61, the hamlet of **Onward** has a historical plaque marking the "birthplace of the Teddy Bear." The original Teddy Bear was inspired by a cub from the woods near Onward: Tied by a noose to a tree in the canebrakes, the cute fellow was found by President Teddy Roosevelt while hunting here in 1903. His refusal to shoot the defenseless animal, publicized in an editorial cartoon, garnered such popular approval that a New York firm requested the president's permission to name a stuffed toy after him. The only rub is, T. R. didn't actually refuse to shoot—because, in fact, he wasn't there. But neither was the cub! According to members of the hunting party, the president's guide, Holt Collier, an African-American veteran of the Confederate cavalry, was challenged to prove he could lasso a bear. So he did, when one came along through the swamp—an old and rather weak one, as it turned out, that splashed around in a slough before they cut him loose. T. R., however, having tired of waiting for game, had returned to camp and missed the whole episode.

Robert Johnson (1911–1938) is remembered by a burial marker in Itta Bena; B. B. King was born in Indianola, and is honored in an annual festival the first weekend in June; while south on US-61, Rolling Fork was the birthplace of **Muddy Waters** (1915–1983).

Vicksburg stands at the junction of the Great River Road and our **Southern Pacific** tour along US-80 (see page 759). This route runs from San Diego to Savannah, and is described on pages 724–780.

Vicksburg

The "Red Carpet City of the South," **Vicksburg** (pop. 26,407) didn't roll one out for the Union army during the Civil War; rather, the city so stubbornly opposed Union efforts to win control of the Mississippi River that it became the target of one of the longest sieges in U.S. military history. After the war ended, Vicksburg suffered once again in 1876, when the city woke up to face a mud flat of flopping fish after the Mississippi River found itself a new streambed—overnight. Thanks to the diligence of engineers who redirected the Yazoo River, Vicksburg has its waterfront back, now complete with several modern-day sharks, whose slot machines and roulette wheels spin 24 hours a day for your entertainment.

Many of the city's posh **antebellum houses** survived the Civil War with varying degrees of damage, and during the post-war Reconstruction several additional mansions were added to the bluffs overlooking the river. Most of these homes are open to the public (for around $6 each), and during the fortnight-long "Pilgrimages" in late March and mid-October, slightly discounted multiple-house tours are available. The architecturally varied mansions, many of which double as B&Bs, and their copious inventories of fine antiques are more fascinating to decorative arts aficionados than to history buffs, who may find tours illuminating more for what is omitted than included. Stories of deprivation and Union plundering, cannonballs in parlor walls, and other wartime relics are religiously enshrined, yet never a word is spoken about slavery.

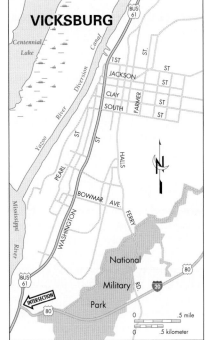

The most famous of Vicksburg's antebellum homes is **Cedar Grove** (daily; 601/636-1000), south of downtown at 2200 Oak Street, which has a spectacular panorama over lush gardens down the bluffs to the broad Mississippi River. Ironically, Cedar Grove was built for a cousin of General Sherman, who used it as a military hospital. Another grand old mansion, **Anchuca** (601/661-0111), at 1010 E. 1st Street, preserves a more-complete picture of antebellum life, with well-preserved gardens and slave quarters. Dozens more, including some dating from the 1870s up through the early 1900s, are found throughout Vicksburg's pleasantly cobblestoned residential areas.

The downtown commercial district, on the bluffs above the river, offers another, more contemporary glimpse into Southern culture. If you've ever tried to imagine a world without Coke, step into the **Biedenharn Museum of Coca-Cola Memorabilia**, smack downtown at 1107 Washington Street, and see where one man's ingenuity slew all hopes for such a world. Here, in 1894, Joseph Biedenharn conceived of putting the strictly regional soda-fountain drink into bottles, the better to reach new markets; the rest, as they say, is history. Toast worldwide domination with some of the classic stuff, straight up or over ice cream, or pay $2 to view galleries full of old promotional serving trays and the like.

To escape from Vicksburg's indoor onslaught of Chippendale claw feet, stop by **Margaret's Grocery** (601/638-1163), right on the GRR (old US-61) on the north side of town at 4535 N. Washington Street, where an assemblage of huge hand-lettered signs preach biblically-inspired words of wisdom at passersby.

Vicksburg National Military Park

Though the engineering feat that redirected the Mississippi River, and brought Vicksburg more civil engineers per capital than any other U.S. city, is impressive, it's the story of the Civil War campaign to split the Confederacy in half that dominates history here. The battle for Vicksburg, which was known as the "Gibraltar of the Confederacy," reached its dramatic conclusion on July 4, 1863, amid the strategic heights and ravines of the 1,800-acre **Vicksburg National Military Park.** The ins and outs and strategizing behind the 47-day Siege of Vicksburg, and the story behind the 1,300-odd markers and monuments, becomes emotionally compelling after some accounting of the anecdotes of individual valor, of odd courtesies amid the bloodshed, and of the tragedy and humanity that lie behind the 16 winding miles of stone. The **visitors center** (daily; $8 per car; 601/636-0583), on the east side of Vicksburg via Clay Street or off I-20 exit 4, has exhibits, maps, brochures, and audio tours with narration and sound effects. Or, you can hire a guide to accompany you in your car and explain everything from battle tactics to the symbolism of the monuments. The advantage to a live guide is the opportunity to ask questions and to delve into whatever suits your curiosity, be it stories of the many women who fought incognito, or of the immigrants who enlisted to win citizenship.

*Late in the year when the pecan crop is in, you can buy **pecans** from vans or shacks beside the highway. But buy pre-shelled ones, or spend hours struggling with a nutcracker.*

While Vicksburg's surrender allowed President Lincoln to declare that "the Father of Waters now flows unvexed to the sea," local whites stayed vexed for over 80 years: Because the surrender occurred on July 4, until the end of World War II Independence Day in Vicksburg was celebrated only by African Americans.

One of the most unusual sights in the Vicksburg Military Park is the USS *Cairo,* an ironclad paddlewheel battleship that was sunk by a torpedo during the Civil War. Preserved for a century by the Mississippi mud, it was recovered and restored, and is now on display in its own museum, above the river at the west end of the park.

Vicksburg also has two military cemeteries, one for each side. The Union cemetery is the largest Civil War burial ground in the country, holding the remains of more than 17,000 soldiers who died here and all over the south; more than 12,000 of the dead are simply marked "unknown." Another 5,000 Confederate dead are buried in the Vicksburg City Cemetery.

Vicksburg Practicalities

Vicksburg has an enormously compelling history, but it's also a very pleasant place to spend some time. For a traditional Southern feast, sit down to the communal round table at **Walnut Hills** (601/638-4910) at 1214 Adams Street and dig into the endless supply of classic regional dishes, from fried pork tenderloin to okra; given the fresh ingredients and depending on how much of a pig you can be, the moderate prices are a great value. Deep-fried tamale addicts should seek out **Solly's Hot Tamales** (601/636-2020), near the "Cedar

*The icon of Southern gentility and refreshment, the mint julep, was allegedly born in Vicksburg: Water from fragrant **Mint Springs** in what is now the National Military Park was mixed with good Kentucky bourbon brought to town by riverboat captains. It goes without saying that Kentuckians and Tennesseeans consider this to be pure fiction.*

"Church of the Golden Hand"

Grove" mansion on US-61 Business at 1921 Washington Street. Barbecue lovers will want to sample the offerings at **Goldie's Trail** (601/636-9839), 4127 S. Washington Street.

Vicksburg motels, found at the south edge of town along I-20 between the Mississippi River and the Military Park, include a wide selection of the national chains and their local imitators; one of the nicest is the **Battlefield Inn** ($50–75; 601/638-5811), at the I-20/US-61 junction.

If you're in the mood, you can play Rhett and Scarlett for a night, pampering yourself with canopied beds in one of the dozen camellia-draped antebellum mansions (including Cedar Grove and Anchuca) that double as plush $120-a-night B&Bs. Any will have you whistling "Dixie," but true history buffs will want to request the Grant Room at Cedar Grove, which is still furnished with the very bed the general used after Union forces occupied Vicksburg. The staff claims ol' Sam was a bedridden drunk for his entire stay, but pay no attention—he was probably a poor tipper at the bar, and folks around here bear grudges for generations over things like that.

For thorough and concise information on lodging and attractions, contact the friendly **Vicksburg Convention and Visitors Bureau** (601/636-9421 or 800/221-3536) at 1221 Washington Street, or visit their **tourist information center** opposite the entrance to the National Military Park. If your visit falls during Pilgrimage, don't expect easy pickings on rooms: Most B&Bs are booked up to *two years* in advance for those weeks.

You won't notice many people lolling about on grassy lawns or parks in the southern Delta, for the simple reason that this has become the realm of the **fire ant**, whose stinging bite would shame a wasp into adopting some other line of work.

Port Gibson

One of the many little gems of the GRR is 30 miles south of Vicksburg: **Port Gibson**, the town General Grant found "too beautiful to burn." As they did with Savannah, Georgia, the Union Army spared Port Gibson during the Civil War, and decades of economic doldrums have spared the town from the Wal-Mart sprawl that at times seems to have enveloped the rest of the South. Fine homes still grace the pleasantly shaded main drag, but most eye-catching is the giant Monty Python prop known as

For an overview of a nearly vanished Southern culture, spend some time at the **Museum of the Southern Jewish Experience** (601/362-6357). Based at a former Jewish summer camp in **Utica**, a half hour to the northeast of Port Gibson, the museum also has a branch exhibit in the basement of **Temple B'nai Israel** in Natchez, 213 S. Commerce Street (by appointment only; 601/442-1321).

the "**Church of the Golden Hand**" because its steeple is topped by a gold-leafed hand, its index finger pointing the way to Heaven. Actually, this is the circa-1859 First Presbyterian Church, whose interior is lit by the gasoliers of the famous steamboat *Robert E. Lee,* the record-setting winner of the Great Steamboat Race of 1870. Newspapers of the day reckoned that millions of dollars were wagered on the outcome of the New Orleans-to-St. Louis race, which attracted international attention. The *Lee*'s three-day, 18-hour, and 14-minute victory was an upset for the favored title holder, the *Natchez.*

Across the street from the Golden Hand, next to an Exxon station, stands another unusual building, **Temple Gemiluth Chassed,** an elaborate Moorish-arched temple built in 1891 by Port Gibson's then-large and prosperous Jewish community.

Just up the street, **Grant's Place** (601/437-4351), at 1091 N US-61, serves great fried chicken, authentically served up southern style, with turnip greens, pepper sauce, and cornbread. Yum.

Ruins of Windsor and Emerald Mound

From Port Gibson, you can race along the 70-mph US-61 to Natchez, or follow a quietly scenic 50-mile detour along kudzu-lined country backroads and the serene Natchez Trace Parkway. The great Mississippi writer Willie Morris said "there is no more haunted, complex terrain in America" than this, and traveling through here you can't help but be aware of the region's many ghostly remnants. The looping first part of this route leaves Port Gibson next to the Exxon station, heading west on Rodney Road (Hwy-552) toward the Mississippi River past abandoned homesteads, and picturesque old cemeteries rotting in the woods. After about 13 miles, look for a small sign and follow a short gravel road until you spot giant stone columns poking through the treetops. This is the **Ruins of Windsor.** Once the state's most lavish Greek Revival mansion and landmark to river pilots, it was reduced by an 1890 fire to its bare Corinthian ribs.

Another enigmatic remain is further south, nearly invisible in the lush growth: **Emerald Mound,** a prehistoric platform over 400 feet wide and 35 feet tall. The second-largest mound in North America, it was built around 1250 AD and was still in use as a ceremonial center when the first Europeans arrived; Emerald Mound is open daily, and located on Hwy-553 just west of Natchez Trace Parkway milepost 10.3.

Ruins of Windsor

Natchez

Before the Civil War, **Natchez** (NATCH-iss, rhymes with "matches") had the most millionaires per capita in the United States, and it shows. If luxurious antebellum houses make your heart beat faster, Natchez (which has more than 500 antebellum structures inside the city limits), with its innumerable white columns and rich smorgasbord of Italian marble, imported crystal, and sterling silver, might just put you in the local ICU. That so much antebellum finery still exists is because Natchez, unlike Vicksburg, surrendered to Grant's army almost without a fight. Anti-Yankee sentiment may in fact run higher now than during the war, for Natchez was vehemently opposed to the Confederacy, and outspokenly

Natchez Trace Parkway

A mile or so south of Port Gibson, US-61 and the GRR cross the much more relaxed Natchez Trace Parkway, which, like the Blue Ridge Parkway, is a scenic route managed by the National Park Service. The Parkway follows the route of the old Natchez Trace, a pre-Columbian Indian path that grew into the major overland route between the Gulf Coast and the upper Mississippi and Ohio River Valleys in the years before steamboats provided a faster alternative. The Natchez Trace appeared on maps as early as 1733, and from the 1780s to the 1820s, when steamboats made it obsolete, the Natchez Trace was one of the nation's most traveled routes. Farmers and craftspeople in the Ohio River Valley would transport their products by raft downstream to Natchez or New Orleans, then return on foot, staying at the dozens of inns along the route while doing battle with swamps, mosquitoes, and bands of thieves.

The entire 430-mile length of the Parkway, which runs from Nashville south to the edge of Natchez, with a short break around Jackson, is well-paved and makes a delightful driving or riding route, with places of interest marked every few miles. Just north of Port Gibson at milemarker 41.5, the Sunken Trace preserves a deeply eroded, 200-yard-long section of the trail, the canopy of moss-laden cypress trees offering one of the most evocative five-minute walks you can imagine. Between Port Gibson and Natchez, sights along this short (and eminently bicycleable) stretch include the prehistoric **Emerald Mound,** the second-largest prehistoric structure in the United States, which dates from around 1400 AD and offers a commanding view of the woodlands. **Mount Locust** at milemarker 15.5 is a restored Trace roadhouse and the best place to pick up parkway information; if you're fortunate, you might get a tour guided by park ranger Eric Chamberlain, who was born in the house, and whose family lived there for five generations.

The National Park police keep the parkway under very thorough radar surveillance, by the way, so try to stay within the posted speed limit, often 35 mph with a maximum of 50 mph.

Across the Mississippi from Natchez, the town of **Ferriday, Louisiana,** was where rocker **Jerry Lee "Great Balls of Fire" Lewis** and his cousin, evangelist **Jimmy Swaggart,** grew up. The Lewis family home is now a museum (daily; $7 donation; 318/757-2460), with 11 rooms full of old photos, baby clothes and other mementos.

There are no cotton fields around Natchez, because all the cotton that paid for these mansions was grown across the river in the Louisiana bottomlands.

against Mississippi's secession from the Union. Since Natchez was second only to New Orleans as social and cultural capital of a region with two-thirds of the richest people in America, most of whom owed their wealth to slave-picked cotton, its support of the Union might seem a little incongruous.

Of course, such apparent contradictions should come as no surprise from a community raised with genteel cotillions and the Mississippi's busiest red-light district side by side. (Once-disreputable Natchez Under-the-Hill, where the most famous brothel in the South was destroyed by a fire in 1992, is today but a single gentrified block of riverfront bars and restaurants lined up alongside a permanently moored riverboat casino.

As befits the place that originated the concept, the annual Natchez Pilgrimages (held in late Spring, October, and at Christmas) are twice as long as the typical 10–15 days done elsewhere. The number of **antebellum mansions** open to the public more than doubles, hoop skirts and brass-buttoned waistcoats abound, and musical diversions like the **Confederate Pageant** are held nightly. Among the most fascinating homes open year-round is the one that didn't get finished: **Longwood,** on Lower Woodville Road, is the nation's largest octagonal house, capped by a red onion dome. Its grounds are fittingly gothic, too, with moss-dripping tree limbs, sunken driveway, and the family cemetery out in the woods. Information on the "pilgrimages," other house tours (about $8 per house), and the chance to stay in one of many historic B&Bs, all comes from the same group, Natchez Pilgrimage Tours (601/446-6631 or 800/647-6742), who also run horse-drawn carriage tours.

Southern history doesn't merely comprise those Greek Revival heaps and their *Gone With the Wind* stereotypes. Natchez, for example, had a large population of

Mammy's Cupboard, Natchez

free blacks, whose story is told in downtown's **Museum of Afro-American History and Culture** (call for hours; 601/445-0728), in the old Post Office at 301 Main Street, where you'll also find interesting Black Heritage walking-tour brochures. Large Jewish sections in the **City Cemetery** (follow signs for the National Cemetery, and the city's is along the way) also furnish evidence of the South's tapestried past. The marble statuary and decorative wrought iron offer a pleasant outdoor respite for weary mansion-goers, too.

One last Natchez landmark deserves special mention: **Mammy's Cupboard** (601/445-8957), a roadside restaurant in the shape of a five-times-larger-than-life Southern woman, whose red skirts house the small dining room and gift shop. Having survived many incarnations and abandonments, Mammy's is once again open for business, offering rather refined lunches (cups of tea and dainty sandwiches) from 11 AM to 2 PM Monday–Saturday. She can be found along the east side of four-lane US-61, roughly five miles south of town.

Natchez Practicalities

As befits a place with a strong tourism trade, Natchez has some great places to eat. Natchez is almost the southern extremity of the Tamale Belt, and you can sit down to a paperboard dish of them (a dozen for $6) at **Fat Mama's** (601/442-4548), in a little log cabin at 500 S. Canal Street. Fat Mama's has a large shady patio out back, and also serves killer "Knock You Naked" margaritas, a combination which draws large crowds on summer nights (and earned the place a role in Jill Conner Browne's novel *Sweet Potato Queens' Book of Love*).

If you prefer fried catfish, po' boys, and chocolate shakes, head down to the **Malt Shop** (601/445-4843), where Martin Luther King Street (US-61 Business) dead-ends into Homochitto Street. For a change of pace, try **Pearl Street Pasta** (601/442-9284), just off Main Street at 105 S. Pearl Street, whose short, dinner-only menu is eclectic, reasonably priced, and laced with vegetables that haven't been boiled to oblivion.

Accommodations in Natchez include a half-dozen familiar names scattered along US-61 and US-84 both north and south of downtown. For a more memorable experience, consider staying the night in one of those historic mansions, many of which do double-duty as B&Bs. The circa-1890 **Highpoint** ($100 and up; 601/442-6963 or 800/283-4099), on the north side of downtown at 215 Linton Avenue, is a good example, with comfortable rooms, a generous "plantation" breakfast, evening mint juleps, and friendly hosts whose political, Southern, and Confederate connections would make any storyteller green with envy. Top-of-the-line is probably **Monmouth Plantation** ($175 and up; 601/442-5852), 36 Melrose Avenue, preserved as it was in its circa-1818 heyday, and set amidst 25 acres of lush gardens. Keep in mind the enormous popularity of Pilgrimage requires seriously advanced bookings during those times.

For an illustrated B&B guide and other useful information contact the **Natchez Convention and Visitors Bureau** (800/647-6724), which operates a large orientation center near the Mississippi River bridge (US-84) at 640 S. Canal Street.

Woodville: Rosemont Plantation

Rolling and curving past hay fields and woods, the distinctively red earth of southern Mississippi crowding the soft shoulders, the GRR passes quickly over the 45 miles between Natchez and the Louisiana state line. You won't see it from the highway, but just across the Mississippi is possibly the most significant piece of engineering anywhere along its length: the **Old River Project**. More than mere flood control, the project is designed to keep the Mississippi going down to Baton Rouge and New Orleans, rather than finding a new route to the Gulf via the Atchafalaya River. This actually happened during the 1948 flood, and there are hydrologists who predict it is only a matter of time before it will happen again—a potential catastrophe for downstream cities along both rivers. About 10 miles north of the border, an unprepossessing intersection of gas stations marks the turnoff west for **Woodville** (pop. 1,393), where a lovely old courthouse sits at the center of a green square full of stately old oak trees, and a trio of historic churches line the somnolent streets.

The biggest attraction of Woodville, however, is a mile east of the GRR on US-24, where a small sign along the highway marks the entrance to **Rosemont Plantation** (daily 10 AM–5 PM Mar.–Dec.; $6; 601/888-6809), the boyhood home of Confederate President Jefferson Davis. Built in 1830 with wooden pegs holding together hand-hewn posts and beams, the house is surrounded by a grove of live oaks and a large rose garden, planted by Davis's mother, after which the plantation takes its name.

LOUISIANA

As the GRR approaches its southern end, land and river begin to merge. With giant levees on one side and standing water on the other, it's easy to imagine the land is sinking—and indeed, by the time you roll off elevated I-10 into New Orleans, you will be four to six feet *below* sea level.

From the St. Francisville ferry to the Interstate bridge just west of New Orleans, the GRR crosses the Mississippi four times, threading along rough back roads past a series of fine antebellum plantation homes along what's sometimes called **Plantation Alley.** The GRR also runs among a barrage of industrial giants whose toxic discharges have earned the region another sobriquet: "Chemical Corridor." The Great River Road across Louisiana is not without its charms—a vividly painted church out in a field, or wrought iron gates framing exquisitely gnarled live oaks festooned with Spanish moss—but these are all too often overshadowed by the specter of a land being poisoned for profit. End of sermon.

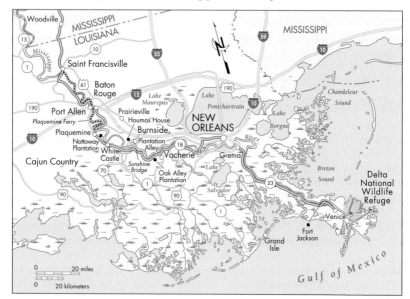

St. Francisville

Louisiana is divided into parishes rather than counties, one of many subtle reminders of the original French Catholic settlement of the state. The past is ever-present in this part of the country, so turn west off US-61 at **St. Francisville**, and explore the myriad tales of this fascinating community, which grew up around the graveyard of a frontier-era monastery. Pick up an anecdotally rich walking-tour brochure at the **West Feliciana**

Greenwood Plantation, St. Francisville

Historical Society Museum (225/635-6330), at 11757 Ferdinand Street, for a sample of the architectural charms that draw visitors to this curious little town. All around St. Francisville, there are grand old manor homes, most notably at **Rosedown Plantation** (daily; $10; 225/635-3332), on Hwy-10 just east of US-61, where a 370-acre state-run historic site preserves an 1830s main house, a pair of slave cabins, and lush formal gardens. About five miles southeast of St. Francisville on Hwy-965, off US-61 at the "Roadside BBQ" stand, is the **Audubon State Historic Site** (daily; 225/635-3739) also known as the Oakley House, where in 1821 naturalist and illustrator John James Audubon came to work as a resident tutor while he compiled his comprehensive "Birds of America."

Along with the rich history, St. Francisville also has one compelling, contemporary attraction: the **Magnolia Cafe** (225/635-6528), a wonderful little restaurant housed in the old 3V motor court complex at the corner of Commerce and Ferdinand Streets. The café moved here when its original home (a gas station) burned down in 2003, but it's better than ever, still serving some of the best-tasting po' boys in the state that invented them. The Magnolia doubles as one of the coolest little nightclubs anywhere, drawing big-name alt-folk performers like Dave Alvin and the Bottle Rockets, who stop here in between big-city gigs. There's also a coffee house-cum-art gallery, occasional cabins for overnight guests; there's no better place to get a feel for this part of Louisiana.

Heading on from St. Francisville, race south down US-61 to Baton Rogue, or snake west along Ferdinand Street for about a mile until the road dead-ends at the large car ferry (on the hour and half hour; $1) that shuttles across the Mississippi toward Lousiana's legendary "Cajun Country."

A dozen miles west of St. Francisville and the Great River Road along Hwy-1, the small town of **Morganza, Louisiana,** was the place where the character played by Jack Nicholson was beaten to death in his sleeping bag in the classic 1960s road movie *Easy Rider.* North of St. Francisville via Hwy-66 is **Angola**, location of a state prison that holds a famous annual rodeo and Louisiana's "Death Row," which was featured in the book and movie *Dead Man Walking.*

Baton Rouge

From the lofty vantage point of the I-10 bridge over the Mississippi River, **Baton Rouge** (pop. 227,818) appears to be a largely industrial city, its skyline dominated by smokestacks, a WW II destroyer, a mock–Mississippi Riverboat casino, and the nation's tallest state capitol—essentially a 34-story monument to the populist demagoguery of Huey "Kingfish" Long. Just south of the towering Capitol, a lifesize animatronic figure of Long, the state's legendary Depression-era governor, dominates the **Old State Capitol** (daily; $4), that clearly visible white Gothic-style castle—the only thing missing is a moat. Inside the restored 1847 edifice are engaging computer-aided history exhibits, including one about Huey Long's unresolved 1935 assassination: Was the patronage-dealing, road-building, vote-buying potentate the target of premeditated murder, or was then-U.S. Senator Long the victim of his five trigger-happy bodyguards' "friendly fire," aimed at a man who merely punched the boss? Review the evidence and draw your own conclusions.

Another lesson in Louisiana history can be yours at the wonderful **Rural Life Museum** (daily; $7; 225/765-2437), managed by Louisiana State University and located at 4600 Essen Road, east of downtown off I-10 exit 160. This expansive collection of shotgun houses, barns, farming equipment, riverboats, donkey carts, hand tools, and appliances—basically, anything that might have been seen in the state 100 years ago—was assembled on a former plantation by artist Steele Burden. The rest of the plantation is now a picturesque garden that covers 25 acres.

Baton Rouge hosts a **National Balloon Festival** early in August. Besides being a beautiful sight, the hundreds of colorful balloons take part in a target competition, trying to drop bean bags onto a bulls-eye from 1,000 feet in the air.

The popularity of college football shouldn't be underestimated in Baton Rouge: Motel No Vacancy signs light up all over town whenever the **LSU Tigers** play. Basketball, baseball, and other sports are big, too; for tickets, call LSU (800/960-8587).

Along with po' boys and boiled crawdads, Louisiana's roadsides offer another local specialty, the **daiquiri bar**. Like a high-octane version of a Dairy Queen slush, daiquiris come premixed in a variety of sticky fruit flavors and sizes up to the quart that kick: yes, an eye-crossing 32-ouncer. If that isn't enough, many of these bars have drive-up windows. In the eyes of the law, that piece of masking tape across the cup's lid makes it a "sealed container"; seems the law doesn't care about the straw.

Baton Rouge Practicalities

If you're looking for a place to eat and absorb a little Baton Rouge ambience, the **Pastime** (225/343-5490), a few blocks from the Old State Capitol at 252 South Boulevard, right under the I-10 interchange, is one of those windowless, smoky sports bars ideally suited for discussing political chicanery over po' boys, fried fish, and beer. Best pizzas in town, too; try the one topped with crawfish tails for some local flavor. Another excellent place to eat a fine meal and get filled in on local lifeways is world-famous **Jay's Barbecue** (225/343-5082), 4215 Government Street, open 10 AM–10 PM every day but Sunday for real good ribs, beef, pulled-pork sandwiches—and, if you're lucky and ask nicely, smoked alligator.

Another bunch of good eating and drinking prospects are clustered around the Highland Avenue entrance to Louisiana State University, a couple of miles south of I-10. **Louie's Cafe** (225/346-8221), 209 W. State Street across from the Super Fresh shopping plaza, is open 24 hours, so there's no excuse to miss it. Facing the LSU gates at 3357 Highland is **The Chimes** (225/383-1754), a restaurant and oyster bar with "100 beers from 24 countries" and frequent live music. Several other bars in the vicinity offer music with some regularity, but be warned that undergraduate projectile vomiting is a serious hazard.

While there are a number of hotels in downtown Baton Rouge, and along the highways south and east of town, most of the inexpensive accommodations cluster around exit 151 on I-10, two miles west of the Mississippi in Port Allen.

The Baton Rouge **visitor information center** (504/383-1825 or 800/527-6843), in the State Capitol complex, should be able to satisfy your informational and glossy brochure needs.

The bridge that now carries US-190 over the Mississippi was built during the gubernatorial reign of the notorious "Kingfish," Huey P. Long. The structure was designed to be low enough to prevent oceangoing freighters from passing, thus snuffing out the chances of Vicksburg and other upstream cities to compete with the port of Baton Rouge—now the nation's fifth-busiest.

Cajun Country

West of New Orleans and Baton Rouge, a world away from the grand houses of lining the Mississippi River, the watery world known as "Cajun Country" spreads along the Gulf of Mexico. If you have the time to explore, the region offers an incredible range of delights for all the senses: antebellum plantation houses and moss-covered monuments set amidst groves of stately old oak trees, with all manner of wildlife (from birds to gators) chirping and squawking away in the oddly still bayous, and the sound of accordions and the aroma of boudin sausages and boiling crawfish emanating from what can seem like every other doorway. Cajun Country is also sugarcane country: over half a million acres are cultivated each year, rising to 10-feet in height by the end of summer, when the cane is chopped down and made into molasses at the many aromatic mills. The name "Cajun" comes from the French-speaking Catholic Acadians, 10,000 of whom were chucked out of Canada when the English took over in 1755. The Acadians were refused entry by the American colonies on the East Coast, and had to make their way to this corner of still-French Louisiana, where they absorbed many other cultural influences while retaining their distinct identity.

US-90, the main route through Cajun Country, follows the route of the Old Spanish Trail, the historic cross-country highway that, in the early days of the automobile, linked San Diego and St. Augustine. Though the main route has been widened and "improved" countless times in the past century (it is often signed as "Future I-49"), many wonderful stretches of old country road still wind along shady bayous. Wandering aimlessly, getting lost and found amidst

For a dramatic perspective, cross the Mississippi on the Hwy-70 **Sunshine Bridge,** which runs between the GRR at Donaldson and I-10 exit 182. A quick link between Plantation Alley and New Orleans, the Sunshine Bridge was named in honor of **"Singing Governor"** Jimmy Davis's most famous song, "You Are My Sunshine," now the state's official song.

the many small backwater towns is half the fun of spending time here, but there are a number of places where the whole Cajun Country experience comes together in a concentrated dose. One of your main stops should be the historic town of **St. Martinville,** where the **Church of St. Martin de Tours**($1; 337/394-7334), 103 Main Street, stands at the center of many blocks of ornate buildings and majestic oak trees, including the one featured in the Cajun-flavored Longfellow poem "Evangeline". St. Martinville is just north of **New Iberia,** the home of Tabasco sauce, perhaps Cajun Country's most identifiable product, and just south of another great stop in Cajun Country: **Breaux Bridge,** the "Crawfish Capital of the World," located just off the I-10 freeway, a quick half-hour west of Baton Rouge. Next to the bridge in Breaux Bridge, look for **Café des Amis** (337/332-151), 140 E. Bridge Street, renowned for its Saturday morning "Zydeco Breakfast," starting at 8 AM.

Plantation Alley

Between Baton Rouge and New Orleans, if you don't have a stomach strong enough to bear miles of industrial blight, hop onto the I-10 freeway, but if your senses can handle the constant juxtaposition of refined domestic design alongside satanic industrial complexes, with a few trailer parks, upscale vacation homes, and photogenic above-ground cemeteries thrown in for good measure, the Great River Road is full of treats, and this 100-mile traverse of what is promoted as "Plantation Alley" may well be a highlight of your trip. To 19th-century passengers aboard the packet steamboats traveling the lower Mississippi, the great mansions adorning the river bends between Baton Rouge and New Orleans must have made an impressive sight. The houses are no less grand today but, sadly, their surroundings have been degraded by the presence of enormous petrochemical refineries. These have, by and large, replaced the antebellum sugar-cane fields as the region's economic engine, but in late summer when the cane is 10 feet tall and the smell of molasses fills the air, you can *almost* pretend nothing has changed.

Giving directions along Plantation Alley is complicated by the winding Mississippi, with its bridges and ferry boats, by the numerous roads and highways, and by the fact that the region is equally easy to explore from Baton Rouge or New Orleans, but it's as good place as many to get lost and found again, so take your time and enjoy the ride. We recommend 3 or 4 of the most popular and memorable plantation estates, but there are many along the way, in varying stages of restoration and decay.

Nottoway

Heading north to south, as the river flows, the first of these riverside manors is **Nottoway** (daily; $10; 225/545-2730), whose 64 rooms place it among the largest plantation homes in the South. Built in the 1850s, it was also one of the last "big houses" to be built. On the western shore of the Mississippi, along Hwy-1 about two miles north of the town of White Castle, Nottoway is a bright white Greek Revival structure enclosing over an acre of floor space, so you'll be glad you don't have to pay the air-conditioning bills or do the dusting.

Two miles south of White Castle, a state-run ferry jogs across the river (every 30 mins, during commute hours only) to Carville on the other side.

Burnside: Houmas House

The most familiar (and easiest to reach) of Louisiana's plantation homes, **Houmas House** (daily; $10; 225/473-7841), stands on the east bank of the Mississippi amid 12 acres of manicured grounds. Another of Louisiana's *grandes dames*, Houmas House is a dignified complex of buildings constructed over many generations, mainly between the 1780s and 1840s. The main is composed of white columns and rich red-ochre walls supporting a central belvedere (like a cupola) from which the antebellum owners could survey their domain; today, the endless seas of sugar cane have been replaced by the monstrous sprawl of the neighboring Du Pont plant. Once the seat of a massive, 20,000-acre sugarcane plantation, Houmas House may well look strangely familiar: the stately home was used as the setting for Robert Aldrich's 1965 gothic Southern horror film, *Hush, Hush, Sweet Charlotte*, starring Bette Davis, Olivia de Havilland, Joseph Cotten, and Bruce Dern. B&B rooms, and a restaurant, are also available.

Driving along the river near Houmas House, you may pass the remains of another old plantation home, **Tezcuco**, which was built in 1855 and burned to the ground in 2002; all that remains are the chimneys and a number of outbuildings. Yet another local landmark, the 7,500-square-foot, 1820s-era **Bocage House**, was recently up for sale-for a cool $5.5 million.

Located at 40136 River Road (Hwy-942) near the hamlet of Darrow, Houmas House is just 4 miles west of the I-10 freeway via Hwy-22 or Hwy-44, and is about a dozen miles north of the "Sunshine Bridge" (Hwy-70) over the Mississippi.

Vacherie: Oak Alley and Laura

Traveling along the GRR, moldering concrete mausoleums, houses with loud colors and louvered French doors, insouciant pedestrians along the levee (not to mention the dangerously large potholes), all may arrest your attention briefly, but **Oak Alley** (daily; $10; 225/265-2151) will probably stop you in your tracks. This place is to antebellum plantations what Bora Bora is to islands, or the Golden Gate is to bridges: Even if you've managed to avoid seeing Oak Alley on tourist brochures, or in the movies *Interview with a Vampire* or *Primary Colors*, it will look familiar—or rather, it will look exactly like it ought to. Plus, no cooling tower or gas flare mars the immediate horizon. For the full effect of the grand quarter-mile-long allée of arching live oaks, which were

Oak Alley

New Orleans

Royal Street in New Orleans' French Quarter

Royal Street in the French Quarter

Long famous for its easy-going, live-and-let-live personality, and for placing a high value the good things in life—food, drink, and music, to name a few—New Orleans was shocked by the destruction that followed in the wake of Hurricane Katrina. No doubt the Big Easy will take some time to recover from the $200+ billion worth of damage, but no one who knows and loves New Orleans can have any doubt that the city will get its groove back before too long.

With deep roots going back to the earliest days of European settlement in North America, New Orleans is very proud of its multicultural heritage: Its people, its ornate buildings, and especially its food all reflect a uniquely diverse and resilient culture. The focus of New Orleans, for visitors and locals alike, is the **Vieux Carré**, in the French Quarter, which sits on the highest ground in the city and thus escaped the worst of Katrina's floods. Centering on Bourbon Street, lined with tacky souvenir stalls and strip clubs catering to conventioneers, this square mile is full of wrought-iron balconies on picturesque brick buildings. Yes, it's a huge tourist attraction, but it's also the heart of old New Orleans. At the center of the quarter is **Jackson Square,** where a statue of the victor of the Battle of New Orleans, Andrew Jackson, stands in front of St. Louis Cathedral, which was rebuilt in 1850 on top of an original foundation dating back to 1724. The nearby **Old U.S. Mint** (daily; $5; 504/568-6968), at 400 Esplanade, has the famous "Streetcar Named Desire" on display in the courtyard, and holds excellent collections tracing the history of two New Orleans institutions: jazz and Mardi Gras.

After dark, there's live music aplenty in all styles and modes, but one stop you have to make is at **Preservation Hall** (nightly from 8 PM; $5), 726 St. Peter Street, for the redolent ambience and the live traditional Dixieland jazz.

Practicalities

New Orleans has some of the best and most enjoyable places to eat in the world, so plan to take the time to enjoy yourself here. In the French Quarter, the informal **Acme Oyster House** (504/522-5973), at 724 Iberville Street, is the place to go for the freshest bivalves, but it closes early by New Orleans standards—around 10 PM nightly. At the other end of the spectrum is expensive, formal **Antoine's** (504/581-4422), at 713 St. Louis Street, one of the oldest restaurants in the world, serves classic French-Creole cuisine to a who's who of New Orleans society. Another very popular spot is **K-Paul's Louisiana Kitchen** (504/524-7394) at 416 Chartres Street, where Chef Paul Prudhomme, who popularized Cajun-style "blackened" food all over the country, saves the very best examples for his own place. Another world-famous place that merits a meal or two: **NOLA** (504/522-6652), at 534 St. Louis Street, a comparatively casual setting for celebrated chef Emeril Lagasse's finely crafted Creole fare.

No visit to New Orleans is complete without a stop for coffee and beignets (and some serious people-watching) at busy **Cafe du Monde** (504/525-4544), open 24 hours a day on the river side of Jackson Square at 800 Decatur Street. A wider range of beverages, and even more immersive history, is on tap at the legendary **Napolean House** bar (504/524-9752), 500 Chartres Street.

Except during Mardi Gras, Jazzfest, or Superdome football games, places to stay in New Orleans aren't *all* that expensive. The **Radisson Hotel** ($100 and up; 504/522-4500 or 800/824-3359), at 1500 Canal Street, has 15 floors of bland but comfortable rooms within walking distance of the French Quarter. In the French Quarter at 828 Toulouse Street, the charac-

terful **Olivier House** ($90 and up; 504/525-8456) is a quirky, family-run hotel filling a pair of French Quarter townhouses. Another good bet: **Place d'Armes Hotel** ($90 and up; 504/524-4531 or 800/366-2743) at 625 St. Ann Street, right off Jackson Square at the heart of the French Quarter, with rooms facing onto a quiet courtyard.

Antoine's Restaurant, 713 St. Louis St., New Orleans

The best visitor information is provided by the **New Orleans Metropolitan Convention and Visitors Bureau**, at the base of the Superdome at 1520 Sugar Bowl Drive (504/566-5011) and also at 529 St. Ann Street (504/566-5031) in the French Quarter.

The word "Cajun" comes from the French-speaking Catholic **Acadians**, 10,000 of whom were chucked out of Canada when the English took over in 1755. The Acadians were refused entry by the American colonies on the East Coast, and had to make their way to still-French Louisiana, where they absorbed many other cultural influences while retaining their distinct identity.

To get a real feel for Louisiana's extensive bayous, you have to get out of the car. A number of outfits offer "swamp tours," including **Alligator Bayou** (225/642-8297) and **Munson's Tours** on Chacahoula Swamp (985/851-3569) near Morgan City.

Because the Mississippi in its natural, pre-Corps state created a raised channel for itself between embankments of silt, the river sits higher than a third of Louisiana. Much of New Orleans, for example, is below sea level, and the river has been dredged to a depth of more than 200 feet.

planted in the 1700s, nearly a century before the current house was built in the late 1830s, drive past the entrance a short ways. Besides the obligatory tour, there's lodging and a restaurant in buildings on the grounds in back of the main house.

Oak Alley stands on the west bank of the river, 3 miles north of Vacherie at 3645 Hwy-18/Great River Road. The house is about 15 miles south of the Sunshine Bridge, and 8 miles north of the Veteran's Memorial Bridge (Hwy-3213). There's a ferry nearby, too, between Edgard and Reserve, but this runs at very limited hours.

As a colorful antidote to the grand, white-washed privilege on display at Oak Alley, set aside some time for a tour of nearby Laura plantation as well. Smaller, but seeming more in touch with the realities of sugar-cane plantation life, **Laura** (daily; $10; 225/265-7690) presents itself as a Creole plantation, and plays up the myriad of ethnicities and cultures that came together in Louisiana. Laura is 9 miles downriver from Oak Alley, south of Vacherie at 2247 Hwy-18 (Great River Road).

Continuing south from Vacherie, scattered housing begins to invade the sugarcane, and traffic starts to pick up as the GRR (Hwy-18) works its serpentine way past a pair of ferry landings, a nuclear power plant, and a huge chemical plant with a photogenic cemetery felicitously occupying its front yard. By the time the GRR is within sight of the stylish, rusty-red I-310 bridge, the tentacles of New Orleans's bustle are definitely apparent. Hop on the Interstate eastbound and inside of 25 miles you can be hunting for parking in New Orleans's Vieux Carré, or searching for a Sazerac to celebrate the journey.

Driving New Orleans

Assuming you resisted the industrial-strength charms of US-61 and opted to take the I-10 freeway into town, stay on it until you reach downtown, then get off and park the car as soon as can, and get out and walk. New Orleans rivals Boston for the discomfort it causes drivers, and there are no driving routes that let you see anything you can't see better on foot—or from the St. Charles trolley. Parking in and around the French Quarter is a nightmare, and the small print on the signs can set you up for a ticket or a tow, so play it safe and park in one of many in the nearby lots, which typically charge around $10 a day.

Hwy-23: To the Gulf

From downtown New Orleans, if you really, really want to follow the Mississippi River all the way to its mouth at the Gulf of Mexico, you can. (Well, almost . . .) From the Superdome, take the US-90 bridge south across the river to Gretna, where you can join the Belle Chasse Highway (Hwy-23), which follows alongside the river for about 75 miles, ending up at Venice, still a dozen miles from the Gulf, on the fringes of the Delta National Wildlife refuge. Apart from swamps and giant freighters, the main sight along the route is old **Fort Jackson** (daily 7 AM–6 PM; donations; 985/657-7083), six miles northeast of Venice, which was built in the 1830s to protect the river from invasion.

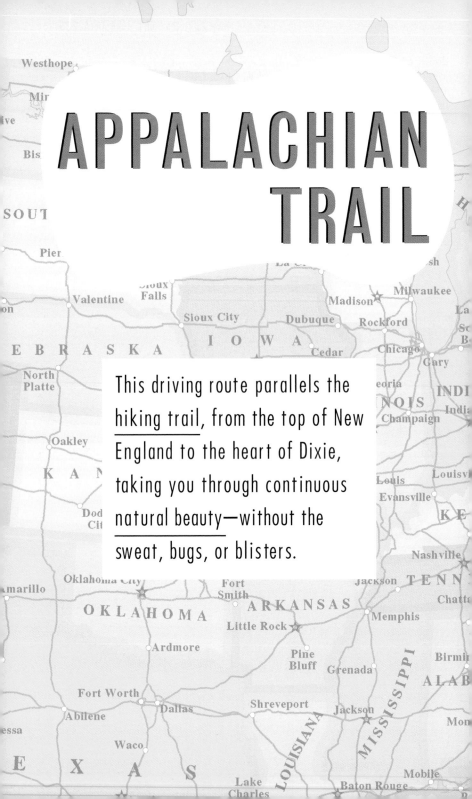

APPALACHIAN TRAIL

This driving route parallels the hiking trail, from the top of New England to the heart of Dixie, taking you through continuous natural beauty—without the sweat, bugs, or blisters.

See Live
Bears!

pg.
297

Gettysburg

◀560 mi▶

pg.
336

◀60 mi▶

Dinosaur Land

pg.
342

◀350 mi▶

Blue Ridge
Parkway

pg.
348

◀115 mi▶

pg.
367

Talullah
Gorge

Between the North Woods of Maine and Atlanta, Georgia

The longest and best-known hiking trail in the country, the **Appalachian Trail** winds from the north woods of Maine all the way south to Georgia. While you won't earn the same kudos driving as you would by walking, the following scenic roads come very close to paralleling the pedestrian route, taking you through the almost continuous natural beauty without the sweat and blisters. Best of all, this driving route follows magnificently scenic two-lane roads all the way from the top of New England to the heart of Dixie, running past a wealth of fascinating towns and historic sites.

The Appalachian landscape holds some of the wealthiest, and some of the most needy, areas in the entire country. These contrasting worlds often sit within a few miles of one another: Every resort and retirement community seems to have its alter-ego as a former mill town, now as dependent upon tourism as they once were upon the land and its resources.

After an extended sojourn through the rugged and buggy wilds of northern **Maine,** where the hiker's route winds to the top of Mt. Katahdin, our Appalachian Trail driving tour reaches an early high point atop windswept Mt. Washington in the heart of **New Hampshire's Presidential Range.** From these 6,000-foot peaks, the tallest mountains in New England and some of the hardest and most durable rocks on earth, the route winds through **Vermont's Green Mountains,** taking in the idyllic charms of rural New England, with its summer homes and liberal-arts college communities. Beyond the **Berkshires,** the summer destination of the Boston and New York culture vultures and intelligentsia for most of two centuries, towns become even more prissy and pretty as we approach within commuting distance of New York City.

Skirting the Big Apple, our route ducks down through the **Delaware Water Gap** to enter the suddenly industrial Lehigh Valley, former land of coal and steel that's now struggling to find an economic replacement. South of here, we pass through the heart of the world-famous **Pennsylvania Dutch Country,** where the simple life is under the onslaught of package tourism.

South from Pennsylvania, nearly to the end of the route in **Georgia,** the Appalachian Trail runs through continuous nature, with barely a city to be seen. Starting with Virginia's **Shenandoah National Park,** then following the **Blue Ridge Parkway** across the breathtaking mountains of western **North Carolina,** it's All-American scenic highway all the way, with recommended detours east and west to visit such fascinating historic sights as Thomas Jefferson's home, Monticello, outside Charlottesville, Virginia; the most opulent mansion in America, Asheville's Biltmore; the real-life town that inspired TV's *Mayberry RFD*—Mount Airy, North Carolina; or the whitewater that was featured in the film *Deliverance,* north Georgia's Chattooga River.

All in all, the Appalachian Trail is an amazing drive, whether or not you come for fall color.

NEW HAMPSHIRE

"Live Free or Die" is the feisty motto of tiny New Hampshire, the state that hits the national limelight every four years when its political primaries launch the horse race for the White House. During the presidential campaign's opening stretch, locals have to turn into hermits to avoid having their votes solicited by every candidate running and their opinions polled by every reporter. Some of New Hampshire's million residents take the state's motto to heart, however, and when you see the ruggedness of the landscape you'll appreciate how easy it is to find isolation from the madding crowd.

Despite its apparent brevity, the route across New Hampshire provides a hearty sampling of the topographic spectrum from its start at New England's highest peak, Mt. Washington, to neighboring Vermont amid the rolling farmland of the Connecticut River Valley.

Mt. Washington

The star attraction of the White Mountains' Presidential Range, 6,288-foot **Mt. Washington** stands head and shoulders above every other peak in New England. East of the Mississippi, only Mt. Mitchell in North Carolina's Blue Ridge and Clingman's Dome in Tennessee's Great Smokies are taller. Despite its natural defenses—such as notoriously fierce storms that arise without warning—Mt. Washington is accessible to an almost unfortunate degree. The **Mount Washington Auto Road** (daily, weather permitting, May to mid-Oct.; $18 car and driver, $7 each additional adult; 603/466-3988) was first opened for carriages in 1861, and still switchbacks up the eastern side,

Though the Appalachian Trail runs within day-hiking distance of over 50 million people, most of the route is intensely solitary—only some 200 people manage to hike the entire 2,144-mile trail each year.

Although clear-day views from the summit of Mt. Washington are amazing, 9 days out of 10 the summit is socked in and cold, and snow can fall any month of the year.

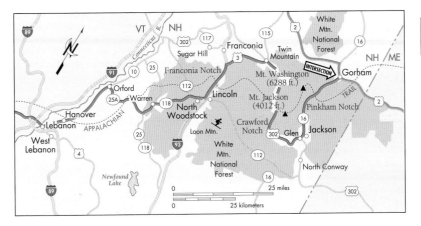

Severe Weather on Mt. Washington

A mountain barely over 6,000 feet hardly deserves the same respect as the 20,000-footers in the Patagonian Andes, yet people die from exposure on the slopes of New Hampshire's Mt. Washington every year. Easy access invites complacency and a tendency to ignore trailside warnings advising retreat if you're unprepared for bad weather. But do respect the facts of nature: Simply put, the Presidential Range of the White Mountains experiences some of the worst weather in the world, rivaling both Antarctica and the Alaska-Yukon ranges for consistently raw and bone-numbing combinations of gale-force winds, freezing temperatures, and precipitation. Lashings by 100-mph winds occur year-round on Mt. Washington, whose summit holds the title for highest sustained wind speed on the face of the planet (231 mph in April 1934). Cloudy days outnumber clear ones on the peak, where snowstorms can strike any month of the year, and even in the balmiest summer months the average high temperature at the summit hovers around 50°F. Compounding the weather's potential severity is its total unpredictability: A day hike begun with sunblock and short sleeves can end up in driving rain and temperatures just 10 degrees above freezing, or worse, in a total whiteout above tree line, even as a group of hikers a couple miles away on a neighboring peak enjoys lunch under blue skies and warm breezes.

The bottom line is, listen to what your mother always told you: Be careful, and don't take chances. Learn to recognize and prevent hypothermia. Figure out how to read your trail maps and compass before you get caught in pelting sleet above tree line. Better to feel foolish packing potentially unnecessary wool sweaters and rain gear for a hike in July than to have your name added to the body count.

climbing some 4,700 feet in barely eight miles. A marvel of engineering, construction, and maintenance, the Mount Washington Auto Road offers a great variety of impressions of the mountain, and wonderful views from almost every turn.

If the weather's clear, you can see the Atlantic Ocean from the top of the mountain; in summer, mornings tend to be clearer, and sunny afternoons turn cloudy and stormy on the summit, complete with lightning and thunder. At the top, be prepared for winter weather any time of year (it can and does snow here every month of the year), and be sure to have a look inside the Summit House, which has displays on the historic hotels and taverns that have graced the top over the years. Visited by hundreds of people

The first automobile ascent of Mt. Washington was made in 1899 by none other than **F. O. Stanley**, piloting one of his namesake **Stanley Steamers**.

every day throughout the summer, since the 1850s the summit of Mt. Washington has sprouted a series of restaurants and hotels—even a daily newspaper. The most evocative remnant of these is the tiny, recently restored **Tip Top House**, "the oldest mountaintop hostelry in the world," still open for tours, if not food and drink (which is available, dully and expensively, in the Summit House cafeteria).

historic Tip Top House at the summit of Mount Washington

Cyclists and runners regularly race each other up the road to the summit, but there is another "easy" ride to the top: the **Mount Washington Cog Railway,** which climbs slowly but surely on its steam-powered, coal-fired way, straight up and down the mountain's western slope from Bretton Woods (see below for more).

Along the northeast side of the White Mountains, between Grafton Notch and Mt. Washington, the Appalachian Trail parallels the **Great Northern** route of US-2 (see page 520). Full coverage is on pages 446–528.

North to Mt. Katahdin

North and east of Mt. Washington, the Appalachian Trail runs through one of its toughest sections, rambling through Mahoosuc Notch into Maine, then passing through Grafton Notch State Park. There are no real roads anywhere near here, so drivers wanting a quick taste of this impenetrable country will have to join US-2 for the drive through Gorham and Bethel (see the US-2: The Great Northern chapter for more), then wind along the Bear River on scenic Route 26. Beyond Grafton Notch, the hiker's Appalachian Trail passes through ever more extensive wilderness, with fewer services (and many more mosquitoes and black flies!) the closer you get to the trail's northern finish, atop **Mt. Katahdin.**

Though the hiking trail and the nearest roads are like strands of a double helix, both routes take you through some memorable country, especially around Rangeley Lakes and Moosehead Lake, in the deep Maine woods. The rest of the Appalachian Trail journey, and many more great backroads adventures around the region, are covered in detail in the companion guidebook *Road Trip USA: New England.*

Pinkham Notch

South from the turnoff for the Mount Washington Auto Road, Route 16 passes through **Pinkham Notch,** a mostly undeveloped stretch of the White Mountains lined by forests and a few ski areas. First of these is **Great Glen** (603/466-2333), a cross-country ski area and summertime mountain bike center, which also serves as a convenient base for hiking around Mt. Washington.

Continuing down Route 16, about four miles south of the Auto Road is the **Wildcat Mountain ski area,** across from which is Grand Central Station for

In New England, locals call their highways "routes," and we've followed suit, using Route as a generic term (Route 100 for example, rather than Hwy-100). The Interstates (I-93) and federal highways (US-3) are abbreviated as usual.

Pinkham Notch, the **Pinkham Notch Camp.** Operated by the venerable Appalachian Mountain Club (AMC), the year-round trailhead facility offers topographical maps, guidebooks, weather updates, and precautionary advice, as well as limited gear. The camp also offers snacks, a cafeteria, a 24-hour hikers' pack room with bathrooms and showers, scheduled shuttle van service, and the **Joe Dodge Lodge** (about $65 bed and board; 603/466-2727), a modern hostel with shared bunk rooms, a few private doubles, and great views from the library. For extended stays be sure to inquire about the significantly discounted package rates, or consider AMC membership, which yields an additional discount on all overnight stays at any AMC property.

Mt. Washington Valley: Jackson

Dropping sharply away to the south of 2,032-foot Pinkham Notch is the Ellis River, along whose banks sits the northern gateway to the Mt. Washington valley, resort-dominated **Jackson** (pop. 678). Given the number of lodgings among the attractive century-old clapboard homes, it seems the principal village occupation is innkeeper. The quantity of porches, gables, and chimneys hint at standard country B&B charms: lazy breakfasts in summer, nooks and crannies brimming with cabbage roses, and crackling fires in your room at night. A covered bridge beside Route 16, taverns filled with antiques, and winter sleigh rides complete the postcard image of Merry Olde New England.

To park a car at any trailhead in the White Mountains National Forest, you'll need to buy a pass from one of the information centers; these passes cost about $5 and are good for seven days.

The Jackson area is not only pretty, but also has a couple of northern New Hampshire's best places to eat, drink, and sleep. Just outside the southern edge of Pinkham Notch, at the junction of Route 16 and Route 16B, the **Shannon Door Pub** (603/383-4211) is usually just the right side of crowded—full of skiers, hikers, and other hungry folks enjoying hearty food, good beers, and frequent live folksy, bluesy music in a jovial setting. The grand hotel in Jackson is the stately **Wentworth** ($80 and up; 603/383-9700) at the heart of the village, welcoming travelers since it was established back in 1880.

Glen

A half mile South of Jackson along Route 16 or Route 16A you pass the picturesque Jackson Covered Bridge, where the two alternates rejoin at the north edge of tiny **Glen**, which, in the short stretch between the bridge and the junction with US-302, has one of the more concentrated barrages of roadside clutter in the White Mountains. Glen is best known not for hiking or sightseeing but as home to the children's theme park **Storyland** (daily in summer only; $21, under 4 free; 603/383-4186), where among its many playfully designed and carefully coifed acres, the highlights include a boat ride, a raft ride, and a fake fiberglass cow that gives fake milk when you squeeze its fake udders. Next to Storyland, and operated by the same people, the simulated realities of **Heritage–New Hampshire** feature slightly animated mannequins that act out episodes from New Hampshire's past—from initial immigration to the

New World, through the Revolutionary War, to a steam train ride through Victorian-era White Mountains. If you like Disneyland attractions (especially "Great Moments with Mr. Lincoln") you may well love it; if not . . . well, the White Mountains are right outside the gates.

A half mile south of these twin attractions, Route 16 links up with US-302 at a cluster of shops, a grocery store, and a bank ATM. This jumble is also home to the **Red Parka Pub** (603/383-4344), a jolly, moderate-to-inexpensive place to eat and drink, with live music most weekend nights.

North Conway

If you're overdue for a little retail therapy you might consider continuing south on Route 16 from the US-302 junction toward **North Conway** (pop. 2,069), one of the cornerstones of New England's factory-outlet circuit. City dwellers be warned: Horrible flashbacks to your commute may result if you venture into the shopping mall zone, where half-hour (or longer) crawls along a five-mile stretch of highway are not unheard-of on holidays, weekends, and afternoons, or during summers, springs, and autumns.

If you can turn a blind eye to all the retail frenzy, North Conway's central park offers one of the best views of Mt. Washington, and the baseball diamond here hosts some pretty intense games.

Besides factory-outlet stores, North Conway is also home to New Hampshire's most popular scenic railroad, running steam engines throughout summer and during the fall color season. Based out of Conway's downtown depot, the **Conway Scenic Railroad** ($10 and up depending on trip; 603/356-5251) runs historic trains south to Conway, through Bartlett, and all the way to Crawford Notch via the historic Frankenstein Trestle, with special excursions available in addition to these frequent trips.

Just over the Maine border, about 10 miles east of North Conway via US-302, the town of **Fryeburg** hosts a weeklong **agricultural fair** during the first week in October that's one of the most popular in New England—packed with tractor pulls, horse racing, lots of music, even a pig scramble (a contest, not an egg dish).

Although all the tourists may well drive you away from North Conway, the town does have some good places to eat and drink, like **Horsefeather's,** a lively bar with a good restaurant on Main Street right across from the depot. If this is a bit rowdy (as it can be during Red Sox–Yankees games), head up the street to **Elvio's Pizza,** where you can get slices or full pies, submarine sandwiches, and big salads, plus wine and beer.

There are lots of accommodations on and off Route 16, from old cabin courts to anodyne motels, but the most interesting place has to be the **Cranmore Inn** ($60 and up; 603/356-5502), a quick walk east of Route 16 at 24 Kearsarge Street, which has been welcoming travelers since 1863.

Conway

Conway, five miles down Route 16 from North Conway at the south end of the scenic railroad line, is a nicer, littler town, with a couple of restaurants, a post office, and the very clean and very friendly **HI White Mountains Hostel**

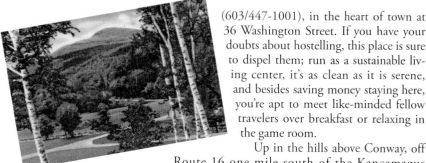

(603/447-1001), in the heart of town at 36 Washington Street. If you have your doubts about hostelling, this place is sure to dispel them; run as a sustainable living center, it's as clean as it is serene, and besides saving money staying here, you're apt to meet like-minded fellow travelers over breakfast or relaxing in the game room.

Up in the hills above Conway, off Route 16 one mile south of the Kancamagus Highway at the edge of the White Mountains National Forest, the **Darby Field Inn** ($100 and up; 603/447-2181) is a B&B open year-round for skiing, hiking, and great après-outdoors meals.

Kancamagus Highway

Running east-to-west from Conway over the mountains to Lincoln, the 34-mile **Kancamagus Highway** (Route 112) is one of the most incredible drives in the White Mountains. Much shorter and a lot less traveled than the prime tourist route along US-302 and US-3 through Crawford and Franconia Notches, the Kanc, as it's often called, takes you up and over the crest of the peaks, giving grand vistas over an almost completely undeveloped landscape—great for fall-color leaf-peeping. Fall is definitely prime time for the drive, but any time of year (except maybe winter, when it can be a bit hairy) it's a lovely trip, lined by lupines in early summer and raging waterfalls in the spring.

Near the midpoint of the Kanc, the **Russell Colbath Historic House** dates from the early 1800s and now houses a small museum (daily 9 AM–4 PM; free) with exhibits describing the lives of the White Mountains' early settlers. From the house, a short loop trail explores the effects loggers had on this region in the 1890s, when everything you see along the Kanc (and most everywhere else) was devastated by clear-cuts.

Three miles further west, just east of the crest and an easy half-mile walk from the well-signed parking area, **Sabbaday Falls** is a lovely little waterfall roaring through a narrow gorge. In a series of noisy, splashing cascades, the river drops down through a polished pink granite gorge, barely 10 feet wide but surrounded by dense forest. It's an ideal picnic spot, and only 10–15 minutes from the road.

Crawford Notch

US-302 between Glen and Twin Mountain winds west around the southern flank of the Presidential Range, then heads north through **Crawford Notch**, another of the White Mountains' high passes and centerpiece of the

*Fall foliage is at its best when warm clear days are followed by cold nights that stop the essential pigment-producing sugars from circulating out of the leaves. Sugar production is low on cloudy days, when warm nights allow the sugars to disperse before the brightest colors are produced. For **New Hampshire Fall Foliage Reports** (Sept. and Oct. only), call 800/258-3608.*

The name Kancamagus honors the local Indian chief who controlled the area when the first European settlers began arriving at the White Mountains in the 1680s. The roadway was not paved until 1964 and was declared a National Scenic Byway in 1989.

Crawford Notch State Park. The road closely follows the Saco River through new-growth forest; the oaks and white pine of the lower valley give way to more birch and spruce as you gain elevation.

Crawford Notch offers good **day hikes** to various waterfalls and vantage points such as **Frankenstein Cliff,** named for an artist whose work helped popularize the White Mountains, and 200-foot **Arethusa Falls,** the state's highest waterfall.

For ambitious and well-prepared hikers, the north end of Crawford Notch is the start of the oldest and perhaps grandest walking trail in the country, the eight-mile **Crawford Path** up towering Mt. Washington. A strenuous, demanding, and potentially dangerous route, the Crawford Path is also breathtakingly beautiful, and a walk along it gives an almost complete picture of the White Mountains—sparkling brooks, fields of wildflowers, and glorious mountaintop panoramas.

> The first known ascent of Mt. Washington was made in 1642 by **Darby Field** of Durham, New Hampshire, who historians believe followed a route near that of today's Crawford Path.

> Parking along New Hampshire highways is illegal, so don't be tempted to leave your car beside the road while you take a hike up that nearby hill—you may return to find it's been towed to some town 20 miles away.

Mount Washington Hotel and Cog Railway

North of Crawford Notch, the highway joins the Ammonoosuc River headwaters as they flow toward the Connecticut River, passing **Bretton Woods** and the access road for the Mount Washington Cog Railway. The giant **Mount Washington Hotel** ($195 and up; 800/258-0330) dominates the surrounding plain, its Victorian luxury no longer standing in such grand isolation below the peaks of the Presidentials now that a ski resort sits across the highway, and motels and condos squat around its skirts. Built at the turn of the 20th century by Pennsylvania Railroad tycoon Joseph Stickney, the Mount Washington Hotel received its most lasting recognition as host of the 1944 United Nations International Monetary Conference, the historic meeting of financiers from 44 nations that established the World Bank and chose the dollar as the global standard for international trade.

Climbing the mountains behind the hotel, the **Mount Washington Cog Railway** was built in 1869 and has a maximum grade of 37.5 percent, surpassed by only one other non-funicular railway in the world, high up in the Swiss Alps. Burning a ton of coal with each trip, the cinder-spewing engines of this historic "Railway to the Moon" take over an hour to ratchet up the three-mile track to the often windy, cold summit. Trips ($50; 603/846-5404) run year-round; you can ride up and hike (or ski) back down.

Franconia

Between Twin Mountain (at the junction of US-302 and US-3) and where US-3 merges with I-93, you'll find the aging face of the area's long association with tourism: a variety of motel courts and "housekeeping cottages" at least as old as you are. Despite their outward dowdiness, several make a virtue of the rustic, but given their prime location most are hardly the bargains you might hope for.

More interesting and historic lodging may be had on a 200-acre working farm in **Franconia** (pop. 811), where, since 1899, the friendly Sherburn family's **Pinestead Farm Lodge,** on Route 116 south of town, has offered simple rooms and warm hospitality at reasonable rates ($50 and up with shared bath and kitchen; 603/823-8121).

Also dating back to the same early-1800s era is **The Homestead** ($75 and up; 603/823-5564 or 800/823-5564), a country inn just west of Franconia on Route 117 in **Sugar Hill.** The township is aptly named: The sugarbush (a grove of sugar maples) on Hildex Maple Sugar Farm, also on Route 117, contributes its unforgettable essence to breakfasts at the very popular **Polly's Pancake Parlor.** Polly's is located in the farm's thrice-expanded 1830 carriage shed (open weekends only April–mid-May and late Oct., daily rest of the year; 603/823-5575). Warning: After trying real maple syrup, you may never be able to go back to Aunt Jemima's or Mrs. Butterworth's again.

*Cannon Mountain, home slope of World Cup ski champion **Bode Miller,** was the location of the first aerial tram for skiers in the United States. One of the original aerial tram cars has been preserved among the many attractions at Clark's Trading Post, near Lincoln at the south end of Franconia Notch.*

The most famous farm in the vicinity is certainly the **Frost Place** (Sat.–Sun. 1–5 PM Memorial Day–June, Wed.–Mon. 1–5 PM July–Columbus Day; $3; 603/823-5510) on Route 116 south of the Franconia village intersection. Besides the 1.5-mile Poetry Trail and the displays of Robert Frost memorabilia from his 11-year residency here, there's a regular program of readings by the current poet-in-residence.

Franconia Notch

Franconia Notch is the tourist Grand Central of the White Mountains. I-93 offers easy access, and a host of attractions—an aerial tram, the state's own "little Grand Canyon," covered bridges, a powerful waterfall called the Flume, even a trading post with trained bear s—make it a great place to linger; if you include the time to hike around or sit still by a mountain stream, you could easily spend a week or more enjoying it all.

The main draw in Franconia Notch used to be one of the most famous landmarks in New England: the **Old Man of the Mountain,** a series of five granite ledges 1,200 feet above the valley, which, when viewed from certain angles, seemed to resemble an old man's profile. After years of reconstructive surgery, being held together by epoxies and steel reinforcement, the Old Man came tumbling down on May 3, 2003.

The other well-known feature of Franconia Notch is still there: **The Flume** is a granite gorge, 15 feet wide and nearly 100 high, carved by roaring waters at the south end of the notch. To get there, head to the large **visitors center** (603/745-8391), pay the admission fee ($8), and take a short bus ride to near the start of the wooden boardwalk, which runs the length of the 800-foot-long gorge and ends up at the ear-pounding rumble of Avalanche Falls.

The hiker's Appalachian Trail crosses the Franconia Notch Parkway and Pemi Trail at Whitehouse Bridge, in between the Basin and the Flume.

Though less famous than the Old Man and the Flume, in between the two sits another favorite Franconia Notch stop:

the **Basin,** where a lovely waterfall in the thundering Pemigewassett River has polished a 25-foot-round pothole. Thoreau visited in the 1820s and thought it was remarkable; it's still a peaceful place to sit and picnic and be soothed by the natural white noise.

Clark's Trading Post

Just south of Franconia Notch along US-3, a barrage of deliciously tacky tourist attractions and old-fashioned roadside Americana awaits you. Well-maintained 1930s motor courts line the highway, setting the stage for one of New England's greatest "Roadside Attractions:" **Clark's Trading Post** (daily in summer; $12; 603/745-8913), where you can enjoy a slice of good ol' cornpone kitsch. At Clark's, you can ride on a genuine old wood-burning railroad over an authentic 1904 covered bridge (and be chased all the way by a hairy, hilarious Wolfman); admire an im-

maculate 1931 LaSalle in a vintage gas station; or tour a haunted mansion.

For the past 50 or so years, the main draw at Clark's has been the chance, according to the sign, to **"See Live Bears!"** House-trained black bears perform a series of entertaining tricks—rolling barrels, shooting basketballs through hoops, and riding scooters—and they clearly seem to enjoy their work (not to mention the ice cream cones they're rewarded with). The trainers and caretakers crack jokes and make wry comments about "bear facts" and how the animals are "bearly" able to behave themselves, but they smile and beam every time the bears do what they're supposed to, giving the performances a feel more akin to a school play than to a professional circus. Many of the bears are born and reared here at Clark's, and although they're captive, they have a much longer life expectancy than wild bears. Across from the enclosure where they perform you can pay respects to the graves of favorite bears who've performed here over the years. Spend any time at Clark's and you'll begin to realize that the bears are regarded as family members (albeit seven-foot-tall, 500-pound family members).

Take those **moose-crossing** signs seriously. Dozens of collisions occur annually, and you can bet your car won't fare too well if it hits an animal that weighs well over a half ton.

Clark's has been in business since 1928, when it was known as Ed Clark's Eskimo Dog Ranch, and everything about it is very much a family affair. More than a dozen Clarks and close relatives work here throughout the summer, doing everything from training and caring for the bears to making milk shakes. The bear shows at Clark's Trading Post start every two hours or so (roughly at noon, 2, and 4 PM), and you could happily spend most of a day here, making it well worth the price of admission. If you're just racing through, be sure to at least visit the gift shop, which is stocked with all the wonderfully tacky stuff (wind-up toys, funky postcards, snow domes, and the like) retro-minded road-trippers drive miles to find.

You Can't Get There from Here

One of the first things first-time visitors to New England notice is its compact size: A crow flying 100 miles from almost any treetop outside of Maine will end up in the next state, if not Canada. But map distances bear absolutely no relation to travel time, thanks to the mountain ranges pitched up across northern New England. So if you're sitting in your motel room in New Hampshire or Vermont wondering how far to drive for dinner, look to towns north or south. As a rule these will share the same valley since the rivers and mountains are generally aligned north-to-south, like compass needles. In contrast, that next town to the east or west may as well be on the opposite side of the state so far as convenience is concerned: Whether winding along erratic streambeds or stitching their ways up the sides of passes between high peaks, east–west roads tend to be a slow grind in even the best weather, truly as tortuous as the wiggling lines on the map suggest. Heavy vehicles, cautious drivers, and foul weather make the going doubly difficult. Keep this in mind as you consider outings and side trips or you, too, will learn to say, "You can't get there from here."

Lincoln sits at the west end of Route 112, the amazing Kancamagus Highway, which is described above.

In case you're wondering what North Woodstock is north of, there is a much smaller hamlet called **Woodstock**, little more than a collection of cabins, about three miles south of North Woodstock along US-3.

Lincoln and North Woodstock

Three miles south of Franconia Notch, tiny **North Woodstock** (pop. 700) is a good example of what White Mountains towns used to look like before vacation condos popped up like prairie dog colonies; neighboring **Lincoln** (pop. 1,229) is the portrait of "after." North Woodstock is a handful of mostly unpretentious businesses at the junction of US-3 and Route 112, while Lincoln seems to be nothing but a strip of ski-clothing stores, malls, and motels east of I-93 at the base of the Loon Mountain ski resort. When Loon's condo-covered foothills fill to capacity during fall and winter holidays, the weekend population can mushroom more than 20-fold to more than 30,000.

Diner fans will want to check out the **Sunny Day Diner** (closed Tues.; 603/745-4833), a stainless-steel 1950s icon at the north edge of North Woodstock on US-3. A classic breakfast and lunch place, the Sunny Day makes some fine French toast (including a deeply flavored banana variation that goes great with local maple syrup). The Sunny Day, which is just south of Clark's Trading Post, also serves delicious dinners on Friday and Saturday.

Lost River Gorge

With five main roads and countless minor ones connecting the Franconia Notch area with the Connecticut River Valley, there are nearly endless ways to get between these two places while staying more or less on the path of the hiker's Appalachian Trail, which disappears into the woods for most of the way. All of the roads are partly pretty and partly yucky in about equal degrees, but one of the easiest to follow is Route 112, which runs west from North Woodstock along the Lost River, hopping over the crest and dropping down along the Wild Ammonusuc. The main stop along this route is the privately owned gorge known as the **Lost River** (daily mid-May–Oct.; $11; 603/745-8031), where you can explore the jumble of glaciated granite boulders that seem to swallow up the river, giving it its name. Many of

the big, moss-covered boulders have been given names (Guillotine Rock and Lemon Squeezer, to name two), and you can see these (and smell the fragrant pine trees) from the comfort of a wooden boardwalk or go wild and explore some of the many caves formed by the huge piles of rocks.

Continuing west from Lost River Gorge, which sits at the top of Route 112's spectacular run through wild Kinsman Notch, the highway drops down into the Connecticut River watershed toward the Vermont town of Wells River, which happens to be home to the best truck stop in all New England: the **P&H Truck Stop Cafe** (802/429-2141) at I-91 exit 17, where you can enjoy fine chowder, charbroiled cheeseburgers, and great pies (and walls covered with images of Peterbilts and Mack trucks)—24 hours a day. After eating here, backtrack four miles to the river and follow scenic Route 10 along its east bank, winding south toward Hanover. A parallel route along the Vermont side of the river, along old US-5 through the town of Fairlee (which has a nice diner and a unique drive-in movie theater/motel), is another nice alternative to the I-91 freeway.

Route 10: North Haverhill and Lyme

While hikers along the Appalachian Trail have to struggle up and over several mountaintops, we drivers get to amble along a few miles to the west, following scenic Route 10 along the east banks of the lazy Connecticut River. Winding past pastures and cornfields, Route 10 is a nonstop pleasure to drive (or cycle); uneventful perhaps, but giving seemingly endless pastoral views framed by white rail fences, occasional farmhouses, and the voluptuous peaks that rise to the east and west. The first hamlet you reach along this part of Route 10, **North Haverhill,** is a real museum piece, with a necklace of distinctive colonial-era homes flanking an oval town green, and one of New Hampshire's oldest cemeteries close by.

Further south spreads Loch Lyme, where the fine restaurant, rustic lodge, and cabins of **Loch Lyme Lodge** ($80 and up; 603/795-2141 or 800/423-2141) have been welcoming generations of New Englanders since 1946. Swim, sail, or float out on the small lake, which has an idyllic location between the mountains and the river.

A mile south of Loch Lyme, eight miles north of Hanover, the tidy town of **Lyme** presents yet another Kodak-worthy scene, with a Soldiers and Sailors Monument

In case you're worried, Lyme, New Hampshire, is not the place the tick-borne disease was named for; that Lyme is in Connecticut. That said, you still need to be on the lookout for these devilish little creatures.

standing at the center of a slender green, a large church at one end and an equally large stable at the other.

Lyme, which feels more like a part of the Virginia hunt country than New England, also has a fully stocked general store and a pair of nice places to stop for a night or three. The 1809 **Alden Country Inn** ($100 and up; 603/795-2222) has period-decorated rooms, a very fine restaurant, and a cozy pub with a heartwarming fireplace. If you want to build up an appetite before dinner, the innkeepers will rent you a bike and point you toward some of the area's best routes. The equally pleasant white clapboard **Dowd's Country Inn** ($100 and up; 603/795-4712) is right across the green.

Although Ivy League Dartmouth has a $2 billion endowment and a conservative reputation, it also has had some interesting students, including children's stars **Dr. Seuss**, **Captain Kangaroo**, and **Mr. Rogers**, the latter two both dropouts. The poet **Robert Frost** was another famous nongraduate.

A few years after New Hampshire and the other 12 American colonies began their revolt against mother England, Hanover and a handful of neighboring towns divorced themselves from New Hampshire to join Vermont. That short-lived association fell apart in 1782, leaving the towns independent for four years before they reunited with New Hampshire.

Hanover: Dartmouth College

Dartmouth College is the principal resident of attractive little **Hanover** (pop. 9,212), and the Ivy League influence shows in the local architecture, fashions, and cultural diversions. When school is in session, the cafés hum with undergraduate discourse, the downtown teems with students, and a varsity air envelops the historic campus and its sturdy neighbors. Between terms, however, the town's metabolism drops toward hibernation levels, which means there's no line for espresso.

Standing out from all the Georgian-style brick buildings is Dartmouth's **Hood Museum of Art** (closed Mon.; free; 603/646-2808), on the southeast side of the Green. Housed in a modern gallery designed in part by Charles Moore, the Hood shows a changing selection from its permanent collection, but mainly hosts visiting exhibitions.

More contentious art can be experienced at the very center of Dartmouth where, in the lower level reading room of Baker Library, the walls are covered with a set of politically-charged frescoes by **José Clemente Orozco**: "An Epic of American Civilization."

If it's too nice a day to stay indoors and contemplate society's ills, rent a bike and ride north to Lyme and back, or borrow a canoe or kayak from Dartmouth's **Ledyard Canoe Club** ($5/hour; 603/643-6709), located on the river just north of the Route 10A bridge, and play Huck Finn for an afternoon. Or you can take a hike: the Dartmouth Outing Club maintains hundreds of miles of trails, including a part of the Appalachian Trail that runs right through town. There's an AT marker embedded in the sidewalk in front of the Hanover Inn, from where the trail runs west across the bridge to Vermont, and east down Main and Lebanon streets to the town of Etna, before climbing the 2,280-foot peak of Moose Mountain.

Hanover Practicalities

Generations of Dartmouth students have survived their college years thanks in part to the generous portions served up at **Lou's** (603/643-3321), 30 S. Main Street. Hardly changed since it opened in 1947, and famed for its magical strawberry rhubarb and other fresh-baked pies, Lou's does great big breakfasts, lunchtime soups and burgers, and early dinners (they close at 5 PM, 3 PM on Sun.). Best of all, there's not a fluorescent light to be seen. For a nice dinner, try the pasta at **Café Buon Gustaio** (603/643-5711), 72 S. Main Street.

The
Hanover Inn

For accommodations around Hanover, there's the stately, Dartmouth-run **Hanover Inn** facing onto the Green ($250–350; 603/643-4300); for affordable rooms, however, look in nearby West Lebanon or across the river in White River Junction, Vermont.

Into the Mountains: Norwich, West Hartford, and Pomfret

From the Hanover area, into **Norwich, Vermont,** the most direct driving tour approximation of the hiker's route is to follow US-4 west through Woodstock toward Killington. The hiking trail, however, runs further north, and passes through a series of pretty foothill villages that are well worth searching out on your way to the heart of the Green Mountains.

At Norwich, just uphill from where the Appalachian Trail crosses the Connecticut River along Route 10A on a broad low bridge from Hanover, you might want to while away a rainy afternoon at the interesting **Montshire Museum of Science** (daily; $7; 802/649-2200), which has more than 100 educational exhibits focusing on natural history, as well as aquariums showcasing fresh- and saltwater creatures. The next town the AT passes through is West Hartford, on the banks of the White River upstream from I-91 along Route 14.

From West Hartford, you can circle around (on unnumbered and rather rough-surfaced country roads) through **North Pomfret, Pomfret,** and **South Pomfret,** passing dairy farms, quaint barns, and one post office per town, coming in through the backdoor to upscale Woodstock, where this AT route links up with US-4. From South Pomfret, a quaint little hamlet that's also home to the Suicide Six ski area, the hiker's Appalachian Trail heads up into the mountains through a long, roadless stretch before crossing Route 100 at Sherburne Pass. The only real driving equivalent follows Route 12 south into Woodstock.

Lebanon and West Lebanon

Sitting rather quietly a couple of miles south of Hanover, east of the Connecticut River near the point where US-4 gets submerged beneath the I-89 freeway, historic **Lebanon** (pop. 12,183) has a town green so spacious it seems more like the outskirts of a city park than the center of a town. Near the northwest corner is the main commercial area, or what's left since the malls arrived, kept alive in part by a tasty establishment: **Sweet Tomatoes** (603/448-1711), facing the park

Diners: Fast Food Worth Slowing Down For

Aaaah, the local diner! Throughout New England, these brightly lit establishments are magnets for folks weary of the dull predictability of the fast-food mega-chains. In contrast to the impersonal nature of those billions-serving burger factories, diners are low-key gathering spots where community gossip is shared and politics debated by a gang of regulars assembling each morning. Where motherly waitresses (frequently named Mildred, Blanche, and Edna, wearing lace hankies pinned to their aprons) are quick to offer refills on coffee. Where UPS drivers, Methodist clergy, morticians, and middle-school principals perched on adjacent stools know they can score decent hot roast-beef sandwiches or a great piece of fresh fruit pie. And where autumn leaf-peepers and other passers-through can inquire about local attractions or find out which nearby motels or B&Bs might still have empty rooms for that night.

The diner's lineage can ultimately be traced back to horse-drawn lunch carts selling sandwiches and hot coffee along the streets of cities like Providence and Boston beginning in the 1870s. However, the prototypical New England diners are those built from the 1920s through the 1950s by the Worcester Lunch Car Company: barrel-roofed with colorful porcelain panels on the exterior and plenty of varnished hardwood inside. Other diners came from manufacturers headquartered in New York (DeRaffele) and especially New Jersey (Mountain View, Fodero, Kullman, Paramount, Silk City, O'Mahony, and many more). Each diner-maker trumpeted its own design innovations: Streamlined metal exteriors, artful tilework, bits of elegant stained glass, distinctive built-in clocks, and more efficient floor plans. Some even included all necessary crockery, flatware, and cooking equipment, so that new owners could begin serving hungry locals on the very day set-up was complete.

Aficionados will be quick to inform you that real diners are roadside eateries whose component parts were fabricated in a factory, then shipped

at 1 Court Street, is an ever-popular trattoria whose gourmet pasta and wood-fired pizzas pull in crowds from miles around.

Right along the bonny banks of the Connecticut River, three miles south of patrician Hanover, the commercial busybody of **West Lebanon** has everything you probably try hard to avoid: shopping plazas, traffic tie-ups, and familiar fast *everything,* all clustered around the two local exits off the I-89 freeway.

VERMONT

Vermont is quintessential New England: picturesque villages still served by cluttered country stores, small farms nestled among the granite ridges of the Green Mountains, and needle-sharp white church spires ris-

by road or rail for assembly on-site. Real diners, they'll insist, always have counters, with at least some cooking done within view of patrons. There'll almost certainly be booths, too, and a definite blue-collar, no-frills ambience. Unlike their urban or roadside truck stop equivalents, few diners are open 24 hours; many in fact serve breakfast and lunch only, opening very early in the morning (around 6 AM) and closing around 2 or 3 PM. But not every place with the word "diner" in its name is the genuine article. Many places that call themselves diners are as far removed from the classic prefab as IKEA furniture is from a handcrafted antique, and mavens regard diner-themed restaurants (like the current generation of Denny's) with considerable scorn. The smaller, the better, they say, with points deducted for any remodeling that disfigures the original design.

You needn't care about any of this lore, of course, to enjoy yourself. But after visiting your third or fourth diner, you may begin to notice similarities and differences among them. Curious about a particular establishment's history? Quiz the owner—more often than not, he or she will be happy to tell you all about the place, which may have started life with a different name in another town and been moved three or more times before it found its current home. Look for a "tag," the small metal plate (often affixed to the wall over the entry door) listing manufacturer, date, and serial number. The best and most enjoyable way to get to know diners and diner culture is simply to spend time in them, but if you want to learn more, check the authoritative volume, *American Diner Then and Now* by Richard Gutman, published by Johns Hopkins University Press.

For more details on any of the dozens of diners described in this book, see the Diner entry in the index. Enjoy!

ing above forests ablaze with autumn colors. Precocious from birth—its constitution was the first in the United States to prohibit slavery and establish public schools—Vermont is known for its independent-minded politicians like Jim Jeffords and Bernie Saunders and strong liberal traditions (think: Howard Dean).

From the Connecticut River, this route across Vermont follows the contours of the land, tagging along fast-running mountain streams or keeping to the valleys between the steep surrounding ridges that carry the Appalachian Trail ever southward.

White River Junction

Across the river from Hanover and Dartmouth, turn-of-the-20th-century **White River Junction** (pop. 2,582) used to echo with the sounds of some 50 trains a day traveling over six separate rail lines. The demise of the railroads and arrival of the Interstate cloverleaf on the outskirts of town effectively moth-balled the downtown area, but like good vintage clothing, the photogenic historic center has been rediscovered by an art-smart crowd that doesn't mind the holes and missing buttons.

Freight trains still rumble through White River Junction a few times a day, and Amtrak stops here on its mainline Vermonter route along the Connecticut River between New York City and Montreal. Apart from the trains, the main signs of life here are at breakfast and lunch, when the ancient-looking **Polka Dot Diner** (daily 5 AM–7 PM; 802/295-9722) at 7 N. Main Street serves the usual unpretentious, inexpensive grilled and fried foods. Or try the delicious fresh pastries and croissants that come out of the **Baker's Studio** (802/296-7201), a 30-second walk away from the Polka Dot at 7 S. Main Street.

If you're looking for lodging with more character than the chain motels (Super 8, etc.) along the interstates, consider downtown's **Hotel Coolidge** ($65/night, $225/week; 802/295-3118 or 800/622-1124) at 39 S. Main Street. In business since the 1920s, it has a nice café downstairs, an opera house next door, and is clean, friendly, and definitely good value. Even better value are their HI-hostel bunks, which go for around $20.

Quechee and Quechee Gorge

West from White River Junction, US-4 climbs upstream into the valley of the Ottauquechee River (auto-KWEE-chee) near **Quechee,** a second-home community to country-clubbing executives from Connecticut and Boston. You cross **Quechee Gorge** almost without warning, but adjacent parking on both sides of the gorge gives you a chance to take a longer look at the dramatic little canyon or to stretch your legs along the rimside hiking trails. East of the gorge there's a tacky Quechee Village souvenir shop, which boasts a tiny train and a well-preserved streamline-style 1946 Worcester pre-fab that's been incorporated into the **Farina Family Diner** (802/296-7911), a retro all-American roadhouse serving up the usual standards.

Quechee Gorge

West of the gorge, you can turn north into old Quechee, a quaint town with a lumber mill-cum-art gallery selling Simon Pearce glassware. A Norman Rockwell-esque rope swing hangs under a covered bridge, and on lazy summer afternoons, local youths drop from it into the river below.

East of the gorge, **Quechee State Park** (802/295-2990) provides access to the Ottauquechee River and also has **camping** with hot showers. Next to the park is the new nature center of the **Vermont Institute of Natural Science** (daily; $8; 802/457-2779), an outdoor museum dedicated to local wildlife, especially raptors: Enclosures let you get up close and personal with hawks, eagles, owls and falcons.

> If you're in the area around mid-June, check out the **Quechee Hot Air Balloon Festival**, held during Father's Day weekend.

Woodstock

"The good people of Woodstock have less incentive than others to yearn for heaven," said a 19th-century resident. It's a sentiment readily echoed today. Originally settled in the 1760s, **Woodstock** (pop. 3,232) remains an exceedingly well-preserved example of small-town New England—tidy federal-style homes, built by wealthy professionals of the newborn American republic, still ring the classic village green. Now the historic village is home to wealthy retirees and their fortunate sons and daughters. You'll see the signs of this old money throughout the town: well-stocked wine racks at the general store, shady basketball courts along the river, excellent performing arts at the Town Hall Theater, and, most importantly, the wherewithal to refuse any compromising commercial development. Having financially generous, conservation-minded residents like Laurance Rockefeller around hasn't hurt, either. To put it mildly, expansion of the tax base is *not* a pressing issue for this community.

> Notice, as you approach Woodstock Village Green, that there are no overhead power lines on the two main downtown streets, Central and Elm. **Laurance Rockefeller** paid to have the lines buried back in 1973.

During summer and fall, walking tours are an excellent way to take stock of the town's history and architecture. Call or visit the **Information Booth** (802/457-3555) on the Green for a schedule. Hiking trails lead up both the summits overlooking the town. A community blackboard, aka the Town Crier, at the corner of Central and Elm, lists local events and activities all year. Even if you're racing through Woodstock, bound for the mountains, be sure to stop in Woodstock long enough to enjoy this quick tour: From the oblong green, cross the Middle Covered Bridge, and follow the Ottauquechee downstream along River Street. Then work your way back via Elm Street past F. H. Gillingham & Sons, Vermont's oldest country store.

If you've admired the rolling fields and weathered wooden fences, savored the local apples and sharp cheddar, and enjoyed the scent of mown hay or boiling maple sap, you'll appreciate an even closer look at New England's farms with a visit to the **Billings Farm & Museum** (daily in summer, weekends rest of year; $10; 802/457-2355), on Route 12 north of the village. Frederick Billings, better known as the builder of the

Northern Pacific Railroad (Billings, Montana is named for him), began this working dairy farm in the late 19th century. Its restored farmhouse and huge barns illustrate the rural life in galleries, demonstrations, and hands-on activities.

Across the road, another historic farm has recently been opened to the public as the **Marsh-Billings National Historical Park** (tours daily; $6; 802/457-3368), Vermont's only national park. The property, which includes the former home of Laurance Rockefeller (who married Billings's granddaughter), is a study in conservation practice, and its dense woodlands are living proof of the merits of sustainable agriculture.

Woodstock Practicalities

Hungry travelers will find plenty of choices around town, although some eateries assume you have a private endowment. The burgers at **Bentley's** (802/457-3232), across from the Town Crier at 3 Elm Street, are a tad high-priced, but consider the accompaniments: Vermont microbrews, oriental carpets, Victorian sofas, and a casual, cheerful, talkative crowd. If you'd pay as much for good vibes as you'd tip for good service, it's worth a visit. Another agreeable and not-too-pricey place is the **Village Inn** (802/457-1255) at 41 Pleasant Street, which is semi-famous for its roast turkey dinners.

There are also two bare-bones road-food haunts bookending the town along US-4. At the east end of town, you'll find the white shack housing **WASP's Snack Bar** (802/457-9805), 57 Pleasant Street. On US-4 a half mile west of the green at 462 Woodstock Road is the open-air (which in Vermont means "summer-only") **White Cottage Snack Bar** (802/457-2968), serving up ace burgers and deep-fried clams. Next to the White Cottage is a healthier alternative, the **Woodstock Farmer's Market,** with top-quality produce and full meals available.

Accommodations run the gamut from moderate motels to deluxe inns; at all of them, expect rates to increase during high season, which in Woodstock is most of summer and fall, along with the winter holidays. The main place right in town, the 144-room, Rockefeller-built **Woodstock Inn** ($150 and up; 802/457-1100) sits on the south side of the green, and although it tries hard to look like a stately old place, the inn was actually built from scratch in 1969. The modest **Braeside Motel** ($70–120; 802/457-1366), along US-4 on the eastern outskirts of town, is about as budget-friendly as you're going to get.

Bridgewater and Killington

The tiny town of **Bridgewater** (pop. 895), stretching along the banks of the Ottauquechee, seems well on the way to the middle of nowhere. But that's what lures many visitors to this region—the fact that so much of it seems to have contentedly hung back with Rip van Winkle. That said, Bridgewater *is* a gateway to one of the state's most important somewheres: the ski resorts of central Vermont. The large woolen mill here has been converted into the Old Mill Marketplace, its water-powered turbines and textile machines replaced by small shops selling a typically Vermont mix of antiques, ski apparel, New Age books, and gift-packaged Vermont foods to visitors heading for the mountains.

Through the Bridgewater area, US-4 is generously wide-shouldered and level, making it a popular cycling route, especially during the fall color season, when the dense hardwood forests that climb the slopes above the roadway are blazing with autumn hues. When the leaves have fallen and been replaced by snow, this scenic stretch changes character completely, becoming one of the East Coast's most prominent ski resorts, **Killington.** The permanent population of Killington is maybe 50 people, but on winter weekends as many as 10,000 skiers flock to its seven different mountains and many miles of trails (lift tickets around $70; snow info 800/621-6867). The skiers also support a plethora of real estate agencies, restaurants, and bars, especially off US-4 on the main road to the slopes, Killington Road.

Compared to the rest of Vermont, Killington is not an especially attractive place to be in summer, when the parking lots of the time-share condo complexes are empty and the hills are scarred by clear-cut ski trails, but the lack of crowds also means lower prices for accommodations. Everywhere from roadside motels to upscale resorts like the **Inn at Six Mountains** offer their lowest rates when the temperatures are highest.

Vermont holds over 100 covered bridges, several good examples of which are to be seen between Quechee and Bridgewater. Look for the 1836 **Taftsville bridge** west of Quechee, the **Middle Bridge** in Woodstock (which was totally rebuilt way back in 1969), and the 1877 **Lincoln Bridge** four miles west of Woodstock. The nation's longest covered bridge crosses the Connecticut River at Windsor, about 15 miles southeast of Woodstock, with a 460-foot span built in 1866.

In the Killington area, tune to "The Mountain," **WEBK 105.3 FM,** for the best in alternative pop music—everything from the Grateful Dead to Beck and Bela Fleck.

Gifford Woods State Park

Sitting in the scenic heart of the Green Mountains, at the junction of US-4 and Route 100 **Gifford Woods State Park** (802/775-5354) protects one of the few virgin forests left in New England, with 7 acres of massive sugar maple, birch, and ash trees, some of which are more than 300 years old. There's a nice **campground** with hot showers, and access to many fine trails, including the Appalachian Trail and the Long Trail, which run together across US-4 just west of 2,190-foot Shelburne Pass.

Route 100: Rochester, Hancock, and Granville Gulf

Route 100 runs north–south through the geographical and spiritual heart of Vermont, winding from curve to curve past cornfields and fat cows lazing in impossibly green pastures, alongside gurgling streams, up and down switchbacking passes, and generally setting the standard for what scenic roads ought to be.

Route 100 runs right at the edge of the Green Mountains National Forest, parallel to Vermont's beloved crestline Long Trail, and every so often passes by a picturesque gas station-cum-general store, selling everything you'll need to keep you on the road, from gas to maple-syrup milk shakes. Up and down the whole state of Vermont, Route 100 is a wonderful drive, as are just about all of the roads that intersect it.

North of US-4, the first place you come to along Route 100 is **Pittsfield**, an all-in-white hamlet set in a pastoral valley and surrounded by hayfields and acres of corn. From here Route 100 edges east into the White River Valley, passing through Stockbridge, which centers on an ancient-looking Ford dealership, and a couple more places that seem to exist solely on maps. The next stop is **Rochester,** at the junction with Route 73, which heads west over scenic Brandon Gap. Rochester is a proper Vermont town, with a village green and a bandstand. A mile north of town is the main **ranger station** (802/767-4261) for this part of the **Green Mountains National Forest,** where the friendly staff will tell you all about the best day hikes, campgrounds, and historic sites in the area. Two miles south of Rochester, across the river and away from Route 100, the **Liberty Hill Farm B&B** ($85; 802/767-3926) is a family-friendly farmstay B&B and has a working 100-plus-acre dairy where you can hike, bike, fish, or help feed the cows (and the ducks and chickens and cats).

The biggest town in these parts, **Hancock** is a lumber town with a small hardwood mill and a showroom for White River Timber Frames home builders and designers. Stop for a vegetarian meal at the **Sweet Onion** (802/767-3734), which also has B&B rooms. Or go inside the old **Hubbard's General Store** at the Route 125 junction, pick up some aged cheddar and a soda or a beer, and watch the world go by. North of Hancock, Route 100 passes through what is still a working landscape, with ski club cabins sharing the roadside scene with a few barns and remnants of historic sheep pens.

The one don't-miss highlight of this middle section of Route 100 is **Granville Gulf State Preserve,** five miles north of Hancock and about 30 beautiful miles north from US-4. The Green Mountains rise steeply to either side of the road, and just off the west side of the road, delicate **Moss Glen Falls** tumble down through craggy cliffs to a gurgling stream. A short boardwalk, built using recycled wood products, including supermarket plastic bags, leads to the foot of the falls from a small parking turnout.

Plymouth and Plymouth Notch:
Calvin Coolidge Country

Running a twisty seven miles south from US-4 and Bridgewater, Route 100A passes through beautiful scenery and **Plymouth Notch,** birthplace of Calvin Coolidge, the only U.S. president born on the 4th of July. The small hilltop clutch of buildings is so little changed by modern times, it's a wonder there aren't horses with carriages parked behind the visitors center instead of Subarus. One of the most evocative and simply beautiful historic sites in New England, **the Coolidge homestead** has been restored to its 1923 appearance when Colonel John Coolidge administered the oath of office to his vacationing son, the vice president, after President Harding died unexpectedly in San Francisco. The house, the general store, and the cheese factory are three of the ten buildings open to the public (daily in summer; $7.50; 802/672-3773). There's also a mile-long nature trail offering fine views of Plymouth Notch and its Green Mountain surroundings.

COLONEL JOHN COOLIDGE, FATHER OF PRESIDENT CALVIN COOLIDGE AND CALVIN JR.
PLYMOUTH, VERMONT

Route 100: The Skiers' Highway

Known as the Skiers' Highway, serpentine Route 100 manages to pass the base of nearly every major ski resort in southern Vermont. From Ludlow south through Jamaica, Stratton, and West Dover, any doubt that skiing is the cash cow of the state's most lucrative industry—tourism—is quickly dispelled by the wall-to-wall inns, sportswear shops, vacation real estate offices and restaurants along the way.

In recent years, downhill mountain-bikers and inn-to-inn cyclists riding Route 100 have made the region more of a year-round recreation center, but overall you still get the sense that, pretty as they are with their village greens, old homes, and hand-carved wooden signs, many of these Route 100 towns spend the warm months convalescing.

"Silent Cal" Coolidge was famous—perhaps unjustly—for being a man of few words. A White House dinner guest is said to have bet that she could make the president address her with at least three words; when confronted with this challenge, Coolidge replied, "You lose."

Wilmington and Route 9

Route 100 catches a panoramic view of Mt. Snow as it descends into **Wilmington** (pop. 1,968), a picturesque village of 18th- and 19th-century shops and houses built along the Deerfield River. For delicious pancakes served with a half-dozen toppings, stop at earthy **Sonny's Cup 'n' Saucer** (802/464-5813) at 159 N. Route 100. The chamber of commerce is named after the local ski resort rather than the town, so you know who pays the bills around here. Nevertheless, the warmer months see a fair bit of activity in the galleries and antique shops, and for classical music lovers, the **Marlboro Music Festival** (802/254-2394 in summer only) marks summer's zenith at Marlboro College, a dozen miles east toward Brattleboro on Route 9. Between mid-July and mid-August several score of the world's finest classical musicians perform here in one of the nation's most distinguished annual chamber music series.

Heading westward toward Bennington, you can continue west on Route 9 to Bennington and follow US-7 south through Williamstown, or you can make your way south through the much less developed areas along Route 8 and Route 100, which take you through the heavy-duty mill town of North Adams.

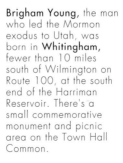

Brigham Young, the man who led the Mormon exodus to Utah, was born in **Whitingham,** fewer than 10 miles south of Wilmington on Route 100, at the south end of the Harriman Reservoir. There's a small commemorative monument and picnic area on the Town Hall Common.

Bennington

By far the largest Vermont town south of Burlington, **Bennington** (pop. 16,451) is a bustling little manufacturing and commercial center. It was the site of a significant victory against the British-paid Hessians in 1777 during the American Revolution, a sweet morale-booster that contributed to the defeat of General "Gentleman Johnny" Burgoyne's army of Redcoats at Saratoga. In the subsequent centuries, Bennington's name became synonymous with art: the decorative arts of the antebellum **United States Pottery Company**; the liberal arts of **Bennington College**, one of the nation's most expensive and exclusive private colleges; and the folk art of **Mary Robertson "Grandma" Moses.**

Whether or not you need gas, those interested in old cars and automobilia will want to stop by the full-service, re-created Sunoco filling station and antique car collection at **Hemmings Motor News** (800/227-4373), at 215 Main Street in Bennington.

The largest public collection of Grandma Moses's beguiling work is on display in the **Bennington Museum** (closed Wed.; $8), whose white-columned, ivy-covered edifice is found up the hill on West Main Street (Route 9) in the graceful old part of town. Along with 30 Grandma Moses paintings and the rural schoolhouse she attended two centuries ago, the museum also has a wide variety of historical artifacts, examples of early Bennington pottery, and the sole survivor of the fabulous motor cars once made here in Bennington: a 1925 **Wasp.**

From the Bennington Museum, walk north toward the 306-foot obelisk that towers over the town: the **Bennington Battle Monument,** erected in 1891 to commemorate the Revolutionary War victory, which actually occurred west of town, over the New York border. For $2, mid-April–November 1, an elevator will take you to an observation room near the top of the tower for a great view up and down the valley.

Bennington is also the final resting place of poet Robert Frost, whose tombstone in the burial ground alongside the Old First Church, at Church and Monument Streets, says: "I had a lover's quarrel with the world."

If anyone starts erecting monuments to good dining instead of old wars or dead poets, this town would have another tower of stone beside the **Blue Benn Diner** (802/442-5140), north of town at 314 North Street. The fact that it's a vintage 1940s Silk City certainly gives this cozy, nonsmoking joint character. But what earns the seven-days-a-week (from 6 AM) loyalty of its patrons is the top-notch short-order cooking: From baked meat loaf

When garnished with Vermont-made **Ben & Jerry's** ice cream, apple pie á la mode is certainly nothing to sneer at, but if you really want to try apple pie the Vermont way, ask for a slab of sharp cheddar on the side instead of ice cream.

and roast pork to broccoli stir-fry and multigrain pancakes, the food's good, cheap, and served up so fast you'll barely have time to choose your song on the wall-hung jukebox at your table.

Most of Bennington's accommodations are strung along Route 7A to the north and US-7 to the south of downtown, all local names but for the Ramada and Best Western inns found on 7A. If you are in the market for a distinctive B&B, check out the central and historic **Four Chimneys Inn** ($135 and up; 802/447-3500), on Route 9 at 21 West Road.

MASSACHUSETTS

Hemmed in by the daunting topography of its surrounding mountains, the Berkshire region of western Massachusetts is a world apart, blessed with abundant nature and an easygoing small-town character. The region's relaxed, rural charms, and its location equidistant from Boston and New York City, have long made it a magnet for writers and artists as well as a playground for the rich, so be prepared to experience a little of everything from natural splendors to high-society display. And remember, it never takes more than a few strategic turns to trade plush restaurants and music festivals for splendidly rural forests as deep and undisturbed as any in New England.

By the early 19th century, farmland had replaced 75 percent of Berkshire County's forests. Now forests have reclaimed that 75 percent and more, but innumerable drystone walls serve as reminders of the once vast cultivated fields.

North Adams

If you've grown accustomed to the typical tourist New England of village greens and clapboard B&Bs, industrial **North Adams** (pop. 14,681) may come as something of a shock. Nearly from its inception, North Adams tied its fortunes to major manufacturing plants, churning out printed cotton until textiles went south, then rolling out electronics for everything from the first atomic bomb to the television sets of the 1950s and 1960s. When electronics went solid-state and overseas, North Adams nearly died clinging to the belief that some new assembly line would come fill its sprawling complex of massive Victorian-era mill buildings. Finally, the town's long-awaited salvation seems to be taking shape, in the form of art: the Massachusetts Museum of Contemporary Art. Better known as **Mass MoCA** (daily in July & Aug., closed Tues. rest of year; $10; 413/664-4481), the museum galleries fill some 200,000 square feet of heavy-duty industrial buildings with an ever-changing array of cutting-edge art (plus the inevitable shop and a very nice café, Eleven).

For those more interested in the olden days, the region's historic gravy train is faithfully recollected in the **Western Gateway Heritage State Park** (daily; free; 413/663-8059). Occupying the former freight-yard of the Boston and Maine

North Adams is five miles north of the quaint town of **Adams**, the birthplace of voting rights activist Susan B. Anthony (1820–1906). Adams is also home to another American classic: the **Miss Adams Diner** (413/743-5303), at 53 Park Street, serving very good "funky comfort food" in a lovingly preserved 1949 Worcester.

Railroad, the park highlights the landmark construction of the five-mile-long Hoosac Tunnel and North Adams's front-row seat on the Boston-to-Great Lakes rail connection it made possible.

In northwestern Massachusetts, this Appalachian Trail crosses the **Oregon Trail** transcontinental road trip along US-20 and other highways (see page 615). Heading east from North Adams along Route 2 (the Mohawk Trail to Boston and Cape Cod), and west from Williamstown through Albany and beyond, the entire coast-to-coast journey is covered beginning on page 532.

Williamstown

To the visitor it appears as if stately **Williamstown** (pop. 4,754) is simply a nickname for the immaculate and graceful campus of Williams College—even the main commercial block is basically the corridor between dorms and gym. From their common 18th-century benefactor, Ephraim Williams (who insisted the town's name be changed from its original West Hoosuck), to the large number of alumni who return in their retirement, "Billsville" and its college are nearly inseparable. The town-gown symbiosis has spawned an enviable array of visual, performing, and edible arts, yet fresh contingents of ingenuous youth keep all the wealth and refinement from becoming too cloying.

Singer Sewing Machine heir Robert Sterling Clark's huge art collection ended up in Williamstown in part because of the Cold War. In the late 1940s and early 1950s, the threat of a Russian nuclear attack seemed real enough that being as distant as possible from likely bomb targets was a critical factor in choosing a permanent repository. Today **Clark Art Institute** (daily July & Aug., closed Mon. rest of year; $10 in summer, free rest of year; 413/458-2303), at 225 South Street, is the town's jewel, displaying display paintings by Winslow Homer and an extraordinary collection of Impressionist works, including more than 30 Renoirs. Also worth a look is the excellent and wide-ranging **Williams College Museum of Art** (closed Mon.; free; 413/597-2429) on Main

It was during the blasting of the **Hoosac Tunnel** that nitroglycerin was first used as a construction explosive. And just so you know, the river is the Hoosic, the mountain range is the Hoosac.

Street opposite Memorial Chapel (that mini Westminster Abbey).

Williamstown can claim another gem, this time in the natural art of relaxation. Luxurious Cunard Lines used to serve its ocean-going passengers water exclusively from Williamstown's **Sand Springs** (Memorial Day–Labor Day; $7.50; 413/458-5205). Since the 1950s, a family-friendly swimming pool complex has opened on the site, on the north side of town at 158 Sand Springs Road, all summer long.

Williamstown Practicalities

For breakfast, head to US-7 on the north side of town, where the popular **Chef's Hat** (413/458-5120) at 905 Simonds Road preserves a 100-year-old counter and other parts of its original diner incarnation. Also good, the **Clarksburg Bread Company** (closed Sun. and Mon.; 413/458-2251) at 37 Spring Street serves up soups, sandwiches, and a wealth of delicious baked goods until 4 PM. The hands-down best takeout pizza joint is **Hot Tomatoes** (413/458-2722), at 100 Water Street, and in mild weather the nearby streamside park is well-suited to lolling picnickers.

Tony continental dining suitable for starched alumni banquets abounds in Williamstown, but if you're looking for truly fresh, interesting food, skip the inns and go to **Mezze** (413/458-0123) at 16 Water Street.

A drive along Main Street (Route 2) will give you a view of most of Williamstown's accommodations, from the on-campus **Williams Inn** ($150 and up; 413/458-9371), 1090 Main Street, to the small motels out on the eastern edge of town like the **Maple Terrace** ($60 and up; 413/458-9677) at 555 Main Street. For a real treat, consider **Field Farm** ($125 and up; 413/458-3135) at 554 Sloan Road in South Williamstown, five miles south along either Route 7 or scenic Water Street (Route 43). Occupying the 254-acre former estate of Pacific Northwest lumber tycoon Lawrence Bloedel, the main house, designed in 1948, is a striking example of American modern architecture. If you have any love of Frank Lloyd Wright or Charles and Ray Eames, you'll be delighted by this live-in museum of contemporary design, with its huge picture windows, proto-Scandinavian furniture, and meadow-side swimming pool.

Additional information is available from the Chamber of Commerce **Information Booth** (413/458-9077) at the center of town.

Mt. Greylock

South of Williamstown, Massachusetts' tallest peak is the centerpiece of 12,500-acre **Mount Greylock State Reservation,** one of the state's largest and most popular possessions. More than 50 miles of trails, including some thigh-burning mountain-bike routes, wander along the reforested slopes, most of which were heavily logged for fuel and pulp back in the 19th century. Rock ledges provide great views of the Hoosic River Valley to the east and the

Hancock Shaker Village

Just five miles west of Pittsfield on old US-20, Hancock Shaker Village is one of the best-preserved remnants of the religious sect known popularly as Shakers, but formally as the United Society of Believers in Christ's Second Appearing, whose utopian communities flourished in the years before the Civil War. Shakers, as outsiders called them because of their occasional convulsions during worship, were dedicated to a communal life conspicuous in its equality between men and women, a natural corollary to their belief in parity between a male God and a female Holy Mother Wisdom.

The English-born leader of the group, Ann Lee, was in fact regarded by Shakers as the female, and second, incarnation of Christ. Although Puritan theocracy was ending, preaching this gospel did not endear her to many New Englanders in the decade following her arrival just prior to the American Revolution. During that war, Lee and her "children" sought their "Heaven on Earth," as seen in her visions. Mother Ann died near Albany, New York, in 1784, before any communities based on her precepts could be founded.

Hancock Shaker Village, third among the 24 settlements built in the nation by Lee's followers, was founded in 1790 and survived 170 years,

Housatonic Valley to the south, when the namesake mists aren't keeping the 3,491-foot summit wadded up in a damp ball of dingy cotton. During warm months access is a cinch: Century-old Notch Road snakes its way up through the birch and spruce from Route 2 on the north side, while Rockwell Road ascends more gently from US-7 along the flanks of Greylock's southern neighbors. Combine these roads' 17 miles and you'll enjoy the most scenic, driveable mountain ascent in New England, although keep in mind that both roads are narrow, rumble-stripped with frost-heaves, enlivened by occasional hairpin turns, and—especially at dusk—prone to wandering wildlife. If you want to see over the forest, climb the 105-foot **War Memorial Tower** on the summit. If the weather is good, you'll have a panoramic view from New Hampshire to Connecticut.

A stone's throw from the granite tower is the AMC's **Bascom Lodge** (mid-May–late Oct. only; $40 and up; 413/443-0011), a beautiful old stone and timber structure with private rooms, shared bunk rooms, and cold-water baths.

Pittsfield

Compared to the carefully preserved Norman Rockwell simplicity of many of the surrounding small towns, the aging industrial cityscape of **Pittsfield** (pop. 48,000) has made it the place most Berkshire weekenders strenuously try to avoid, despite the fact that its size and the valley's topography make this nearly impossible unless you have a resident's familiarity with the backroads.

Despite Pittsfield's anything-but-quaint appearance, there are actually some good reasons to pay the place a

outlasting all but two other Shaker communities. It's been preserved as a living museum (daily April–Oct.; $15.00; 413/443-0188 or 800/817-1137), with exhibits, tours, and working artisans interpreting the rural lifestyle and famous design skills of the Shakers. Appreciation of the efficiency, simplicity, and perfect workmanship consecrated within the "City of Peace" can quickly fill a couple of days if you let it. For a special treat, secure a place at the candlelight Shaker dinners held on Saturday evenings; you can also sample Shaker cuisine in the Village Cafe.

The center of Shaker activities was just west of Hancock, along US-20 across the New York border at New Lebanon, where a few buildings still stand today. Other large Shaker communities in New England included Sabbathday Lake in Maine (the only one still "alive"), one at Enfield, New Hampshire (east of Hanover), and another at Canterbury, New Hampshire (south of Franconia Notch).

Arrowhead

visit. Head out to Holmes Road, at the city's rural southern edge, and maybe you will see the resemblance between a leviathan and the imposing outline of Mt. Greylock, particularly if you view it from the study window of Herman Melville's **Arrowhead** (daily in summer; $10; 413/442-1793). That salty masterpiece, *Moby Dick,* was indeed written in this landlocked locale, where Melville moved in 1850 to be near his mentor, Nathaniel Hawthorne. While foremost a literary shrine, the spacious farm is also home to the **Berkshire County Historical Society,** whose well-curated exhibits are always interesting. Serious pilgrims on the path of Ishmael and the great white whale will also want to visit the **Melville Memorial Room** on the upper level of the Berkshire Athenaeum, Pittsfield's public library.

As with its other attractions, Pittsfield has some real out-of-the-way gems when it comes to food. In the acute angle between East and Elm Streets at 503 East Street, for example, is the semicircular facade of the **Pittsfield Rye Bakery** (413/443-9141), a 1950s flying saucer of glass and blue tile with big bright cases of fresh muffins, bagels, and breads beckoning within. For excellent pasta, pizza, and pub grub at a great small-town price, step around the corner to the **East Side Cafe** (413/447-9405), at 378 Newell Street, a neighborhood bar whose comfort food and convivial atmosphere attract a family clientele.

You may not know that all of the paper used in all of the money printed in the United States comes from a mill here in the backwoods of Massachusetts, but it does. In fact, **Crane & Co.** of **Dalton** makes the 100 percent cotton paper used in United States currency at a series of historic mills along Route 8 just east of Pittsfield.

Places to stay include a large **Holiday Inn Crowne Plaza** ($119 and up; 413/499-2000) at 1 West Street and other chains, plus the pleasant **Berkshire Inn** ($75 and up; 413/443-3000), on US-20 a half mile west of US-7 at 150 W. Housatonic Street.

Lenox

During the late-19th-century Gilded Age, the Berkshires were the inland equivalent of Newport, Rhode Island, with dozens of opulent "cottages" constructed here by newly rich titans of American industry. Built for an era in which "society" was a respectable, full-time occupation for folks with names like Carnegie and Westinghouse, some 75 of these giant mansions still stand, especially around the genteel town of **Lenox** (pop. 5,100). Many of the houses have been converted to palatial B&B inns, full-service health spas, or private schools; others are home to organizations whose presence has made Lenox a seasonal mecca for the performing arts.

The lives and times of the Gilded Age elite were well chronicled by Edith Wharton, who lived in Lenox for many years in a 42-room house she designed and built for herself called **The Mount** (daily in summer only; $16; 413/637-6900). Recently restored, and set in 3 acres of Italianate gardens, The Mount is just south of central Lenox, well-signed off Plunkett Street. Wharton, who considered herself better at gardening than writing, was the first woman to win a Pulitzer Prize (for her 1920 novel *The Age of Innocence*). She drew upon local people and incidents in many of her works, including two of her most famous: *House of Mirth* and *Ethan Frome*.

Lenox is also connected with another great American writer, Nathaniel Hawthorne, who lived here with his family around 1850 and wrote *The House of Seven Gables* at what is now the summer home of the Boston Symphony and many visiting performers, **Tanglewood** (tickets $20 and up; 888/266-2100). Besides Tanglewood, the Lenox area also hosts the Jacob's Pillow dance festival in Becket (413/243-0745) and the Berkshire Theatre Festival in Stockbridge (413/298-5576), so you can understand why such a small town is such a big magnet for East Coast culture vultures.

Lenox Practicalities

The annual influx of cosmopolitan concert-goers affects everything in southwestern Massachusetts, most obviously the local restaurants, half of which cater to seasonal immigrants from Boston and New York. If you aren't counting nickels, try the eclectic American menu at the **Church Street Cafe** (413/637-2745), at 65 Church Street, where the tastes from the kitchen and accents from the diners are unmistakably reminiscent of some big-city bistro. Other major contenders for the town's gourmet dining crowd lie within the same two-block area. At the other end of the price spectrum is **Salerno's Gourmet Pizza** (413/637-8940), across the street at 50 Church Street, whose plain fast-food–style decor masks a practitioner of the delicious *abbondonza* school of pizza.

Lenox brims with more than 20 handsome B&B inns attractively situated amid wide lawns and gardens. Try the historic **Birchwood Inn** ($100 and up; 800/524-1646), at 7 Hubbard Street, opposite the Church on the Hill; or the

Brook Farm Inn ($125 and up; 413/637-3013) on Hawthorne Street, which offers more than 700 volumes of poetry in the library, poetry on audiotape, poetry readings on Saturday, and poems *du jour* for perusal before breakfast. Another popular option, right at the center of Lenox, is the **Village Inn** ($100 and up; 413/637-0020), 16 Church Street, built in 1771 and featuring clean, comfortable rooms and a very good restaurant.

Of course, if you prefer the anonymity of your favorite **chain motels** you'll find them scattered along US-20 between the Pittsfield-Lenox line and the I-90 interchange in neighboring Lee.

For a complete list of these local accommodations, or for help with last-minute lodging or tickets to performances, contact the **Lenox Chamber of Commerce** (413/637-3646), 75 Main Street.

Stockbridge's Main Street hasn't always been the exclusive province of boutiques for coffee, curtains, and AARP members. Once upon a time it was also home to the eatery immortalized by **Arlo Guthrie** as the place where "you can get anything you want" in his 1967 folk song, "Alice's Restaurant Massacree."

Stockbridge

On the south side of the I-90 Mass Turnpike from Lenox, the other main center of Berkshires cultural life is **Stockbridge** (pop. 2,276). If Main Street feels familiar, perhaps it's because the town made its way onto Norman Rockwell canvases during the final decades of his career, when he lived and worked here. You may dismiss his illustrations as the epitome of contrived sentimentality, but only people with hearts of solid flint won't find themselves grinning after a stroll through the collection of **The Norman Rockwell Museum** (daily; $12; 413/298-4100). The modern museum is on Route 183 two miles west of town, and the town itself is well worth a stroll, too, particularly past the grand houses along Main Street that seem frozen in an idyllic past.

Know that **Rockwell** painting of the runaway kid with the policeman? The lunch-counter setting was inspired by **Joe's Diner** (413/243-9756) at 85 Center Street in nearby Lee, a Berkshire institution favored by everybody from local factory workers to New York celebrities.

While most of the large estate homes around Stockbridge are not open to the public, one of the county's more extravagant "cottages" is **Naumkeag** (daily in summer only; $10), an 1885 mansion on Prospect Hill Road less than a mile north of downtown. The mansion, designed by Stanford White for Joseph Choate, a lawyer who later served as U.S. ambassador to Britain, amply illustrates why this region was regarded as the state's Gold Coast a century ago. The impressively landscaped grounds are an attraction in their own right.

Sculpture is the highlight of **Chesterwood** (daily in summer; $10), off Route 183 just south of the Rockwell Museum. The residence was the summer home of **Daniel Chester French**, one of the most popular contributors to the fin-de-siècle American renaissance. French arrived on the art scene with a bang, sculpting Concord's *Minute Man* statue at age 25, but he is best remembered for his statue of the seated president in Lincoln Memorial in Washington, D.C. A tour of French's studio and house (now a property of the National Trust), or a walk around the 122 wooded acres graced with works of contemporary sculptors, quickly confirms why the sculptor once called his seasonal visits "six months . . . in heaven."

Tyringam

Route 8, US-20, and the Mass Turnpike all cross the Appalachian Trail at Greenwater Pond east of Lee, but a much more scenic stretch of the trail can be accessed south of here in the village of **Tyringham** (pop. 370). Site of a Shaker community in the 1800s, and later a popular artist colony, this small hamlet is situated in a delightfully rural landscape of small farms and

Museum & Gardens

rolling pastures. The main sight here is an odd one: **Santarella** (daily; $4), the hand-hewn home and studio of British sculptor Sir Henry Kitson, whose many works include the Pilgrim monument at Plymouth and the *Minute Man* at Lexington Green. His house is a place where *The Hobbit's* Bilbo Baggins would feel at home, with its sculpted rocks, twisting beams, and organic-looking pseudo-thatched roof.

South of Santarella, beyond the ever-quaint center of Tyringham, a signed parking area marks the crossing of the Appalachian Trail, which you can follow on a short (three-mile round-trip) hike through fields of wildflowers up through Tyringham Cobble to a ridge giving a good view over this pastoral valley, which feels far more remote than it really is.

The first black man ever to earn a Ph.D. from Harvard, writer **W. E. B. DuBois,** was born in Great Barrington in 1868.

Great Barrington

While most South County towns have been spruced up like precious antiques, **Great Barrington,** with as many hardware stores as chic boutiques, is like grandma's comfortable old sofa, still too much in daily use to keep under velvet wraps. The town doesn't deplore the few tacky commercial lots around its fringes, perhaps because they can't detract from the handsome buildings at its core. Prime among these buildings, which include stone churches on wide Main Street and imposing Searles Castle, a former Berkshire cottage turned private academy, is the landmark **Mahaiwe Theater** (413/528-0100) at 14 Castle Street, all marble and gilt trim behind its marquee. Built for vaudeville, and recently restored, it still hosts frequent theater and musical theater productions.

When people think of electricity they think of Thomas Edison and light bulbs, but the roots of your local utility lie here in the nation's first commercial electrical system, created by transformer inventor **William Stanley** for Great Barrington's downtown in 1886.

Besides architecture and history, Great Barrington has a lot to offer hungry travelers. Fussy early-risers seeking their cappuccino and muffins, or picnickers needing the makings of a great spread will want to check out the **Berkshire Coffee Roasting Company,** at 286 Main Street, which serves up espresso drinks, teas, and bakery items, with the added benefit of the South County's best let's-hang-out atmosphere. **Bev's Homemade Ice Cream,** around the corner at 5 Railroad

Street, is another source of caffeine, light lunch fare, and sugar, too, by the rich and creamy coneful.

Across from Bev's is **20 Railroad Street,** *the* place for burgers, sandwiches, and soups; its lively bar is the closest native example of a honky-tonk.

Sheffield

Between Great Barrington and the Connecticut state line, US-7 winds through **Sheffield** and is lined by dozens of antique stores, earning this stretch the nickname Antique Alley. Sheffield also has a faded gray covered bridge, just 100 yards east of US-7 on the north side of town. At the south edge of Sheffield, just west of US-7 off Weatogue Road, the natural rock garden of **Bartholomew's Cobble** rises up above the west bank of the Housatonic River. Geology and weather have conspired to produce an outstanding diversity of plants and birds—more than 700 species, including beautiful wildflowers—within a relatively small pocket of fern-covered limestone outcrops and broad meadows. At the center of the 300-acre reserve, a very pleasant walk up Hulburt's Hill gives a broad view over the surrounding Berkshire scene.

South Egremont: Bash Bish Falls

While US-7 gets the most tourist traffic, a more pastoral way south into Connecticut follows Route 41 via **South Egremont,** another of those well-preserved villages entirely ensconced in the National Register of Historic Places, which is hardly a rare honor in Massachusetts.

At the center of town, **Mom's Country Cafe** (413/528-2414) is a friendly choice for a bite before or after a hike; you'll find country breakfasts, burgers, pasta, and soups.

South Egremont also has a wonderful B&B inn, the **Weathervane** ($115 and up; 413/528-9580), which has 10 acres of gardens and grounds (including a swimming pool) and 10 rooms in a white clapboard farmhouse built in 1783.

South Egremont is the gateway to the state's remotest corner, the 4,000 forested acres of **Mount Washington State Forest.** Within its wooded boundaries are miles of hiking trails, including a stretch of the Appalachian Trail climbing up to the 2,602-foot summit of Mt. Everett, but the highlight here is photogenic **Bash Bish Falls,** the highest in Massachusetts. A whopping 80-foot drop, splashing down in a V-shaped pair of cascades, Bash Bish Falls is no Niagara, but it's a nice place to while away a hot summer's afternoon.

The mountainous section of US-20, north of the Mass Turnpike between Huntington and Lee, is one of the oldest auto roads in New England, originally called **Jacob's Ladder.** Older, and in some ways prettier, than the busier and much more famous Mohawk Trail across the state's northwestern tier, Jacob's Ladder is centered on the quaint town of **Chester.**

The last battle of **Shay's Rebellion,** an uprising of farmers demanding reforms to prevent foreclosures after the American Revolution dried up English credit, was fought in a field south of the village on Sheffield Road. A small stone obelisk marks the spot, coincidentally adjacent to the Appalachian Trail.

Bash Bish Falls

CONNECTICUT

Anyone who drives its interstates will appreciate why Connecticut enjoys a solid reputation among New Englanders as "the drive-through state." The high-speed route between Boston and New York City, I-95, is something endured rather than enjoyed, but our route through the scenic northwest corner is as different from the coastal megalopolis as a tulip is from a truck tire. Like the neighboring Berkshires, Connecticut's Litchfield Hills are a traditional retreat for discerning city dwellers. The area is rich in forests, farms, and picturesque little towns laden with antiques and great restaurants. Fast food and discount shopping are as alien to this landscape as affordability, so if your purse strings are tight you'll want to keep moving; otherwise, linger a while and enjoy some of the rural charm so prized by those people you see on the cover of *Business Week.*

North Canaan and Salisbury

Crossing into Connecticut from the north on US-7, the first thing that will catch your eye is the stainless-steel siding of **Collin's Diner** (860/824-7040) in the heart of **North Canaan**. A classic 1940s prefab O'Mahony diner, Collin's has all the usual diner standards, and its big parking lot (shared with the neighboring historic railroad depot) is frequently full of equally classic cars, whose owners congregate here on summer afternoons. The rest of North Canaan—a couple of clothing stores and an old movie theater—is anything but prissy, a refreshing change of pace from the overly tidy tourist towns that dominate the surrounding region.

Salisbury's **Lakeville Furnace** was the armory of the American Revolution, supplying George Washington's troops with almost their entire arsenal of artillery and ammunition for the duration of the war.

From North Canaan, US-44 winds east toward Hartford, stopping after 15 miles at another gem of a small town, **Norfolk**; if any town has capitalized on being far removed from trading floors and board meetings, it's this one. With three public parks and the largest private forest in the state, Norfolk has considered its sheer scenic beauty a stock in trade for nearly a century; the town green is worth the drive, so you can see the folksy road sign that points the way with pictures of rabbits and other cute creatures.

After extensive touring around New England, you risk taking white columns, wide porches, picket fences, and the obligatory Congregational steeple for granted. Even then, prim little **Salisbury**, a half-dozen miles west of US-7 at the junction of Route 41 and US-44, still may elicit reveries about what small-town America would look like if strip malls ceased to exist. Spend an after-

Collin's Diner in Cornwall

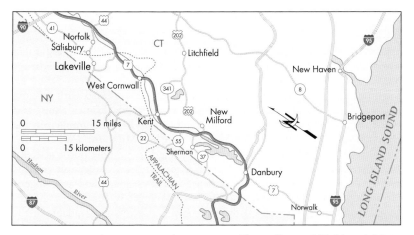

noon sipping cardamom-scented tea in tiny **Chaiwalla**, on US-44 at 1 Main Street, or step over to Academy Street to nosh on a stylish lunch at the **Harvest Bakery**, while regulars banter with the owner as they stock up on the delicious breads and desserts, and see if you don't conclude that franchising of fast food should be declared a misdemeanor.

West Cornwall

Rivers are consistently some of the most attractive driving companions you could ask for, a fact proven once again as US-7 rejoins the Housatonic River south of Lime Rock. The highway's scenic miles are further enhanced by the sudden appearance of a barn-red covered bridge, which since 1837 has served as the one-lane gateway to idyllic **West Cornwall**. This is the kind of place that would tar and feather the first vinyl-siding salesperson to walk into town, lest harm befall its antiquarian bookshop or other clapboard buildings bearing signs from previous commercial lives (although the old meat market *is* now a video store).

LIME ROCK PARK

South of town, **Housatonic Meadows State Park** offers riverside **camping** (mid-April–mid-Sept.; $10), perfectly situated for anyone considering a canoe or kayak rental from adjacent **Clarke Outdoors**, on US-7 a mile south of that covered bridge. Their 10-mile canoe trips (around $50 for 2 people; 860/672-6365) include a boat, life-vests and all the gear, plus van shuttles and hot showers. Remember to bring bug repellent if you're planning to spend time near the water.

Housatonic Meadows State Park also includes a short, three-mile round-trip trail up 1,160-foot Pine Knob, which offers fine views from its summit. Just south of the park boundary, the hiker's Appalachian Trail crosses US-7 and the Housatonic River at the hamlet of Cornwall Bridge, then runs alongside the river for some eight miles, the longest riverside cruise in the trail's entire 2,100 miles.

On Route 112 a couple of miles west of US-7, you'll find **Lime Rock Park** (860/435-0896 or 800/722-3577), an automobile racetrack made famous in part by classic car rallies, a mid-May **Grand Prix**, the Skip Barber Racing School (800/221-1131), and the occasional appearance of celebrity drivers like Paul Newman and Tom Cruise. The sharp, twisting descent from nearby Lakeville to the raceway is one of many pretty back-road drives in the area.

Kent

Like many of its Litchfield-area neighbors, **Kent** (pop. 2,918) had a thriving iron industry until competition from larger Pennsylvania mines—with better access to post–Civil War markets—forced the local furnace to close. Now it's a bustling, upscale market town, its main street (US-7) lined with antique shops, galleries, and boutiques that have replaced blacksmith shops and wheelwrights. The area's transition from industry to leisure is implicit in the unusual displays inside the **Sloane-Stanley Museum** (Wed.–Sun. 10 AM–4 PM; $4; 860/927-3849), located along US-7 a mile north of Kent, near the ruins of an early-American iron foundry. The collection consists mainly of old tools—planes of all shapes and sizes, plus handsaws, augers, clamps, and other woodworking devices—all arranged by local artist and author Eric Sloane (1905–1985), whose books and prints are available in the gift shop. The "Stanley" in the museum's name comes (surprise, surprise) from the famous Stanley tool company, based in nearby New Britain, which donated the land and the museum building. Stanley tools make up a significant portion of the collection, but many others are handmade tools, some of which date back to days when colonial-era craftsmen forged their own tools to suit their specific needs.

Kent Falls State Park, along US-7 about four miles north of the museum, is a nice place to take a break from behind the wheel. Along with the namesake cascade, which is most impressive after a rain, the park includes a short path through dense woods.

Running south of Kent, parallel to US-7 for about six miles along the west bank of the Housatonic River, Schagticoke Road is a slower, much more scenic route that gives an up-close look at the rugged geology beneath the trees. The route crosses the Schagticoke Indian Reservation and passes an old Indian cemetery before rejoining US-7 via a covered bridge on Bulls Bridge Road, three miles north of Gaylordsville.

The Appalachian Trail crosses the New York state line near Bull's Bridge south of Kent, and so should you, making your way west to Route 22 or the Taconic State Parkway if you want to enjoy a landscape that offers more fields and trees than guardrails and parking lots. Technically speaking, there's still a large swath of New England between New York and New Milford, but most of this has more in common with the Indianapolis beltway than with the Vermont countryside.

NEW YORK

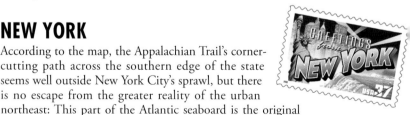

According to the map, the Appalachian Trail's corner-cutting path across the southern edge of the state seems well outside New York City's sprawl, but there is no escape from the greater reality of the urban northeast: This part of the Atlantic seaboard is the original megalopolis. The map may not make it obvious that some tens of millions of people live within an hour's drive of this route, but the volume of traffic will.

Bear Mountain Bridge carries the Appalachian Trail across the Hudson River.

Between the Connecticut border and the Hudson River, many of the roads along the route of the Appalachian Trail have become heavily developed corridors of suburban malls and Park 'n' Ride lots for Manhattan commuters.

The hiker's Appalachian Trail, and our driving equivalent along old US-6, both cross the Hudson River near West Point, the Army's famous military academy, located at a point on the west bank of the Hudson, naturally. West and south of West Point, the two routes stay together for a scenic foray through Harriman and Bear Mountain State Parks before heading west toward Pennsylvania.

Even if you're racing across New York on the I-84 freeway, there's one place you should stop: the town of **Hyde Park**, where the homes of **Franklin D.** and **Eleanor Roosevelt** offer a look back at their admirable lives and challenging times.

Harriman State Park and Bear Mountain

Rising out of the Hudson Valley, **Harriman State Park** is a mountainous oasis with 30 lakes and some 200 miles of hiking trails; the first section of the Appalachian Trail was opened here in 1923. In utter contrast to the get-out-of-my-way style of later highway construction, the roads across the

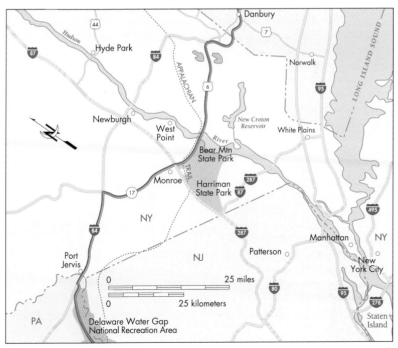

New York City

STATUE OF LIBERTY, NEW YORK CITY

Some people avoid New York City like the plague, but seven million others can't bear to leave the glorious buzzing mosaic that makes New York unique in the world. Love it or hate it, New York is New York, and this great metropolis is undeniably the capital of the capitalist world, with some of the best museums, the best shops, the best sights, and the best restaurants in the world.

There's not much point in our recommending a select few of New York's huge spectrum of attractions, so we'll get straight to offering some practical help. For drivers, to whom all roads must seem to converge upon—and become gridlocked in—New York City, there are a number of semi-painless ways to deal with the city without driving miles out of the way, or driving yourself mad. The best way to experience New York in passing is on I-95; this gives you a brief glimpse of the city's gritty glamour and a distant view of Manhattan's spires to the south.

If you value your sanity and your shock absorbers, park your car in a long-term lot (not on the streets; city parking regulations are arcane and the fines huge) and walk or take public transportation. New York's subway system, one of the most extensive in the world, is relatively safe and usually the fastest way to get around town; it's also inexpensive ($2 per ride, or $7 a day, payable via electronic Metrocard). City buses are generally slower, but you see more of the sights. Taxis are ubiquitous—except when you want one.

The key to a successful visit to New York City is finding a place to stay. Ideally, you'll have an expense account, a friend, or a rich aunt, but lacking that, here are a few suggestions, most in the low-to-moderate range. It's hard to beat the **Holiday Inn** ($150 and up; 212/966-8898) at 138 Lafayette Street for convenience, as it's equidistant from Chinatown, Little Italy, SoHo, and TriBeCa. For families, another good option is the **Embassy Suites** ($199 and up; 212/945-0100) at Battery Park City, 102 North End Avenue, with views

of the Statue of Liberty. The least expensive place in town is the very large and popular **HI New York Hostel** (212/932-2300), on the Upper West Side at 891 Amsterdam Avenue at 103rd Street, with private rooms (around $70) plus dorm beds for $25 a night. One of the many fabulous hotels in New York City is the small but stylish **Morgan's** ($250 and up; 212/686-0300) at 237 Madison Avenue.

Eating out is another way to blow a lot of money very quickly, but there are some great places where you can get both a good meal and a feel for New York without going bankrupt. One such place is **Katz's Delicatessen** (212/254-2246), 205 E. Houston Street, a Lower East Side landmark that's been serving up man-sized sandwiches (including great pastrami) "since 1888." (For movie buffs, Katz's is where Meg Ryan did her famous fake-orgasm scene in *When Harry Met Sally.*) And if you like diners, check out the **Empire Diner** (212/243-2736), at 210 10th Avenue at 22nd Street in the Chelsea neighborhood—all black enamel and gleaming stainless steel, and open 24 hours, 7 days a week. The well-prepared food is the usual burgers and meat loaf, etc., enlivened by frequent live jazz. There are dozens of world-class restaurants in Gotham City, but at least one serves excellent food in stylish surroundings without breaking the bank: On the Upper East Side, between the Metropolitan and Whitney museums, Michelin-starred chef Daniel Boulud serves up exquisitely prepared French bistro fare at his **Cafe Boulud** (212/772-2600), 20 E. 76th Street. The ever-changing menu features a wide variety of traditional favorites and contemporary inventions, available for lunch and dinner at (comparatively) moderate prices. It's very popular, so make reservations as soon as you can.

About 30 miles northwest of Port Jervis, Max Yasgur's farm outside **Bethel, New York,** welcomed revelers to the August 1969 "Woodstock Festival of Music and Art", starring Jimi Hendrix, Crosby Stills and Nash, and some 300,000 mud-soaked hippies.

Off I-87 and Hwy-32 on the north side of the expansive U.S. Military Academy at West Point, stretch your legs and broaden your mind at the **Storm King Art Center** (daily Apr.—mid-Nov. only; $10; 845/534-3115), a fabulous 500-acre sculpture park.

park, designed in the 1920s for Sunday afternoon family outings in the new-fangled motor car, maximize exposure to the surrounding forests, and even the rustic Romanesque stone arch bridges manage to harmonize with local rock outcroppings.

Closer to the Hudson River, an adjacent state park, **Bear Mountain,** is even more full of old-fashioned pleasures, and draws more annual visitors than Yellowstone National Park (no doubt thanks to its location at the north end of the Palisades Parkway). A scenic drive leads near the top of Bear Mountain itself, where a New Deal–era lookout tower gives views over the entire region, and an interior mural traces local history. In season, there are pedal boats for rent, plus a large swimming pool (or an ice-skating rink). Meals and accommodations are available in a rustic, circa 1915 lodge (845/786-2731).

Local literary trivia: At the beginning of Jack Kerouac's *On the Road,* the main character, Sal Paradise, sets off from New York City on an ill-fated attempt to follow US-6 all the way to the West Coast. Hoping to hitch a ride along the "one red line called Route 6 that led from the tip of Cape Cod clear to Ely, Nevada, and there dipped down to Los Angeles," Sal got caught in a rain storm here at Bear Mountain and had to head home, giving up on the "stupid hearthside idea that it would be wonderful to follow one great line across America instead of trying various roads and routes."

Monroe and Port Jervis

West of Harriman State Park, the Appalachian Trail and US-6 cross the busy I-87 New York Thruway, then wind through the exurbs of the Big Apple, where town after town seems unsure whether this is country living or not. Outside **Monroe,** for example, a country store, a one-room schoolhouse, and a log cabin have been collected together in a roadside living-history "Museum Village" (daily in summer; $10). Right in Monroe, the very cool, very kitsch, green-glass **Monroe Diner** (845/783-8916), at 1797 US-6/Hwy-17, serves great burgers.

Further west, along I-84 on the tri-state (NY/NJ/PA) border, **Port Jervis** is a curious mixture of small-town dereliction and commercial bustle. Transportation has clearly been a major historical force here, with the influence of successive eras—the river, the railroad, and the highway—inscribed in the very layout of the town. For a

glimpse of the long reign of the iron horse, check out the intriguing artifacts and photos in the restored waiting room of the old **Erie Lackawanna Depot** on Front Street, or stop inside the old **Erie Hotel** next door, which has an ornate bar, a lively restaurant and rooms upstairs ($60; 845/858-4100).

Port Jervis clearly still believes in the virtues of home cooking: **Homer's Coffee Shop** (845/856-1712), unmissable at 2 E. Main Street, is a prime example, with its democratic social club of elderly regulars, young tie-wearing businessmen, and tradespeople with company names stitched on their shirt pockets, all drawn to the bargain meals. Despite the acoustic tile and too-new counter and seating, it's a welcoming spot, with the added attraction of a soda fountain in case you need to wash down that turkey club or beef stroganoff with a Tin Roof Sundae.

PENNSYLVANIA

The hikers' Appalachian Trail runs across southern New York and western New Jersey, but our road route avoids the Garden State almost entirely, crossing instead the natural chasm of the **Delaware Water Gap,** whose forests, waterfalls, and wildlife are popular with city-dwellers escaping the New York-to-Philly megalopolis. In its 150-mile length, this route across Pennsylvania passes through a succession of strikingly different places, starting with the densely populated industrial regions of the Lehigh Valley and the historic little town of **Bethlehem,** which plays up its Christmas connections more than its role as a formerly vital steelmaking center. Farther south, modern industry gives way to the traditional agriculture of **Pennsylvania Dutch Country,** world-famous for its anti-technology, Old Order Christian communities. Continuing southwest across the Susquehanna River, you'll follow the route of the old Lincoln Highway through historic **York,** early capital of the United States, now home to the Harley-Davidson motorcycle assembly plant. The last stop on the Pennsylvania leg of the route is the Civil War battlefields at **Gettysburg,** just shy of the Maryland border.

Lackawaxen

The tiny town of **Lackawaxen** (pop. 125), along the Delaware River 20 winding, scenic miles northwest of Port Jervis via Hwy-97, holds two fascinating attractions: the preserved home of writer Zane Grey, and a unique suspension bridge built in 1847 by Brooklyn Bridge designer John Roebling. It comes as something of a surprise to find out that Zane Grey, author of the classic Western novel *Riders of the Purple Sage,* was in fact a fly-fishing, baseball-loving Pennsylvania dentist, but he was. His home at 135 Scenic Drive was preserved by his family as the **Zane Grey Museum** (Fri.–Sun. 10 AM–5 PM; free; 570/685-4871), and now offers an intimate look into his life and works. Zane Grey and his wife (and childhood sweetheart) Dolly are buried side-by-side in the small Lackawaxen graveyard.

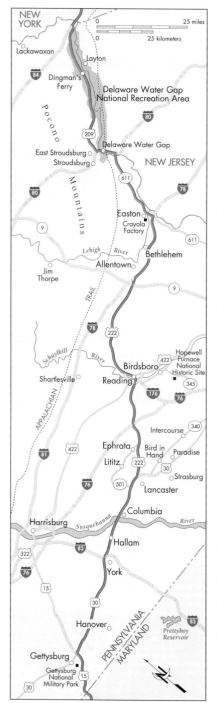

The Roebling Bridge is about 100 yards upstream from Zane Grey's home and has been preserved by the National Park Service—though it's now used by cars instead of canal boats. For the full experience, stay the night in the circa-1860 canal office, now housing the **Roebling Inn** (570/685-7900).

Milford

At the west end of US-6's very pleasant run along the river from Port Jervis, just off I-84 at the northern end of Delaware Water Gap National Recreation Area, **Milford** (pop. 1,400) is a cute little town cashing in on the hordes of rafters, campers, and B&Bers who make the weekend journey to the surrounding Pocono Mountains from New York or Philadelphia. Drive slowly when passing through Milford's deceptively peaceful central business district, because the local police maintain carefully concealed **speed traps** that result in heavy fines for even the most minor speed limit violation.

Milford was the longtime home of forestry pioneer and two-term Pennsylvania Governor Gifford Pinchot, whose **Grey Towers** estate off US-6 is often open for tours ($5; 570/296-9630).

The unsurpassed people-watching perch is the front porch of the historic **Tom Quick Inn** (rooms $80 and up; 570/296-6514), which serves lamb chops and prime rib dinners in the heart of downtown Milford at 411 Broad Street. Less-expensive rooms are available at the **Blue Spruce Motel** motor court ($50–75, 570/491-4969) on the northeastern outskirts of town on US-6 at the US-209 junction.

Delaware Water Gap National Recreation Area

Totaling some 70,000 acres of forest on both banks of the Delaware River, the **Delaware Water Gap National Recreation Area** stretches for 35 miles south of the I-84 freeway along two-lane US-209. Established in 1965, the park is still very much under development, though numerous hiking trails lead through hardwood forests to seasonal waterfalls, and the river itself offers abundant canoeing, swimming, and fishing. Though far from pristine, the natural beauty is surprisingly undisturbed considering the park lies only 50 miles west of New York City.

A few remnants of the area's historic agricultural villages have been preserved under the aegis of the park service, but the main attraction is the oddly named Delaware Water Gap itself, a deep cleft carved by the river into the solid rock of the Kittatinny Mountains. Artists, sightseers, and rock-climbers have admired this unique feat of geology for centuries, but unfortunately the natural passageway is crisscrossed by all manner of road and railroad, including the six-lane I-80 freeway that runs right through it.

The tiny tourist town of **Delaware Water Gap,** south of I-80 at the far southern end of the park, provides the best views of the gap. A **visitors center** (908/841-9531 or 570/588-2435) sits along the river, just off I-80 at the first/last New Jersey exit, and offers exhibits on the geology and history of the region, as well as information on sundry recreational opportunities. **Pack Shack Adventures** (570/424-8533) rents canoes, if you want to get out on the water and stretch your arms and legs.

A 25-mile stretch of the Appalachian Trail cuts along a 1,200-foot-high ridge at the southeast corner of the park, crossing the Delaware River on an old bridge at the town of Delaware Water Gap. Get a feel for the trail at the full-service, AMC-run **Mohican Outdoor Center** (908/362-5670), outside Blairstown, New Jersey.

The Poconos

The **Pocono Mountains,** which rise to the west of the Delaware River, hold a number of traditional summer resort hotels spread among the golf courses and ski areas. Like the Catskills "Borscht Belt" of southern New York, the Poconos had their glory days in the 1950s, but some resorts still thrive thanks to the invention here in the 1960s of the couple-friendly, heart- or champagne glass–shaped bath tub, which has turned many a Pocono hotel into a pseudo-Roman honeymoon destination (the *Baltimore Sun* called one a "mini Playboy Mansion"). Many of these passion pits tend to feature all-inclusive package deals (free archery lessons, so you and your beloved can play Cupid with real arrows, etc). If you're interested, try **Caesars Pocono Palace** (570/588-6692) off US-209 five miles northeast of Stroudsburg. By contrast, a classic "old-school" Pocono resort—the rightly named **Skytop** (800/345-7759)—is about 20 miles northwest of Stroudsburg, via Hwy-447. This very grand yet family-friendly 1920s hotel, with just 150 rooms but full resort facilities, sits on 6,000 acres of mountaintop forest, with its own golf course, hiking trails, and hunting preserve.

At the southern edge of the Delaware Water Gap park, **Stroudsburg** has the Poconos' most extensive tourist facilities, clustered along the I-80 freeway corridor.

Easton and Nazareth

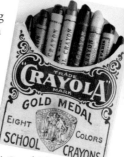

South of the Delaware Water Gap, Hwy-611 runs along the Delaware River until its confluence with the Lehigh River, near the town of **Easton**. This historic industrial center is now home to one of the Poconos' most popular family attractions: the **Crayola Crayon Factory Tour** (closed Mon.; $9; 610/515-8000), at 30 Center Square, where you can watch colorful crayons being made and packaged, then scribble away to your heart's content. The main Crayola factory is actually a half-dozen miles away, and not open to the public; this tourist-oriented mini-factory shares a waterfront building with the **National Canal Museum**, which traces the history of the Delaware and Lehigh Canal and other man-made waterways all over the United States. Occasional canal boat trips are offered. Opening hours and admission fees are the same as the Crayola factory.

The historic center of Easton is worth exploring, not only for art galleries, espresso bars, bookshops—and the unique **PEZ Dispenser Museum** (610/253-9794), at 15 S Bank Street—but also for a chance to enjoy a genuine slice of Americana: Center Square's **Sweet Shop Luncheonette**.

Along with Martin Guitars, Nazareth is home to **Nazareth Speedway**, home track of the Andretti racing family. Another sporting hero, boxer Larry Holmes, lives in nearby Easton.

Another more historic American factory tour is in nearby **Nazareth**, where the venerable **Martin Guitar Company** (610/867-0173 or 800/633-2060) has been in business since 1833. If you've ever enjoyed strumming a six-string, you'll want to take one of the wonderful tours (Mon.–Fri. at 1:15 PM; free) of the family-owned factory at 510 Sycamore Street. The tours include both a look inside the workshops—where you can watch workers as they bend, carve, inlay, and polish the instruments—and displays of classic Martin guitars.

Bethlehem

Upstream from Easton along the Lehigh River and US-222, the remarkable small city of **Bethlehem** (pop. 71,329), famous for its Christmas festivals and as a fun place from which to mail Christmas cards, was originally established in 1741 by a group of Moravian missionaries. The missionaries' original circa-1803 chapel still stands at the heart of the compact, gas-lighted downtown district, its cemetery full of 200-year-old headstones laid flat so as not to offend God.

The **Moravian Museum**, at 66 W. Church Street, is housed inside the circa 1741 *Gemeinhaus,* the oldest building in Bethlehem; besides showcasing historic artifacts, the museum also offers guided walking tours of the downtown area. Another engaging historic site is the **Sun Inn** at 564 Main Street, a well-preserved former tavern "where the leading figures of the Revolutionary era were entertained," says a plaque on the wall; it's now a nice German restaurant.

Across the Lehigh River from the tidy homes and shops of downtown Bethlehem, Lehigh University stands above the rusting remains of the **Bethlehem Steel Company.** Famous for fabricating engineering marvels such as the towers of the Golden Gate Bridge—cast here in sections, then shipped through the Panama Canal and assembled in San Francisco—the mill was in business for over a century before being closed down in the 1990s. The hulking structure, and most of the machinery and equipment, is still intact and in place, but the future of this historically important industrial site is very much up for grabs.

Back in downtown Bethlehem, the sidewalk tables outside **Viennese Pastry,** 500 Main Street, are a great place to enjoy a wickedly rich piece of cake or a light lunch; another good spot is the **Apollo** (610/865-9600), 85 W. Broad Street, a bistro-style sandwich and pasta place.

For dinner, try the aforementioned **Sun Inn** on Bethlehem's Main Street, or the more down-to-earth **Chicken and Ribs,** a local favorite at 2 W. 3rd Street (610/866-1212). On 4th Street across the river from downtown, **Godfrey Daniel's Coffee House** (610/867-2390) hosts a range of live folk and jazz music most nights.

For a place to stay, the large **Radisson Hotel Bethlehem** ($110–135; 610/625-5000 or 800/333-3333), on Main Street overlooking the river, is centrally located. For further information, contact the Bethlehem **visitors center** (610/868-1513) at 52 W. Broad Street.

> Every May, Bethlehem hosts a hugely popular **Bach Festival,** rated as one of the best in country. For details, contact the visitors center at 610/868-1513.

Allentown

The seat of Lehigh County, **Allentown** (pop. 106,632) spreads west of Bethlehem, across a bend in the Lehigh River. The downtown area has two very worthwhile stops, the bigger and better of which is the **Allentown Art Museum** (closed Mon.; $6; 610/432-4333) at 31 N. 5th Street. Here you'll find a good general collection of paintings and photography as well as an entire library moved from the Frank Lloyd Wright–designed Little House. Allentown's other main attraction lies two blocks west at Church and Hamilton Streets: the **Liberty Bell Shrine** (Mon.–Sat. noon–4 PM; free), an old church which houses a replica of the famous bell that was hidden here for safekeeping during the Revolutionary War battles at Philadelphia.

Allentown boasts some great places to eat, thanks to the multiple branches of **Yocco's: The Hot Dog King;** these local landmarks, like the one at 625 Liberty Street (610/433-1950), have been serving up wieners (and a few burgers) bathed in a top-secret chili sauce since 1922. Allentown also has one of the country's oldest, largest collections of roller

> The town of **Jim Thorpe,** in the Lehigh Valley 30 miles northwest of Allentown off the Pennsylvania Turnpike (Hwy-9), 10 miles north of the Appalachian Trail, is a former coal-mining town with many 19th-century buildings. The town changed its name from Mauch Chunk in 1954 to honor the great Olympic athlete Jim Thorpe, whose remains lie in a granite mausoleum along Hwy-903 on the northeast side of town.

Roadside America

One of the quirkiest tourist attractions in the United States, Roadside America (daily in summer; $5; 610/488-6241) stands alongside the I-78 freeway, 20 miles northwest of Reading in the village of Shartlesville. Built by Reading native Laurence Gieringer, Roadside America is a giant 3/8-to-the-inch scale model of bygone Americana, fleshed out with animated scenes that trace a typical day in the life of the country—circa 1941, when Roadside America first opened to the public. As you walk around the edges of the 8,000-square-foot exhibit, you can push buttons to make wheels spin, lights flash, and pumps pump, and you'll see a little of everything rural: an 1830s New England village featuring a church and choral music; a canyon and lake complete with waterfalls and resort cabins; a model of Henry Ford's workshop in Dearborn, Michigan, where he built one of the first "horseless carriages"; various turnpikes, canals, highways, and railroads; a coal mine; and a mock-up of the San Francisco Bay Bridge, the closest Roadside comes to a city scene.

Though it's definitely a fine example of kitsch, Roadside America is also an oddly compelling place, and only the hardest-hearted road-tripper will be able to hold back the tears when, every half-hour or so, the sun sets and Kate Smith bursts into "God Bless America."

coasters (and a fine old carousel), in Dorney Park (daily in summer; around $35; 610/398-7955). There's a water park, too.

Reading

Standing along the eastern banks of the Schuylkill River, **Reading** (pop. 81,207) is more interesting than its frightening title, "Factory Outlet Shopping Capital of Southeastern Pennsylvania," would lead you to expect. Ornately turreted row houses line 5th Avenue (US-222 Business) through the residential districts, downtown holds a number of well-maintained businesses and signs from the first half of the century, and a 85-foot, 100-year-old pagoda offers panoramic views from the summit of Mt. Penn, east of town. Perhaps the best place to stop is along US-222, at 2738 Penn Avenue on the north side of town, where **Schell's Hot Dogs, BBQ, and Miniature Golf** (610/678-8333) offers everything a road-tripper could ask for. (Well, almost.)

For history buffs, two worthwhile places to visit sit southeast of Reading along the Schuylkill River. The closer of these is at **Birdsboro**, 10 miles from town and a mile north of US-422. The **Daniel Boone Homestead and Birthplace** (closed Mon.;

Midway between Allentown and Reading, every June and July the week-long **Kutztown Folk Festival** celebrates the arts, crafts, and culture of the local Pennsylvania Dutch communities, which are less austere than their Lancaster County counterparts.

$4; 610/582-4900) marks the site where the great frontiers-man was born in 1734. Back in Birdsboro on US-422 at 668 Ben Franklin Highway, **Gregory's Diner** (610/385-7900) is open daily 5 AM–10 PM for the usual fare plus very good pies.

Well worth the winding five-mile drive south of Birds-boro via Hwy-345, the **Hopewell Furnace National Historic Site** (daily; $4) preserves intact an entire iron-making community that thrived here from the colonial era until the mid-1880s. Park rangers fire up the furnace and demon-strate the primitive foundry (melting aluminum rather than iron to take the "heat" off the ancient tools), and exhibits trace the iron-making process—mining the ore, making charcoal, and fabricating the finished product, which here at Hopewell was primarily pig iron and stoves.

The Monopoly "Chance" card "Take a Ride on the Reading—Collect $200," commemorates the railroad that formerly ran between Reading and Philadelphia.

Ephrata and Lititz

South of Reading, US-222 runs along the western edge of the Amish- and Mennonite-influenced Pennsylvania Dutch Country. The heart of this region is due east of Lancaster, but the area north of Lancaster also holds a number of related sites often missed by visitors. The most appealing of these is the **Ephrata Cloister** (daily; $7), at 632 W. Main Street just west of the town of Ephrata. Founded in 1732 by a commu-nal society of religiously celibate German Pietists, the Ephrata Cloister consists of a half-dozen well-preserved 250-year-old wooden buildings, which housed dormitories, bakeries, and a printing shop where the commune produced some of the finest illustrated books of the colonial era. Across Main Street from the entrance, the **Cloister Restaurant** (717/733-2361) serves very good home-style food for breakfast, lunch, and dinner in an overgrown 1940s diner.

Lititz is the unlikely final resting place of **John Sutter**, the Swiss immigrant who owned huge chunks of pre—gold rush California. He died here in Pennsylvania while battling the Washington, D.C., bureaucracy, hoping to receive compensation for his confiscated land.

If you happen, or can manage, to be in Ephrata on a Friday, there's no more "Authentic Amish" experience than the once-a-week **Green Dragon Farmers Market** (717/738-1117), a chaotic complex of some 400 different fresh fruit and vegetable sellers, sausage and hotdog stands, pizza places and bakery outlets, covering 30 acres in 7 buildings, just over a mile north of town at 955 N. State Street. Many people here are truly Amish, so obey the 2nd commandment and resist the urge to take their photo.

West of Ephrata, eight miles north of Lancaster via Hwy-501, the delightful though tiny town of **Lititz** (pop. 8,280) is dominated by the huge **Wilbur Chocolate** candy factory at 48 N. Broad Street, which liberally perfumes the air with the smell of hot chocolate. Lititz, which is packed full of stone buildings and carefully tended gar-dens, also holds the nation's oldest operating pretzel factory, the **Sturgis Pretzel House** at 219 E. Main Street, where you can twist your own.

Ephrata Cloister

The Pennsylvania Dutch Country

East of Lancaster, toward Philadelphia, the old Lincoln Highway (US-30) runs through the heart of what has become internationally famous as the Pennsylvania Dutch Country. This is a very pretty, almost completely rural region, unremarkable apart from the presence here of various "Old Order" Anabaptist Christian sects, including Amish and Mennonite groups, who eschew most of the trappings and technological advances of the 21st century, including cars, electricity, and irrigation, and retain their simple ways. Long before the Peter Weir movie *Witness* gave Amish low-tech lifestyle the Hollywood treatment, visitors have been coming here to see these anachronistic descendants of German immigrants (Deutsche = Dutch) who settled here in the early 1700s, and to whom all outsiders are known simply as "English."

The best way to get a feel for the Amish and Mennonite ways of life is to follow back roads, by bike if possible, through the gently rolling countryside of Lancaster County, keeping an eye out for their horse-drawn buggies (Amish ones are gray, the Mennonites' are black). You can buy produce, breads, cakes, or "Shoo Fly Pie" from the many roadside stands marked by hand-lettered signs. For a thorough overview, stop at **The People's Place**

Amish Boys Out for a Drive, Lancaster County, Pa.

Lancaster

The only place approaching an urban scale in this part of Pennsylvania, **Lancaster** (pop. 56,438) is the region's commercial center, a bustling city that, for a single day during the Revolutionary War, served as capital of the country. Though most visitors view it as little more than a handy base for exploring nearby Pennsylvania Dutch Country, Lancaster does have a couple of attractions in its own right, such as the redbrick, pseudo-Romanesque **Central Market** at King and Queen Streets in the center of town. It hosts the nation's oldest publicly owned, continuously operating Farmer's Market, currently held all day Tuesday and Friday, as well as Saturday mornings. A block south on Queen Street, the ground-floor windows of the local newspaper trace local history through headlines, starting back in 1794 and continuing up through the present day.

Two miles northeast of Lancaster, the state-run and well-signed **Landis Valley Museum** (daily; $9) is a popular 40-acre living history park preserving and interpreting traditional rural lifeways of eastern Pennsylvania.

A word to the wise: In Dutch Country, remember that anything claiming to be "authentic Amish" definitely isn't. Also, please respect the Amish you see and refrain from taking photographs. Drive carefully, too.

(Mon.–Sat. 9:30 AM–5 PM; $8; 717/768-7171), at 3513 Main Street in Intercourse (so named because it sits at the junction of two roads), which presents a multimedia show outlining the beliefs and culture of the Amish and Mennonite peoples, along with displays of quilts and other handicrafts. More amusing is the restored one-room **Weavertown Schoolhouse** ($4), populated by "authentic" audio-animatronic Amish schoolkids, along Hwy-340 a mile east of the town of Bird-in-Hand, 2.5 miles west of Intercourse.

Most of the many Amish-style restaurants in the region are huge and for-biddingly full of bus-tour hordes; one exception is **Stoltzfus Restaurant** (Mon.–Sat. 11 AM–8 PM, May-Nov. only; 717/768-8156) on Hwy-772 a mile southeast of Intercourse. A less Amish but very good road food place is **Jennie's Diner** in Ronks, open 24 hours every day on the north side of US-30, just east of the Hwy-896 intersection.

Though it won't give you any great insight into the Amish, one unique place to stay is the **Red Caboose Motel and Restaurant** ($80 and up; 717/687-5000), a mile east of Strasburg on Paradise Lane. All the rooms are built inside old railroad cars, and the on-site restaurant simulates a train journey, with whistles blowing and a gentle rocking vibration to ease your digestion. Strasburg is also home to the **Village Greens** miniature golf, which is so fun and challenging that it was featured in a recent *Sports Illustrated*.

For complete listings of attractions, restaurants, and hotels, or to pick up handy maps and other information, stop by the helpful **Pennsylvania Dutch visitor center** (717/299-8901 or 800/PA-DUTCH), on US-30 just east of Lancaster.

Hallam: The Shoe House

Many oddball attractions grew up along the old Lincoln Highway, the great cross-country highway that ran coast-to-coast beginning in 1915, and one of the best-beloved is the **Haines Shoe House**, which stands above the modern four-lane US-30 freeway, west of the town of Hallam. This landmark of pro-grammatic architecture was built in 1948 by Mahlon "The Shoe Wizard" Haines, who owned a successful shoe company that proudly claimed to make boots "hoof-to-hoof," from raising the cattle to selling the finished products. The seven-room structure is shaped like a giant cartoon boot, and can be reached by following Hwy-462 (the old Lincoln Highway, which runs just south of cur-rent US-30), to Shoe House Road, then winding north for a quarter mile. (The turnoff is easy to miss, so keep an eye out for the Shoe House Mini-Storage, which stands on the cor-ner.) The Shoe House has been bought and sold a number of times over the years. If you're lucky, the owners will be there to let you tour the interior.

Two of the main tourist stops in the Dutch Country region are the towns of **Intercourse** (source of many snickeringly allusive postcards) and **Paradise** (the Paradise post office, just north of US-30 at the east end of town, is a popular place from which to send mail).

Midway between Lancaster and York, the town of **Columbia** holds what is arguably the country's best collection of timepieces in the **Watch and Clock Museum** at 514 Poplar Street. Also in Columbia is a beautiful multi-arched concrete bridge that used to carry the old Lincoln Highway (US-30) across the broad Susquehanna River.

Just east of Hallam on US-30, **Jim Mack's Ice Cream** (717/252-2013) at 5745 Lincoln Highway has been attracting fans for its ice cream—and its adjacent mini–golf course and mini-zoo, complete with a pair of rather sad-looking brown bears. Next door: a bowling alley.

York

Though it doesn't look like much from the highway, bypassed by both US-30 and the I-83 freeway, the medium-sized town of York (pop. 40,862) claims to be the first capital of the United States: Late in 1777, the Articles of Confederation were adopted here by the 13 newly independent former colonies, and (arguably) it's in that document that the name "United States of America" was first used. A significant number of historic buildings still stand in the quiet, low-rise downtown area, including the medieval-looking, circa-1740 Golden Plough Tavern and other colonial-era structures along Market Street at the west edge of the business district.

For all its historic importance, York is best known for its industrial prowess, which is saluted at the **Harley-Davidson assembly plant and museum** (Mon.–Fri. 9 AM–2 PM; free; 717/848-1177), a mile east of town off US-30 on Eden Road. The guided tours take about two hours, and begin with a brief history of the company, which is still based in Milwaukee. The tour then takes you past a lineup of some 40 Harleys past and present, culled from the corporate collection of over 200 motorbikes, then proceeds to the shop floor for a close-up (and very noisy) look and listen as the bikes get put together: Sheets of steel are pressed to form fenders and fairings, and, once assembled, each bike is "road-tested" at full throttle on motorcycling's equivalent of a treadmill. A souvenir store is stocked with all manner of things with the Harley-Davidson logo, from T-shirts to leather jackets.

Downtown York has a handful of cafés and restaurants, and on the west edge of town, where the US-30 bypass rejoins the old Lincoln Highway (Hwy-462), **Lee's Diner** (717/792-1300), at 4320 W. Market Street, is a classic early 1950s Mountain View pre-fab diner, still serving up hearty road food.

The town of **Hanover**, south of US-30 between York and Gettysburg, is a prime producer of snack foods, from potato chips to the famed pretzels baked by **Snyder's of Hanover**, 1350 York Street, which offers free factory tours.

Gettysburg

Totally overwhelmed by the influx of tourists visiting its namesake battleground, the town of **Gettysburg** (pop. 7,490) has survived both onslaughts remarkably unscathed. Despite the presence of sundry tourist attractions—wax museums, various multimedia reenactments of the battle and President Lincoln's Gettysburg Address, even a Lincoln Train Museum displaying over a thousand model trains that include a scale replica of the one Lincoln rode here in—once the day-tripping crowds have dispersed Gettysburg is actually a very pleasant place, with rows of brick-fronted buildings lining Baltimore and York streets out from the circle at the center of town.

There are, not surprisingly, quite a few places to eat, including the atmospheric and inexpensive **Dobbin House,** south of town at 89 Steinwehr Avenue, serving above-average pub food in Gettysburg's oldest building. The same building doubles as the **Gettystown Inn** ($95 and up; 717/334-2100), a moderately priced and pleasant B&B. The dozens of other places to stay include all the usual national chains, plus the circa-1797 **Gettysburg Hotel** ($95 and up; 717/337-2000) on Lincoln Square right at the center of town.

Gettysburg National Military Park

Site of the most famous two-minute speech in U.S. history, and of the bloody Civil War battle that marked the high tide of Confederate fortunes, **Gettysburg National Military Park** surrounds the town of Gettysburg, protecting the scenes of the struggle as they were July 1–3, 1863, when 50,000 of the 165,000 combatants were killed or wounded. Over a thousand monuments mark the various historic sites around the 6,000 acres of rolling green pasture that form the park. Take advantages of tape-recorded **tours** ($10–20) or park-approved **Battlefield Guides** (about $40 per car), who will take you along a well-marked route past such places as Little Round Top, The Angle, and Cemetery Ridge, site of fabled Pickett's Charge.

Most of the guided tours start and finish at the **visitors center** (daily; free; 717/334-1124) on Taneytown Road a mile south of town, where an extensive museum puts the battle into context and displays a huge array of period weaponry. You can learn more by watching the battle unfold on the **Electric Map** ($4), which looks a lot like a boxing ring. Unfortunately, the famous circular **Cyclorama,** a 26- by 356-foot painting that accurately portrays the events of the final day's battles, is undergoing restoration and won't be seen again until 2007. Across the road, the **Gettysburg National Cemetery** is the place where President Abraham Lincoln delivered his famous address on November 19, 1863.

Abraham Lincoln
Robert E. Lee
George Gordon Meade

A 230-acre farm on the southwest fringe of the Gettysburg battlefields was home to U.S. Army general and later-president **Dwight D. Eisenhower** and his wife, **Mamie,** and is now open for guided **tours** (daily; $7; 717/338-9114) that leave from the Gettysburg visitor center.

The Lincoln Highway

The main east–west route through Pennsylvania Dutch Country, US-30 is also one of the best-preserved stretches of the old Lincoln Highway, the nation's first transcontinental route. Planned and named in 1915, linking New York City's Times Square with the Panama Pacific International Exposition in San Francisco, the Lincoln Highway followed over 3,000 miles of country road across 12 states. A thousand miles of the original "highway" were little more than muddy tracks, scarcely more visible on the ground than they were on the still-nonexistent road maps, but by the early 1930s the road was finally fully paved, following present-day US-30 as far as Wyoming, then bending south to follow what's now US-50, "The Loneliest Road in America," along the route of the Pony Express across Nevada and most of California.

Originally marked by telephone poles brightly painted with red, white, and blue stripes and a large letter "L," in 1928 the Lincoln Highway was blazed by more discreet concrete mileposts carrying a small bust of Lincoln; 3,000 of these were placed, one every mile, by Boy Scout troops across the land, but only around a dozen still stand. As with the later Route 66, the Lincoln Highway was replaced by the interstates, but it does live on, in folk memory as well as the innumerable "Lincoln Cafes" and "Lincoln Motels" along its original route, much of which still bears the name "Lincolnway."

For an overall discussion of this old road's significance and legacy, read Drake Hokansen's excellent *Lincoln Highway: Main Street Across America* (University of Iowa Press, 1987), and become a member of the **Lincoln Highway Association** (PO Box 8117, St. Louis, MO 63156; 630/466-4382), whose top-quality quarterly magazine is well worth the annual dues. For help finding the many roadside landmarks that survive in the Keystone State, pick up a copy of *Pennsylvania Traveler's Guide to the Lincoln Highway* by Brian A. Butko (Stackpole Books, 1996). And if you like what you see here, take a trip west to Iowa, another state with substantial reminders of the Lincoln Highway heyday.

MARYLAND

Crossing the Mason-Dixon Line from Gettysburg into Maryland on US-15, our route veers west into the Appalachian foothills of **Catoctin Mountain Park**, site of the presidential retreat Camp David. The landscape here is quite rugged, and signs of life few and far between—an oasis of peace and quiet, under an hour by road from Baltimore or Washington, D.C. Winding south through the mountains of the Maryland Panhandle, the thin strip of land that stretches for some 75 miles between Pennsylvania and West Virginia, this route again meets the hikers' Appalachian Trail, then detours to visit the

The Maryland state motto, *Fatti Maschii, Parole Femine,* is translated roughly as "Manly Deeds, Womanly Words."

battlefield of **Antietam**, the well-preserved site of the worst carnage of the Civil War.

Catoctin Mountain Park: Camp David

US-15 continues south from Gettysburg across the Maryland border, and there's little to stop for until **Thurmont** (pop. 5,588), "Gateway to the Mountains," where the route heads west on Hwy-77 into the green expanse of **Catoctin Mountain Park.** Fully recovered after centuries of logging activity, the park protects some 10,000 acres of hardwood forest, a handful of 1,500-foot peaks, and the presidential retreat at Camp David, hidden away in the woods and strictly off-limits to visitors; for security reasons it doesn't even appear on park maps. The park **visitors center** (daily; 301/663-9388) along Hwy-77 two miles west of US-15 provides information on **camping** and maps of the many hiking trails, including a short trail from the visitors center to the preserved remains of the Blue Blazes whiskey still, where rangers demonstrate moonshine-making on summer weekends.

Spreading along the south side of Hwy-77, Maryland-run **Cunningham Falls State Park** offers more natural scenery and a very pleasant swimming area in Hunting Creek Lake. There's a snack bar and boats for rent.

In Gathland State Park, on the Appalachian Trail east of Gapland off Hwy-67, the 50-foot terra-cotta arch of the **War Correspondents Memorial** was erected in the late 1880s in honor of journalists killed while covering the Civil War.

Washington Monument State Park

From Catoctin Mountain Park, our route heads south on undivided Hwy-6 and two-lane Hwy-17 along the hikers' Appalachian Trail, winding up at **Washington Monument State Park** between the I-70 freeway and the small town of **Boonsboro.** A 35-foot-tall, bottle-shaped mound dedicated to the memory of George Washington stands at the center of the park; Boonsboro citizens completed the monument in 1827, making it the oldest memorial honoring the first U.S. president.

Atop a hill south of the park, across an old alignment of the National Road (US-40), the **South Mountain Inn** (301/432-6155) has

the "original" Washington Monument

operated as a tavern and inn since 1732, and now serves dinner nightly (closed Mon.) and lunch on weekends.

Antietam National Battlefield

Between Boonsboro and the Potomac River, which forms Maryland's border with West Virginia, **Antietam National Battlefield** preserves the hallowed ground where over 23,000 men were killed or wounded on the bloodiest day of the Civil War—September 17, 1862. Atop a shallow hill at the middle of the park, a scant mile north of **Sharpsburg** off Hwy-65, the **visitors center** (daily; $5 per car; 301/432-5124) offers films, museum exhibits, and interpretive programs that put the battle into military and political context. Though there was no clear winner, Antietam is said to have convinced Lincoln to issue the Emancipation Proclamation, officially freeing slaves in Confederate states and effectively putting an end to British support for the southern side.

Clara Barton tended the wounded during and after the Civil War's bloodiest battle at Antietam

WEST VIRGINIA

In its short run across the eastern tip of West Virginia, US-340 passes through one of the most history-rich small towns in the United States: **Harpers Ferry**, located at the confluence of the Shenandoah and Potomac Rivers. Lovely mountain scenery surrounds Harpers Ferry, especially during early autumn when the hardwood forests rival Vermont's for vibrant color. South of Harpers Ferry, the hikers' Appalachian Trail runs directly along the Virginia–West Virginia border, east of the Shenandoah River atop the roadless crest of the Blue Ridge Mountains. The best route to follow by car, US-340 swings to the west through the historic mountain resort of **Charles Town** before entering Virginia.

Harpers Ferry

Climbing the steep slopes of the Blue Ridge Mountains, **Harpers Ferry** (pop. 300) embodies the industrial and political history of the early United States. Protected since 1963 as a national park, its many well-preserved wood, brick, and stone buildings are palpable reminders of early American enterprise: Besides the country's first large factory, first canal, and first railroad, scenic Harpers Ferry saw abolitionist John Brown's 1859 rebellion against slavery, and was later a strategic site during the Civil War.

*Harpers Ferry is the national headquarters of the **Appalachian Trail Conference**, the nonprofit group that oversees the entire 2,144-mile footpath. For information, contact them at (304/535-6331).*

Small museums, housed in separate buildings along Shenandoah and High Streets along the riverfront in the "Lower Town," trace the various strands of the town's past. From the Shenandoah River, the Appalachian Trail winds south down what the third president called "one of the most stupendous scenes in Nature," Jefferson's Rock. Crossing the Potomac River to the north, the AT climbs up to Maryland Heights for more spectacular vistas.

Especially in summer, when cars are banned from lower Harpers Ferry, the best first stop is the small **visitors center** (daily; $5; 304/535-6223) above the town along US-340. Park here and take one of the frequent free shuttles down to the historic area. Although most of Harpers Ferry is preserved as a historic site, the eastern portions along the Potomac riverfront are still in private hands, and here you can indulge your taste for fast food, wax museums, and schlocky souvenirs. A couple of companies offer whitewater rafting trips, and for another sort of adventure you can hop onboard one of the **Amtrak/MARC** trains, which serve Washington, D.C., on a very limited schedule. Back up the hill along US-340, near the visitors center, there's a **Comfort Inn** ($50–75; 304/535-6391).

Charles Town

Founded in 1786, the former colonial resort of **Charles Town** (pop. 2,907) was named in honor of George Washington's younger brother Charles, who surveyed the site on behalf of Lord Fairfax. Many of the streets are named after other family members, over 75 of whom are buried in the cemetery alongside the **Zion Church,** on Congress Street on the east side of town. Charles Town, which shouldn't be confused with the West Virginia state capital, Charleston, later played a significant role in John Brown's failed raid on Harpers Ferry. After Brown was captured, he was tried and convicted of treason in the Jefferson County Courthouse at the corner of George and Washington Streets, and hanged a month later. With his last words, Brown noted the inevitable approach of Civil War, saying he was "quite certain that the crimes of this guilty land will never be purged away but with blood." A small **museum** (Mon.–Sat. 10 AM–4 PM; donations) operates in the basement of the town library, a block from the old courthouse on Washington and South Samuel Street.

South of Charles Town, US-340 winds along the western slopes of the Appalachians for a dozen miles before entering Virginia east of Winchester.

East of Winchester, Virginia, the Appalachian Trail crosses the transcontinental US-50 highway, the **Loneliest Road** in America (see page 713). Full coverage is found on pages 636–721.

VIRGINIA

The Appalachian Trail covers more ground in Virginia than it does in any other state, following the crest of the Blue Ridge Mountains from Harpers Ferry in West Virginia all the way south to the Tennessee and North Carolina borders. In the northern half of the state, the road route closely follows the hikers' route, and the two crisscross each other through the sylvan groves of **Shenandoah National Park.** Midway along the state the two routes diverge, and hikers turn west while the motor route follows the unsurpassed Blue Ridge Parkway along the top of the world.

Most of the time the route follows the mountain crests, though in many places you'll find fascinating towns and cities a short distance to the east or west. Best among these is **Charlottesville,** a history-rich Piedmont town that's best known as the home of Thomas Jefferson and the University of Virginia. Other suggested stops include the Shenandoah Valley town of **Lexington,** the "natural wonder" of **Natural Bridge,** and the engaging city of **Roanoke.**

Dinosaur Land

Located at the intersection of US-340 and US-522, eight miles southeast of Winchester near the hamlet of White Post, **Dinosaur Land** (daily; $5; 540/869-2222) displays an entertaining and marvelously kitschy collection of manmade sharks, cavemen and, of course, dinosaurs. It's especially fun for kids, who are welcome to climb on and around the concrete menagerie, and wry-humored adults will enjoy searching through the very large gift shop, which has all manner of cheesy souvenirs.

White Post, by the way, got its name from—you guessed it—a white post, placed here by a young surveyor named George Washington. The post marked the road to the country estate of Lord Fairfax, which was destroyed in 1858.

Front Royal and Little Washington

The town of Front Royal takes its name, perhaps apocryphally, from a Revolutionary War drill sergeant who, since his troops were unable to tell their left from their right, was forced to shout out "Front Royal Oak" to get them to face the same way. **Front Royal** (pop. 13,589) sits just south of I-66 at the entrance to Shenandoah National Park. Because of its key location, Front Royal has grown unwieldy in past decades but retains some semblance of its 19th-century self along Chester Street, a well-maintained historic district at the center of town, a block east of US-340. You can also rent a boat and float along the South Fork of the Shenandoah River, thanks to the friendly folks at the **Front Royal Canoe Company** (540/635-5440).

You'll find walking-tour maps and other information at the **visitors center** (540/635-5788 or 800/338-2576) at 414 E. Main Street, which is housed in an old train depot. The usual battery of fast-food franchises line US-340 from the freeway south through town, as does **Sandy's Diner** (540/635-2911), 1718 Shenandoah Avenue just south of the Shenandoah River bridge; and motels like the **Twi-Lite** (540/635-4148) at 53 W. 14th Street or the **Twin Rivers** (540/635-4101), 1801 Shenandoah Avenue, a mile south of I-66/Hwy-7.

At the foot of the Blue Ridge Mountains, 26 miles southeast of Front Royal via US-522, pristine, colonial **Washington** (pop. 200) was surveyed by the future father of the United States, George Washington, who named many of the streets after friends and family. The main

Housed in an old feed store off I-81 in **Middletown**, the **Route 11 Potato Chip Factory** (Mon.–Sat.; 540/869-0104), at 7815 Main Street, is said to be the smallest in the country. When it's open, you can watch the spudmasters at work and sample the freshly made chips.

Fall foliage in the Blue Ridge Mountains can be stunning, though it is not usually as intense as it is in New England.

Pollution from metropolitan areas and from so many car-borne visitors has caused serious problems at Shenandoah National Park, both for the trees—many of which have been poisoned—and for the views people come to see. On an average summer day, visibility is impaired and the surrounding valleys are often shrouded in smoggy haze.

Along with multicolored leaves, the autumn months bring hundreds of hawks, eagles, and other birds of prey to the mountains on their annual migration. You'll spot the greatest numbers of raptors in late September, when birdwatchers congregate for a **Hawk Watch** in the parking lot of the Holiday Inn, off I-64 along the crest.

attraction here is the **Inn at Little Washington** at Main and Middle Streets (540/675-3800), one of the few Mobil five-star resort hotels in the country, though with room rates starting at over $350 a night and dinners averaging $100 a head (plus wine and tip), it's definitely a special-occasion place to stay or eat. It's worth it though: A critic for *The New York Times* said his dinner there was "the most fantastic meal of my life."

Shenandoah National Park

One of the most popular national parks in the east, especially during the fall foliage season when seemingly everyone in the world descends upon the place to "leaf-peep," **Shenandoah National Park** protects some 300 square miles of hardwood forest along the northernmost crest of the Blue Ridge Mountains. Though the landscape looks natural now, it was in fact heavily cultivated until the 1920s; when the soils were depleted, nearly 4,000 farmers and their families moved out, and the government began buying up all the land to return it to its original state.

Most people experience the park from the top, by driving along the famously beautiful Skyline Drive (see sidebar). This road climbs up from the Shenandoah Valley, but mostly runs along the crest, offering grand vistas (when the air is clear, at least). Besides the hardwood forests, the park also protects numerous waterfalls, wildflower meadows, and understory plants like azaleas and mountain laurels, which bloom brightest in late spring. There is considerable development in the park, with a pair of rustic lodges and enough gas stations and restaurants and campgrounds to handle the thousands of visitors who flock (especially in October, for the autumn foliage). Despite the crowds, it's not hard to find peace and quiet, especially if you venture off on even the briefest of hikes.

There is a ranger station at each entrance to the park, where you pay your $10 per-car fee (or show your pass). There is a **visitors center** (540/999-3500) at each end of the Skyline Drive, and one in the middle, at Big Meadows (milepost 51). Trails at Big Meadows lead past herds of very tame deer to Dark Hollow Falls, which drops 70 feet over greenish volcanic stone. The Big Meadows Lodge was built in 1939, and retains its cozy feel; this is also where the park's largest campground is located. There's another lodge to the north, at Skyland, the highest point on Skyline Drive. There are full-service restaurants at both lodges; all food and lodging (and most everything else in the park) is managed by a private concession, Aramark (540/743-5108 or 800/778-2851).

Skyline Drive

Most people experience Shenandoah National Park by driving the spectacular Skyline Drive. The drive opened in 1939 and runs (at 35 mph!) along the crest over 100 miles between the I-66 and I-64 freeways, giving grand vistas at every bend in the road. Mileposts, arranged in mile-by-mile order from north to south, mark your progress along Skyline Drive. While such scenic driving is definitely memorable, by far the best way to really see the park is to get out of the car and walk along the many miles of trails that lead through the dense green forests to innumerable waterfalls and overlooks.

A helpful map and brochure is handed out at entrance booths along the route (one at either end and two mid-way). Here are some more great places to stop:

Milepost 31.5: Thornton Gap; historic Panorama restaurant is being converted into a visitor center.

Milepost 32.4: Mary's Rock Tunnel, a 13-foot bore cut through the granite in 1932.

Milepost 50.7: Near Big Meadows, under a mile from the well-marked trailhead, Dark Hollow Falls drops over a 70-foot cliff.

Milepost 56.4: A short, steep hike scrambles up to the 3,300-foot-high summit of Bearfence Mountain for a 360-degree panorama.

Milepost 84.1: A parking area marks the trailhead for the rewarding 3.6-mile hike to Jones Run Falls, tumbling over a mossy 45-foot cliff.

Milepost 98.9: Near the southern end of Skyline Drive, Calf Mountain provides a grand panorama over the Shenandoah Valley.

Detour: Charlottesville

From the southern end of Shenandoah National Park, it's a quick 20 miles east on I-64 to **Charlottesville** (pop. 45,049), a richly historic college town that's one of the most enjoyable stops in the state. From the rolling green lawns of the University of Virginia campus to neoclassical Monticello on the hills above it, the legacy of Thomas Jefferson dominates Charlottesville. Jefferson lived and worked here for most of his life—when he wasn't out founding the country or serving as its president.

West of the compact downtown district, the **University of Virginia** campus was Jefferson's pride and joy. Not only did he found it (in 1819) and fund its early years, he planned the curriculum and designed the original buildings, a quadrangle of redbrick Palladian villas that the American Institute of Architects declared the most perfect place in the country. Edgar Allan Poe lived and studied here briefly before dropping out in 1826. Poe's room, appropriately, is No. 13 in the West Range, and it's decorated to look like it did a century ago, with a few period belongings visible behind the glass door. When school is in session, free campus tours are offered five times a day by the **University Guides** (434/924-3239).

Charlottesville's other key site is Jefferson's home, **Monticello**—the domed building that fills the back of the nickel coin—well-signed off I-64, exit 121. Recently restored and open for tours (daily; $14; 434/984-9800), Monticello embodies the many different traits of this multifaceted man. The house was designed and built by Jefferson over a period of 40 years (1769–1809), and holds various gadgets he invented—including a double-pen device that made a copy of everything he wrote—and odd things he collected over the years, from elk antlers to recipes for home-brewed beer. Jefferson died here at Monticello on July 4, 1826, and the grounds, which in Jefferson's time formed an extensive plantation worked by slaves, hold his mortal remains in a simple tomb beyond the vegetable gardens.

Down in the valley below Monticello, **Michie Tavern** (daily; $8 adults, $3 children; 434/977-1234) is a touristy but interesting inn that

Monticello, home of Thomas Jefferson

opened in 1784 and was moved to the present site in the 1920s. Admission includes a tour of the parlors, bars, and upstairs rooms, as well as a dairy and a grist mill. Michie Tavern is also a restaurant serving "Olde Worlde foode" for the bus-tour hordes, at $15 a head (plus dessert!) for a "colonial buffet" lunch. (Just so you know, Michie is pronounced MICK-ee, as in Mantle.)

Practicalities

Like most college towns, Charlottesville provides a broad range of good places to eat, from bare-bones cafés like the **White Spot** (434/295-9899), right across from campus at 1407 University Avenue —this is the place to satisfy those midnight cravings for a cheeseburger with a fried egg on top— to more upscale places ranged along Elliewood Street around the corner. On the downtown "Mall" are an increasing number of trendy places like **Rapture** (434/293-9526) at 303 E. Main Street, which offers eclectic Asian dishes alongside steaks and fish-and-chips. It's also a very popular nightclub, with pool tables, dancing, and a modish bar.

There's more great live music at **Miller's** (434/971-8511) at 109 W. Main Street, where alt-rock pop star Dave Matthews used to tend bar, or at **Starr Hill** (434/977-0017), 709 W. Main Street, which has good food and its own brewery.

Most of Charlottesville's motels line up along Emmett Street (US-29 Business), including the well-placed **Best Western Cavalier Inn** at 105 Emmett Street ($75 and up; 434/296-8111). For more detailed information on visiting Charlottesville, contact the **visitors center** (434/293-6789 or 877/386-1102), which is hard to miss on Hwy-20, off I-64 at exit 121.

Luray Caverns

Halfway through Shenandoah National Park, US-211 runs west down to **Luray Caverns** (daily; $18 adults, $8 children; 540/743-6551), the largest and most impressive of the many caverns in the limestone Blue Ridge region—a single room measures 300 by 500 feet and is over 140 feet high. It also boasts the "World's Only Stalacpipe Organ," where rubber mallets make music by banging on the stone stalactites. There's also a large antique car museum and a garden maze (included in caverns admission).

Near the caverns, along US-211 a half mile west of town, the **Luray Zoo** (daily; $8; 540/743-4113) is home to one of Virginia's largest collections of scaly creatures, both extinct and living. Cobras, alligators, and 20-foot pythons coexist with tropical birds and a monkey; for young children and herpetophobes, there's also a petting zoo of farmyard animals.

Earl Hamner Jr. based his famous 1970s TV series *The Waltons* on vivid memories of growing up during the Depression in the rural village of Schuyler, a half-hour southwest of Charlottesville. Fans of the show will enjoy visiting the **Walton's Mountain Museum** (Mar.–Nov. daily; $5; 434/831-2000), which re-creates the Waltons' kitchen and living room (and John-Boy's bedroom) in the Schuyler Community Center—once the town's elementary school.

The Blue Ridge Parkway: From Shenandoah National Park to Roanoke

Starting at the southern end of Shenandoah National Park, and winding along the crest of the Blue Ridge Mountains all the way to Great Smoky Mountains National Park some 469 miles away, the Blue Ridge Parkway is one of the country's great scenic drives. This is especially true during autumn, when the dogwoods and gum trees turn deep red, and the hickories yellow, against an evergreen backdrop of pines, hemlocks, and firs. Spring is wildflower time, with abundant azaleas and rhododendrons blooming orange, white, pink, and red throughout May and June, especially at the higher elevations.

First proposed in the 1920s, the Blue Ridge Parkway was constructed during 1935–1967, when it grew from a network of local roads to the current route, along which billboards and commercial traffic are both banned. While the Parkway avoids towns and commercial areas to concentrate on the scenery, many interesting towns and other places along the way are well worth a detour. For ease of use, we've divided the Blue Ridge Parkway into three main sections, starting with the drive between Shenandoah National Park and Roanoke. (For the Roanoke-to-North Carolina section, see page 354; for the final run south to the Great Smoky Mountains, see page 358.)

Mile 0: Rockfish Gap, at the southern end of Shenandoah National Park's Skyline Drive, marks the northern start of the Blue Ridge Parkway.

Staunton

West of the mountains from the south end of Shenandoah National Park on I-64, tidy **Staunton** (pop. 23,853; STANton) was founded in 1732 as one of the first towns on the far side of the Blue Ridge. Unlike much of the valley, Staunton was untouched during the Civil War, and now preserves its many 18th- and early 19th-century buildings in a townscape so perfect it was rated among the dozen most distinctive destinations in the United States by the National Trust for Historic Preservation.

*Just east of the Skyline Drive, 3 miles northeast of I-64 exit 107, "Virginia's Best Pizza" has been served up for the past 25-plus years inside barn-red **Crozet Pizza** (434/823-2132) on Hwy-240 at 5794 Three Notched Road.*

One of Staunton's many sizeable historic districts surrounds the boyhood home of favorite son Woodrow Wilson. Son of a Presbyterian minister, Wilson was born in 1856 in a stately Greek Revival townhouse at 18–24 N. Coulter Street, now established as the **Woodrow Wilson Birthplace and Museum** (daily; $8; 540/885-0897), with galleries tracing his life as a scholar—he was president of Princeton University—and as U.S. President during World War I.

Milepost 6.1: Humpback Rocks has a short but strenuous trail (45 minutes each way), leading through a reconstructed historic farmstead and a visitors center (540/943-4716), ending with a 270-degree view over the mountains.

Milepost 34.4: Yankee Horse parking area has an exhibit on an old logging railroad, part of which has been restored, and a short trail to Wigwam Falls.

Milepost 63.6: James River Visitor Center (804/299-5496), exhibits, and trails along the James River and Kanawha Canal. Lowest point on the Parkway, at 649 feet; it is also the junction with US-501, which runs west along the James River for 15 miles to Natural Bridge (see below).

Milepost 76.5: Great views over both valleys from the highest point on the Parkway in Virginia, at 3,950 feet.

Milepost 84–87: The most popular—and most developed—stretch of the Parkway, the Peaks of Otter section includes a visitors center, gas station, restaurant, and very pleasant lodge ($60–90; 540/586-1081), which is open year-round. Three peaks rise above a small lake, and give great sunrise and sunset views; many good trails, including a two-mile loop to Fallingwater Cascades, let you escape the sometimes sizeable crowds.

Milepost 105: The city of Roanoke.

Staunton is also the home of the unique **Frontier Culture Museum** (daily; $10; 540/332-7850), right off I-81 exit 222 on the east side of town. A rural version of Williamsburg, this living history museum consists of four resurrected working farms, incorporating buildings brought over from Germany, England, and Ireland. The fourth farm, dating from antebellum Virginia, shows how various "Old World" traditions blended in America. The farms are inhabited by interpreters dressed in (very clean) period costumes busily husking corn, spinning wool, or working in the fields.

Staunton holds one of the best places to eat in the Shenandoah Valley, on US-250 just east of I-81 exit 222, near the frontier museum: **Mrs. Rowe's Family Restaurant** (540/886-1833), which has been serving excellent, home-style cooking, from pork chops to banana cream pies, for the past 50 years. It's open every day (since 1947) for breakfast, lunch, and dinner—go for their world-famous fried chicken, which is well worth the 25-minute wait. Staunton is also home to another classic: **Wright's Dairy-Rite** (540/886-0435), at 346 Greenville Avenue, with great burgers, hot dogs, and onion rings, served up in your car or a dining room decorated with old menus and a free Wurlitzer jukebox.

All the usual motels cluster around the I-64/I-81 junction, but you'll find the region's most pleasant accommodations at the rambling Victorian-era **Belle Grae Inn** ($100 and up; 540/886-5151), at 515 W. Frederick Street in the center of Staunton, with B&B rooms, a lovely garden, and a fine restaurant.

While in Staunton, check out the wares available at the **Jolly Roger Haggle Shop**, a fascinating junk shop ("over 1,000,000 items") across from the train station at 27 Middlebrook Avenue.

Lexington

Founded in 1778, and named for the then-recent Revolutionary War battleground, photogenic **Lexington** (pop. 6,959) is home to an estimable pair of Virginia institutions, the Virginia Military Institute (VMI) and Washington and Lee University, which meld into one another at the center of town. Numerous old brick buildings, including a typically southern lawyer's row around Courthouse Square, still stand around the town, which you can tour on foot or in one of the horse-drawn carriages (about $10/hr) that leave from the downtown visitors center.

Animated by an unusually crew-cut version of typical college-town energy, Lexington is redolent with, and intensely proud of, its military heritage. Generals, in fact, have become the town's stock-in-trade: From 1859 until his death in 1863, **Gen. Thomas "Stonewall" Jackson** lived at 8 E. Washington Street, now a small museum (daily; $6; 540/463-2552); he is buried in the small but well-tended cemetery a short distance west of downtown. **Gen. Robert E. Lee** spent his post–Civil War years teaching at Washington and Lee, which was named after him (and his wife's ancestor George). Lee is entombed in a crypt below the chapel, under a famous statue of his recumbent self, with his trusty horse, Traveller, buried just outside. Another influential old war-horse, **Gen. George C. Marshall,** is honored in a large eponymous museum (daily; $3) on the VMI campus; the museum traces General Marshall's role in World War II and salutes his Nobel Prize–winning "Marshall Plan" for postwar reconstruction.

Spend a summer night in Lexington at the community-run **Hull's Drive In** (540/463-2621), at 2367 N. US-11, a much-loved local "ozoner" still showing Hollywood hits.

If you've tired of fried food and meat, Lexington offers respite from the usual road fare: the **Blue Heron Cafe** (540/463-2800) serves healthy and delicious soups and sandwiches at 4 E. Washington Street, in the center of town. For truly fine "New American" dining—anything from Chesapeake Bay crab to creations like a pecan-crusted pork loin with ginger sauce—try the smoke-free **Wilson-Walker House** (closed Mon.; 540/463-3020), 30 N. Main Street.

There are a number of comfortable and captivating places to stay in and around Lexington, such as the **Alexander Winthrow House** ($120–160; 540/463-2044) at 3 W. Washington Street, or the **Llewellyn Lodge** ($100–120; 540/463-3235 or 800/882-1145) at 603 S. Main Street, both friendly B&Bs within easy walking distance of the campuses and the historic town center.

To get a sense of life in the Shenandoah Valley, tune to **WSVA 550 AM** in Harrisonburg, which broadcasts updated farm and livestock prices every hour on the hour, and Rush Limbaugh during lunch.

For walking-tour maps, general information, or further listings, contact the Lexington **visitors center** (540/463-3777), located at 106 E. Washington Street.

Natural Bridge

Held sacred by local Monacan Indians, and bought from King George in 1774 by Thomas Jefferson, the 215-foot-high notch of Natural Bridge is a remarkable piece of geologic acrobatics. Spanning some 90 feet, the thick stone arch bridges Cedar Creek at the bottom of a steeply walled canyon. To see the Natural Bridge, which is heralded as one of the Seven Natural Wonders of the World (others on the list include Niagara Falls, Yellowstone, and Giant's Causeway in Northern Ireland), you have to buy a ticket (daily; $10; 800/533-1410) from the unbelievably huge souvenir shop that fills the bottom of the old hotel. Natural Bridge is the focus of a once-plush resort complex that has definitely seen better times but still offers some 200 rooms in two hotels, as well as a large cave ($8) and a wax museum ($8) of Virginia history in which you can watch the wax figures being made, dressed, and posed.

The **Natural Bridge Inn,** located next to the Natural Bridge entrance, has rooms ($50–90; 800/533-1410) and 4- to 6-room cottages across the road for $50–70. There's also an Olympic-sized pool, and the colonial dining room serves all meals daily, with outdoor dining on the veranda and popular weekend buffets.

Explore Park

Depicting life at various points in Virginia's long history, the living-history **Explore Park** (closed Mon. & Tues.; $8; 540/427-8508 or 800/842-9163) sits off the Blue Ridge Parkway at milepost 115, near Roanoke's Mill Mountain. Interpreters portraying Native Americans and frontier families tend the working farm and its crops and animals, but are happy to demonstrate colonial skills, including loading and firing flintlock muskets, flint-and-steel firemaking, crafts, and cooking. Eight miles of hiking and mountain bike trails loop past the recreated buildings into the surrounding countryside. You can stop for lunch or dinner at the **Brugh Tavern,** a restored inn that once served travelers on the Great Wagon Road in the early 19th century.

Mountain passes throughout the Blue Ridge are known as "gaps."

Roanoke

Apart from Asheville at its southern end, **Roanoke** (pop. 94,911) is the only real city that can claim it's actually *on* the Blue Ridge Parkway. With block after block of brick-fronted business buildings, most of them adorned with neon, metal, and painted signs that seem unchanged since the 1940s, Roanoke contrasts abruptly with the natural verdancy of the rest of the Parkway, but you may find it a welcome change after so many trees. Once a busy, belching, industrial Goliath supported by the railroads, Roanoke has evolved into a sophisticated, high-tech city—the commercial, cultural, and medical center of southwest Virginia.

Roanoke's main visitor attractions lie right downtown in the **Center in the Square** complex (540/342-5700), a restored warehouse that holds a wide variety of cultural offerings, including theaters, an art museum (free), a kid-friendly science museum ($6), and a local history museum. Also worth a look is the **Virginia Museum of Transportation** (daily; $7.50; 540/342-5670),

three blocks west of Center in the Square at 303 Norfolk Avenue, which displays lots of old cars and trucks, steam and diesel locomotives, and horse-drawn carriages, plus a complete traveling circus—minus the performers, of course. Steam trains, as documented by Roanoke-based photographer O. Winston Link, are the real highlight of the museum, and a short walk away at 101 Shenandoah Avenue, inside Roanoke's streamlined 1930s-era Norfolk & Western Railroad passenger station, the new **O. Winston Link Museum** (daily; $5; 540/982-LINK) displays more than 200 of the photographer's indelible black-and-white images. There's also a neat gallery devoted to the building's legendary designer, Raymond Loewy, who created the Coke bottle, the logo for Lucky Strike cigarettes, and hundreds of other all-American icons.

"World's Largest Man-Made Star," on Roanoke's Mill Mountain

On Mill Mountain high above Roanoke, the 100-foot-tall "**World's Largest Man-Made Star**" shines nightly, lit by 2,000 feet of neon tubing. You can drive up to the base of it and get a grand view over Roanoke.

For NPR news and non-commercial arts programming, tune to **WVTF 89.1 FM** in Roanoke.

Roanoke Practicalities

The town's most popular place to eat is **The Roanoker** (540/344-7746), "The Home of Good Food since 1941," which serves traditional Virginia dishes and also does a tasty bowl of chili, a mile south of downtown off US-220 (Wonju Street exit) at 2522 Colonial Avenue. There are also a number of good cafés downtown, like the unexpectedly world-beat cuisine at **Carlos' Brazilian and International Cuisine** (540/345-7661) at 312 Market Street near Church. If you're planning a picnic up in the mountains, be sure to stop first at the historic **Farmer's Market** (closed Sun.; free), downtown next to the Center in the Square and active since 1874.

Southeast of Roanoke, the **Booker T. Washington National Monument** (540/721-2094) preserves the site of the plantation cabin where the influential African American leader was born. Other buildings on the 225-acre site, 20 miles from Roanoke via Hwy-116 and Hwy-122, have been reconstructed.

On the west edge of Roanoke, near I-81 on Hwy-311 in Salem, excellent home cooking (fresh biscuits, fried chicken, incredible fresh fruit cobblers) is served Thursday–Sunday, for dinner only, at **The Homeplace** (540/384-7252).

Places to stay range from the usual Interstate motels, lined up along Orange Avenue (US-460), to a pair of grand hotels. Oldest and best of these is the **Hotel Roanoke** ($90 and up; 540/985-5900 or 800/222-8733), at 110 Shenandoah Avenue, which has anchored downtown for over a century. It has outlasted the railroads that financed it, and even if you stay elsewhere, the lobby, with its Florentine marble floors and vaulted ceiling, is worth a look. Another downtown landmark, the **Patrick Henry Hotel** ($100 and up; 540/345-8811 or 800/537-8483) at 617 S. Jefferson Street, is listed on the National Register of Historic Places, and renovations have preserved the wrought iron, brass, wood, and crystal accents in the lobby area.

The handy **visitors center** (540/342-6025 or 800/635-5535), downtown inside the Link Museum, offers lots more listings and information.

Floyd

One of the more offbeat corners of the state, the town and county of **Floyd**, south of Roanoke, shelters a small pocket of the 1960s that's apparent in subtle but distinct signs. Earthships (houses made of recycled materials and earth), gasohol, and tie-dyed T-shirts in crafts stores all reflect a counterculture legacy that combines and contrasts intriguingly with the surrounding rural lifestyle. There's only one stoplight in the town of Floyd itself, which makes it easy to find the **Floyd General Store** ($3; 540/745-4563), which is famous for its weekly Flatfoot Jamboree: every Friday at 7 PM, the display cases are pushed aside and the floor given over to *real* country music and shuffling feet.

The soft drink **Dr. Pepper**, which originated in Waco, Texas, was named for a pharmacist who worked in the town of **Rural Retreat**, Virginia, along I-81 near its intersection with the AT.

The Blue Ridge Parkway: Roanoke to North Carolina

South from Roanoke, the Blue Ridge Parkway winds another 100 miles before crossing the North Carolina border. This midsection of the Parkway, especially the first 25 miles south of Roanoke, runs at a lower elevation across a more settled and cultivated landscape than the rugged ridge tops followed elsewhere. In place of the spectacular vistas, you'll see many more houses and small farms, a few pioneer cabins (preserved and not), miles of split-rail fences, and some picturesque cemeteries. The southern reaches, approaching the North Carolina border, get better and better.

Milepost 122: The city of Roanoke.

Milepost 154.5: A two-mile loop trail leads to a pioneer cabin overlooking the Smart View for which it's named. Blooming dogwoods abound in May.

Milepost 165.2: At Tuggles Gap, the junction with Hwy-8 has a motel, a restaurant, and a gas station, also a small cemetery right along the Parkway.

Mileposts 167–174: The 4,800-acre Rocky Knob area contains a campground (540/745-9664), a visitors center near the Meadows of Dan (540/745-9662), and a 10-mile roundtrip trail at Milepost 167.1 leading down through Rock Castle Gorge.

Milepost 176.1: A short trail leads to Mabry Mill, in use 1910–35. In summer, interpreters demonstrate blacksmithing and milling skills. A coffee shop (open May–Oct. only) sells old-fashioned pancakes made from stone-ground flour, plus country hams and hamburgers.

Milepost 189: Near the midpoint of the Parkway, atop Groundhog Mountain, the Doe Run Lodge (276/398-2212) offers spacious, modern, chalet-style cabins (with a pool and tennis courts) and a "fine dining" restaurant.

Milepost 199–200: Junction with US-52, which runs south to Mount Airy, North Carolina, and with I-77 freeway, running south to Charlotte.

Milepost 216.9: Virginia/North Carolina border.

NORTH CAROLINA

Running along the crest of the Blue Ridge Mountains at the far western edge of the state, this route across North Carolina takes in some of the most beautiful scenery east or west of the Mississippi. Though not as immense as the Rockies or other western landscapes, this part of North Carolina abounds with rugged peaks and deep valleys, pastoral meadows, and ancient-looking mountain villages, some dating back to colonial times. It's all linked by the magnificent Blue Ridge Parkway, perhaps the country's greatest scenic drive.

The border between Virginia and North Carolina was surveyed in 1749 by a team that included **Thomas Jefferson's** father, Peter.

The region's sole city, **Asheville**, is a proud old resort dominated by the ostentatious Biltmore Estate, "the world's largest private house," but everywhere else nature predominates—especially in the majestic **Great Smoky Mountains National Park** in the state's far southwestern corner.

Mount Airy: Mayberry, RFD

Along the Virginia–North Carolina border, 12 miles southeast of Blue Ridge Parkway milepost 200 via US-52, **Mount Airy** (pop. 7,156) was the boyhood home of **Andy Griffith**, who based much of his long-running TV show *The Andy Griffith Show* and the spin-off sitcom *Mayberry, RFD* on the region. If you have fond memories of Opie, Andy, Barney, and Aunt Bea, you'll definitely want to visit Mount Airy, which has effectively re-created itself in the image of the show. Eat an ever-tender pork chop sandwich, raved about by *Gourmet Magazine* and Oprah, at the very popular **Snappy Lunch** (closed Sun.; 336/786-4931), at 125 Main Street in the compact downtown business district, and admire the 8x10 glossies of Mayberry actors and their local lookalikes at Floyd's Barber Shop, next door. Or head a few blocks west to **Aunt Bea's BBQ**, 425 Old US-52, and stay the night at the comfortable, clean and inexpensive **Mayberry Motor Inn** ($50 and up; 336/786-4109) across the highway—just look for the black-and-white Mayberry sheriff's car parked out front.

In the valley below Mount Mitchell, off I-40 northeast of Asheville, **Black Mountain College** was a lively intellectual and artistic nexus during the 1930s and 1940s, when the likes of Charles Olson hung out here.

the sheriff's car, parked outside Mayberry Motor Inn

The Mayberry mania reaches a peak during **Mayberry Days** in late September; details on this (and anything to do with Andy Griffith) can be had from the Mount Airy **visitors center** (336/789-4636 or 800/576-0231), at 615 N. Main Street.

Along with *Mayberry RFD*, Mount Airy is also home to the world's largest open-face granite quarry.

Blowing Rock

A quick two miles south of the Blue Ridge Parkway via US-221 from milepost 291.9 lies the delightful little resort community of **Blowing Rock** (pop. 1,418)—the place to stop if you're only stopping once. The cool summer temperatures have been attracting visitors for centuries, and once you get past the hideous factory outlet mall that welcomes you to town, quaint old Main Street is a great place to stretch your legs while taking in the eclectic range of late Victorian buildings, including some delightful churches. Blowing Rock takes its name from a nearby cliff overlooking John's River Gorge, where updrafts can cause lightweight objects to be blown upwards rather than down; this effect, which earned Blowing Rock a mention in *Ripley's Believe It or Not!* as the only place "Where Snow Falls Upside Down," also inspired the Native American legend of a Cherokee brave who, rather than be forcibly separated from his Chickasaw lover, leapt off the cliff, only to be blown back into the arms of his sweetheart.

North Carolina's oldest tourist attraction, the **Blowing Rock** itself, two miles east of town via winding US-321 (daily; $6), is worth the admission, whether or not the "magic wind" is blowing. Check out the tremendous views from a platform suspended 3,000 feet above the valley below. The nearby area also offers a couple of enjoyable tourist traps, including an apparently gravity-defying **"Mystery Hill"** just off the Parkway, and the scenic, coal-fired steam trains of the **Tweetsie Railroad** four miles north of town on US-321.

Downtown Blowing Rock has a number of good places to eat lined up along the quaint few blocks of Main Street downtown. For good food at fair prices, try **Sonny's Grill**, 1119 Main Street, and for a front deck that overlooks the town, it's hard to beat the **Speckled Trout Cafe**

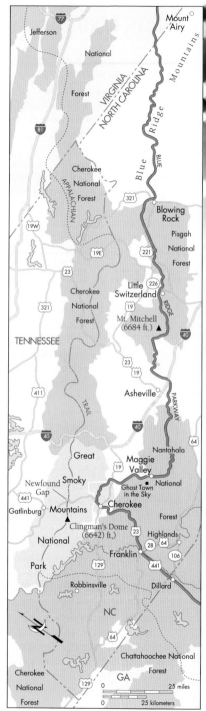

(828/295-9819), open for breakfast, lunch, and dinner at 922 N. Main Street. Across US-321 from the Blowing Rock, the storybook **Green Park Inn** ($100–150; 828/295-3141) is a large historic resort hotel built in 1882, with a golf course. More modern conveniences are available at the **Cliff Dwellers Inn** ($80 and up; 828/295-3121), right off the parkway on US-321.

Little Switzerland

Another classic mountaintop vacation spot, located midway between Blowing Rock and Asheville, Little Switzerland was founded in 1910 around the **Switzerland Inn** (828/765-2153 or 800/654-4026), a stately old chalet-style resort that also operates a very popular restaurant right off the Blue Ridge Parkway at milepost 334.

The inn stands on a crest, but the rest of Little Switzerland sits in the deep canyon to the east, spread out along Hwy-226 and a number of smaller side roads. The main stop is **Emerald Village** (daily April–Nov.; $5; 828/765-6463), on McKinney Mine Road 2.5 miles from the Parkway, where you can tour an old gemstone mine (above and below ground) and museums displaying everything from gemstones to mechanical music makers.

Asheville

What the English country town of Bath was to King George's London, the mountain resort of **Asheville** (pop. 68,889) was to the pre–jet set, pre-air-conditioned Deep South. When summer heat and humidity became unbearable, the gentry headed here to stay cool while enjoying the city's many grand hotels and elaborate summer homes.

The presence here of the world's biggest vacation house, the Vanderbilt family's **Biltmore Estate** (daily; $39; 828/274-6333 or 800/543-2961), is a testament to Asheville's primary position in the resort pantheon. The estate now covers 8,000 acres on the south side of town, though at one time it stretched up to the Blue Ridge Parkway. Surrounded by a series of flower gardens planned in part by Frederick Law Olmsted, the estate centers on a truly unbelievable French Renaissance–style mansion built in 1895. The 250-plus rooms hold everything from a palm court and a bowling alley to Napoleon's chess set to paintings by Renoir, Singer Sargent, Whistler, and others. Signs aplenty direct you to the estate, which stands just north of the I-40 exit 50 off Biltmore Avenue, across from the shops and restaurants in **Historic Biltmore Village**, which originally housed the estate's staff and workshops—it's a true "model village," designed in gothic style by Richard Morris Hunt.

The hikers' Appalachian Trail winds west of the Blue Ridge Parkway along the North Carolina/Tennessee border.

A dozen miles west of the Blue Ridge Parkway via US-321 and Hwy-194, the village of Valle Crucis holds the original **Mast General Store**, a one-of-a-kind survivor that sells a little of everything, from gasoline to Gore-Tex parkas. They now have a branch in Blowing Rock.

The Blue Ridge Parkway: North Carolina to the Smokies

The highest and most memorable parts of the 469-mile Blue Ridge Parkway are the 250 mountainous miles leading along the backbone of North Carolina. Following the southern Blue Ridge Mountains as they fade into the taller and more massive Black Mountains, the Parkway skirts three other mountain ranges before ending up at Great Smoky Mountains National Park on the Tennessee border. Spring flowers (including massive rhododendrons), fall colors, songbirds and wild turkeys, numerous waterfalls, and occasional eerie fogs that fill the valleys below all make this an unforgettable trip no matter what the time of year. Take your time and drive carefully, however hard it is to keep your eyes on the road.

A couple of worthwhile detours—to the mountain hamlets of Blowing Rock and Little Switzerland, and to the city of Asheville—are covered in greater detail in the main text. From north to south, here are the mile-by-mile highlights along the North Carolina portion of the Blue Ridge Parkway:

Milepost 216.9: Virginia/North Carolina border.

Milepost 217.5: A very easy half-mile trail leads to the top of 2,885-foot Cumberland Knob. A visitors center marks the location workers began construction of the parkway in 1935.

Mileposts 238.5–244.7: Doughton Park, named for one of the politicians who made the Parkway possible, has a gas station, a nice café, a campground, and the small **Bluffs Lodge** (336/372-4499).

Milepost 260.6: An easy mile-long trail leads to the top of Jumpinoff Rocks for a sweeping view.

Mileposts 292–295: Moses H. Cone Memorial Park is a 3,600-acre former private estate, with many miles of mountaintop hiking trails. At Mile 294, Southern Highlands Crafts Guild members demonstrate various Appalachian crafts throughout the summer, on the front porch of the former Cone mansion, which is now the nonprofit Parkway Craft Center.

Milepost 304: The marvelous engineering feat of the Linn Cove Viaduct carries the Parkway around rugged Grandfather Mountain. Completed in 1987, this was the last part of the Parkway to be built. Dense walls of rhododendrons border the Parkway south of the viaduct.

Milepost 305.1: US-221, which used to carry the Parkway before the viaduct was built, leads a mile south to 5,837-foot Grandfather Mountain, the highest peak in Blue Ridge, now a private park (daily; $14) with trails, a zoo, and the famous "Mile-High Swinging Bridge."

Milepost 308.2: A half-mile nature trail leads to 3,995-foot Flat Rock for a view of Grandfather Mountain.

Milepost 316.3: Linville Falls crashes through a rugged gorge; short trails lead to scenic overlooks.

Milepost 331: At the junction of Hwy-226, the **Museum of North Carolina Minerals** (daily 9 AM–5 PM; free) displays all kinds and sizes of local gemstones, which you can watch being polished.

Milepost 355.4: West of the Parkway, the 1,650 acres of Mount Mitchell State Park include a mountaintop observation tower. Drive to within 200 yards of the weather-beaten 6,684-foot summit, the highest point east of the Mississippi River.

Milepost 364.6: Best seen in late spring when the rhododendrons are in full bloom, the lush greenery of Craggy Gardens feels like an Appalachian Shangri-la.

Milepost 382: You can check out exhibits and demonstrations of Appalachian arts and crafts in the Folk Art Center.

Milepost 431: At the highest point on the Parkway (6,047 feet in elevation), a self-guided nature trail leads through a first-growth spruce and fir forest.

Milepost 469: Southern end of Blue Ridge Parkway, at the junction with US-441 and the entrance to Smoky Mountains National Park.

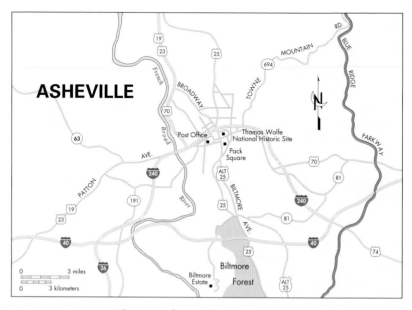

ASHEVILLE

The rest of Asheville can't compete with the nouveau riche excess of the Biltmore Estate, and in fact it's a surprisingly homespun city, with a downtown commercial district filled with 1930s-era storefronts housing thrift stores and off-beat art galleries. One truly worthwhile place to see in downtown Asheville is the nondescript old boardinghouse where author Thomas Wolfe grew up from 1900 to 1920, preserved as it was when Wolfe lived here. The rambling house, at 48 Spruce Street across from the beige modern Radisson Hotel, is officially known as the **Thomas Wolfe Memorial State Historic Site** (daily, closed Mon. in winter; $1; 828/253-8304); unfortunately, the house suffered a major fire in 1998, but after restoration is still one of the most evocative of all American literary sites. In the details and, more importantly, in general ambience, it's identical to the vivid prose descriptions of the house he called "Dixieland," the primary setting of his first and greatest novel, *Look Homeward, Angel.* After Wolfe's death from tuberculosis in 1938, the house was made into a shrine to Wolfe by his family, who arranged it to look as it did during his youth; one room contains his desk, typewriter, and other mementos of his life and work. An adjacent museum tells more of his story.

Two blocks south of the Wolfe memorial, where Broadway becomes Biltmore Avenue, **Pack Square** is the center of Asheville, surrounded by the county courthouse, the city hall, a small art museum, and the public library.

This is where Thomas Wolfe's father ran a stonecutting shop, on whose porch stood the homeward-gazing angel, now recalled by a statue standing on the square's southwest corner.

Asheville Practicalities

The streets around Pack Square hold many good places to eat, including a trio of bistro-type places with outdoor dining areas, lined up side by side around the **Bistro 1896** (828/251-1300), at 7 S. Pack Square. There are more good places around the magical, art deco–era Grove shopping arcade west of the square, including **Margie's Battery Park Café** (828/255-2688), at 1 Battle Square, for great pies; and the **Laughing Seed Cafe** (828/252-3445), serving health-conscious "international vegetarian cuisine" at 40 Wall Street. Yet more cafés and bakeries line Biltmore Avenue south of Pack Square, where you'll also find Asheville's best nightlife. The **Orange Peel** (828/255-5851), at 101 S. Biltmore Avenue, gets an enviable array of nationally known musicians in all genres, while the **Fine Arts** cinema across the street shows the latest art-house releases. North of downtown, near the UNC-Asheville campus, good microbrews (and $1 evening movies) are available at **Asheville Pizza and Brewing** (828/254-1281), 675 Merrimon Avenue.

Profits from Grove's Tasteless Tonic paid for the ultra-tasteful Grove Park Inn.

The usual chain hotels cluster along the Interstates, and some more characterful older, neon-signed motels line old US-70 between downtown and the Blue Ridge Parkway. For a true taste of Americana, you may prefer the classic 1930s **Log Cabin Motor Court** ($50–85; 828/645-6546), six miles north of Asheville off at 330 Weaverville Highway. To complete the retro experience, there's a roller-skating rink next door.

When Vanderbilt types come to Asheville today, they probably stay at **Grove Park Inn Resort** ($250 and up; 828/252-2711 or 800/438-0050), at 290 Macon Avenue north of I-90, a lovely rustic inn built in 1913. Newer wings contain the most modern four-star conveniences, but the original lodge boasts rooms filled with authentic Roycroft furniture, making the Grove Park a live-in museum of arts-and-crafts style. There's also a very plush **Inn on Biltmore Estate** ($275 and up; 828/225-1600), for the full Biltmore Estate experience.

For further information on the Asheville area, contact the **visitors center** (828/258-6101 or 800/257-1300), at 151 Haywood Street off I-240 exit 4C.

Maggie Valley

The Blue Ridge Parkway swings south from Asheville through Transylvania County on the approach to Great Smoky Mountains National Park, though you'll save an hour or more by following the I-40 freeway to the junction with US-19, which links up with the south end of the parkway.

Novelist **F. Scott Fitzgerald** lived at Asheville's Grove Park Resort while visiting his wife, **Zelda**, who had been committed to the Highland Hospital sanitarium, where she died in a fire in 1948.

20 miles southwest of Asheville, the eponymous peak featured in the book *Cold Mountain* rises amidst the Pisgah National Forest, but the Academy Award–winning movie version was filmed on location—in distant Romania.

You can spot the wild mountains southeast of Asheville in numerous movies including *Last of the Mohicans*, much of which was filmed around Chimney Rock, east of town along scenic US-64. **Chimney Rock** (800/277-9611) is a great destination, and features fabulous views and a 26-story elevator carved through solid granite.

This stretch of US-19, winding through the Maggie Valley over the foothills of the Great Smokies, is a very pretty drive, and absolutely packed with roadside Americana—miniature golf courses, trout farms, souvenir shops, lookout towers alongside pancake houses, BBQ shacks . . . you name it, it's here.

For years, the biggest and best of many great places to stop in Maggie Valley was **Ghost Town in the Sky,** a real, old Appalachian "ghost town"-themed amusement park, with roller coasters, bumper cars, and all the usual suspects, high on the side of the Great Smoky Mountains. Alas, the park closed in 2003, and has been for sale since.

Cherokee

West of Maggie Valley, the Blue Ridge Parkway and US-19 join up 40 miles west of Asheville at touristy **Cherokee** (pop. 5,971), commercial center of the 56,000-acre **Cherokee Indian Reservation,** which was established here by a small band of Cherokee Indians in 1866, long after the rest of this once-mighty tribe had been forcibly exiled to Oklahoma on the Trail of Tears. Cherokee is a last gasp of commercialism at the edge of the national park, a traffic-clogged gauntlet of places where you can See Live Bears, Eat Boiled Peanuts, Pan For Gold, or ride the "Rudicoaster" at the kid-friendly Santa's Land amusement park. The biggest draw hereabouts is the ever-expanding Harrah's Casino.

The upscale casino, the region's biggest draw, looms over a fading roadside lined by tacky old-time souvenir stands like the "Big Chief," but amidst the tourist-taunting sprawl is at least one worthwhile stop: the **Museum of the Cherokee Indian** (daily; $9), which traces tribal history from pre-conquest achievements— the Cherokee used a natural version of aspirin centuries before western chemists "discovered" it, for example—to their forced removal after gold was discovered here in the 1830s.

For many years, **Cherokee Chief Henry** was known as "The World's Most Photographed Indian," his image gracing countless postcards.

Great Smoky Mountains National Park

The most popular park in the United States, **Great Smoky Mountains National Park** offers a taste of wilderness to some nine million visitors annually. Knoxville, Nashville, and Atlanta are all within a two-hour drive, and day-trippers visit mostly during late October for the annual display of fall color. The park covers 520,460 acres along the 6,000-foot-high crest of the Great Smoky Mountains, so named for the fogs that fill the deep valleys. Before the park was established, its lands were extensively logged—70 percent of the trees had been clear-cut by 1934, when the lands were protected as a national park. Fortunately, the forests have grown back to obscure any sign of past degradations, and the uncut portions form the most extensive stands of primeval forest in the eastern United States.

Biologists estimate that some 500 native **black bears** live in the backcountry (and campgrounds!) of Great Smoky Mountains National Park.

The main route through the park is Newfound Gap Road (US-441), which runs northwest from Cherokee to the even

more tourist-traveled Gatlinburg and Pigeon Forge in Tennessee. The road winds steeply through dense forests packed with magnificent giant hardwoods, flowering poplar, dogwood, azalea, and rhododendron, and evergreen pines and firs at the highest elevations. Where the highway reaches the crest, a spur road runs parallel to the Appalachian Trail five miles west to 6,642-foot **Clingman's Dome,** the highest point in the park, where you can take a short but steep trail up to a lookout tower.

One of the most extensive "natural" areas—unlogged, old-growth forest, full of the park's oldest and tallest trees—lies at the very center of the park, off Newfound Gap Road on the north side of the crest. Starting at the popular Chimney Tops picnic area, the well-marked, three-quarter-mile **Cove Hardwood nature trail** winds through a sampling of the park's most stately maples and other broad-leafed trees—the ones responsible for the best of the fall colors.

Along Little River Road, west of the Sugarlands Visitor Center off US-441 at the park's northern entrance, stands another group of ancient trees. Midway along, trails lead to two marvelous waterfalls, Laurel Falls and Meigs Falls. Little River Road ends up at **Cades Cove,** where the preserved remnants of a mountain community that existed here from the early 1800s until the 1930s give a strong sense of Appalachian folkways. A church and a number of mills still stand, and interpretive staff offer guided walks and other programs explaining the history and culture of these "hillbilly" people—some 6,000 of whom used to live within the park boundaries. **Bike rentals** are available at the Cades Cove campground, and you'll find plenty of opportunities for rides along the old country lanes.

The Appalachian Trail runs along the crest of the Great Smoky Mountains, crossing **Newfound Gap Road** at the center of the park.

The many different **salamanders** native to the Great Smokies range from the tiny pygmy to the massive hellbender, which grows up to two feet long, head to tail. These crawling critters have earned the Great Smokies a reputation as the "Salamander Capital of the World."

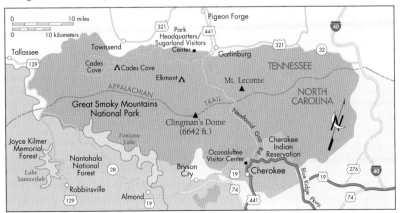

Another popular park destination is **Grotto Falls,** southeast of Gatlinburg via the Roaring Fork Road, where a short, flat trail to the tumbling cascade leads through lush hemlock forest—an ideal environment for mushrooms, and for the 27 different species of salamanders that slither around underfoot.

Just over the mountains on the Tennessee side of the Great Smokies, Dolly Parton owns, runs, and stars at Dollywood (800/DOLLYWOOD), the country's biggest autobiographical theme park.

The only beds available in the park are at the historic **LeConte Lodge** (865/429-5704), built in the 1920s atop 6,593-foot Mt. LeConte, and located a six-mile hike from the nearest road. There are no phones, no TVs, little privacy, and no indoor plumbing, but the $90 and up nightly rates do come with "family-style" breakfast and dinner. Ten fairly basic **campgrounds** (no showers or hookups) operate in the park, with reservations taken only for the largest and most popular ones at Cades Cove, Elkmont, and Smokemount (800/365-2267). These last three are accessible to RVs up to 35 feet long; for hikers, there are also bear-proofed backcountry shelters along the Appalachian Trail.

For more information, or to pick up the handy brochures (35 cents each) describing the park's array of flora, fauna, trails, and other features, stop by either of the two main visitors centers. North of Cherokee at the south entrance, the **Oconaluftee Visitor Center** (828/497-1900) stands alongside a restored pioneer farmstead, where crafts demonstrations are given in summer. From the **Sugarlands Visitor Center** (865/436-1200), two miles south of Gatlinburg, Tennessee, you can take a short hike to Cataract Falls.

South to Georgia: Franklin

South from Cherokee and the Great Smoky Mountains, US-441 runs through the giant **Nantahala National Forest,** which stretches all the way to the Georgia border. It's a fast road, mostly divided, four-lane freeway, passing through a fairly developed corridor of towns and small cities.

The biggest town in this part of North Carolina, **Franklin** (pop. 3,490) was founded in the mid-1800s on a shallow ridge overlooking the Little Tennessee River. Along with lumber milling, Franklin's main industry has long

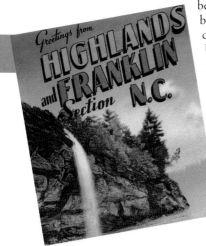

been the mining of gemstones—garnets, rubies, and sapphires. Now a light industrial center, spread out around the intersection of US-441 and US-64, Franklin has a compact downtown area packed with gemstone and jewelry shops like **Ruby City,** 44 N. Main Street, which also has a small free museum. The **Franklin Motel** ($50; 828/524-4431 or 800/433-5507), at 17 W. Palmer Street, has clean, comfortable rooms and a swimming pool.

US-441 races south to Georgia from Franklin, while Hwy-28/US-64 heads southeast through the heart of **Transylvania County,** known as the "Land of Waterfalls" because of its many cascades. The biggest of these is 13 miles from Franklin and named, for some unknown reason, **Dry Falls.** From the well-signed parking area, follow a short trail that ends up underneath and behind the impressively raging torrent, a powerful white-noise generator you can hear long before you reach it. Another waterfall, known as **Bridal Veil Falls,** is a mile south from Dry Falls. Bridal Veil is much smaller than Dry Falls, but spills right along the road; the overhang is so deep that you can drive underneath it.

Two miles south from Bridal Veil Falls, US-64 enters the resort community of **Highlands** (pop. 900). Here Hwy-106 loops back to the southwest, giving grand panoramic views over the forested foothills before rejoining US-441 across the Georgia border in Dillard.

One of the few radio stations you can hear in mountainous western North Carolina, Franklin's **WVFC 1480 AM** plays an entertaining combination of local news and contemporary Christian country music.

Between Franklin and Highlands, US-64 passes by several waterfalls and has been designated a Mountain Waters Scenic Byway.

GEORGIA

If Georgia brings to mind endless, flat cotton or peanut plantations, you'll be pleasantly surprised by the mountainous wilds of the state's northern tier. The great Appalachian ridge that runs along the East Coast has its southern foot here, high up in the forests of Rabun County, which packs natural wonders, outdoor adventures, and down-home Appalachian spirit into the state's small, isolated corner. Chattooga River whitewater—made famous by the movie *Deliverance,* and rated among the top 10 river runs in the United States—is the biggest draw, and sightseers can take in the spectacular waterfalls of Chattooga's Tallulah Gorge. Christmas-tree farms, dairies, and car graveyards dot the old-time mountain towns, but the ongoing "improvement" of US-441 into a four-lane freeway has resulted in a development boom of golf courses and mountain-view estates, increasing exponentially as the route approaches Atlanta's endless suburbs.

Dillard

Just south of the North Carolina border, the highway hamlet of **Dillard** (pop. 199) is a mini-fiefdom of the Dillard family, whose name dates back to the 1700s in these parts. For generations, the Dillards have run a local hospitality empire based around the sprawling set of bungalows, lodges, and dining rooms all going by the name **Dillard House** (706/746-5348), on a hill above US-441 at the south edge of town. Heading up the complex is the Dillard House restaurant, famous for its all-you-can-eat country cooking and its glass-walled patio, where diners can enjoy plates of classic country ham, fried chicken, pan-fried trout, vegetables, cornbread, and assorted relishes and desserts. The legendary institution may today impress you as more institution than legend—bus tours dominate the clientele—but you never leave hungry. Rooms (around $75) are around back in low-slung lodges scattered near a swimming pool and tennis courts.

In addition to the rambling inn, the family oligarchy operates a row of roadside businesses off US-441, selling collectible and keepsake souvenirs.

The hikers' Appalachian Trail crosses the Georgia/North Carolina border roughly 10 miles west of Dillard, then veers southeast, coming to a finale at the 3,782-foot summit of **Springer Mountain**, where a photogenic sign marks the end (or the beginning, since most of the 200 or so annual thru-hikers travel south to north) of the 2,144-mile trail.

The rocky crest of Black Rock Mountain marks the eastern **Continental Divide**—from here waters part to follow a path to either the Atlantic Ocean or the Gulf of Mexico.

Black Rock Mountain State Park

At the wind-worn summit of 3,640-foot Black Rock Mountain, a flagstone terrace looks out over a grand Appalachian panorama: If there's no fog, you can see clear to the South Carolina piedmont 80 miles away and as far as the Great Smokies to the north. The highest state park in Georgia, **Black Rock Mountain State Park** offers hiking trails and accommodations in addition to the splendid vistas. Set off in a ring at the top of the mountain, 10 spacious cottages are removed from lowland civilization—no phones, no TVs, just fireplaces and porch rockers. The cottages cost $90–125 a night, sleep up to 10 people, and are available for rent year-round—a nice snowy winter retreat. There's also a pair of campgrounds. The park is three miles north of Clayton, well-signed to the west of US-441. For information, or for reservations for the cabins or the campgrounds, contact the **visitors center** (706/746-2141) near the summit.

Mountain City: Foxfire Museum

The monolith of Black Rock Mountain imposes an early twilight on **Mountain City** (pop. 784), the community that stretches along US-441. Tucked away on the west side of US-441 just south of the turnoff to Black Mountain State Park, the modest **Foxfire Museum** (Mon.–Fri.; $5; 706/746-5828) is part of a radical cultural and educational movement that began here in the mid-1960s when local schoolteacher Eliot Wigginton, frustrated in attempts to motivate his uninspired high-school students, assigned them the task of interviewing their elders about how things were in "the old days." The students, inspired with the newly discovered richness of their Appalachian heritage, assembled the written interviews into a magazine, which they named *Foxfire* after a luminescent local fungus.

The magazine expanded to a series of *Foxfire* books, and more than eight million copies have been sold worldwide. The program's twofold success—educational innovation and folklife preservation—further broadened as the then-emerging back-to-the-land movement seized upon these books as vital how-to manuals for subsistence farming and generally living off the grid. The Foxfire organization still runs classes and summer programs on a 110-acre campus in the hills above town.

Deliverance: Clayton

Slicing through the Appalachian wilderness along the Georgia–South Carolina border, the Chattooga River rates among the nation's top 10 whitewater river adventures, attracting some 100,000 visitors a year for rafting, canoeing, kayaking, tubing, swimming, fishing, and riverside hiking. The "Wild and Scenic" river was seen in the movie *Deliverance,* based on the book by Georgia poet and novelist James Dickey; ever since the movie was released, authorities have been pulling bodies out of the river—not toothless mountaineers but overconfident river-runners who underestimate the whitewater's power.

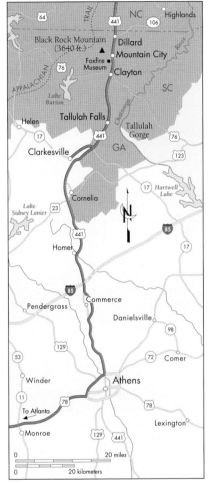

The largest town in the area, the down-home mountain community of **Clayton** (pop. 2,019) is a popular base for excursions into the wild forest and Chattooga River areas. US-441 has grown into an exurban morass of Wal-Mart sprawl, but Main Street, a three-block length of wooden storefronts on a sunny rise just west of US-411, still looks like you could hitch a horse at the curb without attracting much attention. The **Old Clayton Inn** (706/782-7722) at the center of town has been open for a century or so, though it's been tidied up considerably in the years since Burt Reynolds and crew stayed here while filming *Deliverance* on the raging Chattooga.

The smaller **Clayton Cafe,** 50 Main Street, slings down-home breakfasts, burgers, and other basic diner fare, while south of town the **Cookie Jar Café** (706/782-6810) at 621 S. US-441 is run by Billy Redden who, in the movie, played one of the porchfront "Duelin' Banjos."

Tallulah Falls and Gorge

Balanced precariously over the precipitous gorge that once held the thundering cascades of the Tallulah River, tiny **Tallulah Falls** (pop. 147) has an illustrious history. As word of the natural wonder spread, crowds were drawn to the breathtaking sight, and by the turn of the century Tallulah Falls was a fashionable resort, with several elite hotels and boardinghouses catering to lowland sightseers. Fortunes changed when the falls were harnessed for hydroelectricity, but recent

Atlanta

With a youthful and energetic metropolitan population rapidly approaching three million people, Atlanta has emerged as one of the most dynamic communities in the country. State capital of Georgia, and world headquarters of that flagship of American culture, Coca-Cola, Atlanta is the financial and cultural heart of the "New South," having recovered from its total destruction during the Civil War. Despite the sprawling scale of the place, in general people here are gracious and welcoming, so much so they could seem like walking parodies of Southern hospitality—if they weren't so darn sincere.

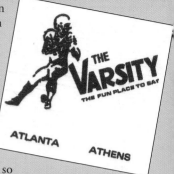

Atlanta began as a railroad junction (its original name was simply "Terminus"), and the early streetscape has been preserved and restored in Underground Atlanta, a warren of shop fronts underneath the center of the modern city. Abandoned in the 1920s, the buildings here were restored in the late 1980s to form a successful shopping and entertainment district. Numerous plaques and artworks commemorate the area's past, while two blocks to the east stands the gold-domed Georgia State Capitol.

Across the wide I-975 freeway, a half-mile east of downtown, the **Martin Luther King Jr. National Historic Site** (daily; free; 404/331-5190), at 450 Auburn Avenue, sits at the heart of the predominantly black Sweet Auburn neighborhood. The four-block area holds many important landmarks in the life of Dr. King: his birthplace at 501 Auburn Avenue; the recently renovated Ebenezer Baptist Church, 407 Auburn Avenue, where he, his father, and his grandfather all served as pastor; and his tomb, emblazoned with the words "Free at Last, Free at Last," sitting on the grounds of the Center for Non-Violent Social Change, 449 Auburn Avenue.

Atlanta's main museum district is north of downtown in the upscale Buckhead neighborhood, where the **Atlanta History Center** (daily; $12.50; 404/814-4000), at 130 W. Paces Ferry Road, is a don't-miss introduction to the city. Back downtown, building on the mixed success of the 1996 Olympics, Atlanta has developed Centennial Park as its new center, opening the $200 million **Georgia Aquarium** (daily; $23), the country's largest aquarium, in 2005. Next door, a new showcase for the city's most successful product, **World of Coca Cola** (daily; $10; 800/676-COKE), is due to open soon.

On the southwest side of downtown, near the I-20/I-85 junction, the powerhouse **Atlanta Braves** (800/326-4000) play at Turner Field, aka "The Ted."

Practicalities

Atlanta's airport, Hartsfield International, one of the busiest in the country, is a dozen miles south of downtown Atlanta, at the junction of the I-85 and I-285 freeways. All the usual rental car companies have branches there, and taxis and shuttle vans are supplemented by the extensive network of Metro Atlanta Rapid Transit Authority (MARTA) trains.

The I-75/I-85 freeway cuts through the center of Atlanta, while the I-20 freeway skirts its southern edge. Sliced by freeways and spreading Los Angeles–like in a low level ooze of mini-malls and housing tracts, Atlanta's outlying areas are impossible to make sense of, but the downtown area is compact and manageable. Note also that seemingly every other thoroughfare includes the word "Peachtree" in its name, so check twice before getting completely lost.

Centrally located places to stay include the **Hotel Indigo** ($119 and up; 404/874-9200), at 683 Peachtree Street NE, a historic 1920s building upgraded into boutique status by the InterContinental chain, in a handy Midtown location across from the landmark Fox Theatre. The adjacent all-suite **Georgian Terrace** (404/897-1991), at 659 Peachtree Street NE, is characterful and spacious.

A few blocks east, the **Atlanta International Hostel** ($20; 404/875-9449), at 223 Ponce de Leon, is a circa 1915 Midtown house with dorm beds, across the street from **Mary Mac's Tea Room** (cash only; 404/875-4337), 224 Ponce de Leon Avenue—an ideal combination for hungry budget travelers.

On the same street, the **Majestic Diner** (404/875-0276) at 1031 Ponce de Leon Avenue is a large, lively (and just a little bit seedy) 1940s-style cafe, open 24 hours for great waffles, burgers, and endless cups of java.

One more north-of-downtown Atlanta landmark deserves mention: **The Varsity** (404/881-1706), at 61 North Avenue near Georgia Tech alongside I-75, is the world's largest drive-in, serving up very good junk food: chili dogs, onion rings, and more Coca-Cola than anywhere else on this earth. Further north, off I-85, carnivores and blues fans flock to **Fat Matt's Rib Shack** (404/607-1622) at 1811 Piedmont Avenue NE. In the upscale Buckhead neighborhood, a mile south of I-85, the **Colonnade** (cash only; 404/874-5642), 1879 Cheshire Bridge Road, has been serving Southern food (baked ham, fried chicken, and more) since 1962. After dark, enjoy an alfresco movie at the **Starlight Six** ($6; 404/627-5786), 2000 Moreland Avenue SE. Double features are shown every night, rain or shine, starting at 8:45 PM.

The usual barrage of tourist information can be had from the **Atlanta Convention and Visitors Bureau** (404/521-6688 or 800/ATLANTA), located at 233 Peachtree Street.

When you take in the sight of Tallulah Gorge, imagine walking a tightrope suspended 1,200 feet above the ground across its breadth. "Professor Leon" managed it (despite a stumble) in 1886, and in 1970, the flying Karl Wallenda replicated the feat, walking across on a wire suspended from the Tallulah Point Overlook, where postcards and photos document his effort.

compromises have brought the falls back to occasional life. On weekends, usually in spring and fall, the waters are again released, and can be admired from **Tallulah Gorge State Park** (706/754-7970), a very pleasant park with a local history museum, camping, showers, hiking trails and a very cool suspension bridge over the river and gorge.

Downstream from Tallulah Falls, the dramatic sheer walls of Tallulah Gorge have both haunted and attracted people for centuries. The wary Cherokee heeded legends that warriors who ventured in never returned, and many a curious settler had a waterfall or pool named in his honor—posthumously, after an untimely slip.

Tallulah Gorge is best seen staircase-trails leading from the state park, or from the mile-long scenic route (old US-441), which loops off east of the modern highway. Drivers can pull over at numerous parking areas and take one of several rough trails along the gorge's rim, though the best views are from the historic **Tallulah Point Overlook** (daily 9 AM–6 PM; free), a privately owned concession stand midway along the loop.

Clarkesville

The charming little town of **Clarkesville** (pop. 1,248) retains a sophistication dating back to its founding over 150 years ago by lowland Carolina and coastal Georgian plantation families seeking refuge from the oppressive summer heat.

In the mountains northwest of Clarkesville, 15 miles along Hwy-17 and Hwy-75, the tiny town of **Helen** (pop. 355) turned itself into a tourist draw in 1969 by remodeling all the buildings in mock-Bavarian decor and repaving the streets in cobblestones.

Best known as the home of the renowned country resort Glen-Ella Springs Inn, Clarkesville sits at the lower slope of a river valley that stretches northwest to the faux-Bavarian town of Helen, and is surrounded by countryside perfect for a leisurely drive or bike tour past an old mill here, a covered bridge there, and old-time country stores in wooden cabins.

Clarkesville tucks urbane delights into its rustic country setting, with over 40 buildings, most of them former summer homes, listed on the National Register of Historic Places. Downtown, three blocks of wooden storefronts, centering around a shaded plaza where numerous festivals take place, hold cafés and crafts shops.

Hundred-year-old **Glen-Ella Springs Inn** ($125–195; 706/754-7295), eight miles north of Clarkesville on Bear Gap Road off US-441, is northern Georgia's premier country inn. Set on 17 lush acres, the historic two-story lodge holds 16 guest rooms, each of which opens to a porch with rocking chairs.

Athens

If you've got the time and inclination, one of Georgia's most enjoyable destinations is just a slight veer to the east off our route: Athens, the coolest college town in the South. Famed for its lively music scene which gave the world the "alternative rock" bands B-52s and R.E.M., Athens is the home of the University of Georgia, whose Greek Revival campus sits at the center of town, bordered on the north by a half-dozen blocks of cafés, bars, and book and record stores. Besides the dozens of super-sized Bulldogs (the UGA mascot) around town, Athens also holds a classic Road Trip destination: **"The Tree That Owns Itself,"** a second-generation mighty oak tree standing on a small circle of land at the corner of Finley and Dearing Streets west of campus, whose legal autonomy earned it a place in *Ripley's Believe or Not!*.

The main music venue is the **40 Watt Club** (706/549-7871), at 285 W. Washington Street, where R.E.M. played their second gig. Good, cheap food is available on the east side of town at **Weaver D's Soul Food BBQ** (706/353-7797), at 1016 E. Broad Street, whose enigmatic slogan "Automatic for the People" was enshrined as an R.E.M. album title. R.E.M.'s Michael Stipe owns the gourmet vegetarian **Grit** (706/543-592) at 199 Prince Avenue. The best restaurant in Athens, and one of the Top Ten in the USA according to *Food & Wine Magazine,* is the **5 & 10** (706/546-7300), at 1653 S. Lumpkin Street, off Milledge Street southwest of downtown. The 5 & 10 is open for dinner nightly and Sunday brunch, serving a range of Southern favorites enlivened by inventive, international touches. (Shrimp 'n' grits with andouille sausages, anyone?)

For listings of hotels or for more **information,** contact the Athens **visitors center** (706/357-4430 or 800/653-0603), located at 300 N. Thomas Street.

Cornelia, the southernmost Appalachian town, is known for its **Giant Apple Monument** on Hwy-23 downtown, and if you're here in fall you can sample them fresh from the tree.

On to Atlanta: Stone Mountain

From the foothills of northern Georgia, it's only an hour by freeway southwest to Atlanta, the cultural and commercial center of the New South, and a fascinating (and fun) place to explore. Unfortunately, Atlanta is surrounded by miles and miles of mega-freeway sprawl, so you'll have to endure some of the country's craziest driving to get there.

From Athens, Hwy-316 merges into I-85 for the quickest route there, but for a more interesting route follow old US-78 southeast, approaching Atlanta by way of **Stone Mountain,** 16 miles east of downtown. A Confederate Mt. Rushmore and historic KKK rallying point, Stone Mountain (daily; $8 per car; 770/498-5690 or 800/317-2006) consists of the 20-times-larger-than-life figures of Robert E. Lee, "Stonewall" Jackson, and Jefferson Davis carved into an 800-foot-high hump of granite. At the base are 3,200 acres of the tackier tourist traps going (riverboat cruises, a scenic railroad, a cable car "Skylift" to the summit—all of which charge separate fees of around $8 each), plus the velodrome from the 1996 Olympics and Atlanta's best **campground.**

ATLANTIC COAST

Starting at the Statue of Liberty, and winding up at free-wheeling Key West, these almost two thousand miles of two-lane country roads run within earshot—if not sight—of the Atlantic Ocean.

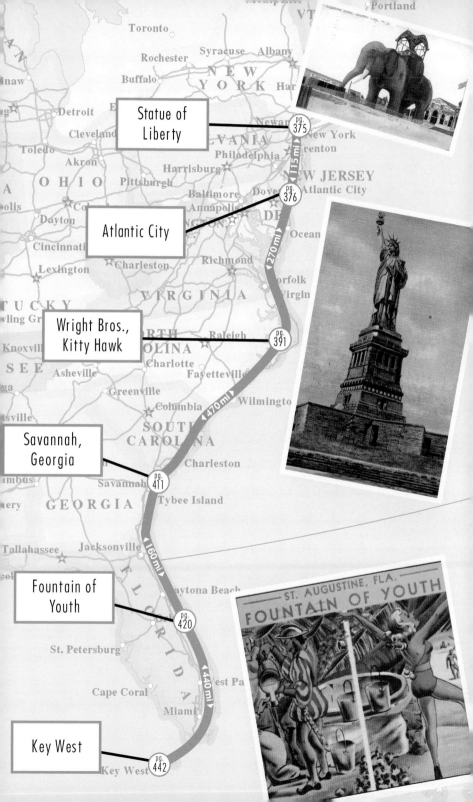

Statue of
Liberty

pg.
375

Atlantic City

pg.
376

115 mi

270 mi

Wright Bros.,
Kitty Hawk

pg.
391

470 mi

Savannah,
Georgia

pg.
411

160 mi

Fountain of
Youth

pg.
420

440 mi

Key West

pg.
442

ST. AUGUSTINE, FLA.
FOUNTAIN OF YOUTH

Between New York City and the Tip of Florida

If your impressions of the East Coast come from driving along the I-95 corridor through nearly nonstop urban and industrial sprawl, following our Atlantic Coast route will open your eyes to a whole other world. Alternating between wildly differing beach resort areas and lengthy stretches of pristine coastal wilderness, the route runs along almost 2,000 miles of two-lane country roads, within earshot, if not sight, of the Atlantic Ocean almost the entire way. In place of the grimy concrete and soulless netherworld of the interstate, this route passes through innumerable quirky seaside towns and timeless old fishing villages, interspersed with huge swathes of beaches, wetlands, and woodlands that have hardly changed since the first explorers laid eyes on them four centuries ago.

Starting in the north at that all-American icon, the **Statue of Liberty**, and winding up in the south at free-wheeling **Key West**, this route truly offers something for everyone. Those searching for photogenic lighthouses or beachcombing solitude will love the undeveloped and usually deserted strands that stretch for miles along the low-lying islands that make up most of the coast, much of which, as at **Assateague Island** or **Cape Hatteras,** has been protected as national seashore parks. In contrast, the many beach resorts that dot the in-between areas vary from the grand Victorian charms of Cape May to the funky old Coney Island–style attractions of **Ocean City, Maryland,** and **Myrtle Beach, South Carolina,** with their boardwalks full of roller coasters, wax museums, and saltwater taffy stands. And let's not forget the glitzy casino resorts of **Atlantic City.**

Alongside the contemporary attractions are many evocative historic sites, including such unique places as **Roanoke Island, North Carolina,** where the first English-speaking colony in North America vanished without a trace in 1587. Lying south of the Mason-Dixon Line for almost all of its length, the route also visits many important Civil War sites, including **Fort Sumter,** where the first shots were fired, and the vital naval battlegrounds at **Hampton Roads** at the mouth of Chesapeake Bay. Midway along, we also pass one of the key sites of modern history: the windy sand dunes at **Kitty Hawk** where the Wright Brothers first proved that humans could fly.

Though this Atlantic Coast route will bring you to many well-known sights, its real attraction is the traveling, stopping off for fried chicken or barbecue at one of the hundreds of roadside stands, watching the shrimp boats pull into a sleepy dock and unload their day's catch, or simply chatting with locals at the general store or post office in a town that may not even be on the map.

NEW JERSEY

Being so close to New York and Philadelphia, it's not surprising that New Jersey has among the busiest and most densely developed stretches of coastline in the country. It *is* surprising, however, that beyond the boardwalk amusements and flashy gambling casinos of **Atlantic City**, the New Jersey shore offers a whole lot more. As with most of the East Coast, the "shoreline" is actually a series of barrier islands separated from the mainland by wildlife-rich estuaries; these provide fishing and bird-watching opportunities, as well as a break from the ceaseless commercial and residential development along the ocean beaches. Bustling in summer, these beachfront communities—starting with **Margate** near Atlantic City, and running south through vibrant **Wildwood** before winding up at the dainty Victorian-era beach resort of **Cape May**—offer something for everyone, all within a 150-mile stretch of shoreline.

Inspired by the end of slavery following the Civil War, the Statue of Liberty took nearly 20 years to complete. "Lady Liberty" was sculpted in France, then the 300-plus pieces were put in crates and shipped across the ocean. The statue is just over 150 feet tall, but including her 150-foot stone pedestal, it was the tallest building in New York when dedicated in 1886.

The Statue of Liberty

Raising her lamp beside New York City's immense harbor, the **Statue of Liberty** is one of the most vivid emblems of America. Despite the fact she is French, given to the American people to celebrate the 100th anniversary of the Declaration of Independence, the statue has come to symbolize the Land of the Free and the Home of the Brave. Its spirit has long been evoked by the poem Emma Lazarus wrote in 1883 to help raise funds for installing the Statue of Liberty. Called "New Colossus," the poem ends with these famous words:

> Keep ancient lands, your storied pomp!" cries she
> With silent lips. "Give me your tired, your poor,
> Your huddled masses yearning to breathe free,
> The wretched refuse of your teeming shore.
> Send these, the homeless, tempest-tost to me,
> I lift my lamp beside the golden door!"

The Statue of Liberty sits on a 12-acre island, and can be visited by ferry only (daily; $10; 866/STATUE4). It's about a mile from Manhattan, via the Circle Line ferry from Battery Park, but it's much easier to reach from **Liberty State Park** in Jersey City, off New Jersey Turnpike exit 14B. (Both ferry routes also visit Ellis Island, where some 12 million immigrants entered the United States.) There is no admission fee for the Statue of Liberty, but to avoid waiting in line, visitors should order a time pass ($1.75), which gives access to the statue at an appointed time. Visitors can explore the base of the Statue of Liberty, and gaze up inside, but her torch and crown are off-limits.

The New Jersey Shore

The northernmost stretches of the New Jersey shore are not exactly appetizing, and visitors bound for the beaches and vacation spots farther south turn a blind eye to the industrial blight. From **Perth Amboy** (Vaseline) to **Asbury Park** (Bruce Springsteen), the region has given the world many distinctive products, and there are a couple of intriguing Victorian-era resorts like **Spring Lake** and **Avon-by-the-Sea,** but to be honest, the attractions increase the further south you go.

The middle stretch of the Jersey shore is actually the quietest, with the million-acre **Pinelands National Preserve** covering the inland area with forest and wetlands, and the coastal **Long Beach Island** dotted with sleepy little fishing and retirement communities. The biggest sight hereabouts is at the northern tip of the island: **Barnegat Lighthouse** (daily; free; 609/494-2016), "Old Barney," whose image appears on personalized New Jersey license plates.

Atlantic City

Midway along the Jersey Shore, the world-famous beach resort of **Atlantic City** (pop. 40,517) has ridden the ups and downs of history. Home of the world's oldest beachfront boardwalk and the first pleasure pier, Atlantic City also spawned the picture postcard and the Miss America beauty contest. Perhaps most significant of all, the street names for Monopoly were taken from Atlantic City, although the city's layout bears little resemblance to the board game (and there's no "Get Out of Jail Free" card, either).

Atlantic City reached its peak at the turn of the 20th century, when thou-

sands of city-dwellers flocked here from New York and Philadelphia each weekend. Later on, as automobiles and airplanes brought better beaches and more exotic locales within reach, Atlantic City went into a half-century of decline until **gambling** was legalized in the 1970s and millions of dollars flowed into the local economy from speculating real-estate developers like Donald Trump, whose name is emblazoned on the massive **Taj Mahal.**

These days, the boardwalk of Atlantic City has been transformed from a derelict relic into a glitzy gambling resort, attracting some 35 million annual visitors and millions of dollars daily to its casinos. It's no Las Vegas, but the clattering of slot machines and the buzz of the craps tables continues 24 hours a day year-round. The **Boardwalk,** backed by a wall of 25-story casino/hotels, is still the main focus, running along the beach for over two miles. Few of the remaining pleasure piers offer much of interest: **Ocean One,** located opposite **Caesars Atlantic City** casino at the foot of Arkansas Avenue, is an anodyne shopping mall on the site of the legendary Million Dollar Pier. Only the rebuilt **Steel Pier,** located opposite Trump's Taj Mahal, holds the traditional seaside rides and arcade games. At the heart of Atlantic City, on the Boardwalk a block south of Park Place, stands the stalwart art deco Convention Center. The largest auditorium in the world when it was built, the convention center was recently revamped and renamed the **Boardwalk Hall Arena,** and is best known as the home of the Miss America beauty pageant.

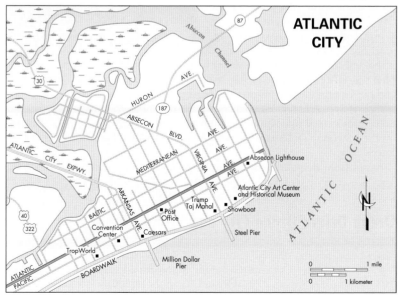

To enjoy a day on the sands at many of New Jersey's beaches, you need to buy (and wear) a beach badge, which costs around $2 a day and is available at local tourist offices, shops, and fast-food stands.

To take the pulse of the Jersey shore's nightlife, tune to **WZXL 100.7 FM,** which advertises nightly events and plays a proven mix of alternative rock hits, from Lou Reed to R.E.M.

Besides comprising Atlantic City's main attractions, the casinos hold most of the places to eat, apart from the dozens of fast-food stands along the Boardwalk. That said, a couple of old favorites stand out from the seedy crowd of ramshackle businesses that fill the nearby streets. One is the birthplace of the "submarine" sandwich, the chrome **White House Sub Shop** (609/345-1564), open until midnight every day at 2301 Arctic Avenue. A block away, but at the other end of the aesthetic and budgetary spectrum, is **Dock's Oyster House** (609/345-0092) at 2405 Atlantic Avenue, a white-linen, dinner-only restaurant that's been serving great seafood since 1871. Along with a number of national chains, the casinos also control accommodation options—expect to pay upwards of $150 a night, since bargains can be hard to find even midweek, midwinter. The newest and most luxurious of the casino resorts is the celebrity-friendly **Borgata** ($180 and up; 609/317-1000), which has plush rooms and a truly fine Italian restaurant, **Specchio**.

For complete listings and more detailed information, contact the Atlantic City **visitors center** (800/262-7395), off the Boardwalk at 2314 Pacific Avenue.

Margate: Lucy the Elephant

Immediately south of Atlantic City, tidy **Margate** (pop. 8,400) fans out along the shore, its solidly suburban streets lined by grand houses. Margate utterly lacks the reckless seaside qualities of its larger neighbor, but does include one classic remnant of the Jersey shore's glory days: **Lucy the Elephant** (daily in summer, limited hours rest of the year; $3; 609/822-6519). The six-story

wood-and-tin pachyderm, a curiosity built by a Philadelphia real-estate speculator in the 1880s to draw customers to his newly laid-out community, looms over the beach at 9200 Atlantic Avenue. The landmark architectural folly was used around the turn of the century as a tavern, and now holds a small museum of local history. Visitors walk through the museum on the way up to an observation deck, which is disguised as a canopied seat on Lucy's back.

Saved from demolition and restored by community efforts in the 1970s, Lucy is ever in need of repair, kept alive by tour monies, donations, and sales of Lucy souvenirs in the small gift shop.

Ocean Drive: Ocean City and Stone Harbor

A series of local roads collectively known as Ocean Drive runs along the south Jersey coast, passing through a number of family-oriented beach resorts, starting at Ocean City, "The Greatest Family Resort for a Vacation, or a Lifetime," 10 miles south of Atlantic City. **Ocean City** (pop. 15,500) was founded as a religious retreat in the late 1870s, and hasn't strayed far from its roots: Every summer morning, life on the Boardwalk promenade comes to a standstill as "The Star-Spangled Banner" blares out from loudspeakers and the American flag is raised at the beachfront amusement park. Located at 6th Street, and known as **Wonderland Pier** (daily in summer, weekends only spring and fall; free admission, fee per ride; 609/399-7082), this old-time funfair has over 30 rides, including a giant Ferris wheel and a 1920s carousel. A block south, you can cool off on a hot summer's day at **Gillian's Water Wonderland.**

Vacation homes, marinas, miniature golf courses, and a pair of toll bridges mark Ocean Drive for the next 20 miles. At **Stone Harbor,** five miles north of Wildwood, the **Wetlands Institute** (daily in summer, closed Sun. & Mon. rest of year; $7; 609/368-1211), at 1075 Stone Harbor Boulevard, is one of the best places to experience the abundant natural life of the New Jersey shore. An observation tower looking over 6,000 acres of saltwater marshland provides excellent bird-watching opportunities, and there's also a museum with a touch-tank and aquarium.

Wildwood

On the Jersey Shore, fun in the sun reaches a peak at raucous **Wildwood,** a trio of interconnected towns housing dozens of nightclubs and New Jersey's biggest beachfront amusement parks. The largest of all, **Mariners Landing** on the pier at Schellenger Avenue, has 35 rides including the largest Ferris wheel on the East Coast. At 25th Street is **Morey's Pier,** which has a miniature golf course that takes you through the history of the New Jersey shore. A little farther south is **Morey's Adventure Pier,** which has the Unites States' only wooden roller coaster built on a pier. All three of these are jointly owned by the Morey family, prime movers behind Wildwood's retro-rediscovery, and an all-ride, all-pier pass (around $40; 609/522-3900) is available for a full day's fun.

Away from the sands in the low-key downtown district at 3907 Pacific Avenue, Wildwood's local history **museum** (free; 609/523-0277) is worth a look for its one unique feature: the **National Marbles Hall of Fame,** featuring thousands of glass balls and more marble-shooting paraphernalia than you've ever seen. The museum, which hosts the National Marbles Championship every June, also has a fascinating and informative display of postcards, documenting the region's recent past.

For many visitors, the best reason to spend time in Wildwood is that the area boasts an extensive collection of 1950s roadside architecture—mainly motel after motel, all sporting exuberant Las Vegas–style neon signs. You can stay the night in one of these classic "Doo Wop" motels—like the **Mango Motel** (609/522-2067) at 209 E. Spicer Avenue, or the renovated **Lollipop Motel** (609/729-2800) at 2300 Atlantic Avenue—or stop for a meal at the chrome-and-glass **Big Ernie's Diner** (609/522-8288), a block south of the main pier at 3801 Atlantic Avenue.

For more details of places to stay and things to do—like October's massive **Thunder on the Beach** monster truck rally—contact the Wildwood **visitors center** (800/992-9732), 3601 Boardwalk.

Cape May

A world away from the carnival atmosphere of the Wildwoods, **Cape May**, the oldest and most serene of the New Jersey beach towns, sits at the southern tip of the state. First settled in the early 1600s, Cape May's glory years ran from the 1850s to the 1890s as an upper-crust summer resort, when it rivaled Newport, Rhode Island, as the destination of choice for the power brokers of Philadelphia and New York City.

A few modern motels and miniature golf courses spread along Cape May's broad beaches, while the compact downtown district retains all its overwrought Victorian splendor. Century-old cottages now house cafés, boutiques, and art galleries, and it seems as if every other building has been converted into a quaint B&B. The town's ornate gingerbread mansions were constructed in the aftermath of a disastrous 1878 fire; among the better examples is the elaborate **Emlen Physick House**, eight blocks north of downtown at 1048 Washington Street, designed by noted Philadelphia architect Frank Furness. It now houses the nonprofit, preservation-oriented **Mid-Atlantic Center for the Arts** and is open as a museum of late Victorian life (daily in summer, weekends only in winter; $8; 609/884-5404).

Pick up walking-tour maps of some of the town's 600 listed historic buildings, and do a taste-test of Cape May's many architecturally magnificent, mostly Victorian-era **bed-and-breakfasts.** These include the mansard-roofed **Queen Victoria** ($95 and up; 609/884-8702) at 102 Ocean Street, and the **Mainstay Inn** ($120 and up; 609/884-8690) at 735 Columbia Avenue, which has a spacious verandah opening on to gorgeous gardens. Cape May's

Cape May Lewes Ferry

Running between the tip of the New Jersey shore and the heart of the Delaware coast, the Cape May–Lewes Ferry carries cars and passengers on a relaxing ride across the mouth of Delaware Bay. The trip costs about $25 for a car and one passenger, plus $6.50 for each additional passenger; bikes are $7, $12.50 round-trip. Schedules change seasonally, with boats leaving about every two hours in summer and every three hours in winter. Crossings take about 90 minutes, and if the seas are calm you can often see porpoises playing in the swells.

For up-to-date times and other information, call 609/886-9699 or 800/643-3779. Reservations ($5 extra) are a very good idea at peak travel times, and should be made at least one day in advance.

oldest and most atmospheric place to stay is the Southern gothic **Chalfonte Hotel** ($80–140; 609/884-8409), located at 301 Howard Street. What the Chalfonte lacks in TVs, telephones, and air-conditioning, it more than makes up for with a bank of rocking chairs, full breakfasts, and huge, down-home dinners—all included in the rates.

Places to eat, including a dozen or so bakeries, cafés, restaurants, and bars, can be found along the pedestrian-friendly few blocks of Washington Street at the center of town. The best seafood restaurants, naturally enough, are near the marina on the north edge of town, off US-9.

DELAWARE

Across Delaware Bay from Cape May, the Delaware shore is considerably quieter and more peaceful than New Jersey's. Both shores, originally settled by Scandinavian whalers who established port colonies here in the early 1600s, share a common history. But because the Delaware shore is that much farther from the urban centers, it has been spared the overdevelopment of much of the rest of the coast. Nevertheless, Delaware's statewide population of half a million doubles in summer as visitors from Baltimore and Washington, D.C., descend upon its coastal resorts, from historic **Lewes** to lively **Rehoboth Beach** to the untouched sands of **Delaware Seashore State Park**, stretching south to the Maryland border.

Lewes and Cape Henlopen

Sitting at the southern lip of Delaware Bay, **Lewes** is a sportfishing center that traces its roots back to 1631, when it was settled by the Dutch West India Company as a whaling port. Though this colony lasted only two years, Lewes calls itself the "First Town in the First State," commemorating its history in the false-gabled brick **Zwannendael Museum** at the center of town (closed Mon.; free). Lewes also harbors huge sand dunes, a fine stretch of beach, and a **campground** with showers in 3,000-acre **Cape Henlopen State Park,** east of town at the mouth of Delaware Bay. Expect relative peace and quiet here, since most visitors, arriving off the Cape May ferry, simply rush through Lewes to the beach resorts farther south. Three meals a day, the best food is at the **Blue Plate Diner** (302/644-8400), near the ferry terminal at 329 Savannah Road.

Rehoboth Beach

Fronting the open Atlantic, **Rehoboth Beach** was founded in the 1870s when church groups bought beach-front land, established the town, and extended a railroad line south from Lewes. The highway frontage along Hwy-1 is over-full of franchise food and factory outlet malls, but the heart of town along Rehoboth Avenue is the place to go. With its small but lively **Funland Amusement Park,** where the rides include bumper cars and a night-time haunted house, and a tidy boardwalk running along the broad beach, Rehoboth has somehow retained a small-town feel despite the many thousands of bureaucrats and power brokers who descend upon the place during the summer, escaping the sweltering heat of Washington, D.C.

The D.C. connection helps explain the town's profusion of very good (and some very expensive) restaurants. Lining the main drag are casual, kid-friendly places like **Dogfish Head** (302/226-BREW) at 320 Rehoboth Avenue, which has great food and killer beers in Delaware's oldest microbrewery. More grown-up palates will be drawn to the gourmet places a block south, where the outrageously kitsch **La La Land** (302/227-3887) at 22 Wilmington Avenue fills a pair of old beach houses alongside the eclectic, Mediterranean-inspired and unfailingly yummy **Espuma** (302/227-4199) at 28 Wilmington Avenue. There are also the more mainstream delights of **Thrashers French Fries,** and sundry beer-and-burger stands along the Boardwalk.

Ever wonder what happens to all those pumpkins that don't get bought by Halloween? In Delaware, they end up as fodder for a unique competition, the **Punkin' Chunkin',** in which the helpless gourds get launched hundreds, even thousands of feet through the air by a variety of mechanical devices. Thousands turn out for the event, which is usually held the first weekend in November; for details, call 302/856-1444.

Places to stay include a barrage of B&Bs and motels, like the **Beach View** ($150; 800/288-5962), on the boardwalk at 6 Wilmington Avenue. There are also weekly cottage rentals and a couple of old-fashioned guesthouses like the **Gladstone Inn** ($80; 302/227-2641) at 3 Olive Drive, with rocking chairs on a cozy front porch that's just 20 yards from the beach.

For more detailed information, stop in at the Rehoboth **visitors center** (302/227-2233 or 800/441-1329), in the old train depot at 501 Rehoboth Avenue.

Delaware Seashore State Park

South from Rehoboth stretches one of the most pristine lengths of beach on the northern East Coast: **Delaware Seashore State Park** (302/227-3071), which contains six miles of open beach with golden-flecked white sand and acres of marshland estuary, thronged in season with migrating birds—and bird-watchers (and campers and anglers, too.) The park's many beaches are all easily accessible from beachfront Hwy-1.

The park has camping and nice new cottages (costing $1,500 a week in summer!), and is book-ended by a pair of beachfront resort towns. **Dewey Beach** in the north draws a younger, collegiate crowd, while **Bethany Beach** in the south attracts more families. Approaching Maryland, the 1858 **Fenwick Island Lighthouse,** on the bay side of Hwy-1 just south of Hwy-54, marks the state border. This lighthouse is a local landmark, but the waist-high white marker in front of it may be more significant: Placed in 1751, it marked the boundary between Maryland and Pennsylvania, of which Delaware was then a part. Showing respect to the colonial proprietors, the more than 250-year-old marker has the Calvert Family coat of arms on the Maryland (south) side, and William Penn's family crest on the other.

MARYLAND

Maryland, the most oddly shaped of the lower 48 states, shares the broad "DelMarVa" peninsula with Delaware and a small piece of Virginia. The inland area along the eastern shore of Chesapeake Bay, with its many inlets and tributary rivers, is filled with dozens of small colonial-era towns and fishing villages, while the Atlantic Coast is completely taken up by two very different beasts: the gloriously kitschy beach resort of **Ocean City** and the untrammelled wilds of **Assateague Island National Seashore.** Heading inland around Assateague, the highway passes by a number of historic small towns, including **Berlin** and captivating **Snow Hill.**

Running west from Ocean City across the Eastern Shore, and across the country to California is the US-50 route (see page 721). This **Loneliest Road** in America is covered on pages 636–721.

Ocean City

About the only place left on the entire East Coast that retains the carnival qualities of classic seaside resorts, **Ocean City** (pop. 7,173, swelling to some 400,000 in summer) has by far the best array of old-time fun-fair attractions in the Mid-Atlantic (well, south of Wildwood, New Jersey, at least). On and around the main **Ocean Pier** at the south end of the island, there are enough merry-go-rounds, Ferris wheels, roller coasters (including "The Hurricane," which is illustrated with scenes from Ocean City storms past), mini-golf courses, haunted houses, and bumper cars to divert a small army. A block inland, **Trimper's Amusements,** in business since the 1890s, has two more roller coasters, plus a Tilt-a-Whirl, a 100-year-old Hershell carousel, and a spooky haunted house.

To go along with its great beaches, Ocean City has a radio station, the excellent **WOCM 98.1 FM** playing classic rock 'n' roll and broadcasting details of Ocean City's nightclub scene.

From the pier north, Ocean City stretches for over two miles along a broad, clean, white-sand beach. A wide, part-wooden boardwalk lines the sands, packed with arcades full of video games and a few nearly forgotten old amusements like skee-ball and pokerino, not to mention midway contests—the kind where, for $1 a try, you can win stuffed animals and other prizes by shooting baskets or squirting water into clowns' mouths. A ramshackle collection of fortune-tellers, T-shirt stands, and burger-and-beer bars completes the scene, forming a busy gauntlet that is among the nation's liveliest promenades.

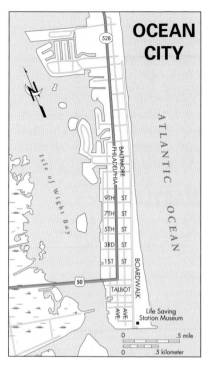

On summer weekends, Ocean City becomes Maryland's second-largest city, and most of the fun is simply in getting caught up in the garish human spectacle of it all, but there are a couple of specific things worth searching out. For the price of a bumper car ride, you can enjoy the quirky collections of the **Life-Saving Station Museum** (daily May–Oct., weekends only in winter; $3), at the south end of the boardwalk, where alongside displays of shipwrecks and bathing suits you can compare and contrast bowls full of sand from 100 different beaches around the world. The museum also marks the starting point for the open-air **trams** ($2.50) that run north along the boardwalk for over two miles.

Much of Ocean City's charm is decidedly lowbrow, but the **food** is better than you might expect, with numerous places offering plates full of shrimp and pitchers of beer for under $10, and fresh-fried chicken or crab cakes available from boardwalk stands like **Dayton Brothers Chicken House**, across from the Life Saving Station. **Thrashers Fries** are available (no ketchup; salt and vinegar only!) from a number of counters along the boardwalk, and you can top them off with a cone or milkshake from **Dumser's Ice Cream**, near the Wax Museum at the south end of the boardwalk.

Places to stay are also abundant. Of the grand, older hotels, only the **Atlantic Hotel** ($60–115; 410/289-9111 or 800/328-5268), on the oceanfront at Wicomico Street, is still open for business; modern motels like the **Oceanic** (410/289-6494), looking across the inlet to Assateague Island from 106 S. 1st Street, charge as much as $200 a night for a room that goes for less than $50 off-season.

For complete listings of lodgings and restaurants, contact the Ocean City **visitors center** (410/289-2800 or 800/OC-OCEAN), in the Convention Center at 4001 Coastal Highway.

Assateague Island National Seashore

At one time, Assateague Island, the long thin barrier island on which Ocean City sits, stretched in an unbroken line all the way into Virginia. In 1933, a major storm created the broad inlet that now divides Ocean City from the near-wilderness of **Assateague Island National Seashore.** One of the few areas of the Atlantic coast protected from commercial development, Assateague Island offers some 37 miles and 10,000 acres of hiking, swimming, camping, canoeing, clamming, and bird-watching. Swarms of voracious mosquitoes, and a lack of fresh water, keep the crowds to a minimum.

To reach the island from Ocean City, follow US-50 west for two miles and turn south on Hwy-611, which loops around Sinexpunt Bay before arriving at the **visitors center** (daily; 410/641-3030). The center has a small aquarium as well as maps, guides, and up-to-date information about the national seashore.

Berlin and Snow Hill

From Ocean City, the route turns inland around Assateague Island and Chincoteague Bay, following US-50 west for eight miles, then turning south on US-113 through the dark cypress swamps along the Pocomoke River. Just southwest of the US-50/113 junction, the remarkably well-preserved town of **Berlin** offers a look back at a slower-paced era. Redbrick buildings house antique shops around the 1890s

landmark **Atlantic Hotel** ($95 and up; 410/641-0189) at 2 Main Street, where the row of rocking chairs along the open-air front porch all but demand you to sit and stay a while.

Another 15 miles southwest of Ocean City, detour west from the highway to take a look at the 250-year-old town of **Snow Hill** (pop. 2,200). The **Julia A. Purnell Museum** (Tues.–Sun. April–Nov. only; $2), housed in an old church at 208 W. Market Street, features a range of exhibits tracing Eastern Shore history. Pick up a walking-tour map of Snow Hill's many significant structures, or if the weather's fine, paddle a canoe through the surrounding wild cypress swamps with the **Pocomoke River Canoe Company** (410/632-3971), at 312 N. Washington Street, next to the drawbridge.

VIRGINIA

Virginia's Eastern Shore is among the most isolated re-gions of the country, and its dozens of small towns and villages remain much as they have for centuries. Everything on the Eastern Shore is on a much smaller scale than on the mainland, and the many stands selling fresh corn and tomatoes along the roadside attest to the important role farming plays in the local economy. Although fast-food places, chicken-processing plants, and a couple of modern malls dot US-13, the main route through Virginia's Eastern Shore, the area is still mostly rural and undeveloped, with business loops turn-ing off through the many well-preserved old towns. The numerous historic sites include colonial-era plantations and archaeological remnants of Native American tribes.

The highlight for most visitors is **Chincoteague**, a small commercial and sportfishing port sitting at the entrance to massive **Chincoteague National Wildlife Refuge**, which faces the Atlantic Coast and offers the only ocean beaches in this part of the state. South of Chincoteague, US-13 runs down the center of the narrow Eastern Shore peninsula, giving access to the Chesapeake Bay waterfront at **Onancock**, then passing through numerous small towns like **Accomac** and **Eastville**, neither of which has changed much since Revolutionary times. Crossing the mouth of the Chesapeake Bay via a 23-mile-long bridge

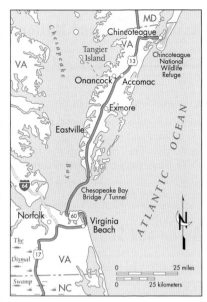

and tunnel brings you to maritime Norfolk and the state's main Atlantic resort, Virginia Beach, before the route turns inland and south into North Carolina.

Chincoteague

The drive into **Chincoteague** (pop. 4,317; SCHINK-a-teeg), a low-key fishing village, takes you across miles of glowing gold and blue marshlands through a gauntlet of quirky billboards advertising local motels, restaurants, and sportfishing charters. This mix of natural beauty and tacky tourism aptly reflects the character of the town, which is totally dependent upon summertime visitors but seems to wish that we'd all just leave and let the locals go fishing.

A small bridge along Hwy-175, which runs 10 miles east from US-17, drops you at the heart of town, where casual seafood restaurants like the **Landmark Crab House** (757/336-5552) line the small wharves that stretch along the bay. For oysters, go to **Capt. Fish's** (757/336-5528) at 3865 Main Street and sample them for around $8 a dozen. For breakfast, head south of town to the end of Ridge Road, where the popular **Island Family** (757/336-1198) serves up hearty meals across from the "pony swim" landing.

Among the many places to stay are several nice B&Bs and a handful of standard motels like the friendly and central **Birchwood** (757/336-6133) at 3650 N. Main Street.

For more-complete listings and other information, contact the Chincoteague **visitors center** (757/336-6161), located at 6733 Maddox Boulevard.

Chincoteague National Wildlife Refuge

The **Chincoteague National Wildlife Refuge** is one of the largest nature preserves along the Atlantic flyway, attracting hundreds of species of birds, including egrets, herons, geese, and swans, and thousands of migrating ducks. A

continuation of the Assateague Island National Seashore across the Maryland border
(see above), the refuge contains hundreds of
acres of marshland, excellent beaches, and a
number of hiking and cycling trails. The
refuge **visitors center** (daily; 757/336-6122)
has detailed information on park activities as
well as special exhibits on Chincoteague's famous **wild ponies,** which can usually be seen
from the Woodland Trail that loops south
from Beach Road.

South of town at the end of Main Street, just outside the
refuge boundary, you can pitch a tent or park an RV at the
privately owned **Tom's Cove Campground** (757/336-6498).

Accomac

One of the most photogenic spots on the Eastern Shore, **Accomac** (pop. 547) is centered around an ancient-looking redbrick courthouse, flanked by a series of wooden sheds
converted into professional offices. The old library next door
dates from the 1780s and was used for years as a debtor's
prison; the library, courthouse, and surrounding buildings
comprise one of the more extensive collections of colonial-era
buildings in the country. By way of contrast, Accomac is also
home to a huge Perdue Chicken processing plant, right along
US-13.

The children's story
Misty of Chincoteague
is set in the area and
tells how wild ponies—
whose ancestors were
sent here by English
settlers in the late
1600s—are rounded up
from the wildlife refuge
on Assateague Island for
a forced swim across to
Chincoteague. The
annual roundup, swim,
and auction benefits
local firefighters and
attracts thousands of
spectators. The swim
takes place the last
Wednesday in July, and
the auction follows the
next day.

Onancock and Tangier Island

The picturesque harbor town of **Onancock** (pop. 1,525, o-
NAN-cock), on the Chesapeake Bay two miles west of US-13
via Hwy-179, is one of the nicest towns on the Eastern Shore.
A short walking tour of over a dozen historical homes and
churches begins at perhaps the finest mansion on the Eastern
Shore, the **Kerr Place** (Tues.–Sat. 10 AM–4 PM; $3) at 69
Market Street, built in 1799 and now home to the offices and museum of the
Eastern Shore Historical Society (757/787-8012). Another historic curiosity is
the 150-year-old **Hopkins and Bros. General Store,** on the wharf at 2 Market
Street, which in the past has sold everything from sweet potatoes to postcards—
and now serves as a sort of mini welcome center. A great taste of Onancock life
awaits inside the **Corner Bakery** (757/787-4520), at 36 Market Street, where
great doughnuts and fresh coffee are served up to a mostly local crowd, while a
great place for dinner is **Armando's** (757/787-8044) at 10 North Street, serving
a mix of Italian and South American food that's good enough to plan a weekend
around. After dinner, catch a flick at Onancock's nifty 1950s movie theater, the
Roseland (757/787-2209) on Market Street; and to savor it all, stay the night at
the lovingly restored Victorian-era **Montrose House** ($90 and up; 757/787-
8887), set in gorgeous Italianate gardens, off Market Street near Hwy-13.

In summer, stands
selling fresh fruit and
vegetables—particularly
sweet corn and
tomatoes—dot
roadsides all over
the Eastern Shore.

Onancock was born and grew up around its natural deep-water harbor, and the town wharf is still the place to catch the seasonal ferry across Chesapeake Bay to **Tangier Island,** an evocative old place where things seem to have hardly changed since colonial times. The few hundred people who live here year-round have a unique and almost indecipherably archaic accent—which some trace back to 17th-century Cornwall, England—and earn their livelihoods catching crabs and the occasional oyster from Chesapeake Bay. Tangier Island is best known for its soft-shell crabs, which are sold all over the eastern United States.

Visiting Tangier Island is easy, but takes some advance planning. Boats leave once a day from Onancock Wharf ($24; 757/891-2240); travel time is one hour and 15 minutes each way, leaving around 10 AM and returning around 3 PM. This means visitors returning on the ferry have only about two hours on the island, though **Shirley's Bay View Inn** (757/891-2396) and **Hilda Crockett's Chesapeake House** (757/891-2331) make an overnight stay possible (each charges around $100 a night), which is about the only way to have any kind of close encounter with the tourist-shy locals. Hilda's also serves meals, and good seafood is available at the **Fisherman's Corner Restaurant** (757/891-2900). Bike rentals are available on the island, no part of which of which is more than 5 feet above sea level.

Eastville

You can get a good idea of just how rural and quiet life is on Virginia's Eastern Shore by visiting **Eastville** (pop. 185), the seat of Northampton County. A mile west of US-13 on a well-marked business loop, Eastville centers on the redbrick courthouse and old county jail, with a handful of even older buildings dating back to the mid-1700s. Eastville also has a couple of roadside crab shacks along US-13: "**Just Seafood**" on the north edge of town sells crab cakes and fish-and-chips, while the **Great Machipongo Clam Shack** has crabmeat sandwiches and fresh steamed clams, grown and picked by the owners.

Before the Chesapeake Bay Bridge/Tunnel was completed in 1964, ferries linking the Eastern Shore with the mainland docked at **Cape Charles,** west of US-13 eight miles south of Eastville. Barges still use the harbor, ferrying freight trains across the bay.

Chesapeake Bay Bridge/Tunnel

One of the more impressive engineering feats on the East Coast is the **Chesapeake Bay Bridge/Tunnel,** which opened in 1964 at the mouth of the Chesapeake Bay, and was effectively doubled in 1997 by the addition of an extra set of driving lanes. Almost 18 miles long and charging a $10 toll, the structure consists of one high-level bridge, two deep tunnels, four islands, and many miles of raised causeway. At the north end of the bridge, there's the large and very pleasant **Sunset Beach Resort** ($80; 757/331-4786), and two miles from the southern end of the bridge, a fishing pier and restaurant operate on a man-made island.

CHESAPEAKE BAY BRIDGE – TUNNEL

Virginia Beach

From the toll plaza at the southern end of the Chesapeake Bay Bridge, US-60 heads east along Atlantic Avenue, passing through the woodland waterfront of **First Landing State Park** before winding up at the ocean and **Virginia Beach** (pop. 435,000), the state's most populous (and fastest-growing) city, and its one and only beach resort. Ten-story hotels line the main drag, Atlantic Avenue, which is plastered with large signs banning cars from "cruising" the mile-long array of fun-fairs, surf shops, and nightclubs.

Unlike many coastal towns, Virginia Beach also boasts a significant history. Virginia's first colonists landed at Virginia Beach on April 26, 1607, before settling upriver at Jamestown; the site is marked by a stone cross at Cape Henry, at the southern lip of Chesapeake Bay. The **visitors bureau** (800/822-3224), on the west side of town at 2100 Parks Avenue, has walking- and driving-tour maps of Virginia Beach's many historic houses, and can point you toward the area's excellent **Virginia Marine Sciences Museum** (daily; $12; 757/425-3474), at 717 General Booth Boulevard, which has nearly a million gallons of sharks, sting rays, barracudas, and sea turtles, and an IMAX theater.

Dining options tend toward seafood restaurants hidden away in the resort hotels, though the **Maple Tree Pancake House** (757/425-6796), at 2608 Atlantic Avenue, is a great breakfast stop and the **Jewish Mother** (757/422-5430) at 3108 Pacific Avenue serves up good deli sandwiches, and doubles as a popular nightclub.

Perhaps the best reason to stop at Virginia Beach is that accommodations are much cheaper here than elsewhere in the area: Dorm beds at **Angie's Guest Cottage HI Hostel** (757/428-4690) at 302 24th Street cost under $20 a night, and a room at a locally run place like the **Golden Sands Inn** ($80–130; 757/428-1770), at 1312 Atlantic Avenue, will be cheaper than any of the national chains. Campers will appreciate the fine facilities at **First Landing State Park** (757/412-2300).

Norfolk

During colonial times, **Norfolk** (pop. 234,403; NAW-fik) was the largest city in Virginia and one of the busiest ports in North America. It's still very much connected with the water, which you can experience first-hand at the **Nauticus National Maritime Center** (daily in summer, closed Mon. rest of year; $9.95; 757/664-1000), where the engaging displays inside are dwarfed by the massive hulk of the battleship USS *Wisconsin* moored alongside. Away from the waterfront, Norfolk has a couple more worthwhile destinations, including the lovely **Chrysler Museum** (closed Mon. & Tues.; $7; 757/664-6200), on the north side of downtown off Olney Road and

The two deepwater harbors near Norfolk at the mouth of the Chesapeake Bay, **Newport News,** and **Hampton Roads,** are the headquarters of the U.S. Navy's Atlantic Fleet and together form the world's largest naval base.

If you see or hear warnings about **shark attacks,** take them seriously. In recent years many swimmers have been badly injured or killed by sharks, even in very shallow water.

Virginia Beach is home to the **Association for Research and Enlightenment** (800/333-4499), at 67th and Atlantic, which is dedicated to continuing the legacy of early American psychic Edgar Cayce, offering classes in ESP—but you already knew that, didn't you?

DOUGLAS MacARTHUR

6¢ US

stop for a bite at Doumar's

Duke Street. The personal art collection of Walter Chrysler, the self-educated engineer who created one of the "Big Three" car companies and built New York's Chrysler Building, is displayed inside a commodious Italianate building. Norfolk, a staunch Navy town, also holds the final resting place of controversial U.S. Army Gen. Douglas MacArthur, preserved alongside his personal papers (and his 1950 Chrysler Imperial limousine) at the **MacArthur Memorial** (daily; free), inside Norfolk's old City Hall building at Bank and Plume Streets downtown.

Even if you're just racing through, bound for the beach, Norfolk has one place where you really ought to stop and eat: **Doumar's Cones and BBQ** (757/627-4163), a half mile north of downtown at 19th Street and Monticello Avenue. Besides being a real old-fashioned drive-in, this place stakes a claim to having invented the ice cream cone, since the owner's uncle, Abe Doumar, sold the first ones at the 1904 St. Louis World's Fair. They still sell great handmade cones, very good BBQ sandwiches, and a thirst-quenching limeade. Pass by at your peril. . . .

The **Norfolk Tides** (757/622-2222), Class AAA farm team of the New York Mets, play at beautiful Harbor Park, off I-264 at Waterside Drive, where you can watch big ships sail past. Games are broadcast on **WGH 1310 AM.**

For a stylish but inexpensive place to stay, try the historic **Clarion James Madison** ($79–139; 757/622-6682), at 345 Granby Street.

From Norfolk, you can take US-17 south across the aptly named Great Dismal Swamp, or follow the faster Hwy-168, which takes you past a feast of roadside fruit stands, BBQ shacks, and junk shops, straight down to Kitty Hawk and the Outer Banks of North Carolina.

NORTH CAROLINA

Wild Atlantic beaches, a handful of tiny fishing villages, and some of the country's most significant historic sites make coastal North Carolina a great place to visit. A highlight for many vacationers is the **Outer Banks,** miles of barrier islands where busy resort towns like **Nags Head** contrast with the stretches of pristine beaches protected on the **Cape Hatteras National Seashore.** Besides golden sands, the Outer Banks area includes two evocative historic sites: the dunes at **Kitty Hawk,** where the Wright Brothers first took to the air, and **Roanoke Island,** site of the first ill-fated English effort to colonize the New World. Farther south, beyond the quirky, small city of Wilmington, a movie-making mecca, the 300-mile coastal route turns inland around **Cape Fear,** heading toward the South Carolina border.

Kitty Hawk: The Wright Brothers National Memorial

Alternately known as Killy Hauk, Kitty Hock, and Killy Honk before its current name came into general use, **Kitty Hawk** to most people means one thing: the Wright Brothers' first powered airplane flight more than a century ago, on December 17, 1903. Lured by the steady winds that blow in from the Atlantic and by the high sand dunes that cover the shore, Wilbur and Orville Wright first came to the Outer Banks in 1900, and returned every year thereafter with prototype kites and gliders built out of bi-

cycle parts that they fine-tuned to create the world's first airplane. Their tale is truly one of the great adventure and success stories of the modern age, and the site of their experiments has been preserved as the **Wright Brothers National Memorial.** First stop is the **visitors center** (daily; $3; 252/441-7430), which includes a number of exhibits tracing the history of human efforts to fly. Every hour, rangers give engaging talks alongside a full-sized replica of the Wright Brothers' first plane.

The most affecting aspect of the memorial is the unchanged site where the brothers first flew. Each of the first four flights is marked by stones set on the grassy field. The first flight, with Orville at the controls flying into a 25-mph headwind, lasted 12 seconds and covered just 120 feet—barely more than a

Orville and Wilbur Wright

brisk walking pace. The 90-foot-high sand dune where Wilbur and Orville first took to the air has been planted over with grasses to keep it from blow-

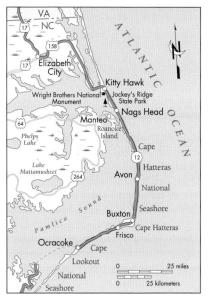

ing away. A series of paths climbs to the top of the dune, where a 60-foot, wing-shaped granite pylon is inscribed with the words:

In commemoration of the conquest of the air by the brothers Wilbur and Orville Wright. Conceived by genius, achieved by dauntless resolution and unconquerable faith.

The park is off US-158, on the inland side of the highway, two miles south of the Wright Memorial Bridge from the mainland. Though the memorial is definitely worth an extended visit, the towns around it are a bit disappointing—both Kitty Hawk and Kill Devil Hills are little more than narrow strips of commercial development.

The Outer Banks

The geography of the Outer Banks, a series of barrier islands stretching for over 200 miles along the coast of North Carolina, has changed dramatically over time, thanks to hurricanes and winter storms, not to mention human hands. Until a series of lighthouses was built beginning in the late 18th century, the islands and the offshore shoals were so treacherous they became known as the "Graveyard of the Atlantic."

Nowadays, the same places where pirates once plundered are given over to wind-surfing, hang-gliding, kite-surfing, sportfishing, and beachcombing, as the Outer Banks (sometimes abbreviated "OBX") have become a tourist and recreation destination par excellence. The resident population of some 30,000 swells to accommodate over six million annual visitors, but unlike its nearest comparison, Cape Cod, the Outer Banks area boasts only a few colonial towns. Instead, substantial development during the ongoing building boom has covered the sands with an ugly sprawl of vacation homes and time-share condos perched—often on stilts to protect them from storm damage—directly on the broad Atlantic beaches. Most of the development has taken place in the north along two parallel roads: US-158, usually called "The Bypass" but also known as "Croatan Highway"; and oceanfront Hwy-12, aka "Virginia Dare Trail" and "Beach Road." Mileposts on both roads mark distances from north to south. There's plentiful lodging in the many little towns along Hwy-12; gas stations and fast-food restaurants line US-158. The exception to the commercial sprawl is the magical 75 miles of the Cape Hatteras National Seashore.

Along the northern Outer Banks, bridges link Nags Head and Kitty Hawk with the mainland, though access to the less-developed southern parts of the Outer Banks is limited to ferry boats, all of which carry cars. For detailed listings and other visitor info, contact the Outer Banks **visitors bureau** (877/OBX-4-FUN).

Jockey's Ridge State Park

The windswept 110-foot-high twin sand dunes of **Jockey's Ridge State Park** (daily; free; 252/441-7132) tower over US-158 between Kitty Hawk and Nags Head. The highest sand dunes on the East Coast, Jockey's Ridge barely survived being bulldozed in the 1970s to form yet another Outer Banks resort; it's now one of the prime hang-gliding spots in the country—remember the Wright Brothers! Jockey's Ridge is also a nice place to wander the short boardwalk nature trail that points out the diverse plants and animals of the dune community. You may want to take your shoes off and scamper around the sands barefoot. If you feel especially daring, **Kitty Hawk Kites** across the highway at milepost 10.5 dubs itself the "World's Largest Hang-Gliding School" and offers **lessons** ($65 and up; 252/441-4124 or 800/334-4777) and equipment, plus anything else you might need to make the most of your time here.

Nags Head

The towns of the northern Outer Banks overlap each other so much it can be hard to tell you are in **Nags Head**, six miles south of Kitty Hawk. One of the oldest and most popular resorts in the region, Nags Head also offers the widest range of visitor facilities. Good places to spend a night or two include a beachfront roadside classic at Milepost 16.5: the historic **Sea Foam Motel** ($65–150; 252/441-7320), at 7111 S. Dare Trail, one of the last surviving 1940s motels on the Outer Banks. The pine-paneled walls, vivid tiles, and slamming screen doors will take you back to a simpler time. Nearby, the even more atmospheric **First Colony Inn** ($75–200; 252/441-2343), along US-158 at milepost 16, was moved from its valuable oceanfront location to the middle of the island and completely renovated in 1988, and now offers oodles of old-fashioned charm along with a delicious breakfast and afternoon tea.

One more long-standing local landmark, **Sam & Omie's** (252/441-7366), near the east end of US-64 at milepost 16.5, has featured inexpensive but well-prepared family fare, three meals a day, for over 50 years.

If you're traveling along the Carolina coast in summer, be aware that the hurricane season begins in June and lasts through the end of November. These are deadly serious storms, so take heed of any warnings, and follow the evacuation instructions broadcast over radio and TV networks.

The name Nags Head is derived from the practices of Outer Banks pirates, who tied lanterns around the heads of their horses to simulate boats bobbing at anchor. The lanterns lured passing ships onto shore, where they ran aground on the offshore sandbars.

Roanoke Island: Fort Raleigh National Historic Site

From an area known as Whalebone Junction at the south end of Nags Head, US-64 runs west over a causeway and bridge to **Roanoke Island,** site of the first English settlement in North America. The legendary "Lost Colony" was first established in 1585 by Sir Walter Raleigh, but the effort was not a success, and the survivors returned to England. In 1587, a larger expedition of 110 colonists arrived, including 17 women and nine children, but because of the difficulties involved in crossing the Atlantic Ocean, there was no further contact with England until 1590. By that time, the settlers had disappeared without a trace, which prompted numerous theories about their fate. Now, amidst an eerily dark forest, the colony's original earthwork fortress has been excavated and reconstructed as the centerpiece of the **Fort Raleigh National Historic Site.** Exhibits inside the visitors center (daily; free; 252/473-5772) include a few rusty artifacts and dry displays explaining the historical context of the colonial effort. There are also copies of the many beautiful watercolors and drawings of native plants, animals, and people produced by the

Raleigh's flagship, *Ark Raleigh*

Hundreds of ancient ships and unfortunate sailors met their watery end in the shallow waters off Cape Hatteras. The remains of over 2,000 vessels lie along the entire Carolina coastline; a few are visible from shore at low tide.

Throughout the summer, a waterfront theater adjacent to Fort Raleigh presents a popular production of *Lost Colony,* which dramatizes the events of the ill-fated settlement. Call for details or tickets ($16–20 adults, $8 under 11; 252/473-3414 or 800/488-5012).

original expedition's two immensely talented scientists, John White and Thomas Hariot.

The historic port of **Manteo** (pop. 1,052; MAN-tee-o), in the middle of Roanoke Island between Fort Raleigh and the beach resorts of the Outer Banks, was named for the Native American who helped Sir Walter Raleigh and the Lost Colony. Manteo is the only county seat in North Carolina that's located on an island. You can still sense the town's proud seagoing history as you walk along the quiet streets near the tidied-up waterfront. Surrounded by pleasure boats, the main attraction here is the *Elizabeth II* (daily in summer, closed Mon. rest of the year; $3), a full-sized, square-rigged replica of the type of ship that carried colonists here from England 400-odd years ago.

Cape Hatteras National Seashore

The first piece of coastline to be protected as a national park, **Cape Hatteras National Seashore** stretches for 75 miles along the Atlantic Ocean. Starting in the north at Nags Head, and continuing south along slender Bodie, Hatteras, and Ocracoke Islands, the area preserved within Cape Hatteras National Seashore is the largest undeveloped section of coastline on the East Coast, providing an increasingly rare glimpse of nature amidst ever-encroaching development. The few old fishing villages that stood here when the seashore was set aside in the 1930s are unfortunately exempt from the anti-development prohibitions of the National Seashore, and have grown ugly and unwieldy. Nevertheless, the many miles in between remain almost entirely untouched.

Warmed by the Gulf Stream currents, the Outer Banks beaches are some of the best in the world, but the waters do not warm up appreciably until south of Oregon Inlet, and swimming in the northern stretches remains quite invigorating until July.

For many visitors, the highlight of the National Seashore is the historic Cape Hatteras Lighthouse, a mile west of Hwy-12 at the south end of Hatteras Island. Others come here to enjoy the warm waters and strong, steady winds—two areas of Pamlico Sound on the inland side of Cape Hatteras have been set aside for windsurfers, dozens of whom flock here on summer days to what's considered one of the finest board-sailing and kite-surfing spots in the United States. And of course, there are miles of open beaches, perfect for aimless strolling.

At the north end of Cape Hatteras, eight miles south of Nags Head, there's a National Seashore **visitors center** (daily; 252/473-2111) and a nature trail winding along Pamlico Sound at the foot of **Bodie Island Lighthouse,** the first of three historic towers along the Hatteras coast. On the ocean side of Hwy-12, **Coquina Beach** has a broad strand, lifeguards and showers in summer, and the remains of a wooden schooner that was wrecked here in the 1920s.

Cape Hatteras Lighthouse, Cape Hatteras, N. C.

Continuing south, across the Oregon Inlet (where there's a first-come, first-served campground), Hwy-12 runs through the 6,000-acre **Pea Island National Wildlife Refuge,** which was established in 1938 to protect the nesting grounds of loggerhead sea turtles, as well as the coastal wetlands essential to the survival of the greater snow goose and other migratory waterfowl. South of the refuge, a few short barrages of vacation condos and roadside sprawl—go-cart parks, mini-golf courses, and a KOA Kampground—line the highway between Rodanthe and Salvo, before the road reaches the heart of the park, where high sand dunes rise along 15 miles of undeveloped oceanfront.

The section of Pamlico Sound known as **Canadian Hole,** between the towns of Avon and Buxton, is rated as one of the best windsurfing spots on the East Coast.

Hurricanes!

If you're traveling along the East Coast in late summer, be aware that the farther south you go the more likely you are to encounter one of Mother Nature's most powerful phenomena, the hurricane. All across the southeastern United States, hurricane season begins in June and lasts through November, and the threat of a storm can put a sudden end to the summer fun. Hurricanes are tropical storms covering upwards of 400 square miles, with winds reaching speeds of 75 to 150 mph or more. These storms form as far away as Africa, and sophisticated warning systems are in place to give coastal visitors plenty of time to get out of harm's way. Radio and TV stations broadcast storm watches and evacuation warnings, and if you hear one, heed it and head inland to higher ground.

Even more dangerous than the high winds of a hurricane is the storm surge—a dome of ocean water that can be 20 feet high at its peak, and 50 to 100 miles wide. Ninety percent of hurricane fatalities are attributable to the high waves of a storm surge, which can wash away entire beaches and intensify flooding in coastal rivers and bays many miles upstream from the shore. The strongest hurricane recorded in the United States was the Labor Day storm of 1935, which killed 500 people and destroyed the Florida Keys Railroad. More recent hurricanes include Hurricane Andrew in 1992, which killed 54 people and caused more than $25 billion worth of damage, and the multiple 'canes that pounded Florida in 2004. More recent hurricanes include Hurricane Andrew in 1992, which killed 54 people and caused more than $25 billion worth of damage, and the multiple 'canes that pounded Florida in 2004. The levee breaks which flooded New Orleans made Hurricane Katrina by far the most costly hurricane, but the deadliest hurricane on record hit Galveston Island, Texas in 1900, killing more than 6,000 people—the worst natural disaster in United States history.

Blackbeard the Pirate

Wandering around the idyllic harbor of Ocracoke, it's hard to imagine that the waters offshore were once home to perhaps the most ferocious pirate who ever sailed the Seven Seas—Blackbeard. The archetypal pirate, even in his day, when piracy was common, Blackbeard was famous for his ruthlessness and violence as much as for his long black beard and exotic battle dress, wearing six pistols on twin gunbelts slung over his shoulders and slashing hapless opponents with a mighty cutlass. His pirate flag featured a heart dripping blood, and a skeleton toting an hourglass in one hand and a spear in the other.

For all his near-mythic status, Blackbeard's career as a pirate was fairly short. After serving as an English privateer in the Caribbean during Queen Anne's War, in 1713 Blackbeard (whose real name was Edward Teach) turned to piracy, learning his trade under the pirate Benjamin Hornigold. Outfitted with four stolen ships, 40 cannons, and a crew of 300 men, Blackbeard embarked on a reign of terror that took him up and down the Atlantic coast of the American colonies. After five years of thieving cargoes and torturing sailors, Blackbeard was confronted off Ocracoke by forces lead by Lt. Robert Maynard of the Royal Navy, and during a ferocious battle on November 22, 1718, the pirate and most of his men were killed. Blackbeard himself was stabbed 25 times, and his head was sliced off and hung like a trophy on the bowsprit of his captor's ship.

Though there is no evidence that he ever buried any treasure anywhere near Ocracoke, Blackbeard's ship, the *Queen Anne's Revenge,* was discovered in 1996 off Bogue Bank, and objects recovered from it are being preserved by the North Carolina Maritime Museum in Beaufort. Blackbeard's legend, to be sure, lives on.

Avon and Buxton: Cape Hatteras Lighthouse

At the rough midpoint of Hatteras Island, the vacation town of **Avon** stretches for a couple of miles along Hwy-12 before the road hits the Canadian Hole windsurfing area, two miles south of town. After another few miles of natural dunes, the road bends sharply to the west; continuing south here brings you to the main Cape Hatteras **visitors center** (daily in summer only; 252/995-4474), and the famous **Cape Hatteras Lighthouse.** At 208 feet, the black-and-white-striped lighthouse is the tallest brick lighthouse in the United States, visible from as far as 25 miles. However, because the ocean here has been slowly eroding away the beach (when the lighthouse was built in 1870, it was a quarter mile from the waves; by 1995 the coast was a mere 120 feet away from its base), in 1999 the National Park Service succeeded in lifting the 3,000-ton lighthouse onto rails and shifting it a quarter mile inland. If you feel fit, climb ($6) the stairs (12 stories' worth, each way) to the top of the lighthouse for a grand view—one that gives the clearest sense of just how narrow and transitive the Outer Banks really are.

Farther along, at the end of this road, there's a summer-only, first-come, first-served **campground.**

From the Cape Hatteras Lighthouse, Hwy-12 bends west and south through **Buxton** and **Frisco,** where you will find a gauntlet of motels, gas stations, and fast-food restaurants at the commercial center of Cape Hatteras. The very popular **Fish House** (252/995-5151) is on the main highway next to Cape Hatteras High School. Buxton's motels, like the **Lighthouse View** (252/995-5680 or 800/225-7651) or the **Falcon** (252/995-5968 or 800/635-6911), are reasonably priced (under $100 in summer) and clean. Ocean beaches here at the very tip of the cape are among the most spectacular anywhere; south-facing, they tend to pick up some of the most extreme surf—especially when hurricanes hit—which is why Buxton and Frisco are the local surfing capitals.

More restaurants and motels (including a Holiday Inn Express) await you in **Hatteras,** at the southern end of the island. From here, state-run **ferries** (5 AM–midnight; free) shuttle every half hour across to Ocracoke Island, another mostly unspoiled barrier island where you'll find great beaches and the pretty village of Ocracoke, at the island's southern tip.

The village of Frisco, five miles north of the Hatteras ferry terminal, holds the small but surprisingly good **Native American Museum** (closed Mon.; $2; 252/995-4440), which boasts an extensive collection of artifacts from several tribes including those from the Cape Hatteras area, and Hopi and Navajo crafts.

Ocracoke

About the only Outer Banks town that hasn't lost its small-scale charm, **Ocracoke** is a great place to spend an afternoon or two, walking or cycling along unpaved back streets lined by overgrown gardens and weathered old homes. Since it's easy to reach from the mainland, via ferries from Swan Quarter and from Cedar Island, Ocracoke is a popular destination, but the tourism here is so low-key it still feels like a place you can discover for yourself.

The ferries from the mainland drop you at the heart of town, but coming in from the north on Hwy-12, you pass through a short strip of real estate agencies and restaurants like **Howard's Pub** (252/928-4441), a local institution whose rooftop, ocean-view deck is a very pleasant place to eat fresh local seafood and sample one or more of its 200 different beers.

From Hwy-12, a number of small back roads (including oak-lined Howard Street, and another called simply "Back Road," which runs past **Teach's Hole,** a shop dedicated to the pirate Blackbeard) are worth exploring—especially by bike, the best way to get around Ocracoke. Just south of the harbor, Point Road runs west to the squat, whitewashed 1823 Ocracoke Lighthouse, while the harbor itself is ringed by restaurants, bike rental stands, hotels, bars, and B&Bs.

Ocracoke Practicalities

Many of the restaurants ringing the Ocracoke harbor morph into bars after dark. All are friendly and informal, and most have some kind of live music during the summer season, making wandering around town a prime visitor activity. Right on the water, the **Jolly Roger Pub** (252/928-3703) is a prime

The carnivorous **Venus Flytrap**, which Charles Darwin called "the most wonderful plant in the world," does not grow wild in any part of the world except the seacoast Carolinas.

sunset-viewing spot, while **The Pelican** (252/928-7431) serves full meals in an oak-shaded Victorian home, with a lively patio. Away from the harbor, the **Back Porch** (252/928-6401) on Back Road is rated as one of the Outer Banks' best restaurants.

There are no chain hotels on Ocracoke (which may in itself be reason enough to visit), and local places are generally down-to-earth, not ritzy. The oldest lodging option is **Blackbeard's Lodge** ($80 and up; 252/928-3421), a rambling old motel on Back Road. Another characterful place is the **Island Inn** (65 and up; 252/928-4351), near the harbor. Right across from the ferry landing, there's a very helpful **visitors center** (252/928-4531) that has complete information on Ocracoke and the rest of Cape Hatteras. Running between Ocracoke on Cape Hatteras, and two places on the North Carolina mainland (Cedar Island and Swan Quarter), the state-run ferry departs approximately every two hours (every three hours in winter) and takes close to two and a half hours each way. The cost is $15 per car; call 800/BY-FERRY for current schedules and further information.

North Carolina's beaches are prime nesting grounds for endangered **loggerhead sea turtles**. These huge turtles come ashore mid-May to late August by the light of the full moon. Each female lays over 100 eggs that hatch at the end of summer.

From Cedar Island, it's close to an hour's drive along US-70 to the next big city, Beaufort.

Cape Lookout National Seashore

If you liked the look of Cape Hatteras but want to avoid the crowds, plan a visit to the much wilder **Cape Lookout National Seashore**, another series of barrier islands, which stretch for 55 miles from Ocracoke to the south near Beaufort. It's accessible only by boat, and there are few roads or services once you're there, but it's a lovely place to hike or camp, collect seashells, or just wander along the peaceful shore. Day trips to Point Lookout leave from Beaufort on the "World's Largest Speedboat," the *Lookout Express* ($15; 252/728-6997). For more information, contact the park **headquarters** (252/728-2250), at 3601 Bridge Street in Morehead City.

Not surprisingly, Beaufort, North Carolina is often confused with Beaufort, South Carolina. The former is pronounced BO-fort; the latter is pronounced BYOO-furd.

Beaufort and Morehead City

Known as Fishtown until it was renamed in 1722, the charming 18th-century town of **Beaufort** (pop. 3,800) has quiet streets lined with churches, cemeteries filled with weather-stained monuments, and whitewashed houses with narrow porches. The nautical-themed shops and restaurants along the water on busy Front Street, three blocks south of US-70, attract tourists and boaters traveling along the Intracoastal Waterway. The spacious **North Carolina Maritime Museum** (daily; free; 252/728-7317), at 315 Front Street, features many informative exhibits on the region's nautical and natural history, as well as a truly impressive display of over 1,000 beautiful seashells. The museum also sponsors the annual **Wooden Boat Show,** held the last weekend in September.

Beaufort has one great place to eat: **Clawson's** (252/728-2133), a burger and seafood place housed in an old grocery store at 425 Front Street, that's been in business "since 1905."

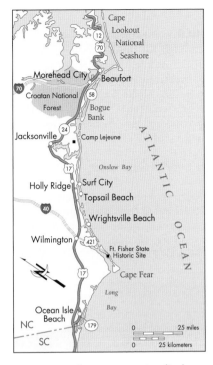

While Beaufort may be prettier, you'll find the best food in burly **Morehead City,** three miles west of Beaufort and across the bridge. Try the homemade seafood-cocktail sauce and Tarheel hush puppies at the **Sanitary Fish Market & Restaurant** (252/247-3111) at 501 Evans Street; it's easy to find amidst the sportfishing boats a block south of US-70.

Bogue Bank: Fort Macon

More barrier island beach resorts line **Bogue Bank,** which runs south of Morehead City in a nearly east–west orientation for some 25 miles. The half-dozen family-oriented resort towns have freely accessible—but quite often crowded—beaches. The largest, **Atlantic Beach,** across a bridge from Morehead City, has a boardwalk backed by a go-cart track and a small amusement arcade. The **State Aquarium** (daily; $3), five miles west of town on Hwy-58, features extensive displays on the local loggerhead sea turtles.

At the northeast end of Bogue Bank stands **Fort Macon State Park** (daily; free), which centers on a massive pre–Civil War fortress overlooking the harbor entrance. The pentagon-shaped masonry fort, completed in 1834, was captured early in the Civil War by the Confederacy. In April 1862, Union forces retook Fort Mason after a bombardment, and controlled Beaufort for the rest of the war.

Camp Lejeune and Jacksonville

Midway between Beaufort and Wilmington, much of the coastline is taken over by the 100,000-acre U.S. Marine Corps base of **Camp Lejeune.** Established during World War II, and now home to the crack rapid deployment forces and an urban combat training center, Camp Lejeune is open to visitors interested in a nose-to-nose encounter with tanks, humvees, and other lethal machines. Sentries will check you in and out at both ends of the surprisingly scenic 25-mile drive across the base along Hwy-172, which serves as a shortcut to looping US-17.

At the northwest corner of Camp Lejeune, **Jacksonville** (pop. 66,715) is little more than a civilian adjunct to the base, with all the gas stations, fast-food franchises, and tattoo parlors Lejeune's 45,000 Marines and their dependents could want. One sobering sight is on the edge of town, just off Hwy-24 (opposite a Sonic Drive-In): the 50-foot-long granite wall of the **Beirut Memorial** remembers the more than 250 Camp Lejeune marines killed in Beirut in 1983 by a suicide bomber. Alongside a list of their names are the words "They Came in Peace."

Surf City to Wrightsville Beach

South of Camp Lejeune, US-17 runs through the lushly forested lowlands around Holly Ridge, while Hwy-210 cuts across a series of narrow barrier islands. The waterfront is mostly private, backed by beach house after beach house with a few parking areas in between. One of the few commercial areas along here is **Surf City,** where the inviting **Sea Star Motel** ($90; 910/328-5191) snuggles up against the sands. The clean strands and clear blue waters continue through sleepy Topsail Beach, which is home to the nation's only hospital for injured loggerhead turtles. The 20-odd "patients" are cared for by volunteers at 822 Carolina Boulevard downtown, across from the water tower.

Most of this stretch of coastline is dedicated to low-key, by-the-week family vacations, but the town of **Wrightsville Beach** has a bit more going on. Located 10 miles east of US-17 via US-74 or US-76, it's not all that different from dozens of other coastal vacation communities, but proximity to the lively city of Wilmington makes it a great place to stop. Places to stay along the beach include the comfortable **Blockade Runner Resort** ($99–300; 910/256-2251) at 275 Waynick Boulevard, which has a good restaurant, two bars, and bicycle rentals.

In the book and movie *Gone With the Wind,* dashing southern hero Rhett Butler spent the Civil War as a Wilmington-based blockade runner, evading the U.S. Navy.

Wilmington

Though it's surrounded by the usual miles of highway sprawl, the downtown business district of **Wilmington** (pop. 75,838) is unusually attractive and well-preserved, its many blocks of historic buildings stepping up from the Cape Fear River waterfront. The largest city on the North Carolina coast, Wilmington was of vital importance to the Confederate cause during the Civil War, when it was the only southern port able to continue exporting income-earning cotton, mostly to England, in the face of the Union blockade. Wilmington also played an important role before and during the Revolution, first as a center of colonial resistance, and later as headquarters for British Gen. Cornwallis.

Despite its lengthy and involved military history, Wilmington itself has survived relatively unscathed and now possesses one of the country's more engaging small-town streetscapes. Cobblestoned wharves and brick warehouses line the Cape Fear River, which also provides moorage for the massive 35,000-ton battleship USS *North Carolina* (daily; $9), across the river. A couple of the warehouses, like the Cotton Exchange at the north end, have been converted to house boutiques and restaurants. A block inland, Front Street is the lively heart of town, a franchise-free stretch of book and record stores, cafés, and other businesses that's often used by film crews attempting to re-create a typically American "Main Street" scene. Films like *Blue Velvet,* and TV's teenage

Wilmington waterfront

soap opera *Dawson's Creek,* were shot at Wilmington's massive Screen Gems studio and in surrounding locales.

Thanks in large part to its significant TV and movie-making business, Wilmington has a number of excellent places to eat, like the comfortable **Caffé Phoenix** (910/343-1395) at 9 S. Front Street, an excellent Italian bistro serving fresh pasta dishes and pizzas. Within stumbling distance are bars like the rough-hewn **Barbary Coast,** 116 S. Front Street.

Rates at Wilmington's many chain motels and hotels are refreshingly low; try the riverfront **Hilton** ($90 and up; 910/763-5900).

For more information on visiting the Wilmington area, contact the **Cape Fear Convention & Visitor Bureau** (910/341-4030 or 800/222-4757), in the 100-year-old courthouse at 24 N. 3rd Street.

Transcontinental I-40 starts in Wilmington, and runs west to Southern California. The first stretch is named in honor of local basketball superstar **Michael Jordan,** and another sign gives the road's western destination: "Barstow, Calif. 2,554".

Cape Fear

Though it has lent its name to two of the most terrifying movies ever made, **Cape Fear** is not at all a scary place. The name was given to it by sailors who feared its shipwrecking shoals. Hundreds of vessels have been wrecked off the cape, including dozens of Confederate blockade-runners sunk during the Civil War embargo of Wilmington harbor.

Between the east and west banks of the Cape Fear River, a **ferry** (800/BY-FERRY) runs about once an hour between Fort Fisher and Southport.

South of Wilmington, US-421 runs along the east bank of the Cape Fear River through typical barrier island beach resort towns like Carolina Beach and Kure Beach. Near the south end of the island, **Fort Fisher State Historic Site** features the earthwork fortification that enabled Wilmington harbor to remain open to ships throughout most of the Civil War. The fortress looks more like a series of primitive mounds than an elaborate military installation, but its simple sand piles proved more durable against Union artillery than the heavy masonry of Fort Sumter and other traditional fortresses. A **visitors center** (daily; free; 910/458-5538) describes the fort's role, with details of the war's heaviest sea battle, when Union ships bombarded Fort Fisher in January 1865.

On the west bank of the Cape Fear River, Hwy-133 winds up at the pleasure-craft harbor of **Southport,** which is the halfway point between New York City and Miami, attracting sailors traveling the Intracoastal Waterway. It's also the site of the large Brunswick nuclear power plant.

Cape Fear itself is formed by **Bald Head Island,** at the mouth of the Cape Fear River, reachable only by boat from Southport. The **Old Baldy Lighthouse** on the island is the state's oldest, built in 1817.

Hwy-179: Ocean Isle Beach

South of Wilmington, US-17 runs inland, so if you want to stick close to the coast, take Hwy-179, which curves along the shore past the rambling towns of **Ocean Isle Beach** and **Sunset Beach** before rejoining US-17 at the South Carolina border. Amid the roadside shrimp stands and seafood restaurants, one place that's worth searching out is **Big Nell's Pit Stop** (910/579-6461), at 6393 Live Oak Drive, which has attracted Myrtle Beach–bound travelers

South of the Border

If the Grand Strand and Myrtle Beach haven't satisfied your need for road-side kitsch, or if you're bombing along I-95 looking for a place to take a break, head to South of the Border, the world's largest and most unapologetic tourist trap. Located just south of the North Carolina state line at I-95 exit 1, South of the Border is a crazy place with no real reason to exist, yet it draws many thousands of visitors every day to a 250-acre assembly of sombrero-shaped fast-food stands, giant video arcades, souvenir shops, and innumerable signs and statues of the South of the Border mascot, Pedro, including one that's nearly 100 feet tall.

Many roadside businesses suffered when a new Interstate or bypass left them high and dry, but in the case of South of the Border, the opposite is true. It started as a fireworks and hot dog stand along US-301 in the early 1950s, but when highway engineers decided to locate I-95 here, its middle-of-nowhere acres suddenly became prime highway frontage, and owner Alan Shafer (who died in 2001 at the age of 87) made playful use of its location (50 feet south of the state line) to create this pseudo-Mexican "South of the Border" village-cum-roadside rest stop. Though the complex itself is hard to miss, with its sombrero-clad concrete brontosaurus and 20-story "Sombrero Tower" giving a panoramic view of the Interstate, I-95 drivers from both directions get plenty of notice of their approach, thanks to the hundreds of garish billboards that line the road, saying silly things like "Chili Today, Hot Tamale," the subliminal messages all but forcing you to pull off and chow down on a taco or three and buy some mass-produced keepsake you'll throw away as soon as you get home.

South of the Border is open 24 hours every day, and, along with the myriad of tourist tack, it also has two gas stations and a pleasant, 300-room motel ($50 and up; 843/774-2411 or 800/845-6011).

with huge breakfasts, tasty vinegar-based barbecue, and their Brunswick Stew. Another good place to eat is at the north end of Hwy-179, in the town of Shalotte: **Joe's Old-Fashioned BBQ** (910/754-8876), a large, family-friendly place with a big buffet and well-smoked ribs, on the Main Street at the US-17 junction.

SOUTH CAROLINA

Just beyond the border into South Carolina, you suddenly hit the exuberant mega-tourism of the "Grand Strand," a 25-mile-long conglomeration of resort hotels, amusement arcades, and Coney Island–style Americana that centers on **Myrtle Beach,** the state's number-one tourist destination. South of here things quiet down considerably, as coastal US-17 winds past the lush lowland marshes, passing through historic **Georgetown** and numerous preserved plantations before reaching **Charleston,** one of the most gracious and engaging cities in the southern United States.

Myrtle Beach: The Grand Strand

Standing at the center of the Grand Strand, **Myrtle Beach** (pop. 32,000) is one of the largest and most popular beach resorts in the country, attracting some 13 million visitors every year. It's a huge place, with mile after mile of motels, Wal-Marts, and fast-food franchises lining all the main roads. Long famous for its golf courses (and for having the world's biggest collection of miniature golf courses), in recent years Myrtle Beach has refashioned itself as a coastal version of Branson, Missouri, with numerous new theaters offering everything from medieval pageants to a mini Grand Old Opry.

So, if you want to wallow in beachfront Americana, there are few better places to head. Myrtle Beach grew up around **The Pavilion** amusement park, at the east end of US-501 along Ocean Avenue at 9th Avenue, which started in the 1920s as a dance hall (where the dance craze "The Shag" began). The pay-as-you-ride park, a block inland from the beach, offers a classic array of roller coasters, Ferris wheels, and a circa-1915 Herschell merry-go-round, plus go-cart tracks and multiple midway arcade games. From spring break until the end of summer, the surrounding blocks are jammed with people showing off their well-formed bodies, though after school starts up again things get suddenly quiet.

The spring- and summer-blooming crepe myrtle trees, with long branches of purple and red flowers, gave Myrtle Beach its name. Myrtle Beach is also known as the 1950s birthplace of **"The Shag,"** a sexually explicit slow jitterbug that is now the official South Carolina state dance.

Myrtle Beach boasts more **golf courses,** including a bewildering array of miniature golf courses, than anywhere else in the country. Most have castaway or pirate themes; one's based upon the TV show *Gilligan's Island.*

Myrtle Beach Practicalities

The Myrtle Beach area is a mecca for fans of "themed" restaurants: Planet Hollywood, NASCAR Café, Hard Rock, Margaritaville, and Caddyshack all vie for attention in the massive Broadway-at-the-Beach complex on Kings Highway, north of US-501; this is the biggest attraction in Myrtle Beach, but despite the name, Broadway-at-the-Beach is over a mile from the ocean.

Some of the best places to eat are in Murrells Inlet (see below), but one very nice "old-time" Myrtle Beach restaurant is the **Sea Captain's House** (843/448-8082) at 3000 N. Ocean Boulevard, serving three delicious meals a day since 1954. The seafood is great, and just about every table has an ocean view. There are also a number of all-you-can-eat seafood buffets along "Restaurant Row"; the oldest, biggest, and best of the bunch is **Original Benjamin's** (843/449-0821) at

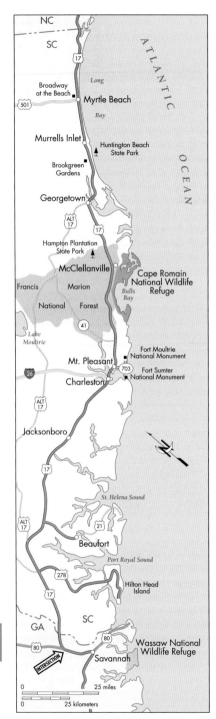

9301 N. King's Highway.

Across from The Pavilion, grab a bite from the **Peaches Corner** burger stand on Ocean Avenue.

Accommodations in and around Myrtle Beach range from roadside motels to flashy resorts; rates vary tremendously depending upon the time of year. Across from the Pavilion, the independently owned **Holiday Inn** ($45–125; 843/448-1691 or 800/465-4329) at 1200 N. Ocean Boulevard offers two pools and beach-front rooms. The nearby **Chesterfield Inn** ($85–175; 843/392-3869), at 700 N. Ocean Boulevard, is a redbrick, Georgia-style escape from the surrounding concrete.

For complete listings and other information, contact the **visitors center** (843/626-7444 or 800/356-3016), at 1301 N. King's Highway.

Murrells Inlet

There *may* be more picturesque places elsewhere in the state, but the as-yet unspoiled fishing village of **Murrells Inlet**, 12 miles south of Myrtle Beach, is definitely worth a stop for the chance to sample the dozens of excellent seafood restaurants lining a short business loop off US-17. For the best and freshest seafood, head to **Nance's Creekfront** (843/357-8277), right on the water at 4883 US-17; other good bets range from **Flo's Place** (which has great key lime pie) at the north end to the rustic **Oliver's Lodge** a mile south, in business since 1910. And if you've got the time and inclination to catch your own seafood, sportfishing charter boats run from the marina, or you can put on some waders and head into the waters in search of clams, mussels, oysters, and crabs.

Brookgreen Gardens and Huntington Beach State Park

One of the most popular and pleasant gardens in South Carolina, **Brookgreen Gardens** (daily; $12), 16 miles south of Myrtle Beach, is a privately owned, 4,000-acre park on the lushly landscaped grounds of four colonial-era indigo and rice plantations. Oak trees laden with Spanish moss stand alongside palmettos, dogwoods, and azaleas, as well as hundreds of sculptures, including many done by the owner, Anna Hyatt Huntington, who developed the site in the 1930s. Alligators and otters play in the simulated swamp and many species of birds fly around enclosed aviaries in a section of the gardens set aside as a wildlife park.

Across the highway is the 2,500-acre **Huntington Beach State Park** ($4 per car; 843/237-4440), which sits on land carved out of the Huntington estate that is leased to South Carolina. Besides a nice beach and a popular campground, it features the Moorish-style castle "Atalaya," Anna Huntington's studio.

Carry insect repellent and be prepared for **mosquitoes,** especially late in the afternoon, almost everywhere along the muggy South Carolina coast.

Pawleys Island and Hobcaw Barony

South of the commercial chaos of Myrtle Beach, travelers in search of serene tranquility have long appreciated **Pawleys Island.** The rope hammocks for which the island is best known aptly symbolize this generally relaxed, weather-worn community, where a few traditional tin-roofed shacks mix with ever-increasing numbers of multi-million-dollar mock-antebellum mansions. It's mostly private, apart from the plush environs of **Litchfield Plantation** ($160 and up; 843/869-1410), a 600-acre resort on the grounds of a colonial-era plantation. The poet and novelist James Dickey, author of *Deliverance,* liked it so much he lived here for his last 25 years, and is buried in the small Pawleys Island cemetery.

An even more extensive and intimate (and affordable) taste of the old-fashioned Lowcountry life is available just down the road from Pawleys Island. Spreading along the north bank of the Pee Dee River, a mile north of Georgetown on US-17, **Hobcaw Barony** is a 17,500-acre estate that was once the winter home of 1920s financier and New Deal–era statesman Bernard Baruch and his daughter, Belle. The extensive, mostly undeveloped grounds are home to two university research centers specializing in coastal ecology, and the main homes and plantation buildings have been kept in original condition, complete with one of very few surviving slave streets. Along with preserving these historic quarters and the regional history they represent, the nonprofit

One of the more unusual radio stations in the country, WLGI 90.9 FM, is operated by the Ba'hai faith and broadcasts a commercial-free mix of classic 1970s soul, contemporary jazz, and messages of peace, love, and understanding. To learn more, call 800/228-6483.

educational foundation that runs Hobcaw Barony offers half-day tours to school groups and individuals (Tues.–Fri.; $15; 843/546-4623). Tours start at the visitors center and museum (Mon.–Fri.; free) along US-17.

Georgetown

Site of a short-lived Spanish settlement in 1526, the first European outpost in North America, **Georgetown** later became the rice-growing center of colonial America. Bounded by the Sampit and Pee Dee Rivers and the narrow inlet of Winyah Bay, Georgetown is one of the state's few deepwater harbors and home to two huge steel and paper mills along US-17, but its downtown district along Front Street is compact and comfortable, with dozens of day-to-day businesses and a few cafés and art galleries filling the many old buildings.

The original lyrics to **Stephen Foster's** song "The Old Folks at Home" began "Way down upon the Pee Dee River..." though he quickly changed it to the more sonorous "Suwanee."

Three blocks south of US-17, at the east end of Front Street, there's a pleasant waterfront promenade, where the clock-towered old town market now houses the **Rice Museum** (closed Sun.; $5). A series of dioramas traces South Carolina's little-known history as the world's main rice and indigo producer, a past often overshadowed by the state's later tobacco and cotton trade. The rest of town holds many well-preserved colonial and antebellum houses, churches, and commercial buildings.

Another South Carolina musical connection: **Chubby Checker** (of "The Twist" fame) was born inland from Georgetown in Spring Gully, SC, near the town of Andrews.

A couple of good places to eat in Georgetown include the locals' favorite **Thomas Cafe** (843/546-7776), next to the Rice Museum at 703 Front Street. For more information, or to pick up a self-guided-tour map of town, contact the Georgetown County **Chamber of Commerce** (843/546-8436 or 800/777-7705), on the waterfront at 1001 Front Street.

Hampton Plantation and McClellanville

The Santee Delta region along US-17 between Georgetown and Charleston once held dozens of large and hugely profitable plantations. One of the best preserved of these is now the **Hampton Plantation State Park** (Thurs.–Mon. 9 AM–6 PM; free), located 15 miles south of Georgetown, two miles west of US-17. Spreading out along the northern edge of Francis Marion National Forest, the 320-acre grounds feature a white wooden Greek Revival manor house (tours Thurs.–Mon. 1–4 PM; $4) that once welcomed George Washington. The manor house was later home to Archibald Rutledge, poet laureate of South Carolina from 1934 until his death in 1973.

South from Hampton Plantation along US-17, a small sign marks the turnoff to the quaint Lowcountry fishing village of **McClellanville** (pop. 383). A short drive past moss-draped oak trees brings you to the town dock, where a substantial portion of South Carolina's shrimp and crab catch gets unloaded and shipped to market.

Cape Romain National Wildlife Refuge

Dense forests stretch west from the highway, while the unspoiled **Cape Romain National Wildlife Refuge** stretches south of McClellanville nearly to

Charleston, forming one of the largest and most important sanctuaries for migratory birds on the East Coast. Thousands of great blue herons, pelicans, terns, and ducks join the resident population of wild turkeys, feral pigs, deer, and alligators. To get a glimpse of the diverse life protected here, visit the **Sewee Visitor Center** (daily; free; 843/928-3368), on US-17 at Awendaw. Exhibits inside explain the natural and human history of the region, and trails outside lead to a boardwalk viewing area and an enclosure that's home to native red foxes.

Directly across from the refuge entrance on US-17, you can appreciate other aspects of the area's culture at the homey **SeeWee Cafe** (843/928-3609), a general store turned restaurant serving homemade specialties, including a fabulously rich she-crab soup (served with a shot of sherry on the side). The ambience is perfect—tin cans still fill the shelves, and local fishermen stop by to offer their catches—and the low prices and friendly people make it worth planning your trip around.

Fort Moultrie and Mount Pleasant

Sitting at the entrance to Charleston harbor, across from its better-known sibling, Fort Sumter, **Fort Moultrie** (daily; $3) overlooks the Atlantic with good views of passing ships and the city of Charleston. The location alone would make Moultrie well worth a visit, but most come because of its vital role in American military history. Originally built from palmetto logs during the Revolutionary War, and since rebuilt many times, the fort is a testament to the development of coastal defenses. Its well-preserved sections date from every major U.S. war between 1812 and World War II, when Fort Moultrie protected Charleston harbor from roving German U-boats. But the fort is most famous for its role in the events of April 1861, when Fort Moultrie touched off the Civil War by leading the bombardment of Fort Sumter.

Fort Moultrie is easy to reach. From Mount Pleasant, a suburban community on the north bank of the Cooper River, across from Charleston, turn south from US-17 onto Hwy-703 then follow signs along Middle Street to the fort.

Along with Fort Moultrie, **Mount Pleasant** itself is worth visiting for the many African sweetgrass basketmakers who set up shop along US-17. While the roadside is rapidly filling up with suburban tract-house "plantations," in the warmer months women sit and weave these intricate baskets at their ramshackle stands. Like so many other Lowcountry traditions, sweetgrass weaving may soon be a lost art, as younger women are increasingly reluctant to take on this low-paid work; it can take four to five hours to weave a basket that may sell for less than $30.

African sweetgrass basket

Fort Sumter National Monument

Commanding an island at the mouth of Charleston Harbor, **Fort Sumter National Monument** marks the site of the first military engagement of the Civil War. On April 12, 1861, a month after Abraham Lincoln's inauguration and four months after South Carolina had seceded from the United States, Confederate guns bombarded the fort until the federal forces withdrew. The structure was

a Grumman E-1B Tracer on the deck of the USS Yorktown, at Patriot's Point

badly damaged, but no one was killed and the fort was held by the Confederates for the next four years, by which time it had been almost completely flattened. Partly restored, but still a powerful symbol of the destruction wrought by the War Between the States, Fort Sumter is a key stop on any tour of Civil War sites.

The only way to visit Fort Sumter is by tour boat ($14; 843/722-1691); they leave from the north side of Charleston Bay at Patriot's Point, just off US-17 at the foot of the soaring new cable-stayed bridge across the Cooper River. (Other boats to Fort Sumter dock at Liberty Square in downtown Charleston.) Patriot's Point is also the anchorage of the aircraft carrier USS *Yorktown* (daily; $14), centerpiece of a floating maritime museum that also includes WW II–era fighter planes, a Coast Guard cutter, and a Cold War–era submarine.

Charleston

Established in 1670 as the capital of South Carolina, **Charleston,** more than any other Deep South city, proudly maintains the aristocratic traditions established during the plantation era. Then the elite would flee the heat, humidity, and mosquitoes of their lowland fiefdoms and come here to cavort in ballrooms and theaters. Still ruled by old money, though no longer the state capital, Charleston is both pretentious and provincial; locals like to say that Charleston is the place where the Ashley and Cooper Rivers meet to form the Atlantic Ocean. Though there are clear divides between the haves and have-nots, Charleston is also surprisingly cosmopolitan, accommodating a historic ethnic mix of French Huguenots, Catholic Acadians, and Afro-Caribbeans, who collectively introduced the wrought-iron balconies and brightly colored cottages that give the city much of its charm. George Gershwin's opera *Porgy and Bess,* for example, was inspired by life in Charleston's Creole ghetto, specifically Cabbage Row, now a tidy brick-paved alley off Church Street.

Having suffered through a devastating earthquake, two wars, and innumerable hurricanes, Charleston has rebuilt and restored itself many times, yet it remains one of the South's most beautiful cities. Impressive neoclassical buildings line the streets, especially in the older, up-

market sections of town south of Broad Street and along the waterfront Battery. Charleston's many small, lush gardens and parks make it ideal for aimless exploring on foot rather than by car.

Many of the mansions and churches are open to visitors, but it's the overall fabric of Charleston, rather than specific sites, that is

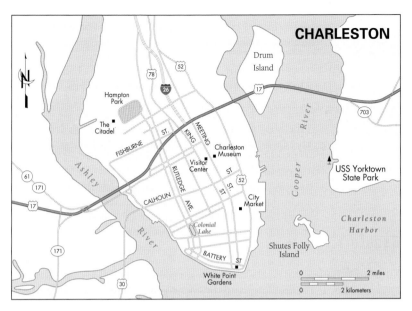

most memorable. That said, the 1828 Greek Revival **Edmonston-Alston House** (daily; $8) at 21 E. Battery is definitely worth a look, as is the beautiful spire of **St. Michael's Episcopal Church** (daily; donations) at 78 Meeting Street, which was modeled on the London churches of Sir Christopher Wren. A quarter mile north, at Church and Market Streets, is the open-air **City Market,** known as the "Ellis Island of Black America," since over a third of all slaves arrived in the colonies here. Once the commercial center of Charleston, the market now houses a range of souvenir shops and touristy restaurants.

The Charleston accent is famous throughout the South. The word "garden" here is characteristically pronounced "gyarden," and "car" is "kyar," while the long "a" of Charleston (usually pronounced "Chaaahrleston") is as distinctive as JFK's "HAAH-vahd."

Charleston Practicalities

Thanks to its considerable tourist trade, Charleston supports a number of excellent eateries at all price ranges. Great breakfasts (as well as lunch, dinner, and Sunday brunch) are available at the very popular **Hominy Grill** (843/937-0930) at 207 Rutledge Street. Around the City Market, choose from the very popular **Hyman's Seafood** (843/723-6000) at 215 Meeting Street, which has a variety of basic but good-value fresh fish entrées for around $10; expect a wait. More sedate and expensive dinner places nearby include the stylish, Mediterranean-inspired **Blossom Cafe** (843/722-9200) at 171 E. Bay Street, and the upscale and usually crowded **Magnolias** (843/577-7771) next door, serving locally-inspired Lowcountry food in a 250-year-old customs house. Both are open until 11 PM or later.

Like its restaurants, Charleston's accommodation options tend toward the luxurious and expensive. Of the dozens of

Charleston's annual arts-and-opera **Spoleto Festival USA** (843/722-2764) is held over two weeks in May and June.

old-fashioned but well-appointed B&Bs (all of which charge around $150 a night), the elegant **John Rutledge House** (843/723-7999 or 800/476-9741) at 116 Broad Street offers four-star comfort in a converted 1763 house. The romantic, Queen Anne–style **Two Meeting Street Inn** (843/723-7322) at 2 Meeting Street has been welcoming guests for over 50 years. Hotels in and around the historic district are similarly expensive, though you'll find a very handy **Days Inn** ($100 and up; 843/722-8411) downtown at 155 Meeting Street.

Outside the historic area a half mile south of US-17, the **Charleston Visitor Center** (daily; 843/853-8000) at 375 Meeting Street is a good first stop; watch the 21-projector multi-image slide show *Forever Charleston* and pick up a **day pass** to ride the DASH shuttle buses that loop around town.

Beaufort

The second-oldest town in South Carolina, **Beaufort** (pop. 12,950; BYOO-furd) is a well-preserved antebellum town stretching along a fine natural harbor. Established in 1710, Beaufort stands on the largest of some 75 islands near the Georgia border; the town is perhaps best known as the home of the massive U.S. Marine Corps Recruit Depot at nearby Parris Island, where new marines undergo their basic training (graduation ceremonies, held Fri., are open to the public). Dozens of colonial-era and antebellum homes line Beaufort's quiet, small-town streets, but only two, the **Verdier House** and the Greek Revival **Elliott House**, a block apart on Bay Street along the waterfront, are open to visitors.

As recently as 1960, the population of South Carolina's Sea Islands was predominantly African American—10 to 1 on average. Now, with all the recent "plantation-style" vacation resorts, the proportions have effectively been reversed. As a last defense against the dark arts of developers, traditional African American **"Gullah" culture** is celebrated in summer festivals and tourism literature promoting the "Gullah-Geechee Heritage Coast."

Beaufort is a very enjoyable place to wander around and explore, and has at least one great place to eat: **Blackstone's** (843/524-4330), off the main street at 205 Scott Street, where fans of the shrimp 'n' grits and corned beef hash include local writer Pat Conroy. Places to stay include the waterfront **Best Western Sea Island Motel** (843/524-4121 or 800/528-1234), 1015 Bay Street, and the state's only four-star B&B: the lovely **Rhett House** ($160 and up; 843/524-9030) at 1009 Craven Street, where the film of Conroy's *Prince of Tides* was shot on location.

South to Savannah: Hilton Head

From Beaufort, the easiest way south is to follow Hwy-170 all the way to Savannah, or to detour east onto I-95. Otherwise, a pleasant but potentially confusing series of two-lane run around Hilton Head Island across the lowlands toward Georgia.

Near the southern tip of South Carolina, **Hilton Head Island** is the largest ocean island between Florida and New Jersey. It was first settled in 1663, but only since the late 1950s, when a bridge to the mainland was completed, has it really been on the map. Now Hilton Head's deluxe **Sea Pines Resort** ($175 and up; 888/807-6873) is a major international destination, and upscale golf courses and plantation-style estates abound the island's 30,000 acres, as do mini-malls and all the trappings of suburban America.

The "success" of Hilton Head has caused developers to set their sights on the rest of the Lowcountry, as shown by the opening of the super-plush **Palmetto Bluff** resort ($350 and up; 843/706-6500) at nearby Bluffton, where each of 50 waterfront cottages is outfitted with plasma TVs and a Sub-Zero fridge for that quintessential Lowcountry experience.

Along the Savannah River, which marks the boundary between South Carolina and Georgia, **Eli Whitney** invented the cotton gin in 1793 at Mulberry Grove plantation.

The beautiful city of Savannah marks the junction of our Atlantic Coast route with the **Southern Pacific** road trip along US-80 (see page 778). Full coverage of US-80 is on pages 724–780.

GEORGIA

The marshes and barrier islands that line the Atlantic Ocean along the Georgia coast are among the lesser-known treasures of the eastern United States. Geographically, the coastline consists of mostly roadless and largely unconnected islands, which makes coastal driving nearly impossible; the nearest north–south routes, I-95 and the older US-17, run roughly 15 miles inland, and only a few roads head east to the Atlantic shore. The lack of access has kept development to a minimum and has also been a boon to wildlife—well over half the coastline is protected within state and federal parks, preserves, and refuges.

The "you-can't-get-there-from-here" aspects can make it more than a little frustrating for casual visitors, but if you have the time and inclination, they also make the Georgia coast a wonderful place to explore. The two main car-friendly destinations along the Georgia coast are **Tybee Island** in the north, east of Savannah and forming the end of our cross-country road trip along US-80, and the beautiful and history-rich **Golden Isles,** east of Brunswick. Both are great places to visit, and they offer an appetizing taste of the 100 miles of isolated shoreline Georgia otherwise keeps to herself.

Savannah

Named "the most beautiful city in North America" by the style-arbiting Parisian newspaper *Le Monde,* **Savannah** (pop. 130,000) is a real jewel of a place. Founded in 1733 as the first settlement in Georgia, the thirteenth and final American colony, Savannah today preserves its original neoclassical, colonial, and antebellum self in a welcoming, unself-conscious way. Famous for having been spared by General Sherman on his destructive "March to the Sea" at the end of the Civil War, it was here that Sherman made his offering of "40 acres and a mule" to all freed slaves.

Before and after the war, Savannah was Georgia's main port, rivaling

Charleston, South Carolina, for the enormously lucrative cotton trade, but as commercial shipping tailed off, the harbor became increasingly recreational—the yachting competitions of the 1996 Olympics were held offshore. Savannah, home of writer Flannery O'Connor and songsmith Johnny Mercer, also served as backdrop to the best-selling book *Midnight in the Garden of Good and Evil,* and for numerous movies, most famously *Forrest Gump,* but has resisted urges to turn itself into an "Old South" theme park; you'll have to search hard to find souvenir shops or overpriced knickknack galleries. Mainly, March is when things get crazy here: Thousands of visitors come to the bars along Congress Street for what has grown into the world's second-largest **St. Patrick's Day** celebration—only New York City's is bigger.

At the center of Savannah, midway down Bull Street between the waterfront and spacious Forsyth Park, **Chippewa Square** was the site of Forrest Gump's bus bench (the movie prop was moved to the visitors center and may one day be erected in bronze). **Reynolds Square,** near the waterfront, has a statue of John Wesley, who lived in Savannah in 1736–1737 and established the world's first Sunday School here. **Wright Square** holds a monument to Chief Tomochichi, the Native American tribal leader who allowed Oglethorpe to settle here, and **Forsyth Park,** at the south edge of the historic center, is modeled after the Place de la Concorde in Paris, surrounded by richly scented magnolias.

Another great place to wander is **Factor's Walk,** a promontory along the Savannah River named for the "factors" who controlled Savannah's cotton trade. This area holds the Cotton Exchange and other historic buildings, many of them constructed from 18th-century ballast stones. Linked from the top of the bluffs by a network of steep stone stairways and cast-iron walkways, **River Street** is lined by restaurants, and at the east end there's a statue of a girl waving: This was erected in memory of Florence Martus, who for 50 years around the turn of the 20th century greeted every ship entering Savannah harbor in the vain hope that her boyfriend would be on board.

Savannah Practicalities

Getting around is blissfully easy: Savannah is the country's preeminent walker's town, with a wealth of historic architecture and a checkerboard of 22 small squares shaded with centuries-old live oak trees draped with tendrils of Spanish moss, all packed together in a single square mile. The sensible and very attractive modified grid plan of Savannah makes finding your way so simple that it's almost fun to try to get lost. Parking in town isn't hard to find, but if you're staying a while, the visitors center sells a $5 visitor's parking pass, which lets you disregard *almost* all the parking restrictions for two days.

For an unforgettable breakfast or lunch, be sure to stop at **Mrs. Wilkes Boarding House** (912/232-5997) at 107 W. Jones Street, a central Savannah home that's no longer a boarding house but still offers up traditional family-style Southern cooking—varying from fried chicken to crab stews, with side dishes like okra gumbo; sweet potato pie; red, green, or brown rice; and cornbread muffins. Worth a trip from anywhere in the state, don't leave Savannah without eating here. On the south side of town on old US-80 at 1651 E. Victory Drive, **Johnny Harris** (912/354-7810) is Savannah's oldest restaurant, and one of the fanciest BBQ places in the world.

Road-food fans may want to head a half mile south of downtown to the **Streamliner Diner**, at 102 W. Henry Street, a gorgeously restored 1938 Worcester diner operated by (and across the street from) the Savannah College of Art & Design (SCAD), which has taken over many of the city's older buildings and converted them into art studios, galleries, and cafés.

There are also many good places cheek-by-jowl in the old City Market, like the lively **Vinny Van Go Go's** pizza joint (912/233-6394), facing Franklin Square at 317 W. Bryan Street.

The nicest place to eat in town is probably **Elizabeth on 37th** (912/236-5547), housed in a moss-draped mansion at 105 E. 37th Street. Open for dinner every night, for over 20 years chef Elizabeth Terry has been earning international acclaim for her "New Southern" cooking, using the freshest possible ingredients to revitalize traditional Savannah specialties.

Places to stay in Savannah vary from quaint B&B inns to stale high-rise hotels. For the total Savannah experience, try the **Bed and Breakfast Inn** ($99 and up; 912/238-0518) at 117 W. Gordon Street, which has very nice rooms in an 1853 townhouse off Monterey Square. At the **River Street Inn**

One of Savannah's more unusual tourist attractions is the **Juliet Gordon Low Birthplace,** at 142 Bull Street, a circa-1820 house that was the childhood home of the woman who introduced Girl Scouts to America in 1912. Current Girl Scouts gain a merit badge just by walking in the door.

The Class A **Savannah Sand Gnats** (912/351-9150), a Washington Nationals farm club, play at WPA-built Grayson Stadium, off US-80 on the south side of town.

Along US-17, a small sign on the east side of the highway (a mile south of I-95 exit 67) welcomes travelers to **"The Smallest Church in America,"** a 12-seat cabin that's open 24 hours. Turn the lights out when you leave.

($150 and up; 912/234-6400 or 800/253-4229), at 115 E. River Street, well-appointed rooms fill a converted antebellum cotton warehouse, right on Factor's Walk at the heart of the Savannah riverfront. Nearby at 201 W. Bay Street, the large **Days Inn** ($125 and up; 912/236-4440 or 800/325-2525) has standard rooms, right across from Factor's Walk.

The **Savannah Visitors Center** (912/944-0456 or 877/728-2662), at 301 Martin Luther King Boulevard in the old Georgia Central railroad terminal just west of the historic center, has free maps and brochures and other information on the city.

US-17: Midway

The section of US-17 south of the Ogeechee River, off I-95 between exits 14 and 12, offers shunpikers a 24-mile taste of old-style Lowland Georgia. Sometimes called the Old Atlantic Highway, it is a textbook example of how traveling the two-lane highways is superior in almost every way to hustling down the interstates. Midway along, the coincidentally named town of **Midway** (pop. 1,100) was founded back in 1754 by a band of New England colonists, two of whom (Lyman Hall and Button Guinett) went on to sign the Declaration of Independence as Georgia's self-declared representatives to the Continental Congress. The centerpiece of Midway, then and now, is 200-year-old **Midway Church,** which preserves the original pulpit and slave gallery; keys for the church are available at the adjacent **Midway Museum** (closed Mon.; $3; 912/884-5837).

Though redolent with ghosts of Georgia's past, Midway is still a living, breathing little place, with a great little 1930s-era road-food restaurant, **Ida Mae & Joe's** (912/884-3388), serving up plates of fresh-fried catfish, chicken fingers, and fresh-made pies at 817 N. US-17.

Sapelo Island and Darien

A compelling non-fiction account of 1970s Darien, **Melissa Fay Greene's** *Praying for Sheetrock* describes how locals and legal activists used federal lawsuits to overcome the corrupt regimes of local government and law enforcement officials.

For an unforgettable taste of the *real* pre–tourist industry Georgia coast, make your way east to **Sapelo Island,** which stretches offshore between Midway and Darien. The island is a sparsely populated, mostly undeveloped and generally fascinating place to spend some time, a truly wild landscape where alligators and ferocious feral pigs live free among remnants of colonial-era plantation agriculture and native Creek Indian shell middens dating back 6,000 years. Once a cotton plantation, worked by slaves whose 70-odd descendents live in Hog Hammock, Sapelo's only permanent community, the island is now owned by the state of Georgia and used as a marine biology research center. There is no real commercial development—no stores, and no restaurants, so bring your own food and drink—just miles of beaches, marshlands, and open sea. Get there from the mainland hamlet of **Meridian,** where you can catch the state-run ferry for a four-hour guided tour (reservations required; adults $10, under 18 $6; 912/437-3224), which gives a full introduction to Sapelo Island life. For a more memorable experience, stay overnight at **The Wallow** (912/485-2206), a small Hog Hammock B&B run by lifelong Sapelo Island resident Cornelia Bailey.

South of Sapelo Island near the mouth of the Altamaha River, which formed the rough and frequently fought-over boundary between British and Spanish parts of the New World, **Darien** (pop. 1,800) looks a lot like most other coastal Deep South towns, but it boasts a history to match many bigger or more famous destinations. After a small, 16th-century Spanish mission near here was destroyed by Native Americans, Darien was founded in 1736 by Scottish colonists (many named McIntosh, now the name of the surrounding county) near Fort King George, the first British outpost in what became Georgia. Darien later became a center of the lucrative early-19th-century rice trade, surrounded by plantations where the abuse of slaves inspired British actress Fanny Kemble's book-length indictment, *Journal of a Residence on a Georgia Plantation in 1838–39,* an influential abolitionist text.

Despite the many claims it could make to importance, Darien preserves its past in a matter-of-fact manner. The main attraction is the reconstructed **Fort King George**, a state historic site, a mile east of US-17 on Fort King George Drive (closed Mon.; $5).

Another intriguing place to visit is the **Hofwyl-Broadfield Plantation** (daily; $5; 912/264-7333), five miles south of Darien along US-17, where a well-preserved plantation home is surrounded by 1,200 acres of one-time rice fields that have reverted to cypress swamps. Displays inside the visitors center tell the story of how slaves were forced to labor in the sweltering, mosquito-plagued summer heat, building levees, and doing the back-breaking work of planting, growing, and harvesting the rice.

Brunswick: The Golden Isles

Along the southeast Georgia coast, a patchwork of islands known as the Golden Isles offer a wide range of images and experiences. The largest and best-known, **St. Simon's Island** is a mini Hilton Head, with many vacation resorts and a sizeable year-round community. The center of activity on St. Simon's is at the south tip of the island, where the "village" consists of a central plaza and a few blocks of shops, saloons, and restaurants along Mallory Street, which leads down to the waterfront pier and a circa-1872 lighthouse. Sea kayaks, bicycles, and boats can be rented here, and there are a number of reasonable motels; for food try the popular **Fourth of May Café** (912/638-5444), off Mallory at 444 Ocean Boulevard.

Georgia's most famous 19th-century poet, **Sidney Lanier,** settled near Brunswick after contracting tuberculosis as a POW during the Civil War. He wrote his most famous poems, including "The Marshes of Glynn," while he sat under an oak tree that stands along US-17, a mile north of town.

The one real "sight" on St. Simon's Island is the **Fort Frederica National Monument,** at the northwest edge of the island, which protects the remains of the village surrounding what was once the largest fortress in the British colonies. Built in 1736 and abandoned in 1763, Fort Frederica played a vital role in keeping Georgia British, rather than Spanish; in 1742, a key battle was fought six miles south of the fort, at a site known as "Bloody Marsh."

For the total Golden Isles experience, splurge on a night or two at one of the country's plushest resorts, the four-star **Cloister Hotel** ($450 and up; 912/638-3611 or 800/732-4752), which covers adjacent Sea Island with 36 holes of golf courses and 264 Spanish-style rooms. Presidents from Coolidge to Bush have

vacationed here, the late JFK Jr. got married here, and the G8 economic summit was held here in 2004, which should give you some idea of the elite character of the place.

Back on the mainland, heavily industrialized **Brunswick** (pop. 16,500) feels about as far from the genteel pleasures of the Golden Isles as you can be. Most vacationers pass through quickly on their way to and from the Golden Isles, but there is one great place to stop: the **Georgia Pig** (912/264-6664), southwest of town at the US-17/82 junction, just east of I-95 exit 29. Tucked away next to a gas station in a scruffy woodland, it looks like it's been there forever; the bare-bones decor—log rafters, pine picnic tables, and creaking front door—disappears when you bite into the absolutely perfect ribs and fabulous pulled-pork sandwiches, which are smoked in a hickory-fired oven right behind the counter.

Jekyll Island

Southeast of Brunswick, and developed in the late 1880s as a private, members-only resort for New York multimillionaires, **Jekyll Island** now offers a chance for those *not* in control of a Fortune 500 company to enjoy a generous slice of Golden Isles life. Now

owned by the state of Georgia, a grand hotel and dozens of palatial vacation "cottages" that would look equally at home in Newport, Rhode Island, are accessible to the general public after a long life spent catering to the richest of the rich.

At the center of the island, and the best place to start a visit, is the landmark **Jekyll Island Club Hotel** ($160 and up; 912/635-2600 or 800/535-9547). The very pleasant rooms here aren't *all* that expensive, considering the luxury you're swaddled in, and the setting is superb. Majestic oak trees dangling garlands of Spanish moss cover the 200-acre grounds, and within a short walk, many of the grand old mansions are now open for guided tours ($10). The nearby stables have been converted into a nice little **museum** (daily; free), which tells the whole Jekyll Island story.

> Around the turn of the 20th century, the 50-odd members of the Jekyll Island Club, which included such names as Rockefeller, Carnegie, Morgan, and Vanderbilt, controlled as much as 20 percent of the world's wealth.

Less than a mile east, the Atlantic oceanfront is lined by **Beachview Drive** and a five-mile-long beach—with the least developed stretches at the north and south ends of the island. Bike rentals—which really provide the best way to see the island—are available from the mini-golf course midway along Beachview Drive ($4/hr; 912/635-2648).

Cumberland Island National Seashore

Right on the Florida border, and once the private reserve of the Carnegie family, the **Cumberland Island National Seashore** is a 99-percent uninhabited barrier island with miles of hiking trails and primitive backcountry camping along beaches and in palmetto forests. Also here is the unique **Greyfield Inn**

(904/261-6408), the Carnegie family mansion that's now operated (by Carnegie heirs) as an unpretentious 17-room historic lodge that runs around $400 a night for two people, including gourmet meals and transportation from the mainland. (Bring your own bug spray!)

Unless you're a guest at the Greyfield, Cumberland Island is only accessible by a twice-daily ferry ($12 round-trip) from the town of St. Marys, 10 miles east of I-95 exit 1. For further details, contact the Cumberland Island National Seashore information and reservations center at 912/882-4336.

St. Marys, Georgia, the main access to Cumberland Island, is also home to a huge U.S. Navy Base, home port of the nuclear-powered and -armed submarine fleet.

FLORIDA

Stretching some 600 miles between the Georgia border and Key West at its far southern tip, Florida offers something for everyone, from unsullied nature to the tackiest tourist traps in the land, and everything imaginable in between. More than anywhere else in the United States, the Florida landscape has been designed for tourists, and no matter what your fancy or fantasy, you can live it here, under the semi-tropical sun. The many millions who visit Disney World or flock to fashionable Miami Beach each year are doing exactly what people have come to Florida to do for over a century—enjoy themselves.

In the 1920s and 1930s, when car travel and Florida tourism were both reaching an early peak of popularity, the roadside landscape was, in the words of the WPA *Guide to Florida,* lined by

. . . signs that turn like windmills; startling signs that resemble crashed airplanes; signs with glass lettering which blaze forth at night when automobile headlights strike them; flashing neon signs; signs painted with professional touch; signs crudely lettered and misspelled. They advertise hotels, tourist cabins, fishing camps, and eating places. They extol the virtues of ice creams, shoe creams, cold creams; proclaim the advantages of new cars and used cars; tell of 24-hour towing and ambulance service, Georgia pecans, Florida fruit and fruit juices, honey, soft drinks, and furniture. They urge the traveler to take designated tours, to visit certain cities, to stop at certain points he must see. Alas, most of these signs are long gone, but their spirit lives on.

Two men who made millions in the automobile industry have had immeasurable influence over the evolution of the Florida coast. Standard Oil baron **Henry Flagler** constructed the first railroad and built a chain of deluxe resort hotels from St. Augustine to Miami, while **Carl Fisher,** the developer of car headlights, promoted Florida's "Route 66," the Dixie Highway, and later helped to found Miami Beach. Their names reappear frequently wherever you travel along the Atlantic coast.

Despite the modern gloss of tourist attractions, golf course estates, and sprawling retirement communities, which tend to overshadow the substantial stretches of wide open beaches and coastal forest, Florida has a lengthy and fascinating history, with significant native cultures and, in **St. Augustine,** some of the oldest signs of European presence in North America, including the legendary Fountain of Youth. At the other end of the state, on the fringes of the Caribbean, **Key West** is a tropical paradise, founded by pirates four centuries

ago, and still one of the most lively and anarchic places in the United States. In between, our road-trip route passes through such diverse places as **Daytona Beach,** mecca for race car fans and a magnet for college kids on spring break; the launch pads and mission control centers of the **Kennedy Space Center;** the multicultural melting pots of **Miami** and **Miami Beach;** and, of course, the "Happiest Place on Earth," **Disney World.**

There are three main routes running north–south along Florida's Atlantic coastline, and your travels will likely make use of at least a little of each one. The fastest route is the **I-95** freeway, which races uneventfully along, linking the major cities. The most scenic route is **Hwy-A1A,** a mostly two-lane highway that runs as close as possible to the shoreline, linking many gorgeous beaches but, because of the very flat topography and the extensive beachfront development, only rare glimpses of the open ocean. In between I-95 and Hwy-A1A runs historic **US-1,** part of the old Dixie Highway, which is lined by reminders of Florida's rich roadside heritage, but which also passes through some of the state's less salubrious corners, especially in and around the larger cities. Our suggested route primarily follows coastal Hwy-A1A, but directions from other, faster routes are also given, so you can alternate freely and easily among them all.

Of all the American colonies, only Florida remained loyal to the British crown during the Revolutionary War. After the war, the British ceded Florida to Spain, which eventually swapped it to the United States in 1821 in exchange for $5 million in assumed debt.

Amelia Island

Entering Florida from Georgia across the St. Marys River, which flows east out of the Okefenokee Swamp to the Atlantic Ocean, you may want to skirt around the metropolitan sprawl of Jacksonville by following old US-17, or getting off I-95 at exit 129, to Hwy-A1A, which runs due east to the brilliant white-sand beaches and picturesque historic buildings of **Amelia Island.** The main community on the island is **Fernandina Beach** (pop 10,549), once the main port in northeast Florida. The eastern terminus of the first trans-Florida railroad, and long a popular tourist destination, Fernandina Beach retains many late-Victorian buildings, collected together in a wanderable 30-block historic district along the waterfront.

Among the many nice B&Bs here, you'll find the **Florida House Inn** ($99 and up; 904/261-3300 or 800/258-3301), at 22 S. 3rd Street, a historic hostelry that's been welcoming travelers since 1857. Florida's oldest hotel, it also serves traditional southern family-style meals (closed Sun.). At the center of town, the lively **Palace Saloon** (904/261-6320) at 117 Centre Street is another of "Florida's Oldest," with a lovely carved wood bar, very good burgers,

FLORIDA HOUSE INN

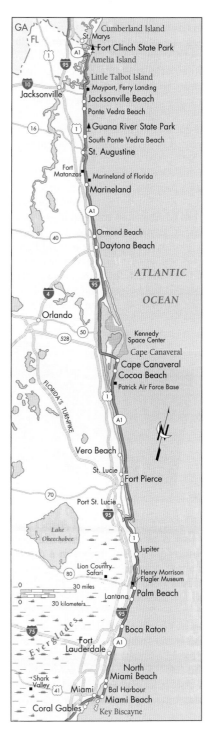

and regular live reggae and other warm-weather music.

More history has been preserved at the north end of Amelia Island, adjacent to Fernandina Beach, where the well-preserved remnants of a pre–Civil War brick fortress stand in **Fort Clinch State Park** (daily; $2; 904/277-7274), with 250 acres of marshes, sand dunes, and coastal hammock forests, plus a nice campground, along the edge of Cumberland Sound.

South of Fernandina Beach, Hwy-A1A follows Fletcher Avenue along Amelia Island's gorgeous white beaches, passing upscale resorts (including the Ritz-Carlton) before crossing over a bridge onto Talbot Island. Four miles south of the bridge, there's a turnoff west to the 3,000-acre **Kingsley Plantation State Historic Site** (daily; free; 904/251-3537), the last remaining antebellum plantation in Florida, where you can explore the elegant old lodge and remains of more than 20 slave cabins.

Continuing south, Hwy-A1A winds across the dense native jungles of **Little Talbot Island,** where a large **state park** (daily dawn–dusk; $3.50; 904/251-2320) has hiking and cycling trails, a nice campground, and a magnificent beach. The scenic road, which has been dubbed the "Buccaneer Trail," eventually ends up at the terminal for the ferry to Mayport (every 30 min.; no RVs) across the St. Johns River.

Jacksonville Beach

East of Jacksonville, at the mouth of the St. Johns River, Hwy-A1A curves around a large U.S. Navy base, past the Bath Iron Works shipyard and the sizeable fishing port of **Mayport,** where you can enjoy a quick bite at a

Host of the 2005 Super Bowl, Jacksonville, which covers over 840 square miles, is the largest city by area in the continental United States.

seafood shack (try **Singleton's,** 100 yards west of the ferry landing) while watching the ferry shuttle back and forth. From Mayport, Hwy-A1A zig-zags inland south and east, reaching the water again at **Jacksonville Beach,** a welcoming, family-oriented community with the usual gauntlet of cafés, mini-golf courses, and video arcades, and a nice beachfront centering on a small pier.

South of Jacksonville Beach spreads the enclave of **Ponte Vedra Beach,** where country club resorts replace roadside sprawl. Hwy-A1A bends inland through here, so if you want to keep close to the shore (most of which is private), follow Hwy-203 instead, rejoining Hwy-A1A on the edge of town.

South of Ponte Vedra, Hwy-A1A passes a pair of beachfront state parks (the marvelous 12,000-acre **Guana River** and smaller **South Ponte Vedra**), both of which give access to usually uncrowded sands. About 30 miles south of Jacksonville Beach, across the water from St. Augustine in the town of **Vilano Beach,** Hwy-A1A passes by a real historic Florida landmark, **Oscar's Old Florida Grill** (closed Mon. and Tues.; 904/829-3794), at 614 Euclid Avenue, east of the highway at milemarker 52. Built in 1909 and hardly changed since, this funky little shack has great fresh seafood, steaks, and burgers, and you can listen to live bluegrass and other good music while watching the sun set over the Tolomato River, the slow-flowing stream that doubles as the Intracoastal Waterway.

Fountain of Youth

Between Vilano Beach and St. Augustine, Hwy-A1A cuts inland from the shore, crossing a bridge over the North River, then following San Marco Avenue south past the Fountain of Youth and into the center of St. Augustine. That's right, the Fountain of Youth. Though its efficacy has never been proven in court, there is an actual site where Spanish explorer Ponce de León, searching for a fabled spring that would keep him forever young, came ashore in 1513. Now a  pleasant 20-acre park, facing Matanzas Bay about a mile north of central St. Augustine, the **Fountain of Youth** (daily 9 AM–5 PM; $6; 800/356-2222) preserves a naturally sulphurous spring (which you can drink from using Dixie cups— though there are no guarantees of immortality!), a burial ground, and remnants of a native Timucuan village and an early Spanish settlement.

St. Augustine

If you like history, architecture, sandy beaches, bizarre tourist attractions—or any combination of the above—you'll want to spend some time in St. Augustine. The oldest permanent settlement in the United States—though Santa Fe, New Mexico, makes a strong counterclaim to this title—**St. Augustine** was founded in 1565, half a century after Ponce de León first set foot here in 1513, looking for the Fountain of Youth. Under Spanish control, the town's early history was pretty

Henry Flagler: Father of Florida Tourism

You can't travel very far along the east coast of Florida without coming under the influence of Henry Flagler, who almost singlehandedly turned what had been swampy coastline into one of the world's most popular tourist destinations. After making a fortune as John D. Rockefeller's partner in the Standard Oil Company, in the early 1880s Flagler came to St. Augustine with his wife, who was suffering from health problems. He found the climate agreeable, but the facilities sorely lacking, so he embarked on construction of the 540-room Hotel Ponce de León, which opened in 1888. The hotel, the first major resort in Florida, was an instant success, and Flagler quickly expanded his operations, building the first railroad along the coast south to Palm Beach, where he opened the world's largest hotel, the now-demolished Royal Poinciana, in 1894, joined by The Breakers in 1901, and his own palatial home, Whitehall, in 1902.

Meanwhile, Flagler was busy extending his railroad south, effectively founding the new city of Miami in 1897 when he opened the deluxe Royal Palm Hotel (which stood on the waterfront, where the Inter-Continental does today). From Miami, he decided to extend his Florida East Coast Railway all the way to Key West, which at the time was Florida's most populous city, and the American deep-water port closest to the proposed Panama Canal. At a cost of $50 million and hundreds of lives, this amazing railroad was completed in 1912, but lasted only two decades before a hurricane destroyed the tracks in 1935. The remnants of Flagler's railroad were used as the foundation for today's Overseas Highway, US-1, but Flagler himself never lived to see it: In 1913, a year after his railroad reached Key West, Henry Flagler fell down a flight of stairs and died at age 84.

lively, with Sir Francis Drake leveling the place in 1586. The British, after trading Cuba for Florida at the end of the Seven Year's War, took control in 1763, and held St. Augustine throughout the American Revolution—during which Florida was staunchly loyal to King George. It served for many years as capital of Florida under both the British and Spanish, but after the Americans took over St. Augustine, the city lost that status to Tallahassee, subsequently missing out on much of Florida's 20th-century growth and development, which has allowed the preservation of its substantial historical remnants.

The heart of St. Augustine is contained within a walkably small area, centered around the Plaza de la Constitución, which faces east onto Matanzas Bay. Pedestrianized St. George Street runs north and south from here through the heart of historic St. Augustine, while two blocks west stands the city's most prominent landmarks, two grand, early 1900s hotels—the **Ponce de Leon** and the **Alcazar**.

They were originally owned and operated as part of Henry Flagler's Florida empire but now respectively house **Flagler College** and the decorative arts collections of the **Lightner Museum** (daily; $6). Both are full of finely crafted interior spaces and well worth a look.

Though it's the compact size and overall historic sheen of St. Augustine that make it such a captivating place to spend some time, there are lots of individual attractions hawking themselves as important "historic sites," usually the oldest this-or-that in Florida, or even in the whole United States. The **Oldest Wooden Schoolhouse,** at 14 St. George Street in the heart of historic St. Augustine, dates from 1750 and now features a push-button wax dummy of a schoolteacher, while the **Oldest Store,** a block south of the main plaza at 4 Artillery Lane, has 100,000 items, all of them well past their turn-of-the-century sell-by date. At the north end of St. George Street, an original city gate leads across San Marco Avenue (Hwy-A1A) to another must-see tourist trap: the original **Ripley's Believe It or Not!** museum (daily; $12.95; 904/824-1606), an elaborate Spanish Revival mansion filled since 1950 by Robert Ripley's personal collection of oddities. Outside, in the parking lot, is a four-room "tree house," carved out of a California redwood tree in 1957.

Across the street from the Ripley's Believe It or Not!, a coquina stone ball known as the **Zero Milepost** marks the eastern end of the **Old Spanish Trail,** one of the earliest transcontinental highways. Marked and promoted from here west to San Diego, the Old Spanish Trail, like the Lincoln Highway and the Dixie Highway, preceded the system of numbered highways (Route 66 et al.), and provided a popular cross-country link.

These are fun in a tongue-in-cheek way, but the most impressive historic site is the remarkable **Castillo de San Marcos** (daily; $5), which dominates the St. Augustine waterfront. Built by Spain between 1672 and 1695, the Castillo saw its first battle in 1702, when British forces laid siege for 50 days but were unable to capture it, though they did once again level the adjacent town of St. Augustine. The Castillo was later used by the British to house American POWs during the Revolutionary War, and by the United States to house Native American prisoners captured during the Seminole War of 1835–1842 as well as during the later Indian Wars of the Wild West. Since 1924 it's been a National Monument and is open for walks along the ramparts, and for frequent ranger-guided tours.

St. Augustine Practicalities

One of many attractive things about St. Augustine is the almost total lack of franchised fast-food restaurants, at least in the historic downtown area. Instead, you can choose from all sorts of local places, like the **Florida Cracker Cafe** (904/829-0397) at 81 St. George Street, a casual seafood grill where you can sample the local delicacy, alligator tail. For fish-and-chips, try the **White Lion Cafe and Pub** (904/829-2388), off St. George Street on Cuna Street; or **Milltop Tavern,** at the north end of St. George Street, which boasts a block-long bar. (Yes, it's a short block.) Another fun place to while away an evening is **Scarlett**

O'Hara's, offering beers, burgers, and live music a block from Flagler College at 70 Hypolita Street.

Away from the historic core, head north up Hwy-A1A to historic **Oscar's Old Florida Grill** (described in the Jacksonville Beach section above). Heading south toward St. Augustine Beach, Hwy-A1A passes a series of roadside restaurants: **Capt. Jack's,** 410 Anastasia Boulevard, is a family-friendly, deep-fried fish place; while the **Gypsy Cab Company,** 828 Anastasia, is more urbane—and more expensive. On St. Augustine Beach itself, **Po-Mar's** is a very popular sandwich and beer stand.

Unfortunately for present-day visitors, the grand old Ponce de Léon Hotel no longer welcomes overnight guests, but contemporary St. Augustine does offer a wide variety of accommodations, including the only B&B on Florida's Atlantic beachfront, the imaginatively named **Beachfront B&B** ($129 and up; 904/461-8727) at 1 F Street in St. Augustine Beach, where you can spend the night in one of six tastefully decorated suites in a historic home, then wake up to watch the porpoises cavorting offshore. In the historic district, the **Kenwood Inn** ($95 and up; 904/824-2116) at 38 Marine Street has rooms in a Victorian-era hotel along the Matanzas River.

For additional listings, maps, and general information, your first stop should be the St. Augustine **visitors center** (904/825-1000 or 800/OLD-CITY), across from the Castillo.

Alligator Farm

From the heart of St. Augustine, Hwy-A1A crosses over the Matanzas River on the lovely, historic Bridge of Lions to Anastasia Island, bound for the Atlantic beaches three miles to the east. On the way to the beach, just two miles south of Old Town St. Augustine on Anastasia Boulevard (Hwy-A1A), sits one of the greatest of Florida's many tourist traps, **Alligator Farm** (daily; $15; 904/824-3337). Touted as the world's only complete collection of crocodilians, this was the first and is now one of the last of many such roadside menageries. A legitimate historical landmark, Alligator Farm is also a fun and informative place to spend some time—great for kids and anyone who finds 'gators and crocs (and turtles, iguanas, monkeys, and tropical birds, all of which are here) to be captivating creatures. Start at the largest enclosure, a mossy pond seething with hundreds of baby 'gators (which you can feed), and be sure to pay your respects to Gomek, the Alligator Farm's massive taxidermied mascot, and to Maximo, a 16-foot Aussie crocodile who's still growing ever-larger.

Across from Alligator Farm, a road turns east from Hwy-A1A to **Anastasia State Recreation Area,** the site

About three miles north of Marineland, on the inland side of Hwy-A1A, you can see the 16-foot-thick stone walls of **Fort Matanzas**, built by the Spanish around 1736, and never conquered. Now a national historic site, it's open for free tours.

The town of Ormond Beach, which adjoins the north side of Daytona Beach, was also used by early speed-seekers, and prior to that was a winter playground of the rich and famous, richest and most famously **John D. Rockefeller,** who wintered here for years before his death in 1937, aged 97. His mansion, called **The Casements,** is now a **museum** (386/676-3216), along the east bank of the Halifax River at 25 Riverside Drive.

where the stone for Castillo de San Marcos was quarried, and where in addition to beaches there's an inlet set aside for windsurfing, hiking trails through coastal hammock forests, and a nice campground (904/461-2033) amidst stately live oaks and magnolia trees.

Marineland

Eighteen miles south of St. Augustine, 35 miles north of Daytona Beach, the original sea-creature amusement park, **Marineland** (daily except Tues.; $14; 904/460-1275) opened with a "splash" in 1938, and closed down suddenly in 1998, declaring bankruptcy after struggling for years to compete with the much-larger likes of Sea World and Disney World. Marineland, which is credited with the first performing dolphins (and with playing a key role in the sci-fi movie *Creature From the Black Lagoon*), reopened in 2005 on a much smaller scale, with an "edutainment" focus on offering intimate encounters with its famous dolphins.

Continuing along the coast south of Marineland, you start to see roadside fruit stands advertising "Indian River Fruit"—something you'll see more of as you travel south. This stretch of Hwy-A1A, around the town of Flagler Beach, is also one of the few where you can actually see the ocean from the road.

Daytona Beach

Offering a heady barrage of blue-collar beach culture, **Daytona Beach** (pop. 61,900) is a classic road-trip destination in every way, shape, and form. The beach here is huge—over 20 miles long, and 500 feet wide at low tide—and there's a small amusement pier at the foot of Main Street (with a Sky Ride that dangles you over the fishermen below), but the rest of Daytona Beach is rather rough at the edges, with boarded-up shops and some lively bars and nightclubs filling the few blocks between the beach area and the Halifax River, which separates the beach from the rest of the town.

Besides being a living museum of pop culture, Daytona Beach has long played an important role in car culture: In the first decades of the 20th century, a real Who's Who of international automotive pioneers—Henry Ford, R. E. Olds, Malford Duesenberg, and more—came here to test the upper limits of automotive performance. The first world land-speed record (a whopping 68 mph!) was set here in 1903, and by 1935 the ill-starred British racer Malcolm Campbell had raised it to 276 mph.

The speed racers later moved west to Bonneville Salt Flats in Utah (see page 136), and Daytona became the breeding ground for stock car racing—today's Daytona 500 started out as a series of 100- to

200-mile races around a rough four-mile oval, half on the sands and half on a paved frontage road. The circuit races, both for cars and motorcycles, really came into their own after World War II. In 1947, NASCAR (the National Association for Stock Car Auto Racing) was founded here as the nascent sport's governing body, but the races soon outgrew the sands, and in 1958 were moved to the purpose-built **Daytona International Speedway,** on US-92 six miles west of the beach, right off I-95 exit 87. Except during the run-up to a race, you can take a guided tour (daily; $6; 386/947-6800) of the triangular track, cruising down the back straight and around the steeply banked turns—in a bus, at a modest 20 mph.

On the speedway grounds, the racing experience is brought to life at the very enjoyable **Daytona USA** ($16), part museum and part amusement park, where you can learn the history of stock car racing, take part in a simulated pit stop, play video games, and watch a loud and totally thrilling big screen movie that lets you experience the pace and power of Daytona—without having to wear seat belts. (After a visit, you may want to spend some time practicing your skills at the go-cart track across the street.)

Daytona Beach Practicalities

Daytona Beach is party central during March and April, when some 300,000 college kids escape from northern climes to defrost and unwind with a vengeance. There has been a concerted effort to keep a lid on things recently, but if you're after peace and quiet you should head somewhere else. The same is true of the springtime "Bike Week" before the Daytona 200 in March, and again in fall during "Bike-toberfest," when thousands of motorcycling enthusiasts descend upon Daytona for a week or more of partying in between races at Daytona Speedway. The grandaddy of all stock car races, the Daytona 500, is held around Valentine's Day, but getting one of the 110,000 tickets is all but impossible for casual fans.

A world apart from the spring break, biker, and race car scenes, but just a mile from the beach, the **Cuban Sandwich Shop** (386/255-6655), at 722 Mason Avenue, serves inexpensive Cuban food and great fresh fruit smoothies. There are tons of high-rise hotels along beachfront Atlantic Avenue, many advertising off-season or midweek deals, and one unusual place to stay: the **Traveler's Inn** ($45–60; 386/253-3501) at 735 N. Atlantic Avenue, where the motel rooms are all decorated with murals of movie stars (from Marilyn Monroe to John Wayne) and biker chicks.

Adding to Daytona's already broad mix of pop culture icons is the **Hamburger Hall of Fame** (386/254-8753). This wacky collection of burger-related memorabilia is displayed in a private home, but is open for tours by appointment.

Between Orlando and the Space Coast, the Beeline Expressway (Hwy-528) is a fast, flat toll road, with only three exits in the 30 miles between I-95 and greater Orlando.

For a Disneyfied view of the ideal American town, visit the Walt Disney Company's retro-Victorian planned community of **Celebration** (pop. 700 and growing), south of US-192 at the I-4 junction. Contrary to popular belief, this is not the town seen in the Jim Carrey movie *The Truman Show* (that was Seaside, in the Florida Panhandle), but it could have been.

Detour: Orlando and Walt Disney World

Entire guidebooks are devoted to covering the mind-boggling array of tourist attractions in and around Orlando, but three words would probably suffice: **Walt Disney World.** Over 100,000 people come here every day to experience the magic of the Magic Kingdom, which is divided into four main areas—the Magic Kingdom amusement park, a new "Animal Kingdom" animal park, the futuristic EPCOT Center, and the Disney-MGM studio tours. Entrance to any of these will set you back around $60; to see all of them, get a "park-hopper" pass, which is valid from four days (about $225) or longer. For further information on admissions and lodging packages call 407/824-4321.

At the time of writing, there's still no law that says you have to go to Disney World just because you've come to Florida, but it is a cultural phenomenon and more than a little fun. While you're here, you may want to visit the other big-time attractions like Sea World and Universal Studios, but Orlando also has some funky, pre–Disney era tourist traps, with ad budgets small enough that you won't have to fight the crowds.

To watch a space shuttle or other launch at Kennedy Space Center, you can get passes from the visitors center, or simply watch from the many good vantage points: **Playalinda Beach,** in the Canaveral National Seashore at the west end of Hwy-402 from Titusville; across the Indian River, along US-1 in Titusville; or the beaches west of Hwy-A1A in **Cocoa Beach**.

The Space Coast: Cape Canaveral

It's more than a little ironic that one of the most extensive sections of natural coastal wetlands left in Florida is home to the launch pads of the nation's space program. Though the natural aspects—thousands of seabirds and wide open stretches of sandy beaches—are attractive enough in their own right to merit a visit, most people are drawn here because the undeveloped landscape allows clear and generally unobstructed views of missile launches, and Space Shuttle take-offs and landings, at Cape Canaveral's **Kennedy Space Center.** All the big milestones in the history of the U.S. space program—the Mercury, Gemini, Apollo, and Space Shuttle launches—happened here, and if names like Alan Shepard, John Glenn, or Neil Armstrong mean anything to you, set aside time for a visit.

The Kennedy Space Center itself, eight miles west of US-1 via the NASA Parkway (Hwy-405), is open to the public, but only on guided tours. These tours require advance tickets, and all leave from the large **visitors complex** (daily; $18–37; 321/452-2121) where a pair of IMAX theaters show films of outer space to get you in the mood. There are also some small museums, a simulated Space Shuttle mission control center, a half-dozen missiles in the Rocket Garden,

Best of this bunch is probably **GatorLand** (daily; $19; 407/855-5496), 14501 S. Orange Blossom Trail, where thousands of alligators, crocodiles, snakes, and other reptiles are gathered together in a cypress swamp. You enter through a gator's gaping jaws, and inside can see such sights as live chickens being dangled over a pond, taunting the hungry carnivorous gators just of out reach below. Continuing south along US-441, past the world headquarters of Tupperware, another sight of offbeat interest is the 100-year-old historic district at the heart of **Kissimmee** (pop. 38,200), where a 50-foot stone and concrete pyramid, constructed in 1943 with rocks from most states, as well as 21 countries, stands in Lake Front Park.

It doesn't take a Boy Genius to figure out the customer base of the Jimmy Neutron–themed **Nickelodeon Family Suites** ($180 and up; 866/462-6485), a kid-friendly Holiday Inn with multiple bedrooms near Disney World. Another movie spinoff: Disney's extraordinary **Animal Kingdom Lodge** ($199 and up; 407/939-7429), where a 30-acre savannah landscape offers families and Lion King fans the chance to take an African safari—without the jet lag.

and an actual Space Shuttle, which you can walk through. The visitors center also has a couple of fast-food restaurants and a kennel for pets.

To see the Kennedy Space Center up close, board a bus for a tour; these leave every few minutes, and visit the Apollo and Space Shuttle launch pads and other sites, including a mock-up of the International Space Station. On other tours, you can visit the Cape Canaveral Air Force station; the Cape Canaveral Air Station, site of many early "Space Race" adventures; or even "have lunch with an astronaut," and talk about outer space with someone who's actually been there (glass of Tang not included).

One of the best places to eat in this part of Florida is west of the Space Center, in the town of Titusville: **Dixie Crossroads** (daily; 321/268-5000), at 1475 Garden Street, an immense (and immensely popular) place to eat seafood, especially massive plates of shrimp. All-you-can-eat piles of small shrimp cost $20, while jumbo shrimp cost around $1 apiece. The Crossroads is away from the water, two miles east of I-95 exit 220.

At the entrance to the Kennedy Space Center visitors center, the **Astronaut Memorial** is a huge black granite block backed by high-tech mirrors that reflect sunlight onto the surface of the stone, illuminating the engraved names of the men and women who have given their lives exploring space.

Cocoa Beach

The town of **Cocoa Beach,** familiar to anyone who ever watched the 1960s Space Age sitcom *I Dream of Jeannie,* sits south of the Kennedy Space Center, and the town pier that juts out into the Atlantic Ocean at the north end of town is a

East from Hwy-A1A on the south side of Cocoa Beach, "I Dream of Jeannie Lane" leads down to a nice beachfront park.

prime spot for viewing Space Shuttle and other rocket launches. Long before there were Space Shuttles, or even NASA, Cocoa Beach was home to the Cape Canaveral Air Station, the launch site for the unmanned space probes of the late 1950s, including the first U.S. satellite (Explorer 1), and the famous "astro chimps" (Gordo, Able, and Miss Baker, who were sent into orbit to test the effects of weightlessness). The Air Station has historical exhibits and dozens of missiles, from today's Patriots back to German V2s (which were fired at England during World War II and provided the engineering basis for the American rockets of a decade later). The small on-site museum includes early computers and other equipment, housed inside the blockhouse from which the first launches were controlled.

Though travel to outer space is clearly on the minds of many residents, especially personnel stationed at Patrick Air Force Base here, another focus is catching the perfect wave: Cocoa Beach is surf center of the Space Coast. Along with a clean, 10-mile-long beach, the town also holds a batch of good-value motels, located within a short walk of the waves. Choose from chains (including a Motel 6), or check out the garish **Fawlty Towers** (321/784-3870), at 100 E. Cocoa Beach Causeway, which is sadly devoid of John Cleese or put-upon Juan. It is, however, next door to Cocoa Beach's main event, the massive **Ron Jon Surf Shop** (321/799-8888), open 24 hours every day at 4151 Atlantic Avenue, and *the* place to buy or rent surfboards, body boards, or bicycles.

Spring Training: Grapefruit League Baseball

Every February and March, hundreds of baseball players at all levels of expertise head to Florida to earn or keep their places on some 20 different Major League teams and their minor league farm club affiliates. The informality and ease of access during this spring training, which is known as the Grapefruit League, attracts thousands of baseball fans as well. Though they're not necessarily played to win, Grapefruit League games are played in modern 10,000-seat stadia that approach the major leagues in quality, and the smaller size allows an up-close feel you'd have to pay much more for during the regular season. (And your chances of snagging balls during batting practice are infinitely better, too.)

Most of the teams make their springtime homes on the Gulf Coast, but many others locate in cities and towns along Florida's Atlantic coast, as the Los Angeles Dodgers do in Vero Beach. Three teams are in the Orlando area, including the Atlanta Braves and the Houston Astros. Back on the coast, the New York Mets train in Port St. Lucie, the Washington Nationals in the Space Coast town of Viera, the St. Louis Cardinals and Florida Marlins play in Jupiter, and the Baltimore Orioles can be found in Fort Lauderdale.

Vero Beach

As a boy growing up in sunny Los Angeles, I could never understand why the Dodgers felt they had to disappear to distant Florida to get in shape during Spring Training. I knew the weather couldn't be so much better there (after all, didn't L.A. have the heavenly climate?), and I never quite figured out what the big attraction of Vero Beach, the Dodgers' off-season home, could be. But when I discovered that the Dodgers had started playing here way back in 1948—back when they still called Brooklyn home—it all began to make sense. And it still does, once you see the spacious grounds of **Dodgertown**, their Florida training complex, which spreads amidst the grapefruit orchards on the west side of town at 4001 26th Street. The Dodgers train here in February and March, when the place is packed with thousands of baseball fans from all over the country.

Besides baseball, Vero Beach also has a really nice beach, in South Beach Park at the end of the Palmetto Causeway. This South Beach is family-friendly and about as far as you can get from Miami's South Beach and still be in Florida: the sands here are clean, grainy, and golden, the waves are good-sized, and there are showers and free parking.

Vero Beach also has a nice place to stay and eat: the **Driftwood Resort** (772/231-0550) at 3150 Ocean Drive, which has funky 1950s-style motel rooms, and the fun and good-value **Waldo's**, a poolside café and bar overlooking the ocean.

The Dodgers' Class A farm team, the **Vero Beach Dodgers**, play in Dodgertown all summer long, drawing fans to sunny Holman Stadium ($4–6; 772/569-4900). Games are broadcast on **WTTB** 1490 AM.

South of Fort Pierce, Port St. Lucie is the spring training home of the **New York Mets** (561/871-2100), who play at 525 NW Peacock Boulevard, off I-95.

Fort Pierce

South of Vero Beach, Hwy-A1A continues along North Hutchinson Island past the **UDT Navy SEALs Museum** (closed Mon.; $5; 772/595-5845), which describes the various roles played by underwater divers in demolishing enemy property during wartime. Among the displays of wetsuits and explosives is an Apollo capsule—it's Navy SEALs who rescued returning astronauts after they "splashed down" in the ocean. On either side of the museum, undeveloped stretches of the coast have been preserved in a pair of parks, where you can enjoy uncrowded beaches or wander along boardwalks through thickly forested mangrove swamps.

Bending inland across the North Bridge, Hwy-A1A links up briefly with US-1, the old Dixie Highway, through the town of **Fort Pierce** (pop. 37,516), a market center of the famous "Indian River" produce-growing district. After this half-mile detour, Hwy-A1A returns to the shore, passing along the way by the very good **St. Lucie County Historical Museum** (closed Mon.; $4), at the east end of the South Bridge, where broad-ranging displays tell the history of the region, showing off a hand-carved canoe and explaining the "fort" in Fort Pierce (it was built in 1835, during the Seminole Wars).

South of Fort Pierce, Hwy-A1A embarks on a nearly 30-mile run along Hutchinson Island, where dense stands of pines block the views of largely undeveloped beachfront. On the coast just north of Palm Beach, the town of Jupiter has long been home to movie star Burt Reynolds; the park surrounding the town's excellent **Loxahatchee River Historical Museum** (closed Mon.; $4), off Hwy-A1A at 805 N. US-1, is named in Burt's honor, though he himself is absent from the museum's displays.

Palm Beach

A South Florida sibling to the conspicuous consumption that once defined Newport, Rhode Island, **Palm Beach** (pop. 10,468) has been a winter refuge for the rich and famous since Henry Flagler started work on his fashionable (but long-vanished) resort hotel, the 1,150-room Royal Poinciana. It was the world's largest wood building when completed in 1894, but the site is now an upscale shopping district at the center of town. Away from here, most of Palm Beach is well-guarded private property, off-limits to most mere mortals. The best way for anyone not named Kennedy or Pierpont to get a look at Palm Beach life is to spend some time at the Hearst Castle of the East Coast, the **Henry Morrison Flagler Museum** (closed Mon.; $10; 561/655-2833), on the inland side of downtown Palm Beach, at the north end of Cocoanut Row. Officially known as Whitehall, this opulent 60,000-square-foot mansion was Flagler's private home, and the 50-plus rooms (many of which were taken from European buildings and re-installed here) contain historical exhibits tracing the life of Flagler, the Standard Oil baron (John D. Rockefeller's right-hand man) who made a fortune while making Florida into an immensely popular vacation destination.

Inland from Palm Beach, you can wave at rhinos, lions, and wildebeest in a 500-acre, drive-through simulation of African ecosystems at **Lion Country Safari** *(561/793-1084), 18 miles west of I-95 via US-98. No convertibles allowed!*

The town of **Lantana**, *on the coast between Palm Beach and Boca Raton, is the home of the* **National Enquirer** *tabloid.*

Even bigger and better than Whitehall is **The Breakers**, a stately resort hotel that faces the ocean at the east end of Palm Beach and retains much of its 1920s Mediterranean style and grace. Rooms will set you back around $500 a night (much more for suites), but you can enjoy the lobby, have a drink or afternoon tea, or take a tour (Wed. at 3 PM only; free; 561/655-6611).

Not surprisingly, there are some very good and very expensive restaurants in and around Palm Beach, but happily there's also a very nice, normal, all-American luncheonette just two blocks north of The Breakers: **Green's Pharmacy** (561/832-4443), at 151 N. County Road, serving very good diner-style meals.

Boca Raton

Whoever named **Boca Raton** (pop. 74,764), which translates literally as the "Rat's Mouth," clearly didn't have an ear for future promotional bonanza, but despite the awkward name the town has become one of the more chichi spots in the state. As in Palm Beach, Coral Gables, and Miami's South Beach, the best of Boca dates from the 1920s, when architect and real estate promoter Addison Mizner, flush from his success building Mediterranean-style manors in Palm Beach, created a mini Venice of resorts and canals, which survives mainly in the shocking pink palazzo of the **Boca Raton Resort** ($200 and up; 561/447-3000), on the southeast side of town at 501 E. Camino Royal.

Downtown Boca has been turned into a massive stucco shopping mall, but it's worth braving for a look inside the ornate Mizner-designed Town Hall, on US-1 (old Dixie Highway) in Palmetto Park downtown, which now houses the local historical museum (closed Mon.; free).

US-1, the main route through town, also holds the very popular **Boca Diner** (561/750-6744), serving above-average coffee shop fare at 2801 N. Federal Highway; the early evening "Early Bird" scene here is straight out of *Seinfeld*.

Hwy-A1A misses most of Boca Raton, cruising past along the densely pine-forested coast. The beaches are accessible but hard to find; one well-marked stop along the way is the **Gumbo Limbo Nature Center** (Mon.–Sat. 9 AM–4 PM, Sun. noon–4 PM; free; 561/338-1473) on the inland side of the highway, a mile north of Mizner Park. A variety of native Floridian landscapes have been re-created here, letting you wander at will past coastal dunes, mangrove wetlands, and rare sabal palm hammocks. Across Hwy-A1A, **Red Reef Park** is a popular surfing beach.

Fort Lauderdale

Once famed for wild spring break frolics that saw thousands of college kids descending here for an orgy of drunken round-the-clock partying, **Fort Lauderdale** (pop. 162,800) is a surprisingly residential city, brought to a more human scale by the many waterways that cut through it. One of the largest cargo ports in the state, Fort Lauderdale also boasts more boats per capita than just about anywhere else in the United States, and over 165 miles of canals, inlets, and other waterways flow through the city.

Fort Lauderdale is said to be one of the points that form the **"Bermuda Triangle,"** so of course there are numerous beachside bars where college kids try to simulate its supernatural effects by imbibing too many margaritas.

Downtown Fort Lauderdale has a few big, dull office towers, but along the New River there are some well-preserved historic buildings dating back to 1905, when the city first emerged from the swamps. Find out more by visiting the **Historical Museum** (Tues.–Fri. 10 AM–4 PM; $2), west of US-1 at 231 S.W. 2nd Avenue, which has lots of old photos and walking-tour maps, or the nifty **Stranahan House** (closed Mon. & Tues.; $6), off US-1 at 335 S.E. 6th Avenue, a circa-1901 trading post and house, with broad verandahs and a high ceiling to help cool down in the days before air-conditioning. Still owned by the same family that built it, the Stranahan House is one of the most evocative historic places in the state.

Fort Lauderdale's main beachfront bar and nightclub district is along Atlantic Avenue and Las Olas Boulevard, where you'll find some nice sidewalk cafés and fast-food restaurants. One culinary landmark: **Johnny V.'s** (954/761-7920), 625 E. Las Olas, a popular and stylish haunt where traditional American dishes are enlivened by a canny blend of exotic ingredients. For a change of pace from the frenetic tourism, or simply to enjoy good basic fried seafood, cold beer, and live blues, head south down US-1 to **Ernie's BBQ Lounge** (954/523-8636) at 1843 S. Federal Highway, famous for its conch fritters, calamari rings, and rooftop deck.

Miles of inexpensive motels line Hwy-A1A north of Fort Lauderdale, and unless there's something big going on you shouldn't have trouble finding a room for under $100—half that in summer. For complete listings of restaurants and accommodations, contact the **visitors bureau** (954/765-4466 or 800/356-1662), located at 1850 Eller Drive.

North of Fort Lauderdale, Hwy-A1A winds in along the coast through a series of funky, friendly beachside communities. South of Fort Lauderdale, Hwy-A1A heads inland and merges into US-1, returning to the coast for the run south to Miami Beach.

North Miami Beach

Between Fort Lauderdale and Miami Beach, Hwy-A1A runs along the shore, first as Ocean Drive and later as Collins Avenue, while US-1 runs inland parallel to the old Dixie Highway. There's nothing here to compare with the attractions farther south, but the town of **North Miami Beach** does have one oddity: the **Ancient Spanish Monastery** (daily 10 AM–4 PM; $5), at 16711 W. Dixie Highway, a 12th-century monastery bought in the 1920s by William Randolph Hearst, who had it dismantled and shipped to the United States for his Hearst Castle. However, it was confiscated by U.S. Customs, and finally rebuilt here as an Episcopal church.

On the coast, Hwy-A1A runs past a number of indistinct beach towns before hitting **Bal Harbour,** home to one of Miami's biggest and best shopping malls, and one of its biggest beaches, **Haulover Beach.** From here south to Miami Beach, the road is lined with towering concrete condos and hotels.

At the far north end of Miami Beach, one place you'll want to stop, especially if you're hungry, is **Wolfie Cohen's Rascal House** (daily 6:30 AM–2 AM; 305/947-4581), on Hwy-A1A at 17190 Collins Avenue, a super-sized NYC-style deli done up in Miami's favorite colors: shocking pink and turquoise green. The portions here are good and huge—big enough to feed two or more—and the conversation is more entertaining than *Seinfeld* reruns.

Miami Beach

Covering a broad island separating downtown Miami from the open Atlantic Ocean, **Miami Beach** (pop. 87,933) has long been a mecca for fans of 1930s art deco architecture and design. More recently, it's also become one of the world's most fashionable and bacchanalian beach resorts, with deluxe hotels and high-style nightclubs and restaurants lining the broad white sands of South Beach, the relatively small corner of Miami Beach that gets 99 percent of the press and tourist attention. Here, along beachfront Ocean Drive and busier Collins Avenue (Hwy-A1A) a block inland, you'll find dozens of glorious art deco hotels, many lighted with elegant neon signs. Guided walking tours (Wed.–Sun.; $20) of the district leave from the **Art Deco Welcome Center** (daily; 305/531-3484) at 1001 Ocean Drive, which also sells guidebooks, posters, postcards, and anything else you can think of that has to do with the art deco era.

No matter how intoxicating the architecture, beach life, and nightlife along South Beach are, while you're here be sure to set aside an hour or two to explore the fascinating collection of pop culture artifacts on display two blocks

Carl Fisher: Father of Miami Beach

Fisher Park, on the bay side of Miami Beach on Alton Road at 51st Street, holds a small monument to the fascinating Carl Fisher, the man most responsible for turning Miami Beach from a mangrove swamp into America's favorite resort. Before building up Lincoln Avenue into Miami Beach's first commercial district, Carl Fisher had played an important role in America's early automotive history. Called the "P. T. Barnum of the Automobile Age," Fisher made millions through the Prest-O-Lite company, which in the early 1900s developed the first functioning car headlight. Around 1910, he invested this fortune in building and promoting the Indianapolis Motor Speedway, then went on to plan and publicize both the Lincoln Highway, America's first transcontinental road, and the Dixie Highway, the first main north–south route in the eastern United States. He invested heavily in Miami Beach property, but was ruined by the Great Depression and the sudden drop in land values. He died here, nearly penniless, in 1939, just as the economy was rebounding and the art deco hotels of South Beach were bringing new life to Miami Beach.

inland at the **Wolfsonian** (closed Wed.; $5; 305/531-1001), at 1001 Washington Avenue. One of the odder highbrow museums you'll find, the Wolfsonian (officially the Mitchell Wolfson Jr. Collection of Decorative and Propaganda Arts) fills a retrofitted 1920s warehouse with four floors of furniture, sculpture, architectural models, posters, and much more, almost all dating from the "Modern Era," roughly 1885 to 1945. Two areas of excellence are drawings and murals created under the New Deal auspices of the WPA, and similar agitprop artifacts created in Weimar, Germany. Only a small portion of the extensive collection is on display at any one time, and most of the floor space is given over to changing exhibitions—on anything from World's Fairs to Florida tourism to William Morris chairs—but it's a fun and thought-provoking place, with an unexpressed but overriding theme of how art can counterbalance, or at least respond to, the demands of industrial society.

Miami Beach Practicalities

Not surprisingly, there are scores of cafés and restaurants in and around Miami Beach; some, like exotic **Wish** (305/674-9474) in The Hotel at 801 Collins Avenue, are rated among the best in the world. More down to earth, and just two blocks west of the beach, the **11th Street Diner** (305/534-6373) on 11th and Washington is a 1948 Paramount pre-fab diner, plunked down in 1992 and open 24 hours ever since.

Miami

Equal parts jet-set glitz and multicultural grit, and with more than half its population coming here from other countries around the globe, Miami (pop. 372,000) really embodies the transitive state of the nation at the beginning of the 21st century. Having sprung up from swampland in the 1920s, Miami has weathered hurricanes and race riots, real estate booms and busts, drug running and endless political intrigue to become one of America's most energetic cities.

Approaching from Miami Beach past the cruise ship docks along the MacArthur Causeway, or the older and more leisurely Venetian Causeway, you experience the view of Miami made famous by Miami Vice—downtown towers rising above Biscayne Bay. West of downtown, Miami's most engaging district is Little Havana, which focuses along SW 8th Street (aka "Calle Ocho") between 12th and 16th Avenues. Since the 1950s and 1960s, when the first refugees fleeing Castro's regime fetched up here, this neighborhood has been the heart of Cuban-American Miami. Hang out for a while with the old men who congregate in the Domino Park on 8th Street and 14th Avenue, or visit the Martyrs of Giron (aka Bay of Pigs) Monument along 8th Street between 12th and 13th Streets; you'll definitely get a feel for it. Better yet, stop for something to eat or drink at one of Little Havana's many great Cuban cafes, like **La Esquina de Tejas** (305/545-0337), at 101 SW 12th Avenue; or **Casa Panza** (305/643-5343), at 1620 SW 8th Street, which turns into a lively dance club on Tuesday and Thursday nights. To watch the power brokers at work, try **Versailles** (305/444-0240), at 3555 SW 8th Street, and enjoy a bowl of *ropa vieja* (tender threads of garlicky beef in a black bean soup).

In downtown Miami, a fun place to stay is the characterful and historic **Miami River Inn** ($70–199; 305/325-0045), 118 SW South River Drive, a well-preserved circa-1908 hotel with B&B rooms (all with private baths). Miami Beach still has the best range of stylish hotels, but Miami itself has the stunning **Four Seasons** ($250 and up; 305/358-3535) at 1435 Brickell Avenue, offering stunning views from a 70-story tower. Back down to earth, the major chains all have locations on the downtown waterfront; as at all South Florida accommodations, room rates tend to increase considerably during the peak season (Jan.–April).

The **Florida Marlins** (305/930-4487) play at Pro Player Stadium, 2267 NW 199th Street.

The best source of information on greater Miami, including Miami Beach, is the Greater Miami **visitors bureau** (305/539-3063 or 800/283-2707) at 701 Brickell Avenue.

For an unforgettably hedonistic experience, check into one of South Beach's great old art deco hotels, or at least saunter through the lobby and stop for a drink. The **Delano** ($180 and up; 305/672-2000), at 1685 Collins Avenue, is a high-style symphony in white; while the **Raleigh** ($180 and up; 305/534-6300), 1775 Collins Avenue, has the coolest pool in South Beach. Dozens of these 1930s divas stand out along Ocean Drive and Collins Avenue, but the wonderful architecture, alas, doesn't always manage to mask their elderly bones, nor is the 24-hour hubbub that surrounds them especially conducive to a good night's sleep. Ocean Drive, by the way, is undriveable on weekend nights, since so many cars cruise up and down it, stereos blasting.

Less than a mile north of bustling South Beach, comfortable and reasonably priced accommodation options in the rest of Miami Beach include the friendly **Abbey Hotel** ($120 and up; 305/531-0031), a nicely restored art deco hotel, three blocks from a nice broad beach at 300 21st Street.

Stylish though it is, South Beach is not frequented by many locals, who instead tend to spend time on **Lincoln Road,** a half mile north of South Beach. The Mediterranean Revival–style commercial district along Lincoln Road, developed in the 1920s by promoter Carl Fisher, was the original main drag of Miami Beach; it has been pedestrianized and nicely landscaped and is now packed with dozens of lively sidewalk cafés like the iconoclastic **SushiSambaDromo** (305/673-5337) at 600 Lincoln Road and the highly regarded **Pacific Time** (305/534-5979), 915 Lincoln Road.

Across Miami

The I-95 freeway, and the old main route, US-1, both enter Miami north of downtown in the very rough Little Haiti neighborhood, while the infinitely more scenic Hwy-A1A crosses Biscayne Bay from Miami Beach. Around downtown, Biscayne Boulevard winds along the waterfront, merging into historic Brickell Avenue, now lined by flashy postmodern bank and condo towers. From here, detour west on the one-way system along 7th and 8th Streets through Little Havana, then south through Coral Gables, joining the old Dixie Highway (US-1) for the drive south through Homestead to the Florida Keys.

Coral Gables

South of Miami's Little Havana neighborhood, accessible through grand gates off the Tamiami Trail (8th Street), the stately community of **Coral Gables** is one of the few Florida resort towns that survives fairly unchanged since the boom years of the 1920s. Coral Gables boasts many grand boulevards, fine fountains, plazas, and lush gardens, but the landmark to look for is the 26-story **Biltmore Hotel** ($150 and up; 305/445-1926 or 800/727-1926), at 1200 Anastasia

The stately Mediterranean Revival manor where fashion designer **Gianni Versace** lived and was murdered sits at the heart of South Beach, on Ocean Drive just north of 11th Street.

In her 1987 book *Miami*, **Joan Didion** describes the city as an economically schizophrenic place where it's possible "to pass from walled enclaves to utter desolation while changing stations on the car radio."

The Latin American influence on Miami is evident everywhere you go, but for proof of just how deep the connections run, consider the fact that two of Cuba's deposed presidents, **Gerardo Machado** and **Carlos Prio,** are buried in Miami's **Woodlawn Park Cemetery,** a mile west of Little Havana. Former Nicaraguan dictator **Anastasio Somoza** is buried there, too.

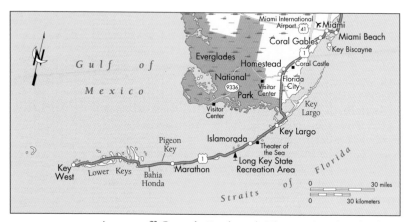

In 1983, the
Bulgarian artist **Christo**
wrapped 11 Biscayne
Bay islands in bright
pink plastic as part of
his Surrounded
Islands installation.

Avenue off Granada Boulevard. This opulent hotel, which opened in 1926 and boasts the world's largest swimming pool (Johnny Weismuller was the original lifeguard!), has been restored to its original glory.

The southern edge of Coral Gables is occupied by the drab campus of the University of Miami, which is bounded by US-1, the old Dixie Highway.

Homestead: Coral Castle

One of the most diverting stops between Miami and the Florida Keys has to be the **Coral Castle** (daily; $10; 305/248-6345), 28655 S. Dixie Highway, an amazing house hand-carved out of huge blocks of oolitic coral in the 1930s. Located right along the highway, two miles north of Homestead, the house is filled with furniture also carved from stone—a 3,000-pound sofa and a 500-pound rocking chair—and no one has figured how its enigmatic creator (Ed Leedskalnin) did it all without help or the use of any heavy machinery.

Homestead, along with neighboring Florida City farther south, forms the main gateway to Everglades National Park, and there are tons of reasonably-priced motels hereabouts—all the usual suspects line up here along US-1, including the very nice **Best Western Gateway to the Keys** (305/246-5100).

Florida's other big national park, **Biscayne National Park**, stretches east of Homestead from near Miami to the top of the Florida Keys, but is almost completely underwater. Privately run snorkeling and diving tours (around $30–35) leave from near the main Convoy Point visitors center (305/230-7275), 9 miles east of US-1 at the end of 328th Street—near the huge Homestead Motorsports Complex (and a nuclear power plant).

Everglades National Park

Covering over 1.5 million acres at the far southwestern tip of mainland Florida, **Everglades National Park** protects the largest subtropical wilderness in the United States. A fair portion of the park is actually underwater, and the entire Everglades ecosystem is basically a giant, slow-flowing river that is 50 miles wide but only a few inches deep. Fed by Lake Okechobee, and under constant threat

by irrigation in-flows and out-flows, and by the redirection of water to Miami and other cities, the Everglades still seem to vibrate with life. Some 300 species of birds breed here, as do 600 different kinds of fish and animals, ranging from rare manatees to abundant alligators. (Not to mention the gazillions of mosquitoes.)

The backcountry parts of the Everglades can be visited by boat, but by road there are only two main routes. In the north, the Tamiami Trail (the "Tampa to Miami Trail," aka US-41) heads west from Miami to misnamed **Shark Valley**, where you can rent bikes or take a tram tour on a 15-mile loop through the "sawgrass" swamps that make up the heart of the Everglades. Gazing at the gators, eagles, and hawks here, it's hard to believe you're barely a half hour from South Beach. Just west of Shark Valley, the **Miccosukee Indian Village** is a reminder of the Everglades native peoples, the Seminoles, some of whom now wrestle alligators, run souvenir shops, and give airboat tours of their ancestral lands.

The main road access to the Everglades is via Palm Drive (Hwy-9336) from the Florida Turnpike or US-1. This route takes you past the main visitors center, where interpretive displays and a pair of nature trails give an appetizing taste of the Everglades (and almost guaranteed sightings of alligators). The road continues nearly 40 miles west to the former town of Flamingo, where both the residents and the namesake birds have all moved on, leaving a few tour boat operators and the Everglades' only eating and accommodation option, the **Flamingo Lodge** ($70 and up; 239/695-3101).

The main Everglades National Park **visitors center** (305/242-7700) is west of Florida City, just inside the park boundary.

Key Largo

The Overseas Highway (US-1) officially starts in Florida City, near the Everglades some 50 miles south of Miami, but doesn't really come alive until it leaves the mainland and lands at **Key Largo**, the first and largest of the dozens of "keys" (from the Spanish word *cayos,* meaning small islands) the highway links together. The Overseas Highway reaches Key Largo at the very popular **John Pennecamp Coral Reef State Park** (daily; $4; 305/451-1202), at MM 102.5. The first place where you can really get a feel for life on the Keys, the park is the starting point for a variety of **guided tours** (scuba diving, snorkeling, or in glass-bottomed boats) that offer up-close looks at the only tropical coral reef in the continental United States, and all but guarantee that you'll see enough sealife to fill a photo album or two. Along with

In the Everglades, and anywhere in Florida, **mosquitoes** are intensely annoying pests, so if you're here at any time but the dry middle of winter, bring strong insect repellent—and lots of it. In parts of the Everglades, the bugs are so bad that full-body cover is recommended, in addition to the most potent sprays and lotions you can lay your hands on.

Key Largo is home to the **Key Lime Products** store (305/853-0378) at milemarker 95, selling all manner of key lime pies, juice, cakes, cookies, suntan lotions— even key lime trees, though commercial key lime orchards are a thing of the past. (Most key limes today come from Mexico and Honduras.)

Between milemarker 106 and milemarker 86, a hiking and bicycling path parallels US-1— sometimes very closely— but it's a rare long-distance route on these tiny islands.

The Overseas Highway

Imagine a narrow ribbon of asphalt and concrete hovering between emerald seas and azure blue skies, and lined by swaying palm trees and gorgeous, white-sand beaches. Add a generous taste of exotic wildlife, including alligators and dolphins, the country's only tropical coral reefs, and a romantic history rich with tales of buccaneering pirates and buried treasure. Hang it off the far southern tip of Florida, and you have the Overseas Highway, one of the country's most fascinating scenic drives.

Running for over 125 miles from the Everglades to the edge of the Caribbean, the Overseas Highway is the southernmost section of US-1, the historic route that winds for over 2,400 miles along the full length of the East Coast. From its very inception, the Overseas Highway has been unique. It was built on top of the legendary Florida and East Coast Railroad, which at the turn of the century linked the great resort hotels of St. Augustine and Palm Beach with Key West and Cuba. An engineering masterpiece, the railroad cost $50 million and hundreds of lives to complete in 1912, but lasted only two decades before the century's most powerful hurricane destroyed the tracks in 1935. The state of Florida bought the remnants

There are a number of places in the Florida Keys where you can pay to swim with dolphins, including: **Dolphins Plus** (305/451-1993) in Key Largo; **Theatre of the Sea** (305/664-2431) in Islamorada; and the **Dolphin Research Center** (305/289-1121) in Marathon. Each charges around $100 for a short but memorable swim.

the adjacent **Key Largo Coral Reef National Marine Sanctuary,** the park gives access to more than 175 square miles of diving spots, including reefs, shipwrecks, and a nine-foot-high bronze statue called "Christ of the Deep." The visitors center has a replica reef in a 30,000-gallon aquarium full of colorful fish, allowing a quick look at the fascinating underwater world without getting your feet wet; the park also has other on-land attractions, like a boardwalk over a mangrove swamp and a pleasant campground.

Film fans will know that Key Largo was the title and setting of a great 1948 film noir movie starring Bogie, Bacall, and Edward G. Robinson; these days, it's also home to the co-star of another classic, the boat from the *African Queen,* which is moored next to the Holiday Inn at MM 100. Most of Key Largo today, however, is a rather tawdry four-mile stretch of seashell stands, dive shops, boat shops, and margarita bars; there are many good restaurants, including **Mrs. Mac's Kitchen** (305/451-3722) at MM 99.4, a small and friendly place with inexpensive food all day, and more beers to drink than seats to sit on. Also popular: the **Crack'd Conch,** at MM 105.

of the railroad for $650,000, and proceeded to convert it into a two-lane highway, the Overseas Highway, which opened to traffic in 1938. Most of the old road has since been superseded by a more modern highway, but many old bridges and causeways still stand as evocative remnants of an earlier era.

As in much of Florida, ramshackle roadside development has uglified much of the route—in the larger Keys towns, like Key Largo, Islamorada, and Marathon, signs hawking restaurants, motels, and snorkel tours are more common than pelicans—but you can't help but be hypnotized by the scenic beauty of what pockets of "nature" still remain. Many of the best views are from the road itself, and specifically from the bridges, such as the Long Key Bridge and soaring Seven Mile Bridge, which run north and south of Marathon. Two state parks, John Pennecamp on Key Largo and Bahia Honda in the Lower Keys, offer a respite from the commercialism, and all along the Overseas Highways, unmarked roads and driveways lead across the narrow keys down to the waterside, where all manner of sportfishing marinas and Margaritaville-type bars give you another outlook on the true "Key" experience.

All the way along the Overseas Highway (US-1), the roadside is lined by milemarker posts counting down the miles from Florida City to Key West, starting at MM 127 and ending up at MM 0; addresses usually make reference to these numbers. Though it's only about 160 miles, be sure to allow at least four hours for the drive between Miami and Key West—plus however many hours you manage to spend out of the car, of course.

Key Largo also has many good places to stay, from the funky **Sunset Cove Motel** ($80 and up; 305/451-0705) at MM 99.5, to the boutique **Azul del Mar** ($125 and up; 305/451-0337), a relaxing small resort at MM 104.3. Also here: the unique **Jules' Undersea Lodge** (packages from $300; 305/451-2353), a two-room motel that's 22 feet beneath the sea—a quick scuba dive down from 51 Shoreland Drive, off MM 103.2.

Entering Islamorada from the north, you are welcomed to town by the "World's Largest Lobster," standing at milemarker 87 in front of the Treasure Village gift shop. He hasn't yet been boiled or grilled, so he's a naturally greeny-brown color, not bright red.

Islamorada

Continuing south on US-1, Key Largo blends into **Islamorada** (EYE-la-mo-RA-da), the self-proclaimed "Sportfishing Capital of the World," where anglers from all over the world come to try their hands at catching the elusive, hard-fighting bonefish that dwell in the shallow saltwater "flats," and the deep-sea tarpon, marlin, and sailfish. Though now famous for its fishing and fun-in-the-sun, Islamorada (which means "purple island") used to be synonymous with death and destruction: On September 2, 1935, a huge tsunami, whipped up by 200-mile-per-hour hurricane winds, drowned over 400 refugees trying to escape on what turned out to be the last train ever to travel along the old Florida East Coast Railway. Most of the dead were WW I veterans, members of the "Bonus Army" who had marched on Washington, D.C., in 1934 and had been given jobs working to build the Overseas Highway. A stone pillar at the south end of Islamorada, along US-1 at MM 81.6, was erected by the WPA to remember the event.

At the center of Islamorada sits one of the older tourist traps in south Florida: the **Theater of the Sea** (daily; $25; 305/664-2431), at MM 84.5, a funky, friendly place where you can watch performing sea animals or even swim with dolphins.

Islamorada is also home to two of the plushest accommodation options in the Keys. The large and prominent **Checca Lodge** ($200 and up; 305/664-4651 or 800/327-2888) has 200 spacious rooms, two pools, a pier, a palm-lined beach, and a golf course at MM 82.5. Harder to find, but delightful, **The Moorings** ($150 and up; 305/664-4242) is on the ocean side of MM 81.5 at 123 Beach Road. The Moorings is an idyllic and much-loved retreat, with 18 self-sufficient wooden cottages on 18 acres, alongside a beautiful 1,100-foot white sand beach.

The Moorings also has a nice restaurant, **Morada Bay,** serving urbane renditions of traditional Key favorites on US-1 at MM 81.6. For a more down-to-earth taste of the Keys, try the nearby **Green Turtle Inn,** or the waterfront dive known as **Papa's Joe's** (305/664-8109), a popular bar and fish restaurant at the southern tip of Islamorada (MM 79.7) that has good food, cold beers, and incredible sunset views.

For more information on Islamorada, stop by the little red caboose (at MM 82.5) that holds the **visitors bureau** (305/664-4503 or 800/322-5397). Outside, in the parking lot, informational plaques tell the story of the ill-fated railroad that became the **Overseas Highway.**

Long Key State Recreation Area

South of Islamorada, up and over the high "Channel 5" bridge, the roadside scene gets pretty again very fast, especially at the **Long Key State Recreation Area** at MM 67.5, where boardwalks wind through coastal "hammocks"—dense stands of mahogany and dogwood trees that bunch together on the small humps of land that lie above the tide line. There's a **campground** (305/664-4815) in the park, with showers, and some nice but narrow beaches. There's also a full-service **KOA Kampground**at MM 70 on Fiesta Key.

Marathon and Pigeon Key

The second-longest of the many bridges that make up US-1, the elegant multi-arched Long Key Bridge supports a long, flat causeway where the road finally earns its other name, the Overseas Highway. Unobstructed views of the distant horizon are yours in all directions, with the narrow ribbon of highway seemingly suspended between the sky and the sea. Fortunately, turnouts at both ends of the causeway let you take in the vista without worrying about oncoming traffic.

The Long Key Bridge marks the northern end of **Marathon,** a sprawling community that's the second-largest in the keys, stretching between MM 65 and MM 47 over a series of islands. One of the visitor highlights of Marathon is at MM 59, on Grassy Key, where the **Dolphin Research Center** (daily; $18; 305/289-1121), a rest home for dolphins who've been kept in captivity for too long, is marked by a 30-foot-tall statue of a leaping dolphin. You can swim with a dolphin for around $175.

Accessible by tram from a visitors center in Marathon at MM 48, **Pigeon Key** (daily; $8.50; 305/743-5999) is one of the least famous but perhaps most fascinating spots along the Overseas Highway. A National Historic District, preserving substantial remnants of the clapboard construction camp that housed some 400 workers employed on the original Seven Mile Bridge from 1912 to 1935, Pigeon Key offers a glimpse of blue-collar Keys history the likes of which you'll find nowhere else.

Lower Keys: Bahia Honda

The old Seven Mile Bridge, which carried first the railroad and later US-1 over Pigeon Key between Marathon and Big Pine Key, was replaced in the early 1980s by a soaring new bridge that gives another batch of breathtaking ocean-to-Gulf views. (The old bridge, which was seen in the Arnold Schwarzenegger/Jamie Lee Curtis movie *True Lies,* still stands below the new one, but is now used as a very long fishing pier.)

On Bahia Honda Key, near milemarker 37, you can see a double-decker remnant of the original Keys railroad, with the 1938 **Overseas Highway** supported atop the trestle. Widening the rail bed to accommodate cars was impossible, so a new deck was added to the top of the bridge.

The south end of the Seven Mile Bridge, near MM 40, marks the start of the "Lower Keys," which are considerably less commercial than the others. The best of the Lower Keys is yours to enjoy at MM 36.5, where the entrance to **Bahia Honda State Park** (daily; $4 per car plus 50¢ per person; 305/872-2353) leaves the highway behind and brings you back to the way the Keys used to be: covered in palms and coastal hardwood hammocks, with white sand beaches stretching for miles along blue-water seas. Facilities are limited to a few cabins, a general store, and a snorkel rental stand, but it's a great place to spend some time fishing, beachcombing, sunbathing, or swimming in the deep, warm waters of the Atlantic Ocean or Gulf of Mexico. **Camping** overnight, the best way to enjoy the sunset, sunrise, and everything in between, costs an additional $25 a night.

From Bahia Honda, US-1 bends along to Big Pine Key, second-largest of the keys and suffering from a bout of suburban mini-mall sprawl. Though it looks about as far from natural as can be, Big Pine Key happens to be part of the **National Key Deer Refuge,** set up to protect the increasingly rare Key Deer, the "world's smallest deer" at around three feet tall. Some 250 Key deer now live on the island.

The last big key before Key West is Sugarloaf Key, formerly full of pineapple plantations but now known for its **Perky Bat Tower,** a National Historic Landmark alongside US-1 at MM 17. Built by a man named Perky in 1929, the 35-foot tower was designed to house a colony of bats, who were supposed to feast

At sunset over the Gulf of Mexico, keep your eyes open for the visual effect known as the "green flash," when the sky and the sea seem to explode in a bright flash of green.

on the plentiful mosquitoes here; however, the bats stayed away, and the mosquitoes stayed put. Sugarloaf Key is also home to the wild **Mangrove Mama's** (305/745-3030), a roadhouse tucked away south of the bridge at MM 20. The seafood and key lime pie is as good as it gets, and there's often live music in the evenings.

Next stop, Key West.

Key West

Closer to Cuba than to the U.S. mainland, and still proudly preserving the anarchic spirit of a place that was founded by pirates, **Key West** (pop. 25,478) is definitely a world unto itself. The main drag, Duval Street, has been overrun by tacky souvenir shops, but the rest of Key West is still a great place for aimless wandering.

Just so you know, the seashell that's been adopted as a Key West emblem, the **conch**, is pronounced "konk."

Just a block from the official "Mile Zero" end of US-1, one of Key West's most popular stops is the **Hemingway House** (daily 9 AM–5 PM; $9), an overgrown mansion on Hwy-A1A at 907 Whitehead Street where the burly writer produced some of his most popular works, including *To Have and Have Not* and *For Whom the Bell Tolls*. Writing in a small cabin connected to the main house by a rope bridge, and spending his nights in the roughneck bar (originally called "Sloppy Joe's," now known as "Captain Tony's") that still survives at 428 Greene Street, "Papa" Hemingway lived in Key West for about 10 years until his divorce in 1940, when he moved to Havana.

Though Key West is the southwestern end of the Overseas Highway, the name is thought to derive from a corruption of the Spanish Cayo Hueso, or "Island of Bones." When the first explorers set foot here, they found piles of human bones.

A half mile away, at Whitehead and South Streets, a brightly painted buoy marks the "Southernmost Point in the USA"; next to this is the "Southernmost House." (There's also a "Southernmost Motel.")

At the other end of Duval Street, one place you ought to go—especially if you can time it to be there around sunset—is Mallory Square, which faces west across the Gulf of Mexico and the open Caribbean Sea. Street performers juggle and play music on the broad, brick-paved plaza all day and much of the night. This historic waterfront area is lined by old warehouses and the **Mel Fisher Maritime Museum** (daily; $9), at 200 Greene Street, which displays many millions of dollars worth of jewels, silver, and gold recovered from a pair of 17th-century Spanish shipwrecks.

Key West Practicalities

Amid the tourist clutter, Key West holds a range of fabulous restaurants, enough to suit all tastes and budgets. Capturing the eccentric Key West spirit for over 20 years, kid-friendly **Camille's** (305/296-4811), at 1202 Simonton Street, serves crisp waffles, sandwiches, and delicious dinners every day. Up the street, another oddball: "The Southernmost One-hour Photo Lab" shares space with the fabulous **Conch Cupboard** luncheonette (305/294-1577) at 1229 Simonton, where you can enjoy Cuban food or cheeseburgers while sitting on the turquoise-green stools. At the other end of the price and style spectrum, swanky

Antonia's (305/294-6565) at 615 Duval has great fresh pastas and grilled meats. But for a real taste of Key West, you can't beat **B.O.'s Fishwagon** (305/294-9272), a ramshackle fish stand a block from the water and three blocks north of Duval at 801 Caroline Street—softshell crab and oyster po' boys, fresh mahi fish-and-chips, cold beer, and frequent live blues bands make this a great place to soak up Key West's party-hardy-at-the-end-of-the-world ambience.

The aforementioned **Southernmost Motel in the USA** ($95 and up; 305/296-6577), at 1319 Duval Street, has a poolside bar and AAA-rated rooms. A surprisingly desirable option is the **Crowne Plaza** ($150 and up; 305/296-2991) at 430 Duval Street, which plasters its chain-like name on the facade of the La Concha Hotel, one of Key West's oldest and largest hotels, but otherwise preserves the historic 1920s character intact; you can't get more central than this. Gay male travelers (and there are many in Key West) flock to the **Atlantic Shores** ($95 and up; 305/296-2491) at 510 South Street, a lavender-painted motel with a lively, clothing-optional poolside scene and an on-site, all-night café called Diner Shores (geddit?). There are also many nice old B&Bs around Key West, like the landmark **Eaton Lodge** ($150 and up; 305/292-2170), at 511 Eaton Street, an 1880s Greek Revival mansion with a gorgeous garden.

For more information on Key West, contact the **visitors bureau** (305/296-4444 or 800/527-8539), located at 3840 N. Roosevelt Boulevard, at the north edge of town near MM 4, where the Overseas Highway lands on Key West island.

Key West is the end of the Overseas Highway, but it's not the end of the sightseeing opportunities, so if you don't want to turn around and head home just yet, you don't have to. You can board a sunset cruise, or take a seaplane tour of historic **Fort Jefferson**, a 150-year-old fortress and prison located on an island in **Dry Tortugas National Park**, 68 miles west of Key West. Prisoners held here included the hapless doctor Samuel Mudd, who set the broken leg of Lincoln assassin John Wilkes Booth.

The official end of US-1 is marked by a zero milepost sign in front of the Key West post office, on Truman Avenue.

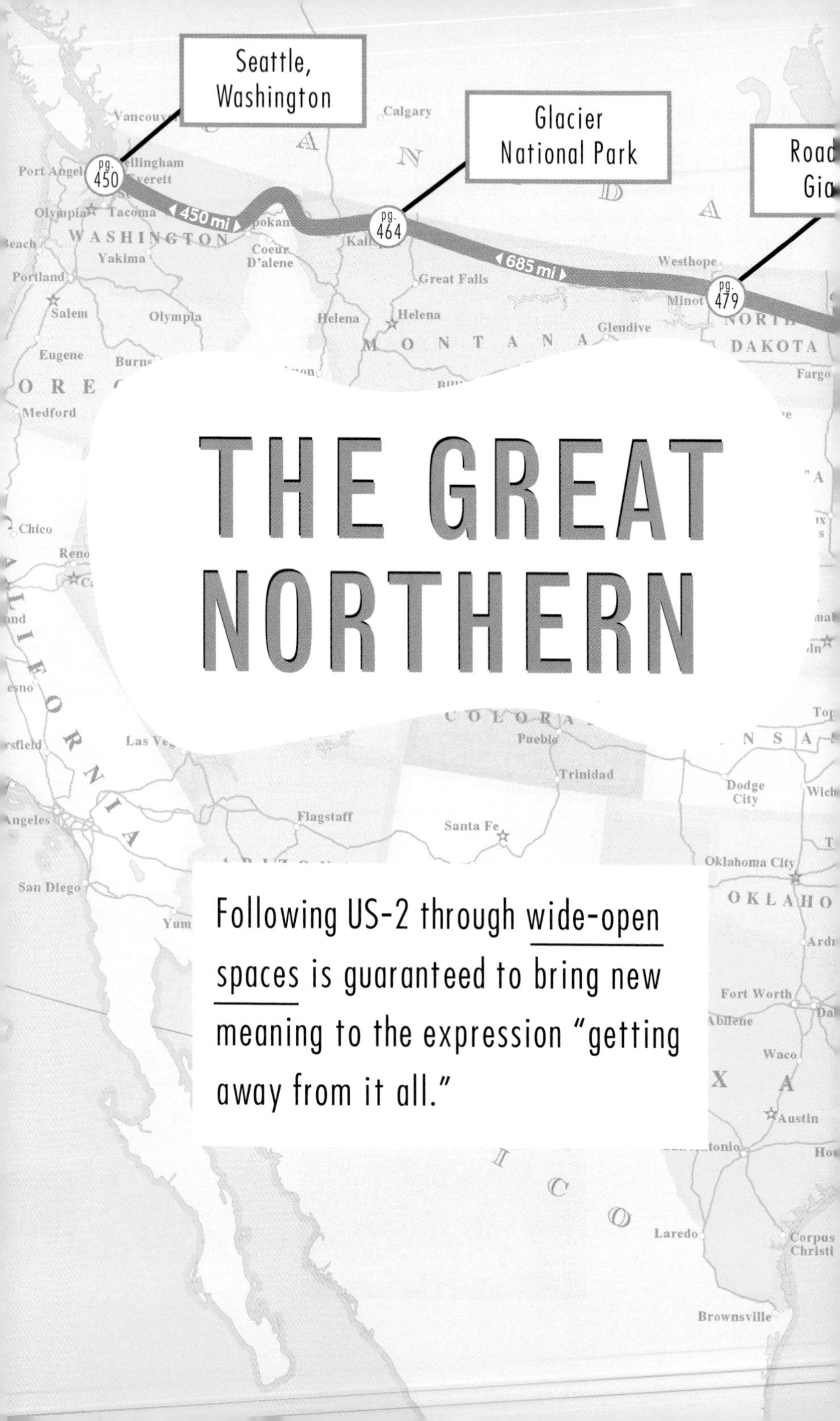

Seattle, Washington
pg. 450

450 mi

Glacier National Park
pg. 464

685 mi

Road
Gia
pg. 479

THE GREAT NORTHERN

Following US-2 through wide-open spaces is guaranteed to bring new meaning to the expression "getting away from it all."

Michigan's
Upper Peninsula

The Big Nickel

Acadia
National Park

605 mi

pg. 488

◄ 375 mi ►

pg. 500

◄ 700 mi ►

pg. 527

Houlton

Bar Harbor

Sault Ste. Marie

Montréal

ME

Augusta

MICHIGAN

Marquette

Escanaba

Montpelier

VT NH

Portland

WISCONSIN

St. Paul

Green Bay

Oshkosh

Toronto

Concord

Boston

Provincetown

La Crosse

Milwaukee

Saginaw

Rochester

Syracuse

Albany

MA

Madison

Lansing

Buffalo

NEW

Hartford

Providence

RI

Dubuque

Rockford

South Bend

Detroit

Erie

YORK

CT

Cedar Rapids

Chicago

Gary

Toledo

Cleveland

Akron

Warren

Des Moines

INDIANA

OHIO

Columbus

Dayton

Cincinnati

Lexington

KY

Green

Greetings from MAINE

Asheville

Fayetteville

Greenville

Wilmington

Columbia

SOUTH

Atlanta

CAROLINA

Charleston

Macon

Savannah

GEORGIA

Tybee Island

Talla

St.

Lafayette

New Orleans

Venice

Key

Between Seattle, Washington and Acadia National Park

Though many come close, no other cross-country route takes in the variety and extremity of landscape that US-2 does. Dubbed the Great Northern in memory of the pioneer railroad that parallels the western half of the route, US-2 is truly the most stunning and unforgettable, not to mention longest, of all the great transcontinental road trips.

Starting in the west near the beautiful Pacific port city of Seattle, US-2 runs steeply up and over the volcanic **Cascade Range**, climbing from sea level to alpine splendor in around an hour. From the crest, the road drops down onto the otherworldly **Columbia Plateau**, a naturally arid region reclaimed from sagebrush into fertile farmland by New Deal public works projects like the great **Grand Coulee Dam**, one of the largest pieces of civil engineering on the planet. From **Washington**, US-2 bends north, clipping across the top of the **Idaho Panhandle** before climbing up into western **Montana**, a land of forests, rivers, and wildlife that culminates in the bold granite spectacle of **Glacier National Park**.

On the eastern flank of the Rockies, the route drops suddenly to the windswept prairies of the northern **Great Plains**. Though empty to look at—especially when you're midway along the 1,000-mile beeline across Montana and **North Dakota**, wondering how long it will be until you see the next tree or peak—this is a land rich in history, where the buffalo once roamed freely, where Plains tribes like the Shoshone, Blackfeet, Sioux, and Cheyenne reigned supreme, and where the Lewis and Clark expedition followed the Missouri River upstream in search of a way west to the Pacific.

Midway across the continent, the Great Plains give way to the **Great North Woods** country of **Minnesota**—birthplace of both Paul Bunyan and Judy Garland—and then to the rugged lumber and mining country of **Wisconsin** and **Michigan's Upper Peninsula**. Continuing due east, the route crosses the border into **Ontario, Canada**, through the capital city of **Ottawa**, and the francophile environs of **Montreal** before returning to the United States near lovely **Lake Champlain** in upstate **New York**.

From there, US-2 passes through the hardwood forests of **Vermont's Green Mountains** and the rugged granite peaks of **New Hampshire's White Mountains**, two very different ranges, though only 50 miles apart. The route winds down to the coast of **Maine**, reaching the Atlantic Ocean at Bar Harbor and **Acadia National Park**.

Landscapes, rather than cities and towns, play the starring roles on this route. Between Seattle and Montreal, the biggest cities along the route are Spokane and Duluth. Still, after a few days spent following US-2 through small towns and wide-open spaces, you'll probably consider Duluth bustling and fast-paced; driving even a short stretch of the Great Northern highway is guaranteed to bring new meaning to the expression "getting away from it all."

WASHINGTON

The 350 miles of US-2 across Washington State contain enough contrasting landscapes to fill many states. West to east, the route begins at the industrial fringes of Seattle and the Puget Sound, passing through a couple of Victorian-era towns before climbing steeply up toward the towering peaks, dense forests, and pristine lakes of the **Cascade Mountains.** East of the Cascade crest, the rugged volcanic landscape suddenly becomes drier and much more sparse, the dense forests fading first into lush farmlands and orchards reclaimed from the natural desert, then continuing across increasingly barren sagebrush plains into Idaho.

Though traffic can be heavy on long summer weekends, and also in winter in the Cascades section, along US-2 it is usually light, since most of the 18-wheelers and other heavy vehicles follow the parallel I-90 freeway, 25 miles to the south.

Midway between Seattle and Everett, the town of Edmonds has frequent Washington State Ferry service (206/464-6400 or 800/843-3779) across Puget Sound to the Olympic Peninsula, start of our **Pacific Coast** road trip, which begins on page 10.

Everett

Thirty-odd miles north of downtown Seattle via the I-5 freeway or the older, funkier Hwy-99, at the west end of transcontinental US-2, busy **Everett** (pop. 91,488) is a thoroughly blue-collar place that feels a lot farther from Seattle's high-tech flash than the mere half hour it is. A heavy industry center economically dependent upon two of the largest livelihoods in the Pacific Northwest—wood products and aircraft manufacturing—Everett has a few large turn-of-the-century mansions overlooking the all-business waterfront, where a Kimberly-Clark paper mill shares space with a big U.S. Navy base that's home port to the carrier USS *Abraham Lincoln.* The old-fashioned downtown, a half mile west of I-5 around Hewitt and Colby Avenues, has some neat antique and junk shops, a dozen or so roughneck bars and taverns, and a very nice brewpub, the **Flying Pig** (425/339-1393), next to the historic Everett Theatre at 2929 Colby Avenue. For milk shakes or great fish-and-chips, stop by **Ray's Drive-In** (425/252-3411) at 1401 Broadway.

Everett's one big tourist draw is the huge **Boeing assembly plant** on the southwest edge of town, well-marked from I-5 exit 189, at the west end of Hwy-526. The factory, where they make the world's biggest planes—747s through 7E7

If a Boeing tour doesn't get your blood flowing, maybe a baseball game will: The always-entertaining **Everett Aquasox** (425/258-3673), Class A affiliate of the Seattle Mariners, play at 39th and Broadway, off I-5, exit 192. Games are broadcast on **KKRO 1380 AM.**

East of Monroe, just west of the town of **Sultan,** a dollhouse-sized church stands along US-2 as a roadside rest stop and mini shrine. Sultan is also home to an annual **Summer Shindig and Logging Show** every July.

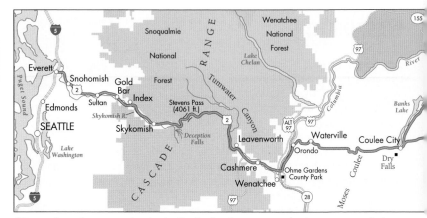

"Dreamliners"—is worth a look if only for the 11-story-high, quarter-mile-long building, which is the largest in the world by volume. Tours (Mon.–Fri. 9 AM–3 PM; $5; 800/464-1476) leave on the hour and last 90 minutes, but they fill up quickly, so get tickets as early as you can.

US-2 leaves Everett on Hewitt Avenue, which crosses I-5 then takes a historic old drawbridge over the Snohomish River before winding for a half-dozen miles across low-lying fields toward the town of Snohomish.

Snohomish

Though they're spreading fast, Seattle's suburbs haven't yet reached the tidy Victorian town of **Snohomish** (pop. 8,535), a century-old former logging center that lines the north bank of the Snohomish River, 25 miles upstream from Puget Sound. Six blocks of well-preserved warehouses and commercial buildings stand along First Street, across the river from a whining old sawmill, while the blocks above hold dozens of charming homes and quite a few impressively steepled churches. One of these old homes has been restored and now houses the **Blackman Museum** (daily in summer, weekends only in winter; $1; 360/568-5235). Located at 118 Avenue B, the museum features period-style furnishings and displays on the town's early history. The range of antique shops, taverns, and cafés in the historic center has made Snohomish a popular day-trip from Seattle, but the town has maintained an admirable balance of history and commerce, and is well worth a short stop if you're passing by.

Around Snohomish, the old US-2 road has been replaced by a four-lane freeway that loops around to the north, so follow signs for the "historic center."

Gold Bar and Index

Surprisingly little of the route traversed by US-2 on its way between the flatlands and Stevens Pass high up in the Cascades is given over to ski shops, bike shops, and espresso stands—except for the section around Munroe, where a mile-long gauntlet of mega-malls and fast-food franchises catering to Seattleites racing to and from the slopes comes as a shock to the system. East of Munroe, the one-time mining, logging, and railroad camp of **Gold Bar** stretches along US-2, halfway between Stevens Pass and Puget Sound. Besides all the gas sta-

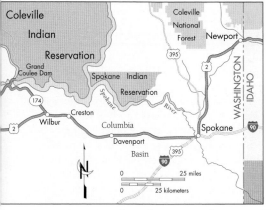

tions and cafés you could want, Gold Bar also holds the well-posted trailhead (follow First Street north from the center of town) for the 3.5-mile hike to 250-foot **Wallace Falls,** one of the tallest in the northern Cascades, tantalizingly visible from US-2.

Farther east, **Index,** on a side road a mile north of US-2, sits at the western foot of the Cascade Mountains at the point where the scenery changes suddenly from pastoral to alpine. Besides a riverfront tavern, a general store/post office, a neat little historical museum featuring Great Northern Railroad photographs, and constant trains rumbling over the swimmably deep (but often freezing cold) Skykomish River, Index offers good food and comfortable lodging at the 100-year-old **Bush House Inn** ($85 and up; 360/793-2312).

In a park at the center of Index, a giant saw blade is a reminder of the town's early industry: a granite quarry that cut the steps used in the state capitol. High above here, another reminder of the town's rocky past is the so-called "Index Town Wall," a 400-foot sheer granite cliff that attracts Seattle rock climbers.

Deception Falls

Lining the busy Burlington Northern Santa Fe railroad tracks, a block south of US-2, **Skykomish** is a quirky and engaging place that seems to belong somewhere else, some long time ago. Around eight miles east of Skykomish, a well-marked turnout along US-2 gives access to one of the region's prettiest and most historically significant sites. On the north side of the highway, the parking area's interpretive exhibits tell the story of the Great Northern Railroad, the transcontinental railroad which was completed on this spot in 1893. A plaque displays a photograph showing the driving of the traditional golden spike, while other exhibits discuss the construction and importance of the railroad in the growth of Puget Sound.

If you're not interested in railroad lore, head along the 100-yard-long paved trail that loops back under the highway to the powerful cascade of **Deception Falls.** If you can stand the usually bone-chilling snowmelt, you'll be pleased to find a number of deep and clean swimming holes in the area.

Stevens Pass

At the crest of the Cascades, US-2 climbs over 4,061-foot **Stevens Pass,** the highest and northernmost Cascade pass that's kept open year-round. Stevens Pass was also a historically vital railroad crossing, though Amtrak and other trains now avoid the pass, detouring instead through an eight-mile-long

Stevens Pass was named in honor of John F. Stevens, the Great Northern Railroad engineer who also plotted the Panama Canal.

Seattle

An engaging and energetic combination of scenic beauty, blue-collar grit, and high-tech panache has made Seattle one of the most popular cities in the United States, for visitors and residents alike. A young city, historically and demographically, Seattle has managed to preserve much of its heavy industrial heritage as parks and museums, if not as economic engines. The eco-conscious, civic-minded city spreads over a series of hills, surrounded by the waters of Puget Sound (be sure to ride a ferry or two!), with a backdrop of the snow-capped Cascade and Olympic Mountains. The evergreen Seattle can be an entrancing city—at least when the sun comes out, which no matter what people say is likely to happen at least once during your stay.

The heart of downtown Seattle, **Pike Place Market** is a raucous fish, crafts, and farmers market with some 250 different stalls and stores filling a 1930s municipal-feeling building that steps along the waterfront. For a respite from the hubbub, head two blocks south to the postmodern **Seattle Art Museum** (closed Mon.; $7; 206/654-3100), 100 University Street, and enjoy the amazing collection of regional Native American art and artifacts on display. Downtown's other piece of noteworthy new architecture is the shiny **Seattle Central Library,** a fantastic (and free!) high-tech public space whose multi-faceted glass diamond exterior steps down between Fifth and Fourth Avenues.

Microsoft millionaire Paul Allen has indulged his taste for Space Age adventure by subsidizing the private rocketship SpaceShipOne, and closer to home by renovating the world's last intact **Cinerama Theatre** (206/441-3080), an early 1960s icon at 2100 Fourth Avenue.

The Two Sentries,
The 42 story L. C. Smith Building and Mt. Rainier,
SEATTLE
U.S.A.

At the south edge of downtown, a half-mile from the Pike Place Market, the 30-block Pioneer Square historic district preserves the original core of the city, which boomed in the late 1890s with the Klondike Gold Rush. Another essential place-to-go is the **Seattle Center** (206/684-8582), north of downtown at Broad Street and 5th Avenue North, built for the 1962 World's Fair. Take the elevator to the top of the landmark Space Needle, or ride the Windstorm roller coaster, bumper cars, or a dozen other funfair attractions at the summer-only Fun Forest (noon–midnight; pay-per-ride). The Seattle Center is also home to the intriguing Experience Music Project (206/367-5483), a hand's-on musical exploration and living memorial to the city's native-born guitar genius, Jimi Hendrix. A don't-miss photo opportunity: A statue of Chief Seattle with the Space Needle rising behind him.

Spectators enjoy downtown views and Puget Sound sunsets at SAFECO Field ballpark, south of Pioneer Square, where the **Seattle Mariners** (206/346-4001) play.

Practicalities

Seattle's main airport is Seattle–Tacoma International ("Sea-Tac"), a half-hour drive south of downtown Seattle via the I-5 freeway. Seattle's freeways are often filled to capacity most of the day, but the best drive-through tour of Seattle follows old US-99 along the Alaska Way Viaduct, a concrete freeway that cuts along the downtown waterfront, runs through a tunnel, then follows Aurora Avenue on a soaring bridge over the Lake Union Canal. (By the way, under the Aurora Bridge sits one of Seattle's biggest pieces of auto-art: the **Aurora Troll,** caught in the act of eating an old VW Beetle.)

Fortunately, most everything of visitor interest is within the walkably compact downtown, where an extensive bus system runs in a fare-free zone; there's also a mile-long monorail ($1), linking 5th and Pine Streets downtown with the Seattle Center and Space Needle.

The niftiest place to stay is the **Hotel Andra** ($180 and up; 206/448-8600), at 2000 4th Avenue, a fully modernized 1920s hotel three blocks from Pike Place Market. The cheapest place to stay has to be the **HI Seattle Hostel** (206/622-5443) at 84 Union Street, which offers clean and comfortable dorm beds for around $18, right along the waterfront next to Pike Place Market.

Seafood, not surprisingly, is the thing Seattle restaurants do best, and the city is full of great places to eat fish (the sushi here is as good as it gets, outside Japan). For fish-and-chips or cheap, fresh oysters (and Washington produces more oysters than anywhere else in the United States), head down to **Emmett Watson's Oyster Bar** (206/448-7721) at the north end of Pike Place Market; more down-home fare is served up for breakfast, lunch, and dinner at the **5 Spot** (206/285-7768), at 1502 Queen Anne Avenue in the residential Queen Anne district, a mile northwest of downtown high above Lake Union.

The best source of advance information on visiting Seattle is the **Seattle–King County Convention and Visitors Bureau** (206/461-5840), 666 Stewart Street.

tunnel cut through the mountains in 1929. In 1910, before the completion of the tunnel, which is the longest still in use in the western hemisphere, the pass was the site of the worst avalanche disaster in U.S. history: 96 passengers and railroad workers were killed by a mile-long snow slide.

Besides providing grand views of the nearby peaks and more distant valleys, Stevens Pass is also a popular **ski area**, with 10 chair lifts and a 1,800-foot vertical drop.

Tumwater Canyon

Heading east through the Cascades from Stevens Pass, US-2 runs through the forests of **Tumwater Canyon,** a breathtaking place when fall color sweeps through it, and quite scenic any other time of year. Much of the surrounding wilderness was badly burned by wildfires in 1994 and again in 2001, but much of the area along US-2 survived pretty much unscathed.

All along this stretch, US-2 winds along the raging Wenatchee River through evergreen conifer forests highlighted by occasional aspens. The roadside is pretty much undeveloped, with one exception: At Coles Corner, 15 miles west of Leavenworth, the '59er Diner is a popular road-food restaurant, with great juicy burgers and crispy fries.

Leavenworth

Leavenworth's faux-European reconstruction was inspired in part by Danish-flavored Solvang, California.

Sitting in the eastern foothills of the Cascades, 125 miles from Seattle, **Leavenworth** (pop. 2,074) has successfully transformed itself from an economically depressed railroad town into one of the most popular day-trip destinations in the Pacific Northwest. After the local lumber mills closed down in the mid-1960s, the town took advantage of its spectacular location and re-created itself as an ersatz Bavarian village and has been drawing huge crowds of tourists ever since—over a million visitors annually. Check out the old photographs on the walls of **Der Markt Platz** shopping center, on the corner of Eighth and Commercial Streets, for the whole story.

Over a dozen blocks of half-timbered pseudo-chalets and Tyrolean shopping malls house a range of low-budget craft galleries and T-shirt stores, which you can escape by walking two blocks south to an attractively landscaped park along the Wenatchee River. Eat and drink at the **Heidel Burger Drive-In,** or **Gustav's** sausage-beer-and-burger garden, both on US-2 at the west end of town, or at the elaborate mock-Bavarian McDonald's, on US-2 farther east. The pleasant and moderately priced **Evergreen Inn** ($75 and up; 509/548-5515), a block south of US-2 at 1117 Front Street, has quiet rooms and bike rentals. For more-complete listings, contact the **visitors center** (509/548-5807).

Cashmere

At the heart of the Wenatchee Valley, surrounded by apple orchards and bare-brown eastern Cascade foothills, **Cashmere** (pop. 2,965) has an attractive downtown district, its unusual red columns and brown-shingled awnings both shading the sidewalks and giving the town some visual identity. The main sight here is the large **Chelan County Historical Museum** (daily; $4), off US-2 at the east end of town, with an excellent collection of Native American artifacts and a free outdoor Pioneer Village made up of 18 different historic structures from around the county.

Cashmere is also the home of **Aplets and Cotlets** fruit-and-nut candy, started here in the 1920s by two Turkish brothers. These sweet treats are so dominant in the local scheme of things that the main route into town has been renamed Aplets Street. The Liberty Orchards factory, across from the railroad depot, is open daily for free tours and samples.

For road food, stop by **Rusty's Drive-In**, at the east edge of town near the big Tree Top apple juicery, or head to the block-long downtown district, where you'll find a handful of cafés and taverns, and the quiet **Village Inn** ($50 and up; 509/782-3522) at 229 Cottage Avenue.

> Two miles northwest of Cashmere, right along US-2, the sandstone slabs and spires of **Peshastin Pinnacles State Park** provide a popular rock-climbing spot—but no camping.

Ohme Gardens County Park

Overlooking the confluence of the Wenatchee and Columbia Rivers on a bluff above the US-2/US-97 junction, **Ohme Gardens County Park** (daily April 15–Oct. 15; $6; 509/662-5785) maintains nine acres of immaculate greenery that offer a cool contrast to eastern Washington's arid terrain. Created beginning in 1929 by the Ohme family, the lush plantings of ferns and evergreens have transformed an otherwise rugged Cascade crest. Stone pathways wind past waterfalls and rocky pools, culminating in a rustic lookout that gives sweeping views of Wenatchee and the surrounding Columbia River valley.

Wenatchee

Just south of US-2, **Wenatchee** (pop. 27,856) is the commercial center of the Wenatchee Valley, one of the world's most productive apple- and pear-growing regions—it's responsible for about half the nation's annual crop. The **Washington Apple Commission Visitor Center,** a block north of US-2 below the Ohme Gardens, is the place to go to find out all about the state's apple industry, and to enjoy free apples and apple juice (not to mention potent air-conditioning).

Wenatchee stretches south from US-2, with three miles of shopping malls, car dealerships, and anonymous highway sprawl before you reach the downtown business district. Many large fruit warehouses and a nice park line the railroad tracks along the riverfront; one place worth stopping is the excellent **North Central Washington Museum** (closed Sun.; $3), at 127 S. Mission Street, which contains extensive displays tracing the region's prehistoric and pioneer past, from native rock art to a working model of the railroad route over the Cascades. An adjacent building houses a large exhibit on Washington's apple industry, including an antique but fully functioning apple sorting and packing line.

Along with every fast-food franchise known to humankind, Wenatchee also has some great local haunts, including **Dusty's In-N-Out** (509/662-7805), at 1427 N. Wenatchee Avenue, famous for burgers and shakes (and words of wisdom on their sign) since 1949; one block north is the **Windmill** (509/665-9529), a dinner-only western steakhouse at 1501 N. Wenatchee Avenue. There are also lots of motels, ranging from the low-budget **Travelodge** ($50; 509/662-8165) at 1004 N. Wenatchee Avenue to the business-oriented **West Coast Wenatchee Center Hotel** ($75–100; 509/662-1234) at 201 N. Wenatchee Avenue.

Lake Chelan

From Wenatchee, US-97A runs north along the west bank of the Columbia River to beautiful Lake Chelan, at the southern edge of the North Cascades National Park. Edged by wilderness and surrounded by tall mountain peaks, fjord-like Lake Chelan offers quick and comfortable escape from the modern world, thanks to the *Lady of the Lake* **tour boat** (daily March–Nov; $35 round-trip; 509/682-4584), which crosses the waters to the peaceful hamlet of Stehekin, on the lake's road-free northern shore.

From Stehekin, where there is a National Park visitor center (360/856-5700), you can hike deep into the volcanic wilds of the North Cascades, ride bikes along old mining trails, fish or swim in the glacial lake, and stay the night at the 28-room **Stehekin Lodge** ($80-150; 509/682-4494), one of a handful of tourist facilities in this delightfully isolated neck of the woods.

Waterville

Standing at the center of fertile wheat fields 10 miles east of the Columbia River, the compact farming town of **Waterville** (pop. 1,163) was laid out in 1886 around the stately, whitewashed brick **Douglas County Courthouse**, which still stands at Birch and Rainier Streets. Most of downtown Waterville has been declared a National Historic District, and the four franchise-free blocks of attractive brick buildings still house banks, cafés, and grocery stores—making it a very nice place to stop on a journey across the state. There's a photogenic, sign-painted barn at the west end of town, and midway along US-2's zig-zag through town, the **Douglas County Historical Museum** at 124 W. Walnut Street has an intriguing display of objects tracing regional history, including Native American artifacts and a perfectly preserved pioneer post office.

Across US-2 from the museum, the attractive **Waterville Historic Hotel** ($49–149; 509/745-8695) has recently been nicely restored and offers characterful and comfortable accommodations.

Moses Coulee

One of the last vestiges of eastern Washington's natural, unirrigated landscape, **Moses Coulee** is an 800-foot-deep gorge bounded by vertical walls of ruddy brown volcanic basalt, brightened by splashes of green and orange lichen. From the rolling plains above, US-2 cuts down into the coulee, then back up the other side, passing through some of the Columbia River Basin's sole surviving sagebrush and giving a strong sense of how profoundly irrigation has changed the region.

Coulee City and Dry Falls

A shipping center for the wheat farms of eastern Washington, **Coulee City** (pop. 600) calls itself the "Friendliest Town in the West." Despite this claim, there's no more reason to stop now than there was during the pioneer days of the 1860s, when it was said that transfer times on stagecoaches and trains were arranged so that travelers were forced to spend the night in Coulee City, like it or not. If you find yourself here, you can choose from a pair of motels and three gas stations.

Northwest of Coulee City, the large **Dry Falls dam** impounds Columbia River water to form Banks Lake; Hwy-155 runs along its sluggish shores on the way to the Grand Coulee Dam. Though you can see the coulee's towering basalt walls from this road, to get a sense of what the Grand Coulee looked like before the dams were built, follow Hwy-17 four miles south from Coulee City to where the **Dry Falls** escarpment stands out as the most impressive reminder of the region's tumultuous geology. Interpretive exhibits along the highway explain that during the last ice age, when the Columbia River flowed over the falls, this was the most powerful waterfall on the planet: twice as high as Niagara, and over three miles across.

Grand Coulee Dam

The centerpiece of the massive project of dams and canals that have "reclaimed" the Columbia Basin, the **Grand Coulee Dam** is one of the civil engineering wonders of the world. Built from 1933 to 1942 under the auspices of FDR's New Deal, at a cost of many millions of dollars and 77 lives, the dam is one of the largest concrete structures in the world: 550 feet high, 450 feet thick at its base, and nearly a mile across. The combined generating capacity is more than 6,450 megawatts—half of which comes from the Third Powerplant, added in 1975. Exhibits on the construction and impact of the dam fill the large, modern **Visitor Arrival Center** (daily; free; 509/633-9265) just downstream. On summer evenings a half-hour laser light show (May–July nightly at 10 PM, Aug. at 9:30 PM, Sept. at 8:30 PM; free) is projected onto the spillway of the dam.

In Electric City, along Hwy-155 a mile southwest of Coulee Dam, take a look at the **Gehrke Windmill Garden**, a whimsical collection of whirligigs and windmills made by folk artist Emil Gehrke, who lived here until his death in 1979.

There are three small towns—Coulee Dam, Grand Coulee, and Electric, respectively, east to west from the dam—all of which service the needs of boaters, anglers, and other visitors. The best place to see the Grand Coulee Dam light show is the very pleasant **Columbia River Inn** ($90 and up; 509/633-2100) across from the visitors center.

The Columbia Basin: Davenport

The 150 miles of rolling farmland that lie to the east of the Cascades are a natural desert, receiving an average of 10 inches of annual rainfall. Though small-scale farming limped along here for over a century, the region underwent a wholesale change after World War II, when irrigation water from reclamation projects along the Columbia River and its many tributaries turned the sagebrush plains into the proverbial amber waves of grain, spreading toward the horizon against an (almost) always-clear blue sky.

US-2 runs directly across the heart of this sparsely populated, nearly treeless region, passing through a few very small towns. In **Wilbur**, at the turnoff to Coulee Dam, an old service station has been brought back to life as a drive-by espresso stand; eight miles east is the blink-and-you'll-miss-it community of **Creston** ("Home of 1982 and 1984 Girls State B Champions").

Twenty miles east of Creston, **Davenport**, one of the oldest towns in eastern Washington, has a nifty old courthouse on a hill just north of US-2, a handful of quaint old houses, as well as the small **Lincoln County Historical Museum**, located a block south of US-2 at Park and 7th Streets, with a circa-1879 log cabin schoolhouse preserved across the street. Davenport also boasts a pair of burger-and-shake places along US-2 at either end of town.

Spokane

The only real city in eastern Washington, **Spokane** (pop. 195,629) feels even bigger than it is, thanks to its location amidst the prosperous agricultural hinterlands of the Columbia River Basin. First established as a fur-trading outpost around 1810, Spokane began to grow when railroads arrived in the 1870s, and has boomed since the advent of irrigation in the 1940s. The second largest city in Washington, and the biggest between Seattle and Minneapolis, Spokane is economically dependent on warehousing and transportation, taking advantage of its busy railroads as well as its location at the junction of US-2, US-395, and I-90.

In summer, enjoy a Class A **Spokane Indians** (509/535-2922) baseball game at Avista Stadium, on the county fairgrounds off Broadway. Games are broadcast on KFAN 790 AM.

Though downtown Spokane boasts a number of grand buildings—one recent guidebook called Riverside Street between Jefferson and Lincoln "the loveliest three blocks in the Pacific Northwest"—Spokane really came of age when it hosted the 1974 World's Fair, for which much of the riverfront was cleared and converted to the attractive, 100-acre **Riverfront Park.** Designed, but never implemented, by Frederick Law Olmsted a mere century earlier, the park gives good views of tumbling **Spokane Falls,** which form a deep canyon at the center of downtown. Besides an opera house and a convention center, other remnants of the fair include numerous kiddie rides, a summer-only **gondola** sky ride (daily; $5) which drops down to the base of the falls, a 1909 **Looff carousel** ($2) complete with hand-carved wooden horses, and a landmark sandstone clock tower that's the sole reminder of the Great Northern rail yards that lined the

riverfront for most of the previous century.

Riverfront Park is right at the heart of downtown, and a quick walking tour can take in dozens of well-preserved, creatively reused architectural treats, like the Spokane **City Hall**, which faces the southwest corner of Riverfront Park at 808 Spokane Falls Boulevard—the only government I know of that's housed in a

converted Montgomery Ward department store, a terra-cotta gem dating from 1929. Another worthwhile stop is **Auntie's Bookstore**, a full service independent bookstore with a popular café at 402 W. Main Avenue.

Northeast of downtown, across the Spokane River via Division Street (US-2), the best known dropout of **Gonzaga University**, Bing Crosby, is fondly remembered in a museum in the Crosby Library at the heart of the small campus.

Spokane's other center of visitor interest is **Browne's Addition**, a turn-of-the-century residential district a mile or so west of downtown with many stately homes. The highlight here is the wonderful "MAC," the **Northwest Museum of Arts and Culture** (closed Mon.; $7; 509/456-3931), at 2316 W. First Avenue, which houses the Cheney Cowles collections of artifacts tracing Native American and regional history and culture.

Spokane Practicalities

There's no shortage of good places to eat in Spokane, from hearty and homespun to eclectic and expensive. One of the former is **Frank's Diner** (509/747-8798), near downtown at 1516 W. 2nd Avenue, where very good, inexpensive meals are served in an elegant old 1906 railroad car, moved here from Seattle in 1991. An example of the latter is **Patsy Clark's** (509/838-8300), one of Washington's finest restaurants, housed in an opulent old Browne's Addition mansion at 2208 W. 2nd Avenue. In between are brewpubs aplenty, and many reliably good places downtown like **Fugazzi** (509/624-1133), an upscale bistro near Riverfront Park at 1 N. Post Street; and the local favorite **Someplace Else** (509/747-3946), at 518 W. Sprague Avenue. In Browne's Addition, another good bet is the **Elk Public House** (509/363-1973) at 1931 W. Pacific Avenue, with bistro-style food (and a soda fountain).

One of Spokane's most popular roadside attractions is the giant-sized **Radio Flyer** wagon, 12 feet tall with a slide down the "handle," near the clock tower in Riverfront Park.

Some people in Spokane insist that, rather than dying in a shootout in South America, Wild West legend **Butch Cassidy** actually lived for years in Spokane, under the name William Phillips, until his death at age 70 in 1937.

Bing Crosby

Motels line the main highways in and out of Spokane, especially along I-90, but Spokane does have at least two great places to stay. At the heart of downtown stands the fabulous **Davenport Hotel** ($125 and up; 800/899-1482), at 10 S. Post Street; while out in Browne's Addition the **Fotheringham House B&B** ($95 and up; 509/838-1891), at 2128 W. 2nd Avenue, is a lovely Queen Anne Victorian (with flower garden, porch swing, and a turret!) very near the MAC museum.

For further information on visiting Spokane, contact the **visitors center** (509/624-1341), 801 W. Riverside Main Avenue.

Heading northeast from Spokane, US-2 crosses a few miles of suburban sprawl before winding through 35 miles of beautiful forested uplands and occasional crossroads communities on the way to Newport, on the Idaho border.

Newport

Straddling the Idaho–Washington border, **Newport** (pop. 1,921) began as a small trading post on the Idaho side in 1889, then moved to Washington when the Great Northern Railroad arrived in 1892. The original town site, overlooking the Pend Oreille (PON-doo-ray) River, holds most of the modern shopping malls, while the railroad legacy still defines much of the main part of town. Two depots face each other along US-2 at the south end of the three-block main street, Washington Avenue, one holding the offices of a lumber company, the other housing the small but enjoyable **Pend Oreille County Historical Museum** (daily; $1), which has farming and mining artifacts—plus a pencil collection. Overlooking the river on the northeast edge of town, technically in Old Town, Idaho, **The Riverbank** has reliable American food.

To get a feel for local life in Newport, tune in to **KMJY 700 AM**, which broadcasts country music, CNN news, and an hour-long "Swap and Shop" on-air flea market, daily 11am–noon.

IDAHO

Even though the route zig-zags for some 75 miles along the Kootenai and Pend Oreille Rivers, it doesn't take long for US-2 to cross the narrow neck, known as the Panhandle, of northern Idaho. Following the Pend Oreille River east from Washington, the route passes through the resort community of **Sandpoint** before threading the deep gorge of the Kootenai River upstream toward Montana.

Priest River

Roughly five miles east of the Washington border, and taking its name from the renowned trout-fishing stream that flows into the Pend Oreille River nearby, **Priest River** (pop. 1,754) is a supply center for hunters, anglers, and river-runners, as well as a busy lumber town, with two huge Louisiana Pacific mills dominating the local economy.

Priest River may not look like much from the highway, but the three blocks of Main Street running south from US-2 hold an interesting mix of hardware stores, antique stores, and taverns. The popular **River Pigs** restaurant

(208/448-1097) is at 114 Main Street, and there's also a small historical museum and ad hoc visitors center in the nearby **Keyser House** (208/448-2721).

Sandpoint

Located at the junction of US-2 and US-95 at the northern end of Idaho's largest lake, Pend Oreille, **Sandpoint** (pop. 6,835) is a resort community with a relaxed, welcoming feel. The highly regarded **Schweitzer Mountain Resort** (208/263-9555 or 800/831-8810) north of Sandpoint attracts skiers in winter and mountain bikers in summer. The mix of Rocky Mountain scenery and abundant recreation has made Sandpoint a popular place to visit and live; despite the dozens of real estate agents and other signs of potential despoilation, it still feels like a small town.

As you might guess from the name, Sandpoint boasts a fine, quarter-mile-long beach: **City Beach,** just a few blocks' walk from downtown at the east end of Bridge Street, complete with volleyball courts and a dock where you can board tour boats to cruise the lake.

The main business district along 1st Avenue fills a half-dozen blocks around the landmark **Panida Theater** (208/263-9191), where big names and locals still perform. You'll find a number of good cafés here, plus **Eichardt's** (208/263-4005), a beer-drinker's delight with great food (burgers, sandwiches, fish-and-chips) at 212 W. Cedar Street. Two blocks east, the **Cedar Street**

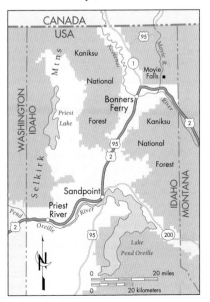

Bridge was rebuilt as a shopping mall in the mid 1970s and now houses the HQ and showcase store of Coldwater Creek, an outdoorsy clothing company. Besides the $150-a-night rooms and condos at Sandpoint's resorts, there are many more moderate motels, including national chains like **Super 8, Quality Inn,** and **Best Western.**

For more information, or for details of Sandpoint's festivals, contact the **chamber of commerce** (208/263-2161 or 800/800-2106).

Naples and Bonners Ferry

North from Sandpoint, US-2 and US-95 run together through broad flat valleys dotted with small timber towns. The largest of these, **Naples,** draws travelers to its friendly **HI Hostel** (208/267-2947), housed above the general store. Next door, the **Northwoods Tavern** is a great place to meet locals over a beer and a game of pool (or three).

Ten miles north of Naples, and named after a ferry service across the Kootenai River that started here in 1864, **Bonners Ferry** (pop. 2,515) is a busy blue-collar town with a natural resource–based (read: logging and farming, especially hop-growing) economy. The **Kootenai River Inn** ($65 and up; 208/267-8511) is an Indian-run casino and Best Western.

> The Idaho–Montana line marks the boundary between the Pacific and Mountain time zones, so adjust your clocks and watches accordingly.

One roadside sight to see is the **Barber Ship,** on US-2 at the center of town, not a typo but a land-locked houseboat now housing a barber shop. Away from the highway, there's an equally unusual accommodation option, too: the **Shorty Peak Fire Lookout,** way up in the wild Selkirk Mountains, where two people can spend the night and take in the panoramic views for a bargain $20 a night. For reservations, and information on hiking in the surrounding wilderness, contact the USFS **ranger station** (208/267-5561) on US-2/95 at the south edge of town.

Between Bonners Ferry and the Montana state line, US-2 crosses the once-wild, now-dammed Moyie River on a 450-foot-high bridge.

MONTANA

Crossing northern Montana roughly 30 miles south of the Canadian border, US-2 gives an up-close look at two very different parts of this huge state. The western quarter, on the slopes of the Rocky Mountains, offers incredible scenic beauty and innumerable options for outdoor recreation, culminating in magnificent

> How big is Montana? It stretches for over 650 miles east to west, covering an area larger than New England and New York put together, but has a total population smaller than that of Hartford, Connecticut.

Glacier National Park. East of Glacier, it's like a completely other world as two-lane US-2 (popularly known as the "Hi-Line") races across glaciated Great Plains range lands along the many tributaries of the broad Missouri River. A few low buttes and cylindrical grain silos rise up in sharp silhouettes, but the horizon is the dominant aspect, stretching for what feels like hundreds of miles in all directions. Apart from dozens of one-side-of-the-road blink-stops, the towns along US-2 in the eastern stretches of Montana—**Culbertson, Wolf Point, Glasgow, Malta,** and **Havre**—are few and far between. It's here you realize what the "Big Sky Country" is all about: cruising along at 70 mph, pacing a freight train and waving at the engineer, and *never* passing a gas station when the tank's less than half-full.

> The many roadside crosses you'll see while driving through Montana each mark a traffic fatality. They have been placed along the roads over the past 35 years by the American Legion; many are now elaborate shrines to lost loved ones.

Troy: Kootenai Falls

On the banks of the broad Kootenai (KOOT-nee) River, 14 miles east of the Idaho border, the mining and lumber-milling town of **Troy** (pop. 957) is at very nearly the state's lowest elevation—1,892 feet above sea level. There's not a lot to the place, apart from a short stretch of motels, gas stations, taverns, churches, and cafés—the best of which is the family-friendly **Silver Spur,** right on US-2—plus a small **historical museum** at the east end of town. Some seven miles west of Troy, there's a nice USFS campground at the confluence of the Yaak and Kootenai Rivers.

Though the only sign says simply "Historic Point," the nicest spot to stop is nine miles west of Libby, two miles east of Troy, where the thundering cascade of **Kootenai Falls** drops down a half-mile-long series of terraces. A pair of hiking trails leaves from the well-marked roadside parking area, one leading 400 yards upstream to the main falls, the other heading downstream to a rickety old swinging bridge that sways from cables suspended 50 feet above the green water.

Writer and resident **Rick Bass** has documented the isolated Yaak River Valley, north of US-2 via the scenic Hwy-508, in a trio of compelling books: the nonfiction titles *Winter: Notes from Montana* and *The Book of Yaak,* and a 1998 novel, *Where the Sea Used to Be.*

For most of the way between Troy and Libby, US-2 is bordered by marked turnouts where trails lead to the narrow, twisting old highway, preserved as a hiking and cross-country skiing trail through the dense forest.

Libby

The lumber town of **Libby** (pop. 2,626) was first founded as a gold-mining camp but grew into its present, elongated form after the Great Northern railroad came through in 1892. On the south bank of the Kootenai River, Libby is just downstream from the Libby Dam, which was built in 1972 and forms the Lake Koocanusa Reservoir, stretching north into Canada. Despite the fact that Libby is the hometown of Montana governor and Republican Party national chairman Mark Racicot, the town has suffered one of the worst cases of toxic pollution in recent U.S. history. From the 1940s up until 1990, mining company W. R. Grace dug millions of tons of asbestos-laced vermiculite rock out of a local mountain, covering Libby in toxic dust that has caused more than 1,200 people to suffer from serious lung diseases. The EPA has spent over $50 million to clean up Libby's streets, gardens, and houses, and in 2005 company officials were indicted on criminal charges.

Despite the occasional media interest in the asbestos case, Libby looks like a pretty typical Montana mountain town. Alongside the railroad tracks, Libby strings for a few miles along US-2 frontage, where you can find casinos and gas stations galore (the Conoco station offers **hot showers**), a half dozen motels, including the **Sandman** ($40 and up; 406/293-8831), and places to eat like **Beck's Montana Cafe,** 2425 W. US-2 at the west end of town; the old center of town, along Mineral Drive north of US-2 toward Libby Dam, holds the **Pastime Saloon,** serving beer since 1916.

A number of pleasant **campgrounds** operate in and around Libby, including excellent spots in the nearby **Cabinet Wilderness.** Libby's most interesting accommodation option: spending a night or two in the **Baldy Mountain Fire Lookout,** 20 miles north of town. The popular lookout sleeps up to six people and costs $25 a night; for details contact the Libby ranger station (406/293-8861).

Between Libby and the busy mini-metropolis of the Columbia Falls/Whitefish/Kalispell area, US-2 traverses 70 miles of **Kootenai National Forest,** an all but uninhabited area, sections of which have been badly charred by forest fires. A small display at milepost 63 explains the role of fire in the natural scheme of things.

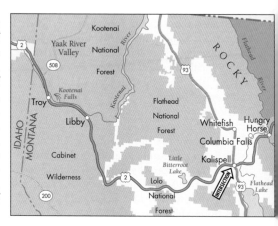

West of Glacier National Park, US-2 crosses US-93, the **Border to Border** route, which runs through the towns of Whitefish and Kalispell (see page 120). This road trip is described fully on pages 106–157.

Columbia Falls and Hungry Horse

Two intriguingly named towns line US-2 between Kalispell and Glacier National Park. A roadside collection of gas stations and industrial plants, including a massive Plum Creek lumber mill, make up the much larger town of **Columbia Falls** (pop. 3,645) where, despite the name, there are no falls. There are, however, a ton of entertaining roadside attractions, from go-carts to mini-golf.

If you like this sort of thing, you're in for an even bigger treat as you head east along US-2. The town of **Hungry Horse,** a service center for the large reservoir to the southeast, proclaims itself "The Friendliest Dam Town in the Whole World," and boasts ever bigger roadside attractions, starting with the **House of Mystery** ("Montana's Only Vortex"), on the north side of US-2 (daily April–Oct. only; $4; 406/892-1210). Located along the Flathead River at the mouth of Bad Rock Canyon (which Native Americans thought was haunted), this is among the more credible of these places where, to quote from the brochure, "the laws of physics are bent, if not broken altogether . . . where birds won't fly and trees grow at odd angles. Could it be a bearing point for extraterrestrial visits centuries ago? . . . Nobody knows!" It's as fun as these places get (which is to say, very, if you get into the "spirit" of the place), and well worth the minimal admission fee; there's a good gift shop, too.

The stretch of US-2 between here and the turnoff to Glacier National Park holds one "attraction" after another, including a **Drive-Thru Bear Park** and a wildlife museum marked by a pair of neon polar bears.

Even if you're appalled by the brashness of all this hucksterism, you'll want to stop in Hungry Horse for a piece of pie or a milk shake at the **Huckleberry Patch** (406/387-

If you're a fan of local newspapers, do what you have to do to get a copy of the *Hungry Horse News* (50 cents), organ of record for stories of mountain lion maulings and other events in the Glacier National Park region.

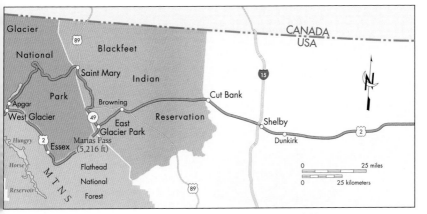

5000), at the center of town at 8868 E. US-2. It's a full-service restaurant, boasting over 25 different fresh berry and cherry concoctions.

West Glacier

Like many tourist towns on the edges of our national parks, **West Glacier** has its share of tackiness, but here it's on a tolerably small scale and limited to the approach along US-2 from the west. After all the billboards advertising scenic helicopter rides, taxidermy museums, and "The World's Greatest Maze," the actual town of West Glacier seems serenely quiet and peaceful, with little more than a couple of restaurants and comfortable motels, including the **West Glacier** (406/888-5662), right on the Flathead River, and the **Vista** (406/888-5311 or 800/831-7101), which is open all year. There's also a large **visitors center** for **Glacier National Park** (406/888-7800).

For many visitors, especially those who love trains, the main highlight in West Glacier is the landmark **Belton Chalet** ($120 and up; 406/888-5000), built by the Great Northern in 1910 and fully, lovingly restored in 2000. Rooms are small but have balconies with nice views, and the restaurant is one of the best in the Glacier region.

Essex: The Izaak Walton Inn

Avoiding the most extreme alpine scenery and the heavy winter snows, US-2 winds around the southern edge of Glacier National Park, climbing over the Continental Divide at 5,216-foot **Marias Pass,** the lowest of the Rocky Mountain passes. Though the road and the railroad are kept open year-round, there's very little visible development, and numerous trailheads access the southern reaches of the Glacier National Park backcountry.

One place that's well worth a stop, or better yet an extended stay, is the **Izaak Walton Inn** ($115 and up; 406/888-5700), midway between East and West Glacier, a half mile south of US-2 in the railroad village of Essex. Especially in winter, when the inn overlooks miles of cross-country ski trails, this is one of the best (and least-known) stops in the state. A more humble version of the grand Glacier Park lodges, the inn was built to house

Glacier National Park

102—GOING-TO-THE-SUN MOUNTAIN AS SEEN FROM EAST TUNNEL.

GOING-TO-THE-SUN HIGHWAY, GLACIER NATIONAL PARK, MONT.

The wildest and most rugged of all the Rocky Mountain national parks, Glacier National Park protects some 1,500 square miles of high-altitude scenery, including the glaciers for which the park is named, more than 200 lakes, and countless rivers and streams. Knifelike ridges of colorful sedimentary rock rise to over 10,000 feet, looming high above elongated glacier-carved valleys. Grizzly bears, black bears, bighorn sheep, mountain lions, and wolves roam the park's wild backcountry, which is criss-crossed by some 700 miles of hiking and riding trails.

The park's main features are reached via 50-mile-long **Going-to-the-Sun Road,** a magnificent serpentine highway that is arguably the most scenic route on this planet. Climbing up from dense forests to the west and prairie grasslands to the east, this narrow road (built in 1932, and rebuilt in 2005) is the only route across the park's million acres. Note that the road's middle section—everything east of Lake McDonald, basically—is usually closed by snow from late October until early June. In May, before the road is open, the park service hosts "Show Me Day," when shuttle buses bring interested visitors near to where the snowplows are working, shooting the fluffy stuff hundreds of feet through the air. RV drivers note: No vehicles or combinations over 21 feet are allowed on the Going-to-the-Sun Road.

On the west side of the park, lovely Lake McDonald is Glacier's largest lake, and also the most developed area, with an attractive lodge, two restaurants, a gas station, and a nice campground. A boat offers hour-long narrated cruises throughout the summer. Between the lake and Logan Pass, five miles east of the Lake McDonald Lodge, Avalanche Creek is the most beautiful short hike in the park, winding through dense groves of cedar and fir alongside a creek that cascades noisily down a sharp cleft in the deep red rock. The two-mile trail ends up at Avalanche Lake, hemmed in by 1,500-foot-high cliffs.

The heart of the park is Logan Pass, a 6,680-foot saddle straddling the Continental Divide, which comes alive when the snow melts to reveal a rainbow of brightly colored wildflowers. Two very popular trails run from the large visitors center: The shorter but more strenuous one heads south on a wooden boardwalk across an alpine meadow to a viewpoint overlooking Hidden Lake, while the fairly flat High Line Trail runs north, high above the Going-to-the-Sun Road.

Along with the extensive facilities along US-2 at West Glacier, East Glacier, and St. Mary, you'll find a couple of rustic lodges and motels within the park. All lodging (and everything else) in Glacier National Park is run by the same concessionaire (406/892-2525); rooms start around $100 a night. The nicest place to stay is the intimate, comfortable, Lake McDonald Lodge, with a lovely lobby filled with comfy chairs arrayed around a fireplace, and lots of

bearskin and buffalo rugs; it also serves the park's best food. In the park's northeast corner, the Many Glacier Lodge is a circa-1917 pseudo-Swiss chalet on the shores of Swiftcurrent Lake, looking up at Grinnell Glacier. There are over a dozen campgrounds in Glacier, but they fill up fast.

Besides the grand lodges, a few other relics of Glacier Park's early days as a "Grand Tour" destination still survive: bright red, open-top 1920s vintage touring cars (recently and expensively overhauled to be as eco-friendly as possible) run along the Going-to-the-Sun Road, providing enjoyable guided tours as well as a shuttle service for hikers.

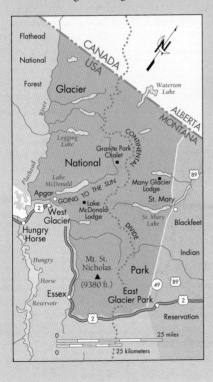

Admission to the park is $20 per car for a seven-day pass, and the required backcountry camping permits are an additional $4 per person per night. For a more complete overview of the park, stop in at one of three main visitors centers, located in West Glacier, at Logan Pass (summer only), and at the eastern entrance in the town of St. Mary. For information in advance, call the park headquarters (406/888-7800).

At **Marias Pass**, a roadside rest area holds an obelisk marking the old Roosevelt Highway and a statue of Great Northern Railroad engineer **John Stevens**.

railroad workers (which it still does) and is now a popular, year-round alternative to the often-overbooked accommodations within the park. The inn also serves very good food for breakfast, lunch, and dinner (try the huckleberry pie).

Another place worth a stop in early summer is the so-called **Goat Lick** on US-2, near milepost 182 about five miles east of the Essex turnoff, where dozens of shaggy white mountain goats regularly congregate around a mineral-rich spring.

East Glacier Park

Situated along US-2 at the southwest edge of the Blackfeet Indian Reservation, the town of **East Glacier Park** is, as the name suggests, the eastern gateway to Glacier National Park. It's a tiny place, barely more than a wide spot in the road, with a couple of general stores and gas stations, plus **Serrano's**, a good Mexican restaurant; and **Blondie's**, a bar, grill, and pizza place.

With the main park entrance over 30 miles to the northeast at St. Mary, East Glacier Park is not an especially convenient base, though it does have one compelling attraction: the **Glacier Park Lodge** (406/892-2525), the grandest of all the historic park lodges. Built by the Great Northern Railroad to attract visitors to the park (and to their trains), the lodge centers on a magnificent lobby built of 60-foot-tall Douglas fir logs—each of which runs floor to ceiling, with the bark still on it. It's an impressively rustic space, and well worth a look.

St. Mary

Located on the Blackfeet Indian Reservation, 30 miles north of US-2 at the east entrance to Glacier National Park, the town of **St. Mary** makes a great alternative to the in-park lodges. At the east end of the historic Going-to-the-Sun Road, St. Mary has a large visitors center, and the clean modern **St. Mary's Lodge** ($99 and up; 406/732-4431) resort has a nice café, the **Snowgoose Grill**, serving buffalo burgers and huckleberry pie. Another great little place, the **Park Cafe and Grocery** (406/732-4482), serves mega-breakfasts and yet more great berry pies, a half mile north of the park entrance.

St. Mary makes an especially handy base for visiting the comparatively quiet Many Glacier section of Glacier National Park, and for seeing the sights of adjacent **Waterton National Park**, across the border in Canada.

Blackfeet Indian Reservation

The 1.5-million-acre **Blackfeet Indian Reservation**, stretching north to the Canadian border along the eastern border of Glacier National Park, is a weather-beaten land home to 7,500 members of what was once the most powerful tribe on the Northern Plains. The Blackfeet, whose nomadic lives took them all over the plains in pursuit of buffalo, were feared and respected for their fighting and hunting abilities, though contact with white traders brought smallpox, alcoholism, and other diseases that devastated the tribe. Their strength in battle won the Blackfeet concessions from the encroaching U.S. government, including a huge swath of land that, in 1855, included everything north of the Yellowstone River between the Dakotas and the Continental Divide. Much of this land, including what's now the eastern half of Glacier National Park, was later bought back or simply taken away; the tribe now earns most of its income from ranching, and from oil and natural gas leases.

The Blackfeet's tribal headquarters and main commercial center is **Browning** (pop. 1,065), located on US-2 near the eastern entrance to Glacier National Park. Like many reservation towns, Browning has a desolate and depressing feel to it, but there are a couple of places worth stopping, including the **Museum of the Plains Indian** (daily in summer, Mon.–Fri. rest of the year; $4), near the west end of town at the junction of US-2 and US-89. Operated by the U.S. government's Bureau of Indian Affairs, the bland building contains a small collection of Plains Indian arts and crafts, mostly blankets and jewelry. Also in Browning: the stuffed menagerie of the **Montana Wildlife Museum**, plus a couple of cafés and a pair of concrete tepees.

Cut Bank

It's hard for travelers heading west along US-2 to believe that, despite having covered over 1,000 miles of undulating Great Plains, they have yet to reach the mountains. It isn't until **Cut Bank** (pop. 3,105) that the see-forever glaciation looks like it might be waning. You crest a hill and suddenly there they are: the rugged Rocky Mountains. Popularly known as the coldest city in the United States, as measured at the local U.S. Weather Service monitoring station, Cut Bank is a friendly and pretty enough place, bisected neatly by US-2 and the railroad tracks.

Downtown, on US-2, the **Golden Harvest Cafe** (406/873-4010), at 13 W. Main Street, is great for rubbing shoulders with the locals at breakfast, lunch, or dinner. The best spots are a little east: The **Point Drive-In** (406/873-2431), 1119 E. Main Street, is a classic roadster drive-up, while across the highway a **27-foot-tall penguin** stands next to the **Glacier Gateway Inn** (406/873-5544 or 800/851-5541) at 1130 E. Main Street, the town's nicest motel.

Shelby

Despite what a quick map-read would indicate, or local tourist boosters would proclaim, the fact that **Shelby** is bustling is due solely to the busy I-15 Interstate freeway, which crosses US-2 here, 25 miles south of the Canadian border. Even so, Shelby's activity—typical truck-jockey, blue-smoke activity—is relegated to the area immediately around the I-15 exit, and to the busy "multi-modal" depot along the Burlington Northern tracks. Otherwise, it's an oversized version of all the other Great Northern Railroad towns, one that extends farther than most along the

Thirteen miles east of Browning, or 22 miles west of Cut Bank, a much-abused monument along US-2 points out the most northerly point reached by **Lewis and Clark** on their cross-country expedition. On July 23, 1806, Meriwether Lewis, searching for the headwaters of the Marias River, made it to a spot four miles north of US-2, which he called **Camp Disappointment,** before turning back because of bad weather.

tracks, with wide streets and a much-appreciated hill flaring up to the south of downtown.

Shelby is not rowdy, but neither does it roll up its sidewalks by 8 PM. Shelby has an impressive lineup of bars along Main Street (The Mint, the Mountain Club, the Alibi Lounge, and the Tap Room, to name a few), but the town's major claim to fame is that it hosted the 1923 world heavy-weight fight between Jack Dempsey and Tommy Gibbons, a 15-round decision for Dempsey that was closer than it should have been. The match was produced as a publicity stunt to lure people to the oil boomtown, and Shelby built a 40,000-seat arena, but after Dempsey's managers hemmed and hawed about canceling the bout, only 7,000 showed up.

For great shotgun-seat reading along the way, William Least Heat-Moon's Blue Highways *contains an honest, lyrical account of the highs, lows, and endless in-betweens along this stretch, including a brief account of a day in Shelby.*

A replica arena and a room full of artifacts from the fight are among the many intriguing items on display at the **Marias Museum of History and Art** (closed Sun.; donations; 406/434-2551), in a former residence at the corner of 12th Avenue and 1st Street North. It feels much more like a home than a museum, which adds a welcome amount of weirdness to the usual battery of dusty old stuff. Best of all, the museum is across the street from the local **swimming pool,** an essential rest stop on a hot mid-summer afternoon.

There are a handful of cafés along Main Street, and an absolutely huge "Motel" sign marks the entrance to **O'Haire Manor** ($40 and up; 406/434-5555) at 204 S. 2nd Street, one of Shelby's better motels.

Shelby boasts the last good range of services for the 100-plus miles between here and Havre, so be sure to fill up the tank before setting off. Heading east, US-2 crosses bare plains broken by cattle ranges, wheat farms, and the occasional remnants of Cold War–era missile silos. It's a thumb-on-wheel, greased-lightning, straight-shot road, miles and miles of your own wandering thoughts.

Havre

The largest town along eastern US-2, **Havre** (pop. 9,621; HAV-ver) was founded by the Great Northern Railroad and named, for no good reason, after the French port Le Havre, though you'd never tell by the pronunciation. Havre re-

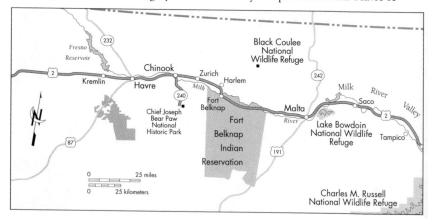

tains more than a little of its Wild West feel and has enough unusual attractions to merit an extended stop. West of town is a large area of eroded **badlands**, and just north of US-2, behind the Holiday Village Shopping Center, is **Wahkpa Chu'gn Archaeological Site** (daily May–Sept.; $6). Dating back to prehistoric times, the area has been used by many cultures, including Plains Indian tribes, to drive bison to their deaths. Many of the artifacts recovered from the area are displayed inside nearby **H. Earl Clack Memorial Museum** (daily May–Sept.; donations), which manages the site.

The town itself is engaging and rowdy. Numerous poker clubs (everything has "casino" tacked onto it) and cowboy bars line the compact downtown area, underneath which is a defunct underground world of illicit bordellos and opium dens—all part of the whiskey trail that flourished a century ago and again during Prohibition, when bathtub gin—copious quantities from Canada, a stone's throw north—was run through. Tours ($10) are available through **Havre Beneath the Streets** at 120 3rd Avenue, next door to Norman's Ranch Wear.

Up until the oil crisis of 1974, when federal lawmakers enacted a national speed limit of 55 mph, Montana law stipulated only that drivers should travel at a reasonable and prudent speed, with no legal maximum. In 1996 federal legislation returned speed-limit control to the states, and for a few years, until Montana set a statewide 70-mph limit in 1999, this meant you could drive as fast as you wanted.

Along 1st Street (US-2) you'll find all the usual fast-food suspects, and Chinese at **Canton Restaurant** (406/265-6666), at 439 W. 1st Street. There's also the smaller, fresher **Lunch Box** deli/café (406/265-6588) at 213 3rd Avenue. For a place to stay, the plushest of Havre's handful of motels is the **Great Northern Inn** ($60 and up; 406/265-4200), at 1345 1st Street.

For further listings or other information, contact the **chamber of commerce** (406/265-4383), right downtown at 518 1st Street.

Chinook and Chief Joseph

Chinook (pop. 1,386) takes its name from the Northwest intertribal patois for the warm southerly winds that rip through the area in January and February, raising temperatures some 50°F in a matter of hours, melting the winter snow, and allowing cattle to forage. Now a small cattle-ranching town, Chinook is best known for its proximity to the surrender site of Nez Percé Chief Joseph to the U.S. Army in 1877—which effectively marked the end of the Indian Wars of the Plains. The very good **Blaine County Museum** (free; 406/357-2590), four blocks south of US-2 at

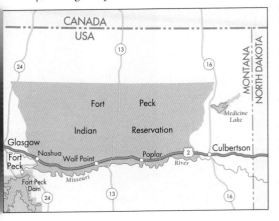

Chief Joseph and the Nez Percé

The odyssey of Chief Joseph and his 600 followers is perhaps the most familiar tale of the final days of freedom of the North American Indians. Having led his band over 1,000 miles throughout the summer from their lands in Idaho, from which they were forcibly removed by the U.S. government (which had "re-negotiated" an initial treaty, in effect reducing the Nez Percé's holdings by 90 percent), Joseph and the ragtag, exhausted Nez Percé, thinking the cavalry farther south and Canada closer north than either really were, chose to camp and rest near Chinook, Montana, in 1877.

The U.S. Army, in hot pursuit, sent ahead a 400-man contingent, which reconnoitered the tribe and camped 12 miles to the southeast on September 28. The Nez Percé

Chief Joseph

501 Indiana Street, includes an impressive collection of fossils and local pioneer artifacts, as well as an informative multimedia presentation on the events leading up to the final surrender of Chief Joseph.

If the weather's fine and you can spare half a day, the actual site where the Nez Percé were captured is now preserved (with an interpretive trail and a few plaques, but otherwise unchanged) as **Chief Joseph Bear Paw Battlefield National Historic Park**, 16 miles south of Chinook via Hwy-240.

Fort Belknap Indian Reservation

Between Chinook and Malta, US-2 runs along the northern border of the **Fort Belknap Indian Reservation**, which covers some 650,000 acres stretching south to near the Missouri Breaks, a rock-and-sagebrush landscape that provided perfect hiding spots for outlaws like Kid Curry, Butch Cassidy, and the Hole-in-the-Wall Gang.

The Fort Belknap reservation was established in 1887 to contain the surviving members of the once-feared Gros Ventre and Assiniboine Indians who, before siding with the U.S. Army against the Blackfeet, were one of the major powers on the northern Plains. The tiny town of **Fort Belknap**, just south of US-2 about 25 miles east of Chinook, is the main reservation crossroads. The town hosts the annual **Milk**

Butch Cassidy

awoke to attack on September 30. The Army, expecting to prevail on the basis of surprise, instead met fierce resistance, and a five-day siege ensued. After losing their herd of horses, 30 warriors, and three chiefs, and suffering high casualties among the women and children, the Nez Percé gave up. Chief Joseph's words upon surrendering were an eloquent and tragic encapsulation of the Native American experience:

Our chiefs are dead; the little children are freezing to death. My people have no blankets, no food . . . I want to have time to look for my children and see how many I can find . . . Hear me, my chiefs. I am tired. My heart is sick and sad. From where the sun now stands, I will fight no more forever.

After receiving promises from the U.S. commanders that the Nez Percé would be allowed to return to Idaho, Chief Joseph instead suffered the government's forked-tongue duplicity. Most of the Nez Percé were dispersed to several reservations, eventually winding up in Oklahoma. In 1885, through the Herculean efforts of Chief Joseph and with help from his old nemesis Colonel Miles, some 120 Nez Percé were allowed to return to Idaho. Chief Joseph, however, was never allowed to see his homeland again, finishing out his days in exile on the Colville Reservation in Washington, where he is buried.

River Indian Days at the end of July, featuring athletic contests as well as dances and country-fair festivities.

Malta

Twenty miles east of the Fort Belknap reservation is **Malta,** named for the Mediterranean island but otherwise just another ranching town that grew up along the Great Northern Railway. Along with the above-average **Philips County Historical Museum** in the old Carnegie Library at 133 S. 1st Street W, Malta holds the region's best place to eat, drink, and sleep: the landmark **GN Hotel** ($60 and up; 406/654-2100) at 2 S. 1st Avenue E, which has a bar-cum-steak house and a café with good breakfast specials.

Malta, where the eastbound and westbound trains of Amtrak's Empire Builder pass each other, is just one of dozens of flyspeck US-2 Montana towns with names borrowed at random by Great Northern Railway promoters from all over the globe. Heading along the highway, you pass near or through Dunkirk, Kremlin, Havre, Zurich, Harlem, and Tampico, all of which were founded by the railroad and settled in the main by Northern and Eastern European immigrants enticed here around the turn of the 20th century by the railroad's offers of farmlands and homesteads.

At the tiny farming town of **Saco,** 28 miles east of Malta, pride of place is given to the one-room schoolhouse where TV journalist **Chet Huntley** received his education.

Milk River Valley

East of Malta, the road and the railroad cross and recross the banks of the sluggish and narrow Milk River. Highway signs proclaim your entrance to "Beef Country"; just check out the menu options in the cafés and you'll know you've arrived. US-2 continues its jaunt over the Milk River tributaries, winding along the swampy **Lake Bowdoin National Wildlife Refuge,** once the state's best duck-hunting grounds and now warm-weather home to pheasants, grouse, and sage hens as well as pelicans, ibis, and herons.

Unless you're a keen bird-watcher, the main place worth stopping along this stretch is 10 miles west of Saco and four miles north of US-2. Here, the large and enticing **Sleeping Buffalo Hot Springs** resort ($50 and up; 406/654-2100) offers a huge (60 by 80 feet) naturally heated swimming pool as well as hot tubs—as hot as 106°F!

Roughly 20 miles north of US-2, the 15,500-acre **Black Coulee National Wildlife Reserve** (daily 8am–4:30pm; free) shelters one of the few nesting areas of the white pelican in the northwestern United States.

In winter, northeastern Montana suffers some of the worst weather in the lower 48 states, as arctic storms cause wind chills to drop as low as -80°F.

In the premier issue of *Life* magazine (Nov. 23, 1936), documentary photographer **Margaret Bourke-White** profiled the town of Fort Peck as well as the other 18 boomtowns that sprang up in the surrounding area during construction of Fort Peck Dam.

Glasgow

Glasgow (pop. 3,253), on the north banks of the Milk River 50 miles west of Wolf Point, is one of the few Hi-Line towns that's more than a collection of grain elevators, though its own dominant visual aspects are spreads of combines and threshers. Founded as a railroad town by the Great Northern Railroad in 1889, Glasgow is now the largest town in northeastern Montana. In Summer, stop in for a look at the tremendously cluttered, diorama-filled **Valley County Historical Museum** on US-2 at 8th Avenue, worth a look for its bar room exhibit. **Johnnie's Cafe** (406/228-4222) at 433 S. 1st Avenue serves great road food.

Fort Peck and Fort Peck Dam

Fifteen miles south of Glasgow and US-2 via Hwy-24, the enormous Fort Peck Lake collects the waters of the Missouri River behind massive **Fort Peck Dam,** one of the largest construction projects of the New Deal era and still the world's second-largest earthen dam. From 1933 until 1940, a friendly invasion of ultimately 10,000 civilian workers, earning between 50 cents and $1.20 per hour, hacked, dug, poured, sweated, and wrested a sea out of High Plains desolation. As a result, 20-million acre-feet of water can be impounded behind the nearly four-mile-long dam, corralled to a maximum depth of 220 feet and with a serpentine shoreline longer than California's—1,600 miles! Ongoing drought since 1998 means levels are well below average, hurting recreation and leaving boat ramps high and dry; the lake is also home to a huge array of wildlife, including elk, bighorn sheep, pronghorn, and migrating waterfowl, all protected within the **Charles M. Russell National Wildlife Refuge.** The Fort Peck area also has one of the world's biggest concentrations of fossils; dinosaur bones, including skulls of a triceratops and T. rex, can be seen inside the Fort Peck Dam Interpretive Center, (daily in summer; free; 406/526-3411), at the base of the dam. Fort Peck Lake is most easily approached via Hwy-117, 15 miles south from US-2 at the town of Nashua; you can also reach it from Glasgow via Hwy-24.

Besides the dam and lake, the area's best surviving example of New Deal spirit is the snug town of **Fort Peck** (pop. 300), built from scratch to house the construction workers, though its current population is but a small fraction of the number that once called it home. A few of the old buildings still stand, including the landmark **Fort Peck Theater** (406/228-9219) on Hwy-24, a huge draw in the area with its summertime plays and musicals. The **Fort Peck Cafe** has basic but good food, while one of the greatest places to stay near US-2 in Montana is the original **Fort Peck Hotel** (closed Jan.–Mar.; 406/526-3266), long dormant but recently taken over and touchingly (with nary an ounce of avarice) brought back into a semblance of its classic old self. Rates are very reasonable, and the restaurant is by far the best in the area.

Because trees are scarce on the eastern Montana plains, early settlers built homes by impaling slabs of sod over thin poles. A few of the museums in towns along US-2 display mock-ups of these **sod houses**.

Fort Peck Indian Reservation

The sprawling **Fort Peck Indian Reservation**, Montana's second-largest, stretches for nearly 100 miles along US-2, and for 50 miles north. Home to 6,800 Assiniboine and Yanktonai Sioux, but co-owned by non-Indians as a result of unscrupulous land dealings encouraged by the 1887 Dawes Act, the reservation offers few sights or services to outsiders. Travelers interested in tribal life can best experience it at weekend events like the annual **Red Bottom Day** celebrations (held every June in Frazer, west of Wolf Point); the **Wild Horse Stampede** rodeo in July, the oldest rodeo in Montana; or the **Wadopana Pow Wow** (early August). The latter two events are held in Wolf Point, the reservation's largest town.

120 miles south of US-2, the tiny town of **Ismay** (pop. 26) unofficially changed its name to **Joe Montana**, in honor of the retired 49ers football superstar.

Slated to become the site of the Montana Cowboy Hall of Fame, **Wolf Point** is halfway across the reservation, and home to cafés and motels like the **Sherman Motor Inn** ($40–60; 406/653-1100) at 200 E. Main Street, which has clean rooms and a decent restaurant. Another 55 miles east of Wolf Point down US-2, nearly at the North Dakota border, **Culbertson** (pop. 796) is a quiet town with a disproportionate number of farm-implement and feed dealers—the tourist brochures brag about the "ever-expanding SVO Oilseed processing plant." Located a mile east of town, the **Montana Visitor Center** houses a good local history museum. There are also a couple of cafés in town, including the classic three-meals-a-day **Wild West Diner** (406/787-5374) right on US-2 at 20 E. 6th Street. The **King's Inn** ($40 and up; 406/787-6277), at 408 E. 6th Street, is a clean, modern motel.

Fort Peck Theater

NORTH DAKOTA

Apart from the likeable small city of **Grand Forks**, at the state's eastern border, much of North Dakota's landscape lives up to those nondescript clichés from childhood family trips: It hems and rolls and yawns *forever.*

Montana may be Big Sky Country, but North Dakota sure seems to be High Sky Country, the land where, if you tire of watching dancing golden wheat mirages, you can exercise your finger channel-surfing on the radio. It's a long, flat, and (dare we say it?) dull drive across the state, with little but plains or pseudo-prairie, and even the most epic side trip offers minimal relief. The state has done what it can to help out bored travelers by eliminating roadside mowing for most of the trip across, opting for native prairie and a potential refuge for wildlife—and road kill.

Crossing between Montana and North Dakota, you switch between Central and Mountain time zones, so set your clocks and watches accordingly.

That said, the 300 miles across the state do hold a few points of interest, including Fort Union, an evocative outpost of the early frontier; popular Devil's Lake recreational areas; and the geographical center of North America, marked by a stone monument in the town of Rugby.

Fort Union National Historic Site

Astride the Montana–North Dakota border, standing proud atop the banks at the confluence of the Yellowstone and Missouri Rivers, the **Fort Union Trading Post National Historic Site** was once the largest and busiest outpost on the upper Missouri River. Despite the "fort" in its name, it was never a part of the U.S. military; it was, however, the most successful and longest-lived of all the frontier trading posts. In 1804, Lewis and Clark visited the site, which they called "a judicious position for the purpose of trade." Twenty-five years later, John Jacob Astor's American Fur Company proved them right, establishing an outpost here in a successful attempt to end the Hudson Bay Company's monopoly on northwest trade. Linked by steamboat with St. Louis some 1,800 miles

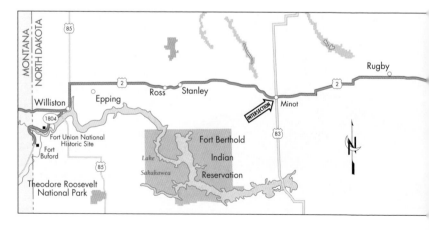

away, Fort Union reigned over the northern plains. Its bon vivant overseer, Kenneth McKenzie, the "King of the Missouri," kept the fine china polished and the wines cool in the cellar, offering a taste of displaced civilization to such luminary explorers as George Catlin, Prince Maximilian, and James Audubon.

The fort was abandoned as the fur trade declined in the 1850s, and portions of original buildings and walls were taken down by the U.S. Army in 1867 to construct Fort Buford, a mile to the east. In the late 1980s, the park service reconstructed the buildings atop the original foundations, giving a palpable if somewhat overly polished idea of how the old fort looked. McKenzie's old home and office, **Bourgeois House,** is now a **visitors center** (daily; donations; 701/572-9083) with some surprising artifacts. The fort hosts occasional reenactments of boisterous frontier life: Mid-June, for example, brings the annual

Kenneth McKenzie

Fort Union Rendezvous, a rollicking re-creation of fur-trapper gatherings to trade, talk, and compete in wilderness skills.

Fort Buford

Built in 1866 and now a state historic site, **Fort Buford** is eerily quiet, with only the stone powder magazine and a museum in an original soldiers' quarters open for viewing. Home to a company of "Buffalo Soldiers," as the Sioux called the black cavalrymen, the fort is best known for its sad contribution to the U.S. extermination campaign of Native Americans: It was here that Chief Sitting Bull surrendered to the U.S. Army in 1881, and here that Chief Joseph of the Nez Percé was brought after his "I will fight no more forever" surrender in Montana (see sidebar).

Williston

Just north of the Missouri River, a dozen miles east of the Montana line, **Williston** (pop. 12,512) is a classic, just-big-enough, one-movie-theater town. Always a boom or bust kind of place, Williston revolves around the wheat-growing and oil-pumping industries, but the downtown area is an all-American scene straight out of *Our Town.*

Apart from filling the tank before a trip to Fort Union or farther afield, there's not a lot to do in Williston except eat. Responding to an impromptu breakfast poll, locals will likely recommend **Gramma Sharon's** (702/572-1412) as the eatery of choice; it's located right on US-2 on the east edge of town—attached to a Conoco station, as most good cafés in the northern Great Plains seem to be. At the junction of US-2 and Hwy-85 is a **Super 8** motel (701/572-8371), one of many highway motels offering decent rooms from under $40 a night.

Epping

Like many other North Dakota rural communities, the old Great Northern railway town of **Epping** (pop. 55) has all but disappeared thanks to automobiles, changes in farming practices, the railway's move to diesel instead of steam, and sundry other common complaints. Here, however, the rapidly vanishing Great Plains lifeways have been partially preserved, thanks to the efforts of a local preacher who single-handedly preserved the abandoned buildings and artifacts as the **Buffalo Trails Museum** (daily except Mon. in summer only; $2; 701/859-4361), which has grown to encompass almost the entire town. Main Street is still dusty dirt, lined by a general store, a hardware store, a pool hall, the Sons of Norway Hall, and other essential elements. Most of these old buildings have been converted to house an amazing array of animated dioramas (papier-mâché dummies dressed up like dentists and patients) and the usual old tools and other junk, but the best reason to stop may be the **Buffalo Inn Cafe** across from the museum entrance, serving good food daily but especially popular on Sunday, when farming families come from near and far to enjoy the buffet lunch.

In the past, the historic sites of Fort Buford and neighboring Fort Union used to be more easily reached from Montana, though recent roadwork has made them accessible from either side of the border. Signs point the way south from US-2.

Roughly 65 miles southeast of Williston via US-85, the north unit of **Theodore Roosevelt National Park** preserves one of the largest contiguous areas of semi-natural Great Plains landscape.

Across western North Dakota, tune to **KMHA 91.3 FM** for commercial-free country music and community news and features from the Fort Berthold Indian Reservation, home to descendants of the Native American Mandan, Arikara, and Hidatsa tribes.

Ross and Stanley

East of Epping toward Minot, US-2 twists up and through a hundred miles of gentle, chocolate-drop hillocks, residuals of the great Ice Age glaciers, with some beautiful rises and plateaus capped by an occasional abandoned squad of dwellings. Along the way, podunk villages whiz by: **Ross** (pop. 61), for example, is a typically funky old town with some dilapidated, boarded-up buildings and huge grain elevators that look more like spacecraft engines.

The one sizeable place, **Stanley** (pop. 1,279), resting along the horizon-straight railroad tracks seven miles east of Ross and 47 miles west of Minot, is worth a stop to sample the world's last working Whirl-a-Whip machine at the old-fashioned soda fountain inside the **Dakota Drug Store** on Main Street, north of US-2. There's also a free municipal **campground** at the north end of town.

Minot marks the junction of US-2 and US-83, **The Road to Nowhere**, which runs from Canada to Mexico, and is described on pages 160–211. Minot is discussed on page 161.

Rugby: Geographical Center of North America

The landscape along the North Dakota stretch of US-2 consists of immense stretches of hay fields typical of the Great Plains, and only occasional highlights of miniature cattails, goldenrod, and sunflowers. The place names here are decidedly Anglocentric, with towns named Leeds or York after the hometowns of English investors who, during the 1880s, pumped the fledgling towns full of cash. The general population, however, has always been decidedly Scandinavian.

Midway between Devil's Lake and Minot, **Rugby** (pop. 2,939) is an important agricultural hamlet, known to road wanderers as the town nearest to the **geographical center of North America**. The exact spot is marked with a two-story stone cairn along the south side of US-2, in front of the Conoco station. Nearby is the **Pi-**

the geographic center of North America

oneer Village Geographical Center Museum (summer only; $3), featuring 27 restored buildings—train depot, schoolhouse, even a a reconstruction of a railroad hobo camp—relocated here from around the county, as well as an exhibit on the life of a 8-foot-plus-tall local man, Clifford Thompson. The **Cornerstone Cafe**, inside the Conoco station, and the **Hub of America Motel** ($40; 701/776-5833), across US-2, complete the list of reasons to stop.

Midway between Minot and Rugby, the tiny town of **Denbigh** is the burial site of **Sondre Norheim**, a Norwegian national hero who invented the telemark turn in cross-country skiing. Royalty have paid their respects—you can too.

Devil's Lake and Fort Totten

The wetlands south of the eponymous town of **Devil's Lake** (pop. 7,222), 60 miles east of Rugby and 85 miles west of Grand Forks, are one of the biggest natural draws in the state, with bird-watching, hunting, and fishing opportunities aplenty. However, the waters of what is the largest body of water in North Dakota have no natural outlet, and, true to its name, in recent years Devil's Lake has been wreaking havoc: flooding farmland, threatening towns, and forcing the raising and rebuilding of US-2 into a sort of causeway. Despite the threat, the town still takes good care of its blocks of tidy brick

Many places along the Missouri River are named for the intrepid and enigmatic Shoshone woman who guided explorers Lewis and Clark across the Plains in 1804. **Sacagawea** is alternately rendered as "Sakakawea" or "Sacajawea" and translated either as "Bird-Woman" or "Boat-Launcher."

buildings (including a truly beautiful circa-1909 Carnegie Library), and the whole community, cheery to a fault, seems done up in Sunday best, especially during the annual summer-long **North Dakota Chautauqua,** a reminder of the days when Devil's Lake was a major stop on the educational, recreational, and religious chautauquas that traveled across the country until the 1920s.

The local **visitors center** (701/662-4903), on US-2 at the south edge of town, can provide information on the area's recreation, pioneer history, and uncertain future. Downtown Devil's Lake also holds a number of places worth a stop, like the cutesy **Liquid Bean** café at 316 4th Avenue.

Historic **Fort Totten** (daily; free), 14 miles south of town on Hwy-57, is one of the country's best-preserved 19th-century military forts, with numerous restored buildings set around a spacious central square, as well as a museum and a theater (productions Thurs., Sat., and Sun. in July and Aug.). A rodeo and pow-wow, featuring highly competitive Native American dances, are held during **Fort Totten Days** the last weekend in July. Next to the fort is **Sully's National Game Preserve,** a 1,600-acre refuge for bison, elk, deer, and other wildlife, which you may spot while hiking the nature trail.

Both the fort and the nature preserve are located on the 137,000-acre **Fort Totten Sioux Indian Reservation,** centering around the mission village of **St. Michael's,** four miles east of the fort. The main attraction is the **Dakotah Sioux Casino,** "North Dakota's First and Finest," standing 18 miles southeast of downtown Devil's Lake.

Driving around Devil's Lake, tune your radio to 530 AM to hear all about the rising waters and plans to reengineer US-2 over them.

Grand Forks

The oldest and second-largest community in North Dakota, and frequently rated one of the "Top 10 Most Livable Places" in the country, **Grand Forks** (pop. 49,321) gained a place in the national headlines during the terrible floods that devastated the city in April 1997. Following one of the worst winters on record, during which blizzard after blizzard dumped over eight feet of snow and ice on the surrounding plains, Grand Forks prepared for the worst floods the Northern Plains had ever seen. The Red River of the North, which forms the state border between North Dakota and Minnesota, was expected to crest at more than twice its usual peak. In the aftermath of a hurricane-force rain- and snowstorm, the river rose an inch every hour, two feet a day, day after day, while volunteers and relief workers struggled to protect the town.

Under the watchful eyes of the national news media, the river continued to rise, finally breaching its sand-bagged banks and inundating the town. The entire population was evacuated, and over 75 percent of the homes and buildings were flooded; many were partially submerged for more than a month until the waters finally receded and cleanup could begin. The worst destruction occurred in the downtown core, where electrical short-circuits set off fires that raged for days and turned historic landmarks into scorched, empty shells. Total damage reached over $1 billion, but, miraculously, not a single death was attributed to the floods. Signs of flood and fire are still visible everywhere in Grand Forks, but what is most remarkable is how quickly and energetically

Roadside Giants of North Dakota

It may be the long cold winters, the endless flat landscape, or the incredible solitude of life on the northern Great Plains, but there's something about North Dakota that makes people do strange things. The most obvious signs of this odd behavior are the many giant sculptures that stand along the roadside all over the state. Bigger and better than their cousins elsewhere in the United States, the Roadside Giants of North Dakota quite simply have to be seen to be believed. The following are a few of the biggest and best:

World's Largest Turtle: Nicknamed Wee'l, this giant turtle is made out of more than 2000 old car wheels and stands along Hwy-5 near Dunseith, north of Rugby along the Canadian border.

World's Largest Buffalo: This 60-ton giant looms over I-94 in Jamestown, 100 miles south of Devil's Lake.

World's Largest Cow: "Salem Sue" stands along I-94 in New Salem, 30 miles west of Bismarck.

the community set about rebuilding itself. A lone obelisk along the riverside shows the high-water mark.

Many century-old downtown buildings have been renovated, including the landmark **Empire Theater** (701/746-5500), now an arts center at 416 DeMers Avenue; but one of Grand Forks' liveliest institutions is the 11,000-student University of North Dakota, whose pretty brick campus spreads north of DeMers Avenue (old US-2). A former campus gym is now home to the **North Dakota Museum of Art** (daily; donations; 701/777-4159), which survived the flood unscathed and houses the state's only contemporary art collection. Also on campus you'll find the acoustically exquisite (Tony Bennett has raved about it) **Chester Fritz Auditorium**, the local venue for touring national and international acts, as well as the aeronautically-minded **Center for Aerospace Studies**.

Grand Forks Practicalities

For weary road-trippers, one place you'll definitely want to stop is legendary **Whitey's Cafe and Lounge** (218/773-1831), across the river on the new "boardwalk" of East Grand Forks at 121 DeMers Avenue. Though legally in Minnesota, this is a true Grand Forks institution, a genuine speakeasy dominated by the fabulous art deco–styled "Wonderbar"—a horseshoe-shaped, stainless steel sculpture, surrounded by comfy booths with individual jukeboxes. The food and drink—try the pan-fried walleye, best washed down with a bottle of microbrewed Summit Ale—is excellent, but the ambience alone would be worth the visit. Another characterful old Grand Forks landmark, **The Kegs** (701/775-4993) is an outdoor root-beer stand supported by, you guessed it, a massive pair of bright orange wooden-looking kegs. Look for them north of downtown at 901 5th Street; order a Sloppy Joe and a side of onion rings, and people will think you belong here.

*Long the commercial center of northern Great Plains agriculture, Grand Forks became the birthplace of **Cream of Wheat** cereal in 1893.*

Right downtown, the best bet for food and drink is **Bonzer's,** a popular sandwich and beer bar that's open 11 AM–1 AM at 420 DeMers Avenue, across from the landmark Empire Theater. Downtown Grand Forks also houses a great natural foods grocery, the **Amazing Grains Natural Food Market,** on the west side of the Red River bridge at 214 DeMers Avenue, where you can pick up organic foods, baked goods, and even prepared foods for a quick-fix picnic lunch.

Accommodation options include the usual range of national chain motels out around the junction of US-2 and I-29; close to downtown there's also the very attractive **Best Western Town House** ($65–85; 701/746-5411 or 800/867-9797), at 710 1st Avenue North, with an indoor pool and on-site miniature golf course.

For the latest information, contact the Grand Forks **visitors bureau** (701/746-0444 or 800/866-4566), at the US-2/I-29 junction.

MINNESOTA

In its trek across northern Minnesota, US-2 offers nearly 250 miles of open road before winding up in the busy but surprisingly attractive lakefront city of **Duluth.** Midway across the state, after the endless wheat fields of the west, the scenery turns slightly turbid with the remnants of old iron mines and a series of still-busy lumber and paper mills. Opportunistic little cells of roadside community crop up to serve the beer-and-bait needs of those bound for the myriad recreational opportunities of Minnesota's "Lake Country" along the headwaters of the mighty Mississippi River. At either edge of this summertime playground, two largish towns, **Grand Rapids** and **Bemidji,** serve as gateways to the gaping spreads of **Chippewa National Forest** and many of Minnesota's 10,000 lakes.

Fisher

The first town east of the North Dakota state line, tiny **Fisher** (pop. 413) doesn't look like much, but was once a bustling frontier port, thanks to its location at the navigational headwaters of the Red River of the North. River traffic has all but disappeared, but the local sugar-beet industry pulls in a billion dollars a year, which may explain the town's prosperous air. For good food, stop at the **Fisher Cafe,** across the street from the spindly water tower, three blocks south of US-2.

Near Fisher stretches the **Malmberg Prairie,** one of the few extant virgin prairies left. Protected by the Nature Conservancy, 80 acres of wild prairie roses, blue gentians, and bright yellow sunflowers shine in late summer; once home to herds of bison, the land here has never been plowed. To reach the preserve from US-2, take US-75 south to Hwy-9, then turn south onto Hwy-56 and drive for two miles until you see Nature Conservancy sign.

The **Minnesota Welcome Center,** 11 miles east of the North Dakota border on US-2, has a full range of maps and information on both states.

Crookston

Crookston (pop. 8,192), 25 miles east of the North Dakota border, has a series of bridges over the meandering and tree-lined Red Lake River, which winds along the south side of the compact downtown business district. There's a statue of pioneer Joe Roulette in front of the community center on US-2, and a small **Polk County Museum** (daily May–Sept.; donations), containing the usual slew of 19th-century stuff with the addition of the world's largest ox-cart, but that's about it as far as sights go.

There are also two rather big festivals in Crookston: August's **Ox-Cart Days,** and **Red River Valley Winter Shows and Rodeo.** The latter draws up to 40,000 visitors from the United States and Canada.

The tiny town of **Fosston,** midway between Erskine and Bagley, holds one of two stoplights on this 100-mile stretch of US-2. Fosston also marks the sudden switch between the Great Plains and the Great North Woods; the town motto is unusually appropriate: "Fosston, Where the Plains Meet the Pines."

Erskine and Bagley

In the 100 miles east of the North Dakota border, US-2 spreads into a divided four-lane highway, climbing out of the fecund Red River Valley of the North (not to be confused with the *other* Red River Valley, down in Texas) onto the flat glaciated plains, while the roadside colors alternate between the dark reds and greens of sugar beets and the buff and leafy tones of the wheat, soy beans, and potatoes for which the area is known.

Continuing east, US-2 passes occasional isolated pockets of trees, planted as windbreaks amidst the furrowed fields. In the tiny village of **Erskine** (pop. 422), a classic one-horse Midwest town, you'll find **Joe DiMaggio's Pizza** (218/687-2100) at 124 S. Vance Avenue, which is neither a misprint nor the genuine article. (The owner, Mr. D., used to get oodles of wrong numbers for the legendary Yankee Clipper. Not surprisingly, his place is full of baseball memorabilia.) Erskine also has a municipal swimming beach on Lake Cameron, and takes civic pride in being the home of the "World's Largest Northern Pike."

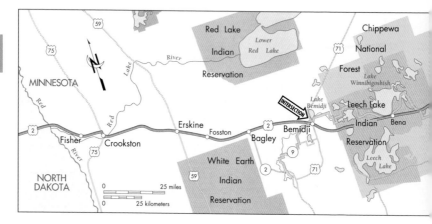

Thirty miles east of Erskine, at the western turnoff to Lake Itasca, **Bagley** (pop. 1,388) features a large wildlife museum packed with stuffed polar and Kodiak bears, among some 750 other creatures, right on US-2 at the western edge of town.

Between Bemidji and Grand Rapids, US-2 runs parallel to the slower but more scenic **Great River Road**, which winds along the Mississippi River, from Lake Itasca all the way south to New Orleans (see page 217). The entire route, including the towns of Bemidji and Grand Rapids, is detailed on pages 214–285.

Skyline Parkway and Hwy-61

One of the greatest loop trips in the country, **Skyline Parkway** is a 25-mile (over 30 with side trips) bucolic wind along the bluffs above Duluth. Accessed from West Duluth off I-35, the parkway takes in numerous historical sites, but it's mostly just jaw-dropping scenery, especially **Hawk Ridge**, which offers perfect wind conditions for viewing up to 30,000 hawks, eagles, and falcons daily in fall; also along the ridge is a fantastic network of trails, boarding stations, and observation posts. The parkway, which was started in 1889 and completed in 1929, connects at its north end with famed Hwy-61, which, if you've got the time to spend, is an even more beautiful jaunt along Lake Superior's granite cliffs to Grand Portage and Canada, 150 miles to the northeast. Along the way are some of the region's best places to eat: numerous **smokehouses** touting their smoked fish, plucked from the frigid waters of the great lake.

On Hwy-33, 11 miles south of US-2 and 15 miles west of Duluth on the edge of the Fond Du Lac Indian Reservation, the town of **Cloquet** boasts the only gas station ever designed

THE STEAMER
WILLIAM A. IRVIN

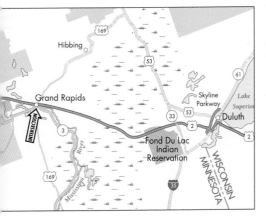

by famed architect Frank Lloyd Wright. Cloquet also has a large, Fond du Lac Indian–owned casino.

Duluth

Though it doesn't get a lot of positive press, **Duluth** (pop. 86,918) has to be one of the most beautiful and underappreciated travel destinations in the Midwest, "a Lilliputian village in a mammoth rock garden," the old WPA *Guide to Minnesota* aptly noted.

Gracefully etched into the side of tough, 800-foot granite slopes and gazing over the dark harbor hues, Duluth, from the attractively redone redbrick paving of gentrified Superior and Michigan Streets downtown to the grittier heights atop the bluff, quietly goes about its business, usually with foghorns belching in the background. It is a city of maritime and timber history, but it is a city of stunning, pervasive, pristine, *healthy* wilderness as well.

Tracts of forest, harbor preserves, shoreline, and parks flourish in the city, and there are dozens of interesting Great Lake or historical museums, mansions, lakefront walks, boat or foot tours, and festivals—from Native American powwows (mid- August) to midwinter dogsled races. Many visitors start at Duluth's landmark, the **Aerial Lift Bridge**, a 385-foot-tall monster connecting the mainland to the mouth of the harbor. The waterfront around here has been gently redeveloped, with an Omnimax theater and the **Lake Superior Maritime Visitor Center** (daily; free; 218/727-2497) within a short stroll. Best of all is another landmark of Great Lakes maritime industry, the truly huge hulk of the **SS *William A. Irvin*** (daily; $7; 218/722-7876), a former U.S. Steel ore ship that stretches over two football fields long.

Hwy-61 north of Duluth is the road that inspired the title of **Bob Dylan's** album *Highway 61 Revisited*. Dylan himself was born in Duluth and grew up in the nearby iron-mining town of **Hibbing,** which is also where **Greyhound Bus Lines** got its start, shuttling between the mines and the town. Home-run hitter **Roger Maris** was another Hibbing product.

The Aerial Lift Bridge over Duluth's harbor can be raised 138 feet in under a minute in order to let ships pass underneath. When it's down, cross the bridge and continue for a quarter mile for a real treat: a long, clean, sandy beach stretching along the shores of Lake Superior.

Another good stop, the **St. Louis County Heritage and Arts Center**, aka "The Depot,"

103-D Bird's-Eye View from Skyline Drive, Duluth, Minn.

across I-35 but walkably close to the waterfront at 506 W. Michigan Avenue, is an enormous, magnificently restored example of early city architecture as well as home to many of the city's artistic and cultural centers. Around it are the historic locomotives of the Lake Superior Museum of Transportation, and two dozen shops re-creating early 20th-century Duluth, right down to the old ice cream parlor.

A fun and filling place to eat, **Grandma's Saloon** (218/727-4192), at 522 S. Lake Avenue, serves up heaps of Italian-American food at the foot of the Aerial Lift Bridge. Stay overnight on the lakefront at the **Inn on Lake Superior** ($120 and up; 218/726-1111). For more information on Duluth, contact the main **visitors center** (218/722-4011 or 800/438-5884), located near the bridge at 100 Lake Place Drive. There's also a **ship watcher's hotline** (218/722-6489) if you want to head down to the harbor and check out the ore-boat traffic.

> In Minnesota and Wisconsin, the "On and Off" and "Off Sale" signs on many bars and roadhouse restaurants designate whether they can sell beer and wine for consumption on or off the premises.

WISCONSIN

US-2's briefest stint in any state, the route through Wisconsin nevertheless navigates wisely, for it takes in the far, Lake Superior cap of Wisconsin's northern region, and includes a majestic 140-mile detour along the rough-and-tumble Lake Superior shoreline, home of rich history, gorgeous boreal forest, and pastoral and littoral scenery. All of these provide outstanding opportunities to stop and explore.

Superior

Both rival and best friend of bigger Duluth across the harbor, despite the "superior" name, **Superior** (pop. 27,368) is often the butt of jokes, usually regarding its comparatively lower geography (which means Superior catches all of Duluth's flotsam), its hardy, blue-collar mentality, its forests of grain elevators (rather than trees), and its mountains of coal. It is also proud, along with Duluth, of being one of the busiest harbors in the nation, shipping millions of tons of ore a year from the nation's most-inland port.

> Northern Wisconsin is in the heart of big snow country, a promontory jutting into the maw of bad-tempered **Gitcheegumee**, where 35 inches of snow a month during the winter don't begin to crease a frown on a native Wisconsinite's face. Play it safe if you're traveling along Lake Superior then.

Superior's lack of pretense is perhaps its biggest attraction. The route on US-2 through the city is decidedly industrialized, featuring a seemingly endless amount—almost 30 miles—of bay shore crowded with trains, tracks, elevators, and spindly working piers jutting out into the lake almost to the horizon. The city itself is sedate but offers a few things of historical or Great Lake interest, including its biggest draw, **Fairlawn Mansion** (daily; $5), the sprawling 42-room ex-residence of a lumber and mining baron, now the main local-history museum. The main stretch of US-2 through town is looked over by a stern statue of an early industrial magnate, James J. Hill, "The Empire Builder," who made a fortune

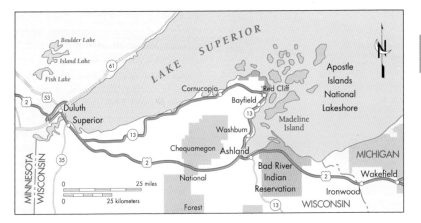

building and running the Great Northern railroad whose tracks still parallel US-2 west to Puget Sound.

There are plenty of places to stay along the main strip through town, including a nice **Days Inn** ($60; 715/392-4783) a couple of blocks north of the junction of US-2 and Hwy-53. For food, try the **Town Crier,** a full service, family-oriented café at 4927 E. 2nd Street. For more information, contact the **visitors center** (715/392-2773 or 800/942-5313), on US-2 at the west end of town, giving superior views both of the lake and town.

In 1979, *Terminator* movie star and California Governor **Arnold Schwarzenegger** got a BA degree from the UW-Superior business school.

Hwy-13 Loop: Cornucopia

One of the best alternative routes on the Upper Midwest stretch of US-2 is Hwy-13's 100-mile loop along the shores of Lake Superior. The 45 miles that this loop adds to your journey across the state are without question worth it, taking in the superlative Apostle Islands, charming peninsula communities, and unbeatable roadside vistas. Each little hill you climb reveals a new view of the expansive lake, groves of trees, or mosaics of farmland bordered by vacation cabins and archaic farming equipment. An occasional black bear may cross the road as you whiz by tottering, one-eyed cabins hardly larger than hunting shacks, their grainy, weather-beaten shingled siding obscured by weeds.

Starting in the west at the blue-collar harbor town of Superior, Hwy-13 zigzags northeast to the lakeshore and follows it to picturesque **Cornucopia,** the northernmost community in Wisconsin. If you're here on a Friday evening, be sure to stop for the traditional Scandinavian fish boil, held at the **Village Inn Restaurant** (715/742-3941), which also has rooms from around $60. Across the highway, tip a beer or two at **Fish Lipp's** (715/742-3378), and enjoy the incredible Lake Superior sunsets.

East of Cornucopia, the road veers away from the water, emerging again onto the lakefront at the peninsula's main Ojibwa Indian town, **Red Cliff**, which has a marina and boat slip, a lakeside **campground** within view of Basswood and Madeline Islands, a big casino, and an annual 4th of July **powwow**. The outskirts of Red Cliff include some lake views and some great views of open pastureland meshed with dense evergreen forests on what appears to be slight tableland. Boats and canoes are ever-present, scattered among rural jetsam, decades-old Chevys and Ford pickups, their sculpted sheet metal rusting mutely in the cattails.

From Red Cliff Hwy-13 turns south, immediately entering the outskirts of Bayfield.

Bayfield and Apostle Islands National Lakeshore

The nerve center of Hwy-13's sinuous trip through the Apostle Islands region is the diminutive, laid-back resort village of **Bayfield** (pop. 775). Bayfield itself dates from 1856 and looks at first glance about as Lilliputian as you can get, with a curvy (10 mph on the corners) narrow road winding beside impeccably tailored cottages and modest local-brownstone mansions. Virtually every hairpin turn offers an outstanding glimpse of the Apostle Islands and the boats plying the waters, especially on the far northern edge of town. While the waterfront area draws most visitors, the best views of the town and lake can be had from the blocks of dainty Victorian homes that line the hills above.

There are plenty of classy or quaint places to stay in Bayfield, from cottages and motels to the ritzy **Old Rittenhouse Inn** ($99–249; 715/779-5111), at 301 Rittenhouse Avenue, which is famed for its comfy rooms and multi-course gastronomic feasts. Hearty meals for the common man and woman have been served up since the Civil War at **Greunke's** (715/779-5480), across from the marina at 17 Rittenhouse Avenue, which is famous throughout the state for its whitefish livers, weekend fish boils, and generally funky feel. From the marina, there are also plenty of **ferries** (windsleds over the ice in winter!) to Madeline Island or some of the Apostle Islands, which are sprinkled out to the north across the chilly waters of Lake Superior. The HQ of the Apostle Islands National Seashore (daily; 715/779-3397), located in the old Bayfield Town Hall, offers the best introduction to these undeveloped islands, which are served by the **Apostle Island Cruise Service** (715/779-3925). The islands offer hiking trails, photogenic lighthouses, and wilderness camping. If you don't have time for an extended visit, you can hike along the Lakeshore Trail on the mainland, which runs along the northern tip of the Bayfield Peninsula, starting from Little Sand Bay Visitor Center, midway between Cornucopia and Red Cliff.

A unique draw in the summer is Washburn's **Big Top Chautauqua** ($5–25; 715/373-5552 or 888/244-8368), a revival of old traveling tent shows that offers great concerts, plays, and musical revues most evenings.

The Bayfield **visitors bureau** (715/779-3335) has complete listings of things to do and places to stay in the Apostle Islands area.

South of Bayfield, Washburn is a pleasant little community, less pretty than Bayfield, perhaps, but with cheaper accommodations: Try the **Super 8** ($40–75; 715/373-5671). Washburn also has a great road-food restaurant: **It's a Small World** (715/373-5177), on Hwy-13 at the heart of town. The menu changes constantly, reflecting different regional cuisines, but always includes some veggie-friendly choices, plus great big breakfasts and a chance to sample the locally famous Oddball Burger. To work off some of the calories, downtown Washburn's parks offer great lake vistas and a lakeshore walking trail.

In Northern Wisconsin, tune your radio to **WOJB 88.9 FM,** *run by the Lac Court Oreille Ojibwa Nation and featuring excellent, eclectic music as well as National Native and NPR news.*

Ashland

As you enter Ashland on US-2, some 40 miles west of the Michigan border, Lake Superior finally pokes its great nose at you. **Ashland** (pop. 8,620), a big fish in sparsely populated north-woods Wisconsin, likes to call itself the "Garland City of the Inland Seas," but it's really a town full of trestles, all the roads dipping and drooping under the mud-brown wood framework or plain faded steel of Soo Line bridges. Built up on an ever-so-slight rise above the lake, the town has an attractive Main Street with many well-preserved old buildings and a lakeshore lined with great parks, frigid-looking beaches and gritty pull-offs where you can gaze at the gargantuan **Ashland Soo Line Ore dock,** the largest of its kind in the world.

Listed on the National Register of Historic Places, **The Depot** (715/682-4200) at 400 W. 3rd Avenue is a luxurious restaurant inside a restored Soo Line depot, with great—but pricey—regional fare, and a downstairs brewpub. The nicest hotel in town—with a fine restaurant to boot—is the grand **Hotel Chequamegon** (shuh-WAH-muh-gun; $100 and up; 715/682-9095), on the lakeshore at the junction of US-2 and Hwy-13. Following a 1955 conflagration that destroyed the structure, the reconstruction has managed to capture the decorative charm and original grandeur.

Another big attraction, in interest if not actual size, is the newish **Northern Great Lakes Interpretive Center** (daily; free; 715/685-2680), 2.5 miles west of downtown, along US-2 at the Hwy-13 junction. The spacious building is full of interpretive exhibits tracing local history and industry; outside there's a nature trail through 180 acres of mixed forest and wetlands, and a 5-story tower gives a panoramic view.

For a change of pace, head 50 miles south from Ashland to Phillips, where the **Wisconsin Concrete Park** (free; 715/339-6475), 8236 N. Hwy-13, preserves the hundreds of creative concrete-and-glass sculptures of Paul Bunyan, Abe Lincoln, and lots of farm animals, all made in the 1950s by former logger and self-taught artist Fred Smith.

Just west of the border with Michigan, a Wisconsin liquor store proffers travelers a giant corkscrew statue, beckoning you to imbibe.

Bad River Indian Reservation and Superior Falls

Home to one of Wisconsin's six Ojibwa communities, the **Bad River Indian Reservation** encompasses 56,697 acres owned by approximately 1,800 descendants of the original Ojibwa Loon Clan who settled near the delta confluence of the Bad and White Rivers. The tribe holds its annual **Manonin Powwow** in late August, their wood-products factory builds log-home kits, and of course there's a large casino.

From the eastern edge of the reservation, it's another 20 miles to the Michigan border. The main highlight of this stretch is about midway along: a very nice vista point, overlooking the lakeshore from a parking area just west of the Hwy-122 junction. If you're up for a short detour, follow Hwy-122 north for a half-dozen miles to the shores of Lake Superior, where beautiful **Superior Falls** plummet more than 50 feet at the end of the Montreal River. There's a parking area near the small power plant, and the sunsets here can be spectacular.

MICHIGAN

There are two main routes across Michigan's Upper Peninsula (the "U.P."), which stretches for nearly 300 miles between Canada and Wisconsin, wedged between Lake Superior and Lake Michigan. Between Ironwood in the west and Sault Ste. Marie on the Canadian border in the east, you can choose between **US-2** along the north shore of Lake Michigan, or the slightly more direct option, **Hwy-28**, which runs near the south shore of Lake Superior near Pictured Rocks National Lakeshore. Either way takes most of a day, and this is not a place to try and make up time.

In either case, you're privy to one of the greater finds of the Midwest, the sparsely populated and thoroughly underappreciated (especially by the "trolls" of southern Michigan) land of the "Yoopers," as the proud residents have christened themselves, many still ensconced in the logging and mining enclaves their forebears founded. The U.P. is a surprisingly mountainous and larger-than-it-looks place, dotted with boom-to-bust towns relying on summer tourism and one or more of the industrial triumvirate up here: timber, mining, and fishing. More than three quarters of the land here is protected to varying degrees within national and state parks and forests, and it's no surprise that the best places tend to be farthest away from the main roads; though the roadside scenery is plenty pretty, the more remote areas are as wild and ruggedly beautiful as anywhere in North America.

Ironwood and Environs: The Gogebic Range

The westernmost U.P town is **Ironwood** (pop. 6,800), which, along with sleepy Bessemer and rough-and-tumble Hurley over the Wisconsin border, was the center of the Gogebic Range iron-mining district. The area's population now is about a fifth of what it was during the 1920s peak, and these mountain towns have moved on from mining to a more leisurely occupation: downhill skiing. Within a few miles are some of the Midwest's largest ski resorts, all benefiting from the vertiginous topography and the average 200 inches of annual snowfall. Most of these ski areas, like Indianhead (800/346-3426), double as summer mountain biking centers, and rental shops line US-2.

The center of Ironwood is easy to miss, but it's worth the quick trip along the US-2 Business Loop to see the old-fashioned business district, which fills a few blocks around the art deco Ironwood Theater movie palace. In a small hillside park just south of downtown, don't miss the absolutely huge, 52-foot-high statue of **Hiawatha**, the fictional hero of Henry Wadsworth Longfellow's famous poem.

The place to eat in Ironwood is **Joe's Pasty Shop,** two blocks off US-2 at 116 Aurora Street, serving pasties since 1946; it's open daily for breakfast (try the pasties filled with eggs and cheese) and lunch. Ironwood is the only town along US-2 to keep the U.P. Finnish tradition of sauna alive; many of the motels strung along US-2, including the **Sandpiper Motel** ($45 and up; 906/932-2000) right on the highway on the east side of town, boast real cedar saunas like the old country—bring your own birch twigs for self-flagellation in the snow banks.

All over the U.P. you'll see signs advertising pasties. The quintessential miner food, the Cornish **pasty** (which rhymes with nasty, not tasty—hang onto the vowel a bit, like a true Yooper) was introduced to Copper Country 100-odd years ago by immigrant Cornish miners. These dense, baked crust-pockets, stuffed with minced meat and vegetables, are ubiquitous in U.P. cafes and restaurants.

Across Michigan, Hwy-28 is often referred to as "M28."

Black River Road and the Porcupine Mountains Wilderness

From Hwy-28 at Bessemer, Hwy-513 heads north towards the shores of Lake Superior forming one of the U.P.'s many lovely scenic drives. Best-known as the **Black River Road,** this 15-mile-long, densely wooded two-laner runs along the banks of the Black River, which drops over a series of well-signed waterfalls as it approaches the lakeshore; a good trail starts at a parking area about 13 miles from Bessemer. Nearby, the **Copper Peak Ski Flying Hill,** the world's tallest ski-jumping facility, towers nearly 800 feet above the forest. In summer, visitors with no fear of heights can ride a chairlift, then an elevator, then take stairs to the top for a great view of the forest, Lake Superior, three states, and Canada ($10; 906/932-3500).

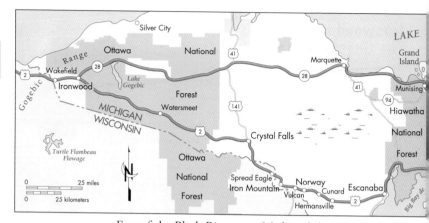

East of Ironwood, at the town of **Wakefield**, our route divides: US-2 runs south along Lake Michigan, while Hwy-28 veers north along Lake Superior.

East of the Black River area, Michigan's largest state park, the **Porcupine Mountains Wilderness,** covers 60,000 acres of serrated ridges and dense pine forests, including the largest swathes of virgin forest in the Midwest. The main outpost of civilization here (motels, restaurants, bars, etc.) are the lakefront towns of **Silver City** and **Ontonagon;** the latter is home to the park HQ (906/885-5275). Both towns are about 20 miles north of Hwy-28, via Hwy-64 or US-45, respectively.

US-2: Crystal Falls

At the eastern edge of the vast Ottawa National Forest, **Crystal Falls** (pop. 1,950) is a charming, postcard kind of place built into a bluff near a rivulet waterfall on the Paint River. Time seems to stand still here, the town sporting original (read: *old*) street signs still pointing the way, and huge trees overhanging US-2 as it slowly hairpins through town. The only "sights" here are the local courthouse, won in a poker game in the 1880s, and a water-filled old pit mine outside of town.

Southeast from Crystal Falls, US-2 passes numerous rock and ore formations jutting out of the hillsides. The road sweeps into the **Copper Country State Forest,** which gives every appearance of symmetrical reforestation, then flits through 15 miles of northern Wisconsin before re-entering the U.P. just west of Iron Mountain.

Iron Mountain and Norway

Though separated by a half-dozen blacktop miles of US-2, the sister towns of Norway and Iron Mountain both grew up with the lumbering and iron-mining industry, producing over 300,000 tons annually from three big mines. The larger of the two towns, **Iron Mountain** (pop. 8,154), backs up against the easy grade of its eponymous mountain and seems casually strewn about in parts: The east side is mini-mall sprawl, while the west side is older, traditional "downtown." The must-

see here, everyone will tell you, is the **Cornish Pump and Mining Museum** (daily May–Oct.; $4; 906/774-1086), two blocks off US-2 on Kent Street. This comprehensive local-history museum has as its star attraction the most enormous steam-driven pump engine you could imagine—it's 54 feet tall and weighs in at over 700 tons. There are also displays on the old Ford Motor Company factory complex in Kingsford, which fabricated such innovations as the "Woody" station wagon as well as WW II gliders. The *real* must-see is the freebie, the **Majestic Pine/Roosevelt Mountain Ski Jump,** west of town off US-2 along Pine Mountain Road. This 90-meter jump hosts annual international competitions in February and is the site of the current U.S. distance record.

The mines at **Norway** (pop. 2,959) were so close together and so active that the village once caved in and they had to re-build it down the hill. Gritty Norway—which once produced more wood shingles than anywhere else, as shown by the numerous houses still coated with them—also boasts the beautiful **Piers Gorge,** a couple of miles south via US-8, where the raging whitewater of the Menominee River scraped out this fascinating, 70-foot-deep gorge on the border between Michigan and Wisconsin. West of Iron Mountain, the Menominee River also provides a backdrop to one of the area's most pleasant places to stay: the **Edgewater Resort** ($80–130; 906/774-6244), 10 family-friendly one-, two-, and three-bedroom log cabins with kitchens, right on the river at 4128 N. US-2.

Around Iron Mountain in the 1920s, car maker **Henry Ford** created an industrial complex named **Kingsford** that supplied, among other products, fuel for his factories. This came in the form of charcoal briquettes, the same ones now essential for summer BBQs.

Besides ski areas, **Bessemer** is also home to what a large plaque claims is "The Most Scenic Little League Baseball Stadium in America," located just a block north of US-2.

Escanaba

Midway along US-2's route across far northern Michigan, **Escanaba** (pop. 13,740)—with picture-perfect placement where the Escanaba River pours into the Little Bay de Noc—was born in typical U.P. fashion, out of the country's insatiable need for timber and ore. At one time its docks contributed to the largest ore-shipping operation of its kind in the United States, work that continues today as Escanaba feeds the steel mills of Illinois

and Indiana across Lake Michigan. To get a feel for lake life, head to the renovated 1867 **Sandpoint Lighthouse** ($1) along the lushly landscaped waterfront. The annual **U.P. State Fair,** held here the third week in August, is great fun; for more on the fair and most anything to do with Escanaba, contact the **visitors bureau** (800/437-7496).

Hiawatha National Forest: Fayette State Park

Between Escanaba and Manistique, US-2 broadens into a fast four-lane highway along both Big and Little Bay de Noc, where you'll pass through a slew of lakefront "resorts," some with their own beaches and all famous for their fishing. Between the bays, the landscape reverts to trees and more trees in the chevroned conifers of the 879,000-acre **Hiawatha National Forest.** The flyspeck communities here haven't changed much—ubiquitous flashing yellow lights, matchbox dwellings attached to bulbous propane gas tanks, and, in a few communities, forlorn old Soo Line railcars aging gracelessly on the tracks right off the highway.

*Fifteen miles west of Escanaba, at the eastern edge of tiny **Potawatomi Indian Reservation,** you pass between the Central and Eastern time zones. Adjust your clocks and watches accordingly.*

Jutting south from US-2, two quiet peninsulas stick their thumbs out into Lake Michigan. Both have forests, fruit orchards, and a few lighthouses, but the best destination here has to be **Fayette State Park,** the extant ghost of an iron smelting community with a few dozen stone and wooden buildings kept almost totally in their original 1890s condition, not renovated but preserved in varying states of repair. The park is an impressive, sometimes eerie place, situated on sheer limestone cliffs along Hwy-183, 17 miles south of US-2 from the crossroads community of Garden Corners.

Manistique

The only sizeable town between St. Ignace and Escanaba, **Manistique** (pop. 3,583) tends to underwhelm, apart from its Lake Michigan frontage. Mountains of gravel and mini-smokestacks line the road into town on the east side, and the sweetly pungent smell of paper permeates the air. Despite that, Manistique does have an offbeat sleepy tourist draw: old US-2 (now Hwy-94) crosses the Siphon Bridge, which was featured in *Ripley's Believe It or Not!* for being partially supported by water, and having a roadway four feet below the water level.

US-2: Along Lake Michigan

The route that US-2 follows along Lake Michigan between Escanaba and St. Ignace is one of the U.P.'s best autumn scenic drives. The true heart of U.P. lies here, with patches of pine or birch woodland followed by brief lakeshore, then a dormant ore-mine, a trailer park, or a long-abandoned fishing camp.

*From the flyspeck town of **Gulliver,** 13 miles east of Manistique, a road leads southeast to Michigan's most picturesque lighthouse, at **Seul Choix Pointe.***

The first hint of anything special comes in tiny **Blaney Park,** 22-odd miles east of Manistique, which boasts two grand B&Bs: the **Celibeth House B&B** (906/283-3409), an 1895 mansion with eight rooms; and the posher **Blaney Lodge B&B** (906/283-3883), which June–October maintains one of the best dining rooms in the U.P.

East of here, as you approach St. Ignace, the scenery becomes increasingly gorgeous. Bay views give way only occasionally to small towns or groves of trees, but most of the way the lake breaks through fully as US-2 skims along a beach-side causeway bordered by huge sand dunes with green tufts of mixed grasses.

St. Ignace

Coming into St. Ignace from the west along US-2, travelers are tempted by a number of "scenic overlooks" west of town, all proffering a chance to stretch and view the often fog-shrouded Mackinac Bridge over blue Lake Michigan. Picturesque **St. Ignace** (pop. 2,678; IG-nus) lies east of, and down a hill from, the concrete river of the I-75 freeway. This little town, at one time 70 percent French-Canadian, is more important than its obviously tourism-contrived loveliness would indicate, situated as it is at the crossroads of the upper and lower regions of Michigan, with Mackinac Island just across the bay. The town is busy and cheerful, in places gentrified and meticulously maintained; downtown you can stroll along a bright lake promenade lined with gift shops, motels, and restaurants.

Downtown, the city-run **Museum of Ojibwa Culture** (daily May–Oct.; $2) traces over three centuries of life along the Straits of Mackinac, detailing the native Ojibwa and Huron lifeways. The museum, on the site of Father Marquette's original mission, also hosts a number of summer powwows; the largest takes place over Labor Day weekend, and attending one is an unforgettable way to experience the tribe's heritage.

For concentrated kitsch, don't miss **Paul Bunyan Pasties** on US-2, eight miles west of the Mackinac Bridge; they're in the *Guinness Book of World Records* for having baked a 223-pound monster.

St. Ignace sits at the north end of what locals like to call the "Eighth Wonder of the World," the **Mackinac Bridge**, one of the longest suspension bridges in the world at 7,400 feet (with its approaches, the total length is over five miles). Lots of scenic views are found throughout St. Ignace and from **Straits State Park**, west of town.

Mackinac Island

The main attraction around St. Ignace is anachronistic **Mackinac Island**, one of the top draws in the Midwest. Pronounced "Mackinaw," this flyspeck island is almost completely car-free, and walking and cycling trails loop around its 2,200 acres (even UPS delivers parcels by bike!). Now billed as a sort of bygone-days living museum, during the early 19th century Mackinac Island was the headquarters of John Jacob Astor's early fur-trading empire. For two centuries before then, its coveted position at the heart of the Great Lakes meant that French, British, and later Americans frequently fought over it. Historic sites and beauty spots abound, so be sure to move quickly through the Main Street commercial area around the ferry landing, which is oversupplied with fudge shops (an island specialty since Victorian times).

Apart from slabs of fudge, the biggest "tourist attraction" on Mackinac has to be the aptly named **Grand Hotel**, which

GRAND HOTEL AND GROUNDS, MACKINAC ISLAND, MICH.

has been in business since 1887. Famous for its 660-foot-long "World's Longest Front Porch," packed with potted plants and comfy chairs, the hotel is definitely deluxe; room rates are pretty high (around $350 a night, including dinner; 906/847-3331), but you can explore the place and enjoy a drink or high tea, or pay for a self-guided tour ($7). Room rates elsewhere on the island start well above $100 at most of the many nice hotels and B&Bs—for details, call the Mackinac Island **visitors bureau** (906/847-3783 or 800/454-5227)—but it's a great place to rent a bike (or take a horse-and-buggy ride), cruise around, and forget about your daily grind.

Passenger ferry services (about $15 round-trip) from the docks in St. Ignace are fast (20 minutes each way) and frequent from April through October; call Arnold Line (800/542-8528) or Star Line (800/638-9892) for times and rates.

Hwy-28: Marquette

Midway across the Upper Peninsula along Hwy-28, the U.P.'s biggest and, in many ways, most attractive city is **Marquette** (pop. 23,000), a Lake Superior ore port with a lovely lakeside setting. Blocks of 100-year-old beaux arts–style buildings fill the business district above the heavy industrial harbor, and the presence of government offices and the region's main college (Northern Michigan University) has given it a lively, prosperous feel.

Other aspects of U.P. life are documented down the road in neighboring Negaunee, 8 miles west along Hwy-28/US-41, where the excellent **Iron Industry Museum** (daily May–Oct.; free; 906/475-7857) tells the full story of the $48 billion Michigan iron mining industry. Further west, the lighter side of U.P. lifeways is the theme of **Yooperland** (daily; free; 800/628-9978), aka "Da Yooper Tourist Trap," a gigantic gift shop-cum-cultural museum along Hwy-28/US-41. (Just look for the "World's Largest Snowplow" parked out front.) If you're looking for comic postcards of giant pasties and similar oddities, this is the place to come.

World's Largest Rifle at Yooperland

The Huron Mountains

Stretching north and west from the Marquette region, the **Huron Mountains** hold the highest point in Michigan (1,979-foot Mt. Arvon), but almost all of this rugged 50- by 25-mile area is privately owned and pretty much off limits. It's also among the wildest corner of a wild part of the country; the private owners (with last names like McCormick, founders of International Harvester, and

Miller, of Miller Beer infamy) keep it pretty much as it has always been—before the miners and loggers had their way with the rest of the U.P. The best place to get a feel for the Huron Mountains region is at the **Thunder Bay Inn** ($80–130; 906/345-9376), in the hamlet of Big Bay on Lake Superior, 25 miles northwest of Marquette.

Pictured Rocks National Lakeshore

If travel time is not an issue for you, there is at least one excellent reason to bypass US-2 across the Upper Peninsula and to follow Hwy-28 instead. **Pictured Rocks National Lakeshore,** a lovely, 40-mile-long stretch of undisturbed sand

Every February, Marquette hosts the start and finish of the **UP 200,** a sled dog race to Escanaba and back that draws some 30,000 spectators.

dunes, beaches, and colorful bluffs, lines Lake Superior in the northeastern quadrant of the U.P. For casual visitors, the lakeshore is best visited by boat, since roads here are few, far between, mostly unpaved, and all but invisible; in summer, three-hour **cruises** leave about every two hours from the pier in **Munising,** right on Hwy-28 at the west edge of the park. Even better, if you're feeling fit, is a self-powered kayak trip; try **Northern Waters** (906/387-2323), 129 E. Munising Avenue, who offer day-long guided tours (9 AM; $95).

Besides being the gateway to the Pictured Rocks, Munising is also the main departure point for glass-bottomed-boat tours of the many shipwrecks that lie along this treacherous stretch of coastline. Well-preserved by the cold Lake Superior waters, the wrecks are also legally protected within the 113-square-mile **Alger Underwater Preserve.**

For more information, contact the Pictured Rocks **visitors center** (906/387-3700), located in Munising at 400 E. Munising Avenue.

Tahquamenon Falls State Park and Paradise

East of the Pictured Rocks National Lakeshore, about 40 miles west of Sault Ste. Marie, you come to a real gem: **Hwy-123,** a must-do loop road (particularly during autumnal color sweeps) that heads north from Hwy-28 past the outstanding—and popular—**Tahquamenon Falls State Park** ($4 per car). The 50-foot-high, 200-foot-wide Upper Falls here were mentioned in Longfellow's *Song of Hiawatha.* Hwy-123 also passes through the lakefront vacation village of **Paradise,** where Whitefish Point Road runs 11 miles north up to some of the best and most isolated beaches in the U.P., and the oldest lighthouse (circa 1849) on the Great Lakes.

From Longfellow to Lightfoot: In Whitefish Point, north of Paradise, visit the **Great Lakes Shipwreck Historical Museum** (daily May–Oct.; $8.50; 877/SHIP-WRECK), to learn about the wreck of the 725-foot lake freighter *Edmund Fitzgerald,* subject of Canadian balladeer Gordon Lightfoot's 1970s pop song. Twenty miles offshore is the point where the ship suddenly went down—without a distress call, but with all 29 crew members on board—in November 1975.

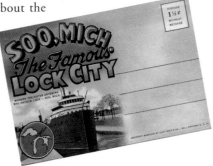

Sault Ste. Marie, Michigan

Michigan's oldest community, **Sault Ste. Marie** (pop. 16,542; SOO-SAYNT-ma-REE) was home to an Ojibwa Indian community for hundreds of years before the first fur-trappers and French-Catholic colonists arrived in the late 17th century. Known historically for the tussles over the area between the French and British, and as the closest land link between the United States and Canada for hundreds of miles, "The Soo" is a great place to break a journey and catch up on the region's complicated past, present, and future.

Beneath the steel-span International Bridge that links this Michigan town with Ontario's twin "Soo," the raging torrents that impelled French Fr. Jacques Marquette to dub the newly established mission *Le Sault de Sainte Marie,* literally "falling waters of Saint Mary," are no longer readily apparent. The U.S. Army Corps of Engineers long ago corralled and tamed the rapids between 20-foot-higher Lake Superior and Lake Huron with four enormous locks, the largest and busiest in the world. During their 1920s mining heydays, the locks conveyed many times the tonnage of the Panama and Suez Canals combined—with no tolls paid. The locks area is worthy of at least an hour's siesta; lush parks and a walkway line the locks, with observation points letting you get within a few feet of the massive lake freighters that pass through around the clock. If you want to "lock through" yourself, join a Soo Lock boat **tour** ($19; 800/432-6301).

A handful of nice cafés and restaurants line Water Street and Portage Avenue within a few blocks of the locks; this is also where you'll find the art deco **Ramada Ojibway Hotel** ($80–150; 906/632-4100), at 240 Portage Avenue. For more information, the local **visitors center** (906/632-3301 or 800/647-2858) is at 2581 Ashmun Street (Business I-75).

CANADA

Between Sault Ste. Marie and Ottawa, the capital of Canada, our route winds along the north shore of Lake Huron then cuts inland to follow a series of broad rivers. The main highway here, Hwy-17, is a section of the busy Trans-Canada Highway; it is also part of the "Voyageurs Trail," roughly retracing the route taken by the early fur-traders between their winter trapping grounds—the wilderness of forests, lakes, and streams to the northwest—and Montreal, the summer fur market. The scenery varies from rivers and forests to paper mills and coal mines, and most of the way Hwy-17 is a two-lane road with a 90-kph (55 mph) maximum and occasional passing lanes to help you get around the timber trucks. Towns here tend to sprawl along the roadside, with a few "chip stands" selling fried potatoes amongst the franchised American fast-food joints, but there are expansive sections of natural wilderness within easy reach.

East of Ottawa, it's a short run to French-speaking Montreal, Canada's second-largest city and one of the most European places in North America. The change between bilingual Ontario and French-speaking Quebec is sudden and sometimes surreal, as if England and France were divided by a river, not the Channel.

Driving in Canada

Between the United States and Canada, the rules of the road don't really change, but the measurements do. Both countries drive on the right, and the speed limits are similar: In Canada it's generally 90 kilometers (55 mi) per hour on two-lane roads, 100 kph (63 mph) on freeways. All cars are required to have their headlights illuminated night and day; to the unaccustomed, a daytime traffic jam can look like a massive funeral procession. Other rules: All passengers must wear seat belts, and turning right on red is illegal in the Province of Quebec; in the rest of Canada, it is legal after stopping first. Deciphering parking zones, especially in French-speaking Quebec, can really test your interpretive abilities.

Gas in Canada tends to be more expensive than in the States, and it's priced by the liter (3.785 liters equal 1 U.S. gallon). Some gas stations accept U.S. currency (and almost all accept credit cards) but often give you a less-than-favorable rate of exchange.

Crossing the border, there are brief checkpoints (and sundry duty-free shops) on both sides. Customs officers usually do a cursory check, asking your address, reason for travel, when you last visited the country, and whether you are carrying firearms, tobacco, or alcohol. The rules are subject to change, but generally for U.S. or Canadian citizens a passport is not legally necessary, but it is the best proof of citizenship and identity. People of other nationalities should confirm their visa status well before attempting to cross the border; it may be difficult (or impossible) to return to the United States, and border officials may confiscate vehicles and arrest people they suspect are trying to enter the United States illegally.

Sault Ste. Marie, Ontario

Across the busy harbor from Michigan, the "other" **Sault Ste. Marie** (pop. 81,000) is a much bigger, much grittier, and comparatively depressed Canadian sibling. Graffiti on a railway bridge proclaims: "This is Indian Land," and since the big Algoma Steel mill here began laying off workers, many locals seem tempted to let them have it back. The main visitor attraction, right downtown, offers a quick escape: the Algoma Central Railway Terminal, well-signed at 129 Bay Street, from which the **Agawa Canyon Wilderness Tours** (daily at 8 AM; $C65; 705/946-7300 or 800/242-9287) depart throughout the summer and early fall (fall color season is the prime time to come). These day-long train trips take you north through a roadless wilderness featuring

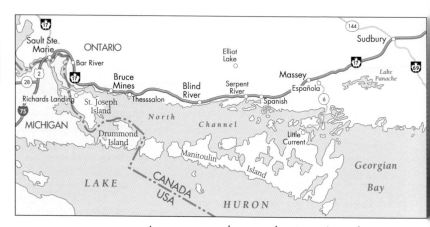

narrow river canyons and spectacular views. A two-hour stop above the canyon lets you get out and have a picnic, or stretch your legs with a walk to a waterfall. From January through March there is also a "Snow Train" for the hardy, and there's also an "End of the Line Tour" (to Hearst, Ontario), which takes two days (and does return, despite the name).

Sault Ste. Marie also has a mile-long waterfront boardwalk (though all the big ships travel on the U.S. side), and a pleasant HI **youth hostel** in the old Algonquin Hotel, 864 E. Queen Street ($C20; 705/253-2311 or 888/269-7728). The Soo is something of a culinary wasteland, but there are a surprising number of very cheap greasy-spoon diners.

St. Joseph Island

East of Sault Ste. Marie, Hwy-17 winds along Lake Huron's North Channel waterfront for most the way to Sudbury. South and east of Bar River, a turnoff heads south to St. Joseph Island, part of the Manitoulin Island chain. The main sight here lies at the island's south end: **Fort St. Joseph National Historic Park.** When the fort was built by the British in 1796, it was the westernmost outpost of their Canadian empire. At first the fort protected the fur trade; it then served as a base for attacking the Americans during the War of 1812. The Americans burned the fort in 1814, and the park is built around its scenic remains.

At the island's north end is the tiny town of **Richards Landing**; the general store at the dock serves good burgers and soft ice cream.

Along Lake Huron

Twelve miles east of the St. Joseph Island turnoff lies the town of **Bruce Mines**, founded in 1846 around some small copper mines. The earliest settlers were miners from Cornwall in England. The road then runs slightly inland, returning to the lakeside a dozen miles later at **Thessalon**, where

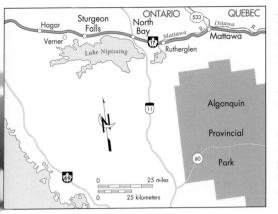

you can stay the night along the beachfront at **Carolyn Motel** ($C70; 705/842-3330); the on-site restaurant is open all day and always has fresh fish on the menu.

Following Hwy-17 east along the lakeshore toward Massey, the landscape is generally flat with occasional rocky outcrops. Just west of the settlements of Spanish and Serpent River, you have a great view across the North Channel, an arm of Lake Huron, to Manitoulin Island in the distance.

Massey and Manitoulin Island

Massey, "The Home of Chutes Provincial Park and Lots of Friendly People," sits at the confluence of the Sauble and Spanish Rivers. The main attraction hereabouts is just north of Hwy-17: **Chutes Provincial Park,** which offers swimming, camping, picnicking, and several scenic waterfalls along the Sauble River.

> Manitoulin Island is one of the largest freshwater islands in the world, and it still has a substantial aboriginal "First Nation" population.

Twenty miles east of Massey, 40 miles west of Sudbury, Hwy-17 intersects with Hwy-6, which heads south toward **Manitoulin Island,** the world's largest freshwater island, set in the northern end of Lake Huron. Manitoulin is a popular vacation spot, ringed with picturesque harbors at Meldrum Bay, Providence Bay, and South Baymouth.

Sudbury

The biggest city between Ottawa and Duluth, **Sudbury** (pop. 163,000) lies in the middle of a geological basin that contains one of the world's largest concentrations of nickel, as well as numerous other precious metals. Originally an Ojibwa tribal settlement, the town began to develop after the 1883 arrival of the railway, and boomed when nickel and copper were discovered here three years later. Uncontrolled development followed, mines and processing plants sprang up all over the landscape, and soon the area was a classic industrial-era ecological disaster. No trees grew for miles around, and a haze of toxic smoke choked the inhabitants, who lived in narrow valleys below the mine heads.

In the early 1950s, Sudbury undertook a massive urban renewal and land reclamation project to return at least a vestige of the original beauty and unpolluted air to the area, with considerable success. For older residents, the city has changed

> Around Sudbury, a rare alternative to the often over-earnest CBC (Canadian Broadcasting Corporation) radio is offered by Laurentian University's **CKLU 96.7 FM**—wacky, ad-free, and often very funny college radio.

> East of Sudbury, Hwy-17 enters the narrow **Veuve River Valley,** lined with scraggly pines and picturesque rock outcroppings. Apart from a couple of very small towns, it's mostly dairy farming country for the 130 kilometers (80 mi) of Hwy-17 between Sudbury and North Bay.

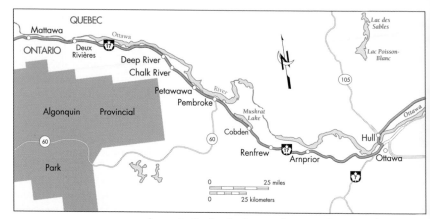

The highway town of Bar River is home to the **Big Loonie,** a very large statue of the Canadian dollar coin, right along Hwy-17.

dramatically for the better; the air is cleaner and trees dot the landscape. Today, Sudbury is still Canada's most important mining community, producing as much as 85 percent of the world's nickel and operating the country's largest copper mine, INCO, west of town, but it's an infinitely healthier place than its past may suggest.

As it passes around Sudbury, the Trans-Canada Highway (Hwy-17) bypasses the city's center, so turn north onto Hwy-80 toward Sudbury's real visitor draw: **Science North.** Located at the edge of downtown Sudbury, along manmade Lake Ramsey, Science North is a state-of-the-art science and technology museum featuring many hands-on displays for kids and adults (daily; $C16–40; 705/522-3700 or 800/461-4898). Inside the snowflake-shaped structure, you can experience a simulated hurricane, watch flying squirrels fly, enjoy a butterfly aviary, talk to ham radio operators around the world, enjoy a show (most recently featuring grizzly bears) in the IMAX theater ($C12), or take a "virtual reality" voyage to Mars ($C7).

Science North also has one of Sudbury's better places to eat—the **Snowflake Restaurant**—which says a lot about the town's culinary offerings. The newest attraction here is **Dynamic Earth,** which simulates an underground mine. Outside, you can see Sudbury's famous **"Big Nickel,"** moved here in 2003—it's exactly what it sounds like, a 30-foot-tall replica of a Canadian nickel.

Among the better Sudbury hotels are the downtown **Peter Piper Inn** ($C90–120; 705/673-7801) at 151 Larch Street, and the **Travelodge Hotel Sudbury** ($C60; 705/522-1100) at 1401 Paris Street a block from Science North. For more complete information, contact the Sudbury **visitors center** (705/671-2489).

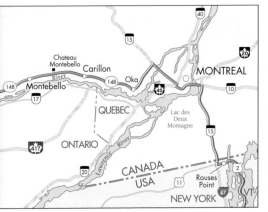

North Bay

North Bay (pop. 55,000; "Gateway to Opportunity") was originally a fur-trading post that boomed after the 1882 arrival of the railway. These days North Bay is still a trade and transportation center, and its fur auctions are among the largest in the world. Many tourists use the city as a jumping-off point for wilderness expeditions.

Just southeast of town, Hwy-17 joins Hwy-11, which runs south to Toronto. Near the junction there's a **visitors center** and the **Dionne Quintuplets Museum** (daily in summer only; $C3), housed in the cabin that was their 1934 birthplace.

Apart from the Dionne Quintuplets, the main attractions of North Bay line up along the Lake Nippising waterfront park; from here, the *Chief Commanda II* cruises (705/494-8167) follow the old voyageurs' route across the water. In midsummer, the guided tour will likely tell you all about the locally famous **shad flies,** mouthless, fish-smelly bugs that swarm out of the water and make a nuisance of themselves on North Bay sidewalks in their short, 24-hour lives.

Many motels are along Lakeshore Drive, such as a **Comfort Inn** (705/494-8461) and the moderate **Lincoln Motel** (705/472-3231). The fancy restaurant in town is **Churchill's Prime Rib House** (705/476-7777) at 631 Lakeshore Drive.

> For more information, tune in to North Bay Tourism Radio, **CKTR 104.9 FM**, "a ray of sunshine highlighting our beautiful city," featuring an hour-long program of driving tours, local events, and things to do.

Mattawa and the Ottawa River

East of North Bay, Trans-Canada Hwy-17 runs through its wildest and least populated stretch: scenic country largely empty of human habitation. The road hugs the riverside while rolling over steeper hills, past birch and pine forests and many lakes and ponds. In the midst of all this wilderness, the attractive and relatively large town of **Mattawa** (pop. 2,300; "There Is a Story Here Where Rivers Meet") lies at the confluence of the Ottawa and Mattawa Rivers. Surrounded by dense green forest, the riverfront is lined by a very pleasant park (with free hot showers), and the town center is quaint and quiet—two blocks of brick-fronted buildings, along the river just north and west of the main highway.

The Mattawa River is the focus of the expansive **Samuel de Champlain Provincial Park** which offers campgrounds, canoeing, and hiking trails.

> The Ottawa River marks the border between Ontario and Quebec, the bluffs of which may be seen across the water.

Algonquin Provincial Park

Between Mattawa and Deep River, Hwy-17 runs along the northern boundaries of the enormous **Algonquin Provincial Park,** which stretches for many miles to the south. Ontario's oldest and most popular park, Algonquin protects 3,000

Ottawa

Originally an Algonquin settlement, Ottawa (pop. 775,000) was a small fur-trading and lumber-milling outpost until the 1850s, when Queen Victoria chose the city to be the national capital, a compromise answer to the bitter rivalry between Montreal and Toronto. Construction of the Parliament buildings began the following year, but government only became the largest employer after World War II, when the lumber mills began to decline. Today the train tracks and factories have been replaced by telecom and computer companies, and the miles of parks and greenbelts make Ottawa one of the most peaceable and pleasant of the world's capitals.

Orientation within Ottawa is easy: **Parliament Hill,** which holds the most prominent buildings, is on the north edge of town, with its back turned on the Ottawa River and the French-speaking province of Quebec. Getting around is easy, since most of the sights are gathered together around Parliament Hill and the adjacent Byward Market. To see Ottawa, you should definitely park the car, get out, and walk (or bike, or rollerblade . . .) around town.

Parliament Hill is home to the three buildings that comprise Parliament, Canada's seat of federal government. The architecture is reminiscent of England's Houses of Parliament as redesigned by the cartoonist Charles Addams: Elegant, Gothic-style carved stone walls rise to copper mansard roofs topped with fantastically filigreed wrought iron. On the lawns of the Parliament buildings, the **Changing of the Guard** ceremony (daily at 10 AM, late June–late Aug.; free) is extremely popular with tourists, as is the firing of the Noonday Gun (daily at noon, May–Aug.), which you can watch from the bluffs above the Ottawa River.

East of Parliament Hill stands the **National Gallery of Canada** (daily May–Oct., Wed.–Sun. Oct.–April; free), at 380 Sussex Drive. Along with many floors of painting and sculpture from colonial times up to the present, including George Segal's automobilia assembly *The Gas Station,* there's also a large collection of Asian and Inuit art. Another striking piece of modern architecture stands upstream, just west of Parliament Hill: the new riverfront **Canadian War Museum** (daily; $C10), which documents Canadian soldiers' bravery in war- and peace-making.

ROYAL CANADIAN MOUNTED POLICE, CANADA

Practicalities

Ottawa's airport, with flights from most major U.S. hubs, is 20 minutes south of the city. The major east–west access is via Hwy-17, the Trans-Canada Highway; within town, this becomes the Hwy-417 free-way. From the south, Hwy-31 links up with Hwy-401, the Interstate freeway along the north shore of Lake Ontario.

Ottawa's Chateau Laurier hotel

Byward Market, east of Parlia-ment Hill across the Rideau Canal, is the place to go for food. The market stalls offer a variety of fresh produce, cafés are abundant (try **Cafe Wim** at 537 Sussex Drive), and the restaurants and bars lively and pretty good. **Blue Cactus Bar & Grill** (613/241-7061), 2 Byward Market, is one of many good restaurants here, featuring Tex-Mex food in a cheery ambience, and a late-night supper club. There's a popular Stream-line-style American diner, **Zak's** (daily; 613/241-2401), open 24 hours on weekends at 16 Byward Market, and a very nice East Indian place, **Cafe Shafali** (613/789-9188), at 308 Dalhousie Street.

Places to stay in Ottawa are centrally located and not all that expen-sive—the capital of Canada is not really a major tourist destination. **Château Laurier** ($C150 and up; 613/241-1414), 1 Rideau Street, situat-ed in an opulent tower directly across from Parliament Hill, is luxurious but not all that expensive. **Albert House** ($C90 and up; 613/236-4479), at 478 Albert Street, is a large mansion converted into one of Ottawa's nicest bed-and-breakfast inns. One of the most interesting budget options anywhere has to be the **Ottawa HI Hostel** ($C21; 613/235-2595), 75 Nicholas Street, which occupies the old Ottawa jail a 10-minute walk from Parliament Hill. Guests sleep in cell bunks; solitary confinement is now the laundry room.

An overwhelming quantity of visitor information on Ottawa is available from the **Capital Infocentre** (613/239-5000), 90 Wellington Street.

The Dionne Quintuplets

In 1934, during the depths of the Great Depression, in a small house deep in the wilds of north Ontario, five baby girls were born to the Dionnes, a poor rural family. The fact that all the babies—Annette, Cecile, Yvonne, Marie, and Emilie—were born healthy despite being two months premature is noteworthy enough, but what happened in later years verges on the incredible. The babies were cared for at home for the difficult first weeks, but after that, the Ontario government took the infants away from their destitute family. Across from the family home, the government built a zoo-like environment called Quintland, and raised them in public—selling tickets for three "shows" daily and effectively doing everything possible to keep them from having a "normal" childhood. At age five (of course) they were introduced to the King and Queen of England and later appeared in movies and "wrote" their own autobiography, *We Were Five.* The quints also did product endorsements, promoting soap, toothpaste, cereal, and Carnation milk. During the 1930s, the quintuplets were Canada's number-one tourist attraction—bigger than Niagara Falls, it was said—and by the time they turned 10 years old they had been visited by more than 3 million people.

After a long and bitter custody battle, the girls were eventually returned to their parents, and faded from the public eye. The Ontario government, which earned an estimated $1 billion marketing the Quints, paid the surviving three girls a settlement of $4 million in 1998. The house where they were born has been moved from Corbeill to North Bay, where it has been rebuilt as the Dionne Quintuplets Museum and filled with toys, dresses, baby carriages, and photographs that trace their youthful fame. (Continuing the quintuplets' lifelong exploitation, there's a nifty gift shop on the museum premises.)

square miles of almost untouched wilderness, offering a wide variety of wildlife (including moose, bears, beavers, and timber wolves), dozens of lakes, and hundreds of miles of backcountry hiking and canoeing trails. The main **visitors center** (705/633-5572) is at the park's far southwest corner, south of North Bay or west of Pembroke and Renfrew via Hwy-60, the "Parkway Corridor," the only road through the park. Here you can get details on the park's abundant camping and cabins, and pick up all the necessary permits.

Deep River and Chalk River

The first real town east of Mattawa is **Deep River** (pop. 4,200), Canada's first "Atomic Town," a planned community built for employees of the Chalk River labs just downstream. The **Diplomat Motor Hotel** (613/584-1234) on Hwy-17 dates to the Cold War era and would be equally at home in the former Soviet Union, but the real attraction is the **Laurentian View Dairy Bar** (613/584-3777) a few blocks west, featuring homespun Canadian country cooking and homemade ice cream.

Nine miles farther east, you enter **Chalk River**. In 1945, this tiny logging center became the home of the first atomic reactor outside of the United States. Seven years later, Atomic Energy of Canada, Ltd. (AECL), a government-owned nuclear research organization, was founded here; they design and sell commercial and research nuclear reactors around the world, and produce most of the world's radioactive isotopes for medical use. At the **Chalk River Laboratories**, you can "tour the atomic age" and clamber around a research reactor (Mon.–Fri. summer only; free; 613/584-3311, ext. 4965).

Petawawa and Pembroke

Southeast of Chalk River, Hwy-17 crosses the namesake river of the town of **Petawawa**, home since 1905 to a Canadian Forces base. You can visit a number of small military museums on the base; the largest, the **Canadian Forces Airborne Museum**, traces the history of Canadian paratroopers. There's also a riverfront beach and campground, but otherwise the area is strictly off limits, as the numerous signs along the road warn.

The rather quaint, redbrick town of Petawawa itself is two miles north of Hwy-17 via Hwy-41, well worth the short trip through what seems like one big light-industrial park.

Wrapping around the eastern edge of Algonquin Provincial Park, Hwy-17 nears **Pembroke**, another timber town along the Ottawa River, north of the highway. The main sights here are the many history-themed murals painted on downtown buildings, the **"World's Tallest Totem Pole"** along the river, and the **Champlain Trail Museum** (June–Sept. only; $C5), with exhibits on local history at 1032 E. Pembroke Street.

Arnprior

Midway between Pembroke and Renfrew, you can see the Ottawa River loop north around Cobden, a little town on Muskrat Lake. **Renfrew**, another of Ontario's many Scots-founded towns, is now a center of high-tech industry.

Twenty-seven miles east of Renfrew, Hwy-17 approaches the banks of the Ottawa near **Arnprior**, founded in 1823 by Archibald McNab, a despotic Scottish lord who imported dozens of his countrymen and -women to the settlement and ruthlessly exploited them. This reign of terror ended when the townsfolk banded together and drove him away. There's a **museum** in the old stone post office building, and downtown boasts some moderately priced motels and, best of all, **Wes' Chips** (Mar.–Oct. only; 613/623-5492) at 198 Madawaska Boulevard, an open-air chip stand selling the exquisite Canadian delicacy Americans call "french fries."

Hockey fans may want to make a pilgrimage here in November and December, when Pembroke hosts "North America's largest hockey tournament," the **Silver Stick** (613/732-1364); Renfrew was home to one of the first professional hockey teams, the Renfrew Millionaires.

Hwy-17 is fairly boring between Ottawa and Montreal, and you're better off taking the much faster Hwy-417, called the **Queensway**, or following our two-lane route across Quebec, along the north bank of the Ottawa River.

Montreal

Dominion Square, Montreal

Located on an island in the St. Lawrence River, and first settled as a frontier outpost by fur-trapping French voyageurs, Montreal (pop. 1,016,376) has grown into Canada's second-largest city, and today is easily the most European city in North America, with the largest French-speaking population outside La France. Hotbed of the separatist movement, Montreal tolerates the polyglot federalism of Canada, but the accent here is most definitely on the "French" in French-Canadian; in a wide variety of gourmet restaurants, stylish boutiques, nightclubs, museums, and theaters—you can half-close your eyes and pretend you're in Paris.

The city takes its name from a 700-foot-high hill, now the very pleasant tree-covered **Mount Royal Park** just north of downtown. Planned by Frederick Law Olmsted and opened in 1876, the park's stairs and paths lead up to a belvedere, from which you have a sweeping view of the city, the St. Lawrence River, the southern suburbs and, on the eastern slope, a huge steel cross that's lit up at night.

At the foot of Mount Royal Park runs Sherbrooke Street, Montreal's most prestigious and majestic street, lined with grand 1920s buildings as impressive as any on Park Avenue. Among the many posh boutiques (Chanel, Armani, et al.) and luxury hotels (like the Ritz-Carlton, where Richard Burton married Elizabeth Taylor), you'll find the **Montreal Museum of Fine Arts** (closed Mon.; free, special exhibits $C15; 514/285-1600), at 1380 Sherbrooke Street. The oldest museum in Canada, the Museum of Fine Arts has a large permanent collection of European, Canadian, and American art, as well as an extensive display of Eskimo artifacts. A half mile east, the **McCord Museum of Canadian History** (closed Mon.; $C7; 514/398-7100) at 690 Sherbrooke Street has a wonderful collection of art and artifacts related to Montreal, Quebec, and Canada—everything from Victorian evening gowns to "First Nation" masks and carvings. South of the Museum of Fine Arts, the elegantly modern **Canadian Center for Architecture** (closed Mon. & Tues.; $C10; 514/939-7026), at 1920 Rue Baile, mounts fascinating shows devoted to the built environment.

About a mile southeast of Mount Royal, just off the riverfront, the two-block-long, cobblestoned square of Place Jacques Cartier is the heart of Old Montreal, a picturesque neighborhood that was the site of the earliest European settlement. In the summer the square is transformed into an open-air market, and all year-round you can sample the area's excellent cafés and restaurants.

Practicalities

Montreal's airport, known as Dorval, lies 13 miles west of downtown. Numerous freeways criss-cross Montreal, and driving around is pretty easy (though all signs, including the complicated parking rules, are in French), but if you want to escape from your car for a day or two, the city is eminently walkable.

For food, Montreal has something for everyone, thanks to the city's truly international population—sizeable immigrant communities make Montreal a dining adventure. At lunchtime, workers from the Montreal financial district cram into **Chez Delmo,** 211 Notre Dame Street, a very traditional Old Montreal seafood restaurant where dishes are always fresh, simple, and reasonably priced. Nice oyster bar, too. You really must eat French at least once while in Montreal, and French restaurants do not come more traditional than **Le Paris,** at 1812 St. Catherine Street. Another reliable (but fairly expensive) bet is **L'Express,** at 3927 St. Denis Street. One unexpected local specialty is a taste of NYC: the deli sandwich. **Ben's** (514/844-1000), a cavernous deli at 990 de Maisonneuve on the corner of Metcalfe Street, serves a classic version of Montreal's beloved "smoked meat," aka corned beef. Ben's is near the McCord Museum, and open early until late, from 6 AM daily till 3 or 4 in the morning. Another great old deli is **Schwartz's Charcuterie Hebraique** (514/842-4813), at 3895 Boulevard St. Laurent.

The best budget place to stay is the large **Montreal Youth Hostel** ($C25–65; 514/843-3317), at 1030 Mackey Street, which has dorm beds and private rooms a five-minute walk south of Mount Royal Park. For something a bit more special, **Château Versailles** (514/933-3611), 1659 Sherbrooke Street, is composed of four Victorian townhouses converted into one charming, antique-filled hotel; doubles from $C120. The **Four Seasons** (514/284-1100), 1050 Sherbrooke Street, is about as fancy as it gets in Montreal, and that is pretty fancy: whirlpools in the rooms and a gourmet "spa cuisine" restaurant; doubles from $C300.

For tourist information, contact the **Greater Montreal Convention and Tourism Bureau** (514/873-2015 or 800/363-7777), 1555 Peel Street.

A quick Quebecois sampler for travelers: "Arrêt" = "Stop" "Cul de Sac" = "Dead End" "Bar Latiére" = "Ice Cream Stand" "Poutine" = "Chili Cheese Fries."

East of Arnprior, Hwy-17 continues its trek toward Ottawa with a 90-kph (55-mph) maximum speed posted; occasional passing lanes help you get around the timber trucks. The highway curves gradually southward, away from the Ottawa River, through mostly flat woodlands and a few farms, then converts to freeway for the run into Ottawa.

Hull

Offering the best views of Ottawa's dramatic riverside setting, the francophone town of **Hull** (pop. 62,339) is a nice change of pace from the Canadian capital. Older than Ottawa, French-speaking despite having been founded in 1800 by an American Loyalist (Philemon Wright) fleeing the Revolution, and named after an English port despite being miles from any ocean, Hull has managed to retain its traditional identity in the face of the multicultural federalizing of its cross-river neighbor.

The best thing about Hull, apart from the chance to walk across the bridges and wander the riverside parks that link it to Ottawa, is the **Canadian Museum of Civilizations** (daily in summer, closed Mon. Oct.–April; $C10–17; 819/776-7000), a huge and fascinating institution, housed in a sinuously curving 3,200-square-meter (35,000-square-foot) complex on the banks of the Ottawa River at 100 Rue Laurier, directly across the water from the Parliament Buildings at the foot of the Alexandria Bridge. The main lobby is filled with historic totem poles and canoes made by Canada's diverse native peoples, and galleries elsewhere in the building highlight everything from whaling communities in Labrador to life on the vast western prairies. It's a fun and educational place, well worth half a day at least.

A quiet town and provincial park along the Ottawa River, 32 kilometers (20 mi) west of Montreal, **Oka** gained international prominence in 1990, when native Mohawk Indians, protesting plans to turn a burial ground into a golf course, blocked the main highway to and from Montreal.

Across the street from the museum is one of Hull's, and Ottawa's, most enjoyable French restaurants, **Cafe Henry Burger** (819/777-5646), at 69 Rue Laurier.

Montebello and Carillon

East from Hull, Hwy-50 runs as a fast freeway along the north bank of the Ottawa River before calming down into a two-lane sojourn along Hwy-148. About an hour east of Ottawa, 80 miles west of Montreal, the town of **Montebello** holds one of the region's most famous landmarks: **Fairmont Château Montebello** (819/423-6341), an enormous octagonal palace built of red cedar logs that has evolved into one of Canada's most exclusive hotels, frequently hosting international conferences by the likes of NATO, G7, and similar power brokers. The grounds of the hotel hold an even more historic landmark, Papineau Manor, a manor house built in 1850 by a notable French-Canadian politician.

Farther east, 72 kilometers (45 mi) west of Montreal via sinuous Hwy-344, the roaring rapids at **Carillon** (pop. 193) have been harnessed by a massive hydropower facility and a lock system that provides the largest single lift of any in Canada—20 meters (65 ft). East of Carillon, Hwy-344 winds through sleepy farming country along the Ottawa River before ending up at the edge of the Montreal metropolis.

Driving across Montreal

Montreal is as scythed by freeways as any U.S. city, and it helps to be prepared to deal with the sudden shift from quiet countryside to confusing urban madness. If you've followed the rural route across Quebec from Ottawa, you enter the city from the northwest, on the Hwy-640 Autoroute; the freeway route from Ottawa brings you in on the Hwy-40 Autoroute, straight into downtown.

Any east–west freeway you find yourself on will cross the Hwy-15 Autoroute, the main route between Montreal and the U.S. border. Vermont is a quick 30 miles south of Montreal; after crossing the U.S. border, take the second exit off the I-87 freeway, and head east along US-11/US-2 to Rouses Point, New York, at the north end of Lake Champlain, to rejoin our two-lane road trip route. Between Vermont and the Canadian border, US-2 nips briefly and uneventfully across the northeast corner of New York State, crossing the international border on the I-87 freeway between the United States and Quebec.

VERMONT

Starting at the state's northwestern corner, US-2 crosses the heart of verdant Vermont. From the shores of Lake Champlain, our route winds south to the university town of Burlington, then east past Montpelier, the state capital, all the way to New Hampshire, some 150 miles in all. Paralleled for much of the way by the modern I-89 freeway, US-2 makes a slower but much more diverting alternative to the fast lane, passing through some of the state's most attractive small towns and giving an up-close look at its rural charms, not to mention Vermont's untrammelled mountains, forests, lakes, and rivers.

Lake Champlain Islands

After its brief jaunt across New York from the Canadian border, US-2 winds across the sleepy **Lake Champlain Islands.** Pancake-flat and covered with cows, orchards, and pick-your-own fruit farms, this trio of islands is very pretty to drive across, with the Adirondacks rising up to the west and the Green Mountains to the south and east, but there's not a lot to do; far more farm animals than people populate the route, and tractors clog the road, flinging clods of mud and manure (here pronounced man-OO-ah) with abandon.

From the middle of the Alburg Peninsula, where US-2 crosses from New York into Vermont, a turn west onto Route 129 leads to **Isle La Motte,** home of the first French settlement in

The roaring waterfalls that powered the **Champlain Mill** have been adapted with a fish lift; in spring and fall you can watch trout and salmon make their way upstream.

Vermont, established in 1666. The site is now occupied by **Saint Ann's Shrine,** a popular pilgrimage destination featuring daily outdoor masses in summer and a granite statue of the explorer Samuel de Champlain, for whom the lake is named.

Continuing south on US-2, the town of **North Hero** (pop. 502) has a gas station, a stone courthouse, a number of quietly luxurious vacation homes dating from the early decades of the 20th century, and the very handy **Hero's Welcome,** a café-cum-gift shop at the center of the two-block-long town. A mile south along US-2, **Shore Acres Resort** ($90 and up; 802/372-8722) offers tennis courts, boating and swimming, moderately priced lakeside rooms, and a restaurant famed for its chocolate pie—served at dinner only.

Seven miles and another bridge to the south, the town of **Grand Isle** (pop. 1,642) ambitiously claims to be "The Beauty Spot of Vermont." A well-marked turn leads to tiny **Grand Isle State Park,** on the shores of the lake, where there's a nice campground. At the other end of the island, connected by a causeway to the mainland, **South Hero** is another quaint little place; it and North Hero were named after those famous Vermont Revolutionary War heroes, the Green Mountain Boys, Ira and Ethan Allen.

From South Hero, US-2 rejoins the mainland at the entrance to **Sand Bar State Park,** set in a forest with picnic tables and bathing beaches, surrounded by sprawling, wildfowl-rich marshes on either side. From here US-2 heads east through rolling hills, linking up with the I-89 freeway for the fast route into Burlington, 10 miles to the south.

Winooski

If you have a little time or an abiding interest in America's industrial heritage, get off I-89 at exit 15, or follow Riverside Street (old US-2) north from Burlington to the center of

---

One of the more unlikely institutions located on the Lake Champlain Islands is the summer home of the world-famous **Royal Lippizaner Stallions** (802/372-5683), Austrian dressage horses that perform in an arena along US-7 near North Hero.

ETHAN ALLEN HOMESTEAD TRUST

Another reason to visit Winooski is to tour the restored farm of Vermont patriot Ethan Allen, preserved as the **Ethan Allen Homestead** (daily in summer; $5; 802/865-4556) along Route 127 two miles northeast of Winooski.

Winooski, an old woolen mill town now focusing on the restored Champlain Mill, downtown at 1 Main Street. This
former woolen mill now houses more than 20 cafés and specialty shops, and the rest of town provides a blue-collar balance to Burlington's somewhat upscale airs. The town green
is marred by a bank and large parking lot, but the surrounding buildings hold some interesting spots, including **Sneakers
Bistro** (802/655-9081), at 36 Main Street, which serves great
breakfasts and lunches every day. Another popular spot for
"homecooked food and friendly, upbeat service" is **Libby's
Blue Line Diner** (802/655-0343) north of Winooski on
Main Street in Colchester, just off I-89, exit 16. The usual
diner menu of breakfasts and burgers is enhanced by grilled
eggplant and fresh fish.

Winooski's historic
Centennial Field is
home to the Class A
Vermont Expos ($3–6;
802/655-4200).
Games start Sundays at
5pm and weekdays at
7pm.

Burlington

After the original French settlers were ejected from the Lake
Champlain region in 1760 at the end of the French and Indian Wars, English settlers soon arrived, and **Burlington** (pop.
39,150) was chartered in 1763. The area was abandoned during the Revolutionary War. Afterward, Ethan Allen, leader of
the famous Green Mountain Boys band of guerrillas, and his
brothers were granted huge tracts of land along the eastern
shore of Lake Champlain. The Allen brothers were ambitious. Not only did they encourage settlement and industry
in Burlington, but in 1791 they founded the University of
Vermont here. The town boomed, aided by its strategic position on Lake Champlain, which was the quickest route between New York's Hudson River and Montreal. Burlington quickly became the
center of Vermont industry, finance, education, and culture—a position it has
held ever since.

US-2/US-7 passes right through the center of Burlington, following Winooski Avenue to the north, then along Main Street, lined by motels and restaurants
on the outskirts but eventually crossing the lively, sprawling campus of the **University of Vermont** (UVM), which stands on a shallow hill on the east side of
town. Along Colchester Avenue on the north edge of campus, the **Robert Hull
Fleming Museum** (closed Mon.; $3; 802/656-0750) is the main visitor attrac-
tion, with a small but varied collection of fine and applied arts from ancient
Egypt to the present.

Midway between Lake Champlain and the UVM campus,
downtown Burlington is anchored by the **Church Street
Mall,** a pedestrianized and increasingly chain-dominated
shopping district that lies perpendicular to Main Street, north
from Burlington's stately old City Hall. From City Hall,
Main Street continues west to Lake Champlain, where the
Burlington Waterfront Park has a strollable boardwalk linking up with **Battery Park,** home to a collection of cannons

Burlington was the home
of **Dr. Horatio Nelson
Jackson,** who, in 1902
(along with his chauffeur
and a stray dog they
picked up along the
way), became the first
person to cross the
country by automobile.

The Shelburne Museum and Shelburne Farms

One of the most popular and enjoyable stops in the state of Vermont sits just five miles south of downtown Burlington, on the shores on Lake Champlain: the **Shelburne Museum** (daily 10 AM–5 PM, mid-May–mid-Oct. only; $17.50; 802/985-3346). The museum presents perhaps the best, and certainly the most unusual, agglomeration of fine art, folk art, and general oddities you'll find anywhere. These toys, dolls, trade signs, and weathervanes (and much, much more) really do defy classification, but there's more here than a riot of garage-sale stuff. Assembled over a lifetime by heiress Electra Havemeyer Webb, whose parents introduced America to the art of the French Impressionists, the Shelburne collection includes paintings by European and American masters (Rembrandt, Monet, Manet, and Winslow Homer, to drop a few famous names). However, it is most interesting for its unique Americana: old fire trucks, handmade quilts, and a world-class collection of cigar-store Indians (not to mention a model of a circus parade that's more than 500 feet long).

There are also some three dozen historic buildings brought here from all over New England: a covered bridge, a round barn, a lighthouse, a railroad depot, even a complete side-wheeled Lake Champlain steamboat, the *Ticonderoga*. The buildings, which all house different parts of the expansive collection, are spread over 40 acres of lawns and formal gardens, and there's so much to see you may want to save some for another visit, which you can do, since tickets are good for two days.

Northwest of the Shelburne Museum, just over a mile from US-7 via Bay and Harbor Roads, **Shelburne Farms** is a 1,400-acre farm and nonprofit environmental center with eight miles of hiking trails on a promontory jutting out into Lake Champlain. The grounds were laid out by landscape architect Frederick Law Olmsted to take full advantage of the natural topography (and to maximize views across the lake toward the Adirondack Mountains). In recent years, Shelburne Farms has become a leading force in the movement toward sustainable agriculture, and you can taste the results in their fabulously flavorful cheddar cheeses, available nationwide. Free tastings are available here at the Farm Store, where you can also join a 90-minute guided **tour** ($10; 802/ 985-8442) and explore the entire property. Included on the tour is a stop at the old mansion at the center of the estate, now the **Inn at Shelburne Farms** (May–Oct.; $90–175; 802/985-8498), where you can stay overnight or enjoy a wonderful meal (or three). There are also concerts, children's programs, and a variety of educational workshops held at Shelburne Farms throughout the summer.

pointing menacingly across the lake. In 1813, these cannons were used against British warships that bombarded the town. Bands frequently play here on summer evenings, and a bike path runs along the water. If you feel like getting out on the water, you can rent a boat from the **Community Boathouse** (802/865-3377), or take a sunset cruise on board the *Spirit of Ethan Allen* (802/862-8300). (Keep an eye out for Champ, Vermont's version of the Loch Ness Monster, who dwells deep in the waters of Lake Champlain.)

Burlington Practicalities

A mile north of the town of Grand Isle, along US-2 next to a school, stands the **Hyde Log Cabin**, considered by many to be the country's oldest log cabin, dating from 1783.

Downtown Burlington offers all the delights of a typical college town: bookstores, bars, ethnic food, and trendy shopping. For food, two local favorites—the Asian **Five Spice Cafe** (802/864-4045) at 175 Church Street and the **Daily Planet** (802/862-9647) behind Church Street at 15 Center Street—both feature international fusion food, from pastas to Latin American dishes. Also nearby are the mid-1950s stainless-steel **Oasis Diner** (802/864-5308), at 189 Bank Street, and the tasty **Ahli Baba's Kabob Shop** (802/862-5752), at 163 Main Street.

Thanks to the many students and Vermonters' general love of live music, Burlington has some great nightclubs, ranging from the juke joint ambience of **Nectar's** (802/658-4771), at 188 Main Street, where the band Phish was born and bred, to the high-style art deco of the **Flynn Theater** (802/863-5966), at 153 Main Street, across from City Hall, where bigger-name bands perform.

Places to stay, alas, don't come particularly cheap, unless you opt for the dorm beds at the very friendly **Mrs. Farrell's HI Home Hostel** ($20; 802/865-3730), at 27 Arlington Court, three miles northwest of town near the Ethan Allen Homestead. The historic and central **Willard Street Inn** ($125 and up; 802/651-8710), 349 S. Willard Street, is a very nice B&B in an 1880s home, and there are also many motels along US-7 south of downtown Burlington, including locally owned ones like the **Town and Country Motel** ($50 and up; 802/862-5786), 490 Shelburne Road.

For additional information on the Burlington area, contact the **visitors bureau** (802/863-3489), located at 60 Main Street.

Richmond and Williston

Between Montpelier and Burlington, US-2 follows the Winooski River Valley lined with dairy farms. For most of the way, the road parallels the less-than-attractive concrete expanse of I-89, but a few sights along the "old road" make the two-lane route preferable. First and foremost of these is **Al's French Frys** (802/862-9203), east of downtown on US-2 at 1251 Williston Road, which has been churning out great fries (sold by the quart!), burgers, hot dogs, and shakes since the 1940s.

To escape the highway chaos, turn south from US-2 at the only stoplight in Richmond, where the unique **Old Round Church,**, a 16-sided, two-story white clapboard structure, stands just east of the road. The church was built in 1813 and is the communal effort of five different Protestant denominations. They eventually parted ways, of course, and the structure lapsed into civic use, becoming the town hall. Today it is used as a meeting house, and on summer weekends the local historical society (802/434-6070) gives guided tours.

Williston (pop. 4,887) sits roughly 10 miles east of Burlington and less than a mile north of the freeway. Although large by local standards, Williston is a classic northern New England town, its streets lined by towering maple trees and white clapboard houses.

Waterbury Center: Ben & Jerry's

Though it's known for beautiful mountains and the brilliant fall color of its hardwood forests, Vermont's number-one tourist attraction is none other than **Ben & Jerry's Ice Cream Factory,** a kind of hippie Disneyland in **Waterbury Center,** on the hillside above Route 100, a mile or so north of I-89. The grounds of the brightly painted factory include a number of large cartoonish artifacts strewn outside to play on—weird vehicles, whimsical picnic tables, and the like. Ben and Jerry began making ice cream in 1978, and became internationally famous for their ultra-rich ice cream and for their activism, donating a percentage of profits to philanthropies supporting "progressive social change." Now part of Anglo-Dutch conglomerate Unilever, Ben & Jerry's is still a Vermont icon.

If **Ben & Jerry's** trademark black-and-white splotched ice cream packaging gets you interested in the different bovine breeds, here's a short primer to help you tell them apart: black-and-white splotches = Herefords; brown-and-white splotches = Guernseys; brown all over = Jerseys.

You can tour the factory (daily; $2; 866/BJ-TOURS), although production is halted on Sundays, holidays, and company celebration days—when you get a video presentation. The premises also feature a gift shop and the "Scoop Shop," featuring all of Ben & Jerry's ice cream, frozen yogurt, and sorbet flavors. Outside are many picnic tables where you can enjoy the ice cream and a view over the valley.

Camp Meade

North of Waterbury Junction on Route 100, the ski resort of **Stowe** was the post-WW II home of the musical **von Trapp family,** whose escape from the Nazis inspired *The Sound of Music.* Running south, Route 100 travels through the heart of the Green Mountains all the way south to Massachusetts, and is one of the state's most popular "leaf-peeping"

Back on US-2, midway between Montpelier and Waterbury just west of Middlesex, stands **Camp Meade** ($65 and up; 802/223-5537), a Depression-era Civilian Conservation Corps camp that once housed workers building dams and flood control projects, and has since been turned into a summer-only restaurant and motel. It is also a shrine to America in the 1930s and 1940s, from the New Deal to D-Day, mostly the latter: A fighter plane, a tank, and military trucks adorn the grounds. A gift store sells army-surplus goods, the restaurant sports camouflage tablecloths and a bomb suspended from the rafters, and the cabins are named after notables such as Gen. Patton and Col. Oliver North. Primarily, Camp Meade draws a nostalgic crowd of retired folk swapping war stories, but it's a fascinating and definitely unique place to stop.

Montpelier

The smallest capital in the country, and the only one without a McDonald's, Vermont's **Montpelier** (pop. 8,200) was settled in 1787 and designated the state capital in 1805. Today, Montpelier's economy is based on government, insurance, and tourism.

As you follow US-2 Business into town, the gold dome of the capitol building hovering over the valley ahead signals your arrival in Montpelier. Constrained by the Winooski River on one side and the narrow valley on the other, Montpelier is so compact that you can park your car and find all the sights within a 10-minute walk. (Thankfully, the I-89 freeway and the main US-2 bypass are well away from downtown.) A quick poll of shops along State and Main Streets reveals the cosmopolitan nature of the town: the magical **Bear Pond Books** (802/229-0774), at 77 Main Street, along with coffee bars, wine merchants, and multiple combinations of the same.

The north side of State Street opens up into a broad lawn fronting the **capitol dome,** the focal point of the Republic of Vermont—like Texas, the state takes some pride in the fact that it was an independent "country" before joining the rest of the United States. The state legislature is only in session from January to April—being a Vermont politician is a part-time job. The rest of the year they go about being farmers, businesspeople, and so on, but you can tour the building year-round (Mon.–Fri. only).

Above the capitol rises **Hubbard Park,** a 100-year-old, 154-acre green space, with seven miles of hiking trails and a 54-foot observation tower atop the summit, the highest point in Montpelier.

Just west of the capitol is the **Vermont Historical Society Museum** (closed Mon.; $5), where permanent and temporary displays illustrate different aspects of Vermont's history, and you can also find lots of 19th-century furniture and a small bookstore and gift shop. Rising up a hill a few blocks further west, the **Green Mount Cemetery** is filled with impressive granite monuments. Many of these were carved by the immigrant stonecutters of nearby Barre for their own family plots, and the well-groomed grounds make ideal picnic spots, especially on a summer afternoon.

In the Montpelier region, alternative music fans will want to tune their car radios to the "The Point," broadcasting Phish, Everclear, Lucinda Williams, Neil Young, and other rowdy rockers at **WNCS 104.7 FM**.

Near Montpelier, watch sap being turned into delicious maple syrup at the **Morse Farm and Sugarhouse,** three miles northeast from the capitol dome along Main Street.

Montpelier thrived off the granite quarries of the nearby town of Barre. The **Rock of Ages quarry** (daily in summer; free; 802/476-3119), four miles southeast of Barre, is the world's largest.

Montpelier Practicalities

Montpelier residents take their eating seriously. Very good and very inexpensive food is readily available, thanks to the local presence of the New England Culinary Institute, a cooking school that operates the **Main Street Bar and Grill** (802/223-3188) and **Chef's Table** (802/229-9202), both at 118 Main Street. Another great local place is the **Farmers Diner,** 240 N. Main Street in neighboring Barre. A full range of healthy deli food and drink is available at the **State**

Street Market (802/229-9353), at 20 State Street, and the nearby **Coffee Corner** (802/229-9060), on the corner of State and Main Streets, offers breakfast with hometown ambience.

For upscale lodgings in period surroundings, go to the **Inn at Montpelier** ($120 and up; 802/223-2727), two renovated 19th-century homes that have been joined into one hotel. The best moderate choice is the **EconoLodge** ($65; 802/223-5258) on Route 12 south of the river.

Plainfield

Hitchhikers are common on US-2 between Montpelier and Plainfield, thanks to the presence of **Goddard College,** one of the nation's most renowned countercultural institutes of higher learning. The tiny town of **Plainfield** also boasts a bookstore, a pair of huge barns, a fly-fishing shop, and the **Maple Valley Country Store,** a combo deli-café-pizzeria that's the local hangout (tie-dye welcome; 802/454-8626). The soups are fantastic, as are the veggie burgers. The store's parking area is built on a foundation of recycled granite, leftovers from the nearby quarries and stonecutters. Plainfield also has a great place to eat breakfast: the **River Run** (closed Mon. & Tues; 802/454-1246) at 3 Main Street, where you can get a great heap of pancakes studded with fresh blueberries for around $5. Lunch and dinner take on more of a Deep South flavor: As prepared by the Mississippi-born chef, the BBQ and plates of catfish caused playwright David Mamet to call it "the best place on earth." If you want to linger, consider a night on the farm: at **Hollister Hill Farm** ($85 and up; 802/454-7725), 2193 Hollister Hill Road east of town, they make their own maple syrup (and serve it over pancakes at breakfast) and raise all sorts of organic produce (from vegetable to "beefalo" hybrids).

portrait of Abe Lincoln, made out of 6,399 dried insects by a man named John Hampston in 1916

West Danville: Joe's Pond

West Danville, a summer community 20 lovely miles east of Plainfield on the edge of Joe's Pond, is ringed by rustic vacation cabins. The pond, which at sunset in summer is one of the more idyllic spots imaginable, was originally called Indian Joe's Pond, which explains the presence of Indian Joe Court, a set of roadside cabins dating from the pre–politically correct era. At the junction of US-2 and Route 15 in the center of town, you'll see a micro-sized covered bridge and the **Hastings Store** (802/684-3630), the local "if we ain't got it, you don't need it" emporium, selling cheddar cheese, maple syrup, fishing supplies, and other Vermont essentials.

At the hilltop cabins of **Indian Joe Court** ($45 and up; 802/684-3430), guests can borrow pedalboats or canoes from a 300-foot beach and hang out on the water. You can also stay at the one- or two-bedroom cabins of **Point Comfort** ($55–65; 802/684-3379). Both establishments have weekly rates if you're lucky enough to linger here a while. Indian Joe has a few RV sites, too.

Danville and Peacham

Heading east, the next place you'll pass is **Danville**, yet another picture-postcard Vermont town, set on a hill surrounded by farmland. The center of Danville is a classic New England village green, with a general store and the customary churches. Just off the green you'll find the headquarters of the **American Society of Dowsers** (Mon.–Fri.; 802/684-3417), whose members have refined their talents for finding water or mineral deposits using a dowsing rod. The building houses a small exhibit on the history and practice of the art, and a shop where you can buy dowsing books and rods.

South of US-2 from the center of Danville, enjoy the lovely pastoral drive toward **Peacham,** a perennial contender for the title "prettiest village in Vermont." During the fall color sweeps, the mountaintop village is likely to be crowded with sightseeing tourists, but most of the time it's a somnolent little place. In fact, Peacham is so timeless that the producers of the movie version of Edith Wharton's Victorian fable *Ethan Frome* filmed here (without having to remove any streetlights or other signs of modern life!).

St. Johnsbury

In the 19th century, the economy of **St. Johnsbury** (pop. 7,600) was based on maple products and the manufacture of platform scales. Fairbanks Scales, founded by the inventor of platform scales, still operates a plant here. Today it is the pleasantly peaceful commercial center of Vermont's Northeast Kingdom, at the junction of the US-2 and US-5 highways, the I-91 and I-93 freeways, and the Canadian Pacific and old Maine Central railroad tracks. The economy never regained its Victorian-era prosperity, so the town's extensive stock of historic landmark architecture has been preserved almost totally unchanged. Elegant (and often empty) four- and five-story brick buildings line the riverfront and railroad line along US-2 and US-5. On the hill above the riverfront, a more genteel commercial district surrounded by massive trees and dozens of grand Victorian homes is highlighted by two of the most fascinating institutions in the state, both funded by the largess of the Fairbanks family.

All along US-2, and all over New England for that matter, the old roads are lined by 1940s-style knotty-pine cabins and motor courts, like the photogenic **Wallinda Cabins** east of Plainfield.

At the center of town, at 1171 Main Street, stands the **St. Johnsbury Athenaeum, Art Gallery, and Public Library** (Mon.–Fri.; free) in a red-brick 1871 building. The building houses a surprising collection of 19th-century paintings, the jewel of which is Albert Bierstadt's monumental *Domes of Yosemite.*

A block east down Main Street, you'll find my very favorite museum in all New England: the **Fairbanks Museum** (daily; $5; 802/748-2372), a charmingly quirky Victorian-era center of knowledge established by Franklin Fairbanks in 1889. A pair of menacing stuffed bears greets visitors inside the entrance, followed by a seemingly endless display of taxidermied wildlife—a veritable Noah's ark of North American fauna. Climb the spiral stairs to the mezzanine of the main gallery, a grand Richardsonian Romanesque space topped by a coffered barrel vault and furnished with fireplaces and other homey touches. You'll find more fascinating oddities: arrowheads and other anthropological artifacts, rocks and fossils, and art made out of bugs (including a portrait of Gen. Pershing made out of flies and moths!). View exhibits on local history, a set of dollhouse furniture made by author Mark Twain, and a very funny letter written by Robert Louis Stevenson in which he wills his birthday (which he said he was too old to need anymore) to Fairbanks' daughter (whose own birth fell on Christmas, meaning she effectively missed out).

St. Johnsbury's eating options include **Hilltopper Restaurant** (802/748-2241), across the street from the Athenaeum, and **Anthony's Diner** (802/748-3613), 50 Railroad Street at the US-5/US-2 junction. For motels, try the **Fairbanks Motor Inn** ($50–75; 802/748-5666) on US-2 at 32 Western Avenue.

Maple Grove Farms

Taking a scenic alternative to the I-93 freeway east from St. Johnsbury, US-2 passes over the Memorial Bridge (1943) spanning the Passumpsic River. One mile east of the bridge you'll find the **Maple Grove Farms** complex. Highlights include the maple museum (and tasting room!), and the so-called world's largest maple candy factory. Vermont is the heart of maple-sugaring territory, which runs all the way from Maine to Michigan and up into Canada. Maple Grove Farms has been in business here since 1915, and it is the largest packager of maple syrup in the United States. In front of the store, you can have your picture taken in front of the World's Largest Can of Maple Syrup (which is, alas, empty).

Concord and Lunenburg

Near the New Hampshire border, US-2 heads across rolling rocky hills covered with forests, largely pine and birch, with a few scattered farms. This corner of the state, a recreational paradise of hills and lakes and few year-round residents, is known as the Northeast Kingdom. The road drops down into the narrow, pastoral valley of the Moose River before reaching **Concord**, which features a country store and a small historical society.

Fifteen miles east of Concord, along the banks of the broad Connecticut River, **Lunenburg** is a perfect New England village of white clapboard houses clustered around a church—Vermont specializes in this species of quaintness.

From Lunenburg, you can take a highly recommended detour across the Connecticut River on the 266-foot-long Mt. Orne covered bridge, then proceed north along Route 135, rejoining US-2 at Lancaster.

NEW HAMPSHIRE

Crossing the broad Connecticut River, which forms Vermont's 200-mile-long border with New Hampshire, US-2 makes a short but scenic run across the state. From the historic commercial center of **Lancaster,** just east of the state border, US-2 winds along the wide valley of the Israel River before reaching **Jefferson,** home to two of the state's biggest tourist traps. Continuing east, US-2 curves around the northern flank of towering **Mt. Washington** and the rugged White Mountains, an area rich in outdoor recreation and scenic splendor. At **Gorham,** US-2 reaches the valley of the Androscoggin River, which it follows east into Maine.

> A marker along US-2 points out the site, in nearby Concord Corner, where the **First Normal School,** America's first teachers' academy, was founded in 1823.

Lancaster

Across the Connecticut River from Vermont, **Lancaster** (pop. 3,550) is a market town that was first settled in 1764. US-2 becomes Main Street through Lancaster, lined with dozens of attractive old homes and churches, a cemetery on a knoll to the north, and on the south side, a heroic redbrick courthouse that dates from 1887.

> A roadside marker along US-2 just west of Jefferson commemorates the birth nearby of inventor **Thaddeus Lowe,** who pioneered balloon aviation during the Civil War.

Two miles south of Lancaster via US-3, the mountaintop estate of the man who saved New Hampshire's forests from the lumber industry has been preserved as **John Wingate Weeks Historic Site** (Wed.–Sun. 10 AM–6 PM in summer only; $2.50), complete with a tourable mansion and an observation tower giving grand views of Mt. Washington and Vermont's Green Mountains.

If you weren't thrilled by the modern bridge that carries US-2 into Lancaster, there are two historic covered bridges in Lancaster that will renew your appreciation of civil engineers. Five miles south of US-2 via Hwy-135 the Mt. Orne covered bridge spans the Connecticut River to Vermont (see above), while just east of US-2 in Lancaster village there's a nifty 140-year-old, 90-foot-long **covered bridge** that spans the Israel River along Mechanic Street.

Jefferson

High above the Israel River on the slopes of the White Mountains, the small resort town of **Jefferson** (pop. 1,003) is good base for the exploring the surrounding peaks, and is home

Your welcome to New Hampshire is a sign—"Brake for Moose." Apparently, moose are hard to see at night and are involved in many serious collisions because headlights shine through the legs of this towering beast, rather than reflecting off its body.

to two big tourist draws, both ideal for the truly masochistic parent. About a mile west of Jefferson is **Santa's Village** (daily in summer, weekends in Dec.; $20; 603/586-4445), with candy canes looming threateningly at the entrance, a Ferris wheel, a roller coaster, the Yule log flume and, of course, Santa himself. Just east of town is **Six Gun City** (daily in summer; $17.95; 603/586-4592), an ersatz Wild West town featuring cowboy skits ("Come on out, you varmints!"), frontier shows, a carriage museum, a roller coaster, and a pair of water slides.

Outside the town, along US-2 on a crest between Jefferson and Gorham, the **Grand View Lodge** ($65 and up; 603/466-5715) has nice rooms and truly grand views. Two other accommodations in Jefferson deserve mention, starting with the historic **Jefferson Inn** ($90 and up; 800/729-7908), which has panoramic views and a swimming pond, right on US-2. A half mile south of Jefferson along Route 115A, the friendly **Applebrook B&B** ($65 and up; 800/545-6504) sits on 35 acres and offers full Victorian splendor gilded with summer raspberries and a hot tub under the stars.

East of Jefferson the road ascends, the valley narrows, and the scenery becomes more spectacular with every mile, as the Presidential Range looms larger and larger to the south.

Eight miles south of Gorham, towering Mt. Washington marks the start of our **Appalachian Trail** route, which follows along these landmark mountains all the way south to Atlanta. See page 291.

Gorham

Gorham (pop. 3,173), incorporated in 1836, was another early tourist town. Its boom began when the railroad came through in 1851; the train's, and the town's, story is told at the **Gorham Historical Society** (daily 1–5 PM May–Nov.; donations), which stands in the old depot at 25 Railroad Street, a half-block off Main Street.

Just east of Gorham, the road passes through a famous grove of birch trees, the "world-renowned Shelburne Birches." Here you find the big but pleasant **Town & Country Motor Inn** ($65 and up; 603/466-3315) with some spa and resort facilities, such as saunas, a golf course, and a good restaurant. This is also where the **Appalachian Trail,** which runs from Maine's Mt. Katahdin to northern Georgia, crosses US-2.

West of Gorham, right off US-2, the summer-only **Moose Brook State Park** (603/466-3860) has a campground and a swimming hole built back in the 1930s by the New Deal CCC.

MAINE

Following the Androscoggin River across the New Hampshire border, US-2 enters Maine at the forested eastern flank of the **White Mountains.** Winding east along the river, the route passes through alternating mountain resorts and mill towns, starting at sedate **Bethel** and ending up 135 miles later at **Bangor**, once one of the wildest lumber towns in the country. From Bangor the route veers south toward the coast, hitting the Atlantic Ocean at beautiful **Acadia National Park.**

Bethel

At the far west end of its run across Maine, US-2 winds along the south bank of the Androscoggin River through the dense pine and birch forests of the White Mountain National Forest. Ten miles east of the New Hampshire border, along a placid stretch of the Androscoggin, **Bethel** (pop. 2,329) was first settled in 1774. At the tail end of the Revolutionary War, the town, then named Sudbury, suffered the last Indian raid inflicted on New England. The Gould Academy, one of Maine's oldest prep schools, was established at the west end of town in 1836, and after the railroads came through Bethel quickly became a center for White Mountain–area tourism. Founded in 1913, the **Bethel Inn** ($99 and up; 207/824-2175 or 800/654-0125) was one of New England's early health resorts, and it continues that tradition today. The inn is surrounded by 200 acres (including an 18-hole golf course), and if you're looking for upscale lodging and dining or spa treatments, this is the place to go. Information on Bethel's many other well-preserved old buildings can be found in the 200-year-old **Mason House**, facing the town common at 15 Broad Street, which doubles as a small, summer-only museum (closed Mon.; $3).

> Just east of the Maine border, 10 miles west of Bethel, a sign marks a turn south from US-2 onto Route 113 toward Evans Notch. This narrow, winding, motorcycle-friendly road runs along the **Wild and Cold Rivers** up to a stunningly scenic mountain pass.

For outdoor enthusiasts, the **Sunday River Ski Area** (800/543-2SKI), six miles northeast of town, draws thousands of visitors to the area for skiing in winter and hiking and mountain biking in summer (there's also a popular "wife-carrying" contest in October). Near the well-marked turnoff to Sunday River, there's a nice picnic area with a covered bridge, along US-2 and the Androscoggin River. If you head north from here a mile or so past the ski area, another sign will point you toward the intricately constructed **Artist's Covered Bridge**, which spans the Sunday River.

Back on US-2, the **Sunday River Brewing Company** (207/824-3541) is a popular brewpub serving good food, very good beer, and frequent live music; if you like peace and quiet, come for lunch or an early dinner—as it gets later it gets rowdier.

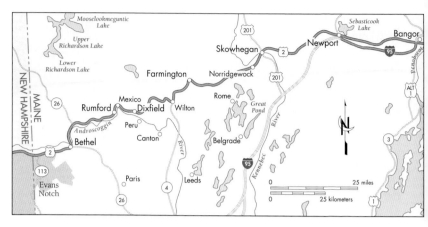

Rumford

Rumford's main claim to fame is as the birthplace of **Edmund Muskie,** governor, U.S. Senator, Secretary of State, and vice-presidential and presidential candidate in 1968 and 1972, respectively.

The biggest and brawniest place along otherwise rural US-2, **Rumford** (pop. 7,078) is a definite change from the leisure-time orientation of many other places in New England. A historic paper-pulp mill town with low brick buildings and a downscale downtown along Waldo Street, Rumford grew up around Androscoggin Falls, which provided the hydropower that led to the original settlement of the town. Now, enormous steam-puffing smokestacks loom large at the Mead Publishing Paper Division, New England's largest paper mill, surrounded by huge piles of logs, chips, and wood residue; tours are available (207/369-2589).

At a junction in **Dixfield,** a single sign points the way toward Peru and Mexico. Paris, Leeds, Canton, Madrid, Belgrade, and Rome are also within 30 miles—only in America!

The hard-working, perpetually under-paid realities of Rumford (and its next-door neighbor, Mexico, where the mill is located) are in many ways what makes it remarkable. Clearly this isn't a town designed for tourists, but if you're interested in how Americans live, work, and drink too much in places where heavy industry still rules the roost, Rumford is worth investigating.

To jump in at the deep end, have breakfast at the 1930s **Freddie's Restaurant** (207/364-3069), near the paper mill at 105 Congress Street, where gruff guys in Carhartt caps and union jackets can clue you in to what's going on in town.

From US-2 at Bethel, Route 26 runs southeast toward Portland and the coast, passing through the spa town of **Poland Spring** and the world's last-remaining intact Shaker community at **Sabbathday Lake,** where a small **museum** gives tours (Mon.–Sat. in summer; $7.50; 207/926-4597).

Away from the center of town, the Rumford area is suddenly semi-pastoral and very pretty. US-2 winds around the valley as the Androscoggin makes an oxbow, and an even nicer route heads north following Route 17 and the Swift River toward the popular Rangeley Lakes resort area.

Wilton

West of Farmington and just north of US-2, the town of **Wilton** was the longtime home of famous shoemaker G. H.

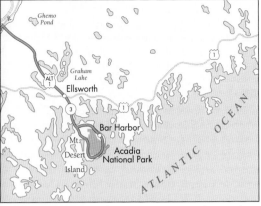

Bass Company, makers of those leather "Weejuns" so loved by preppies. In 1998 the Bass Company abandoned Wilton for the lower-wage Dominican Republic, but their old mill is still standing. Next to the mill, an old boarding house holds the **Wilton Farm and Home Museum** (by appointment only; donation; 207/645-2261), a fascinating museum with exhibits on G. H. Bass, its shoe-making operations, and everything from old bottles to the life of the Wilton-born "Maine Giantess," Sylvia Hardy, an 8-foot-tall, 400-pound woman who was a star of P. T. Barnum's famous freak shows. Across the street from the mill and museum is the nice little **Curiosity Book Shop** (207/645-4122), at 285 Main Street.

Wilton is also home to a large windmill marking the **Dutch Treat** restaurant and ice cream stand right on US-2 east of town.

Farmington

Like many other northern Maine towns, **Farmington** (pop. 4,200) was first settled by soldiers who fought in the Revolutionary War. The rolling hills that surround it still hold a few farms and orchards, but as elsewhere, the economy revolves around trees—both as tourist fodder during the fall color sweeps and as pulp for paper mills (there's a big pulp mill just south of town on US-201). US-2 bypasses the center, but the downtown area has a few blocks of tidy brick buildings housing barbershops, bookstores, and cafés, supported in large part by the presence of the large Farmington campus of the University of Maine.

On the south edge of downtown, at the US-2/Route 4 junction, a pair of neighboring places offer local culinary treats. A classic streamlined prefab, the smoke-free **Farmington Diner** (207/778-4151), at 313 Main Street, has become a bit shabby, but it is still open dawn to dusk for the usual greasy spoon delights. Across the road, **Gifford's Ice Cream** (207/778-3617) serves cones and foot-long hot dogs all summer long.

Between Skowhegan and Farmington, US-2 passes through a pair of quietly quaint places. **Norridgewock** is a historic hamlet, now home to a New Balance shoe factory, and **New Sharon** has a rusty old bridge spanning the Sandy River. The region's real draw is south of US-2: the **Belgrade Lakes,** a chain of seven lakes circled by ageless vacation cabins and summer camps. It was this idyllic location that inspired

In the town of Rangeley, an hour northwest of Farmington via Route 4, the **Wilhelm Reich Museum** (207/864-3443) preserves the flat-roofed final home and tomb of the iconoclastic psychoanalyst, who died in 1957.

Farmington's main claim to fame is that way back in 1873 a local teenager, **Chester Greenwood**, rigged up a pair of beaver-skin pads on a piece of bent wire to create the world's first earmuffs.

Ernest Thompson to write the play *On Golden Pond,* later made into that weepy Fonda-family movie. The movie was filmed at New Hampshire's Squam Lake off US-3 in the White Mountains, but you can re-enact real-life scenes here in Maine by taking a ride on the **Great Pond Mailboat,** which departs from the boat house in the village of Belgrade Lakes, along Route 27.

Skowhegan

In 1976, the Kennebec River at Skowhegan was the site of the last log drive in Maine.

During the second week of August, Skowhegan is home to the **Maine State Fair.** Celebrated annually since 1818, it is one of the oldest state fairs in the country.

First settled in 1771 on an island in the Kennebec River, the mid-sized mill town of **Skowhegan** (pop. 8,725) was the birthplace of Margaret Chase Smith (1897–1995), one of Maine's most renowned politicians and a 36-year veteran of the U.S. House and Senate. Her home, set on 15 riverside acres, is now the **Margaret Chase Smith Library Center** (Mon.–Fri.; donations; 207/474-7133). Northwest of town at 54 Norridgewock Avenue, the complex includes a museum depicting her life and Cold War times.

Skowhegan's other larger-than-life character can be visited off US-201, just north of US-2: the **Skowhegan Indian,** a 62-foot statue sometimes billed as the Largest Wooden Indian in the World, which stands unloved and unmarked in a parking lot behind a gas station.

North from Skowhegan, US-201 runs along the Kennebec River, offering some of Maine's greatest fall foliage vistas. One of the prettiest stretches is around the town of **Bingham,** about 25 miles north of Skowhegan. On US-201 a mile south of town, you can catch an alfresco movie at the **Skowhegan Drive-In** (207/474-9277) on weekend nights all summer long.

East of Skowhegan, US-2 veers away from the river across low, rolling hills covered with pine and birch forests, the only signs of habitation a few trailer homes and scraggly farms.

Bangor

Built on the banks of the Penobscot River, **Bangor** (pop. 33,200; BANG-gor) is the largest city in northern Maine. This site was an important rendezvous for local tribes, who called it Kendusbeag or "eel-catching place." In 1604 Samuel de Champlain sailed up the Penobscot River as far as Treats Falls here, but long-term settlement did not begin until 1769. Throughout the next century, Bangor was the most important lumber town in the eastern United States. It also developed into a shipbuilding center, and Bangor's lumber circled the globe. The people of Bangor were devoted to providing amusement for the loggers and sailors who would arrive in town with free time and fat wallets. In a riverside neighborhood called the Devil's Half Acre, dozens of bars, bordellos, and gambling dens competed to empty the men's pockets, but now the most prominent sign of life along the water is the **Sea Dog Brewery** (207/947-8004), at 26 Front Street, one of Bangor's most popular bars and restaurants.

Bangor is home to best-selling horror writer **Stephen King,** who lives in a suitably Gothic and surprisingly visible mansion at 47 W. Broadway.

In the 19th century, Bangor was as wide open as any town in the Wild West, but traces of rougher days have all but disappeared. Modern Bangor, once a supply center for the northern half of Maine, is still a center for the lumber industry. Coming into town across the Penobscot River, you'll turn right onto Main Street and see a 31-foot statue of a smirking **Paul Bunyan,** erected in 1959. The compact downtown area, impressive redbrick 19th-century buildings interspersed with church spires, lies a few blocks to the east of Paul Bunyan.

The **Bangor Museum** (Tues.–Sat. noon–4 PM; free), housed in an 1836 Greek Revival mansion downtown at 159 Union Street, has exhibits, furnishings, and paintings reflecting 19th-century life. Away from the center of Bangor, car, truck, and tractor fans flock to the **Cole Land Transportation Museum** (daily May–Nov.; $6), off I-95 and I-395 at 405 Perry Road, which displays more than 200 historic vehicles, from wooden wagons to modern 18-wheelers.

Bangor Practicalities

Thanks to the nearby University of Maine, Bangor has a wide variety of places to eat and drink. Unexpectedly, there are a couple of inexpensive Indian and Pakistani places, including **Taste of India** (207/945-6865) at 68 Main Street. For whiling away an evening, head down to the aforementioned **Sea Dog Brewery,** or for something a little more cerebral, the **Whig and Courier Pub** (207/947-4095), at 18 Broad Street at the center of Bangor, serves good food and even better beer.

On the west edge of Bangor, off I-95 exit 180, soothe your white-line fever at the trucker's favorite stop, **Dysart's** (207/942-4878). This around-the-clock fuel stop and café offers a place to rest where you can dig in to the world's largest sundae, the 18-scoop "18-Wheeler."

The pick of area lodging is the **Charles Inn** ($80 and up; 207/992-2820), a restored 1873 hotel at 20 Broad Street downtown; a good local motel is the **Main Street Inn** ($50 and up; 207/942-5282) at 480 Main Street. The national chains are out on US-2 near the airport and I-95, a mile or so west of town, which is where the fast food is, too.

From Bangor, US-2 winds northeast along the Penobscot River, ending up near the Canadian border at Houlton. We've opted to head "Down East," ending our cross-country odyssey at Acadia National Park.

For more information on Bangor, contact the **visitors bureau** (207/947-0307), next to Paul Bunyan at 519 Main Street.

Ellsworth and Trenton

Ellsworth, chartered in 1763, began as a lumber town but is now a thriving commercial center, located southeast of Bangor at the junction of Route 3 and US-1. Downtown is marked by lots of redbrick buildings and the **Riverside**

Mount Desert Island

Mount Desert Island is an idyllic, 11- by 14-mile chunk of dense forests, barren peaks, and rocky inlets just off the coast of Maine. (The "desert" in Mount Desert Island is pronounced "dessert.") The island was first inhabited by the Penobscot people and was not explored by Europeans until 1609, when Samuel de Champlain named it Isle de Monts Déserts ("Isle of Bald Peaks") and claimed it for France. In 1844, Hudson River School artist Thomas Cole painted a stunning series of scenes featuring Mount Desert Island, which soon became a summer playground for elite Eastern families, many of whom built massive vacation "cottages" here, largely around Bar Harbor. In 1916, the Mount Desert colony, led by the Pulitzer and Rockefeller families, donated most of the island to the federal government to establish the first national park east of the Mississippi—Acadia National Park. The Great Depression and World War II effectively put an end to the Bar Harbor high life, and most traces of the summer colony were either torn down or destroyed by a huge fire that raged through Bar Harbor in 1947.

Today about half of Mount Desert Island remains in private hands, including the villages of Bass Harbor, Northeast Harbor, Seal Harbor, and Southwest Harbor, all of which are exclusive enclaves. These locales offer a much quieter version of island life than you'll get in Bar Harbor. Northeast Harbor is perhaps the most welcoming, with two public gardens, the genteel old **Asticou Inn** ($175–275; 207/276-3344) on Route 3, and some surprisingly affordable cafés like the **Docksider** (207/276-3965) on Sea Street, where you can munch a crab sandwich while waiting for the ferry boats that shuttle across to the picturesque Cranberry Isles. For more on these less-visited corners of Mount Desert Island, contact the ever-friendly Northeast Harbor **visitors bureau** (207/276-5040).

For local weather and good music, tune in to **WMDI 107.7 FM** in Bar Harbor.

At 1,532 feet, **Cadillac Mountain** on Mount Desert Island is the highest point on the Eastern seaboard of North America. It also shares a namesake with the classy automobile marque.

Cafe (207/667-7220), an upscale retro diner at 151 Main Street that's famous for weekend brunch and its fine slices of pie. The rest of Ellsworth is full of malls (Wal-Mart, et al.), car lots, chain motels, and gas stations—harsh reminders of the sprawling suburban America many Maine visitors are trying to escape.

Between Ellsworth and Trenton, gateway to Mount Desert Island and Acadia National Park, there's a short but bittersweet six-mile parade of tacky roadside attractions along Route 3. If you've got kids with you or are in the mood to act like one, you can choose from such questionable pleasures as the **Great Maine Lumberjack Show** in Trenton, plus go-carts, trading posts, miniature golf courses—even a zoo. Just before the bridge, you pass many lobster pounds on this stretch of highway, the best of which is the **Trenton**

Bridge Lobster Pound (207/667-
2977), open daily (May–mid-Oct.
only) since 1956; just look for the
billowing clouds of steam.

Bar Harbor

Once a semiprivate enclave of the
very rich (can you say Rockefeller?), the town of **Bar Harbor**
(pop. 4,400), the largest and
busiest on Mount Desert Island, has turned to catering to
the less-well-heeled visitor as the old money has
retreated to more discreet settlements to the west, such as
Northeast Harbor—aka Philadelphia on the Rocks. Bar
Harbor's principal thoroughfares, lined with gift shops, art
galleries, bike rental stands, hotels, and restaurants, intersect at the lively and pleasant Village Green. Since most of
Bar Harbor's old mansions were destroyed in a 1947 fire,
there aren't all that many sights to search out, although the
Tiffany windows of lovely little **St. Saviour's Church** on the
west side of the Village Green give some sense of the wealth
that once lingered here.

    There are dozens of generally good and relatively inex-
pensive restaurants clustered together in Bar Harbor's few
short blocks, so wander around and take your pick. Many
are clearly aimed at the tourist trade, none more so than
the amiable **Freddie's Route 66 Restaurant** (207/288-
3708), at 21 Cottage Street, a pseudo-1950s diner that's
absolutely packed with nostalgic memorabilia—jukeboxes,
gas pumps, neon signs, you name it. Another fun place is
Reel Pizza (207/288-3811), at 33 Kennebec Place across from the Village
Green, where you can watch a classic or art-house film while kicking back in
a recliner, waiting for your pizza. Lobsters, of course, are at the core of Maine
cuisine: Sample them at **Fisherman's Landing** (207/288-4632), on the West
Street Pier.

    The classic place to stay is the **Bar Harbor Inn** ($80 and up; 207/288-3351),
which has a lovely historic inn and standard motel rooms right on the water.
Other reasonable accommodations include the **Cadillac Motor Inn** (207/288-
3831) at 336 Main Street, and the hilltop **Wonder View Motor Lodge**
(207/288-3358) on Route 3 northwest of town.

Acadia National Park

Mount Desert Island's natural glories are preserved in **Acadia National Park,**
occupying 41,634 acres of the island's most scenic areas. Route 3 runs through
the heart of the park, but the best way to appreciate Acadia is to track the 20-
mile-long **Park Loop Road,** which circles the eastern side of the park. (Note

Bar Harbor is the
terminus for the ferry
(888/249-7245) to
Yarmouth, Nova Scotia,
a six-hour cruise each
way that will save you
hours of driving time if
you are continuing east.
The boats also turn into
casinos when crossing
international waters.

The upscale environs of
Seal Harbor are also
home to one of the
country's great luxury car
collections, on display
inside the **Seal Cove
Auto Museum** (daily in
summer only; 207/244-
9242) on Route 102.

SCENE ON CADILLAC MOUNTAIN ROAD, ACADIA NATIONAL PARK, MT. DESERT ISLAND, MAINE

that large campers and trailers are prohibited.) Midway along, the loop road pauses at Sand Beach, one of the few sandy beaches in Maine (get here early to find parking in summer), then passes the Thunder Hole tidal cavern before winding inland past Jordan Pond. If you want to get out and stretch your legs, the best way to see the fantastic ocean views and breathe the fresh ocean air is to walk along the two-mile trail that links Sand Beach, the Thunder Hole, and the 110-foot-high Otter Cliffs. From Jordan Pond, the loop road continues past the turnoff (also accessible directly from Bar Harbor) for the drive to the top of Cadillac Mountain. Here, you'll experience a truly breathtaking panorama over Mount Desert Island, the surrounding inlets and islands, and (on a fog-free day) miles and miles of the Maine coast.

In the summer and fall, when thousands clog the loop road and the streets of Bar Harbor, the most sensible visitors head to the park's hiking trails, which wind among the beautiful inland lakes and mountains. Approximately 57 miles of the unpaved, car-free "carriage roads" constructed (well, paid for) by Edsel Ford and John D. Rockefeller Jr. are open to walkers, bikers, wheelchairs, and baby strollers. Many of these roads leave directly from the main park visitors center, but some of the best (and least crowded) start from Jordan Pond, in the southwest corner of the park. Jordan Pond is also the site of the only restaurant within the park boundary, **Jordan Pond House** (207/276-3316), where you can

reserve a table for an idyllic afternoon tea. In winter, when the park is virtually dormant, the carriage roads are kept open for cross-country skiing or snowshoeing, a magical way to get a feel for the place.

Acadia National Park also protects some exemplary places beyond Mount Desert Island, including the southern tip of Isle au Haut, tiny Baker Island (which you can visit on a ranger-guided tour), and the unforgettable Schoodic Peninsula across Frenchman Bay, accessible via US-1 just north of Ellsworth.

Three miles northwest of Bar Harbor, on the edge of Hulls Cove, the main **Acadia National Park Visitors Center** (daily; 207/288-3338) is a good place to start.

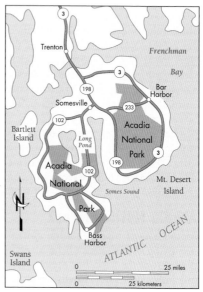

COOLER

NORTHERN VACATION
ROUTE

U S

2

Lake St. Mary — Glacier National Park, Montana

**THEODORE
ROOSEVELT
HIGHWAY**

U. S. HIGHWAY 2 ASSOCIATION

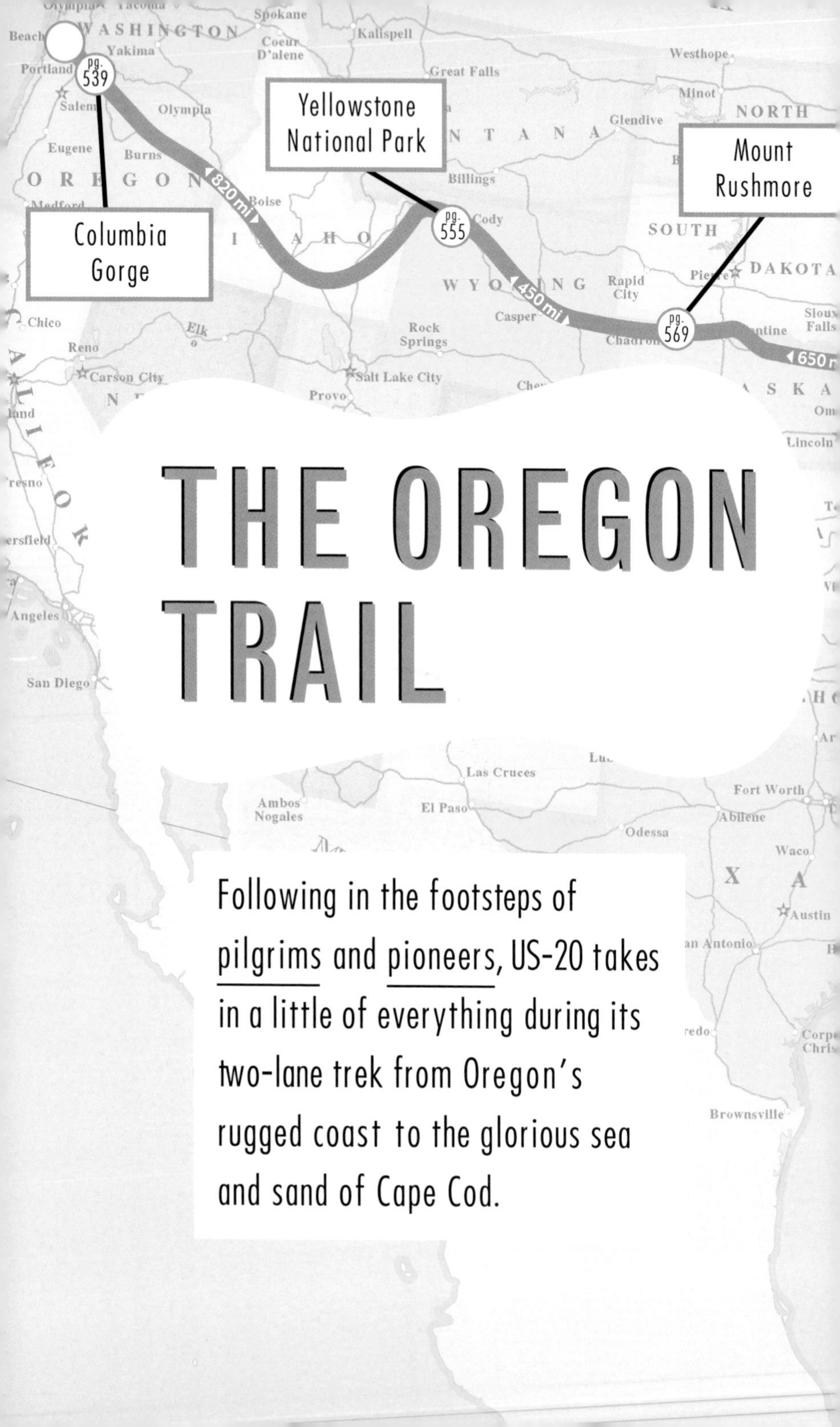

THE OREGON TRAIL

Columbia Gorge

Yellowstone National Park

Mount Rushmore

pg. 539

820 mi

pg. 555

450 mi

pg. 569

650 m

Following in the footsteps of pilgrims and pioneers, US-20 takes in a little of everything during its two-lane trek from Oregon's rugged coast to the glorious sea and sand of Cape Cod.

Field
of Dreams

Niagara Falls

Cape Cod

pg.
576

pg.
604

pg.
630

◄ 480 mi ►

◄ 740 mi ►

GREETINGS from PORTLAND OREGON

Between the Oregon Coast and Provincetown, Massachusetts

From the wide-open spaces of the West to the dense urban chaos of the East, this route offers the longest and most-involved road trip in this book. Connecting an exceedingly diverse range of places and totaling over 3,200 miles—many more if you count all the potential detours, side trips, and parallel routes—US-20 takes in a little of everything during its two-lane trek from Oregon's rugged coast to the glorious sea and sand of Cape Cod. Superlative sights include at least two wonders of the world, New York's **Niagara Falls** and Wyoming's **Yellowstone National Park;** the great cities of **Boston** and **Chicago;** and two halls of fame, one in Cleveland celebrating rock 'n' roll, the other in Cooperstown idolizing the national pastime, baseball. Odd museums, classic diners, idyllic towns, and poignant post-industrial decay—you'll find it all along this great cross-country highway.

Starting in the West, the route parallels, and in places runs right on top of, the broad path that formed the Oregon Trail. The landscape across **Oregon, Idaho,** and **Wyoming,** along US-20 and parallel to US-26, is still as lonesome as it was 150 years ago when pioneer families followed this one-way route west to the promised lands of the Pacific coast. Midway across the country you can visit two notable monuments, **Mt. Rushmore** and **Carhenge.** You also can test the wisdom of Walt Whitman, who wrote, "While I know the standard claim is that Yosemite, Niagara Falls, the upper Yellowstone and the like afford the greatest natural shows, I am not so sure but the Prairies and Plains last longer, fill the aesthetic sense fuller, precede all the rest and make North America's characteristic landscape." Drive across the Sand Hills of northern **Nebraska** on your way past Iowa's "Field of Dreams," and see for yourself what's so great about the **Great Plains.**

Crossing the Mississippi River at Dubuque, which along with Galena on the Illinois side are two of the oldest settlements on what was once the nation's western frontier, US-20 stops off for a look at Chicago before winding east through the newly resurgent, former "Rust Belt" along the Great Lakes. This densely populated region also holds some perfectly preserved historic sites, including Amish farmlands, and the automobile plants responsible for the country's classiest cars.

In upstate **New York**, we follow US-20 across a historical middle ground, in between the slow boats of the Erie Canal and the high-speed toll road of the I-90/New York Thruway, winding along the north edge of the lovely **Finger Lakes** before crossing the Hudson River into the Berkshires of western **Massachusetts.** The historic Mohawk Trail carries us past Lexington and Concord and into Boston, retracing Paul Revere's historic ride—in reverse—before following old US-6 to the tip of **Cape Cod** at the lovely and lively resort of Provincetown, where the Pilgrims *really* arrived in America, way back in 1620.

OREGON

Starting at one of the state's most enjoyable small towns, the arts-and-craftsy Pacific Ocean resort community of **Cannon Beach,** this route traverses the heart of Oregon. From the salty cow pastures along the Pacific Ocean, over the evergreen mantle of the Coast Range to culturally vibrant **Portland** and the lush Willamette Valley, the route starts where history says we should end up— amid the bountiful land at the west end of the Oregon Trail. From Portland, the state's largest city, you'll climb into the **Cascade Mountains,** through the amazing Columbia Gorge alongside its signature peak, Mt. Hood. East of the Cascades, the route drops down into the suddenly dry and desert-like landscape of the otherworldly **Columbia Plateau,** across which the highway rolls and rocks for 300 miles through old mining camps, fossil beds, and wide open rolling ranch lands before crossing the Snake River into Idaho.

INTERSECTION

Canon Beach is also part of our **Pacific Coast** trip. Scenic US-101's winding route is covered more fully on pages 10–103.

Cannon Beach

Unlike most Oregon coast towns, **Cannon Beach** (pop. 1,588) is hidden from the highway, but it's one place you won't want to miss. Though it has long been known as an artist's colony, and has grown considerably in recent years thanks to its popularity as a weekend escape from Portland, Cannon Beach retains a rustic quality, a walkably small size, and a coastline that rates second to no other in the state. (For full coverage of Cannon Beach, see page 28).

Cannon Beach marks the farthest point reached by the **Lewis and Clark** expedition to the West Coast. From here, they retreated back to their outpost at Fort Clatsop, near the mouth of the Columbia River, where they spent the winter of 1805–1806.

Sunset Highway: Saddle Mountain State Park

Running over the coastal mountains between Cannon Beach and Portland, US-26 is known as the Sunset Highway. Climbing up from the coastal plain, two miles east of US-101, our first stop is the old-growth spruce and fir forest preserved in **Klootchy Creek Park.** Among the many huge firs and spruce trees is the "World's Largest Sitka Spruce." More than 215 feet high, almost 16 feet in diameter, and thought to be over 700 years old, the tree is pointed out by a sign along the north side of the highway.

About 10 miles east of US-101, an eight-mile side trip to the northeast, along well-signed (but unpaved) Saddle Mountain Road, will lift you quickly above the frequent coastal clouds and fog. Named for a geographical saddle that sits high above the surrounding forests, **Saddle Mountain State Park** surrounds the highest point in the Coast Range. A very

By state law, there is no self-service gasoline in Oregon; all stations have attendants who pump the gas for you. There's no sales tax, either.

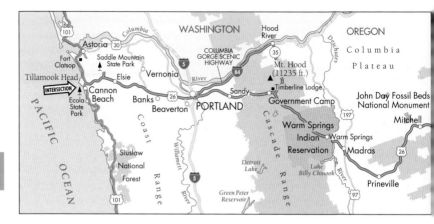

steep 2.5-mile hiking trail climbs to the summit, with opportunities to view bleeding heart, Indian paintbrush, monkey flowers, and other rare plants and wildflowers. From the 3,283-foot peak, you can often see the mouth of the Columbia River and the spine of the Coast Range. On a clear day, the panorama may include 50 miles of Pacific coastline and Mounts Hood, St. Helens, and Rainier (with more than a few ugly acres of clear-cuts in between). Primitive campsites are open mid-April to October; RVs should avoid this narrow road.

Camp 18

Continuing east on US-26, about 18 miles from the coast highway and a mile west of the hamlet of Elsie, the remarkable **Camp 18 Restaurant** (daily; 503/755-1818 or 800/874-1810) draws travelers for a variety of reasons. Some people come for the absolutely massive portions of very good food, from the gigantic fresh-baked cinnamon rolls and liter jugs of coffee at breakfast, to the steaks, chicken, and seafood served up at lunch and dinner. Others are drawn by the playful, Paul Bunyanesque scale of the place: The front door handle is a hefty old ax, the spacious dining room roof is

held up by a single massive Douglas fir log—85 feet long, eight feet thick, and weighing 40,000 pounds—and many of the tables are made from foot-thick planks of planed and polished wood.

The whole room is packed with an amazing collection of old logging gear, but best of all is the setting, overlooking a babbling brook, with

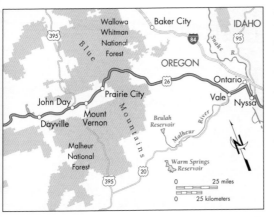

dozens of birdfeeders attracting flocks of finches and other colorful songbirds. Outside, an extensive museum in the parking lot lets visitors examine more old logging equipment to get a feel for a bygone era of misery whips, 20-foot handsaws, and steam donkeys. (Surprise, surprise: There's also a good gift shop.)

Banks-Vernonia Linear State Park

Midway between the coast and Portland, US-26 reaches the 1,635-foot crest of Sunset Summit, then winds east through the verdant delights of the leeward Coast Range, zipping through tunnels and sliding down slopes to the farm country of northwest Willamette Valley. **Banks-Vernonia Linear State Park,** 20 miles from downtown Portland, is a 21-mile stretch of abandoned railroad that runs north from US-26 between the town of Banks and the tucked-away timbertown of Vernonia. Six well-marked trailheads along Hwy-47 provide access to the fairly level gravel trail, Oregon's first rail-to-trail park.

Across Portland

Coming in from the west on the Sunset Highway (US-26), our route enters Portland next to sylvan Washington Park, then crosses the downtown area along Jefferson and Columbia Streets. Crossing the Willamette River, US-26 follows Powell Boulevard across East Portland.

Mount Hood Highway

Starting out along Powell Boulevard east from Portland, US-26—now dubbed the **Mount Hood Highway**—follows, albeit in reverse, the final leg of the historic Oregon Trail. Passing first through the comically named photo-stop town of Boring, the road some 20 miles east of Portland reaches **Sandy,** a boisterous gateway to the mountains. Nestled in berry-farm country, Sandy is full of ski shops, pizza parlors, and other enterprises geared for outdoor enthusiasts, who fuel up at places like the **Elusive Trout** (503/668-7884), at 39333 Proctor Boulevard, a pub/restaurant serving gourmet hamburgers and homemade soup. After Sandy's lively commerce, the road ambles through pastureland and into the foothills of the Cascades.

East of Sandy, oddly named towns along US-26 hold good places to eat and drink before or after a day out in the mountains. The **Inn Between** (503/622-5400) in **Wemme,** one of the little wide spots clustered at the base

South of US-26 on the western fringes of Portland, the mega-suburb of **Beaverton** is base camp for the high-tech companies of **Silicon Forest** and, most famously, corporate headquarters for **Nike,** the international sports apparel giant.

Portland

Portland, Oregon's largest city, is located inland from the coast near the confluence of the Willamette and Columbia Rivers. Due to its strategic location, the pioneer municipality grew so fast it was nicknamed Stumptown for the hundreds of fir stumps left by early loggers, and while railroad tracks and other heavy industrial remnants are still highly visible around town, Portland's riverfront park and numerous winding greenways show that this mini metropolis is not a smokestack town but a community that values art and nature as highly as commerce. Along with the largest (5,000-acre Forest Park) and the smallest (24-inches-in-diameter Mill Ends Park) urban parks in the nation, and one of the coolest urban skate parks anywhere (under the Burnside Bridge), Portland also has more movie theaters, restaurants, microbreweries, and bookstores per capita than any other U.S. city.

The oldest part of Portland has, over the past few years, been renovated into a lively Old Town district, where cast-iron facades of 120-year-old buildings hold some of the city's most popular bars, clubs, and cafés. South of Old Town along the river, an ugly freeway has been torn down to form the mile-long Tom McCall Waterfront Park, and west of the river, downtown Portland centers on lively Pioneer Courthouse Square, at 6th Avenue and Yamhill Street. South of the square, the South Park Blocks between Park and Ninth Avenues were set aside as parklands in the original city plan and are now bounded by Portland's prime museums. One essential Portland place is north of the square: **Powell's Books** (503/228-0540), at 1005 W. Burnside Street across from the Blitz-Weinhard Brewery, is the largest (and certainly among the best) new-and-used bookshop in the world. South of town, **Oaks Park** (503/233-5777) is a wonderful circa-1905 amusement park, with ancient and modern thrill rides all packed together in a sylvan, oak tree–dotted park.

One of the largest and oldest ballparks in the minor leagues, the circa-1926 Civic Stadium, downtown off Burnside at 1844 SW Morrison, has been fully renovated and redubbed PGE Park, home to the **Portland Beavers** (503/553-5400), the San Diego Padres' top farm club.

Practicalities

Air travelers can land at Portland International Airport (PDX), but most long-distance flights here come and go via Seattle's Sea-Tac, which is only about two hour's drive to the north, via the I-5 freeway. Getting around public-spirited Portland is a breeze thanks to the combination of an efficient bus system and a light rail train (called MAX; 503/238-7433).

Though it doesn't have a trendy reputation, Portland does have some great restaurants in all stripes and sizes. **Esparza's Tex-Mex** (503/234-7909), 2725 SE Ankeny Street, hidden away behind a hole-in-the-wall facade a block south of E. Burnside Street, is worth searching out for its smoky pork tacos and a jukebox featuring Tejano, norteño, and Marty Robbins hits. For more traditional Portland fare, head to **Jake's Famous Crawfish** (503/226-1419), at 401 SW 12th Street, which for over a century has been the place to go for the finest, freshest seafood. For meat, nothing beats the **Ringside** (503/223-1513), near PGE Park at 2165 W. Burnside Street, long famous for its great beef, fine fried chicken, monster Walla Walla sweet onion rings, and Hemingway-esque ambience. If your taste happens to run more to Marilyn Manson than to Marilyn Monroe, you'll probably prefer to eat across town at **Dots Cafe** (503/235-0203), at 2521 SE Clinton Street, a late-night hangout that has comfy dark booths, great black-bean burritos, microbrews, and pool tables.

There are all sorts of places to stay in Portland, starting with a pair of popular HI youth hostels, one east of downtown at 3031 Hawthorne Boulevard (503/236-3380) and a newer one in the Northwest District, at 1818 NW Glisan (503/241-2783). The comfortable, close-to-downtown, and moderately priced **Mallory Motor Hotel** ($90 and up; 503/223-6311 or 800/228-8657), at 729 SW 15th Avenue, offers reasonable room rates and free parking; and if you feel like splurging try the im-peccably restored downtown landmark, the **Heathman Hotel** ($199 and up; 503/241-4100 or 800/551-0011), at 1009 SW Broadway, is the poshest of Portland's posh, with an elegant lobby and sumptuously appointed rooms.

The best source of visitor information on Portland is the **Portland Visitors Association** (800/962-3700), at 25 SW Salmon Street.

of Mt. Hood, has affordable eats varying from teriyaki chicken to macho nachos.

The other suggested stop is the **Mount Hood Visitor Center** (daily; 503/622-4822), in Welches at 65000 E. US-26, operated by the USFS and loaded with maps, brochures, and other information on the mountain and surrounding recreational hotspots.

Government Camp

Just off US-26 at the southern foot of Mt. Hood, **Government Camp** is but another wide spot in the road with a range of food and drink options. For espresso, microbrews, sandwiches, pizzas, and pastas, stop at the **Mount Hood Brewing Company** (503/272-3724), at the west end of town. Another good stop is the **Huckleberry Inn** (503/272-3325), open 24 hours a day, seven days a week, and famous for its wild huckleberry pies, huckleberry pancakes, and huckleberry shakes. If you're unable to move after a berry feast, the inn also offers low-priced rooms.

Government Camp's main attraction is the **Mount Hood Ski Bowl** (503/222-2695), a year-round recreation center with skiing and snowboarding in winter and mountain biking in summer, plus guided horseback trips, go-carts, paintball games, and a 100-foot bungee jump.

Timberline Lodge

East of Government Camp, near the junction of US-26 and Hwy-35, which comes from Hood River and the Columbia Gorge, be sure to turn off north toward Mt. Hood to visit **Timberline Lodge** ($135–250; 503/231-5400 or 800/547-1406), an elegantly rustic national landmark built in 1937 by the Depression-era artisans of the Works Progress Administration. The actual hotel seen (from the outside, not the inside) in Stanley Kubrick's creepy 1983 film, *The Shining,* Timberline Lodge is an unforgettable place, with a humongous fireplace in the three-story main lobby, grand dining rooms, and cozy guest rooms decorated in characterful Pacific Northwest motifs, not to mention an unbeatable setting high atop the Cascade Mountains. Even if you don't stay, check out the Cascade Dining

Enticing though it is, snowcapped **Mt. Hood** is also a difficult and dangerous peak to climb—there is no trail to the 11,239-foot summit, and all routes require a high degree of technical ability and specialized equipment. There are lots of fine hikes around its base, however.

The **Columbia Gorge Scenic Highway** was built by millionaire lawyer Sam Hill, who built the road to link Portland with the pacifist agricultural colony he planned at his 7,000-acre estate at Maryhill, Washington. Maryhill is now a fascinatingly eclectic **museum** (daily; $7; 509/773-3733), near the I-84/US-97 junction. Three miles east of Maryhill, Hill also constructed a concrete replica of Stonehenge, in memory of local men killed in World War I.

Detour: Columbia Gorge

Though our route across Oregon generally follows scenic US-26, the fastest route east from Portland is I-84, which races along the Columbia River, rejoining US-26 at the Idaho border. Freeway the whole way, I-84 is worth considering for its one incredible feature: the **Columbia Gorge**, the deep, verdant basalt canyon through which the mighty river, and the freeway, not to mention a busy railroad, all run. The heart of the Columbia Gorge is between the small towns of Sandy and Cascade Locks, some 15 and 35 miles east of Portland respectively, and is best experienced by driving the historic **Columbia Gorge Scenic Highway**—the oldest scenic route in the country, built beginning in 1913, and still retaining all its old-road character.

The highlight (and approximate midpoint) of this historic highway is the aptly named **Vista House**, built in 1917 to mark the completion of the road, which here rises over 700 feet above the Columbia River. East of Vista House, a series of tremendous waterfalls drop down along the road: First comes **LaTourell Falls**; then the 242-foot cascades of **Wahkeenah Falls**; then, saving the best for last, famous **Multnomah Falls**, which drops 620 feet into a densely forested canyon, bridged by a delicate concrete arch. Each of these waterfalls is within a short walk of parking areas along the scenic highway, and many smaller falls can be seen cascading from canyon walls.

The Columbia Gorge Scenic Highway rejoins I-84 a few miles east of Multnomah Falls, at the town of **Cascade Locks**. Another 20 miles east, at the east end of the Columbia Gorge, the lively town of **Hood River** is packed with brewpubs, espresso bars, bookshops, cafés, and moderate motels. Along the river, the historic **Columbia Gorge Hotel** (541/386-5566) preserves its Jazz Age elegance, with comfortable rooms and an excellent restaurant.

Mushroom Rock along the Columbia River Highway, Ore.

Room's award-winning cuisine, the more-casual pizza and sandwiches at the Blue Ox, and the Ram's Head Bar, which has locally brewed beers and ales.

Warm Springs Indian Reservation

East of the Cascades crest, US-26 becomes the Warm Springs Highway as it angles down out of the mountains across the sage and juniper country of eastern Oregon. Most of the land between here and Madras is part of the 600,000-acre **Warm Springs Indian Reservation**, home to

The Columbia Gorge west of Hood River is one of the world's best windsurfing spots, and throughout the summer dozens of brightly colored sails can be seen racing along the river.

Around the Warm Springs Reservation, tune to **KWSO 91.9 FM** for an intriguing array of music (from The Eagles to talking drums) and National Native News.

the Confederated Tribes of Warm Springs (Wasco, Paiute, and Warm Springs).

From US-26, follow signs to **Kah-Nee-Tah** (ca-NEE-da, all run together despite the odd spelling), a resort complex that cheerfully blends modern and ancient lifestyles. You can soak in the famously soothing hot springs, camp in a tepee, play golf along the banks of the Warm Springs River, and savor salmon fillets cooked over an alderwood fire. The resort also includes the large Indian Head casino. Room rates vary tremendously (541/553-1112 or 800/554-4SUN).

Back on US-26, the real attraction of the reservation is the modern, 27,000-square-foot **Museum at Warm Springs** (daily; $6; 541/553-3331). Check out exhibits of more than 20,000 artifacts, replicas of a Paiute mat lodge and a Wasco plank house, recordings of tribal languages, and a pushbutton-activated Wasco wedding scene. Across the highway, a stylized mini-mall holds a gift shop and the very good **Indian Trail Restaurant.**

A mile east, at the edge of the reservation where US-26 bridges the deep canyon of the Deschutes River, the **Deschutes Crossing Cafe** (541/553-1300), at 2198 US-26, offers good food including Indian fry bread, best followed by a slice of fresh huckleberry pie.

Madras

One of eastern Oregon's landmarks, and a celebrated challenge to rock climbers, **Smith Rock State Park** (541/548-7501) stands 17 miles south of Madras along US-97.

After crossing the Deschutes River from the Warm Springs reservation, US-26 climbs up a deep canyon, then plateaus at **Madras** (pop. 5,078), birthplace of the late actor River Phoenix. Contrary to what you might expect from the town's East Indian name, few of its hardworking residents wear plaid, and the beatific followers of a certain Indian guru are red-clad memories: It's been nearly 30 years since Bhagwan Shree Rajneesh and his disciples lived on their 175,000-acre commune, 30 miles to the northeast at the village of Antelope.

There's not a lot to see or do in Madras, which stands at the junction of US-26 and busy US-97, but there are stores and gas stations and at least one good place to stay: **Sonny's Motel** ($65; 541/475-7217), at 1539 SW US-26/97, which has clean rooms and a pool, plus an adjacent restaurant famed for its steaks.

Prineville

East of the Mt. Hood hamlet of Zigzag, US-26 drops to an old-fashioned, undivided two-lane road. Summer-only Lolo Pass Loop (Hwy-18) cuts off north from here on a scenic half-circle around the base of Mt. Hood to Hood River, on the Columbia River and I-84.

From Madras, US-26 veers farther away from the Cascades, crossing the **Crooked River National Grasslands,** which mark the geographical center of Oregon. Strolling the streets of **Prineville** (pop. 7,356), a town with a vivid heritage of cattle and sheep ranching, you'll notice plenty of cowboy hats (or "gimme" caps, emblazoned with the logos of the wearer's favorite fertilizer or tractor company) atop the heads of dusty citizens piloting dusty pickup trucks. It's been a rip-snorter of a town since Barny Prine built his blacksmith shop

End of the Oregon Trail

After long months of hardship and danger, pioneers nearing the end of the Oregon Trail had two choices when they reached the narrow gorge of the Columbia River: They could float their wagons down the perilous river to Fort Vancouver, or climb over the Cascades to the Willamette Valley via the Barlow Road, a route that parallels today's US-26. While much safer than the river route, the Barlow Road had its own precarious moments—emigrants struggled down muddy declines, hanging onto ropes hitched around trees to keep wagons from runaway destruction. Such moments assuredly gave the pioneers second thoughts about their choice of passage. At $5 per wagon and 10 cents a head for cattle, horses, and mules, following the privately owned Barlow Road was also expensive. Nonetheless, in 1845, the first year of operation, records report that 1,000 pioneers in 145 wagons traveled the route.

Heading east, you're going backwards along the Barlow Road, so bear that in mind as you take in a few historical sites that record the struggles of pioneers on the last stretch of their 2,000-mile overland journey. The steepest section of the road was the **Laurel Hill "Chute,"** where wagons skidded down a treacherous grade; a sign and pull-out five miles east of Rhododendron mark the start of a short, steep hike up to the chute. Just west of Laurel Hill, at Tollgate Campground, you'll find a reproduction of the **Barlow Road Tollgate,** where the road's owner, Sam Barlow, stood with his hand out.

Look for other markers depicting Barlow Road history on Hwy-35, the loop road that traverses the eastern slope of Mt. Hood down to Hood River. The first, **Pioneer Woman's Grave,** is a quarter mile north of the junction with US-26; a sign marks a right turn onto Forest Road 3530 and points toward a gravesite with a brass plaque commemorating the women who traveled the Oregon Trail. Two miles north of the junction is 4,161-foot **Barlow Pass,** where ruts grooved in the Barlow Road lead downhill from a parking area, mute testament to the perseverance of westward-driven settlers.

The "official" western end of the Oregon Trail is at Oregon City, 10 miles south of Portland in the Willamette Valley.

In every U.S. presidential election since Oregon became a state (in 1859), the people of Crook County around Prineville voted for the winner; until, that is, they voted for George Bush in 1992, putting an end to their reputation as the national bellwether.

and saloon here in 1868 following the discovery of gold in nearby hills. These days, the people of Prineville are ranchers, loggers, miners, and employees of the Les Schwab tire company, which has its HQ here, though tourism is slowly but surely taking its place as an economic force.

You can learn more about the region's history at the **A. R. Bowman Museum** (closed Sun.; 541/447-3715), two blocks north of the landmark Crook County Courthouse at 246 N. Main Street. Two floors of exhibits include a campfire setup, a moonshine still, and a country store with a pound of Bull Durham tobacco. If you hanker after a sit-down meal, check out the **Ochoco Inn and Cinnabar Restaurant** (541/447-3880) at 123 E. 3rd Street, known for its generous and eclectic menu. **Barr's Cafe** (541/447-5897), at 887 N. Main Street, serves coffee-shop food. Besides the Cinnabar Restaurant, the Ochoco Inn also has an inexpensive motel, and other lodging choices include the **City Center Motel** ($45–65; 541/447-5522), at 509 E. 3rd Street, in the middle of the city in the middle of the state, and eminently in the middle of the motel price range.

The drive along US-26 east of Prineville takes you up into the Ochocos, a low-slung gem of a mountain range once the heartland of the Paiutes. Seven miles from Prineville, US-26 skirts **Ochoco Lake,** a popular recreational reservoir with fishing, boating, hiking, camping, and a picnic bench or two for travelers—but not a lot of shade. The rest of the Ochoco Range, which reaches heights of nearly 7,000 feet, holds acres and acres of lovely meadows, clear streams, pristine pine forests, and views of the jagged Cascade Range, rising on the western horizon.

Mitchell

The only concentration of human habitation near the John Day Fossil Beds National Monument is **Mitchell,** a semi-ghost town 40 miles east of Prineville and two miles east of the turnoff for the Painted Hills section of the fossil beds. The main "town" of Mitchell lines up along the short stretch of old road signed as the "Business Loop," just south of US-26, where the old-fashioned general store

Wheeler County Mercantile captures the flavor of the 1870s. Mitchell also holds one of the more atmospheric old places to stay in this part of eastern Oregon, the **Oregon Hotel** ($45 and up; 541/462-3027) at 104 Main Street, with a comfy front porch, a resident border collie for company, and B&B rooms.

John Day Fossil Beds National Monument

East of the Ochocos, midway across Oregon, the **John Day Fossil Beds National Monument** documents many millions of years of prehistoric life, from thundering dinosaurs to delicate plants. Discovered

ammonite fossil

in the 1860s by a frontier preacher and amateur geologist named Thomas Condon, the beds contain one of the world's richest and most diverse concentrations of mammalian and dinosaur fossils. Offering a complete and easily accessible record of life on earth, spanning some 50 million years, the monument is made up of three distinct units, totaling some 14,000 acres. Needless to say, fossil collecting is strictly prohibited in the park.

There's also a more distant section of the John Day fossil beds at the **Clarno Unit**, along the John Day River some 50 miles northwest of Painted Hills, between the towns of Antelope and Fossil. This area includes the most ancient rocks—ranging from 37 to 54 million years old.

The eerie, empty moonscape can be easily toured from US-26. Start in the west with the **Painted Hills Unit,** just west of Mitchell, then six miles north of US-26, where trails and overlooks offer views of striated hills and bluffs formed by fallen ash and brilliantly colored in bands of red, pink, black, and bronze. A life-sized Georgia O'Keeffe landscape, Painted Hills is a popular spot with photographers and painters, especially the short Painted Cove trail, which winds through the most intensely colored section.

About 30 miles east of Mitchell, six miles west of Dayville along US-26, then three miles north on Hwy-19, the **Sheep Rock Unit** is the best place to see fossils in their natural state; the monument headquarters and a small museum are also here, housed inside the **Cant Ranch Visitor Center** (541/987-2333). East of the turnoff to the Sheep Rock fossil beds, US-26 runs right along the John Day River through the 500-foot-deep basalt canyon of Picture Gorge, so named because of the abundance of Native American pictographs.

Dayville and Mount Vernon

After gazing at striped hillsides and fossilized remains, regain some perspective by strolling through any of the towns that line the John Day River along this part of US-26—Dayville, Mount Vernon, John Day, Canyon City, or Prairie City. Founded as miners' camps after gold was discovered here in 1862, many now cater mostly to local ranchers—but offer a warm welcome to the few visitors who brave a trip through this uninviting but unforgettable part of the world.

The namesake of the fossil beds, **John Day,** was a fur trapper hunting along the Columbia River in 1810 when he was attacked by Indians. He turned up two years later at Astoria on the coast, but never again went anywhere near the river, the town, or the region that now bear his name.

Starting in the west, the **Dayville Diggins** in Dayville will take care of your dust-choked palate; **Dayville** (pop. 185) also has a great roadside "antiques" store, and what has to be among the world's smallest city halls—a one-room shack at the east edge of town. The **Fish House** ($50–65; 541/987-2124), a 1908 bungalow turned antique-bedecked B&B at 110 Franklin, will cater to both your appetite and road-weariness. Farther east, at the junction of US-26 and US-395, **Mount Vernon** is home to **The Wounded Buffalo,** a local landmark known for its Buffalo Bill Burger and juicy rib eye steaks.

John Day: Kam Wah Chung Museum

The town of **John Day** (pop. 1,821), the metropolis in this chain of ghostly gold towns, holds the area's one not-to-be-missed attraction: **Kam Wah Chung Museum** (daily May 1–Oct. 31 only; $3; 541/575-0028), 250 NW Canton, run by the state and located in a nice park just north of US-26 at the center of

John Day's one and only radio station, **KJDY 1400 AM,** broadcasts country-tinged Top 40 music and local news across eastern Oregon. For truly twangy C&W—á la Waylon, Hank and Merle—tune to **KFXD 580 AM.**

John Day. Built as a trading post in 1866–1867, in the late 1880s the Kam Wah Chung building became a general store and medical center for the Chinese workers who toiled in the mines, and for 60 years it continued to be the center of the almost exclusively male Chinese community of eastern Oregon, which at times made up a majority of the regional population. Most of the building is preserved intact, displaying a fascinating collection of items ranging from herbal remedies and ornate red Taoist shrines to gambling paraphernalia and ancient canned goods. There's also a bedroom with bunks and a wood stove left as they were by the last residents, Ing Hay and Lung On, the herbalist and storekeeper who lived and worked here until the 1940s.

Right next to the museum is the John Day **swimming pool,** much appreciated on a hot summer afternoon. For food, the **Grub Steak Mining Company** (541/575-1970), at 149 E. Main Street, has a sumptuous menu of rib eyes and other beef entrées. The **Dreamers Lodge Motel** (541/575-0526) at 144 N. Canyon Boulevard, and a **Best Western** (541/575-1700) at 315 W. Main Street, both have reasonable rates.

Prairie City

Back on US-26, the first town east of John Day is tidy little **Prairie City** (pop. 1,080), an old-fashioned ranching community that is fast becoming a western false-front photo-opportunity. For a taste of local life, stay at the 100-year-old **Riverside Schoolhouse** (541/820-4731), a B&B located on a working cattle ranch.

Leaving the John Day River watershed, US-26 heads east, climbing over mile-high Dixie Pass (which is exactly one mile high—5,280 feet above sea level) while rambling through the Malheur and Wallowa-Whitman National Forests, where campgrounds, cool mountain lakes, natural hot springs, and dense forests abound.

Halfway between Prairie City and Vale is the dividing line between Pacific and Mountain time zones. Adjust clocks accordingly as you head over Eldorado Pass.

East of the crest, dropping down from the mountains across the Snake River plain, US-26 crosses another 75 miles of rolling sagebrush, with little more than an occasional cattle ranch, or a golden eagle sitting atop a telephone pole, to attract your attention. Tiny little tavern-and-post-office towns like Unity, Ironside, Brogan, and Willow Creek will make you slow to 45 mph (or risk a ticket), while on a hot summer's day the smell of juniper and sage is so potent it perfumes the dry desert air, unmistakable even if you cruise through at 70 mph with the a/c blasting away.

Vale

The seat of Malheur ("Bad Smell" or "Bad Luck," depending upon who tells it) County, **Vale** (pop. 1,701), sits on the banks of the Malheur River at the junction of US-20 and US-26. The comparatively easy river crossing and the presence of a natural hot spring made it a prime stopping place on the Oregon Trail. Murals and markers around town explain something of the history, and point out sights like the **Malheur Crossing,** next to the bridge on the eastern edge of

the town, where pioneers dunked their aching bods in the still-hot Malheur River Springs; and **Keeney Pass,** just south of downtown Vale on Enterprise Avenue, where 150-year-old wagon ruts can still be seen along the roadside. There's more to see inside the **Stone House Museum** (closed Sun. and Mon.; free; 541/473-2070), at 255 Main Street, housed inside a frontier-era stagecoach stop and hotel.

Towns in eastern Oregon have taken to decorating their buildings with large and colorful murals, usually with historical or outdoorsy themes.

Taking a breather at Vale is an honored tradition—it was here that pioneers rested before climbing out of the Snake River Valley into the Blue Mountains. Today's travelers can opt for a night at the **Bates Motel** ($40; 541/473-3234), on US-20 at 1101 A Street W; it has nothing to do with Hitchcock's *Psycho,* but has been run by the Bates family (no Normans among them) for over 30 years, offering clean showers, a pizza restaurant, and a good night's sleep. Another unusual option is the **1900 Sears & Roebuck Home** (541/473-9636), at 484 N. 10th Street, a B&B originally ordered from the Sears catalog back around the turn of the 20th century.

Toward Idaho: Ontario & Nyssa

Approaching the Idaho border, you have two choices: to follow I-84, heading east via **Ontario** (pop. 10,985), the largest of many mid-sized farming and ranching communities in the surrounding area; or to continue along the more atmospheric older roads. The official **Oregon Trail Auto Route** (US-20/26) bends to the south along the Snake River, passing one last Oregon town, **Nyssa,** before crossing into the Land of Famous Potatoes. Nyssa calls itself the "Thunderegg Capital of the World" because of the many geodes found there, but it's primarily a shipping point for the tons of spuds, onions, and sugar beets grown nearby—the different crops are even labeled along the highway for your edification. While Nyssa doesn't have a lot else to offer, it does have a very large riverfront sugar beet refinery, and the more enjoyable **Sugar Bowl,** a bowling alley off US-20/26 on the north edge of town.

IDAHO

US-20's route across southern Idaho cuts through one of the most magnificently empty American spaces, an arid, volcanic region cut by life-giving rivers and isolating mountain ranges, with strange geological outcrops that encourage travelers to stop and explore the inhospitable terrain. Irrigation has altered the look of the land considerably, so much so that vineyards and lush fields now thrive in the otherwise barren, gray-green sagebrush plains, but little else has changed since this region provided the greatest challenge to pioneers crossing the country along the Oregon Trail. The provision of visitor services may have improved considerably in the intervening 150 years, but southern Idaho is still a wild and demanding land. Like much of the West, it's also addictively satisfying.

Parma and Fort Boise

Just as US-20/26 does today, the historic Oregon Trail crosses between Idaho and Oregon at the confluence of the Boise and Snake Rivers, southwest of I-84 at the town of **Parma**. Sugar beets and onions fill the fields around the tiny town, which takes pride in its replica of **Fort Boise,** one of the first European outposts in the Pacific Northwest. Originally established in 1834 by the Hudson's Bay Company, Fort Boise was famous for its frontier hospitality, entertaining and supplying travelers and traders until the mid-1850s, when it was closed because of declines in demand and an increase in Indian hostilities. The original Fort Boise stood along the banks of the river and was washed away long ago. The site is marked today by an odd, horse-headed stone obelisk festooned with the Hudson's Bay Company flag, which stands along the Snake River at the end of Old Fort Boise Road, two miles west of US-20/26. The less-than-authentic steel-and-stucco reconstruction of the old fort that stands along US-20 near the center of town is the site of the annual **Old Fort Boise Days** in early May.

The quickest route across Idaho is the I-84 freeway, though the historic Oregon Trail route, marked by large highway signs, follows a much more scenic route along the Snake River.

Caldwell

East of Parma, US-20/26 runs along the north bank of the Boise River for a dozen miles before crossing I-84 at the city of **Caldwell**—home of the mid-August **Caldwell Night Rodeo** (208/459-2060). A century ago, Caldwell was the site of the 1905 bomb-blast murder of former Idaho Governor Frank Steunenberg. Blamed on "Wobbly" left-wing union activists, including "Big Bill" Haywood, who'd been organizing Idaho's miners and loggers, the murder was the story behind Anthony Lukas's sprawling book *Big Trouble.*

*One fun spot out between Caldwell and Boise is the **Western Idaho Fairgrounds,** home to year-round events and the Class A baseball games of the **Boise Hawks** (208/322-5000). Games are broadcast on KTIK 1350 AM.*

From Caldwell, you can follow the freeway into Boise, but it's more interesting, and depending on traffic possibly even quicker as well, to stay on US-20/26 (aka Chinden Boulevard), which runs right atop the old Oregon Trail

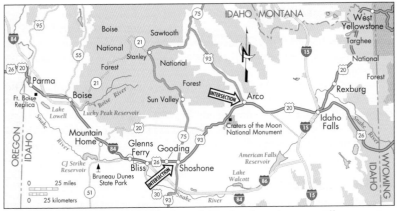

into downtown, past corn and wheat fields that have been rapidly sprouting golf course estates, a Hewlett-Packard factory, car parts stores, and the usual Asphalt Nation sprawl.

Boise

Capital of Idaho and perennial contender for the title of "most livable" city in the United States, **Boise** (pop. 187,000) is still a very pleasant, medium-sized city, despite growing at a rate of 25 percent per decade. A lush green oasis in the middle of the barren lava lands of the Snake River plain, Boise was so named by fur-trappers for its dense groves of cottonwood trees (*bois* is French for "wood"), which made the area an especially welcome respite before irrigation turned the brown desert much greener than it naturally would be. The presence of the state government and the 12,000 students at Boise State University lend a degree of sophistication and vitality mixed in with the more usual Idaho trappings—more than anywhere else for miles, roller blades and mountain bikes compete with pickup trucks as the main method of transportation here, and bookshops and espresso bars line the downtown streets.

Downtown Boise focuses on the **state capitol** (closed Sun.; free), three blocks north of Main Street between 6th and 8th Streets, a typically grand, neoclassical structure, built of local sandstone with a giant eagle atop its landmark dome. The usual exhibits of the state's produce fill display cases, and free guided tours are given upon request.

South of the capitol, restaurants and cafés have reclaimed the blocks of 100-year-old brick buildings around 6th and Main Streets, the historic center of Boise. In the heart of this lively, pedestrian-friendly neighborhood, a block south of Main at 611 Grove Street, the small but intriguing **Basque Museum** (closed Sun. & Mon.; 208/343-2671) documents the culture of the Basque people who work in Idaho's ranching industries. A block west stands **The Grove,** Boise's

convention center and main shopping complex, featuring a large fountain through which daredevils like to skate and cycle. Don't miss **Taters** (208/338-1062), at 249 S. 8th Street, which sells all manner of Idaho souvenirs, from postcards and fridge magnets to cookbooks describing 100 things you can do with potatoes.

Farther east, where Main Street turns into Warm Springs Road, the **Old Idaho Penitentiary** (daily; $5; 208/368-6080) served as the main state prison for over 100 years from its construction in 1872. High sandstone walls, cut by prisoners, surround the complex, and the old cell blocks are now filled with displays on prison life—from collections of tattoos to the gallows where many prisoners met their end.

Boise Practicalities

By Idaho standards, Boise has a truly exciting range of restaurants, with many good places around 6th and Main Streets and elsewhere in the compact downtown area. For a huge breakfast, or an out-of-this-world milk shake, stop by **Moon's Cafe** (open until 3 PM; 208/385-0472), in the back room of a gift shop that used to be a gun shop at 815 W. Bannock Street. Another favorite stop is the **Gernika** (208/344-2175), near the Basque Museum on the corner of Grove and Capitol Avenues, which serves up delicious tastes of Basque-inspired food (lamb sandwiches, chorizo *tapas,* and out-of-this-world shoestring fries), plus wines and beers, in a friendly, unpretentious room—with a sidewalk seating area in summer. And if this doesn't hit the spot, within a few blocks are the excellent **Guido's Pizzeria** (208/345-9011), at 235 N. 5th Street; the upscale **Grape Escape** wine and *tapas* bar at 800 W. Idaho Street, and maybe a million coffeehouses and juice-and-smoothie bars.

Boise's downtown restaurant district doubles as its nightlife zone as well, so after a meal you can stagger between old-fashioned, carved-wood bars like Pengilly's, at 513 Main Street, and nightclubs like the excellent **Blues Bouquet**, at 1010 Main Street.

Boise's one great place to stay, the wonderful old **Idanha Hotel** at 928 Main Street—built in 1901 and featuring ornate corner turrets, opulent public spaces, and Idaho's oldest elevator—has, alas, been converted into apartments, but the **Owyhee Plaza** ($95 and up; 208/343-4611), at 1109 Mian Street, is almost as nice. For a cheap but still restful sleep, head to the **Cabana Inn** ($50; 208/343-6000), on the west side of downtown at 1600 Main Street. West of Boise, there's an **HI Hostel** ($19; 208/467-6858) at 17322 Can Ada Road in Nampa.

the Idanha Hotel

Mountain Home and Bruneau Dunes

Across southern Idaho, the I-84 freeway has effectively replaced the older highways, especially in the area southeast of Boise. The huge **Mountain Home Air Force Base**, 35 miles southeast of Boise, is the only thing for miles, which is no doubt by design: The base is a testing ground for the latest high-tech weapons systems and aircraft. One of the more contentious side effects of Mountain

Home's presence is that the powers-that-be have decreed that much of the surrounding wilderness, including the wild Owyhee Mountains and almost the entire southwest corner of the state, should be closed to the public and turned into a bombing range—so pilots can gain experience firing missiles and dropping live munitions.

Northeast from Boise, Hwy-21 makes a very scenic trip through the Sawtooth Mountains to Stanley.

Eighteen miles south of Mountain Home and the I-84 freeway via Hwy-51, **Bruneau Dunes State Park** (208/366-7919) protects the highest free-standing sand dune in North America—rising over 400 feet above the Snake River plain. Since the temperatures can hit 100° throughout the summer months, mornings or sunsets are the best times to exercise your legs by climbing up and careening back down the white sands.

Glenns Ferry

The tiny town of **Glenns Ferry**, 28 miles southeast of Mountain Home on the Snake River and I-84, would hardly rate a mention were it not the site of one of the most important crossings on the old Oregon Trail. This site, now preserved as **Three Island State Park**, a mile southwest of town, gives one of the strongest impressions of the tough going for Oregon-bound pioneers. A very good **visitors center** (daily; 208/366-2394), with a Conestoga wagon out front, has displays of trail lore and history, and every August enthusiasts get together to reenact the river crossing. Go for a swim to cool off, and feel the powerful currents—more placid here than most anywhere else, which is why it was considered the best place to ford the river. This is also a fine place to camp; the usually clear night sky makes for excellent stargazing, and there's even a very docile herd of buffalo.

At Mountain Home, US-20 cuts off northeast from I-84, following a branch of the Oregon Trail known as Goodale's Cut-off across the harsh volcanic plains. Bliss marks the turnoff onto US-30, which follows the old Oregon Trail along the banks of the Snake River along a lovely, waterfall-rich route known as **Thousand Springs Scenic Byway**, rejoining I-84 at Twin Falls.

Bliss and Hagerman

Along with providing the chance to add to your collection of city limits signs, or to send a postcard saying you're in **Bliss** (pop. 186), this idyllically named town is worth a stop to see the deep canyon of **Malad Gorge State Park** (daily dawn–dusk; free; 208/837-4505), well-signed southeast of town, off I-84 exit 147. It doesn't look like much until you get out of the car and walk 100 feet down the trail, where you suddenly come upon a truly awesome sight: a 250-foot-deep gorge with a crashing waterfall. The freeway passes overhead, oblivious to the natural wonder directly below.

Across the Snake River from Malad Gorge, **Hagerman Fossil Beds National Monument** contains what's been called "the richest known deposit of Pliocene Age terrestrial fossils," mainly horses (Equus simplicidens) that roamed the area some three million years ago. The undeveloped monument also preserves one of the longest sections of visible wagon ruts in the entire length of the Oregon Trail. The visitors center (208/837-4793) is in Hagerman, 5 miles south of Bliss and across the river from the fossil beds. The center also has information on visiting the area's other national monument: the **Minidota Interment Camp**, north of Twin Falls (see page 132).

The Oregon Trail

In 1993, the 150th anniversary of the opening of the Oregon Trail renewed interest in this best-known of emigrant trails across the Wild West. History buffs got together for summer-long reenactments of the arduous crossing, building authentic wagons and eating, dressing, and sleeping as the pioneers did—with the inestimable comfort of knowing that they, unlike their predecessors, could easily return home at any point.

From 1843 until the 1860s, some 400,000 men, women, and children followed this 2,000-mile trail, averaging four months to make the cross-country journey. Long followed by fur-trappers and traders, and first charted by a series of U.S. Army expeditions led by Kit Carson and John C. Fremont in the early 1840s, the Oregon Trail followed the path of least resistance across the western half of the continent. Beginning at various points along the Missouri River, the trail followed the valley of the Platte River across the Great Plains, crossed the Rockies at Wyoming's gentle South Pass, then set off across the desert of southern Idaho. The most difficult parts were saved for the end, when emigrants had a choice of floating downstream on the turbulent Columbia River or struggling over the rugged Cascades to reach the Willamette Valley. Nearly half of the travelers who set off along the Oregon Trail from Missouri actually had other destinations in mind: More than 100,000 turned off south toward the California gold mines, and some 30,000 Mormons followed the route west to their new colony at Salt Lake City.

The Oregon Trail had many variants and shortcuts and was never a sharply defined track, but clear traces survive in a number of places along the route. Many evocative sites also survive, often as reconstructions of pioneer forts, trading posts, and river crossings. There are also many fine museums along the way.

Many Oregon Trail sites are covered in more detail under our Road Trip routes. As shown on the map, some of the most interesting Oregon Trail sites are:

Oregon City: Western end of the Oregon Trail, 10 miles south of downtown Portland along the Willamette River. A visitors center and museum off I-205 at 1726 Washington Street (daily 9 AM–5 PM; $7; 503/657-9336) tells the whole saga.

The Barlow Road: To avoid the treacherous falls of the Columbia Gorge, many emigrants opted to follow this difficult toll road that cuts inland around Mt. Hood (see page 541).

The National Oregon Trail Interpretive Center: In eastern Oregon, off I-84 near Baker City, Oregon's biggest and most developed Oregon Trail historic site (daily 9 AM–4 PM, till 6 PM in summer; free; 541/523-1843) has an original "Meeker Marker" and a 15-mile-long set of well-preserved wagon ruts.

Fort Boise: This fortress, a reconstruction of a fur-trapping post built nearby in 1834, stands along the banks of the Snake River (see page 546).

Three Island State Park: One of the best places to get a feel for life as an Oregon Trail pioneer: Camp where they camped and swim where they swam, at one of the most important crossings of the Snake River (see page 549).

Fort Caspar: A credible reconstruction of a frontier fort houses a good museum and the remains of an early ferry and bridge over the Platte River, while a new building in town houses the National Historic Trails Interpretive Center (see page 563).

Fort Laramie: Located 40 miles southeast of Douglas, Wyoming, this restored fort is among the best stops on the contemporary trail. The most impressive set of preserved wagon ruts survive in an evocative state park outside Guernsey, upstream from the fort (see page 565).

Santa Fe Trail Junction: For the first few miles, the Santa Fe and Oregon Trails coincided, and a sign here pointed the way: right to Oregon, left to Santa Fe (see page 686).

Independence, Missouri: Where most travelers on the Oregon Trail began, this is also the site of one of the best museums on the subject of the westward migrations. (see page 687).

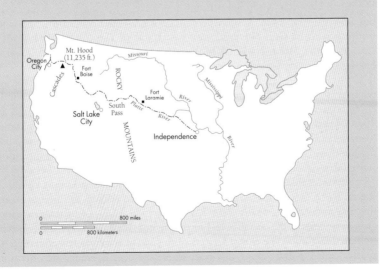

Shoshone Falls, Idaho.

US-26: Gooding and Shoshone

In the midst of inhospitable volcanic badlands, a pair of small towns that grew up along the railroad tracks have somehow survived to the present day. Coming from the west along US-26 from Bliss, the first one you reach is **Gooding** (pop. 2,820), named for local sheep rancher Frank Gooding, who went from being mayor to Idaho governor to ending his days in 1928 as U.S. Senator.

A straight shot east along the tracks brings you to **Shoshone** (pop. 1,398), another ranching and railroad center—with Amtrak service—and a number of buildings that have been constructed from local volcanic rock. Though it's a fairly timeworn place, Shoshone looks great at sunset, when its steel water tower glows and places like the neon-signed **Manhattan Cafe** (208/886-2142), along the railroad tracks, look especially appealing.

If you're hungry, thirsty, or low on gas, be sure to fill up here, as services are rare between Shoshone and Arco, 75 miles to the east.

Shoshone sits at the junction where US-26 crosses Hwy-75, which runs north to Sun Valley, and US-93, which runs south to Twin Falls (see page 131). For more on our **Border to Border** route, see pages 106–157.

Craters of the Moon National Monument

Described by writer Washington Irving as a place "where nothing meets the eye but a desolate and awful waste, where no grass grows nor water runs, and where nothing is to be seen but lava," the vast tracts of volcanic fields known as **Craters of the Moon National Monument** aren't totally devoid of life—they just look that way. Covering some 60,000 acres at an average altitude of 6,000 feet, the lava fields are but a small part of the extensive Snake River volcanic plain, which forms a 100-mile-wide swath across southern Idaho. The rounded cinder cones and acres of glassy black stone were formed between 2,000 and 15,000 years ago, and, despite first impressions, they do shelter a wide variety of plant and animal life, from pines and prickly pears to various raptors and a population of mule deer. May and June see abundant wildflowers, and temperatures stay cool, so it's altogether an ideal time to visit.

Easily accessible from a seven-mile loop road that runs south from US-20/26, the most striking remnants of the region's volcanic activity are the huge cones that rise above the generally flat plain. These huge knolls of lightweight cinder give great views of the overall area, but they're not volcanoes, and there's no crater to look down into. The closest Craters of the Moon comes to real craters are the **spatter cones** midway along the loop, where the deep openings are often filled with snow late into summer. The most interesting section of the monument is at the end of the loop, where—provided you have a flashlight—you can wander through sub-surface **lava tubes** like Beauty Cave and Indian Tunnel. At 830 feet, Indian Tunnel is the longest in the park.

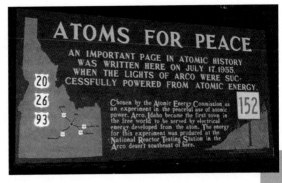

For further information or to pick up the useful park brochures, stop by the small **visitors center** (daily; 208/527-3257), where you ought to pay the entry fee. A basic, 52-site **campground** offers water and restrooms but no showers, hookups, or dump station.

Arco

"The first city in the free world to be powered by nuclear-generated electricity," **Arco** (pop. 1,026) sits on the banks of the Big Lost River, so-called because it disappears a few miles downstream, vanishing into the volcanic labyrinth of the Snake River plain. Arco itself, a crossroads town straddling

*Northwest of Arco, the highest peak in Idaho, 12,662-foot **Mt. Borah**, was epicenter of a powerful 1983 earthquake that registered 7.3 on the Richter scale.*

the junction of US-20 and US-93, is a handy stop for food (try **Pickles Place**, at 440 S. Front Street on the east side of town), gas, or supplies. All over town, signs and historic plaques point out Arco's connections with the early days of nuclear power.

If you have more than a passing interest in nuclear fission, you'll want to check out the anonymous-looking redbrick structure 18 miles southeast of Arco on the south side of US-20, which holds the inoperative remains of **Experimental Breeder Reactor Number One**. Sitting at the edge of the massive Idaho National Engineering Lab (INEL), the deactivated reactor is open for self-guided **tours** (daily in summer only; free; 208/526-0050), on which you can get an up-close glimpse of the turbines and control room, even the fuel rods that first produced nuclear power on December 20, 1951. (To put all this in context, the first reaction produced enough electricity to power four small lightbulbs.) By 1953 the reactor here was finally able to produce more power through nuclear reactions than it consumed, a much more important achievement. Some 50 years later, INEL is now one of the nation's de facto repositories for nuclear waste, and will remain so for the foreseeable future—12 million years or so, by some estimates.

Idaho Falls

Taking its name from the wide but short waterfall completely tamed to form a pleasant green lake at the center of town, **Idaho Falls** (pop. 50,730), at the junction of US-20 and I-15, is a busy, big city with a very attractive, Middle American downtown set along the banks of the Snake River. Grain elevators and stockyards stand along the railroad tracks, train whistles blow throughout the

Summer fun in Idaho Falls: an **Idaho Falls Chukars** Pioneer League baseball game (208/522-8363), at McDermott Field along West Broadway (US-20), west of I-15. Games are broadcast on **KUPI 980 AM**.

night, and all manner of neon signs line the highways, offering a concentrated dose of rural Americana, while its hotels, supermarkets, and restaurants make Idaho Falls a handy last stop before heading on to the diverse wilderness areas that rise to the north, east, and west. Apart from the chance to wander around a business district that's hardly changed since 1956, you can stroll along the waterfront park, feeding the geese or just watching the waters tumble over the weirs.

Though it's rich in small town Americana, Idaho Falls also has a few pockets of big-city sophistication, no doubt thanks to the well-paid engineers employed at INEL west of town, and the skiers bound for Grand Targhee in the mountains to the east. Cafés and bakeries crowd together around Park Avenue and A Street downtown, serving a wide enough range of pastries, coffees, and sandwiches to suit any palate. For a place to stay, try the well-placed **Red Lion Inn** (208/523-800 or 800/432-1005), overlooking the falls at 475 River Parkway.

Rexburg

First settled by Mormon homesteaders in the 1880s, the town of **Rexburg** (pop. 17,257) still has a pronounced Mormon feel, but it is best known for the near-disaster of 1976, when the huge Teton Dam collapsed and unleashed eight billion gallons of floodwater onto the valley below. Fortunately, engineers noticed the warning signs and were able to evacuate the area beforehand; though damage was extensive, fatalities were few. Housed in the basement of the old Mormon tabernacle, the **Teton Flood Museum** (closed Sun.; $2; 208/359-3063), at 51 W. Center Street across from city hall, has the usual displays of quilts and cattle brands tracing the history of the region, plus a large section devoted to the great flood of 1976. A short film shows the actual collapse of the dam. There's also an exhibit on the terrible forest fires that burned much of Yellowstone National Park in 1988.

West of US-20, 15 miles north of Idaho Falls, the sleepy town of **Rigby** played a hugely important role in the development of contemporary culture: It was here that young **Philo T. Farnsworth**, the inventor of the cathode-ray television, grew up and went to school.

From Rexburg, US-20 runs northeast through the **Targhee National Forest**, climbing from the Snake River plain along Henry's Fork River—one of the country's top fishing streams, loaded with cutthroat trout as big as 10 pounds—into the heart of the Rocky Mountains. On the Idaho–Montana border, 7,072-foot Targhee Pass marks the **Continental Divide**.

Rising to the east of Idaho Falls, the serrated crest of the Grand Tetons stands out along the Idaho–Wyoming border. Though the US-20 route through Yellowstone National Park is closed in winter, you can get across the Rockies by detouring via US-26 through Jackson Hole, Wyoming—a beautiful route.

West Yellowstone, Montana

Western gateway to Yellowstone National Park, the Montana town of **West Yellowstone** (pop. 1,177; elev. 6,667) sits just over the Idaho border, offering all the motels, gas stations, and cafés you could ever want, plus a lot more. The primary access point for early tourists visiting Yellowstone on the Union Pacific Railroad, West Yellowstone preserves a great deal of old-style tourist facilities. The rustic old railroad station is now the engaging **Museum of the Yellowstone** ($6; 406/646-1100), and the town's many roadside motels (there are more motel rooms than residents!) display a mouthwatering assembly of nifty neon signs while still serving the food-and-fuel needs of today's travelers.

> In 1808, when fur-trapper **John Colter** described the scenes he saw in what's now Yellowstone—gurgling, spouting steam vents, prismatic pools of sulfurous boiling water—nobody believed him, and many thought he was mad, calling the fantastic land "Colter's Hell."

There's also a huge **IMAX theater** ($9; 406/646-4100), at 101 S. Canyon Street, in case you prefer the Memorex version to real-life Yellowstone. The theater (recently offering a somewhat surreal triple bill: *Yellowstone, Wolves,* and *Michael Jordan!*) is adjacent to a contentious wildlife theme park that intends to collect "problem" bears and wolves and put them on display—rather than kill them as is currently done.

West Yellowstone's main drag, Canyon Street (US-20), is lined by cafés and Wild West souvenir shops. The excellent **Book Peddler** (406/646-9358), at 106 Canyon Street, boasts an espresso and sandwich bar along with a wide array of fiction and nonfiction titles.

Most of West Yellowstone's enviable collection of historic motels are off the main highway frontage, so drive around the back streets and take your pick; the Arts-and-Crafts-style **Stage Coach Inn** ($50–150; 406/646-7381), at Madison and Dunraven Streets, has been charming visitors for more than half a century.

WYOMING

Most visitors to Wyoming have one thing in mind: Yellowstone National Park. This amazing spectacle, which our route takes us right through, is deservedly the state's premier visitor attraction, but the rest of Wyoming holds a surprising variety of interesting places, from Wild West cow towns to the wide open spaces of the Great Plains.

The least populated of the 50 states, Wyoming has more wide-open space than just about anywhere else. If you like the idea of traveling for miles and miles without seeing anyone, then coming upon a crossroads outpost where the post office shares space with the general store and gas station, you'll want to take the time to explore Wyoming.

Yellowstone National Park

Sitting astride the Continental Divide, high up in the northern Rockies at the northwest corner of Wyoming, **Yellowstone National Park** is one of the true wonders of the natural world. A veritable greatest hits of Mother Nature, the park is packed full of burbling geysers, magnificent canyons, raging waterfalls, and still-wild wildlife. The country's (and the world's) oldest national park, established in 1872, Yellowstone was first explored by frontiersman John Colter, who passed through in 1808; it's also one of the largest parts of the lower 48 states never to be farmed or fenced.

You probably already know something about what Yellowstone has in store for you: The one essential Yellowstone sight is **Old Faithful Geyser,** in the

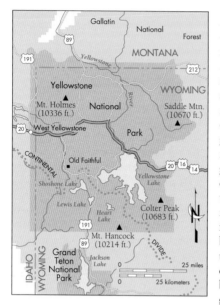

southwest quarter of the park. One of the world's most famous natural features, Old Faithful is known for its clockwork eruptions, in which some 5,000 gallons of boiling water are sent 150 feet into the air, forming a solid, steamy column. Hundreds of people line up around the geyser waiting for it to blow, and rangers are able to predict it with a good deal of accuracy—the visitors center will list the expected times of the day's eruptions, which occur roughly every 75 minutes and last for another two to five minutes. In between eruptions, take the chance to wander around to the dozens of other features in the Old Faithful basin, including a number of other geysers (the Old Faithful area has the greatest concentration in the world), as well as colorful pools and other geothermal features, all linked by well-marked boardwalks and trails along the Firehole River.

The other main sight is the **Grand Canyon of the Yellowstone River,** where a pair of powerful waterfalls cascade into a 20-mile-long, half-mile-wide, and 1,000-foot-deep canyon of eroding yellow stone. Parking areas line the north and south rims of the canyon, allowing access to trails along the edge of the gorge. A personal favorite is **Uncle Tom's Trail,** leaving from the south side of the falls. More a staircase than a trail, this route zig-zags steeply down the walls of the canyon, bringing you face to face with the falls. Farther along the south rim is **Artist's Point,** which gives the classic view of the canyon. Also, two "**Brink of the Falls**" routes lead from the north side down to where the waters plunge.

Along with these two main attractions, there are many more sights to see, so take the time to visit the visitors centers, talk to the rangers, and find out what other wonders await. Covering a roughly 100- by 100-mile square, Yellowstone is a big place, plenty big enough to absorb the many tourists who come here during the peak summer season. Whatever you do, don't try to see it all in a day or two; if time is tight, choose one or two places and spend all your time there. Get out of the car, hike a few trails, and enjoy.

Old Faithful

Yellowstone Practicalities

Yellowstone's visitor facilities book up well in advance (sometimes up to a year), so if you want the complete experience, it's best to plan ahead as much as possible. **Accommodations** are the main thing you ought to sort out as soon as you can, as bed space is at a premium. The first choice is the wonderful **Old Faithful Inn**, next to the famous geyser. Built of split logs and huge boulders and exuding rough-hewn elegance, this delightful inn was completed in 1904 and fully renovated in 2005. Rooms in the old lodge, without baths, start at about $45; a newer wing has larger rooms and modern conveniences for $100–250 a night—some of these rooms have Old Faithful views. Another historic lodge, at Yellowstone Lake, is plusher but architecturally less distinctive; a half dozen other inns, cabins, and motels are scattered around the park. All rooms are handled through a central service (307/344-7311), which also handles reservations for the park's campgrounds, most of which operate on a first-come, first-served basis and fill up by noon daily.

Places to eat include the usual cafeteria-type restaurants at all of the park's hotels and lodges, plus a truly remarkable restaurant at the classic Old Faithful Inn, with a three-story log-cabin dining room and food that's as good as it gets in the national parks.

You'll find gas stations, gift shops, and general stores at just about every road junction in the park. There are **ranger stations** at most main features, and large **visitors centers** at Mammoth Hot Springs, Old Faithful, and the Canyon. For further information, contact **park headquarters** (307/344-7381).

One rarely mentioned aspect of life in Yellowstone is the profusion of bison (aka buffalo) droppings: Everywhere you look—all around the geysers, hot springs, etc.—they've made their mark. And though they may seem placid, bison can be dangerous, so keep your distance.

Note that the Yellowstone visitor season is very short—roads are usually blocked by snow from November until April, May, or even June. To find out current road conditions, phone 307/344-7381. US-26 is a year-round alternative through the Grand Tetons and Jackson Hole.

Between Yellowstone and Cody, US-20 drops steeply through lovely **Wapiti Valley**. Teddy Roosevelt supposedly called this area "the most scenic 50 miles in America." Another scenic route, the **Beartooth Highway** (US-212), runs northeast to Red Lodge, Montana, and was rated by Charles Kuralt as "the most beautiful roadway in America."

BUFFALO BILL'S WILD WEST
CONGRESS, ROUGH RIDERS OF THE WORLD.

MISS ANNIE OAKLEY,
THE PEERLESS LADY WING-SHOT.

Cody

Eastern gateway to Yellowstone National Park, and an enjoyable overnight stop in its own right, **Cody** is a self-conscious frontier town and a busy center for local ranching and wood products industries. The outskirts are lined by Wal-Marts, Kmarts, and all the fast-food franchises you could name, but the town center along Sheridan Avenue (US-20) still looks like the Wild West town Cody was built to be.

Sitting on the Bighorn Basin plains at the foot of the mountains, Cody was founded in the late 1890s by Wild West showman "Buffalo Bill" Cody, whose name graces most everything in town, including the **Buffalo Bill Historical Center** (daily in summer, closed Mon. rest of the year, closed Dec.–Feb.; $15; 307/587-4771). One of the country's great museums, and certainly the best in the Wild West, this place tells all you could want to know about the American frontier. The center is divided into five main collections. First stop should be Buffalo Bill's home, which was moved here from LeClair, Iowa in 1933; then move on to the Buffalo Bill Museum, which includes a battery of movies and artifacts from his famous "Wild West Show," a circus-like extravaganza that toured the world. The Whitney Gallery of American Art, one of the country's most extensive collections of western art, displays important works by George Catlin, Thomas Moran, Albert Bierstadt, and Frederic Remington, plus some fine contemporary works. Gun freaks will enjoy the Cody Firearms Museum, which displays more than 5,000 historic weapons. Saving the biggest and best for last, the Plains Indian Museum has an amazing collection of art and artifacts created by the diverse Plains Indian peoples, from beadwork dresses to a reconstructed Sioux tepee. Pride of place is given to an extraordinary buffalo robe painted with scenes of the legendary Battle of Little Big Horn.

At the west edge of Cody is **Trail Town** (daily mid-May–mid-Sept.; $6; 307/587-5302), a low-key but engaging collection of old buildings moved here from northwestern Wyoming and southern Montana. Wagons, buffalo robes, and other relics are on display. A memorial cemetery holds the remains of Wild West figures, including Jeremiah Johnson, played by Robert Redford in the 1972 movie named for the man.

The **Cody Nite Rodeo** (nightly at 8:30pm; $14; 307/587-5155) at the huge rodeo grounds at the west end of town has been held June–September since 1938, making it the nation's longest-running rodeo. Get a seat in the "Buzzard's Roost," close to the chutes where the cowboys mount those bulls and buckin' broncos.

Cody Practicalities

You'll find most of Cody's good places to eat on Sheridan Avenue, the main drag. **Silver Dollar Bar and Grill** (307/527-7666), at 1313 Sheridan Avenue, serves great burgers and bottles of beer. A block away at 1227 Sheridan Avenue, the **Proud Cut Saloon** (307/527-6905) has a range of sandwiches at lunch and great steaks at dinner.

The historic **Irma Hotel** ($50 in winter, $75 and up in summer; 307/587-4221), at 1192 Sheridan Avenue, was built by Buffalo Bill and named for his daughter and features a lovely cherrywood bar given by Queen Victoria, and an evening gunfight on the front porch. At the heart of Cody at 1701 Sheridan Avenue, **Buffalo Bill Cabins** ($100 and up; 307/587-5544) started life in 1914 as a cowboy camp-out, and has grown into a full-service family resort.

There are also lots of motels along US-20, ranging from under $50 to over $150 depending upon seasonal demand; for help, contact the **visitors center** (307/587-2297), located at 836 Sheridan Avenue.

> Though Buffalo Bill gets most of the publicists' ink, another famous Cody figure is the abstract impressionist "action painter" **Jackson Pollock,** who was born here.

Meeteetse

East of Cody, Hwy-120, a prettier alternative to US-20, angles south over the rugged foothill badlands of the Absaroka (ab-SOR-ka) Mountains, historic homeland of the Crow Indians but now equal parts cattle ranches and oil wells. Thirty miles along this lonely highway brings you to **Meeteetse** (pop. 375), one of the oldest settlements in central Wyoming and still much the same after 125 years. The broad Greybull River—and an occasional cattle drive—runs right through town, which still retains wooden boardwalks and hitching posts for cowboys' horses.

Besides being wonderfully evocative of an earlier era, Meeteetse also has a great museum documenting diverse aspects of the region's past: the **Charles J. Belden Museum** (daily 9 AM–5 PM; free; 307/868-2264) at 1947 State Street, which holds an extraordinary collection of cowboy photography that includes the first "Marlboro Man" ads, shot on the nearby Pitchfork Ranch by Mr. Belden, a local rancher and commercial photographer. The Belden Museum also has the stuffed remains of an 8-foot-tall **grizzly bear,** one of the largest ever found in the area.

Along with an old but fully stocked general store, tiny Meeteetse has a few restaurants and the **Oasis Motel** ($35–50; 307/868-2551), at 1702 State Street, with camping and a Conestoga wagon.

> Aviator **Amelia Earhart** was having a ranch home built for her near Meeteetse along the Greybull River in 1934, but construction stopped after she disappeared on her round-the-world flight.

Legend Rock

One of Wyoming's most significant collections of petroglyphs, **Legend Rock** contains over 250 images dating back some 2,000 years, carved into sandstone cliffs in the oil-rich foothills of the Owl Creek Mountains. To get there, follow US-120 for 21 miles from Thermopolis, or 33 miles from Meeteetse, then turn south at the Hamilton Dome turnoff and follow the dirt road for eight miles to a locked gate. The petroglyphs are a quarter-mile beyond the gate. The Thermopolis **visitors center** has detailed information.

Thermopolis

Despite the highfalutin' resonance of its classical-sounding name, **Thermopolis** (pop. 3,172) is a sleepy little retirement town, surrounded by red rock canyons and centered among a remarkable set of natural hot springs. The land was bought in 1896 from local Shoshone chief Washakie on the understanding that the spring waters be kept open to the public, white and Indian alike. This spring, which flows at a rate of 4 million gallons of 135°F water daily, was the basis of Wyoming's first state park, Hot Springs State Park, which still covers the east bank of the Bighorn River. A state-run **bathhouse** (daily; free) has showers and changing rooms—you can rent towels and bathing suits for a nominal charge. There is also a pair of commercial enterprises in the park—the **Hot Springs Water Park** and **Star Plunge**—with water slides, saunas, and so on.

Across the river in the center of town, the enjoyable **Hot Springs Historical Museum** (daily; $4; 307/864-5183), at 700 Broadway, has a wide-ranging collection of historic photos, farming and oil-drilling implements, and even the cherrywood bar from the Hole-in-the-Wall Saloon where Butch and Sundance supposedly bellied up for a drink or two. The final big draw in Thermopolis—and I mean BIG—is the **Wyoming Dinosaur Center** (daily; $6; 307/864-5522 or 800/455-3466), on the east side of town at 100 Carter Ranch Road. Follow the green dinosaur footprints from the center of town to a paleontology dig that's open to the public; finds on display include a full T. rex and a Triceratops.

The friendly Thermopolis **visitors center** (307/864-3192 or 800/786-6772), in the same building as the Hot Springs Historical Museum at 700 Broadway, has listings of motels and campgrounds and other information on the area.

Wind River Canyon

South of Thermopolis, US-20 winds through **Wind River Canyon**, one of the most memorable drives in a state of memorable drives. The 2,500-foot-deep canyon, with the highway on one side of the broad river and the railroad on the other, reveals millions of years of sedimentary rock. As you drive along heading south, you reach deeper and deeper into the earth; each layer is labeled with signs explaining its geological age and significance, with the oldest layers dating back to the Precambrian era, some 2.5 billion years ago.

Due in part to the visual effect of the uplifted sedimentary layers, the river at times gives the illusion of flowing uphill; this may explain why Indians and early explorers thought there were two distinct rivers, and called the canyon itself the "Wedding of the Waters." The river still has two distinct names: Upstream from Wind River Canyon, it is called the Wind River; downstream from the canyon, it's called the Bighorn River.

Driving along US-20 between the Wind River Canyon and Shoshoni, keep an eye out for the many pronghorn antelope that play on the rolling rangeland.

At the south end of the river, Boysen Reservoir, a popular place for fishing and waterskiing, backs up behind Boysen Dam, which was completed in 1961. The land west of the reservoir forms the two-million-acre **Wind River Indian Reservation**, home to descendants of the Eastern Shoshone and Northern Arapahoe tribes; a woman thought by some to be Sacagawea (the Shoshone guide of Lewis and Clark fame) is buried on the reservation, along the Wind River near Fort Washakie.

Jackson Hole

In winter, Yellowstone is closed to cars, and the only road kept open is US-212 between Gardiner and Cooke City, Montana, at the northern edge of the park. But if you're here anytime but summer, don't despair: US-26, a very different but still unforgettable route, is open year-round, running south of Yellowstone between Idaho Falls and Casper, through the Wild West town of Jackson Hole and the spectacular scenery of Grand Teton National Park.

Climbing up from Idaho Falls along the banks of the Snake River, US-26 crosses into Wyoming on a sinuously scenic route, past cottonwood trees and whitewater-running kayakers, before linking up with north–south US-89. The tourist mecca of Jackson Hole, one of the country's most popular "wilderness" destinations, takes its name from the main town, **Jackson** (pop. 8,647), which sits at the center of a broad, mountain-ringed valley. Drawing upwards of 35,000 visitors on a summer day, Jackson isn't exactly an idyllic spot, but it has managed to retain its Wild West character, especially in the few blocks around the lively Town Square. Here, false-fronted buildings linked by a raised wooden sidewalk hold upscale boutiques and the wonderfully kitsch likes of the **Million Dollar Cowboy Bar,** on the west side of the square, a huge and always lively hangout with silver dollars implanted in the bar top and real leather saddles instead of bar stools.

Jackson has many very good (and very expensive) restaurants, like the art deco–style **Cadillac Grill** (307/733-3279), which has grilled ahi tuna and similarly sophisticated fare on the Town Square at 55 N. Cache. The Cadillac Grill shares space with Jackson's best burger spot, **Billy's Giant Burgers,** which burger-loving Bill Clinton rated as the best he'd ever tasted. Jackson caters to so many visitors that accommodations, however plentiful, can be booked solid in summer. There's something for everyone here: campgrounds and RV parks, B&Bs and highway motels—including a Motel 6 and the nifty log cabins of **Wagon Wheel Village** ($90 and up; 307/733-2357), at 435 N. Cache Street—and $4,000-a-week guest ranches.

The Jackson Hole area, which suffered from terrible wildfires in the summer of 2001, is one of the country's most exclusive winter resorts, with world-class ski areas including **Grand Targhee** (800/827-4433), powder-hound heaven on the Idaho border; and **Jackson Hole Ski Resort** (800/450-0477), which boasts the longest vertical drop in the United States: an astounding 4,139 feet!

Grand Teton National Park

North of Jackson, south of Yellowstone, the silver peaks of **Grand Teton National Park** cut into the sky, their slopes offering some of the best hiking and mountaineering in the lower 48 states. US-26/89 runs right along the base of the mountains,

From Grand Teton National Park, US-89 runs north to the heart of Yellowstone National Park.

giving grand views and tempting travelers to stop and explore. West of the main highway, Teton Park Road winds past Jenny Lake, where you can board a boat ($5) and ride across to a short trail that leads up past Hidden Falls to **Inspiration Point,** at the foot of 13,770-foot Grand Teton.

Details on the abundant hiking, skiing, fishing, and other recreational activities, as well as camping and lodging options, are available by contacting the main Grand Teton National Park **visitors center** (307/739-3600), a mile west of US-26 on Teton Park Road.

Dubois and the National Bighorn Sheep Center

Between Casper and the Grand Tetons, US-26 is a mostly scenic highway, crossing the Continental Divide at 9,644-foot Togwotee Pass before winding along the Wind River through the multi-colored badlands that surround the town of **Dubois** (pop. 1,100; dew-BOYS). A low-key ranching and logging center that's still in its infancy as a tourist destination, Dubois does have one unique attraction: the **National Bighorn Sheep Center** (daily; $2; 307/455-3429), right on US-26 at the west edge of town, documenting the life and times of the thousands of bighorn sheep that congregate in the winter months around Whisky Mountain, south of Dubois. At the center of Dubois, another unique sight is inside historic **Welty's General Store** (free; 307/455-2377), on US-26 at 113 W. Ramshorn, where you can see a Colt .44 revolver with the name "Butch Cassidy" carved in the handle; Butch lived and rustled horses here back in the 1880s.

On US-26, 18 miles west of Dubois, a roadside monument remembers the work of the "tie hacks," who, from the 1870s until World War II, cut down lodgepole pines to form railroad ties.

There are a few saloons, steak houses, and fly-fishing shops, and one great place to stay in Dubois: the log-cabin **Twin Pines Lodge** ($50 and up; 307/455-2600), at 218 Ramshorn.

Shoshoni

Named for the Shoshone Indians who once held sway over this part of the Great Plains, the forlorn town of **Shoshoni** (pop. 635) sits at the junction of US-20 and US-26, at the southeast edge of the Boysen Reservoir. Though it doesn't look like much if you just race through, Shoshoni does have one excellent reason to stop: the **Yellowstone Drug Store** (307/876-2539), 127 Main Street, at the center of Shoshoni's block-long business district. It sells the state's best milk shakes and ice cream floats at the ancient-looking soda fountain.

The Mushroom, Hell's Half Acre, Wyoming.

Between Shoshoni and Casper, the only attraction worth mentioning is the odd geology of **Hell's Half Acre,** a 300-acre concentration of grotesquely eroded stone south of US-20 amid the arid badlands landscape. (Scenes in the movie *Starship Troopers* were filmed here in 1996.)

Casper

Like other towns in southern Wyoming, Casper began as a way station on the many frontier trails that followed the North Platte River, first as a ferry crossing (log rafts were run by Salt Lake City–bound Mormons from 1847 to 1852; non-Mormons were charged $1.50) and later toll bridges, culminating with an elaborate plank bridge built by Louis Guinard in 1859. The second-largest city in Wyoming, only slightly smaller than capital city Cheyenne, **Casper** (pop. 49,644) is still dependent upon passing trade; its key location along the I-25 corridor has enabled Casper to survive the boom-and-bust variations in its other main industry, oil.

Most of the places of interest in Casper (which was originally spelled Caspar) have to do with the westward migration. **Fort Caspar** (daily; free; 307/235-8462), west of downtown off Hwy-220, is a New Deal–era replica of the original rough log fort and Pony Express station. There's also a reconstruction of the Mormon-operated ferry, and displays of pioneer artifacts in the small museum. Just off I-25 exit 189 at 1501 Poplar Street, the new **National Trails Interpretive Center** (daily; $6; 307/261-7700) is designed to resemble a Conestoga wagon, and exhibits inside tell the stories of the 3,623 miles of historic pioneer trails all over the western United States preserved under the auspices of the federal Bureau of Land Management (BLM).

Casper was the heart of the oil fields that led to the notorious **Teapot Dome** scandal of the 1920s, in which Secretary of the Interior Albert Fall went to prison for accepting a $100,000 bribe. It is also the hometown of oil magnate Vice President **Dick Cheney** and his high school sweetheart (and wife), **Lynne**.

While the rest of the city has a definite roughneck feel, downtown Casper is also rich in 1920s Americana, with a pair of great old movie theaters, rusty neon signs and art deco storefronts, plus one of the country's largest cowboy clothing stores: **Lou Taubert's** (307/234-2500) has over 10,000 pairs of boots and three floors of blue jeans, rhinestones, and other essential range-riding gear at 125 E. 2nd Street.

East of downtown, the one place you really ought to visit is the **Nicolaysen Art Museum** (closed Sun. & Mon.; free; 307/235-5247), housed in an imaginatively converted old power plant at 400 E. Collins Street, along the railroad tracks. The finest contemporary art museum in Wyoming, the Nicolaysen also has a permanent collection of Plains Indian arts and crafts, plus a hands-on art center for children.

The Pioneer League **Casper Rockies** (307/232-1111) play baseball at community-built Mike Lansing Field, north of I-25 via the Poplar Street exit. A 500-foot home run here would end up in the North Platte River. Games are broadcast on **KWYY 95.5 FM**.

On the west side of downtown, **First Street Bakers** (307/472-0255), at 260 W. 1st Street, has good coffees, teas, and baked goods. Casper's accommodation options along the I-25 frontage include most of the national chains, where rooms run $40–75.

Glenrock

Midway between Casper and Douglas along the south bank of the North Platte River, **Glenrock** (pop. 2,231) was a vital rest stop and supply station on the Oregon and other emigrant trails. Several downtown buildings have endured since its heyday, when Glenrock was known as Deer Creek Station and some

Jackalopes 'R' Us

Traveling around the Great Plains, you're bound to come across all sorts of oversized wildlife—giant fish, giant cows, giant bison—plus some more that defy anatomical description. Most of the latter—fur-bearing trout, in particular—are seen primarily on post-cards, but at least one species can usually be found mounted on the wall of any self-respecting saloon or taxi-dermist's shop: the jackalope. So rare that one has never been seen in the wild, the jackalope has the body of a jackrabbit and the horns of an antelope; dozens of ex-amples are displayed around the Wyoming town of Douglas, with the "world's largest" standing over eight feet head-to-tail in Jackalope Square at 3rd and Center Streets downtown. The enigmatic creature is also cele-brated during Jackalope Days in the middle of June.

20,000 migrants came through each year, many of them camping overnight at the "rock in the glen" on the west side of town, where a sandstone boulder still holds the names of passing pioneers. Nowadays Glenrock is known for its mas-sive coal-fired power plant, one of the largest in the country.

Between Casper and Glenrock, US-26 winds along the river, but between Glenrock and Douglas the old road has been replaced by the I-25 freeway.

Douglas

Situated far enough off I-25 to retain its Wild West cowboy character, the en-joyable town of **Douglas** (pop. 5,288) was founded in 1886 across the river from Fort Fetterman, which for the previous 25 years had protected traffic on the old Oregon and Bozeman trails along the North Platte River. The setting of Owen Wister's genre-inventing Western novel *The Virginian,* and more recently birthplace of that other Wild West icon, the **jackalope** (see sidebar), Douglas is a quietly picturesque small town with a wild history, and a great place to break your long-distance road trip.

Douglas's own KKTY 99.3 FM (1470 AM) plays local news, country hits, and Colorado Rockies baseball games.

The **Wyoming State Fairgrounds**, along the river at the west end of Center Street, host a livestock-frenzied fair at the end of August, and also features the year-round **Pioneer Mu-seum** (Mon.–Fri. only; free; 307/358-9288), packed full of artifacts from the late 1800s—everything from rifles and a roulette table to fos-sils and farm implements. It also houses a Sioux-style hide tepee made for the movie *Dances with Wolves.* The wilder side of Douglas history is perhaps most vividly apparent in tombstones in the **cemetery** on the east edge of town at the end of Pine Street, where legendary cattle rustler George Pike is interred be-neath a marker that reads, in part:

> *Underneath this stone in eternal rest sleeps*
> *the wildest one of the wayward west.*

Lusk

A cattle-ranching and farming center, **Lusk** (pop. 1,500) is the largest town in the least-populated county in the country's least-populated state. It also boasts the only traffic light on US-20 between Douglas, Wyoming, and Chadron, Nebraska. And if those claims to fame don't make you want to stop, the **Stagecoach Museum** (closed Sun.; $2; 307/334-3444) at 322 S. Main Street definitely will, if only to see the sole authentic 1880s Cheyenne-Deadwood Stagecoach—the one Doris Day sang about in *Calamity Jane*. (The only other stagecoach from this legendary route is now in the Smithsonian.) Behind the museum building is another frontier icon—a one-room schoolhouse—and along US-20 at the east edge of town, a plaque points out a redwood water tower dating from 1886, when steam locomotives still chugged across the plains.

Lusk also has a good range of motels, including the **Best Western Covered Wagon Motel** ($60–90; 307/334-2530 or 800/341-8000), at 730 S. Main Street.

Guernsey: Oregon Trail

A worthwhile detour from Douglas or Lusk via I-15 and US-26 takes you 40-plus miles south to the town of **Guernsey** on the North Platte River, where you can visit two of the most evocative Oregon Trail historic sites. The Oregon Trail passed through along the south bank of the river, and a well-signed but otherwise undeveloped park, a mile south of town via Wyoming Avenue, holds the best surviving set of Oregon Trail **wagon ruts**, cut shoulder-deep in the soft sandstone. Nearby is a small obelisk marking the grave of an unfortunate pioneer, and three miles to the southeast along the same road, **Register Cliff** is carved with the names of over a thousand pioneers and explorers, many dating back to 1840–60, the heyday of the trail.

For maps and more details, contact the Guernsey **visitors center** (307/836-2715), on Wyoming Avenue a block south of US-26. **Fort Laramie National Historic Site**, another frontier landmark, is a dozen miles east of Guernsey via US-26.

A dozen miles west of Douglas, five miles south of I-25 via Natural Bridge Road, **Ayers Natural Bridge** arches 30 feet above La Prele Creek.

A marker on the south side of US-20, a mile east of Lusk, stands where US-20 intersects the **Texas Trail**—in the 1870s over 500,000 head of cattle were driven each year between Fort Worth and the open range of Wyoming and Montana along this route.

Oregon Trail wagon tracks across Guernsey

NEBRASKA

In its 454-mile trek across Nebraska, US-20 passes through a surprising variety of landscapes. In the west, the highway skirts the edge of the huge and desolate **Sand Hills,** where North America's largest system of sand dunes underlies a grassy pastoral scene. Across the midsection, the road runs parallel to the broad Niobrara River, one of the few rivers in the Great Plains not blocked behind a dam, before reaching the bluffs above the Missouri River.

One of the last reaches of the country to be settled and domesticated, northern Nebraska is still sparsely populated, and looks like the Great Plains are *supposed* to look. Towns are few and far between, and come and go in the proverbial blink of an eye; the rolling ranch lands are marked every mile or so by spinning Aermotor windmills pumping up water for wandering cattle herds, while historical plaques point out the sites where, barely a century ago, cowboys rode and Indians did battle with the U.S. Cavalry. Besides being rich in Wild West history—and in prehistoric fossil beds—the region has a strong literary tradition, thanks to writers such as Mari Sandoz and John G. Neihardt. All in all, few corners of the country pay back time spent with as much interest as does northern Nebraska; hard to believe, perhaps, but true.

Nebraska publishes a handy free booklet about US-20's route across the state. Copies are available at most visitors centers, or through the Nebraska US-20 Association (402/582-3798), R.R. 1, Box 218, Plainview, NE 68769.

Harrison and Agate Fossil Beds National Monument

The US-20 highway alignment through Harrison was still unpaved as recently as 1941.

Just over the Wyoming border, the tiny town of **Harrison** is an attractive wide-spot-in-the-road, worth a stop to sample the huge (up to two-pound!) burgers and silky milk shakes at **Sioux Sundries** (308/668-2577), at the corner of Main and

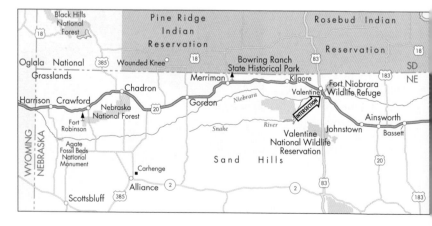

2nd Streets. On the banks of the Niobrara River 23 miles south of Harrison, the **Agate Fossil Beds National Monument** (daily; $5 per car; 308/668-2211) contains the 20-million-year-old remains of bison-sized pigs, twin-horned proto-rhinos, and other vanished creatures.

Fort Robinson

Fort Robinson (308/665-2919), 30 miles from the Wyoming border, was established in 1874 to control the 15,000 restless natives of the Red Cloud and Pine Ridge Sioux Indian agencies. Now a state park, and planted with groves of mature trees where 100 years ago all was grassland prairie, Fort Robinson has perhaps the most tragic and uncomfortable history of all the many old forts on the Wild West frontier: This is where the unarmed Sioux chief Crazy Horse was stabbed to death with bayonets while in the custody of the U.S. Army; it's where the controversial Red Cloud Treaty, in which the Sioux gave up the Black Hills, was signed; and it's where the last of the Cheyenne under Chief Dull Knife were killed in battle rather than transported south to a reservation in Oklahoma.

Knowing this history, it can be hard to take Fort Robinson as the enjoyable respite it is today. The hundreds of hardwood trees make it an oasis on the generally treeless plains, and the whitewashed wooden barracks, many now converted to cultural centers and museums, give it the air of a college campus—especially on summer weekends, when the park turns into a living history museum, complete with cookouts and evening melodramas.

The only part of the park open year-round is the **Fort Robinson Museum** in the old headquarters building, with full displays on the fort's history, plus walking-tour maps of the entire post. Accommodations are offered in the officers' quarters, and there are many good camping spots.

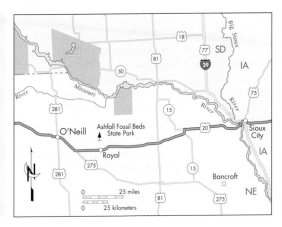

Crawford

Three miles east of Fort Robinson, **Crawford** has settled into a sedate life as a ranching and farming center. Pines and cottonwoods line the White River at the foot of the weirdly eroded Legend Buttes, making a pretty scene. Even prettier are the **Oglala National Grasslands**, which start six miles north of Crawford via Hwy-2 and occupy

Buttes looking west, Crawford, Neb.

nearly 100,000 acres along the Nebraska–Wyoming–South Dakota borders. The grasslands are home to hawks, eagles, and antelope, and highlighted by the eerie landscape of **Toadstool Geological Park**, where ancient fossils can be found amongst weirdly eroded figures. The grasslands also protect an archaeological site known as the **Hudson-Meng Bison Bone Bed**, a shallow arroyo holding the enigmatic remains of over 600 bison, plus stone tools and arrowheads dating from approximately 10,000 years ago, and a small garden growing native, pre-conquest crops. For details on either place, contact the USFS **ranger station** (308/432-4475) in Chadron.

Chadron: Museum of the Fur Trade

The largest town in northwest Nebraska, **Chadron** (pop. 5,634) sits at the northern edge of the Sand Hills region, bounded by pine forests to the south and the Pine Ridge Sioux Reservation to the north, across the South Dakota border. The highway frontage along US-20 isn't especially inviting, but the two-block town center preserves its turn-of-the-20th-century character with sandstone and brick-fronted buildings along the south side of the still-used railroad tracks.

There's not a lot to do in Chadron, but it does make a handy base for trips north to the Pine Ridge lands and the Black Hills, or south to the marvelous Carhenge. Motels include a Best Western and a Super 8, but the most characterful place to stay is the **Old Main Street Inn** ($65–85; 308/432-3380), at 115 Main Street. Part old railroad hotel, part cozy B&B, the inn has rooms, a popular restaurant and saloon downstairs, and Chadron's only espresso machine. (In 1890, General Miles stayed at this hotel before heading north to massacre Sioux women and children at Wounded Knee.)

If you're anywhere nearby, don't miss the excellent **Museum of the Fur Trade** (daily June–Sept., by appointment rest of the year; $5; 308/432-3843), on US-20 three miles east of downtown Chadron. One of the great small museums in the United States, this privately run collection focuses on the material culture of the North American frontier. Its extensive displays bring to life the first few centuries of interaction between Native Americans and Europeans. Besides giving the overall historical context of the fur trade and its many related enterprises, the collection emphasizes the day-to-day realities of life on the Great Plains in the 18th and 19th centuries. Walls decked with weapons and bottles of whiskey (from the Americans), rum (from the English), and brandy (from the French) document the better-known aspects, but what captures your attention are the little things: packs of playing cards, a checkerboard—even a waterproof parka made out of seal intestines by the Inuit.

In 1893, Chadron's early boosters found a perfect way to get their town in the news: They sponsored a 1,000-mile horse race from Chadron to Chicago, which made front pages across the country. A plaque in front of the black-and-white **Blaine Hotel**, a block east of Main Street, marks the start of the race.

Mt. Rushmore, Crazy Horse, and Carhenge

Three of the nation's most distinctive outdoor sculptures stand along US-385 within a manageable drive from US-20. One is perhaps the best-known artwork in the United States: the giant presidential memorial at Mt. Rushmore. Roughly 100 miles north from Chadron, at the far eastern side of the beautiful Black Hills, Mt. Rushmore is graced by the 60-foot heads of four U.S. Presidents—Washington, Jefferson, Lincoln, and Teddy Roosevelt—carved into a granite peak. It's equal parts impressive monument and kitschy Americana, and one of those places you really have to see to believe.

On the way to Mt. Rushmore, be sure to stop and see the ambitious Crazy Horse Memorial, a work-in-progress along US-385 four miles north of Custer, South Dakota, which, when completed, will be over 500 feet tall and 600 feet long—10 times the size of Mt. Rushmore.

Another newer, less-famous monument to America sits in a flat field off US-385, outside the town of Alliance, 62 miles south of Chadron. Built in 1987 as part of a local family reunion, Carhenge is a giant-sized replica of the famous Druid ruin, Stonehenge; this one, however, is built entirely out of three dozen late-model American cars, stacked on top of one another to form a semi-circular temple.

Gordon: Mari Sandoz Country

The tiny town of **Gordon**, midway between Merriman and Chadron, is a typical northwestern Nebraska ranching town with a strong connection to the "Storycatcher of the Plains," Mari Sandoz (1896–1966), whose many books document the lives and times of the surrounding Sand Hills region. Sandoz, who wrote about growing up on a nearby ranch in her first book, the haunting classic *Old Jules,* captured the spirit and history of the Great Plains in her many works of fiction and nonfiction, all of which are available in the **Mari Sandoz Room** (closed Sun.; free; 308/282-9972), 117 Main Street, north of US-20 beyond the grain elevators and railroad tracks at the center of town. The **Sandoz**

In north-central Nebraska, an interesting radio alternative is the commercial-free music and news broadcast from the Pine Ridge reservation on KILI 90.1 FM—"The Voice of the Lakota Nation."

museum, which shares space with the Ad-Pad stationery store, has extensive displays of her personal effects, and free pamphlets describing a driving tour of Sandoz-related sites in the area. For aficionados of her work, a local woman, Sybil Berndt, offers guided **tours** (308/282-2133); and Mari Sandoz's sister, Caroline Sandoz Pifer, has a small museum and bookshop at her home, 20 miles south of Gordon via Hwy-27, then six miles east on a gravel road. For details and hours, phone 308/282-1687.

Gas stations line the US-20 frontage in Gordon, and the one-stop **Hacienda Motel** (308/282-1400), on the west side of town, has rooms and a popular restaurant and bar.

Merriman

In Merriman, a block south of US-20, a roadside display shows the many different cattle brands used by Sand Hills ranches.

East of Gordon, US-20 winds along the northern edge of the Sand Hills, coming within a few miles of the South Dakota border. The town of **Merriman** (pop. 151) may not look like much, but it does mark the turnoff north to the nearby **Arthur Bowring Sand Hills Ranch State Historical Park** (daily; $3 per car; 308/684-3428), a working cattle ranch preserved pretty much as it was at the turn of the 20th century. The site is lovely, with a sod house surrounded (in springtime, at least) by rolling green hills. A modern visitors center has displays on windmills and other facts of Sand Hills life, plus biographical displays on the politically powerful Bowring family, who lived and worked here from 1895 until 1985. To get there, head 1.3 miles north of town on Hwy-61, then two miles northeast following good signs.

Between Merriman and Valentine, US-20 passes through flyspeck former railroad towns including Kilgore (pop. 71), Crookston (pop. 99), and Cody (pop. 177).

Valentine marks the junction with US-83, **The Road to Nowhere,** which begins on page 160. The town and surroundings are fully described on pages 181–182.

Johnstown

In the village of **Johnstown,** 40 miles southeast of Valentine and eight miles west of Ainsworth, a block of wooden storefronts and boardwalks were gussied up as a backdrop for a TV production of Willa Cather's *O Pioneers!* Behind the contrived facades you'll find a dusty old general store, and a beer bar and pool hall complete with backyard privy.

Kilgore marks the dividing line between Central and Mountain time zones; adjust your clocks and watches accordingly.

On Norden Road, 16 miles north of Johnstown, the Nature Conservancy protects the 50,000-acre Niobrara Valley Preserve, which has both Sand Hills and riparian ecosystems. Self-guided trails wind through the preserve past a small but expanding herd of bison.

Ainsworth

Roughly the midway point of US-20's long cruise across Nebraska, **Ainsworth** (pop. 1,800) has something of an identity problem, if its slogans ("Welcome to the Middle of Nowhere" and "Where the Sandhills Meet the Niobrara") are any guide. Ainsworth also calls itself the state's "country music capital" and hosts a popular concert and festival in early August.

Ainsworth's **Middle of Nowhere Festival,** held in June, is celebrated with a Wild West–style trail ride and a black powder rendezvous—where "living history" fans re-enact the muzzle-loading, fur-trapping frontier era. For details on either of these events, contact the town's **visitors center** (402/387-2740).

Eat big burgers at **Big John's,** along US-20 at 1110 E. 4th Street, and stay the night at the tidy, white clapboard **Upper Room B&B** ($45–75; 402/387-0107), in a quiet location on the west side of town at 409 N. Wilson Street.

The grounds of Ainsworth's **Brown County Historical Museum** preserve the weatherbeaten shell of a tiny old filling station, with a vintage Phillips 66 pump, right on US-20.

O'Neill

East of Ainsworth, US-20 runs through an especially scenic section of the Sand Hills around the artsy hamlet of Bassett before following the Elkhorn River to the town of O'Neill, 66 miles downstream. Nebraska's official "Irish Capital," **O'Neill** (pop. 3,774) hosts a very popular St. Patrick's Day parade and celebration (the town paints shamrocks on the side of the police station and at the intersection of US-20 and US-281), but also has a fascinating history: The town was founded in 1874 by Irish settlers led by John O'Neill, who commanded a brigade of black infantrymen during the Civil War, and afterwards became involved in the Fenian invasions of still-British Canada.

Northeast Nebraska

Because it's a fascinating part of the country, fairly detailed coverage has been directed at the places along US-20 across most of northern Nebraska. The same, however, cannot be said of Nebraska's far northeast quarter, but there are a couple of interesting detours.

Six miles north of US-20 via Hwy-59, from a well-signed junction two miles west of the tiny village of Royal, you can watch paleontologists at work uncovering giant fossils at **Ashfall Fossil Beds State Park** (daily; $3 per car; 402/893-2000). Unusual for a fossil bed, the skeletons here are preserved completely intact because the original residents—including prehistoric herds of rhinoceros, camels, and saber-toothed deer—got caught in a volcanic eruption some 10 million years ago. Since the bones haven't been disturbed, you can get a clear sense of the creatures' size and the sheer numbers of their populations around a prehistoric watering hole.

When completed, the 321-mile-long **Cowboy Nature & Recreation Trail** will be the nation's longest rails-to-trail conversion, following the bed of the old Chicago and Northwestern Railroad along US-20 between Chadron and O'Neill. Major sections are already open, especially around Valentine.

If you want to learn more about the fascinating human histories and cultures of the Great Plains, head south of US-20 across the Winnebago and Omaha Indian Reservations to the tiny town of Bancroft, where the **John G. Neihardt Center** (daily; free; 402/648-3388) exhibits the personal collection of Nebraska's poet laureate and writer of the Native American classic *Black Elk Speaks.*

IOWA

US-20 cuts straight across the midsection of Iowa between the Missouri and the Mississippi Rivers, running along the invisible border that divides the flat, agricultural tableland that distinguishes the northern half of the state from the more heavily industrialized south.

The first industry here was lead mining in the 1840s, but the predominant activity these days is livestock raising. Cows and pigs feed on the abundant corn that grows in fields all along the highway. Popcorn is also a major crop.

More than on any other section of its cross-country trek, US-20 across Iowa is being "upgraded" into a fast four-lane freeway, so you may well want to consider alternate routes like old US-30, which preserves some fine stretches of the historic Lincoln Highway, the country's first transcontinental road.

Sioux City

The honey-producing and hog-butchering center of **Sioux City** (pop. 85,013) is not most people's idea of a vacation treat, but it does offer a few diversions to the road-tripping traveler. Grain elevators and huge brick warehouses fill the riverfront district, an immaculately restored City Hall dominates downtown, and the gorgeous brick and glass-block **Sioux City Art Center** (daily; free; 712/279-6272) at 2nd and Nebraska includes pieces by Grant Wood, Salvador Dali, David Hockney, and James McNeill Whistler. The **Sioux City Public Museum** (daily; free; 712/279-6174), a mile north of downtown at 2901 Jackson Street, fills an 1890s mansion with all the usual displays tracing the Native American, pioneer, and agricultural histories of the area.

Over 95 percent of Iowa is cultivated farmland—the highest percentage of any U.S. state.

Sioux City's favorite daughters are the sisters and advice columnists **Ann Landers** and **Abigail "Dear Abby" Van Buren**.

Lewis and Clark buffs will also want to stop south of Sioux City at the **Floyd Monument,** where a 100-foot stone obelisk marks the place where expedition member Sgt. Charles Floyd—the Corps of Discovery's only fatality—died of appendicitis

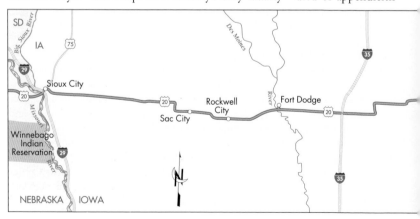

in August 1804, two months after setting off from St. Louis. Besides the historical homage, the site offers a great panorama of the Missouri River. Fact collectors might want to know that this little-known marker was the first official National Historic Landmark in the United States.

Sioux City Practicalities

Part of the general renaissance of American downtowns, the newly renovated, two-block section of town known as **Historic Fourth,** just east of the railroad yards around the intersection of 4th and Court Streets, boasts a large selection of restaurants, brewpubs, live-music clubs, and specialty shops in a restored commercial district built between 1889 and 1915, many in the Richardson Romanesque style. Grab a burger and browse the used LPs and CDs at **Uncle John's Music Cafe and Records** (712/277-3922) at 1101 4th Street, a one-time head shop which now dishes up inexpensive meals and hosts live music several nights a week.

Away from Historic Fourth, one long-standing local favorite, **Green Gables Restaurant** (712/258-4246), a half mile north of downtown at 1800 Pierce Street, has bountiful, cheap food and very good desserts.

The **Best Western City Centre** ($70; 712/277-1550), at 130 Nebraska Street across from the Sioux City Art Center, is the best in-town option. Otherwise, the usual chains line the I-29 exits north and south of town.

Sac City and Rockwell City

East of Sioux City, US-20 alternates between four-lane freeway and rapidly disappearing two-lane highway, passing acres of farmland and occasional towns. **Sac City** (pop. 2,492) is one of the few places along this stretch of road that tries to preserve its past, with a log cabin and preserved Chautauqua

Sioux City's unaffiliated Northern League baseball team, the **Explorers**, plays throughout the summer in modern Lewis & Clark Park, where you can sometimes get standing room tickets ($3; 712/277-9467) and linger on the grass along the foul lines. Games are broadcast on KSCJ 1360 AM.

Hall along US-20 and a small historical museum on Main Street. It also has the nicely maintained **Sac City Motel** (712/662-7109), right on US-20.

Twenty miles farther east, in **Rockwell City** (pop. 1,981, "The Golden Buckle on the Corn Belt"), the **Leist Oil Company** has an incredible collection of old neon and enameled metal roadside signs advertising cars, car parts, soda pop, and sundry other things. Downtown also has a nice old Carnegie Library, a railroad station, and some nifty little shops, well worth a few minutes of wandering.

Fort Dodge

Founded in the 1850s to protect settlers from roving bands of Sauk and Black Hawk Indians, **Fort Dodge** is today a sleepy Midwestern town, economically dependent upon local farms, gypsum wallboard plants, and a huge Friskies cat food factory. Amid many stately homes on the south side of downtown, one place really worth a look is the **Blanden Memorial Art Museum** (closed Mon.; free), at 920 3rd Avenue South. Housed inside a grand neoclassical 1930s building, the collections include examples of pre-Columbian pottery, Renaissance sculpture, and Japanese prints. Modern paintings include works by people you wouldn't expect to find in the middle of Iowa—Max Beckmann, Marc Chagall, and Rufino Tamayo, to name three—along with works by Grant Wood and other Iowa artists.

The famous **Cardiff Giant**, a seven-foot-tall skeleton supposedly unearthed in New York in 1868, was thought by experts to be the bones of a prehistoric man. However, the skeleton, which was kept on prominent display by showman P. T. Barnum for the next 35 years, was later proven to be a hoax, carved from a slab of gypsum quarried at Fort Dodge. A replica is on display at the **Fort Museum and Frontier Village** ($6) on US-20.

Cedar Falls and Waterloo

US-20 turns to fast, four-lane freeway around **Cedar Falls,** a historic industrial town founded in the 1850s along the Cedar River. Now home to the University of Northern Iowa, Cedar Falls preserves the remnants of its manufacturing heritage and has some surprisingly upscale bistros tucked away in its sleepy but tidy downtown district. The **Olde Broom Factory** (319/268-0877), at 125 W. First Street, serves up American and Cajun cuisine in a renovated broom factory; and **Montage** (319/268-7222), at 222 Main Street, lives up to its fran-

cophone moniker by presenting a *nouvelle* variety of Latin, Southwestern, and Asian dishes. For die-hard road-food types, there is a vintage **Maid-Rite** diner (319/277-9748) a few blocks away at 116 E. 4th Street, in the small industrial section of downtown "CF," and the **Cup of Joe**, a 1950s-style chrome diner on Main Street. For a place to stay, check out the lovely **Blackhawk Hotel** (319/277-1161) at 115 Main

Waterloo is worth a look if you can be here on Memorial Day, when vintage car enthusiasts from around the Midwest participate in the Fourth Street Cruise.

Street, which has a great lobby and oodles of charm.

Downstream from Cedar Falls, and similarly bypassed by the modern US-20 freeway, **Waterloo** (pop. 68,747) is a bigger and busier city, with an almost urban feel and yet more good museums, including the **Grout Museum**(closed Mon.; $4.50; 319/234-63570). (Despite the name, it's a general science and history museum—not a collection of great tile-setting materials!). Waterloo is also home to the massive **John Deere Tractor** assembly plant on the outskirts of town at 3500 E. McDonald Street, which is open for free tours (Mon.–Fri. only; 319/292-7697). There's also a small shop where you can stock up on their trademark caps and souvenirs.

> Waterloo was the hometown of the **Fighting Sullivan Brothers,** five young men who were all killed at the World War II battle of Guadalcanal. The U.S. Navy has named a series of ships after them.

In keeping with its blue-collar character, Waterloo's favorite place to eat is **Moosie's Loosemeat Sandwich Shop** (319/232-5030), at 518 Jefferson Street, which prides itself on thick soft-serve malts and three types—beef burger, buttered turkey, and BBQ pork—of Iowa-style loosemeat sandwiches, a sort of Midwestern Sloppy Joe.

Quasqueton: Cedar Rock

Midway between Waterloo and Dyersville, the tiny town of **Quasqueton** (pop. 579) holds **Cedar Rock,** a wonderful riverside house completed in 1950

The Lincoln Highway in Iowa

Iowa may not be everybody's idea of a vacation destination, but fans of old highways are in for a treat here: The state has some of the best-preserved remnants of the nation's first cross-country route, the Lincoln Highway. Running between New York and San Francisco, the Lincoln Highway was the main transcontinental road from its opening in 1915 until 1927, when it was converted to the less-inspiring US-30, which, improvements notwithstanding, it still is today. Much of the original alignment survives, especially in small towns, and the old road makes a fascinating alternative across the state.

Thanks to its many dedicated devotees, the old route is well-marked all across Iowa—just keep an eye out for the red, white, and blue blazes, and the giant "L." Two of the many evocative sites on the Lincoln Highway in Iowa are in the midsection, between Ames and Cedar Rapids. The city of **Belle Plaine,** for example, has hardly changed since its 1915 heyday, and in the town of **Tama** a historic bridge, with the words "Lincoln Highway" spelled out in the concrete guardrails, has been preserved as a riverside park, on 5th Street a block west of the US-30 bypass.

by architect Frank Lloyd Wright for local-boy-done-good businessman Lowell Walter, who got rich by developing and patenting a method of sealing highway surfaces. One of seven houses Wright built in Iowa, and one of only 17 of the 1,000-plus houses Wright built that he "signed" with a signature tile, Cedar Rock is an excellent and complete example of his "Usonian" ideals, and everything in the house—from the soaring roof, the smooth flow of interior space, and the signature hearth, right down to the designs of the carpets and cutlery—embodies Wright's idealized vision of middle-class American houses, designed for simple if stylish living in close accord with nature.

Carved into a limestone ridge overlooking a bend in the Wapsipinicon River, Cedar Rock is seven miles south of US-20, and surrounded by acres of rolling woodland. The house and grounds are now owned and managed by the state of Iowa and are open in summer only for guided **tours** (closed Mon.; free; 319/934-3572).

Dyersville: The Field of Dreams

"If you build it, they will come. . . ." Ever since the movie *Field of Dreams* came out in 1989, some 60,000 people have flocked each year to **Dyersville** (27 miles west of Dubuque) to reenact the fairy tale baseball movie, major scenes from which were filmed just outside of town. Acres of cornfield surround the rather municipal-looking diamond, where people can play for free. Though privately owned, the attraction is "open" daily April–November; to get there, take Hwy-136 north from US-20, then follow signs northeast along 3rd Avenue and Field of Dreams Road for about 3.5 miles from US-20. Alongside the playing field, there are two rival souvenir stands: one along the right field line, one along the left.

Field of Dreams

Considering it's such a small town, Dyersville has a lot in store. Besides the Field of Dreams, the town boasts one of only 36 Catholic basilicas in the United States (St. Francis Xavier, that can't-miss gothic pile in the center of town). The **National Farm Toy Museum** (daily; $4), right off US-20 at 1110 16th Avenue, has over 30,000 miniature tractors and plows showcasing 100 years of toys—from horse-drawn wooden ones to die-cast modern ones—many of them made here in Dyersville by the Ertl Toy Company, which has recently moved its factory overseas.

Dubuque marks the junction with our road trip along the **Great River Road**, which begins on page 214. The town and surroundings are fully described on pages 233–234.

ILLINOIS

US-20 angles across northern Illinois from the Mississippi River to Lake Michigan, bringing you from the unglaciated scenery of the "Driftless Region" to the towering city of Chicago in less than 200 miles. The western stretches pass through hill-and-valley regions where water power and mineral deposits were harnessed by early industry. The old two-lane road is still in use, climbing onto stony ridges, then dropping into hardwood-forested valleys across the undulating region that stretches east from the Iowa border. This stretch of old road has as great a variety of barns and grain bins as anywhere in the country; however, there's considerable pressure to widen and "improve" it into a four-lane freeway, so enjoy it while you can.

Galena

If ever there's a place where you can truly step back in time, **Galena** (pop. 3,647) is it: Pass through the floodgates that protect the town from the namesake river (and the US-20 highway), and it's like entering Brigadoon. Spawned by Wisconsin's mid-19th-century lead-mining rush, Galena became the social and cultural capital of the Upper Mississippi basin. In the 1840s, while Chicago was still a mean collection of tents in a swamp around Fort Dearborn, and the Twin Cities were but a trading post in the woods around Fort Snelling, Galena was producing upwards of 75 percent of the world's lead, and the town was filled with bankers, merchants, and speculators who built mansions, hotels, and emporiums stuffed with fine goods and furnishings from around the world. This part of the Driftless Region saw some of the greatest wealth and commerce of the upper Mississippi, with Galena alone higher in population—some 15,000 lived here during the Civil War—than the entire Minnesota Territory.

But the California gold rush, played-out lead mines, a river silting up from miner-induced erosion, and a national economic panic all drove Galena to become a handsome ghost town that nobody bothered to tear down. For 100 years it slumbered, but beginning in the 1960s Galena was resurrected as a quaint tourist town. The brick warehouses were converted into shops and galleries, and anything but the most subtle, hand-carved signage was banned: In Galena, preserving the historical complexion of the streetscape isn't just a good idea, it's the law. The outskirts, especially along the US-20 frontage, are fairly typical roadside sprawl, and there are still a few everyday businesses in the historic core (including a funeral parlor and a large and busy metal foundry), but the overall feel is of a long-ago era. Even the

Northwestern Illinois was the site of many skirmishes between settlers and Indians during the **Black Hawk War** of the early 1830s.

Along US-20, 12 miles east of Galena just west of historic **Elizabeth,** a 75-foot-tall lookout tower gives tourists a "Tri-State View" over the hilly **Driftless Area,** so-called because the landscape here was never smoothed out by Ice Age glaciers.

Mrs. Grant didn't like the fact that her late husband's statue in Galena's **Grant Park** showed the general with his hand in his pocket. Not that she wanted it changed. "Oh, no!" she told the sculptor, "Leave it as it is, but dear me, I've told that man 20 times a day to take his hand out of his pocket."

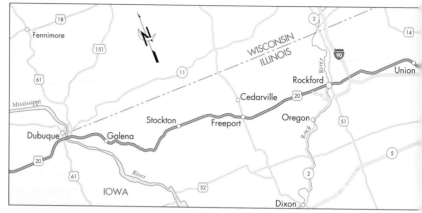

Commander of the Union Army and President of the United States
1822 - 1885

innumerable galleries and shops selling T-shirts and "collectibles" can't spoil the remarkable effect of the place. One essential: Park the car and *stroll*.

Besides the integrity of its mid-19th century buildings, Galena is famous as the town that saw a local store clerk win both the Civil War and the presidency. The modest **Ulysses S. Grant Home** (daily 9 AM–5 PM except major holidays; $2 donation; 815/777-0248) sits up Bouthillier Street in a quiet residential neighborhood across the river from downtown. Given to the general by a grateful group of local Republicans, the house is now a state historic site restored to the period immediately preceding Grant's move to the White House. A small museum behind the house traces Grant's life, from the Civil War to the presidency to his burial in Grant's Tomb.

Galena Practicalities

Even if you're blind to Galena's manifold aesthetic and historical delights, you'll probably enjoy its wide variety of food and lodging options—the clearest proof of the town's tourism dependency. The downside of this is that most of the longstanding local cafés have given way to knick-knack boutiques and fancy bistros. Unless you're staying at a B&B, the only place to get a good breakfast is a half mile west of downtown along US-20, at **Emmy Lou's** (815/777-4732). There is, fortunately, still one great old downtown place for a good, fairly cheap, and always cheerful dinner: the **Log Cabin** (815/777-0393), at 201 N. Main Street. Galena's oldest restaurant, with a great big green-and-red sign that predates the town's anti-neon ordinance, the Log Cabin is also known as "The House of Plenty," and has been serving up a mix of industrial-strength Greco-Italian food, plus steaks and seafood, since 1935.

The multinational corporation **Kraft Foods** got its start in Stockton, Illinois, and thanks to the three large cheese plants along US-20, Illinois is the top-ranked Swiss cheese producer in the United States.

There are some 60-odd hotels, guest homes, and historic inns here in "the B&B capital of the Midwest." The central **DeSoto House** ($100–250; 815/777-0090), at 230 S. Main

Street, was U. S. Grant's headquarters during his 1868 presidential campaign; the entire place was tastefully modernized during a recent $8 million renovation. Away from downtown, the spacious and comfortable **Belle Aire Mansion** ($95 and up; 815/777-0893) stands along US-20 walkably west of town. If you're just passing through, the cheapest decent sleep in town is at the **Grant Hills Motel** ($65; 815/777-2116) along US-20 east of town.

The Galena/Jo Daviess County Convention and Visitors Bureau operates an excellent **visitors center** (815/777-0203 or 800/747-9377), across the river via a pedestrian-only bridge, in the old Illinois Central Railroad depot at the base of Bouthillier Street. Stacks of brochures cover everything from accommodations to bike tours. This is also the best place to **park** the car, as spaces are at a premium in the often-crowded downtown area.

Freeport

Midway between Galena and Rockford, the oddly named town of **Freeport** (pop. 26,443) is neither a port nor even near any body of water. According to the WPA *Guide to Illinois,* the name was bestowed by the wife of an early settler to satirize his fondness for providing free room and board to passersby.

> Jane Addams (1860–1935), founder of Chicago's reform-minded Hull House and winner of the 1931 Nobel Peace Prize, was born and is buried in the town of **Cedarville**, six miles north of Freeport.

There's no free lunch here today, but Freeport does offer at least one good reason to stop: the **Alber Ice Cream Parlour,** at 126 E. Douglas Street two blocks north of the US-20 Business Loop. Enjoy a creamy, cool milk shake or sundae, then step next door to the small park, where an oddly distorted statue marks the site of the second **Lincoln-Douglas debate,** held here on August 27, 1858. A plaque quotes both men equally, with Lincoln's "This government cannot endure permanently half-slave and half-free" opposing Douglas saying, "I am not for the dissolution of the Union under any circumstance."

Rockford

Spreading haphazardly along the leafy banks of the Rock River, **Rockford** (pop. 150,115) is a big, somewhat sprawling, post-industrial city five miles west of the busy I-90 toll road from Chicago. US-20 bypasses the down-at-heel downtown area that, if the denizens wore more hats, would look like a film set on Main Street of industrial America circa 1949. Unfortunately, many of the classy office buildings and storefronts here have been abandoned in favor of anonymous

Chicago

Night in Chicago

New York may have bigger and better museums, shops, and restaurants, and even Los Angeles has more people, but Chicago is still the most all-American city, and one of the most exciting and enjoyable places to visit in the world. Commerce capital of Middle America, where something like 80 percent of the nation's agricultural produce is bought and sold, Chicago's location at the crossroads between the settled East and the wide-open West has helped it to give birth to many new things we now take for granted: the skyscraper, the blues, and the atomic bomb.

Away from The Loop, the skyscraper-spiked lakefront business district that holds the world's tallest and most impressive collection of modern architecture in its oblong square mile, much of Chicago is surprisingly low-rise and residential. Also surprising, considering its inland location, is that Chicago has the highest percentage of immigrants of any American city—300,000 Poles form the largest community outside Warsaw, and Hispanics constitute 20 percent of Chicago's population of three million—with a multi-ethnic character readily apparent in numerous enclaves all over the city. Whatever their origin, however, residents take a particular pride in identifying themselves as Chicagoans, and despite the city's rusting infrastructure, their good-natured enthusiasm for the place can be contagious.

For an unbeatable introduction to Chicago, hop aboard a river cruise offered by the **Chicago Architecture Foundation** (daily May–Nov. only; $25; 312/922-3432). Departing from where the Michigan Avenue Bridge crosses the river and Wacker Drive, these informative and enjoyable tours offer an unusual look up at the city's magnificent towers. Enthusiastic expert guides give the city's general historical background as well as pointed architectural history. North from the river, the "Magnificent Mile" of Michigan Avenue is a bustling shopping strip that holds yet more distinctive towers, along with many of the city's top shops, restaurants, and hotels. Starting with the gothic-style Tribune Tower—decorated with bits of famous buildings stolen by Tribune staffers from around the globe—and running past the circa-1869 Historic Water Tower at its midpoint, the "Mag Mile" ends in the north with the 95-story John Hancock Center.

Along the lakefront at the heart of downtown, the **Art Institute of Chicago** ($12, free Tues.; 312/443-3600), 111 S. Michigan Avenue, boasts one of the world's great collections of 19th- and 20th-century French painting, and a broad survey of fine art from all over the world. Among its many fine paintings, the Institute also demonstrates a pride of place with

Grant Wood's *American Gothic*, which he painted as a student and sold to the Institute for $300. North and east of the museum is Chicago's latest great claim to fame: **Millennium Park,** a 25-acre public garden full of fabulous sculptures and a magical, Frank Gehry–designed outdoor concert pavilion that's home to numerous summer concerts and events.

More than just another baseball game, watching the **Chicago Cubs** play at Wrigley Field (773/404-2827), 1060 W. Addison Street, is a rite of passage that taps into the deepest meanings of the national pastime. It's also a hugely pretty scene, with ivy covering the redbrick outfield walls, and Chicagoans of all stripes rooting on the perennial not-quite winners. The "other" Chicago baseball team, the World Series–winning **White Sox,** play at modern new US Cellular Field (312/674-1000), south of the Loop alongside I-94 at 333 W. 35th Street.

Practicalities

Chicago is home to America's busiest and most infuriating airport, O'Hare (ORD), 17 miles northwest of the Loop and well-served by Chicago Transit Authority (CTA) subway trains, shuttle services, and taxis. Chicago's other airport, Midway, is closer to the center of town, and Chicago is also the hub of the national Amtrak system, with trains pulling in to Union Station from all over the country. To get around, you'll really be better off leaving the car behind and riding the CTA elevated train—better known as the "El" (312/736-8000). It serves the entire city around the clock.

Chicago has all sorts of top-quality, cutting-edge-cuisine restaurants, but to get a feel for the city you'll be better off stopping at the many older places that have catered to Chicagoans forever. The **Berghoff** (312/427-3170), at 17 W. Adams Street, is one of these, a picture-perfect turn-of-the-20th-century saloon and steakhouse, serving up excellent food (sandwiches at lunch, hearty roast beef at dinner); cash only, often crowded. At **Little Al's Italian Beef BBQ** (312/226-4017), 1079 W. Taylor Street, step up to the counter and chow down on a juicy mess of shredded beef soaked with garlicky gravy; truly good food. Near the start of old Route 66, **Lou Mitchell's,** 565 W. Jackson Street, is one of the greatest breakfast and lunch places on the planet.

Places to stay in Chicago include the moderate likes of the **Best Western River North** ($99 and up; 312/467-0800), at 125 W. Ohio Street, in the trendy River North gallery district, within a quick walk of the "Magnificent Mile" along Michigan Avenue. Top of the line is the **Drake Hotel** ($200 and up; 312/787-2200), 140 E. Walton Place, Chicago's classiest hotel, with elegant public areas and gracious staff. The most fabulous place to stay has to be the **InterContinental** ($175 and up; 312/944-4100), at 505 N. Michigan Avenue, housed in an exuberant space that used to be a Shriner's health club.

The best source of information in advance is the **Chicago Office of Tourism** (877/CHICAGO).

office parks and shopping malls closer to the I-90 corridor.

After exploring Rockford's nooks and crannies, including many nice parks, reward yourself with lunch or dinner at one of Illinois' great road-food haunts, the **Rathskeller** (815/963-2922) at 1132 Auburn Street, off Main Street a mile north of downtown Rockford. Since 1931, this Teutonic institution has been serving up skillets of sausage and potatoes, corned beef sandwiches, and very good desserts. If you'd prefer something a bit more healthy and contemporary, try the new downtown bistro, **Paragon on State** (815/963-1660) at 205 W. State Street, which has great pastas and grilled meat dishes, a *nouvelle* sense of style—and microbrews at reasonable prices.

Rockford has lots of places to stay, from all the main chains along the Interstate to old US-20's characterful **Sweden House Lodge** ($55 and up; 815/398-4130) at 4605 E. State Street, a still-thriving icon of 1950s roadside Americana.

Dixon and the Rock River

If you have the time, Hwy-2 follows a lovely route from Rockford along the Rock River southwest to the quaint old town of **Dixon**, where the **Ronald Reagan Boyhood Home** (815/288-3404) at 816 S. Hennepin Avenue preserves the house where the late Great Communicator spent his teenage years. Midway along, a rather majestic statue of the great Indian chief Black Hawk stands above the river outside the town of Oregon.

Union: Illinois Railway Museum

young Ronald Regan

Between Rockford and Chicago, US-20 is a slow, winding, and poorly signposted alternative to the high-speed I-90 toll road. It's a leisurely route, with few identifiable attractions except for the road itself, which cruises through small towns surrounded by farmlands and lined by fruit-and-vegetable stands. The one real draw here is a mile east of the tiny town of **Union**, where the sprawling **Illinois Railway Museum** (daily; $8; 815/923-4000) displays a great range of track-based transportation: streetcars, interurban trolleys and railroad cars, with historic engines running weekends throughout the year.

Oak Park

Running parallel and south of the I-90 Northwest Tollway, old US-20 approaches Chicago from the northwest past Schaumberg and O'Hare Airport, before bending south near **Oak Park**, Chicago's most interesting suburb. Just 10 miles west of the Loop, easily reachable at the end of the Lake–Dan Ryan CTA "El" line, this sleepy but well-heeled neighborhood was the home and proving ground of America's best-known architect, Frank Lloyd Wright. Visit the **Frank**

Lloyd Wright Home and Studio (daily; $8; 708/848-1976), at 951 Chicago Avenue, for a fascinating look into the life and work of the great architect. Take a guided tour of the house he designed, remodeling almost constantly between 1890 and 1910 as his practice, and his family, grew. He also completed many other buildings in this turn-of-the-20th-century suburb, including the austere classic Unity Temple.

> The small town of **Woodstock**, 10 miles northeast of Union, stood in for the Pennsylvania town of Punxsutawney in my favorite Bill Murray movie, *Groundhog Day.*

Oak Park was also the boyhood home of Ernest Hemingway, and of contemporary writer Dave Eggers, author of *A Heartbreaking Work of Staggering Genius.*

US-20 Across Chicago

From Oak Park, US-20—which somehow has managed not to be diverted onto one of Chicago's many Interstate freeways—crosses the Des Plaines River and the "Sanitary Canal," then bends east onto 95th Street, following that road all the way across Chicago to the Lake Michigan waterfront. East of downtown, US-20 bends south along Lake Michigan into Hammond, Indiana, and the industrial districts along the Calumet River.

INDIANA

So close and yet so far away from the excitement of Chicago, northern Indiana can't help but seem a little bit boring. In the northwest, the state is bounded by Lake Michigan, along whose shores Rust Belt hulks of derelict heavy industry stand side by side with the pristine sands of the fascinating and beautiful **Indiana Dunes National Lakeshore.** The northeastern corner, even in the estimation of the state tourist office, offers little more than a few lakes and the so-called "muck lands" around the Fighting Irish homeland of **South Bend.** In between stretch endless acres of rolling farmland, Amish homes, and other tourist-attractive agricultural communities, as well as some of the most important sites in early American (meaning, pre-Detroit "Big Three") automotive history: the homes of Studebaker, Cord, Duesenberg, and other now-defunct car companies.

Gary

If you ever watched and enjoyed the Hollywood musical *The Music Man*—in which the song "Gary, Indiana" paints a picture of idyllic homespun Americana—you'll be surprised by the reality of the place. In contrast to the rural rest of the state, this far northwest corner of Indiana is among the most heavily industrialized and impoverished areas of the country. In and around **Gary** (pop. 106,000), massive petrochemical refineries and factories (including a huge U.S. Steel mill) are surrounded by decaying communities, and the streets are lined by strip malls, strip clubs, stripped-down cars—and

signs directing you toward the big new waterfront casinos. During the region's heyday around the turn of the 20th century, the mills, foundries, and factories along the Calumet River pumped out millions of dollars' worth of products every day. The town's more recent products include musical family The Jackson 5, born and bred here in the 1950s, but nowadays economic times are so hard that local authorities have had to call in the National Guard to police the streets.

Indiana Dunes National Lakeshore

Though its etymology sparks heated debates, the nickname "Hoosier" has come to connote all that is Middle American about Indianans—their independence, their practicality, and their thrift (or is it their cussedness, conservatism, and cheapness?).

Covering 15,000 acres along 15 miles of Lake Michigan shoreline, 25 miles east of Chicago, **Indiana Dunes National Lakeshore** is a striking and surprising collection of golden sand dunes, freshwater beaches, and dense forests. Chicago poet Carl Sandburg said the dunes "are to the Midwest what the Grand Canyon is to Arizona." Formally established in 1972, the park includes a huge variety of plant life—groves of maples and red oaks, pine tree and prickly pear cactus, grasslands and berry bushes—linked by many miles of hiking trails and highlighted by 125-foot Mt. Baldy at the far northeast corner of the park.

Three huge steel mills and a number of small vacation home communities share space among the dunes. Also here, two miles northeast of the main visitors center, is the unusual **Beverly Shores**, a model community constructed for the "Century of Progress" World's Fair in Chicago in 1933 and reassembled here soon after in an attempt to attract buyers to a new resort community. Six of these then-futuristic structures survive along Lakefront Drive, including three steel-framed, enamel-paneled "Lustron" houses, designed to provide low-cost housing during the Great Depression. Next door is the "House of Tomorrow," an ordinary-looking house designed with an additional garage to hold the private plane every future family was sure to have.

Pick up maps, guides, and other information at the **visitors center** (daily; free; 574/926-7561) on Kemil Road between US-20 and US-12.

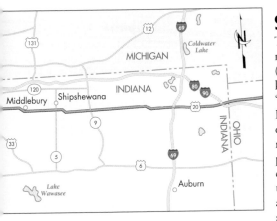

South Bend

The largest city in Indiana's northern tier, **South Bend** (pop. 107,789) is best known as the home of the "Fighting Irish" of Notre Dame University, and home of the car- and carriage-making Studebaker Company. The Notre Dame campus is most visitors' destination, whether or not it's a Saturday during football season. The 1,250-acre campus, along Michigan Street a mile north of downtown, is worth a stroll to see its many Catholic icons, including a replica of the grotto of Lourdes and the famous "Touchdown Jesus."

And if that's not enough, South Bend is also home to the **College Football Hall of Fame** (daily; $9; 574/235-9999) at 11 S. St. Joseph Street. Inside the 60,000-square-foot museum (bigger than a football field), you can watch videos of classic college games, experience a player's perspective in the 360-degree "Stadium Theater," or giggle at the antics of mascots and cheerleaders in the "Pigskin Pageantry" section.

On the south side of downtown, the **Studebaker National Museum** (daily; $7; 574/235-9714) at 525 S. Main Street displays a comprehensive survey of carriages and motor vehicles produced by the South Bend–based company before it closed in 1963.

One of South Bend's best restaurants, **Tippecanoe Place**, at 620 W. Washington Street, is housed in the old Studebaker Mansion. Across the street is the **Book Inn** (574/288-1990), a secondhand bookstore and B&B.

Behind the Studebaker museum, the 5,000-seat Coveleski Stadium hosts Midwest League Class A baseball games of the **South Bend Silver Hawks**. Tickets to see these potential Arizona Diamondbacks cost $3–6 (574/235-9988).

1958 Golden Hawk

Indianapolis

1911: the first Indy 500

Before Detroit came to dominate the industry, **Indianapolis**, a two-hour drive south of South Bend, was an early center of American automobile manufacturing, home to such classy marques as Stutz, Marmon, and Duesenberg, and of course the Indianapolis 500, perhaps the most famous car race in the world. Held the Sunday before Memorial Day almost every year since 1911, the Indianapolis 500 is still the biggest thing in town, drawing upwards of a half-million spectators to "The Brickyard," the oldest racetrack in the country. The rest of the year, the speedway is open for tours ($3), on a bus that cruises around the legendary oval. Tours leave from the excellent **Indianapolis Motor Speedway Hall of Fame Museum** (daily; $3; 317/484-6784), which displays some 75 racing cars, from the Marmon "Wasp," which won the inaugural Indy 500 race, to the latest Indy champions. The museum is located on the speedway grounds at 4790 W. 16th Street in the city of **Speedway** (pop. 13,092), in the northwest quarter of Indianapolis's pancake-flat sprawl.

Trickle-down improvements from Indy racing to passenger cars have included inflatable "balloon" tires, rear-view mirrors, and high octane gasoline.

Elkhart

A light industrial center, once famous for producing over half the brass-band instruments made in America, **Elkhart** now makes RVs and pharmaceutical products: Drug giant Miles Laboratories was founded here in 1884 and still has a major presence. In many ways it's a sleepy little Midwest town, home to the energetic little **Midwest Museum of American Art** (closed Mon.; $1; 574/293-6660), downtown at 429 S. Main Street in a restored bank building.

*The small town of **Peru**, on US-31 midway between South Bend and Indianapolis, was the home base of many traveling circuses during the mid-19th century, an era remembered in the **Circus City Museum** (317/472-3918), downtown at 154 N. Broadway. Peru was also the birthplace of songwriter **Cole Porter**, who is buried in the town's Mount Hope Cemetery.*

Northern Indiana is one of the country's main centers for the manufacture of recreational vehicles, so don't be surprised to find that Elkhart is home to the **RV Hall of Fame** (Mon.–Fri. only; free; 574/293-2344 or 800/378-8694), at 801 Benham Avenue, which tells the industry side of the travel trailer/RV/mobile home/manufactured housing story.

Indiana's Amish Country: Middlebury and Shipshewana

East of South Bend, US-20 again becomes a road worth traveling, especially through the quiet agricultural expanses around the towns of **Middlebury** and

Shipshewana, heartland of Indiana's sizeable Amish population. As in other Amish areas, it's the general look of the land, rather than specific attractions, that make it enjoyable to visit; as elsewhere, the few attractions that offer an "authentic Amish experience" leave a lot to be desired. One of the largest tourist traps, **Das Dutchman Essenhaus**, sits along US-20 at the west edge of Middlebury. Rather than fight your way through the bus-tour hordes, turn north here into the quiet town center, and stop by the **Village Inn** (574/825-2043) at 107 S. Main Street. The country café is run by, and popular with, local Amish and Mennonites, who, along with everyone else, enjoy the hearty coffee-shop food—not to mention great homemade pies for around $1 a slice.

Ten miles south of Shipshewana via Hwy-5, the tiny town of **Topeka** holds the **Yoder Popcorn Shop** (800/537-1194), one of many popcorn sellers whose signs you'll see all around this part of Indiana.

Back on US-20, seven miles east of Middlebury, Hwy-5 runs north just short of a mile to the intriguing **Menno-Hof Mennonite-Amish Visitor Center** (closed Sun.; $4 donation; 260/768-4117), outside the hamlet of Shipshewana. Operated by the local Amish and Mennonite communities, who built the large barn that houses the center during a six-day "barn-raising," the center gives an overall introduction to the Amish and Mennonite beliefs and lifeways. Surprisingly high-tech multimedia exhibits also tell of their resistance to modern technology, their long struggle for religious freedom, and their love of peace, which has helped them through centuries of torture and abuse—often at the hands of other Christians.

Auburn: Auburn-Cord-Duesenberg Museum

Though it's a bit out of the way (20 miles south of US-20 via the I-69 freeway), lovers of vintage American cars will want to make the effort to visit the elegant **Auburn-Cord-Duesenberg Museum** (daily; $8; 260/925-1444), in a lovely art deco showroom at 1600 S. Wayne Street in the town of Auburn. Considered by most aficionados the finest, most innovative, and most all-around gorgeous automobiles ever produced in America, these instant classics were the brainchild of Auburn industrialist Errett Cord. During the 1920s and 1930s, Cord's company designed and produced the covetable cruisers right here in Indiana— Auburns and the front-wheel-drive Cords were produced in Auburn, while the "Dusies" were made in Indianapolis—and they're now on display inside the original showroom, built in 1930 and immaculately preserved.

The collection includes beautifully restored examples of all these classic makes, plus representatives of other classic roadsters—Packards, Cadillacs, even a Rolls-Royce or two—numbering around 150 altogether, and making this one of the top auto museums in the world. It also hosts an annual classic car festival every Labor Day weekend, attended by as many as 200,000 people.

Another lost American industry is remembered near Auburn in Kendallville, along US-6: the **Mid-American Windmill Museum** (closed Mon; $3; 260/347-2334), where 40 acres of grounds display over 100 whirring Aermotors—the largest collection in the country.

Detroit

Though Detroit (pop. 956,266) is a ways off our route, no guidebook enamored with American car culture could feel complete without covering the "Motor City," heart of America's automotive industry. Once among the biggest, brawniest and busiest American cities, Detroit has lost more than half its population to suburban sprawl. Numerous efforts to "renew" the city by replacing the historic urban fabric with megalithic casinos and sports stadiums have resulted in a cityscape that at times resembles a war zone—the post-apocalyptic *Robocop* movies, for example, were set and filmed in downtown Detroit without much need for an art director. That said, the city's energy is undeniable, and hosting the 2006 Super Bowl put Detroit back in the international spotlight.

One of the best places to get a sense of Detroit, past and present, is at the huge **Detroit Institute of the Arts** (closed Mon. & Tues.; $6 donation; 313/833-7900), two miles north of downtown at 5200 Woodward Avenue. Along with its massive collection of art from around the world—the fifth-largest in the USA—the "DIA" is well worth a look for its huge and powerful Diego Rivera mural, *Detroit Industry,* celebrating the workers behind the wheels. The other must-see in Detroit is the **Motown Historical Museum** (closed Sun. & Mon.; $8; 313/875-2264), located about 3 miles northwest of downtown at 2648 W. Grand Boulevard. Dubbed "Hitsville USA," the Motown Museum is contained in the very house where Berry Gordy Jr. produced so many great dance hits in the 1960s. It's surprisingly small and homey, considering the quantity and quality of the music that was born there. Memorabilia galore documents the making of the Motown Sound by the likes of Smokey Robinson, Martha Reeves, Marvin Gaye, Stevie Wonder, the Temptations, and Diana Ross and the Supremes.

Sports fans may want to take in a **Detroit Tigers** (313/471-BALL or 248/25-TIGER) game. The team has abandoned historic Tiger Stadium for the faux-retro surrounds of downtown's Comerica Park, where a Ferris wheel and a carousel entertain fans even when the baseball doesn't. Detroit also remembers Joe Louis, the "Brown Bomber," with **The Big Fist,** a 25-foot-high fist looming over the city's main thoroughfare, in the middle of Woodward Avenue at Jefferson Avenue, across from the Renaissance Center downtown.

In the southwestern suburbs of Detroit, pay homage to the man who made your car affordable at the **Henry Ford Museum & Greenfield Vil-**

lage (daily; $20 each or around $45 for all; 313/982-6001), located just off US-12 in Dearborn, about 10 miles southwest of downtown Detroit, at 20900 Oakwood Boulevard. The complex has been officially renamed "The Henry Ford: America's Greatest History Attraction," and its incredible collection of cars and car-related objects certainly illustrates the massive impact the automobile has had on American history and American life. The adjacent open-air complex of Deerfield Village is a virtual microcosm of American history, holding everything from Abe Lincoln's law office to Thomas Edison's workshop, arranged by Henry Ford and his heirs to form an ideal village of American creativity. Henry Ford's notorious white-supremacist politics are downplayed, but the collection does includes one icon of multicultural American history: the bus on which the late, great Rosa Parks refused to give up her seat in 1955, sparking the Civil Rights–era Montgomery Bus Boycott. There's also an IMAX theater showing big-screen films. One of the newest attractions is the chance to tour Ford's landmark River Rogue automobile factory, home of everything from the Model T to today's F150 pickups. Once the world's largest factory, "The Rogue" is still a state-of-the-art assembly plant, where you can witness all eras of car-making under one eco-friendly "Living Roof."

Practicalities

The downtown riverfront has been the focus of much of Detroit's re-invention, but the best places to stay, eat, and generally spend time are north of there along Woodward Avenue, in the emerging midtown "Cultural District" near the DIA and lively Wayne State University. To gain a deeper appreciation of Detroit's past, stay overnight at one of the restored Victorian-era homes that comprise the **Inn on Ferry Street** ($120-up; 313/871-6000), a very comfortable B&B at 84 E. Ferry Street. The same neighborhood also holds **Union Street** (313/831-3965) an old-fashioned tavern at 4145 Woodward Avenue with good food (huge portions) for lunch and dinner and a welcoming if often noisy ambience. For more detailed Detroit information, contact the city's **visitors bureau** (800/DETROIT).

PENOBSCOT BUILDING

OHIO

The many routes across Ohio along the Lake Erie shore have long been major thoroughfares. Traders and war parties of Iroquois and other Native American tribes regularly passed this way hundreds of years before European and American pioneers started coming through in Conestoga wagons. Nowadays, historical survivors, including a number of colonial-era taverns and other early roadside Americana, and a rapidly decreasing number of vegetable farms and greenhouses fill the flatlands, threatened by ever-expanding suburbia. All over northern Ohio you'll also see Rust Belt remnants of massive industrial activity that took place here from the 1880s to the 1950s, when the Great Lakes were the "Anvil of America," producing the bulk of the nation's—and the world's—iron, steel, and petroleum products.

On I-90 at the Indiana–Ohio border, a very large **World's Largest Fireworks Stand** also hypes itself as the "8th Wonder of the World."

Rather than try to follow one or another of the many old roads that crisscross the state, it's best to alternate between a variety of routes to either side of the part-tollway, part-freeway known as I-90. In the western half of the state, we follow US-20 from **Toledo** through a rural landscape of gambrel-roofed, red-painted barns, daubed with "Chew Mail Pouch" signs and made immortal by Sherwood Anderson's classic portrayal in his book *Winesburg, Ohio*. In the middle, we detour north to the lakeshore along US-6, which passes through idyllic summer home communities, gritty old ports, and one of the country's great old amusement parks, **Cedar Point**. East of the metropolitan **Cleveland** area, US-20 veers north along the **Lake Erie** shore, while US-6 zig-zags south through the fertile farming country of northeastern Ohio—a region accurately described by the 1939 WPA *Guide to Ohio* as an "enchanting country of tumbling hills, valleys, and forests."

Toledo

One of Ohio's most important industrial centers, **Toledo** (pop. 313,619) is the third-busiest Great Lakes port, with many miles of docks, bridges, warehouses, factories, refineries, and power plants lining the mouth of the Maumee River. That may not sound like a good reason to visit, but Toledo is a fascinating place, big enough to be impressive but small enough to get around and get a feel for. Downtown Toledo has long been a rather anonymous place that empties after 5 PM (that world-renowned expert on tedium, the late John Denver, went so far as to write a song saying, "Saturday night in Toledo, Ohio, is like being nowhere at all"), but the streets just south hold dozens of gorgeous old cast-iron warehouses and commercial buildings around the new "Fifth Third Field" baseball stadium, home of the loveable **Toledo Mud Hens.**

A mile west of downtown, among the stately homes of the Old West End neighborhood, Toledo's pride and joy is the excellent **Museum of Art** (closed

Mon.; free), at 2445 Monroe Street, where works by El Greco (who lived and worked in Toledo, Spain) highlight a survey of European painting. The real strength of the collection is its glassware, with dozens of beautiful goblets and vases dating back to Roman times, housed in a lovely new pavilion.

Another truly not-to-be-missed Toledo stop offers a very different feast for the senses: **Tony Packo's Cafe** (419/691-6054), across the river at 1902 Front Street. Packo's addictive chili dogs, made famous by Corporal Klinger (played by real-life Toledo native Jamie Farr) on the long-running TV series *M.A.S.H.*, still pack the crowds into this East Toledo haunt—despite its location near a huge Toledo Edison coal-fired power plant. A good-value place to stay in the region is the **Toledo Hilton**($100; 419/381-6800), at 3100 Glendale Avenue on the southwest edge of downtown.

In **Monroe, Michigan** (between Toledo and Detroit), you can kick back in a selection of easy chairs past and present at the **La-Z-Boy Museum,** in the company headquarters! It's free, but by reservation only (734/242-1444).

Maumee and Perrysburg

South of Toledo along the Maumee River, a pair of towns preserve important parts of western Ohio's early history. On the west bank of the river, **Maumee** (pop. 15,237; MAH-mee) was founded in 1817 at the western edge of settled territory, and holds remnants of the Miami and Erie Canal.

Across the river, **Perrysburg** (pop. 16,945) is a pretty little town of white colonial-style houses, with a nice waterfront park and a short strip of restaurants and bars running east along Louisiana Street (US-20). A mile upstream from town, past the cemetery and a set of expensive-looking tract houses, **Fort Meigs** (Wed.–Sun. in summer; $4) is a full-scale reconstruction of the wooden fortress that played a key role in defending the frontier against British and Indian attack during the War of 1812.

The Class AAA International League affiliate of the Detroit Tigers, the **Toledo Mud Hens** (419/725-HENS) play at delightful Fifth Third Field in the old downtown Toledo warehouse district. The stadium is located not at Fifth and Third Streets (the name comes from a Cleveland bank), but along Huron and Washington Streets; games are broadcast on **WLQR 1470 AM.**

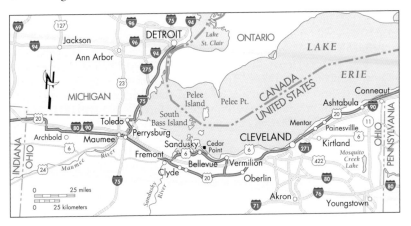

Fremont

In **Fremont** (pop. 17,600), where in the 1700s native Wyandot Indians established a village along the main trail between Pittsburgh and Detroit, the main attraction is the **Rutherford B. Hayes Presidential Center** (daily; $6; 419/332-2081), south of US-20 at 1337 Hayes Avenue, which encompasses the 25-acre estate of Civil War general and former U.S. President Rutherford B. Hayes, who lived here 1873–93 and served as president 1877–81. The nation's first presidential library, the Hayes center includes the rather plain, redbrick family house and a large museum displaying his public and private papers, sundry mementos, and his daughter Fanny's dollhouse collection. Hayes is buried on a wooded knoll on the grounds, alongside his wife and their favorite horses.

Clyde: Winesburg, Ohio

Five miles east of Fremont, the town of **Clyde** (pop. 6,064) is a perfect little place, still very much the typical farm town that the New Deal–era WPA *Guide to Ohio* said might well have served as a model for one of Thomas Hart Benton's murals of rural America: "Old Indian paths and sand ridges are now angular streets; cheek by jowl with an odd assortment of business houses is the railroad cutting across Main Street, gyved with station, elevator, and spur track; around the decorous houses are gardens, flower beds, and shrubbery tended by friendly and loquacious folk."

While downtown "Winesburg" is still a low-key place, the US-20 frontage west of Clyde is dominated by a truly massive factory and distribution center for **Whirlpool** appliances.

Clyde's brick-paved streets are still quiet, lined by mature trees and most of the same houses as when writer **Sherwood Anderson,** who was born in southern Ohio in 1876, grew up here in the 1880s and 1890s. Because the people of Clyde took offense at Anderson's sharply drawn and only slightly disguised portraits of them in his groundbreaking book, *Winesburg, Ohio*—which was published in 1919, 20 years after Anderson left Clyde for Chicago—the town doesn't celebrate him in any obvious way. The only real sign of him is in the local **library** at 222 W. Buckeye Street, a block west of the town center, where visitors can check out a collection of his books and a short documentary video of his life and times. The library is also the best place to pick up the pamphlet that points out Anderson's home and the sites of many scenes from *Winesburg.*

Beside the Winesburg legacy, Clyde also offers a couple of very good road food stops: **Bogey's Diner** (419/547-9947) at 222 W. McPherson Highway; and nearby, the photogenic **Twistee Treat,** shaped like an ice-cream cone and serving great shakes. To complete the Sherwood Anderson tour, stay at the AAA-recommended **Winesburg Motel** (419/547-0531), 214 E. McPherson Highway.

In Clyde, the McPherson Cemetery along US-20 holds the remains of Brigadier Gen. James "Birdseye" McPherson, the highest-ranking Union officer killed in the Civil War.

Sandusky and the Lake Erie Islands

Midway between Toledo and Cleveland, a fine natural harbor has enabled **Sandusky** to remain a busy port, albeit now more for recreational ferries to the offshore islands than for the coal and iron ore it once handled. The waterfront is good for a short stroll, and the town is rich in elaborate mid-1800s houses like the **Follett House Museum** (daily 1–4 PM; free) at 404 Wayne Street, a well-preserved 1827 Greek Revival house filled with period artifacts and a few displays on the area's history. Stop for a bite to eat at **Markley's** (419/627-9441), a classic little 1950s diner on the corner of Market and Wayne Streets, a block east of Columbus.

On **South Bass Island** in Lake Erie, 15 miles by boat from Sandusky, a stone column commemorates the victory of Adm. Oliver Perry, who defeated a British fleet here on September 10, 1813, announcing his success with the laconic words, "We have met the enemy, and they are ours." The second biggest thing on the island, which is a very popular vacation spot, may well be the "World's Longest Bar," a 406-footer running inside the **Beer Barrel Saloon.**

If the weather's too bad to brave a boat trip, or the coasters of Cedar Point, families may want to head to the **Great Wolf Lodge** ($175 and up; 419/609-6000), a kid-friendly hotel and massive indoor water park (guests only), south of Sandusky at 4608 Milan Road.

Cedar Point

Northern Ohio's number-one summer attraction is the wonderful, old-time amusement park of Cedar Point (hours vary; $45 adults, $9.95 for children under four feet tall; 419/627-2350), just north of Sandusky. Cedar Point has the country's biggest and best collection of roller coasters, 16 in all, ranging from fragile-looking old wooden ones to high-speed modern monsters like the **Magnum,** a 15-story colossus, the terrifying **Raptor,** in which riders swing on benches hanging upside down from the track, and the 90-plus-mph **Millenium Force,** which features a stomach-levitating 300-foot drop. It's definitely one of the most popular destinations in the Midwest, so expect crowds if you come on summer weekends. The 360-acre park sits on a peninsula across the water from downtown Sandusky, and has animal shows, a Lake Erie beach, and a water park called Soak City, as well as restaurants and on-site camping and hotel accommodations.

Vermilion

One of the more attractive resorts on Ohio's Lake Erie frontage, **Vermilion** took its name from the rich red clay that colors the soil. Along with a fine beach backed by dozens of attractive summer homes, the town also holds the **Inland Seas Maritime Museum** (daily; $6), along the waterfront at 480 Main Street. The museum's usual array of scale models and

The lovely little town of **Milan,** two miles south of I-90 via US-250, was the birthplace in 1847 of the great inventor **Thomas Edison.** His childhood home at 9 Edison Drive is preserved as a **museum.**

paintings of ships is augmented with preserved timbers from Perry's ship *Niagara,* and a 62-foot-tall replica of a Lake Erie lighthouse.

A great old-fashioned ice cream and sandwich parlor, **Ednamae's,** stands at 5598 Liberty Avenue at the center of town; for a more complete meal, try the comfortable **Old Prague Restaurant** next door. A reliable place to stay is the **Motel Plaza** ($50; 440/967-3191), at 4645 Liberty Avenue.

Oberlin

Away from the lakeshore, 25 miles west of Cleveland between I-90 and US-20, the attractive college town of **Oberlin** (pop. 8,195) serves up an idyllic slice of Middle Americana. Founded along with the surrounding town in 1833, Oberlin College has a history of being at the leading edge of American education, despite (or perhaps because of) its location far from the madding crowds. In 1837 Oberlin became the country's first co-educational college. It was also among the first to embrace the education of African Americans: In the 19th century, Oberlin awarded more degrees to black students than all other mainstream American colleges combined.

The Oberlin College campus spreads west of the town's green main square, which is also graced on the east side by the neoclassical facade of the **Allen Art Museum** (closed Mon.; free), which displays an overall survey of world art—Japanese prints, Islamic carpets, and modern painting by the likes of Cézanne and Diebenkorn. Architecture fans should take note: The old gallery was designed by Cass Gilbert, who also planned a handful of Romanesque buildings on campus; a new wing was added in 1977 by Robert Venturi. The museum also offers guided **tours** ($5) of a nearby house designed in 1947 by Frank Lloyd Wright.

The town of Oberlin seems preserved in a time warp, mostly avoiding the trend-swapping café culture of many college towns. Its few blocks are lined by an old five-and-dime, an Army surplus store, a hardware store, and a bookstore, all along the south side of the broad town square. Another block south holds a spacious, modern library (with free Internet access); and a very nice Mediterranean-flavored café, **Feve** (440/774-1978), at 30 S. Main Street, which has fresh falafel, good coffee, and cold Guinness on draught. South of town, **Cecil's Trackside Diner** (440/647-0334) at 194 W. Herrick Avenue in Wellington. For a place to stay, try the no-frills **Sunset Motel** ($40; ($40; 440/774-1629) at 44077 Old Route 20.

Much of Oberlin's endowment comes from the bequest of Oberlin graduate **Charles Hall**, *who in 1886, a year after graduating, discovered a viable process for refining aluminum and later founded Alcoa Corporation.*

In the past 30 years, much of Ohio has been turned from farmland to suburbia, a development that inspired Pretenders singer and Ohio native **Chrissie Hynde** *to write "My City is Gone"— which, coincidentally, is the theme song for Rush Limbaugh's radio program.*

I went back to Ohio/but my pretty countryside/ Had been paved down the middle/by a government that had no pride/The farms of Ohio/had been replaced by shopping malls/And Muzak filled the air/from Seneca to Cuyahoga Falls

US-20 across Cleveland

The nicest old road route into Cleveland from the west is US-6, which winds along Lake Erie as Sandusky Road, Lake Avenue, and Clifton Boulevard. Running right through downtown, past "The Flats" along Shoreway, then east along Superior Avenue, US-6 gives a great taste of the city.

US-20, on the other hand, diverges slightly east of downtown Cleveland, following Euclid Avenue past the Museum of Art, then crosses to the north of US-6, following the lakeshore all the way into Pennsylvania.

The Cleveland Municipal Airport, Cleveland, Ohio

Kirtland

The rolling farmlands of northeastern Ohio around **Kirtland** were, from 1831 to 1837, the center of the Mormon religion. Joseph Smith Jr., along with 1,000 of his followers, settled here and built a large temple—the first Mormon temple anywhere—and developed industries and a bank (known as the "Kirtland anti-BANK-ing Company"). The bank failed in 1838 and Smith fled, first to Liberty, Missouri, and later to Nauvoo, Illinois, where in 1844 he was killed by a mob.

The **Kirtland Temple** at 9020 Chillicothe Road (Hwy-306) is surrounded by pleasant gardens and open to the general public on guided **tours** (daily; free; 440/256-3318). The stately Greek Revival structure has a gleaming white interior built in part by Brigham Young, with elaborately crafted woodwork pulpits (one at each end) and an upstairs classroom with more of the unusual double pulpits. The temple and most of the town have been preserved under the auspices of the Reorganized Church of Jesus Christ of Latter-day Saints, now called "Community of Christ," which was set up in 1852 by Joseph Smith Jr.'s oldest son and the Mormons who didn't go west to Salt Lake City with Brigham Young.

Ashtabula

On the shores of Lake Erie, 18 miles from the Pennsylvania border, **Ashtabula** (pop. 20,962) is a large and busy pleasure-boating port, first dredged at the mouth of the Ashtabula River in 1826 and later home to some of the biggest shipyards on the Great Lakes. Now primarily recreation-oriented, Ashtabula still has a few signs of its industrial past, including the lakefront coal conveyor that forms an archway over the river, next to a squat lighthouse and a small local history **museum** housed in the old lighthouse keeper's quarters. The town's lakeside location made it a key transit point for escaping slaves on the Underground Railroad, a history recounted inside the **Hubbard House Museum,** on the corner of Walnut and Lake. Both museums are open Friday–Sunday afternoons in summer only.

A block south of the lakefront, pride of place goes to a burly bascule drawbridge and to the many turn-of-the-20th-century industrial and business premises along Bridge Street

North of I-90 along US-20, a half mile from the center of **Mentor,** a large white house is preserved much as it was when **James Garfield** lived here before assuming the presidency. Ten miles northeast, at 792 Mentor Avenue in Painesville, the **Rider Tavern** was built in 1818 along the stagecoach route between Buffalo and Cleveland.

Cleveland

Poor Cleveland. Home base of John D. Rockefeller's Standard Oil, for decades on either side of the turn of the 20th century Cleveland was one of the biggest and heaviest of all the Great Lakes heavy industrial giants. Despite losing half its population, and spending much of the past 60 years reeling from Rust Belt decay, the city does seem to be coming back to life, energized by the sporting success of LeBron James's Cavaliers and baseball's fan-friendly Jacobs Field.

Cleveland's old heavyweight lakefront industrial district, known as "The Flats," has undergone a successful facelift: overlaid by a network of bridges (drawbridges, lift bridges, swing bridges, all kinds of bridges) that form a feast for the eyes of any post-industrial amateur archaeologist, with water taxis running back and forth across the river, linking the bars and restaurants that now fill gigantic old mills, factories, and warehouses. The primal force behind the area's rebirth has been the **Rock and Roll Hall of Fame and Museum** (daily; $21; 888/764-ROCK), housed in a striking modern I. M. Pei–designed building; 50,000 square feet of galleries fill a 165-foot tower with a barrage of multimedia exhibits tracing the roots and branches of the rock family tree. (Q: Why Cleveland? A: The Hall of Fame was located here because it's a Cleveland DJ, Alan Freed, who is credited with naming the music "rock and roll," way back in 1951.)

At the heart of downtown, Jacobs Field is the place that made Cleveland feel like a winner: the **Cleveland Indians** (216/420-4200) baseball team won the American League championship for the first time in two generations the year the stadium opened, and success has inspired a general renaissance of civic pride. "The Jake" is packed full every game, so buy tickets as far in advance as possible.

Practicalities

The Cleveland airport, Hopkins International, is 12 miles southwest of downtown, linked by I-71 and the RTA subway (216/621-9500) to central Cleveland. To get a feel for the place, a car is hard to beat, especially since the city tends to sprawl sideways rather than concentrate vertically. In the downtown area, finding your way around the Cuyahoga River waterfront takes patience, as many roads dead-end and some of the old bridges are closed to traffic; on foot, the Ohio City RTA stop is a good place to start exploring.

For food, the **Great Lakes Brewing Company** (216/771-4404), at 2516 Market Avenue in Ohio City, west of the Cuyahoga River in an artsy low-rent district, has good food, great beer, and a generally convivial crowd. While here, check out the **West Side Farmer's Market,** and **Allstate Barber College,** across the street on 26th and Lorain Avenue—20 chairs, no waiting!

Night Scene, Hotel Cleveland and Terminal Tower.

Cleveland, Ohio

In a light industrial and warehousing district east of I-90, a half mile from downtown, **Slyman's** (216/621-3760), at 3106 St. Clair Avenue, has the best corned beef in Cleveland, bar none. For real good road food, **Ruthie & Moe's Diner** (216/881-6637), at 4002 Prospect Avenue, is a pair of vintage diners joined together, now serving road-food classics like meatloaf, macaroni and cheese, and milk shakes, plus unusual specials: Hungarian goulash, Louisiana gumbo, and matzo ball soup. The diner is open Monday–Friday, for breakfast and lunch only.

For a place to stay, **the Holiday Inn–Lakeside** ($129 and up; 216/241-5100), 1111 Lakeside Avenue, is hard to beat. It offers the usual Holiday Inn comforts and is very near the Rock and Roll museum. Right downtown, across from Claes Oldenburg's "World's Largest Rubber Stamp" statue, the **Renaissance Cleveland Hotel** ($175 and up; 216/696-5600), 24 Public Square, is a 1920s classic which has been immaculately updated into the city's nicest place to stay.

For complete visitor information, contact the **Cleveland Convention and Visitors Bureau** (216/621-4110 or 800/321-1004), 3100 Terminal Tower, 50 Public Square.

that form a three-block parade of gift shops, bars, and restaurants, including the **Doxsie Deli and Ice Cream Parlour** (440/964-9888) at 1001 Bridge Street, open daily for sandwiches and sundaes.

Conneaut

A dozen miles east of Ashtabula, just west of the Pennsylvania border, the historic port town of **Conneaut** (pop. 13,200; KAH-nee-ut) has an art director's dream of a great road-food restaurant, the **White Turkey Drive-Inn** (440/593-2209), on US-20 at 388 E. Main Road. Owned and run by the Tuttle family since 1952, this place is famous for two things: turkey sandwiches and root beer floats. Between Mother's Day and Labor Day, sit outside under the red canopy on a warm summer evening watching the fireflies, and everything's guaranteed to feel right with the world. Conneaut also supports two great breakfast and lunch places: **Johnson's Drive-In** and the turquoise-green **State Street Diner,** facing each other across US-20 downtown.

PENNSYLVANIA

US-20 takes little more than the proverbial blink of an eye to cross the 45 miles of northwestern Pennsylvania, which is part of Pennsylvania only because the country's founding fathers thought it was unfair to deny the Keystone State a share of the Lake Erie shoreline. I-90 is most travelers' route of choice, but US-20 does have a couple of worthwhile stops. Twelve miles east of the Ohio border, the town of **Girard** (pop. 4,722) has the nifty little **Hazel Kibler Museum,** 522 E. Main Street, documenting local history and the life of circus clown Dan Rice, who posed as Uncle Sam in the famous "I Want You" posters. Girard also has one of the country's oldest Civil War memorials, an eagle-topped obelisk dedicated with great fanfare in November 1865.

In **Erie,** the big city in these parts (pop. 101,175), a replica of Commodore Perry's flagship *Niagara* is moored along the waterfront at 164 E. Front Street. The art deco Union Pacific depot is now home to a popular brewpub and res-

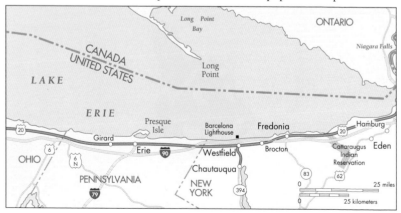

taurant, **Porter's** (814/452-2787), at 123 W. 14th Street; the even more opulent **Warner Theater** is a picture palace par excellence, its 2,300-seat auditorium still in regular use along State Street. One more reason to spend time here, especially in the depths of winter: **Splash Lagoon,** a trio of chain hotels ($90 a night) attached to a 75,000-square-foot indoor water park ($40 866/3-SPLASH), just south of the I-90 Erie exit.

Erie also has a Class AA baseball team, the Detroit Tigers-affiliated **Erie Seawolves** (814/456-1300), who play at a nice and neighborly new downtown stadium, on 10th Street two blocks east of State Street. Games are broadcast on **WLKK 1400 AM.**

NEW YORK

From inauspicious beginnings in the marshlands and vineyards of the Lake Erie "grape belt" at the state's far western tip, the portion of US-20 that runs across upstate New York cuts a wide scenic swath through a diverse terrain of flatlands, rippling hills, and spring-fed lakes. This well-maintained, mostly four-lane road glides surreptitiously through four centuries of history, slicing through vast Dutch patroonships, serene Shaker colonies, blood-soaked Revolutionary War battlefields, Native American hunting grounds, the birthplace of the women's movement, Underground Railroad hideouts, and the long-calmed waters of the once-mighty Erie Canal. Sparkling baseball diamonds, dairy bars by the dozen, petrified creatures, stately longhouses, abandoned motor courts, prancing wooden horses, off-key nose whistles, and succulent, grill-toughened hot dogs are just a few of the countless other reasons to slow down and pull over early and often as you cross the Empire State.

The "Romance Road," as labeled by a 1940s travel writer, follows several old Iroquois Indian trails as it nudges its way through the western Niagara Frontier, then traces the 19th-century Great Western Turnpike through the Finger Lakes region before easing down into the historically rich Hudson Valley near Albany, where it begins a gradual ascent of the Taconic Mountains and Berkshire foothills that hug the Massachusetts border. All the way across the state, US-20 roughly parallels the crowded, rumbling I-90 New York Thruway toll road—a necessary evil that lures most of the diesel-spewing, view-obscuring 18-wheel traffic away from placid US-20 with a 65-mph speed limit and the promise of uneventful, predictable fast-food rest-stop dining experiences and fluorescent-lit motels.

Westfield: New York's Wine Country

The salt-whitened, snowplow-scraped roadway and endless, slightly hilly expanse of shaggy, kudzu-like vineyards on the south side of the road continue for a dozen monotonous miles between the state line and proud, hardworking **Westfield** (pop. 3,500), known locally as Vine City because of its large Italian American grape-growing community and its proximity to some of Chautauqua County's finest wineries.

The tangy Concord grape was introduced to the region in 1859, but it wasn't until 1897 that Dr. Charles Welch and his father moved to Westfield

MUSEUM

Comedian **Lucille Ball** grew up in Jamestown, at the southeast end of Chautauqua Lake. A museum-cum-gift shop at 212 Pine Street ($5; 716/484-0800) displays lots of *I Love Lucy* memorabilia.

Chautauqua was founded in 1874 by **Lewis Miller,** inventor Thomas Edison's father-in-law.

and founded the factory that led to Westfield's long-standing nickname, the "Grape Juice Capital of the World." Though many of the canneries have since vanished, **Welch Foods** still maintains a large plant and its corporate offices on N. Portage Street, on the western edge of Westfield's compact downtown.

Westfield's no-frills **Main Diner** (716/326-4351), at 40 E. Main Street in the heart of downtown, is a pleasant place to grab a cup of coffee and sandwich while watching the pickup trucks cruise past; it's open daily 6 AM–3 PM, plus evenings Thursday–Saturday. Great homemade pies. (For all you diner mavens, the building is a 1929 Ward & Dickinson, originally fabricated in neighboring Silver Creek.)

Across I-90 from Westfield along waterfront Hwy-5, Lake Erie's Barcelona Harbor is home to the landmark **Barcelona Lighthouse,** which was the first lighthouse in the world to be lit by natural gas when constructed in 1830.

Fredonia

East of Westfield, US-20 trucks through cherry orchards, vineyards, and dozens of "U-Pik-Em" fruit stands before ebbing into the center of neatly maintained **Fredonia** (pop. 10,706), the namesake of the Marx Brothers' beloved *Duck Soup* homeland. Site of the first natural gas well in the United States (1825), Fredonia was also—ironically, for a town in the heart of the western New York Wine Belt—the birthplace of the Women's Christian Temperance Union (1873).

Downtown Fredonia boasts the gracefully shaded, New England–style town square, bordered by a restored opera house and a host of Greek Revival, Italianate, Victorian, and gothic 19th-century commercial buildings. A stroll down tree-lined Central Avenue to the north of Main Street (US-20) reveals an equally diverse array of turn-of-the-20th-century homes, which stand in marked contrast to the sterile modernity you encounter up the road in the several I. M. Pei–designed buildings that define the State University of New York (SUNY) Fredonia campus.

West of Fredonia, in the town of **Brocton** ("Home of Don Reinhoudt, World's Strongest Man"), a unique green dome has been hovering over US-20 at the main downtown intersection since 1910.

The veranda-fronted **White Inn** ($95 and up; 716/672-2103) at 52 E. Main Street has very nice rooms, and its restaurant has been open so long it still boasts of recommendations by 1940s road-food writer Duncan Hines.

East of Fredonia, the vineyards vanish, replaced by the thick stands of scruffy pine trees, used car lots, and cheap-cigarette stands that crowd the roadside along US-20's two-mile passage through the northeastern corner of the Cattaraugus Indian Reservation.

Detour: Chautauqua

One of the few utopian-minded 19th-century communities to survive to the present day, **Chautauqua** (pop. 4,554) is an idyllic Victorian village of quaint pastel cottages, tidy flower gardens, and pedestrian-friendly streets— a genteel model of middle-class, small-town civilization. Established as a summer training ground for Methodist Sunday school teachers, and now preserved as a nonprofit, nonsectarian cooperative foundation, in the first decades of the 20th century Chautauqua had an immeasurable effect on American culture, sponsoring correspondence courses and cross-country lecture tours that brought liberal arts education to the masses, especially in the rural Midwest.

idyllic Chautauqua

Chautauqua, which is located along Hwy-394 about 20 miles south of West-field on US-20 (off I-90 exit 60), has hardly changed since its heyday, and still welcomes all comers to its summer-long series of lectures and concerts, which are held in a delightful old open-air am-phitheater. Though the emphasis is on education, Chautauqua is not entirely academic: In between broadening their minds, visitors can relax on the white sand beaches that line the lakeshore. Day visitors to Chautauqua have to pay admission (about $10, free on Sun.) and pass through a set of ancient turn-stiles, as if entering a mind-improving amusement park. Others come for a week or two, renting a cottage or staying at the wonderful old **Athenaeum Hotel**, built in 1881. Along with dozens of quaint Victorian cottages is the Machine Age "Steel Away," a 3-bed "Lustron" pre-fab (716/357-3851).

For further information, or to request a schedule of Chautauqua classes, lectures, and events, call 716/357-6200 or 800/836-2787.

Eden: Original American Kazoo Company

US-20 bumps up north along the lakeshore through several miles of scraggly for-est, and you won't miss a thing by taking the I-90/NY Thruway to exit 57A, which lands you on a two-lane back road bound right for sleepy downtown **Eden** (pop. 3,579). Eden, a make-your-own-music-lover's paradise that lays claim to an annual summer Corn Days festival, is home to the one-and-only **Original American Kazoo Company** museum, gift shop, and factory (daily; free; 716/992-3960) at 8703 S. Main Street—just look for the "World's Largest Kazoo" on the roof. Established in 1916, the company boasts the world's only still-operating metal kazoo factory (most of the plastic ones are made in China and Hong Kong). A restored, two-story clapboard house contains a gift shop and museum offering an up-close-and-personal view of the factory's belt-and-pulley metal

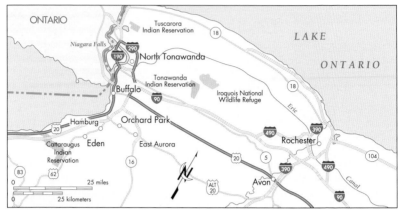

kazoo production line and the opportunity to sign a petition aimed at getting the kazoo declared America's national instrument.

After viewing a video extolling the virtues of one of the few musical instruments invented in the United States, visitors can gaze at a display of antique kazoos, ranging from an original wooden model to the bottle-shaped kazoos churned out to celebrate the repeal of Prohibition. A large sign chimes in with some fascinating kazoo-related trivia, describing the most popular kazoo (the slide trombone), the largest kazoo ever made (the 43-pound Kazoophony), and the number of kazoo bands registered in the United States (15,000 and still counting). You can pick up an adenoid-popping nose flute, a trombone kazoo, and a variety of noisemakers in the gift shop on your way out, or grab some wax paper, rubber bands, and an empty toilet paper roll and create your own kazoo.

Buffalo

Founded as a Niagara frontier outpost in the early 1800s, **Buffalo** (pop. 292,648) exploded into a bustling shipping, manufacturing, and railroad center after the 1825 opening of the Erie Canal. For over a century, especially around World War I, Buffalo was the commercial and industrial linchpin between the Great Lakes, Canada, and the eastern United States. A shrinking population, and the continuing departure of many factories and corporate headquarters to warmer, cheap-labor climes, has dented Buffaloans' self-confidence over the past several decades, but the optimistic made-in-Buffalo spirit captured so eloquently in Verlyn Klinkenborg's portrait of Polish-American bartender Eddie Wenzek, *The Last Fine Time,* lives on.

A 15-minute drive from downtown up tree-lined Elmwood Avenue takes you to Buffalo's premier attraction, the extensive collection of Picassos, de Koonings, Pollocks, and other important modern masterpieces inside the **Albright-Knox Art Gallery** (closed Mon.; $8; 716/882-8700). This world-class museum stands amidst the grassy expanses and ponds of **Delaware Park,** designed by Frederick

Law Olmsted, the landscape architect of New York City's Central Park and Brooklyn's Prospect Park. Across the road you'll see the marble neoclassical structure that has housed the Buffalo and Erie County Historical Society **museum** (daily; $6; 716/873-9644) since its construction in 1901 for the historic Pan-American Exposition. The non-air-conditioned gallery can be a bit stifling on hot summer afternoons, but the wonderful "Made in Buffalo" and "Dividing the Land" local manufacturing and immigration exhibits should satisfy most of your local-history thirsts.

The **Buffalo Bisons**, the Cleveland Indians top farm team, play right downtown at 21,000-seat **Dunn Tire Park** ($7 and up; 716/846-2000). Games are broadcast play-by-play on **WWKB 1520 AM.**

A short walk from the Delaware Park brings you to the Frank Lloyd Wright-designed **Darwin D. Martin House** (tours $10; 716/856-3858), 125 Jewett Parkway, currently undergoing restoration but well worth a look for anyone interested in American architecture.

Between Buffalo and Niagara Falls, **North Tonawanda** is a tough-looking factory town concealing one of the Buffalo area's best-kept secrets, the **Herschell Carousel Factory Museum** (daily in summer; $4; 716/693-1885) at 180 Thompson Street a half mile to the east of Hwy-265. Creators of much-loved landmarks at amusement parks from the Jersey Shore to Santa Monica, the barn-like factory houses a restored 1916 pulley-driven carousel and a stable of immaculately painted wooden steeds, zebras, roosters, ostriches, frogs, bears, and bulls hand-carved by the factory's immigrant artisans for the countless carousels and kiddie rides turned out by the factory in its 1920s to 1940s heyday.

Buffalo Practicalities

Most of Buffalo's many local clubs, films, and offbeat attractions are found in the funky, historic Allentown neighborhood around the junction of Elmwood Avenue and Allen Street, just north of downtown.

The infamous **Anchor Bar** (716/886-8920), "Birthplace of Buffalo Wings," is a short walk away at 1047 Main Street. Skip the bland Italian entrées in favor of the bar's much-hyped specialty—the saucy, fiery, deep-fried chicken wings born here in 1964. A long way out Main, about three miles from downtown near the SUNY Buffalo campus, is another even more perfect only-in-Buffalo pit stop: **Parkside Candy** (716/833-7540), at 3208 Main Street, where you can feast on delicious hot fudge sundaes or housemade candies in an opulently decorated 1930s space that looks like a ballroom out of some Jane Austen novel.

Southeast of downtown, another unique Buffalo treat—the "Beef on Weck" sandwich, a moist and meaty version of a French Dip, best eaten with a dash of horseradish—can be sampled at **Schwabl's** (716/674-9821), at 789 Center Road in West Seneca.

The south Buffalo suburb of **Hamburg**, "The Town That Friendship Built" and one of many supposed birthplaces of the hamburger, holds the retro **Uncle Joe's Diner**, open daily 6 AM–11 PM at 4869 SW Boulevard (US-20).

For a place to stay, most of the national chain motels are clustered east of town around I-90 and the Buffalo airport. The in-town **Best Western** ($85 and up; 716/886-8333), at 510 Delaware Avenue, is a bit higher-priced, but its central location saves driving time and grounds you smack in the middle of the city's Allentown bar, restaurant, and club district. An even better value, especially for solo travelers, is the immaculate **HI Buffalo Hostel** (716/852-5222) at 667 Main Street, with dorm beds in a historic downtown building. If money is less of a concern, consider an arts-and-crafts treasure tucked away in the south Buffalo suburb of East Aurora. In the early 1900s this was home of Roycroft Campus, a turn-of-the-20th-century arts-and-crafts community of furniture shops and studios, the crown jewel of which was recently restored and opened as the **Roycroft Inn** ($120–220; 716/652-5552), a hotel and restaurant at 40 S. Grove Street.

For additional information and maps of Buffalo's wealth of significant architecture (Louis Sullivan, H. H. Richardson, Eliel Saarinen, and Frank Lloyd Wright all completed major buildings here), contact the Buffalo/Niagara County **visitors center** (716/852-0511 or 800/283-3256), 107 Delaware Avenue.

Niagara Falls

One of the most famous sights in the world, **Niagara Falls** are a quick trip upriver from Buffalo. They're not the biggest or most powerful in the world, but they're easy to reach and very easy to get up close and personal with. Once you venture underneath the falls on the famous *Maid of the Mist* boat ride ($12; 716/284-8897), or even stand on the brink at Prospect Park or Goat Island, you won't soon forget the awesome force of the water tumbling in twin, 180-foot-tall torrents.

The power of Niagara Falls was first used to generate electricity by the remarkable inventor **Nikola Tesla** in 1896. A monument to him stands near the falls in Prospect Park.

Much to the despair of the tourism authorities on the American side, where the surprisingly post-industrial town has long suffered from economic decline, the best view and the biggest tourist attractions are across a bridge on the Canadian side, where the Las Vegas–scale **Fallsview Casino Resort** ($100–250; 888/325-5788) recently joined the traditional wax museums, water parks, aquarium, and a Ripley's Believe It or Not! Museum fronted by a statue of King Kong.

Avon: Tom Wahl's

East of Buffalo, US-20 makes a rigidly straight run through the flat corn and hay fields that climb the gradually rising plateau toward the Finger Lakes. This 40-mile stretch is virtually devoid of traffic, thanks to the faster-moving NY Thruway and serpentine Hwy-5, which links up with US-20 at **Avon**. Splash some cold homemade root beer down your throat to wake up and address the burning sensation left by the grilled, vinegar-doused, chili-drenched Texas Hot and Pork Hot Zweigle-brand hot dogs that are family staples at **Tom Wahl's** (585/226-2420) at 283 E. Main Street, two blocks east of Avon's leafy green central park. Birthplace of a regional favorite with locations all over western New York, this rambling Avon institution has been a required tour-bus stopover since 1955 thanks to its soft ice cream, frosty mugs, and gut-busting Wahlburgers (ground steak on a six-inch bun, topped with a slice of grilled Virginia ham and Tom's special, mayonnaise-based sauce).

Near the conservatory in Rochester's F. L. Olmsted-designed Highland Park, the 1898 memorial to anti-slavery activist **Frederick Douglass** was the first public statue of an African American erected in the United States.

Rochester

There's plenty of culture in the sprawling Genesee River manufacturing center of **Rochester** (pop. 219,700), and the best of it is of the vernacular variety, making the 25-mile detour off US-20 well worth your time and effort. With impressive **High Falls,** a mini Niagara right at the center of town; numerous historic sights (the Erie Canal passed right through Rochester, and Susan B. Anthony and Frederick Douglass both lived here for many years); and an expansive Lake Ontario shoreline boasting long beaches and the historic **Seabreeze Amusement Park** (585/323-1900), complete with the ancient wooden Jack Rabbit rollercoaster, Rochester is a fine example of how much fun one can have in a "minor league" U.S. city.

The **Rochester Red Wings** Class AAA baseball team play at friendly Frontier Field (585/454-1001) downtown. The team has been the Baltimore Orioles' prime farm team since the 1960s (ironman Cal Ripken played for Rochester as a teenager); games are broadcast on **WHTK 1280 AM.**

Start your visit with the vast holdings of the Americana-rich **Strong Museum** (daily; $7), clearly marked off I-490 downtown. This 500,000-item collection of Victorian-era toys, appliances, dolls, perfume bottles, marbles, salt-and-pepper shakers, and classic board games is a must-visit for closet pack rats, pop culture fanatics, and anyone with children in tow. Just inside, but accessible without paying admission, is a lovely circa-1918 Herschell hand-carved carousel (made in nearby North Tonawanda), and the fully restored **Skyliner Diner,** a 1956 Fodero serving lunch all day.

South of Rochester, I-390 runs alongside a still-intact section of the original **Erie Canal** waterway. In other places, the freeway runs right over the old canal, with the old stone locks still visible on the side of the road.

The **George Eastman House** (daily; $7; 585/271-3361) at 900 East Avenue, is a 10-minute drive along Rochester's fashionable mansion-lined main boulevard. In addition to relaying the Horatio Alger–like story of workaholic Eastman's success and philanthropy as the founder of the Eastman Kodak Company, the 50-room Georgian mansion in which he lived before his 1932 suicide also houses a fascinating exhibit ("Enhancing the Illusion") on the history of photography.

STRONG MUSEUM • ROCHESTER, NY

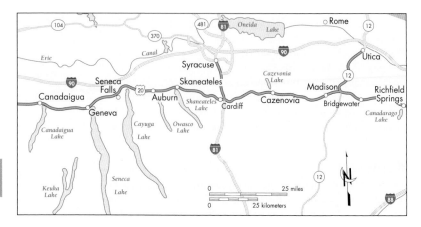

Geneva and Waterloo

Iroquois legend has it that the **Finger Lakes** (five of which—Cayuga, Onondaga, Oneida, Seneca, Tuscarora—bear names of the Six Nations of the Iroquois Confederacy) were created by the handprint of God.

Geneva (pop. 14,100) sits at the head of Seneca Lake, the largest of the Finger Lakes, and is linked to this sailboat-flecked jewel by a long, green linear park. For a worthwhile detour off the busy four-lane highway, take a quick pass through the lively downtown along Main Street, perhaps wandering around the twin campuses of Hobart and William Smith Colleges to take in a more long-distance view of the lake. The waterfront is dominated by a solitary high-rise housing the **Ramada Inn** ($80–130; 315/789-0400), but a much more interesting place to stay is a half mile south of town: the historic **Belhurst Castle** ($120 and up; 315/781-0201), a 100-year-old, 14-room B&B at 4069 S Hwy-14.

Picturesque, flag-draped downtown Waterloo has an all-American feel, befitting its contentious claim of holding the nation's first observance (in May 1866) of **Memorial Day**.

Ten miles east of Geneva, at the edge of **Waterloo**, the unprepossessing **Mac's Drive-In Curb Service Restaurant** (315/539-3064) at 1166 Waterloo-Geneva Road has been open every summer since 1961, dishing out creamy Richardson's root beer floats, frosty 16-ounce mugs of Pabst Blue Ribbon, butter-dipped sweet corn, and burgers-in-a-basket at an awning-covered counter or right at your car window.

Seneca Falls: Women's Rights National Historical Park

You'd never think that the diminutive redbrick, blue-collar town of **Seneca Falls** saw the birth of the American women's movement, but it did; the first women's rights convention, spearheaded by Lucretia Mott and Elizabeth Cady Stanton, took place here in July 1848. The remains of the Wesleyan Chapel where the convention was held can still be viewed at the center of town, on a guided tour from the **Women's Rights National Historical Park** (daily; free; 315/568-2991), right on US-20 at 136 Fall Street. A brief exhibit on the scandalous pants-like "bloomers" popularized in 1851 by local feminist Amelia Bloomer combines

organizers of the first women's rights conference, 1848

with displays on transcendentalism, abolitionism, temperance, and phrenology to place the rise of this revolutionary movement in historical context.

A block away, the **National Women's Hall of Fame**, 76 Fall Street, is a reading-intensive monument to the likes of Georgia O'Keeffe, Harriet Tubman, Emily Dickinson, Billie Jean King, and Jane Addams. You can listen to a saucy blues selection from Bessie Smith while dodging an endless stream of group tours.

Auburn

Auburn (pop. 28,574) is a proud industrial city with a solid, hilly downtown and a rich stock of historical homes, including that of William H. Seward, the anti-slavery Whig governor of New York, founder of the Republican Party, and secretary of state under presidents Abraham Lincoln and Andrew Johnson, who single-handedly negotiated the purchase of Alaska from Russia in 1867. The **Seward House** (Tues.–Sat. 1–4 PM; $4), on Hwy-34 a block south of US-20 at 33 South Street, contains all the original furniture and many fascinating historic exhibits. Down the street from the Seward home, you can also tour the home of escaped slave and underground railroad heroine **Harriet Tubman**, who, between the end of the Civil War and her death in 1913, lived in the tidy white house at 180 South Street (Tues.–Fri. only; donations). Seward and Tubman are both buried in the town's Fort Hill cemetery, west of South Street between the two homes.

Right downtown, the sparkling, streamlined **Hunter's Dinerant** (315/255-2282), a 1950s O'Mahony at 18 Genesee Street, offers great greasy-spoon breakfasts (24 hours a day Thurs.–Sat.), slices of thick lemon meringue pie, and a panoramic view of the aging Genesee Beer sign that watches over the wide streets of the hill-hugging downtown.

At the west edge of Seneca Falls, the emblematic landmark of the long-vanished 1920s-era **Windmill Tourist Camp** has been kept alive as the local chamber of commerce and visitor information center.

Along US-20 on the western outskirts of Auburn, keep your eyes peeled and your camera at the ready as you pass the **Finger Lakes Drive-In Theater** (summer only; 315/252-3969). North of town, the Class A **Auburn Doubledays** (315/255-2489) play at friendly Falcon Park.

Skaneateles

Roughly midway across New York State, **Skaneateles** (pop. 2,700; scan-e-AT-less) is a pristine, sun-dappled resort nestled on the north shore of shimmering Skaneateles Lake. This popular summer family escape houses arts, crafts, and antique stores along its immaculate Genesee Street (US-20), which fronts a lovely lakeside park where you can enjoy free summer concerts (Fri. at 7 PM) on the quaint bandstand, watch the boats come and go, or hop on board a historic lake steamer for a scenic tour offered by Mid-Lakes Navigation (315/685-8500). A stroll up the main downtown north–south drag leads you past the unadorned **Skaneateles Bakery** (315/685-3538) at 19 Jordan Street to the Skaneateles Historical Society's petite **Creamery Museum** (1–4 PM Thurs.–Sat.; donation; 315/685-1360) and elm-lined side streets full of well-maintained Greek Revival homes.

If you're hungry for more than a pastry or piece of cake, wait in line at the high-quality but self-effacing **Doug's Fish Fry** (315/685-3288) at 8 Jordan Street, "not famous since 1962" for its fried haddock sandwiches ("2,987,000 sold"), fried clams, Coney Island hot dogs, and ice cold beer. Doug's also has creamy, thick Perry's ice cream and milk shakes, plus fresh strawberry sundaes in season. Buy a postcard for a nickel, and Doug's will slap on a stamp and send it on its way.

For something a bit more sit-down and soothing, one of the country's oldest restaurants, **Kreb's Inn** (315/685-5714), has been open since 1899 at 53 W. Genesee Street, and will empty your wallet with its pricey-but-hearty lobster, roast beef, and chicken specialties. One of the finest restaurants in upstate New York is the dining room at **Mirbeau Inn** (315/685-5006) at 851 W. Genesee Street, serving classic French meals for around $100 a head; the deluxe inn also has a small number of rooms ($125 and up).

Along US-20 just west of the I-81 interchange, the tiny crossroads of Cardiff is where the 10-foot, 2,700-pound "fossil" of the P. T. Barnum–hyped **Cardiff Giant** was "unearthed" in 1869.

A number of motels line US-20 east and west of Skaneateles; stay at the **Hi-Way Host** (315/685-7633), west of downtown at 834 W. Genesee Street, and you can eat at the family-friendly **Hilltop Restaurant,** across the highway, then go bowling in the adjoining **Cedar House Bowling Center.** Another nice place, the **Sherwood Inn** ($90 and up; 315/685-3405), is along US-20 at 26 W. Genesee Street.

Syracuse and Utica

A short, 25-minute side trip from US-20 north to **Syracuse** (pop. 149,435) via I-81 yields an informative tour of the fascinating **Erie Canal Museum** (daily; free; 315/471-0593) at 318 E. Erie Boulevard in the shadow of I-690. Housed in an 1850 weighlock building straddling the mostly paved-over canal bed, the museum has a 65-foot restored 1850s canal boat, and offers free guided walking tours of the city that gave birth to the electric typewriter, the loafer, and the turn-of-the-20th-century, arts-and-crafts-style furniture of Gustav Stickley. A short film describes the staggering impact of the canal's 1825 opening on the city, an impact also visible in the cast-iron commercial districts of the historic and still-lively downtown, south and west from the museum around Clinton and Armory Squares.

East of Syracuse down the I-90 NY Thruway, hilly **Utica** (pop. 60,651) is another good detour. Beer fans in particular will want to make the trip: Since 1888, the old West End Brewery **F.X. Matt Brewing Co.** ($3; 315/624-2400), at 811 Edward Street on Brewhouse Square, has pumped out barrels of Matt's trademark Utica Club and Matt's Premium regional beers alongside its more heavily promoted Saranac line of premium microbrews. In-depth tours of the compact, family-owned facilities take you through the entire production process—where you are apt to spy some contract-brewed Brooklyn Lager, New Amsterdam, Dock Street Ale, or Olde Heurich slipping out the door—and drop you off in a velvet-lined Victorian tavern for your complimentary glasses of Saranac or frothy root beer.

Shake off your post-lager drowsiness with a thick, delicious cheeseburger, coffee, and slice of lemon meringue pie at the timeless **Triangle Coffee Shop** (315/735-4692), at

With roots going back to the building of the Erie Canal, the sizeable Irish immigrant population of Syracuse once insisted that traffic lights in their neighborhoods be turned upside-down so that the "British" red did not sit above the "Irish" green.

One of the oldest baseball clubs in existence, the **Syracuse SkyChiefs** (315/474-7833) have been around in various forms since 1885. Now the top farm club for the Toronto Blue Jays, they play at modern P&C Stadium north of downtown off I-81 exit 25. Games are broadcast on **WFBL 1390 AM.**

Northwest of Utica, the decidedly nonclassical city of **Rome** was the site of **Fort Stanwix**, which played a decisive role in the struggle for control of upstate New York during the Revolutionary War.

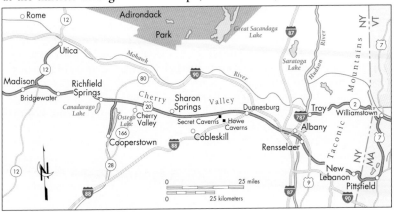

244 Genesee Street downtown, which manages to cram four sit-down tables, seven counter stools, and a hungry crowd of professionals into its tiny, bright, triangular space.

Cherry Valley

East of I-81, all the way to Albany, US-20 follows the route blazed by the old Great Western Turnpike over gradually steepening roller-coaster hills, past sweet-corn stands, dairy bars, and cabbage fields, and into the western reaches of pic-ture-perfect Cherry Valley. Refuel for the rolling road ahead at the ramshackle **Gatesdale Dairy Bar** in **Bridgewater,** which sports a cooler full of creamy, rich ice cream and a sagging neon sign featuring a dripping milk bottle under the portrait of a satisfied heifer in a floppy chef's hat. Another tempting place to pause is **West Winfield**, its streets lined by big trees and well-maintained Victorian-era homes.

Midway between Syracuse and Albany, 15 miles northwest of Cooperstown, **Richfield Springs** (pop. 1,565) is a peaceful crossroads that offers a calmer and less-expensive base for exploring the area. A rustic bandshell stands in the center of its grassy town square, and right across 20-mph US-20 you can enjoy a Hoff-man's hot dog or a Hershey milk shake at the friendly, family-run **Village Snack**

Detour: Cooperstown

The neat, prosperous village of **Cooperstown** (pop. 2,200), founded in 1786 by the father of *Last of the Mohicans* novelist James Fenimore Cooper, was transformed into a family tourist mecca thanks to the **National Baseball Hall of Fame** (daily; $15; 607/547-7200), at 25 Main Street, which opened here in 1939. Recently expanded and upgraded, the Hall of Fame revolves around a beautifully organized time line of dioramas and display cases that walk you through the sport's great-est—and most embarrassing—moments. You'll see Babe Ruth's bat, the pair of cracked, black leather shoes worn by the ill-fated and latterly famous 1919 "Black Sox" player Shoe-less Joe Jackson, and rows and rows of bronze plaques naming all the greats of the game. Special exhibits highlight the Negro Leagues, women in baseball, and, of course, baseball cards, all amid a voluminous collection of uniforms, periodicals, programs, player records, scrap-books, and film and audio holdings. The combination admission ticket (around $30) to the Baseball Hall of Fame also gains you entrance to the other Cooperstown museums.

Cooperstown's many attractions are augmented by the subtler delights of the **Fenimore House Museum** (daily in summer, weekends only in winter; $9), which, along with memorabilia of the writer, has engaging displays of Native American artifacts, folk art, and Hudson River School paintings.

Bar (daily in summer; 315/858-3988), open since 1953. Behind the snack bar, and built at the same time, is the equally pleasant, AAA-rated **Village Motel** ($80–100; 315/858-1540).

On the south side of US-20, several miles east of Richfield Springs at the crest of a large hill, a private home does double-duty as the **Petrified Creatures Museum of Natural History** (daily July & Aug., hours vary rest of year; $8, $4 for under-12s; 315/858-2868), an outdoor tour of real 300-million-year-old Devonian-era fossils, plus garishly painted, life-sized "talking" dinosaur sculptures. An added attraction is the option of using a pickax to hack out and take home a few fossilized keepsakes from the slate pit—where most of the "petrified creatures" come from. The admission is a bit steep, but the gift shop—packed full of prehistoric-themed knick-knacks—is free.

East of Richfield Springs, US-20 makes a roller-coaster ride through the patchwork of hillside cornfields and dairy farms that drape the bubbling landscape through the fertile Cherry Valley region. Just south of the highway, attractive little **Cherry Valley** (pop. 600) contains a small local history **museum** that recalls this tiny crossroads' early-19th-century boom period as a rowdy turnpike stagecoach stop. A small obelisk in the village

The Fenimore House is on Lake Street a mile north of town along the shores of Otsego Lake—the source of the Susquehanna River, known locally as "Glimmerglass" for its spectacular, sparkling appearance.

Near the Fenimore House, the **Farmer's Museum** (daily in summer, weekends only in winter; $9; 607/547-1450) has illuminating exhibits on 19th-century rural life, with dignified agricultural and local history exhibits occupying most of the sturdy stone structures speckling this 1918 farm. The "remains" of the previously encountered Cardiff Giant lie in stony silence.

Avoid the in-town parking hassles and stash your car in one of the free lots near the Fenimore House. Then catch a city-operated trolley ($2 for an unlimited day pass) to downtown.

In the several-block central business district, every other bookstore, restaurant, and variety store seems to be cashing in on their tourist customers' insatiable appetite for baseball-related camp and nostalgia. For example, the **Doubleday Cafe** (607/547-5468) at 93 Main Street has above-average food and a Father-of-the-National-Pastime theme.

There are literally dozens of motels from which to choose in the Cooperstown area, and the Hall of Fame offers many package deals; be sure to make your reservations far in advance to beat the summer rush. The **Lake Front Motel** ($80–140; 607/547-9511) has a lakefront beach within walking distance of downtown, while in-town accommodation options include the grand **Hotel Otsego** ($120–180; 607/547-9931), at 60 Lake Street.

For more information on Cooperstown, including details on the very popular summertime **Glimmerglass Opera Festival**, contact the **visitors bureau** (607/547-9983), 31 Chestnut Street.

cemetery on S. Main Street pays homage to the residents killed in 1779 in the Cherry Valley Massacre, a British-backed Iroquois raid during the Revolutionary War.

Cherry Valley also holds a more recent landmark: **The TePee** (607/264-3987), a 50-foot-tall, tepee-shaped attraction, which has lured souvenir-starved travelers since 1950 with its array of Native American trinkets, famous "TePee Taffy," and "Grand Panoramic View" telescope. A snack bar has hot dogs and very good chili.

Sharon Springs

The 19th-century spa and resort community of **Sharon Springs** (pop. 543), 20 miles west of Albany, was once on a par with Saratoga Springs, but for most of the past 75-plus years the silent streets have been lined by the slowly crumbling remains of once-grand wooden Victorian-era hotels. In its pre–Civil War heyday, the spas here attracted as many as 10,000 visitors at a time, but for the past decades Sharon Springs has been kept alive thanks to its unlikely role as a seasonal escape for Orthodox Hasidic Jews fleeing the heat of New York City summers. Throughout the ups and downs, the sulfurous, supposedly health-giving waters have continued to flow, bubbling up into a small fountain in the small park at the center of town, and into large tubs at the public Imperial Baths bathhouse farther down Main Street. Most of the patrons at the Imperial Baths are Russian or Eastern European, giving the place a totally foreign, time-warped feel.

In recent years, Sharon Springs has seemed set for a revival. On Main Street, the white-columned hotels have been undergoing total overhauls; the stately **American Hotel** ($120 and up; 518/284-2105) now has a very good dining room, with a stylish cocktail bar, and guests can settle into comfy chairs lined up along the spacious front porch and watch the world go by.

There's also a nice pizza place (Geno's), a general store, a kosher hotel (the Adler), and an intriguing local-history museum, with plaques all over town telling the story of Sharon Springs' varied incarnations.

Cobleskill: Iroquois Indian Museum

If you're interested in the native history of upstate New York, detour southeast along I-88 to tidy **Cobleskill** (pop. 4,533) and the **Iroquois Indian Museum** (daily 10 AM–5 PM; $5; 518/296-8949). The imposing, long-house-shaped structure contains artifacts, arrowheads, and more recent works of art associated with the Native Americans descended from the Six Nations of the Iroquois Confederacy, as well as an interactive, hands-on children's museum. The museum's collection of contemporary Native American painting and sculpture also asks tough, probing questions about the one-dimensional casino culture that has recently come to dominate reservation life across the United States.

All over this part of New York, massive roadside billboards blare out the competitive presence of Howe Caverns (marked

Sharon Springs offers a high-contrast picture of American architectural history: The characterful hotels and landscaped parks of the old town, just north of US-20, are neighbors to the massive and anonymous beige shed of a Wal-Mart distribution center, on a hill just east.

by simple, yellow-and-black "Howe Caverns" directional signs) and Secret Caverns (on which a Deadhead-ish wizard beckons you onward with pesky lines like "If you haven't seen the underground waterfall, you ain't seen guano!"). Though located within two miles of each other, these two tourist attractions are about as far apart as Pat Boone and Jimi Hendrix.

The sanitized-for-your-protection **Howe Caverns** (daily; $16; 518/296-8900) boast a well-lit, guided elevator and flat-bottomed boat tour of a 156-foot-deep underground cave. Along the same road, you know you're in for something completely different the moment you approach the dark, foreboding **Secret Caverns** (daily in summer; $12; 518/296-8558)—entering through the mouth of a giant, leering bat. Don't let the "Abandon hope all ye who enter here" sign scare you off from taking the twisting (and twisted) one-and-a-half hour guided trek down into the clammy 180-foot-deep innards along a narrow, randomly lit footpath, which terminates at an impressive, 100-foot waterfall.

Albany

The New York state capital, **Albany** (pop. 95,658) was founded in 1609 when Dutch traders traveling up the Hudson River from New Amsterdam on Henry Hudson's ship *Half Moon* went ashore and established a fur-trading post. As the gateway between upstate New York and the increasingly powerful New York City port, Albany remained a powerful trading center through the 1820s and 1830s, extending its reach with the opening of the Erie Canal and the city's growth as a central railroad terminus and manufacturing center. Nowadays, the legendary canal has long since vanished, and the glamorous New York Central railroad's French renaissance–style, turn-of-the century Union Station, at Broadway and Clinton Street, has been transformed into the sleepy corporate headquarters of the Fleet banking group—Amtrak passenger trains now stop at a lonely platform on the opposite side of the Hudson River.

As the seat of the New York state government, however, Albany still wields obvious political power. Its rich array of museums, parks, and tree-lined boulevards—plus a few barely preserved historical neighborhoods that survived the wrecker's balls in the early 1960s—confirm the fact that the Capital City is still very much alive and well. The towering granite slabs and flying saucer–like structures that stick out at the heart of the 100-acre Empire State Plaza government center hold exhibition halls, theaters, a 44-story observation tower, and the excellent **New York State Museum** (daily; 518/474-5877), which includes a sensitively organized exhibit on the state's Iroquois and Mohawk Native American cultures, centering around a reconstructed longhouse. The huge area devoted to the history of the metropolitan New York City area is as good or better than anything in "The City That Never Sleeps," with a re-created Upper West Side Hispanic barber shop, a Horn and Hardart Automat food dispenser, a restored 1940s car from the A-train subway line, and a solemn gallery documenting the September 11, 2001, destruction of the

Uncle Sam

Troy's prominent Uncle Sam monument, along the waterfront at River and Front Streets, memorializes bearded local meat-packer Samuel Wilson, who supplied beef to the soldiers quartered at the local Watervliet Arsenal during the War of 1812. Wilson's donations were quickly dubbed "Uncle Sam's beef," and the nickname and character have become the finger-pointing stuff of legend. Wilson himself is buried in the macabre, gothic hillside Oakwood Cemetery, at the head of 101st Street north of Troy via Oakwood Avenue. A health food store around the corner from the monument admonishes passersby with an "I want you . . . to enjoy good health" window poster.

World Trade Center. Exhibits on the rest of the Empire State fill the rest of the museum, highlighted by a fully-functioning (and rideable!) Herschell carousel.

Albany Practicalities

If all the high culture and power politics leave you hungry for a back-to-basics road-food experience, head a mile or so west from downtown to **Jack's Diner** (518/482-9807) at 547 Central Avenue. This New Jersey–built 1930s chrome-plated diner car attracts a diverse batch of families, local crazies, beat cops (the police station is across the street), and fellow travelers who come for its hearty meat loaf and burgers, bottomless cups of coffee, and friendly, loquacious staff. Albany's other great old diner, the **Miss Albany** (518/465-9148), is a 1941 Silk City (aka "Lil's") on the National Register of Historic Places and in the flesh at 893 Broadway.

In between the downtown museums and the green spaces of Washington Park, the blue-collar bohemian Lark Street neighborhood is Albany's answer to Greenwich Village, sporting several cafés, some tattoo parlors, and a number of good restaurants. The roadhouse-style **Lark Tavern** (518/463-9779), at 453 Madison Avenue at Lark Street, serves hearty food and big mugs of cheap beer in a cavernous, dark setting thronged with an eclectic mix of yuppies, old-timers, and artsy types.

Albany's motels congregate off the I-90 Everett Road exit, but one very nice, centrally located place to stay is the **Mansion Hill Inn** ($120–160; 518/465-2038), near the Governor's Mansion at 115 Philip Street, which doubles as a fine restaurant.

Downtown Troy's cast-iron buildings are popular with set designers, who transform them into backdrops for films like **Martin Scorsese's** 1992 adaptation of **Edith Wharton's** The Age of Innocence.

Troy

The grave of Uncle Sam and the birthplace of the detachable shirt collar are both across the river in **Troy** (pop. 49,170), 10 minutes north via the I-787 freeway. A world removed from downtown Albany, this narrow riverfront city was strategically situated at the point where the Erie Canal headed west from the Hudson River. It rose to national promi- nence as a manufacturing center in the 19th century, when its foundries and factories cranked out iron for stoves, stage- coaches, bells, and battleships.

Troy's burly factories have given way to a quietly pic- turesque college town, with Rensselaer Polytechnic Institute rising on the steep hill to the east above the cast-iron busi- ness district downtown. In addition to its many impressive buildings, Troy's dense downtown has two great road-food finds: **Manory's Restaurant** (518/272-2422) at 99 Congress Street, doles out stuffed combo sandwiches, home-cooked pasta, meat and seafood dinners, and really, really big breakfasts; **The Famous Lunch** (518/272-9481), at 111 Congress Street, is a de- lightfully worn-down greasy spoon with hand-lettered signs, tall wooden booths, and an eye-opening clientele of cops, winos, RPI students, and local businesspeople—nearly all of whom, from noon until late every day but Sun- day, chow down on multiple four-inch-long, chili-doused hot dogs served on Styrofoam plates with cold RC Colas on the side.

*Troy's Astros-affiliated Class A **Valley Cats** (518/629-2287), transplanted from Pittsfield, MA, and the oldest stadium in the minor leagues, play in a nice new stadium on the campus of Hudson Valley Community College.*

Mount Lebanon Shaker Village

Heading east from Albany across the Hudson River toward the Massachusetts state line, US-20 follows Columbia Av- enue through the warehouse and factory town of Rensse- laer, then climbs a long, retail-lined hill past innumerable liquor stores, mini-marts, gas stations, and motels into the Taconic Mountains. Also here: the full-throttle oval of the **Lebanon Valley Raceway** (518/794-9806), with racing throughout the summer.

After this 25-mile barrage of contemporary culture, the tranquil hillside remains of **Mount Lebanon Shaker Village,** on the south side of US-20 a few hundred yards west of the Massachusetts border, come as a welcome relief. Of the 20 Shaker communities once scattered over the eastern United States, practicing a passionate but celibate form of Christianity, Mount Lebanon was the head min- istry, founded here in 1785. The community endured until 1947, and some two dozen historic buildings still stand, including a 192-foot stone barn—the largest stone barn in the world when constructed in 1859—and a no-frills, but cleverly constructed, 1854 washhouse boasting hidden wall drawers and perfectly fitted floorboards. All of which is testimony to the Shaker edict, "Hands to work, hearts to God."

*If you're interested in the Shakers, you'll want to make the short detour south of I-90 from Albany or New Lebanon to **Old Chatham**, where an excellent **museum** (Thurs.–Mon. in summer only; $8; 518/794- 9100) has the world's most extensive collection of Shaker-related items, everything from pieces of Shaker furniture to the woodworking tools and devices used to make them.*

INTERSECTION

The quickest route east from Troy is Hwy-2, a rural back road across the Taconic Mountains to Williamstown, Massachusetts. Alternately, you can follow old US-20 east through New Lebanon to Pittsfield, Massachusetts, then follow a short stretch of the **Appalachian Trail** route along US-7 north to Williamstown and North Adams (see page 312). For details on the full route, see pages 288–371.

MASSACHUSETTS

The leafy amble from New York State, up and over the
ridge of the Taconics, brings you through a beautiful
region dense with visitor appeal, including the Shaker
communities along US-20 and the industrial and literary sites of
the Berkshires, not to mention Williamstown, a New England poster town if
ever there was one. (For full coverage of this region, see pages 312–313.)

    Across Massachusetts, we follow the very scenic Route 2, also known as the
"Mohawk Trail," across the state's northern tier, rather than US-20, which runs
more or less underneath the Massachusetts Turnpike, I-90. Passing across some
of the least-populous and most deeply forested acres in the whole Common-
wealth of Massachusetts, you can easily imagine you're in Vermont rather than
the so-called Bay State. Picking its way over the flattened summits of the
Hoosac Range foothills to the Green Mountains in the north, Route 2 follows
rock-strewn trout streams flecked with whitewater and shaded by boreal forests
of hemlock, yellow birch, and red spruce—including some of the state's only remaining stands of old growth. Midway across Massachusetts, Route 2 bridges
the Connecticut River above Turners Falls, lopes through the trees, and emerges
at historic Lexington and Concord, at Boston's back door.

The Mohawk Trail

Running east from North Adams toward Greenfield and I-91, and taking its
name from the warpath used for raids against Algonquian settlements along the
upper Connecticut River Valley, the **Mohawk Trail** (Route 2) was one of the nation's first scenic highways, improved and paved as early as 1914 as part of a
massive state effort to lure tourists into this cash-deprived farm belt of New
England. If you're driving an overloaded or underpowered vehicle, you'll appreciate the thrill and radiator-popping risks that once attended the slow switch-
back grind up around the attention-getting Hairpin Turn at the edge of the
Western Summit. The turn is so tight that signs insist on a 15-mph speed limit,
and people who don't abide by the rules are likely to find themselves screeching

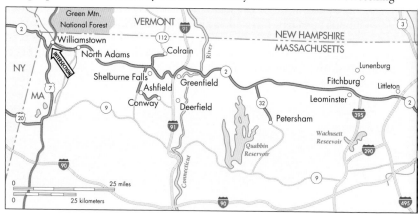

around past the sightseers at the **Golden Eagle Restaurant.** Further up, at the top of the hill, the tidy **Wigwam Summit Motel** ($50–80; 413/663-3205), one of many photogenic old motor courts along the route, has been taking in guests since the road was built. Don't be fooled by the short stretch of gentle ups and downs east of the summit over the glacier-flattened mountain peaks:

The route east along the tortuous Cold River ravine quickens the pulse, even in these days of power steering and anti-lock brakes, especially if you get sandwiched between a pair of 18-wheelers, whose burning brake pads sometimes scent the air all the way down the valley.

East of the summit, dropping down into the valley of the Deerfield River, you pass groups of kayakers and some roadside stands offering rentals of inner tubes—the whitewater equivalent of a recliner, and the preferred mode of transport for those interested in relaxing and enjoying the ride. More serious river runners may want to sign up for one of the trips offered by **Zoar Outdoors** (413/339-4010). There are also some enticingly kitschy old Indian trading posts, packed full of postcards, plastic tomahawks, and moccasins; my personal favorite is the Big Indian, fronted by a historically inaccurate, politically incorrect, and photogenically irresistible 35-foot-tall statue of a Plains Indian. Another giant Indian statue, a half-ton bronze entitled *Hail to the Sunrise,* stands along Route 2 just west of the town of Charlemont.

> In Massachusetts and the rest of New England, we have adopted the use of "Route" instead of "Hwy-," in keeping with regional practice.

Shelburne Falls

Travelers in search of variety should head west from Greenfield along the historic Mohawk Trail, Route 2, and take a turn at the signs for the lively, artsy little town of **Shelburne Falls,** which is actually two towns, Shelburne and Buckland, facing one another across the Deerfield River. The two are linked

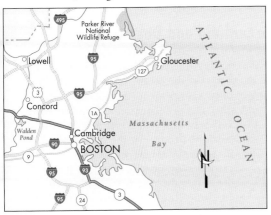

by the **Bridge of Flowers,** a former electric trolley bridge that was converted to a linear display garden after the trolleys closed down in the 1920s. Four score and a few years later, there are mature trees growing out of the concrete arches, and every spring local gardeners add rich displays of annual color. The story of the trolleys is told, and rides

Northeast of Deerfield, near the Vermont border, the town of **Northfield** had the first youth hostel in the United States in 1934. Unfortunately, the hostel closed in 1998, taken over as dormitories by a local college.

are sometimes offered, at the **Shelburne Falls Trolley Museum** (413/625-9443) at 14 Depot Road, walking distance south of the bridge.

Nearby food and beverage options include espresso concoctions from Bridge Street's **Shelburne Falls Coffee Roasters,** or the vegetarian-friendly deli selections at the rear of **McCusker's Market,** facing the south end of the iron bridge. The best cheap grub in town is served up at the homey **Fox Town Coffee and Sandwich Shop** on Bridge Street, where you can feast on a short stack of pancakes with real maple syrup ($2), or enjoy a fresh BLT with a packet of potato chips and a pickle on the side for $2.55.

Scenic Route 116: Ashfield and Conway

Come fall, the sugar maples in the surrounding mixed hardwood forest add a blaze of brilliant orange to the landscape, making Route 2 a favorite of leaf-peepers between the end of September and Columbus Day weekend. But if sharing the two-lane road with thousands of rubbernecking drivers becomes wearisome, consider taking a road less-traveled. Almost any road will do, but a loop along Route 116 through **Ashfield** and **Conway,** a few miles south of Route 2, passes over several historic covered bridges and offers enough pastoral beauty to more than compensate for the detours.

You'll find excellent wooded streamside campsites in **Mohawk Trail State Forest** (413/339-5504) just above where the Cold River empties into the Deerfield. There are five year-round rustic log cabins, too, but make reservations well in advance if you have your heart set on staying in one.

Shunning the main highway doesn't require skipping meals, either. For instance, there are thin-crust whole pizzas and slices at the **Countrypie Pizza Company** (open daily till 9 PM; 413/628-4488), at 343 Main Street across from Ashfield's public library. Given the fresh fancy toppings available, the prices are a real steal. Or coast down Route 116 to **Baker's Country Store** (413/369-4936), just east of Conway's old water tower, and sit down to a simple soup or sandwich amid the fishing tackle and canned goods. If you like your pastry crusts short and white, be sure to sample the fresh pies, particularly in the summer during berry season.

Greenfield and Deerfield

As Route 2 speeds down into the Connecticut River Valley, it veers along I-91 just long enough to skirt the county seat of Greenfield, a place once known for its cutlery, tap-and-die, and other metals-related manufacturing. The proximity of the Interstate has endowed Greenfield with some of the only chain motels in western Massachusetts.

A world away from the modern Interstate aesthetic, but just three miles south of Greenfield along Route 5, **Historic Deerfield** (daily; $15; 413/774-5581) is an immaculately preserved ensemble of architecture and agroculture dating back over 350 years. More than a dozen clapboard buildings, shaded by a canopy of stately old elm trees, form a mile-long reminder of the time when this part of Massachusetts formed the frontier of western "civilization," and English settlers waged bloody war against the native Pocumtuck Indians. The adjacent town of Deerfield, and the famous Deerfield Academy prep school, hardly intrude, leaving Historic Deerfield to stand as it was—fanlight windows, wrought iron, well-worn stones, and all. Inside each house, guides discuss the lives, belongings, and historical contexts of the former inhabitants, often with such parental intimacy that you half-expect these long-dead Ebenezers, Jonathans, and Marys to be napping upstairs. One of the finest surviving colonial townscapes in America, Historic Deerfield is well worth a visit, no matter how brief, especially since there's no admission charge if you just want to stop and walk around.

Historic Deerfield also offers the **Flynt Center of Early New England Life** at the edge of a field behind Main Street. The 27,000-square-foot museum, designed to look like a colonial tobacco barn, displays thousands of "fancy goods" and other consumer treasures—pewter teapots, silk waistcoats, and the like—that were keys to civilized life here on the edge of wilderness. For the full historic experience, stay for dinner or overnight at the **Deerfield Inn** ($140 and up; 413/774-5587), right in the historic core.

Although early spring is aptly known as mud season throughout New England's back country, it's also when the sugar maple sap starts to flow. Boil away nearly 98 percent of the sap and you have genuine **maple syrup** delicious enough to make muddy, frost-heaved farm roads positively inviting.

Route 2: Gardner

About 10 miles east of I-91, Route 2 crosses high over the Connecticut River atop the huge, art deco French King Bridge, giving grand views over the surrounding landscape. From here east, the route becomes a mini freeway as it launches into a 40-mile stretch of almost nothing but forest; though nearly unimaginable today, some two thirds of the landscape you see out your windows was totally deforested in the early 1800s. After some 150 years, that statistic has been reversed, although much of the forest along this stretch is relatively young, having grown up since a devastating hurricane in 1938 blew down nearly every pine tree in its path.

For most of the way across this part of central Massachusetts, the older two-lane alignment of the Mohawk Trail (Route 2) is still in use as Route 2A, running through a series of small towns like Orange, Athol, Templeton, and **Gardner,** which was once one of the busiest chair-making centers in the United States. The area's industrial history is remembered by the town's pride and joy, the one-time **World's Largest Chair,** which sits on the front lawn of Gardner's Elm Street elementary school.

Leominster and Harvard

As you approach the Tri-Town area of **Leominster** (LUH-minster), Fitchburg, and Lunenburg, rooftops begin to supplant treetops and Boston radio stations crowd the dial. Although "the Hub" is still some 30 miles away, its gravitational attraction seems to compel a majority of cars to exceed the speed limit. If you already know that you would rather walk barefoot over hot coals than be caught driving in Boston, you can start looking for accommodations now, as you are within the sphere of the **MBTA Commuter Rail** service to downtown (617/722-3200 or 800/392-6100). Purely by way of an example, the 80-minute journey from end-of-the-line Fitchburg to Boston's North Station, made 10 times daily on weekdays, five times daily on weekends, costs around $12 roundtrip—equivalent to a couple hours' parking in most Boston lots.

Accommodations here, along I-495 on the perimeter of the Boston metropolitan area, are largely geared toward business travelers, though the aptly named **Friendly Crossways Retreat** (978/456-3649), at 247 Littleton County Road, just north of the Route 2/I-495 junction in the hamlet (not the college) of Harvard, has dorm beds and a few private rooms, too.

Practicalities aside, one very positive reason to spend time out here is the presence of **Fruitlands**, (daily May–Oct.; $10; 978/456-3924), 102 Prospect Hill Road, the Harvard College museum of American arts and crafts.

Lowell

At "five o'clock of a red-all-over suppertime" on March 12, 1922, **Jack Kerouac**—baptized John L. (Jean-Louis) Kirouac by his French Canadian parents—was born in **Lowell** (pop. 100,500), a city sincerely regarded as one of the wonders of the world back when the Industrial Revolution was as fascinating as the Internet is now. Although this original dharma bum is more widely remembered for hanging out with Ferlinghetti in San Francisco, and Ginsberg in New York, and for pasting the beat generation firmly across the map of American culture, Kerouac also wrote five novels based on friends and familiar places in his native city. His fictional work, from *On the Road* on, is that much more interesting when read in the context of his real life in this Merrimack River mill town, a dozen miles but a world away from quaint little Concord.

Reciprocating Kerouac's lifelong love for Lowell, the National Park Service publishes a walking-tour brochure on Jack and his life in Lowell. They also help sponsor the annual **Lowell Celebrates Kerouac!** festival the first full weekend in October. Maps and guides to the man and the town are available from the visitors center (978/970-5000) at 246 Market Street.

If you want to pay your respects to Kerouac, who died in Florida in 1969, he is buried in Edsom Cemetery, two miles south of downtown Lowell via Gorham Street. Fans by the hundreds beat a path to his grave, which is on Lincoln Avenue between 7th and 8th Streets, marked by a pile of beer cans and other ritual offerings.

Patriots and Poets

One of the more enjoyable rites of springtime in and around Boston is the annual celebration of the events leading up to the American Revolution. Now held on the third Monday in April, but originally occurring on April 18, the state holiday known as Patriot's Day sees all kinds of special events. Most famous is the Boston Marathon, which since 1897 has been run from Hopkinton southwest of the city through Newton to its finish at Copley Square. Although the marathon follows a very different route, it is held on the anniversary of another famous race, the one between British soldiers and patriot Paul Revere, who made his legendary ride on the night of April 18, 1775, to warn his fellow minutemen of the British march on Lexington and Concord.

At the end of his ride, on the morning of April 19, Paul Revere reached the Buckman Tavern in Lexington, where fellow revolutionaries John Hancock and Samuel Adams (he of boutique beer fame) were asleep, awaiting word of the British advance. Revere woke them (and some 70 others), and at 5:30 AM they assembled to meet the redcoats. Although the minutemen backed off, shots were fired and eight Americans were killed. Three hours later, when the British moved on to Concord, they were met by a much larger and better organized force of minutemen, who fired back and started what we now know as the Revolutionary War. This battle, which raged all day and followed the overwhelmed British all the way back to Boston, was remembered in another oft-recited patriotic poem by Concord writer Ralph Waldo Emerson, words from which are inscribed on the base of Concord's minuteman statue.

> By the rude bridge that arched the flood,
> heir flag to April's breeze unfurled,
> Here once the embattled farmers stood,
> And fired the shot heard round the world.

These events and many related ones are all reenacted each year, either on their actual anniversary or on Patriot's Day, and usually at the historically accurate crack of dawn.

Even without the Kerouac connection, Lowell—with its working water-powered looms, canal tours, and engaging interpretive tours—would deserve attention. Befitting its blue-collar past, Lowell is home to several classic diners—best of which is the excellent **Arthur's Paradise** (978/452-8647), a 1937 Worcester diner at 112 Bridge Street, where the house specialty is the great big Boot Mill sandwich (which consists of. . . ?)

Lowell's other blue-collar landmarks include the **Club Diner** (978/452-1679) at 145 Dutton Street, and the **Four Sisters' Owl Diner** (978/453-8321), open every day at 244 Appleton Street.

Concord: The Shot Heard Round the World

Route 2 feels increasingly freeway-like the closer you get to Boston, but there are a few things in the neighborhood you may want to check out if you're not in a hurry to hit the "Hub." A good example is lovely little **Concord,** the destination of British Redcoats that fabled day in April 1775 when the war for American independence began. A reconstructed **Old North Bridge,** site of the "shot heard round the world," still arches over the placid Concord River next to open fields and drystone walls. The superb setting draws artists and picnickers as well as history buffs, and if the crowds aren't too bad, the scene ranks among the most evocative in New England. The **Minute Man National Historical Park** maintains a free year-round visitors center (978/369-6993) on the hillside overlooking the famous site. Stop in and pick up a guide to the rest of the park's holdings along the "Battle Road" (aka Lexington Road and Route 2A) between Concord and Lexington (and try to turn a deaf ear to the constant stream of small planes flying in and out of nearby Hanscom Field).

Although it often seems as if you can't toss a stick anywhere in eastern Massachusetts without hitting something of historic significance, this is especially true in and around Concord, where some of the most influential American writers— Ralph Waldo Emerson, Nathaniel Hawthorne, Henry David Thoreau, and

Louisa May Alcott, to name the most famous four—lived and/or worked. To get a sense of the lives of these influential and interconnected writers, head to that ancient-looking parsonage alongside the famous Old North Bridge, **The Old Manse** (daily April–Oct.; $7.50; 978/369-3909), whose study window views are not so very different from what they were when Ralph Waldo Emerson and Nathaniel Hawthorne lived here. And if the mood strikes you, you can visit the final resting place of these literary lions along Author's Ridge in **Sleepy Hollow Cemetery,** off Bedford Street northeast of the town center.

Visitors may be struck by the quantity of No Parking signs lining the streets of Concord, but the reason for this barrage of apparent inhospitality may be seen on any sun-drenched summer weekend, when long columns of cars bound for the beach at nearby **Walden Pond** jam Route 126. Serious fans of Henry David Thoreau and his little experiment of simple living may be able to overlook its overstressed condition, but more than likely you'll be taken aback by the erosion, the crowds, and the racket of passing commuter trains. Of course, there is still some magic to the place, although

standing guard at Minute Man National Historical Park

it usually takes a near-dawn in late spring or near-dusk in late fall to find any hint of transcendence along the pond's well-worn peripheral path.

For a quick introduction to all this and more, stop by the **Concord Museum** (daily; $7; 978/369-9609), just east of the town green, where the collection contains everything from the lantern used in Paul Revere's famous ride to dozens of household objects (beds, chairs, desks, etc.) belonging to Emerson and Thoreau.

If you want to linger in Concord long enough to have some transcendent moments of your own, stay the night at one of many nice B&Bs like the **Hawthorne Inn** ($160–220; 978/369-5610), at 462 Lexington Road across from Hawthorne's home, the Wayside.

For more information about the Concord area, contact the historic Wright Tavern **visitors center** (978/369-3120) at 2 Lexington Road, by the east end of the town common.

> Perhaps you haven't got a week—like Thoreau did—to paddle down the Concord River. You can still make your own, albeit abbreviated, journey with a summer or fall canoe rental from **South Bridge Boat House** (978/369-9438), at 496-502 Main Street in Concord.

Cambridge

One last stop before you hit Boston proper is erudite Cambridge (pop. 95,802), an inseparable sibling to the big city but very much a place in its own right. Best known for its top universities, Harvard and Massachusetts Institute of Technology, Cambridge is a liberal, earthy, and open-minded foil to the big money and social pretension that so often characterize its big brother across the water.

The two universities and their many fine museums (especially Harvard, which boasts world-class collections in the Fogg Art Museum, the Sackler Gallery of Far Eastern Art, and the Peabody Museum of Archaeology) are the main draws for visitors, but the "town" away from the "gown" is equally worth exploring, despite the recent outbreak of chain-store disease around Harvard Square. For an antidote, head two stops north on the T subway to Davis Square in neighboring Somerville, where a classic 1940s Worcester diner, **The Rosebud** (617/666-6015), off Elm Street at 381 Summer Street, serves up the highest quality meals all day, with nary a Starbucks in sight.

> Not far from Thoreau's reconstructed cabin at Walden Pond, a very different philosophy of simplicity may be found in the design of the **Gropius House** (Wed.–Sun. 11am–4pm in summer; $8; 781/259-8098), on Baker Bridge Road in Lincoln. Built between 1937 and 1938 by and for Bauhaus founder Walter Gropius, this small showcase blends Bauhaus form-is-function precepts with traditional New England simplicity.

Driving Across Boston

From Concord, the remaining dozen miles to Boston are most quickly devoured along Route 2, although you can take slower Route 2A if you wish to follow the footsteps of those retreating British redcoats. Either way will bring you to the same gateway for the metropolitan area. Following US-3 will bring you in through wealthy Winchester and eventually onto Memorial Drive

Rosebud Diner

Car Talk

Ever tuned in to your local national public radio station, and instead of hearing breaking news and informed commentary, you got two guys laughing their heads off and making jokes about cars and mechanics? Well, you probably tuned in to *Car Talk,* the Cambridge-based call-in show featuring a pair of MIT-trained auto mechanics, Click and Clack, the Tappet Brothers, otherwise known as Tom and Ray Magliozzi. From its humble beginnings back around 1977, *Car Talk* has become the most popular program at the left edge of the radio dial, reaching more than 2 million listeners every week. In between bouts of sarcasm and scandal-mongering, Tom and Ray do actually give advice about cars—advice that occasionally helps people—so if you're having trouble with your car, give them a call at 1-888-CAR-TALK, or send a message through their website, www.cartalk.cars.com. Either way, it's free. And you're safe from the public humiliation for a while at least. The show is not broadcast live but cunningly edited together in a darkened room off Harvard Square (look for a sign saying Dewey, Cheatham, and Howe), with the help of sophisticated technology and an ever-expanding team of contributors with names like Zbigniew Chrysler, Orson Buggy, Rusty Steele, Denton Fender, Alan Greasepan, and Francis Ford Cupholda.

If you're in Cambridge ("Our Fair City") and happen to need some car repair, *Car Talk*'s Ray Magliozzi runs the **Good News Garage** (617/354-5383), at 75 Hamilton Street, off Brookline Street midway between Central Square and the BU Bridge over the Charles River.

along the Charles River, past the campuses of Harvard and MIT. But unless it's 3 AM and the roads are all clear, you would be well-advised to leave your car in the gigantic Alewife T subway station commuter parking garage (about $8 a day) at the Route 2/US-3/Route 16 junction in Arlington, and use the subway to get around the city. (Cyclists note: From the Alewife T, the very nice **Minuteman Bikeway** follows the bed of the old Boston & Lowell Railroad between Cambridge and the edge of Concord—11 idyllic, car-free miles.)

Driving directions across downtown Boston are basically a waste of paper; signs are few and traffic is chaotic, so you'll need to keep your eyes firmly on the road.

One of the most beautiful gardens in the Boston area is **Mount Auburn Cemetery,** along the Charles River in western Cambridge. Landscaped by F. L. Olmstead, it has 172 acres of trees, hills, paths, and memorials marking the mortal remains of such luminaries as Henry Wadsworth Longfellow, Winslow Homer, and Buckminster Fuller.

Quincy: The Adams Family

South of Boston, Route 3 reemerges from the I-93 freeway at **Quincy** (pop. 84,985), home of the Adams family, the political dynasty that helped shape the early republic. John Adams (1735–1826) signed the Declaration of Independence, served as a diplomat during the Revolutionary War, helped negotiate the Treaty of Paris, then returned home to become

George Washington's vice-president and successor. His son, John Quincy Adams (1767–1848), served as president from 1825 to 1829. Rather than quit politics after losing the election in 1828, he returned to Washington, serving in the House of Representatives for the next 16 years. The rather modest houses where both men were born, plus a nice garden and a historic church, are preserved as part of the **Adams National Historic Site** (daily; $3; 617/770-1175), which covers 13 downtown acres starting at a visitors center at 1250 Hancock Street.

More recently, Quincy has been home to granite quarries and the truly huge Fore River Shipyard, on Route 3A at the south edge of town, where the massive battleship **USS** *Salem* (daily; $6; 617/479-7900) is berthed as part of a nascent shipbuilding museum. This dense forest of cranes, derricks, and scaffolding rises along the south side of the 1930s Fore River Bridge, along Route 3A at the south edge of town.

Playing on the common perception of the Pilgrims as thrifty, reliable, and stead-fast, in 1928 the automobile company **Chrysler** named its now-defunct line of low-priced cars "Plymouth."

Plymouth Rock and Plimoth Plantation

There's little evidence to back up the story of **Plymouth Rock,** the supposed landing site of those weary *Mayflower* passengers back in 1620, but like the Liberty Bell and Mt. Rushmore, it's something every red-blooded American tourist has to see.

Now protected by a neoclassical granite portico and inscribed with the date 1620, **Plymouth Rock** is right on the waterfront, off Water Street at the south end of North Street in **Plymouth**. The rock is part of a pleasant park, which also includes the *Mayflower II* (daily; $8), a replica of the Pilgrim's ship, where an on-board exhibit describes the Pilgrims' two-month transatlantic journey.

On a hill across the street from Plymouth Rock is the **Plymouth National Wax Museum** (daily; $7; 508/746-6468), where the light-and-sound show depicting the landing at Plymouth Rock is *almost* worth the price of admission. The wax museum is the only sign of Plymouth being such a potential tourist trap; the whole place is actually fairly low-key, with a couple of gift shops and snack bars across from the Rock. Two blocks inland, downtown Plymouth looks like any other very pleasant New England suburb, with no tacky T-shirt shops to be found.

Further south, two miles from Plymouth Rock along Route 3A, or off the Route 3 freeway at exit 5, **Plimoth Plantation** (daily; $20; 508/746-1622) is a living history re-creation of the original Pilgrim colony and features costumed interpreters taking part in planting, harvesting, and other daily chores.

If you happen to be around Boston before Christmas rather than in mid-April, you may want to take part in another historical reenactment: the **Boston Tea Party.** Every year, on the Sunday nearest to the anniversary of the original event (December 16, 1773), volunteers dress up as Indians (mimicking the colonists who disguised themselves as Native Americans) and throw bales of tea into the harbor from the decks of the *Boston Tea Party Ship* (617/338-1773).

Boston

In the 360-plus years since its founding, Boston (pop. 589,000) has witnessed more historically significant events than any American city even twice its size. The youthful energy of the city's many college students certainly helps cloak it's traditional Puritan parochialism, while the high-tech economic boom (and the breaking of the "Curse of the Bambino" by the 2004 World Series champion Boston Red Sox baseball team) have helped loosen up a city previously best known for baked beans and banning sexy books.

There are lots of places to start a Boston tour, but a personal favorite is the **Old North Church**, (daily; $3; 617/523-6676), at 193 Salem Street, a Boston landmark since well before Paul Revere set off on his midnight ride. The steeple has been rebuilt, but almost everything else dates back to colonial times. Paul's house, the oldest in Boston, is a few blocks away at 19 North Square, and the surrounding neighborhood, the predominantly Italian North End, is the city's oldest and most pedestrian-friendly quarter, its narrow streets jutting out toward Boston harbor.

With its abundance of universities, museums, and cultural centers, Boston is packed with places to improve your mind. One of the nicest has to be the **Isabella Stuart Gardner Museum**, (closed Mon.; $11; 617/566-1401) at 280 The Fenway. In the late 19th century, "Mrs. Jack" Gardner built her home in the style of a Venetian palazzo, crammed it with exquisite art, and then opened it as a museum. Her idiosyncratic taste is part of the charm of this place, along with the lushly landscaped interior courtyard. (Note: Anyone named "Isabella" gets in free!). The much bigger **Museum of Fine Arts**, (daily; $15; 617/267-9300; $15) at 465 Huntington Avenue is only a short walk away, and has more than 200 world-class galleries of just about every type and era of fine art, including perhaps the best Japanese art collection in the United States.

Of course, for baseball fans, Boston's must-see is **Fenway Park** (tickets 617/267-1700), home of the Red Sox. Located off Boylston Street at 4 Yawley Way, this is the oldest, smallest, and arguably most entertaining stadium in the nation.

Practicalities

Boston, a.k.a. "The Hub," sits spider-like at the center of a web of major highways. Air travelers get to deal with the chaos and malfunction of Logan

International Airport, the major gateway to New England for U.S. and foreign flights. Logan is very central—just a seven-minute ride across Boston Harbor to downtown if you take the Water Shuttle. Logan is also connected to the city by the Blue Line subway run by Massachusetts Bay Transportation Authority (617/722-3200), the "T," a well-run and nearly comprehensive network of subways, buses, trams, ferries, and commuter trains (617/722-3200). Despite the completion of the $15 billion "Big Dig," Boston's 21st-century traffic and 17th-century streets are not for faint-hearted drivers. Narrow, often unidentified, poorly maintained, and laid out in irregular patterns conforming to long-buried topography, the streets of Boston are also home to aggressive, bumper-riding red-light-runners. So park your car, take public transit, and walk.

While nightly rates at top-end hotels run well over $400 a night, places to stay in Boston start with the budget **HI Boston Hostel**, ($33 per person; 617/536-9455), centrally located near the Green Line's Hynes/ICA station at 12 Hemenway Street. It's a standard urban hostel, which is to say that if the person in the next bunk snores, good luck catching a good night's rest. Private rooms (around $70 for two) are also available, as is an additional, summer-only HI hostel. For a moderate price and a great location, right at the Copley Square finish line of the Boston Marathon, try the popular **Charlesmark Hotel**, ($150; 617/247-1212) at 655 Boylston. Many steps up the comfort scale is the well-appointed and very central **Beacon Hill Hotel**, (around $250; 617/723-7575), a boutique B&B with a popular bistro and rooftop terrace at 25 Charles Street.

Thanks no doubt to Boston's Puritan past, the city has never had a great reputation for its food, but things have definitely changed. If you really have to have an old-fashioned Boston meal, go to **Durgin Park**, (617/227-2038) in Faneuil Hall. Open since 1827, this New England eatery serves up Yankee Pot Roast, clam chowder, and baked beans at shared tables to a mix of tourists and masochistic locals. Boston also has more than few great Mexican, Japanese, and Chinese places, but for another only-in-Boston experience head to the **Daily Catch**, (617/523-8567) at 323 Hanover Street, in the old North End within walking distance of the Haymarket T. This 30-year-old joint is so tiny that the cook could shake hands with half his customers without leaving his stove. Calamari (squid) is the house specialty, but the menu's mainstay is Sicilian seafood over linguine (with red or white sauce), served in sauté pans instead of on plates. They take cash only, but don't take reservations, so expect a wait after 6 PM. For breakfast, head across the Charles River to Cambridge and neighboring Somerville (see page 623).

For further information, contact the Greater Boston Convention and Visitors Bureau (617/536-4100 or 800/888-5515), located at 2 Copley Place.

New Bedford

Predominantly Portuguese **New Bedford** (pop. 93,768) is remembered as a capital of the whaling industry back in the days when spermaceti candles and whale oil lamps were necessities, not antiques. The city's harbor at the mile-wide mouth of the Acushnet River was home port for the East Coast's largest commercial fishing fleet until nearly two decades of flagrant overfishing brought the industry to collapse. The **New Bedford National Historical Park** showcases the cobblestone streets and brick facades, virtually unaltered since Herman

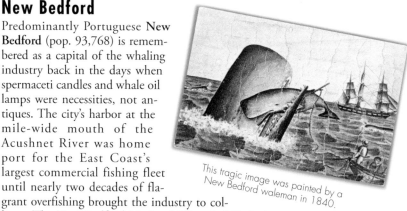

This tragic image was painted by a New Bedford waleman in 1840.

Although the Pilgrims are often given credit for establishing the first permanent white settlement in what later became the United States, they arrived a dozen years after other English settlers established Jamestown, Virginia.

New Bedford's Acushnet Avenue has a significant place in the world of late-19th-century American art: **Albert Pinkham Ryder,** visionary "painter of dreams," was born here, across from the childhood home of **Albert Bierstadt,** Romantic painter of the American West.

Melville shipped out of here in 1847 aboard a whaler bound for the Pacific. For a good orientation, drop by the well-stocked **visitors center** (508/996-4095), at the corner of William Street and North 2nd Street, and join one of their free hour-long guided **walking tours.** Before or after a stroll around town, head to the top of Johnny Cake Hill and visit the excellent **Whaling Museum** (daily; $8; 508/997-0046). Scrimshaw (carved whale ivory), tools of the whaling trade, historic photos, special maritime exhibits, and an 89-foot ship model are a few of the artifacts found in the not-to-be-missed museum collection maintained by the Old Dartmouth Historical Society. Across the street from the museum, the gorgeous little **Seamen's Bethel,** built in 1832 and featuring a pulpit shaped like a ship's bow, was featured in a chapter of Herman Melville's classic, *Moby Dick.*

Diner fans will appreciate New Bedford's offerings, too. The easiest diner to find is **Angelo's Orchid Diner** (508/993-3172), at 805 Rockdale Avenue, a 1953 O'Mahony serving solid short-order cookery enlivened by—you guessed it—a Portuguese influence. Or check out another 1950s O'Mahony, the pristine **Shawmut Diner** (508/993-3073), at 943 Shawmut Avenue at Hathaway near Route 140, open daily from 5 AM; the neon Indian alone makes it worth a visit. (For more on diners, see the sidebar in the Appalachian Trail chapter.)

Cape Cod: Sandwich

Although it rides the ridge of Cape Cod's glacial moraine, the forest-clad US-6 freeway (called Mid-Cape Highway) affords few good vistas. Traffic willing, you'll sail between the Sagamore Bridge and the Outer Cape in about 30 minutes, surrounded by more green than blue. One preferred route is parallel Route

6A. Never more than a mile or two away from US-6, this slower road is a good introduction to a part of the Cape that does its utmost to stay quaint without being too cute. Generally, it succeeds.

Take **Sandwich,** for example. When you reach the center of town, you'll come across a small, irregular green bordered by a tall, white church, a stately carriage-stop inn, and the Historical Society's **Sandwich Glass Museum** (daily April–Oct., Wed.–Sun. only Nov.–March; $4). Although the town's various glassworks could and did produce consummate extravagant vases and other artistic pieces, they mostly created inexpensive, mass-market stuff—such as 10-cent oil-lamp chimneys, and pressed plates and saucers, hundreds of which are on display.

Nearby on Pine and Grove Streets (follow signs from Route 130) is a more diverse collection of Americana, the **Heritage Plantation of Sandwich** (daily mid-May–mid-Oct.; $9; 508/888-3300). Here nearly 80 landscaped acres surround collections of Currier & Ives prints, military miniatures, antique cars, cigar store figures, American primitive portraiture—more unflattering likenesses of children have never been conceived—and even a working 1912 carousel.

Bayside Route 6A

In total contrast to the high-speed US-6 freeway or the traffic-clogged, overdeveloped, and frequently ugly Route 28 along the south shore, Route 6A along Cape Cod Bay shows off the Cape as it should be seen. Route 6A's winding backroads pass through small historic town after small historic town, and are lined by seafood shacks, ice cream stands, high-style restaurants, colonial-era homes, village greens, and stately churches—backed all the way by miles of bayfront beaches.

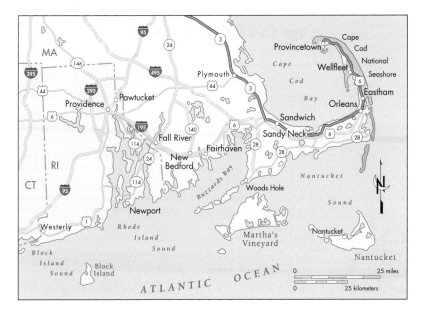

From Sandwich in the west to Brewster in the east, Route 6A offers a taste of what the Cape is all about. **Barnstable,** for example, is the second-oldest community on Cape Cod (founded in 1639), and has managed to retain its historic core through the years. A series of quaint villages line the bay between here and **Brewster** (pop. 8,440), which has the 80-acre **Cape Cod Natural History Museum** (daily; $7) at 869 Main Street and the old-fashioned **Brewster Store,** 1935 Main Street, in business since the 1850s.

Midway along, **Dennis,** the terminus of the Cape Cod Rail Trail to Wellfleet, is also the setting for the nation's oldest professional summer-stock theater, the **Cape Playhouse** (box office 508/385-3911), on Route 6A just east of the gas station. If you prefer film over stage, the **Cape Cinema** (508/385-2503), on the grounds behind the Playhouse, specializes in movies you won't find at the mall. If you arrive late, stick around until the lights go up after the credits or you'll miss one of the Cape's best public artworks, the Rockwell Kent mural of Prometheus on the cinema's ceiling.

Dennis also offers the chance to take in excellent Cape Cod views from atop **Scargo Tower;** turn toward South Dennis at the gas station, then follow signs along Scargo Hill Road.

Massachusetts is one of two states that recognizes private property ownership down to the low tide line, which is why you should respect the No Trespassing signs you may encounter on some beaches. Fortunately, plenty are amended with "Walkers Welcome."

To learn more than you ever thought possible about thermometers, pay a visit to the world's largest thermometer collection, proudly on display in the basement of Dick "The Thermometer Man" Porter's home in Onset; call 508/295-5504 for directions (and to make sure he's home).

Cape Cod National Seashore

The outermost stretch of Cape Cod, from Orleans to Provincetown, are protected from commercial development within the **Cape Cod National Seashore,** a 40-mile-long National Park Service property encompassing the whole of the coast.

The park's highlights include miles of gorgeous beaches, harbor seals, and some of the Cape's best waves, which occur here because the south-facing beaches are blocked by the islands of Nantucket and Martha's Vineyard, and the bayside is sheltered by the Cape itself. Pick up information detailing the various nature trails and interpretive programs at the **Salt Pond Visitor Center** (daily; free; 508/255-3421).

Wellfleet

The town of **Wellfleet** (pop. 2,493) is one of the Cape's most picturesque communities, favored for some reason by writers, psychiatrists, and oysters. Although home to a cluster of fine art galleries, crafts and clothing shops, and pricey restaurants,

A Cape Cod Primer

To avoid frustration and confusion when visiting Cape Cod, it helps to understand its basic directions and seasons. The compass isn't your friend here, as you will discover when faced with highway signs stubbornly directing you south to Provincetown—when heading south would bring you sooner to Venezuela than to the Cape's northernmost town. Instead, the principal directions are up and down: "Up-Cape" means generally westward, toward the mainland, while "Down-Cape" means roughly east, toward the Outer Cape and Provincetown. Further confusion arises with the distinctions among the various coasts: "Bayside" faces inward onto Cape Cod Bay, the "South Shore" faces Nantucket Sound, and the "Backside" braves the open Atlantic to the east.

It's a little easier to keep track of Cape Cod's seasons. High season, when Cape-bound traffic can be bumper-to-bumper from near Boston all the way to Hyannis, is basically from Memorial Day to Labor Day. The summer vacation months of July and August see the highest hotel rates, the most crowded beaches, and abysmal traffic on Fridays especially, when most vacation rentals "turn over." That said, even at the worst of times you can still find peace and quiet if you're willing to walk, paddle, or bike a little way from your car.

the place succeeds handsomely in finding a niche between self-conscious quaintness and residential seclusion. It's also blessed by a Cape Cod rarity: **Mayo Beach** just west of the town pier, a public beach with year-round free parking.

Wellfleet also has some of the Outer Cape's more affordable rooms, at the historic **Holden Inn** ($125 and up; 508/349-3450), 140 Commercial Street, where you share bathrooms, the front porch, and the bay views.

Truro

One of the finest biking or scenic driving routes on Cape Cod is the stretch of Old County Road that winds between Wellfleet and Truro, on the bay side of US-6. Topography is very varied, with hills and dunes, and traffic is minimal, so you can get a full sense of what the Cape is like beyond parking hassles and bijou restaurants. Like Wellfleet, **Truro** is well off the beaten track, and has very little commercial development. From the 1940s through the 1960s, Truro attracted a significant summer artists' colony whose members included painter Edward Hopper. These days, Truro is perhaps best known for the **Head of the Meadow** beach, just north of the landmark Highland Lighthouse on the Atlantic side of the Cape.

The Truro area also has a pair of unique accommodation options. The **HI Truro Hostel** (late June–early Sept. only; 508/349-3889) is beautifully situated between cranberry bogs and ocean beach in a former Coast Guard station on N. Pamet Road. On the calmer bay side, the 1930s beachfront cabins at **Days Cottages** ($75–120; 508/487-1062), along Route 6A in North Truro, are photogenic and very welcoming.

Provincetown

If not for its lack of freshwater, **Provincetown,** not Plymouth, would be the place we immediately equate with the Pilgrims. Way back in 1620, the band of religious travelers and fortune-seeking shipmates aboard the *Mayflower* landed here, expecting warm weather (in November, of all times) and good water. Neither was to be found, and the Pilgrims sailed on, disembarking across the bay at Plymouth Rock. Thus, P-town (as natives and in-the-know locals call it) lost its chance to be enshrined as the cornerstone of Anglo-American civilization and has had to butter its bread with something other than the national creation story.

So P-town took to the water. For much of its history, the sea sustained the town, which became a trading spot, whaling village, and fishing port. As those industries tapered off, new ones arose to take their place. Art and tourism now keep P-town busy.

In 1901 Charles Hawthorne opened an art school here, and the town earned art colony status that persists to this day. Bohemians followed. Among the artists and writers were John Reed, Eugene O'Neill, and George Cram Cook, whose Provincetown Players made theater history. And on the heels of Greenwich Village's fashionable flock came the car-borne tourists, who have proven themselves as faithful as Capistrano swallows, returning year after year to this tip of the Cape. Provincetown is a particularly strong magnet for East Coast gays and lesbians, so don't be surprised to see as many rainbow flags as Stars and Stripes waving in the breeze.

The summer trade prompts P-town to do its beach-boardwalk strut, as boatloads of day-trippers from Boston mob aptly named Commercial Street each afternoon, tanned couples mingle among the restaurants and outdoor cafés each evening, and fun-seekers fill up the bars and clubs each night. During any other season, however, the beach shuttle becomes a school bus, the wait for a table is negligible, and there's actually a chance that you'll find a place to park. Meanwhile, the off-season sunsets are still worth a visit to Race Point or Herring Cove Beach, even if they come at an earlier hour and require extra layers of clothing.

Provincetown Practicalities

After a day spent cycling amid dunes speckled with wild roses and beach grasses, or admiring the handiwork of windowbox gardeners in P-town's cottage-lined lanes, you'll probably get hungry. Snackers may want to try the sugar-coated *trutas* (sweet potato fritters) from the **Portuguese Bakery** at 299 Commercial Street. However, if you have a bigger appetite and want a harborside table, consider the moderately priced **Lobster Pot** (enter through the kitchen; 508/487-0842) at 321 Commercial just east of MacMillan Wharf for heaping portions of time-tested local favorites such as cioppino or *sopa do mar,* veggie pastas, and of course, lobster every which way you want it. It's open year-round, too—an exception in these parts.

For livelier, less-expensive dining, check out the multicultural menu—one of the few to please vegetarians—at **Napi's** (508/487-1145), tucked away behind Tedeschi's at 7 Freeman Street. **Spiritus Cafe & Pizzeria** (508/487-2808), at 190 Commercial Street, is another good, low-cost savior, dishing up pizza, focaccia sandwiches, ice cream, and lattes to a steady clientele of tattooed young smokers and slackers until 2 AM on summer weekends.

Planning to spend the night? If it's a summer weekend, make reservations or you may spend your time searching for a bed rather than basking on the beach. If you don't mind the occasional bout of late-night laughter from Commercial Street carousers, the **Somerset House** ($150 and up; 508/487-0383) at 378 Commercial Street has comfortable rooms and a very central location in an old Cape Cod manse. Quieter and calmer, the **Inn at Cook Street** ($135 and up; 508/487-3894), in the "East End" at 7 Cook Street, offers relaxing decks and gardens, and a great breakfast. Rounding out the lodging options are the bargain-priced shared little cottages of the **Outermost Hostel** (May–Oct.; $14; 508/487-4378) on Winslow Street past the Pilgrim Monument parking lot.

For help with anything to do with Provincetown, from a

place to stay to the perfect beach for kite-flying, contact the **visitors bureau** (508/487-3424) office on Lopes Square at the foot of the wharf.

Because Cape Cod juts out into the Atlantic, Provincetown is one of the best spots on the East Coast for **whale-watching trips.** From April through mid-October, boats leave many times a day on 4-hour trips (508/349-1900), traveling out to feeding areas off Stellwagen Bank to see humpback, minke, and finback whales.

That 252-foot tower jutting up over Provincetown is the **Pilgrim Monument and Museum** (9am–5pm, mid-March–Nov.; $7), with the best panorama on the Cape: In clear weather the entire peninsula can be seen, as well as the Massachusetts coast at Plymouth.

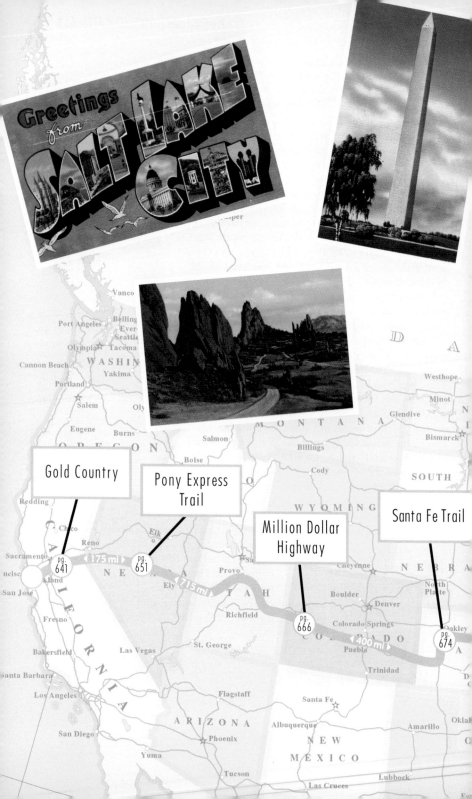

Greetings *from* SALT LAKE CITY

Gold Country

Pony Express Trail

Million Dollar Highway

Santa Fe Trail

pg. 641
pg. 651
pg. 666
pg. 674

175 mi

715 mi

400 mi

LONELIEST ROAD

The backbone of America runs from sea to shining sea, passing through eleven states, and some of the country's most magnificent landscapes.

Independence, Missouri
pg. 687

Louisville, Kentucky
pg. 698

Annapolis, Maryland
pg. 717

485 mi

530 mi

Between San Francisco and the Chesapeake Bay

Running coast-to-coast through the heart of America on a 3,200-mile odyssey from sea to shining sea, US-50 passes through a dozen different states and four state capitals, as well as the nation's capital, Washington, D.C. Along the route are some of the country's most magnificent landscapes: the **Sierra Nevada** and the **Appalachian** and **Rocky Mountains,** the endless farmlands of the **Great Plains,** and the desiccated deserts of **Utah** and **Nevada.** It follows the footsteps of pioneers, and gives a reverse time line of national development. Heading west to east, you can travel back in history from the cutting-edge high tech of contemporary Silicon Valley, across the Wild West frontier of the mid-1800s, and through lands the likes of Daniel Boone and countless others pioneered in the 1700s, before arriving at the Atlantic Ocean near some of the oldest and best-preserved colonial-era landscapes in the United States.

All the way across the country, US-50 passes through literally hundreds of timeworn small towns, the great majority of which have survived despite the modern onslaught of Wal-Marts and fast-food franchises. *Blue Highways* author William Least Heat-Moon writes about US-50, "for the unhurried, this little-known highway is the best national road across the middle of the United States." The route offers such a compelling cross-section of the nation that *Time* magazine devoted nearly an entire issue (July 7, 1997) to telling the story of the road it called the "Backbone of America."

From its start at **San Francisco,** the route cuts across California's midsection, passing the state capital at Sacramento before following the route of the old Pony Express up into the Sierra Nevada to the shores of **Lake Tahoe** and into Nevada. The Nevada portion of the route, dubbed "The Loneliest Road in America" by travel writers and tourist boards, is one of the most compelling long-distance drives in the country—provided you find miles and miles of little more than mountains, sagebrush, and blue sky compelling. The Great Basin desert continues across half of Utah, but then the route climbs over the Wasatch Front and onto the national park–packed red-rock country of the **Colorado Plateau.**

Continuing east, you cross the Continental Divide atop the Rockies, then follow the Arkansas River along the historic Santa Fe Trail. For fans of vanishing Americana, the route really comes into its own here across the Great Plains, with its hypnotically repetitive landscape of water towers, windmills, railroad tracks, and one small town after another.

After bisecting **Missouri** from Kansas City to St. Louis, US-50 crosses the Mississippi River into a much older and more settled landscape, through the agricultural heartlands of **Illinois, Indiana,** and **Ohio.** After climbing into the Appalachian backwoods of **West Virginia,** US-50 emerges suddenly into the wealth and power of downtown **Washington, D.C.,** before passing through the still perfectly picturesque fishing and farming communities of **Maryland's Eastern Shore.**

CALIFORNIA

Heading east from San Francisco across the heavy-duty Oakland Bay Bridge, the route across California starts off along the busy I-80 freeway through the urbanized San Francisco Bay Area. Passing diverse bayfront towns, including blue-collar **Oakland** and collegiate **Berkeley,** the busy and often congested eight-lane highway heads northeast across the historically important but increasingly suburbanized flatlands of the Sacramento Delta. Beyond **Sacramento,** the state capital of California, US-50 finally emerges, first as a freeway but later as a two-lane mountain road climbing through the heart of the **Sierra Nevada** foothills, where many of the small towns slumber in a gold-rush dream of the 1850s. Continuing east, US-50 winds through endless tracts of pine forest before cresting the Sierra to reach alpine Lake Tahoe, a year-round resort lying astride the California–Nevada border.

San Francisco is also a stop along our **Pacific Coast** road trip, which is described on pages 10–103. For particulars on what to see and do in the City by the Bay, see pages 60–61.

Oakland

Though many dismiss it as the West Coast equivalent of Newark, New Jersey, the hardworking city of **Oakland** (pop. 400,000) is actually a lively and intriguing place. The main attraction for visitors is its waterfront **Jack London Square,** honoring the city's favorite prodigal son. Covering a few blocks at the foot of Broadway, the complex contains a large bookstore, a couple of restaurants, an ancient log cabin supposedly lived in by Jack London in the Yukon Territory, and last but not least, the truly funky **Heinold's First and Last Chance,** a rickety old saloon that's the only survivor from the waterfront's wild past.

Oakland's other main draw is the excellent **Oakland Museum** (closed Mon. & Tues.; $6; 510/238-2200), housed in a landmark modernist ziggurat on the east edge of downtown, at 1000 Oak Street. Inside, exhibits cover everything from California's natural history to the photography of Dorothea Lange. An in-depth look at the state's popular culture is highlighted by a lively display of Hollywood movie posters, neon signs, jukeboxes, and classic cars and motorcycles.

Oakland's native son, Jack London

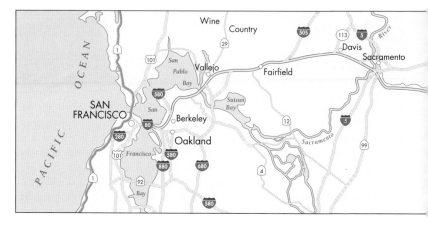

Berkeley

The intellectual, literary, and political nexus of the San Francisco Bay Area, left-leaning **Berkeley** (pop. 102,743) enjoys an international reputation that overshadows its suburban appearance. The town grew up around the attractively landscaped University of California campus, which, during the 1960s and early 1970s, was the scene of ongoing battles between "The Establishment" and unwashed hordes of antiwar, sex-and-drugs-and-rock-and-roll-crazed youth. Today, Berkeley maintains a typical college town mix of cafés and CD stores, and its site is superb, looking out across the bay to the Golden Gate and San Francisco.

The square-mile **University of California** Berkeley campus sits at the foot of eucalyptus-covered hills a mile east of the University Avenue exit off the I-80 freeway. Wander along Strawberry Creek, admiring the mix of neoclassical and postmodern buildings. Berkeley's cacophonous main drag, Telegraph Avenue, runs south from the heart of campus in a crazy array of tie-dye and tarot, lined by a half-dozen good cafés and some of the country's best bookstores.

There are dozens of great places to eat and drink in Berkeley, including one of the best breakfast joints on the planet, **Bette's Oceanview Diner** (510/644-3230), two blocks north of the I-80 University Avenue exit at 1807 4th Street, at the center of a boutique shopping district. Berkeley also has many top-rated restaurants, including world-renowned **Chez Panisse** (reservations essential; 510/548-5525), birthplace of California cuisine, located in the heart of Berkeley's gourmet ghetto at 1517 Shattuck Avenue.

The busy section of I-80 east from San Francisco has been improved by two new bridges; One is under construction to replace the earthquake-endangered **Bay Bridge**, while another new span crosses the **Carquinez Straits**.

To help ease the pain of his baby son's arthritis, in the 1940s a Berkeley machinist named **Candido Jacuzzi** created the air-bubbling hydrotherapy device that bears his name.

The big "C" above the **University of California** campus is over 100 years old. It was the first of these giant letters, which have since been repeated on hillsides all over the country.

Vallejo

On the north side of the Carquinez Straits, through which the Sacramento and San Joaquin Rivers flow into San Francisco Bay, **Vallejo** is a blue-collar maritime town still reeling

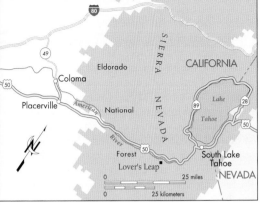

from the closure of its huge and historic Mare Island naval shipyard, which from 1854 to 1994 built and maintained many of the country's fighting ships and submarines. The town served as California's state capital on two different occasions in the gold rush years of the early 1850s. Vallejo's bona fide attraction these days is the **Six Flags Marine World** theme park (hours vary, daily in summer; $45; 707/643-6722), on the north side of town just west of I-80, with 160 acres of elephants, tigers, sea lions, and killer whales, all trained to perform tricks on cue. The adjacent amusement park is the largest in Northern California, with a huge array of thrill rides.

Vallejo also marks the turnoff for Hwy-12, which runs north and west through the Wine Country of the Napa and Sonoma Valleys.

I-80 Towns

Between the San Francisco Bay Area and Sacramento, I-80 passes through an ever more suburbanized corridor of towns like **Fairfield** (pop. 96,178), home of Travis Air Force Base, the "Jelly Belly" jelly bean factory (800/522-3267), and a large Anheuser-Busch beer refinery (closed Sun. & Mon.); the last two are open for free tours. Running across an unstintingly flat landscape of farmland and "big box" shopping centers, just before Sacramento I-80 races past **Davis**, a friendly former farming town that's now home to a University of California campus renowned around the world for its wine-making school.

East of Davis, I-80 is raised on stilts across the Yolo Bypass wetlands, one of the last signs of the natural delta that covered this part of California before the natural water supply was diverted south to Los Angeles.

Sacramento

Spreading for miles at the heart of California's 500-mile-long, agriculturally rich Central Valley, **Sacramento** (pop. 415,000) is not what most would expect of the capital of the Golden State. Green and suburban, with only the state capitol and a few modern towers rising over fine Victorian houses that line the leafy downtown streets, Sacramento is a relatively quiet backwater that effectively embodies California's bipolar politics, forming a sort of neutral ground between the liberal urban centers, which contain 90 percent of the state's population, and the conservative, rural

California's capitol as it appeared in the early 1900s

rest, which covers 90 percent of the land.

Now scythed by freeways, and stretching for miles along the banks of the Sacramento and American Rivers, the city was chosen as the state capital during the Gold Rush era, when Sacramento was the main jumping-off point for the Sierra Nevada mines. Dozens of buildings dating from that era have been restored to form **Old Sacramento,** a diverting shopping complex and tourist trap along the riverfront, where ersatz paddle-wheel steamboats offer sightseeing cruises, and the **California State Railroad Museum** (daily; $4; 916/445-6645), boasting one of the world's largest collections, documents the history of western railroads. Along with the wealth of Gold Rush architecture, "Old Sac" also has memorials to the Pony Express and the Transcontinental Railroad, both of which had primary stations here.

Two other museums are nearby. The **Crocker Art Museum** (closed Mon.; $6; 916/264-5423), two blocks from the riverfront at 216 O Street, is the oldest gallery west of the Mississippi, with a broad range of European and Californian paintings. A half mile south of Old Sacramento, underneath the I-80/I-5 interchange at Front and V Streets, the **Towe Automobile Museum** (daily 10 AM–6 PM; $7; 916/442-6802) displays hot rods, muscle cars, and examples of just about every Ford made before 1952, from Model Ts to massive Ford V-8s.

A half mile inland from the riverfront, standing at the west end of a pleasantly landscaped park, the impressive **California State Capitol** (daily 9 AM–5 PM; free; 916/324-0333) has publicly accessible legislative chambers of the state's Senate and Assembly, hallways full of exhibits on the Golden State's diverse counties, and of course the office of the "Governator," Arnold Schwarzenegger.

3034 - Monument to John Marshall at Coloma. Where Gold was first discovered in California.

Two miles east of the waterfront, at 27th and L Streets, Sacramento's main historic attraction is **Sutter's Fort** (daily; $4; 916/445-4422), a reconstruction of the frontier outpost established here in 1839 by Swiss settler Johannes Sutter. The first commercial, as opposed to religious, settlement in Alta California, Sutter's Fort played a vital role in early West Coast history—this is where the Donner Party was headed, and where the Gold Rush really began, when Sutter's employee James Marshall discovered flakes of gold at Sutter's Mill, in the Sierra Nevada foothills above Sacramento. The grounds of Sutter's Fort also hold the small but interesting **California State Indian Museum** ($2), which has displays of baskets and other California Native American handicrafts.

Sacramento Practicalities

The Old Sacramento area has some good but touristy restaurants and bars, but the Midtown neighborhood south of Sutter's Fort holds Sacramento's best range of restaurants, including the tasty but inexpensive **Cafe Bernardo** (916/443-1180) at 2726 Capitol Avenue, with fresh salads, pizza, and pasta dishes, and great fruit smoothies; **Paesano's** (916/447-8646), at 1806 Capitol, has great cheap pizzas and a nice sidewalk terrace.

During Memorial Day weekend, Old Sacramento hosts the **Sacramento Jazz Jubilee** (916/372-5277), which draws an enormous crowd intent on hearing the dozens of very different jazz bands—everything from Dixieland and "trad" bands to cutting-edge contemporary players.

Another lively spot is the **Tower Cafe** (916/441-0222), attached to the landmark 1920s Tower Theater (which plays art-house hits) at 1518 Broadway, and serving healthy, multi-ethnic food with a world-beat attitude. (The café is where the Sacramento-based **Tower Records** CD and bookstore company got its start; both have stores across the street, open till midnight every night.)

Though Sacramento can't compete with San Francisco for cutting-edge cuisine, it does excel in one culinary niche: **hamburgers.** There are some truly great old burger places in and around downtown Sacramento, like **Ford's Real Hamburgers** (916/452-6979), at 1948 Sutterville on the south side of expansive Land Park; and funky little **Jim Denny's** (916/443-9655), a 1930s burger stand at 816 12th Street, downtown between H and I Streets.

Places to stay include the wonderful **HI Sacramento International Hostel** (916/443-1691), in a fabulous Victorian mansion right downtown at 925 H Street, with beds from $15/night for members, $18/night non-members; early in 2002, the entire hostel was picked up and moved a block away, to make room for a new office building. For an unusual experience, how about staying the night in a 1920s paddlewheel riverboat? The *Delta King* ($120–175; 916/444-KING) is permanently moored near Old Sacramento.

Between Sacramento and Placerville, US-50 is an eight-lane freeway—and one of the California Highway Patrol's most lucrative speed traps, especially for westbound (downhill) travelers.

Placerville and Coloma: Gold Country

The main US-50 stop in the Sierra Nevada foothills, **Placerville** (pop. 9,010; elev. 1,860) takes its name from the placer gold deposits recovered from the South Fork of the American River, which flows just north of town. The historic core of Placerville is well-preserved, with a few cafés and bars paying homage to its rough-and-tumble past. A reminder of the town's gold-rush heritage is the nation's only municipally owned gold mine: **Gold Bug Mine** (daily in summer, weekends only rest of the year; $3; 530/642-5207), a mile north of US-50 off the Bedford Avenue exit. A stamp mill and other mining equipment stand outside the entrance to the mine tunnel, which you can explore on a self-guided tour.

Throughout the gold-rush era, Placerville was known as Hangtown, with a reputation for stringing up petty thieves and other law-breakers. An effigy still hangs at the center of town, in front of a bar.

If you want to explore the region's many evocative gold rush-era remnants, Placerville makes a good base, with its handful of motels (including a Best Western and a Days

Inn) fronting the highway. North and south of Placerville, Hwy-49 runs along the Sierra Nevada foothills through the heart of the Gold Country. Starting in the north beyond beautiful Nevada City, Hwy-49 winds through one historic town after another, all the way to the gates of Yosemite National Park, 150 miles to the south.

The original site of the discovery of gold, **Sutter's Mill,** has been reconstructed as part of **Gold Discovery State Historic Park** (daily; $4 per car; 530/622-3470) in **Coloma,** now an idyllic place along the banks of the American River, nine miles north of Placerville along Hwy-49. The 275-acre park, set aside in 1890 as the state's first historic monument, is also a prime spot for whitewater rafting and kayaking, especially on weekends, so don't be surprised to find the place thronged with wet-suited and Teva-shod hordes. For a restful or romantic place to stay, try the Gold Rush-era **Coloma Country Inn** ($120 and up;

530/622-6919), set in five acres of gardens at 345 High Street.

One great old Gold Country haunt can be reached within a short drive of US-50 from Placerville. The ancient and very popular **Poor Red's Barbecue** (530/622-2901), housed in a Gold Rush–era stagecoach station in the hamlet of El Dorado, five miles south of Placerville on Hwy-49, has full lunches and dinners (and great margaritas) for very little money.

The American River and Lover's Leap

Some 20 miles east of Placerville, US-50 changes suddenly from a four-lane freeway into a twisting, narrow, two-lane road over the crest of the Sierra Nevada. The usually busy highway, which every year is battered and frequently closed by winter storms, runs right alongside the steep banks of the American River. The lushness of the western Sierra Nevada is immediately apparent as the road passes luxuriant groves of pine, fir, and cedar, with numerous old resorts and vacation cabins lining the highway.

About six miles west of the summit, the towering granite cliff of **Lover's Leap** stands out to the south of the highway, its 1,300-foot face attracting rock climbers, while to the north the delicate cascade of **Horsetail Falls** offers a more serene pit stop. Climbing east up US-50's steepest set of hairpin turns, you'll reach 7,365-foot Echo Summit, which gives great views of the Lake Tahoe basin—the shining blue waters beckoning you along another steep stretch of US-50, downhill to the lakeshore itself.

South Lake Tahoe

One of the biggest (12 miles wide, 22 miles long, and 72 miles of coastline) and deepest (over 1,000 feet in places) lakes in the country, straddling the Nevada–California border at 6,220 feet above sea level, Lake Tahoe is a beautiful sight from any angle—from the crest of the alpine peaks surrounding it, from a car or bicycle as you cruise along the shoreline roads, or from a boat out on the lake itself.

Sitting, as the name suggests, at the southern end of Lake Tahoe, the ungainly resort community of **South Lake Tahoe** is a place of multiple personalities. On the California side, low-rise motels line the US-50 frontage, and the atmosphere is that of a family-oriented summer resort, with bike-rental stands and T-shirt shops clogging the roadside. Across the Nevada border, glitzy 20-story casinos rise up in a sudden wall of concrete and glass, ignoring the surrounding beauty in favor of round-the-clock "adult fun"—gambling, fine dining, racy nightclub revues, and more gambling. (For more on the attractions of Nevada's half of Lake Tahoe, see below.) A few strategically placed pine trees work hard to retain a semblance of the natural splendor, but in peak summer season it's basically a *very* busy stretch of road, on both sides of the state line.

To get away from it all, head along Hwy-89 around the west side of the lake to the magnificent state parks around Emerald Bay. Acres of shoreline forest and numerous mansions built as summer resorts back around the turn of the 20th century, like the **Tallac Historic Site** (free; 530/573-2600) three miles west of US-50, have been preserved and are open for tours. In winter, the Tahoe area turns into an extremely popular ski resort—**Heavenly** (775/586-7000) on the south shore and **Squaw Valley** (530/583-6985) in the north are among the largest and busiest ski areas in the United States; both have sightseeing chair lifts in summer.

Despite the lake's great popularity, year-round prices for Tahoe accommodations are surprisingly low; with three **Travelodges** and dozens of others to choose from, you shouldn't have trouble finding something suitable. For a carbo-loading breakfast head to the **Red Hut Waffle Shop** (530/541-9024) on US-50 at 2749 Lake Tahoe Boulevard.

NEVADA

Between Lake Tahoe in the west and Great Basin National Park on the Utah border, US-50 crosses more than 400 miles of Nevada's corrugated country, climbing up and over a dozen distinct mountain ranges while passing through four classic mining towns and the state capital, **Carson City.** Early explorers mapped this region, Pony Express riders raced across it, and the long-distance Lincoln Highway finally tamed it, but the US-50 byway has always played second fiddle to the I-80 freeway, the more popular northern route across the state. Besides being a more scenic alternative to the mind-numbing, and therefore accident-prone, I-80, US-50 across Nevada has gained a measure of notoriety in its own right—it's known as the "Loneliest Road in America." As you travel

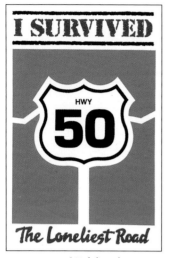

along it you'll see road signs, T-shirts, and bumper stickers proclaiming it as such.

Inspired by the July 1987 story in *Life* magazine that dubbed US-50 "The Loneliest Road," the state-run Nevada Commission on Tourism (800/237-0774) sponsors a tongue-in-cheek promotion in which trans-Nevada travelers can earn themselves a certificate saying "I Survived the Loneliest Road in America." Get your official US-50 travel passport stamped at visitors centers along the highway.

Stateline

Right where US-50 crosses from California into Nevada, the casino complex at **Stateline** forms, for a few short blocks, a mini Las Vegas, with four 20-story resort hotels towering over the lakeshore. **Harvey's** ($120 and up; 775/588-2411), the largest with over 650 lakeside rooms, started it all in the 1940s with six nickel slot machines, still in use in a corner of the casino. **Harrah's** ($135 and up; 775/588-6611), across US-50, is the most opulent, with luxurious 500-square-foot suites. Altogether, over 2,000 rooms are available, combined with at least that many more across the California border. The multitudes of game-hungry visitors that converge here create a definite charge in the rarefied atmosphere when the casino tables are turning at full speed, and it's also a great place to catch your favorite music and comedy performers (particularly ones whose popularity peaked in the 1980s), or a Vegas-style floor show.

Nevada Beach and Zephyr Cove

From the casino district at Stateline, US-50 winds along Lake Tahoe's southeastern shore for over 20 miles, passing by a pair of waterfront parks at Nevada Beach and Zephyr Cove, where you can ride the faux paddle wheeler **MS *Dixie II*** on a variety of cruises ($25 and up; 775/589-4906) across the lake. Otherwise, lakeshore access is severely limited, since most of the waterfront is privately

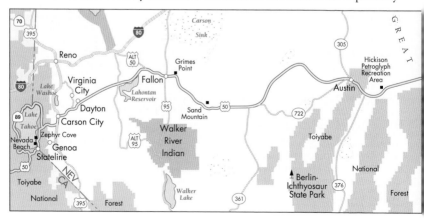

owned, though numerous roadside turnouts (most easily accessible to westbound, lakeside travelers) offer ample opportunities to take in unforgettable views.

Midway along the lake's eastern shore, US-50 turns sharply and begins climbing up and over the 7,140-foot crest of Spooner Summit, all the way giving great views of the tantalizing blue gleam below. At the summit, stretch your legs by taking a quick hike on the Tahoe Ridge Trail, a work-in-progress that will eventually circumnavigate the entire Lake Tahoe basin. Dropping down swiftly from Spooner Summit into the Great Basin desert, US-50 links up with US-395 for the final few miles into Carson City.

Genoa

Between Stateline and Carson City, a delightful little back-door route takes you through **Genoa,** the oldest city in Nevada. Founded by Mormon farmers way back in 1851, Genoa still retains its rural frontier feel, especially since most of the 20th-century development was focused elsewhere, leaving Genoa pleasantly far behind the times—for the time being, at least, though new faux-Victorian houses for Carson City commuters have been springing up around the historic downtown.

At the center of town is **Mormon Station State Park** (daily; 775/782-2590), which has a small museum and a stockade dating back to the 1850s. Across the way, at Main and 5th streets, the **Genoa Courthouse Museum** (daily; 775/782-4325) has more comprehensive displays of historical items—everything from Native American baskets to the keys of the old jail, with an especially interesting exhibition on Wild West legend John A. "Snowshoe" Thompson, who carried the mail over the mountains between Genoa and Sacramento. There's also a little tidbit on mining engineer and native son George Ferris, who designed and built the first of his namesake Ferris wheels for the 1893 World's Fair in Chicago. Much of old Genoa has burned down over the years, but the very **Genoa Bar** (775/782-3870), 2282 Main Street, is full of character, and fairly claims to be the oldest bar in the state.

A nice place to stay is the **Genoa House Inn** ($120 and up; 775/782-7075), at 180 Nixon Street, a quaint historical B&B. A mile south of town via Foothill Road, Genoa's other great overnight attraction is **Walley's Hot Springs** (775/782-8155), a resort hotel complex built around natural 160-degree hot springs. Thriving on the tourism Genoa's charm generates, there are also some good shops and restaurants around town.

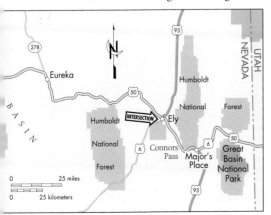

The **Genoa Bar,** a block south of downtown Genoa at 2282 Foothill Road, is the oldest licensed premises in the state, in operation since 1863.

To get to Genoa from Stateline and Lake Tahoe, go east on Hwy-207, down the very steep Kingsbury Grade, then turn north on Hwy-206. From Carson City, turn off US-395 south of the US-50 junction onto Jack's Valley Road (Hwy-206), and follow that for 12 miles.

Carson City

Nevada's state capital and third largest city, **Carson City** (pop. 52,457) was named in honor of Wild West explorer Kit Carson. Nestled at the base of the sheer eastern scarp of the Sierra Nevada, the city was founded in 1858—just a year before the discovery of the Comstock Lode riches, and six years before Nevada became a state.

Carson City is a hard place to characterize. Considering it's the capital, life is very slow, with the main buzz being the **Carson Nugget** (775/882-1626), at 507 N. Carson Street on the main US-50/395 route through town, which has a million-dollar collection of raw, unprocessed gold on display, along with roulette, craps, and blackjack tables, and an army of old ladies feeding banks of slot machines.

Gambling aside, the one place to stop in Carson City is the excellent **Nevada State Museum** (daily; $3), which stands across the street from the stately capitol—and catercorner from the Nugget—at 600 N. Carson Street. Housed inside the solid old U.S. Mint, built in 1870 to make coins from Comstock silver, are displays on mining (including a large, full-scale mock-up of a working mine), as well as on Nevada and Great Basin natural history. Also worth a look are the **Stewart Indian Museum** (daily; 775/882-6929), which has Native American artifacts and a great collection of Edward Curtis's anthropological photography, on the former campus of a Bureau of Indian Affairs school, off US-395 south of town at 5366 Snyder Avenue; and the old Virginia & Truckee steam engines at **Nevada State Railroad Museum,** farther south along US-50/395.

Good Mexican meals are the order of the day at **El Charro Avitia**, south of town at 4389 S. Carson Street, and the specials at the **Carson Nugget** can be incredibly cheap ($2 steak sandwiches). However, the best and most expensive fare is served at **Adele's** (775/882-3353) at 1112 N. Carson Street, where power brokers broker their power. Motels line Carson Street north and south of the capitol; try the classic 1950s-style **Frontier** (775/882-1377) at 1718 N. Carson.

Virginia City

In 1859, prospectors following the gold deposits up the slopes of Mt. Davidson discovered one of the richest strikes in world history: the **Comstock Lode.** Almost overnight, the bustling camp of Virginia City grew into the largest settlement between Chicago and San Francisco, and over the next 20 years nearly a billion dollars in gold and silver (in 19th-century money!) was grubbed from deep underground. Afterward the town very nearly dried up and blew away, but thanks in part to the 1960s TV show *Bonanza,* in which Hoss and company were always heading over to Virginia City for supplies or to fetch the sheriff, tourists discovered the town and gave it a new lease on life.

These days **Virginia City** (pop. 800) is both a tacky tourist trap and one of the most satisfying destinations in the state. Reachable via a very steep (grades in excess of 15 percent) eight-mile drive up Hwy-341 from US-50, dozens of hokey but enjoyable attractions—like the amiable **Bucket of Blood Saloon,** which offers a panoramic view down the mountain—line the five-block-long main drag, C Street. The streets above and below—and I do mean above and below: The town clings to such a steep slope that C Street is a good three stories higher than neighboring D Street—hold some of the most authentic sites. B Street, for example, has the elegant **Castle,** Nevada's premier mansion, with all the original furnishings and fittings, a block south of the ornate Victorian **Storey County Courthouse** and the landmark **Piper's Opera House.** Down the hill on D Street was once a more raucous quarter, where brothels and opium dens shared space with railroad tracks, cemeteries, and the mines themselves: the Gold & Curry, the Ophir, and the Consolidated Virginia.

Before or after a wander around town, be sure to stop in to the excellent museum on the ground floor of the **Fourth Ward School** (daily; 775/847-0975), the Victorian gothic landmark at the south end of C Street. Exhibits inside recount the lively history of Virginia City, from mining technology to Mark Twain, who made his start as a

In 1861, **Orion Clemens** was appointed secretary to the governor of Nevada Territory, and his younger brother Sam came with him to Nevada. Sam submitted dispatches of his mining and travel adventures to Virginia City's largest daily newspaper, the *Territorial Enterprise,* and began perfecting his unique brand of humor under the pen name Mark Twain.

The dress of the Silver Queen in Virginia City contains over 3,000 silver dollars.

journalist with Virginia City's *Territorial Enterprise*. An intact classroom is preserved as it was in 1936 when the last class graduated.

Another not-to-be-missed spot is the **Red Light Museum** (daily; 775/847-9288), which displays an amazing barrage of antique condoms, pornographic postcards, opium pipes, and other sexually explicit historical oddities. The museum is in the basement of the former Julia C. Bulette Saloon, now the Mandarin Gardens Chinese restaurant, at 5 C Street.

Unless you're tempted by the many places to eat hot dogs and drink sarsaparilla along C Street, food options in Virginia City are very limited, though the **Brass Rail** and the **Delta Saloon** are both above par. For complete listings, contact the Virginia City **chamber of commerce** at 775/847-0311.

Reno

Nothing helps heighten the contrast between the rest of the world and life along the "Loneliest Road" than making a stop in **Reno** (pop. 180,480), "The Biggest Little City in the World," as the bold archway over Virginia Street downtown proclaims. An ancient city by Nevada standards, dating back to pioneer days (the Donner Party camped here on their ill-fated way west), Reno first came to national prominence in the 1930s as a center for quickie divorces, and now has all the gambling of its much-larger sibling, Las Vegas, with a pleasantly homey, settled-down feel.

Besides taking advantage of Reno's cheap hotel rooms, cheap food deals ($1 hot-dogs-and-Heinekens!) and 24-hour fun, car culture fans will want to visit the $10 million, 100,000-square foot **National Automobile Museum** (daily; $8; 775/333-9300), on the south bank of the Truckee River at 10 S. Lake Street, perhaps the best and probably the most extensive car collection in the country, assembled primarily by casino magnate William Harrah. (Over 220 classic cars, and a great gift shop, too.) Reno's other national attraction: the **National Bowling Stadium**, a state-of-the-art 80-lane extravaganza, at Center and 4th Streets.

Reno's famous arch, which spans Virginia Street at 3rd Street downtown, was first erected in 1926 to mark the Lincoln Highway route through town. The current arch, the fourth to stand on the site, was built in 1987; an older version has been rebuilt next to the National Auto Museum.

For a taste of old-time Reno and a look at some of the oldest slot machines in existence, stop by the **Liberty Belle Casino** (775/825-1776) next to the Convention Center at 4250 S. Virginia Street. Tiny by contemporary standards, and more of a restaurant than a gambling emporium, the Liberty Belle is owned by the heirs of slot machine inventor Charlie Fey, whose original machines are on display amidst a fascinating collection of gambling ephemera.

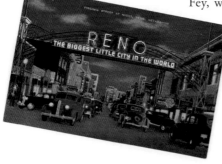

Reno is located at the eastern foot of the Sierra Nevada, on I-80 about 30 miles north of Carson City, 25 miles from Virginia City. There's a nice little mom-and-pop motel, the **Heart O'Town** ($40 and up; 775/322-4066), right in the heart of it all at 520 N. Virginia Street.

Dayton

Though the roadside east of Carson City is increasingly lined by trailer parks and convenience stores, just a half block north of the highway sits **Dayton,** one of the oldest settlements in Nevada. Gold was first discovered here in 1849, and later the town's massive stamp mills pounded the ore carried through the massive Sutro Tunnel from the fabulous Comstock Lode in the mountains above. The historic town center is little more than the two blocks of Main Street north from the traffic light on US-50; choose from a couple of combination café-saloons, including the **Old Corner Bar** (775/246-7984) at 30 Pike Street, a favorite hangout of John Huston, Arthur Miller, Marilyn Monroe, and company when they were in Dayton in 1960 to film *The Misfits.*

Fallon

Coming into Fallon, especially after crossing the Great Basin deserts of Utah and Nevada that stretch to the east, can be a shock to the system. First, relative to Nevada's other US-50 towns, **Fallon** is big: upwards of 7,000 residents, with all the attendant shopping malls, traffic lights, and fast-food franchises. Second, but perhaps more striking, Fallon is green: alfalfa, onions, garlic, and cantaloupe as far as the eye can see. Otherwise, Fallon offers ATMs, gas stations, and motels lining US-50, as well as the usual Pizza Huts and Subways, and a handy 24-hour Safeway.

About the only radio station along this stretch of US-50 is Fallon's **KBLB 980 AM,** which plays a standard array of country hits.

Besides agriculture, Fallon's main employer is the U.S. Navy, whose air base and target range is an important training center for carrier-based fighters and bombers—the "Top Guns" of Tom Cruise fame.

While it's not an especially attractive place, Fallon does have what they accurately call "The Best Little Museum on the Loneliest Road in America," the eclectic and engaging **Churchill County Museum** (daily; free; 775/423-3677) at 1050 S. Maine Street, less than a mile south of US-50. Filling an old Safeway supermarket, the exhibits contain native Paiute basketry, clothing and hunting gear, and the usual array of pioneer quilts and clothing, plus a player piano, and the gift shop sells a wide range of books and historical postcards.

Forty-five miles east of Fallon, Hwy-361 heads south to the magnesium-mining company town of Gabbs. East of Gabbs lies fascinating **Berlin-Ichthyosaur State Park** (775/964-2440), which holds an only-in-Nevada combination: the 100-year-old ghost town of Berlin and a 225-million-year-old marine fossil quarry. Camping is available year-round, and guided tours of the town and the fossil beds are given weekends in summer.

Grimes Point and Sand Mountain

The 110 miles of US-50 between Fallon and Austin, the next town to the east, look pretty empty on most maps, but there's more to see than you might think. In the midst of a U.S. Navy target range, where supersonic fighters play electronic war games across the alkali flats, there are historical plaques marking Pony Express and Butterfield Stage way stations, a dusty old brothel, and two unique attractions—a singing sand dune and an extensive petroglyph site.

Ten miles east of Fallon, the extraordinary grouping of petroglyphs at **Grimes Point** is not to be missed. Just 100 yards north of US-50, a self-guided trail

Grimes Point petroglyphs

leads past hundreds of images etched into the lichen-covered, espresso-brown basalt boulders. Some 8,000 years ago, when the carvings were made, Grimes Point was on the shores of now-vanished Lake Lahontan, a prime hunting and fishing ground for prehistoric Great Basin peoples. These days, fast and fierce lizards, and the occasional antelope, share the arid setting with the shiny rocks, into which a huge array of abstract and figurative images have been pecked and chiseled. If you're intrigued and want to know more, stop by the excellent Churchill County Museum in Fallon (see above); guided tours (every other Sat.) are available of nearby **Hidden Cave,** where significant archaeological remains have been uncovered.

Sand Mountain, 15 miles east of Grimes Point, 84 miles west of Austin, and just a half mile north of US-50, is a giant sword-edged sand dune that makes a deep booming sound when the cascading crystals oscillate at the proper frequency—somewhere between 50 and 100 hertz. On weekends you're more likely to hear the sound of unmuffled dirt bikes and dune buggies, but at other times the half-hour trudge to the top is well worth making to watch the swirls of sand dance along the ridges.

Austin

Some 110 miles east of Fallon and 70 miles west of Eureka, tiny **Austin** (pop. 300) huddles well above 6,000 feet on the north slope of the mighty Toiyabe Mountains. The steep incline of Main Street (US-50) as it passes through town attests to the precariousness with which Austin has clung to life since its 10-year mining boom ended—in 1873. Unlike Fallon or Eureka, which wear their prosperity on their sleeves, Austin hangs on to the rustic, steadfastly un-whitewashed nature that was once—and in some places, remains—central to Nevada's character. Austin takes its central assignment seriously, since the state's exact geographical center is a mere 12 miles to the south.

According to local legend, a Pony Express rider accidentally discovered silver ore here in 1862, and the rush was on. Prospectors fanned out from Austin, which was named after the Texas hometown of one of its founders, to establish Belmont, Berlin, Grantsville, Ione, and dozens of other boomtowns-turned-ghost towns; roughly $50 million in gold and silver was shipped out over the next 10 years. Since then Austin has experienced a long, melancholy decline, though

At the turn-off to Sand Mountain, a battered sign marks the official (solar-powered!) "Loneliest Phone on the Loneliest Road in America."

If the "Loneliest Road" nickname makes you think that road maintenance may have suffered, it hasn't; the road surface is actually mostly all smooth champagne asphalt, much to the delight of the hundreds of motorcyclists who ride the road every summer.

The Pony Express

Of all the larger-than-life legends that animate the annals of the Wild West, none looms larger than that of the Pony Express. As is typical of frontier adventures, accounts of the Pony Express are often laced with considerable exaggeration, but in this case the facts are unusually impressive. Beginning in April 1860, running twice a week between St. Joseph, Missouri, and Sacramento, California, where it was linked with San Francisco by steamship, the Pony Express halved the time it took to carry news to and from the West Coast, making the 1,966-mile trek in just 10 days. Eighty riders (including teenaged William "Buffalo Bill" Cody, who made the record single run of 322 miles) were employed to race between the 190 stations en route, switching horses every 10–15 miles and averaging 75 miles per run—day or night, in all kinds of weather, across 120°F deserts or snowbound Sierra passes.

Covering nearly 2,000 miles of the wildest and ruggedest land on the frontier, the Pony Express established the first high-speed link between the two coasts. At a time when the nation was divided against itself, with the Civil War looming on the horizon, the Pony Express connection played a key role in keeping the valuable mines of California and Nevada in Union hands. A private enterprise that lasted just 18 months and lost considerable amounts of money before being put out of business for good, the Pony Express proved that overground connections across the still-wild western United States were both necessary and possible.

The completion on October 28, 1861, of the transcontinental telegraph made the Pony Express obsolete overnight, and not so much as a saddle survives from this legendary endeavor, apart from a few postmarked letters. Along with the various statues and plaques marking the Pony Express route, the most evocative sites survive in the dry Nevada desert, within easy access of the US-50 highway. East of Fallon, for example, the highway runs right on top of the old Pony Express route, and the remains of two relay stations can still be seen. One is at **Sand Springs,** at the foot of Sand Mountain. More substantial remains survive at **Cold Springs,** 32 miles east, where plaques recount the history and a trail brings you to what was once among the most isolated and dangerous of the Pony Express stations.

Every June, Wild West aficionados recreate the era in the **Pony Express Reride,** in which a team of 500 riders follow the old route as closely as possible, alternating direction each year.

recent efforts to mine the abundant turquoise and barium in the region have met with some success.

A two-minute drive (at 10 mph) along Main Street takes you past all there is to see in Austin today, but you could easily spend hours wandering around the place, or hanging out in its quirkily populated junk shops, cafés, and bars. The impressive steeples of the Catholic, Methodist, and Baptist churches dominate the townscape, while at the western (downhill) end of town you can glimpse **Stoke's Castle,** a three-story stone sentinel built in 1897 and lived in for all of a month. It looks best from a distance, looming over the nearby cemeteries, but if you want to get closer, follow Castle Road for about a half mile south from US-50.

Another good way to get a sense of Austin is to rent a mountain bike from **T-Rix Bikes** (775/964-1212) at 270 Main Street, the self-proclaimed "Loneliest Bike Shop on the Loneliest Road," and tour the many rugged old mining tracks and trails around the town.

For its 300 residents, Austin has three gas stations (it's a very long way to the next town, so fill up here), three motels—including the **Lincoln Motel** ($40; 775/964-2698) at 728 Main Street, whose name recalls the road's early role as part of the cross-country Lincoln Highway—and a pair of cafés: the ancient **International,** moved here board by board from Virginia City in 1863, and the **Toiyabe Cafe.** Both are right on Main Street, and open early (around 6 AM) and close around 9 PM.

Hickison Petroglyph Recreation Area

Bookended by 7,000-foot mountain ranges at either end, the route between Austin and Eureka is perhaps the longest, flattest, straightest stretch of the entire trans-Nevada length of US-50, over 70 miles of Great Basin nothingness. Cattle ranches fill the plains, which were crisscrossed by early explorers like John C. Fremont, who passed through in 1845, as well as by the Pony Express and the Butterfield Stage. Such recent history, however, pales in comparison to the relics from the region's prehistoric past, particularly the fine petroglyphs carved into the rocks on the eastern side of 6,594-foot Hickison Summit, 28 miles east of Austin and 46 miles west of Eureka.

Now protected as part of the BLM-operated **Hickison Petroglyph Recreation Area,** the petroglyphs stand in a shallow sandstone draw on the north side of the highway. A half-mile trail loops through sagebrush, junipers, and piñon pines from the parking area-cum-camp-

ground past dozens of these enigmatic figures, some of which are thought to date back as far as 10,000 BC. Somewhat surprisingly, so far they are graffiti-free.

Eureka

Right in the middle of a 100-mile stretch of spectacular Great Basin scenery, **Eureka** is one of the most engaging and enjoyable stops in the state. Unlike a lot of places along the Loneliest Road, Eureka is fairly thriving, thanks to numerous gold mines still in operation in Eureka County.

The four blocks of 100-year-old buildings lining the steeply sloping, franchise-free Main Street (US-50) are a mix of well-restored brick and wood storefronts alongside less fortunate ruins, some merely sets of cast-iron pilasters holding up false fronts. The focal point, the grand 1879 **Eureka County Courthouse,** is still in use, and behind it the **Eureka Sentinel Museum** (daily; free; 775/237-5010) has displays tracing the lively local history as well as typesetting equipment and printing presses of the newspaper published here from 1870 to 1960.

Besides being an intriguing place to stroll around (walking-tour booklets are available from the Sentinel Museum and many local shops), Eureka is also a good place to break a journey. The most characterful place to stay is the historic **Jackson House** hotel ($70; 775/237-5247) on Main Street; reservations are handled by the Best Western motel two blocks away, which has modern rooms for $10 cheaper. The liveliest place to drink and be merry is the **Owl Club** café and casino, down Main Street; fast food can be had from **DJ's Drive-In Diner,** at the east end of town.

> **INTERSECTION**
>
> Ely marks the junction of US-50 and our **Border to Border** route along US-93 (see page 138). Running between the Canadian Rockies and the desert Southwest, US-93 is covered beginning on page 106.

Ely

Ely (pop. 4,756; E-lee, as in Robert) is a sprawling cross-roads community where US-6, US-50, and US-93 all intersect. For nearly 100 years, Ely was a boomtown flush with

Across Nevada, US-50 follows the route of the Lincoln Highway, the nation's first transcontinental route.

the wealth from the massive Kennecott-owned Liberty Pit copper mines, Nevada's largest and longest-lived mining venture, which produced over a billion dollars' worth of ore while employing nearly 10,000 people at its peak during the 1950s. After the main mines closed down in 1982, the railway that had shuttled pay dirt from the mines to the smelter was abandoned—track,

macho miners in Ely

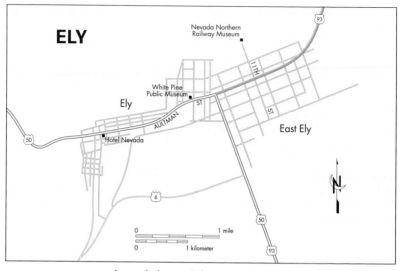

The world's oldest known bristlecone pine, dubbed **Prometheus**, was cut down on Wheeler Peak in 1964 by a graduate student researcher who discovered too late that, at 4,900 years old, the tree had been the oldest living thing on earth. A cross-section of the trunk is displayed at the **Bristlecone Convention Center,** at 150 6th Street in Ely.

Mountains of mine tailings tower over US-50 west of Ely, and five miles west of town a short detour south takes you to **Ruth,** which sits alongside the huge crater where hundreds of tons of ore were dug. A mining company is currently leaching the metal out of the previously discarded ore, so there's no longer access to the crater itself.

stock, and depot. The entire operation was turned into **Nevada Northern Railway Museum** (Wed.–Sun. in summer only; 775/289-2085) in 1985, and now you can take a 2-hour tour aboard the "Ghost Train," pulled by a 1910 Baldwin Steamer locomotive. The train leaves from the depot at the north end of East 11th Street and uses a ton of coal and 1,000 gallons of water; tickets cost around $20.

Ely's other main stop is the **White Pine Public Museum** (daily; free; 775/289-4710), 2000 Aultman Street (US-50), which has a wide-ranging collection of minerals, mining implements, and Pony Express memorabilia on display.

Along with extensive mining history, Ely has motels, gas stations, the only supermarket for the next 250 miles east, and dozens of vivid, building-sized **murals** depicting various aspects of the town's heritage. The heart of town is a neon-rich few blocks of Aultman Street (US-50) west of the US-93 junction, centering upon the landmark **Hotel Nevada** ($30 and up; 775/289-6665), with its giant cowboy and neon-lit slot machines. Inside there are real (as opposed to video) slot machines, pool tables, a café, and a bar with nightly live music. Another place worth stopping is the **Ramada Copper Queen Casino** ($65; 775/289-4884), on the south side of Ely, where motel rooms open directly onto a lobby shared by banks of slot machines and a small swimming pool. Also nice is the quiet **Four Sevens Motel** ($35 and up; 775/289-4747), a block north of Aultman at 500 High Street.

For food, Ely has three coffee shop–style restaurants along US-50, plus the chance to down a milk shake at the soda fountain inside **Economy Drug**, Aultman and 7th Streets.

The route east of Ely toward Great Basin National Park is an official "scenic route," rolling across sagebrush plains and climbing over the Schell Creek and Snake mountain ranges through dense groves of pine and juniper.

Connors Pass and Major's Place

East of Ely, US-50, spliced together with US-6 and US-93 into a single two-lane highway, continues for 25 miles before crossing the narrow waist of the Schell Creek Range at 7,722-foot **Connors Pass.** As you ascend toward the pass, the air cools and freshens, the single-leaf piñon and Utah juniper appear and increase and, cresting the summit, the mighty Snake Range, including 13,063-foot Wheeler Peak, comes into view.

East of the pass, at **Major's Place** (where there's a roadhouse with cold beer and "loose slots," but no reliable gas), US-93 cuts due south, heading 80 long, solitary miles to the next contact with humans at Pioche, while US-50 heads east across open rangelands toward Great Basin National Park.

Great Basin National Park

Approaching Nevada from the east, travelers are greeted by the towering silhouette of **Wheeler Peak,** at 13,063 feet the second-highest and most impressive mountain in the state; from the west, similarly sheer escarpments tower over lush green open range for miles and miles along US-50. In 1987 the 77,000 acres around Wheeler Peak were designated **Great Basin National Park,** but its remote location has made it one of the least-visited national parks in the United States. Hikers and campers will have no trouble finding solitude amidst the alpine forests, ancient bristlecone pines, delightful annual wildflowers, glacial lakes, and small ice field.

Thanks to the well-maintained **Wheeler Peak Scenic Road** climbing to over 10,000 feet, the wilderness areas are easily accessible to people willing to take a short hike, though many visitors go no farther than the park's centerpiece, **Lehman Caves.** Geological forces have been sculpting Lehman Caves for roughly 70 million years, but they weren't noticed until homesteader Absalom Lehman stumbled upon the small entrance to the caves in 1885. They were declared a national monument in 1922, and since then only minor improvements have been made, leaving the mind-bending limestone formations alone—no flashy light-and-sound show, just hundreds of delicate stalagmites, stalactites, helictites, aragonites, and the like. A variety of guided tours ($2–8) are conducted at intervals throughout

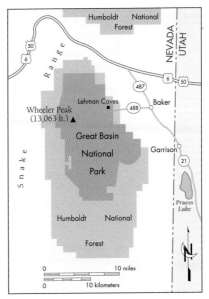

the day; on some summer evenings at 6 PM there's a memorable candlelight tour. Tours leave from the small **visitors center** (775/234-7331), which has details of hiking and camping options as well as exhibits on Great Basin wildlife—from birds and bats to mountain lions. There's even a small summer-only café.

If you're not camping and self-relying, or if you are and want a break, the nearest food and drink are at the foot of the park in tiny **Baker** (pop. 55), which boasts one gas station, the seven-room **Silver Jack Motel** (40; 775/234-7323), and the friendly, homey **Outlaw Cafe and Bar,** which serves breakfast, burritos, and beer from early till late.

Back on US-50, straddling the Utah–Nevada border, the **Border Inn** is a café/gas station/motel, open 24 hours a day (775/234-7300). From here, the only other reliable services are in Ely, 70 miles west, or in Delta, 85 miles to the east, so pass by at your peril.

UTAH

For most of the way across Utah, the high-speed I-70 freeway has replaced US-50, but if you have time to take a couple of detours you'll be rewarded with some of the most incredible scenery in the world. Most of this is concentrated in the southeastern corner of the state, where a number of national parks, including Canyonlands and Arches, preserve the sandstone "Canyon Country" of the Colorado Plateau. In the west a few old mining towns stand amidst the arid desert of the Great Basin. Distances are huge and services few and far between, but if you have the time and plan ahead, this is one of the most satisfying and memorable corners of the country.

Delta

About 85 miles east of the Nevada border, the landscape changes suddenly from barren desert to lush pastures around the town of **Delta,** which is irrigated by the green Sevier River. Delta bills itself the "Gateway to Great Basin National

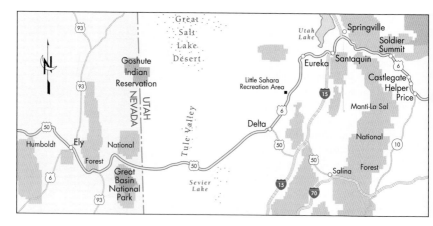

Park," and it does have a **Best Western** and other motels, gas stations, and a large supermarket—but very little else to attract visitors. One place worth a stop is the small **Great Basin Museum** (Tues.–Sat. only; free; 435/864-5013), a block north of Main Street at 328 W. 100 North Street. The museum features minerals, arrowheads, and local history exhibits, including a display of artifacts relating to **Topaz Camp,** an internment camp set up in the desert west of Delta by the U.S. government to imprison Americans of Japanese descent during World War II.

For a bite to eat, join the locals at the counter or a booth at **Top's City Cafe** (435/864-2148), 313 W. Main Street, open 6 AM to 9 PM for breakfasts, burgers, soups, salads, and creamy milk shakes.

North of Delta, the horizon is split by the belching smokestack of the coal-fired **Intermountain Power Plant.**

From Delta, US-50 officially cuts southeast across I-15, linking up with I-70 at Salina for the trip east to Grand Junction. Our route, however, follows US-6 (old US-50) toward the Great Salt Lake area, then east over the Wasatch Front, rejoining official US-50 (now I-70) at Green River.

Little Sahara Recreation Area

From Delta, the route follows the Sevier River northwest, racing across the featureless desert for 32 miles before reaching the well-posted turnoff north to the **Little Sahara Recreation Area.** Visible from the highway, to the north of US-6, the Little Sahara Recreation Area holds 60,000 acres of sand dunes and sagebrush flats, the prettiest parts of which are preserved for hikers and campers, though motorcyclists and ATVers can overwhelm any sense of peace and tranquility, turning it into a campground from hell.

Eureka

Fifty miles east of Delta, 20 miles west of the I-15 freeway, the weather-beaten town of **Eureka** (pop. 750) climbs steeply up surrounding mountainsides at the heart of the once-thriving Tintic Mining District, where, as recently as the 1930s, thousands of miners dug millions of dollars' worth of gold, silver, copper, and lead out of the ground every year. Now the massive wooden headframes of long-closed mine shafts stand high above the houses and prefab trailers that cling to the slopes, while fading signs advertise abandoned businesses along Main Street.

Though diehard residents still speak of plans to reopen one or more of the mines, prosperity seems a distant dream in Eureka, and while it's not quite a ghost town, it seems well on its way there. The glory days are recounted in the small **Tintic Mining Museum,** next to city hall on Main Street, and at the west edge of town a historical plaque stands alongside the heavy timber

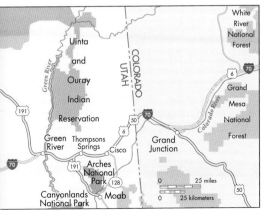

Detour: Salt Lake City

With no other city for some 500 miles in any direction, **Salt Lake City** (pop. 181,743), an hour north of Springville via the I-15 freeway, seems like the oasis it naturally is. Taking its name from the undrinkable alkaline Great Salt Lake, the city is actually blessed with abundant fresh water, thanks to the rain- and snow-making properties of the Wasatch Range, which rises knife-like to the east. Founded by Mormons in 1847, and effectively controlled by Mormon elders ever since, Salt Lake City is clean and pleasant, and unusual enough to merit a detour. Most of what there is to see has to do with the Mormons, better known as the Church of Latter-day Saints, which has its worldwide headquarters at **Temple Square** downtown (street numbers and addresses are measured from here, not the nearby State Capitol, which goes to show just how predominant the LDS church is in local life). On the west side of Temple Square are the amazing genealogical libraries the Mormons maintain; a block east of Temple Square is the **Beehive House**, preserved as it was in the 1850s, when Brigham Young lived here.

Given its Mormon roots and Midwest temperament, Salt Lake City is not exactly a food-lover's paradise, but there are a number of good restaurants. One truly fine place to dine is **Bambara** (801/363-5454), 202 S. Main Street, whose eclectic menu and stylish decor would feel at home in New Orleans or San Francisco. A nice place to stay, for comfort, convenience and character, is the very central **Inn at Temple Square** ($99 and up; 801/531-1000), 71 W. South Temple Street.

For more information, contact the Salt Lake City visitors bureau (800/541-4955).

head-frame of the Bullion-Beck Mine, one of the area's most productive.

Heading east from Eureka, our route bends across rock-strewn sagebrush hills around the southern shore of Utah Lake toward I-15. **Utah Lake,** which is freshwater in contrast to the briny expanse of the Great Salt Lake to the north, used to be much larger than it is now, before so much of it was diverted to water the apple, peach, and cherry orchards that line US-6 around **Santaquin**—whose three gas stations are the last reliable source of fuel for westbound travelers until Delta, 70 miles to the southwest. From Santaquin, follow the I-15 freeway north to **Springville,** from where the Salt Lake City megalopolis stretches north along I-15 for nearly 100 miles.

Castlegate and Helper

Heading east from Springville, the drive along US-6 (old US-50) up and over 7,477-foot **Soldier Summit** is truly beautiful, as the two-lane highway twists alongside pines and cottonwoods to the crest, then passes through bright red sandstone canyons along the stark eastern side of the towering Wasatch Range. The summit itself, where there's a handy Conoco gas station-cum-general store (their motto: "Radiators Filled, Bladders Emptied"), marks the boundary between the Colorado River drainage and the Great Basin. Dropping down from Soldier Summit, US-6/191 winds along the Price River through **Castlegate**, a steeply walled sandstone canyon lined with working coal mines, many of which you see from the highway. While most now rely on heavy machinery to do the dirty work of digging out the coal, the Castlegate area has been the site of the two worst mining disasters in Utah history: 173 men and boys killed in a 1924 explosion, and another 200 killed at nearby Scofield on May Day, 1900.

> **Park City,** in the mountains above Salt Lake City, is home to the annual **Sundance Film Festival,** and nearby ski resorts hosted the 2002 Winter Olympics.

> Helper earned its name in 1892 when the Denver and Rio Grande Railroad built a depot and roundhouse here to hold the "helper" engines that were added to trains to help push them over Soldier Summit, 25 miles to the west.

Tiny **Helper** (pop. 2,025), at the downstream edge of Castlegate, six miles northwest of Price, is a classic railroad town preserved almost unchanged for nearly a century. The six-block downtown area, fronting onto the tracks, includes so many turn-of-the-20th-century brick- and stone-fronted buildings that it's been declared a National Historic District—though the sad truth is that most of these have stood abandoned since the railroad switched to diesel power in the 1950s.

Relive the glory days at the excellent **Western Mining and Railroad Museum** (closed Sun.; 435/472-3009) at 296 S. Main Street, which contains enough raw material on railroading and coal mining, not to mention the region's diverse immigrant cultures, to keep you occupied for an hour or more. There's also a display recounting the exploits of Butch Cassidy and his gang, who raided banks and rustled cattle throughout the region in the late 1890s, hiding out in the surrounding hills. Behind the museum, an outdoor lot displays some of the giant machines used in the coal mines, which, unlike the railroad, still employ a large number of local people.

Price

The largest city in eastern Utah, **Price** (pop. 8,402) is located roughly midway between the I-15 and I-70 freeways, 65 miles northwest of Green River. Coal is so prevalent in the area that roadcuts reveal solid black seams, but the town itself is lush and green, thanks to irrigation provided by the Price River, which flows south from town into the Green and Colorado Rivers.

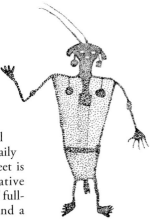

Coal mining, and to a lesser extent agriculture, still power Price, where the small **Prehistoric Museum** (daily in summer; $3; 435/637-5060) at 155 E. Main Street is worth a look for its extensive displays on the Native American cultures of the region, and for its range of full-sized dinosaur skeletons, including a stegosaurus and a

Butch Cassidy and the Hole in the Wall Gang

Long before Paul Newman played him alongside Robert Redford's Sundance Kid, Butch Cassidy was one of the great outlaw legends of the Wild West. Thanks to his habit of sharing the proceeds from his crimes with the widows and children of men killed or ruined by bankers and cattle barons, Butch Cassidy earned a reputation as the "Robin Hood of the Wild West." That, plus the fact that he never killed anyone while committing his crimes, gained him popular admiration from the cowboys, miners, and homesteading pioneers among whom he worked his trade.

Born Robert Leroy Parker to a family of Mormon farmers in Beaver, Utah, on Friday the 13th of April, 1866, the man who came to be known as Butch Cassidy spent his youth as a ranch hand in Utah, Colorado, and southern Wyoming. The first major crime attributed to Butch Cassidy is the robbery of a bank in Telluride, Colorado, in 1889, which netted him and his three accomplices some $20,000. From 1894 to 1896 he was imprisoned in Wyoming for cattle theft, and following this he joined up with Harry Longabaugh (aka The Sundance Kid) and the rest of the gang. Together they robbed over a dozen banks, trains, and stagecoaches throughout the West, netting an estimated $350,000 in five years. One of their many daring heists was the daylight robbery of a coal-mining company in Castlegate, Utah, in April 1897; while the payroll was being taken from a train, Butch simply grabbed the satchel and rode off in a cloud of dust, $9,000 richer.

According to many sources, Butch and Sundance died in 1909, in a shoot-out in South America (as depicted in the 1969 movie *Butch Cassidy and the Sundance Kid*). But some people (including his sister, who lived until the 1970s) say that Butch survived to a ripe old age, living in Spokane, Washington, under the name William T. Phillips until his death in 1937.

mammoth. Many of these were reassembled from fossils collected from the **Cleveland-Lloyd Dinosaur Quarry,** 30 miles south of town.

Price also has all the highway services travelers might need: numerous gas stations, places to eat, and six motels.

Southwest from Price, bound for Green River and the I-70 freeway, US-6/191 runs alongside the busy Denver and Rio Grande mainline railroad through a region of arid plateaus highlighted every few miles by brilliantly colorful, weirdly sculpted sandstone mesas. Though barren and empty at first glance, the region is particularly rich in two things: coal mines and, more unusually, dinosaur bones. (Why do you think they call them fossil fuels?)

In June 1925, Price saw the lynching of a black man, **Robert Marshall,** an itinerant miner who was hanged by vigilantes for allegedly killing a coal company guard. A crowd of over 1,000 people witnessed the lynching, but no one was arrested; in 1998 a small memorial, describing Marshall as "A Victim of Intolerance—May God Forgive" was erected on his grave.

Green River

Straddling the eponymous river on the north side of I-70, **Green River** (pop. 973) makes a handy base for exploring southeastern Utah, but it offers very little in and of itself. The town holds numerous 24-hour gas stations, a handful of motels, and a couple of good places to eat—try the **Tamarisk** (435/564-8109), overlooking the Green River at 870 E. Main Street.

Just south of Main Street, the most characterful place to eat and drink in Green River is **Ray's Tavern** (435/564-3511), 25 S. Broadway, with good beers, a pool table, and dining tables made out of tree trunks.

Even if you don't need fuel, food, or a place to sleep, Green River offers one very compelling reason to stop: the spacious, modern **John Wesley Powell River History Museum** (daily; $2; 435/564-3427), above the east bank of the river at 885 E. Main Street. In 1869 Powell and his crew were the first to travel the length of the Colorado River through the Grand Canyon; though the legendary explorers started their epic adventure in Green River, Wyoming, not here in Utah, the spacious modern museum, on old US-50 along the east bank of the Green River, is the best single repository of artifacts relating to their feat. The collection concentrates on Powell in particular and on waterborne transport in general, but there are also displays chronicling the adventures of other early explorers (including Juan de Oñate in 1605 and the Domínguez and Escalante expedition of 1776), and of fur-trappers, miners, and Mormons—all of whom contributed to the exploration and mapping of the American West.

The otherworldly aspects of the Utah landscape south of Green River have tempted **NASA** to establish the **Mars Desert Research Station** here, to test equipment and train would-be Mars-bound astronauts.

To get some sense of what Powell and crew experienced, take a raft, canoe, or kayak trip down the Green or Colorado Rivers. Dozens of outfitters offer equipment rentals, shuttles, and guided trips, from all-day to week-long tours.

Canyonlands National Park

The largest and least-visited park in the Southwest, **Canyonlands National Park** is both breathtakingly beautiful and totally inhospitable, an arid wilderness of high plateaus and deep canyon carved by the mighty Green and Colorado Rivers. The park is divided into several very different areas, each of

Uranium mined from Temple Mountain, west of Canyonlands, was used to make the first atomic bombs.

which is at least a 100-mile drive from the others, so it pays to plan ahead. The most popular section, the **Island-in-the-Sky,** stands high above the confluence of the rivers and gives the most sweeping panoramas—100 miles in every direction from over 6,000 feet above sea level. South of the rivers, **The Needles** district holds 50 square miles of spires, arches, and canyons and is the best place to undertake lengthy hikes. One trail leads from the end of the road down to the mouth of Cataract Canyon on the Colorado River. Another area of Canyonlands, **The Maze,** is west of the rivers and virtually inaccessible.

There's one **visitors center** near the entrance to Island-in-the-Sky, and another near the entrance to The Needles. The Canyonlands **headquarters** (435/259-7164) at 125 W. 200 S in Moab also has extensive information. Adjacent to Canyonlands are two state parks, **Dead Horse Point** in the north and **Newspaper Rock** in the south, both of which are also well worth a look.

Arches National Park

Taking its name from the hundreds of naturally formed sandstone arches scattered here, **Arches National Park** is the most feature-packed of southern Utah's national parks. Ranging in size from around three feet to nearly 300 feet in span, the arches are the result of erosion over millions of years, the same agent that formed the thousands of brilliantly colored spires, pinnacles, and canyons that cover southeast Utah. Piñon pines and junipers add a splash of green to the red and brown backdrop, but mostly what you see are red stone and blue sky—lots and lots of both.

The park's highlights can be easily reached from the 20-mile paved road that runs through the center of the park. A **visitors center** (daily; 435/259-8161) at the entrance, east of US-191 and five miles north of Moab, has maps, pamphlets, and displays on the geology and natural history of Arches.

From the entrance, the road switchbacks uphill past the sandstone skyline of **Park Avenue** before reaching a turnoff east to **The Windows,** whose dense concentration of arches and spires is required viewing, no matter how little time you have. Four miles beyond The Windows, a dirt road leads east to **Wolfe Ranch,** trailhead for **Delicate Arch,** the park's most postcard-worthy feature, a three-mile

Delicate Arch at Arches National Park

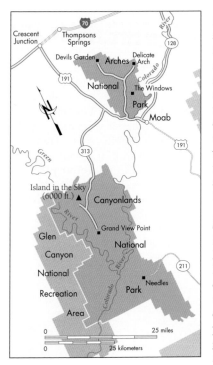

round-trip hike. Three miles farther along the main road, **Fiery Furnace** is an otherwordly collection of narrow canyons, that, despite the name, is quite cool and shady; park rangers give guided walks here throughout the summer. At the far end of the road there's a two-mile trail leading to **Devil's Garden**, where you can see **Landscape Arch**, the park's largest (and the world's second-largest)—291 feet across and 105 feet high.

Moab

Driving across southern Utah, you have two main options: Race along I-70 and get somewhere else in a hurry, or slow down and search out the truly unforgettable scenery the state has to offer. One of the best places to base yourself for an exploration of the region is **Moab** (pop. 4,779), an old uranium mining town that's located 30 miles south of the freeway, surrounded by two national parks (Arches and Canyonlands) and hundreds of thousands of acres of desert wilderness.

Thanks to *Outside* magazine and the recent mania for outdoor athleticism, Moab has experienced a massive tourist boom in the past decade—Edward Abbey, cantankerous poet of the Southwest who wrote his first book, *Desert Solitaire,* about a season he spent at nearby Arches National Park, would probably turn in his grave if he saw the gangs of Lycra-clad mountain bikers milling around Moab's Main Street T-shirt stores and brewpubs. But despite the addition of fast-food franchises and hundreds of new motel rooms, Moab is still a dusty little back-of-beyond hamlet, albeit one that gives easy access to the wilds nearby.

If you're not prepared to camp out in the backcountry (if you are, the nearby state and national parks have a full range of possibilities), Moab has the usual national motels plus local ones like the **Apache** ($50 and up; 435/259-5727 or 800/228-6882), at 166 South 400 E, where John Wayne slept while filming *Rio Bravo* here in 1950.

For breakfast, try the **Jailhouse Café** (435/259-3900) at 101 N. Main Street. After a day on the trails, treat yourself to a gourmet dinner at the **Center Cafe** at 60 N. 100 West Street (435/259-4295).

For more information on visiting the Moab area, including all the surrounding parks, contact the very helpful

The annual **Fat Tire Festival**, held the week before Halloween, brings mountain bikers from all over the world to Moab.

A word of warning: Even if you're not planning to venture from your car, it's a good idea to carry at least a gallon of water per person when traveling in the desert.

Moab Information Center (daily; 435/259-8825 or 800/635-6622) at Main and Center in the middle of town.

The prettiest route east from Moab, Hwy-128, winds along the broad and brown Colorado River past 25 miles of swimming, kayaking, and camping spots. Hwy-128 links up with I-70 23 miles west of the Colorado border at junction 212, near the former sheep-ranching center of **Cisco,** a ghostly old US-50 crossroads abandoned after completion of the interstate, where old gas station buildings are slowly decaying into a post-apocalyptic art installation.

Fifteen miles south of Moab along US-191, one of Utah's oddest attractions is the **Hole 'n The Rock** (daily; $5; 435/686-2250) a 5,000-square-foot home carved out of a sandstone cliff over a 20-year period, beginning in the 1940s, by Albert and Gladys Christensen. Now open to tourists, the site also includes a large carving of FDR's face.

COLORADO

Driving across southern Colorado on US-50 takes you through almost every landscape landlocked North America has to offer. From the geological wonderland of the Colorado River plateau, which stretches west into Utah, the route climbs up and over the 14,000-foot Rocky Mountains, which form a formidable wall down the center of the state. Continuing east, the alpine meadows, deeply etched river canyons, and snow-covered peaks of the southern Rockies fade away into the flat, agricultural prairies that stretch east across the middle of the country. While there is considerable ranching and farming, outdoor recreation—fishing, hiking, skiing, and mountain biking—is the basis for the economy, and the region is well-provided with tourist facilities, especially in the mountainous middle.

Grand Junction

Thirty miles east of the Utah border, US-50 diverges from high-speed I-70 at the city of **Grand Junction** (pop. 41,986) on the Colorado River. After all the desert that surrounds it, Grand Junction feels much bigger than you'd expect, with its thriving old downtown, complete with cobblestoned streets, odd bits of outdoor sculpture, great antique shops, neon signs—and tons of free parking. Catering to passing traffic, Grand Junction's I-70 frontage has all the motels and places to eat you could want, but downtown holds one really nice older place, the clean and comfortable **Hotel Melrose** ($30–50; 970/242-9636), a block south of Main Street at 337 Colorado Avenue —just look for the red neon sign.

Like the rest of western Colorado and eastern Utah, the Grand Junction area is rich in two things: the scenic splendor of rivers and red-rock canyons, and fossilized dinosaurs. The scenery is everywhere, and a fine array of the latter are on display west of town along I-70 at Fruita, in the Museum of Western Colorado's wonderful **Dinosaur Journey** (daily; $6; 970/242-0971). Kids can have fun pushing buttons to control gigantic audio-animatronic mechanical critters, while learning a little about Triassic, Jurassic, and other period details.

Colorado National Monument

Rising south and west of Grand Junction, nearly 2,000 feet above the Colorado River, the brilliantly colored cliffs of **Colorado National Monument** are simply impossible to miss. Deep canyons, alive with piñon pines and cottonwood trees, nestle at the foot of sheer rock walls, at the top of which you get panoramic views over miles and miles of the Colorado Plateau. The 23-mile-long **Rim Rock Drive** winds along the tops of the cliffs, giving quick access to numerous trails for up-close looks at the various layers and hues of sandstone and shale, which have eroded over the eons into masses of sculpted stone.

There's a large **visitors center** (970/858-3617) at the main entrance, four miles southeast of town, and there's another entrance off I-70 in Fruita, at the northern end of the park.

Delta

From Grand Junction, US-50 briefly becomes a four-lane freeway, then reverts to two lanes following the Gunnison River as far as **Delta** (pop. 6,400). The half-dozen building-sized murals of elk and local agricultural products support Delta's claim that it is "The City of Murals," but the biggest attraction to travelers is the reconstructed **Fort Uncompahgre** (un-com-PA-gray; Mon.–Fri. Apr.–Oct. only; $5; 970/874-8349), at the confluence of the Gunnison and Uncompahgre Rivers on the northwest side of town. One of the most authentic living history museums in the country, the small, city-sponsored fort re-creates the lifestyles of trappers and traders who first settled in the western Rocky Mountains in the early 1820s. The fort's well-versed guides take you around the small palisaded compound, discussing the historical context of the fur trade while demonstrating (and encouraging visitors to take part in) the arts and crafts necessary for frontier life: metalworking, tanning, and tomahawk-throwing, not to mention hunting, shooting, and fishing.

Delta has one great old landmark, the 1920s **Egyptian Theater** movie palace (970/874-9770) at 452 Main Street, along with its fair share of motels (including a **Best Western**) and fast-food places. It's also home to a classic piece of roadside Americana: the log-and-stone cabins of the **Westways Court Motel** ($55; 970/874-4415), 1030 Main Street, on US-50 in the center of town.

Southeast of Delta, US-50 runs along the banks of the Uncompahgre River, passing lots of farms and one very large Louisiana-Pacific lumber mill at Olathe, midway to Montrose.

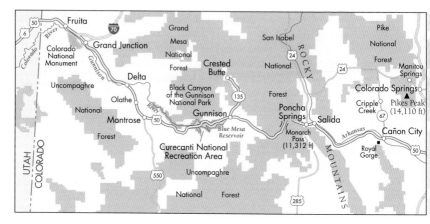

Montrose

With the San Juan Mountains standing out to the south, and Black Canyon just up the road, **Montrose**, a farming community of some 12,000 souls that spreads from the heart of the fertile Uncompahgre Valley, makes a good base for exploring the region. The town itself has an appealing, still-in-business business district, and a historical museum housed in the old railroad depot, and the US-50 frontage has plenty of motels and places to eat, especially east of downtown. **Sicily's** (970/240-9199) at 1135 E. Main Street, has good Italian food served up (in summer . . .) on the terrace. *The* place to stay, for fans of old roadside Americana, has to be the 1930s-era **Log Cabin Motel** ($40 and up; 970/249-7610), across the street at 1034 E. Main Street, which is exactly what it sounds like.

Eight miles east of Montrose, Hwy-347 turns off north toward the Black Canyon of the Gunnison National Park.

memorial to snowplow drivers killed on the Million Dollar Highway

US-550: The Million Dollar Highway

No matter what you want from a scenic drive, Colorado's famous **Million Dollar Highway** has it in spades. Loaded with sublime natural scenery, historically fascinating and visually appealing small towns, and, most of all, sheer driving pleasure, the Million Dollar Highway more than lives up to its name. One of the best-loved roads in the country, this classic stretch of two-lane blacktop forms a swirling ribbon through the San Juan Mountains, the wildest and ruggedest peaks in the Colorado Rockies. Marked on maps and by road signs as US-550, which runs south from the Gunnison River ranchlands around Montrose to the Southern Ute Indian Reservation, the "Million Dollar" tag

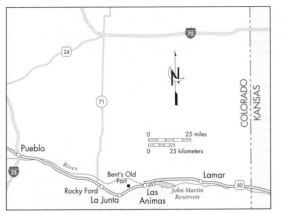

is generally applied to the 25 steep and twisting miles that link Ouray and Silverton, a pair of remote gold and silver mining communities, but it's also an appropriate nickname for the entire 110 miles of US-550 that link US-50 with Ouray and Durango.

As you might expect of a road born in a Wild West mining country animated by tales of million-dollar fortunes earned, lost, and hoped-for, the history of the Million Dollar Highway is rife with legend. The route was first blazed by the so-called "Pathfinder of the San Juans," a five-foot-tall Russian immigrant named Otto Mears who was working as a U.S. mail carrier between Silverton and Telluride. By 1882 Mears had created a lucrative toll road that he parlayed into a sizeable empire of roads and railroads, but his original hand-carved route through the mountains formed the basis of today's Million Dollar Highway.

Even the origin of the "Million Dollar" name is clouded in myth. Some say it was first used after an early traveler, complaining of the vertigo-inducing steepness of the route, said, "I wouldn't go that way again if you paid me a million dollars." Others claim that it derives simply from the actual cost of paving the route in the 1930s. But the favorite explanation is also the most likely: When the highway was first constructed, the builders used gravel discarded by nearby gold and silver mines, only to find out later that this dirt was actually rich in ore and worth an estimated "million dollars."

The New Deal–era documentary photography project, which produced many indelible images from the likes of **Walker Evans** and **Dorothea Lange,** was directed by **Roy Stryker,** who spent his youth on a ranch outside Montrose.

Black Canyon of the Gunnison National Park

Some of the hardest and oldest rocks on earth form the sheer walls of 2,000-foot-deep **Black Canyon of the Gunnison,** the deepest and most impressive gorge in the state. The river cutting through the canyon falls faster than any other in North America—dropping 2,150 feet in under 50 miles—and the canyon bottom is so rugged that there are no trails along it. Unless you're a serious mountaineer, you'll have to content yourself with looking down into it from the rim, which is accessible on the north side via Hwy-92, and from US-50 on the south via Hwy-347. The **visitors center** (970/641-2337) on the south rim provides details on hiking trails and camping, and can tell you more than you ever wanted to know about the canyon's unique geology: For instance, unlike the Grand Canyon with its layers of exposed rock, the Black Canyon is basically one solid hunk of stone, a half-mile-thick chunk of two-billion-year-old Precambrian gneiss (pronounced "nice").

Upstream from the Black Canyon, US-50 parallels the Gunnison River, renowned for its excellent trout and landlocked salmon fishing, though sadly the once-raging waters have been backed up behind dams to form a series of reservoirs, jointly managed as the **Curecanti National Recreation Area.**

For a non-commercial, "wide-spectrum" audio taste of Crested Butte, tune in to **KBUT 89.9 FM** and **90.3 FM.**

Gunnison and Crested Butte

A crossroads cattle town with a rapidly-growing recreational aspect and the only commercial airport for miles, **Gunnison** (pop. 5,409, elev. 7,707) is made livelier than many Colorado towns by the presence of Western State College, whose ski-bumming students are responsible for the many bike shops and Internet cafés, not to mention the huge "W" that marks a mountainside south of town. To get a feel for Gunnison, stop by the lively **Bean** coffeehouse, a half-block north of US-50 along Hwy-135, which runs through the redbrick heart of old downtown Gunnison. For food, pig out at the **Trough** (970/641-3724), on US-50 a mile west of downtown. Motels line up along US-50, making Gunnison a handy base for exploring the region.

If you're taken with the scenery around Gunnison and want to see more, head north along Hwy-135 and the Gunnison River to the area's skiing and mountain biking center, **Crested Butte** (pop. 898), 25 miles away. As in Telluride and Aspen, this 100-year-old gold-mining camp won a second lease on life thanks to tourism, though compared to other Colorado places Crested Butte is low-key and somewhat off the beaten path. Skiers in search of solitude flock here in winter to cruise the 1,100-plus acres of Mt. Crested Butte, while in summer Crested Butte is a mountain bike mecca, with miles and miles of mining roads and single-track trails winding through the mountains. (The ski lifts convert to bike lifts, to save you suffering on the climb back uphill.)

Relax while you recharge your batteries with a burger and a beer or two at the **Wooden Nickel** (970/349-6350), at 222 Elk Street, or the adjacent **Idlespur Brewpub** (970/349-5026), at 226 Elk Avenue.

The first European explorers to pass through this part of the Rockies were the Spanish missionaries **Domínguez** and **Escalante**, in 1776.

Three blocks north of Elk Avenue, the **HI Crested Butte International Hostel** (970/349-0588), 615 Teocalli Avenue, has dorm beds for around $20 a night. There are also hotels and chalets available through the ski resort (970/349-2262 or 800/544-8448).

Monarch Pass and Poncha Springs

East of Gunnison, the landscape changes swiftly as US-50, and a few masochistic cyclists, climb steeply through a gorgeous alpine landscape of meadows and cattle ranches toward 11,312-foot **Monarch Pass.** The pass marks the highest point on US-50 and straddles the Continental Divide: The 30 feet of annual snowfall on the east side of the pass end up in the Atlantic, while (in theory, at least) moisture falling farther west makes its way to the Pacific. There's a ski and snowboarding area here in winter, and in summer you can ride a **tram** or hike to a nearby summit for a 360-degree view over the Rocky and Sangre de Cristo Mountains.

At the eastern foot of Monarch Pass, the tiny town of **Poncha Springs** has a pair of places perfect for weary travelers: a truck stop featuring great Mexican food, and the historic **Jackson Hotel** (719/539-4861), at 6340 US-285, a recent-ly restored 1870s stage stop that has hosted every Wild West figure from Billy the Kid to Teddy Roosevelt, and is now a restaurant serving outstanding steaks.

Movie Manor and Colorado Gators

Some 75 miles southwest of Poncha Springs, the potato-farming town of Monte Vista is home to the **Movie Manor** (719/852-5921 or 800/771-9468), a combi-nation drive-in movie theater, restaurant, and Best Western motel at 2860 W. US-160. You can watch movies (for free!) from the comfort of your motel room, though the screen is so far away it's about the same size as watching movies on TV. Fun, though, and unique, for sure; where else can you snuggle down beneath the covers, gazing out the window as the sun sets and the lights come up on the big-screen figures swaggering through their latest Hollywood hits against a backdrop of snow-capped, 14,000-foot peaks?

Other good reasons to loop south from US-50 include the **Great Sand Dunes National Park,** and the even more unlikely sight of hundreds of alliga-tors enjoying the geothermal hot springs at **Colorado Gators** (daily; $6; 719/378-2612), an hour south of Poncha Springs on Hwy-17, near the turnoff east to the Great Sand Dunes.

Salida

Sitting alongside the Arkansas River east of Monarch Pass, **Salida** (pop. 5,504; elev. 7,038) is a riverfront railroad town gradually switching over to the tourist trade. Close your eyes to the sprawl of Wal-Mart and McDonald's along US-50, and head a dozen blocks north to the historic downtown. Here along the riverfront, a half-dozen brick buildings along 1st Street house slightly hippyish cafés—like the **Laughing Ladies** (719/539-6209) at 128 W. 1st Street—and outdoor recreation shops, including **Headwaters** (719/539-4506), at 228 N. F Street, which rents and sells mountain bikes and kayaks and is the best source of information on the area's wealth of recreational opportunities.

Salida Hot Springs, next to the visitors bureau on Rainbow Avenue (US-50) at 1st Street, is the largest in the state. The naturally heated, WPA-built indoor pool and baths are open year-round; call 719/539-6738 for times and prices.

East of Salida, river rafters can be seen riding the rapids of the Arkansas River for most of the next 45 miles; over a dozen different rafting companies have operations along this beauti-fully scenic stretch. Steeply walled sandstone gorges alternate with broad meadows and sagebrush plains all the way to Royal Gorge and Cañon City, and campers may want to avail themselves of a nicely sited **KOA Kampground,** along the riverside at Cotopaxi.

Every December, Salida lights up a tree on **Christmas Mountain** with 10,000 bulbs. Another unusual sight: West of town along US-50, a large pet cemetery lies next door to a veterinarian's office.

Royal Gorge

It would be easy to object to the rampant commercialism of **Royal Gorge** (daily; $20; 719/275-7507), but if you don't mind seeing impressive works of hu-mankind amidst a stupendous show of nature's prowess, I heartily recommend a visit. The gorge itself is unforgettable, its sheer, red granite cliffs dropping over

1,000 feet straight down to the Arkansas River, and the experience is enhanced by a barrage of civil engineering feats, including aerial trams, incline railways, and an impossibly delicate suspension bridge, all enabling visitors to experience the area in diverse ways. You can look down from the rim, dangle from a gondola on your way across to the other side, and from there follow a short nature trail that offers good views of Pike's Peak. Walk back across the wooden planks of the bridge—the highest in the world, feelin uncomfortably like a rickety old seaside pier—then drop down on a funicular to the gorge's bottom, where you can stand alongside the raging river, listening to the roar or admiring the famous Denver and Rio Grande Railroad line that passes through the gorge, in places suspended out over the river from the solid rock walls.

The only problem with Royal Gorge, apart from the steep admission fees, is that to get there you have to run a gauntlet of some of the tackiest tourist traps in creation, worst of which is the self-proclaimed "Real Historic Buckskin Joe—Gunfights and Hangings Daily." Similarly hyped outfits line the well-marked, two-mile-long road to Royal Gorge, which cuts south from US-50 eight miles west of Cañon City.

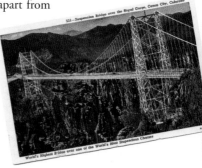

Cañon City

One of the last remaining Wild West towns in the lower 48 states, **Cañon City** (pop. 15,431) is carved out of the eastern flank of the Rocky Mountains. Over a mile high and surrounded by a ring of 14,000-foot peaks, Cañon City's short Main Street, a block north of US-50, is lined by work-a-day saddle shops, gun shops, bookshops, and saloons (eight in four blocks!). But the local economy prospers not so much from tourism as from prisons: 14 in all, including Colorado's newest maximum-security penitentiary, nicknamed "Supermax," and its oldest, the **Territorial Prison** (daily in summer, weekends only in winter; $5) at the west end of Main Street, in which 32 cells have been preserved as a somewhat gruesome but compelling museum. The Territorial Prison's most famous guest was Alferd Packer, a miner and Wild West gunslinger convicted of cannibalism and other crimes; the top-security Supermax prison has held some of the nation's most notorious inmates, including Atlanta Olympics bomber Eric Rudolph, Unabomber Ted Kaczynski, and actor Woody Harrelson's alleged hit-man dad, Charles.

convicted cannibal
Alferd Packer

Despite the notoriety of its many prisons, Cañon City's main attraction is the surrounding scenery, particularly the views along **Skyline Drive**, accessible from just west of town. It's a three-mile, one-way drive across the top of an

800-foot hill, as close to riding a roller coaster as you're ever likely to get while inside a passenger car. Royal Gorge to the west (which the city owns and operates; see above) is another major draw, and Cañon City makes a good base for explorations, with a few moderately priced motels like the **Pioneer** ($45; 719/269-1745), at 201 Main Street next to the old prison. The best place for cheap food and drink is **The Owl**, 626 Main Street, a combo cigar store, soda fountain, diner, and pool hall at the heart of the lively Main Street business district north of US-50. Also worth a look: the historic **St. Cloud Hotel** ($70 and up; 719/276-2000), at 631 Main Street, which has a friendly bar and grill on its ground floor.

Pike's Peak and Manitou Springs

One of the highest points you can drive to in the continental United States, **Pike's Peak** has been a road trip destination since 1901 when the first car (a two-cylinder Locomobile Steamer) made its way to the 14,110-foot summit. Opened as a toll road in 1915, the Pike's Peak Highway now winds its way to the top—climbing nearly 7,000 vertical feet in under 20 miles, with no guardrails to comfort you or block the amazing 360-degree Rocky Mountain panorama. The road is now owned and operated by the city of Colorado Springs, which charges a $10 per person toll; go early, before the clouds and haze build up, for the best long-distance views.

And if the views aren't enough, another good reason to climb Pike's Peak is that to get there you pass through the delightful old resort town of **Manitou Springs**. A National Historic District, Manitou Springs has all the grand hotels, hot springs, tourist traps, and cave tours you could want, plus my very favorite pinball arcade in the entire world—dozens of ancient machines in perfect working order, and still charging the same nickel or dime that they did in the 1920s, '30s, and '40s.

Besides places to play, Manitou Springs also has some classic places to stay, like the historic motor court cabins of the **El Colorado Lodge** ($50 and up; 719/685-5485) at 23 Manitou Avenue, arrayed around four acres of pine trees, with fireplaces, a pool, and a horseshoe pit!

North of Manitou Springs, the 1,350-acre **Garden of the Gods** (daily; free) is a photogenic geological outcropping of red sandstone spires, some rising to heights of 300 feet.

All along US-50 west of Cañon City, you can see rafters racing along the wild Arkansas River. Many companies offer guided trips, including **Arkansas River Tours** (800/321-4352).

According to the WPA *Guide to Colorado*, the poet **Joaquin Miller,** who served as mayor, judge, and minister in Cañon City's early days, wanted to change its name to Oreodelphia, to highlight the region's many gold mines. Local miners, however, protested, insisting that "the place is a canyon, and it's goin' to be called Cañon City."

The **Pike's Peak Hill Climb** has been held around the 4th of July almost every year since 1916. Top drivers often compete, hitting speeds of up to 100 mph on the twisting mountain road. After a visit to the top of Pike's Peak in 1893, Katharine Lee Bates wrote the words to "America the Beautiful."

Detour: Denver

Though it's 100 miles north of Pueblo via the I-25 freeway, **Denver** (pop. 554,636) has the biggest, newest, and coolest airport in the Rockies, which may make it a handy starting or stopping point. The airport, which opened in 1996, is in the middle of nowhere, 25 miles northeast of town. The main lobby has a soaring fabric roof that from the outside looks like a Plains Indian encampment; inside is a pair of artworks, called "America: Why I Love Her," which trace artist Gary Sweeney's childhood memories of road trips to see the "World's Largest Ball of Twine" and other all-American icons.

Other reasons to visit Denver include the **U.S. Mint** (Mon.-Fri.; free), right downtown at 320 W. Colfax Avenue, where you can watch and hear coins being pressed into shape; **Coors Field** (303/762-5437), lively home of the Colorado Rockies baseball team; and **Lakeside Park** (303/477-1621), off I-70 at 4601 Sheridan Boulevard, a nifty old summer-only amusement park with art deco architecture, a wooden Cyclone roller coaster, and other rides dating back to 1908.

In downtown Denver, eat at **Dixon's Downtown Grill** (303/573-6100), a family-friendly haunt serving great breakfasts, afternoon sandwiches (try the Reuben), and drinks all night long in a historic building at 1610 16th Street. There are the usual range of hotels and motels in and around Denver, plus one unforgettable classic dating from 1890s: President Dwight Eisenhower's favorite hotel, the **Brown Palace** ($150 and up; 303/297-3111), 321 17th Street. The lobby is worth a look even if you stay the night somewhere else.

For details on these or anything else to do with Denver, contact the visitors bureau (303/892-1112 or 800/645-3446), located at 1555 California Street.

Pike's Peak and Manitou Springs are along US-24, just west of Colorado Springs. From US-50, Hwy-115 runs north from just outside Cañon City to Colorado Springs, where you can take I-25 north to reach US-24. For more information, contact the **visitors bureau** (719/685-5089 or 800/642-2567) at 354 Manitou Avenue.

Pueblo

At the foot of the mountains, 38 miles east of Cañon City and 150 miles west of the Kansas border, the heavily industrialized city of **Pueblo** (pop. 102,121) spreads to both sides of the Arkansas River. Colorado's third-largest city, Pueblo was founded by legendary black fur-trapper **Jim Beckwourth** in 1842, but the town really grew in the 1870s following the arrival of the railroad and the discovery nearby of vast amounts of coal. Steel mills, including some of the largest west of the Mississippi, still stand around the fringes of the pleasant, tree-lined downtown area, but Pueblo is increasingly more bucolic than brawny, and the historic areas are slowly filling up with artsy cafés, bookshops, and antique stores, especially along Union Avenue on the south side.

La Junta

For eastbound travelers, **La Junta** (pop. 7,568), a busy railroad town on the banks of the Arkansas River, is where we begin tracing the historic Santa Fe Trail. The name La Junta, which means "the junction," is apt, since the town has long been a key crossroads, first on the Santa Fe Trail and now as the division between the main line and the Denver branch of the Santa Fe Railroad, and as the junction of US-50 and US-350. Besides gas stations and a good range of places to eat (Mexican restaurants are a particular strength), a two-screen movie theater, and an ancient-looking barber shop, La Junta also offers the excellent **Koshare Indian Museum** (daily; $2), on the campus of Otero Junior College on the south side of town. Sleep cheap at the **Mid-Town Motel** ($40; 719/384-7741), 215 E. 3rd Street.

La Junta also marks the spot where the "Mountain Branch" of the Santa Fe Trail finally cuts away to the south, following what's now US-350 through the Comanche National Grassland and continuing over Raton Pass into New Mexico and on to Santa Fe. Eastbound travelers are in luck, as we follow this historic route all the way to the other side of Kansas City.

From US-50, one of the West's most scenic (unpaved but easily passable) drives, Phantom Canyon Road, 25 miles west of Pueblo and seven miles east of Cañon City, winds north to the old mining camp, now prosperous gambling town, of Cripple Creek.

On the west side of the Colorado State Capitol, a benchmark at the unlucky 13th step lets you stand exactly 5,280 feet above sea level—a mile high.

Bent's Old Fort

From La Junta, an interesting quick detour off US-50, Hwy-194 runs along the north bank of the Arkansas River to one of Colorado's most evocative historic sites, **Bent's Old Fort** (daily; $3; 719/383-5010). It lies eight miles east of La Junta, or 15 miles west of Las Animas. From 1833, when it was built by the fur-traders William and Charles Bent, until 1848, when war with Mexico and increasing unrest among the local Arapahoe, Apache, and Cheyenne tribes put an end to their business, Bent's Fort was the Southwest's most important outpost of American civilization, and a stopping place for travelers, trappers, and explorers including John C. Fremont, Francis Parkman, and just about every other Wild West luminary.

Though it was abandoned and left to decay for over 100 years, the large adobe fort was authentically rebuilt by the National Park Service in 1976, and now stands as a palpable

William Bent

Santa Fe Trail

For over half a century, beginning in the 1820s and lasting until the railroads were completed in the 1880s, the Santa Fe Trail was the primary link between the United States and the Spanish and Mexican Southwest. Running from the Missouri River ports around present-day Kansas City, the trail angled along the banks of the Arkansas River, splitting west of what's now Dodge City into two routes: the Mountain Branch, which US-50 follows, and the quicker but more dangerous Cimarron Cut-Off, across the arid plains of the Jornado del Muerto. The two branches rejoined before climbing the Sangre de Cristo Mountains into what was then, as it is now, the capital of the Southwest, Santa Fe.

Unlike many of the routes across the Wild West frontier, the Santa Fe Trail was established by commercial traders rather than emigrant pioneers, and travel along it was active in both directions: Merchants from the United States brought manufactured goods by the wagon load, which they exchanged for Mexican silver. First blazed by trader William Becknell in 1821, the year the newly independent Republic of Mexico opened the border (which Spain had kept closed), the 750-mile-long trail was surveyed by the U.S. government in 1826, and traffic increased slowly until the Mexican-American War brought Santa Fe, and all the land in between, under U.S. control. Military forts were established to protect traders from the marauding Comanche and other native tribes; at the time of the Civil War, commerce along the trail reached at peak, with over 5,000 wagons making the trek to Santa Fe, carrying over $50 million worth of trade goods. The extension of the railroads across the Great Plains in the 1870s diminished the importance of the trail, and by 1880, when the Santa Fe railroad reached Santa Fe itself, the trail became a part of history.

Though US-50 follows the Santa Fe Trail almost exactly, from Las Animas east to Kansas City, very little remains, apart from outposts like Bent's Fort and Fort Larned and a few all-but-invisible stretches of old wagon ruts. Numerous plaques mark historic sites, and it's still possible to get a powerful sense of what the trail might have been like—provided you take the time to park the car and walk even a few hundred yards in the footsteps that crossed here a century ago.

The following are some of the most evocative sites along the Santa Fe Trail, west to east.

Santa Fe, NM: The second-oldest city in North America, preserving a vivid taste of its Spanish, Mexican, and American past (see page 810).

Bent's Old Fort, CO: A reconstructed adobe trading post along the banks of the Arkansas River in the Rocky Mountain foothills (see page 673).

Dodge City, KS: One of the best-preserved remnants of the original Santa Fe Trail wagon ruts stretches across the rolling farmlands just west of this Wild West landmark town (see page 678).

Fort Larned, KS: A well-preserved U.S. Army fortress, intact since the 1850s and protecting a fine set of wagon ruts (see pages 679–680).

Council Grove, KS: The last American town on the trail west, hardly changed since the heyday of the trail (see pages 683–684).

Westport, MO: Now surrounded by suburban Kansas City, this was the real start of the trail from the 1840s on.

Independence, MO: The original start of the Santa Fe and the Oregon Trails, with a fine museum detailing the westward frontier movements (see page 687).

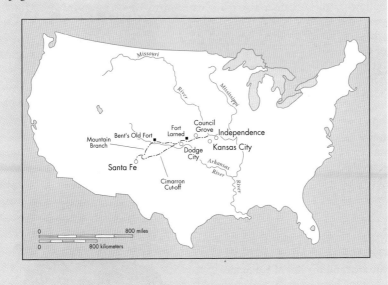

reminder of the early years of the frontier era. Thick adobe walls, 15 feet tall with circular bastions at the corners, protect a roughly 100-square-foot compound. Rangers dressed in period clothing work as wheelsmiths, coopers, and carpenters, or process the many buffalo robes and beaver pelts piled up in storerooms.

Las Animas

The farming community of **Las Animas** (pop. 2,758) takes its name from the Arkansas River tributary originally known as **Río de las Animas Perdidas en Purgatorio**—the River of Lost Souls. Las Animas is also the place where, on November 15, 1806, Lt. Zebulon Pike first laid eyes on the Rocky Mountain peak that now bears his name—Pike's Peak, 120 miles to the northwest.

Beyond Las Animas, US-50 continues its gradual descent across the Rocky Mountains foothills. The area was first known as Big Timbers for the tall cottonwoods that grew here along the Arkansas River, though most of these trees were cut down soon after the arrival of white settlers. In the 1840s and 1850s, local Cheyenne, Arapaho, Kiowa, and Apache tribes bartered bison hides at William Bent's trading post, and Wild West explorer **Kit Carson** died here on May 23, 1868, in his family home at what was then the U.S. Army's Fort Lyon, south of present-day US-50. Carson's remains were later moved to Taos, New Mexico, and his lands were flooded after the Arkansas River was dammed to form the large John Martin Reservoir, which stretches most of the way downstream to Lamar.

Lamar

Following the Arkansas River downstream toward the Kansas border, US-50 runs along what was known as the "Mountain Branch" of the Santa Fe Trail, a longer but safer alternative to the main route along the Cimarron Cut-Off. There's little to see here apart from acres and acres of irrigated farmlands, feedlots, and cattle ranches, though the region's main town, **Lamar** (pop. 8,869), is worth a quick stop. Very good Mexican-American food is available all day long at the **Main Cafe,** at 114 S. Main Street in the center of town. A block away, the handy state-run **Welcome Center** (719/336-3483) in the old Santa Fe depot on the east side of Main Street (US-50) has reams of information on the area and the rest of Colorado.

At the heart of town, next to the old depot, a stately *Madonna of the Trail* stands as a reminder of the indefatigable spirit of the pioneers. Standing

Lamar's *Madonna of the Trail*

nearly 20 feet tall atop an engraved plinth, this statue is one of 12 identical memorials erected in the 1920s by the Daughters of the American Revolution (D.A.R.). From Bethesda, Maryland, to Upland, California, the memorials were placed along the original National Old Trails Highway, which followed the National Road (US-40) and later Route 66 on the westward path of Manifest Destiny.

Lamar's **KLMR 93.3 FM** plays a broad mix of chart-topping pop and country music, and broadcasts Colorado Rockies and Broncos games.

KANSAS

In its nearly 500 miles across Kansas, US-50 and its selected variants pass across the agricultural heartland of America, winding through dozens of small farming towns that dot the generally level landscape. (Locals definitely seem to prefer the word "level" to the equally accurate "flat," if only because it sounds less boring.) This is the heart of the "Wheat Belt," where most of the country's grain is grown—as much as half the bread baked in America is made from Kansas wheat—and it's also prime cattle country, with towns like Dodge City and many less famous ones maintaining their historic dependence on cows and cowboys.

All the way across Kansas, we follow almost exactly in the footsteps of the trappers and traders who braved the Santa Fe Trail along the western frontier, stopping at preserved old outposts like Fort Larned and Council Grove while tracking the few more evocative remnants of this pioneer Wild West corridor.

Holcomb

Apart from numerous feedlots fattening cattle for slaughter, and a few wheat, corn, and beet farms fed by water diverted from the Arkansas River, there's not much to see in the 120 miles of barren plains that stretch east from the Colorado border. On the western outskirts of Garden City, the region's biggest town, US-50 runs through the meat-packing town of **Holcomb**, notorious as the site of the *In Cold Blood* murders documented by Truman Capote. In 1959, Perry Smith and Richard Hickock ruthlessly killed the entire Clutter family during a robbery attempt. Both killers were eventually captured, convicted, and executed.

The dividing line between Central and Mountain time zones is 15 miles west of Garden City. Set your clocks and watches accordingly.

At Garden City, 50 miles west of Dodge City, US-50 crosses US-83, **The Road to Nowhere**, which follows the 100th Meridian from Canada to Mexico. See pages 160–211 for details on this route. Garden City is described on pages 191–193.

Santa Fe Trail Tracks

One of the best-preserved sections of Santa Fe Trail **wagon ruts** is along this stretch of US-50, nine miles west of Dodge City. Marked by a large sign, just west of the Howell grain elevator, these wheel tracks, or ruts, lie in a rolling field

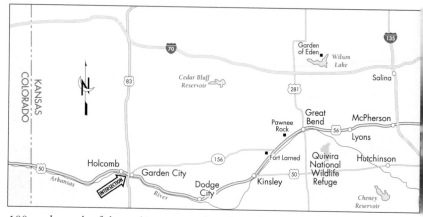

100 yards north of the parking area and are basically a broad depression in the soil, approximately 800 yards wide and two miles long. Farther west, at Cimarron, 32 miles east of Garden City and 16 miles west of Dodge City, the main track of the Santa Fe Trail crossed the Arkansas River and headed southwest across the waterless plain of the Jornada del Muerto on what was known as the **Cimarron Cut-Off.** This desolate region is also where, in 1831 during the earliest days of the trail, legendary mountain man **Jedediah Strong Smith** was killed by a band of Comanche warriors.

Dodge City

One of the most notorious places on the Wild West frontier, **Dodge City** (pop. 26,176) can be something of a disappointment if you come here looking for a rip-roaring frontier town. In its heyday, which lasted roughly from 1872, when the railroad arrived, to 1884, when the cattle drives were effectively banned, Dodge City was the undisputed capital of the buffalo-hunting, cattle-driving Wild West, with as many as 100 million bison hides and seven million head of cattle shipped out from here in that decade alone. At the same time, Dodge City was known as "Hell on the Plains," famous for its gunfights and general lawlessness, despite marshals like **Bat Masterson** and **Wyatt Earp** keeping order and planting bad guys in the Boot Hill cemetery above town.

However, almost nothing in Dodge City survives from that era. Boot Hill, for example, was bought by the city and is now the site of a small office building. (A statue of a cowboy, erected in 1927, says somewhat mournfully: "On the ashes of my campfire this city is built.") Most of what you see in Dodge City dates from the 1920s at the earliest, and Dodge City is by and large a busy farming and cattle-ranching community, with extensive stockyards surrounding the small downtown area. Because of the low-profit economics of the beef industry, most of the 4,000–5,000 peo-

ple who work in the feed-lots and slaughterhouses today are immigrant workers from Mexico—which explains the predominance of Mexican cafés and grocery stores around town.

For travelers, there's little here apart from one of the Midwest's more heavily-hyped tourist attractions, the fake but fun **Boot Hill Museum** (daily; $8; 620/227-8188) and its recreated Front Street, where actors stage gunfights and "medicine shows" throughout the day. There's also an evening burlesque show, featuring "Miss Kitty and her Can Can Girls;" a reconstructed sod house; the old (circa-1865) jail; and a one-room schoolhouse. A historic Santa Fe locomotive completes the Boot Hill collection; not surprisingly, Boot Hill is hard to miss, well-marked on the west side of town, just north of the railroad tracks along Wyatt Earp Boulevard (US-50/56), the main route through town.

Wyatt Earp Boulevard (US-50) holds most of Dodge City's eating options, like the **Hitch 'n Post** truck stop at the east end of town, along with a half dozen motels.

Kinsley: Midway USA

Paralleling the mainline Santa Fe Railroad across the flattest, emptiest 50 miles of Kansas cornfields, east of Dodge City we follow US-50 as far as **Kinsley,** where we switch onto US-56 (which used to be known as "US-50 North") to follow the Santa Fe Trail. Kinsley, which calls itself **"Midway USA,"** lies equidistant from New York and San Francisco: 1,561 miles from either place. This geographical fact is pointed out by a large sign outside the entertaining (and free!) **Edwards County Historical Museum,** at the US-50/56 junction on the west side of town, surrounded by an old locomotive and a variety of old farming and ranching equipment.

Fort Larned

One of the best-preserved vestiges of the Santa Fe Trail, **Fort Larned** (daily; $3; 620/285-6911), six miles west of US-56 via Hwy-156, was established in 1859, and for the next 20 years troops stationed here protected travelers on the Santa Fe Trail from the threat of attack by local Arapahoe and Cheyenne tribes. The fort also served a vital role in the many Indian Wars of 1860s, but by 1878, when the trail was no longer in active use, the fort was deactivated. It was sold

Tornadoes

Driving across the Great Plains heartland, especially in late spring and early summer, be prepared to encounter Mother Nature's most potent force: a **tornado**, whose swirling winds can reach from 150–300 mph or more. The Midwest has been dubbed "Tornado Alley," for the frequency of storms that can hit the region. While the tornado at the start of *The Wizard of Oz* touched down in Dorothy's home state, Kansas, they are just as likely to occur in Oklahoma, Missouri, or Mississippi.

Each year about a thousand tornadoes touch down in the United States, and 50 or so people are killed as a result. Tornadoes can last from several seconds to more than an hour, but most last around 10 minutes. You can greatly reduce the chance of injury by doing a few simple things. Be aware of the possibility of severe weather; most tornado-related deaths and injuries happen to people who are unaware and uninformed. Tune into local radio stations for current information. If a **tornado watch** has been issued, it means that a tornado is possible. If a **tornado warning** is issued, it means that a tornado has actually been spotted, and you should seek shelter immediately.

If you are in a car, do not try to escape from a tornado by driving away from it. Tornadoes have been known to blow cars off the road, or hurl them away. If there is no time to get indoors, get out of the car and lie in a ditch or low-lying area away from the vehicle. Do not seek shelter under a highway overpass, which act like wind tunnels, making the winds even stronger.

and used as a ranch until 1960, but has survived the intervening years in excellent condition. Careful restoration by the National Park Service has made Fort Larned an excellent place to experience what the frontier really looked like, albeit from the military perspective.

Sandstone buildings, which replaced the original adobe after the end of the Civil War, surround a 400-square-foot parade ground, and interior rooms have been filled with accurate reproductions of original fixtures and fittings, ranging from barracks to blacksmith's shops to a large storehouse. A nearby farm preserves a set of ruts surviving from the Santa Fe Trail days, though you really need to have an active imagination to get much from them.

In between Fort Larned and US-56, the **Santa Fe Trail Center** (closed Mon.; $4; 620/285-2054) is a private, nonprofit museum focusing on the overall history of the Santa Fe Trail region. Diorama-like exhibits feature full-scale mock-ups of wagons and frontier trading posts, and behind the main building are a sod house and a one-room schoolhouse.

Pawnee Rock

Just eight miles northeast of Larned, a half mile north of US-56 and the Arkansas River, **Pawnee Rock** was once one of the most important landmarks on the Santa Fe Trail. However, so much of the original 60-foot-high tower of Dakota sandstone has been quarried—to build houses as well as the roadbed of the Santa Fe railroad—that it's little more than a stubby hump. But you can still get a grand view of the surrounding countryside from the easy trail that leads to the rock's much-diminished summit.

Great Bend

Spreading along the northern bank of the Arkansas River at the northernmost point on its sweep across central Kansas, **Great Bend** (pop. 15,345) was originally established as a fort along the Santa Fe Trail, but really began to grow after the railroad came through. As with Dodge City to the southwest, the arrival of the railroad in 1872 attracted cattle drovers from the Chisholm Trail, who turned Great Bend into a raucous Wild West town. It's now a quiet, rural city, earning its livelihood from wheat farms and, since the 1930s, oil.

Great Bend was the boyhood hometown of **Jack Kilby**, the Texas Instruments electrical engineer who helped invent the integrated circuit and the pocket calculator. Kilby was awarded the Nobel Prize for Physics in 2000, and died in 2005.

Downtown Great Bend has a number of building-sized **murals,** especially the blocks along Main Street perpendicular to US-56, and the outskirts of town have the engaging **Barton County Historical Society Museum** (closed Mon.; $2; 620/793-5125), just south of the railroad tracks and the river along US-281. Farther afield, the Great Bend area holds two of the largest wildlife refuges in Kansas, **Cheyenne Bottoms** to the northeast and **Quivira** to the southeast, both of which offer excellent bird-watching (and hunting . . .) opportunities.

Great Bend does have a fairly good range of places to eat, with franchise fast food supplemented by a handful of local restaurants like **Granny's Kitchen** (620/793-7441), at 925 10th Street.

Along with the national chains, one reliable place to stay in Great Bend is the **Traveler's Budget Inn** ($40; 620/793-5448), at 4200 W. 10th Street.

The Garden of Eden

If you're one of those bi-coastal types who thinks that the Midwest is full of conventional-minded folks leading ordinary lives as contented consumers, you owe it to yourself to visit the **Garden of Eden** (daily; $5; 785/525-6395), one of the country's oldest and oddest folk-art environments. Located in the tiny town of **Lucas, Kansas** (pop. 436), the Garden of Eden is the sort of place that puts the gothic back in American Gothic, a front-yard forest of Biblical scenes and Populist political allegories—Adam and Eve, Cain and Abel, and the Crucifixion of Labor at the Hands of Preachers, Bankers, and Lawyers—created out of concrete from around 1910 to 1930 by one Samuel Dinsmoor. An Ohio native and Civil War veteran, Dinsmoor actively promoted his Garden as a tourist attraction, managing to draw many hundreds of visitors to this distant and fairly inaccessible corner of Kansas. Dinsmoor died at age 89 in 1932 and is buried in a glass-covered tomb on the property, yet carried on his hucksterism even after death, insisting in his will that no one be allowed "to go in and see me for less than $1."

The next town east of Great Bend along US-50 is Ellinwood, where a couple of antique shops mark the historic downtown area. Ellinwood sits atop a series of tunnels used as tornado shelters and occasionally as storerooms for contraband. They are sometimes open for guided tours by **Underground Ellinwood** (620/564-2218).

The Garden of Eden is at the corner of 2nd and Kansas in Lucas, which is on Hwy-18, north of Great Bend and 15 miles north of I-70. Homespun Lucas is also home to the **Grassroots Art Center** (785/525-6118), at 213 S. Main Street, a gallery showing and selling artworks created by other self-taught "outsider" artists; outside the gallery is a courtyard full of carved limestone masonry sculptures, many salvaged from demolished buildings around the area.

> If you happen upon one, check out a **public auction,** held irregularly in towns across the rural Midwest. Fast-talking auctioneers take bids on various lots, ranging from real antiques to boxes of junk and cast-off clothes.

> The central Kansas farmlands around **Goessel** are home to one of the largest Mennonite communities in the United States.

Lyons

The farming, oil-drilling, and salt-mining town of **Lyons** (pop. 3,732), 30 miles due east of Great Bend, doesn't look much different from most other Kansas towns, but it has an unusually impressive history—and a very nice courthouse square downtown. There's a 150-foot-long intaglio serpent carved into the prairie eight miles northeast of town, and some Santa Fe Trail ruts, but the most compelling remains are those left behind by Coronado's expedition through the region in 1541, in search of the fabled Golden City of Quivira. Exhibits on all of these, as well as on Indian and pioneer American cultures, are displayed inside the modern, pur-pose-built **Coronado-Quivira Museum** (daily; $2; 620/257-3941) at 105 W. Lyon Street, two blocks south of the landmark county courthouse off US-56.

Two miles west of Lyons along US-56, a large cross marks the site where Fa-ther Padilla, who accompanied Coronado on his expedition and returned the following year to convert the natives, was killed by unreceptive Indians, thereby becoming the first "Christian martyr" in the present-day United States.

For a place to stay, try the **Lyons Inn** ($40; 620/257-5185), on US-56 at 817 W. Main Street.

US-50: Hutchinson

If you've opted to follow US-50 rather than the Santa Fe Trail tour along US-56, be sure to check out **Hutchinson** (pop. 40,787), a large and lively city that's home to the world's longest grain elevator (over a half mile long). The town's old salt mines, some 600 feet below ground, are now used for storage of impor-tant archives, including the original negatives of many classic Hollywood films. The mines, not surprisingly, aren't open to visitors, but Hutchinson does have another surprising attraction: the **Kansas Cosmosphere and Space Center** (daily; $13; 620/662-2305 or 800/397-0330), at 1100 N. Plum Street. The center boasts a great collection of historic air- and spacecraft, including Mer-cury, Gemini, and Apollo capsules; a Lockheed SR-71A "Blackbird" spy plane; and a pair of German V-1 and V-2 rockets; plus two planetarium shows and an IMAX theater.

McPherson

From a distance across the flat plains, the towering grain elevators make **McPherson** (pop. 13,770), 35 miles east of Lyons and marking the junction of US-56 and I-135 between Salina and Wichita, look more impressive than it really is. You can fill the gas tank or get a bite to eat (all the usual franchise food places and gas stations are here) or just stretch your legs wandering around the four-block Main Street business district.

The small **McPherson Museum** (Tues.–Sun. 1–5 PM; donations; 620/241-8464), well-marked in a residential district at 1130 Euclid Street, displays rooms furnished in typical turn-of-the-20th-century Kansas style. It also holds the world's first manmade diamond, produced by Willard Hershey, a local chemistry teacher.

Hillsboro and Herrington: Mennonite Country

One of the centers of the sizeable local Mennonite community, **Hillsboro** (pop. 2,854), 13 miles west of US-77, serves as market center for the area's highly productive farmlands. Tabor College, on the east side of town, is the most visible sign of the Mennonite presence; although it's a coed nondenominational college, about half the students are local Mennonites.

The tidy town of **Goessel** (pop. 506), 15 miles southwest of Hillsboro, was also founded by Mennonite farmers, and now holds the worthwhile **Mennonite Heritage Center** (daily; $3; 620/367-8200), at 200 N. Poplar Street, where numerous buildings, including two schools, a barn, and a bank, have been moved for preservation. The flat, black earth around Goessel is among the world's greatest producers of wheat, in particular the hearty hybrids able to withstand the Midwest winter. The original seed, known as "Turkey Red," was brought to Kansas in the early 1870s by Russian Mennonites who immigrated here after their 100-year exclusion from military service was rescinded.

Zig-zagging east from Hillsboro and then north along US-77/US-56, after another 37 "level" miles US-56 reaches the town of **Herrington,** whose central square holds a monument to Father Padilla, who passed through southern Kansas in search of the mythical Golden City of Quivira as part of Coronado's expedition.

Council Grove

Just 75 miles southwest of the suburban sprawl of Kansas City, 25 miles west of the I-335 Kansas Turnpike, **Council Grove** (pop. 2,321) still looks much as it did over a century ago when, from the 1830s to the 1860s, it was the most important of all way stations on the Santa Fe Trail. Council Grove's lush maples and oaks were the last hardwoods available on the long route west across the treeless plain, which meant traders and travelers could make final repairs and stock up on spare axles and other essentials. It was also the western extent of "safe territory"; beyond here travelers were subject to frequent attacks by hostile Indians.

Nowadays the town proudly preserves its many historic sites, and in many ways serves as the most not-to-be-missed stop for modern travelers heading along the Santa Fe Trail. The sites of two of the most important trail icons, the **Council Oak** under which, in 1825, the native Kansa and Osage Indians agreed to allow Americans to cross their territory, and the **Post Office Oak** that served as a natural message center for

The **Kaw Mission State Historic Site,** in Council Grove five blocks north of Main on Mission Street, was built by Methodist missionaries in 1851 as a school for local Indian children. Students included **Charles Curtis,** who served as U.S. vice president from 1929 to 1933.

early travelers, are marked along Main Street (US-56), east of the bridge over the small Neosho River. Four blocks west, the **Last Chance Store** at Main and Chautauqua Streets has served as a bank and a post office since it was built in 1857.

In between, the banks, cafés, and stores along Main Street, which the Santa Fe Trail followed through town, make little obvious effort to cater to tourists, and the town basically goes about its day-to-day business without forgetting its extraordinary past. The **Hays House** (620/767-5911), in the center of town at 112 W. Main Street, lays fair claim to being the oldest restaurant west of the Mississippi; originally built as a frontier home, and later serving as a saloon, supply post, courthouse, and hotel, it has stood on this site since 1847. Now modernized, it is still the focus of the town's social and political life and is open all day—with excellent fried chicken. Across Main, the soda fountain inside the **Aldrich Apothecary** has good milk shakes. The best place to stay is the comfortable **Cottage House Hotel** ($65–95; 620/767-6828) at 25 N. Neosho.

Further information is available from the Council Grove **visitors center** (620/767-5882 or 800/732-9211), 212 W. Main Street.

US-50: Tallgrass Prairie National Preserve

The delights of the Flint Hills landscape are pastoral in the extreme, with few roaring waterfalls or towering cliffs to take your breath away or make you pull out the camera, but the unique ecosystem has enough admirers that a section of it was recently set aside as the **Tallgrass Prairie National Preserve.** Located along Hwy-177 about 17 miles south of Council Grove, or two miles north of Strong City and US-50, the 11,000-acre preserve protects the largest remaining portion of the extensive tallgrass prairie which once covered over 400,000 square miles of the Great Plains—most of the present-day Midwest. Interpretive facilities are housed in an old stone barn, on a hill above the highway, which has a **visitors center** (daily; 620/273-8494) with exhibits and videos on the natural flora, fauna, and geography of the area. A 1.5 mile nature trail starts here, winding along to the historic one-room Fox Creek Schoolhouse while giving an up-close look at the head-high (or taller) flowering grasses that

Cottonwood Falls courthouse, the oldest operating courthouse in Kansas

give the tallgrass prairie its name. Park rangers also guide bus tours of the grassland ecosystem.

The best base for a visit to the Tallgrass Prairie National Preserve is **Cottonwood Falls,** two miles south of Strong City and US-50 via Hwy-177. The town boasts the beautiful Chase County Courthouse, the oldest still in use in the state, standing like a French château at the south end of a sleepy

Blue Highways to PrairyErth

Writing about US-50, author William Least Heat-Moon has said that "for the unhurried, this little-known highway is the best national road across the middle of the United States." After traveling 13,000 miles of back road through the nooks and crannies of 38 states to write his first book, the road-trip classic *Blue Highways*, Heat-Moon began work on a very different study. Straying no farther than the 744 square miles of Chase County, Kansas, he embarked upon what he termed a "deep map" of the area that sits atop the lush rolling Flint Hills, the nation's last remaining grand expanse of tallgrass prairie, split by US-50 and the Santa Fe Railroad.

The result was the 1991 book *PrairyErth,* a 600-plus-page evocation of history and contemporary life in this otherwise unremarkable corner of the country, which Heat-Moon describes as being "five hours by Interstates from home, eight hours if I follow a route of good café food." Combining folk history and contemporary anecdotes with captivating quotes from sundry novels, Native American legends, travel guides, essays, and old newspaper clippings, this unique project—which has been described as the nonfiction equivalent of the Great American Novel—manages to capture the rhythms of ranching life here in the middle of the great American nowhere.

Main Street business district, where you'll also find a couple of cafés and crafts shops, and the elegant 10-room **Grand Central Hotel** ($140 and up; 620/273-6763), at 215 Broadway, which has a fine, subtly Western-themed restaurant. For a night out in the country, consider the **1874 Stonehouse on Mulberry Hill** (620/273-8481; $95), located on 60 rolling acres just outside town, on the banks of the Cottonwood River.

Burlingame and Baldwin City

Between Council Grove and Kansas City, US-56 passes through the lovely cattle-ranching grasslands of the northern Flint Hills, zig-zagging at 90-degree angles through one-time coal-mining towns like Worden, Overbrook, and Scranton. **Burlingame** (pop. 2,735), the largest of this bunch, is noteworthy for its very broad, brick-paved, 20-mph Main Street (US-56), lined by diverse 100-year-old buildings painted with a barrage of signs advertising player pianos as well as the usual liquor, food, and auto parts.

At the northeast edge of the Flint Hills, 13 miles west of the I-35 freeway from Kansas City, US-56 skirts the leafy, brick-paved streets of **Baldwin City** (pop. 2,961), a small town that was once a main rest-and-repair stop on the Santa Fe Trail—four days' travel west of Independence, Missouri. In 1858, the first college on the western frontier was founded here in a three-story sandstone building now preserved as "The Castle," alongside a combination general store and post office on the east side of the pleasant campus of Methodist-run **Baker University**. The library (Mon.–Fri. only; free) three blocks west displays the **Quayle Collection** of rare religious texts, including clay tablets dating from Old

Testament times, and a range of hand-bound bibles, arranged to trace the development of printing techniques and typography styles.

For the rest of the way east to Kansas City, US-56 parallels I-35 across lush rolling grassland pastures and farms, marked in places by signs reading "Old US-50." Along this route, two miles west of Gardner, a historical marker stands on the site where the Santa Fe and Oregon Trails once divided. For many years, a crude wooden sign pointed westbound travelers in the proper direction: left to Santa Fe, right to Oregon.

MISSOURI

From Kansas City, and its noteworthy neighboring towns of Independence and Liberty, US-50 makes a lazy trek across Missouri's rolling-prairie farmlands, stopping at the historic railroad town of **Sedalia** before reaching the state capital, **Jefferson City,** roughly midway across. Continuing east, climbing through hardwood forests of the Ozark uplands, US-50 leads to a number of similarly slow but more interesting old roads like Hwy-100, which winds through a number of historic towns along the banks of the Missouri River before approaching **St. Louis,** at the eastern edge of the state.

US-50: Across Kansas City

US-50 is now submerged beneath the Interstates and runs west–east around Kansas City via I-35, I-435, and I-470. The older, pre-Interstate route also avoided downtown, following what's now signed as US-169 along Park Avenue and 47th Street, past the Country Club Plaza and the Nelson-Atkins Museum of Art, before dipping south again on the Swope Parkway to Lee's Summit, where the old alignment rejoins the current US-50 routing.

To reach the downtown area from US-50, you can follow any of many north–south streets, like Troost Avenue, the down-at-heel old main drag, or the parkway-like El Paseo.

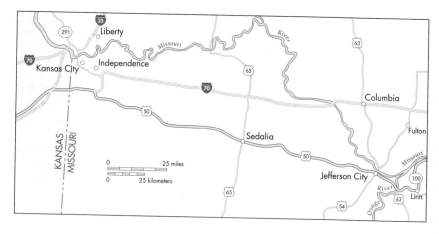

Independence

A quiet suburb lying on the eastern fringe of greater Kansas City, **Independence** (pop. 113,288) doesn't look like a special place, but it is. One of the country's most history-rich small cities, Independence came to life during the early years of the westward expansion, serving as the jumping-off point for the Santa Fe, and later, Oregon and California Trails. A century later, Independence again gained prominence as the hometown of U.S. President Harry Truman, who lived here from boyhood until his death in 1972.

The city-run **National Frontier Trails Center** (daily; $4), four blocks south of the town square at 318 W. Pacific Street, is one of the best museums dedicated to America's pioneers. Beginning with a brief account of Lewis and Clark, the exhibits explore the heyday of the Santa Fe Trail, which throughout the 1820s and 1830s made Independence the leading town on the western frontier. The later Oregon Trail, on which some 300,000 people left Independence for the West Coast, is recounted through an engagingly displayed series of diary entries and drawings made by pioneers.

While very little remains from the pioneer days, Independence has hardly changed since Harry Truman grew up here around the turn of the 20th century. The soda fountain where he held his first job, and the courtroom where he presided as judge, still stand in the town square. His home, northwest of the square at 219 N. Delaware Street, is open for **tours** (daily; $4), and the large **Harry S Truman Library** (daily; $5) four blocks north contains his presidential papers, a replica of his White House office, and the gravesites of Truman and his wife, Bess.

Clinton's Soda Fountain ("Where Harry Had His First Job"; 816/833-2625), at 100 W. Maple Street, still serves milk shakes and sandwiches. For a place to stay, try the historic **Serendipity B&B** ($45–85; 816/833-4719), at 116 S. Pleasant Street, within a short walk of all the Independence attractions.

For more information, contact the Independence **visitors bureau** (816/325-7111), located at 111 E. Maple Street.

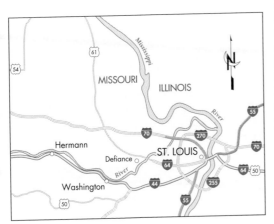

Kansas City

Walnut St. looking North from 10th St., Kansas City, Mo.

Though it covers a huge area, stretching for some 20 miles on both sides of the Missouri–Kansas border, and nearly 30 miles north to south, Kansas City (pop. 450,000) never really feels like a big city. It's more like a conglomeration of small towns, once separate from each other but now joined together by tract-house sprawl and the 100-mile-long I-435 Beltway. The historic center of Kansas City lines the south bank of the Missouri River, where 30-story skyscrapers stand above hefty brick warehouses, huge stockyards, railroad tracks, and banks of grain elevators all testifying to Kansas City's role as the main distribution point for Midwestern farm products.

Southwest of the city center, off Main and 40th Streets, **Westport** is the birthplace of Kansas City. Before the Kansas River switched course and left it high and dry, Westport was the westernmost steamboat landing in the United States, and quickly grew into a prime supply point on the Santa Fe and Oregon Trails. For a better taste of old-time riverfront Kansas City, head downtown to the **Steamboat Arabia Museum** (daily; $9.50; 816/471-4030), in the historic City Market at 400 Grand Boulevard, which displays the fascinating contents of a steamboat that sank in 1856: hardware, guns, clothes, booze, canned and bottled food, and all sorts of things that made life on the western frontier livable.

Located on the south side of Westport, the remarkable **Nelson Atkins Museum of Art** (closed Mon.; free; 816/561-4000), at Main and 47th Streets, would do any city proud, with strong surveys of both Asian and American art, including in-depth coverage of K.C.-based Thomas Hart Benton. Two blocks west, **Country Club Plaza** was one of the country's first shopping malls, and its opulent Spanish Revival styling still attracts the up-scale likes of Gucci, Saks, and the Body Shop.

Right downtown, the **Hallmark Visitors Center** (closed Sun.; free; 816/274-5672) is at Main and 25th Streets, on the top floor of the Crown Center Mall. It is much better, or at least much less nauseatingly saccharine, than you might expect: 14 galleries trace the history of the Hallmark company, which started here in 1910, and explain the design and production processes behind the 50,000 different types of greeting cards (more than $4 billion worth!) they sell each year.

A mile east of downtown K.C., in the revitalized 18th and Vine neighborhood, the heartland of Kansas City's post-war jazz scene is the marvelous **Negro Baseball Leagues Museum** (closed Mon.; $6; 816/221-1920), at

1616 E. 18th Street. The newly renovated building houses an outstanding new museum dedicated to documenting the players and culture of the various professional baseball leagues that existed side-by-side with the majors before the color barriers began to be broken down in the late 1940s. An extra $2 gets you in to the adjacent **American Jazz Museum**, documenting K.C.'s prolific jazz heritage. The city's big band golden age (1930s–1940s) spawned jazz greats Charlie Parker, Lester Young, Count Basie, and Jo Jones, all of whom are honored alongside national jazz greats like Louis Armstrong and Duke Ellington in a series of listener-friendly exhibits.

The **Kansas City Royals** (816/921-8000 or 800/676-9257) play at the very pleasant, 40,000-seat Kauffman Stadium off I-70 at the I-435 junction. Games are broadcast on **WHB 810 AM.**

Practicalities

To get around Kansas City, drive. As in Los Angeles, which Kansas City resembles more than residents of either city are likely to admit, cars rule the roads. Distances are huge and public transportation is basically nonexistent.

In downtown Kansas City, the anonymously named **Historic Suites of America** ($80–180; 816/842-6544), two blocks from the City Market at 612 Central Avenue, offers spacious accommodations in a nicely converted 100-year-old warehouse. Budget-conscious travelers can also stay a bit closer to Midtown, Westport, and the Plaza area at the **Rodeway Inn–Center City** (816/531-9250), at 3240 Broadway.

For food, there's no better introduction to the delights of K.C. cuisine than **Arthur Bryant's** (816/231-1123), east of downtown at 1727 Brooklyn Avenue. Meat-eaters drive for miles to eat at this classic, no-frills rib shack, located near the Negro Baseball Leagues Museum, where heavenly BBQ sauces come in plain plastic bottles. Way away from downtown, but not far from old US-50 in a photogenic roadhouse on the south side of the city (take the Holmes Road exit off I-435), **Stroud's** (816/333-2132), at 1015 E. 85th Street, serves simply perfect fried chicken, rated by *Gourmet* magazine critics Jane and Michael Stern as the very best in the country. With huge portions of mashed potatoes, peppery gravy, and sweet cinnamon buns, it's certainly hard to beat.

Kansas City's once-vaunted nightlife is nothing like it was during the jazz and R&B heyday of the 1940s and 1950s, though a few good places remain. The best bet for blues (and beer!) is the **Grand Emporium** (816/531-7557), near Westport at 3832 Main Street. The historic **Kelly's Westport Inn** (816/561-0635) at 500 Westport Road is a great place to enjoy a budget-priced beer while soaking up some old K.C. ambience.

For complete information, contact the Kansas City **visitors center** (816/691-3800) at 1100 Main Street.

Outlaw Jesse James grew up near Liberty.

Liberty

Another ideally named small town on the suburban fringes of Kansas City, **Liberty** (pop. 26,232) is worth a visit for rather different reasons. This is where, having finished fighting for the Confederacy in the Civil War, on February 13, 1866, **Jesse James** and his brother Frank staged the first-ever daylight bank robbery, getting away with over $60,000. The bank building itself, at 103 N. Water Street on the northwest corner of the preserved-in-amber town square, is pretty much as it was, complete with the vault, safe, and banknotes; it's now a small **museum** (daily; $2).

A block north of the square stands another historic site, the oxymoronic **Liberty Jail** (daily; free) at 216 N. Main Street, where Mormon prophet Joseph Smith and his followers were imprisoned during the winter of 1838–39. It's a significant site for Mormons, and has been faithfully reconstructed.

Liberty also has a good place to eat: the **Hardware Cafe** (816/792-3500), housed in a characterful old 1880s hardware store, just east of the square at 5 E. Kansas Street, serving hearty, home-style pasta, steaks, chops, and salads, plus old-fashioned soda-fountain drinks.

Sedalia

East of Kansas City, the roadside along fast, four-lane US-50 is endless open, rolling prairie, most of it planted in wheat and corn. As in most of the West, early development here occurred along the railroad lines, which were constructed beginning in the 1850s. Towns boomed when the trains arrived, but most went bust as the tracks were extended westward to Kansas City and beyond.

Twenty miles west of Sedalia, south of US-50 near the town of Knob Noster, **Whiteman Air Force Base** is the home of the 509th Bomb Wing, which operates and maintains the entire fleet of B-2 "Stealth" bombers. Whiteman AFB was named after 2nd Lt. George A. Whiteman, a Sedalia resident and fighter pilot who was killed in action during the attack on Pearl Harbor.

Sedalia (pop. 20,339), 75 miles east of Kansas City, was one of the few that survived, growing into a small city thanks to its position straddling the main line between St. Louis and Kansas City. Sedalia reached its peak of prosperity around 1900, an era evoked by the ragtime music of Sedalia's own Scott Joplin. The tracks through town, and most of the way across Missouri, have been converted into the hiking and bicycling Katy Trail.

Along with ragtime music and railroad history, Sedalia offers many great places to stop and eat (all of them are cash-only). **Eddie's Drive-In** (660/826-0155), on US-50 at 115 W. Broadway, has been a Sedalia establishment since 1937, serving steak burgers—with meat ground fresh each day. **Le Maire's Cajun Seafood** (660/827-3563), at 3312 S. US-65, has great fried catfish, boiled shrimp, crab legs, frog legs, crayfish, and other swamp, creek, and seafood fare; for a taste of Cajun country, it saves the 600-mile drive down US-65 to the Louisiana bayous. Last but not least is the **Wheel Inn Drive In** (660/826-5177), at 1800 Broadway at the US-50/US-65 junction, which since 1947 has been serving the unique specialty "Guberburgers"—hamburgers slathered with peanut butter.

> In 1867, the militant prohibitionist **Carry Nation** moved to the village of **Holden**, nine miles south of US-50 via Hwy-131, with her alcoholic first husband, Dr. William Gloyd, who died the following year.

At the heart of the historic downtown, a few blocks from the Katy Trail, the **Hotel Bothwell** ($60 and up; 660/826-5588), 103 E. 4th Street, is a nicely restored 1920s hotel, now part of the Clarion Hotel group.

The old railroad depot downtown has been brought back to life as the town's **visitors center** (660/826-2222), at 600 E. 3rd Street.

Jefferson City

Roughly at the center of the state, 130 miles west of St. Louis and 140 miles east of Kansas City on the south bank of the Missouri River, **Jefferson City** (pop. 39,636) is a strangely small and somnolent place. The handsome neoclassical **state capitol** (daily; free), modeled on the U.S. Capitol and completed in 1918, is the central landmark, rising above the river at the heart of town. Inside, the rotunda and ground floor area is packed with informative exhibits tracing the state's political and natural history, while hourly **guided tours** take in the entire building, including a famous mural by Thomas Hart Benton on the walls of the third-floor House Lounge.

> It was at Westminster College in the town of **Fulton**, 20 miles northeast of Jefferson City, that **Winston Churchill** made his famous "Iron Curtain" speech in 1946.

The small, surprisingly quiet downtown area has one place worth searching out: **Arris Pizza** (573/635-9225), at 117 W. High Street, which has been serving great pizzas and a range of Greek specialties since 1961. Right downtown, a block off US-50, the family-run **Hotel Deville** ($75 and up; 573/636-5231) at 319 W. Miller Street is the closest Jeff City comes to a boutique hotel.

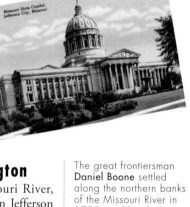

Missouri State Capitol, Jefferson City, Missouri

Hwy-100: Hermann and Washington

Running along the south bank of the Missouri River, Hwy-100 is the most interesting route between Jefferson City and St. Louis. Midway along, the town of **Hermann** (pop. 2,674) was founded by German immigrants in 1837. Surrounded by small wineries and standing right on the riverfront, Hermann reminds some visitors of a Rhine Valley village, its German heritage kept alive at the **German School Museum** (closed Mon.; 573/486-2017) at 4th and Schiller Streets downtown.

Roughly 50 miles from the Gateway Arch at downtown

> The great frontiersman **Daniel Boone** settled along the northern banks of the Missouri River in 1799, and lived near what's now the town of **Defiance** for the next 20 years until his death in 1820. His home, five well-signed miles outside town, is now owned by his descendants and is open for tours (daily 9am–5pm; $7; 636/798-2005).

Scott Joplin: the King of Ragtime

Music is among the most mobile of the arts, equally affecting anywhere and anytime, but many forms are strongly identified with a given place and era. New Orleans means jazz, the Delta has the blues, Detroit will always be equated with the Motown sound, and if credit were given where credit is due, Sedalia, Missouri, would join the above places as the source of another classic African American music—ragtime. The first ragtime tunes, so-called because of their ragged, syncopated rhythms, were played in the early 1890s, but later came into full flower out of the musical mind of Scott Joplin, the universally acclaimed king of ragtime.

Born in 1868 near Texarkana, Texas, to a former slave and freeborn mother, Scott Joplin was one of six children in a musical family. After moving around the Midwest throughout his youth, in the late 1890s Joplin settled in Sedalia, which was then a raucous railroad town, where he studied music theory at Sedalia's small black college. To pay his way, Joplin played piano at many of the clubs that lined Main Street in Sedalia, which had a reputation both for multiracial harmony and as an adult playground of bars and brothels catering to the many itinerant men passing through. One of

these nightclubs gave its name to the "Maple Leaf Rag," the composition that made Joplin's reputation and which, at a penny-per-sheet royalty, earned around $500 a year—enough to support him, but far from a fortune. As late as 1940, *Life* magazine said Sedalia still had one of the "most notorious red-light districts" in the Midwest, but very little remains here today to give a taste of the rowdy, ragtime era. Sedalia remembers its favorite son with a **Scott Joplin Ragtime Festival** (660/826-2271) every June. There's also a Scott Joplin mural, downtown at Ohio and 2nd Streets, near the site of the Maple Leaf club.

St. Louis, the redbrick town of **Washington** (pop. 13,243) rises on narrow streets above the broad Missouri River. Like Hermann, the town was settled by German immigrants in the mid 1800s, and is now full of restaurants and B&B inns catering to weekend visitors—the **visitors center** (636/239-7575), at 323 W. Main Street, has extensive listings.

The small **Washington Historical Society Museum** at 4th and Market streets has exhibits on early settlers and the town's current main industry (after tourism, that is): manufacturing **corn-cob pipes**.

Driving St. Louis

West of St. Louis, Hwy-100 and US-50 merge into the high-speed I-44 freeway in Eureka, very near the massive Six Flags amusement park ($42; 636/938-4800), which has great roller coasters and various "theme" areas evoking aspects of Missouri's past. For most of the way across St. Louis, old US-50 follows **Route 66**, which is covered on pages 000–000. The two diverge in East St. Louis, and the old US-50 alignment follows St. Clair Avenue, just south of present-day I-64.

St. Louis is the only city where three of our routes coincide—US-50, the **Great River Road** (page 251), and **Route 66** (page 833). For details on visiting St. Louis, see pages 252–253.

ILLINOIS

US-50 runs straight across over 150 miles of Southern Illinois' pancake-flat farmlands—acres of corn and soybeans as far as the eye can see, with small towns dotting the roadside every 10 or so miles. For much of the way, US-50 follows the "Trace Road," a slightly raised causeway originally traced across the swampy marshlands by the same prehistoric people who built the enigmatic mounds at Cahokia, which still stand in the eastern suburbs of St. Louis. Midway across Illinois, US-50 passes through the quirkily historic town of Salem (birthplace of two American icons: William Jennings Bryan and Miracle Whip), then crosses over the Wabash River into Indiana.

Lebanon

US-50 follows I-64 east from St. Louis across the flat prairie, whose fertile alluvial soil has earned it the nickname "Little Egypt." The highway parallels the Illinois Central Railroad through a dozen small towns, the most significant of which is **Lebanon** (pop. 3,523), 20 miles east of the Mississippi River. An attractive town, with a number of stately, mansard-roofed, Victorian-era commercial buildings now housing antique shops along Main Street and St. Louis Street (US-50), Lebanon grew up around the bucolic campus of McKendree College, founded here in 1828, making it one of the oldest in Illinois.

Bible-packing 18th-century settlers of the uplands opposite St. Louis referred to their chosen homesteads as "Goshen" and the flood-prone flats to the south as "Egypt." Comparisons between the Mississippi and Nile rivers were reinforced with place-names like Karnak, Joppa, Thebes, and Cairo; for generations now, all of Southern Illinois has borne the nickname "Little Egypt."

The best reason to stop, however, is the small **Mermaid House Hotel**, on US-50 at 114 E. St. Louis Street. Charles Dickens, who visited the area to see the rich but muddy prairie east of town, stayed here for a night in 1842, and described it in *American Notes* as comparing "favorably with

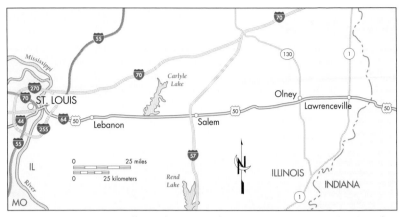

any village ale house of a homely kind in England." After spending most of the past 150 years as a private home, the building is now undergoing restoration, but is open for tours (Sat. and Sun. 10 AM–4 PM; donations).

Miracle Whip was created at **Max Crosset's Cafe** on Main Street before being sold to Kraft Foods (for $300!) in 1931. The birthplace of Miracle Whip is now a parking lot at the center of Salem.

Salem

Halfway across Illinois, just east of the busy I-57 freeway, US-50 cuts through the center of **Salem** (pop. 7,470), a historically fascinating if visually less-than-thrilling city best known as the birthplace and boyhood home of William Jennings Bryan. The turn-of-the-20th-century politician and orator, who served as leader of the Democratic Party for 15 years, prosecuted the so-called "Monkey Trial" of 1925 and led the successful attack on Tennessee schoolteacher John Scopes (who, coincidentally, was also born and raised in Salem) for breaking a local ban on teaching evolution. Bryan was born in 1860 in the small frame house at 408 S. Broadway, four blocks south of Main Street (US-50). It has been preserved as a small **museum** (daily except Thurs. 1–5 PM; free). There's a statue of Bryan, crafted by Mt. Rushmore sculptor Gutzon Borglum, on Broadway a half mile north of Main Street, in front of the Roller Palace skating rink.

WILLIAM JENNINGS
BRYAN

1860 1925

YOU SHALL NOT PRESS
DOWN UPON THE BROW
OF LABOR THIS CROWN
OF THORNS YOU SHALL
NOT CRUCIFY MANKIND
UPON A CROSS OF GOLD

Besides William Jennings Bryan, and the sandwich spread Miracle Whip, Salem has given America the **G.I. Bill of Rights.** Also known as the G.I. Bill, this law entitles military veterans to subsidized education and other services. It was first proposed by the local American Legion branch before being signed into law in 1944.

Salem has a good place to eat, **Austin's Restaurant** (618/548-0084), at 1419 W. US-50; and an inexpensive motel, the **Continental** ($40–60; 618/548-3090), on US-50 at 1600 E. Main Street.

Olney and Lawrenceville

The flat farmlands of southeast Illinois are dotted with occasional oil wells and signs painted on barn sides encouraging travelers to "Chew Mail Pouch Tobacco" or "See Rock City," but towns are few and far between. The first of these is the attractive town of **Olney** (pop. 8,664). Besides boasting a large number of grand old mansions set behind broad green lawns along quiet, leafy streets, Olney has the singular attraction of **albino squirrels,** which were set loose in town around the turn of the 20th century. By 1940, the WPA *Guide to Illinois* noted that "thousands of the little animals now scamper about the parks and courthouse square, and frisk over lawns, trees, and rooftops," though these days you're most likely to see them if you head to the **city park** north of the courthouse square.

Olney is famous for its large but elusive population of albino squirrels.

Perhaps the best reason to detour through Olney is to sample the incredibly good cheeseburgers, onion rings, and milk shakes at **Hovey's** (618/395-9144), on old US-50 at 412 E. Main Street—look for the Mike's Ice Cream sign.

East of Olney, US-50 reverts to two-lane highway, running for 23 miles before passing by **Lawrenceville** (pop. 4,745), which was named for U.S. Navy Capt. James Lawrence, best remembered for his dying words, "Don't give up the ship," during the War of 1812.

East of Lawrenceville, follow the old road south of the modern freeway, crossing the Wabash River into Indiana at historic Vincennes.

INDIANA

From the Wabash River at its western end to the Ohio River in the east, the 170 miles of southern Indiana that lie in between present an immensely varied landscape. The hilly eastern sections are surprisingly rugged, though the central and western reaches are comparatively flat and largely agricultural. Besides numerous well-preserved historic Ohio River towns like **Madison** and **Aurora**, there are a number of unlovely industrial sections, especially around Bedford and the famous limestone quarries in the central parts of the state.

On the east side of **Carlyle,** 22 miles west of Salem, a very delicate suspension bridge built in 1860 has been preserved in a riverside park, on the northeast side of where US-50 crosses the Kaskaskia River.

The Wabash River between Indiana and Illinois marks the boundary between the Central and Eastern time zones. Subtract an hour heading east, add an hour heading west. At the west end of the bridge over the river, a roadside memorial recounts the westward migration of young **Abraham Lincoln** and his family.

George Rogers Clark Memorial

Vincennes

First settled by the French in 1732, and intensely fought over during the Revolutionary War, **Vincennes** (pop. 18,701) remained a lawless frontier until 1803, when it was named the territorial capital. A handful of early buildings, including a bank, a church, and a newspaper office, have been restored at 1st and Harrison Streets in the historic downtown area. Nearby, overlooking the Wabash River, the **George Rogers Clark National Historical Park** ($3) is a classical dome honoring Revolutionary War general George Rogers Clark, who led local militiamen in the capture of Vincennes from the British in 1779. (George Rogers Clark was the older brother of William Clark, of Lewis and Clark fame.)

The monument, built as a WPA project during the Great Depression, wouldn't look out of place in D.C., but the rest of Vincennes is decidedly down-to-earth, with grain elevators, five-and-dime stores, and cafés along the busy railroad tracks.

The area around Vincennes is very flat farming country, notable for its large Amish communities (and numerous roadside "Amish Kountry Korner" stores and cafés), especially around **Loogootee,** 30 miles east of Vincennes.

French Lick and Mitchell

Between Vincennes and Bedford, US-50 winds its way through the hilly groves of the **Hoosier National Forest,** but a worthwhile detour heads south through the hometowns of two of Indiana's best-known sons. The first of these, on Hwy-56 just south of US-150, is **French Lick** (pop. 1,941), where Boston Celtics star (and Indiana Pacers head coach) Larry Bird, "The Hick

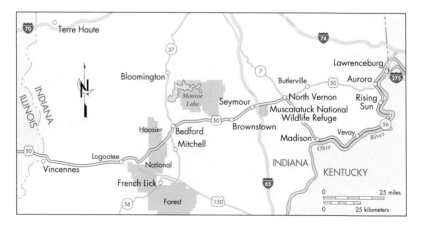

from French Lick," learned his game. The town itself is little more than a two-block-long business district, but around the turn of the 20th century, the surrounding area was a popular vacation resort, as thousands of Midwesterners (including Al Capone and other Chicago mobsters) came here to stay at the monumental, 500-room **French Lick Springs Resort** ($99 and up; 812/936-9300) and take the mineral-rich waters that still flow from local artesian springs. The even larger **West Baden Springs Hotel** closed decades ago but is open for fascinating guided **tours** ($10; 812/936-4034).

One thing to see along US-50 is 10 miles east of North Vernon, in **Butlerville**, where a roadside plaque marks the 1885 birthplace of Hannah Milhous Nixon, Richard's mother.

The other famous hometown, **Mitchell**, is about six miles south of Bedford and was the boyhood home of astronaut Virgil "Gus" Grissom, who captained Mercury and Gemini space flights before dying in the Apollo 1 disaster. There's an impressive memorial—a 30-foot-high limestone statue of a Titan rocket—to Grissom south of Main Street on 6th Street, next to the police station.

Bedford

Nicknamed "Stone City" because it holds some of the largest and most famous limestone quarries in the country, **Bedford** (pop. 13,768) is a busy, industrial-looking city, the largest on the Indiana stretch of US-50. The quarries that earned Bedford's reputation are still in use, producing the durable stone that has clad many high-profile structures, including the Empire State Building. Though you can see the limestone *in situ* at many road cuts along US-50, perhaps the most prominent examples in Bedford are the monuments and gravestones in the cemeteries lining the highway through town.

Bedford's main hard-rock attraction is **Bluesprings Caverns** (daily May–Oct. only; $10; 812/279-9471), five miles west of downtown on US-50, where you can descend into a cave and take an hour-long boat tour along the largest underground river in the United States.

Brownstown, Seymour, and North Vernon

Roughly 27 miles east of Bedford and 10 miles west of the I-65 freeway, **Brownstown** (pop. 2,978) is an unusually pretty Indiana town set around a large central square shaded by 100-year-old maple trees—and a war surplus tank. An old-fashioned general store and a couple of down-home restaurants make it worth a brief stop, particularly during the annual **Watermelon Festival** in late August.

East of Brownstown, it's a scenic 10 miles to **Seymour** (pop. 18,101), with its many motels (including a Holiday Inn and an EconoLodge), fast-food

Detour: Louisville

Home of the world's greatest horse race (the Kentucky Derby), the world's biggest baseball bat (a 120-foot-tall Louisville Slugger), and the man who was and is simply "The Greatest" (boxer Muhammad Ali, who was born and grew up here), Louisville (LOO-avil) is a characterful mid-sized city on the south bank of the Ohio River. During Kentucky Derby week, the mint julep–fueled party leading up to the first Saturday in May, the whole city comes alive, but Louisville is an enjoyable place to explore any time of year. Along with some well-above-average art museums and high-culture institutions, Louisville also has some top pop-culture destinations, best of which is the **Louisville Slugger Museum** (daily; $6; 502/588-7228), at 800 W. Main Street, marked by that giant baseball bat, and full of memorabilia on big hitters from Babe Ruth to Hank Aaron. Thanks to the Louisville Slugger connection, the local baseball team is called the **Louisville Bats** (502/212-2287), a Class AAA farm club for the Cincinnati Reds. The Bats play at Louisville Slugger Field, right downtown on Main Street. Games are broadcast on **WGTK 970 AM.**

Outside Louisville, along US-31 30 miles to the southwest, you can cruise past another icon: **Fort Knox,** and dream about the 150 million ounces of gold locked inside; at current prices, Fort Knox is worth *almost* as much as Bill Gates.

Louisville is also home to one of the better BBQ places you'll find anywhere: **Vince Staten's** (502/228-7427), northeast of downtown at 9219 US-42. Owner Vince Staten is also a noted historian of hardware, having written the excellent *Did Monkeys Invent the Monkey Wrench?* Stop by and say hi.

Another distinctive local product, bourbon, is best sampled at the rooftop **D. Marie Lounge**, where 100 bottles of bourbon frame views over the Ohio River. The bar is atop the landmark **Galt House** hotel (800/626-1814). For more information, contact the **visitors bureau** (502/584-2121 or 800/626-5646), in the convention center at 3rd and Market Streets.

franchises, 24-hour gas stations, and an absolutely HUGE Wal-Mart distribution center marking the junction with I-65. Blue-collar Seymour is the birthplace of rock star John "Don't Call Me Cougar" Mellencamp, and you can get a good feel for the place by stopping for a meal at the **Town House Cafe** (812/522-1099) at 206 E. 4th Street.

Twelve miles east of Seymour, turn south from US-50 at neat little **North Vernon** onto Hwy-7, which runs toward the Ohio River town of Madison across miles of rolling farmland, closely paralleling the route of Morgan's Raid, when Gen. John Morgan and 2,000 Confederate soldiers invaded Indiana during the Civil War.

The quaint town of **Vevay**, 20 miles east of Madison, was the birthplace of **Edward Eggleston**, author of *The Hoosier Schoolmaster*. Another important area native was engineer **Elwood Mead**, the man for whom Lake Mead is named.

Madison and the Ohio River Towns

The route east along US-50 is uneventful, so if you have some time, loop to the south along **Hwy-56,** which curves along the north bank of the broad Ohio River. The riverside here is rich in history, and the 60-mile drive passes by modest tobacco farms and timeless small towns, the pastoral scene marred only by occasional power plants, most of them across the water on the Kentucky side.

Though the drive is nice enough in itself, it's most worthwhile because it brings you to **Madison** (pop. 12,006), one of the best-preserved historic Ohio River towns, thanks in large part to the National Trust for Historic Preservation, which used Madison as a case study in how to keep small-town America alive and well in the modern age. Now a popular vacation destination, especially during the **Chautauqua Arts Festival** in late September and the rowdier **Madison Regatta** around the 4th of July, when 200-mph hydroplanes race along the river, Madison has managed to stay alive economically without sacrificing its small-town charms. Wandering around a few blocks of the franchise-free Main Street, you can enjoy a milk shake at the soda fountain in the back of **Rogers Drug Store,** listen to the town gossip while getting a haircut at the chrome and red-leather barber shop, or tour the many **historic homes.** The best of these is the impressive Greek Revival mansion of Civil War financier James Lanier, near the river at 511 W. 1st Street. Also worth a look is the perfectly preserved **doctor's office** at 120 W. 3rd Street, which served as the only hospital between Cincinnati and Louisville from 1882 to 1903.

Besides the wealth of Americana, Madison has a number of good places to eat along the three blocks of Main Street, including **Hinckle's,** open 24 hours (closed Sun.) for great greasy-spoon burgers and round-the-clock breakfasts. Places to stay range from the 1847 federal-style **Schusser House B&B** ($90 and up; 812/273-2068 or 800/392-1931) at 514 Jefferson Street to the motel-type rooms at the **Clifty Inn** ($80; 812/265-4135) in wooded Clifty Falls State Park, a mile west of town.

For complete information on Madison, contact the **visitors center** (812/265-2956 or 800/559-2956) at 301 E. Main Street, across from the landmark Jefferson County Courthouse.

Rising Sun

Farther along Hwy-56, nine miles south of Aurora and US-50, the village of **Rising Sun** holds a handful of frontier-era structures as well as one of the state's biggest riverboat casinos, the **Grand Victoria** (800/472-6311), which opened in 1996 and actually cruises out onto the river so you can play its 1,300 slot machines. The adjacent hotel offers 200 rooms($90 and up). The historic parts of town have managed to stay quaint despite the influx of gamblers, and the old-fashioned (but newly repaved) downtown area has the very good **Ohio County Historical Museum** at 212 S. Walnut Street.

Aurora and Lawrenceburg

Our Ohio River detour along Hwy-56 rejoins US-50 at **Aurora** (pop. 9,192), a small riverside town that's well worth at least a brief stop. The highlight here is the handsome **Hillforest Mansion** (closed Mon.; $5) at 213 5th Street, an exuberant survivor from the steamboat era whose colonnaded facade is topped by a circular lookout tower from which residents could gaze out at river traffic up and down the Ohio. Built in 1852 and preserved in fine condition, the hillside mansion gives a strong sense of how comfortable and sophisticated life was for the wealthy, even on the so-called frontier.

East from Aurora, approaching the Ohio state line, US-50 forms a seedy gauntlet of roadside motels, diners, cut-rate liquor stores, and fireworks stands, all competing with giant billboards for the tri-state trade. **Lawrenceburg** (pop. 4,685), along the I-275 freeway three miles west of the Indiana–Ohio–Kentucky border, seems to revolve around the sale of cheap booze, perhaps because the main employer is the massive redbrick **Seagram's** distillery at the north end of Main Street—one of the oldest and largest in the United States.

Apart from a wonderfully photogenic collection of old auto-related advertising signs in a used-car lot on the west side of town near the Wal-Mart, the view of Lawrenceburg from US-50 is unpromising, with railroad tracks and a huge levee cutting off the town from the waterfront. However, the historic town center, south of the highway along Walnut Street, holds a number of interesting old buildings dating from the steamboat era of the early 1800s, when Lawrenceburg was a favorite Ohio River port of call. Among the many church spires competing for preeminence is that of the Presbyterian church, where in 1837 orator Henry Ward Beecher (father of Harriet Beecher Stowe, she of *Uncle Tom's Cabin* fame) held his first pastorate.

Places to eat in old-town Lawrenceburg emphasize the 80-proof aspects of local life: **Whisky's** (812/537-4239), at 334 Front Street, for example, serves steaks in an old button factory on Front Street.

Lawrenceburg's signs of the old road

OHIO

Winding along the Ohio River from Indiana, US-50 cuts east from Cincinnati across the hill-and-valley country of southern Ohio before finally crossing the Ohio River into West Virginia. The 220 miles US-50 takes to cross the state are a fairly constant mix of upland forest and bottom-land farms, with a single industrial district in the middle, around **Chillicothe,** and a refreshing small college town, **Athens,** farther east.

North Bend

East from the Indiana line, US-50 winds along the partly industrial, partly rural Ohio River waterfront, without much to detain you before Cincinnati. The one place really worth a stop is the hamlet of **North Bend** (pop. 603), five miles east of the state border. A tall sandstone obelisk, overlooking the river and US-50 amidst a 14-acre park, marks the final resting place of William Henry Harrison (1773–1841), the ninth president of the United States, who lived here for many years when North Bend was a thriving frontier port. Born in Virginia, Harrison came to fame fighting Shawnee tribes in and around the Ohio Valley, and served in Congress for many years before he was elected president; he died of pneumonia after only a month in office. His grandson Benjamin Harrison, who became president in 1889, was born in the nearby family home in 1833.

Continuing along US-50, five miles west of downtown Cincinnati and just three miles north of the main Cincy airport, the tiny **Anderson Ferry** ($3 per car, 25 cents for foot passengers) has been chugging back and forth since 1817, though the broad Ohio River is nothing like the busy river it was back then. But as recently as 1940, the WPA *Guide to Ohio* wrote that "fleets of barges pushed by snub-nosed towboats crawl along the motionless water; and now and then appears one of the Greene Line packets, all white and triple-decked."

US-50: Across Cincinnati

US-50 survives pretty much intact across Cincinnati, though most of its former traffic now follows the freeways that loop around and cut through the city. West of downtown, US-50 follows the Ohio River along River Road, but the old alignment veers away from the freeway-sliced waterfront along State Avenue, running through downtown along 7th, 8th, and 9th Streets. East of downtown, old US-50 rejoins the riverfront around Mt. Adams, then follows the Columbia Parkway east to the garden city of Mariemont, where we rejoin it.

Mariemont

From Cincinnati, US-50 follows surface streets through the warehouse and residential districts along the Ohio River, before becoming a freeway for the quick drive east to **Mariemont** (pop. 3,408). Built in the mid-1920s as one of the nation's first planned "Garden City" communities, Mariemont's mock-Tudor downtown centers around the historic and very comfortable **Best Western Mariemont Inn** ($80; 513/271-2100), right on US-50 at 6880 Wooster Pike. Across the street there's a branch of the excellent local ice-cream chain,

Cincinnati

Spreading along the north bank of the Ohio River, Cincinnati, whose nicknames range from "Queen City" to "Porkopolis," was once the largest and busiest city on the western frontier. During the heyday of steamboat travel in the first half of the 19th century, the city's riverside location made it a prime transportation center, but as the railroad networks converged on Chicago, Cincinnati was eclipsed as the prime gateway to the western United States. Procter & Gamble, the world's largest consumer products company, started here in the 1830s, making soap out of the abundant animal fat from the city's hundreds of slaughterhouses. In recent years, the city has welcomed some cutting-edge art and architecture, but has been best known for a variety of less salubrious things: race riots, the fall from grace of baseball hero Pete Rose, and the TV antics of former mayor Jerry Springer. Cincinnati's declining population, now barely over 300,000 people, ranks it just ahead of Toledo as Ohio's third largest city, which from a traveler's point of view makes it an easily manageable and usually stress-free place to visit.

A good first stop in Cincy is the **Museum Center** (daily; $10; 513/287-7000 or 800/733-2077), in the former Union Terminal on Ezzard Charles Drive, off I-75 exit 1. This 1930s art deco railroad station has been converted into one of the best museum complexes in the country. The city's most interesting neighborhood, Mount Adams, is east of downtown, high above the Ohio River. This 300-foot-high hilltop neighborhood was once connected to downtown by an incline railway, but is now somewhat cut off by the I-71 freeway. It has emerged from years of neglect as an artsy district of craft shops and cafes. Nearby Eden Park holds the respected **Cincinnati Art Museum** (closed Mon.; free; 513/721-5204), as well as a planetarium and conservatory amidst acres of greenery. Along the Ohio River downtown, the **"Great American Ballpark"** (513/765-7400) is home to the Cincinnati Reds.

Unfortunately, most of Cincinnati's once vibrant waterfront area, known as "The Basin," has been torn down in the name of urban renewal. What the 1940 WPA Guide to Ohio called "a museum of city history and the building styles of the past century," has been eliminated in favor of a stadium each for the Reds and Bengals and a contentiously flashy museum on the anti-slavery Underground Railroad. The sole survivors of old

45:—Aeroplane View, Ohio River and Bridges connecting Kentucky and Cincinnati, Ohio.

Cincinnati are found across the river in Covington, Kentucky. You can get there by crossing the Roebling Bridge, built in 1865 as a precursor to the more famous Brooklyn Bridge. East of the bridge, a line of well-preserved 1820s houses, many of which served as way stations on the actual Underground Railroad, overlook the historic Ohio River boundary between "slave" and "free" states.

Practicalities

Most major airlines fly into the Greater Cincinnati International Airport, which lies southwest of downtown in Kentucky. Getting around town is best done by car, if only so you can drive back and forth across the Ohio River on the Roebling Bridge. There are hundreds of rooms available in national chain motels along the I-71 and I-75 freeways. The handy and spacious **Embassy Suites** ($139-159; 859/261-8400) overlooks the Ohio River from the Kentucky side of the Roebling Bridge. But the nicest place to stay is the classic art deco **Hilton Netherland Plaza** (513/421-9100 or 800/843-6665; $90 and up), at 35 W. 5th Street. One of the country's grandest old hotels, its lovely lobby is often clogged with ad execs courting Procter & Gamble business.

No road-tripper in his or her right mind should pass through Cincinnati without sampling its excellent road food—mounds of chili and/or stacks of melt-in-your-mouth ribs, finished off with a scoop or two of Graeter's ice cream, (available all over the city, both at their own parlors and at most good restaurants). Cincinnati-style chili is poured over spaghetti and served either "3-Way" (spaghetti, chili, and grated cheese); "4-Way" (add onions); or "5-Way" (add beans). One road food landmark, **Camp Washington Chili** (513/541-0061), three miles north of downtown at 3005 Colerain, right off I-75 exit 3, is famous for it. Over 100 other places around town serve this subtly spiced local specialty—there's even a 3-Way Pentecostal Church! Downtown, **Arnold's** (513/421-6234), at 210 E. 8th Street, is a fine old place, a cozy circa 1860 tavern and deli that also features good live music. East of downtown along the river, **Montgomery Inn at the Boathouse** (513/721-7427), at 925 Eastern Avenue, serves what Bob Hope, Billy Carter, and Bill Clinton agree are some of the best BBQ ribs in America. The original **Montgomery Inn** (513/791-3482) can be found at 9440 Montgomery Road, about 12 miles northeast of downtown, off I-71. In tandem, these two restaurants manage to serve over 200 tons of ribs annually, more than anywhere else in the country.

The main source for visitor information is the Greater Cincinnati Visitors Bureau, on Fountain Square downtown (513/621-2142 or 800/246-2987).

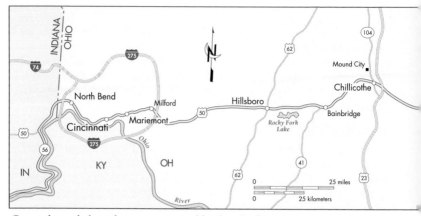

Graeter's, and the sole surviving neighborhood of Mariemont's original 1920s half-timbered arts-and-crafts homes is an easily walkable block to the southeast.

East of Mariemont, US-50 crosses the Little Miami River at the scenic, 25-mph town of **Milford**—where there's a **Frisch's Big Boy** (513/831-0111) restaurant at 840 Lila Avenue with a great old "Big Boy" sign, straight out of *American Graffiti*—before racing east across 40 miles of flat and sparsely settled farming country to Hillsboro.

Hillsboro

Hillsboro (pop. 6,368), 60 miles east of Cincinnati and 40 miles west of Chillicothe, is the biggest and busiest town along the way. Besides the Greek Revival landmark Highland County Courthouse, second-oldest in Ohio, Hillsboro has a unique, alcohol-related history: During Christmas in 1873, the town's 13 saloons were closed down by one of the country's earliest temperance movements, and more recently, late great country singer Johnny "Take This Job and Shove It" Paycheck did time in prison for shooting a man in Hillsboro's North High Saloon. (Even more recently, that saloon was torn down to make way for a new city office building.)

Serpent Mound

East from Hillsboro toward Chillicothe, US-50 winds past whitewashed farmhouses and broad cornfields flanked by low hills. The region also holds two fascinating remnants of the "mound builder" people who once lived here. Just west of the sleepy village of Bainbridge, heading 20 miles south onto Hwy-41 (or following Hwy-73 south from Hillsboro) brings you to the **Serpent Mound** (in summer Wed.–Sun. 9 AM–5 PM, weekends only rest of year; $7 per car; 937/587-2796), which stretches in seven sinuous curves alongside a creek for nearly a quarter mile. There's a small museum on the site, and to see the snake-shaped earthworks—the largest and finest effigy mound in the country—visitors climb up a turn-of-the-20th-century vintage lookout tower.

Midway between Chillicothe and Hillsboro, the nice little town of **Bainbridge** was the site of the first dental school in the United States, now a **dental museum** along US-50 at 208 W. Main Street.

Another of these prehistoric sites, the **Seip Mound,** two miles east of Bainbridge and 14 miles west of Chillicothe, is over 200 feet long and 30 feet tall, surrounded by 10 acres of pasture. To prevent early farmers from plowing them into oblivion in the 1880s, many of these evocative monuments were purchased and preserved through the efforts of Harvard University archaeologists. Harvard owned the land for many years, and later donated the sites to the state of Ohio. Recent state budget problems have made these sights subject to closure, so phone ahead (800/283-8905) if you can.

For more on the enigmatic creators of these burial mounds, see the sidebar that follows, "The Mound Builders."

Chillicothe and Mound City

In the middle of the state, **Chillicothe** (pop. 21,796; chill-a-COTH-ee) comes as a sudden surprise after the pastoral landscape that surrounds it. It is one of the state's oldest industrial centers; since 1812 Chillicothe's economy has revolved around the massive Mead Paper mill on the south side of town, whose red-and-white striped smokestack belches a pungent white cloud around the clock.

Chillicothe served as capital of the Northwest Territory from 1800 to 1802, and later as the first capital of Ohio.

Heavy industry aside, Chillicothe has done an admirable job of preserving its history, most notably in the recently spruced-up "First Capital" district along Main Street (US-50) downtown. Dozens of elaborate, late-Victorian commercial buildings and Greek Revival–style mansions, mostly dating from the mid-1850s, surround the overwrought Ross County Courthouse, which has a different entrance for each government department.

While the downtown area is worth a quick stroll, specific sites are few, and the area's real attraction is three miles north of town via Hwy-104. Officially known as the Hopewell Culture National Historical Park, but usually called **Mound City,** this complex of prehistoric burial sites sits on the west bank of the Scioto River, just beyond a huge prison complex. Two dozen distinct, grass-covered mounds, the largest of which is about 15 feet high, are reachable on a mile-long trail that starts at the **visitors center** (daily; $3; 740/774-1125) at 16062 Hwy-104, where films and exhibits explore aspects of this 2,000-year-old culture.

Chillicothe makes a good place to break a journey. **Johnny's** (740/772-5570), at 1247 Western Avenue, on

The Mound Builders

The broad area between the Mississippi River and the Appalachian crest is rich in early American history, but the human story here goes back way beyond Daniel Boone and Abraham Lincoln to an era not often discussed in textbooks. From around 800 BC until AD 1500, this region was home to two successive prehistoric cultures which were roughly simultaneous with the legendary Mayans and Aztecs of Mexico, but are now all but forgotten, remembered solely for the massive earthen mounds they left behind.

The older of these two prehistoric peoples is known as the Hopewell culture, since the first scientific studies were conducted in 1891 at a farm owned by a man named Hopewell. Some 50 years earlier, the mounds had already become famous, as stories spread tracing their construction back to a "lost race" of mysterious origin, not unlike the Anasazi of the desert Southwest. As the Hopewell culture began to decline, around AD 500, another culture, called the Mississippian, came into being. Similarities between these two hunter-gatherer cultures, with their far-flung trading networks and hierarchical societies, are much greater than their differences, but archaeologists consider them to be completely distinct from one another. A key difference: Almost all of the Hopewell mounds were rounded or conical, and built as burial sites, while Mississippian sites tended to be more rectilinear, with the mounds serving not as interments but as bases for long-

US-50 next to McDonald's a mile west of downtown, serves very good fried chicken but closes at 8 PM. The **Chillicothe Inn** ($40–60; 740/774-2512) lies a half block north of US-50 at 24 N. Bridge Street.

Chillicothe is known throughout Ohio as the site of *Tecumseh*, an outdoor pageant dramatizing the life of the Shawnee Indian warrior. Shows are at 8 PM Monday–Saturday in summer only (740/775-0700). More fun, and cheaper, are the baseball games played by the Frontier League **Chillicothe Paints** (bleacher seats $5; 740/773-8326), who play from June through August near Mound City.

Athens

East of Chillicothe, US-50 passes through Vinton County, one of the state's poorest and least-developed regions. Hidden amidst forested hills, the remains of coal mines and overgrown, rail-fenced cornfields line the next 50 miles, and little has changed (for the better, at least) since the WPA *Guide* described the scene in 1939: "Abruptly the road sweeps into a rock-bound gorge dotted with the rickety houses of hill-folk . . . who make a living by seasonal mining, moonshining, trapping, or on Government relief projects."

After all this rural poverty, US-50 finally arrives at **Athens** (pop. 21,265), one of the most attractive small

vanished wooden structures built atop them. In Hopewell sites, buried along with the usually cremated human remains, archaeologists and treasure hunters have recovered a compelling array of artifacts—obsidian tools (from the Pacific Northwest), shell beads (from the Gulf of Mexico), and silver and copper objects (from the Great Lakes)—which give some hint of the quality of ancient Native American life.

Ohio is particularly well-provided with these enigmatic earthworks; at the **Hopewell Culture National Historic Park** near Chillicothe (see page 705), over two dozen burial mounds have been preserved by the National Park Service. West of Chillicothe, the low-lying **Serpent Mound** stretches for a quarter-mile along a river, and over 100 other sites have been identified across the state.

Further west on US-50, along the Mississippi at **Cahokia Mounds State Historic Site** (see page 834), the remnants of the largest prehistoric city in North America now sit across the river from St. Louis. North along the river, the **Effigy Mounds National Monument** in Iowa across from Prairie du Chien (see page 231) preserves yet more burial mounds, while down south, the Natchez Trace Parkway features the prehistoric **Emerald Mound** (see page 272). Macon, Georgia, has the major mounds of **Ocmulgee National Monument** (see page 777); and in Louisiana, perhaps the most extensive site of all is being excavated at **Poverty Point**, north of Monroe (see page 758).

towns in Ohio. Set, like its classical namesake, on a series of hills, Athens is an idyllic little town that has grown up around the leafy campus of Ohio University, which opened here in 1809 and has developed a reputation as the liveliest small party school in the country. Brick-paved streets lined by bookstores, copy shops, and clothing stores, mostly catering to the college's 18,000 well-groomed twentysomethings, fill the eight-block "Uptown" neighborhood along College and Court Streets on the north side of the neoclassical College Green, a National Historic Landmark dating from 1816.

US-50 follows the Hocking River and bypasses the heart of town, so follow Stimson Avenue or State Street from the highway, past the cafes and shops that fill the few blocks around the campus. **The Pub** (740/592-2699), 39 N. Court Street, has Athens's best burgers (and happy hour specials), while the best live music is played at **The Union** (740/593-5060), 18 W. Union Street. By most accounts, the best food is four miles east of Athens at the **Big Chimney Baking Company** (740/592-4147), in the historic Canaan Coal Company building just off US-50. Accommodations in Athens include a **Days Inn** and other motels along Columbus Road (US-33) on the north side of town.

East of the Athens area, US-50 passes through 40 miles of scrubby second-growth forests and the abandoned but enticingly named coal-mining towns of Guysville and Coolville, before reaching the West Virginia border at the Ohio River and Parkersburg.

Southeastern Ohio has one of the country's greatest concentrations of barns painted with "Chew Mail Pouch Tobacco" signs.

WEST VIRGINIA

The slowest part of US-50's transcontinental crossing is the 150-mile section across West Virginia, which twists and turns its way over the rugged Allegheny Mountains. Starting along the Ohio River in the western, more-developed half of the state, US-50 runs briefly as a fairly fast freeway before beginning its climb into the rugged hill country. Though there are many fine hardwood forests and whitewater rivers, including some of the most extensive semi-wilderness areas left in the eastern states, this part of West Virginia is mostly rural, with more than a few corners where things seem straight out of a Depression-era Walker Evans photograph. Rusting appliances and broken-down cars fill more than a few front yards, but around the next bend you may come across a lovely old covered bridge, or a waterfall that takes your breath away. The few towns along the route, formerly bustling thanks to the railroads or coal mines, are still dominated by the empty remnants of industries that have vanished, never to return, and most places are populated by people who seem to have lived there forever. The self-reliant, "Mountaineer" ethos still runs strong, and right-wing militia types may lurk in the hills and hollows, but the lingering impression West Virginia leaves behind is of taking a step back in time to a world where men work hard in mines and mills, women raise the kids, and everybody goes to church on Sunday.

Parkersburg

Northern West Virginia's largest and most heavily industrialized city, **Parkersburg** (pop. 33,099) is located strategically at the junction of the Ohio and Little Kanawha Rivers. The town's economy is based around an unusual pair of employers: the federal Bureau of the Public Debt, which redeems U.S. Savings Bonds, and a massive DuPont Teflon factory.

Though the first impression can be fairly bleak, Parkersburg does merit a closer look. The **Blennerhasset Museum** (closed Mon.; $2; 304/420-4800), housed in a turn-of-the-20th-century brick warehouse at 2nd and Juliana Streets, traces

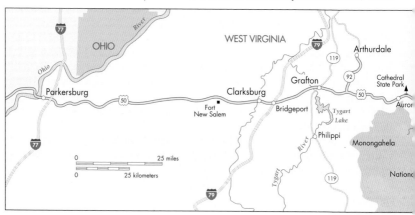

regional history, with a focus on the escapades of the Irish aristocrat Harman Blennerhasset, who in 1806 conspired with Aaron Burr to establish an independent fiefdom in Texas and the Southwest. If you're interested, you can ride a paddle wheeler to and from the Ohio River island on which Blennerhasset built the palatial home where the plot was hatched. The house has been reconstructed as a state park (tours $2), and **boats** ($8) leave hourly for the island from Point Park, which is two blocks west of the museum, under the railroad bridges and on the far side of the 25-foot concrete flood walls at the confluence of the rivers.

Parkersburg also has a good range of motels and a couple of coffee shops along US-50, like the 24-hour **Mountaineer Family Restaurant** (304/422-0101), at 4006 E. 7tth Street, near I-77 on the east side of town.

Fort New Salem

Between Parkersburg and Clarksburg, US-50 winds along as a fast, four-lane freeway through a mountainous one-time oil- and gas-producing region dotted with tiny, all-but-forgotten towns. The small farms are cultivated by descendants of Scotch-Irish immigrants who settled here in the late 18th century. One place that's well worth a stop is **Fort New Salem** (Wed.–Sun.; $4), 14 miles west of Clarksburg. Just south of US-50, on the campus of half-Japanese Salem-Teikyo University, the fort is a credible reconstruction of the frontier outpost erected near here in 1795.

Clarksburg

Birthplace of Confederate Civil War hero Thomas "Stonewall" Jackson, and now a national center for law enforcement biometric data analysis, **Clarksburg** (pop. 16,743) is a tidy railroad town sitting on a branch of the Monongahela River. The downtown area is a sampler of turn-of-the-20th-century commercial buildings, great for taking pictures of old signs and brick walls, and the town's large Italian population, estimated at around 40 percent, supports numerous good restaurants like **Minard's Spaghetti Inn** (304/623-1711), 813 E. Pike Street on old US-50, at the Joyce Street exit off the US-50

The house where "Stonewall" Jackson was born is marked by a plaque at 326 Main Street in Clarksburg. Across the street is the FBI's national center for fingerprint and high-tech biometric security operations, located here thanks to the machinations of West Virginia's long-serving U.S. Senator **Robert Byrd**.

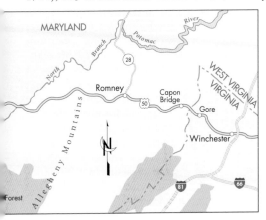

freeway. Another good old-fashioned place to eat is the **Ritzy Lunch** (304/842-7388), at 465 W. Pike Street, selling famous chili dogs since 1933.

On the east side of Clarksburg, US-50 climbs a steep hill before becoming suddenly busy at **Bridgeport**, which straddles the I-79 freeway, around which the highway is lined by a two-mile sprawl of motels and fast food.

The Grafton area saw the first fatality of the Civil War, when Union soldier **Bailey Brown** was killed by Confederate forces during the battle of Philippi.

South of Grafton, US-119 passes through the town of Philippi, where the largest **covered bridge** in West Virginia spans the Tygart River. Originally constructed in 1852, the 285-foot-long red-and-white bridge was badly burned in 1989 but has been totally restored.

Across West Virginia, US-50 follows the approximate route of the colonial-era **Northwest Turnpike**, which was surveyed in 1748 by a 16-year-old George Washington.

Grafton: Mother's Day Shrine

Grafton (pop. 5,489), the first large town west of Winchester, Virginia, grew up as a bustling B&O railroad town beginning in the 1850s but is now among the most economically and socially depressed places in the state. Dozens of architecturally interesting but run-down houses and churches drop on brick-paved streets down the steep hills to the Tygart River and the railroad tracks, where a monumental station and a grand but boarded-up hotel are grim reminders of Grafton's formerly busy self.

Besides its impressive physical setting, Grafton's main claim to fame is as the birthplace of Mother's Day, first celebrated here in 1908 in a Methodist church that's been converted into the **International Mother's Day Shrine** (Mon.–Fri.; donations), at 11 E. Main Street across from the old train station.

East of Grafton, the landscape becomes more mountainous, and isolated villages replace the small towns that line the western half of the route.

Arthurdale

Northeast of Grafton, a half hour north of US-50 via Hwy-92, the homestead community of **Arthurdale** was the first and perhaps the most important of the many anti-poverty rural resettlement projects initiated during the Depression-era New Deal. Though not the largest, Arthurdale was prominent because of the personal involvement of then–First Lady Eleanor Roosevelt, who not only helped plan the project but also visited many times, handing out diplomas at school graduations.

Beginning in 1934 with the construction of some 165 homes, plus schools and factories, a cooperative farm, a health center, and a small hotel, Arthurdale was an ideal community set up to relieve the dire living conditions of unemployed Morgantown coal miners. Most of the houses are still intact and still inhabited by the original homesteaders or their descendants. The old community center is being restored and now holds a small **museum** ($5; 304/864-3959) that chronicles the whole story.

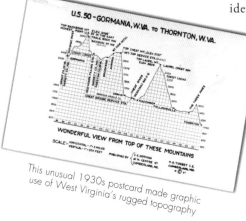

This unusual 1930s postcard made graphic use of West Virginia's rugged topography

Cathedral State Park

Four miles west of the Maryland border, US-50 runs right through **Cathedral State Park,** where over 130 acres of stately maples and hemlocks constitute one of the few first-growth stands left in this lumber-hungry state. Beyond here, US-50 makes a quick seven-mile jaunt across a corner of Maryland before crossing the north branch of the Potomac River back into West Virginia.

Midway across western Maryland's short stretch of US-50, around a mile east of Redhouse next to an immaculate "Chew Mail Pouch Tobacco" barn, the **Route 50 Quilt House** has hundreds of high-quality handmade quilts for sale.

From the bridge, US-50 climbs steeply up the densely wooded Alleghenies, twisting over 3,000-foot-high ridges with turns so tight the posted speed limit is 15 mph—the going is very slow, and not much fun if you're prone to car sickness.

Romney and the Eastern Gateway

The oddly shaped arm of eastern West Virginia, which juts between Maryland and Virginia at the headwaters of the Potomac River, is promoted as the "Eastern Gateway" and offers quick access to the mountainous wilderness of Monongahela National Forest that stretches south of US-50, and to the raging whitewater of the Cheat and Gauley Rivers. Originally inhabited by Shawnee Indians, the region was settled during colonial times as part of the six-million-acre Virginia estate of Lord Fairfax.

The B&O railroad came through in the 1850s, which made the region strategically important during the Civil War, nowhere more so than around **Romney** (pop. 1,940), the Eastern Gateway's largest town, which changed hands over 50 times in four years of fighting. In the center of Romney, at the corner of Main Street and Bolton, the **Davis History House** (hours vary; 304/822-3342) is a well-restored log cabin packed full of pioneer and Civil War artifacts.

Heading east toward Winchester, US-50 passes through mountain hamlets like Capon Bridge (on the West Virginia side) and Gore (on the Virginia side), which consist of little more than a gas station, a tavern, and a post office, plus one or two antique stores selling everything from colonial-era furniture to old highway signs. It's hard to help feeling light years from the modern world, even though Washington, D.C., is only 90 miles away.

VIRGINIA

Dropping from the Allegheny and Appalachian Mountains of West Virginia, US-50 enters Virginia at the northern tip of the **Shenandoah Valley,** passing through the center of the quietly attractive small city of **Winchester.** Continuing east, in short order the road climbs

the foothills of the Blue Ridge Mountains and crosses the Shenandoah River, delighting John Denver fans and carrying travelers through the heart of the ultra-wealthy "Hunt Country" of northern Virginia, a rural and unspoiled landscape of small towns, horse farms, and vineyards that's home to more well-connected millionaires than just about anywhere in the United States.

Approaching the outer suburbs of the nation's capital, however, US-50 swiftly loses its luster, and while you *can* follow it through miles of suburban sprawl on both sides of the I-495 Beltway, you might prefer to follow the misleadingly numbered I-66 freeway—which has nothing at all to do with the *real* Route 66—into the city. US-50's final approach takes you past the powerful Iwo Jima Memorial statue, arriving in D.C. at the Lincoln Memorial.

Winchester

Patsy Cline (September 8, 1932–March 5, 1963)

Northern Virginia's largest city, **Winchester** (pop. 24,750) is a surprisingly quiet and very pleasant small city, best known for the extensive apple orchards that fill the surrounding countryside, producing some 250 million pounds of fruit each year. The I-81 freeway, complete with the usual sprawl of shopping malls and fast-food franchises, cuts across US-50 along the east side of Winchester, but the downtown district is eminently strollable, especially the pedestrianized Old Town area around Loudon Street, between Piccadilly (US-50) and Cork Street, where you can visit George Washington's office or Stonewall Jackson's Civil War headquarters.

After apples and American history, Winchester is probably most famous as the hometown of **Patsy Cline,** the inimitable country singer who died in a plane crash on March 5, 1963, at age 30. Cline, whose greatest hits include "Crazy," "Sweet Dreams," and "Walking After Midnight," lived in Winchester from age 3 to age 16 in a small house at 608 S. Kent Street near downtown, and dropped out of high school to earn money making milk shakes at **Gaunt's Drug Store,** south of downtown at Loudon Street and Valley Avenue. She's buried in **Shenandoah Memorial Park,** a mile southeast of town.

Other sites associated with Patsy Cline are included in the handy brochure "Celebrating Patsy," available inside the **Kurtz Cultural Center** (daily; free; 540/722-6367), in Old Town Winchester at 2 N. Cameron Street, which also has extensive displays on local and Civil War–era history and culture.

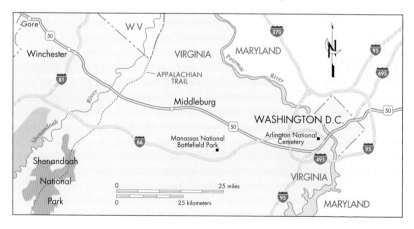

US-50 crosses our **Appalachian Trail** route near 1,100-foot-high Ashby Gap, 15 miles east of Winchester (see page 341). Harpers Ferry, West Virginia, 26 miles north of US-50 via US-340, and Shenandoah National Park, just south of US-50, are covered in detail on pages 340 and 344, respectively.

Middleburg

Located at the heart of northern Virginia's "Hunt Country," where senators, ambassadors, and aristocrats mix at multi-million-dollar country estates, **Middleburg** (pop. 632) is a small but immaculate town with a four-block business district packed with antique shops, art galleries, and real estate agencies.

Many of Middleburg's brick- and stone-fronted buildings date from colonial times, including the **Red Fox Inn** ($150–175; 540/687-6301 or 800/223-1728), at 2 E. Washington Street, on US-50 at the center of town. Originally built in 1728 as a coach inn and tavern, it's now a comfortable and upscale B&B and restaurant. There's a couple of other good places to eat, including the zesty Italian cooking at the **Backstreet Cafe** (540/687-3122) at 4 E. Federal Street; and the **Upper Crust Bakery** (540/687-5666) at 2 N. Pendleton Street, a local favorite offering cookies and sandwiches among the usual array of baked goods.

East of Middleburg, US-50 winds through gently rolling farmlands for a dozen miles before hitting the outlying suburbs of Washington, D.C.

Manassas National Battlefield Park

Site of the first major land battle of the Civil War, **Manassas National Battlefield Park** has been preserved intact despite the suburbanizing pressures of the surrounding towns. The prospect of battle-view executive homes still looms in the future, but for now, Manassas (which in the North was also known as Bull Run) is among the most evocative of all the Civil War sites, its five square miles of rolling hills and woodlands kept as they were, with few intrusions of modern life.

Manassas, which controlled transportation links between Washington, D.C., and the Shenandoah Valley, was the site of two major battles. The first battle, fought here on July 21, 1861, was strategically inconclusive, though the fact that the Confederate "rebels" forced the overconfident Union army into a panicked retreat surprised the many onlookers who had traveled out from Washington to watch the fighting, and foreshadowed the next four years of war. The second battle, fought August 28–30, 1862, followed the instatement of Robert E. Lee as commander of the Confederate forces. That conflict marked the beginning of the bloodiest year of fighting, culminating in the battle of Gettysburg the following July.

On Winchester's town square you'll find the "World's Largest Apple," a 5,200-pound rival to another "world's largest apple" in Cornelia, Georgia (which was actually a 1927 gift from the city of Winchester).

Washington, D.C.

Even if you slept through high school civics and have less than zero interest in national politics, visiting Washington, D.C. (pop. 565,000) is still an unforgettable experience. The monuments and monoliths that line the city's many grand avenues embody nearly two centuries of American political history, and museums show off everything from ancient art to the first flying machines. Best of all, almost everything is free, though there are a few caveats every would-be tourist should know. Parts of D.C. can be dangerous after dark, and the weather here varies tremendously, from freezing cold in winter to sweltering-ly hot and humid in summer (though both spring and fall can be lovely).

Sometime during your visit to D.C., you ought to spend a few hours at the **National Museum of American History** (daily; free; 202/357-2700), on Constitution Avenue between 12th and 14th Streets. Part of the huge Smithsonian Institution, this huge and endearingly quirky museum is the best example of its role as the "Nation's Attic," displaying a little of everything: the giant flag that inspired Francis Scott Key to write the "Star-Spangled Banner," the ruby slippers Judy Garland wore in *The Wizard of Oz*, even a 40-foot stretch of historic Route 66, part of the massive "America on the Move" transportation exhibit.

In recent years, a trio of impressive and sometimes controversial museums and monuments have opened along the National Mall, ranging from the stunning new **National Museum of the American Indian**, closest to the Capitol, through the somber **National World War II Memorial** at the base of the **Washington Monument**. At the west end of the Mall, the eight-acre **FDR Memorial** traces the journey of our longest-serving U.S. President from his elite childhood through his mid-life affliction by polio, up through the Great Depression and World War II.

If you're not the most serious student of historical globalpolitik, your favorite memory of visiting Washington may turn out to be the same as mine: watching workers pushing wheelbarrows full of money across the floors of the **Bureau of Engraving and Printing** (Mon.–Fri. 9 AM–2 PM; 202/622-2000; free), south of the Mall at 14th and C Streets SW. This high-security printing plant is where all your hard-earned cash—some $300 billion a year—is born. Postage stamps, too.

After many decades, major league baseball returned to the capital in 2005 when the former Montreal Expos moved here to become the **Washington Nationals** (202/675-NATS).

Practicalities

Ronald Reagan National Airport (DCA) is D.C.'s main airport, very near downtown and easily accessible on the Metro subway system. The second D.C. airport is Dulles (IAD), way out in the western suburbs, which handles most international flights (and has a large branch of the Smithsonian Air and Space Museum nearby). Often the cheapest D.C.-area airport is Baltimore/Washington International (BWI), midway between D.C. and Baltimore to the northeast. By road, D.C. lies on the busy north-south I-95 corridor, encircled by the I-495 Beltway. US-50, redubbed "I-595" east of D.C., and supplemented in the west by the I-66 freeway, is the main east-west artery.

The basic layout of D.C. is fairly simple, as the entire diamond-shaped city is divided into four quadrants (NE, NW, SE, and SW) with the Capitol at the center. However, because of D.C.'s baroque street plan, with its extensive one-way systems, driving can be very confusing. To get around, you'll do well to avail yourself of the handy Metro subway, which serves most of the places you'll want to go. It may also help to know that the Mall, where most of the museums and memorials are located, is roughly two miles long, from the Capitol west to the Potomac River.

The cheapest and most convenient place to sleep is the modern **HI Hostel** (202/737-2333), at 1009 11th Street NW, within walking distance of the White House. It has dorm beds, private rooms (and air-conditioning!). At the plushest end of the price and comfort spectrum, the **Hay Adams Hotel** ($250-up; 202/638-6600), at 1 Lafayette Square NW directly across from the White House, is a well appointed old hotel, with a grand lobby full of expense-account lobbyists. The nicest mid-range place to stay has to be the **Kalorama Guest House** ($65–120; 202/667-6369), 1854 Mintwood Place, which has clean, nicely furnished rooms in a number of historic houses north of downtown near the National Zoo and trendy Adams-Morgan neighborhood.

To wine and dine with the movers, shakers and wanna-bees of Washington, head to Wisconsin Avenue in **Georgetown,** at the northwest edge of the district, or take a giant leap back to a time when polished wood bars and brass spittoons were the order of the day at the **Old Ebbitt Grill,** east of the White House at 675 15th Street NW (202/347-4800). Open early until late, this casual grill serves everything from breakfasts and burgers to oysters and filet mignon. For a more down-home taste of D.C., head north on the Green Line Metro to the U Street station, near which you can choose between Bill Cosby's favorite chili dogs (at **Ben's Chili Bowl,** right at the station entrance) or the flavorful soul food at the ever-popular **Florida Avenue Grill,** two blocks north at 1100 Florida Avenue NW (202/265-1586).

For more information, contact the Washington, D.C. **visitors bureau** (800/422-8644).

Hundreds of monuments and memorials, along with rows of artillery set up along battle lines, dot the grassy hills and point out the many key moments of the battles. A loosely structured 1.4-mile walking tour begins at the small **Henry Hill Visitor Center** ($3; 703/361-1339), where audiovisual displays and collections of military artifacts give a sense of what the war was like.

To reach Manassas Battlefield, follow the I-66 freeway from Washington, D.C., or the Lee Highway (US-29) west from Fairfax. From US-50, follow US-15 or the smaller Hwy-659 south.

Arlington National Cemetery

Across the Potomac River from Washington, D.C., one of the most compelling and thought-provoking places in the capital region is **Arlington National Cemetery** (daily; free), a 600-acre hillside that contains the mortal remains of over 250,000 U.S. soldiers, sailors, and public servants. Row after row of nearly identical, unadorned white tablets cover most of the cemetery, but special plots are dedicated to the most prominent people, such as John F. and Jacqueline Kennedy, who are buried together beneath an eternal flame, 200 yards straight beyond the main gate. Bobby Kennedy's grave is adjacent.

Located high on a ridge at the top of Arlington Cemetery, the neoclassical mansion of **Arlington House** was the antebellum home of Confederate General Robert E. Lee. Besides providing great views of the Mall and the heart of monumental Washington, the house serves as a vivid reminder of the deep rift caused by the Civil War. During the war, the grounds of the house were made into a cemetery for war dead, which formed the basis for Arlington National Cemetery. Washington, D.C.'s French-born designer, Pierre L'Enfant, lies in front of the mansion in a tomb marked by his plan for the city. The somber **Tomb of the Unknowns** is a quarter-mile south of Arlington House, where a U.S. Army honor guard is formally "changed" every half hour during hot summer days, every two hours on cold winter nights.

To explore the cemetery more completely, stop first at the **visitors center** (703/607-8000) near the cemetery entrance for a map of the grounds that identifies the gravesites of many other famous people interred here, including boxer Joe Louis, explorer Robert Peary, civil rights martyr Medgar Evers, and writer

Confederate hero **Thomas "Stonewall" Jackson** earned his nickname at the first battle of Manassas, where his steadfastness under fire helped rally rebel troops.

One place worth stopping in the D.C. suburbs is the **29 Diner** (703/591-6720), off US-50 on US-29 (hence the name), in Fairfax at 10536 Lee Highway. A National Landmark chrome-and-blue enamel 1947 Mountain View diner, it's open 24 hours every day.

As much as half of all Internet traffic is routed through Fairfax County in D.C.'s western suburbs.

Dashiell Hammett. Arlington is ideal for wandering around, but if it's hot and humid (as it often is in D.C.'s swampy summers), you might want to hop on a Tourmobile tram (unlimited rides for $6; free for those over 65) and take a guided ride up the hill.

Driving D.C.

Following US-50 across Washington, D.C., takes you through the heart of the nation's capital. Starting in the west, alongside Arlington National Cemetery at the **Iwo Jima Memorial** (which sits in the middle of a traffic circle and is all-but-impossible to reach), US-50 crosses the Potomac River, entering "The District" on the Theodore Roosevelt Bridge—making a beeline toward the State Department. US-50 then follows Constitution Avenue along the north side of The Mall, running past the Lincoln and Vietnam Veteran's memorials and between the White House and the Washington Monument, before zig-zagging to the northeast along 7th Street and New York Avenue, which turns into a freeway and runs east to Annapolis and the Chesapeake Bay.

MARYLAND

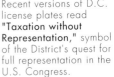

Racing out of Washington, D.C., on a high-speed multi-lane freeway, US-50 accesses one of the state's most popular destinations, the colonial Chesapeake Bay port town of **Annapolis**. From Annapolis, heading toward the Atlantic coast and the massively popular beach resort of **Ocean City**, the final leg of US-50's 3,200-mile transcontinental trek is a mad dash across 100 miles of Maryland's Eastern Shore. This is one of the more captivating areas in the northeastern United States, but the four-lane US-50 freeway doesn't encourage sightseeing, so if you want to get a feel for the *real* Eastern Shore of piney woods, cornfields, and fishing fleets, you'll have to follow the many back roads and search out the many historic towns and villages—many of which we point out as worthwhile detours, including some that are among the oldest and most carefully preserved in the nation.

Annapolis

State capital of Maryland, and one of the most attractive and well-preserved historic cities in the United States, **Annapolis** (pop. 36,500) is one place you won't want to miss. First settled in 1649 and chartered in 1708, Annapolis makes fair claim to being the oldest city in the country. The nation's first capital, it's now best-known for its maritime heritage, both as a yachting center and as home of the U.S. Naval Academy, which stands guard along the Chesapeake Bay waterfront.

   The historic center of Annapolis is just south of US-50 via Hwy-70, which leads straight to the **State House** (daily; free), where the U.S. Congress met in 1783–84 and ratified the Treaty of Paris, thus ending the Revolutionary War. This is

Between D.C. and Annapolis, the town of **Bowie** is home to the Baltimore Orioles' Class AA farm team, the **Bowie Baysox** (301/805-6000).

In Annapolis, **WRNR 103.1 FM** is an anarchic modern rock station, playing everything from The Animals to Frank Zappa.

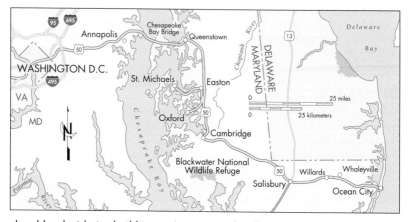

the oldest legislative building in America, and well worth some time. From the State House, Main Street drops downhill to the City Dock waterfront, where a **visitors center** has walking-tour maps and guides to the wealth of historic buildings, including the beautiful colonial-era **Hammond Harwood House** (closed Mon.; $6; 410/263-4683) at 19 Maryland Avenue.

Annapolis has a number of good places to eat, including the venerable **Chick & Ruth's Delly** (410/269-6737), a longstanding local fave at 165 Main Street.

To fully absorb the colonial-era ambience, stay a night or two at the historic **Maryland Inn** ($129 and up; 410/263-2641 or 800/847-8882), right across from the State House.

Bay Bridge

Before the four-mile-long **Bay Bridge** was completed in the early 1950s, Maryland's Eastern Shore was physically and spiritually an island, protected by the broad Chesapeake Bay from the sprawling modern cities of Washington and Baltimore, and cut off at its neck by the Chesapeake and Delaware Canal. Despite the completion of a parallel span in the 1970s, the bridge gets clogged solid each summer by vehicles headed for coastal resorts like Rehoboth Beach ("The Beltway by the Bay") and Ocean City.

At the west end of the bridge, US-50 lands at **Sandy Point State Park,** where you can swim, hike, or launch a boat. At the eastern end, US-50 is joined by US-301, and together the two roads race along as a six-lane freeway as far as **Queenstown,** a busy port in the early 1800s but now little more than an upscale suburb of the greater Baltimore/Washington urban area.

Easton

Maryland's **Eastern Shore** is excellent bicycling country, with generally flat, quiet roads winding through farmlands, forests, and waterfront fishing villages.

Midway across Maryland, 20 miles southeast of the Chesapeake Bay Bridge, turn off the freeway and head a half mile west to explore the well-preserved heart of **Easton** (pop. 11,708), where the stately Talbot County Courthouse overlooks a compact business district that could easily pass as an English country High Street. Besides the many 18th-century

Detour: Baltimore

The best description I've ever heard of Baltimore's quirky charms came from film director John Waters, who has drawn considerable inspiration from his offbeat hometown. In his book *Shock Value,* Waters wrote: "I would never want to live anywhere but Baltimore. You can look far and wide, but you'll never discover a stranger city with such extreme style. It's as if every eccentric in the South decided to move north, ran out of gas in Baltimore, and decided to stay." Signs of this can be seen at the **American Visionary Art Museum** (closed Mon.; $9; 410/244-1900), at 800 Key Highway, which displays an array of works by "outsider" and "self-taught" artists in every medium imaginable—painted packing crates, "art cars," and so on. The museum, which is near the popular Inner Harbor waterfront redevelopment, also has the very good, "ultra-organic" **Joy America Cafe.**

For more typically Baltimorean food and drink, head to historic **Fell's Point,** a mile east of the Inner Harbor. Location for the TV show *Homicide,* it's not as gritty as that might sound; one of a dozen good places to eat here is **Bertha's** (410/327-5795) at 734 S. Broadway, a friendly little café famed for (grit-free!) mussels and other seafood specialties. To sample the other local specialty, Chesapeake Bay crab, head to **Obrycki's** (410/732-6399), at 1727 E. Pratt Street.

If you're interested on catching a ballgame, the very popular **Baltimore Orioles** play at always-packed Camden Yards (410/685-9800) right downtown.

For more information, contact the Baltimore **visitors bureau** (410/837-4636 or 800/282-6632) at the Inner Harbor.

structures, including a federal-style townhouse at 25 S. Washington Street that's been converted into the Talbot County historical society **museum** (closed Mon.), the most interesting place to stop is the white wood-frame **Third Haven Meeting House,** on the edge of town on South Washington Street, built in 1684 and still in use by a Quaker congregation.

The most impressive place to stay in Easton is the stately **Tidewater Inn** ($90 and up; 410/822-1300 or 800/237-8775), a recently restored landmark in the center of town at 101 E. Dover Street, which offers guests free carriage rides around town and the option of a 4:30 AM breakfast—designed for early-rising duck-hunters. Easton also holds the comfortable **Bishop's House** B&B ($80 and up; 410/820-7290), at 214 Goldsborough Street, and the usual range of motels and fast-food places along the US-50 frontage.

St. Michaels and Oxford

The pride and joy of the Eastern Shore is the Chesapeake Bay village of **St. Michaels,** a colonial-era shipbuilding center turned yachting haven that's home to the excellent **Chesapeake Bay Maritime Museum** (daily; $9; 410/745-2916). Located right on the waterfront at the center of town, the museum has extensive

West of St. Michaels, at the far end of Hwy-33, **Tilghman Island** is home port for Chesapeake Bay's sole surviving fleet of skipjacks, the unique sail-powered vessels used to harvest oysters from the bay.

displays of skipjacks and other historic sailing vessels, which you can watch being restored in the museum workshops. There are also diverse pieces of fishing and hunting gear, plus a working lighthouse, all displayed to conjure up traditional Eastern Shore maritime life.

Though full of lovingly maintained old houses and commercial buildings as well as working wharves, chandlers, and sail lofts, St. Michaels, it has to be said, is definitely a major tourist trap, with the usual array of souvenir shops, overpriced restaurants, and overquaint B&Bs.

After seeing the museum and wandering around the town, if you want to get a feel for the unspoiled Chesapeake follow the signs southeast from St. Michaels to the historic **ferry** (daily 7 AM–sunset; $6/car, $1.25/pedestrian each way) that shuttles across the Tred Avon River every half hour or so between Bellevue and Oxford. **Oxford** (pop. 700), a truly sleepy little Eastern Shore town, has hardly changed since the 1760s, when it was one of two authorized ports-of-entry into colonial-era Maryland. Wander along the waterfront or south along Morris Street to the village center, through what may be the best-preserved colonial townscape left in America. There are no museums or displays proclaiming Oxford a special place, though no less an authority than James Michener (who lived in St. Michaels for many years) did go so far as to say that the crab cakes served inside the circa 1710 **Robert Morris Inn** ($110 and up; 410/226-5111) opposite the ferry dock were among the best he'd ever tasted.

Cambridge

Founded in 1684 on the south bank of the broad Choptank River, unlike sleepy Oxford, busy **Cambridge** (pop. 10,911) is a market town for the surrounding farmlands. Still somewhat industrial in feel, thanks to its now-closed canning and packing plants, Cambridge does have some attractive corners, though its one apt but unique sight is the decaying old **Cape Charles ferry,** which once sailed south to Norfolk but has long since been abandoned on the northwest side of the US-50 bridge over the Choptank River.

US-50 through Cambridge is the **Harriet Tubman Highway.** Her birthplace is eight miles west of town.

Cambridge is also home to the Eastern Shore's most bizarre range of annual festivals, from the winter **National Muskrat Skinning Championship** to powerboat and antique-airplane fairs held throughout the summer; for details, contact the **visitors center** (410/228-1000).

Throughout the summer, Salisbury is home to the popular **Delmarva Shorebirds,** the Baltimore Orioles' Class A farm team, who play at the modern Perdue Stadium (410/219-3112) off US-50 on Hobbs Road.

Salisbury

Though largely modern and commercial, **Salisbury** (pop. 23,734) has preserved part of its older townscape in a pedestrianized downtown shopping district and in the Newton Historic District, a collection of dainty Victorian-era houses along Elizabeth Street. The one place to stop is the **Ward Museum of Wildfowl Art** (daily; $7), 900 S. Schumaker Drive, which has a comprehensive collection of carved decoys and other hunting-related arts and crafts.

Crossing the coastal wetlands and estuaries, US-50 races east from Salisbury, bypassing a few small towns like Willards and Whaleyville, which are best seen by following the Hwy-346 frontage road. The two routes run parallel, joining each other 30 miles east in the old-time beach resort of Ocean City.

Ocean City is also a stop along the **Atlantic Coast** route, covered on pages 374–443. Full coverage of Ocean City can be found on page 383.

Greetings from SAVANNAH BEACH GEORGIA

Oil Well in West Texas

Desert View Tower

Felicity: Center of the World

The Thing!

Buddy Holly Monument

pg. 727

pg. 729

pg. 735

pg. 750

92 mi

325 mi

615 mi

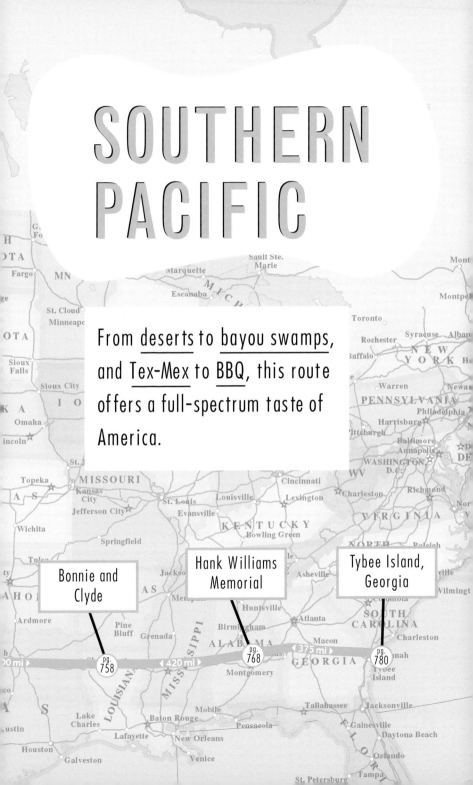

SOUTHERN PACIFIC

From deserts to bayou swamps, and Tex-Mex to BBQ, this route offers a full-spectrum taste of America.

Bonnie and Clyde

pg. 758

Hank Williams Memorial

pg. 768

Tybee Island, Georgia

pg. 780

◀ 420 mi ▶

◀ 375 mi ▶

Between San Diego, California and Savannah, Georgia

Following old US-80 and its contemporary equivalents across the nation's southern tier takes you through more varied cultural and physical landscapes than you'll find along any other cross-country route. Throughout this 3,000-mile journey you can shift from one world to another in the time it takes to watch a football game. Heading east from the golden sands of San Diego, within a few hours you reach the harshly beautiful Southwest deserts, their trademark saguaro (SWA-row) cacti creating a backdrop straight out of a Roadrunner cartoon. The route's central segment crosses the thousand-mile, "you can see for two days" plains of **New Mexico** and **Texas,** where pumpjacks jig for oil and cattle graze beneath a limitless sky. To the east spreads another land, starting at the cotton-rich **Mississippi Delta** and continuing along the foot of the **Appalachians** to the bayous and sea islands surrounding the country's grandest little city, **Savannah.**

Especially memorable is the diversity of people and prevailing customs along the route, all highlighted by a range of accents and lingos. For travelers, this cultural diversity is perhaps most accessible in the food. Many regional American cuisines—Tex-Mex, Cajun, Creole, and BBQ, to name a few—were originally developed somewhere along this route, and roadside restaurants continue to serve up local specialties that lend new meaning to the word "authentic." Along the open borders between Texas and New and old Mexico, in unself-conscious adobe sheds with corrugated metal roofs, chile-powered salsa accompanies roast-steak fajitas; in Louisiana, entrées featuring catfish fillets or bright red boiled shrimp grace most menus; and everywhere you turn, roadside stands dish out reputedly the best BBQ in the universe. We've noted favorite places along the route, but all you really need do is follow your nose, or look for a line of pickup trucks, and you'll find yourself in culinary heaven.

On an equal footing with the fine food is the incredible variety of music you'll hear, whether it's in a Texas honky-tonk or in the juke joints and gospel-spreading churches of Mississippi and Alabama. Along the Mexican border, from San Diego well past El Paso, radio stations blast out an anarchic mix of multi-lingual music, part country-western, part traditional Mexican, with accordions and guitars and lyrics flowing seamlessly from one language to the other and back—often in a single line of a song. Along the way, you can visit the hometowns of Buddy Holly, Little Richard, and Otis Redding, or pay your respects at the final resting places of Hank Williams, Jimmie Rodgers, and Duane Allman. After dark, listen to the current and next generation making music in roadside bars and clubs.

A wealth of distinctive literature has grown out of these regions, and you can visit dozens of characteristic literary scenes, live and in the flesh: Carson McCullers's "Ballad of the Sad Cafe" and other tales, which capture 1920s life in Columbus, Georgia; Cormac McCarthy's wide-open tales of the Texas frontier;

the diner from *Fried Green Tomatoes;* and the original God's Little Acre and Tobacco Road. But there's also sober history, from Wild-West Tombstone and Bonnie and Clyde's death site, to the Dallas intersection where JFK was assassinated, to the streets of Selma, where the civil rights movement burst forth onto the nation's front pages. Best of all, many of the most fascinating places along the way remain refreshingly free of the slick promotion that greets you in more-established tourist destinations. The relatively low profile of tourism here, and the fact that only a few big cities lie in wait to swallow your vacation dollars, help make this particular trip a relatively inexpensive one—but even at twice the price, it would be well worth experiencing.

CALIFORNIA

From the Pacific bays and golden beaches of San Diego, you can choose between two routes as you head east across Southern California: the high-speed I-8 freeway up and over pine-forested mountains, or a winding drive along the Mexican border. We've covered the slower, more southerly route that follows the remnants of old US-80 through sleepy border towns and past a pair of unique roadside attractions—the funky old Desert View Tower, and the oddly endearing "Official Center of the World" at tiny **Felicity**. Also included is a quick side trip south of the border to beer-making **Tecate**. But no matter which way you choose, eventually you'll have to cross many monotonous miles of the **Mojave Desert,** a barren, dry, and inhospitable land.

Point Loma: Cabrillo National Monument

The sturdy headland that protects San Diego's extensive harbor from the open Pacific Ocean, Point Loma has long been occupied by the military, whose many fences, radio towers, and gun emplacements all seem to disappear at the very tip, where the **Cabrillo National Monument** (daily 9 AM–5 PM; $5 per car; 619/557-5450) protects a breathtaking 150 acres of cliffs and tidepools. Set aside in 1913 to remember the efforts of Portuguese sailor Juan Cabrillo, who explored the California coast in 1542, there's also an old lighthouse, some nice trails, and a visitors center describing the whole shebang.

San Diego is at the southern end of our **Pacific Coast** road trip, which is described on pages 10–103. For details on visiting San Diego, see pages 100–101.

Across San Diego: Old US-80

From Point Loma and the Pacific Ocean, old US-80 bends south past the airport (named for Charles Lindbergh, and featuring one of the most hair-raising landing patterns of any big American airport) and through downtown along

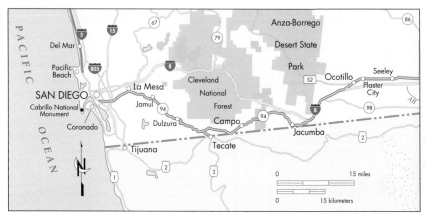

12th Avenue and Market Street, then veers north again along the Cabrillo Freeway (one of the oldest in the country) through historic Balboa Park, home to the San Diego Zoo, a replica of London's old Globe Theater, and many grand Spanish Colonial–style buildings that have been standing here since the 1915 Panama International Exposition.

East of San Diego, old US-80 follows El Cajon Boulevard past San Diego State University and a dozen miles of unsightly but surviving motels, cafés, and gas stations before it reaches the foothill town of **La Mesa,** where you can leave old US-80 (which runs alongside the high-speed I-8 freeway), and turn onto the two-lane blacktop of Hwy-94. Twisting to the southeast around the 4,000-foot peaks of the **Cleveland National Forest,** Hwy-94 traverses classic Southern California landscape: rolling, chaparral-covered hillsides rising above grassy ranch lands and stately valley oaks.

Tecate

After passing through **Jamul** and **Dulzura,** two quiet ranching towns that appear on the verge of extinction due to San Diego's rapidly approaching sprawl, some 40 miles east of downtown San Diego along Hwy-94, you'll spot a sign marking the turnoff south to the Mexican border town of **Tecate** (pop. 48,000). Known around the world as the source of tangy Tecate beer—by most accounts, the brew that started people drinking beer with a squeeze of fresh lime—Tecate is in the top tier of enjoyable border towns, if only by virtue of being cleaner, quieter, and much less "touristy" than Tijuana. Potential stops include the usual restaurants, cantinas, and souvenir shops. Because of insurance concerns, it's a good idea to leave your car on the U.S. side of the border and cross into Mexico on foot.

East of the Tecate area, Hwy-94 runs along the U.S. side of the border for 41 miles before joining the I-8 freeway.

Campo marks the southern end of the **Pacific Crest Trail,** which winds for 2,638 miles between Canada and Mexico.

Campo

Set in a broad valley midway between Tecate and the I-8 freeway, tiny **Campo** (pop. 1,102) has one main attraction, the **San Diego Railroad Museum** (Sat.–Sun. and holidays

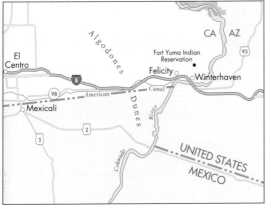

9 AM–5 PM; free; 619/595-3030), well-posted at the west end of town on Forest Gate Road. Along with an extensive outdoor collection of old locomotives and carriages, the museum offers rides (11 AM and 2:30 PM; $10) on restored steam- and diesel-powered trains, including a 16-mile round trip through the surrounding countryside. Occasionally, the museum also offers all-day trips south to Tecate, Mexico.

Jacumba and the Desert View Tower

South of the I-8 freeway on a surviving stretch of the old US-80 highway, **Jacumba** is a former spa and resort town where Clark Gable, Marlene Dietrich, and countless others soaked themselves silly in the free-flowing natural hot springs. Established in 1852 as a station on the stagecoach mail route across the desert, Jacumba had its heyday during the 1920s, and while little remains apart from the water, it makes a great place to stop. The mineral-rich hot springs still flow into outdoor pools and private hot tubs at **Jacumba Hot Springs Spa** (619/766-4333), at 44500 Old US-80, which includes motel rooms for around $40, a good on-site restaurant, and a popular "locals" bar.

Southern gateway to the splendid, 600,000-acre **Anza-Borrego State Park,** the largest and wildest desert park in the country, the Jacumba area is also home to one of the great road-trip stops in southern California: the **Desert View Tower** (daily 9 AM–dusk; $2.50; 619/766-4612). The four-story, cut-stone structure was built in 1922 to commemorate the pioneers who struggled across the arid desert.

Inside the tower, a small but interesting museum displays a haphazard collection of desert Americana such as Navajo blankets and Native American artifacts, with similar items on sale in the gift shop. You can't beat the price of admission, and at the top of the tower, an observation platform offers views across 100 miles of desert landscape, sliced by the I-8 freeway. (You can also see places where the excavations for I-8 have left

For more information on visiting **Anza-Borrego State Park,** which covers some 600,000 acres of desiccated desert, contact the ranger station in Borrego Springs (760/767-5311).

When driving in the desert, always keep the gas tank as full as possible, and always carry at least one gallon of drinking water per person. In case of trouble, stay with your car. Don't walk off in search of help; let it find you.

El Centro is the winter home of the aerial acrobats of the U.S. Navy's **Blue Angels,** who can sometimes be spotted practicing their loops and rolls in the skies around the city. It is also the birthplace of **Cher**.

sections of the old US-80 roadway stranded on manmade mesas, 50 feet or higher than the modern freeway.)

Across the parking lot from the Desert View Tower, a hillside of quartzite granite boulders has been carved with dozens of three-dimensional figures. Most of the figures are of skulls, snakes, and lizards—with real lizards sometimes racing each other across the rocks—the whole ensemble was created during the Depression by an out-of-work engineer named W. T. Ratliffe.

The Desert View Tower stands at a cool 3,000 feet above sea level, three miles east of Jacumba, on the north side of I-8 at the In-Ko-Pah Road exit; billboards point the way.

El Centro

Located some 50 feet below sea level, midway across California at the heart of the agricultural Coachella Valley, **El Centro** (pop. 37,835) was founded in 1905 and has since bloomed into a bustling small city, thanks to irrigation water diverted from the Colorado River. Melons, grapefruit, and dates are the region's prime agricultural products, along with alfalfa grown to feed the many dairy cows. There's not a lot here that doesn't depend upon farming.

Though not much of a destination, El Centro is still the best place to break a journey between San Diego and the Arizona border, so fill your gas tank if nothing else. All the national food and lodging chains are here, along with neon-signed local ones along the I-8 Business Loop.

Algodones Dunes

In the middle of the southern Mojave Desert, 42 miles east of El Centro, a rest area south of the I-8 freeway at the Gray's Well Road exit gives access to the enticing pink-hued sands of the **Algodones Dunes,** which stretch to both sides of the freeway for over 50 miles. The slender dunes, which measure at most 10 miles across and reach heights of 200 feet, often cover the highway in blowing sandstorms. Though you can amble around on foot, be aware that the dunes themselves are under constant abuse from hordes of motorcycles and dune buggies.

If you're really, really interested in old highways, you won't want to miss the reconstructed remnants of a **wooden plank road,** built across the sands in 1914 and later used as part of the original US-80

highway. Preserved by the dry desert air, and arranged to form a 100-foot section across the dunes, this fenced-off museum piece is along the south side of I-8, two miles west of the Gray's Well Road exit. The All-American Canal, which waters the Coachella Valley, snakes alongside the freeway.

Felicity: The Center of the World Pyramid

One of the odder sites in the Southwestern deserts—and competition for this title is pretty fierce—sits just north of the I-8 freeway in the tiny but happily named town of **Felicity** (pop. 4). Local resident Jacques-Andres Istel—author of a children's fairy tale concerning a scholarly, fire-breathing dragon named Coe who lives at the center of the world reading fireproof books and eating the nearby Chocolate Mountains—convinced France, China, and Imperial County that Felicity is, legally and officially, the center of the world.

From 1858 to 1861 the original **Butterfield Stage,** which carried mail and passengers from St. Louis to San Francisco, followed the approximate route of I-8 across Southern California. The route was originally blazed by Spanish explorer **Juan de Anza,** on his way to found San Francisco in 1775.

A 25-foot-high pink terrazzo pyramid stands above the exact spot, which you can visit on regular guided **tours** (daily late Nov.–mid-April only; $1; 760/572-5000); the fee also buys a certificate saying you've stood at "The Official Center of the World." You can climb a set of stairs that used to belong to the Eiffel Tower and sift through sundry souvenirs in the gift shop.

Winterhaven

The last California town before the Colorado River, **Winterhaven** is the modest center of the Quechan community on 44,000-acre Fort Yuma Indian Reservation. A few reminders of its pre- and post-colonial past are displayed inside the small **Fort Yuma Indian Museum** (Mon.–Fri. 7 AM–noon, 1–4 PM; $1) alongside the white-walled St. Thomas missionary church. Both structures overlook the Colorado River from atop Indian Hill off the end of 1st Street. From the church, you can walk across a historic bridge to Yuma, Arizona (see below).

ARIZONA

Between the Colorado River, which divides Arizona from California, and the Phoenix–Tucson megalopolis in the middle of the state, there is not very much to attract the traveler off the freeway. However, the rather complete absence of interesting places in southwestern Arizona is more than made up for by the wealth of fascinating things to see in the state's southeast corner. Here you'll find such legendary sites as Tombstone—home of the OK Corral—and other finely presented reminders of the state's Wild West heritage, along with some of Arizona's most beautiful natural scenery.

The Colorado River forms the border between California and Arizona, and marks the line between the Pacific and Mountain time zones. Arizona, however, doesn't observe daylight saving time, so in summer both states are on the same time.

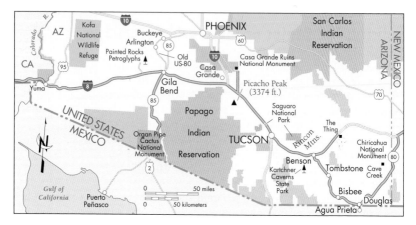

Yuma

Among the hottest, driest, and fastest-growing areas in the country, **Yuma** (pop. 135,000) was first settled in 1779 at the site of one of the few good crossings along the Colorado River. Dozens of decaying old adobe buildings around town testify to Yuma's lengthy history, and a select few places are preserved as historic parks. The **Yuma Crossing** (daily; $4; 928/329-0471), along the river and I-8 at the north end of 4th Avenue, has been restored to its appearance prior to the arrival of the railroad in 1876, when supplies for U.S. troops throughout the Southwest arrived here by steamboat from the Gulf of California.

Around the time the railroad arrived, a full century after its founding by Spanish missionaries, Yuma was the site of Arizona Territory's main prison. Built out of stone and adobe by convicts struggling in the 120° heat, over the next 33 years until it was closed in 1909, the prison earned a reputation as the "Hellhole of Arizona," due in large part to the summer heat and the brutality of its regime, though park rangers emphasize the fact that prisoners had access to a library and other facilities unusual at the time. Now preserved as the state-run **Yuma Territorial Prison** (daily; $4; 928/783-4771), well-posted along the north side of I-8 at the 4th Avenue exit, the site consists of a few of the cells and the main gate, as well as a small museum.

From the prison, a rickety pedestrian-only steel bridge (formerly part of US-80) leads across the Colorado River to California and the **St. Thomas mission church** on the Quechan Fort Yuma Indian Reservation.

Along with the usual national franchises, Yuma has a number of decent places to eat, ranging from the big breakfasts and afternoon BBQ at **Brownie's Cafe** at 1145 S. 4th Avenue (old US-80); to the pool tables, burgers, and sandwiches at ancient **Lutes Casino** (928/782-2192), at 221 S. Main Street in the historic old downtown area. Voted the "Best Place to Stop in

Yuma" by the *Arizona Republic* newspaper, Lutes is a barn-like hall full of old photos, political posters, street signs, and all manner of junk, well worth a look at least for its passionately played domino games.

Along with the national chains, places to sleep in Yuma include the pleasant **Yuma Cabana** ($40; 928/783-8311 or 800/874-0811), at 2151 S. 4th Avenue, with palm trees, a nice pool, and a recliner in every room.

Along with dozens of Spanish-language stations north and south of the Mexican border, Yuma's **KBLU 560 AM** plays oldies and local news.

Yuma to Gila Bend: I-8

Spanning 110 miles of barren desert east of Yuma, between the U.S. Air Force's 14-million-acre Barry M. Goldwater Bombing Range and a U.S. Army Proving Ground, the I-8 freeway follows the route of early Spanish explorers and settlers on the flat but forbidding Camino del Diablo, along the banks of the usually dry Gila River.

East of 767-foot-high Telegraph Pass, 20 miles outside Yuma, the old US-80 highway reappears along the north side of the freeway, running through old-time desert outposts. If you're hungry, the flyspeck ranching community of **Tacna** has a great place to eat burgers, lamb chops, and a full menu of other Mexican and American dishes: **Basque Etchea** (closed Mon.; 928/785-4027). Take I-8 exit 42, then head north across the railroad tracks. **Dateland,** 25 miles farther east along I-8, has a café and gift shop selling dates in all possible forms, including refreshing milk shakes.

Gila Bend

The only place approaching a town between Yuma and Phoenix or Tucson, **Gila Bend** (pop. 1,980) is regularly the "Hottest Spot in the Country"—a title of which it is so proud that, more than once, it's been caught inflating the numbers. First settled as a main stop on the Butterfield Stage route, Gila Bend doesn't offer much relief for the senses, though it does have some photogenic old motels and all the gas stations, restrooms, and restaurants you could reasonably expect to find in the middle of the Arizona desert.

Twenty-two miles west of Gila Bend, off I-8 at exit 102, **Painted Rocks Road** leads 11 miles north to a BLM-managed site where an array of petroglyphs, carved into the boulders by the Hohokam people around AD 1400, covers the rocks.

One place to eat is the **Outer Limits Coffee Shop** at 401 E. Pima Avenue, downtown off exit 115. Marked by a flying-saucer-shaped sign, it's part of the **Best Western Space Age Lodge** motel ($70; 928/683-2273 or 800/528-1234). Both are essential stops for any Jetsons-aged traveler, though the refurbishment after a fire has diminished the Space Age charm.

From Gila Bend, Hwy-85 runs south to the beautiful and totally deserted **Organ Pipe Cactus National Monument,** before linking up with Hwy-86 to loop east to Tucson.

If you're interested in following the route of old US-80 across California and western Arizona, pick up a copy of the entertaining and informative *Old US-80 Highway Traveler's Guide*, by Eric J. Finley.

Old US-80 via Phoenix

I-8 is by far the fastest way east from Gila Bend to Tucson and beyond, but if you have the time and inclination to follow the old road, it took the long way around: From Gila Bend US-80 veers north across the usually dry Gila River along what's now an unmarked county road, then east through the towns of Arlington, Palo Verde, and **Buckeye**, where a 40-odd-foot statue of "Hobo Joe" stands along Baldy Street downtown. US-80 runs through downtown Phoenix on Van Buren Street (which was also US-60 and US-70), before heading south to Tucson.

Between Phoenix and Tucson, I-10 parallels our US-93 **Border to Border** road trip route, which runs about 20 miles to the east, along Hwy-79 (see page 154). From Phoenix, the route passes such enticing desert oddities as the famous Biosphere 2, and a memorial to cowboy actor Tom Mix. Phoenix and Tucson, and the alternate route between them, are covered on pages 150–157.

Picacho Peak

Looming like a giant battleship alongside the I-10 freeway, 75 miles southeast of Phoenix and 45 miles northwest of Tucson, 3,374-foot **Picacho Peak** has served as a Sonora Desert landmark for as long as there have been people here. Native Americans, Spanish explorers, American pioneers, you name it, they've used the volcanic peak to keep them on track. Now a state park, Picacho Peak also played a role in the Civil War, as the official westernmost battlefield of the War Between the States fought here on April 15, 1862, when a dozen Union soldiers skirmished with 17 Confederate cavalrymen. These days, people come here to enjoy the saguaro cactus and the desert wildflowers (in March mainly, when they're at their most colorful), or to hike to the summit for a desert panorama (two miles each way, with a roughly 1,500-foot elevation gain). The park ($6 per car; 520/466-3183) is open for day use and camping.

Along the freeway at the foot of Picacho Peak, a sprawling ostrich farm lets you feed the ungainly beasts or purchase a variety of ostrich-derived products.

Saguaro National Park: Tucson Mountain

Northwest of Tucson, the more popular half of **Saguaro National Park** protects extensive stands of saguaro cactus as well as ancient petroglyphs, spring wildflowers, and generally gorgeous desert scenery. From I-10 at Cortaro (exit 246), a loop road runs southwest, then back east through rugged, mountainous terrain, which, though popular, is a great place to get a feel for the Sonora Desert landscape. A **visitors center** (daily; 520/733-5158) has details of the many hikes here, the longest of which winds its way to the 4,687-foot summit of Wasson Peak.

There's more hiking, plus camping, in the adjacent county-owned **Tucson Mountain Park** where **Old Tucson Studios** ($14.95) has movie sets used to film more than 300 movies and TV shows; these days, the "action" is mostly staged gunfights and dance-hall revues.

Tucson Mountain Park is also home to the excellent **Arizona Sonora Desert Museum** (daily; $9–12; 520/883-2702). Apart from spending a lifetime in the desert itself, there's really no better place to get a sense of the abundant flora and fauna of the Sonora Desert than this creatively presented zoological park.

The saguaro cactus, whose creamy white blossoms are the Arizona state flower, blooms in May.

From Tucson Mountain Park, Gates Pass Road drops down into Tucson's main east–west road, Speedway Boulevard.

Across Tucson: Old US-80

From the north and west, the best old road introduction to Tucson is the so-called **Miracle Mile**, a few blocks of old neon-signed motels, right off the I-10 freeway exit 255. From here, old US-80 follows a series of one-way surface streets into compact downtown Tucson, first following 5th Avenue, then 6th Avenue, the pre-interstate main highway.

Tucson marks the junction with our **Border to Border** road trip along US-93, covered on pages 106–157. Tucson and nearby attractions are covered on pages 156–157.

The Boneyard: Davis-Monthan Air Force Base

On the southeast side of Tucson, off I-10 at the Kolb Road exit, Davis-Monthan Air Force Base holds one of the very strangest sights in the entire Southwest desert: rows and rows and rows of surplus military aircraft, lined up for what seems like miles. The official name for this desert facility is the "Aerospace Maintenance and Regeneration Center" (AMARC), but it's best known as **"The Boneyard"** because of its role as a salvage yard for aircraft long past their production era. You can glimpse dozens of the planes from the highway, but for the full experience you have to sign up for one of the very popular **tours** (hours vary; $6; 520/618-4800). The tours are offered by the Pima Air and Space Museum, which has another extensive exhibit of aircraft, including JFK's Air Force One, near the Boneyard. They also operate the unique Titan Missile Museum south of Tucson (see page 154).

Saguaro National Park: Rincon Mountains

A dozen miles east of Tucson, on the slopes of the Tanque Verde and Rincon Mountains, the eastern half of **Saguaro National Park** covers 57,000 acres of rolling desert landscape. Named in honor of the anthropomorphic saguaro cactus, which here reaches heights upwards of 40 feet and lives as long as 200 years, the monument is best seen by following eight-mile Cactus Forest Drive, along which numerous hiking trails give close-up looks at the multi-limbed succulents. For more information and details of hiking opportunities, stop at the **visitors center** (daily; 520/733-5153).

Colossal Cave

Beyond the Rincon Mountains section of Saguaro National Park, 14 miles from downtown Tucson via the Old Spanish Trail, **Colossal Cave** (daily; $7.50, plus $3 per car; 520/647-7275) is another great place to stop. A huge old limestone cavern that offers a cool (in every sense of the word!) escape from the sweltering summer heat, this is one of the state's most enduring tourist attractions. (Avid cavers will appreciate comparing Colossal Cave, which is a "dry" cave, with the newly opened Kartchner Caverns (see below), a "wet" cave where the humidity will have you dripping with perspiration.) Colossal Cave was used in Wild West times by train robbers who escaped here with $62,000; the money bags were recovered, but not the money. Most of the very limited "development" here (footpaths, the museum and gift shop) was done as a CCC project during the New Deal 1930s.

The surrounding ranch land has been opened as a nature reserve with hiking and mountain-bike trails, and the ranch buildings have been preserved as a museum of early Arizona life.

Kartchner Caverns State Park

On the other side of I-10 from Colossal Cave, one of Arizona's most long-awaited "openings" has been that of **Kartchner Caverns State Park**, a massive limestone cavern—over two miles long—that is rated by experts as one of the 10 most beautiful in the world. Discovered by a pair of avid cavers back in 1974, it took 25 years of negotiation and $27 million worth of careful construction of tunnels and facilities before the cave was opened to the general public. Advance reservations for one of the mandatory tours ($19–24) are all but required if you want to see the 150-foot-square Throne Room, with its 60-foot ceiling, or the larger but less lofty Rotunda, or any of the other phantasmagorical sights. The caverns, which are kept at near 100 percent humidity by a set of airlocks at the entrance, are remarkable for their diverse and delicate formations, including over 30 different types of stalactites, stalagmites, columns, draperies, shields, and helictites, not to mention the longest "soda straw" in the United States—a thin tube of limestone over 21 feet long but only a quarter-inch in diameter.

Kartchner Caverns State Park is just west of Benson, nine miles south of I-10 exit 302, along Hwy-90. If you don't manage to join a tour, it's still worth stopping at the 23,000-square-foot **visitors center** (daily; $5 per vehicle; 520/586-4100), which includes videos of the cave and full-scale replicas of its features (including the famous "soda straw"). There's also an above-ground hiking trail through native hummingbird habitat, and a 63-site campground with full hookups.

> The **Tucson Sidewinders** ($5–8; 520/434-1021), the Class AAA farm club of the Arizona Diamondbacks, play at Tucson Electric Park, southeast of downtown off I-10 at Ajo Way. Games are broadcast on **KTZR 1450 AM**.

Benson and the Amerind Foundation

Off I-10 along the banks of the San Pedro River, **Benson** (pop. 4,711) was founded as a Santa Fe railroad connection to booming Tombstone and the Mexican harbor town of Guaymas. Trains still rumble through town, but there's not much to see apart from fading roadside signs. **Reb's Cafe** (520/586-3856), at 1020 W. 4th Street; and the **Horseshoe Cantina** (520/586-3303), at 154 E. 4th Street across from the

> Benson's radio station **KAVV 97.7 FM** plays lots of good Waylon-and-Willie-type country hits, plus captivating accounts of local news and activities.

railroad tracks, are where locals go to eat. Thanks in part to the popularity of Kartchner Caverns, Benson has a number of motels congregating around I-10 exit 304.

From Benson, our route cuts south on old US-80 (now Hwy-80), while I-10 races east over the mountains that 100-plus years ago were a stronghold of Apache warriors under Geronimo and Cochise. If you're following the interstate, a couple of sights are worth looking for. The more satisfying of these, the **Amerind Foundation Museum** (daily; $5; 520/586-3666), lies 12 miles east of Benson, off Dragoon Road a mile southeast of I-10 exit 318. Started in 1937, the private, nonprofit museum is devoted to the study of local Native American cultures, with everything from ancient arrowheads to contemporary Pueblo pottery on display in the spacious mission-style buildings. Not surprisingly, the best collections are of Hopi, Navajo, and Apache artifacts, with well-presented exhibits of ceremonial and domestic objects—kachina dolls, rugs, and ritual costumes.

I-10: The Thing!

Advertised by signs all along the freeway, one of the country's odder roadside attractions stands atop 4,975-foot Texas Summit, along I-10 at exit 322: **The Thing** ($1; 520/586-2581). A gas station, a gift shop,

and a Dairy Queen stand in front of a prefab shed full of stuff ranging from a Rolls Royce once used by Adolf Hitler to The Thing itself, a mummified corpse whose "secret identity" has yet to be revealed. "What is it?" the signs ask.

Tombstone

While I-10 races east over the mountains, our more scenic route, promoted by tourism authorities as the "Cochise Trail," winds south on old US-80 through the Wild West town of Tombstone, "The Town too Tough to Die." The route loops along the Mexican border before rejoining I-10 across the New Mexico border.

Though it's just 22 miles south of the freeway, and regularly inundated by bikers, RVers, and busloads of tourists, the rough-and-ready mining town of **Tombstone** (pop. 1,504) has kept itself looking pretty much as it did back in the 1880s, when 10,000 miners called it home, and one of the more mythic events of the Wild West took place here: the shoot-out at the OK Corral.

Historians, and everyone in Tombstone, still debate the chain of events of October 26, 1881. Was Wyatt Earp a sharpshooting savior, out to make Tombstone safe for decent society? Or was he really a grandstanding cowboy whom history has romanticized? Decide for yourself after hearing all sides of the story. The **OK Corral** is still there, a block south of Fremont Street (old US-80), on Allen Street between 3rd and 4th Streets, with life-sized, black-leather-clad statues taking the places of Virgil and Wyatt Earp facing down the Clanton brothers. Nearby, in a fenced-off outdoor theater, gunslinging actors stage recreations of the shootout. To see any or all of this, you have to buy a ticket at the entertaining **Historama** (daily; $7.50; 520/457-3456), adjacent to the OK Corral.

About 20 miles southeast of Tombstone, three miles west of Bisbee at the 6,030-foot Mule Pass summit of old US-80, the much-abused stone obelisk of the **Divide Monument** commemorates the convict-laborers who first constructed the road in 1913. The monument stands in a somewhat scruffy parking area directly above the modern tunnel, and from it you get a great panoramic view of the surrounding Mule Mountains.

The dead men, and many hundreds of others, ended up at **Boot Hill Cemetery** (daily; free), along the highway at the northwestern edge of town, where you can wander among 300 wooden grave markers inscribed with all manner of rhyming epitaphs. The Boot Hill Cemetery is the real thing, and the souvenirs in the large gift shop at the entrance are as wonderfully tacky as they come.

Though the OK Corral and Boot Hill are both fun, the best place to learn about Tombstone's real, as opposed to mythic, history is at the **Tombstone Courthouse State Historic Park**, at 3rd and Toughnut Streets. Built in 1882, this old courthouse building holds 12,000 square feet of artifacts documenting and describing the *real* Wild West.

Despite the huge numbers of people who descend upon

Tombstone every day, and the gauntlet of T-shirt and knick-knack shops catering to them, the town is still a very appealing place to visit. Eat breakfast, lunch, or dinner at **Nellie Cashman's** (520/457-2212), off Toughnut at 117 S. 5th Street, Tombstone's oldest eatery. Enjoy a cool drink at the truly historic **Big Nose Kate's Saloon,** right at the center of things on Allen Street, which was named for, owned, and run by Doc Holliday's brothel-keeper girlfriend. Places to stay are not extensive, nor very expensive: Try the centrally located **Tombstone Motel** ($50; 520/457-3478), on the main road at 502 E. Fremont Street.

Every summer, daily and every hour on the hour, historic gunfights are reenacted all around Tombstone, and during the third week in October, the whole town comes alive with a weekend of shoot-outs and parades during **Helldorado Days.**

Bisbee

A classic boom-and-bust mining town, **Bisbee** (pop. 6,090) is one of the most satisfying off-beat destinations in Arizona, combining scenic beauty, palpable history, and a good range of places to eat, drink, and enjoy yourself. Climbing up winding streets lined by 100-year-old structures—Victorian cottages, board shacks, and stately brick churches—Bisbee has attracted a diverse population of desert rats, bikers, working artists, and New Age apostles, all of whom mix amiably in the town's cafés and bars.

The heart of Bisbee lies north of old US-80 along Main Street, stretching west from the **Bisbee Mining and Historical Museum** (daily 10 AM–4 PM; $4), which displays dioramas, old photos, and sundry artifacts inside the old Phelps Dodge company headquarters. Main Street has many cafés, antique shops, art galleries, and restaurants.

For visitors, the main event in Bisbee is the **Queen Mine.** Put on a hard hat and a miner's lamp and take a train ride down into the mine shafts and tunnels, which were in operation until World War II. Hour-long **tours** (daily; $12; 520/432-2071) leave every 90 minutes from the Queen Mine building, just south of downtown along old US-80.

One of Arizona's most unforgettable sights, the massive **Lavender Open Pit** forms a gigantic polychrome crater along Hwy-80, just south of the Queen Mine. Named not for its color—which is more rusty red than purple—but for a mine superintendent, Harry Lavender, this was a true glory hole with ore deposits that provided the bulk of Bisbee's eight billion pounds of copper before being shut down in 1974. The Queen Mine also offers hour-long tours ($7) of this mile-wide, 1,000-foot-deep pit.

Bisbee Practicalities

At the center of Bisbee, the **Copper Queen Hotel** ($90 and up; 520/432-2216), looming over downtown along Howell Street, has been the best place to stay since it opened in 1902. Most of the rooms have been upgraded to include modern conveniences without losing their old-fashioned charm. Another nice place

Fly's Photos

Wild West photographer Camillus S. Fly, whose work forms one of the primary records of life in frontier Arizona, came to Arizona from Michigan in 1879 and opened a portrait studio in Tombstone, now restored as part of the OK Corral Historama complex. His iconic images, displayed in the small gallery, include some of the earliest photos taken of Chiricahua Apache warrior Geronimo, photographed soon after his 1886 surrender. Fly's studio also displays his images of Wyatt Earp, "Doc" Holliday, and many others. What Matthew Brady was to the Civil War, Camillus S. Fly was to Tombstone in its 1880s heyday.

to stay is the **Bisbee Inn** (520/432-5131), at 45 O.K. Street, overlooking Brewery Gulch and offering B&B rooms (shared bathrooms) from about $65 for two.

Bisbee offers what has to be the most unusual accommodations in Arizona: the **Shady Dell RV Park** (520/432-3567) at 1 Douglas Road. Located a mile east of downtown, behind the Chevron station at the Hwy-80/Hwy-92 traffic circle, the Shady Dell welcomes you to stay the night—or longer—in one of seven well-restored 1950s Airstream, Silver Streak, and Spartanette trailers, all filled with period furnishings. Rates are a reasonable $40–75 per night and include use of a VCR stocked with classic B-movies; you can also pitch a tent or pull up your own RV. And if the above is not enough to tempt you; the Shady Dell is also home to **Dot's Diner** (520/432-2046), which serves out-of-this world, Cajun-spiced food for breakfast and lunch Tuesday–Saturday.

Back in Bisbee proper, the Copper Queen Hotel has a good restaurant and popular bar, while the nicest place in town is the gourmet **Cafe Roka** (520/432-5153), at 35 Main Street. Brewery Gulch, which runs north from Main Street at the east side of downtown Bisbee, once held over 50 different saloons and gambling parlors; it's considerably quieter now, but still home to such fun haunts as the **Stock Exchange** bar, inside the old Bisbee Stock Exchange; and **St. Elmo's**, which has live music most weekend nights.

For further information, walking-tour maps, or details of special events, contact the Bisbee **visitors center** (520/432-5421), located at 31 Subway Street.

One of the more infamous events in Bisbee's busy history occurred in July 1917, when over 1,000 miners on strike for better pay and conditions were forcibly deported—literally railroaded out of town and dumped in the desert outside Columbus, New Mexico.

Every summer since 1917, Bisbee has hosted a 4th of July Soap Box Derby.

The Border: Douglas and Agua Prieta

Like Bisbee, the border town of **Douglas** (pop. 14,312) grew up on copper mining, which here lasted until fairly recently: The huge smokestack of the Phelps-Dodge smelter a mile west of town was in operation until 1987, processing ores from mines in Mexico. Now most of the economy revolves around the many *maquiladora* plants in its much larger Mexican neighbor, **Agua Prieta** (pop. 80,000), which feels surprisingly calm and quiet, considering its border-town location.

There's not a lot to see in either Douglas or Agua Prieta, though Douglas does boast one fabulous attraction: the landmark **Gadsden Hotel** ($35 and up; 520/364-4481), at 1046 G Avenue. Rebuilt in 1928 after a fire destroyed the 1907 original, the spacious gold-leafed lobby—one of the grandest public spaces in the state—has a pretty Tiffany-style stained-glass mural decorating its mezzanine. The small and basic rooms are bargain-priced, and there's also a good Mexican-American restaurant and a very popular bar, the Saddle and Spur, its walls decorated with over 200 cattle brands from area ranches.

Across the street from the Gadsden Hotel, a few doors down from the ornate facade of the Grand Theater, the **Grand Cafe** (520/364-2344), at 1119 G Street, is another great place to sample some very good and very cheap border-town Mexican food.

Cave Creek and Chiricahua National Monument

For the 50-odd miles between Douglas and the New Mexico state line, old US-80 cuts diagonally across the southeast corner of Arizona, a rugged country of mountains, canyons, and volcanic outcrops rising above sagebrush plains. There's not much to see along the highway, but to the northwest rise the enticing Pendregosa Mountains, whose forested peaks, now protected as part of the Coronado National Forest, long served as sanctuary to Chiricahua Apaches and sundry outlaws and wanted men.

While you can also reach them from the north off I-10, the best access to the mountains from the south is via the aptly named hamlet of **Portal**, west of old US-80 from the New Mexico border, where the **Portal Peak Lodge, Store, and Cafe** (520/558-2223) is a welcoming oasis, offering fresh food and comfortable rooms.

Above Portal rise the sheer cliffs of **Cave Creek Canyon**, which writer William Least Heat-Moon described in *Blue Highways* as "one of the strangest pieces of topography I've ever seen," its pale sandstone walls looking like a

Travel along the Mexican border is enlivened immeasurably by the many radio stations, varying from the country twang of Douglas's **KDAP 96.5 FM** to the many south-of-the-border stations, like "Radio Sonora" **101.3 FM**, that play a part-English, part-Spanish Tejano mélange typified by songs like "Mama, No Deje Que Sus Hijos Grow Up To Be Vaqueros."

Agua Prieta was the site of skirmishes between revolutionary **Pancho Villa** and the Mexican army.

Much of southeastern Arizona is still open range, so keep an eye out for livestock on the highway.

sun-bleached twin of Utah's Zion National Park. A narrow but passable (except in winter) 20-mile dirt road from Cave Creek climbs over the mountains' pine-covered, 7,600-foot-high crest, ending up in the west at the foot of intriguing **Chiricahua National Monument,** a veritable "Wonderland of Rocks" whose contorted shapes were formed out of soft volcanic stone by eons of erosion.

The **visitors center** (daily; 520/824-3560) near the monument entrance has information on hiking, camping, and wildlife-watching opportunities in the Chiricahuas. Be aware that there are no services—gas, food, or lodging—near the park.

NEW MEXICO

Between Arizona and Texas, the I-10 freeway crosses the part of New Mexico known as the Bootheel, for the way it steps down toward Old Mexico. Until the Gadsden Purchase of 1853, all this was part of Mexico, and the Hispanic influence still dominates the Anglo-American. The few towns here, like **Lordsburg** and **Deming,** were founded and remain primarily based on the railroad, and offer little for the passing traveler. However, at least one place is definitely worth a stop: the historic village of **Mesilla,** set around a dusty plaza just south of the region's one big city, **Las Cruces.**

Lordsburg and Shakespeare

Coming in from southeastern Arizona, old US-80 rejoins I-10 at a crossroads community aptly called **Road Forks** (near the tin-roofed ghost town of Steins), and 15 miles farther east the freeway swerves south to bypass the town of **Lordsburg** (pop. 3,379). Named not from any religious conviction but in honor of the Southern Pacific railroad engineer who plotted it in 1880, Lordsburg has one great attraction—a taste of New Mexican home cooking at the family-run **El Charro** (505/542-3400), open 24 hours at 209 Southern Pacific Boulevard, along the train tracks at the center of town.

Like something out of *The Andromeda Strain,* Lordsburg feels oddly abandoned, as if everyone has just packed up and left town. In fact, the other main draw is New Mexico's best-preserved ghost town, **Shakespeare,** three miles south of Lordsburg on a well-marked dirt road. Briefly home to some 3,000 silver miners during the early 1870s, Shakespeare was abandoned when the mines dried up, only to be reborn during another brief mining boom in the 1880s. By the 1930s it was turned into a ranch by the Hill family, whose descendants still live here, care for the buildings, and conduct irregularly scheduled guided **tours** (weekends 10 AM and 2 PM; $3; 505/542-9034) of the Grant House saloon, a former Butterfield Stagecoach station, and the Stratford Hotel, where Billy the Kid washed dishes as a young boy.

Across New Mexico, towns along the Interstate post road signs that total up their tourist services. Deming, for example, has 27 gas stations, 21 restaurants, and 13 motels.

After delving into Texas at El Paso, you'll enter New Mexico again near Carlsbad Caverns National Park.

Deming

Some 60 miles east of Lordsburg, halfway to Las Cruces, the dusty ranching and farming community of **Deming** (pop. 14,116) advertises itself as "Deming—Home of Pure Water and Fast Ducks." This motto, which is repeated on billboard after billboard along I-10, makes more sense than it may at first seem: Deming's water comes from the underground Mimbres River, and every year at the end of August the town hosts duck races (for living ones, not the rubber kind) with prizes of some $10,000 going to the winners.

All this is little more than a cheap ploy to get hapless (or bored stiff, or both) travelers to turn off tedious I-10 and visit their city. Fortunately, it's not a bad place, boasting the excellent **Deming-Luna-Mimbres Museum** (daily; donations; 505/546-2382), at 301 S. Silver Avenue, three blocks south of Pine Street (old US-80), Deming's main drag. Besides the usual range of old pottery, sparkling rocks, and pioneer artifacts, the museum displays an endearing collection of old toys, dolls, quilts, and dental equipment—well worth a quick look at the very least. Don't be worried by the big tank parked out front—the museum is housed in the old Armory building.

Rooms range from local places like the neon-signed **Butterfield Stage Motel** (505/544-0011) at 309 W. Pine Street to the national chains. The best place to camp is southeast of town in **Rockhound State Park** (505/546-6182), where, besides finding nice sites with hot

Silver City, an evocative old mining town high in the mountains 45 miles northeast of Lordsburg, was another early stomping ground of Wild West outlaw **Billy the Kid** and makes an excellent side trip between Lordsburg and Deming. In the wilderness north of Silver City, the **Gila Cliff Dwellings National Monument** (505/536-9461) is well worth setting aside a full day for.

Deming's own **KNFT 102.9 FM** plays Top 40 country hits of the past 25 years.

showers, you can collect up to 15 pounds of geodes, agates, or quartz crystals—something the rangers urge you to do.

Las Cruces

Along US-70 some 60 miles northeast of Las Cruces, **White Sands National Monument** protects over 60,000 acres of gleaming white gypsum dunes.

Mesilla was founded across the Rio Grande on the Mexican side of the border in 1848, after the agreement of the Mexican-American War gave everything to the north to the Americans. Six years later, Mesilla became (legally at least) American again, after the Gadsden Purchase bought the entire, 30,000-square-mile "Bootheel" region for $10 million.

Spreading along the eastern banks of the Rio Grande, at the foot of the angular Organ Mountains, **Las Cruces** (pop. 74,267) is the commercial center of a prosperous agricultural and recreational region. Named for a concentration of pioneer grave markers, Las Cruces was first settled by Spanish missionaries but is now a thoroughly modern, American-looking place, with all the motels you could want, and a youthful vitality made possible by the presence of the large New Mexico State University campus. One place worth searching out is **Nellie's** (505/524-9982), a Mexican restaurant famed for spicy salsas and delicious green-chile cheeseburgers, housed in a little brown box at 1226 W. Hadley Street, off Valley Boulevard on the northwest edge of downtown. For a unique place to stay, consider the **Inn of the Arts** ($75 and up; 505/526-3327), at 618 S. Alameda Boulevard, which offers B&B rooms in a 140-year-old Spanish Colonial home. One more rare treat: along I-10, the Las Cruces rest area is home to a giant-sized statue of the New Mexico state bird, the **Roadrunner**, crafted entirely from trash.

Mesilla

The best thing about Las Cruces is its nearness to a truly neat little place, the historic village of **Mesilla**, three miles southwest of Las Cruces via Hwy-28. Low-slung adobe buildings set around a shady central plaza include the landmark 1855 adobe church of San Albino, an old jail from which Billy the Kid escaped in 1880, a former Butterfield Stage station that's now home to the biker-friendly **El Patio Cantina,** and the very popular **La Posta** (505/524-3524) restaurant.

Across Hwy-28 from the plaza, the **Gadsden Museum** (daily; $3; 505/526-6293) traces local history from pre-conquest to current times. It's a private collection, pulled together over five generations of the same family; the folk art (dozens of hand-crafted *retablos* and *santos*) is wide-ranging and powerfully evocative of life in the harsh Southwest.

by Any Other Name

C..... ....osole, sopaipillas . . .
M.... ....quarely in the lower
lef...... .... how do you
kn..... ....ng traditional New Mexican
cooking, Southwestern cuisine, or the popular hybrid
known as Tex-Mex? Truth is, they're all hybrids,
launched nearly five centuries ago when the Spanish
brought European spices and domestic animals to
combine with indigenous ingredients. As Spanish
and Mexican settlers followed El Camino Real north
from Chihuahua to Santa Fe, culinary distinctions
grew out of regional variations in locally grown products along the way.

What's new is the categories: A generation ago,
folks just helped themselves to "Mexican food." Tex-
Mex, as its name implies, draws from both sides of
the international border, from grazing lands where
vaqueros roast meat over mesquite fires. In New
Mexico, it's the chiles that set the dishes apart—and
set your taste buds afire. When you order a local specialty, the server may ask, "Red or green?"—referring
to red or green chile. Red chiles are usually sun-dried,
while green chiles are fresh, but the flavor and spici-
ness varies depending on which of the 200 or more
different chile varieties are used to make it. Try a little
of each, and enjoy.

Hwy-28: Juan de Oñate Trail

Southeast from Las Cruces and Mesilla, our route dips
south across the Texas border to El Paso, then continues on
US-180 for some 60 miles east before re-entering New
Mexico at Carlsbad Caverns National Park. For the run to
El Paso you have your choice between I-10 or slower and
more scenic Hwy-28, the **Juan de Oñate Trail**, which
avoids the freeway and runs through the pecan groves,
pepper fields, and dusty small towns that spread along the
west bank of the Rio Grande.

This part of New Mexico is chili country, and there's no
better place to sample the great variety of spicy peppers than
at **Chope's** (505/233-9976), an unpretentious cinderblock café along Hwy-28
in La Mesa, roughly midway between Mesilla and El Paso. House specialty here
is *chiles rellenos*—whole chiles stuffed with cheese and deep-fried.

Juan de Oñate, for
whom Hwy-28 and
numerous other places in
the Southwest are
named, was a Spanish
conquistador and colonial
commander. His name is
infamous in Native
American circles because
of his role in ordering the
mutilation of 24 captive
warriors from Acoma,
whose right feet were cut
off in 1599.

TEXAS AND NEW MEXICO

Mileage-wise, the haul across Texas is the longest part of this coast-to-coast route, but as far as things to see, the state doesn't offer a very high quotient per gallon. In the far-western stretches near El Paso, to maximize scenic interest, follow the slower but significantly more attractive route along US-180 past the beautiful **Guadalupe Mountains,** and veer across a corner of New Mexico to see the remarkable **Carlsbad Caverns.**

From Carlsbad it's a straight shot across the painfully flat **Llano Estacado,** which stretches to both sides of the New Mexico/Texas border; this section of the route is one of the least action-packed in the country—there's almost nothing for miles on end, apart from oil derricks, cattle ranches, and cotton plantations. Only a few of the sporadic towns here have any historic claim or aesthetic interest; it's basically a long day's drive across the open plains. If you're in a hurry, you won't miss much by following the route of old US-80, alongside the I-20 freeway between El Paso and the Dallas/Fort Worth metropolitan area, through roughneck oil towns like **Odessa** and **Midland.**

In eastern Texas, the landscape gradually evolves into that of the Deep South, the dense pine woods doing their best to disguise the historic dependence on the oil industry—with profits far more apparent in the towers of Dallas than here at the often poverty-stricken source. Again, the Interstates offer a faster way across, and you can turn off where you want to visit the few sites of interest, like tiny **Kilgore,** home of the "World's Richest Acre."

El Paso

Part of the largest and fastest-growing international community in North America, **El Paso** (pop. 645,000) was originally settled because of its site at one of the safest crossings of the Rio Grande. It later grew into a vital way station on the transcontinental Butterfield Stage and Southern Pacific Railroad. As its name suggests, for most people El Paso is a place to pass through, but there are many

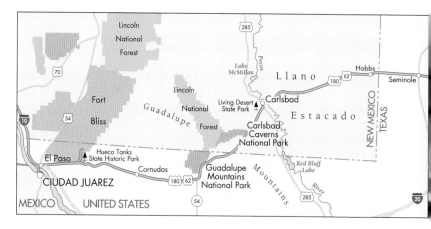

things here for visitors to enjoy.

One of the most interesting aspects of El Paso is the border itself, which for years followed the Rio Grande (known as the Río Bravo in Mexico), whose frequent changes in course caused innumerable problems for the two governments. Finally, in 1963, the river was run through a concrete channel so it could not change course. El Paso has at least three other unique claims to fame: It's the home of Tony Lama boots, which are available at significant discounts at four showrooms around town; the "World's Largest Harley-Davidson Dealership," Barnett's, is along I-10 at Lee Trevino Drive; and the UTEP (University of Texas El Paso) campus, along I-10 west of town, has the only buildings in North America designed to look like Tibetan monasteries. College basketball fans may also know that in 1966 UTEP (then called Texas Western) became the first all-black team to win the NCAA championships.

Hidden away amidst El Paso's horizontal sprawl are the oldest Spanish colonial missions that still stand in what is now the United States. This trio of churches—Ysleta, Socorro, and San Elizario—stand along the well-signed "Mission Trail," southeast of downtown between the Rio Grande and I-10.

Places to eat in and around El Paso tend, not surprisingly, to specialize in Tex-Mex food. One unique stop: breakfast or lunch at the **H&H Coffee Shop** (915/533-1144), just north of downtown at 701 E. Yandell Avenue, where you can enjoy delicious scrambled eggs and chorizo or chile relleno burritos while getting your car cleaned at the adjacent car wash. Another classic is **Forti's Mexican Elder** (915/772-0066), at 321 Chelsea Street east of downtown near the Paisano Avenue exit off I-10.

The **El Paso Diablos** (915/755-2000) play April–August at Cohen Stadium, north of I-10 via the US-54 "Patriot Freeway." Games are broadcast on **KHEY 1380 AM**.

El Paso's hard-to-find **Concordia Cemetery** (it's just northwest of the I-10/US-54 junction) is the final resting place of **John Wesley Hardin**, the "Fastest Gun in the West" before he got killed in 1895.

For the first 35 miles east of El Paso, US-180 runs along the southern edge of gigantic **Fort Bliss**, which stretches north for 50 miles into New Mexico and is home to about 20,000 U.S. troops.

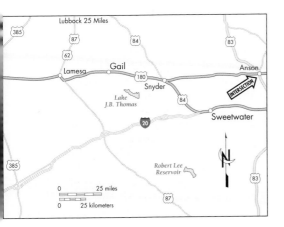

Q: Why do they call it Texas?
A: Because it "Texas" so long to drive across.

The 70-mph section of US-180 east of El Paso is also signed as "Camino Buena Suerte," the "**Good Luck Highway.**"

From 1859 to 1861, the legendary **Butterfield Overland Mail** ran between St. Louis and San Francisco by way of El Paso, carrying mail and passengers across the country in 24 days. Running twice a week in both directions, the Butterfield line had some 140 relay stations along the route, each supplied with a Concord stagecoach and a fresh team of horses.

El Paso's finest place to stay is the grand old **Camino Real Paso del Norte Hotel** ($90 and up; 915/534-3000), at 101 S. El Paso Street, one of the classiest hotels anywhere, with a beautiful bar off the lobby. All the usual mid-range chains are here too: There's a nice old-fashioned **Travelodge** ($40 and up; 915/772-4231), at 6400 Montana Avenue; plus a handy HI-approved youth hostel at the historic **Gardner Hotel** (915/532-3661), downtown at 311 E. Franklin Street.

For maps or more information on El Paso or neighboring Juárez, Mexico, contact the **visitors bureau** (915/534-0696 or 800/351-6024), located downtown at 1 Civic Center Plaza.

Hueco Tanks State Historic Park

In the 100 miles of arid West Texas desert between El Paso and the Guadalupe Mountains, don't miss tiny **Hueco Tanks State Historic Park** (daily 8 AM–dusk; $2; 915/857-1135). Located on the eastern fringes of sprawling Fort Bliss, some 25 miles east of El Paso, then eight miles north on Hwy-2775, the 850-acre park was established to preserve the approximately 3,000 pictographs painted on the syenite basalt boulders. The "tanks" of the title are naturally formed rock basins, which collect rainwater and have made the site a natural stop for passing travelers, from prehistoric natives to the Butterfield stagecoach, which stopped here in the 1850s. Unfortunately, sometimes the "historic" graffiti is overwhelmed by more contemporary spray-paint versions, but the site is pleasant enough, with a popular campground and excellent opportunities for bird-watching and rock climbing.

Some 35 miles east of the Hueco Tanks turnoff, the tiny highway town of **Cornudas** has a nice café—"Home of the World Famous Cornudas Burger"—and a row of false-fronted Wild West buildings.

Guadalupe Mountains National Park

One of the few un-hyped wonders of Texas, **Guadalupe Mountains National Park** covers the rugged peaks that rise along the New Mexico border, 110 miles east of El Paso. Formed as part of the same Capitan Reef of 250 million-year-old limestone as the great caverns of Carlsbad, the Guadalupe Mountains, a cool contrast to the surrounding desert, rise in sheer faces about 2,000 feet above the desert floor and offer the chance to experience many different and contrasting ecosystems side by side, within easy reach of the highway.

Even if you're not prepared to do any serious hiking—which is really the best way to experience the grandeur of the park or to see signs of the abundant wildlife (including mountain lions)—the quickest way

Detour: Ciudad Juárez

Largest by far of the Mexican border cities, **Ciudad Juárez** (pop. 1.2 million, and growing fast) is a compelling, disturbing, exciting, and unforgettable place to visit. Though the city sprawls through miles and miles of some of the worst pollution and direst poverty in Mexico, the downtown areas offer a quick taste of the country, and a half-hour walk can take you very far away from the United States. From the El Paso side, don't drive; park and walk down Stanton Street from downtown and cross the bridge on foot. This crossing drops you at the head of Avenida Juárez, the main drag, lined by cantinas and nightclubs and stalls and stores selling everything from mass-produced "crafts" to knock-off designer goods and Cuban cigars. (The latter items will be confiscated if you try to bring them back into the United States.)

About a half mile south of the border, at the junction with Avenida 16 de Septiembre, Avenida Juárez brings you to the heart of Juárez, where the very good historical museum, housed in the old customs building, and a large, often-packed cathedral give glimpses into the city's history and culture. Among the many restaurants and bars along Avenida Juárez, a couple to check out are the **Kentucky Club**, 629 Avenida Juárez, a 1930s-looking bar that could be used as a set for some Raymond Chandler underworld adventure. Legend has it that Marilyn Monroe got drunk here, celebrating her Juárez divorce from playwright Arthur Miller. Next door, **Martino's** is a very popular Mexican restaurant. Be warned, however, that many Juárez bars double as brothels—these tend to have giveaway names like "The Pink Lady."

Food and drink aside, the best thing about a trip south is the chance to enjoy some **Lucha Libre**—professional wrestling—Mexican style. Dramatic and impassioned bouts (US$5 for a ringside seat) are held Sunday nights in the large municipal auditorium near the cathedral.

to get a feel for the Guadalupes is to walk the half-mile **nature trail** that runs between the main **visitors center** (daily; free; 915/828-3251) and the remains of a Butterfield stagecoach station, passing well-signed specimens of all the major desert flora. If you have more time, head to **McKittrick Canyon**, off US-62/180 in the northeast corner of the park. From the **ranger station** at the end of the road, a well-marked, well-maintained, and generally flat 3.5-mile trail winds along a stream, through a green landscape that changes gradually from the cactus of the Chihuahuan Desert to the oaks, walnuts, and maples of the inner canyon. Rated by many as the most beautiful spot in Texas, it's best in spring, when the

Along with New Mexico, El Paso and the Guadalupe Mountains area are in the Mountain time zone. The rest of Texas is on Central time.

As part of a federal program known as **WIPP—the Waste Isolation Pilot Plant—** the underground potash mines east of Carlsbad have been adapted into a contentious disposal site for the nation's nuclear waste.

desert wildflowers bloom, or in autumn, when the hardwoods turn color.

If you're feeling fit, climb **Guadalupe Peak,** at 8,749 feet the highest point in Texas, via a very steep three-mile trail from the main visitors center. Be aware that the change in elevation makes the mountains subject to serious weather, with great booming thunderstorms in late summer.

Camping is available on a first-come, first-served basis at Pine Springs Campground near the main visitors center, and at numerous sites in the backcountry.

Carlsbad Caverns National Park

Carved out of the solid limestone of Capitan Reef by eons of dripping water, the Carlsbad Caverns contain over 30 miles of underground caves, some over 1,000 feet across. A mile-long trail drops steeply from the large visitors center; or you can board an elevator and ride 750 feet straight down to the "Big Room," where the floor area totals more than eight acres. After wandering among the countless stalactites, stalagmites, and other formations, you can chow down on cheeseburgers at a classic 1950s-style cafeteria. Everyone has to ride the elevator back to the surface. There are also a number of longer guided **tours** available ($7–20; 800/967-2283), if you want to explore some of the more delicate features of the caverns, or clamber around through more-confined reaches of the caves.

The trail down to the Big Room closes early in the afternoon (usually around 3 PM) so that visitors don't interrupt the increasingly popular spectacle of the **"Bat Flight,"** in which hundreds of thousands of Mexican freetail bats swirl out of the caverns at sunset. Every evening (usually around 7 PM, except in winter when the bats have migrated to Mexico), rangers give a brief free talk about bats—proselytizing about how really great and harmless they are—while waiting for them to set off into the night.

The nearest places to stay and eat are in **Whites City** (505/785-2291 or 800/228-3767), a historic complex of motels, restaurants, pinball arcades, and

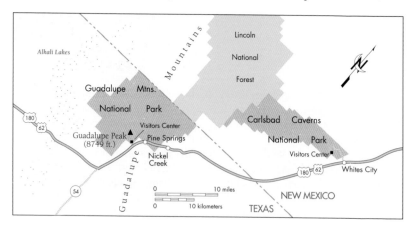

Roswell: UFO Central

Seventy-five miles north of Carlsbad, the New Mexico ranching town of Roswell (pop. 45,293) has become a catch-word for flying saucers, UFOs, extraterrestrials, and a complicated U.S. government cover-up of all the above. The cover-up is the one thing that's pretty much a given, since the Air Force has gone so far as to deny officially that anything ever happened in Roswell—which is equivalent to a confession, in the minds of UFO believers. Everything else about Roswell is, so to speak, up in the air.

The Roswell story goes something like this: In 1947, at the start of Cold War hysteria, something strange and metallic crashed into a field outside town, and the Army Air Corps (teams of tight-lipped operatives wearing special suits and dark glasses, no doubt) came and recovered it. Reports to the effect that a flying saucer had landed in Roswell appeared in the local paper, and quickly spread around the globe, only to be denied by the government, which claimed the "flying saucers" were actually weather balloons. Thirty-one years later, a retired military intelligence officer from the Roswell base sold a story to the National Enquirer, repeating details of the

1947 "flying saucer" crash, and telling of his subsequent capture of extraterrestrial beings. This in turn spawned countless other stories, books, and videos, and spurred the growth of a battery of tourist attractions and souvenir stores in and around Roswell.

The best first stop is the **International UFO Museum and Research Center** (free; 505/625-9495), which fills an old movie theater in downtown Roswell at 114 N. Main Street. There are plenty of motels, and many good places to eat like the friendly **Nuthin' Fancy Café** (505/623-4098), where President George W. Bush raved about the ribs.

souvenir shops along Hwy-180 at the turnoff to the park. Amidst all the tourist clutter of Whites City is the Million Dollar Museum ($3), a bizarre but captivating collection of old typewriters, Texas Longhorns, and the mummified remains of what's labeled an "Alien Baby". (Roswell is just down the road, remember.)

Carlsbad

Twenty miles northeast of the Carlsbad Caverns, the town of **Carlsbad** (pop. 25,000) makes its living from the 750,000 tourists who visit the caves every year. Lining Canal Street (aka US-180, the "National Parks Highway"), the main road through Carlsbad, you'll find most national motel chains and funkier local counterparts like the **Stagecoach Inn** ($35–45; 505/887-1148) at 1819 S.

Lubbock: Panhandle Music Mecca

The largest city in northwest Texas, Lubbock (pop. 199,564) is a busy and unattractive agricultural center, best known for having given the world Buddy Holly, whose songs ("Peggy Sue," "That'll Be The Day," "Rave On") paved the way for rock 'n' roll. Music fans make the trip downtown to pay homage at the statue of Buddy at the corner of 8th Street and Avenue Q, and learn about his life in the **Texas Musicians Hall of Fame** (Tues.–Sat. 10 AM–5 PM; $5; 806/767-2686), which also details the lives and times of other Lubbock boys and girls made good, including Roy Orbison, Waylon Jennings, Tanya Tucker, and Joe Ely. Buddy Holly, who died in a 1959 plane crash at age 22, is buried near the entrance of Lubbock Cemetery, at the east end of 31st Street.

Canal Street. There's also one very good Mexican restaurant, the **Casa de Cortez** (505/885-4747), at 506 S. Canal Street, a plain brown-brick building where locals come for heaping helpings of *frijoles refritos* and *chiles rellenos;* no booze, no credit cards, but great fresh *sopapillas.*

Apart from the caverns, the one other thing to see in the Carlsbad area is the **Living Desert State Park** (daily; $5; 505/887-5516), four miles northwest off US-285, which shows off the plant and animal life of the arid Chihuahuan Desert region. Foxes, wolves, hawks, and eagles are kept in re-creations of their natural environments, and can be seen along a 1.5-mile nature trail.

US-180: The Llano Estacado

From Carlsbad, US-180 crosses the Pecos River, then snakes across the barren **Llano Estacado,** the "Staked Plain," which covers most of eastern New Mexico and the Texas Panhandle. Supposedly named by early explorers who drove wooden stakes into the ground to mark their way, the Llano Estacado area is pretty much the same on both sides of the border—flat, dry, and mostly devoid of settlement. For eastbound travelers, this is the place where oil first becomes noticeably important—pumpjacks can be seen pumping away from here all the way to Alabama.

This is also cowboy country, thanks to the extensive pastures irrigated by water pumped up from aquifers deep underground. For travelers, however, the dominant image is of land stretching out far and wide: mile after mile after mile of endless flat cotton fields, interrupted every now and then by brilliant green alfalfa fields and a few surprisingly large towns like **Hobbs,** New Mexico (pop. 29,115), right on the border, its main street lined by various "Drilling Supply" companies, huge piles of old pipe, and signs for the Black Gold Casino, which opened in 2004.

The Texas part of the drive is dotted with towns like **Seminole** (pop. 6,342) and **Gail**, which has the friendly Caprock Cafe and hosts an annual **Fiddler's Festival.** Midway in between, **Lamesa** (pop. 10,809; la-MEE-sa) has all the All-American makings of a location from the high-school-football movie *Friday Night Lights:* sports-mad families, an intact old Dairy Queen Drive-in, smokey BBQ at **K-Bob's Steakhouse,** and open-air movies at the 60-year-old **Sky Vue Drive In,** said to be the site of Buddy Holly's first show outside his native Lubbock. Each of these small towns seems like a bustling hive of activity after the miles of open, red-earth prairie in between them.

Gail

Midway between Lamesa and Snyder, the tiny town of **Gail** (pop. 189)—which the official *Texas State Travel Guide* describes as a "cow town without bank, theater, railroad, hotel, doctor, or lawyer"—was the site of violent feuds during the land rush of 1902, the history of which is recounted in the tiny **Borden County Museum** (Thurs.–Sun. noon–4 PM; $1). The town and the county are named in memory of pioneer surveyor and newspaper editor **Gail Borden,** who is perhaps best known as the inventor of condensed milk and founder of Borden Foods.

At the town of Anson, US-180 crosses US-83, **The Road to Nowhere.** Anson is described on page 198. The region's biggest city, Abilene, is at the junction of US-83 and the I-20 freeway. It's covered on page 199.

Albany

Albany, one of the more interesting towns in this part of Texas, started as a stagecoach stop on the Butterfield Overland Mail in 1854. It's still a tiny place but it has a lively feel, the oldest County Courthouse in the state, and, more surprisingly, a small but intriguing **art museum** (closed Mon.; free; 325/762-2269) in the Old City Jail at 211 S. 2nd Street. A big surprise in the middle of the ranchlands, the museum contains an outstanding permanent collection of art by Modigliani, Picasso, and others, and also displays Chinese ceramics from the Tang and Ming Dynasties.

I-20: Sweetwater and Cisco

If you've decided to take the high-speed route along I-20, midway across Texas you'll pass **Sweetwater,** where, every March during the **Rattlesnake Round-Up,**

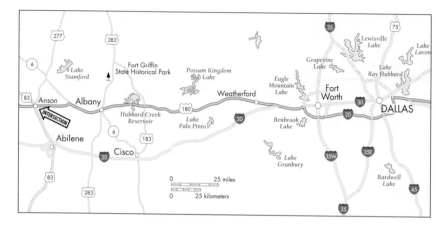

Another highlight of the drive west of Dallas is **Snyder** (pop. 12,195), where a life-sized statue of an albino buffalo stands on the courthouse square.

townspeople get together and collect hundreds of rattlers from the surrounding ranch lands, winning prizes for the biggest, shortest, and most snakes handed in. The town, 25 miles west of Abilene, also has shops selling all manner of rattlesnake-related souvenirs, and any time of year, Sweetwater—which was first settled in the 1850s and now earns its livelihood mining gypsum for use in wallboard—is worth a stop for some of the best fried chicken in West Texas, at **Allen's Family-Style Meals** (325/235-2060), at 1301 E. Broadway, along old US-80.

The I-20 town of **Cisco**, 45 miles east of Abilene, is where **Conrad Hilton** bought and ran his first hotel, the Mobley, in 1919; the hotel is now the chamber of commerce office, and a couple of rooms have been restored to their circa-1919 appearance.

East of Cisco, the town of **Eastland** has two world-class oddities. The middle entrance to the county courthouse displays the embalmed body of "Old Rip" the Horny Toad, who survived 29 years embedded in the cornerstone of the old courthouse before supposedly being discovered, alive, when the building was being torn down. A few blocks away at 411 W. Main Street, the post office contains a huge stamp-themed mural made entirely of 11,217 postage stamps, created over a seven-year period by former postmistress Marene Johnson. (A postcard of the mural is available.)

The salt deposits under **Grand Saline**, 60 miles east of Dallas, are estimated to be over 16,000 feet thick and nearly 10,000 feet across, enough to supply the world's needs for the next 20,000 years.

Old US-80 Across Dallas/Fort Worth

Coming from the west, US-80/180 makes one last small-town stop in **Weatherford**, where an opulent old courthouse anchors a lively town square. Old US-80 enters Fort Worth on Camp Bowie Boulevard (US-377), then bee-lines by The Ballpark in Arlington before reaching Dallas. The old road between Fort Worth and Dallas, now signed as Hwy-180, approaches downtown Dallas on Commerce Street and heads down Main Street before leaving town past the Cotton Bowl.

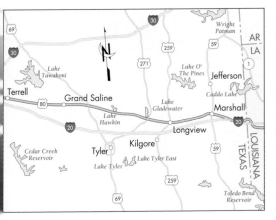

Kilgore: Oil!

The pine-covered, red-earth hills of East Texas are covered with creaking old pumpjacks, still sucking up the crude oil that has kept the region economically afloat since the 1930s. The oil business here has gone through numerous booms and busts since it gushed into existence in December 1930 at a well outside **Kilgore** (pop. 11,301), on the south side of I-20, ten miles southwest of Longview via US-259. This comparatively small and quiet oil town has street lamps disguised as oil rigs and a set of 100-foot-tall derricks standing along the railroad tracks in memory of the "**World's Richest Acre**," a plot of downtown land that produced over 2.5 million barrels of oil through the 1960s. The site was so productive and so valuable that one of the wells was drilled through the terrazzo floor of a local bank, and over a thousand derricks once loomed over the downtown area.

The history of the local petroleum industry is recounted in entertaining detail at the **East Texas Oil Museum** (closed Mon.; $5; 903/983-8295) on the campus of Kilgore College, on Ross Street off US-259. The museum includes displays of drilling equipment and old gas stations, plus a simulated "elevator ride" a mile deep into the earth to show off the oil-bearing geology. Also on the Kilgore College campus is a small free museum devoted to the **Kilgore Rangerettes,** a trained precision drill and dance team that performs at college and professional football games.

Kilgore is decidedly not a typical tourist destination, but it does have a number of handsome if timeworn buildings, and a couple of good food stops, such as **Lupe's** (903/983-1457), serving up traditional Tex-Mex food at 2607 N. US-259, north of downtown. Back on US-80, another good place to eat is Creole-spiced **Johnny Cace's Seafood** (903/753-7691), east of downtown Longview at 1501 E. Marshall Road.

Marshall and Jefferson

North of I-20 some 25 miles west of the Louisiana state line, **Marshall** (pop. 23,935) is one of the older, and once among the wealthiest, towns in Texas. Now a fairly quiet place, in its early years Marshall was the commercial capital of the East Texas cotton country, and during the Civil War two local residences served as the Confederate capital—of Missouri. This anomaly, along with general regional history, is chronicled in

South of I-20, the town of **Tyler** grows thousands and thousands of roses, including the famous yellow ones, the "National Rose of Texas."

Northwest of Fort Worth, 22 miles south of Wichita Falls, writer Larry McMurtry has been turning his hometown of **Archer City** (pop. 1,748) into the world's largest used-book store. Housed in a number of downtown buildings, many of which are featured in McMurtry's *The Last Picture Show* and other works, his **Booked Up** bookstore (940/574-2511) has over 300,000 volumes, mostly rare and out-of-print editions.

Dallas and Fort Worth

Like warring branches of an extended family, Dallas and Fort Worth are inseparable archrivals. Both towns lay fair claim to being capitals of their respective industries: Fort Worth (pop. 535,000) calls itself "Cowtown" but has a surprisingly sophisticated range of cultural centers, and feels like an altogether more "Texan" place; it was founded during the heyday of the Chisholm Trail and still retains much of its Wild West past. Meanwhile Dallas (pop. 1,200,000), which boomed after the discovery of oil in east Texas during the 1930s, plays the role of nouveau riche to the nth degree, home to Neiman Marcus and TV's eponymous soap opera.

In terms of things to see and do, Fort Worth holds the winning hand. The wonderful **Kimbell Art Museum** (closed Mon.; free; 817/332-8451), 3333 Camp Bowie Boulevard, is one of the most perfectly beautiful modern buildings on the planet, designed as a series of vaulted galleries by Louis Kahn. This small museum, which has an impressive collection of pre-Columbian art and some notable Post-Impressionist paintings, stands at the heart of the Fort Worth Cultural District. Adjacent to the Kimbell is another wonderful work of architecture, the Tadao Ando-designed **Modern Art Museum**, and across the street, the **Amon Carter Museum** displays the country's finest collection of Wild West and other American art.

Two miles north of downtown Fort Worth, head to the Stockyards, on Main and Exchange Streets. For a taste of how Texas used to be, spend some time wandering these two short blocks of turn-of-the-20th-century buildings, stretching west from the still-busy Fort Worth Stockyards, and housing some of the city's most popular places to eat, drink, and be merry; after dark, check out **Billy Bob's Texas**, the "World's Largest Honky-Tonk," ($1–35; 817/624-7117).

In Dallas, sightseers head to the **Texas School Book Depository** (daily; $10; 214/747-6660)—"The Sixth Floor"—at 411 Elm Street. Besides the gruesome novelty value of looking out from the very same place where Lee Harvey Oswald shot (or didn't shoot . . .) President John F. Kennedy on November 22, 1963, this extensive museum describes the historical context and discusses the myriad conspiracy theories.

In between Dallas and Fort Worth, off I-30 at the Ballpark Way exit in Arlington, the **Texas Rangers** (817/273-5100) play at Ameriquest Field. Games are broadcast on newstalk **KRLD 1080 AM**.

Practicalities

Linked (or is it divided?) by a trio of fast freeways (I-20, I-30, and Hwy-183), Dallas and Fort Worth lie some 25 miles apart across the plains of northeast Texas. Each city is circled by its own ring road, and two north–south freeways (I-35W through Fort Worth and I-35E through downtown Dallas) complete the high-speed network.

Food in Fort Worth, not surprisingly, tends to the beefy. **Cattlemen's Steak House** (817/624-3945), at 2458 N. Main Street, has steaks of all cuts and sizes, plus BBQ and some seafood. **Joe T. Garcia's** (817/626-4356), at 2201 N. Commerce Street, may or may not be the World's Biggest Tex-Mex restaurant, but it sure can feel like it. Finally, the very friendly **Paris Coffee Shop** (817/335-2041), at 704 W. Magnolia, has great fried chicken and delicious fresh fruit pies.

In Dallas, east of the I-35E Central Expressway from downtown, the café **Green Room** (214/748-7666), at 2715 Elm Street, is a rock 'n' roller's dream of a restaurant serving rooftop pizzas in the heart of "Deep Ellum," a scruffy-looking, post-industrial district of boutiques, bars, restaurants, and nightclubs.

For a place to stay in Fort Worth, the **Ramada Hotel** ($90 and up; 817/335-7000 or 800/272-6232), at 1701 Commerce Street, is centrally located, just across from the convention center and the magical Fort Worth Water Gardens. Bonnie and Clyde (both of whom are buried in Dallas) stayed in the **Stockyards Hotel** ($140 and up; 817/625-6427), at 109 E. Exchange Avenue, a turn-of-the-20th-century hotel that has been restored and redecorated according to various themes, including the aforementioned bank robbers; the downstairs bar has saddles instead of bar stools.

In Dallas, the **Adolphus Hotel** ($150 and up; 214/742-8200), 1321 Commerce Street, is a historic four-star downtown hotel, built in 1912 by beer magnate Adolphus Busch.

For maps and more extensive information, contact the **Dallas visitors bureau** (214/746-6679), 100 S. Houston Street. **Fort Worth** has three visitors centers, including one in the Stockyards at 130 E. Exchange Avenue (817/624-4741).

the **Harrison County Historical Society Museum** (Tues.–Sat. only; $2), housed in the supremely ornate, yellow brick courthouse on the town square.

If you have the time and inclination to get a more palpable sense of the varied culture and history of East Texas, take US-59 15 miles north of Marshall to **Jefferson** (pop. 2,024), an almost perfectly preserved bayou town that looks much as it did during the 1870s when, with a population of nearly 30,000, it was the busiest inland port west of the Mississippi. Among the most prominent of the hundreds of historic structures here is the 1858 **Excelsior House,** 211 W. Austin Street; across the street, you can tour Jay Gould's private railroad car, the Atalanta, or simply explore the many good antique shops, cafés, and restaurants. For more information, contact the Jefferson **tourist office** (903/665-2672) at 118 N. Vale Street.

Back on the main road, just before the Louisiana border, the stretch of old US-80that runs parallel to I-20 is home to the ever-welcoming **New Waskom Café** (903/687-4028), open for breakfast and lunch since the 1920s.

North of Shreveport on Hwy-1, **Oil City** has one of the region's better history museums, housed inside the old railroad depot and displaying a wonderful collection of old postcards.

LOUISIANA

Northern Louisiana, which covers some 200 miles of forested, rolling hills between Texas and Mississippi, is a far cry from the Cajun fun of the southern half of the state. A Baptist-dominated "Bible Belt" heartland, it's

also a very diverse place, part heavily industrial, part poor rural backwater, with a mix of people and products that encapsulates its transitional position between the agricultural Deep South and the petrochemical plants of Texas.

The main city here is the oil town of **Shreveport,** which has recently become a prime place for gamblers, with flashy casinos lining the riverfront. However, you'll mostly find small towns ranging from **Gibsland** (where Bonnie and Clyde met their doom) to the college town of **Ruston** (home to Louisiana Tech and Grambling Universities).

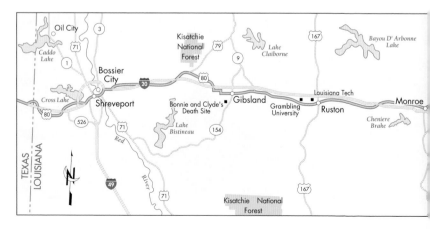

Shreveport and Bossier City

A King Cotton town that thrived in the antebellum years and survived the war physically, though not economically, unscathed, **Shreveport** (pop. 200,145) is now a busy industrial city rising on the west bank of the Red River. Along with its ugly stepbrother, **Bossier City** (BO-zyur) across the river, Shreveport is a center of the Louisiana oil business—which is small only when compared to that of Texas, and is still hugely important. Also, the cities emerged in recent years as two of the hot spots of Louisiana's nascent gambling industry, with a line of major resort-casinos—including the lively **Horseshoe,** a four-story faux riverboat floating in a shallow pond on the Bossier City side—along the riverfront attracting people from all over the tri-state "Ark-La-Tex" region.

Downtown Shreveport is the usual mix of turn-of-the-20th-century brick buildings and boarded-up shopfronts, loomed over by a solitary 10-story glass office tower, with a handful of interesting structures surviving near the riverfront; walking-tour maps of the area are available from the **visitors center** (318/222-9391 or 800/551-8682), a block west of the river at 629 Spring Street. One place car culture fans will want to check out is the **Ark-La-Tex Car Museum** (daily; $6; 318/222-0227), housed in a well-preserved 1920s Dodge Bros. car dealership at 601 Spring Street, which has a futuristic 1948 Tucker on display alongside old fire engines.

The nicest part of town is the leafy Highland district, stretching south from the end of Market Street, south of I-20 between the river and the new I-49 freeway. This is where you'll find the grand old houses of the landed gentry, many of which look like they belong in *Gone With The Wind,* despite the fact

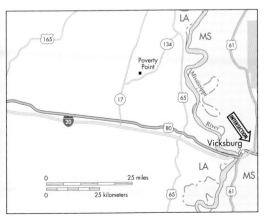

that almost all of them date from the 20th century. The Highland district also holds one of Shreveport's better places to eat: **Don's Seafood House** (318/865-4291), at 3100 Highland Avenue, serving moderately priced Cajun-spiced specialties. All the usual hotel and motel chains line I-20.

Shreveport is named in honor of **Capt. Henry Shreve,** who in the 1830s cleared the Red River of a 165-mile-long logjam that had blocked navigation. He then "bought" the land from native Caddo Indians.

Shreveport and Bossier City have long hosted the **Louisiana Hayride,** a country-western radio program on which Hank Williams and Elvis Presley both started their careers. The same sort of music can still be heard on **KWKH 94.5 FM,** your best bet for late-night bluegrass in northwest Louisiana.

The independent **Shreveport Sports** (318/636-5555) play Central League baseball at the Louisiana State Fairgrounds.

Gibsland: Bonnie and Clyde

East of Shreveport, the old US-80 highway winds through dozens of somnolent little towns, following the rolling land while crisscrossing back and forth under the high-speed I-20 freeway. After passing the pawn shops and girlie bars outside Barksdale Air Force Base, the route parallels railroad tracks along the remains of a historic log turnpike, built in the 1870s to provide all-weather passage across the muddy bogs and bayous.

Apart from the usual barrage of roadside businesses, there's not a lot to stop for until you reach the tiny town of **Gibsland** (pop. 1,119), just south of I-20, 45 miles east of Shreveport. This pleasantly un-

remarkable little hamlet has one unique claim to fame: It was here, in 1934, that the notorious Depression-era gangsters Clyde Barrow and Bonnie Parker (aka **Bonnie and Clyde**) were ambushed and killed. A small, town-run museum tells their story, and sells gruesome postcards of their bullet-riddled bodies, while every May locals dress up and stage gun battles and car chases—more for cops-and-robbers fun than out of any real dedication to historical accuracy.

A battered stone marker, eight miles south of Gibsland along Hwy-154, stands on the site where the desperate duo—who in "real life" were nasty, cold-blooded murderers, nothing like the romantic pair played by Warren Beatty and Faye Dunaway in the Hollywood movie— were shot by state troopers.

Clyde Barrow

Ruston and Monroe

Roughly halfway across the state, **Ruston** (pop. 20,546) calls itself the "Peach Capital" but is best known for its two major colleges: Louisiana Tech (where local boy Terry Bradshaw played his college football), and smaller Grambling University, one of the nation's top African-American schools, three miles west of town, just south of I-20.

One of the oldest, largest, and most significant concentrations of archaeological remains in North America has been protected as **Poverty Point National Monument** ($2; 318/926-5492), 18 miles north of I-20 off Hwy-17 in Epps, Louisiana. These 3,000-year-old burial mounds are jointly managed by federal and state authorities.

Considering that it is one of the largest towns in northern Louisiana, **Monroe** (pop. 53,107) feels strangely abandoned, even though the downtown area has a number of classic commercial buildings dating from the period between the two World Wars, and Victorian-era warehouses and hundreds of ancient-looking "shotgun" shacks line the railroad tracks and US-80.

Apart from its photogenic architecture and fading roadside signs, Monroe doesn't really offer much reason to stop, though the gorgeous greenery of the **Louisiana Purchase Gardens and Zoo** (daily; $4; 318/329-2400), south of I-20 off US-165, makes it a great place to stretch your legs (or take a steam-train or boat ride) among the moss-draped oaks and cypress trees.

East of Monroe, it's an hour's drive across the bayous before you reach the fascinating city of Vicksburg, across the Mississippi River.

MISSISSIPPI

US-80, which for much of the way has been replaced by the I-20 freeway, cuts across the middle of Mississippi, passing through its three largest cities—**Meridian, Jackson,** and **Vicksburg**—whose small sizes show how rural and diffuse the state still is. Only Jackson, the capital and by far the biggest city in the state, is anything like an urban center, with a couple of "skyscrapers" and nearly 200,000 people. Mostly what you see along this stretch is small farms and Civil War battlefields, the most extensive and important of which rises above the Mississippi River in Vicksburg.

The Mississippi River town of Vicksburg marks the junction with our **Great River Road** route, which is described on pages 214–285. Vicksburg's antebellum homes, Civil War sites, and great food are all covered in full detail on pages 268–271.

Clinton and the Natchez Trace

The one-time Choctaw Indian agency of **Clinton,** north of I-20 10 miles west of Jackson, was renamed in 1828 in honor of New York Gov. DeWitt Clinton, who oversaw construction of the Erie Canal. Now a small cotton-growing and shipping center, with a few blocks of "olde towne" around the Baptist-run Mississippi College along Leake and Jefferson Streets, in its early years Clinton sat on the notorious Natchez Trace, now followed by the blissfully pleasant **Natchez Trace Parkway,** which runs southwest to Port Gibson (see page 271) and northeast all the way to Nashville.

Though it survived the Civil War relatively unscathed, Clinton later saw some of the worst Reconstruction-era race riots in the state, with an estimated 50 unarmed blacks killed during a single rampage in 1875. Clinton also suffered through the rapid rise and painful fallout of the MCI/WorldCom scandal. The multinational telecom company had its world headquarters here, and CEO Bernie Ebbers, convicted in 2005 of overseeing a multibillion-dollar fraud, was a Mississippi College graduate.

Jackson

Spreading west from the banks of the Pearl River, **Jackson** (pop. 185,000) was established as state capital in 1822. Named for Andrew Jackson, hero of the Battle of New Orleans during the War of

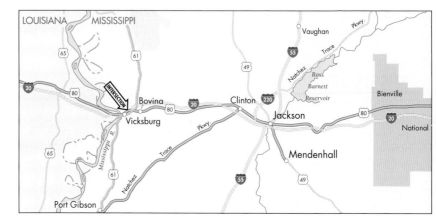

1812 and later president of the United States, it was destroyed during the Civil War but is now Mississippi's political and commercial heart and its biggest city—though you wouldn't know it by the somnolent look of the place.

The very attractive Greek Revival **Old State Capitol,** built in 1838 and used until 1903, rises at the center of town at State and Capitol Streets, and is open for free self-guided **tours** of the building and the well-presented historical exhibits that fill it. Substantial floor space is given over to the 20th century, including a thoughtful (and thought-provoking) examination of the civil rights movement. The few other fine old antebellum buildings—under a dozen altogether—that survive around Jackson were used by Union forces and were thus spared destruction. These include the art-filled **Governor's Mansion** (Mon.–Fri. 9:30–11 AM; free), a short walk east of the old capitol at 300 E. Capitol Street; and **The Oaks** (closed Sun.; $3), at 823 N. Jefferson Street, in which General Sherman lived. Restored to prewar splendor, The Oaks is furnished with period antiques and, surprisingly for the South, a sofa from Abraham Lincoln's law office.

On the south side of downtown Jackson, the **Mississippi Museum of Art** (daily; $5; 601/960-1515) at 401 E. Pascagoula Street has gained international fame by hosting "blockbuster" touring shows like the "Treasures of Versailles" exhibition in 1998. Year-round, the spacious modern galleries also display works by local and international painters and sculptors.

The tiny town of **Vaughn,** 30 miles north of Jackson via the I-55 freeway, was the site of the crash that killed legendary train engineer **Luther "Casey" Jones.** A small museum, a mile east of I-55 exit 133, has exhibits on Casey and the history of railroading in the South.

Away from downtown, the main attraction is the **Mississippi Agriculture and Forestry Museum** (closed Sun; $4; 601/354-6113), a 40-acre complex on Lakeland Drive northeast of downtown, off I-55 exit 98B. Despite the dull name, it's a hugely engaging and entertaining place, with a composite "Crossroads Town" made up of authentic buildings, including a general store, filling station, and sawmill brought here from all over Mississippi.

For more local flavor, try **Franks' World Famous Biscuits** (601/354-5357), open 6 AM–4 PM at 219 N. President Street near the Capitol; or the **Elite Restaurant** (601/352-5606), at

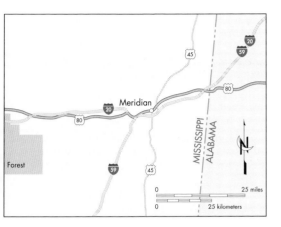

How times change, Mississippi style: Jackson's main streets have been renamed to honor civil rights movement martyrs **Martin Luther King Jr.** and **Medgar Evers**.

After burning Jackson to the ground during the Civil War, **Gen. Ulysses S. Grant** is said to have coined the expression "War is Hell."

Father of Country Music

The collision of Mississippi's rural past with the early stages of industrial development was embodied in the life and work of Meridian's favorite son, Jimmie Rodgers, whose original mixing of black Delta blues and white Appalachian folk songs earned him the title "Father of Country Music." What Elvis Presley was to the 1950s, Rodgers was to the previous generation. Born in Meridian on September 8, 1897, Rodgers worked briefly on the railroad, lost his job after coming down with tuberculosis, then became the original overnight success. After he was discovered by an RCA talent scout in 1927, Rodgers' first record, "Sleep, Baby, Sleep," sold over a million copies. For the next five years he called himself the "Singing Brakeman" and was the world's best-selling recording artist. Rodgers's life and legend are honored in the small **Jimmie Rodgers Museum** (Mon.–Sat. 10 AM–4 PM, Sun. 1–5 PM; $5; 601/485-1808) at 41st Avenue and 19th Street in Highland Park, well-signed two miles northwest of downtown.

It contains all manner of odd Rodgers-related memorabilia, plus his boots and his custom Martin guitar. Jimmie Rodgers died of tuberculosis in May 1933 and is buried alongside his wife in Oak Grove Cemetery, two miles south of Meridian. In 1997, an excellent tribute album of Jimmie Rodgers' songs was recorded by the likes of Bono, Bob Dylan, Jerry Garcia, and Willie Nelson, all of whom rated Rodgers as a major influence on their music.

Roadside Shrines

Among the many pleasures of traveling around rural America is the likelihood of coming upon a striking monument in the middle of nowhere. Winding back roads that for miles and miles have run quietly through woodlands or along cotton fields will be suddenly marked by giant crosses or a pylon of hand-lettered signs. In the Midwest, you'll often see a fiberglass dinosaur or other giant creature constructed by some well-intentioned civic organization and intended to draw highway traffic to local businesses. In the South, however, what you see are intensely personal creations, built by eccentric and often outcast individuals (99 percent of them men), and instead of acting as an advertising gimmick, they usually spout chapter and verse of scripture, warning about the impending Apocalypse or the inevitable coming of Judgment Day.

Among the Deep South roadside shrines, don't miss the one that stands outside **Margaret's Grocery** (601/638-1163), along Business US-61 on the north side of Vicksburg, Mississippi, at 4535 N. Washington Street. At a glance, the assemblage of huge hand-lettered signs atop various red-and-white constructions resembles a fanatical

Margaret's Grocery, north of Vicksburg

141 E. Capitol near the Mississippi Museum of Art. Both are friendly, old-timey local favorites, serving up inexpensive but great-tasting food. For fried catfish (the Mississippi state dish), good beer, and great live music, make your way to **Hal & Mal's** (closed Mon.; 601/948-0888), at 200 S. Commerce Street, in an old warehouse perched along the abandoned railroad tracks above the Pascagoula Street underpass.

Places to stay in Jackson tend to be either rough-but-cheap highway motels lining old US-80, or anodyne chains along the I-20 and I-55 Interstate frontages, like the **Best Western Metro Inn** ($70; 601/355-7483 or 800/528-1234), at 1520 Ellis Avenue off I-20 exit 42B.

The incidents recounted in the film *Mississippi Burning* (the murders of civil rights activists by Ku Klux Klan members in June 1964) took place in the small town of **Philadelphia**, 30 miles northwest of Meridian.

For more complete information, or details on driving the Natchez Trace Parkway (see page 273), which runs north and south from Jackson, contact the **visitors bureau** (601/960-1891 or 800/354-7695), located at 921 N. President Street.

Meridian

At the junction of US-80, I-20, and I-59, the main route to and from New Orleans, modern **Meridian** (pop. 39,968) is a medium-sized industrial center that started from rubble in

Legoland (see page 99). The biblically inspired injunctions are worth at least a pause, but caveat visitor: The friendly owners will talk your ears off if you aren't careful.

Further east, within a short drive of US-80 in Prattville, northwest of Montgomery, Alabama, W. C. Rice constructed an intense **garden of white crosses** that resembles a military cemetery.

The best known of these "Gardens of Revelation," as scholar John Beardsley has called them in his excellent book of the same name, is Howard Finster's **Paradise Garden** (Mon.–Sat. 10 AM–5 PM; donations; 706/857-0323), near Summerville in the Appalachian foothills of northwest Georgia. Recently famous for his primitivist paintings, which appeared on album covers by rock bands like REM and Talking Heads, Finster (who died in 2001) created a series of Gaudi-esque shrines, embedding seashells, bits of tile, and old car parts into concrete forms. Pictures of Henry Ford, Hubert Humphrey, and Hank Williams are arrayed alongside dozens of signs quoting scripture, but the spirit of the place is best summed up by Finster's own verse: "I built this park of broken pieces to try to mend a broken world of people who are traveling their last road." Only two hours from Atlanta, the Paradise Garden is now one of the more popular attractions in the area. To get there, make your way to Summerville, then head north on US-27 for three miles to Pennville.

These roadside shrines are by no means limited to states south of the 35th Parallel; northern states have their share as well, including two of the most intense: the **Garden of Eden** in Lucas, Kansas (see page 681), and the **Dickeyville Grottoes** in Iowa (see page 233).

the aftermath of the Civil War, and owes its existence to strategic geography: After the native Choctaw Indians were removed in 1831, Meridian became a railroad junction and served as a Confederate stronghold until Sherman destroyed it in February 1864, saying afterwards, "Meridian no longer exists." Despite this, the town recovered with a vengeance, and from the 1890s until the 1930s Meridian was the largest and most prosperous city in this very poor state, as shown by the many fine Edwardian and art deco buildings that still stand (in varying stages of repair) around the leafy and clean downtown area.

Two of Meridian's most intriguing stops are two miles northwest of downtown, in **Highland Park** on 41st Avenue at State Boulevard. First is the **Dentzel Carousel** (daily 1–5 PM; 50 cents), a cheerful and historic wooden merry-go-round dating from the 1890s, preserved in its original condition. Nearby is the **Jimmie Rodgers Museum,** described more fully in the "Father of Country Music" sidebar. Another offbeat but interesting Meridian "attraction" is the

Continuing its musical traditions, Meridian is also the birthplace and corporate headquarters of Peavey Electronics, amplifier- and instrument-makers to the stars. The original **Peavey music shop** is still in business downtown at 813 22nd Avenue (601/483-9208).

Meridian was also the birthplace of **Stetson hats,** first made at Dunn's Fall south of town.

gravesite of the **"King and Queen of the Gypsies,"** Emil and Kelly Mitchell, whose circa-1914 plot in Rosehill Cemetery (west of downtown on 40th Avenue between 7th and 8th Streets) is a place of pilgrimage for Gypsies from all over America. Marked by a set of wrought-iron patio furniture and traditional headstones, the grave is often piled high with strands of beads, fruit, and other offerings.

Thanks to its location at the I-20 and I-59 junction, there's no shortage of places to eat and sleep.

ALABAMA

Our route across the midsection of Alabama cuts through the rural Black Belt—a name that comes from the richly fertile but often swampy lowland soil, but which also reflects its predominantly African American population. Prime cotton-growing country, central Alabama was feverishly supportive of slavery and secession—Montgomery, the state capital, was also the first capital of the Confederacy—and later became a crucible in the civil rights battles of the 1950s and 1960s.

Events of both of these historical moments provide most of what there is to see and do in the state, but the intimate scale of things—even the biggest city, **Montgomery,** feels like a sleepy, small town—makes for an enjoyable tour, as does the fact that for most of its 230-odd miles, US-80 alternates between old-style two-laner and newer style four-lane freeway, far away from the anodyne Interstates and passing through some of the South's most interesting places.

For soothing soul or Sunday gospel in west-central Alabama, tune to **WNPT 102.9 FM.**

Demopolis and Faunsdale

Standing just north of US-80 on a bluff above the east bank of the Tombigbee River, **Demopolis** (pop. 7,540) has an interesting history to explain its unusual name—which means "City of the People" in Greek. In 1817, a band of French aristocrats in exile for their allegiance to Napoleon arrived here after the U.S. Congress granted them the land to found a

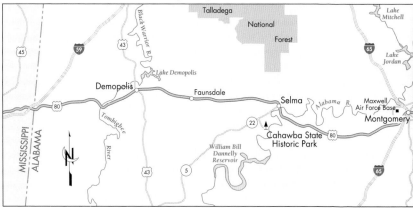

colony based on growing grapes and olives. Not surprisingly, the colonists, a group of soldiers and courtiers whom the WPA *Guide to Alabama* described as "cultured people . . . from the glittering drawing rooms of the French aristocracy . . . none of whom had ever set foot in a plowed field," failed miserably, and survived thanks only to the local Choctaw Indians, who gave them food and taught them to grow viable crops.

By the 1820s the last of the French had quit, and the lands were swiftly taken over by slave-owning American cotton planters, whose mansions still stand in and around town. Though it's not overly imposing from the outside, the biggest and best of these is **Gaineswood** (Tues.–Sat. 9 AM–5 PM; $5; 334/289-4846), at 805 S. Cedar Street E, just north of US-80. The finest antebellum mansion in Alabama, and one of the top three in the country according to the *Smithsonian Guide to Historic America,* Gaineswood began as a rough cabin in 1821 and over the next 40 years grew into a classic Greek Revival manor, built by slaves according to pattern-book designs. Most unusually, it is still decorated with the original furniture, fixtures, and fittings.

The Tombigbee River at Demopolis comes to life the first weekend of December for **Christmas on the River,** when lighted, animated "floats that really float" parade downstream.

Alabama's original state capital, **Cahawba** was founded along the Alabama River in 1820 but was totally abandoned by the 1860s. Its few buildings and other remains are preserved as a state historic park (daily 8am–5pm; free; 334/872-8058), 13 miles southwest of Selma via Hwy-22 and Hwy-9.

The other well-maintained plantation home still standing in Demopolis is **Bluff Hall** (closed Mon.; $5; 334/289-9644), at 405 Commissioners Avenue, overlooking the river at the west edge of town. Smaller than Gaineswood, but more attractively situated, Bluff Hall contains a wider array of furniture, with pieces dating from throughout the 19th century; the kitchen in particular is packed with Victorian-era gadgets.

Demopolis's franchise-free downtown fills four blocks of Washington Street east from Bluff Hall and the river. It's centered upon one of the South's oldest public squares, with a cast-iron fountain and many comfy benches.

The most enjoyable place to eat near Demopolis is about 15 miles east of town in tiny **Faunsdale** (pop. 175), on the south side of US-80. Though little more than a speck on the map, Faunsdale is worth a stop to enjoy the gorgeous home-cooked food and frequent live music at the **Faunsdale Bar and Grill** (Wed.–Sun. 5–9 PM only; 334/628-3240) in the block-long center of town. In April, the restaurant hosts the annual **Faunsdale Crawfish Festival,** which sees hundreds of visitors turn out for bands, beers, and 20 tons of "mudbugs."

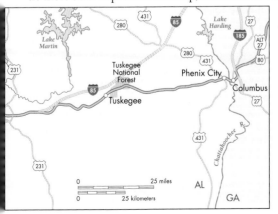

Selma

A full century before it played a seminal role in the civil rights movement of the 1960s, **Selma** (pop. 20,512) was second only to Richmond as an industrial arsenal for Confederate forces—Selma's foundries and forges produced weapons, ammunition, and ironclad warships, including the legendary CSS *Tennessee*—and altogether accounted for nearly half of Confederate-made munitions. As in Richmond, the factories were destroyed by Union forces toward the end of the war in April 1865, but a few blocks of downtown's Water Avenue were spared and now form one of the few intact antebellum business districts left in the South. Hundreds of Civil War–era houses line Selma's streets, marked by blue shields and forming one of the largest collections of historic houses in the country.

Dozens of sites in Selma and Montgomery, and the entire length of US-80 between them, are being documented, preserved, and protected as part of the **Civil Rights Movement National Historic Trail.** One of these sites is the place where **Viola Liuzzo,** a white housewife from Detroit who volunteered to help shuttle marchers between Montgomery and Selma, was murdered by the KKK. A small memorial stands on the site, on the south side of US-80 between Petronia and Lowndesboro.

Along the north bank of the broad Alabama River, Water Avenue's five blocks of well-maintained commercial structures, many now housing antique shops, include the **St. James Hotel,** 1200 Water Avenue, the oldest hotel still standing in the South, built in 1837 and recently restored to its original grand stature. At the west end of Water Avenue, the humpbacked landmark **Edmund Pettus Bridge** still carries old US-80 over the river, and at the north foot of the bridge the small but significant **National Voting Rights Museum** (closed Sun.; $5; 334/418-0800), at 1012 Water Avenue, uses photographs and handbills to tell the story of the civil rights struggles of the 1950s and 1960s. While most accounts focus on the high-profile political leaders, the story here is of the local grassroots activists who struggled for years to win the right to vote. The big names, particularly Rev. Martin Luther King Jr., clearly played key roles, but the sense you get from visiting the Voting Rights Museum is that it was the many brave but uncelebrated heroes who really made the civil rights movement happen.

Five blocks east, at the other end of the Water Avenue historic district, on the site of Selma's largest Civil War foundry, the **Old Depot Museum** (closed Sun.; $4; 334/874-2197), at 4 Martin Luther King Street, traces regional history from before the Civil War up through the civil rights movement, and features a large selection of Confederate currency, much of which was printed in Selma. The depot also marks the juncture of Selma's Civil War history with the more recent battles for civil rights: North along Martin Luther King (formerly Sylvan) Street, markers point out the unchanged sites of key moments in the civil rights movement up to the 1965 March to Montgomery fronted by Dr. King. Twenty different displays explain the significance of Selma and point out the historic importance of such sites as the Brown Chapel AME church, where marchers set off toward Montgomery before being violently turned back at the Edmund Pettus Bridge; and the simple brick public housing of the George Washington Carver Homes, where most of the original activists lived.

Responding to the civil rights marches of 1965, **Pres. Lyndon Johnson** said, "At times, history and fate meet at a single time, in a single place to shape a turning point in man's unending search for freedom. So it was at Lexington and Concord. So it was a century ago at Appomattox. So it was last week in Selma, Alabama."

Selma Practicalities

Along with more vivid history per square foot than just about anywhere else in the South, Selma has a couple of good places to eat: **Ed's Pancake House** (334/872-2736), on US-80 at 1617 Broad Street; and **Major Grumbles** (334/872-2006), off Water Avenue at 1 Grumbles Alley, which serves up fried chicken and steaks in a converted cotton warehouse overlooking the river.

Though luxury accommodations are not exactly in keeping with the suffering and sacrifices of the civil rights movement, you can stay the night at the historic and very central **St. James Hotel** ($75 and up; 334/872-3234), at 1200 Water Avenue, which has wrought-iron balconies, views of the river and the landmark Pettus Bridge, and well-restored rooms and suites arrayed around a gorgeous garden atrium. If there's no room at the St. James, motels along US-80 include a **Holiday Inn** ($65; 334/872-0461), at 1710 W. Highland Avenue.

For further information, including details of the **Alabama Tale Tellin' Festival** held in Selma each October, contact the **visitors bureau** (334/875-7485 or 800/457-3562), at 2207 Broad Street.

Montgomery

Original capital of the Confederate States of America, and now the state capital of Alabama, **Montgomery** (pop. 201,568) is among the more engaging destinations in the Deep South. Not surprisingly, much of what there is to see has to do with the Civil War, which officially started here when Jefferson Davis gave the order to fire on Fort Sumter. Montgomery survived the war more or less unscathed and is now a very pleasant little city with lovely houses lining leafy streets and an above-average range of restaurants, thanks to the presence of politicos and the 6,000 students at Alabama State College.

Montgomery's landmark is the circa-1851 **state capitol** (closed Sun.; free), which served as the Confederate capitol for four months in 1861 and is still in use. A bronze star on the west portico marks the spot where Jefferson Davis took the oath of office as President of the Confederate States of America on February 18, 1861, and a spiral staircase surrounded by historical murals climbs the three-story domed rotunda. Moved to a site across the street from the capitol in 1921, the **White House of the Confederacy** is where Jeff Davis and family lived before moving from Montgomery to Richmond. Yet more Confederate memorabilia is on display next door at the **State Archives and History Museum** (closed Sun.; free), which has displays tracing Alabama history from Creek Indian and pioneer times up through today.

The building behind the Civil Rights Memorial houses the non-profit **Southern Poverty Law Center**, a nationally important force for fighting all forms of racial and religious hatred. Along with numerous legal battles the center has targeted racism on the Internet via its website, www.tolerance.org.

Montgomery's **Maxwell Air Force Base,** established by the Wright Brothers in 1910, is now home to the Air University and War College, national finishing school for fighter pilots and military tacticians. **Tuskegee,** just east, was the training base of the Tuskegee Airmen, black pilots who fought in World War II.

A single block west of the state capitol complex—mind-bogglingly close, considering the historically huge gulf between whites and blacks in Alabama—stands the **Dexter Avenue Baptist Church,** a simple brick building where Martin Luther King Jr. served as pastor from 1954 to 1960. One of the key landmarks of the civil rights movement, it was here that supporters rallied around Rosa Parks in the Montgomery bus boycott of 1955–56, leading to an end to official segregation. Right downtown at 252 Montgomery Street, a small **museum** dedicated to Rosa Parks and the bus boycott opened in the new Troy University library, next to the site of the bus stop where Mrs. Parks refused to give up her seat for a white passenger, sparking off the struggle.

Around the corner from the Dexter Avenue Baptist Church, Montgomery's most powerful site is the **Civil Rights Memorial,** two blocks west of the state capitol at the entrance to the Southern Poverty Law Center, 400 Washington Avenue. Designed by Vietnam Memorial architect Maya Lin, the monument consists of a circular black granite table inscribed with the names of 40 people killed in the struggle for civil rights, with a brief description of how and when they died radiating like the hands of a clock from a central water source, which flows gently over the edges of the stone. Behind the table, a waterfall tumbles over a marble wall inscribed with Martin Luther King's favorite Biblical passage, which says that we will not be satisfied "until Justice rolls down like water, and righteousness like a mighty stream."

Montgomery also has sites to see that have nothing at all to do with the Civil War or the civil rights movement. The first of these is the **Hank Williams Memorial,** marking his final resting place on the northeast side of downtown in Oakwood Cemetery, 1304 Upper Wetumptka Road. Hank Williams was an Alabama native, and singer and writer of such enduring classics as "Your Cheating Heart," "Jambalaya," "Hey, Good Lookin'," "I'm So Lonesome I Could Cry," and "Lost Highway." Williams's last concert in Montgomery took place on December 28, 1952, three days before his death; he died in the back of his Cadillac while en route from Knoxville, Tennessee, to a scheduled New Year's Day concert in Canton, Ohio. His song, "I'll Never Get Out of This World Alive," was rising up the charts at the time of his demise. His grave is on the east side of the central circle, and a small Hank Williams **museum** has opened across from City Hall.

Another notable local was **Zelda Fitzgerald,** who was born and raised in Montgomery and later lived here with her husband F. Scott while he wrote *Tender is the*

Night during the winter of 1931–32. The house they shared, south of downtown at 919 Felder Avenue, has been converted into apartments, one of which (Apt. B, on the ground floor) is now a small **museum** (Wed.–Fri. 10 AM–2 PM, Sat. and Sun. 1–5 PM; donations; 334/264-4222) that details their lives and works through videos and memorabilia—press clippings, first editions, photographs, and more. It's the only museum dedicated to either of them, anywhere.

Montgomery Practicalities

North of I-85 and east of I-65, old US-80 runs right through the historic heart of Montgomery, which is walkably compact and pleasant. At the east end of downtown, there's a clutch of very good "Authentic Southern" restaurants within a short walk of the state capitol: In the Old Alabama Town complex of historic buildings, **Blue Sky at Young House** (334/262-4465), at 231 N. Hull Street, is a popular lunch spot, a half dozen rather dainty dining rooms filling a white clapboard home. The next block west holds the cacophonously huge (and hugely popular) cafeteria-style **Farmers Market Cafe and Pit BBQ** (334/262-1970) at 315 N. McDonough Street.

Places to stay in Montgomery include the usual national chains, plus the pleasant **Riverfront Inn** ($65 and up; 334/834-4300), at 200 Coosa Street, in the historic riverfront district west of downtown. In a residential neighborhood a half mile south of I-85, the very comfortable turn-of-the-20th-century **Lattice Inn B&B** (334/832-9931), at 1414 S. Hull Street, offers a quiet alternative. For more information, contact the **Montgomery Visitor Center** (334/261-1100 or 800/240-9452), located at 300 Water Street.

Tuskegee

Midway between Montgomery and the Georgia border, **Tuskegee** (pop. 11,846) is a medium-sized town that has grown up around the **Tuskegee University**, founded in 1881 by the industrious former slave, Booker T. Washington, in order to help black Americans rise up the economic ladder. Now a National Historic Site, many of the early buildings built by student laborers still stand around the 1,500-acre campus, but the main points of interest are close to the entrance off Old Montgomery Road. Here you'll find the **Carver Museum** (daily; free; 334/727-3200), which traces the career of Tuskegee teacher George Washington Carver, with displays of the various products Carver developed during his lifelong tenure at Tuskegee.

Facing the Carver Museum across the lawn is the strikingly modern Tuskegee Chapel, designed by noted architect Paul Rudolph in 1969. The graves of both Booker T. Washington and George Washington Carver are next to the chapel.

Southeast of the college campus, the center of Tuskegee is a broad square dominated by the large

Macon County Courthouse. At the Rexall Drug Store on the west side of the square, the store windows are filled with lessons in African American history, as illustrated by a "Tuskegee Airman" edition of GI Joe.

East of Tuskegee, the I-85 freeway races up to Atlanta, while US-80 rolls its way east to the engaging old industrial city of Columbus, across the Georgia border.

Phenix City

Across the Chattahoochee River from Georgia, **Phenix City**, apart from being oddly spelled, is interesting for being the site of Fort Mitchell National Cemetery—the "Arlington of the South," holding the graves of soldiers from the Civil War to Operation Desert Storm. Before the cemetery was established, this is where thousands of native Creek Indians were rounded up in 1836 before being sent west on the notorious Trail of Tears to Indian Territory in Oklahoma.

GEORGIA

Running across the middle of Georgia, US-80 follows the "fall line," a geological divide where rivers drop in a series of rapids from the higher Piedmont Plateau to the lower coastal plain. Because the fall line marked the limits of navigation in from the sea, settlements naturally sprung up along it: **Columbus** was founded on the banks of the falling Chattahoochee, while in the middle of the state, **Macon** was built along the Ocmulgee River.

These, the second- and third-biggest cities, respectively, in this still-rural state, are the only real cities our route passes through, and both are fascinating places in very different ways. Apart from these exceptions, however, in its trip across Georgia US-80 takes in more than 300 miles of rolling countryside covered with dozens of dozens of small towns; runs along ancient-looking two-lane blacktop winding through thick hardwood-and-pine forests; and passes stately white-columned farmhouses with wide lawns and run-down tin-roofed shacks with yards full of rusting refrigerators and old bangers-on-blocks.

Especially in the western half of the state, US-80 runs across rolling Piedmont countryside past extensive orchards at the heart of "Georgia Peach" country. Follow You-Pick-'Em signs in early summer for a field-fresh selection, or stop at roadside stands along the route selling this Georgia specialty along with other local fruits and vegetables, including, of course, peanuts.

In the west, you can detour to explore the surprisingly simple homes of two U.S. presidents, Franklin Delano Roosevelt at **Warm Springs**, and Jimmy Carter at **Plains**. At the heart of Georgia, **Macon** is home to the engaging **Georgia Music Hall of Fame**, and a prehistoric Mound City. Continuing east toward Savannah and the Atlantic Coast, US-80 has been replaced by the much faster I-16 freeway, bypassing numerous small towns across an agricultural region that was devastated during General Sherman's Civil War "March to the Sea." Fortunately, Sherman spared the colonial capital, **Savannah**, a lushly verdant gem generally considered to be among the most beautiful cities in North America.

Columbus

Crossing the Chattahoochee River between Alabama and Georgia, look north to see the rushing waterfalls around which the city of **Columbus** (pop. 186,291) grew. Built on the site of a Creek Indian village, Columbus is now Georgia's second-largest city, and home of the brutal Army Ranger training school at Fort Benning. During the Civil War, its iron foundries and water-powered factories converted to munitions production, but Columbus was untouched until Union Gen. James H. Wilson stormed across the Chattahoochee in 1865; unaware that the treaty of Appomattox had already ended the war, "Wilson's Raiders" destroyed much of the city. The huge brick textile mills now lining the river's eastern bank date from the post-Reconstruction years up through the turn of the 20th century, when Columbus emerged as an industrial giant, an era captured in the stories of Columbus author Carson McCullers, and in the recordings of blues singer Gertrude "Ma" Rainey, whose home still stands downtown at 805 5th Avenue.

The Chattahoochee River between Alabama and Georgia officially marks the line between the Central and Eastern standard time zones, though Phenix City, Alabama, also observes Eastern time.

The LA Dodgers Class A **Columbus Catfish** (706/571-8866) play all summer long off Victory Drive at 100 4th Street south of town.

Most city sights are conveniently located in a compact riverside district. Stroll along the Riverwalk promenade for a close-up look at the river, or rumble down the cobblestone lanes of Broadway and Front Street past block after block of graceful old homes and fountain-studded parks. Stop by the Italianate mansion that houses the **Historical Columbus Foundation** (Mon.–Fri. only; 706/323-7979) at 700 Broadway for maps and guided **tours** ($2) of several neighborhood homes, including the former residence of J. S. Pemberton, the inventor of **Coca-Cola.** The elegant little **Springer Opera House,** 103 10th Street, is the highlight of the adjacent commercial district, where beautifully renovated buildings mix with funky shops selling wigs and voodoo trinkets.

On a hill east of downtown, a half mile from the river, the **Columbus Museum** (closed Mon.; free; 706/649-0713), at 1251 Wynnton Road, is the major cultural center for the region, with engaging displays tracing the history of the river valley from the time of the Creek Indians—don't miss the 20-minute movie "Chattahoochee Legacy," which screens frequently throughout the day. A wide-ranging collection of fine and folk art is on display in the spacious galleries. Overall, this is one of the state's more captivating small museums, well worth an hour at least.

On the site of the former Confederate shipyard at Port Columbus, south of downtown at the foot of 4th Street, the **National Civil War Naval Museum** (daily; $4.50; 706/327-9798), 1002 Victory Drive, contains the charred remnants of two Civil War ironclad ships, mock-ups of early submarines and mines, and tons of naval memorabilia.

Columbus Practicalities

At either end of historic downtown, restaurants span the range from down-home to upper-crust. **Country's on Broad** (706/596-8910), at 1329 Broadway,

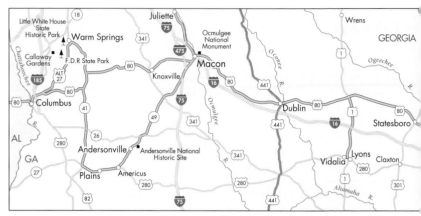

serves up classic country cookin' and fabulous hickory-smoked barbecue in a spruced-up 1940s bus depot. At the other end of town, **Bludau's Goetchius House** (706/324-4863), overlooking the river at 405 Broadway, serves upscale dinners Monday through Saturday—if the seafood and chateaubriand is too rich for your blood, stop for a mint julep at their speakeasy downstairs. On old US-80 west of downtown, the adventurous might try the lunch counter of the **Dinglewood Pharmacy** (706/322-0616), at 1939 Wynnton Road, for their "Scrambled Dog," a hot dog buried under chili, onions, and oysterette crackers.

Most of the national chains line up along the I-185 freeway, but the nicest place to stay in Columbus is the **Wyndham Hotel** ($125 and up; 706/324-1800), downtown at 800 Front Avenue, impressively carved out of a former foundry. The Ironworks next door has been converted into a convention center and performance space and is the site of the city's major festival, the **RiverFest**, in April. Southeast from downtown, Victory Drive winds toward Fort Benning, passing most of Columbus's budget accommodations amidst a gauntlet of strip clubs and pawn shops catering to the young soldiers.

For more information on Columbus, contact the **visitors center** (706/322-1613 or 800/999-1613), 900 Front Avenue.

Warm Springs: FDR's "Little White House"

About 15 miles north of Columbus, an hour southwest of Atlanta, the rising, forested flanks of Pine Mountain attract flatlanders in search of cooler temperatures and an overlook of the surrounding countryside. In 1924, the therapeutic natural hot springs here also drew the future president Franklin Delano Roosevelt who, in between losing the election for vice-president in 1920 and winning the governorship of New York in 1928, was struck with polio and left unable to walk. Roosevelt loved the area so much he built a wooded, three-bedroom retreat here later called the **Little White House** (daily; $7; 706/655-5870). He established a treatment center

Knoxville, Georgia, 25 miles west of Macon and just north of US-80, is built around a typical Southern courthouse square, which holds a unique monument to the local girl, **Joanna Troutman**, who designed the Lone Star flag of Texas. She gave the flag, which featured a blue star on a white background but which was otherwise identical to the current one, to a battalion of Macon volunteers heading west to fight for the Texas Republic.

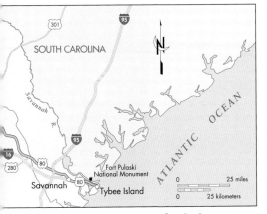

nearby for himself and fellow polio sufferers, funded a charity that grew into today's March of Dimes, and returned regularly over the next two decades. After being elected President in 1932 he formulated much of the "New Deal," and managed the conduct of World War II, while staying here. And on the afternoon of April 12, 1945, FDR collapsed suddenly and died at Warm Springs, leaving an unfinished portrait propped on an easel.

The surprisingly small and unpretentious house is very much as it was when Roosevelt died, with the recent addition of an excellent museum telling all about Roosevelt's life and times. Many of the displays concentrate on his political career, but many of the objects are personal and vividly moving, such as the heavy leg braces FDR wore during public appearances, the wall-full of walking canes crafted for FDR by disabled people all over the world, and the dark blue Ford V-8 convertible (with hand controls) that he drove around the Warm Springs countryside.

At nearby **FDR State Park** (on land donated by Roosevelt) you can take in the terrific views, swim at the pool, hike a portion of the 26-mile Pine Mountain Trail, or stay the night in one of the many state park cabins (800/847-4842 for reservations). In the small town of **Warm Springs** (pop. 400), a half mile north of the "Little White House" park, **Mac's Bar-B-Q** (706/655-2472), at the corner of Spring and Main Streets a block east of Hwy-41, has hickory-smoked ribs and chicken; and homestyle comfort food is on the menu at **Bulloch House** (706/655-9068), at 47 Bulloch Street. The historic **Hotel Warm Springs** ($75–150; 706/655-2114), at 17 Broad Street, offers B&B accommodations. There are also plenty of craft, gift, and antique stores to browse through.

One last area attraction is west of Warm Springs off US-27: **Callaway Gardens** (daily; $13 adults, $6 children; 706/663-2281 or 800/225-5292), which has 14,000 lushly landscaped acres covered in topiary gardens, a lakeside swimming beach, and dazzling displays of colorful flowers. The Day Butterfly Center, a 7,000-square-foot atrium with 100 exotic species of free-flying butterflies, is surrounded by four more acres of butterfly-friendly gardens, and restaurants, a golf course, and overnight accommodations are also available.

In 1975, then-governor of Georgia **Jimmy Carter** announced his bid for the presidency at FDR's Warm Springs cottage.

Plains: Jimmy Carter

Another stop along central Georgia's "Presidential Trail," 45 miles southeast of Columbus via US-285, **Plains** (pop. 637), the home of former President Jimmy Carter, stands as a living monument to small-town America. Here, in a town that's small and remote even by South Georgia standards, the 39th president of the United States was raised, mounted his presidential campaign, and now officiates on matters of international diplomacy—that is, when he isn't teaching Sunday School at the Maranatha Baptist Church. Though the Carter family compound is off-limits, visitors can see Carter's high school, stop by late brother Billy's old

the 39th president and former first lady in their hometown

gas station (the only one in town), and buy a bag of peanuts at the general store.

Much of Plains has been proclaimed the **Jimmy Carter National Historic Site**, and self-guided touring maps are available at the **visitors center** (daily; 229/824-4104), inside the old Plains High School at 300 N. Bond Street. Another major part of the Plains experience is the family farm, preserved in the pre-electricity, circa-1937 state described in Carter's evocative memoir, *An Hour Before Daylight: Memories of a Rural Boyhood*. Finally, there's the old train depot downtown, which served as Carter's campaign headquarters in 1976 and again in 1980, when he was trounced by Ronald Reagan.

In contrast to the luxury of the Windsor Hotel, **Americus** is also worldwide HQ of **Habitat for Humanity**, which helps provide basic shelter for people all over the world.

Ten miles northeast of Plains, in the market town of **Americus** (pop. 16,512), the wealth generated by the region's cotton plantations is embodied in the towering brick **Windsor Hotel** ($95–175; 229/924-1555 or 800/678-8946) at 125 W. Lamar Street. A truly elegant Victorian-era hotel with a three-story atrium lobby—one of the grandest interior spaces in the state—the Windsor is worth a look, and makes a great base for exploring central Georgia.

the elegant Windsor Hotel

Andersonville Prison

Ten miles north of Americus via Hwy-49, the **Andersonville National Historic Site** (daily; free; 229/924-0343) stands on the site of the largest and most notorious Confederate military prison. During the final 18 months of the Civil War, as many as 30,000 Union soldiers were imprisoned here in overcrowded conditions, and 13,000 died as a result of disease, poor sanitation, and exposure. Once this was uncovered after the war, public outrage was so great that the camp's commandant, Capt. Henry Wirz, was convicted of murder and hanged in Washington, D.C., though historians generally agree that there was little he could have done to alleviate the suffering. Thousands of closely packed gravestones fill the Andersonville National Cemetery, just north of the prison site.

Only a few parts of the prison have been reconstructed, but the prisoners' harrowing stories are told in one part of the adjacent **National Prisoners of War Museum,** which was dedicated in 1998 and recounts the stories of American POWs during wars up through the present day. Perhaps surprisingly, the tone of the museum is neither vindictive nor especially patriotic, focusing instead on the instances of individual bravery in the face of impossible difficulties.

Macon

Near the geographic center of the state, the city of **Macon** (pop. 118,000) was founded along the Ocmulgee (oak-MUL-gee) River in 1825, and flourished with the cotton trade. The downtown area holds the modern Georgia Music Hall of Fame (see sidebar "Macon Music") alongside dozens of well-preserved, historically significant public buildings, including a 110-year-old **Opera House** at 639 Mulberry Street and the turn-of-the-20th-century **Douglass Theater** on Broadway west of Mulberry Street, where such Macon-born music legends as Lena Horne, Otis Redding, and Little Richard got their start.

Another aspect of Macon heritage, the city's collection of well-preserved antebellum mansions, stands on a low hill at the north end of downtown, having survived the Civil War unscathed apart from one brief battle: While most of Sherman's troops skirted by to the north, a band of Union soldiers engaged young Confederate soldiers at the city limits and fired a cannonball that landed in the foyer of a stately residence, now known as the **Cannonball House,** 856 Mulberry Street. A small museum (closed Sun.; $5) behind the house displays the usual barrage of Confederate memorabilia, and inside the house you can see the dented floor and original cannonball. A block away, the stunning **Hay House,** 934 Georgia Avenue, is among the most beautiful antebellum houses in the state. You can see these two and many more on a meandering walk led by a Macon tour guide posing as Sidney Lanier, the city's famous 19th-century poet; call the visitors bureau (478/743-3401 or 800/768-3401) for details.

In early spring, Macon's nearly 300,000 cherry trees come into bloom, drawing flower lovers from all over the region.

The **Allman Brothers'** "Ramblin' Man" was "born in the back seat of a Greyhound Bus, rolling down Highway 41," but most of today's traffic follows its modern replacement, I-75. Band members Duane Allman and Berry Oakley are both buried in **Rose Hill Cemetery,** off Riverside Drive; Oakley's epitaph reads "...and the road goes on forever..."

Macon Practicalities

Along with music and architecture, Macon also has a number of good places to eat. Among the very best, and a Macon institution, is **Len Berg's** (Mon.–Fri. 11 AM–2:30 PM only; 478/742-9255), downtown off Broadway and Walnut in Old Post Office Alley. Since 1908, the restaurant has been serving up heaping helpings of fried chicken and other Southern treats, plus platefuls of sweet Vidalia onion rings and fresh-baked pies for dessert. Good coffee, pastries, salads, and sandwiches can be had at **Adriana's,** right downtown at 359 3rd Street.

Macon police officer **Dominick Andrews** has written a book, called *What's Your Excuse?,* which documents the best excuses he's heard from people he's stopped for speeding. If yours is funny enough, he may let you go. Don't count on it, though.

Macon Music

Many people dismissed the creation of Macon's new Georgia Music Hall of Fame as simply another symptom of the state's desperate urge to create tourist attractions to complement Atlanta's hosting of the Olympic Games in the summer of 1996. While Olympic enthusiasm was clearly a key to raising $6.5 million in seed money from the state, the end result is one of the most engaging and enjoyable music museums in the entire country: 12,000 square feet of guitars, amps, albums, posters, costumes, jukeboxes, sunglasses, and blue suede shoes, with just enough curatorial explanation to let you piece together the whole crazy story of Georgia music. The displays are anything but dry, using all manner of artifacts to memorialize their subjects. Best of all, the Hall of Fame is free from the "music industry" bias that says sales equals success—not all of the artists honored here were by any means world-famous or commercial superstars.

Macon may not have the legendary status in music circles as say, Memphis or Detroit, but its claim to fame goes beyond its location at the center of the state. The city's music scene had its heyday in the 1950s and 1960s, when it gave birth to such diverse artists as Ray Charles, Little Richard, Otis Redding, and the Allman Brothers, all of whom are enshrined here. Display cases are packed with instruments and memorabilia donated in many cases by the artists themselves, which lends an air of personality to the place that's missing from many other museums.

Besides telling the musical life and times of Georgia musicians, the museum does an admirable job of evoking the social, racial, and economic contexts in which the different forms of music were created. It also gives overdue credit to the many people working behind the scenes, casting the spotlight on songwriters, producers, and engineers, not to mention diverse promoters, hucksters, and hangers-on. Documenting the contributions of everyone from Ma Rainey to the B-52s, and genres from jazz to rap, the museum makes a strong case for Georgia being the true musical crossroads of America.

The **Georgia Music Hall of Fame** is located at the center of downtown Macon, across from the visitor centers at 5th and Mulberry Streets. It is open Monday–Saturday 9 AM–5 PM, Sunday 1–5 PM, and admission is $8. For further information, call 478/750-8555 or 888/GA-ROCKS.

Little Richard, among others, got his start in Macon.

For a place to stay, choose from the many motels lining Riverside Drive north of town along the I-75 frontage, like the **Comfort Inn** ($70; 478/746-8855), at 2690 Riverside Drive. Or, splurge a little on the very comfortable **1842 Inn** ($140 and up; 478/741-1842) at 353 College Street, a white-columned antebellum mansion converted into a bed-and-breakfast with tons of historical ambience.

For more information on visiting Macon, contact the **visitors bureau** (478/743-3401 or 800/768-3401), at 200 Cherry Street inside the massive old Terminal Station, across from the Georgia Music Hall of Fame.

All across the Deep South, but across Georgia in particular, US-80 is lined by the photogenic remains of long-abandoned filling stations, many of them built with accommodations on the upper floor—right above the old gas pumps.

Ocmulgee National Monument

Across the Ocmulgee River, well-signed from I-16 exit 4, two miles east of Macon along the Emory Highway (US-80), the settlement now preserved as the **Ocmulgee National Monument** was a center of pre-conquest Native American culture. By the time the first colonists arrived, it had been inhabited for over 800 years, with remains dating from AD 900.

From the small, WPA-era **visitors center** (daily; free; 478/752-8257), where you can watch a short film and admire pieces of elaborate pottery found on the site, a short trail leads you to a restored earth lodge (complete with thinly disguised air-conditioning ducts!), where you walk through a narrow tunnel to the center of the circular, kiva-like interior. The trail continues past the excavated remains of a Creek Indian trading post, then crosses a set of railroad tracks before climbing a 45-foot-high "Great Temple Mound," where you can see downtown Macon across the rumbling I-16 freeway—2,000 years of "culture" in one very pleasant half-mile walk.

Juliette: Fried Green Tomatoes at the Whistle Stop Cafe

Tucked away upriver on the Ocmulgee, in the heart of the Piedmont forests of middle Georgia, sits the town of **Juliette**, somewhat revived after a long slumber because of its **Whistle Stop Cafe** (478/994-3670). The café, town, and river were the backdrop for the 1991 film *Fried Green Tomatoes,* based on Fannie Flagg's novel. (The novel, it should be said, was based upon the Irondale Café outside Birmingham, Alabama.)

You can taste Whistle Stop barbecue, along with a plate of fried green tomatoes, every day except Monday. Juliette lies due north of Macon along US-23, or 10 miles east of the I-75 town of Forsyth via Juliette Road.

East Dublin's **WQZY 96 FM** plays popular country and NASCAR, but is most famous for the annual **Redneck Games** it organizes every July.

Around Dublin, you can tune to one of the greatest old-time country stations I've found anywhere: **WXLI 1230 AM**, broadcasting Hank Williams, Hank Snow, Johnny Cash, and other country pioneers "from a little building just off the Interstate."

Off I-16: Dublin and Vidalia

Named by its Irish founders in 1812, **Dublin** (pop. 16,312) continues to celebrate its Irish heritage with shamrocks painted on the center dividers, and an all-out St. Patrick's

North of US-80 via US-1, the town of **Wrens** (pop. 2,414) was the boyhood home of **Erskine Caldwell**, author of the classic stories *Tobacco Road* and *God's Little Acre*, both of which were set in this part of rural Georgia.

Day festival that lasts most of two weeks. The historic district is centered along Bellevue Avenue, where you can note the prominent Confederate Memorial, glimpse the town's many graceful old homes, and look inside the local historical museum (Tues.–Fri. 1–4:30 PM; free) at Bellevue and Academy Streets. Eat at **Ma Hawkins Cafe** (478/272-0941), at 124 W. Jackson Street, which has grits and greens and other Southern specialties.

The Dublin area hosts an increasingly popular, very-tongue-in-cheek annual celebration of rural America: the Redneck Games. Started by local radio DJ Mac Davis as a joking response to Atlanta's preparations for the 1996 Olympics, the Redneck Games competitions include such questionable "country-style" events as a hubcap discus throw, a mud-pit belly-flop contest, bug-zapping, and an armpit serenade in which contestants play TV theme songs by cupping hands under their arms. The games take place in July; admission is around $5 per carload.

East of Dublin, around 15 miles south of I-16, **Vidalia** (pop. 11,078) is known to food-lovers around the world as the home of the delectable Vidalia onion, so sweet it can be eaten raw, like an apple. To the locals, this single crop represents a $30 million industry. In late April and early May, follow the scent to the **Vidalia Onion Festival** (912/538-8687) for taste treats.

Statesboro and Claxton

12 miles north of I-16, **Statesboro** (pop. 22,698) was also one of Sherman's stops on his notorious "March to the Sea." Here in 1864 his troops torched the courthouse; today's historic courthouse dates from the late 19th century. Georgia Southern University, with an enrollment of 16,000, dominates the town, especially during the fall football season.

If you're feeling hungry, generous Southern buffets are served boardinghouse-style (bring your plate to the kitchen when you're through) at the **Beaver House Restaurant** (912/764-2821), in a large white-columned mansion at 121 S. Main Street. For one reasonable price, you get massive servings of fried chicken,

In Statesboro, Main Street runs in four different directions: north, east, south, and west. The town is also famous for having inspired **Blind Willie McTell** to write "Statesboro Blues," later recorded by the Allman Brothers.

vegetables, cornbread, and biscuits. For barbecue, head over to **Vandy's** (912/764-2444), a local landmark at 22 W. Vine Street; or **Boyd's Pit BBQ**, west of town on US-80 at the junction with US-301.

Ten miles south of I-16 at the intersection of US-280 and US-301, the town of **Claxton** bills itself as the **Fruitcake Capital of the World**. In the fall fruitcake-making season, the Claxton Bakery (800/841-4211) in the center of town offers free samples of the 3,000 tons of fruitcake they pound out each year.

The beautiful city of Savannah marks the junction of our US-80 route with the **Atlantic Coast** road trip, which begins on page 374. Savannah is covered in full on pages 411–414.

US-80 across Savannah

Old US-80 comes into Savannah on Louisville Road, past the Savannah International Airport on the northwest edge of town. The old road turns into Bay Street for the final approach, then runs south across the historic downtown area before turning east onto Victory Drive, which runs along the southern foot of Savannah, then across to the barrier islands. If you'd rather save Savannah for another day, you can follow I-16 and Victory Drive around the south side of downtown.

Bonaventure Cemetery

Whether or not you got obsessed with *Midnight in the Garden of Good and Evil,* the book that put Savannah back on the map in the 1990s, you'll enjoy visiting Bonaventure Cemetery, which features prominently in the story. Located east of Savannah proper, north of US-80 via Mechanics Avenue and Bonaventure Road, it is simply one of the most evocative corners of this characterful part of the country, where majestic old trees draped in mossy strands stand over abundant azaleas and all manner of monuments and memorials. No less a figure than naturalist John Muir, who camped here for a while immediately after the Civil War, called it "one of the most impressive assemblages of animal and plant creatures I have ever met." Songwriter Johnny Mercer of "Moon River" fame is buried here, along with centuries' worth of Savannahns.

Fort Pulaski

The drive east from Savannah to the Atlantic Ocean passes through picturesque fishing villages standing out from serene marshlands, where a maze of riverlets and creeks weaves through the tall green reeds, and fishing boats bob along the tidal waters as they head off to harvest shrimp and oysters.

Amid the calm stands **Fort Pulaski National Monument** (daily; $2; 912/786-5787), 15 miles east of Savannah on US-80, a well-preserved stone-and-brick fortress completed in 1848 at a commanding site at the mouth of the Savannah River. Its prominent island site originally held colonial-era Fort Greene, which was demolished by a hurricane in 1804 and replaced by the architecturally impressive, pentagon-shaped bulwark that survives in its battered and breached state today, surrounded by a moat and many acres of grassy lawn.

Near Fort Pulaski, just west of the Bull River Bridge along US-80, **Williams Seafood Restaurant** (912/897-2219) is a popular place to sample local cuisine. Harder to find, but worth the effort to reach, is the waterfront **Crab Shack** (912/786-9857), just across the bridge to Tybee Island on Estill Hammock Road, where "The Elite Dine in Their Bare Feet" on plates of shrimp-and-sausage, "Low Country Boil," and key lime pie raved about by such dignified aficionados as the *New York Times.*

Beginning in 1829, construction of Fort Pulaski, proclaimed "as strong as the Rocky Mountains," took 18 years, used 25 million bricks, and cost just over a million dollars. During the Civil War, its seven-foot-thick walls withstood bombardment by the Union forces' new rifled cannon for only 30 hours, prompting the fort's surrender in April 1862.

Tybee Island

You made it! The Atlantic Ocean at last! The easternmost of many islands filling the delta at the mouth of the Savannah River, the town of **Tybee Island** (pop. 2,842) is a funky old family-oriented resort, with four blocks of burger-and-corn-dog stands, taverns, amusement arcades, thrill rides, and miniature golf courses at the eastern end of US-80, just 18 miles east of central Savannah. Originally known as Savannah Beach, and locally famous for the annual Beach Bum's Parade before Labor Day, Tybee Island's main attraction is its endless, and usually uncrowded, powdery white-sand beaches, which spread to either side of the new pier and pavilion at the end of 16th Avenue.

At the north end of Tybee Island, from whence the Union forces bombarded Fort Pulaski during the Civil War, a centuries-old lighthouse stands next to the WW II-era concrete bunkers that house the **Tybee Museum** (daily; $4; 912/786-5801), which includes the old lighthouse keeper's cottage among its collections tracing the island's history.

Other draws here are the wacky, slightly ersatz, diner-style **Breakfast Club** (912/786-5984), right at the center of things at 1500 Butler Avenue, open daily for breakfast or an early lunch, and the old-time **Sugar Shack** (912/786-4482), at 301 First Street, which serves breakfast, burgers, and great Georgia Peach milkshakes.

Tybee Island's stretch of US-80 also holds the world's first **Days Inn** motel (912/786-4576), upgraded and still in business at 1402 Butler Avenue; rooms go for $50–150 depending on the season. A more characterful, retro-boardinghouse style can be enjoyed at the **17th Street Inn** (912/786-0607) at 12 17th Street.

U.S. 80
SAN DIEGO TO
SAVANNAH
VIA VICKSBURG, MISS.

By Crossing the Mississippi River Via U. S. 80 at Vicksburg, Miss. You have the Benefit of the Only All Year All Weather Route from Coast to Coast. All Paved from San Diego, California, - Savannah, Georgia.

U. S. 80

U. S. 61

COMPLIMENTS
OF
VICKSBURG BRIDGE
COMPANY
VICKSBURG, MISS.

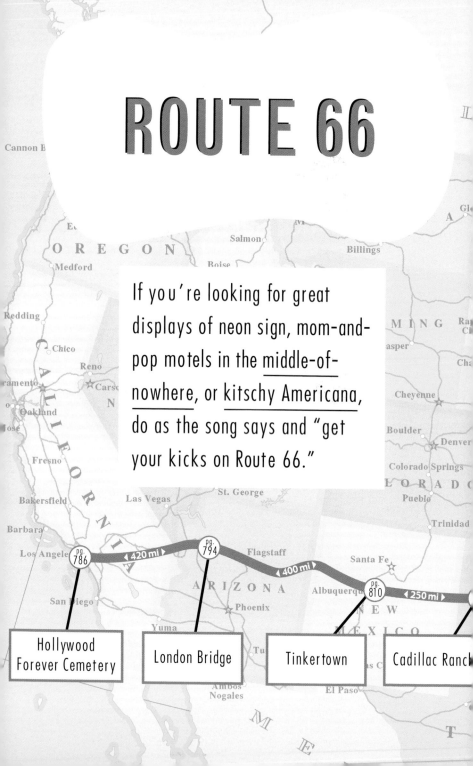

ROUTE 66

If you're looking for great displays of neon sign, mom-and-pop motels in the middle-of-nowhere, or kitschy Americana, do as the song says and "get your kicks on Route 66."

pg. 786

◄ 420 mi ►

pg. 794

◄ 400 mi ►

pg. 810

◄ 250 mi ►

Hollywood Forever Cemetery

London Bridge

Tinkertown

Cadillac Ranch

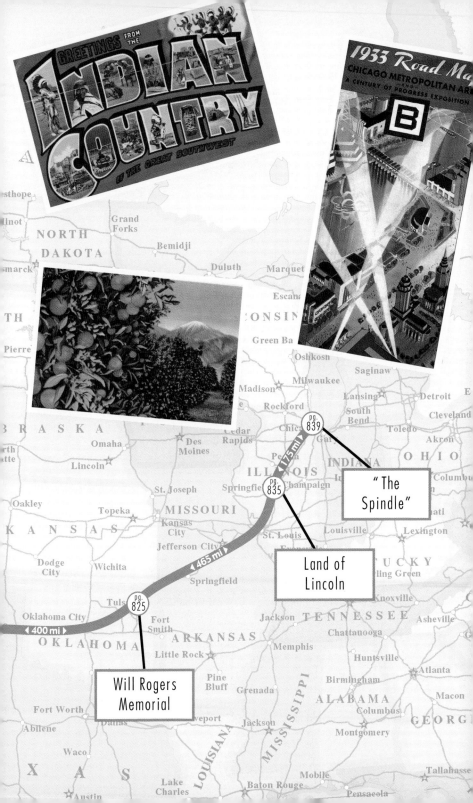

GREETINGS FROM THE INDIAN COUNTRY OF THE GREAT SOUTHWEST

1933 Road Map
CHICAGO METROPOLITAN AREA
AND A CENTURY OF PROGRESS EXPOSITION

pg. 839
"The Spindle"

pg. 835
Land of Lincoln

175 mi

465 mi

pg. 825
Will Rogers Memorial

400 mi

Between Los Angeles and Chicago

The romance of Route 66 continues to captivate people around the world. Running between Chicago and Los Angeles, "over two thousand miles all the way" in the words of the popular R&B anthem, this legendary old road passes through the heart of the United States on a diagonal trip that takes in some of the country's most archetypal roadside scenes. If you're looking for great displays of neon signs, rusty middle-of-nowhere truck stops, or kitschy Americana, do as the song says and "get your kicks on Route 66."

But perhaps the most compelling reason to follow Route 66 is to experience the road's ingrained time line of contemporary America. Before it was called Route 66, and long before it was even paved in 1926, this corridor was traversed by the National Old Trails Highway, one of the country's first transcontinental highways. For three decades before and after World War II, Route 66 earned the title "Main Street of America" because it wound through small towns across the Midwest and Southwest, lined by hundreds of cafés, motels, gas stations, and tourist attractions. During the Great Depression, hundreds of thousands of farm families, displaced from the Dust Bowl, made their way west along Route 66 to California, following what John Steinbeck called "The Mother Road" in his vivid portrait, *The Grapes of Wrath*. After World War II, many thousands more expressed their upward mobility by leaving the industrial East, bound for good jobs in the suburban idyll of Southern California—again following Route 66, which came to embody the demographic shift from the Rust Belt to the Sun Belt.

Beginning in the late 1950s and continuing gradually over the next 25 years, old Route 66 was bypassed section by section as the high-speed Interstate highways were completed. Finally, in 1984, when the last stretch of freeway was finished, Route 66 was officially decommissioned; the old route is now designated Historic Route 66.

Though it is no longer a main route across the country, Route 66 has retained its mystique in part due to the very same effective hype, hucksterism, and boosterism that animated it through its half-century heyday. It was a Route 66 sight, the marvelous Meramec Caverns, that gave the world the bumper sticker, and it was here that the American art of driving tour as first flourished. Billboards and giant statues along the highway still hawk a baffling array of roadside attractions, tempting passing travelers to swim alongside giant blue whales, to see live rattlesnakes and other wild creatures on display in roadside menageries, or to stay at "Tucumcari Tonight—2,000 Rooms."

The same commercial know-how and shameless self-promotion has helped the towns along the old route stay alive. Diners and motels play up their Route 66 connections, and many bona fide Route 66 landmarks are kept in business by nostalgic travelers intent on experiencing a taste of this endlessly endangered American experience. That said, many quirky old motels and cafés hang on by a thread of hope, sit vacant, or survive in memory only—all for want of an Interstate exit. In fact, of all the roads covered in this book, Route 66 has perhaps been the most impacted by the modern Interstate world; for many stretches you'll be forced to leave the old two-lane and follow the super slabs that have been built right on top of the old road.

Route 66 passes through a marvelous cross-section of American scenes, from the golden sands and sunshine of **Los Angeles,** past the **Grand Canyon** and the Native American communities of the desert **Southwest,** to the gritty streets of **St. Louis** and **Chicago.** Whether you are motivated by an interest in its history, feel a nostalgic yearning for the good old days the route has come to represent, or simply want to experience firsthand the amazing diversity of people and landscapes that line its path, Route 66 offers an unforgettable journey into America, then and now.

CALIFORNIA

From the beautiful beaches of Santa Monica, through the citrus-rich inland valleys, over mountains and across the demanding Mojave Desert, Route 66 passes through every type of Southern California landscape. The old road, which survives intact almost all the way across the state, is marked for most of its 315 miles by signs declaring it Historic Route 66; in the Mojave desert the route is also marked as National Old Trails Highway, its title before the national numbering system was put into effect in the late 1920s.

Santa Monica

Old Route 66 had its western terminus at the edge of the Pacific Ocean in **Santa Monica,** on a palm-lined bluff a few blocks north of the city's landmark pier. The pier holds a small amusement park and a lovely old Looff carousel (as seen in the movie *The Sting*). A beachfront walkway heads south of the pier to Venice Beach, heart of bohemian L.A., but near where Santa Monica Boulevard dead-ends at Ocean Boulevard, a brass plaque marks the official end of Route 66, the "Main Street of America," also remembered as the "Will Rogers Highway," one of many names the old road earned in its half century of existence. The plaque remembers Rogers as a "Humorist, World Traveler, Good Neighbor"—not bad for an Okie from the middle of nowhere.

Two blocks east of the ocean, stretch your legs at Santa Monica Place and the adjacent Third Street Promenade, an indoor/outdoor shopping area and icon of

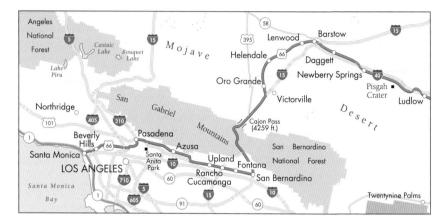

contemporary Southern California (sub)urban culture. The surrounding streets are among the liveliest in Southern California; people actually walk, enjoying street performers, trendy cafés, bookshops, and movie theaters. Right at the center of it all, the **Santa Monica HI Hostel** (310/393-9913) at 1436 2nd Street has 200 dorm beds for under $20 a night—an ideal budget base for seeing Los Angeles.

Route 66 Across Los Angeles

Diehard old-roads fans will be pleasantly surprised to know that Route 66 across Los Angeles still exists, almost completely intact. Heading east from Santa Monica—and now marked by prominent beige road signs as Historic Route 66 1935–1964—old Route 66 follows Santa Monica Boulevard through the hearts of Beverly Hills (where Will Rogers once was mayor) and West Hollywood. In Hollywood itself, Santa Monica Boulevard runs past the cemetery-cum-theme park **Hollywood Forever** (daily; free; 323/469-1181) where such luminaries as Rudolf Valentino and Mel Blanc are entombed, overlooked by the water tower of legendary Paramount Studios. It's a unique experience by day, and even more so on nights when the cemetery is host to "Midnight Movies," outdoor screenings of its residents' works. East from Hollywood, Route 66 merges into Sunset Boulevard for the long winding drive to downtown L.A., ending up at the

historic core of the city: Olvera Street and the Plaza de Los Angeles State Historic Park.

East of downtown L.A., you have your choice of Route 66 routings. You can hop onto the Pasadena Freeway (Hwy-110) for a trip back to freeways past: Opened in 1939, when it was called the Arroyo Seco Parkway, this was California's first freeway and featured such novel (and never repeat-

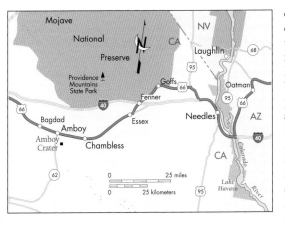

ed) concepts as 15-mph exit ramps and stop signs at the entrances. Or, you can follow Figueroa, which in L.A. lingo is known as a "surface street," running parallel to the freeway past some fascinating pieces of Los Angeles new and old, including the concrete-lined Los Angeles River, hilltop Dodger Stadium, and the nifty **Southwest Museum** (closed Mon.; $6; 323/221-2164), an extensive and unusual collection of Native American art and artifacts from all over western North America, from Arizona to Alaska.

Los Angeles is a stop along our **Pacific Coast** route, which begins on page 10. Some classic L.A. drives are described on pages 92–93.

Pasadena

The Pasadena Freeway (Hwy-110) drops you off unceremoniously short of **Pasadena,** but following Figueroa Street brings you in with a bang on the soaring **Colorado Boulevard Bridge,** an elegantly arching concrete bridge at the western edge of Pasadena, which long marked the symbolic entrance to Los Angeles from the east. Recently restored, the bridge spans **Arroyo Seco** along the south side of the Ventura Freeway (Hwy-134). Arroyo Seco itself is full of significant sights, including college football's Rose Bowl and some of the most important arts-and-crafts–era architecture in Southern California.

Above the arroyo, on old Route 66 at 411 W. Colorado Boulevard, the **Norton Simon Museum** (closed Tues.; $6; 626/449-6840) has a medium-sized but impeccably chosen collection of western and southeast Asian art, ranging from Hindu sculpture to one the world's foremost collections of Degas paintings, drawings, and sculptures. Just a few blocks down old Route 66, Old Pasadena is the new name for the old center of town, where locals congregate for evening fun and daytime shopping, starting their mornings with breakfast at **Marston's** (626/796-2459), at 151 E. Walnut Street.

For more information on Pasadena, contact the **visitors bureau** (626/795-3355), at 865 E. Del Mar.

San Gabriel Valley

East of Pasadena, though effectively swallowed up in Southern California's never-ending sprawl, the **San Gabriel Valley** used to be the westbound traveler's

first taste of Southern California. After crossing the Mojave Desert and the high mountains, Route 66 dropped down into what might have seemed like paradise: Orange groves as far as the eye could see, a few tidy towns linked by streetcars, and houses draped in climbing roses and bougainvillea. The San Gabriel Valley embodied this suburban ideal until the mid-1950s, when Route 66 gave way to high-speed freeways, and the orange groves were replaced by endless grids of tract houses.

If you're willing to search and to close your eyes to mini-mall sprawl, Route 66 still offers a window onto this golden age. Winding between Pasadena and San Bernardino, along the foothills of the sometimes-snowcapped San Gabriel Mountains, the old road links a number of once-distinct communities.

From Pasadena, old Route 66 runs along Colorado Boulevard and then Huntington Drive, turning into Foothill Boulevard around the landmark racetrack at **Santa Anita,** designed by Hoover Dam stylist Gordon Kaufmann. (The Marx Brothers filmed *A Day at the Races* here, but the art deco facades are threatened by the track's ongoing "improvement" into a Las Vegas–style Wild West theme park.) Foothill Boulevard, which is signed as Historic Route 66, jogs along the foothills through **Azusa,** home of the classic Foothill Drive-In, whose marquee was saved when the land was recently developed, then on through collegiate **Claremont.** In **Upland,** where the old road features a number of recently installed retro–Route 66 streetlamps, there's a grass median strip graced by a statue of the pioneer "Madonna of the Trail" that officially marked the western end of the National Old Trails Highway, the immediate precursor to Route 66. The next town, **Rancho Cucamonga** (pop. 125,000), is now best-known as the home of the Epicenter, where the very popular **Cucamonga Quakes** (909/481-5000) play Class A baseball, and a statue of Jack Benny welcomes you through the turnstiles. (If you ever heard his radio show, which featured the tag line "Anaheim, Azusa, and CU-CA-MON-GA," you'll know why he's there.)

At Rancho Cucamonga, Foothill Boulevard crosses the I-15 freeway, which is the quickest route over Cajon Pass; just east of the freeway, Route 66 is remembered by a long-closed "Giant Orange" roadside orange juice stand. The old Route 66 alignment continued east for another 15 miles, passing through Fontana, birthplace of the Hell's Angels' Motorcycle Club (and L.A. culture critic Mike Davis), before bending north at San Bernardino to join I-15 at the summit.

In the 1940s and 50s, **San Bernardino** (pop. 190,000) was where Maurice and Richard McDonald perfected the burger-making restaurant chain that bears their name. In 1961, the McDonald brothers sold their company to Ray Kroc, and the rest is fast-food history; the original location is now an unofficial, ad hoc **"McMuseum"** at 1398 N. E Street (free; 909/885-6324).

Cajon Pass and Victorville

A number of very picturesque but generally dead-end stretches of the old road go over **Cajon Pass,** but the main road is definitely I-15. At the top of the pass, turn off the freeway at the "Oak Hills" exit and stop for a burger and fries at the **Summit Inn** (760/949-1313 or 760/949-8688), one of the few survivors of the old road businesses along this stretch of highway.

East of Cajon Pass, **Hula Ville,** formerly California State Landmark No. 939, bordered old Route 66 on the west side of Victorville. Since the 100-year-old creator and caretaker, "Fry Pan" Miles Mahan, passed away in 1996, some of the hundreds of beer bottles and hand-lettered memorials to sundry bums, hobos, and other travelers he called his friends have been moved to the **California Route 66 Museum,** in downtown Victorville on old Route 66 at 16825 D Street (closed Mon.; 760/951-0436), with a small but growing collection of road signs, photographs, and reminiscences.

Old Route 66 follows 7th Street through town, past a few neon-signed old motels like the **New Corral** ($50; 760/245-9378) at 14643 7th Street with its animated bucking bronco, and the large **Best Western Green Tree Inn** ($80; 760/245-3461), just off the freeway at 14173 Green Tree Boulevard.

Old Route 66 Loop: Oro Grande, Helendale, and Lenwood

Between Victorville and Barstow, old Route 66 survives as an "old roads" trek across the Mojave Desert. The 36-mile route, called the National Old Trails Highway, parallels the railroad tracks and the usually parched Mojave River, passing through odd little towns like **Oro Grande,** which is still home to a huge cement plant and lots of roadside junk shops. Outside Barstow at the west end of Main Street, keep an eye out for the Christian Motorcycle club sign welcoming you to **Lenwood,** a crossroads near where the old road reconnects with I-15.

Midway between Victorville and Barstow is **Helendale,** where you can find the nearly famous stripper's "museum," Exotic World (see the sidebar "Exotic World").

Barstow

Though by population it's under half the size of Victorville, the burly railroad and transportation center of **Barstow** (pop. 21, 495) seems a much bigger place. Located midway between Los Angeles and Las Vegas, at the point where I-15 veers north and I-40 takes the place of old east–west Route 66, Barstow was the first large watering hole west of the Arizona border, a role it still plays, judging by the numerous truck depots arrayed around town. It's scruffy and a little

At the western edge of San Bernardino, a remnant of old Route 66 road culture still survives: the 19 concrete tepees that form the **Wigwam Motel,** at 2728 W. Foothill Boulevard. It's every bit as seedy as the "Do It In A TeePee" sign outside suggests.

San Bernardino County, which covers over 20,000 square miles (most of it desert), is the largest in the United States.

VICTORVILLE

The **Mojave Desert** is one of the driest places on the planet; parts of it receive less than three inches of rainfall in an average year, sometimes going for more than two years without getting a drop.

Exotic World

Victorville is about as far as one could get from the bright lights and bump-and-grind of a big city, but the sprawling desert east of town is the unlikely home of the world's only museum dedicated to the art and craft of striptease dancing—Exotic World. Exotic World fills many rooms in the ranch house of Dixie Lee Evans, a former burlesque dancer who, during the early 1960s, was semi-famous for her striptease impersonations of Marilyn Monroe. Dixie gives each visitor a personally guided tour of the extensive collection, which includes dozens of elaborate costumes as well as posters, photos, props (including one of fan-dancer Sally Rand's famous fans), and rare movies. Most of the items on display were assembled by another burlesque dancer, Jennie Lee, who ran a strip club in San Pedro, California, and who started the collection in order to document the forbidden story of striptease. Jennie Lee's effort to preserve the history of burlesque, and the dancers who made the "hubba-hubba" happen, is carried on by Exotic World's Burlesque Hall of Fame, a wall of 8x10 glossies remembering the shimmying efforts of such striptease luminaries as Lily St. Cyr, Tempest Storm, Blaze Starr, Sally Rand, and Gypsy Rose Lee.

Despite the XXX-rated connotations of striptease, Exotic World (Tues.–Sun. 10 AM–4 PM; donations; 760/243-5261) is a fun place, not at all seedy or licentious, and Dixie's energetic and illuminating presentation makes it well worth the detour. Exotic World is located on a former goat ranch, behind a set of elaborate wrought-iron gates at 29053 Wild Road, just north of old Route 66 in Helendale, about 17 miles east of D Street from Victorville—call Dixie for directions and reservations.

scary in the way railroad towns can be, and along Main Street, the old Route 66 corridor, many of the old cafés and motels are now closed and boarded up.

At the center of town, just north of old Route 66, the circa-1911 Harvey House **Casa del Desierto** hotel next to the train station looks like the Doge's Palace in Venice, its gothic-style arcades a substantial reminder of a time when travel meant more than just getting somewhere. The long-abandoned building was recently brought back to use as a Route 66 **museum** (Fri.–Sun. 11 AM–4 PM; 760/255-1890).

Daggett and Newberry Springs: Bagdad Cafe

East of Barstow all the way to the Arizona border, old Route 66 survives in a series of different stretches alongside the I-40 freeway. The first place of interest,

Northeast of Barstow, **Calico Ghost Town** is an enjoyable resurrection of the silver mining camp that boomed here during the 1890s.

Daggett, is a rusty old mining and railroad town six miles east of Barstow along the north side of the freeway. Old Route 66 runs due east from here, past the region's unique claim to fame: the acres of shiny mirrors at the **Solar One** and **Solar Two** power plants, an experimental, 10-megawatt electricity generating station three miles east of Daggett and north of I-40.

Fifteen miles east of Daggett comes the next I-40 junction and the next small town, **Newberry Springs,** where the popular Percy Adlon movie *Bagdad Cafe* was shot at the town's one and only café, the **Bagdad Cafe** (760/257-3101), open daily for the best food on this stretch of old Route 66. The old road continues along the south side of I-40 for another 25 miles, passing the lava flows of Pisgah Crater before crossing over to the north of the freeway for the final 10 miles into Ludlow, where old Route 66 rejoins the freeway.

Old Route 66 Loop: Ludlow and Amboy

If you want a quick and convincing taste of what traveling across the Mojave Desert was like in the days before air-conditioning and cellular phones, turn south off I-40 at **Ludlow,** 50 miles east of Barstow, and follow the well-signed National Old Trails Highway, one of the many monikers Route 66 has carried over the years, on a 75-mile loop along the old road. At Ludlow, where two gas stations, a coffee shop, and a motel represent civilization between Barstow and Needles, the old road wends slightly southeast, passing first through Bagdad, a turn-of-the-20th-century gold mining town that's now defunct. Continuing east, old Route 66 cuts across another lava flow, this one part of the Amboy Crater, beyond which another road heads south to Twenty-nine Palms and Joshua Tree National Monument.

Midway along the old road loop, **Amboy** (pop. 2) is synonymous with **Roy's Motel and Cafe** (760/733-4263), a museum-worthy assembly of roadside architecture that has survived solely due to the willpower of its longtime lord and master, Buster Burris, who ran the place from 1938 (when he married the daughter of owner Roy Crowl) until 2000, when Buster died at the age of 92. In the late 1940s, Roy's was the prime stop between Needles and Barstow, and as many as 90 people staffed the café, the motel, and the car repair shop, working around the clock to cater to the thousands of passing cars. Roy's fell on hard times after the opening of I-40 in 1974, but the whole town—complete with a huge "Roy's" sign, a classic late-1940s roadside café, a set of simple (but air-conditioned) motor court cabins, and a pair of gas pumps—hung on, and is now a photogenic reminder of the heyday of Route 66.

From Amboy, it's another 48 miles back to I-40 at the town of **Fenner.** If you're keen on traveling as much of

More than 1.5 million acres between I-40 and I-15 have been set aside as the Mojave National Preserve. One of many places here worth the trip is **Mitchell Caverns** ($4; 760/928-2586) at the center of Providence Mountains State Recreation Area, 25 miles north of I-40 at the end of Essex Road. South from Amboy spreads Joshua Tree National Park.

Huge chunks of the Mojave Desert have been used as military training grounds since World War II, when **Gen. George Patton** used this area to prepare his tank battalions for battle in the North African desert. As many as 90,000 soldiers were based here during the war years; the remains of the camp can still be seen in the desert along Crucero Road, just north of the I-40 Ludlow exit.

From Needles, it's a quick 25-mile drive north along the Colorado River into Nevada to visit the gambling center of **Laughlin**. Since the mid-1980s Laughlin has boomed into a sparkling city with huge casinos and over 10,000 cheap rooms.

Needles was the boyhood home of Snoopy and Charlie Brown cartoonist **Charles Schulz**, and is featured in the comic strips as the desert home of Snoopy's raffish sibling, Spike.

the old road as possible, another stretch of Route 66 runs east from Fenner on a roller coaster of undulating two-lane blacktop, parallel to the railroad track through the desert hamlet of **Goffs,** near the spot where comedian Sam Kinison was killed in a car wreck. Fifteen miles east of Goffs, old Route 66 joins up with US-95, which continues north to Las Vegas, 90-odd miles away, and south to I-40, linking up with the freeway 10 miles west of Needles.

Needles

Founded soon after the Santa Fe Railroad came through in 1883, and named for the group of sharp stone spires that stand near where I-40 crosses the Colorado River from Arizona, **Needles** (pop. 4,830) is one of the hottest places in the country, with summertime highs hovering between 100° and 120°F for months on end. Though unbearable in summer, Needles is a popular place with winter snowbirds escaping colder climes; it also has a very rich Route 66 heritage. The magnificent El Garces Hotel is undergoing long-term renovation into a historical museum, while the stretch of old Route 66 through Needles runs along Broadway, alternating along both sides of the freeway.

ARIZONA

If you're not yet a die-hard Route 66 fan, traveling the old route across Arizona is bound to convert you. The high-speed I-40 freeway gives quick access to some of the best surviving stretches of the old road, and these are some of the most captivating parts of Route 66 anywhere. Starting at the Colorado River, the route runs from the arid

Mojave Desert past dozens of remarkable old highway towns along some of the oldest and longest still-driveable stretches of the Mother Road.

Midway across the state, the route climbs onto the forested (and often snowy) Kaibab Plateau for a look at the mighty **Grand Canyon.** East of Flagstaff, the old road is effectively submerged beneath the freeway, which drops down to cross desolate desert, passing through desiccated towns and **Petrified Forest**

National Park. Remnants of numerous old roadside attractions—Indian trading posts, wild animal menageries, and Holbrook's famous "Sleep in a Teepee" Wigwam Village—all survive in varying degrees of preservation along Arizona's section of Route 66.

Lake Havasu City and London Bridge

The first stop east of the Colorado River, nine miles from the border and 23 miles south of I-40, **Lake Havasu City** is a thoroughly modern vacation town built around a thoroughly odd centerpiece: **London Bridge**, brought here stone by stone between 1967 and 1971. Terribly tacky souvenir shops and faux London pubs congregate around the foot of the bridge, which spans a manmade channel to a large island, but the bridge itself is an impressive sight.

Unless you plan to retire here—or simply relax on a houseboat on the river—there's not a lot to do at Lake Havasu; that said, the area has become a popular spring break destination for western college kids, thousands of whom flock to **Lake Havasu State Park** (928/855-2784) for fun-in-the-sun and who-knows-what after dark. For the rest of us—have an English muffin and a cup of tea, pay your respects and take a photograph or two, then hit the road again.

Crossing the Colorado River between Arizona and California, look downstream from the I-40 freeway to see the arching silver steel bridge that carried Route 66 up until 1966. It's still in use, supporting a natural gas pipeline; beyond it, the red-rock spires for which Needles is named rise sharply out of the desert plains.

The crossing over the Colorado River at the California–Arizona border was the site of illegal but effective roadblocks during the Dust Bowl era, when vigilante mobs turned back migrant Okies if they didn't have much money.

Old Route 66: Oatman

One of the most demanding, desolate, and awesomely satisfying stretches of the old road climbs from I-40 along the Colorado River, beginning just east of the California border and rejoining the freeway at Kingman. Following at first along the wildlife refuge that lines the Colorado River, the old road then cuts across a stretch of desert that brings new meaning to the word "harsh." The narrow, roughly surfaced roadway passes few signs of life on this 50-mile loop, so be sure you and your car are prepared for the rigors of desert driving.

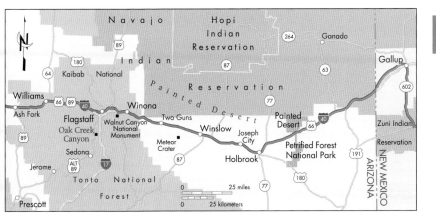

London Bridge

It may not have stood out as the finest piece of engineering art when it spanned the Thames, but London Bridge is a marvelous sight in the middle of the Arizona desert. A replacement for a series of bridges that date back to medieval times, inspiring the children's rhyme, "London Bridge Is Falling Down," this version of London Bridge was constructed in the 1830s. When it was no longer able to handle the demands of London traffic, the old bridge was replaced by a modern concrete span and its stones were put up for sale in 1967.

Bought by property developer Robert McCulloch for $2.4 million, the 10,246 blocks of stone were shipped here and reassembled at a cost of another $3 million. After a channel was cut under the bridge to bring water from the Colorado River, the Lord Mayor of London flew in to attend the re-dedication ceremonies in October 1971; the bridge now stands as the centerpiece of a retirement and resort community that's home to some 25,000 residents. There's no admission charge to see this oddly compelling sight, its finely carved stonework standing in permanent rebuke to the tacky stucco, mock-Tudor souvenir shops lining the base of the bridge.

From I-40 and the California border, take the Park Moabi exit and follow Hwy-95, then Hwy-66, due north; you can also reach Hwy-95 directly from Needles or from Laughlin, Nevada. Westbound drivers have it the easiest—simply follow the well-signed Historic Route 66 west from Kingman, exit 44 off I-40. Whichever way you go, you can't avoid the steep hills that bring you to **Oatman** (elev. 2,700 feet), an odd mix of ghost town and tourist draw that's one of the top stops along Route 66. A gold mining town whose glory days had long faded by the time I-40 passed it by way back in 1952, Oatman looks like a Wild West stage set, but it's the real thing—awnings over the plank sidewalks, bearded roughnecks (and a few burros) wandering the streets, lots of rust, and slumping old buildings. The gold mines here produced some two million ounces from their start in 1904 until they panned out in the mid-1930s; at its peak, Oatman had a population of over 10,000, with 20 saloons lining the three-block Main Street. One of these, the old **Oatman Hotel** (928/768-4408), at 181 N. Main Street, was where Clark Gable and Carole Lombard spent their first night after getting married in Kingman in 1939; you can sample Oatman's highly recommended Navajo tacos, have a beer in the downstairs bar, or peer through a Plexiglas door at the room where Clark and Carole slept, hardly changed for half a century.

For the hits of the1960s, tune to Kingman's "Radio Crazy," **KRCY** 105.9 FM.

Saloons and rock shops line the rest of Main Street, where on weekends and holidays Wild West enthusiasts act out the shoot-outs that took place here only in the movies. Oatman does get a considerable tourist trade, but after dark and out of the peak summer tourist season the town reverts to its rough-and-tumble ways, and the conservative, libertarian bent of most of the local population ensures that nothing is likely to change Oatman's crusty charms.

East of Oatman the road passes the recently reactivated gold workings at **Gol-droad** before climbing up and over the angular Black Mountains. Steep switch-backs and 15-mph hairpin turns make the 2,100-foot change in elevation over a very short eight miles of blacktop; the route then continues for another 20 miles into Kingman, which seems like a bustling metropolis after this hour-plus roller coaster of a drive.

Kingman

The only town for miles in any direction since its founding as a railroad center in 1880, **Kingman** (pop. 20,069) has always depended upon passing travelers for its livelihood. Long a main stopping place on Route 66, and still providing the only all-night services on US-93 between Las Vegas and Phoenix, and along I-40 between Flagstaff and Needles, the town remains more a way station than a destination despite the increasing number of people who have relocated here in recent years, attracted by the open space, high desert air, and low cost of living.

Everything that's ever happened in and around Kingman is documented to some degree at the **Mojave Museum** (daily; $3; 928/753-3195) at 400 W. Beale Street, right on US-93 a block south of I-40. Besides the usual dioramas and displays on regional history, there's an extensive section devoted to local Huala-pai culture and crafts, as well as samples of turquoise mined nearby. There's also a display on the life of local boy Andy Devine and a photograph of Clark Gable and Carole Lombard, who fled Hollywood to get married in Kingman's Methodist church.

Quite a few of the old Route 66 cafés and motels still flourish alongside the old road, now called Andy Devine Avenue, through town; modern development borders I-40. Among the many places to eat are the very good **Mr. D's Route 66 Diner** (928/718-0066), at 105 E. Andy Devine Avenue right downtown and impossible to miss thanks to its bank of neon; and the **House of Chan** (928/753-3232), at 960 W. Beale Street, on US-93 a block north of I-40, which serves a full menu of American food as well as Cantonese specialties. Besides the usual chain motels, accommodation options include the pleasant **Hill Top Motel** ($40; 928/753-2198), at 1901 E. Andy Devine Avenue, forever infa-mous as the place where evil Timothy McVeigh stayed for a week before blow-ing up the Federal Building in Oklahoma City.

The stretch of Route 66 through Kingman has been renamed in memory of favorite son Andy Devine, who was born in Flagstaff in 1905 but grew up here, where his parents ran the Beale Hotel. One of the best-known character actors of Hollywood's classic era, the raspy-voiced Devine usually played a devoted

Peach Springs is the starting point for the 22-mile drive along **Diamond Creek Road**— all the way to the "bottom" of the Grand Canyon. Get a permit and detailed info at the Hualapai Lodge.

Midway between Peach Springs and the Grand Canyon Caverns, Hwy-18 cuts off 65 miles to the northeast toward the Havasupai Indian Reservation, which includes one of the most beautiful and untrammeled corners of the Grand Canyon. No roads, just red rocks, green canyons, cobalt-blue waterfalls, and the **Havasupai Lodge** ($125; 928/448-2111).

sidekick, the sort of role taken by Gabby Hayes, whom Devine replaced in the later Roy Rogers movies. He also did the voice of Friar Tuck in Disney's version of *Robin Hood*, but Devine's most famous role was as the wagon driver in the classic 1939 John Ford western *Stagecoach*. He remained active in films and TV until his death in 1977.

For more information, or to pick up a copy of the town's very good Route 66 brochure, contact the Kingman **visitors center** (928/753-6106), housed alongside a mini museum in an interestingly converted old power plant at 120 W. Andy Devine Avenue.

Hualapai Mountain Park

To escape the summer heat, Kingmanites head south along a well-marked 14-mile road to **Hualapai Mountain Park,** where pines and firs cover the slopes of the 8,417-foot peak. Hiking trails wind through the wilderness, where there's a campground and a few rustic cabins ($25–65) built by the Civilian Conservation Corps during the New Deal 1930s. Contact the ranger station (928/757-3859) near the park entrance for detailed information or to make reservations.

Old Route 66 Loop: Hackberry, Valentine, and the Hualapai Reservation

Probably the most evocative stretch of old Route 66 runs northeast from Kingman through the high-desert Hualapai ("WALL-ah-pie") Valley, along the Santa Fe Railroad tracks through all-but-abandoned towns bypassed by the "modern" Interstate world. Leaving Kingman on a 20-mile-long straightaway, the road (now named Hwy-66) bends back south around the Peacock Mountains through the old railroad town of **Hackberry,** then continues east across a small section of the Hualapai Indian Reservation, centered around the village of **Valentine.** Another 10 miles east brings you to the town of Truxton, where the **Frontier Cafe** (928/769-2238) on the south side of the highway is the one reliable place to eat in this sparsely populated region—good pie and great chat, open daily, with a few rooms as well. **Grandma's Bar** across the highway gives

you another chance to sample local lore and lifeways.

Another mile east is the boundary of the main **Hualapai Reservation** lands. The 700-strong tribe has its community center at the town of **Peach Springs,** which marks the halfway point of this 90-mile, old-roads loop and offers at least one reason to stop: the comfortable **Hualapai Lodge** ($70–115; 928/769-2230) hotel and "River Runners'" restaurant, right on Route 66. Apart from this, Peach Springs is mostly a prefab Bureau of Indian Affairs housing project with few services, though there is a photogenic old Route 66 filling station at the center of town.

Grand Canyon Caverns

A dozen miles east of Peach Springs, 22 miles west of Seligman, a large green sign marks the entrance to **Grand Canyon Caverns** (daily; $12; 928/422-4565), which has somehow managed to survive despite being bypassed by the I-40 superslab. Once one of the prime tourist draws on the Arizona stretch of Route 66, the Grand Canyon Caverns were discovered and developed in the late 1920s and still have the feel of an old-time roadside attraction. Tours start every hour at the gift shop, where you hop on the elevator that drops you 300 feet to underground chambers, including the 18,000-square-foot Chapel of the Ages. Tours last around 45 minutes. There's also a gas station, a motel (with a pool), and a restaurant on the site.

Seligman

At the east end of the long loop of old Route 66, the sleepy little town of **Seligman** (pop. 510; SLIG-man) is a perfect place to take a break before or after rejoining the Interstate hordes. The town retains a lot of its historic character—old sidewalk awnings and even a few hitching rails—and offers lots of reasons to stop, including Angel Delgadillo, the town barber, whose shop at 217 E. Route 66 is a pilgrimage point for old-roads fans. His brother Juan Delgadillo created and ran the wacky **Snow Cap Drive-In** (928/422-3291) a half-block to the east, where the sign says "Sorry, We're Open," and the menu advertises "Hamburgers without Ham." Behind the restaurant, in snow, rain, or shine, sits a roofless old Chevy decorated with fake flowers and an artificial Christmas tree. Juan died in 2004 (at the ripe old age of 88), but his family carries on the Snow Cap traditions, and the burgers, fries, and milk shakes are worth driving miles for.

> Between Seligman and Ash Fork, a nice section of the old Route 66 two-lane runs just north of, and parallel to, the I-40 freeway.

Seligman, 1940s location of Andreas Feininger's classic Route 66 photograph, also has a very good café, the **Copper Cart** (928/422-3241), at 103 W. Chino Avenue in the center of town; a neat old mock-Tudor railroad station that once doubled as a Harvey House hotel and restaurant; and a half-dozen motels including "Unique Motel" (which is now a sign only) and the **Historic Route 66 Motel** (928/422-3204) at 500 W. Route 66. After dark, head to the **Black Cat** saloon, where actor Nicholas Cage has been known to stop in for a drink or two.

Delgadillo's Snow Cap

Grand Canyon National Park

From the east end of Williams, Hwy-64 continues 60 miles due north to one of the wonders of the natural world, the Grand Canyon of the Colorado River. Two hundred miles long, a mile deep, and anywhere from 5 to 15 miles across, the Grand Canyon defies description, and if you're anywhere nearby you owe it to yourself to stop for a look. You could spend a lifetime here and still not get to know it all, but even if you have only half a day be sure to leave the rim and hike down into the canyon to get a real sense of its awesome scale.

Most of what you need to know to enjoy a visit is contained in the brochure you're given at the entrance, where you pay the $20 per-car fee, or can be found at the very good **visitors center** (daily; 928/638-7888).

To make advance reservations for accommodations, a good idea at any time of year but essential in the peak summer months, phone the park concessionaire, **Xanterra** (303/297-2757 in advance, 928/638-2631 for same-day booking). The most characterful and best-value place to stay is the **Bright Angel Lodge**, which overlooks the canyon; there are also many other

nearby motels, and the seriously swanky **El Tovar Hotel**, where rooms cost around $200 a night.

If all the in-park accommodations are full, more rooms are available outside the park's southern boundary at **Tusayan**, where the park service plans to concentrate all future development at the Grand Canyon, if and when cars are finally banned and replaced by the long-proposed light rail.

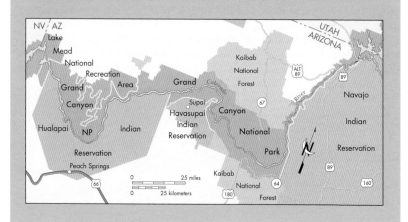

Williams

The last Route 66 town to be bypassed by I-40, **Williams** (pop. 2,842; elev. 6,780 ft) held out until the bitter end, waging court battle after court battle before finally surrendering on October 13, 1984. Despite the town's long opposition, in the end Williams gave in gracefully, going so far as to hold a celebration-cum-wake for the old road, highlighted by a performance atop the new freeway overpass by none other than Mr. Route 66 himself, Bobby "Get Your Kicks" Troup.

Williams today is primarily a gateway to the Grand Canyon, but it also takes full tourist advantage of its Route 66 heritage: The downtown streets sport old-fashioned street lamps, and every other store sells a variety of Route 66 souvenirs, making the town much more than a pit stop for Grand Canyon-bound travelers. Apart from the Route 66 connections, Williams's pride and joy is the vintage **Grand Canyon Railway,** which whistles and steams its way north to the canyon every morning March–December, taking roughly two hours each way. Call for current schedules and fares (round-trip costs around $60; 800/843-8724), or stop by the historic depot, a former Harvey House hotel restored in 1990. Williams is also home to a landmark old Route 66 restaurant, **Rod's Steak House** (928/635-2671), at 301 E. Bill Williams Avenue, in business since 1946.

For a place to stay—and there are many, thanks to the nearby Grand Canyon—there's a nice old motor court motel across from Rod's, now disguised as an **EconoLodge** ($50 and up; 928/635-4085), at 302 E. Route 66. At the upper end of the scale, look into the historic railroad hotel, the **Fray Marcos** ($80 and up; 928/635-4010).

Flagstaff

An old railroad and lumber-mill town given a new lease on life by an influx of students at Northern Arizona University, and by the usual array of ski bums and mountain bikers attracted by the surrounding high mountain wilderness, **Flagstaff** (pop. 52,894) is an enjoyable, energetic town high up on the Coconino Plateau. The natural beauty of its forested location has meant that, compared to other Route 66 towns, Flagstaff was less affected by the demise of the old road. That said, it still takes pride in the past, notably in the form of the **Museum Club** (928/526-9434), at 3404 E. Route 66, an old roadhouse brought back to life as a country-western nightclub and ad-hoc nostalgia museum. There are also dozens of vintage neon signs along the old Route 66 alignment: Check out the Western Hills Motel and the Grand Canyon Cafe downtown, and the Flamingo Motel five blocks west. (The Flamingo has been known as the Flaming Motel since the "o" burned out on the sign.)

Flagstaff also has a pair of non-Route 66 related attractions. First and foremost of these stands on a hill at the west end of Flagstaff, reachable from the west end of Santa Fe Avenue (old Route 66): the **Lowell Observatory,** established in

In his 1945 *Guide Book to Highway 66,* Jack Rittenhouse wrote, "Cowboys and Indians can be seen in their picturesque dress on Flagstaff streets year - round..."

Flagstaff's San Francisco Street was named not for the California city but for the nearby volcanic peaks, so called by early Spanish missionaries and still held sacred by the native Hopi Indians.

Songs of Route 66

If you ever plan to motor west,
Travel my way, that's the highway that's the best,
Get your kicks on Route 66.
It winds from Chicago to L.A.,
More than 2,000 miles all the way,
Get your kicks on Route 66.
Now you go through St. Looey, Joplin, Missouri
And Oklahoma City is mighty pretty.
You'll see Amarillo, Gallup, New Mexico,
Flagstaff, Arizona, don't forget Winona,
Kingman, Barstow, San Bernardino.
Won't you get hip to this timely tip:
When you make that California trip,
Get your kicks on Route 66.
Get your kicks on Route 66.

—Bobby Troup

Flagstaff very nearly became an early movie center, when young **Cecil B. DeMille** stopped here briefly while scouting locations to shoot the world's first feature-length film, a Western called *The Squaw Man*. It was snowing in Flagstaff that day, so he moved on to Los Angeles.

1894 by Percival Lowell and best known as the place where, in 1930, the planet Pluto was discovered. A visitors center (daily in summer, shorter hours rest of the year; $4; 928/774-2096) has descriptions of the science behind what goes on here—spectroscopy, red shifts, and expanding universes, for example—and the old telescope, a 24-inch refractor, is open for viewings 8–10 PM most nights in summer.

The other main draw, the **Museum of Northern Arizona** (daily; $5; 928/774-5213), perches at the edge of a pine-forested canyon three miles northwest of downtown via US-180, the main road to the Grand Canyon; extensive exhibits detail the vibrant cultures of northern Arizona, from prehistoric Puebloans to contemporary Hopi, Navajo, and Zuni.

Downtown Flagstaff has more than enough espresso bars—probably a dozen within a two-block radius of the train station—to satisfy its many multiply pierced, twenty-something residents. There are also ethnic restaurants specializing in Greek, Thai, German, or Indian cuisine, so finding suitable places to eat and drink will not be a problem. For breakfast and lunch, it's hard to beat **Kathy's** (928/774-1951), a cozy café at 7 N. San Francisco Street.

Accommodations, too, are plentiful, and you can pick either the motel with the most appealing sign or step back into an earlier time and stay at the classy old **Hotel Monte Vista** ($50–70; 928/779-6971 or 800/545-3068), right off old Route 66 at 100 N. San Francisco Street. It was good enough for Gary Cooper and has been restored to its Roaring Twenties splendor.

For more-complete listings or other information, contact the **visitors center** (928/774-9541 or 800/842-7293), right downtown at 1 E. Route 66.

One of the most popular road songs ever written, and a prime force behind the international popularity of Route 66, "Get Your Kicks on Route 66" was penned by jazz musician Bobby Troup in 1946 while he was driving west to seek fame and fortune in Los Angeles. Troup consistently credited his former wife Cynthia, with whom he was traveling, for the half-dozen words of the title and refrain. The rest of the song simply rattled off the rhyming place-names along the way, but despite its apparent simplicity, it caught the ear of Nat King Cole, who made it into a hit record and also established the pronunciation as "root" rather than "rout," as repeated in later renditions by everyone from Bob Wills to the Rolling Stones.

If you haven't heard the song for a while, there's a jazzy version by Bobby Troup, along with some lively Route 66–related songs, on the compilation tape and CD, *The Songs of Route 66—Music from the All-American Highway,* available at souvenir stores en route.

Walnut Canyon National Monument

The most easily accessible of the hundreds of different prehistoric settlements all over the southwestern United States, **Walnut Canyon National Monument** (daily 8 AM–4 PM, 7 AM–5 PM in summer; $4; 928/526-3367) is also one of the prettiest places imaginable, with piñon pines and junipers clinging to the canyon walls, and walnut trees filling the canyon floor. On the edge of the canyon, a small visitors center gives the historical background, but the real interest lies below, on a short but very steep path that winds through cliff dwellings tucked into overhangs and ledges 400 feet above the canyon floor.

The entrance to the monument, which contains some 300 identified archaeological sites, lies seven miles east of Flagstaff, accessible from I-40 exit 204.

Don't Forget: Winona

East of Flagstaff, following old Route 66 can be a frustrating task, since much of the roadway is blocked or torn up or both. Unlike the long stretches found in the western half of the state, here the old road exists only as short segments running through towns, and most of the way you're forced to follow the freeway, stopping at exit after exit to get on and off the old road. Among the places worth considering is the one town mentioned out of sequence in the Route 66 song: "Flagstaff, Arizona, don't forget Winona," which, alas, is now little more than a name on the sign at I-40 exit 211.

East of Winona, the route drops swiftly from the cool pines onto the hot red desert, but old-road fanatics will want to take the time to explore what remains of two old-time tourist traps lining the next 20 miles of highway.

First of these is **Twin Arrows**, where a pair of giant but decaying red arrows point toward a long-closed café, right off the freeway at exit 219. Continuing east, approaching exit 230, the freeway crosses deep Diablo Canyon, where an old Route 66 bridge still spans the dry wash, and the walls of a half-dozen bleached buildings are all that's left of the **Two Guns Trading Post**, just south of exit 230. A roadside attraction par excellence, Two Guns had a zoo full of roadrunners, Gila monsters, and coyotes, and one building still has a sign saying Mountain Lions—all for the entertainment of passing travelers. According to various reports down the Route 66 grapevine, Two Guns has been on the verge of reopening in recent years, but most of the time the old road is blocked by a sign reading No Trespassing by Order of Two Guns Sheriff Department. Probably a good thing, since the old buildings are all dangerously close to collapse. It's an evocative site, nonetheless, and photogenic in the right light.

At the west end of Joseph City, right off I-40 exit 274, stop at the **Jackrabbit Trading Post**, the one whose signs you've probably noticed over the past hundred miles, and take a picture or buy a postcard of the giant jackrabbit, one of a long line of creatures who have stood here since 1949.

Meteor Crater

Three miles east of Two Guns, and six miles south of I-40 exit 233, sits **Meteor Crater** (daily; $12; 928/289-2362), Arizona's second-most distinctive hole in the ground. Formed by a meteorite some 50,000 years ago, and measuring 550 feet deep and nearly a mile across, the crater is a privately owned tourist attraction, offering an "Astronauts Hall of Fame," which plays up the crater's resemblance to the surface of the moon (Apollo moon-walkers practiced here). You can't climb down into it, but (weather permitting) you can join a guided "rim tour," walking a half mile there and back across the desert to gaze down into the crater.

Winslow

Winslow, Arizona, didn't make it into Bobby Troup's original Route 66 hit list, but the town more than made it a generation later with the Eagles tune "Take It Easy," which begins, "Standin' on a corner in Winslow, Arizona," a line that has caused more people to turn off in search of the place than anything else.

Winslow and Holbrook are the nearest towns to the **Navajo Nation Indian Reservation**, home of radio station **KTNN 660 AM**, which broadcasts a fascinating mélange of Navajo chants and Jimi Hendrix riffs. It's also the only station in the United States that broadcasts pro football games—in Navajo.

In between I-40 and Route 66, the funky **Old Trails Museum** (closed Sun.; 520/289-5861), at 212 Kinsley Street, sells a range of "Standin' on the Corner" T-shirts, and displays a few reminders of Winslow in its heyday. Down the block, on 2nd and Kinsley, a little sign stakes a claim to being *the* corner the Eagles sang about; in 1994, Eagles songwriter Don Henley donated $2,500 to help beautify the spot with an appropriate monument.

Chain motels and fast-food franchises stand at either end of town around the I-40 exits, but in between is a great landmark of Southwest style: the elegant **La Posada Hotel** ($90 and up; 928/289-4366) at 303 E. 2nd Street. Designed in the late 1920s for Fred Harvey by architect Mary Colter, who considered it her masterpiece, the hotel was closed for 40 years before being restored and reopened in 1998.

Holbrook: Wigwam Village

Holding a concentrated dose of old Route 66 character, **Holbrook** (pop. 4,917) is definitely worth a quick detour off the I-40 freeway. More than the other Route 66 towns in the eastern half of Arizona, it still feels like a real place, with lively cafés and some endearing roadside attractions around the center of town, where Route 66 alternates between Hopi Drive and Navajo Boulevard. Be sure to stop at **Joe and Aggie's Cafe** (928/524-6540) at 120 W. Hopi Drive, or **Romo's Cafe** (928/ 524-2153) across the street; and be sure to check out the huge dinosaur collection outside the **Rainbow Rock Shop**, a block south on Navajo Boulevard near the railroad tracks.

East of Holbrook, along I-40 near exit 289, a series of concrete dinosaurs tempt you toward the **International Petrified Forest Dinosaur Park** (daily; $7; 928/524-6458), a private gallery full of polished petrified rock (and a few Triassic-era fossils), plus a pen of captive bison.

Best of all, stop for the night at the marvelous **Wigwam Village** (928/524-3048), at 811 W. Hopi Drive at the western edge of town, and sleep in a concrete tepee. Based on the original circa-1936 Wigwam Village motor court built in Cave City, Kentucky, Holbrook's was one of seven franchises across the country; this one opened in 1950 but closed down when the Interstate came through in 1974. The family of original owner Chester Lewis fully renovated the buildings and reopened the place after his death in 1988; original bentwood hickory furniture, a small curio shop, and a handful of historic American cars parked outside help complete the ambience of classic roadside Americana. Rooms cost around $35 a night, so you really should stay here at least once in your life.

Another worthwhile place to stop is the **Navajo County Museum** (closed Sun.; free) in the old Navajo County Courthouse, four blocks south of I-40 at the corner of Navajo Boulevard (old Route 66) and Arizona Street. The collections are wide-ranging and include a walk downstairs to the old county jail, in use from 1899 until 1976 (the graffiti is great). The museum hosts Native American dances on summer evenings, and is next door to the **Holbrook Chamber of Commerce** (928/524-6558), which has walking- and driving-tour maps and general information on the town and surrounding area.

The **Hubbell Trading Post National Historic Site** (928/755-3254), 38 miles north of I-40 from exit 333 and a mile west of the town of Ganado, is a frontier store preserved as it was in the 1870s, when trader John Hubbell began buying the beautiful rugs made by local Navajo weavers.

Painted Desert and Petrified Forest National Park

The easternmost 60 miles of I-40 across Arizona are little more than one long speedway, since any sign of the old road has been lost beneath the four-lane interstate. One place that's worth a stop here is **Petrified Forest National Park** (daily dawn–dusk; $10 per car; 928/524-6228). The polished petrified wood on display in the visitors center is gorgeous to look at, but seeing the stuff in its raw natural state is not particularly thrilling. The story of how the wood got petrified is interesting, though: About 225 million years ago, a forest was buried in volcanic ash, then slowly embalmed with silica and effectively turned to stone. You can take a look at 93,000 acres of the stuff outside the visitors center, and at the entrance to the park there's a handy restaurant and gas station.

While the park contains a vast array of prehistoric fossils and pictographs as well as the petrified wood, one of the more interesting sights is the old **Painted Desert Inn**, a Route 66 landmark during the 1920s and 1930s that was converted into a museum and bookstore after the Park Service took it over in the 1960s. The pueblo-style building is perched on a plateau, overlooking the spectacularly colored "**Painted Desert**" that stretches off toward the northern horizon.

East of the park, right along the New Mexico border, Arizona welcomes westbound travelers with an overwhelming display of trading-post tackiness—huge concrete tepees stand at the foot of brilliant red-rock mesas, while gift shops styled after everything from TV's *F Troop* to *Dances with Wolves* hawk their souvenirs to passing travelers. The gift shops themselves may not be all that attractive, but the old Route 66 frontage road along here and east into New Mexico is truly spectacular, running at the foot of red-rock cliffs.

NEW MEXICO

Following old Route 66 across New Mexico gives you a great taste of the Land of Enchantment, as the state calls itself on its license plates. There is less of the actual "old road" here than in other places, but the many towns and ghost towns along I-40, built more or less on top of Route 66, still stand. In **Albuquerque**, Route 66 runs through the center of this sprawling Sun Belt city, while in other places finding the old road and bypassed towns can take some time, though the effort is usually well rewarded.

Stretching for over a dozen miles across the border between the two states, beautiful Hwy-118 runs along the north side of I-40, following old Route 66 between exit 357 in Arizona and exit 8 in New Mexico.

Western New Mexico has the most to see and the most interesting topography, with sandstone mesas looming in the foreground and high, pine-forested peaks rising in the distance. Paralleling the Santa Fe Railroad, the route passes through the heart of this region, and numerous detours—to **Inscription Rock** and **Chaco Canyon**, among others—make unforgettable stops along the way. In the east, the land is flatter and the landscape drier as the road approaches the Great Plains.

Gallup

Though it's not exactly scenic, **Gallup** (pop. 20,209) is a fascinating place. Founded in 1881 when the Santa Fe Railroad first rumbled through, and calling itself "The Gateway to Indian Country" because it's the largest town near the huge Navajo and other Native American reservations of the Four Corners region, Gallup has some of the Southwest's largest trading posts and one of the best strips of neon signs you'll see anywhere on old Route 66.

For travelers intent on experiencing a little of the charms of old Route 66, Gallup also has **El Rancho** ($50 and up; 505/863-9311), at 1000 E. Route 66, a delightful old hotel lovingly restored to its 1930s glory. Built by a brother of movie director D. W. Griffiths, El Rancho feels like a national park lodge, with a large but welcoming lobby dominated by a huge stone fireplace. All the rooms in the old wing are named for the movie stars who have stayed here over the years—the W. C. Fields Room, the John Wayne Room, the Marx Brothers Room (which sleeps six), even the Ronald Reagan Room—and signed glossies of these and many more actors and actresses adorn the halls. El Rancho also has a good restaurant serving regional food, and a gift shop selling souvenirs and locally crafted jewelry, pottery, and rugs.

Gallup also hosts the annual **Inter Tribal Ceremonial**, perhaps the largest Native American gathering in the country, held early in August at Red Rock State Park eight miles east of Gallup, and culminating in a Sunday parade that brings some 30,000 people out to line old Route 66 through town. Festivities include a rodeo, powwows, and a beauty show; call for the latest details (505/863-3896).

In the heart of historic downtown, the old Santa Fe train depot (still in use by Amtrak), houses the **Gallup Cultural Center** (505/863-4131) at 201 E. Route 66; free dance shows are staged here nightly in summer, next to a statue of a WW II Navajo "Code Talker." Another place worth spending some time is **Richardson's Cash Pawn and Trading Post** (505/722-4762), at 222 W. Route 66. Family-run since 1913, this busy but friendly space is crammed to the rafters with arts, crafts, and pawned goods—Navajo rugs and jewelry, ornately tooled leather saddles, pearl-inlaid guitars, and more—that give a better sense of local lifestyles (and all their ups and downs) than any museum ever could. For a taste of this real-life Wild West, stop by the **Eagle Cafe** next door.

Inscription Rock and El Malpais: Hwy-53

Western New Mexico is among the most beautiful places on the planet. South of I-40 and Route 66, one of the best drives through it, Hwy-53, loops between Gallup and Grants across the Zuni and Navajo Nation Indian Reservations. Skirting the southern foothills of the 9,000-foot Zuni Mountains, the route follows ancient Indian trails that Coronado used on his ill-fated 1540 explorations, winding past piñon-covered hills, open grasslands, and the fascinating graffiti collection of El Morro National Monument. Better known as **Inscription Rock,** the 200-foot-high sandstone cliffs of El

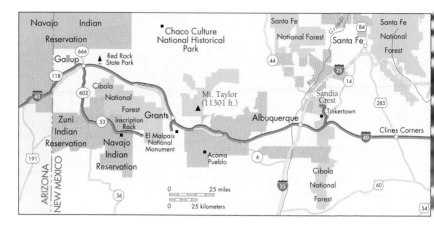

Morro have been inscribed by travelers like Juan de Oñate, who wrote his name with a flourish in 1605, after he "discovered" the Gulf of California.

Atop the cliffs are the partially excavated remains of a small pueblo dating from around AD 1200. A two-mile loop trail to the inscriptions and the ruins starts from a small **visitors center** (daily; $4 per car; 505/783-4226), where exhibits outline the history of the site. The trails are closed an hour before sunset, so get here early enough in the day to enjoy the beautiful scenery. There is also a small campground (no showers, pit toilets) amidst the junipers.

East of Inscription Rock, after crossing the Continental Divide where there's a roadside rest stop, Hwy-53 winds along the edge of the massive **El Malpais** lava flow—thousands of acres of pitch-black, concrete-hard, glassy sharp rock. On the slopes of Bandera Volcano, you can tour the privately-run **Ice Cave** (daily; $9; 505/783-4303) before rejoining I-40 and old Route 66 at Grants.

Grants

Along with the usual Route 66 range of funky motels and rusty neon signs, the former mining boomtown of **Grants** has the unique attraction of the **New Mexico Mining Museum** (closed Sun; $3; 505/287-4802), right downtown on old Route 66 (Santa Fe Avenue) at the corner of Iron Avenue. Most of the exhibits trace the short history of local uranium mining, which began in 1950 when a local Navajo rancher, Paddy Martinez, discovered an odd yellow rock that turned out to be high-grade uranium ore. Mines here once produced half the ore mined in the United States, but production has now ceased. From the main gallery, ride the elevator down (only one floor, but it feels like 900 feet) to the high-

Every bit as impressive and memorable as the cliff dwellings of Mesa Verde, the extensive archaeological remains protected inside **Chaco Culture National Historical Park** are well worth your time. Though it's an hour's drive from I-40 via unpaved roads, the park is one of the wonders of the Southwest desert; for details, call 505/786-7014.

Midway between Grants and Gallup, I-40 crosses the 7,250-foot Continental Divide, where the "Top O' the World" dance hall used to tempt travelers off old Route 66. From here (exit 47), it's possible to follow the old road for 30 miles, running east along I-40 as far as Grants.

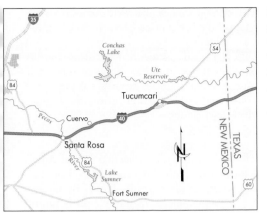

light of the mining museum: a credible re-creation of a uranium mine, complete with an underground lunch room emblazoned with all manner of warning signs.

If you're lucky, the **Uranium Cafe** will still be in business across the street from the Mining Museum, serving up breakfast and lunch every day but Sunday. Just look for the atomic neon sign, a rarely lit Route 66 landmark.

Pie Town and the Lightning Field

A long way south of Grants, an old mining camp was so famous for fine desserts it became known as **Pie Town**. After many years of pielessness, local meringue-lovers lucked out when baker Kathy Knapp opened the **Pie-O-Neer Cafe** (505/772-2900), on old US-60 at milepost 59.

East of Pie Town off US-60, the **Lightning Field** (May–Oct. only; 505/898-3335) is an outdoor "land art" installation by Walter De Maria, who implanted a grid of steel tubes into the New Mexico plain with the intention of attracting lightning strikes. The sculpture consists of 400 stainless steel poles situated in a rectangular grid roughly one mile by one kilometer; the engineering feat here was to set the poles so that their tops form an exactly level plane. For the full Lightning Field experience, you have to stay overnight in nearby cabins, and all meals and transportation to the site are included in the $150/night fee.

Acoma Pueblo: Sky City and Enchanted Mesa

A dozen miles east of Grants and 50 miles west of Albuquerque, one of the Southwest's most intriguing sites, **Acoma Pueblo**, stands atop a 357-foot-high sandstone mesa. Long known as "Sky City," Acoma is one of the very oldest communities in North America, inhabited since AD 1150. The views out across the plains are unforgettable, especially the Enchanted Mesa on the horizon to the northeast.

Few people live on the mesa today, though the many adobe houses are used by Pueblo craftspeople, who live down below but come up to the mesa-top to sell their pottery to tourists. To visit, stop at the visitors center at the base of the mesa, and join a guided **tour** (daily; $10; 505/469-1052). Tours begin with a bus ride to the mesa-top and end with a visit to **San Esteban del Rey Mission**, the largest Spanish colonial church in the state. Built in 1629, the church features

Broadcasting on 530 AM around the Acoma area, actor Ricardo Montalban narrates the story of the pueblo's conquest by the Spanish, and the story of the building of San Esteban church high atop the mesa.

a roof constructed of huge timbers that were carried from the top of Mt. Taylor on the backs of neophyte Indians—a distance of more than 30 miles.

Acoma Pueblo is 15 miles south of I-40, from exit 96 (eastbound) or exit 108 (westbound). Between these two exits, another stretch of old Route 66 survives, passing crumbling tourist courts and service stations across the Laguna and Acoma Indian Reservations.

Albuquerque

Roughly located at the center of New Mexico, the sprawling city of **Albuquerque** (pop. 463,300) spreads north and south along the banks of the Rio Grande and east to the foothills of 10,000-foot Sandia Crest. By far the state's biggest city, Albuquerque is a young, energetic, and vibrantly multicultural community, which, among many features, boasts a great stretch of old Route 66 along Central Avenue through the heart of the city—18 miles of diners, motels, and sparkling neon signs. For an offbeat taste of the city's Route 66 heritage, keep an eye out for the remarkable **Aztec Motel** (505/254-1742), at 3821 Central Avenue, a very funky Pueblo-style 1930s motel kept alive as a live-in sculpture gallery and artists' community.

Albuquerque was also the home of the great travel writer and WW II war correspondent **Ernie Pyle**. His old house, at 900 Girard Avenue, a half-mile south of Central Avenue, is now the city's oldest public library, which includes his collected works and a few personal items in a small display.

One of the best parts of town is **Old Town**, the historic heart of Albuquerque. Located a block north of Central Avenue, at the west end of Route 66's cruise through downtown, Old Town offers a quick taste of New Mexico's Spanish colonial past, with a lovely old church, the 300-year-old **San Felipe de Neri**; as well as shops and restaurants set around a leafy green park. An information booth in the park has walking-tour maps of Old Town and other information about the city. Another Old Town attraction, one that carries on the Route 66 tradition of reptile farms and private zoos, is the **Rattlesnake Museum** (daily; $2.50), southeast of the main square at 202 San Felipe Street, where you can see a range of rattlers from tiny babies to full-sized diamondbacks, about 50 altogether, plus fellow desert-dwellers like tarantulas and a giant Gila monster.

A very different look into New Mexico's varied cultural makeup is offered at the **Indian Pueblo Cultural Center** (daily; $4; 505/843-7270), a block north of I-40 exit 158 at 2401 12th Street. The center is owned and operated by the state's 19 different Pueblo communities; its highlight is a fine museum tracing the history of the region's Native American cultures, from Anasazi times up to the Pueblo Revolt of 1680, with the contemporary era illustrated by video presentations and a mock-up of a typical tourist—camera, shorts, and all. On most weekends ceremonial dances are held in the central courtyard—free and open to the general public. There's also a small cafeteria where you can sample food like fry bread and Navajo tacos, and a smoke-shop selling cut-price cigarettes.

Though most people associate computer giant **Microsoft** with Seattle, the company actually began here in Albuquerque in 1975, in a series of dingy Route 66 motels.

Albuquerque Practicalities

The largest city in New Mexico, Albuquerque makes a very handy point of entry for tours of the Southwestern United States. For old-road fans, the best stretch of Route 66 through Albuquerque is probably the section along Nob Hill, east of downtown and Old Town near the University of New Mexico. Here you'll find vintage neon and some great places to eat and drink, including **Kelly's Service Station** (505/262-2739), a brewpub at 3222 Central Avenue; and the upscale **Monte Vista Fire Station** (505/255-2424), at 3201 Central Avenue. Between Nob Hill and downtown, the excellent **Route 66 Diner** (505/247-1421), at 1405 E. Central Avenue, serves top-quality burgers and shakes, and regional specialties like blue-corn pancakes.

Another good range of places to eat lies within walking distance of Old Town. Enjoy a delicious mix of Mexican and American diner food at **Garcia's** (505/842-0273), at 1736 W. Central Avenue, beneath a glorious neon sign. Another old Route 66 landmark, **Mac's La Sierra** (505/836-1212), serves up "Steak in the Rough" and other beefy specialties in a cozy, dark wood dining room a way's west of town at 6217 W. Central Avenue.

Like most of New Mexico, Albuquerque has a ton of inexpensive accommodations, with all the usual chain motels represented along the Interstate frontage roads. For the total Route 66 experience, stay the night at the **El Vado** ($35; 505/243-4594), 2500 W. Central Avenue, a time-worn but very atmospheric 1930s motel between Old Town and the Rio Grande. The nicest old hotel has got to be the grand **La Posada** ($120 and up; 505/242-9090), a block off old Route 66 at 125 2nd Street, one of the first inns built by New Mexico–born hotel magnate Conrad Hilton.

New Mexico's long relationship with radioactivity is reflected in the name of Albuquerque's very popular Class AAA baseball club, the **Isotopes** (505/924-2255), who play just south of downtown. Games are broadcast on **KNML 610 AM**.

Old Route 66: Bernalillo and Santa Fe

True fans of the full of the Route 66 tour, and anyone interested in the art and architecture (and food!) of the American Southwest, will want to make the detour to the state capital, Santa Fe. The original Route 66 alignment ran north from Albuquerque along the I-25 corridor, then curved back south from Santa Fe, along what's now US-84, to rejoin I-40 west of Santa Rosa.

The best sense of this old route across old New Mexico comes just north of Albuquerque, at the historic town of **Bernalillo**. Route 66 here follows the much older El Camino Real, which linked the Spanish colonies 400 years ago. The heart of Bernalillo contains two great stops, poles apart from each other in ambience but together capturing the essence of the place. First of these is ancient-feeling **Silva's Saloon** (505/867-9976) at 955 Camino del Pueblo, whose walls, coated in layers of newspaper clippings, old snapshots, and other mementos form a fabulously funky backdrop for a cold beer, a burger, or an evening listening to local live music alongside cowboys, bikers, and other characters. Up the street is the stylish **Range Cafe**

the **Range** CAFE

Clines Corners, midway between Albuquerque and Santa Rosa off I-40 exit 218, is a truck stop café that dates back to 1934 and is, as the signs say, Worth Waiting For—for the huge gift shop if not for the unexciting food.

(505/867-1700), at 925 Camino del Pueblo, where a spacious dining room has very good "New New Mexican" food (try the bread pudding!) and a sophisticated, big-city air.

An hour away via I-25 or its old road equivalents, **Santa Fe** itself is one of the most popular and heavily promoted tourist destinations in the country; for further information on the city, contact the Santa Fe **visitors center** (505/984-6760 or 800/777-2489) or see our companion book *Road Trip USA: California and the Southwest.*

Tinkertown and the Sandia Crest

Not that there's any shortage of wacky roadside Americana along what's left of Route 66, but one of the most endearing of them all, **Tinkertown** (daily; $3; 505/281-5233), is a quick 10-minute drive north of the old road. Like an old-fashioned penny arcade run riot, Tinkertown is a marvelous assembly of over a thousand delicately carved miniature wooden figures, arranged in tiny stage sets to act out animated scenes—a circus Big Top complete with side show, a Wild West town with dance-hall girls and a squawking vulture—all housed in a ramshackle building made in part out of glass bottles and bicycle wheels, created over the past 50-odd years by Ross and Carla Ward and family. It's impossible to describe the many odds and ends on show here—one display case holds over 100 plastic figures taken from the tops of wedding cakes, for example—especially since the whole thing is always being improved and "tinkered" with, but the spirit of the place is aptly summed up in the Tinkertown motto: "We Did All This While You Were Watching TV." The Dalai Lama loved it, and so will you.

To get to Tinkertown, turn off I-40 at exit 175, six miles east of Albuquerque, and follow Hwy-14 for six miles, toward Sandia Crest. Tinkertown is on Hwy-536, 1.5 miles west of the Hwy-14 junction, hidden off the highway among the juniper trees.

Sandia Crest itself is another 12 miles uphill at the end of Hwy-536 National Scenic Byway; the ridge offers a phenomenal panorama from an elevation of 10,678 feet. Back on Hwy-14, south of Tinkertown some four miles north of I-40, the **Sandia Mountain Hostel** (12234 N. Hwy-14 in Tijeras; 505/281-4117) offers clean bunks in a ski- and bike-friendly environment.

Santa Rosa

Along the Pecos River via US-84, some 50 miles southeast of Santa Rosa, the gravesite of Wild West legend **Billy the Kid** lies outside the town of **Fort Sumner.** The grave is part of a private museum (daily; $2) adjacent to Fort Sumner, where 7,000 Navajo people were imprisoned from 1864 to 1869.

The I-40 freeway has bisected the town of **Santa Rosa** (pop. 2,744) and cut its old Route 66 frontage in two, but for over 65 years, travelers crossing New Mexico along Route 66 and I-40 made a point of stopping here for a meal at Club Cafe, "The Original Route 66 Restaurant Since 1935." Thanks to signs lining the road for miles in both directions, emblazoned with the smiling face of the "Fat Man," the Club Cafe became nationally famous for its always-fresh food. The Club Cafe closed in 1992, but its legacy (and the Fat Man logo) live on at **Joseph's**

(505/472-1234), at 865 Will Rogers Drive, which has a nifty neon sign and very good food at reasonable prices on old Route 66, a half mile southwest of I-40 exit 275.

On the opposite side of Route 66 from Joseph's, marked by a bright yellow hot rod atop a 30-foot pole, the **Route 66 Auto Museum** (505/472-1966), at 2766 W. Route 66, has a wide-ranging exhibit on "anything to do with wheels," highlighted by some tricked-out old Fords and Chevys and a totally cherry '57 T-Bird convertible.

Santa Rosa's other main attraction is unique: the **Blue Hole,** an 80-foot-wide, 240-foot-deep artesian well filled with water so crystal-clear that it draws scuba-divers from all over the western states to practice their underwater techniques here. The water of the Blue Hole, at around 61°F, is too cold for casual swimming, but in the summer heat it's a great place to cool your heels. The Blue Hole is well-signed at the end of Blue Hole Road, a half mile south of old Route 66.

East of Santa Rosa, along the south side of I-40 as far as Cuervo, you can trace one of the older stretches of Route 66, only partly paved, and best done in a 4WD or on a mountain bike. Here you get an indelible sense of what travel was like in the very early days, when less than half the route's 2,400-odd miles were paved. Another stretch of old (circa 1926–1935) Route 66, off Blue Hole Road just south of the "official" Historic Route 66, now serves as the runway for Santa Rosa's small airport.

> Along I-40 near Cuervo, Ricardo Montalban broadcasts a brief, State of New Mexico-sponsored history of Route 66 on **530 AM**.

Tucumcari

Subject of one of the most successful advertising campaigns in Route 66's long history of roadside hype, **Tucumcari** (pop. 5,989) looks and sounds like a much bigger place than it is. Also known as "the town that's two blocks wide and two miles long" (though Tucumcari Boulevard, which follows the route blazed by old Route 66 through town, stretches for closer to seven miles between Interstate exits), Tucumcari does have a little of everything, including a great range of neon, but it can be hard to explain the attraction of the town that hundreds of signs along the highways once trumpeted as "Tucumcari Tonight—2,000 Motel Rooms." (A new ad campaign plays on this legacy, but signs now say "Tucumcari Tonight—1,200 Motel Rooms.")

Hype or no hype, Tucumcari is a handy place to break a journey, and even if you think you can make it to the next town east or west, you will never regret stopping here for a night. Especially if you stop at the famous **Blue Swallow Motel** ($40; 505/461-9849), at 815 E. Tucumcari Boulevard, which no less an authority than

Buddy Holly, Clovis Man

South of Tucumcari, at the edge of the desolate Llano Estacado that stretches south and east across the Texas Panhandle, the city of Clovis is a large railroad and ranching town that has two unique claims to fame. One is that it was the site of the oldest archaeological remains ever found in North America. In the 1930s, archaeologists dug up bones and arrowheads that proved human habitation dating back as early as 9000 BC; some of these artifacts, belonging to what archaeologists have dubbed "Clovis Man," are on display at the **Blackwater Draw Museum** (daily; $2; 505/562-2202), on US-70 about 10 miles south of Clovis.

Clovis is also semi-famous for having played a part in early rock 'n' roll: Buddy Holly came here from Lubbock, across the Texas border, in the late 1950s to record "Peggy Sue," "That'll Be The Day," and other early classics. You can tour the restored studios, which are located at 1313 W. 7th Street but open only by appointment (505/356-6422).

Smithsonian magazine called "the last, best, and friendliest of the old-time motels." Thanks to the warm hospitality of former owner Lillian Redman, few who stayed there during her long reign would disagree, and the new owners (Dale and Hilda Bakke) have kept up the old spirit while improving the plumbing and replacing the mattresses. Each room comes with its own garage, and the neon sign alone is worth staying awake for.

Across Route 66 from the Blue Swallow stands another survivor, the landmark tepee fronting the historic **Tee Pee Trading Post** (505/461-3773) at 924 E. Tucumcari Drive, where friendly owners Mike and Betty Callens will tempt you to add to your collection of Southwest or Route 66 souvenirs (or "Damn Fine Stuff," as their business cards have it). For a place to eat, try the Mexican food at **La Cita** (505/461-0949), under the turquoise and pink sombrero on the corner of 1st Street and old Route 66.

Two newer additions fill out Tucumcari's roster of attractions: one is a chromed steel **Route 66 sculpture,** welcoming travelers at the west edge of town; the other is the **Mesalands Dinosaur Museum** ($5; 505/461-3466), a block north of Route 66 at 211 E. Laughlin Street. Housed inside Mesa Technical College, the museum boasts "the largest collection of life-sized bronze prehistoric skeletons in the world," plus real fossils, unusual minerals, and the unique *Torvosaurus,* a very rare carnivorous cousin of legendary *Tyrannosaurus rex.*

TEXAS

Known as the Panhandle because of the way it juts north from the rest of Texas, this part of the route is a nearly 200-mile stretch of pancake-flat plains. Almost devoid of trees or other features, the western half, stretching into New Mexico, is also known as the Llano Estacado or "Staked Plains," possibly because early travelers marked their route by driving stakes into the earth. The Texas Panhandle was the southern extent of the buffalo-rich grasslands of the Great Plains, populated by roving bands of Kiowa and Comanche Indians as recently as 100 years ago. Now oil and gas production, as well as trucking and Route 66 tourism, have joined ranching as the region's economic basis.

Even more so than in New Mexico or Oklahoma, old Route 66 has been replaced by I-40 most of the way across Texas, though in many of the ghostly towns like McLean, Shamrock, or Vega, and the sole city, Amarillo, old US-66 survives as the main business strip, lined by the remains of roadside businesses. A select few are still open for a cup of coffee and a sharp taste of the living past.

Adrian: Midpoint Cafe

Between Amarillo and the New Mexico border, the landscape is identical to what lies east of the city: endless flat plains dotted with occasional oil derricks and Aermotor windmills. The main event hereabouts is both a geographical and culinary magnet: the hamlet of **Adrian** (pop. 150) and the unmissable **Midpoint Cafe** (daily; 806/538-6379), one of the route's most enjoyable places to eat, located more or less at the halfway point in Route 66's long ride between Chicago and Los Angeles—both of which are 1,139 miles away. The town's water tower is painted with the "Midpoint" logo, and a more enduring monument to the mileage midpoint is in the works; in the meantime, stop by the café for one of their great steaks, or at least a piece of baked-from-scratch pie. As more than one satisfied customer has said, you can taste the happiness.

Amarillo

At the heart of the Llano Estacado, midway across the Texas Panhandle, **Amarillo** (pop. 175,000; yes, you pronounce the "l"s) is a busy big city that retains its cowboy roots. Center of the local ranching industry that handles some two million head of cattle each year (some 25 percent of the national total), Amarillo is also one of the few places on earth where helium has been found; an estimated 90 percent of the world's supply

---

The border between Texas and New Mexico marks the boundary between Central and Mountain time zones. Set your clocks and watches accordingly.

In Amarillo, radio station **KIXE 940 AM**—"Kicks," as in Get Your—plays a lively variety of 1940s swing and earlier jazz, as well as crooners like Bing and Perry, to help get you in the Route 66 mood. The best alternative is on the other dial, where the local Amarillo College station, **KACV 89.9 FM**, prides itself on playing "less music from dead guys."

In **Glenrio**, just over the border from New Mexico, a rapidly decaying sign advertises the **"First/Last Motel in Texas."**

Most of the Texas Panhandle's 20 inches of annual rain falls during summer thunderstorms that sweep across the plains between May and August.

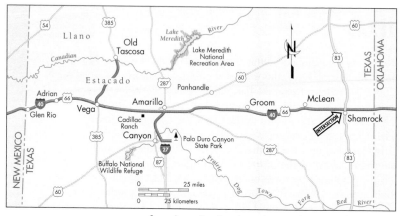

once came from here, but local production has ceased.

Old Route 66 followed 6th Street through Amarillo, past the brick-paved streets of the Old San Jacinto district around Western Avenue, where you can wander amongst ancient-looking gun and saddle shops, numerous Wild West–themed clothing shops, and kitsch-minded antique shops. East of downtown, follow East Amarillo Boulevard past a line of authentic honky-tonks around the 20-acre **Western Stockyards** (806/373-7464) at Grand Avenue and 3rd Street. Livestock auctions are held here Tuesday mornings; visitors are welcome and there's no entry fee.

To eat with the Coors-drinking cowboys and cowgirls of Amarillo, head west to the **Golden Light Cafe** (806/374-9237), at 2908 W. 6th Avenue, a fairly funky roadhouse famed for burgers, homemade hot sauce, green-chile stew, and Frito pies. Amarillo is best known for its many good steakhouses, including the **Iron Horse Cafe**, at 401 S. Grant Street, housed in the old train depot near the stockyards. The most famous has to be the 450-seat **Big Texan Steak Ranch,** which started in 1960 along historic Route 66 and now stands on the east side of Amarillo, off I-40 exit 74, marked by a false-front Wild West town and a giant cowboy atop a billboard. This is the place where they offer free 72-ounce steaks, provided you eat it all—plus a table full of salad, baked potato, and dessert—in under an hour. If you don't finish everything, the cost is around $55; regular meals and very good steaks are available as well.

There's a nice motel featuring a Texas-shaped swimming pool at the **Big Texan** ($40 and up; 806/372-5000), and dozens of moderate chain motels stand along the I-40 and I-27 frontages, so rooms shouldn't be hard to find.

Palo Duro Canyon State Park

Lovely **Palo Duro Canyon,** one of the most beautiful places in all Texas, is just 25 miles southeast of Amarillo, east of the town of Canyon off the I-27 freeway. Cut into the Texas plain by the Prairie Dog Fork of the Red River, Palo Duro stretches for over 100 miles, with canyon walls climbing to over 1,200

On US-60 west of the town of Panhandle, 11 miles northeast of Amarillo, a wire fence on the south side of the road protects the **First Tree in Texas,** planted here on the desolate plains in 1888 by settler Thomas Cree. The trees growing here today are seedlings taken from the original "Bois D'Arc" tree, which was killed by herbicides in 1969.

Cadillac Ranch

No, you're not seeing things—there really are nearly a dozen Cadillacs up-ended in the Texas plain west of Amarillo, roughly midway between Chicago and Los Angeles. Two hundred yards south of I-40 between the Hope Road and Arnot Road exits (numbers 62 and 60, respectively), some six miles west of Amarillo where old US-66 rejoins the interstate, the rusting hulks of 10 classic Caddies are buried nose-down in the dirt, their upended tail fins tracing design changes from 1949 to 1964.

A popular shrine to America's love of the open road, Cadillac Ranch was created by the San Francisco–based Ant Farm artists' and architects' collective in May 1974, under the patronage of the eccentric Amarillo helium millionaire Stanley Marsh 3. The cars were all bought, some running, some not, from local junkyards and used car lots at an average cost of $200 each. Before the Cadillacs were planted, all the hubcaps and wheels were welded on, a good idea since most of the time the cars are in a badly vandalized state. Every once in a while advertising agencies and rock bands tidy them up for use as backdrops during photo shoots. In August 1997, the Cadillacs got another 15 minutes of fame when Marsh decided to dig them up and move them a mile west from where they'd been—to escape the ever-expanding Amarillo sprawl and preserve the natural horizon.

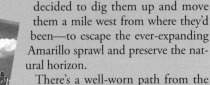

There's a well-worn path from the frontage road if you want a closer look, and visitors are allowed any time, day or night.

feet. Coronado and company were the first Europeans to lay eyes on the area, and numerous Plains tribes, including Apache, Kiowa, and Comanche, later took refuge here.

From the end of Hwy-217, a well-paved road winds past the park **visitors center,** from which a short trail leads to a canyon overlook. Beyond here the road drops down into the canyon and follows the river on a 15-mile loop trip through the Canyon's heart. It's prettiest in spring and fall, and fairly popular year-round; for more information, or for camping reservations, contact the visitors center (daily; $3; 806/488-2227).

On your way to or from Palo Duro Canyon, be sure to stop by the **Cowboy Cafe,** on US-60 west of Canyon, marked by the towering statue of Tex, the giant (47 feet and 7 tons!) cowboy. Not that you need one, but another great reason to visit **Canyon** is the excellent **Panhandle-Plains Historical Museum** (daily; $4; 806/651-2244), at 2401 4th Avenue. One of the state's great museums, this has extensive exhibits on the cultural and economic life of the Panhandle region and its relations with Mexico, the Texas Republic, and the United

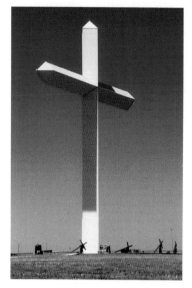

States. The museum, which is housed in a WPA-era building on the campus of West Texas A&M University, has a special section on rancher Charles Goodnight, who once owned a half-million acres here and was also an early advocate of saving the bison from extinction. His cabin is preserved in the "Pioneer Town" behind the museum.

Groom

The town of **Groom** (pop. 587), 40 miles east of Amarillo on the north side of I-40 at exit 113, holds two of the more eye-catching sights along old Route 66. One of these is a water tower that leans like the Tower of Pisa, causing drivers to stop and rub their eyes, then pull out the camera to take some snapshots to show the folks back home. The other landmark is even harder to miss, a gigantic stainless steel cross, erected by a religious group in 1995 and easily 150 feet tall.

East of McLean along the old Route 66 frontage, north of the freeway near exit 148, a skeletal sign still spells out the command: "Rattlesnakes Exit Here."

McLean

Founded around the turn of the 20th century by an English rancher, Alfred Rowe, who later lost his life on the *Titanic* in 1912, **McLean** (pop. 830) is now perhaps the most evocative town along the Texas stretch of Route 66. Bypassed only in the early 1980s, the old main drag is eerily silent, with a few businesses—a barber shop, a boot shop, and some motels, including one with a fine Texas-shaped neon sign—holding on despite the drop in passing trade.

McLean is now headquarters of the state's Historic Route 66 Association, and efforts are being made to preserve the town in prime condition, which explains the lovingly restored Phillips 66 station at 1st and Gray Streets (on the westbound stretch of old Route 66—the pumps price gas at 19 cents a gallon!), and the many other odds and ends on display around town. The center of activity here is the wonderful **Devil's Rope Museum** (daily; free; 806/779-2225), at 100 S. Kingsley Street at the east end of downtown, which has a huge room full of barbed wire—the "Devil's Rope"—and some of the most entertaining and educational collections of Route 66 memorabilia you'll find anywhere. No hype, just lots of good stuff and friendly people telling you all about it.

Midway between McLean and the Oklahoma border, the town of Shamrock marks the junction of Route 66 and US-83, **The Road to Nowhere** along the 100th Meridian, which is described in full on pages 160–211. Shamrock is covered on page 196.

OKLAHOMA

Apart from occasional college football teams, Oklahoma doesn't often get to crow about being the best in the country, but as far as Route 66 is concerned, the state is definitely number one. Containing more still-driveable miles of the old highway than any other state, this is definitely mecca for old-roads fans.

Underneath the promotional hoopla that Route 66 generates everywhere it ever went, all over Oklahoma signs declare that barely a century ago this was Indian Territory, last refuge of Kiowa, Apache, Comanche, and other tribes before the U.S. government took even this land away from them during "land rushes" in the 1890s. A few years later, oil was discovered and the state started on one of a series of boom-and-bust cycles. The Dust Bowl exodus of the 1930s was the greatest down-

Oklahoma has the longest and most intact stretch of old Route 66, and if you really want to explore it to the full, get your hands on a copy of the essential map-packed road guide *Oklahoma Route 66*, by Arcadia's own Jim Ross.

turn, as thousands of Oklahoman families headed west on Route 66. Many of the towns along the road take bittersweet pride in *The Grapes of Wrath* connections.

Texola and Erick

The first town over the Texas border, **Texola** has dried up and all but blown away since it was bypassed by I-40, but a few remnants still stand, awaiting nostalgic photographers. The only signs of life hereabouts are the shouts and swears emanating from the combination pool hall and beer bar housed in the large metal shed on the south side of the old highway, where you're welcome to watch the most passionate domino games this side of Yuma, Arizona.

East from this borderline ghost town, a mile south of the I-40 freeway, a nice stretch of late-model Route 66 continues as a four-lane divided highway, passing through the great little town of **Erick** (pop. 1,083), six miles east of Texola. Along with main streets named for local musical heroes Sheb Wooley and Roger Miller, Erick has another unique draw: the **100th Meridian Museum** (hours vary; donations), on Route 66 at the only stoplight in town. Displays inside trace life on what used to be considered the edge of the habitable world—everything west of the 100th Meridian was officially thought to be the "Great American Desert"—and also explain that Erick used to be on the Texas

border, until the border was realigned. Across the street, check on the status of the proposed Roger Miller Museum, established by the widow of the original "King of the Road".

Sayre

If you want a quick flashback to the dark days of Steinbeck's *The Grapes of Wrath,* turn north off I-40 into sleepy **Sayre** (pop.

Welcome to Texola.

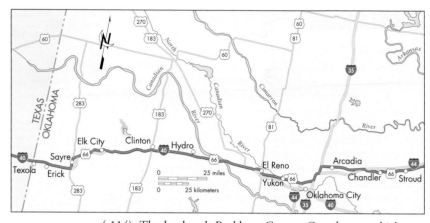

In Jack D. Rittenhouse's original **Guide Book to Highway 66**, published in 1946 and now widely available in reprinted versions, he described Erick as "the first town you encounter, going west, which has any of the true 'western' look, with its wide, sun-baked street, frequent horsemen, occasional sidewalk awnings, and similar touches."

4,114). The landmark Beckham County Courthouse, which looms over the east end of Main Street, was prominently featured in the movie version as Henry Fonda and the rest of the Joads rattled down Route 66 toward California. The Depression era also lives on in the cool and pleasant WPA-era swimming pool in Sayre City Park, in between the old Route 66 alignments. Just off the old road, take a look in the ever-expanding **Shortgrass Country Museum** (hours vary; free), housed in the old Rock Island Line railroad depot at 106 E. Poplar Street, with changing displays documenting regional history from Cheyenne times to the arrival of homesteading settlers during the great Land Rush of 1892. East of the museum stands a giant grain elevator that has rusted into a gorgeous orange glow.

Elk City

The first—or last, depending on your direction—sizeable town east of the Texas border, **Elk City** (pop. 10,510, "Home of Suzanne Powell, Miss America 1981") was a popular stopover on Route 66, as evidenced by the many old motels along the various alignments of the old highway through town.

Long before Elk City had its Route 66 heyday, it was a wild frontier town along the cattle trails from Texas to Dodge City, Kansas. The area's cowboy and pioneer history is recounted in the **Old Town Museum** (daily; $5; 580/225-6266), on the far west side of town, where there's a re-created Wild West town, complete with doctor's office, schoolhouse, "Indian TeePee," and rodeo museum. A newer addition to Old Town Museum is the official **National Route 66 Museum**, which has an old pickup truck decorated to look like the one from *Grapes of Wrath*, and lots of other old road–related memorabilia.

For westbound travelers, El Reno marks the first appearance of one of the longest-running ad campaigns along Route 66: dozens of billboards advertising "Tucumcari Tonight," 350 miles from its New Mexican subject.

During the 1940s oil was discovered underground, and the town experienced another short boom; this aspect of Elk City's past is the focus of the small **Anadarko Basin Museum**

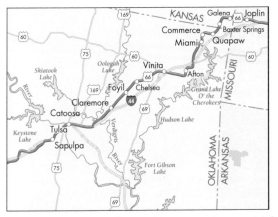

(by appointment; 580/243-0437), housed in the lobby of the old Casa Grande Hotel at 107 E. 3rd Street. The most impressive object here is towering Rig 114, a record-breaking, 180-foot-tall drilling rig, installed after its retirement in the park next to the museum.

Clinton

Named for Judge Clinton Irwin and not for former President Bill, **Clinton** (pop. 8,833) started life as a trading post for local Cheyenne Arapahoe people, and is now in the spotlight as home of the official **Oklahoma Route 66 Museum** (daily, closed Sun. and Mon. in winter; $3; 580/323-7866), near the west end of town at 2229 W. Gary Boulevard. Unlike many other "museums" along the route, this one is a true showcase and not just another souvenir stand. Funded by a variety of state and local sources, the museum reopened in late 1995 after undergoing a massive, million-dollar expansion and improvement, and is one of the better museums of the old road along the old road. Collectors from all over the country, including Clinton's own Gladys Cuthbert, whose husband, Jack Cuthbert, was the primary promoter of Route 66 throughout its glory years, donated signs, artifacts, and memorabilia which have been organized into a comprehensive exhibition of Mother Road history and culture not to be missed by any Route 66 aficionado. (There's a good gift shop, too.)

Clinton also has the very nice McLain Rogers public park, with a swimming pool and water slides, at the center of town along 10th Street (old Route 66), next to the Route 66 Miniature Golf Course.

For food, west of town along the I-40 frontage, just north of exit 62, **Jiggs Smoke House** (580/323-5641) is a tiny cabin selling BBQ sandwiches but specializing in travel-friendly beef jerky. Alas, Clinton's longtime favorite Route 66 restaurant, Pop Hick's, burned to the ground in 1999, with no insurance and no real chance of being rebuilt. Elvis himself stayed four times at the **Tradewinds Best Western** ($50 and up; 580/323-2610), across from the Route 66 museum at 2128 Gary Boulevard. Elvis's room has been "preserved" as a mini shrine, and you can stay in it (for around $90) and experience a time warp back to the mid-1960s.

For more on Clinton's Route 66 connections, contact the helpful **visitors center** (580/323-2222 or 800/759-1397), at 101 S. 4th Street.

Hydro: Lucille's

There's no clearer contrast between the charms of the old road and the anonymity of the Interstate than tiny **Hydro**, midway between Clinton and Oklahoma City on the west bank of the Canadian River. A wonderful length of

Books on Route 66

Considering the old road's great fame, it's hardly surprising that over a dozen different books in print deal with the Route 66 experience. Some are travel guides, some folk histories, others nostalgic rambles down what was and what's left along the Mother Road. Photographic essays document the rapidly disappearing architecture and signage, and at least one cookbook catalogs recipes of dishes served in cafés along the route. The following is a sampling of favorite titles, most of which can be found in stores along the route if not in your local bookstore.

The Grapes of Wrath, John Steinbeck (Viking, 1937). The first and foremost Route 66–related story, this compelling tale traces the traumatic travels of the Joad family from Dust Bowl Oklahoma to the illusive Promised Land of California. Brutally vivid, *The Grapes of Wrath* was an instant bestseller at the tail end of the Depression and was the source of Route 66's appellation, "The Mother Road."

A Guide Book to Highway 66, Jack Rittenhouse (University of New Mexico, 1989). A facsimile reprinting of the self-published 1946 book that the late author sold door-to-door at truck stops, motor courts, and cafés along the route.

Route 66: The Illustrated Guidebook to the Mother Road, Bob Moore and Patrick Grauwels (RoadBook International, 2002). The most-detailed driver's guide to old Route 66, packed with mile-by-mile instructions and information as well as photographs and illustrations. Spiralbound for on-the-road ease of use.

Route 66: The Mother Road, Michael Wallis (St. Martin's Press, 1987). A richly illustrated and thoroughly researched guide to the old road. This is more armchair companion than practical aid, but the book captures the spirit of Route 66, and the writer has been a key promotional force behind the road's preservation and rediscovery.

Route 66 Traveler's Guide, Tom Snyder (St. Martin's Press, 1990). State-by-state description of Route 66, with an emphasis on the stories behind the sights you see. Illustrated with 1930s-era auto club maps adapted to show the path of modern freeways but still evoking the spirit of the old road.

Searching for 66, Tom Teague (Samizdat House, 1996). More personal than other titles on Route 66, this book of vignettes describes the author's interactions with the many people along Route 66 who have made it what it is. As a bonus, the book is illustrated with the fine pen-and-ink drawings of Route 66 artist Bob Waldmire.

old Route 66 runs along the north side of I-40 exit 89, right past the ancient service station and souvenir stand operated by Lucille Hammons from 1941 until her death, at age 85, in August 2000. Though it's just 50 yards from the fast lane of the freeway, visiting Lucille's place to buy a soda or a postcard and have a quick hello with the energetic proprietor was a Route 66 rite of passage.

West of Lucille's, a surviving six-mile stretch of old Route 66 pavement follows the lay of the land up and down, offering a better sense of the landscape than does the faster but duller new road, completed in 1966.

El Reno and Yukon

Established as Fort El Reno in 1874 as part of U.S. Army efforts to subdue the Cheyenne, **El Reno** (pop. 16,212) later saw duty as a POW camp during World War II; more recently it earned a measure of fame as the site of a motel seen in the offbeat road movie *Rain Man*. (In the movie, the motel was in Amarillo, but the "real" one, called the Big Eight, sat along old Route 66 at the east edge of El Reno.)

For hungry road-trippers, another place not to pass by in El Reno is **Johnnie's Grill** (daily; 405/262-4721), at 301 South Rock Island, famed since 1926 for its Fried Onion Burgers. On the first weekend in May, Johnnie's cooks up the "World's Largest Hamburger," a 750-pound behemoth.

East of El Reno, all the way into Oklahoma City (OKC), old Route 66 runs along the north side of I-40; in places it's a three-lane road, with a dangerous passing lane in the center. The last real town beyond the OKC suburbs is Yukon, hometown of country crooner Garth Brooks and of a giant "Yukon's Best Flour" grain mill, whose huge sign lights up the night sky and draws shutterbugs off the highway.

Oklahoma City

Now tragically synonymous with the terrorist bombing carried out by Timothy McVeigh in 1995, **Oklahoma City** (pop. 506,132) has long been one of the primary stops along the Mother Road. In the Bobby Troup song, it was the only place along the route he singled out for praise, no doubt more for the easy rhyme ("Oklahoma City is mighty pretty") than for its less obvious visual charms. The city was the biggest boomtown of the 1889 Land Rush, when Oklahoma was opened for white settlement after being set aside "for eternity" as Indian Territory. Between noon and sundown on April 22, over 10,000 people flocked here to claim the new lands—many of them having illegally camped out beforehand, earning the nickname "Sooner," which is still applied to the state's college football team.

A second boom took place during the Depression years, when oil was struck; there are still producing wells in the center of the city, including some on the grounds of the state capitol. The collapse of the oil industry in the 1980s hit hard, but the shock of the 1995 bombing galvanized the city, which has since

Following old Route 66 across Oklahoma City can be confusing, but keep an eye peeled for the **Route 66 Bowl** on 39th Street; a **bottle-shaped building** on Classen Boulevard at 23rd Street NW; and a **retro McDonald's** featuring a "Speedie" sign and carhop service, on the nearby corner of 23rd Street and Pennsylvania Avenue.

The Class AAA **Oklahoma Redhawks** (405/218-1000) play at ever-pleasant Bricktown Ballpark, south of downtown near the junction of I-35 and I-40. Games are broadcast on **WKY 930 AM.**

revitalized itself with a gorgeous new baseball stadium, a concert arena, and canal-side cafés in the "Bricktown" warehouse district south of downtown.

Right on old Route 66 across from the capitol, a good first stop is the **Oklahoma Museum of History** (closed Sun.; free; 405/521-2491), at 2100 Lincoln Boulevard, which has exhibits tracing the state's history, with special collections on the Native American presence, on pioneers, and on the oil industry. There's also a wide-ranging oral history of the Mother Road.

It can be hard to go about your nostalgic Route 66 tour in the aftermath of the April 19, 1995, bombing of the Alfred P. Murrah Federal Building, where 168 men, women, and children were killed. Between the capitol and Bricktown, the site of the bombing has been preserved as a **memorial park** (open 24 hours; free), landscaped with a shallow pool around which are arrayed a series of 168 sculpted chairs. Each chair represents a person killed in the blast, and the chairs range from very small to full-sized, marking the varying ages of the dead (who included 19 kids from the building's daycare center.) An adjacent **museum** (daily; $7; 405/235-3313) tells the story of the bombing, its perpetrators, and its victims.

Oklahoma City Practicalities

Downtown OKC spreads northwest from the busy I-35/I-40 junction, where a massive new American Indian Cultural Center is under development. On the west side of the freeway, the Bricktown district is home to many fun restaurants and bars like **Tapwerks Ale House** (405/319-9599), at 121 E. Sheridan Avenue, which has great beers, good food, and frequent live music. Oklahoma City also has more BBQ stands and steak houses than just about anywhere else in the country: One old Route 66 landmark, the Kentucky Club speakeasy and roadhouse once frequented by Pretty Boy Floyd, still survives as the **Oklahoma County Line** (405/478-4955), an upscale BBQ restaurant on the northeast edge of town, near the National Cowboy Hall of Fame at 1226 NE 63rd Street. For more great BBQ right on old Route 66, go to **Jack's BBQ** (405/946-1865), a hole-in-the-wall joint at 4418 NW 39th Street Expressway. Another place to check out is the popular **Ann's Chicken Fry House** (405/943-8915), near Jack's BBQ at 4106 NW 39th Street—look for the classic Caddies and fake police cars in the parking lot.

Accommodation options in OKC are limited to the usual motels, including a **Super 8** (405/232-0404), at 1117 N.E. 17th Street across from the capitol.

Old Route 66: Arcadia, Chandler, and Stroud

Northeast of Oklahoma City, one of the state's best surviving stretches of Route 66, known locally as the "Free Road," runs for over 30 miles along the north side of the turnpike, passing by horse and cattle ranches as it rolls across the red earth. The first stop along this idyllic rural cruise is the old highway town of **Arcadia** (pop. 320), which holds a recently restored round, red barn built in 1898. The ground floor of the much-loved landmark is now a mini museum and gift shop (405/396-2761) selling some highly collectible original Route 66 memorabilia. Across the highway, the **Hillbillee's Cafe** (405/396-8177) offers homespun sustenance all day long, in an old Route 66 car repair shop.

The old road runs east from Arcadia along the north side of I-44, crossing under the freeway near the town of Chandler. Near the undercrossing, about four miles west of Chandler, stands a metal-roofed barn emblazoned with a photogenic "Meramec Caverns—Stanton MO" sign.

North of OKC, Route 66 continued through the town of Edmond, the place where aviator **Wiley Post** is buried (he was the pilot killed in the same crash as **Will Rogers**). The town is also notorious for the fact that a disgruntled post office employee killed 14 of his co-workers here in 1986, inspiring the expression "going postal."

Chandler (pop. 2,842) itself is one of the most pleasant old Route 66 towns in Oklahoma; it stands out for a number of good reasons, not least of which is the classic **Lincoln Motel** ($35; 405/258-0200), at 740 E. 1st Street, along old Route 66 at the east edge of town, still as neat and tidy as the day it opened in 1939—two dozen two-room cabins, each with an American flag and a pair of yellow lawn chairs for watching the world whiz by.

Continuing east, old-roads fanatics will probably want to follow the winding alignment of Route 66, which continues along the south side of the turnpike for over 40 miles. On the west side of **Stroud** (pop. 2,758; "Home of Daneka Allen, Miss OK 1999"), check out the **Rock Cafe** (918/968-3990), at 114 W. Main Street, a Route 66 relic built in 1939 out of paving stones from the original highway and still churning out its better-than-average roadside fare.

East of Stroud, old Route 66 zig-zags back and forth along the freeway for the next 25 miles, through Sapulpa and into Tulsa. One stop to keep in mind, **Russ's Ribs** (908/367-5656), at 233 S. Main Street in the brick-paved heart of **Bristow,** is home to some of the best $3 BBQ sandwiches on the planet. A full slab will set you back around $15, and Russ also makes some excellent deli sandwiches and "family packs" with all the fixin's for a roadside picnic.

Between Bristow and Tulsa, old Route 66 snakes back and forth beside I-44 for a dozen miles of eye-blink small towns and abandoned motor courts (most of them built of local rocks). Near the east end of this stretch, three miles west of bustling Sapulpa, the circa-1921 **Rock Creek Bridge** is a reminder of what the old roads were really like: 120 feet long yet only 12 feet wide, the truss is rusty but the bridge still stands as a proud reminder of the original 1920s Route 66. Across the bridge is another evocative

reminder: a drive-in movie theater, now closed but with the screen and the fan-shaped parking lot still intact.

Tulsa

Home to fine art deco buildings built during the 1920s boom years of the Oklahoma oil industry, and the Gilcrease Museum, one of the country's top art museums, **Tulsa** (pop. 385,000) is a bustling big city that doesn't make a song-and-dance out of its many treasures. It's a fascinating place to explore, but if your time is limited, spend it at the **Gilcrease Museum** (daily; 918/596-2700), on the northwest edge of Tulsa. Bought with the fortune benefactor Thomas Gilcrease made when oil was discovered on his land, the collection includes some of the most important works of Western American art and sculpture, with major works by Thomas Moran, George Catlin, and others, plus Native American artifacts and early maps that put the frontier region into its historical contexts. The expansive grounds include a lovely series of gardens and Mr. Gilcrease's old house, now home to the Tulsa Historical Society, which displays photographs and objects related to the evolution of the city.

Tulsa is the home of **Oral Roberts University,** *marked by a futuristic, 15-story tower and an 80-foot-high pair of praying hands along Lewis Avenue, six miles south of downtown.*

One of the country's grand old country-western radio stations, **KVOO 1170 AM,** *"The Voice of Oklahoma," can be heard for miles around Tulsa.*

For dinner or a drink, the liveliest part of Tulsa is the Brookside district, south of downtown around 34th Street and Peoria Avenue, where there's a handful of trendy cafés, nightclubs, and restaurants. For a taste of old Route 66, stop at the retro **Metro Diner** (918/592-2616) at 3001 E. 11th Street, which isn't a *real* pre-fab diner but *is* on old Route 66 and still serves decent diner food.

The usual chain hotels and motels line all the freeways, and there's a big **Ramada Inn** ($60; 918/585-5898) downtown at 17 W. 7th Street.

Catoosa: The Blue Whale

One of Tulsa's premier Route 66 attractions was the giant **Blue Whale,** in the suburb of **Catoosa,** northeast of Tulsa along the stretch of the old road that runs from I-44 exit 240. The park closed down long ago and was left to crumble, but unlike so many other long-suffering Route 66 landmarks, the Blue Whale has been lovingly restored by the family of its original creators, and is sometimes open to visitors.

Catoosa, surprisingly, is also a major port, linked, by way of impressively engineered improvements to the Arkansas River system, to the Gulf of Mexico.

Claremore

Twenty miles northeast of Tulsa, **Claremore** (pop. 15,873) is a bigger-than-average Route 66 town, one that will be forever connected with its favorite son, Will Rogers. Rogers was born nearby in a rough log cabin "halfway between Claremore and Oologah before there was a town at either place," on November 4, 1879. He rose from a vaudeville career as a sideshow rope-tricks artist to become one of the most popular figures in America, thanks to his folksy humor.

Will Rogers starred on Broadway for 10 years in the *Ziegfield Follies,* wrote an immensely popular newspaper column, and acted in over 70 Hollywood movies, but before he could retire back home to Claremore, Rogers was killed in a plane crash in 1935; his land was later turned into the **Will Rogers Memorial** (daily; donations; 918/341-0719), a mile west of downtown Claremore on a hill overlooking the town. A statue of Rogers greets visitors at the front door, and his tomb is here, along with a small archive and museum that recounts his life story, showing off his collections of saddles, lariats, and other cowboy gear.

Will Rogers

Another popular Claremore stop is the **J. M. Davis Arms and Historical Museum** (closed Sun.; donations; 918/341-5707), right off Route 66 at 333 N. Lynn Riggs Boulevard. Besides one of the largest and most comprehensive gun collections anywhere in the world (over 20,000 firearms!), the museum has antique musical instruments, hundreds of posters dating back to World War I, and 1,200 German beer steins.

For great food and out-of-this-world pies, stop by the **Hammett House** (918/341-7333), next to the Rogers Memorial, 1616 W. Will Rogers.

Foyil was the hometown of **Andy Payne**, the Cherokee youth who in 1928 won the **"Bunion Derby,"** a coast-to-coast foot race that followed Route 66 from Los Angeles to Chicago, then headed east to New York City—equivalent to running a marathon and a half every day for the 86 days it took him to finish.

Foyil

Between Claremore and Vinita, old Route 66 survives in regular use, alternating between two-lane and divided four-lane highway. The most interesting wide spot along this stretch of hallowed road is **Foyil,** where in the 1940s and 1950s retired fiddle-maker and folk artist Ed Galloway sculpted an outdoor garden of giant totem poles—the tallest is over 90 feet—and other Native American–inspired objects out of concrete. After fading and weathering for many years, the poles, four miles east of town via Hwy-28A, were restored in 1993–1994 as **Totem Pole Park** (daily dawn–dusk; free), and now it's a fascinating place to stop for a picnic or to simply admire the effort that went into these "Watts Towers of the Plains."

Vinita

Old Route 66 crosses the Interstate again at **Vinita,** where the region's Native American heritage is brought into focus at the **Eastern Trails Museum** (Mon.–Sat. 1–4 PM; free; 918/256-2115), next to the public library at 215 W. Illinois Street. The exhibits center on the Cherokee "Trail of Tears," which brought the tribe here after a forced march from North Carolina

Between Afton and Miami, some of the oldest paved stretches of Route 66 were constructed only one lane wide, because in 1926 the state did not have enough money to build a full-width version. Not surprisingly, these lengths of the road became known as the "Sidewalk Highway," and can still be driven. Look for the "66" shields painted on the pavement; the easiest stretch to find is west of the "Vo-Tech" school.

in the 1830s, but the museum also covers the general history of the surrounding area.

Vinita is home to the **Will Rogers Memorial Rodeo**, held here each August since 1935, the year he died; Rogers attended secondary school in Vinita after growing up near Claremore. Vinita also hosts an annual **Calf Fry Festival** in mid-September. (Calf fries are prairie oysters; otherwise known as beef testicles. Just so you know.) Contact the **visitors center** (918/256-7133) for details on any of these.

Vinita also has a great old Route 66 restaurant: **Clanton's Cafe** (918/256-9053), right at the center of town at 319 E. Illinois Street.

Miami, Commerce, and Quapaw

In the far northeastern corner of Oklahoma, a stretch of old Route 66 leaves I-44 exit 313 from the town of Miami, zigzagging to the Kansas border through a hardscrabble former mining region. The first of these towns, **Miami**, holds the magnificent Spanish Revival–style Coleman Theater, built in 1929 and luxuriating in the riches that came out of the surrounding lead and zinc mines. The next town along, **Commerce** (pop. 2,426), was another old mining town, noteworthy as the boyhood home of the late, great Yankee player Mickey Mantle, in whose honor the old Route 66 alignment down Main Street has been renamed.

Quapaw, the first or last Oklahoma town you visit, depending upon your direction, is worth a look for the many murals painted on the walls of downtown businesses. It's three miles from the Kansas border.

KANSAS

The shortest but perhaps best-signed stretch of Route 66's eight-state run is its 14-mile slice across the southeast corner of Kansas. Be careful not to blink your eyes, or you'll be saying, as Dorothy did in *The Wizard of Oz*, "I think we're not in Kansas anymore."

If you're coming from Oklahoma, **Baxter Springs** is the first town you reach, and **Murphey's Restaurant** (620/856-3263), at 1046 Military Avenue, is famous for its great pies. East of Baxter Springs are a couple of old rainbow-arched concrete bridges and a few other Route 66 relics: In **Riverton**, the next town along, the **Old Riverton Store** (620/848-3330), aka "Eisler Bros.," has been open since the 1920s. Across the highway from a big power plant, the old store is now headquarters of the small but active Kansas Route 66 Association and an essential stop for fans of the old road—and of the old-fashioned milk shakes whipped up there.

One of the Lead and Zinc Mines in the Tri-State Mining District of Missouri-Kansas-Oklahoma

Massive lead mines like this have disappeared from Kansas.

During the Civil War, Baxter Springs saw one of the worst massacres in the country's history, when 87 Union soldiers, held prisoner by William Quantrill's rebel Confederate forces, were killed by gunshots to the back of the head. A monument to the soldiers stands in **Baxter Springs National Cemetery,** the second-oldest military cemetery in the nation, off US-166 two miles west of town.

The last town in Kansas is **Galena,** where the funky **Galena Mining and Historical Museum** (hours vary; 620/783-2192), just off the main drag and marked by a big "Old 66" sign at 319 W. 7th Street, is stuffed with old newspaper clippings and other items that give a glimpse of town life during its 1920s-era mining heyday, and various rusting tools and machines testify to the work that once went on here.

On the Kansas/Missouri border, tune to **KRPS 89.9 FM** for classical music and NPR news.

MISSOURI

The Ozark Highlands of southern Missouri, which Route 66 crosses in its 300-odd-mile journey between Illinois and Kansas, are about the only significant hills the road crosses east of Arizona. This plateau region, though not by any means alpine or breathtaking, is visually dynamic in a way the broad flatlands of Illinois and the Great Plains rarely are. Though the I-44 freeway has replaced the old road all the way across the state, many signs of the old highway line the surviving stretches of the original route, and every exit drops you within a moment's drive of the Mother Road. Missouri also holds one of the greatest of the old Route 66 tourist attractions—Meramec Caverns, an extensive set of limestone caves offering the most over-the-top underground tour you can take.

Joplin

If you travel the old Route 66 alignment across Kansas, you'll also pass through **Joplin** (pop. 45,504), a Missouri border town that's the industrial center of the tri-state region. Formerly a lead- and zinc-mining town, Joplin is not an especially pretty place, better known for its high-quality limestone than for its cultural offerings. Though many of its businesses have fled to the fringes, Joplin's downtown area does hold one unlikely attraction, a vibrant mural by artist Thomas Hart Benton depicting life in Joplin at the turn of the 20th century. The mural, which turned out to be the artist's final complete work, is in the lobby of the banal 1960s-era Municipal Building, east of Main Street at 303 E. 3rd Street.

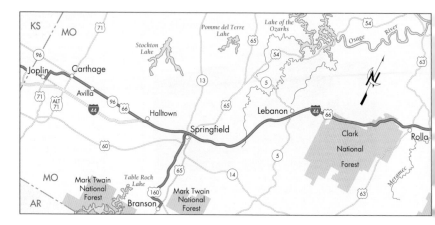

Carthage was the boyhood home of naturalist **Marlin Perkins**, host of *Mutual of Omaha's Wild Kingdom* TV show. A life-sized statue of him stands in Central Park, three blocks southwest of the courthouse square. Carthage was also the girlhood home of Wild West outlaw **Belle Starr**.

If you're feeling the need for a break, stay the night at the homespun **Ko Ko Motel** (417/624-6493), 3102 E. 7th Street.

Carthage

Six miles north of I-44, right on old Route 66, **Carthage** (pop. 12,688) is a perfect little town, looking for all the world like the model for the idyllic though fictional town of Hill Valley from the *Back to the Future* movies. The center of Carthage is dominated by the outrageously ornate, circa-1895, limestone Jasper County Courthouse, which features a local history mural and an open-cage elevator in the lobby. The rest of the town is fairly franchise-free, away from the Interstate at least, and the residential areas hold well-maintained Victorian houses.

For fun on the road, there's a bowling alley, **Star Lanes** (417/358-2144), at 219 E. 3rd Street, just east of the square. A mile or so west of downtown on Old Route 66, enjoy Hollywood blockbusters in the comfort of your car at the recently reopened **66 Drive-In** (417/359-5959), at 17231 Old 66 Boulevard.

If you have a soft spot for hyperbolic sentimentality, one not-to-be-missed monument is the **Precious Moments Chapel** (daily; 417/358-7599), featuring the wide-eyed characters from the religious greeting card series. The chapel is well-signed, west of US-71 on the southwest edge of Carthage; for the full experience, there's a sound-and-light show ($16), the "Fountain of Angels."

A great stretch of old Route 66, renumbered Hwy-96, runs for 50 miles along the north side of I-44 between Carthage and Springfield, passing rolling pastures and little towns like **Avilla** and **Halltown**, with antique shops and abandoned cafés lining the old highway frontage.

The 1940s stainless steel landmark **Iggy's Diner** (daily; 417/237-0212) is not far away, at 2400 Grand Avenue, while downtown Carthage has another good place to eat, the **Carthage Deli** (417/358-8820), 301 S. Main Street, which serves sandwiches and milk shakes in a 1950s-style soda fountain on the northwest corner of the courthouse square. Within a short walk is an elegant B&B, the **Leggett House** ($85; 417/358-0683), at 1106 Grand Avenue, and an old Route 66 landmark: the glowing red-and-green neon sign of

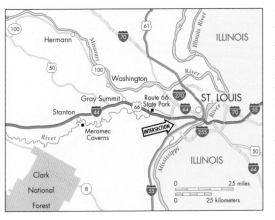

the **Boots Motel**, 107 S. Garrison Street. Clark Gable stayed here, and it remained a welcoming, family-run place until recently, but was closed and "For Sale" at time of writing.

Springfield

The largest city in southern Missouri, **Springfield** (pop. 151,580) doesn't feel nearly as big as it is, though it does sprawl for many miles in all directions. It was here in 1926 that plans for Route 66 were made, and the city preserves much of the old highway frontage along St. Louis Street east of downtown, as well as the grandly named "Chestnut Expressway" west of downtown. The 20-mph speed limit on downtown streets—and tons of free parking—enables Route 66 pilgrims to pay homage to the town's Arabesque landmark **Shrine Mosque** theater (417/869-9164), at 601 E. 1st Street; it still hosts occasional concerts.

Springfield is also celebrated as the place where "Wild" Bill Hickok killed fellow gambler Dave Tutt, apparently because Tutt wore the watch he'd won from Hickok playing cards. A plaque in the central square tells one of many variations on the tale.

One place you have to see to believe—though the bass angler in your family will already know about it, for sure—is "The World's Greatest Sporting Goods Store," **BASS Pro Shops Outdoor World** (417/887-7334), at 1935 S. Campbell Street. Along with acres of floor space, the store has a 140,000-gallon fish tank, a 40-foot waterfall, and even its own McDonald's.

Springfield is home to the Class AA Texas League **Springfield Cardinals**, who play off US-65 at Hammons Field (417/863-2143).

Springfield has at least one fine old Route 66 motel: the **Route 66 Rail Haven** ($55–75; 417/866-1963), at 203 S. Glenstone Avenue on the corner of old Route 66 and US-65. Open since 1938, it has been fully modernized and now is a Best Western affiliate with a railroad theme. A mile away on old Route 66 is one of the earliest and most stylish models of the **Steak and Shake** burger chain (417/866-6109); located at 1158 E. St. Louis Street, and open 24 hours, this is one of the last ones where car hops still bring you your food (during daylight hours).

Detour: Branson

A Middle-American Las Vegas with all the tackiness and none of the exuberant style, Branson is a century-old Ozark resort that hit the big time in the 1980s through clever promotion and cunning repackaging of country-and-western music and God-fearing recreation. There are over 30 major performance venues in Branson, and looking down the list of people who make a living playing here all summer—Jimmy Osmond, Tony Orlando, and Jim "I Don't Like Spiders and Snakes" Stafford— you'd think that anyone who had a hit record or a TV show, or who can sing in a twang and impersonate a country-western star, can have their own showcase theater. Most offer two shows a day plus optional breakfast shows at 10 AM—imagine Hank Williams doing one of those. Bus tours throng and clog the streets and highways around Branson all summer long.

However cruel this assessment sounds, once you visit, you may feel it is, if anything, not biting enough. Branson simply embodies everything that's annoying and disappointing about mass-merchandising of "culture"—a

Lebanon and Waynesville

Between Springfield and St. Louis, I-44 has been built right on top of the old Route 66 corridor, and dozens of old motels, motor courts, gas stations, and other highway-dependent businesses line the remains of the old road, which serves as a frontage road for most of the way. There are plenty of antique shops and cafés to make the journey interesting, but unless you have all the time in the world, you may want to stick to the interstate, which offers a scenic drive through the upland forests of the Ozark plateau.

The two towns on the way grew up along the railroad in the late 1850s, were busy hubs along Route 66, and now boast essential stops for old-roads fans. In **Lebanon** (pop. 12,500), the stretch of old Route 66 running along the north side of I-44 holds the marvelous **Munger Moss Motel** ($30; 417/532-3111), at

1336 Route 66, a landmark since 1949, where Ramona Lehman and family offer clean rooms, a wonderful neon sign, and a swimming pool. Across Route 66 from the Munger Moss is a bowling alley with a set of batting cages, making for a perfect Route 66 destination.

East of Lebanon, I-44 has generated a rash of Wal-Marts and shopping malls in the old Route 66 town of **Waynesville** (pop. 3,500), which stands at the entrance to Fort Leonard Wood U.S. Army base. East of Waynesville, old Route 66 followed the undulating Ozarks through the mountains' most rugged stretch, known as the **Devil's Elbow**. The name comes from a section of the Big Piney River that turns so acutely it caused repeated logjams. Until 1981, through here

cloyingly sentimental version of American music without the slightest sense of humor or moment of sincere feeling. Then again, millions of people like it, so they must be doing something right.

What originally put Branson on the tourist map was not music but a book: *The Shepherd of the Hills,* by Harold Bell Wright. Set in and around Branson and published in 1907, it was a huge bestseller. Adapted in the 1930s into an outdoor stage play (417/334-4191), *Shepherd of the Hills* has been drawing millions here ever since.

But the best thing about Branson is **Silver Dollar City** (daily; $29; 417/338-2611), nine miles west of Branson via Hwy-76, a turn-of-the-20th-century theme park devoted to Ozark arts, crafts, and music—and roller coasters. Nearby: the **Roy Rogers and Dale Evans Museum** (daily; $12.95; 417/339-1900), at 3950 Green Mountain Drive, where it recently moved from its longtime home in Victorville, California, at the other end of Route 66.

The Ozark Mountain area around Branson is still a lovely place to explore; just about any road south, east, or west will take you through beautifully scenic mountain landscapes.

Route 66 followed what's now the very hilly, four-lane **Hwy-Z,** the last sections of the old road to be bypassed by I-44.

Rolla and Cuba

One of the many enduring tourist stops along the Ozark Mountains stretch of Route 66 is the landmark **Totem Pole Trading Post** at the west end of **Rolla** (pop. 14,100; RAW-la). In the center of town, right along old Route 66 on the campus of the University of Missouri at Rolla, another draw is the working replica of that ancient Druidical observatory, **Stonehenge.** If you have trouble finding it, this miniature Wonder of the World stands across Route 66 from the Great Wall of China—a Chinese restaurant. Talk about "small world. . . ."

Along I-44 east of Rolla, the old Route 66 roadside is lined by ramshackle wooden stands which, at the end of summer, sell Concord grapes from local vineyards. The stands are located along the frontage roads (which in many cases are the remnants of the original Route 66), but people park along the freeway and walk to them. At the east edge of this grape-growing district, which is called Rosati, the small town of **Cuba** has a number of local history murals and the friendly old **Wagon Wheel Motel** ($40; 573/885-3411), at 901 E. Washington Street. Another great old roadside stop is the **Route 66 Lounge,** serving the coldest beer on old Route 66 at 1205 W. Washington Street. (There's also a "People's Bank of Cuba," if you're interested in a Fidel-themed photo opportunity.)

Meramec Caverns

The best stop along old Route 66's trek across Missouri, and one of the most enjoyable and charming roadside attractions along the entire Mother Road, **Meramec Caverns** (daily; $14; 573/468-2283 or 800/676-6105) is a set of

Among its many other claims to fame, Meramec Caverns is known as the "Birthplace of the Bumper Sticker."

limestone caves advertised by signs on barns and buildings all along the route, and all over the Midwest. First developed during the Civil War, when the natural saltpeter was mined for use in manufacturing gunpowder, the caves were later popularized as a place for local farmers to get together for dances; the largest room in the caves is still used for Easter Sunrise services and occasional crafts shows and chamber of commerce meetings. Meramec Caverns was opened as a tourist attraction in 1935 by Lester Dill, who guided visitors through the elaborate chambers and, more importantly, was a true master of the art of garnering cheap but effective publicity for his tourist attraction. An example: After World War II, Dill and some friends hung from the top of Empire State Building dressed up as cavemen, and threatened to jump off unless everyone in the world visited Meramec Caverns.

Fact and fiction mix freely at Meramac Caverns, adding to the pleasures of seeing the massive caves. Jesse James used these caverns as a hideout, and at least once took advantage of the underground river to escape through the secret "back door." The natural formations are among the most sculptural and delicate of any cave you can visit, and the manmade additions are all low-tech enough to be charming: The hand-operated sound-and-light show ends with a grand finale of Kate Smith singing "God Bless America," while the red, white, and blue of Old Glory is projected onto a limestone curtain.

Meramec Caverns is near the town of **Stanton**, 55 miles west of St. Louis, three miles south of I-44 exit 230. There's a small café and a motel on the grounds, which spread along the banks of the Meramec River. At the I-44 exit, the odd little **Jesse James Museum** (daily; $5) insists, despite all evidence to the contrary, that a 100-year-old man who turned up in Stanton in 1948 was in fact Jesse James.

Times Beach: Route 66 State Park

There's no plaque or notice marking the spot, but the story of **Times Beach** (pop. 0) deserves mention. Founded in the 1920s as a mountain getaway a dozen miles west of St. Louis along the Meramec River, thanks to Route 66 the town grew into a working-class commuter suburb, with some 2,000 people but no paved streets except for the highway that passed through the center of town. Times Beach remained a quiet hamlet until 1982, when the federal government discovered that the industrial oil sprayed on streets to keep down dust had in fact been contaminated with toxic dioxins. The toxic waste, combined with a flood that buried the town for over a week, made Times Beach uninhabitable.

At Gray Summit, off I-44 at exit 251, a pair of old Route 66 landmarks, the **Diamond Truck Stop** *and the* **Gardenway Motel,** *still stand along the modern freeway. From here, Hwy-100 runs northwest along the Missouri River to the historic towns of Washington and Hermann.*

In 1984 the government paid $33 million to buy Times Beach and tear it down, and 15 years later the cleanup was declared complete. Four hundred acres of what was Times Beach have since been re-opened as the **Route 66 State Park** (daily; free; 636/938-7198) with hiking trails, river access, and a nice little museum on Times Beach and Route 66, housed in a 1930s roadhouse.

West of St. Louis, the best of many Route 66 survivors is on old Route 66, between I-44 exits 253 and 264, a mile east of the town of Pacific. Open since 1935, the **Red Cedar Inn** (636/257-9790) serves dinner every evening in a lovely, warm, woodsy dining room.

Route 66 Across St. Louis

It can be maddening to follow old Route 66 across St. Louis, but its many great spots—Ted Drewe's Frozen Custard Stand, in particular—make it well worth the effort. From the southwest, the old road followed Watson Road and Chippewa Street, which led into Gravois Avenue for the main ride across town. From downtown, the main route crossed the Mississippi River into Collinsville, Illinois (which is covered below), while another "City 66" route headed north along Florissant Avenue and Riverview Drive, crossing the Mississippi on the historic **Chain of Rocks Bridge** (314/741-1211), which has been renovated for use as a mile-long bike and hiking trail, decorated with an array of old gas pumps and neon signs, just south of the modern I-270 freeway.

St. Louis, the only place where three of our Road Trip routes coincide, marks the junction of old **Route 66**, US-50, the cross-country **Loneliest Road** (page 693), and the **Great River Road** (page 251). St. Louis itself is covered on pages 252–253.

ILLINOIS

Heading diagonally across the state between St. Louis and Chicago, what remains of Route 66 is a surprisingly rural cruise through endless fields of corn. Despite the urban conglomerations at both ends, for most of its nearly 300-mile trek here, Route 66 and its modern usurper, I-55, pass along flat prairies with nary a smokestack or skyscraper as far as the eye can see.

The heavy industrial and poverty-stricken suburbs of East St. Louis aren't terribly rewarding for travelers in search of the Mother Road, but a couple of intriguing attractions—one a prehistoric city, the other a water tower shaped like a catsup bottle—are worth searching out. The only real city along the route and the state capital, Springfield, has preserved its sections of Route 66, as have most of the small towns en route. All of them play up their Route 66 connections, and most boast at least one true old-road landmark.

Cahokia Mounds sit in the middle of the American Bottom, a floodplain whose gunpowder-black alluvial soils have long been considered among the richest and most productive in the world—for example, about 80 percent of the world's horseradish supply comes from right here, making the region the official "Horseradish Capital of the World." However, Charles Dickens called it an "ill-favored Black Hollow" after enduring its mud, which had "no variety but in depth."

Collinsville: Cahokia Mounds

Old Route 66 followed today's I-270 from the north side of St. Louis, but one of southern Illinois' biggest attractions sits directly east of the Gateway Arch, off the I-55/70 freeway at exit 6. Clearly visible to the south side of the interstate, the enigmatic humps of **Cahokia Mounds State Historic Site** (hours vary; 618/346-5160) are the remains of the largest prehistoric Indian city north of Mexico. Over 100 earthen mounds of various sizes were built here by the indigenous Mississippian culture while Europe was in the Dark Ages; the largest covers 14 acres—more ground than the Great Pyramid of Cheops.

But don't expect the works of the pharaohs: Symmetrical, grass-covered hills sitting in flat, lightly wooded bottomlands are what you'll find here. The view of the Gateway Arch in distant St. Louis from the 100-foot-top of Monks' Mound lends an odd sense of grandeur to the site, and a sophisticated Interpretive Center is a recommended first stop for its exhibits, award-winning multimedia orientation show, and guided and self-guiding tours.

The nearest town to the Cahokia Mounds is **Collinsville,** a pleasant little place that's famous for its 170-foot-high **World's Largest Catsup Bottle,** which rises high above 800 S. Morrison Avenue (Hwy-159), a quarter mile south of Main Street, on the grounds of what used to be the Brooks Catsup Company. This decorated water tower was constructed in 1949, and restored by the people of Collinsville in 1993.

Mount Olive and Litchfield

East of the Cahokia Mounds and Collinsville, the first really interesting stretch of old Route 66 begins at I-55 exit 41, and runs along the east side of the freeway for over a dozen miles. First stop is the hamlet of **Mount Olive** (pop. 2,126), which in the early 20th century was a bustling coal-mining center. It's now a sleepy little community where the only signs of its mining past are in the Union Miners Cemetery, along old Route 66 at the northwest edge of town. Near the entrance is a granite shaft rising from an elaborate pedestal, which serves as a memorial to Mary Harris "Mother" Jones, the celebrated union activist who died here while helping with a miners' strike in 1930. Famous for her passionate oratory, like the phrase "Pray for the dead, and fight like hell

for the living," her grave is nearby, marked by a simple headstone.

For old-road fans, Mount Olive is also home to the oldest surviving service station on Route 66, the immaculate restored (but no longer in business) Shell station downtown, long owned by Russell Soulsby.

North of Mount Olive, the old road continues for seven miles to **Litchfield**, another old mining center that is home to one of the best of the many good Route 66 restaurants, the **Ariston Cafe** (daily; 217/324-2023), right in the heart of town at the junction of old Route 66 and Hwy-16. The food is a step or two up from the usual roadside fare, and the white linen and refined decor have earned it a spot in the Route 66 Hall of Fame. The rest of Litchfield reeks of the old road, with cafés, motor courts, and old billboards aplenty.

Parts of the old road survive between Litchfield and Springfield, but the route is incomplete and confusing; I-55 makes much shorter work of the 25-mile drive.

Springfield

As the Illinois state capital, **Springfield** (pop. 120,000) embodies the rural small-town character of most of the state and feels much farther away from Chicago than the three-plus-hour drive it actually is, traffic willing. Springfield is also the place that takes the "Land of Lincoln" state's obsession with Abraham Lincoln to its greatest extreme, for it was here that Honest Abe worked and lived from 1837 to 1861. He left Springfield after being elected President, and was buried here after his assassination at the end of the Civil War.

There are all manner of Lincoln sites to see all over Springfield, but the newest and best place to start your homage is at the state-run **Lincoln Presidential Museum** (daily; $7.50; 217/558-8882), which opened in April 2005 at 212 N. 6th Street. Once you've toured this comprehensive, reverential yet thought-provoking $90 million exhibition, other sites to

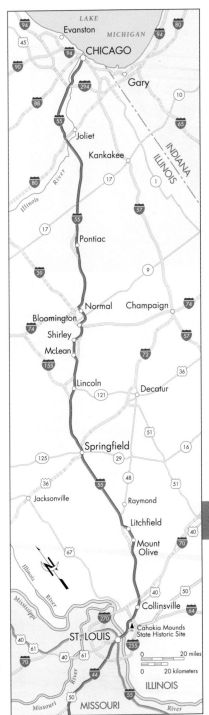

see include the only home Lincoln ever owned, his law offices, and of course his tomb. Located in Oak Ridge Cemetery, two miles north of downtown, his tomb also includes the remains of his wife and three of four children; legend has it that if you touch the nose on the bronze bust of Lincoln, good luck will follow.

Though quite sincere and understated, the Lincoln homage can overwhelm, and one place that lets you escape from Lincoln Land is the beautiful **Dana-Thomas House** (closed Mon. & Tues.; 217/782-6776) at 301 E. Lawrence Avenue, a half mile south of the state capitol. Designed by Frank Lloyd Wright in 1902, it is the most luxurious, best-preserved, and most fully furnished of his houses—and is open for hourlong guided tours. Actually a complete remodel of a house that already stood on the site, the Dana-Thomas house was built for socialite Susan Dana, who lived here until the late 1920s, when it was sold to a publishing company and used as offices until the state of Illinois purchased it in 1981.

Springfield also has a favorite Route 66 watering hole, the **Cozy Dog Drive-In** (217/525-1992), on the old road south of downtown at 2935 S. 6th Street. The birthplace of the corn dog, which here goes by the nicer name "Cozy," was founded in 1949 by Ed Waldmire, father of noted Route 66 artist Bob Waldmire. So come on in, and chow down on a Cozy Dog or two—four dogs, a drink, and a big basket of french fries cost around $5.

CAPITOL AVENUE, LOOKING WEST, SPRINGFIELD, ILL.

Almost all the national chain hotel and motels have operations in Springfield, so you shouldn't have trouble finding a room. For more information, contact the Springfield **visitors center,** 109 N. 7th Street (217/789-2360 or 800/545-7300).

GO FOR COZY DOGS

LOCATED ON HISTORIC ROUTE 66 SINCE 1949, SPRINGFIELD, ILLINOIS

Lincoln

The only town named for Abe in his lifetime, **Lincoln** (pop. 15,418) took his name before he became a famous figure. As a young lawyer, Abraham Lincoln drew up the legal documents for founding the town but warned developers that he "never knew of anything named Lincoln that amounted to much." At the dedication ceremonies, Lincoln supposedly "baptized" the place by spitting out a mouthful of watermelon seeds—hence the plaster watermelon and historical plaque remembering the great event, next to the train station at Broadway and Chicago Streets in the center of town.

> On the stretch of old Route 66 that forms the frontage road at I-55 exit 63, near the town of Raymond, a marble statue of the Virgin Mary forms a shrine that has become known as "**Our Lady of the Highways**."

Funks Grove

Westbound drivers will encounter the towns in the more sonorous order of Shirley and McLean, but wordplay aside, the stretch of Illinois farmland between Bloomington and Springfield is rich in Route 66-related heritage. In McLean, 47 miles from Springfield and 15 miles from Bloomington, old Route 66 emerges from the shadow of I-55 and you can follow old Route 66 along the west side of the freeway for just over four miles north to the delightful anachronism of **Funks Grove** (309/874-3360), where the friendly Funk family has been tapping trees and making delicious maple sirup (that's how they spell it) since 1891. If you're here in the spring you can watch them tap the trees and hammer in the spouts; each tree can produce four gallons of sap a day, but it takes 50 gallons for each gallon of the final product. Free tastings are available, and a full range of bottles is on sale.

From Funks Grove, the old road continues north, rejoining I-55 after four more miles near the town of Shirley, for the run into **Bloomington-Normal.** Hometown of politician Adlai Stevenson (and Col. Henry Blake of TV's *M*A*S*H*), Bloomington-Normal sits at the junction of five different Interstate freeways, surrounded by miles of cornfields. Its main claim to fame is in being the only place in the world where that classic bar snack, Beer Nuts, is made; for a free sample (but no tour, alas), stop by the factory (800/BEER-NUT) at 103 N. Robinson Street.

Pontiac

Some 90 miles southeast of Lake Michigan, the former coal-mining town of **Pontiac** (pop. 11,428) surrounds the stately circa-1875 Livingston County Courthouse. The courthouse's green lawns hold the usual battery of monuments, including one to the namesake Ottawa chief whose visage also graces the General Motors marquee. According to the WPA *Guide to Illinois,* another of these monuments, the Soldier and Sailors Monument, received the shortest presidential dedication in history when, in 1902, it was "dedicated with a few hasty words by President Theodore Roosevelt, before an audience of less than a dozen people, who congregated briefly under a terrific downpour."

Pontiac is also home to a long-lived Route 66 landmark, the **Old Log Cabin Inn** (815/842-2908) on Pontiac Road on the north edge of town. When the

road was rerouted behind the original location, this restaurant was jacked up and flipped around; the old road, which dates from 1918, is still there, behind the café along the railroad tracks.

From the Log Cabin, you can follow old Route 66 northeast through small towns, though the route is obscure and not all that rich in history or aesthetic delights. The final alignment of the old road is now Hwy-53, which runs along the southeast side of I-55. The towns here offer a very pleasant taste of what old Route 66 had to offer: **Dwight** is leafy and quaint, **Braidwood** has a set of Burma-Shave signs and the popular "Polka Dot Drive In," while **Wilmington** is semi-famous for the 30-foot-tall "Rocketman" statue that stands outside the **Launching Pad Drive-In** (815/476-6535), at 810 E. Baltimore Street.

Midewin National Tallgrass Prairie Preserve

Along Route 66 between Joliet and Wilmington, a unique undertaking is working to re-create the natural ecosystem on one of the most environmentally damaged areas imaginable: 19,000 acres of the old Joliet Army Ammunition Plant is being converted into the **Midewin National Tallgrass Prairie Preserve** (limited public access; 815/423-6370). Since 1996, when the land was transferred from the Army to the Forest Service, the change from producing TNT to regrowing the native tallgrass prairie has been slow and steady, and after five-plus years of toxic cleanups and careful husbandry it now offers hiking and biking trails, and frequent guided tours of the site. You get a good feeling for the flora and fauna that would have existed naturally in places like this all over the Midwest.

Joliet

Joliet, the "City of Steel and Stone," has a rough reputation that doesn't really reflect its welter of historic attractions. Route 66 through this once-mighty industrial enclave is a feast for fans of post-industrial scenery: Loads of old warehouses and commercial buildings line the route, while stalwart bridges cross the historic Illinois & Michigan

Canal, which, beginning in the 1840s, connected Chicago with the Mississippi River.

South of Joliet, following old Route 66 (Hwy-53) across the I-80 superslab brings you past the massive **Route 66 Raceway** (815/722-5500), where NHRA drag races, NASCAR stock car races, and occasional pop music concerts are held. North of Joliet, Hwy-53 winds past the high-tech Argonne National Laboratory into the ever-expanding Chicagoland sprawl.

Route 66 Across Chicagoland

Following the first or last leg of Route 66 across Chicago and its hinterlands is really not worth the effort for anyone except the most die-hard end-to-ender—even Jack Rittenhouse, in his original 1946 *Guide Book to Highway 66*, didn't bother to describe the route until it reached Plainfield, 35 miles southwest of the Loop. For a symbolic end point, you can use the grand old Art Institute of Chicago in Grant Park along the lakeshore, since the last US-66 shield used to hang from a streetlight just south of the gallery. If Chicago is your "end of the road," you'll probably prefer to avoid the final few miles of surface streets and make your way to town as quickly as possible via I-55. Starting from Chicago, as the song says you should, you may be more willing to take the time to see what's left of the Mother Road.

At Plainfield, a little piece of highway history happened when the original version of Route 66 crossed the even older Lincoln Highway, America's first transcontinental road.

From Lake Michigan, the old road ran west via Adams Street (take Jackson Boulevard eastbound; both are one-way) before angling southwest along Ogden Avenue—a long, diagonal exception to the city's main grid of streets. Near **Cicero**, which prides itself on having been a haven to Al Capone and other mobsters during the Prohibition era, there's one oddity worth checking out: "**The Spindle**," a tower of ruined cars impaled on a 50-foot steel spike, standing in the parking lot of a shopping mall at the corner of Cermak Road and Harlem Avenue, two miles north of old Route 66. (You may have seen The Spindle in the 1990s comedy *Wayne's World.*)

To continue south and west, you have to follow I-55, which was built right on top of old Route 66. In Willowbrook, off Hwy-83 on the north side of I-55 just a dozen miles from the Loop, **Dell Rhea's Chicken Basket** (630/325-0780) at 645 Joliet Road is a welcoming old roadside tavern, with famously fabulous chicken dinners and frequent live music.

Further west, Route 66 crossed the old Lincoln Highway (US-30) in suburban **Plainfield**, then followed the Des Plaines River and the Chicago Ship and Sanitary Canal as far as Joliet, where Route 66 resurfaces again.

INTERSECTION — Chicago marks the junction of Route 66 and our cross-country route along **The Oregon Trail**, detailed on pages 532–633. The city itself is covered on pages 580–581.

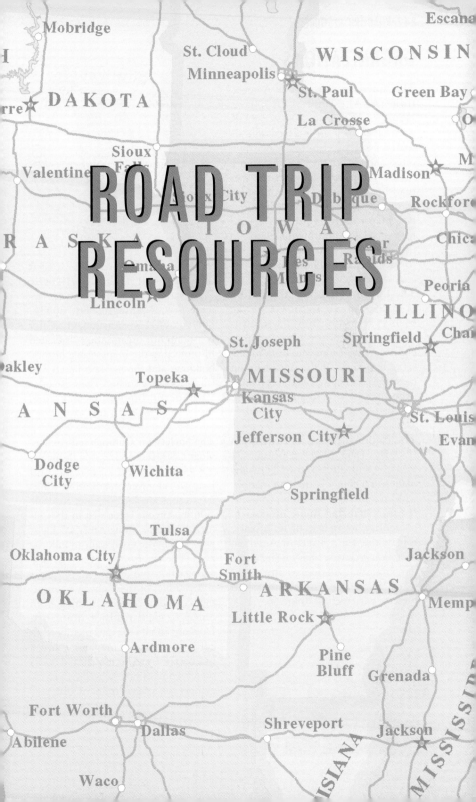

ROAD TRIP
RESOURCES

ORGANIZATIONS

The **American Automobile Association (AAA)** (1000 AAA Drive, Heathrow FL 32746, 800/922-8228, www.aaa.com) is an indispensable resource. No traveler in his or her right mind should hit the road without a membership card. Besides the free roadside assistance (24 hours a day across the country), they also offer free maps, useful guidebooks, and tons of related information. Look in the Yellow Pages for a local office, or contact the national headquarters.

The **Lincoln Highway Association** (111 S. Elm, Franklin Grove, IL 61031, 815/456-3030, www.lincolnhighwayassoc.org) is a group of old-roads aficionados who work to preserve remnants of the nation's first coast-to-coast highway and to promote its memory. They also get together for annual meetings to retrace the route.

The **National Route 66 Federation** (P.O. Box 1848, Lake Arrowhead, CA 92352-1848, 909/336-6131, www .national66.com) is the only nationwide, nonprofit organization committed to revitalizing Route 66, and to promoting awareness of its historic role as the Main Street of America. Members receive a high-quality quarterly magazine. All dues go directly toward lobbying governments to preserve what's left of Route 66.

The **National Trust for Historic Preservation** (1785 Massachusetts Avenue NW, Washington DC 20036, 800/944-6847,www.nationaltrust.org) is a nonprofit organization dedicated to protecting the irreplaceable historic buildings and the neighborhoods and landscapes they anchor. They also offer a wonderful bimonthly magazine, *Preservation,* for $20 a year.

The **Society for Commercial Archaeology** (P.O. Box 45828, Madison, WI 53744-5828, www.sca-roadside.org) is an all-volunteer organization working to preserve and interpret roadside culture. Anyone interested in the cultural landscape lining America's highways and byways will want to join the SCA. The enterprise is geared toward appreciation and enjoyment of quirks and crannies of the highway environment. Studies cover everything from diners to giant roadside dinosaurs. Dues are $35 a year, and members receive a full-color magazine and a quarterly newsletter that details preservation efforts as well as get-togethers for annual tours of different regions.

PRACTICALITIES

Hotel and Motel Chains

Best Western: 800/528-1234
Clarion: 877/424-6423
Comfort Inn: 877/424-6423
Courtyard: 888/236-2427
Days Inn: 800/325-2525
Econo Lodge: 877/424-6423
Embassy Suites: 800/362-2779
Hampton Inn: 800/HAMPTON
Hilton: 800/HILTONS
Holiday Inn: 888/HOLIDAY
Howard Johnson: 800/446-4656
Hyatt: 800/233-1234
Marriott: 888/236-2427
Motel 6: 800/4-MOTEL-6
Radisson: 800/333-3333
Ramada Inn: 800/228-2828
Ritz-Carlton: 888/236-2427
Rodeway Inn: 877/424-6423
Sheraton: 800/325-3535
Super 8: 800/800-8000
Westin: 800/228-3000
W Hotels: 888/625-5144
Wyndham: 800/WYNDHAM

Camping

One essential purchase for anyone traveling around the USA, especially in the western states, is a **National Parks Pass.** This card gives free admission (for an entire family for a full year), to all National Parks and National Historic Sites. The cost is around $50. The **Golden Age Pass**

gives free admission to all of the above sites to any U.S. citizen or permanent resident over the age of 62; other passes offer discounts on campgrounds. For more information, call (888/GO-PARKS) or visit their website at www.national-parks.org. For information on camping and recreation in other federal lands, a great starting point is the www.recreation.gov website.

Car Rental Companies

Alamo: 800/462-5266
Avis: 800/230-4898
Budget: 800/527-0700
Enterprise: 800/325-8007
Hertz: 800/654-3131
National: 800/227-7368
Thrifty: 800/367-2277

US STATE TOURISM AND ROAD CONDITIONS

Alabama
Tourism: 800/ALABAMA

Arizona
Tourism Info: 888/520-3434
Road Conditions: 888/411-7623

Arkansas
Tourism Info: 800/NATURAL
Road Conditions: 800/245-1672

California
Tourism Info: 800/TO-CALIF
Road Conditions: 800/427-7623

Colorado
Tourism Info: 800/COLORADO
Road Conditions: 303/639-1111

Connecticut
Tourism Info: 800/CT-BOUND
Road Conditions: 860/594-2650

Delaware
Tourism Info: 800/441-8846
Road Conditions: 302/760-2080

Florida
Tourism Info: 888/7-FLA-USA
Road Conditions: 800/475-0044

Georgia
Tourism Info: 800/VISIT-GA
Road Conditions: 404/635-6800

Idaho
Tourism Info: 800/635-7820

Illinois
Tourism Info: 800/226-6632
Road Conditions: 800/452-4368

Indiana
Tourism Info: 888/365-6946
Road Conditions: 800/261-7623

Iowa
Tourism Info: 800/345-IOWA
Road Conditions: 515/288-1047

Kansas
Tourism Info: 800/2-KANSAS
Road Conditions: 800/585-7623

Kentucky
Tourism Info: 800/225-TRIP

Louisiana
Tourism Info: 800/33-GUMBO

Maine
Tourism Info: 888/624-6345
Road Conditions: 207/287-3427

Maryland
Tourism Info: 800/543-1036
Road Conditions: 800/327-3125

Massachusetts
Tourism Info: 800/227-MASS
Road Conditions: 617/374-1234

Michigan
Tourism Info: 888/78-GREAT
Road Conditions: 800/381-8477

Minnesota
Tourism Info: 800/657-3700
Road Conditions: 800/542-0220

Mississippi
Tourism Info: 800/WARMEST

Missouri
Tourism Info: 800/877-1234
Road Conditions: 800/222-6400

Montana
Tourism Info: 800/VISIT-MT
Road Conditions: 800/332-6171

Nebraska
Tourism Info: 800/228-4307
Road Conditions: 402/471-4533

Nevada
Tourism Info: 800/NEVADA-8
Road Conditions: 877/687-6237

New Hampshire
Tourism Info: 800/FUN-IN-NH
Road Conditions: 603/271-6900

New Jersey
Tourism Info: 800/JERSEY-7

New Mexico
Tourism Info: 800/733-6396
Road Conditions: 800/432-4269

New York
Tourism Info: 800/CALL-NYS
Road Conditions: 800/847-8929

North Carolina
Tourism Info: 800/VISIT-NC
Road Conditions: 877/368-4968

North Dakota
Tourism Info: 800/435-5663
Road Conditions: 701/328-7623

Ohio
Tourism Info: 800/BUCKEYE
Road Conditions: 614/644-7031

Oklahoma
Tourism Info: 800/652-6552
Road Conditions: 405/425-2385

Oregon
Tourism Info: 800/547-7842

Pennsylvania
Tourism Info: 800/VISIT-PA
Road Conditions: 814/355-6044

Rhode Island
Tourism Info: 800/556-2484

South Carolina
Tourism Info: 800/346-3634

South Dakota
Tourism Info: 800/S-DAKOTA
Road Conditions: 605/367-5707

Tennessee
Tourism Info: 800/GO-2-TENN
Road Conditions: 800/858-6349

Texas
Tourism Info: 800/888-8TEX
Road Conditions: 800/452-9292

Utah
Tourism Info: 801/538-1030
Road Conditions: 801/964-6000

Vermont
Tourism Info: 800/VERMONT

Virginia
Tourism Info: 800/VISIT-VA
Road Conditions: 800/367-7623

Washington
Tourism Info: 800/544-1800
Road Conditions: 800/695-7623

West Virginia
Tourism Info: 800/225-5982
Road Conditions: 877/982-7623

Wisconsin
Tourism Info: 800/432-TRIP
Road Conditions: 800/762-3947

Wyoming
Tourism Info: 800/225-5996
Road Conditions: 307/772-0824

CANADIAN PROVINCIAL TOURISM AND ROAD CONDITIONS

Alberta
Tourism Info: 800/661-8888
Road Conditions: 403/246-5853

British Columbia
Tourism Info: 800/663-6000
Road Conditions: 250/953-9000

Ontario
Tourism Info: 800/668-2746
Road Conditions: 416/235-4686

Quebec
Tourism Info: 800/363-7777
Road Conditions: 418/684-2363

RECOMMENDED READING

Roadside America

American Diner: Then and Now by Richard J. S. Gutman (Johns Hopkins University, 2000): Lushly illustrated, encyclopedic history of that great American roadside institution, from its humble beginnings in the lunch wagons of the late 1880s to the streamlined stainless-steel models so beloved by art directors everywhere.

Asphalt Nation: How the Automobile Took Over America and How We Can Take It Back by Jane Holtz Kay (University of California, 1998): An enthusiastic and informative account of how cars, and the commuter culture they've spawned, have sapped the strength of the nation's communities. Not as histrionic as the title might lead you to believe, this is an engaging and insightful book that aims to help us cut down on the billions of annual hours Americans spend stuck in traffic.

Colossus of Roads: Myth and Symbol along the American Highway by Karal Ann Marling (University of Minnesota Press, 2000): If you're interested in the stories behind America's many roadside giants—Paul Bunyan statues,

super-sized fruits and vegetables, and myriad concrete dinosaurs—you'll love this informative and funny study. Packed with pictures, but a little lacking in details on how to find these giant figures in the flesh, it's bound to inspire more than a few detours.

Flattened Fauna: A Field Guide to Common Animals of Roads, Street and Highways by Roger M. Knutson (Ten Speed Press, 1987): Lighthearted look at that under-studied ecosystem, the highway. Besides being a helpful guide to identifying the sundry dead objects along the roadside, the book also details the natural life and habitats of the unfortunate road-killed creatures.

The Lincoln Highway: Main Street Across America by Drake Hokanson (University of Iowa Press, 1999): The bible of Lincoln Highway history, tracing America's first transcontinental highway from its beginnings in 1915 to its gradual fadeout in the post-interstate world. If you want to travel along the granddaddy of old roads, look for *Greetings From The Lincoln Highway,* a fully illustrated mile-by-mile guide by Brian Butko (Stackpole Books, 2005).

Main Street to Miracle Mile: American Roadside Architecture by Chester H. Liebs (New York Graphic Society, 1985): This lushly illustrated historical survey of roadside design is the best single introduction to the familiar, yet fascinating environment that lines the nation's highways.

Open Road: A Celebration of the American Highway by Phil Patton (Simon and Schuster, 1986): An energetic account of how the American roadside landscape came to look the way it does today, masterfully blending a discussion of the economic and political forces behind the nation's highway network with a contagious enthusiasm for the inherent democracy the automobile embodies.

Pump and Circumstance: Glory Days of the Gas Station by John Margolies (Little, Brown, 1993): Profusely illustrated coffee-table book that uses photographs, advertising, enamel signs, road maps, and brief but revealing text to track the development of that essential feature of the American highway landscape, the gas station. The same author/photographer has produced many other great books, including **Hitting the Road**, about road maps; **Fun Along the Road**, about roadside amusements; and **See the USA**, which explores the graphic world of travel brochures and posters.

Roadside America by Doug Kirby et al. (Fireside Books, 1993): The best guidebook to the wackiest and weirdest attractions along the Great American Roadside. Organized by theme rather than by location, but still an entertaining and agreeable travel companion; check it out "live" at www.roadsideamerica.com .

Travel Guidebooks

American Guide Series: Federal Writers Project Guides to the States: Invaluable documents of the state of the nation during the 1930s and 1940s, these state-by-state, road-by-road, somewhat socialist-minded guidebooks were compiled during the Depression and later by teams of writers put to work under the auspices of the New Deal Works Project Administration (W.P.A.). Many great writers, including Saul Bellow, Richard Wright, Studs Terkel, Ralph Ellison, Kenneth Patchen, Nelson Algren, and Jim Thompson contributed to the series, selected volumes of which have been brought back into print.

The Amusement Park Guide by Tim O'Brien (Globe Pequot, 2003): The subtitle says it all: Coast to Coast Thrills. Contains full descriptions and practical information for 275 small, medium, and large amusement parks all over the United States and Canada.

Ballpark Vacations by Bruce Adams and Margaret Engel (Fodor's, 2002): Enjoyable and informative travel guide detailing the best minor and major league baseball parks in the country, with details on the teams and well-chosen suggestions of places to eat and sleep in 75 different cities and towns. Baseball fanatics should also pick up a copy of the annual Baseball America directory, which gives details of every professional and semi-pro team in the United States and Canada.

Eat Your Way Across the USA by Jane and Michael Stern (Broadway Books,

1997): Handy, cross-country compendium of All-American diners, drive-ins, lobster shacks, and BBQ stands, put together by the road food experts and *Gourmet* magazine correspondents.

Watch It Made In the USA by Karen Axelrod and Bruce Brumberg (Avalon Travel Publishing, 2002): A travel guide that takes you to watch the manufacture of such all-American products as Crayola crayons, Louisville Slugger baseball bats, Hershey's chocolates, and Harley-Davidson motorcycles.

Travelogues

Blue Highways: A Journey Into America by William Least Heat-Moon (Little, Brown and Company, 1982): One of the best-selling travel books ever written, this intensely personal yet openhearted tale traces the path of a part-Indian English teacher who travels the back roads "in search of places where change did not mean ruin and where time and men and deeds connected."

Drive, They Said: Poems About Americans and Their Cars edited by Kurt Brown (Milkweed Editions, 1994): If you like to drive, and like to read or write poetry, you'll love this thick volume of contemporary verse, which samples the work of over 100 poets.

Elvis Presley Boulevard: From Sea to Shining Sea, Almost by Mark Winegardner (Atlantic Monthly Press, 1987): An energetic mix of road trip journal and coming-of-age autobiography, this short book recounts a summer-long tour around the southern and central United States. The Elvis obsession hinted at by the title is only a small

part of the book, which looks at many of the odder corners of America.

Fear and Loathing in Las Vegas by Hunter S. Thompson (Random House, 1972): Subtitled "A Savage Journey to the Heart of the American Dream," this riotous blast of a book starts with the words "We were somewhere around Barstow on the edge of the desert when the drugs began to take hold," and goes on to tell the story of a long lost weekend in Sin City, and much, much more.

Great Plains by Ian Frazier (Farrar, Straus and Giroux, 1989): In-depth, top-to-bottom study of the wide-open land where the buffalo roamed, tracing historical themes like water, cowboys, and Indians, while capturing the contemporary scene.

Let Us Now Praise Famous Men by James Agee, photographs by Walker Evans (Mariner Books, 2001): A classic. The talented collaborators spent the summer of 1936 living with three

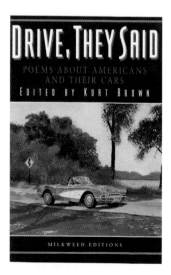

families of poor white cotton share-croppers in the Appalachian foothills of northwest Alabama, and together created a vivid and compassionate portrait of rural America during the depths of the Great Depression.

The Lost Continent: Travels in Small Town America by Bill Bryson (Harper Perennial, 1990): Iowa-born British transplant returns to America in search of material for his sarcastic commentary on contemporary life. Hilariously funny in parts, mean-spirited in others, and packed with trivial truths about life in the land of liberty.

On the Road by Jack Kerouac (Viking, 1957): What the Beatles were to music, the Beats were to literature, and this wild ramble of a road story was Kerouac's first number-one hit, inspiring a generation or two to hightail it along America's highways in the tracks of Sal Paradise and Dean Moriarty.

Out West: American Journey Along the Lewis and Clark Trail by Dayton Duncan (Viking Penguin, 1987): The best travel book since Blue Highways, this marvelous tale retraces the route blazed by the Corps of Discovery on their epic adventure. With a combination of concise history lessons, captivating storytelling, and wry humor, Duncan vividly points out what has and hasn't changed in the 200-odd years since the captains first trekked across the country and back.

Road Trips, Head Trips and Other Car-Crazed Writings edited by Jean Lindamood (Atlantic Monthly Press, 1996): An introduction and description of a road trip along the Mexican border by P. J. O'Rourke sets the tone for this compilation of car-and-driver tales, which also features pieces by Kerouac, Steinbeck, and Hunter S. Thompson.

Spirit of Place: The Making of an American Literary Landscape by Frederick Turner (Sierra Club Books, 1989): A multi-layered tapestry of biography, travel writing, and literary criticism, this wonderful book ex-

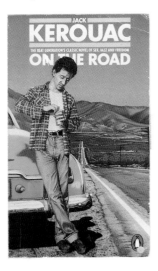

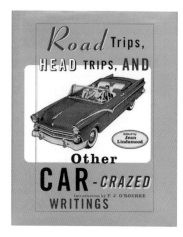

plores how different locales have inspired and defined many of America's greatest writers.

Travels with Charley: In Search of America by John Steinbeck (Viking, 1962): Rambling around "this monster of a land" in his camper Rocinante, accompanied only by the eponymous French poodle, Steinbeck returns to his California haunts from self-imposed exile in New York to find that, even if you can't go home again, there are many intriguing things along the way.

Zen and the Art of Motorcycle Maintenance: An Inquiry into Values by Robert M. Pirsig (William Morrow and Company, 1974): The subtitle points out this big book's more ponderous aspects, but at its best this is a captivating, full-throttle ride down America's back roads in search of meaning in the modern age.

INDEX

Amusement and Theme Parks

Baseball

Diners

Festivals and Events

Roadside Art, Attractions, and Curiosities

Acknowledgments

A proverbial cast of thousands—in ranger stations, visitor centers, libraries, B&Bs, and cafes across the country—has helped shape this book, providing directions, suggestions, story ideas, and endless cups of coffee. I can't thank you enough for your kindness and hospitality. To all the readers who've written in with helpful tips, snapshots, comments, corrections, and compliments—keep those emails, pictures, and postcards a'coming!

For making this book happen in the first place, I am grateful for the support and enthusiasm of the whole crew at Avalon, especially my editors Ellen Cavalli and Kevin McLain, and the entire design team including Jane Musser, Justin Marler, and Stefano Boni. Sincere thanks are also due to Kevin "Roots" Roe (and Debbie and young Nathaniel) for never-ending encouragement, musical accompaniment, and insight into the inner life of the Great Plains. My eternal gratitude goes out to the late great Doug Pappas, whose love for and knowledge of baseball, politics, and these magical old highways still guides me down the road.

So much has happened in the years since I started work on this book that I don't know what to say. I do know I owe many friends and former strangers more kindness and hospitality than I could ever hope to repay. So here's a heartfelt "thank you" for welcoming me when I've dropped in out of the blue, in need of care and feeding. And for coming along for the ride, and being there when I get home, I'd also like to acknowledge the help and enthusiasm of my darling wife Catherine and beloved boys Tom and Alex.

Happy Trails,
Jamie Jensen

PHOTO AND ILLUSTRATION CREDITS